Keys to Economic Prosperity

These keys to the economic prosperity of a nation are highlighted throu

1. **Human Ingenuity.** Economic goods are the result of human i_____, the size of the economic pie is variable, not fixed. [Economics Chapter 2; Macroeconomics Chapter 2; Microeconomics Chapter 2]

2. **Private Ownership.** Private ownership provides people with a strong incentive to take care of things and develop resources in ways that are highly valued by others. [Economics Chapter 2; Macroeconomics Chapter 2; Microeconomics Chapter 2]

3. **Gains from Trade.** Trade makes it possible for individuals to generate more output through specialization and division of labor, large-scale production processes, and the dissemination of improved products and production methods. [Economics Chapter 2; Macroeconomics Chapter 2; Microeconomics Chapter 2]

4. **Invisible Hand Principle.** Market prices coordinate the actions of self-interested individuals and direct them toward activities that promote the general welfare. [Economics Chapter 3; Macroeconomics Chapter 3; Microeconomics Chapter 3]

5. **Profits and Losses.** Profits direct producers toward activities that increase the value of resources; losses impose a penalty on those who reduce the value of resources. [Economics Chapter 3; Macroeconomics Chapter 3; Microeconomics Chapter 3]

6. **Competition.** Competition motivates businesses to produce efficiently, cater to the views of consumers, and search for innovative improvements. [Economics Chapter 22; Microeconomics Chapter 9]

7. **Entrepreneurship.** The entrepreneurial discovery and development of improved products and production processes is a central element of economic progress. [Economics Chapter 23; Microeconomics Chapter 10]

8. **Productivity and Earnings.** In a market economy, productivity and earnings are closely linked. In order to earn a large income, one must provide large benefits to others. [Economics Chapter 26; Microeconomics Chapter 13]

9. **Innovation and the Capital Market.** If the potential gains from innovative ideas and human ingenuity are going to be fully realized, it must be relatively easy for individuals to try their innovative and potentially ingenious ideas, but difficult to continue if the idea is a bad one. [Economics Chapter 27; Microeconomics Chapter 14]

10. **Price Stability.** Maintenance of price stability is the essence of sound monetary policy; price stability provides the foundation for both economic stability and the efficient operation of markets. [Economics Chapter 14; Macroeconomics Chapter 14]

11. **International Trade.** When people are permitted to engage freely in international trade, they are able to achieve higher income levels and living standards than would otherwise be possible. [Economics Chapter 18; Macroeconomics Chapter 18; Microeconomics Chapter 16]

12. **Role of Government.** Governments promote economic progress when they protect individuals and their property, enforce contracts impartially, provide access to money of stable value, avoid high taxes and excessive regulation, and foster competitive markets and free international trade. [Economics Chapter 16; Macroeconomics Chapter 16]

ECONOMICS

PRIVATE AND PUBLIC CHOICE

15TH EDITION

JAMES A. GWARTNEY

Florida State University

RICHARD L. STROUP

Montana State University

RUSSELL S. SOBEL

The Citadel

DAVID A. MACPHERSON

Trinity University, San Antonio TX

CENGAGE
Learning®

Australia • Brazil • Japan • Korea • Mexico • Singapore • Spain • United Kingdom • United States

Economics: Private and Public Choice
Fifteenth Edition

James A. Gwartney

Richard L. Stroup

Russell S. Sobel

David A. Macpherson

Vice President, General Manager, Social Science & Qualitative Business: Erin Joyner

Product Director: Michael Worls

Sr. Product Manager: Steven Scoble

Content Developer: Daniel Noguera

Product Assistant: Anne Merrill

Sr. Marketing Manager: John Carey

Marketing Coordinator: Christopher Walz

Content Project Manager: Jana Lewis

Media Developer: Anita Verma

Manufacturing Planner: Kevin Kluck

Production Service: MPS Limited

Sr. Art Director: Michelle Kunkler

Internal Designer: Ramsdell Design

Cover Designer: Ramsdell Design

Cover Image: franckreporter/E+/Getty Images; © nicoolay/iStockphoto

Rights Acquisitions Specialist: Deanna Ettinger

For product information and technology assistance, contact us at
Cengage Learning Customer & Sales Support, 1-800-354-9706

For permission to use material from this text or product, submit all requests online at **www.cengage.com/permissions**
Further permissions questions can be emailed to
permissionrequest@cengage.com

Library of Congress Control Number: 2013944274

ISBN-13: 978-1-285-45353-8

ISBN-10: 1-285-45353-0

Cengage Learning
200 First Stamford Place, 4th Floor
Stamford, CT 06902
USA

Cengage Learning is a leading provider of customized learning solutions with office locations around the globe, including Singapore, the United Kingdom, Australia, Mexico, Brazil, and Japan. Locate your local office at: **www.cengage.com/global**

Cengage Learning products are represented in Canada by Nelson Education, Ltd.

To learn more about Cengage Learning Solutions, visit **www.cengage.com**

Purchase any of our products at your local college store or at our preferred online store **www.cengagebrain.com**

Printed in the United States of America
1 2 3 4 5 6 7 18 17 16 15 14

BRIEF CONTENTS

CONTENTS

RELATIONSHIP BETWEEN MAIN EDITION AND THE MACRO/MICRO EDITIONS

Chapters

MACRO	MICRO	FULL LENGTH BOOK MACRO— FIRST VERSION	FULL LENGTH BOOK MICRO— FIRST VERSION	
1	1	1	1	The Economic Approach
2	2	2	2	Some Tools of the Economist
3	3	3	3	Demand, Supply, and the Market Process
4	4	4	4	Demand and Supply: Applications and Extensions
5	5	5	5	Difficult Cases for the Market, and the Role of Government
6	6	6	6	The Economics of Political Action
7		7	17	Taking the Nation's Economic Pulse
8		8	18	Economic Fluctuations, Unemployment, and Inflation
9		9	19	An Introduction to Basic Macroeconomic Markets
10		10	20	Dynamic Change, Economic Fluctuations, and the *AD–AS* Model
11		11	21	Fiscal Policy: The Keynesian View and the Historical Development of Macroeconomics
12		12	22	Fiscal Policy, Incentives, and Secondary Effects
13		13	23	Money and the Banking System
14		14	24	Modern Macroeconomics and Monetary Policy
15		15	25	Stabilization Policy, Output, and Employment
16		16	26	Creating an Environment for Growth and Prosperity
17		17	27	Institutions, Policies, and Cross-Country Differences in Income and Growth
18	16	18	16	Gaining from International Trade
19		19	28	International Finance and the Foreign Exchange Market
	7	20	7	Consumer Choice and Elasticity
	8	21	8	Costs and the Supply of Goods
	9	22	9	Price Takers and the Competitive Process
	10	23	10	Price-Searcher Markets with Low Entry Barriers
	11	24	11	Price-Searcher Markets with High Entry Barriers
	12	25	12	The Supply of and Demand for Productive Resources
	13	26	13	Earnings, Productivity, and the Job Market
	14	27	14	Investment, the Capital Market, and the Wealth of Nations
	15	28	15	Income Inequality and Poverty

SPECIAL TOPICS

Core Topic	Topic Title	Macro Topic	Micro Topic
1	Government Spending and Taxation	1	1
2	The Economics of Social Security	2	2
3	The Stock Market: Its Function, Performance, and Potential as an Investment Opportunity	3	3
4	Great Debates in Economics: Keynes versus Hayek	4	4
5	The Crisis of 2008: Causes and Lessons for the Future	5	5
6	Lessons from the Great Depression	6	6
7	The Federal Budget and the National Debt	7	
8	The Economics of Health Care		7
9	Earnings Differences Between Men and Women		8
10	Do Labor Unions Increase the Wages of Workers?		9
11	The Question of Resource Exhaustion		10
12	Difficult Environmental Cases and the Role of Government		11

The lives of many Americans were affected by the economic troubles of 2008–2009 and the weak recovery that followed. What caused these difficulties? Has the political response been helpful or has it made matters worse? Why are so many countries experiencing problems that accompany high levels of debt? Why do some countries grow and achieve high incomes while others stagnate? These are vitally important questions. This text addresses all of them and provides both economic analysis and empirical evidence that will enhance the understanding of these critical issues.

Throughout the life of this text, our goal has been to use the tools of economics to explain how the real world works and to do so in a clear and understandable manner. Perhaps more than ever before, students are seeking to understand the world in which they live and the critical issues we confront. Indeed, this is a teachable moment for economics instructors. This thought was constantly on our minds as we worked on this edition.

ORGANIZATION, SPECIAL FEATURES, AND INSTRUCTOR FLEXIBILITY

The organization of *Economics: Private and Public Choice* is designed to provide instructors with maximum flexibility. Those using the full-length text for a two-semester course can cover either microeconomics or macroeconomics first. As in recent editions, the text is divided into core chapters and a concluding special topics section. The 28 core chapters cover all of the material taught in most principles courses, and they are presented in the usual manner. Examples and data from the real world are used to reinforce the analysis. In addition, "Beyond the Basics" includes 12 relatively short special topic applications on high-profile topics such as Social Security, the Crisis of 2008, the budget deficits and growth of government debt, and the economics of health care. Also included in this section are applications that address questions such as, "Is discrimination responsible for the earnings differences between men and women?" and "Are we running out of resources?" These features are sure to grab the interest of students and are short enough for coverage during a single class period. Our own teaching experience indicates that these applications will enrich an economics course. They will also make it easier for instructors to "pick and choose" and thereby tailor the text readings to fit their own preferences and objectives.

Instructors integrating public choice throughout their course will probably want to cover Chapters 5 and 6 before moving to the core micro or macro material. Others teaching a microeconomics course will want to jump from Chapter 4 directly to the core micro chapters. Correspondingly, some macroeconomics instructors will want to move directly from Chapter 3 or 4 to the core macro material. The chapters have been written so there will be no problem with any of these options.

Substantial changes in both conditions and policies have occurred in recent years. This text fully reflects these changes. Macroeconomic issues have been front-page news during the past several years, and the debate on the impact of fiscal and monetary policy, growth of government debt, and what can be done to speed recovery from recession continues. Economists are not of one mind with regard to fiscal policy, and the core macroeconomic chapters reflect these views. Chapter 11 presents the Keynesian view of fiscal policy and considers its historical development and evolutionary change during recent decades. Chapter 12 presents alternative perspectives that highlight the importance of incentives and secondary effects. Chapter 12 also addresses the "great debates" about the effectiveness of fiscal stimulus and the potential dangers accompanying the growth of government debt. Taken together, these two fiscal policy chapters bring today's news alive and provide a balanced comprehensive analysis of the modern debate about the potential and limitations of fiscal policy.

Chapter 13 on money and banking reflects both the recent changes in how the Federal Reserve controls the money supply and the response of the Fed to the financial crisis and severe recession of 2008–2009. Chapter 14 analyzes the impact of monetary policy and its potential and limitations as a stabilization tool. Chapter 15 on stabilization policy highlights both points of agreement and areas of continuing debate regarding the impact of macroeconomic policy. The last two chapters of the core macro focus on economic growth. They highlight the importance of trade, entrepreneurship and innovation, and investment as sources of growth. Building on the work of Douglass North, Joseph Schumpeter, William Baumol, and Daron Acemoglu, these chapters focus on the institutional foundations of growth and prosperity.

The "Beyond the Basics" special topics will help you make economics come alive for your students. Special Topic 4, "Great Debates in Economics: Keynes versus Hayek," developed around the highly popular video raps on the Keynes–Hayek debates, highlights the alternative views of economists on major issues and illustrates that the study of economics can be fun. Special Topic 5 focuses on the policies and choices underlying the financial crisis of 2008. Special Topic 6 on the Great Depression analyzes the economics of this catastrophic era in a manner that is seldom presented in American history classes. Special Topic 8, "The Economics of Health Care," outlines the major provisions of 2010's Affordable Care Act and considers their expected economic effects. This package of special topic features provides instructors with powerful materials that will enliven their classes.

If you have not integrated the special topic materials into your course, please consider doing so. They will help your students better understand the political economy debates that dominate the daily news of our world.

Take this in consideration. With MindTap it now easier than ever to incorporate the Special Topics in the Course. Special Topics appear not only in the Textbook and e-reader, but they are also shown at the chapter level on MindTap and tied with the most relevant chapter. Activities from the Special Topics can be assigned and graded.

As in the past edition, we worked hard to reduce the length of the text. Several addendums included in past editions have been deleted, but they have been updated in the format of this edition and are available on the open access student Web site. These include the following: "Understanding Graphs" (addendum to Chapter 1); "Incentives and Economic Organization: Who Produces, Who Pays, and Why It Matters" (addendum to Chapter 6); "The Keynesian Aggregate Expenditure Model" (addendum to Chapter 11); and "Consumer Choice and Indifference Curves" (addendum to Chapter 20). These materials are freely available to students on the open access Web site for the text. Thus, instructors can freely assign them if they would like to do so.

The text is accompanied by a robust set of online learning tools designed to support your classroom work. Aplia and MindTap include real-time, interactive tutorials, online experiments, Graphing at a Glance, ConceptClips, Audio Cases with assessments, automatically graded quizzes, and automatically graded problem sets. Likewise, the book's dynamic PowerPoint presentation—considered by many to be the best in the principles market—has been further enhanced with multimedia to facilitate your teaching.

ADDITIONAL TEXT FEATURES

Economics: Private and Public Choice retains several features that make the presentation of economics both more interesting and understandable.

- Keys to Economic Prosperity. Students often fail to appreciate the organizational and institutional factors that are the foundation for economic progress. To help remedy this situation, we have incorporated a "Keys to Economic Prosperity" feature that highlights the importance of factors like gains from trade, secure property rights, competition, and free trade as sources of economic prosperity. In all, 12 key factors that underlie modern economic prosperity are highlighted at appropriate places throughout the text and are also listed inside of the front cover.

- Applications in Economics. "Applications in Economics" boxes apply economic theory to real-world issues and controversies. These features illustrate the importance and power of the principles covered in the text.

- Measures of Economic Activity. The "Measures of Economic Activity" boxes explain how important economic indicators such as the unemployment rate and the index of leading indicators are assembled and what they mean.
- Outstanding Economists. Boxes throughout the text highlight the lives of major economists and focus on how their work has contributed to the development of economics.
- Myths of Economics. These boxed articles dispel commonly held fallacies of economic reasoning. Because they are tomorrow's leaders, we believe that all students should be aware of common economic misperceptions that tend to hamper a nation's economic progress.
- Chapter Focus Questions and Closing Key Point Summaries. Each chapter begins with four or five questions that summarize the focus of the chapter. At the end of each chapter, the Key Points section provides the student with a concise statement of the material covered in the chapter (the chapter learning objectives). These two features help students better integrate the material into the broader economic picture.
- Critical Analysis Questions. Each chapter concludes with a set of discussion questions and problems designed to test the student's ability to analyze economic issues and to apply economic theory to real-world events. Appendix B at the end of the text contains suggested answers for approximately half of these questions.
- Graphing at a Glance. New Graphing at a Glance video tutorials enhance the learning experience by bringing graphs to life, allowing students to see graphs physically move along the axes.
- ConceptClips. New ConceptClips in the interactive eReader address the challenge of understanding economics terminology that students face when first introduced to the subject matter.

SUPPLEMENTARY MATERIALS

FOR THE STUDENT

MindTap MindTap is a fully online, highly personalized learning experience built on Cengage Learning content that combines student learning tools—readings, multimedia, activities, and assessments—into a singular Learning Path that guides students through their course.

Product Support Web Site (www.cengagebrain.com) Valuable resources can be found on the text's Internet support site. Students will find an interactive study center as well as online practice quizzes.

Economic News Videos News video segments from the BBC deliver the "real world" right to students' desktops, giving students a context for how economic topics affect world and national events as well as their own daily lives and helping them learn material by applying it to current events.

FOR THE INSTRUCTOR

We feel sure that many of the features incorporated with this textbook will help you become a better teacher and make your classes more interesting to students. Personally, we have incorporated the Keys to Economic Prosperity series, economics video clips, homework assignments, and online quiz questions into our own classes with great success. The full set of supplements that can accompany the book include the following.

Aplia Aplia™ is an online interactive learning solution that improves comprehension and outcomes by increasing student effort and engagement. Founded by a professor to enhance his own courses, Aplia provides automatically graded assignments that were written to make the most of the Web medium and contain detailed, immediate explanations on every question. Aplia is available in more than 15 disciplines and has been used by more than 2 million students at more than 1800 institutions. Visit www.aplia.com/economics/ for more details.

MindTap MindTap is a fully online, highly personalized learning experience built on Cengage Learning content that combines student learning tools—readings, multimedia, activities, and assessments—into a singular Learning Path that guides students through their course. Instructors personalize the experience by customizing authoritative Cengage Learning content and learning tools, including the ability to add their own content in the Learning Path via apps that integrate into the MindTap framework seamlessly with Learning Management Systems.

Write Experience This technology product allows you to assess written communication skills without adding to your workload. Instructors in all areas have told us it's important that students can write effectively in order to communicate and think critically. Through an exclusive partnership with a technology company, Cengage Learning's. Write Experience allows you to do just that! This new product utilizes artificial intelligence to not only score student writing instantly and accurately but also provide students with detailed revision goals and feedback on their writing to help them improve. Write Experience is the first product designed and created specifically for the higher education market through an exclusive agreement with McCann Associates, and powered by e-Write IntelliMetric Within™. IntelliMetric is the gold standard for automated scoring of writing and is used to score the Graduate Management Admissions Test® (GMAT®) analytical writing assessment. Better Writing. Better Outcomes. Write Experience. Visit http://www.cengage.com/writeexperience to learn more.

Economics CourseMate: Engaging, Trackable, Affordable Economics CourseMate brings course concepts to life with interactive learning, study, and exam preparation tools that support the printed textbook. Watch student comprehension soar as your class works with the printed textbook and the text-specific Web site, Economics Course-Mate goes beyond the book to deliver what you need!

Engagement Tracker How do you know your students have read the material or viewed the resources you've assigned? How can you tell if your students are struggling with a concept? Engagement Tracker assesses student preparation and engagement. Use the tracking tools to see progress for the class as a whole or for individual students. Identify students at risk early in the course. Uncover which concepts are most difficult for your class. Monitor time on task. Keep your students engaged.

Interactive Teaching and Learning Tools Economics CourseMate includes interactive teaching and learning tools:

- Quizzes
- Flashcards
- Videos
- Graphing tutorials

Interactive eBook In addition to interactive teaching and learning tools, Economic CourseMate includes an interactive eBook. Students can take notes, highlight, search and interact with embedded media specific to their book. Use it as a supplement to the printed text, or as a substitute—the choice is up to your students with CourseMate. Go to login.cengage.com to access these resources within CourseMate.

WebTutor™ ToolBox for WebCT, Blackboard, and eCollege WebTutor will allow you to jumpstart your course whether you want to simply Web enable your class or put an entire course online. Using a WebTutor cartridge, it's easy to add, edit, reorganize, or delete content customized for Economics: Private and Public Choice. The content includes media assets, quizzing, Web links, discussion topics, interactive games and exercises, and more. To find out more about WebTutor, contact your local Cengage Learning representative. (Other platform choices are available on request.)

Test Banks The test banks for the 15th edition were prepared by the author team with the assistance of Joe Calhoun. The authors have worked hard to update and improve the test banks for this edition. The three test banks contain approximately 7,000 questions—multiple-choice and short answer. Within each chapter, the questions correspond to the major subheadings of the text. The first 10 questions of each chapter are suitable for use as a comprehensive quiz covering the material of the chapter. Instructors who would like to motivate their students to study will find online practice quizzes on MindTap that can easily be incorporated into their quizzes and exams.

Could-based Test Banks (Cognero) The could-based test banks for this edition have been enhanced significantly. Cognero contains all of the questions in the test bank so you create and customize tests in minutes. You can easily edit and import your own questions and graphics and edit and maneuver existing questions.

PowerPoint We believe our PowerPoint presentation, prepared by Charles Skipton of the University of Tampa, is the best you will find in the principles market. The presentation includes chapter-by-chapter lecture notes with fully animated, hyperlinked slides of the textbook's exhibits. Its dynamic graphs and accompanying captions make it easy for instructors to present (and students to follow) sequential changes. The graphs are also used to highlight various relationships among economic variables. To facilitate classroom discussion and interaction, questions are strategically interspersed throughout the PowerPoint slides to help students develop the economic way of thinking. Instructions explaining how professors can easily add, delete, and modify slides in order to tailor make the presentation to their liking are included. If instructors want to make the PowerPoint presentation available to students, they can place it on their Web site (or the site for their course).

Instructor's Manual The *Instructor's Manual* was prepared by co-author David Macpherson. It contains special sections for Advanced Placement instructors prepared by James Chasey and Francis McMann, two of the nation's leading AP instructors. Information on how to use and modify the PowerPoint material is contained in the front of the instructor's manual. The manual is divided by chapters, and each chapter is divided into three parts. The first part consists of a detailed chapter outline in lecture-note form. It is designed to help instructors organize their notes to match the 15th edition of the book. Instructors can easily prepare detailed, personalized notes by revising the downloadable lecture notes on the book companion website accessed through www.cengage.com. The second part of each chapter contains teaching tips, sources of supplementary materials, and other helpful information. Part 3 of each chapter consists of in-class economic games and experiments. Contributed in part by Professor Charles Stull of Kalamazoo College, the games are highly popular with many instructors. We hope you will try them.

The book companion website contains the key supplements designed to aid instructors, including the content from the instructor's manual, test banks, and PowerPoint lecture and exhibit slides for overhead use.

Support Web Site for Instructors (www.cengage.com) This password-protected Web site includes instructor's manuals and test banks, and the PowerPoint lecture and exhibit slides. To access the site to download these supplements, register online at www.cengage.com.

A NOTE TO INSTRUCTORS

As we try to improve the book from one edition to the next, we rely heavily on our experiences as teachers. But our experience using the book is minuscule compared with that of the hundreds of instructors who use it nationwide. If you encounter problems or have suggestions for improving the book, we urge you to let us know by writing to us in care of Cengage Learning, 5191 Natorp Blvd., Mason, OH 45040.

A NOTE TO THE STUDENTS

This textbook contains several features we think will help you maximize (a good economic term) the returns of your study efforts. Here are some of the things that will help you and a few tips for making the most of them.

- Each chapter begins with a series of focus questions that communicate the central issues of the chapter. Before you read the chapter, briefly think about the focus questions, why they are important, and how they relate to the material in prior chapters.

- The textbook is organized in the form of an outline. The headings within the text (in red) are the major points of the outline. Minor headings are subpoints under the major headings. In addition, important subpoints within sections are often set off and numbered. *Bold italicized* type is used to highlight material that is particularly important. Sometimes "thumbnail sketches" are included to recap material and help the reader keep the important points mentally organized. Careful use of the headings, highlighted material, and the thumbnail sketches will help you master the material.

- A "Key Points" summary appears at the end of each chapter. Use the summary as a checklist to determine whether you understand the major points of the chapter.

- A review of the exhibits and illustrative pictures will also provide you with a summary of the key points of each chapter. The accompanying captions briefly describe the economic phenomena illustrated by the exhibits.

- The key terms introduced in each chapter are defined in the margins. As you study the chapter, go over the marginal definition of each key term as it is introduced. Later, you may also find it useful to review the marginal definitions. If you have forgotten the meaning of a term introduced earlier, consult the glossary at the end of the book.

- The boxed features go into more depth on various topics without disrupting the flow of the text. In general, the topics of the boxed features have been chosen because they are a good application of the theory described in the book or because students tend to be interested in them. The boxed features will supplement the text and enhance your understanding of important economic concepts.

- The critical analysis questions at the end of each chapter are intended to test your understanding of the economic way of thinking. Solving these questions and problems will greatly enhance your knowledge of the material. Answers to approximately half of these questions are provided in Appendix B.

If you need more practice, be sure to ask your professor about Aplia and MindTap.

ACKNOWLEDGMENTS

A project of this type is a team effort. Through the years, numerous people have assisted us in various ways. We are also very much indebted to the excellent team of professionals at Cengage Learning, including Steve Scoble, senior product manager, for his help and support of our efforts; Daniel Noguera, content developer, for his commitment to the development of the project and keeping it on schedule; Jana Lewis, content project manager, for orchestrating the copyediting, proofreading, and indexing; John Hill, rights editor, who helped us locate and obtain permissions for the many photos; and John Carey, marketing manager, who worked hard to inform the marketplace about the advantages of the book.

As with previous editions, the contributions of Amy Gwartney were invaluable. She edited several chapters prior to their submission to the publisher and proofed the text material. Daniel Bennett, Joab Corey, Joe Connors, Joe Calhoun, and Tawni Ferrarini provided us with valuable suggestions for improvement of the text and assistance with supplementary materials. Robert Lawson of Southern Methodist University assisted us with the preparation of several exhibits. The text still bears an imprint of the contributions of Woody Studenmund of Occidental College and Gary Galles of Pepperdine University, who assisted us in numerous ways with past editions.

We have often revised material in light of suggestions made by reviewers, users, friends, and even a few competitors. In this regard, we would like to express our appreciation to the following people for their reviews and helpful suggestions for recent editions:

Barbara Moore, University of Central Florida; Thomas McCaleb, Florida State University; Seth Gershenson, Michigan State University: Gerry Simons, Grand Valley State University; Aaron Lowen, Grand Valley State University; Pete Calcagno, College of Charleston; Joseph Calhoun, Florida State University; Cathy Carey, Bowling Green University; Lee Coppock, University of Virginia; Tawni Ferrerini, Northern Michigan University; Burton Folsom, Hillsdale College; Robert Higgs, Independent Institute; Randall Holcombe, Florida State University; and Ivan Pongracic, Hillsdale College.

We have often revised material in light of suggestions made by reviewers, users, friends, and even a few competitors. In this regard, we would like to express our appreciation to the following people for their reviews and helpful suggestions for recent editions:

Steve Abid, Grand Rapids Community College; Douglas Agbetsiafa, Indiana University, South Bend; James C. W. Ahiakpor, California State University, Hayward; Ali T. Akarca, University of Illinois at Chicago; Ryan C. Amacher, University of Texas at Arlington; Stephen A. Baker, Capital University; Bharati Basu, Central Michigan University; Don Bellante, University of South Florida; Alana Bhatia, University of Colorado at Boulder; Charles A. Booth, University of Alabama at Birmingham; Donald Boudreaux, George Mason University; George Bowling, St. Charles Community College; Robert Brittingham, Christian Brothers University; Byron Brown, Michigan State University; Ford J. Brown, University of Minnesota—Morris; Dennis Brennen, Harper College; James Bryan, Manhattanville College; Darcy R. Carr, Coastal Carolina University; Kathy Clark, Edison College; Jim Cobbe, Florida State University; Mike Cohick, Collin County Community College; David S. Collins, Virginia Highlands Community College; Jim F. Couch, University of North Alabama; Steven R. Cunningham, University of Connecticut; Dusan Curcic, University of Virginia; George W. Dollar, Clearwater Christian College; Jeff Edwards, Collin County Community College; Ann Eike, University of Kentucky; Christina Esquivel, Navarro College; Robert C. Eyler, Sonoma State University; James R. Fain, Oklahoma State University; Kathryn Finn, Western Washington University; Andrew W. Foshee, McNeese State University; Mark Funk, University of Arkansas; Gary Galles, Pepperdine University; Marsha Goldfarb, University of Maryland Baltimore County; Richard

Gosselin, Houston Community College; Darrin Gulla, University of Kentucky; David Harris, Northwood University; Barry Haworth, University of Louisville; Ronald Helgens, Golden Gate University; Robert E. Herman, Nassau Community College/SUNY; William D. Hermann, Golden Gate University, San Francisco; Rey Hernandez, Metropolitan State College of Denver; Brad Hobbs, Florida Gulf Coast University; Randall Holcombe, Florida State University; Jim Hubert, Seattle Central Community College; Katherine Huger, Charleston Southern University; Woodrow W. Hughes, Jr., Converse College; Jeffrey Rogers Hummel, San Jose State University; Tom Jeitschko, Michigan State University, East Lansing; Rob H. Kamery, Christian Brothers University; Derek Kellenberg, University of Montana; Robert Kling, Colorado State University; Frederic R. Kolb, University of Wisconsin, Eau Claire; Barbara Kouskoulas, Lawrence Technological University; David W. Kreutzer, James Madison University; Cory Krupp, Duke University; Jean Kujawa, Lourdes College; George Kuljurgis, Oakland University; Randy W. LaHote, Washtenaw Community College; TsungHui Lai, Liberty University; John Larrivee, Mount St. Mary's University; Robert Lawson, Southern Methodist University; Don R. Leet, California State University, Fresno; George P. Lephardt, Milwaukee School of Engineering; Joe LeVesque, Northwood University; Andrew Light, Liberty University; Stephen Lile, Western Kentucky University; Felix Ling (formerly San Jose State University); Edward J. López, San Jose State University; Dale Matcheck, Northwood University; G. Dirk Mateer, Penn State University; John McArthur, Wofford College; Ed Mills, Kendell College; David M. Mitchell, Oklahoma State University; Hadley Mitchell, Taylor University; Glen A. Moots, Northwood University; Debasri Mukherjee, Western Michigan University; Todd Myers, Grossmont College; John R. Neal, Lake Sumter Community College; Jennifer Offenberg, Loyola Marymount University; Lloyd Orr, Indiana University, Bloomington; Judd W. Patton, Bellevue College; James Payne, Florida State University; Robert Pennington, UCF–Orlando; Claudiney Pereira, Tulane University; Jennifer Platania, Elon University; Robert Reinke, University of South Dakota; Robert C. Rencher, Jr., Liberty University; Dan Rickman, Oklahoma State University; Karin L. Russell, Keiser College; Allen Sanderson, University of Chicago; Lewis F. Schlossinger, Community College of Aurora; Thomas W. Secrest, USC Coastal Carolina; Tim Shaugnessey, Louisiana State University–Shreveport; Ben S. Shippen, Jr., Mercer University; Gerald Simons, Grand Valley State University; Charles D. Skipton, University of Tampa; John Solow, University of Iowa; Ken Somppi, Southern Union State Community College; John Sophocleus, Auburn; William A. Steiden, Jefferson Community College; Edward Stringham, San Jose State University; Marcia Snyder, College of Charleston; David Switzer, St. Cloud State University; Richard D.C. Trainer, Warsaw School of Economics; Bich Tran, San Jacinto College; Scott Ward, East Texas Baptist University; Tom Lee Waterston, Northwood University; Christopher Westley, Jacksonville State University; David Wharton, Washington College; Jim Wharton, Northwood University; Mark Wheeler, Western Michigan University; Janice Yee, Wartburg College; Edward Wolpert, University of Central Florida; and Anthony Zambelli, Cuyamaca College.

ABOUT THE AUTHORS

James A. Gwartney holds the Gus A. Stavros Eminent Scholar Chair at Florida State University, where he directs the Stavros Center for the Advancement of Free Enterprise and Economic Education. His writings have been widely published in both professional journals and popular media. He is the co-author of *Common Sense Economics: What Everyone Should Know about Wealth and Prosperity* (St. Martin's Press, 2010), a primer on economics and personal finance.

Gwartney's current research focuses on the measurement and determination of factors that influence cross-country differences in income levels and growth rates. In this regard he is the co-author (with Robert Lawson and Joshua Hall) of the annual report, *Economic Freedom of the World,* which provides information on the institutions and policies of 152 countries. This data set, published by a worldwide network of institutes in 79 countries, is widely used by scholars investigating topics ranging from economic growth to peaceful relations among nations.

He served as Chief Economist of the Joint Economic Committee of the U.S. Congress during 1999–2000. Gwartney was invited by the incoming Putin Administration in March 2000 to make presentations and have discussions with leading Russian economists concerning the future of the Russian economy. In 2004 he was the recipient of the Adam Smith Award of the Association of Private Enterprise Education for his contribution to the advancement of free market ideals. He is a past President of the Southern Economic Association and the Association for Private Enterprise Education. Gwartney earned his Ph.D. in economics from the University of Washington.

Richard L. Stroup is Professor of Economics Emeritus at Montana State University, as well as a Senior Fellow at the Property and Environment Research Center (PERC) and a Visiting Professor in Economics at North Carolina State University. For the three years before his retirement from Montana State University, he served as head of its Department of Agricultural Economics & Economics. Professor Stroup, who has a PhD in economics from the University of Washington, was one of the originators of the New Resource Economics, the academic approach popularly known as free market environmentalism. He also served as director of the Office of Policy Analysis in the U.S. Department of the Interior and has been published widely in professional journals and popular publications. He is author or contributing editor of numerous books on the economics of resources and the environment and the author of *Economics: What Everyone Should Know about Economics and the Environment* (Cato Institute). Most recently, he co-authored *Common Sense Economics: What Everyone Should Know about Wealth and Prosperity* (St. Martin's Press, 2010) with James Gwartney and Dwight Lee. Stroup has lectured throughout the United States and abroad to professional and general audiences. He also is an adjunct scholar with the Cato Institute.

Russell S. Sobel earned his PhD in economics from Florida State University in 1994. He has published over 150 books and articles, and has received national recognition for his works on Entrepreneurship and FEMA reform. He serves on the editorial board for three academic journals, and on the advisory board for four university centers. He has won numerous awards for both his teaching and his research. He regularly teaches courses in both principles of economics and public economics, and gives lectures at economic education outreach programs. He is a Visiting Scholar in Entrepreneurship in the School of Business at The Citadel.

David A. Macpherson is the E.M. Stevens Distinguished Professor of Economics at Trinity University. Previously, he was Director of the Pepper Institute on Aging and Public Policy and the Rod and Hope Brim Eminent Scholar of Economics at Florida State University, where he has received two university-wide awards for teaching excellence. Professor Macpherson is the author of many articles in leading labor economics and industrial relations journals, including the *Journal of Labor Economics*, *Journal of Human Resources*, and *Industrial and Labor Relations Review*. He is also co-author of *Contemporary Labor Economics*, 10th, as well as the annual *Union Membership and Earnings Data Book: Compilations from the Current Population Survey*. His specialty is applied labor economics. His current research interests include pensions, discrimination, labor unions, and the minimum wage. Macpherson received his undergraduate degree and PhD from Pennsylvania State University.

PART 1

The Economic Way of Thinking

Life is a series of choices

Economics is about how people choose. The choices we make influence our lives and those of others. Your future will be influenced by the choices you make with regard to education, job opportunities, savings, and investment. Furthermore, changes in technology, demographics, communications, and transportation are constantly altering the attractiveness of various options and the opportunities available to us. The economic way of thinking is all about how incentives alter the choices people make. It can help you make better choices and enhance your understanding of our dynamic world.

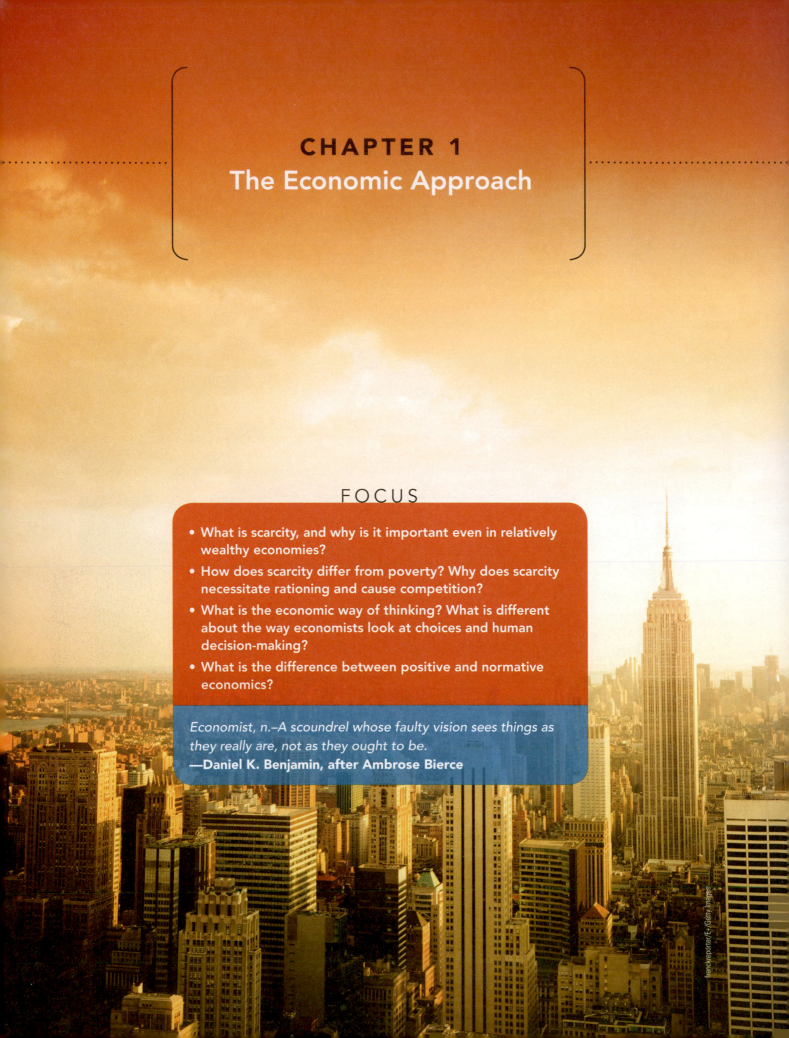

CHAPTER 1
The Economic Approach

FOCUS

- What is scarcity, and why is it important even in relatively wealthy economies?

- How does scarcity differ from poverty? Why does scarcity necessitate rationing and cause competition?

- What is the economic way of thinking? What is different about the way economists look at choices and human decision-making?

- What is the difference between positive and normative economics?

Economist, n.–A scoundrel whose faulty vision sees things as they really are, not as they ought to be.
—Daniel K. Benjamin, after Ambrose Bierce

Welcome to the world of economics. In recent years, economics has often been front-page news, and it affects all of our lives. The housing market's boom and bust, the recession and financial troubles of 2008–2009, the weak recovery and continuation of high unemployment rates, the soaring costs of a college education, and poor job opportunities even for college graduates—all of these have been in the news and have turned the lives of many Americans upside down. Economics will enhance your understanding of all of these topics and many more. You will soon see that economics is about much more than just financial markets and economic policy. In fact, a field trip to the fruits and vegetables section at your local grocery store could well be filled with more economics lessons than a trip to the New York Stock Exchange.

In a nutshell, economics is the study of human behavior, with a particular focus on human decision-making. It will introduce you to a new and powerful way of thinking that will both help you make better decisions and enhance your understanding of how the world works.

You may have heard some of the following statements: The federal government's debt has soared to historic highs, and trouble lies ahead if we do not get it under control. More government spending is necessary in order to speed up economic recovery. Americans would be better off if we did not buy so many things from foreigners. A higher minimum wage will help the poor. Government action is needed to ensure that health care is affordable and available to all. Are these statements true? This course will provide you with knowledge that will enhance your understanding of issues like these and numerous others. It may even alter the way you think about them.

The origins of economics date back to Adam Smith, a Scottish moral philosopher, who expressed the first economic ideas in his breakthrough book, *An Inquiry into the Nature and Causes of the Wealth of Nations,* published in 1776. As the title of his book suggests, Smith sought to explain why people in some nations were wealthier than those in others. This very question is still a central issue in economics. It is so important that throughout this book we will use a special "Keys to Economic Prosperity" symbol in the margin to highlight sections that focus on this topic. A listing of the major keys to prosperity is presented inside the front cover of the book. These keys and accompanying discussions will help you understand what factors enable economies, and their citizens, to grow wealthier and prosper.

OUTSTANDING ECONOMIST

THE IMPORTANCE OF ADAM SMITH, THE FATHER OF ECONOMIC SCIENCE

Economics is a relatively young science. The foundation of economics was laid in 1776, when Adam Smith (1723–1790) published *An Inquiry into the Nature and Causes of the Wealth of Nations.*

Smith was a lecturer at the University of Glasgow, in his native Scotland. Before economics, morals and ethics were actually his concern. His first book was *The Theory of Moral Sentiments.* For Smith, self-interest and sympathy for others were complementary. However, he did not believe that charity alone would provide the essentials for a good life.

Smith stressed that free exchange and competitive markets would harness self-interest as a creative force. He believed that individuals *pursuing their own interests* would be directed by the "invisible hand" of market prices toward the production of those goods that were most advantageous to society. He argued that the wealth of a nation does not lie in gold and silver, but rather in the goods and services produced and consumed by people. According to Smith, competitive markets would lead to coordination, order, and efficiency without the direction of a central authority.

These were revolutionary ideas at the time, but they had consequences. Smith's ideas greatly influenced not only Europeans but also those who developed the political economy structure of the United States. Further, Smith's notion of the "invisible hand" of the market continues to enhance our understanding of why some nations prosper while others stagnate.[1]

[1]For an excellent biographical sketch of Adam Smith, see David Henderson, ed., *The Fortune Encyclopedia of Economics* (New York: Warner Books, 1993), 836–38. The entire text of this useful encyclopedia is now available online, free of charge, at http://www.econlib.org.

1-1 WHAT IS ECONOMICS ABOUT?

Economics is about scarcity and the choices we have to make because our desire for goods and services is far greater than their availability from nature. Would you like some new clothes, a nicer car, and a larger apartment? How about better grades and more time to watch television, go skiing, and travel? Do you dream of driving your brand-new Porsche into the driveway of your oceanfront house? As individuals, we have a desire for goods that is virtually unlimited. We may want all of these things. Unfortunately, both as individuals and as a society we face a constraint called **scarcity** that prevents us from being able to completely fulfill our desires.

Scarcity is present whenever there is less of a good or resource freely available from nature than people would like. There are some things that are not scarce—seawater comes to mind; nature has provided as much of it as people want. But almost everything else you can think of—even your time—is scarce. In economics, the word *scarce* has a very specific meaning that differs slightly from the way it is commonly used. Even if large amounts of a good have been produced, it is still scarce as long as there is not as much of it *freely available from nature* as we would all like. For example, even though goods like apples and automobiles are relatively abundant in the United States, they are still scarce because we would like to have more of them than nature has freely provided. In economics, we generally wish to determine only if a good is scarce or not, and refrain from using the term to refer to the relative availability or abundance of a good or resource.

Because of scarcity, we have to make choices. Should I spend the next hour studying or watching TV? Should I spend my last $20 on iTunes downloads or on a shirt? Should this factory be used to produce clothing or furniture? **Choice**, the act of selecting among alternatives, is the logical consequence of scarcity. When we make choices, we constantly face trade-offs between meeting one desire or another. To meet one need, we must let another go unmet. The basic ideas of *scarcity* and *choice*, along with the *trade-offs* we face, provide the foundation for economic analysis.

Resources are the ingredients, or inputs, that people use to produce goods and services. Our ability to produce goods and services is limited precisely because of the limited nature of our resources.

Exhibit 1 lists a number of scarce goods and the limited resources that might be used to produce them. There are three general categories of resources. First, there are *human resources*—the productive knowledge, skill, and strength of human beings. Second, there are *physical resources*—things like tools, machines, and buildings that enhance our ability to produce goods. Economists often use the term **capital** when referring to these human-made resources. Third, there are *natural resources*—things like land, mineral deposits,

Scarcity
Fundamental concept of economics that indicates that there is less of a good freely available from nature than people would like.

Choice
The act of selecting among alternatives.

Resource
An input used to produce economic goods. Land, labor, skills, natural resources, and human-made tools and equipment provide examples. Throughout history, people have struggled to transform available, but limited, resources into things they would like to have—economic goods.

Capital
Human-made resources (such as tools, equipment, and structures) used to produce other goods and services. They enhance our ability to produce in the future.

EXHIBIT 1

A General Listing of Scarce Goods and Limited Resources

History is a record of our struggle to transform available, but limited, resources into goods that we would like to have.

SCARCE GOODS	LIMITED RESOURCES
Food (bread, milk, meat, eggs, vegetables, coffee, etc.)	Land (various degrees of fertility)
Clothing (shirts, pants, blouses, shoes, socks, coats, sweaters, etc.)	Natural resources (rivers, trees, minerals, oceans, etc.)
Household goods (tables, chairs, rugs, beds, dressers, television sets, etc.)	Machines and other human-made physical resources
Education	Nonhuman animal resources
National defense	Technology (physical and scientific "recipes" of history)
Leisure time	Human resources (the knowledge, skill, and talent of individual human beings)
Entertainment	
Clean air	
Pleasant environment (trees, lakes, rivers, open spaces, etc.)	
Pleasant working conditions	

oceans, and rivers. The ingenuity of humans is often required to make these natural resources useful in production. For example, until recently, the yew tree was considered a "trash tree," having no economic value. Then, scientists discovered that the tree produces taxol, a substance that could be used to fight cancer. Human knowledge and ingenuity made yew trees a valuable resource. As you can see, natural resources are important, but knowing how to use them productively is just as important.

As economist Thomas Sowell points out, cavemen had the same natural resources at their disposal that we do today. The huge difference between their standard of living and ours reflects the difference in the knowledge they could bring to bear on those resources versus what we can.[1] Over time, human ingenuity, discovery, improved knowledge, and better technology have enabled us to produce more goods and services from the available resources. Nonetheless, our desire for goods and services is still far greater than our ability to produce them. Thus, scarcity is a fact of life today, and in the foreseeable future. As a result, we confront trade-offs and have to make choices. This is what economics is about.

1-1a SCARCITY AND POVERTY ARE NOT THE SAME

Think for a moment about what life was like in 1750. People all over the world struggled 50, 60, and 70 hours a week to obtain the basic necessities of life—food, clothing, and shelter. Manual labor was the major source of income. Animals provided the means of transportation. Tools and machines were primitive by today's standards. As the English philosopher Thomas Hobbes stated in the seventeenth century, life was "solitary, poor, nasty, brutish, and short." [2]

Throughout much of South America, Africa, and Asia, economic conditions today continue to make life difficult. In North America, Western Europe, Oceania, and some parts of Asia, however, economic progress has substantially reduced physical hardship and human drudgery. In these regions, the typical family is more likely to worry about financing its summer vacation than about obtaining food and shelter. As anyone who has watched the TV reality show *Survivor* knows, we take for granted many of the items that modern technological advances have allowed us to produce at unbelievably low prices. Contestants on *Survivor* struggle with even basic things like starting a fire, finding shelter, and catching fish. They are thrilled when they win ordinary items like shampoo, rice, and toilet paper.

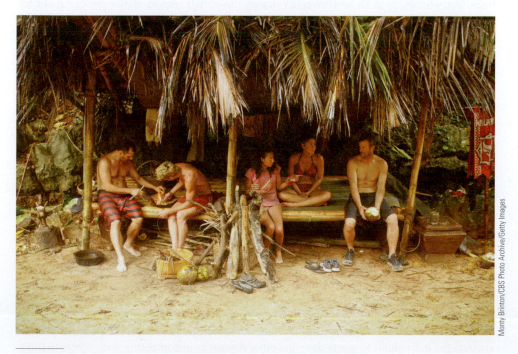

Monty Brinton/CBS Photo Archive/Getty Images

The degree to which modern technology and knowledge allow us to fulfill our desires and ease the grip of scarcity is often taken for granted—as the castaways on the CBS reality series Survivor quickly find out when they have to struggle to meet even basic needs, such as food, shelter, and cleaning their bodies and clothes.

[1]Thomas Sowell, *Knowledge and Decisions* (New York: Basic Books, 1980), 47.
[2]Thomas Hobbes, *Leviathan* (1651), Part I, Chapter 13.

During one episode, a contestant eagerly paid over $125 for a small chocolate bar and spoonful of peanut butter at an auction—and she considered it a great bargain!

It is important to note that scarcity and poverty are not the same thing. Scarcity is an **objective** concept that describes a factual situation in which the limited nature of our resources keeps us from being able to completely fulfill our desires for goods and services. In contrast, poverty is a **subjective** concept that refers to a personal opinion of whether someone meets an arbitrarily defined level of income. This distinction is made even clearer when you realize that different people have vastly different ideas of what it means to be poor. The average family in the United States that meets the federal government's definition of being "in poverty" would be considered wealthy in most any country in Africa. A family in the United States in the 1950s would have been considered fairly wealthy if it had air conditioning, an automatic dishwasher or clothes dryer, or a television set. Today, the majority of U.S. families officially classified as poor have many items that would have been viewed as symbols of great wealth just 65 years ago.

People always want more and better goods for themselves and others about whom they care. Scarcity is the constraint that prevents us from having as much of *all* goods as we would like, but it is not the same as poverty. Even if every individual were rich, scarcity would still be present.

1-1b SCARCITY NECESSITATES RATIONING

Scarcity makes **rationing** a necessity. When a good or resource is scarce, some criterion must be used to determine who will receive it and who will go without. The choice of which method is used will, however, have an influence on human behavior. When rationing is done through the government sector, a person's political status and ability to manipulate the political process are the key factors. Powerful interest groups and those in good favor with influential politicians will be the ones who obtain goods and resources. When this method of rationing is used, people will devote time and resources to lobbying and favor seeking with those who have political power, rather than to productive activities.

When the criterion is first-come, first-served, goods are allocated to those who are fastest at getting in line or willing to spend the longest time waiting in line. Many colleges use this method to ration tickets to sporting events, and the result is students waiting in long lines. Sometimes, as at Duke University during basketball season, they even camp out for multiple nights to get good tickets! Imagine how the behavior of students would change if tickets were instead given out to the students with the highest grade point average.

In a market economy, price is generally used to ration goods and resources only to those who are willing and able to pay the prevailing market price. Because only those goods that are scarce require rationing, in a market economy, one easy way to determine whether a good or resource is scarce is to ask if it sells for a price. If you have to pay for something, it is scarce.

1-1c THE METHOD OF RATIONING INFLUENCES THE NATURE OF COMPETITION

Competition is a natural outgrowth of scarcity and the desire of human beings to improve their conditions. Competition exists in every economy and every society. But the criteria used to ration scarce goods and resources will influence the competitive techniques employed. When the rationing criterion is price, individuals will engage in income-generating activities that enhance their ability to pay the price needed to buy the goods and services they want. Thus, one benefit of using price as a rationing mechanism is that it encourages individuals to engage in the production of goods and services to generate income. In contrast, rationing on the basis of first-come, first-served encourages individuals to waste a substantial amount of time waiting in line, while rationing through the political process encourages individuals to waste time and other resources in competing with others to influence the political process.

Objective
A fact based on observable phenomena that is not influenced by differences in personal opinion.

Subjective
An opinion based on personal preferences and value judgments.

Rationing
Allocating a limited supply of a good or resource among people who would like to have more of it. When price performs the rationing function, the good or resource is allocated to those willing to give up the most "other things" in order to get it.

Within a market setting, the competition that results from scarcity is an important ingredient in economic progress. Competition among business firms for customers results in newer, better, and less expensive goods and services. Competition between employers for workers results in higher wages, benefits, and better working conditions. Further, competition encourages discovery and innovation, two important sources of growth and higher living standards.

1-2 THE ECONOMIC WAY OF THINKING

One does not have to spend much time around economists to recognize that there is an "economic way of thinking." Admittedly, economists, like others, differ widely in their ideological views. A news commentator once remarked that "any half-dozen economists will normally come up with about six different policy prescriptions." Yet, in spite of their philosophical differences, the approaches of economists reflect common ground.

That common ground is **economic theory**, developed from basic principles of human behavior. Economic researchers are constantly involved in testing and seeking to verify their theories. When the evidence from the testing is consistent with a theory, eventually that theory will become widely accepted among economists. Economic theory, like a road map or a guidebook, establishes reference points indicating what to look for and how economic issues are interrelated. To a large degree, the basic economic principles are merely common sense. When applied consistently, however, these commonsense concepts can provide powerful and sometimes surprising insights.

1-2a EIGHT GUIDEPOSTS TO ECONOMIC THINKING

The economic way of thinking requires incorporating certain guidelines—some would say the building blocks of basic economic theory—into your own thought process. Once you incorporate these guidelines, economics can be a relatively easy subject to master. Students who have difficulty with economics have almost always failed to assimilate one or more of these principles. The following are eight principles that characterize the economic way of thinking. We will discuss each of these principles in more depth throughout the book so that you will be sure to understand how and when to apply them.

1. The use of scarce resources is costly, so decision-makers must make trade-offs. Economists sometimes refer to this as the "there is no such thing as a free lunch" principle. Because resources are scarce, the use of resources to produce one good diverts those resources from the production of other goods. A parcel of undeveloped land could be used for a new hospital or a parking lot, or it could simply be left undeveloped. No option is free of cost—there is always a trade-off. A decision to pursue any one of these options means that the decision-maker must sacrifice the others. The highest valued alternative that is sacrificed is the **opportunity cost** of the option chosen. For example, if you use one hour of your scarce time to study economics, you will have one hour less time to watch television, spend social networking, sleep, work at a job, or study other subjects. Whichever one of these options you would have chosen had you *not* spent the hour studying economics is your highest valued option forgone. If you would have slept, then the opportunity cost of this hour spent studying economics is a forgone hour of sleep. In economics, the opportunity cost of an action is the highest valued option given up when a choice is made.

It is important to recognize that the use of scarce resources to produce a good is always costly, regardless of who pays for the good or service produced. In many countries, various kinds of schooling are provided free of charge *to students*. However, provision of the

It [economics] is a method rather than a doctrine, an apparatus of the mind, a technique of thinking which helps its possessor to draw correct conclusions.

—*John Maynard Keynes*[3]

Economic theory
A set of definitions, postulates, and principles assembled in a manner that makes clear the "cause-and-effect" relationships.

Opportunity cost
The highest valued alternative that must be sacrificed as a result of choosing an option.

---

[3]John Maynard Keynes (1883–1946) was an English economist whose writings during the 1920s and 1930s exerted an enormous impact on both economic theory and policy. Keynes established the terminology and the economic framework that are still widely used when economists study problems of unemployment and inflation.

When a scarce resource is used to meet one need, other competing needs must be sacrificed. The forgone shoe store is an example of the opportunity cost of building the new drugstore.

schooling is not free *to the community as a whole*. The scarce resources used to produce the schooling—to construct the building, hire teachers, buy equipment, and so on—could have been used instead to produce more recreation, entertainment, housing, medical care, or other goods. The opportunity cost of the schooling is the highest valued option that must now be given up because the required resources were used to produce the schooling.

By now, the central point should be obvious. As we make choices, we always face trade-offs. Using resources to do one thing leaves fewer resources to do another.

Consider one final example. Mandatory air bags in automobiles save an estimated 400 lives each year. Economic thinking, however, forces us to ask ourselves if the $50 billion spent on air bags could have been used in a better way—perhaps say, for cancer research that could have saved *more* than 400 lives per year. Most people don't like to think of air bags and cancer research as an "either/or" proposition. It's more convenient to ignore these trade-offs. But if we want to get the most out of our resources, we have to consider all of our alternatives. In this case, the appropriate analysis is not simply the lives saved with air bags versus dollars spent on them, but also the number of lives that could have been saved (or other things that could have been accomplished) if the $50 billion had been used differently. A candid consideration of hard trade-offs like this is essential to using our resources wisely.

2. Individuals choose purposefully—they try to get the most from their limited resources. People try not to squander their valuable resources deliberately. Instead, they try to choose the options that best advance their personal desires and goals at the least possible cost. This is called **economizing behavior**. Economizing behavior is the result of purposeful, or rational, decision-making. When choosing among things of equal benefit, an economizer will select the cheapest option. For example, if a pizza, a lobster dinner, and a sirloin steak are expected to yield identical benefits for Mary (including the enjoyment of eating them), economizing behavior implies that Mary will select the cheapest of the three alternatives, probably the pizza. Similarly, when choosing among alternatives of equal cost, economizing decision-makers will select the option that yields the greatest benefit. If the prices of several dinner specials are equal, for example, economizers will choose the one they like the best. Because of economizing behavior, the desires or preferences of individuals are revealed by the choices they make.

Purposeful choosing implies that decision-makers have some basis for their evaluation of alternatives. Economists refer to this evaluation as **utility**—the benefit or satisfaction that an individual expects from the choice of a specific alternative. Utility is highly subjective, often differing widely from person to person. The steak dinner that delights one person may be repulsive to another (a vegetarian, for example).

The idea that people behave rationally to get the greatest benefit at the least possible cost is a powerful tool. It can help us understand their choices. However, we need to realize that a rational choice is not the same thing as a "right" choice. If we want to understand people's choices, we need to understand their own subjective evaluations of their options *as they see them*. As we have said, different people have different preferences. If Joan prefers $50 worth of chocolate to $50 worth of vegetables, buying the chocolate would be the rational choice for her, even though some outside observer might say that Joan is making a "bad" decision. Similarly, some motorcycle riders choose to ride without a helmet because

Economizing behavior
Choosing the option that offers the greatest benefit at the least possible cost.

Utility
The subjective benefit or satisfaction a person expects from a choice or course of action.

they believe the enjoyment they get from riding without one is greater than the cost (the risk of injury). When people weigh the benefits they receive from an activity against its cost, they are making a rational choice—even though it might not be the choice you or I would make in the same situation.

3. Incentives matter—changes in incentives influence human choices in a predictable way. Both monetary and nonmonetary incentives matter.

If the personal cost of an option increases, people will be less likely to choose it. Correspondingly, when an option becomes more attractive, people will be more likely to choose it. This vitally important guidepost, sometimes called the basic postulate of economics, is a powerful tool because it applies to almost everything that we do.

Think about the implications of this proposition. When late for an appointment, a person will be less likely to take time to stop and visit with a friend. Fewer people will go picnicking on a cold and rainy day. Higher prices will reduce the number of units sold. Attendance in college classes will be below normal the day before spring break. In each case, the explanation is the same: As the option becomes more costly, less is chosen.

Because consumers respond to incentives, store owners know they can sell off excess inventory by reducing prices.

Similarly, when the payoff derived from a choice increases, people will be more likely to choose it. A person will be more likely to bend over and pick up a quarter than a penny. Students will attend and pay more attention in class when the material is covered extensively on exams. Customers will buy more from stores that offer low prices, high-quality service, and a convenient location. Senior voters will be more likely to support candidates who favor higher Social Security benefits. All of these outcomes are highly predictable, and they merely reflect the "incentives matter" postulate of economics.

Noneconomists sometimes argue that people respond to incentives only because they are selfish and greedy. This view is false. People are motivated by a variety of goals, some humanitarian and some selfish, and incentives matter equally in both. Even an unselfish individual would be more likely to attempt to rescue a drowning child from a three-foot swimming pool than the rapid currents approaching Niagara Falls. Similarly, people are more likely to give a needy person their hand-me-downs rather than their favorite new clothes.

Just how far can we push the idea that incentives matter? If asked what would happen to the number of funerals performed in your town if the price of funerals rose, how would you respond? The "incentives matter" postulate predicts that the higher cost would reduce the number of funerals. While the same number of people will still die each year, the number of funerals performed will still fall as more people choose to be cremated or buried in cemeteries in other towns. Substitutes are everywhere—even for funerals. Individuals also respond to incentives when committing crimes—precisely the reason why people put signs in their yard saying "This house protected by XYZ security."

4. Individuals make decisions at the margin.

When making a choice between two alternatives, individuals generally focus on the *difference* in the costs and benefits between alternatives. Economists describe this process as **marginal** decision-making, or "thinking at the margin." The last time you went to eat fast food, you probably faced a decision that highlights this type of thinking. Will you get the $1.50 cheeseburger and the $1.00 medium drink, or instead get the $3.00 value meal that has the cheeseburger and drink and also comes with a medium order of fries? Naturally, individual decision-making focuses on the difference between the alternatives. The value meal costs 50 cents more (its marginal cost) but will give you one extra food item—the fries (its marginal benefit). Your marginal decision is whether it is worth the extra 50 cents to have the fries. If you pay attention, you'll notice yourself frequently thinking at the margin. Next time you find yourself asking a salesclerk, "How much *more* is this one?" when you are choosing between two items, you are doing a marginal analysis.

Marginal choices always involve the effects of net additions to or subtractions from current conditions. In fact, the word *additional* is often used as a substitute for *marginal*. For example, a business decision-maker might ask, "What is the additional (or marginal)

Marginal
Term used to describe the effects of a change in the current situation. For example, a producer's marginal cost is the cost of producing an additional unit of a product, given the producer's current facility and production rate.

cost of producing one more unit?" Marginal decisions may involve large or small changes. The "one more unit" could be a new factory or a new stapler. It is marginal because it involves additional costs and additional benefits. Given the current situation, what marginal benefits (additional sales revenues, for example) can be expected from the new factory, and what will be the marginal cost of constructing it? What is the marginal benefit versus marginal cost of purchasing a new stapler? The answers to these questions will determine whether building the new factory or buying the new stapler is a good decision.

It is important to distinguish between *average* and *marginal*. A manufacturer's average cost of producing automobiles (which would be the total cost of production divided by the total number of cars the manufacturer produces) may be $25,000, but the marginal cost of producing an additional automobile (or an additional 1,000 automobiles) might be much lower, say, $10,000 per car. Costs associated with research, testing, design, molds, heavy equipment, and similar factors of production must be incurred whether the manufacturer is going to produce 1,000 units, 10,000 units, or 100,000 units. Such costs will clearly contribute to the average cost of an automobile, but they will change very little as additional units are produced. Thus, the marginal cost of additional units may be substantially less than the average cost. Should production be expanded or reduced? That choice should be based on marginal costs, which indicate the *change* in total cost due to the decision.

People commonly ignore the implications of marginal thinking in their comments, but seldom in their actions. Thus, the concept is far better at explaining how people act than what they say. Students are often overheard telling other students that they shouldn't skip class because they have paid to enroll in it. Of course, the tuition is not a factor relevant at the margin—it will be the same whether or not the student attends class on that particular day. The only real marginal considerations are what the student will miss that day (a quiz, information for the exam, etc.) versus what he or she could do with the extra time by skipping class. This explains why even students who tell others they paid too much for the class to skip it will ignore the tuition costs when they themselves decide to skip class.

Decisions are made at the margin. That means that they almost always involve additions to, or subtractions from, current conditions. If we are going to get the most out of our resources, activities that generate more benefits than costs should be undertaken, while those that are more costly than they are worth should not be undertaken. This principle of sound decision-making applies to individuals, businesses, governments, and for society as a whole.

5. Although information can help us make better choices, its acquisition is costly.

Information that helps us make better choices is valuable. However, the time needed to gather it is scarce, making information costly to acquire. As a result, people economize on their search for information just like they do anything else. For example, when you purchase a pair of jeans, you might evaluate the quality and prices of jeans at several different stores. At some point, though, you will decide that additional comparison-shopping is simply not worth the trouble. You will make a choice based on the limited information you already have.

The process is similar when individuals search for a restaurant, a new car, or a roommate. They will seek to acquire some information, but at some point, they will decide that the expected benefit derived from gathering still more information is simply not worth the cost. When differences among the alternatives are important to decision-makers, they will spend more time and effort gathering information. People are much more likely to read a consumer ratings magazine before purchasing a new automobile than they are before purchasing a new can opener. Because information is costly for people to acquire, limited knowledge and uncertainty about the outcome generally characterize the decision-making process.

6. Beware of the secondary effects: economic actions often generate indirect as well as direct effects.

In addition to direct effects that are quickly visible, people's decisions often generate indirect, or "secondary," effects that may be observable only with time. Failure to consider secondary effects is one of the most common economic errors because these effects are often quite different from initial, or direct, effects. Frédéric Bastiat, a nineteenth-century French economist, stated that the difference between a good and a bad economist is that the bad economist considers only the immediate, visible effects, whereas the good economist is also aware of the **secondary effects**. The true cause of these secondary effects might not be seen, even later, except by those using the logic of good economics.

Perhaps a few simple examples that involve both immediate (direct) and secondary (indirect) effects will help illustrate the point. The immediate effect of an aspirin is a bitter taste in one's mouth. The secondary effect, which is not immediately observable, is relief from a headache. The short-term direct effect of drinking twelve cans of beer might be a warm, jolly feeling. In contrast, the secondary effect is likely to be a sluggish feeling the next morning, and perhaps a pounding headache.

Sometimes, as in the case of the aspirin, the secondary effect—headache relief—is actually an intended consequence of the action. In other cases, however, the secondary effects are unintended. Changes in government policy often alter incentives, indirectly affecting how much people work, earn, invest, consume, and conserve for the future. When a change alters incentives, *unintended consequences* that are quite different from the intended consequences may occur.

Let's consider a couple of examples that illustrate the potential importance of unintended consequences. In an effort to reduce gasoline consumption, the federal government mandates that automobiles be more fuel efficient. Is this regulation a sound policy? It may be, but when evaluating the policy's overall impact, one should not overlook its secondary effects. To achieve the higher fuel efficiency, auto manufacturers reduced the size and weight of vehicles. As a result, there are more highway deaths—about 2,500 more per year—than would otherwise occur because these lighter cars do not offer as much protection for occupants. Furthermore, because the higher mileage standards for cars and light trucks make driving cheaper, people tend to drive more than they otherwise would. This increases congestion and results in a smaller reduction in gasoline consumption than was intended by the regulation. Once you consider the secondary effects, the fuel efficiency regulations are much less beneficial than they might first appear.

Trade restrictions between nations have important secondary effects as well. The proponents of tariffs and quotas on foreign goods almost always ignore the secondary effects of their policies. Import quotas restricting the sale of foreign-produced sugar in the U.S. market, for example, have resulted in domestic sugar prices that have often been two or three times the price in the rest of the world. The proponents of this policy—primarily sugar producers—argue that the quotas "save jobs" and increase employment. No doubt, the employment of sugar growers in the United States is higher than it otherwise would be. But what about the secondary effects? The higher sugar prices mean it's more expensive for U.S. firms to produce candy and other products that use a lot of sugar. As a result, many candy producers, including the makers of Life Savers, Jaw Breakers, Red Hots, and Fannie May and Fanny Farmer chocolates, have moved to countries like Canada and Mexico, where sugar can be purchased at its true market price. Thus, employment among sugar-using firms in the United States is reduced. Further, because foreigners sell less sugar in the United States, they have less purchasing power with which to buy products we export to them. This, too, reduces U.S. employment.

Once the secondary effects of trade restrictions like the sugar quota program are taken into consideration, we have no reason to expect that U.S. employment will increase as a result. There may be more jobs in favored industries, but there will be less employment in others. Trade restrictions reshuffle employment rather than increase it. But those who unwittingly fail to consider the secondary effects will miss this point. Clearly, consideration of the secondary effects is an important ingredient of the economic way of thinking.

THE FAMILY CIRCUS ®   By Bil Keane

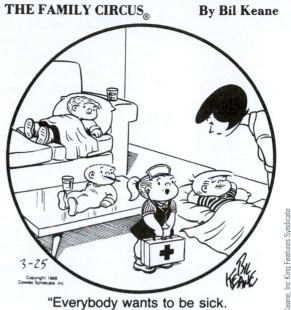

3-25
Copyright 1988
Cowles Syndicate, Inc

"Everybody wants to be sick.
I'm using M&M's for pills."

Bil Keane, Inc King Features Syndicate

Sometimes actions change the incentives people face and they respond accordingly, creating secondary effects that were not intended.

Secondary effects
The indirect impact of an event or policy that may not be easily and immediately observable. In the area of policy, these effects are often both unintended and overlooked.

7. The value of a good or service is subjective. Preferences differ, sometimes dramatically, between individuals. How much is a ticket to see a performance of the Bolshoi Ballet worth? Some people would be willing to pay a very high price, while others might prefer to stay home, even if tickets were free! Circumstances can change from day to day, even for a given individual. Alice, a ballet fan who usually would value the ticket at more than its price of $100, is invited to a party and suddenly becomes uninterested in attending the ballet. Now what is the ticket worth? If she knows a friend who would give her $40 for the ticket, it is worth at least that much. If she advertises the ticket on eBay and gets $60 for it, a higher value is created. But if someone who doesn't know of the ticket would have been willing to pay even more, then a potential trade creating even more value is missed. If that particular performance is sold out, perhaps someone in town would be willing to pay $120. One thing is certain: The value of the ticket depends on several things, including who uses it and under what circumstances.

Economics recognizes that people can and do value goods differently. Mike may prefer to have a grass field rather than a parking lot next to his workplace and be willing to bear the cost of walking farther from his car each day. Kim, on the other hand, may prefer the parking lot and the shorter walk. As a science, economics does not place any inherent moral judgment or value on one person's preferences over another's—in economics, all individuals' preferences are counted equally. Because the subjective preferences of individuals differ, it is difficult for one person to know how much another will value an item.

Think about how hard it is to know what would make a good gift for even a close friend or family member. Thus, arranging trades, or otherwise moving items to higher valued users and uses, is not a simple task. The entrepreneurial individual, who knows how to locate the right buyers and arranges for goods to flow to their highest valued use, can sometimes create huge increases in value from existing resources. In fact, moving goods toward those who value them most and combining resources into goods that individuals value more highly are primary sources of economic progress.

Scientific thinking
Developing a theory from basic principles and testing it against events in the real world. Good theories are consistent with and help explain real-world events. Theories that are inconsistent with the real world are invalid and must be rejected.

8. The test of a theory is its ability to predict. Economic thinking is **scientific thinking**. The proof of the pudding is in the eating. How useful an economic theory is depends on how well it predicts the future consequences of economic action. Economists develop economic theories using scientific thinking based on basic principles. The idea is to predict how incentives will affect decision makers and compare the predictions against real-world events. If the events in the real world are consistent with a theory, we say that the theory has *predictive value* and is therefore valid.

If it is impossible to test the theoretical relationships of a discipline, the discipline does not qualify as a science. Because economics deals with human beings who can think and respond in a variety of ways, can economic theories really be tested? The answer to this question is yes, if, on average, human beings respond in predictable and consistent ways to changes in economic conditions. The economist believes that this is the case, even though not all individuals will respond in the specified manner. Economists usually do not try to predict the behavior of a specific individual; instead, they focus on the general behavior of a large number of individuals.

In the 1950s, economists began to do laboratory experiments to test economic theories. Individuals were brought into laboratories to see how they would act in buying and selling situations, under differing rules. For example, cash rewards were given to individuals who, when an auction was conducted, were able to sell at high prices and buy at low prices, thus approximating real-world market incentives. These experiments have verified many of the important propositions of economic theory.

Laboratory experiments, however, cannot duplicate all real economic interactions. How can we test economic theory when controlled experiments are not feasible? This is a problem, but economics is no different from astronomy in this respect. Astronomers can use theories tested in physics laboratories, but they must also deal with the world as it is. They cannot change the course of the stars or planets to see what impact the change would have on the gravitational pull of Earth. Similarly, economists cannot arbitrarily change the prices of cars or unskilled-labor services in real markets just to observe the effects on quantities purchased or levels of employment. However, economic conditions (for example, prices, production costs, technology, and transportation costs), like the location of the planets, do change from time to time. As actual conditions change, an economic theory can be tested by comparing its predictions with real-world outcomes. Just as the universe is the main laboratory of the astronomer, the real-world economy is the primary laboratory of the economist.

1-3 POSITIVE AND NORMATIVE ECONOMICS

As a social science, economics is concerned with predicting or determining the impact of changes in economic variables on the actions of human beings. Scientific economics, commonly referred to as **positive economics**, attempts to determine "what is." Positive economic statements involve potentially verifiable or refutable propositions. For example, "If the price of gasoline rises, people will buy less gasoline." We can statistically investigate (and estimate) the relationship between gasoline prices and gallons sold. We can analyze the facts to determine the correctness of a positive economic statement. Remember, a positive economic statement need not be correct; it simply must be testable.

> **Positive economics**
> The scientific study of "what is" among economic relationships.

In contrast, **normative economics** is about "what ought to be," given the preferences and philosophical views of the advocate. Value judgments often result in disagreement about normative economic matters. Two people may differ on a policy matter because one is from one political party and the other is from another, or because one wants cheaper food while the other favors organic farming (which is more expensive), and so on. They may even agree about the expected outcome of altering an economic variable (that is, the positive economics of an issue), but disagree as to whether that outcome is desirable.

> **Normative economics**
> Judgments about "what ought to be" in economic matters. Normative economic views cannot be proved false because they are based on value judgments.

Unlike positive economic statements, normative economic statements can neither be confirmed nor proven false by scientific testing. "Business firms should not be concerned with profits." "We should have fewer parking lots and more green space on campus." "The price of gasoline is too high." These normative statements cannot be scientifically tested because their validity rests on value judgments.

Normative economic views can sometimes influence our attitude toward positive economic analysis, however. When we agree with the objectives of a policy, it's easy to overlook the warnings of positive economics. Although positive economics does not tell us which policy is best, it can provide evidence about the likely effects of a policy. Sometimes proponents unknowingly support policies that are actually in conflict with their own goals and objectives. Positive economics, based on sound economic logic, can help overcome this potential problem.

Economics can expand our knowledge of how the real world operates, in both the private and the public (government) sectors. However, it is not always easy to isolate the impact of economic changes. Let's now consider some pitfalls to avoid in economic thinking.

1-4 PITFALLS TO AVOID IN ECONOMIC THINKING

1-4a VIOLATION OF THE *CETERIS PARIBUS* CONDITION CAN LEAD ONE TO DRAW THE WRONG CONCLUSION

Economists often qualify their statements with the words *ceteris paribus*. *Ceteris paribus* is a Latin term meaning "other things constant." An example of a *ceteris paribus* statement would be the following: "*Ceteris paribus*, an increase in the price of housing will cause buyers to reduce their purchases of housing." Unfortunately, we live in a dynamic world, so things seldom remain constant. For example, as the price of housing rises, the income of consumers might also increase for unrelated reasons. Each of these factors—higher housing prices and increasing consumer income—will have an impact on housing purchases. In

> *Ceteris paribus*
> A Latin term meaning "other things constant" that is used when the effect of one change is being described, recognizing that if other things changed, they also could affect the result. Economists often describe the effects of one change, knowing that in the real world, other things might change and also exert an effect.

fact, we would generally expect them to have opposite effects: Higher prices are likely to reduce housing purchases, whereas higher consumer incomes are likely to increase them. We point out this pitfall because sometimes statistical data (or casual observations) appear inconsistent with economic theories. In most of these cases, the apparent contradictions reflect the effects of changes in other factors (violations of the *ceteris paribus* conditions). The observed effects are the result of the combination of the changes.

The task of sorting out the effects of two or more variables that change at the same time is difficult. However, with a strong grip on economic theory, some ingenuity, and enough data, it can usually be done. This is, in fact, precisely the day-to-day work of many professional economists.

1-4b GOOD INTENTIONS DO NOT GUARANTEE DESIRABLE OUTCOMES

There is a tendency to believe that if the proponents of a policy have good intentions, their proposals must be sound. This is not necessarily the case. Proponents may be unaware of some of the adverse secondary effects of their proposals, particularly when they are indirect and observable only over time. Even if their policies would be largely ineffective, politicians may still find it advantageous to call attention to the severity of a problem and propose a program to deal with it. In other cases, proponents of a policy may actually be seeking a goal other than the one they espouse. They may tie their arguments to objectives that are widely supported by the general populace. Thus, the fact that an advocate says a program will help the economy, expand employment, help the poor, increase wages, improve health care, or achieve some other highly desirable objective does not necessarily make it so.

Let's begin with a couple of straightforward examples. Federal legislation has been introduced that would require all children, including those under age two, to be fastened in a child safety seat when traveling by air. Proponents argue the legislation will increase the survival rate of children in the case of an airline crash and thereby save lives. Certainly, saving lives is a highly desirable objective, but will this really be the case? *Some* lives will probably be saved. But what about the secondary effects? The legislation would mean that a parent traveling with a small child would have to purchase an additional ticket, which will make it more expensive to fly. As a result, many families will choose to travel by auto rather than by air. Because the likelihood of a serious accident per mile traveled in an automobile is several times higher than for air travel, more automobile travel will result in more injuries and fatalities. In fact, studies indicate that the increase in injuries and fatalities from additional auto travel will exceed the number of lives saved by airline safety seats.[4] Thus, even though the intentions of the proponents may well be lofty, there is reason to believe that the net impact of their proposal will be more fatalities and injuries than would be the case in the absence of the legislation.

The stated objective of the Endangered Species Act is to protect various species that are on the verge of extinction. Certainly, this is an admirable objective, but there is nonetheless reason to question the effectiveness of the act itself. The Endangered Species Act allows the government to regulate the use of individual private property if an endangered species is found present on *or* near an individual's land. To avoid losing control of their property, many landowners have taken steps to make their land less attractive as a natural habitat for these endangered species. For example, the endangered red-cockaded woodpecker nests primarily in old trees within southern pine ecosystems. Landowners have responded by cutting down trees the woodpeckers like to nest in to avoid having one nest on their land, which would result in the owner losing control of this part of their property. The end result is that the habitat for these birds has actually been disappearing more rapidly.

---

[4]For a detailed analysis of this subject, see Thomas B. Newman, Brian D. Johnston, and David C. Grossman, "Effects and Costs of Requiring Child-Restraint Systems for Young Children Traveling on Commercial Airplanes," *Archives of Pediatrics and Adolescent Medicine* 157 (October 2003): 969–74.

As you can see, good intentions are not enough. An unsound proposal will lead to undesirable outcomes, even if it is supported by proponents with good intentions. In fact, many economists believe that the recent financial crisis was a secondary effect of well-intended government regulations and policies that lowered mortgage lending standards in order to expand homeownership. Sound economic reasoning can help us better anticipate the secondary effects of policy changes and avoid the pitfall of thinking that good intentions are enough.

1-4c ASSOCIATION IS NOT CAUSATION

In economics, identifying cause-and-effect relationships is very important. But statistical association alone cannot establish this causation. Perhaps an extreme example will illustrate the point. Suppose that each November, a witch doctor performs a voodoo dance designed to summon the gods of winter, and that soon after the dance is performed, the weather in fact begins to turn cold. The witch doctor's dance is associated with the arrival of winter, meaning that the two events appear to have happened in conjunction with one another. But is this really evidence that the witch doctor's dance actually caused the arrival of winter? Most of us would answer no, even though the two events seemed to happen in conjunction with one another.

Those who argue that a causal relationship exists simply because of the presence of statistical association are committing a logical fallacy known as the *post hoc propter ergo hoc* fallacy. Sound economics warns against this potential source of error.

1-4d THE FALLACY OF COMPOSITION: WHAT'S TRUE FOR ONE MIGHT NOT BE TRUE FOR ALL

What is true for the individual (or subcomponent) may not be true for the group (or the whole). If you stand up for an exciting play during a football game, you will be better able to see. But what happens if everyone stands up at the same time? Will everyone be better able to see? The answer is, of course, no. Thus, what is true for a single individual does not necessarily apply to the group as a whole. When everyone stands up, the view for individual spectators fails to improve; in fact, it may even become worse.

People who mistakenly argue that what is true for the part is also true for the whole are said to be committing the **fallacy of composition**. What is true for the individual can be misleading and is often fallacious when applied to the entire economy. The fallacy of composition highlights the importance of considering both a micro view and a macro view in the study of economics. **Microeconomics** focuses on the decision-making of consumers, producers, and resource suppliers operating in a narrowly defined market, such as that for a specific good or resource. Because individual decision-makers are the moving force behind all economic action, the foundations of economics are clearly rooted in a micro view.

As we have seen, however, what is true for a small unit may not be true in the aggregate. **Macroeconomics** focuses on how the aggregation of individual micro-units affects our analysis. Like microeconomics, it is concerned with incentives, prices, and output. Macroeconomics, however, aggregates markets, lumping together all 117 million households in this country. Macroeconomics involves topics like total consumption spending, saving, and employment, in the economy as a whole. Similarly, the nation's 28 million business firms are lumped together in "the business sector." What factors determine the level of aggregate output, the rate of inflation, the amount of unemployment, and interest rates? These are macroeconomic questions. In short, macroeconomics examines the forest rather than the individual trees. As we move from the microcomponents to a macro view of the whole, it is important that we beware of the fallacy of composition.

Fallacy of composition
Erroneous view that what is true for the individual (or the part) will also be true for the group (or the whole).

Microeconomics
The branch of economics that focuses on how human behavior affects the conduct of affairs within narrowly defined units, such as individual households or business firms.

Macroeconomics
The branch of economics that focuses on how human behavior affects outcomes in highly aggregated markets, such as the markets for labor or consumer products.

LOOKING AHEAD

The primary purpose of this book is to encourage you to develop the economic way of thinking so that you can separate sound reasoning from economic nonsense. Once you have developed the economic way of thinking, economics will be relatively easy. Using the economic way of thinking can also be fun. Moreover, it will help you become a better citizen. It will give you a different and fascinating perspective on what motivates people, why they act the way they do, and why their actions sometimes go against the best interest of the community or nation. It will also give you valuable insight into how people's actions can be rechanneled for the benefit of the community at large.

KEY POINTS

- Scarcity and choice are the two essential ingredients of economic analysis. A good is scarce when the human desire for it exceeds the amount freely available from nature. Scarcity requires us to choose among available alternatives. Every choice entails a trade-off.

- Every society will have to devise some method of rationing scarce resources among competing uses. Markets generally use price as the rationing device. Competition is a natural outgrowth of the need to ration scarce goods.

- Scarcity and poverty are not the same thing. Absence of poverty implies that some basic level of need has been met. An absence of scarcity implies that our desires for goods are fully satisfied. We may someday eliminate poverty, but scarcity will always be with us.

- Economics is a way of thinking that emphasizes eight points:

  1. The use of scarce resources to produce a good always has an opportunity cost.
  2. Individuals make decisions purposefully, always seeking to choose the option they expect to be most consistent with their personal goals.
  3. Incentives matter. The likelihood of people choosing an option increases as personal benefits rise and personal costs decline.

  4. Economic reasoning focuses on the impact of marginal changes because it is the marginal benefits and marginal costs that influence choices.
  5. Because information is scarce, uncertainty is a fact of life.
  6. In addition to their direct impact, economic changes often generate secondary effects.
  7. The value of a good or service is subjective and varies with individual preferences and circumstances.
  8. The test of an economic theory is its ability to predict and explain events in the real world.

- Economic science is positive; it attempts to explain the actual consequences of economic actions or "what is." Normative economics goes further, applying value judgments to make suggestions about what "ought to be."

- Microeconomics focuses on narrowly defined units, while macroeconomics is concerned with highly aggregated units. When shifting focus from micro to macro, one must beware of the fallacy of composition: What's good for the individual may not be good for the group as a whole.

- The origin of economics as a science dates to the publication of *An Inquiry into the Nature and Causes of the Wealth of Nations* by Adam Smith in 1776. Smith believed a market economy would generally bring individual self-interest and the public interest into harmony.

CRITICAL ANALYSIS QUESTIONS

1. Indicate how each of the following changes would influence the incentive of a decision-maker to undertake the action described.

   a. A reduction in the temperature from 80° to 50° on one's decision to go swimming
   b. A change in the meeting time of the introductory economics course from 11:00 A.M. to 7:30 A.M. on one's decision to attend the lectures
   c. A reduction in the number of exam questions that relate directly to the text on the student's decision to read the text
   d. An increase in the price of beef on one's decision to buy steak
   e. An increase in the rental rates of apartments on one's decision to build additional rental housing units

2. "The government should provide such goods as health care, education, and highways because it can provide them for free." Is this statement true or false? Explain your answer.

3. a. What method is used to ration goods in a market economy? How does this rationing method influence the incentive of individuals to supply goods, services, and resources to others?

b. How are grades rationed in your economics class? How does this rationing method influence student behavior? Suppose the highest grades were rationed to those whom the teacher liked best. How would this method of rationing influence student behavior?

4. *In recent years, the child tax credit has been increased in the United States. According to the basic principles of economics, how will the birthrate be affected by policies that reduce the taxes imposed on those with children?

5. *"The economic way of thinking stresses that good intentions lead to sound policy." Is this statement true or false? Explain your answer.

6. Self-interest is a powerful motivator. Does this necessarily imply that people are selfish and greedy? Do self-interest and selfishness mean the same thing?

7. A restaurant offers an "all you can eat" lunch buffet for $10. Shawn has already eaten three servings, and is trying to decide whether to go back for a fourth. Describe how Shawn can use marginal analysis to make his decision.

8. *"Individuals who economize are missing the point of life. Money is not so important that it should rule the way we live." Evaluate this statement.

9. *"Positive economics cannot tell us which agricultural policy is better, so it is useless to policy makers." Evaluate this statement.

10. *"I examined the statistics for our basketball team's wins last year and found that, when the third team played more, the win-ning margin increased. If the coach played the third team more, we would win by a bigger margin." Evaluate this statement.

11. Which of the following are positive economic statements and which are normative?

a. The speed limit should be lowered to 55 miles per hour on interstate highways.

b. Higher gasoline prices cause the quantity of gasoline that consumers buy to decrease.

c. A comparison of costs and benefits should not be used to assess environmental regulations.

d. Higher taxes on alcohol result in less drinking and driving.

12. Why can't we consume as much of each good or service as we would like? If we become richer in the future, do you think we will eventually be able to consume as much of everything as we would like? Why or why not?

13. Suppose that in an effort to help low-skill workers the government raises the permissible minimum wage to $15 per hour. Can you think of any unintended secondary effects that will result from this action? Will all low-skill workers be helped by the minimum wage law?

14. Should the United States attempt to reduce air and water pollution to zero? Why or why not?

*Asterisk denotes questions for which answers are given in Appendix B.

CHAPTER 2
Some Tools of the Economist

FOCUS

- What is opportunity cost? Why do economists place so much emphasis on it?

- Why do people engage in exchange?

- How does private ownership affect the use of resources? Will private owners pay any attention to the desires of others?

- What does a production possibilities curve demonstrate?

- What are the sources of gains from trade? How does trade influence our modern living standards?

- What are the two major methods of economic organization? How do they differ?

The key insight of Adam Smith's *Wealth of Nations* is misleadingly simple: if an exchange between two parties is voluntary, it will not take place unless both believe they will benefit from it. Most economic fallacies derive from the neglect of this simple insight, from the tendency to assume that there is a fixed pie, that one party can gain only at the expense of another.
—Milton and Rose Friedman[1]

[1]Milton Friedman and Rose Friedman, *Free to Choose* (Harcourt Brace, 1990), 13.

In the preceding chapter, you were introduced to the economic way of thinking. We will now begin to apply that approach. This chapter focuses on five topics: opportunity cost, trade, property rights, the potential output level of an economy, and the creation of wealth. These seemingly diverse topics are in fact highly interrelated. For example, the opportunity cost of goods determines which ones an individual or a nation should produce and which should be acquired through trade. In turn, the ways in which trade and property rights are structured influence the amount of output and wealth an economy can create. These tools of economics are important for answering the basic economic questions: what to produce, how to produce it, and for whom it will be produced. We will begin by first explaining in more detail what opportunity cost is.

2-1 WHAT SHALL WE GIVE UP?

Because of scarcity, we can't have everything we want. As a result, we constantly face choices that involve trade-offs between our competing desires. Most of us would like to have more time for leisure, recreation, vacations, hobbies, education, and skill development. We would also like to have more wealth, a larger savings account, and more consumable goods. However, all these things are scarce, in the sense that they are limited. Our efforts to get more of one will conflict with our efforts to get more of others.

2-1a OPPORTUNITY COST

The choice to do one thing is, at the same time, a choice *not* to do something else. Your choice to spend time reading this book is a choice not to spend the time playing video games, listening to a math lecture, or going to a party. These things must be given up because you decided to read this book instead. As we indicated in Chapter 1, the highest valued alternative sacrificed in order to choose an option is called the *opportunity cost* of that choice.

Opportunity costs are subjective because they depend on how the decision-maker values his or her options. They are also based on the expectations of the decision-maker—what he or she expects the value of the forgone alternatives will be. Because of this, opportunity cost can never be directly measured by someone other than the decision-maker. Only the person choosing can know the value of what is given up.[2] This makes it difficult for someone other than the decision-maker—including experts and elected officials—to make choices on that person's behalf. Moreover, not only do people differ in the trade-offs they prefer to make, but their preferences also change with time and circumstances. Thus, the decision-maker is the only person who can properly evaluate the options and decide which is the best, given his or her preferences and current circumstances.

Monetary costs reflect opportunities foregone, and they can be measured objectively in terms of dollars and cents. If you spend $20 on a new video game, you must now forgo the other items you could have purchased with the $20—a new shirt, for example. However, it is important to recognize that monetary costs do not represent the total opportunity cost of an option. The total cost of attending a football game, for example, is the highest valued opportunity lost as a result of both the time you spend at the game and the amount of money you pay for your ticket. In cases like the online purchase of a video game, for which there is minimal outlay of time, effort, and other resources to make the purchase, the monetary cost will approximate the total cost. Contrast this with a decision to sit on your sofa and play your new video game, which involves little or no monetary cost, but has a clear opportunity cost of your time. In this second case, the monetary cost is a poor measure of the total cost.

---

[2]See James M. Buchanan, *Cost and Choice* (Chicago: Markham, 1969), for a classic work on the relationship between cost and choice.

2-1b OPPORTUNITY COST AND THE REAL WORLD

Is real-world decision making influenced by opportunity costs? Consider your own decision to attend college. Your opportunity cost of going to college is the value of the next best alternative, which could be measured as the salary you would earn if you had chosen to go directly into full-time work instead. Every year you stay in college, you give up what you could have earned by working that year. Typically, students incur opportunity costs of $80,000 or more in forgone income during their stay in college.

But what if the opportunity cost of attending college changes? How will it affect your decision? Suppose, for example, that you received a job offer today for $250,000 per year as an athlete or an entertainer, but the job would require so much travel that school would be impossible. Would this change in the opportunity cost of going to college affect your choice as to whether to continue in school? It likely would. Going to college would mean you would have to say good-bye to the huge salary you've been offered. (See the accompanying illustration on LeBron James for a good example.) You can clearly tell from this example that the monetary cost of college (tuition, books, and so forth) isn't the only factor influencing your decision. Your opportunity cost plays a part, too.

Even when their parents pay all the monetary expenses of their college education, some students are surprised to learn that they are actually incurring more of the total cost of going to college than their parents are. For example, the average monetary cost (tuition, room and board, books, and so forth) for a student attending college is about $10,000 per year ($40,000 over four years). Even if the student's next best alternative were working at a job that paid only $15,000 per year, over four years, that would amount to $60,000 in forgone earnings, So, the total cost of the student's education would be $100,000 ($40,000 in monetary costs paid by the parents and $60,000 in opportunity costs incurred by the student).[3]

Now consider another decision made by college students—whether to attend a particular class meeting. The monetary cost of attending class (bus fare, parking, gasoline costs, and so on) remains fairly constant from day to day. Why then do students choose to attend class on some days and not on others? Even though the monetary cost of attending class is fairly constant, a student's opportunity cost can change dramatically from day to day. Some days, the next best alternative to attending class may be sleeping in or watching TV. Other days, the opportunity cost may be substantially larger, perhaps the value of attending a big football game, getting an early start on spring break, or having additional study time for a crucial exam in another class. As options like these increase the cost of attending class, more students will decide not to attend.

Failure to consider opportunity cost often leads to unwise decision-making. Suppose that your community builds a beautiful new civic center. The mayor, speaking at the dedication ceremony, tells the world that the center will improve the quality of life in your

LeBron James understands opportunity cost. As a high school player, James was already one of the best basketball players in the nation. He had received numerous scholarship offers and was considering attending college at Ohio State, the University of North Carolina, Michigan State, or the University of California. However, after high school graduation, LeBron decided to go directly into the NBA because the opportunity cost of college was simply too high. He was selected as the first pick in the 2003 NBA draft, signing a three-year contract worth almost $13 million, with an option for a fourth year at $5.8 million. Had he decided to go to college instead, James would have incurred an opportunity cost of at least $19 million in forgone income to earn a four-year college degree! Would you have skipped college if your opportunity cost had been that high?

John W. McDonough/Sports Illustrated/Getty Images

---

[3]From the standpoint of the family's total economic cost of sending a child to college, some of the monetary costs, such as room and board, are not costs of choosing to go to college. The cost of living does have to be covered, but it would be incurred whether or not the student went to college.

OUTSTANDING ECONOMIST

THOMAS SOWELL (1930–)

Thomas Sowell, a senior fellow at the Hoover Institution, recognizes the critical importance of the institutions—the "rules of the game"—that shape human interactions. His book *Knowledge and Decisions* stresses the role of knowledge in the economy and how different institutional arrangements compare at using scarce information. Sowell is the author of many books and journal articles and writes a nationally syndicated column that appears in more than 150 newspapers. His writings address subjects ranging from race preferences and cultural differences to the origins and ideology of political conflict.

community. People who understand the concept of opportunity cost may question this view. If the center had not been built, the resources might have funded construction of a new hospital, improvements to the educational system, or housing for low-income families. Will the civic center contribute more to the well-being of people in your community than would these other facilities? If so, it was a wise investment. If not, your community will be worse off than it would have been if decision-makers had chosen a higher valued project.

2-2 TRADE CREATES VALUE

Why do individuals trade with each other, and what is the significance of this exchange? We have learned that value is subjective. It is wrong to assume that a particular good or service has a fixed objective value just because it exists.[4] The value of goods and services generally depends on who uses them, and on circumstances, such as when and where they are used, as well as on the physical characteristics. Some people love onions, whereas others dislike them very much. Thus, when we speak of the "value of an onion," this makes sense only within the context of its value to a specific person. Similarly, to most people an umbrella is more valuable on a rainy day than on a sunny one.

Consider the case of Janet, who loves tomatoes but hates onions, and Brad, who loves onions but hates tomatoes. They go out to dinner together and the waiter brings their salads. Brad turns to Janet and says, "I'll trade you the tomatoes on my salad for the onions on yours." Janet gladly agrees to the exchange. This simple example will help us illustrate two important aspects of voluntary exchange.

1. When individuals engage in a voluntary exchange, both parties are made better off. In the previous example, Janet has the option of accepting or declining Brad's offer of a trade. If she accepts his offer, she does so *voluntarily*. Janet would agree to this exchange only if she expects to be better off as a result. Because she likes tomatoes better than onions, Janet's enjoyment of her salad will be greater with this trade than without it. On the other side, Brad has voluntarily made this offer of an exchange to Janet because Brad believes he will also be better off as a result of the exchange.

People tend to think of making, building, and creating things as productive activities. Agriculture and manufacturing are like this. On the one hand, they create something genuinely new, something that was not there before. On the other hand, trade—the mere exchange of one thing for another—does not create new material items. It is tempting to think that if nothing new is created, the action cannot generate gain. But this is a fallacy, and the motivation for trade illustrates why. An exchange will not occur unless both parties agree to it and they will not do so unless the exchange makes them better off. As the chapter-opening quotation of Milton and Rose Friedman illustrates, many errors in economic reasoning happen when we forget that voluntary trades, like the one between Janet and Brad, make both parties better off.

---

[4]An illuminating discussion of this subject, termed the "physical fallacy," is found in Thomas Sowell, *Knowledge and Decisions* (New York: Basic Books, 1980), 67–72.

2. By channeling goods and resources to those who value them most, trade creates value and increases the wealth created by a society's resources. Because preferences differ among individuals, the value of an item can vary greatly from one person to another. Therefore, trade can create value by moving goods from those who value them less to those who value them more. The simple exchange between Janet and Brad also illustrates this point. Imagine for a moment that Brad and Janet had never met and instead were both eating their salads alone. Without the ability to engage in this exchange, both would have eaten their salads but would not have had as much enjoyment from them. When goods are moved to individuals who value them more, the total value created by a society's limited resources is increased. The same two salads create more value when the trade occurs than when it doesn't.

It is easy to think of material things as wealth, but material things are not wealth until they are in the hands of someone who values them. A highly technical book on electronics that is of no value to an art collector may be worth several hundred dollars to an engineer. Similarly, a painting that is unappreciated by an engineer may be of great value to an art collector. Therefore, a voluntary exchange that moves the electronics book to the engineer and the painting to the art collector will increase the value of both goods. By channeling goods and resources toward those who value them most, trade creates wealth for both the trading partners and for the nation.

2-2a TRANSACTION COSTS—A BARRIER TO TRADE

How many times have you been sitting home late at night, hungry, wishing you had a meal from your favorite fast-food restaurant? You would gladly pay the $5 price for the value meal you have in mind, but you feel it is just not worth the time and effort to get dressed and make that drive. The costs of the time, effort, and other resources necessary to search out, negotiate, and conclude an exchange are called **transaction costs**. High transaction costs can be a barrier to potentially productive exchange.

Transaction costs
The time, effort, and other resources needed to search out, negotiate, and complete an exchange.

Because of transaction costs, we should not expect all potentially valuable trades to take place, any more than we expect all useful knowledge to be learned, all safety measures to be taken, or all potential "A" grades to be earned. Students often discover that finding someone willing to pay an attractive price for a used book at the end of a semester or an unused ticket to a football game is not worth the cost. The cost of information, transportation, and other elements of transaction costs will some times be so great that potential gains from trade will go unrealized.

Reductions in transaction costs will increase the gains from trade. The Internet has significantly lowered transaction costs. The auction Web site eBay helps sellers to reach millions of potential buyers with little effort and few costs. Buyers can easily search eBay for items they want to buy, even if the items are located halfway around the world. Other Web sites, such as Nextag and PriceGrabber, scour online shopping sites for the lowest prices so buyers don't have to. Consumers can also readily find detailed information about products on any number of sites. Amazon.com posts prices, product information provided by manufacturers, and reviews from other buyers. By reducing transaction costs, the Internet creates value and wealth. It expands the number of trades that are made, and makes it faster and easier to make them.

2-2b THE MIDDLEMAN AS A COST REDUCER

Middlemen
People who buy and sell goods or services or arrange trades. A middleman reduces transaction costs.

Because it is costly for buyers and sellers to find each other and to negotiate the exchange, an entrepreneurial opportunity exists for people to become **middlemen**. Middlemen provide buyers and sellers information at a lower cost and arrange trades between them. Many people think middlemen just add to the buyer's expense without performing a useful function. However, because of transaction costs, without middlemen, many trades would never happen (nor would the gains from them be realized). An auto dealer, for example, is a middleman. An auto dealer helps both the manufacturer and the buyer. The dealer helps buyers by maintaining an inventory of vehicles for them to choose from. Knowledgeable salespeople hired by the dealer help car shoppers quickly learn about the vehicles they're interested in and the pros and cons of each. Car buyers also like to know that a local dealer will honor the manufacturer's warranty and provide parts and service for the car. The dealer helps manufacturers by handling tasks like these so they can concentrate on designing and making better cars.

Grocers are also middlemen. Each of us could deal with farmers directly to buy our food—probably at a lower monetary cost. But that would have a high opportunity cost. Finding and dealing with different farmers for every product we wanted to buy would take a lot of time. Alternatively, we could form consumer cooperatives, banding together to eliminate the middleman, using our own warehouses and our own volunteer labor to order, receive, display, distribute, and collect payment for the food. In fact, some cooperatives like this do exist. But most people prefer instead to pay a grocer to provide all of the goods they want rather than trying to trade directly with farmers and other producers.

Stockbrokers, realtors, publishers, and merchants of all sorts are other kinds of middlemen. For a fee, they reduce transaction costs for both buyers and sellers. By making exchanges cheaper and more convenient, middlemen cause more efficient trades to happen. In so doing, they themselves create value.

2-3 THE IMPORTANCE OF PROPERTY RIGHTS

The buyer of an apple, a CD, a television set, or an automobile generally takes the item home. The buyer of a steamship or an office building, though, may never touch it. When exchange occurs, it's really the **property rights** of the item that change hands.

Private-property rights involve three things:

1. the right to exclusive use of the property (that is, the owner has sole possession, control, and use of the property, including the right to exclude others);
2. legal protection against invasion from other individuals who would seek to use or abuse the property without the owner's permission; and
3. the right to transfer, sell, exchange, or mortgage the property.

Private owners can do anything they want with their property as long as they do not use it in a manner that invades or infringes on the rights of another. For example, I cannot throw the hammer that I own through the television set that you own. If I did, I would be violating your property right to your television. The same is true if I operate a factory spewing out pollution harming you or your land.[5] Because an owner has the right to control the use of property, the owner also must accept responsibility for the outcomes of that control.

In contrast to private ownership, common-property ownership occurs when multiple people simultaneously have or claim ownership rights to a good or resource. If the resource is open to all, none of the common owners can prevent the others from using or damaging the property. Most beaches, rivers, and roads are examples of commonly owned property. The distinction between private- and common-property ownership is important because common ownership does not create the same powerful incentives for conservation and efficient use as private ownership. Economists are fond of saying that when everybody owns something, nobody owns it.

Property rights
The rights to use, control, and obtain the benefits from a good or resource.

Private-property rights
Property rights that are exclusively held by an owner and protected against invasion by others. Private property can be transferred, sold, or mortgaged at the owner's discretion.

KEYS TO ECONOMIC PROSPERITY

Private Ownership

Private ownership provides people with a strong incentive to take care of things and develop resources in ways that are highly valued by others.

[5]For a detailed explanation of how property rights protect the environment, with several real-world examples, see Roger E. Meiners and Bruce Yandle, *The Common Law: How It Protects the Environment* (Bozeman, MT: PERC, 1998), available online at www.perc.org.

Clearly defined and enforced private-property rights are a key to economic progress because of the powerful incentive effects that private ownership generates. The following four incentives are particularly important:

1. Private owners can gain by employing their resources in ways that are beneficial to others, and they bear the opportunity cost of ignoring the wishes of others. Realtors often advise homeowners to use neutral colors for countertops and walls in their house because they will improve the resale value of the home. As a private owner, you could install bright green fixtures and paint your walls deep purple, but you will bear the cost (in terms of a lower selling price) of ignoring the wishes of others who might want to buy your house later. Conversely, by fixing up a house and doing things to it that others find beneficial, you can reap the benefit of a higher selling price. Similarly, you could spray paint orange designs all over the outside of your brand-new car, but private ownership gives you an incentive not to do so because the resale value of the car depends on the value that *others* place on it.

Consider a parcel of undeveloped, privately owned land near a university. The private owner of the land can do many things with it. For example, she could leave it undeveloped, turn it into a metered parking lot, erect a restaurant, or build rental housing. Will the wishes and desires of the nearby students be reflected in her choice, even though they are not the owners of the property? Yes. Whichever use is more highly valued by potential customers will earn her the highest investment return. If housing is relatively hard to find but there are plenty of other restaurants, the profitability of using her land for housing will be higher than the profitability of using it for a restaurant. Private ownership gives her a strong incentive to use her property in a way that will also fulfill the wishes of others. If she decides to leave the property undeveloped instead of erecting housing that would benefit the students, she will bear the opportunity cost of forgone rental income from the property.

Consider a second example: the incentive structure confronted by the owner of an apartment complex near your campus. The owner may not care much for swimming pools, workout facilities, study desks, washers and dryers, or green areas. Nonetheless, private ownership provides the owner with a strong incentive to provide these items if students and other potential customers value them more than the costs of their provision. Why? Because tenants will be willing to pay higher rents to live in a complex with amenities that they value. The owners of rental property can profit by providing an additional amenity that tenants value as long as the tenants are willing to pay enough additional rent to cover their cost.

2. Private owners have a strong incentive to care for and properly manage what they own. Will Ed regularly change the oil in his car? Will he see to it that the seats don't get torn? Probably so, because being careless about these things would reduce the car's value, both to him and to any future owner. The car and its value—the sale price if he sells it—belong just to Ed, so he would bear the burden of a decline in the car's value if the oil ran low and ruined the engine, or if the seats were torn. Similarly, he would capture the value of an expenditure that improved the car, like a new paint job. As the owner, Ed has both the

"Their house looks so nice. They must be getting ready to sell it."

A private owner has a strong incentive to do things with his or her property that increase its value to others.

When apartments and other investment properties are owned privately, the owner has a strong incentive to provide amenities that others value highly relative to their cost.

authority and the incentive to protect the car against harm or neglect and even to enhance its value. Private-property rights give owners a strong incentive for good stewardship.

Do you take equally good care not to damage an apartment you rent as you would your own house? If you share an apartment with several roommates, are the common areas of the apartment (such as the kitchen and living room) as neatly kept as the bedrooms? Based on economic theory, we guess that the answer to both of these questions is probably "No."

A few years ago, the student government association at Berry College in Georgia purchased 20 bicycles to be placed around campus for everyone's use.[6] These $200 Schwinn Cruiser bicycles were painted red and were marked with a plate reading "Berry Bike." The bikes were available on a first-come, first-served basis, and students were encouraged to take them whenever they needed them and leave them anywhere on campus for others to use when they were finished. What do you think happened to these bikes? Within two months, most of these high-quality bikes were severely damaged or lost. The campus newspaper reported on the "mangled corpses of twisted red metal that lie about campus." Over the summer break, the student government replaced or fixed the bikes, but despite its pleas to "treat the bikes as if they were your own property," the same thing happened the following fall precisely because the bikes weren't the students' own property. It wasn't that the students at Berry College were inherently destructive; after all, there were no problems on campus with privately owned bikes being lost or abused during this time. It was a matter of the different incentives they faced. The student government association eventually abandoned the program and began leasing the remaining bikes to individual students instead. As you can see, there is no denying the strong incentive that private ownership creates for owners to care for their property (or the lack of the incentive to do so when private ownership is absent.)

3. Private owners have an incentive to conserve for the future— particularly if the property is expected to increase in value. People have a much stronger incentive to conserve privately owned property than they do commonly owned property. For example, when Steven was in college, the general rule among his roommates was that any food or drink in the house was common property—open game for the hungry or thirsty mouth of anyone who stumbled across it. There was never a reason for Steven to conserve food or drinks in the house because it would be quickly consumed by a roommate coming in later that night. When Steven first started living alone, he noticed a dramatic change in his behavior. When he ordered a pizza, he would save some for the next day's lunch rather than eating it all that night. Steven began counting his drinks before he had one to make sure there were enough left for the next day. When Steven was the sole owner, he began delaying his current consumption to conserve for the future because he was the one, not his roommates, who reaped the benefit from his conservation.

Similarly, when more than one individual has the right to drill oil from an underground pool of oil, each has an incentive to extract as much as possible, as quickly as possible. Any oil conserved for the future will probably be taken by someone else. In contrast, when only one owner has the right to drill, the oil will be extracted more slowly. The same applies to the common-property problems involved in overfishing of the sea compared with fisheries that use privately owned ponds.

Without clearly defined private-property rights, there is less of an incentive to take proper care of things—as the student government administration at Berry College found out when it provided common-property bikes to be used around campus.

Courtesy of Berry College, Mount Berry, GA

---

[6]Daniel L. Alban and E. Frank Stephenson, "The 'Berry Bikes': A Lesson in Private Property," *Ideas on Liberty* 49, no. 10 (October 1999): 8–9.

Someone who owns land, a house, or a factory has a strong incentive to bear costs now, if necessary, to preserve the asset's value for the future. The owner's wealth is tied up in the value of the property, which reflects nothing more than the net benefits that will be available to a future owner. Thus, the wealth of private owners is dependent upon their willingness and ability to look ahead, maintain, and conserve those things that will be more highly valued in the future. This is why private ownership is particularly important for the optimal conservation of natural resources.

4. Private owners have an incentive to lower the chance that their property will cause damage to the property of others. Private ownership links responsibility with the right of control. Private owners can be held accountable for damage done to others through the misuse of their property. A car owner has a right to drive his car, but will be held accountable if the brakes aren't maintained and the car damages someone else's property. Similarly, a chemical company has control over its products, but, exactly for that reason, it is legally liable for damages if it mishandles the chemicals. Courts of law recognize and enforce the authority granted by ownership, but they also enforce the responsibility that goes with that authority. Because private-property owners can be held accountable for damages they cause, they have an incentive to use their property responsibly and take steps to reduce the likelihood of harm to others. A property owner, for example, has an incentive to cut down a dying tree before it falls into a neighbor's house and to leash or restrain his or her dog if it's likely to bite others.

2-3a PRIVATE OWNERSHIP AND MARKETS

Private ownership and competitive markets provide the foundation for cooperative behavior among individuals. When private-property rights are protected and enforced, the permission of the owner must be sought before anyone else can use the property. Put another way, if you want to use a good or resource, you must either buy or lease it from the owner. This means that each of us must face the cost of using scarce resources. Furthermore, market prices give private owners a strong incentive to consider the desires of others and use their resources in ways others value.

Friedrich Hayek, the winner of the 1974 Nobel Prize in economics, used the expression "the extended order" to refer to the tendency for markets to lead perfect strangers from different backgrounds around the world to cooperate with one another. Let's go back to the example of the property owner who has the choice of leaving her land idle or building housing to benefit students. The landowner might not know any students in her town nor particularly care about providing them housing. However, because she is motivated by market prices, she might build an apartment complex and eventually do business with a lot of students she never intended to get to know. In the process, she will purchase materials, goods, and services produced by other strangers.

Things are different in countries that don't recognize private-ownership rights or enforce them. In these countries, whoever has the political power or authority can simply seize property from whomever might have it without compensating them. In his book *The Mystery of Capital*, economist Hernando de Soto argues that the lack of well-defined and enforced property rights explains why some underdeveloped countries (despite being market based) have made little economic progress. He points out that in many of these nations, generations of people have squatted on the land without any legal deed giving them formal ownership. The problem is these squatters cannot borrow against the land or the homes they built on it to generate capital because they don't have a deed to it, nor can they prevent someone else from arbitrarily taking the land away from them.

Private ownership and markets can also play an important role in environmental protection and natural-resource conservation. Ocean fishing rights, tradable rights to pollute, and private ownership of endangered species are just some examples. The accompanying Applications in Economics feature, "Protecting Endangered Species with Private-Property Rights," explores some of these issues.

APPLICATIONS IN ECONOMICS

Protecting Endangered Species with Private-Property Rights

© AD Hanekom/Shutterstock.com

Have you ever wondered why the wild tiger is endangered in much of the world but most cats are thriving? Or why spotted owls are threatened in the Pacific Northwest but chickens are not? Why have elephant and rhinoceros populations declined in number but not cattle or hogs? The incentives accompanying private ownership provide the answer.

To understand why many wild animals are scarce, consider what happens with animals that provide food, most of which are privately owned. Suppose that people decided to eat less beef. Beef prices would fall, and the incentive for individuals to dedicate land and other resources to raise cattle would decline. The result would be fewer cows. The market demand for beef *creates* the incentive for suppliers to maintain herds of cattle and to protect them under a system of private ownership.

In some ways, the rhinoceros is similar to a cow. A rhino, like a large bull in a cattle herd, may charge if disturbed. At 3,000 pounds, a charging rhino can be very dangerous to humans. Also like cattle, rhinos can be valuable to people—a single horn from a black rhino, used for artistic carvings and medicines, can sell for up to $30,000. But when hunting rhinos and selling their horns is illegal, rhinos become a favorite target of poachers—people who hunt illegally. Poachers are sometimes even assisted by local people eager to see fewer rhinos present because rhinos make life risky for humans and they also compete for food and water.

However, rhinos are very different from cattle in one important respect: in most of Africa where they naturally range, private ownership of the rhino is prohibited. Since 1977, many nations have outlawed rhino hunting and forbidden the sale of rhino parts. But this approach has only made things worse for the rhino: between 1970 and 1994, the number of black rhinos declined by 95%.[1] According to South African economist Michael 't Sas-Rolfes, the trade ban "has not had a discernible effect on rhino numbers and does not seem to have stopped the trade in rhino horn. If anything, the . . . listings led to a sharp increase in the black market price of rhino horn, which simply fuelled further poaching and encouraged speculative stockpiling of horn."

But what if the powerful incentives created by private ownership were instead brought to bear on the rhino? That ac-

tually happened for a while in Zimbabwe. Landowners were allowed to fence and manage game animals on their property. Because they could profit from protecting the big animals, some ranchers shifted their operations from producing cattle to wildlife protection, ecotourism, and hunting, often in cooperation with neighboring landowners. Under these rules, the black rhino population climbed dramatically. And because ranchers were allowed to cooperate and combine operations, they could reduce fencing between ranches and manage the larger preserves as a unit, better helping not only rhinos but other valued wildlife as well.

Indeed, several parts of southern Africa have a tradition, extending back to the 1960s, of allowing ownership of wildlife. Namibia, for example, gave those rights to private landholders in the 1960s and extended them to communal lands in the mid-1990s. With this policy change, tribal communities began to hold ownership rights over the wildlife in their communal areas and were able to keep all revenues from wildlife. This transformed the incentives in Namibia. By 2007, Namibian communities were receiving $4.3 million from wildlife, says Fred Nelson, a wildlife expert who spent 11 years in Africa developing wildlife management partnerships. The revenues come primarily from trophy hunting and tourism ventures—important new opportunities in semi-arid areas where income-earning options are limited.[2]

To ensure that trophy hunting of elephants, lions, and other animals would be profitable, local communities had to protect the animals and their habitat. These new incentives have led to a natural resurgence in wildlife numbers—lions are returning to areas where they had been overhunted—as well as deliberate restocking of wildlife. Even the number of black rhinos in Namibia has risen from 707 in 1997, to 1,134 in 2004.

Citing the 40 years of progress in Namibia, first by giving private ranchers rights to wildlife on their property and then extending them to tribal communities, Nelson told an interviewer in 2013, "This is an extraordinary achievement due to a very iconoclastic approach to conservation."[3] Clearly, property rights to ownership or use are one key to conservation.

[1]See Michael De Alessi, *Private Conservation and Black Rhinos in Zimbabwe: The Savé Valley and Bubiana Conservancies,* available online at www.cei.org/gencon/025,01687.cfm.

[2]Fred Nelson, "Conservation Can Work: Southern Africa Shows Its Neighbours How," *Swara* (East African Wildlife Society) 32, no. 2 (2009): 36–37.

[3]Interview with Fred Nelson, found on March 14, 2013, at www.iucn.org/about/union/commissions/sustainable_use_and_livelihoods_specialist_group/sulinews/issue_2/sn2_frednelson.cfm

©iStockphoto.com/sorendis

2-4 PRODUCTION POSSIBILITIES CURVE

Production possibilities curve

A curve that outlines all possible combinations of total output that could be produced, assuming (1) a fixed amount of productive resources, (2) a given amount of technical knowledge, and (3) full and efficient use of those resources. The slope of the curve indicates the amount of one product that must be given up to produce more of the other.

People try to get the most from their limited resources by making purposeful choices and engaging in economizing behavior. This can be illustrated using a conceptual tool called the **production possibilities curve**. The production possibilities curve shows the maximum amount of any two products that can be produced from a fixed set of resources, and the possible trade-offs in production between them. The real economy obviously produces more than just two products, but this concept can help us understand a number of important economic ideas.

Exhibit 1 illustrates the production possibilities curve for Susan, an intelligent economics major. This curve indicates the combinations of English and economics grades that she thinks she can earn if she spends a total of ten hours per week studying for the two subjects. Currently, she is choosing to study the material in each course that she expects will help her grade the most for the time spent, and she is allocating five hours of study time to each course. She expects that this amount of time, carefully spent on each course, will allow her to earn a B grade in both, indicated at point *T*. But if she were to take some time away from studying one of the two subjects and spend it studying the other, she could raise her grade in the course receiving more study time. However, it would come at the cost of a lower grade in the course she spends less time studying for. If she were to move to point *S* by spending more hours on economics and fewer on English, for example, her expected economics grade would rise, while her expected English grade would fall. This illustrates an important point: the idea of trade-offs in the use of scarce resources. Whenever more of one thing is produced, there is an opportunity cost in terms of something else that now must be forgone.

You might notice that Susan's production possibilities curve indicates that the additional study time required to raise her economics grade by one letter, from a B to an A (moving from point *T* to point *S*), would require giving up two letter grades in her English class, not just one, reducing her English grade from a B to a D. If, alternatively, Susan were to move from point *T* to point *U*, the opposite would be true—she would improve her English grade by one letter at the expense of two letter grades in economics. You can understand this by thinking about your own studying behavior. When you have only a limited amount of time to study a subject, you begin by studying the most important (grade-increasing) material first. As you spend additional time on that subject, you begin studying topics that are of decreasing importance for your grade. Thus, adding an hour of study time to the subject Susan studies least will have a larger impact on her grade than will taking away an hour from the subject on which she currently spends more time.

EXHIBIT 1

Production Possibilities Curve for Susan's Grades in English and Economics

The production possibilities for Susan, in terms of grades, are illustrated for ten hours of total study time. If Susan studied ten hours per week in these two classes, she could attain a D in English and an A in economics (point *S*), a B in English and a B in economics (point *T*), or a D in economics and an A in English (point *U*).

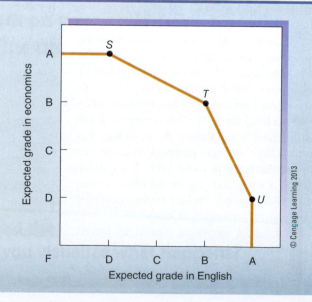

© Cengage Learning 2013

This idea of increasing opportunity cost is reflected in the slope of the production possibilities curve. The curve is flatter to the left of point *T*, and steeper to the right, showing that, as Susan takes more and more of her resources (time, in this case) from one course and puts it into the other, she must give up greater and greater amounts of productivity in the course getting fewer resources.

Of course, Susan could study more economics *without* giving up her English study time, if she gave up some leisure, or study time for other courses, or her part-time job in the campus bookstore. If she gave up leisure or her job and added those hours to the ten hours of study time for economics and English, the entire curve in Exhibit 1 would shift outward. She could get better grades in both classes by having more time to study.

Can the production possibilities concept be applied to the entire economy? Yes. We can grow more soybeans if we grow less corn, because both can be grown on the same land. Beefing up the nation's military would mean we would have to produce fewer nonmilitary goods than we could otherwise. When scarce resources are being used efficiently, getting more of one requires that we sacrifice others.

Exhibit 2 shows a hypothetical production possibilities curve for an economy with a limited amount of resources that produces only two goods: food and clothing. The points along the curve represent all possible combinations of food and clothing that could be produced with the current level of resources and technology of the economy (assuming the resources are being used efficiently). A point outside the production possibilities curve (such as point *E*) would be considered unattainable at the present time. A point inside the production possibilities curve (such as point *D*) is attainable, but producing that amount would mean that the economy is not making maximum use of its resources (some resources are being underutilized). Thus, point *D* is considered inefficient.

More specifically, the production possibilities curve shows all of the maximum combinations of two goods that an economy will be able to produce: (1) given a fixed quantity of resources, (2) holding the level of technology constant, and (3) assuming that all resources are used efficiently.

When these three conditions are met, the economy will be at the edge of its production possibilities frontier (where points *A*, *B*, and *C* lie), and producing more of one good will necessitate producing less of others. If condition 3 above is not met, and resources are being used inefficiently, an economy would be operating inside its production possibilities curve. If the level of resources and technology change (conditions 1 and 2), it will result in an outward shift in the production possibilities curve. We will return to these factors that can shift the production possibilities curve in a moment.

© Cengage Learning 2013

EXHIBIT 2

Concept of Production Possibilities Curve for an Economy

When an economy is using its limited resources efficiently, production of more clothing requires that the economy give up some other goods— such as food in this example. In time, improved technology, more resources, or improvement in its economic organization could make it possible to produce more of both goods by shifting the production possibilities curve outward.

Notice that the production possibilities curve is concave (or bowed out) to the origin, just as Susan's was in Exhibit 1 because of the concept of increasing opportunity cost. Here, the curved shape reflects the fact that an economy's resources are not equally well suited to produce food and clothing. If an economy were using all its resources to produce clothing (point S), transferring those resources least suited for producing clothing toward food production would reduce clothing output a little but increase food output a lot. Because the resources transferred would be those better suited for producing food and less suited for producing clothing, the opportunity cost of producing additional food (in terms of clothing forgone) is low—near point S. However, as more and more resources are devoted to food production and successively larger amounts of food are produced (moving the economy from S to A to B and so on), the opportunity cost of food will rise. This is because, as more and more food is produced, additional food output can be achieved only by using resources that are less and less suitable for the production of food relative to clothing. Thus, as food output is expanded, successively larger amounts of clothing must be forgone per unit of additional food. This is similar to what happened to Susan when she diverted study hours from one course to another. Only this time, we are talking about an entire economy.

2-4a SHIFTING THE PRODUCTION POSSIBILITIES CURVE OUTWARD

What restricts an economy—once its resources are fully utilized—from producing more of everything? Why can't we get more of something produced without having to give up the production of something else? The same constraint that kept Susan from simultaneously making a higher grade in both English and economics: a lack of resources. As long as all current resources are being used efficiently, the only way to get more of one good is to sacrifice some of the other. Over time, however, it is possible for a country's production possibilities curve to shift outward, making it possible for more of all goods to be produced. There are four factors that could potentially shift the production possibilities curve outward.

1. An increase in the economy's resource base would expand our ability to produce goods and services. If we had more or better resources, we could produce a greater amount of all goods. Resources such as machinery, buildings, tools, and education are human-made, and thus we can expand our resource base by devoting some of our efforts to producing them. This **investment** would provide us with better tools and skills and increase our ability to produce goods and services in the future. However, like with the production of other goods, devoting effort and resources toward producing these long-lasting physical assets means fewer resources are available to produce other things, in this case goods for current consumption. Thus, the choice between using resources to produce goods for current consumption and using them to produce investment goods for the future can also be illustrated within the production possibilities framework. The two economies illustrated in **Exhibit 3** begin with identical production possibilities curves (RS). Notice that Economy A dedicates more of its output to investment (shown by I_A) than does Economy B (shown by I_B). Economy B, on the other hand, consumes more than Economy A. Because Economy A allocates more of its resources to investment and less to consumption, A's production possibilities curve shifts outward over time by a greater amount than B's. In other words, the growth rate of Economy A—the expansion of its ability to produce goods—is enhanced by this investment. But more investment in machines and human skills requires a reduction in current consumption.

2. Advancements in technology can expand the economy's production possibilities. **Technology** determines the maximum amount of output an economy can produce given the resources it has. New and better technology makes it possible for us to get more output from our resources. An important form of technological change is **invention**— the use of science and engineering to create new products or processes. In recent years,

Investment
The purchase, construction, or development of resources, including physical assets, such as plants and machinery, and human assets, such as better education. Investment expands an economy's resources. The process of investment is sometimes called capital formation.

Technology
The technological knowledge available in an economy at any given time. The level of technology determines the amount of output we can generate with our limited resources.

Invention
The creation of a new product or process, often facilitated by the knowledge of engineering and science.

EXHIBIT 3

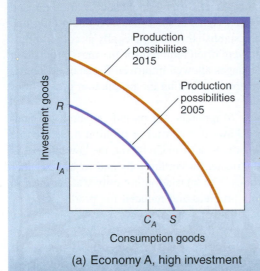

(a) Economy A, high investment

(b) Economy B, low investment

Investment and Production Possibilities in the Future

Here we illustrate two economies (A and B) that initially confront identical production possibilities curves (*RS*). Economy A allocates a larger share of its output to investment (I_A, compared to I_B for Economy B). As a result, the production possibilities curve of the high-investment economy (Economy A) will tend to shift outward by a larger amount over time than the low-investment economy's will.

for example, inventions have allowed us to develop photographs faster and more cheaply, process data more rapidly, get more oil and natural gas from existing fields, and send information instantly and cheaply by satellite. Such technological advances increase our production possibilities, shifting our economy's entire production possibilities curve outward.

The production possibilities of an economy can also be expanded by technological change through **innovation**—the practical and effective adoption of new techniques. Such innovation is commonly carried out by an **entrepreneur**—a person who introduces new products or improved techniques to satisfy consumers at a lower cost. Take, for example, Henry Ford, an entrepreneur who changed how cars were made by pioneering the assembly line. With the same amount of labor and materials, Ford made more cars more cheaply. Another entrepreneur, the late Ray Kroc, purchased a hamburger restaurant from Richard and Maurice McDonald and built it into the world's largest fast-food chain. Kroc revolutionized fast food by offering attractive food at economical prices. He also developed a franchising system that resulted in uniform quality across the many different McDonald's restaurants worldwide. More recently, entrepreneurs like Steven Jobs (Apple Computer) and Bill Gates (Microsoft) helped develop the personal computer and software programs that dramatically increased their usefulness to businesses and households.

Through entrepreneurial discovery and innovation, new products and methods of production are continuously replacing old ones. The great Harvard economist Joseph Schumpeter called this process **creative destruction**. The compact disc, for example, rendered vinyl records obsolete, while the automobile caused the demise of the horse and buggy industry. A modern cell phone can replace more than $1,200 worth of products from the past that would fill a small room, including a portable music player, alarm clock, watch, camera, flashlight, calendar, address book, car GPS system, pedometer, level, ruler, calculator, dictionary, guitar tuner, and many more. Although this process destroys some businesses or industries, it creates new and arguably better ones in their place. Creative destruction is a powerful force leading to economic growth and prosperity.

3. An improvement in the rules under which the economy functions can also increase output.
The legal system of a country influences the ability of people to cooperate with one another and produce goods. Changes in legal institutions that promote social cooperation and motivate people to produce what others want will also push the production possibilities curve outward. However, poor institutions can reduce both the level of resources used (shifting the curve inward) and how efficiently they are used (causing the economy to operate inside its production possibilities curve).

Innovation
The successful introduction and adoption of a new product or process; the economic application of inventions and marketing techniques.

Entrepreneur
A person who introduces new products or improved technologies and decides which projects to undertake. A successful entrepreneur's actions will increase the value of resources and expand the size of the economic pie.

Creative destruction
The replacement of old products and production methods by innovative new ones that consumers judge to be superior. The process generates economic growth and higher living standards.

Historically, legal innovations have been an important source of economic progress. During the eighteenth century, a system of patents was established in Europe and North America, giving inventors private-property rights to their ideas. At about the same time, laws were passed allowing businesses to establish themselves legally as corporations, reducing the cost of forming large firms that were often required for the mass production of manufactured goods. Both of these legal changes allowed improved forms of economic organization and accelerated the growth of output by shifting the production possibilities curve outward more rapidly.

Sometimes governments, perhaps because of ignorance or prejudice, adopt legal institutions that reduce production possibilities. Laws that restrict or prohibit trade are one example. For almost a hundred years following the American Civil War, the laws of several southern states prohibited hiring African Americans for certain jobs and restricted other economic exchanges between blacks and whites. The legislation not only was harmful to African Americans; it also retarded economic progress and reduced the production possibilities of these states.

4. By working harder and giving up current leisure, we could increase our production of goods and services. Hypothetically, the production possibilities curve would shift outward if everyone worked more hours and took less leisure time. Strictly speaking, however, leisure is also a good, so we would simply be giving up leisure to have more of other things. If we were to construct a production possibilities curve for leisure versus other goods, this would be shown as simply a movement along the curve. However, if we restrict our model to only material goods and services, a change in the amount we work would be shown as a shift in the curve.

How much people work depends not only on their personal preferences but also on public policy. For example, high tax rates on personal income may cause people to work less. This is because high tax rates reduce the payoff from working. When this happens, people spend more time doing other, untaxed activities—like leisure activities. This will move the production possibilities curve for material goods inward because the economy can't produce as much when people work less.

2-4b PRODUCTION POSSIBILITIES AND ECONOMIC GROWTH

Within the production possibilities framework, economic growth is simply an outward shift in the curve through time. The more rapidly the curve shifts outward, the more rapid is economic growth. There are other economic models that are used to analyze economic growth; however, they all share the production possibilities curve as a foundation. Economic growth is one of the most important topics in modern economics for good reason. On the one hand, an economic growth rate of 3 percent per year will result in living standards doubling approximately every 23 years. On the other hand, in a country experiencing an economic growth rate of only 1 percent, it will take approximately seventy years for living standards to double.

2-5 TRADE, OUTPUT, AND LIVING STANDARDS

KEYS TO ECONOMIC PROSPERITY

Gains from Trade

Trade makes it possible for people to generate more output through specialization and division of labor, large-scale production processes, and the dissemination of improved products and production methods.

As we previously discussed, trade creates value by moving goods from people who value them less to people who value them more. However, this is only part of the story. Trade also makes it possible for people to expand their output through specialization and **division of labor**, large-scale production, and the dissemination of better products and production methods.

2-5a GAINS FROM SPECIALIZATION AND DIVISION OF LABOR

Businesses can achieve higher output levels and greater productivity from their workers through specialization and division of labor. More than 230 years ago, Adam Smith noted the importance of this factor. Observing the operation of a pin manufacturer, Smith noted that when each worker specialized in a separate function needed to make pins, 10 workers together were able to produce 48,000 pins per day, or 4,800 pins per worker. Smith doubted an individual worker could produce even 20 pins per day working alone from start to finish on each pin.[7]

The division of labor separates production tasks into a series of related operations. Each worker performs one or a few of perhaps hundreds of tasks necessary to produce something. This process makes it possible to assign different tasks to those individuals who are able to accomplish them most efficiently (that is, at the lowest cost). Furthermore, a worker who specializes in just one narrow area becomes more experienced and more skilled in that task over time.

Trading partners can also benefit from specialization and the division of labor. The **law of comparative advantage**, developed in the early 1800s by the great English economist David Ricardo, explains why this is true. *The law of comparative advantage states that the total output of a group of individuals, an entire economy, or a group of nations will be greatest when the output of each good is produced by the person (or firm) with the lowest opportunity cost for that good.*

Comparative advantage applies to trade among individuals, business firms, regions, and even nations. When trading partners are able to use more of their time and resources to produce the things each is best at, they will be able to produce more together than would otherwise have been possible. In turn, the mutual gains they get from trading will result in higher levels of income for each. It's a win–win situation for both.

If a good or service can be obtained more economically through trade, it makes sense to get it that way rather than producing it for yourself. When you think about it, the law of comparative advantage is common sense. If someone else is willing to supply you with a good at a lower cost than you can produce it yourself, doesn't it make sense to trade for it and use your time and resources to produce more of the things you can produce most efficiently? Consider the situation of Andrea, an attorney who earns $100 per hour providing legal services. She has several documents that need to be typed, and she is thinking about hiring a typist earning $15 per hour to do it. Andrea is an excellent typist, much faster than the prospective employee. She could do the job in 20 hours, whereas the typist would take 40 hours.

Because of her greater typing speed, some might think Andrea should handle the job herself. This is not the case. If she types the documents, the job will

Division of labor
A method that breaks down the production of a product into a series of specific tasks, each performed by a different worker.

Law of comparative advantage
A principle that states that individuals, firms, regions, or nations can gain by specializing in the production of goods that they produce cheaply (at a low opportunity cost) and exchanging them for goods they cannot produce cheaply (at a high opportunity cost).

Trade channels goods to those who value them most. Trade also helps disseminate ideas for improved products and makes production methods such as specialization, the division of labor, and mass production more feasible. Over the years, trade has enabled us to produce more with our limited resources, dramatically improving our living standards.

CARLOSBARRIA/Reuters/Corbis

---

[7]See Adam Smith, *An Inquiry into the Nature and Causes of the Wealth of Nations* (1776; Cannan's ed., Chicago: University of Chicago Press, 1976), 7–16, for additional detail on the importance of the division of labor.

cost her $2,000—the opportunity cost of 20 hours of practicing law at $100 per hour. Alternatively, the cost of having the documents typed by the typist is only $600 (40 hours at $15 per hour). Andrea's comparative advantage lies in practicing law. By hiring the typist, she will increase her own productivity for clients and will make more money.

The implications of the law of comparative advantage are universal. Any group will be able to produce more output from its available resources when each good or service is produced by the person with the lowest opportunity cost. This insight is particularly important in understanding the way a market economy works. Buyers will try to get the most for their money. They will not knowingly choose a high-cost option when a lower-cost alternative of the same value is available. This places low-cost suppliers at a competitive advantage. Thus, low-cost producers will generally survive and prosper in a market economy. As a result, the production of goods and resources will naturally tend to be allocated according to comparative advantage.

Most people recognize that Americans benefit from trade among the nation's 50 states. For example, the residents of Nebraska and Florida are able to produce a larger joint output and achieve higher income levels when Nebraskans specialize in producing corn and other grain products and Floridians specialize in producing oranges and other citrus products. The same is true for trade among nations. Like Nebraskans and Floridians, people in different nations will be better off if they specialize in the goods and services they can produce at a low cost and trade them for goods they produce at a high cost. See the addendum to this chapter for additional evidence on this point.

2-5b GAINS FROM MASS PRODUCTION METHODS

Trade also promotes economic progress by making it possible for firms to lower their per-unit costs with mass production. Suppose a nation isolated itself and refused to trade with other countries. In an economy like this, self-sufficiency and small-scale production would be the norm. If trade were allowed, however, the nation's firms could sell their products to customers around the world. This would make it feasible for the firms to adopt more efficient, large-scale production processes. Mass production often leads to labor and machinery efficiencies that increase enormously the output per worker. But without trade, these gains could not be achieved.

2-5c GAINS FROM INNOVATION

Trade also makes it possible to realize gains from the discovery and dissemination of innovative products and production processes. Economic growth involves brain power, innovation, and the application of technology. Without trade, however, the gains derived from the discovery of better ways of doing things would be stifled. Furthermore, observing and interacting with other people using different and better technologies often encourage others to copy successful approaches. People also modify the technology they observe, adapting it for their own purposes. This sometimes results in new, and even better, technologies. Again, gains from these sources would be far more limited in a world without trade.

Can you imagine the difficulty involved in producing your own housing, clothing, and food, to say nothing of computers, television sets, dishwashers, automobiles, and cell phones? Yet, most families in North America, Western Europe, Japan, and Australia enjoy all these conveniences. They are able to do so largely because their economies are organized in such a way that individuals can cooperate, specialize, and trade, thereby reaping the benefits of the enormous increases in output—in both quantity and diversity—that can be generated. In contrast, countries that impose obstacles that retard exchange—either domestic or international—hinder their citizens from achieving these gains and more prosperous lives.

2-6 HUMAN INGENUITY AND THE CREATION OF WEALTH

KEYS TO ECONOMIC PROSPERITY

Human Ingenuity

Economic goods are the result of human ingenuity and action; thus, the size of the "economic pie" is variable, not fixed.

©iStockphoto.com/malerapaso

The size of a country's "economic pie" is most easily thought of as the total dollar value of all goods and services produced during some period of time. This economic pie is the grand total of the wealth (or value) created by each member of the society. It is not some fixed total waiting to be divided up among people. On the contrary, the size of the economic pie reflects the physical effort and ingenuity of human beings. It is not an endowment from nature.

Economic output expands as we discover better ways of doing things. So over time, it is human knowledge and ingenuity—perhaps more than anything else—that limit our economic progress. If Jim, a local farmer who normally produces $30,000 worth of corn each year, finds a better growing method enabling him to produce $40,000 of corn per year, he has created additional wealth. But Jim has actually created more than the $10,000 in extra wealth. The $10,000 is only his share of the gains from the additional trades made possible by the extra corn he grew. Exchange makes both buyer and seller better off, so the total wealth created by Jim includes not only his $10,000 but also the gains of all of the buyers who purchased his additional output of corn.

This highlights an important point: in a market economy, a larger income for one person does not mean a smaller income for a trading partner. In fact, it is just the opposite. When a person earns income, he or she expands the economic pie by more than the amount of the slice that he or she gets, making it possible for the rest of us to have a bigger slice, too. When a wealthy entrepreneur, such as Bill Gates or Stephen King, has an income of, say, $100 million per year earned through voluntary exchanges in the marketplace, he has enlarged the economic pie by an even larger amount. Here's why: Suppose that Linda, a freelance graphic artist, pays $175 for a new software program developed by Bill Gates. As a result, she can do twice as much work in the same amount of time. Because she's more productive, Linda can earn more than enough additional income with the software to justify her purchase. In addition, the businesses she serves are also likely to be better off because the software makes it possible for her to give them more and better service and a lower price. More is produced in total. Thus, while Bill Gates gained, so, too, did Linda and her customers.

Similarly, had Stephen King never written a novel, not only would he not be as rich, but we would also all be poorer for never having had the opportunity to read his novels. When income is acquired through voluntary exchange, people who earn income also help others earn more income and live better, too.

2-7 ECONOMIC ORGANIZATION

Every economy faces three basic questions: (1) What will be produced? (2) How will it be produced? and (3) For whom will it be produced? These questions are highly interrelated. Throughout the book, we will consider how different types of economies solve them. There are two broad ways that an economy can be organized: markets and government (political) planning. Let us briefly consider each.

2-7a MARKET ORGANIZATION

Market organization
A method of organization in which private parties make their own plans and decisions with the guidance of unregulated market prices. The basic economic questions of consumption, production, and distribution are answered through these decentralized decisions.

Capitalism
An economic system in which productive resources are owned privately and goods and resources are allocated through market prices.

Private ownership of productive assets, voluntary exchange, and market prices are the distinguishing features of **market organization**. Market organization is also known as **capitalism**.[8] Under market organization, private parties are permitted to buy and sell ownership rights of their assets at mutually acceptable prices. The government plays the limited role of rule maker and referee. It develops the rules, or the legal structure, that recognizes, defines, and protects private ownership rights. It helps individuals enforce contracts and protects people from violence and fraud. But in this role, the government is not an active player in the economy. Ideally, it avoids modifying market outcomes in an attempt to favor some people at the expense of others. For example, it doesn't prevent sellers from slashing prices or improving the quality of their products to attract customers from other competitors. Nor does it prevent buyers from outbidding others for products and productive resources. No legal restraints limit potential buyers or sellers from producing, selling, or buying in the marketplace.

Under market organization, no single individual or group of individuals guides the economy. There is no central planning authority, only individual planning. The three basic questions are solved independently in the marketplace by individual buyers and sellers making their own decentralized decisions. Buyers and sellers decide on their own what to produce, how to produce it, and whom to trade it to, based on the prices they themselves decide to charge.

In markets, individual buyers and sellers communicate their desires and preferences both directly and indirectly. They communicate directly through their buying and selling choices, by advertising, word of mouth and letters of request and complaint, and other means. They communicate indirectly by exiting or entering exchange relationships, as when they stop purchasing Coca-Cola and switch to Pepsi. The indirect, or "exit," option gives special power to their voiced, or direct, communication.

2-7b POLITICAL ORGANIZATION

Collective decision-making
The use of the political process (voting, taxes, government spending, regulation, political bargaining, lobbying, and so on) to make decisions and allocate resources. In a democratic setting, the votes of citizens and their representatives will determine the actions undertaken.

Socialism
A system of economic organization in which (1) the ownership and control of the basic means of production rest with the state and (2) resource allocation is determined by centralized planning rather than by market forces.

The major alternative to market organization is **collective decision-making**, whereby the government, through the political process, makes decisions for buyers and sellers in an attempt to solve the basic economic questions facing the economy. Sometimes, the government will maintain private ownership but uses taxes, subsidies, and regulations to resolve the basic economic questions. Alternatively, an economic system in which the government also owns the income-producing assets (machines, buildings, and land) and directly determines what goods will be produced is called **socialism**. Either way, individual planning and decisions are replaced by central planning and decisions made through the political process. These decisions can be made by a single dictator or a group of experts, or through democratic voting. Political rather than market forces direct the economy, and government officials and planning boards hand down decisions to expand or contract the output of education, medical services, automobiles, electricity, steel, consumer durables, and thousands of other commodities.

While the market and political process can be used to address the same basic economic questions, there are fundamental differences between the two. The market system relies on voluntary exchange, price signals, and freedom of entry. This results in wider variety of products, a more competitive environment, and more dynamic change. On the other hand, the democratic political process responds primarily to the votes of the majority. In varying degrees, all economies use a combination of both of these methods of economic organization. Even predominantly market economies will still use taxes, subsidies, and some government ownership to direct and control resources. Similarly, predominantly socialist economies will, to some degree, use markets to allocate certain goods and services. As examples, countries such as Venezuela, Zimbabwe, Ethiopia, Angola, Cuba, and North Korea rely predominantly on socialism and government planning to organize economic activity. In contrast, countries such as Singapore, New Zealand, Switzerland, Canada, and

---

[8]*Capitalism* is a term coined by Karl Marx.

Australia rely predominantly on capitalism and market organization. Countries with mixed economies that have significant aspects of both systems include Portugal, Turkey, Mexico, Italy, and Greece.

As we proceed, the tools of economics will be used to analyze both the market and political sectors. We think this approach is important and that you will find it both interesting and enlightening.

LOOKING AHEAD

The next two chapters present an overview of the market sector and explain how demand and supply for goods and services work. Chapters 5 and 6 focus on potential shortcomings of the market and how the collective decision-making process works in a democracy.

KEY POINTS

- The highest valued activity sacrificed when a choice is made is the opportunity cost of the choice; differences (or changes) in opportunity costs help explain human behavior.

- Mutual gain is the foundation of trade. When two parties engage in voluntary exchange, they are both made better off. Trade creates value because it channels goods and resources to those who value them the most.

- Transaction costs—the time, effort, and other resources necessary to search out, negotiate, and conclude an exchange—hinder the gains from trade in an economy. Middlemen perform a productive function by reducing transaction cost.

- Private-property rights motivate owners to use their resources in ways that benefit others and avoid doing harm to them. Private ownership also motivates owners to maintain and care for items they own and conserve valuable resources for the future.

- The production possibilities curve shows the maximum combination of any two products that can be produced with a fixed quantity of resources.

- Over time, the production possibilities curve of an economy can be shifted outward by (1) investment, (2) technological advances,

(3) improved institutions, and (4) greater work effort (forgoing leisure).

- The law of comparative advantage indicates that the joint output of individuals, regions, and nations will be maximized when each productive activity is undertaken by the low-opportunity-cost supplier. When a good can be acquired through trade more economically than it can be produced directly, it makes sense to trade for it.

- In addition to the gains that occur when goods are moved toward those who value them most, trade also makes it possible to expand output through specialization, division of labor, mass production processes, and innovation. These improved production techniques have contributed greatly to our modern living standards.

- The size of the economic pie is variable, not fixed. Human ingenuity can expand output by discovering lower cost methods of production and new products that are highly valued relative to cost.

- Economies can either be organized by decentralized markets (capitalism) or they can be centrally planned by government through political decision-making.

CRITICAL ANALYSIS QUESTIONS

1. "If Jones trades a used car to Smith for $5,000, nothing new is created. Thus, there is no way the transaction can improve the welfare of people." Is this statement true? Why or why not?

2. *Economists often argue that wage rates reflect productivity. Yet, the wages of house painters have increased nearly as rapidly as the national average, even though these workers use approximately the same production methods as they did 50 years ago.

Can you explain why the wages of painters have risen substantially even though their productivity has changed so little?

3. It takes one hour to travel from New York City to Washington, D.C., by air, but it takes five hours by bus. If the airfare is $110 and the bus fare is $70, which would be cheaper for someone whose opportunity cost of travel time is $6 per hour? For someone whose opportunity cost is $10 per hour? $14 per hour?

4. "People in business get ahead by exploiting the needs of their consumers. The gains of business are at the expense of suffering imposed on their customers." Evaluate this statement.

5. What is the major function of the middleman? Would people be better off if there were no middlemen? Why or why not?

6. If you have a private-ownership right to something, what does this mean? Does private ownership give you the right to do anything you want with the things that you own? Explain. How does private ownership influence the incentive of individuals to (a) take care of things, (b) conserve resources for the future, and (c) develop and modify things in ways that are beneficial to others? Explain.

7. What is the law of comparative advantage? According to the law of comparative advantage, what should be the distinguishing characteristics of the goods a nation produces? What should be the distinguishing characteristics of the goods a nation imports? How will international trade influence people's production levels and living standards? Explain.

8. *Does a 60-year-old tree farmer have an incentive to plant and care for Douglas fir trees that will not reach optimal cutting size for another 50 years?

9. *What forms of competition does a private-property, market-directed economy authorize? What forms does it prohibit?

10. Why is exchange important to a nation's prosperity? How does trade influence the quantity of output that trading partners are able to produce? In a market economy, will there be a tendency for both resources and products to be supplied by low-cost producers? Why or why not? Does this matter? Explain.

11. Chick-fil-A's "Eat Mor Chikin" advertising campaign features three cows holding signs that say things like "Save the cows, eat more chicken." If consumers began eating more chicken and less beef, would the cattle population increase or decrease? Explain.

12. *In many states, ticket scalping, or reselling tickets to entertainment events at prices above the original purchase price, is prohibited. Who is helped and who is hurt by such prohibitions? How can owners who want to sell their tickets get around the prohibition? Do you think it would be a good idea to prohibit the resale of other things—automobiles, books, works of art, or stock shares—at prices higher than the original purchase price? Why or why not?

13. Two centuries ago, there were more buffalo than cattle in the United States. Even though millions of cattle are killed for beef consumption each year, the cattle population continues to grow while the buffalo are virtually extinct. Why?

14. Consider the following questions:

   a. Do you think that your work effort is influenced by whether there is a close link between personal output and personal compensation (reward)? Explain.

   b. Suppose the grades in your class were going to be determined by a random drawing at the end of the course. How would this influence your study habits?

   c. How would your study habits be influenced if everyone in the class was going to be given an A grade? How about if grades were based entirely on examinations composed of the end of chapter questions in the textbook?

   d. Do you think the total output of a nation will be influenced by whether or not there is a close link between the productive contribution of individuals and their personal reward? Why or why not?

15. In this chapter, it was stated that a private-property right also involves having the right to transfer or exchange what you own with others. However, selling your organs is a violation of federal law, a felony punishable by up to five years in prison or a $50,000 fine. In 1999, eBay intervened when a person put one of his kidneys up for sale on the auction site (the bidding reached $5.7 million before the auction was halted). Does this lack of legal ability to exchange mean that individuals do not own their own organs? Explain.

16. During the last three decades, entrepreneurs like Steve Jobs, Sam Walton, and Michael Dell have earned billions of dollars. Do you think the average American is better or worse off as the result of the economic activities of these individuals? Explain your response.

17. *As the skill level (and therefore earnings rate) of, say, an architect, computer specialist, or chemist increases, what happens to his or her opportunity cost of doing other things? How is the time spent on leisure likely to change?

18. *This question pertains to the addendum to Chapter 2. The following tables show the production possibilities for two hypothetical countries, Italia and Nire. Which country has the comparative advantage in producing butter? Which country has the comparative advantage in producing guns? What would be a mutually agreeable rate of exchange between the countries?

Italia		Nire	
Guns	Butter	Guns	Butter
12	0	16	0
8	2	12	1
4	4	8	2
0	6	4	3
		0	4

© Cengage Learning

*Asterisk denotes questions for which answers are given in Appendix B.

ADDENDUM

COMPARATIVE ADVANTAGE, SPECIALIZATION, AND GAINS FROM TRADE

This addendum is for instructors who want to assign a more detailed numerical example demonstrating comparative advantage, specialization, and mutual gains from trade. Students who are uncertain about their understanding of these topics may also find this material enlightening. The international trade chapter later in the text provides still more information on trade and how it affects our lives.

We begin with hypothetical production possibilities curves for two countries, Slavia and Lebos, shown in Exhibit A-1. The numerical tables represent selected points from each country's production possibilities curve. To make calculations easier, we have assumed away increasing opportunity costs in production so that the production possibilities curves are linear.

Without trade, each country would be able to consume only what it can produce for itself. Let's arbitrarily assume that for survival, Slavia requires three units of food and Lebos requires six units of food. As can be seen by point *A* in the exhibit, if Slavia were to produce the three units of food it requires, it would have enough

resources remaining to produce two units of clothing. Similarly, if Lebos were to produce the six units of food it requires, it would have enough resources left to produce six units of clothing, again shown by point *A* in the exhibit. As we proceed, we will use this outcome as our benchmark outcome that occurs in the absence of specialization and trade between the countries.

Economic analysis suggests that both countries could gain if each were to specialize in the production of the good for which it has the comparative advantage and then trade for the other. First, let's figure out which country has a comparative advantage in the production of clothing. Doing so requires calculating the opportunity cost of producing clothing for each country. Because, in this example, the opportunity costs are constant at all points along the production possibilities curve, rather than increasing, this can be found by first selecting any two points on the production possibilities curve (or equivalently by comparing any two rows of numbers in the numerical tables given in the exhibit). For Slavia, moving from the point of producing six food units and one clothing unit to the alternative point of producing three food units and two clothing units, we see that Slavia gains one clothing unit but must give up three units of food. For simplicity, the opportunity cost for Slavia can be written as 1C = 3F, where C stands for clothing and F for food. You might note that this same numerical trade-off is true for Slavia anywhere along

EXHIBIT A-1

Production Possibilities for Slavia and Lebos

For Slavia, the opportunity cost of producing one unit of clothing is equal to three units of food (1C = 3F). For Lebos, the opportunity cost of producing three units of clothing is equal to three units of food (3C = 3F or 1C = 1F). The difference in the opportunity costs of production will make possible mutually beneficial trade between the countries, with each specializing in its area of comparative advantage.

SLAVIA		
Food		Clothing
9		0
6	3F = 1C	1
3		2
0		3

LEBOS		
Food		Clothing
12		0
9	3F = 3C	3
6		6
3		9
0		12

© Cengage Learning 2013

its production possibilities curve (for example, beginning from nine food units and zero clothing units, it would also have to give up three food units to gain one unit of clothing).

Using a similar approach (taking any two points or two rows in the table) for Lebos shows that for every three units of clothing the country wishes to produce, it must give up three units of food (3C = 3F). This can be treated as any other mathematical equation, and can be simplified by dividing both sides by three, resulting in an opportunity cost of one clothing unit equals one food unit (1C = 1F). Now, compare this to the opportunity cost for Slavia (1C = 3F). Slavia must give up the production of three units of food for every one unit of clothing it produces, whereas Lebos must give up only one unit of food for every one unit of clothing it produces. Thus, Lebos gives up the production of *less* food for every unit of clothing. Lebos is the low-opportunity-cost producer of clothing, and thus, it has a comparative advantage in the production of clothing.

Because comparative advantage is a relative comparison, if one country has the comparative advantage in the production of one of the products, the other country must have the comparative advantage for the other good. Thus, because Lebos has the comparative advantage in clothing, it will be true that Slavia has the comparative advantage in food. However, it is worthwhile to show this here as well. To produce one unit of food, Lebos must give up one unit of clothing (recall the 1C = 1F opportunity cost). To produce one unit of food, Slavia must give up the production of only one-third of a unit of clothing (recall the 1C = 3F opportunity cost and rewrite the equation as 1/3 C = 1F by dividing both sides of the equation by 3). Thus, Slavia gives up the production of *less* clothing for every unit of food produced. Slavia is the low-opportunity-cost producer of food, and thus has a comparative advantage in the production of food.

Suppose that, according to their comparative advantages, Lebos specializes in producing clothing and Slavia in food. From the last row of the table for Lebos, you can see that it can produce twelve units of clothing (and zero food) if it specializes in producing only clothing. From the top row of the table for Slavia, you can see that it can produce nine units of food (and zero clothing) if it specializes

in producing only food. Note that this joint output (nine food and twelve clothing) is greater than the benchmark joint output (nine food and eight clothing) produced and consumed without trade.

If they are to trade, the countries now must find a mutually agreeable rate of exchange. Any rate of exchange *between* the two opportunity costs of 1C = 3F and 3C = 3F would be mutually agreeable. Here we will use 2C = 3F.

Recall that Slavia requires three units of food for survival. Now, however, they are specializing and producing nine units of food. Using this rate of exchange, Slavia would send its extra six units of food to Lebos in exchange for four units of clothing. After trade, Slavia would then have three units of food and four units of clothing. Compare this to the situation that existed before specialization and trade, in which Slavia had only three units of food and two units of clothing to consume. Specialization and trade have created two additional units of clothing for Slavia that it would not have had without trade.

With specialization, Lebos is producing twelve units of clothing. In the trade with Slavia, Lebos gave up four units of clothing to obtain six units of food. After trade, Lebos has eight units of clothing remaining and six units of food imported from Slavia. Compare this to the situation that existed before specialization and trade, in which Lebos had only six units of food and six units of clothing to consume. For Lebos, specialization and trade have also created two additional units of clothing that it would not have had without trade.

As this simple example shows, total output is greater and *both* countries are better off when they specialize in the area in which they have a comparative advantage. By doing so, each is able to consume a bundle of goods and services that exceeds what it could have achieved in the absence of trade. This concept applies equally to individuals, states, or nations. The typical worker could not begin to produce alone all of the things he or she can afford to buy with the money earned in a year by specializing and working in a single occupation. As our world has become more integrated over the past several hundred years, the gains that have occurred from specialization and trade are at the root of the significant improvements in well-being that we have experienced.

Markets and Government

There are two primary methods of allocating scarce resources: markets and government.

Economics has a great deal to say about how both markets and governments allocate scarce resources. It gives us insight about the conditions under which each will likely work well (and each will likely work poorly). The next four chapters will focus on this topic.

MARKET ALLOCATION OF RESOURCES

Business firms purchase resources like materials, labor services, tools, and machines from households in exchange for income, bidding the resources away from their alternate uses. The firms then transform the resources into products like shoes, automobiles, food products, and medical services and sell them to households. In a market economy, businesses will continue to supply a good or service only if the revenues from the sale of the product are sufficient to cover the cost of the resources required for its production.

GOVERNMENT ALLOCATION OF RESOURCES

Resource allocation by the government involves a more complex, three-sided exchange. In a democratic political setting, a legislative body levies taxes on voter–citizens, and these revenues are subdivided into budgets, which are allocated to government bureaus and agencies. In turn, the bureaus and agencies use the funds from their budgets to supply goods, services, and income transfers to voter–citizens. The legislative body is like a board of directors elected by the citizens. Legislators have an incentive to take action that will attract votes. Voters have an incentive to support legislators who provide them with goods, services, and transfers that are highly valued relative to their tax payments. When decisions are made democratically, political action will require the approval of a legislative majority.

This section will first analyze the operation of markets and then turn to the political process.

franckreporter/E+/Getty Images

CHAPTER 3
Demand, Supply, and the Market Process

FOCUS

- What are the laws of demand and supply?
- How do consumers decide whether to purchase a good? How do producers decide whether to supply it?
- How do buyers and sellers respond to changes in the price of a good?
- What role do profits and losses play in an economy? What must a firm do to make a profit?
- How is the market price of a good determined?
- How do markets adjust to changes in demand? How do they adjust to changes in supply?
- What is the "invisible hand" principle?

I am convinced that if [the market system] were the result of deliberate human design, and if the people guided by the price changes understood that their decisions have significance far beyond their immediate aim, this mechanism would have been acclaimed as one of the greatest triumphs of the human mind.
—Friedrich Hayek, Nobel Laureate[1]

From the point of view of physics, it is a miracle that [7 million New Yorkers are fed each day] without any control mechanism other than sheer capitalism.
—John H. Holland, scientist, Santa Fe Institute[2]

[1]Friedrich Hayek, "The Use of Knowledge in Society," *American Economic Review* 35 (September 1945): 519–30.
[2]As quoted by Russell Ruthen in "Adapting to Complexity," *Scientific American* 268 (January 1993): 132.

Franckreporter/E+/Getty Images

To those who study art, the *Mona Lisa* is much more than a famous painting of a woman. Looking beyond the overall picture, they see and appreciate the brush strokes, colors, and techniques embodied in the painting. Similarly, studying economics can help you to gain an appreciation for the details behind many things in your everyday life. During your last visit to the grocery store, you probably noticed the fruit and vegetable section. Next time, take a moment to ponder how potatoes from Idaho, oranges from Florida, apples from Washington, bananas from Honduras, kiwi fruit from New Zealand, and other items from around the world got there. Literally thousands of different individuals, *working independently*, were involved in the process. Their actions were so well coordinated, in fact, that the amount of each good was just about right to fill exactly the desires of your local community. Furthermore, even the goods shipped from halfway around the world were fresh and reasonably priced.

How does all this happen? The short answer is that it is the result of market prices and the incentives and coordination that flow from them. To the economist, the operation of markets—including your local grocery market—is like the brush strokes underlying a beautiful painting. Reflecting on this point, Friedrich Hayek speculates that if the market system had been deliberately designed, it would be "acclaimed as one of the greatest triumphs of the human mind." Similarly, computer scientist John H. Holland argues that, from the viewpoint of physics, the feeding of millions of New Yorkers day after day with very few shortages or surpluses is a miraculous feat (see the chapter-opening quotations).

Amazingly, markets coordinate the actions of millions of individuals *without* central planning. There is no individual, political authority, or central planning committee in charge. Considering that there are more than 300 million Americans with widely varying skills and desires, and roughly 28 million businesses producing a vast array of products ranging from diamond rings to toilet paper, the coordination derived from markets is indeed an awesome achievement.

The produce section of your local grocery store is a great place to see economics in action. Literally millions of individuals from around the world have been involved in the process of getting these goods to the shelves in just the right quantities. Market prices underlie this feat.

This chapter focuses on demand, supply, and the determination of market prices. For now, we will analyze the operation of competitive markets—that is, markets in which buyers and sellers are free to enter and exit. We will also assume that the property rights are well defined. Later, we will consider what happens when these conditions are absent.

On eBay, sellers enter their reserve prices—the minimum prices they will accept for goods; buyers enter their maximum bids—the maximum prices they are willing to pay for goods. The process works the same way when a person runs a newspaper ad to sell a car. The seller has in mind a minimum price he or she will accept for the car. A potential buyer, on the other hand, has in mind a maximum price he or she will pay for the car. If the buyer's maximum price is greater than the seller's minimum price, the exchange will occur at a price somewhere in between. As these examples show, the buyers' and sellers' desires and incentives determine prices and make markets work. We will begin with the demand (buyer's) side, and then turn to the supply (seller's) side of the market.

3-1 CONSUMER CHOICE AND THE LAW OF DEMAND

Clearly, prices influence our decisions. As the price of a good increases, we have to give up more of *other* goods if we want to buy it. Thus, as the price of a good rises, its opportunity cost increases (in terms of other goods that must be forgone to purchase it).

Law of demand
A principle that states there is an inverse relationship between the price of a good and the quantity of it buyers are willing to purchase. As the price of a good increases, consumers will wish to purchase less of it. As the price decreases, consumers will wish to purchase more of it.

Substitutes
Products that serve similar purposes. An increase in the price of one will cause an increase in demand for the other (examples are hamburgers and tacos, butter and margarine, Chevrolets and Fords).

This basic principle underlies the **law of demand**. *The law of demand states that there is an inverse (or negative) relationship between the price of a good or service and the quantity of it that consumers are willing to purchase.* This inverse relationship means that price and the quantity consumers wish to purchase move in opposite directions. As the price increases, buyers purchase less—and as the price decreases, buyers purchase more.

The availability of **substitutes**—goods that perform similar functions—helps explain this inverse relationship. No single good is absolutely essential; everything can be replaced with something else. A chicken sandwich can be substituted for a cheeseburger. Wood, aluminum, bricks, and glass can take the place of steel. Going to the movies, playing tennis, watching television, and going to a football game are substitute forms of entertainment. When the price of a good increases, people cut back on their purchases of it and turn to substitute products.

3-1a THE MARKET DEMAND SCHEDULE

The lower portion of **Exhibit 1** shows a hypothetical *demand schedule* for pizza delivery in a city. A demand schedule is simply a table listing the various quantities of something consumers are willing to purchase at different prices. When the price of a large pizza delivery is $35, only 4,000 people per month order pizza delivery. As the price falls to $25, the quantity of pizza deliveries demanded rises to 8,000 per month; when the price falls to $10, the quantity demanded increases to 14,000 per month.

EXHIBIT 1

Law of Demand

As the demand schedule shown in the table indicates, the number of people ordering pizza delivery (just like the consumption of other products) is inversely related to price. The data from the table are plotted as a demand curve in the graph. The inverse relationship between price and amount demanded reflects the fact that consumers will substitute away from a good as it becomes more expensive.

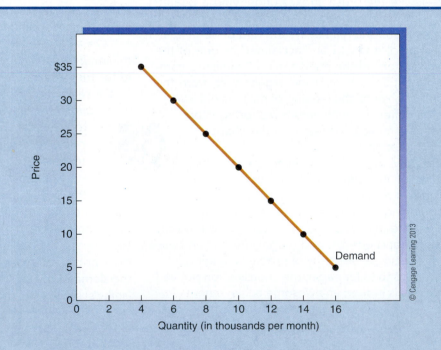

Price	Quantity (in thousands per month)
$35	4
30	6
25	8
20	10
15	12
10	14
5	16

The upper portion of Exhibit 1 shows what the demand schedule would look like if the various prices and corresponding quantities were plotted on a graph and connected by a line. This is called the *demand curve*. When representing the demand schedule graphically, economists measure price on the vertical or *y*-axis and the amount demanded on the horizontal or *x*-axis. Because of the inverse relationship between price and amount purchased, the demand curve will have a negative slope—that is, it will slope downward to the right. More of a good will be purchased as its price decreases. This is the law of demand.

Read horizontally, the demand curve shows how much of a particular good consumers are willing to buy at a given price. Read vertically, the demand curve shows how much consumers value the good. The height of the demand curve at any quantity shows the maximum price consumers are willing to pay for an additional unit. If consumers value highly an additional unit of a product, they will be willing to pay a large amount for it. Conversely, if they place a low value on the additional unit, they will be willing to pay only a small amount for it.

Because the amount a consumer is willing to pay for a good is directly related to the good's value to them, the height of the demand curve indicates the marginal benefit (or value) consumers receive from additional units. (Recall that we briefly discussed marginal benefit in Chapter 1.) When viewed in this manner, the demand curve reveals that as consumers have more and more of a good or service, they value additional units less and less.

3-1b CONSUMER SURPLUS

Previously, we indicated that voluntary exchanges make both buyers and sellers better off. The demand curve can be used to illustrate the gains to consumers. Suppose you value a particular good at $50, but you are able to purchase it for only $30. Your net gain from buying the good is the $20 difference. Economists call this net gain of buyers **consumer surplus**. Consumer surplus is simply the difference between the maximum amount consumers would be willing to pay and the amount they actually pay for a good.

Exhibit 2 shows the consumer surplus for an entire market. The height of the demand curve measures how much buyers in the market value each unit of the good. The price indicates the amount they actually pay. The difference between these two—the triangular area below the demand curve but above the price paid—is a measure of the total consumer surplus generated by all exchanges of the good. The size of the consumer surplus, or

Consumer surplus
The difference between the maximum price consumers are willing to pay and the price they actually pay. It is the net gain derived by the buyers of the good.

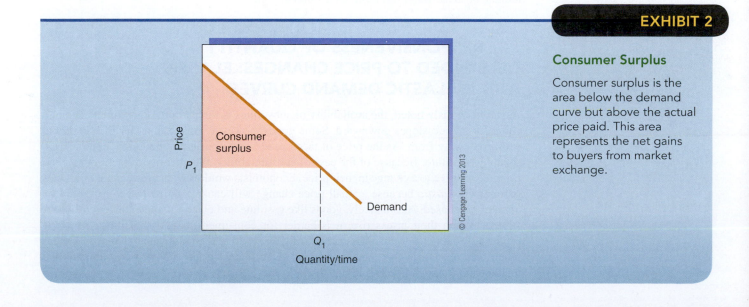

EXHIBIT 2

Consumer Surplus

Consumer surplus is the area below the demand curve but above the actual price paid. This area represents the net gains to buyers from market exchange.

© Cengage Learning 2013

triangular area, is affected by the market price. If the market price for the good falls, more of it will be purchased, resulting in a larger surplus for consumers. Conversely, if the market price rises, less of it will be purchased, resulting in a smaller surplus (net gain) for consumers.

Because the value a consumer places on a particular unit of a good is shown by the corresponding height of the demand curve, we can use the demand curve to clarify the difference between the *marginal value* and *total value* of a good—a distinction we introduced briefly in Chapter 1. Returning to Exhibit 2, if consumers are currently purchasing Q_1 units, the marginal value of the good is indicated by the height of the demand curve at Q_1—the last unit consumed (or purchased). So at each quantity, the height of the demand curve shows the marginal value of that unit, which as you can see declines along a demand curve. The *total value* of the good, however, is equal to the combined value of all units purchased. This is the sum of the value of each unit (the heights along the demand curve) on the *x*-axis, out to and including unit Q_1. This total value is indicated graphically as the entire area under the demand curve out to Q_1 (the triangular area representing consumer surplus *plus* the unshaded rectangular area directly below it).

You can see that the total value to consumers of a good can be far greater than the marginal value of the last unit consumed. When additional units are available at a low price, the marginal value of a good may be quite low, even though its total value to consumers is exceedingly high. This is usually the case with water. The value of the first few units of water consumed per day will be exceedingly high. The consumer surplus derived from these units will also be large when water is plentiful at a low price. As more and more units are consumed, however, the *marginal value* of even something as important as water will fall to a low level. When water is cheap, then, people will use it not only for drinking, cleaning, and cooking but also for washing cars, watering lawns, flushing toilets, and maintaining fish aquariums. Thus, although the total value of water is rather large, its marginal value is quite low.

Consumers will tend to expand their consumption of a good until its price and *marginal value* are equal (which occurs at Q_1 in Exhibit 2 at a price of P_1). Thus, the price of a good (which equals marginal value) reveals little about the *total value* derived from the consumption of it. This is the reason that the market price of diamonds (which reflects their high marginal value) is greater than the market price of water (which has a low marginal value), even though the total value of diamonds is far less than the total value of water. Think of it this way: Beginning from your current levels of consumption, if you were offered a choice between one diamond or one gallon of water right now, which would you take? You would probably take the diamond, because at the margin it has more value to you than additional water. However, if given a choice between giving up *all* of the water you use or *all* of the diamonds you have, you would probably keep the water over diamonds, because water has more total value to you.

3-1c RESPONSIVENESS OF QUANTITY DEMANDED TO PRICE CHANGES: ELASTIC AND INELASTIC DEMAND CURVES

As we previously noted, the availability of substitutes is the main reason why the demand curve for a good slopes downward. Some goods, however, are much easier than others to substitute away from. As the price of tacos rises, most consumers find hamburgers a reasonable substitute. Because of the ease of substitutability, the quantity of tacos demanded is quite sensitive to a change in their price. Economists would say that the demand for tacos is relatively *elastic* because a small price change will cause a rather large change in the amount purchased. Alternatively, goods like gasoline and electricity have fewer close substitutes. When their prices rise, it is harder for consumers to find substitutes for these products. When close substitutes are unavailable, even a large price change may not cause much of a change in the quantity demanded. In this case, an economist would say that the demand for such goods is relatively *inelastic*.

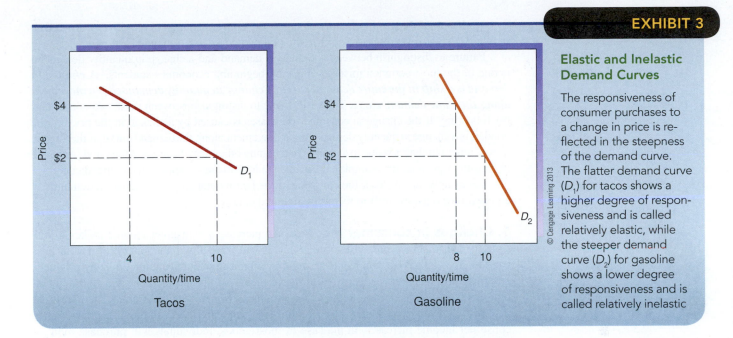

© Cengage Learning 2013

EXHIBIT 3

Elastic and Inelastic Demand Curves

The responsiveness of consumer purchases to a change in price is reflected in the steepness of the demand curve. The flatter demand curve (D_1) for tacos shows a higher degree of responsiveness and is called relatively elastic, while the steeper demand curve (D_2) for gasoline shows a lower degree of responsiveness and is called relatively inelastic

Tacos

Gasoline

Graphically, this different degree of responsiveness is reflected in the steepness of the demand curve, as shown in **Exhibit 3**. The flatter demand curve (D_1, left frame) is for a product like tacos, for which the quantity purchased is highly responsive to a change in price. As the price increases from $2.00 to $4.00, the quantity demanded falls sharply from ten to four units. The steeper demand curve (D_2, right frame) is for a product like gasoline, for which the quantity purchased is much less responsive to a change in price. For gasoline, an increase in price from $2.00 to $4.00 results in only a small reduction in the quantity purchased (from ten to eight units). An economist would say that the flatter demand curve D_1 is "relatively elastic," whereas the steeper demand curve D_2 is "relatively inelastic." The availability of substitutes is the main determinant of a product's elasticity or inelasticity and thus how flat or steep its demand curve is.

What would a demand curve that was perfectly vertical represent? Economists refer to this as a "perfectly" inelastic demand curve, meaning that the quantity demanded of the product never changes—regardless of its price. Although it is tempting to think that the demand curves are vertical for goods essential to human life (or goods that are addictive), this is inaccurate for two reasons. First, in varying degrees, there are substitutes for everything. As the price of a good rises, the incentive increases for suppliers to invent even more substitutes. Thus, even for goods that currently have few substitutes, if the price were to rise high enough, alternatives would be invented and marketed, reducing the quantity demanded of the original good. Second, our limited incomes restrict our ability to afford goods when they become very expensive. As the price of a good rises to higher and higher levels, if we do not cut back on the quantity purchased, we will have less and less income to spend on other things. Eventually, this will cause us to cut back on our purchases of it. Because of these two reasons, the demand curve for every good will slope downward to the right.

3-2 CHANGES IN DEMAND VERSUS CHANGES IN QUANTITY DEMANDED

The purpose of the demand curve is to show what effect a price change will have on the quantity demanded (or purchased) of a good. Economists refer to a change in the quantity of a good purchased in response solely to a price change as a "change in *quantity demanded*." A change in quantity demanded is simply a movement along a demand curve from one point to another.

Changes in factors other than a good's price—such as consumers' income and the prices of closely related goods—will also influence the decisions of consumers to purchase a good. If one of these other factors changes, the entire demand curve will *shift* inward or outward. Economists refer to a shift in the demand curve as a "change in *demand*."

Failure to distinguish between a change in demand and a change in quantity demanded is one of the most common mistakes made by beginning economics students.[3] *A change in demand is a shift in the entire demand curve. A change in quantity demanded is a movement along the same demand curve.* The easiest way to distinguish between these two concepts is the following: If the change in consumer purchases is caused by a change in the price of the good, it is a change in quantity demanded—a movement along the demand curve; if the change in consumer purchases is due to a change in anything other than the price of the good (a change in consumer income, for example), it is a change in demand—a shift in the demand curve.

Let us now take a closer look at some of the factors that cause a "change in demand"—an inward or outward shift in the entire demand curve.

1. Changes in consumer income.

An increase in consumer income makes it possible for consumers to purchase more goods. If you were to win the lottery, or if your boss were to give you a raise, you would respond by increasing your spending on many products. Alternatively, when the economy goes into a recession, falling incomes and rising unemployment cause consumers to reduce their purchases of many items. A change in consumer income will result in consumers buying more or less of a product at all possible prices. When consumer income increases, in the case of most goods, individuals will purchase more of the good even if the price is unchanged. This is shown by a shift to the right—an outward shift—in the demand curve. Such a shift is called an *increase in demand*. A reduction in consumer income generally causes a shift to the left—an inward shift—in the demand curve, which is called a *decrease in demand*. Note that the appropriate terminology here is an increase or a decrease in demand, not an increase or a decrease in quantity demanded.

Exhibit 4 highlights the difference between a change in demand and a change in quantity demanded. The demand curve D_1 indicates the initial demand curve for tablet

---

EXHIBIT 4

Change in Demand versus Change in Quantity Demanded

Panel (a) shows a change in quantity demanded, a movement along the demand curve D_1, in response to a change in the price of tablet computers. Panel (b) shows a change in demand, a shift of the entire curve, in this case due to an increase in consumer income.

(a)

(b)

© Cengage Learning 2013

---

[3]Questions designed to test the ability of students to make this distinction are favorites of many economics instructors. A word to the wise should be sufficient.

EXHIBIT 5

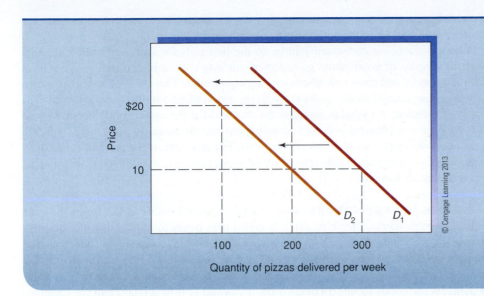

© Cengage Learning 2013

A Decrease in Demand

In college towns, the demand for pizza delivery decreases substantially when students go home for the summer. A decrease in demand is a leftward shift in the entire demand curve. Fewer pizzas are demanded at every price.

computers. At a price of $300, consumers will purchase Q_1 units. If the price were to decline to $100, the *quantity demanded* would increase from Q_1 to Q_3. The arrow in panel (a) indicates the change in *quantity demanded*—a movement along the original demand curve D_1 in response to the change in price. Now, alternatively suppose there were an increase in income that caused the *demand* for tablet computers to shift from D_1 to D_2. As indicated by the arrows in panel (b), the entire demand curve would shift outward. At the higher income level, consumers would be willing to purchase more tablet computers than before. This is true at a price of $300, $200, $100, and every other price. The increase in income leads to an increase in *demand*—a shift in the entire curve.

2. Changes in the number of consumers in the market. Businesses that sell products in college towns are greatly saddened when summer arrives. As you might expect in these towns, the demand for many items—from pizza delivery to beer— falls during the summer. **Exhibit 5** shows how the falling number of consumers in the market caused by students going home for the summer affects the demand for pizza delivery. With fewer customers, the demand curve shifts inward from D_1 to D_2. There is a decrease in demand; pizza stores sell fewer pizzas than before regardless of what price they originally charged. Had their original price been $20, then demand would fall from 200 pizzas per week to only 100. Alternatively, had their original price been $10, then demand would fall from 300 pizzas to 200. When autumn arrives and the students come back to town, there will be an increase in demand that will restore the curve to about its original position. As cities grow and shrink, and as international markets open up to domestic firms, changes in the number of consumers affect the demand for many products.

3. Changes in the price of a related good. Changes in prices of closely related products also influence the choices of consumers. Related goods may be either substitutes or complements. When two products perform similar functions or fulfill similar needs, they are substitutes. Economists define goods as substitutes when there is a direct relationship between the price of one and the demand for the other—meaning an increase in the price of one leads to an increase in demand for the other (they move in the same direction). For example, margarine is a substitute for butter. If the price of butter rises, it will increase the demand for margarine as consumers substitute margarine for the more expensive butter. Conversely, lower butter prices will reduce the demand for margarine, shifting the entire demand curve for margarine to the left.

Gasoline and hybrid cars provide another example of a substitute relationship. As gasoline prices have risen in recent years, the demand for gas–electric hybrid cars has increased. Beef and chicken, pencils and pens, apples and oranges, and coffee and tea provide other examples of goods with substitute relationships.

Other products are consumed jointly, so the demands for them are linked together as well. Examples of goods that "go together" include peanut butter and jelly, hot dogs and hot dog buns, and tents and other camping equipment. These goods are called **complements**. For complements, a decrease in the price of one will not only increase its quantity demanded; it will also increase the demand for the other good. The reverse is also true. As a complement becomes more expensive, the quantity demanded of it will fall, and so will the demand for its complements. For example, if the price of steak rises, grocery stores can expect to sell fewer bottles of steak sauce, even if the price of steak sauce remains unchanged.

Complements
Products that are usually consumed jointly (for example, bread and butter, hot dogs and hot dog buns). A decrease in the price of one will cause an increase in demand for the other.

4. Changes in expectations. Consumers' expectations about the future also can affect the current demand for a product. If consumers begin to expect that a major hurricane will strike their area, the current demand for batteries and canned food will rise. Expectations about the future direction of the economy can also affect current demand. If consumers are pessimistic about the economy, they start spending less, causing the current demand for goods to fall. Perhaps most important is how a change in the expected future price of a good affects current demand. When consumers expect the price of a product to rise in the near future, their current demand for it will increase. Gasoline is a good example. If you expect the price to increase soon, you'll want to fill up your tank now before the price goes up. In contrast, consumers will delay a purchase if they expect the item to decrease in price. No doubt you have heard someone say, "I'll wait until it goes on sale." When consumers expect the price of a product to fall, current demand for it will decline.

5. Demographic changes. The demand for many products is strongly influenced by the demographic composition of the market. An increase in the elderly population in the United States in recent years has increased the demand for medical care, retirement housing, and vacation travel. The demand curves for these goods have shifted to the right. During the 1980s, the number of people aged 15 to 24 fell by more than 5 million. Because young people are a major part of the U.S. market for jeans, the demand for jeans fell by more than 100 million pairs over the course of the decade.[4] More recently, the increased use of cell phones and iPods among teenagers has led to a dramatic reduction in the demand for wristwatches.

6. Changes in consumer tastes and preferences. Why do preferences change? Preferences change because people change and because people acquire new information. Consider how consumers respond to changing trends in popular diet programs. The demand for high-carbohydrate foods like white bread has fallen substantially, whereas the demand for low-carbohydrate foods like beef has risen. This is a major change from the past, when the demand for beef fell because of the "heart-healthy" eating habits consumers preferred then. Trends in the markets for clothing, toys, collectibles, and entertainment are constantly causing changes in the demand for these products as well. Firms may even try to change consumer preferences for their own products through advertising and information brochures.

The accompanying **Thumbnail Sketch** summarizes the major factors that cause a change in *demand*—a shift of the entire demand curve—and points out that quantity *demanded* (but not demand) will change in response to a change in the price of a good.

---

[4]These figures are from Suzanne Tregarthen, "Market for Jeans Shrinks," *The Margin* 6, no. 3 (January–February 1991): 28.

Thumbnail Sketch
Factors That Cause Changes in Demand and Quantity Demanded

This factor changes the quantity demanded of a good:

1. The price of the good: A higher price decreases the quantity demanded; a lower price increases the quantity demanded.

These factors change the demand for a good:

1. Consumer income: Lower consumer income will generally decrease demand; higher consumer income will generally increase demand.
2. Number of consumers in the market: Fewer consumers decreases demand; more consumers increases demand.
3a. Price of a substitute good: A decrease in the price of a substitute decreases the demand for the original good; an increase in the price of a substitute increases the demand for the original good.
3b. Price of a complementary good: An increase in the price of a complement decreases the demand for the original good; a decrease in the price of a complement increases the demand for the original good.
4. Expected future price of the good: If the price of a good is expected to fall in the future, the current demand for it will decrease; if the price of a good is expected to rise in the future, the current demand for it will increase.
5. Demographic changes: Population trends in age, gender, race, and other factors can increase or decrease demand for specific goods.
6. Consumer preferences: Changes in consumer tastes and preferences can increase or decrease demand for specific goods.

3-3 PRODUCER CHOICE AND THE LAW OF SUPPLY

Now let's shift our focus to producers and the supply side of the market. How does the market process determine the amount of each good that will be produced? To figure this out, we first have to understand what influences the choices of producers. Producers convert resources into goods and services by doing the following:

1. organizing productive inputs and resources, like land, labor, capital, natural resources, and intermediate goods;
2. transforming and combining these inputs into goods and services; and
3. selling the final products to consumers.

Producers have to purchase the resources at prices determined by market forces. Predictably, the owners of these resources will supply the resources only at prices at least equal to what they could earn elsewhere. Put another way, each resource the producers buy to make their product has to be bid away from all other potential uses. Its owner has to be paid its opportunity cost. The sum of the producer's cost of each resource used to produce a good will equal the **opportunity cost of production**.

There is an important difference between the opportunity cost of production and standard accounting measures of cost. Accountants generally do not count the cost of assets owned by the firm when they calculate the firm's cost. But economists do. Economists consider the fact that the assets owned by the firm could be used some other way—in other words, that they have an opportunity cost. Unless these opportunity costs are covered, the resources will eventually be used in other ways.

The opportunity cost of the assets owned by the firm is the earnings these assets could have generated if they were used in another way. Consider a manufacturer that invests $100 million in buildings and equipment to produce shirts. Instead of buying buildings and equipment,

Opportunity cost of production
The total economic cost of producing a good or service. The cost component includes the opportunity cost of all resources, including those owned by the firm. The opportunity cost is equal to the value of the production of other goods sacrificed as the result of producing the good.

the manufacturer could simply put the $100 million in the bank and let it draw interest. If the $100 million were earning, say, 5 percent interest, the firm would make $5 million on that money in a year's time. This $5 million in forgone interest is part of the firm's opportunity cost of producing shirts. Unlike an accountant, an economist will take that $5 million opportunity cost into account. If the firm plans to invest the money in shirt-making equipment, it had better earn more from making the shirts than the $5 million it could earn by simply putting the money in the bank. If the firm can't generate enough to cover all of its costs, including the opportunity cost of assets owned by the firm, it will not continue in business. If the firm were earning only $3 million producing shirts, it might be earning profit on its accounting statement, but it would be suffering a $2 million economic loss relative to simply putting the money in the bank.

3-3a THE ROLE OF PROFITS AND LOSSES

KEYS TO ECONOMIC PROSPERITY

Profits and Losses

Profits direct producers toward activities that increase the value of resources; losses impose a penalty on those who reduce the value of resources.

Profit

An excess of sales revenue relative to the opportunity cost of production. The cost component includes the opportunity cost of all resources, including those owned by the firm. Therefore, profit accrues only when the value of the good produced is greater than the value of the resources used for its production.

Loss

A deficit of sales revenue relative to the opportunity cost of production. Losses are a penalty imposed on those who produce goods even though they are valued less than the resources required for their production.

Firms earn a **profit** when the revenues from the goods and services that they supply exceed the opportunity cost of the resources used to make them. Consumers will not buy goods and services unless they value them at least as much as their purchase price. For example, Susan would not be willing to pay $40 for a pair of jeans unless she valued them by at least that amount. At the same time, the seller's opportunity cost of supplying a good will reflect the value consumers place on *other* goods that could have been produced with those same resources. This is true precisely because the seller has to bid those resources away from other producers wanting to use them.

Think about what it means when, for example, a firm is able to produce jeans at a cost of $30 per pair and sell them for $40, thereby reaping a profit of $10 per pair. The $30 opportunity cost of the jeans indicates that the resources used to produce the jeans could have been used to produce other items worth $30 to consumers (perhaps a denim backpack). In turn, the profit indicates that consumers value the jeans more than other goods that might have been produced with the resources used to supply the jeans.

The willingness of consumers to pay a price greater than a good's opportunity cost indicates that they value the good more than other things that could have been produced with the same resources. Viewed from this perspective, profit is a reward earned by entrepreneurs who use resources to produce goods consumers value more highly than the other goods those resources could have produced. In essence, this profit is a signal that an entrepreneur has increased the value of the resources under his or her control.

Business decision makers will seek to undertake production of goods and services that will generate profit. However, things do not always turn out as expected. Sometimes business firms are unable to sell their products at prices that will cover their costs. **Losses** occur when the revenue derived from sales is insufficient to cover the opportunity cost of the resources used to produce a good or service. Losses indicate that the firm has reduced the value of the resources it has used. In other words, consumers would have been better off if those resources had been used to produce something else. In a market economy, losses will eventually cause firms to go out of business, and the resources they previously utilized will be directed toward other things valued more highly, or to other firms who can produce those same goods at a lower cost.

Profits and losses play a very important role in a market economy. They determine which products (and firms) will expand and survive and which will contract and be driven from the market. Clearly, there is a positive side to business failures. As our preceding discussion highlights, losses and business failures free up resources being used unwisely so they can be put to use by other firms providing consumers with more value.

3-3b SUPPLY AND THE ENTREPRENEUR

Entrepreneurs organize the production of new products. In doing so, they take on significant risk in deciding what to produce and how to produce it. Their success or failure depends on how much consumers eventually value the products they develop relative to other products that could have been produced with the resources. Entrepreneurs figure out which projects are likely to be profitable and then try to persuade a corporation, a banker, or individual investors to invest the resources needed to give their new idea a chance. Studies indicate, however, that only about 55 to 65 percent of the new products introduced are still on the market five years later. Being an entrepreneur means you have to risk failing.

Baron Wolman/Getty Images

Entrepreneurs who buy raw land, put in streets and sewer lines, and divide up the land into lots for sale will earn a profit if the revenues derived from the lot sales exceed the opportunity cost of the project. Profit is a reward for increasing the value of the resources.

To prosper, entrepreneurs must convert and rearrange resources in a manner that will increase their value. A person who purchases 100 acres of raw land, puts in streets and a sewage-disposal system, divides the plot into 1-acre lots, and sells them for 50 percent more than the opportunity cost of all resources used is clearly an entrepreneur. This entrepreneur profits because the value of the resources has increased. Sometimes entrepreneurial activity is less complex, though. For example, a 15-year-old who purchases a power mower and sells lawn services to his neighbors is also an entrepreneur seeking to profit by increasing the value of his resources—time and equipment.

3-3c MARKET SUPPLY SCHEDULE

How will producer–entrepreneurs respond to a change in product price? Other things constant, a higher price will increase the producer's incentive to supply the good. Established producers will expand the scale of their operations, and over time new entrepreneurs, seeking personal gain, will enter the market and begin supplying the product, too. *The law of supply states that there is a direct (or positive) relationship between the price of a good or service and the amount of it that suppliers are willing to produce. This direct relationship means that the price and the quantity producers wish to supply move in the same direction. As the price increases, producers will supply more—and as the price decreases, they will supply less.*

Law of supply
A principle that states there is a direct relationship between the price of a good and the quantity of it producers are willing to supply. As the price of a good increases, producers will wish to supply more of it. As the price decreases, producers will wish to supply less.

Like the law of demand, the law of supply reflects the basic economic principle that incentives matter. Higher prices increase the reward entrepreneurs get from selling their products. The more profitable it is to produce a product, the more of it entrepreneurs will be willing to supply. Conversely, as the price of a product falls, so does its profitability and the incentive to supply it. Just think about how many hours of tutoring services you would be willing to supply for different prices. Would you be willing to spend more time tutoring students if instead of $8 per hour, tutoring paid $50 per hour? The law of supply suggests you would, and producers of other goods and services are no different.

Exhibit 6 illustrates the law of supply. The curve shown in the exhibit is called a *supply curve*. Because there is a direct relationship between a good's price and the amount offered for sale by suppliers, the supply curve has a positive slope. It slopes upward to the right. Read horizontally, the supply curve shows how much of a particular good producers are willing to produce and sell at a given price. Read vertically, the supply curve reveals important information about the cost of production. The height of the supply curve indicates both (1) the minimum price necessary to induce producers to supply that additional unit and (2) the opportunity cost of producing that additional unit. These are both measured by the height of the supply curve because the minimum price required to induce a supplier to sell a unit is precisely the marginal cost of producing it.

Supply Curve

As the price of a product increases, other things constant, producers will increase the amount of the product supplied to the market.

© Cengage Learning 2013

3-3d PRODUCER SURPLUS

We previously used the demand curve to illustrate consumer surplus, the net gains of buyers from market exchanges. The supply curve can be used in a similar manner to illustrate the net gains of producers and resource suppliers. Suppose that you are an aspiring musician and are willing to perform a two-hour concert for $500. If a promoter offers to pay you $750 to perform the concert, you will accept, and receive $250 more than your minimum price. This $250 net gain represents your **producer surplus**. In effect, producer surplus is the difference between the amount a supplier actually receives (based on the market price) and the minimum price required to induce the supplier to produce the given units (their marginal cost). The shaded area of Exhibit 7 illustrates the measurement of producer surplus for an entire market.

It's important to note that producer surplus represents the gains received by all parties contributing resources to the production of a good. In this respect, producer surplus is fundamentally different from profit. Profit accrues to the owners of the business firm producing the good, whereas producer surplus encompasses the net gains derived by all people who help produce the good, including those employed by or selling resources to the firm.

Producer surplus
The difference between the price that suppliers actually receive and the minimum price they would be willing to accept. It measures the net gains to producers and resource suppliers from market exchange. It is not the same as profit.

Producer Surplus

Producer surplus is the area above the supply curve but below the actual sales price. This area represents the net gains to producers and resource suppliers from production and exchange.

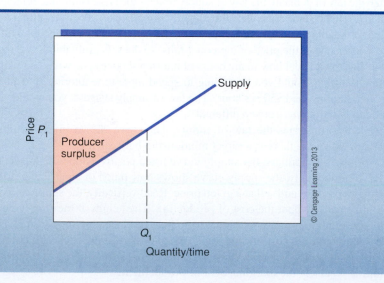

© Cengage Learning 2013

EXHIBIT 8

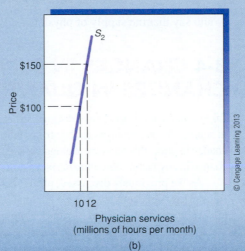

Elastic and Inelastic Supply Curves

Frame (a) illustrates a supply curve that is relatively elastic and therefore the quantity supplied is highly responsive to a change in price. Soft drinks provide an example. Frame (b) illustrates a relatively inelastic supply curve, one in which the quantity supplied increases by only a small amount in response to a change in price. This is the case for physician services.

3-3e RESPONSIVENESS OF QUANTITY SUPPLIED TO PRICE CHANGES: ELASTIC AND INELASTIC SUPPLY CURVES

Like the quantity demanded, the responsiveness of the quantity supplied to a change in price is different for different goods. The supply curve is said to be elastic when a modest change in price leads to a large change in quantity supplied. This is generally true when the additional resources needed to expand output can be obtained with only a small increase in their price. Consider the supply of soft drinks. The contents of soft drinks—primarily carbonated water, sugar, and flavoring—are abundantly available. A sharp increase in the use of these ingredients by soft drink producers is unlikely to push up their price much. Therefore, as **Exhibit 8** illustrates, if the price of soft drinks were to rise from $1 to $1.50, producers would be willing to expand output sharply from 100 million to 200 million cans per month. A 50 percent increase in price leads to a 100 percent expansion in quantity supplied. The larger the increase in quantity in response to a higher price, the more elastic the supply curve. The flatness of the supply curve for soft drinks reflects the fact that it is highly elastic.

In contrast, when the quantity supplied is not very responsive to a change in price, supply is said to be inelastic. Physicians' services are an example. If the earnings of doctors increase from $100 to $150 per hour, there will be some increase in the quantity of the services they provide. Some physicians will work longer hours; others may delay retirement. Yet, these adjustments are likely to result in only a small increase in the quantity supplied because it takes a long time to train a physician and the number of qualified doctors who are working in other occupations or who are outside of the labor force is small. Therefore, as Exhibit 8 (right frame) shows, a 50 percent increase in the price of physician services leads

OUTSTANDING ECONOMIST

ALFRED MARSHALL (1842–1924)

British economist Alfred Marshall was one of the most influential economists of his era. Many concepts and tools that form the core of modern microeconomics originated with Marshall in his famous *Principles of Economics*, first published in 1890. Marshall introduced the concepts of supply and demand, equilibrium, elasticity, consumers' and producers' surplus, and the idea of distinguishing between short-run and long-run changes.

to only a 20 percent expansion in the quantity supplied. Unlike soft drinks, higher prices for physician services do not generate much increase in quantity supplied. Economists would say that the supply of physician services is relatively inelastic.

3-4 CHANGES IN SUPPLY VERSUS CHANGES IN QUANTITY SUPPLIED

Like demand, it is important to distinguish between a change in the *quantity supplied* and a change in *supply*. When producers change the number of units they are willing to supply in response to a change in price, this movement along the supply curve is called a "change in *quantity supplied*." A change in any factor *other than the price* shifts the supply curve and is called a "change in *supply*."

As we previously discussed, profit-seeking entrepreneurs will produce a good only if its sales price is expected to exceed its opportunity cost of production. Therefore, changes that affect the opportunity cost of supplying a good will also influence the amount of it producers are willing to supply. These other factors, such as the prices of resources used to make the good and the level of technology available, are held constant when we draw the supply curve. The supply curve itself reflects quantity changes only in response to price changes. Changes in these other factors shift the supply curve. Factors that increase the opportunity cost of providing a good will discourage production and decrease supply, shifting the entire curve inward to the left. Conversely, changes that lower the opportunity cost of producers will encourage production and increase supply, shifting the entire curve outward to the right.

Let us now take a closer look at the primary factors that will cause a change in supply and shift the entire curve right or left.

1. Changes in resource prices. How will an increase in the price of a resource, such as wages of workers or the materials used to produce a product, affect the supply of a good? Higher resource prices will increase the cost of production, reducing the profitability of firms supplying the good. The higher cost will induce firms to reduce their output. With time, some may even be driven out of business. As **Exhibit 9** illustrates, higher resource prices will reduce the supply of the good, causing a shift to the left in the supply curve from S_1 to S_2. Alternatively, a reduction in the price of a resource used to produce a good will cause an increase in supply—a rightward shift in the supply curve—as firms expand output in response to the lower costs and increased profitability of supplying the good.

2. Changes in technology. Like lower resource prices, technological improvements—the discovery of new, lower-cost production techniques—reduce production costs, and thereby increase supply. Technological advances have affected the cost of almost everything.

EXHIBIT 9

A Decrease in Supply

Crude oil is a resource used to produce gasoline. When the price of crude oil rises, it increases the cost of producing gasoline and results in a decrease in the supply of gasoline.

© Cengage Learning 2013

Thumbnail Sketch
Factors That Cause Changes in Supply and Quantity Supplied

This factor changes the quantity supplied of a good:

1. The price of the good: A lower price decreases the quantity supplied; a higher price increases the quantity supplied.

These factors change the supply of a good:

1. Resource prices (the prices of things used to make the good): Lower resource prices increase supply; higher resource prices decrease supply.

2. Technological change: A technological improvement increases supply; a technological setback decreases supply.

3. Weather or political conditions: Favorable weather or good political conditions increase supply; adverse weather conditions or poor political conditions decrease supply.

4. Taxes imposed on the producers of a good: Lower taxes increase supply; higher taxes decrease supply.

©iStockphoto.com/baianliang

Before the invention of the printing press, books had to be handwritten. Just imagine the massive reduction in cost and increase in the supply of books caused by this single invention. Similarly, improved farm machinery has vastly expanded the supply of agricultural products through the years. The field of robotics has reduced the cost of producing airplanes, automobiles, and other types of machinery. Better computer chips have drastically reduced the cost of producing electronics. Forty years ago, a simple calculator cost more than $100 and a microwave oven almost $500. When introduced in the mid-1980s, a cellular telephone cost more than $4,000. You have probably noticed that the prices of flat-screen computer monitors and plasma-screen televisions have fallen substantially in recent years. Again, technological advances explain these changes.

3. Elements of nature and political disruptions. Natural disasters and changing political conditions can also alter supply, sometimes dramatically. In some years, good weather leads to "bumper crops," increasing the supply of agricultural products. At other times, freezes or droughts lead to poor harvests, reducing supply. War and political unrest in the Middle East region have had a major impact on the supply of oil several times during the past few decades. Factors such as these will alter supply.

4. Changes in taxes. If the government increases the taxes on the sellers of a product, the result will be the same as any other increase in the cost of doing business. The added tax that sellers have to pay will reduce their willingness to sell the product at any given price. Each unit must now be sold for a price that covers not only the opportunity cost of production, but also the tax. For example, a special tax is levied on commercial airline tickets, partially to cover the cost of airport security. This tax increases the cost of air travel and thereby reduces the supply (a shift to the left in the supply curve.)

The accompanying **Thumbnail Sketch** summarizes the major factors that change *supply* (a shift of the entire supply curve) and quantity supplied (a movement along the supply curve).

3-5 HOW MARKET PRICES ARE DETERMINED: DEMAND AND SUPPLY INTERACT

Consumer–buyers and producer–sellers make decisions independent of each other, but market prices coordinate their choices and influence their actions. To the economist, a **market** is not a physical location but an abstract concept that encompasses the forces generated

Market
An abstract concept encompassing the forces of demand and supply and the interaction of buyers and sellers with the potential for exchange to occur.

by the decisions of buyers and sellers. A market may be quite narrow (for example, the market for grade A jumbo eggs), or it may be quite broad like when we lump diverse goods into a single market, such as the market for all "consumer goods." There is also a wide range of sophistication among markets. The New York Stock Exchange is a highly formal, computerized market. Each weekday, buyers and sellers, who seldom meet, electronically exchange corporate shares they own worth billions of dollars. In contrast, a neighborhood market for babysitting services or tutoring in economics may be highly informal, bringing together buyers and sellers primarily by word of mouth.

Equilibrium *is a state in which the conflicting forces of demand and supply are in balance. When a market is in equilibrium, the decisions of consumers and producers are brought into harmony with one another, and the quantity demanded will equal the quantity supplied.* In equilibrium, it is possible for both buyers and sellers to realize their choices simultaneously. What could bring these diverse interests into harmony? We will see that the answer is market prices.

3-5a MARKET EQUILIBRIUM

As we have learned, a higher price will reduce the quantity of a good demanded by consumers. Conversely, a higher price will increase the quantity of a good supplied by producers. The market price of a good will tend to change in a direction that will bring the quantity of a good consumers want to buy into balance with the quantity producers want to sell. If the price is too high, the quantity supplied by producers will exceed the quantity demanded. Producers will be unable to sell as much as they would like unless they reduce their price. Alternatively, if the price is too low, the quantity demanded by consumers will exceed the quantity supplied. Some consumers will be unable to get as much as they would like, unless they are willing to pay a higher price to bid some of the good away from other potential customers. Thus, there will be a tendency for the price in a market to move toward the price that brings the two into balance.

People have a tendency to think of consumers wanting lower prices and producers wanting higher prices. Although this is true, price changes frequently trend toward the middle of the two extremes. When a local store has an excess supply of a particular item, how does it get rid of it? By having a sale or otherwise lowering its price. Firms often lower their prices in order to get rid of excess supply.

In contrast, excess demand is solved by consumers bidding up prices. Children's toys around Christmas provide a perfect example. When first introduced, items such as the Nintendo Wii, Webkinz, and the video game Rock Band were immediate successes. The firms producing these products had not anticipated the overwhelming demand; every child wanted one for Christmas. Some stores raised their prices, but the demand was so strong that lines of parents were forming outside stores before they even opened. Often, only the first few in line were able to get the toys (a sure sign that the store had set the price below equilibrium). Out in the parking lots, in the classified ads, and on eBay, parents were offering to pay even higher prices for these items. If stores were not going to set the prices right, parents in these informal markets would! These examples show that rising prices are often the result of consumers bidding up prices when excess demand is present. A similar phenomenon can be seen in the market for tickets to a World Series game or a popular music group's upcoming concert, as the immediate value of a ticket on the resale market can be much higher than the original retail price if, at that price, the original quantity supplied is not adequate to meet the quantity demanded.

As these examples illustrate, whenever quantity supplied and quantity demanded are not in balance, there is a tendency for price to change in a manner that will correct the imbalance. It is possible to show this process graphically with the supply and demand curves we have developed in this chapter. **Exhibit 10** shows the supply and demand curves in the market for a basic calculator. At a high price—$12, for example—producers will plan to supply 600 calculators per day, whereas consumers will choose to purchase only 450. An excess supply of 150 calculators (shown by distance *ab* in the graph) will result. Unsold calculators will push the inventories of producers upward. To get rid of some of their calculators in inventory, some producers will cut their price to increase their sales. Other firms will have to lower their price,

Equilibrium
A state in which the conflicting forces of demand and supply are in balance. When a market is in equilibrium, the decisions of consumers and producers are brought into harmony with one another, and the quantity demanded will equal the quantity supplied.

EXHIBIT 10

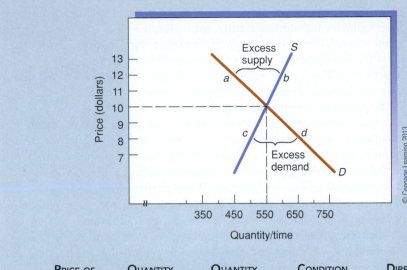

Supply and Demand

The table indicates the supply and demand conditions for calculators. These conditions are also illustrated by the graph. When the price exceeds $10, an excess supply is present, which places downward pressure on price. In contrast, when the price is less than $10, an excess demand results, which causes the price to rise. Thus, the market price will tend toward $10, at which point the quantity demanded will be equal to the quantity supplied.

© Cengage Learning 2013

PRICE OF CALCULATORS (DOLLARS)	QUANTITY SUPPLIED (PER DAY)	QUANTITY DEMANDED (PER DAY)	CONDITION IN THE MARKET	DIRECTION OF PRESSURE ON PRICE
$13	625	400	Excess supply	Downward
12	600	450	Excess supply	Downward
11	575	500	Excess supply	Downward
10	550	550	Balance	Equilibrium
9	525	600	Excess demand	Upward
8	500	650	Excess demand	Upward
7	475	700	Excess demand	Upward

too, as a result, or sell even fewer calculators. This lower price will make supplying calculators less attractive to producers. Some of them will go out of business. Others will reduce their output or perhaps produce other products. How low will the price of calculators go? As the figure shows, when the price has declined to $10, the quantity supplied by producers and the quantity demanded by consumers will be in balance at 550 calculators per day. At this price ($10), the quantity demanded by consumers just equals the quantity supplied by producers, and the choices of the two groups are brought into harmony.

What will happen if the price per calculator is lower—$8, for example? In this case, the amount demanded by consumers (650 units) will exceed the amount supplied by producers (500 units). An excess demand of 150 units (shown by the distance *cd* in the graph) will be the result. Some consumers who are unable to purchase the calculators at $8 per unit because of the inadequate supply would be willing to pay a higher price. Recognizing this fact, producers will raise their price. As the price increases to $10, producers will expand their output and consumers will cut down on their consumption. At the $10 price, equilibrium will be restored.

3-5b EFFICIENCY AND MARKET EQUILIBRIUM

When a market reaches equilibrium, all the gains from trade have been fully realized and **economic efficiency** is present. Economists often use economic efficiency as a standard to measure outcomes under alternative circumstances. The central idea of efficiency is a cost-versus-benefit comparison. On the one hand, undertaking an economic action will be efficient only if it generates more benefit than cost. On the other hand, undertaking an action that generates more cost than benefit is inefficient. For a market to be efficient, all trades that generate more benefit than cost need to be undertaken. In addition, economic efficiency requires that no trades creating more cost than benefit be undertaken.

Economic efficiency
A situation in which all of the potential gains from trade have been realized. An action is efficient only if it creates more benefit than cost. With well-defined property rights and competition, market equilibrium is efficient.

A closer look at the way that markets work can help us understand the concept of efficiency. The supply curve reflects producers' opportunity cost. Each point along the supply curve indicates the minimum price for which the units of a good could be produced without a loss to the seller. Assuming no other third parties are affected by the production of this good, then the height of the supply curve represents the opportunity cost to society of producing and selling the good. On the other side of the market, each point along the demand curve indicates how consumers value an extra unit of the good—that is, the maximum amount the consumer is willing to pay for the extra unit. Again assuming that no other third parties are affected, the height of the demand curve represents the benefit to society of producing and selling the good. Any time the consumer's valuation of a unit (the benefit) exceeds the producer's minimum supply price (the cost), producing and selling the unit is consistent with economic efficiency. The trade will result in mutual gain to both parties. When property rights are well defined and only the buyers and sellers are affected by production and exchange, competitive market forces will automatically guide a market toward an equilibrium level of output that satisfies economic efficiency.

Exhibit 11 illustrates why this is true. Suppliers of bicycles will produce additional bicycles as long as the market price exceeds their opportunity cost of production (shown by the height of the supply curve). Similarly, consumers will continue to purchase additional bikes as long as their benefit (shown by the height of the demand curve) exceeds the market price. Eventually, market forces will result in an equilibrium output level of Q and a price of P. At this point, all the bicycles providing benefits to consumers that exceed the costs to suppliers will be produced. Economic efficiency is met because all of the potential consumer and producer gains from exchange (shown by the shaded area) have occurred. As you can see, the point of market equilibrium is also the point where the combined area showing consumer and producer surplus is the greatest.

When fewer than Q bicycles are produced, some bicycles valued more by consumers than the opportunity cost of producing them are not being produced. This is not consistent with economic efficiency. On the other hand, if output is expanded beyond Q, inefficiency will also result because some of the bicycles cost more to produce than consumers are willing to pay for them. Prices in competitive markets eventually guide producers and consumers to the level of output consistent with economic efficiency.

EXHIBIT 11

Economic Efficiency

When markets are competitive and property rights are well defined, the equilibrium reached by a market satisfies economic efficiency. All units that create more benefit (the buyer's valuation shown by the height of the demand curve) than cost (opportunity cost of production shown by the height of the supply curve) are produced. This maximizes the total gains from trade, the combined area represented by consumer and producer surplus.

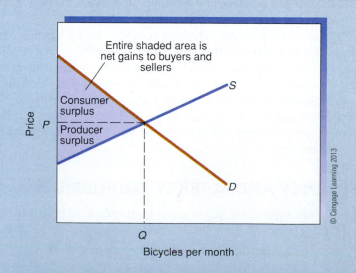

© Cengage Learning 2013

3-6 HOW MARKETS RESPOND TO CHANGES IN DEMAND AND SUPPLY

How will a market adjust to a change in demand? Exhibit 12 shows the market adjustment to an increase in the demand for eggs around Easter. Demand D_1 and supply S are typical throughout much of the year. During the two weeks before Easter, however, consumer demand for eggs rises because people purchase them to decorate, too. This shifts egg demand from D_1 to D_2 during that time of year. As you can see, the increase in demand pushes the price upward from P_1 to P_2 (typically by about 20 cents per dozen) and results in a larger equilibrium quantity traded (Q_2 rather than Q_1—an increase of typically around 600 million eggs). There is a new equilibrium at point b around Easter (versus point a during the rest of the year).

The tradition of coloring and hunting for eggs causes an increase in demand for eggs around Easter. As Exhibit 12 illustrates, this leads to higher egg prices and costly actions by producers to supply a larger quantity during this period.

Although consumers may not be happy about paying a higher price for eggs around Easter, the higher price serves two essential purposes. First, it encourages consumers to conserve on their usage of eggs. Some consumers may purchase only two dozen eggs to color, rather than three; other consumers may skip having an omelet for breakfast and have yogurt instead. These steps on the consumer side of the market help make the eggs that are available around Easter go further. Second, the higher price is precisely what results in the additional 600 million eggs being supplied to the market to satisfy this increased consumer demand. Without the price increase, excess demand would be present, and many consumers would simply be unable to find eggs to purchase around Easter. If the price remained at P_1 (the equilibrium price throughout most of the year), consumers at Easter-time would want to purchase more eggs than producers would be willing to supply. At the higher P_2 price, however, the quantity suppliers are willing to sell is again in balance with the quantity consumers wish to purchase.

Why were suppliers unwilling to supply the additional 600 million eggs at the original price of P_1? Because at the original equilibrium price of P_1, suppliers were already

EXHIBIT 12

Market Adjustment to Increase in Demand

Here, we illustrate how the market for eggs adjusts to an increase in demand such as generally occurs around Easter. Initially (before the Easter season), the market for eggs reflects demand D_1 and supply S. The increase in demand (shift from D_1 to D_2) pushes price up and leads to a new equilibrium at a higher price (P_2 rather than P_1) and larger quantity traded (Q_2)

producing and selling all the eggs that cost less to produce than that price. The additional eggs desired by consumers around Easter all cost more to produce than the old market price of P_1. The higher price of P_2 is what allows suppliers to cover their higher production costs associated with these extra eggs. Around Easter, farmers take costly steps to avoid having the hens molt because hens lay fewer eggs when they are molting. They do this by changing the quantity and types of feed and by increasing the lighting in the birds' sheds—both of which mean higher production costs. Farmers also try to build up larger than normal inventories of eggs before Easter. Eggs are typically about two days old when consumers buy them at the store, but can be up to seven days old around Easter time. Building up and maintaining this additional inventory are costly, too.

In a market economy, when the demand for a good increases, its price will rise, which will (1) motivate consumers to search for substitutes and cut back on additional purchases of the good and (2) motivate producers to supply more of the good. These two forces will eventually bring the quantity demanded and quantity supplied back into balance.

It's important to note that this response on the supply side of the egg market is not a shift in the supply curve. The supply curve remains unchanged. Rather, there is a movement along the original supply curve—a change in *quantity* supplied. The only reason suppliers are willing to alter their behavior (produce more eggs) is because the increased demand has pushed up the price of eggs. Notice that it is the change in demand (a shift of the demand curve) that leads to the change in quantity supplied (a movement along the supply curve). Producers are simply responding to the price movement caused by the change in demand. A movement along one curve (a change in quantity supplied *or* a change in quantity demanded) happens in response to a shift in the other curve (a change in demand or a change in supply).

When the demand for a product declines, the adjustment process sends buyers and sellers just the opposite signals. Take a piece of paper and see if you can diagram a decrease in demand and how it will affect price and quantity in a market. If you've done it correctly, a decline in demand (a shift to the left in the demand curve) will lead to a lower price and a lower quantity traded. What's going on in the diagram is that the lower price (caused by lower consumer demand) is reducing the incentive of producers to supply the good. When consumers no longer want as much of a good, falling market prices signal producers to cut back production. The reduced output allows these resources to be freed up to go into the production of other goods consumers want more.

How will markets respond to changes in supply? **Exhibit 13** shows the market's adjustment to a decrease in the supply of lemons, such as happened during January 2007 when freezing temperatures in California destroyed a large portion of the lemon crop. A reduction

---

EXHIBIT 13

Market Adjustment to a Decrease in Supply

Here, using lemons as an example, we illustrate how a market adjusts to a decrease in supply. Assume adverse weather conditions substantially reduce the supply (shift from S_1 to S_2) of lemons. The reduction in supply leads to an increase in the equilibrium price (from P_1 to P_2) and a reduction in the equilibrium quantity traded (from Q_1 to Q_2).

© Cengage Learning 2013

Thumbnail Sketch
How Changes in Demand and Supply Affect Market Price and Quantity

Changes in Demand

1. An increase in demand—shown by a rightward shift of the demand curve—will cause an increase in both the equilibrium price and the equilibrium quantity.

2. A decrease in demand—shown by a leftward shift of the demand curve—will cause a decrease in both the equilibrium price and the equilibrium quantity.

Changes in Supply

1. An increase in supply—shown by a rightward shift of the supply curve—will cause a decrease in the equilibrium price and an increase in the equilibrium quantity.

2. A decrease in supply—shown by a leftward shift of the supply curve—will cause an increase in the equilibrium price and a decrease in the equilibrium quantity.

in supply (shift from S_1 to S_2) will cause the price of lemons to increase sharply (P_1 to P_2). Because of the higher price, consumers will cut back on their consumption of lemons (the movement along the demand curve from a to b). Some will switch to substitutes—in this case, probably other varieties of citrus. The higher price also encourages the remaining lemon suppliers to take additional steps—like more careful harvesting techniques or using more fertilizer—that allow them to produce more lemons than otherwise would be the case. The higher prices will rebalance the quantity demanded and quantity supplied.

As the lemon example illustrates, a decrease in supply will lead to higher prices and a lower equilibrium quantity. How do you think the market price and quantity would adjust to an increase in supply, as might be caused by a breakthrough in the technology used to harvest the lemons? Again, try to draw the appropriate supply and demand curves to illustrate this case. If you do it correctly, the graph you draw will show an increase in supply (a shift to the right in the supply curve) leading to a lower market price and a larger equilibrium quantity.

The accompanying **Thumbnail Sketch** summarizes the effect of changes—both increases and decreases—in demand and supply on the equilibrium price and quantity. The cases listed in the sketch, however, are for when only a single curve shifts. But sometimes market conditions simultaneously shift both demand and supply. For example, consumer income might increase at the same time that a technological advance in production occurs. These two changes will cause both demand and supply to increase at the same time—both curves will shift to the right. The new equilibrium will definitely be at a larger quantity, but the direction of the change in price is indeterminate. The price may either increase or decrease, depending on whether the increase in demand or increase in supply is larger—which curve shifted the most, in other words.

What will happen if supply increases but demand falls at the same time? Price will definitely fall, but the new equilibrium quantity may either increase or decrease. Draw the supply and demand curves for this case and make sure that you understand why.

3-6a INVISIBLE HAND PRINCIPLE

KEYS TO ECONOMIC PROSPERITY

Invisible Hand Principle

Market prices coordinate the actions of self-interested individuals and direct them toward activities that promote the general welfare.

More than 235 years ago, Adam Smith, the father of economics, stressed that personal self-interest *when directed by market prices* is a powerful force promoting economic progress. In a famous passage in his book *An Inquiry into the Nature and Causes of the Wealth of Nations*, Smith put it this way:

> Every individual is continually exerting himself to find out the most advantageous employment for whatever [income] he can command. It is his own advantage, indeed, and not that of the society which he has in view. But the study of his own advantage naturally, or rather necessarily, leads him to prefer that employment which is most advantageous to society. . . . He intends only his own gain, and he is in this, as in many other cases, led by an invisible hand to promote an end which was not part of his intention. By pursuing his own interest he frequently promotes that of the society more effectually than when he really intends to promote it.[5]

The "invisible hand" to which Smith referred was the pricing system—prices determined by the forces of supply and demand. Smith's fundamental insight was that market prices tend to bring the self-interest of individuals into harmony with the betterment of society. Moreover, when it is directed by market prices, personal self-interest is a powerful force promoting growth and prosperity.

The tendency of market prices to channel the actions of self-interested individuals into activities that promote the prosperity of the society is now known as the **invisible hand principle**. Let's take a closer look at this important principle.

Invisible hand principle
The tendency of market prices to direct individuals pursuing their own interests to engage in activities promoting the economic well-being of society.

3-6b PRICES AND MARKET ORDER

The invisible hand principle can be difficult to grasp because there is a natural tendency to associate order with central direction and control. Surely some central authority must be in charge. But this is not the case. The pricing system, reflecting the choices of literally millions of consumers, producers, and resource owners, provides the direction. Moreover, the market process works so automatically that most of us give little thought to it. We simply take it for granted.

Perhaps an example from your everyday life will help you better understand the invisible hand principle. Visualize a busy retail store with 10 checkout lanes. No one is assigning shoppers to checkout lanes. Shoppers are left to choose for themselves. Nonetheless, they do not all try to get in the same lane. Why? Individuals are always alert for adjustment opportunities that offer personal gain. When the line at one lane gets long or is held up by a price check, some shoppers will shift to other lanes and thereby smooth out the flow among the lanes. Even though central planning is absent, this process of mutual adjustment by self-interested individuals results in order and social cooperation. A similar phenomenon occurs on busy interstate highways as drivers switch between lanes for personal gain, with the end result being the quickest flow of traffic for everyone and for the group as a whole.

The incentive structure generated by markets is a lot like that accompanying the checkout at a busy retail store or driving on the freeway. Like the number of people in a lane, profits and losses provide market participants with information about the advantages and disadvantages of different economic activities. Losses indicate that an economic activity is congested, and, as a result, producers are unable to cover their costs. In such a case, successful market participants will shift their resources away from such activities toward other, more valuable uses. Conversely, profits are indicative of an open lane, the opportunity to experience gain if one shifts into an activity in which the price is high relative to the per-unit cost. As producers and resource suppliers shift away from activities characterized by congestion and into those characterized by the opportunity for profit, they enlarge the flow of economic activity.

Consider the following three vitally important functions performed by market prices.

---

[5]Adam Smith, *An Inquiry into the Nature and Causes of the Wealth of Nations* (New York: Modern Library, 1937), 423.

1. Market prices communicate information to both buyers and sellers that will promote efficient use of resources and proper response to changing conditions. Prices provide producers with up-to-date information about which goods consumers most intensely desire and with important information about the abundance of the resources used in the production process. The cost of production, driven by the opportunity cost of resources, tells the business decision-maker the relative importance others place on the alternative uses of those resources. A boom in the housing market might cause lumber prices to rise. In turn, furniture-makers seeing these higher lumber prices will utilize substitute raw materials such as metal and plastic in their production processes. Because of market prices, furniture-makers will conserve on their use of lumber, just as if they had known that lumber was now more urgently needed for constructing new housing.

Consider another example. Suppose a drought in Brazil severely reduces the supply of coffee. Coffee prices will rise. Even if consumers do not know about the drought, the higher prices will provide them with all the information they need to know—it's time to cut back on coffee consumption. *Market prices register information derived from the choices of millions of consumers, producers, and resource suppliers, and provide them with everything they need to know to make wise decisions.*

2. Market prices coordinate the actions of market participants. Market prices also coordinate the choices of buyers and sellers, bringing their decisions into line with each other. Excess supply will lead to falling prices, which discourage production and encourage consumption until the excess supply is eliminated. Alternatively, excess demand will lead to price increases, which encourage consumers to economize on their uses of the good and suppliers to produce more of it, eliminating the excess demand. Changing market prices induce responses on both sides of the market that will correct imbalances.

3. Market prices motivate economic players. Market prices establish a reward–penalty (profit–loss) structure that encourages people to work, cooperate with others, use efficient production methods, supply goods that are intensely desired by others, and invest for the future. Self-interested entrepreneurs will seek to produce only the goods consumers value enough to pay a price sufficient to cover production cost. Self-interest will also encourage producers to use efficient production methods and adopt cost-saving technologies because lower costs will mean greater profits. Firms that fail to do so will be unable to compete successfully in the marketplace.

At the beginning of this chapter, we asked you to reflect on why the grocery stores in your local community generally have on hand about the right amount of milk, bread, vegetables, and other goods. Likewise, how is it that refrigerators, automobiles, and CD players, produced at different places around the world, make their way to stores near you in approximately the same numbers that they are demanded by consumers? The invisible hand principle provides the answer, and it leads to an amazing degree of social cooperation.

Is the concept of the invisible hand really valid? Next time you sit down to have a nice dinner, think about all the people who help make it possible. It is unlikely that any of them, from the farmer to the truck driver to the grocer, was motivated by a concern that you have an enjoyable meal. Market prices, however, bring their interest into harmony with yours. Farmers who raise the best beef or turkeys receive higher prices, truck drivers and grocers earn more money if their products are delivered fresh and in good condition, and so on. An amazing degree of cooperation and order is created by market exchanges—all without the central direction of any government official.

3-6c COMPETITION AND PROPERTY RIGHTS

As we noted earlier in this chapter, our focus so far has been on markets in which rival firms can freely enter and exit, and private-property rights are clearly defined and enforced. *The efficiency of market organization is, in fact, dependent upon these two things: (1) competitive markets and (2) well-defined and enforced private-property rights.*

Competition, the great regulator, can protect both buyer and seller. It protects consumers from sellers who would charge a price substantially above the cost of production or withhold a vital resource for an exorbitant amount of money. Similarly, it protects employees (sellers of their labor) from the power of any single employer (the buyers of labor). When markets are competitive, both buyers and sellers have alternatives and these alternatives provide them with protection against ill treatment by others.

When property rights are well defined, secure, and tradable, suppliers of goods and services have to pay resource owners for their use. They will not be permitted to seize and use scarce resources without compensating the owners. Neither will they be permitted to use violence (for example, to attack or invade the property of another) to get what they want. The efficiency of markets hinges on the presence of property rights—after all, people can't easily exchange or compete for things they don't have or can't get property rights to. Without well-defined property rights, markets simply cannot function effectively.

LOOKING AHEAD

Although we incorporated numerous examples designed to enhance your understanding of the supply-and-demand model throughout this chapter, we have only touched the surface. In various modified forms, this model is the central tool of economics. The next chapter will explore several specific applications and extensions of this important model.

KEY POINTS

- The law of demand states that there is an inverse (or negative) relationship between the price of a good or service and the quantity of it that consumers are willing to purchase. The height of the demand curve at any quantity shows the maximum price that consumers are willing to pay for that unit.

- The degree of responsiveness of consumer purchases to a change in price is shown by the steepness of the demand curve. The more responsive buyers are to a change in price, the flatter, or more elastic, the demand curve will be. Conversely, the less responsive buyers are to a change in price, the steeper, or more inelastic, the demand curve will be.

- A movement along a demand curve is called a change in quantity demanded. A shift of the entire curve is called a change in demand. A change in *quantity demanded* is caused by a change in the price of the good (generally in response to a shift of the supply curve). A change in *demand* can be caused by several things, including a change in consumer income or a change in the price of a closely related good.

- The opportunity cost of producing a good is equal to the cost incurred by bidding the required resources away from alternative uses. Profit indicates that the producer has increased the value of the resources used, whereas a loss indicates that the producer has reduced the value of the resources used.

- The law of supply states that there is a direct (or positive) relationship between the price of a good or service and the quantity of it that producers are willing to supply. The height of the supply curve at any quantity shows the minimum price necessary to induce suppliers to produce that unit—that is, the opportunity cost of producing it.

- A movement along a supply curve is called a change in quantity supplied. A change in *quantity supplied* is caused by a change in the price of the good (generally in response to a shift of the demand curve). A shift of the entire supply curve is called a change in supply. A change in *supply* can be caused by several factors, such as a change in resource prices or an improvement in technology.

- The responsiveness of supply to a change in price is shown by the steepness of the supply curve. The more willing producers are to alter the quantity supplied in response to a change in price, the flatter, or more elastic, the supply curve. Conversely, the less willing producers are to alter the quantity supplied in response to a change in price, the steeper, or less elastic, the supply curve.

- Prices bring the conflicting forces of supply and demand into balance. There is an automatic tendency for market prices to move toward the equilibrium price, at which the quantity demanded equals the quantity supplied.

- Consumer surplus represents the net gain to buyers from market trades. Producer surplus represents the net gain to producers and resource suppliers from market trades. In equilibrium, competitive markets maximize these gains, a condition known as economic efficiency.

- Changes in the prices of goods are caused by changes in supply and demand. An increase in demand will cause the price and quantity supplied to rise. Conversely, a decrease in demand will cause the price and quantity supplied to fall. An increase in supply, however, will cause the price to fall and quantity demanded to rise. Conversely, a decrease in supply will cause the price to rise and quantity demanded to fall.

- Market prices communicate information, coordinate the actions of buyers and sellers, and motivate decision makers to act. As the invisible hand principle indicates, market prices are generally able to bring the self-interest of individuals into harmony with the general welfare of society. The efficiency of the system is dependent upon two things, however: (1) competitive market conditions and (2) well-defined and secure property rights.

CRITICAL ANALYSIS QUESTIONS

1. *Which of the following do you think would lead to an increase in the current demand for beef?
   a. higher pork prices
   b. higher consumer income
   c. higher prices of feed grains used to feed cattle
   d. widespread outbreak of mad cow or hoof-and-mouth disease
   e. an increase in the price of beef

2. What is being held constant when a demand curve for a specific product (shoes or apples, for example) is constructed? Explain why the demand curve for a product slopes downward to the right.

3. What is the law of supply? How many of the following "goods" do you think conform to the general law of supply? Explain your answer in each case.
   a. gasoline
   b. cheating on exams
   c. political favors from legislators
   d. the services of heart specialists
   e. children
   f. legal divorces

4. *Are prices an accurate measure of a good's total value? Are prices an accurate measure of a good's marginal value? What's the difference? Can you think of a good that has high total value but low marginal value? Use this concept to explain why professional wrestlers earn more than nurses, despite the fact that it is virtually certain that nurses create more total value for society than do wrestlers.

5. What is being held constant when the supply curve is constructed for a specific good like pizza or automobiles? Explain why the supply curve for a good slopes upward to the right.

6. Define consumer surplus and producer surplus. What is meant by economic efficiency, and how does it relate to the gains of consumers and producers?

7. How is the market price of a good determined? When the market for a product is in equilibrium, how will consumers value an additional unit compared to the opportunity cost of producing that unit? Why is this important?

8. *"The future of our industrial strength cannot be left to chance. Somebody has to develop notions about which industries are winners and which are losers." Is this statement by a newspaper columnist true? Who is the "somebody"?

9. What factors determine the cost of producing a good or service? Will producers continue to supply a good or service if consumers are unwilling to pay a price sufficient to cover the cost?

10. *"Production should be for people and not for profit." Answer the following questions concerning this statement:
    a. If production is profitable, are people helped or harmed? Explain.
    b. Are people helped more if production results in a loss than if it leads to profit? Is there a conflict between production for people and production for profit?

11. What must an entrepreneur do to earn a profit? How do the actions of firms earning profits influence the value of resources? What happens to the value of resources when losses are present? If a firm making losses goes out of business, is this bad? Why or why not?

12. *What's wrong with this way of thinking? "Economists claim that when the price of something goes up, producers increase the quantity supplied to the market. But last year, the price of oranges was really high and the supply of them was really low. Economists are wrong!"

13. What is the invisible hand principle? Does it indicate that self-interested behavior within markets will result in actions that are beneficial to others? What conditions are necessary for the invisible hand to work well? Why are these conditions important?

14. What's wrong with this way of thinking? "Economists argue that lower prices will result in fewer units being supplied. However, there are exceptions to this rule. For example, in 1972, a very simple 10-digit electronic calculator sold for $120. By 2000, the price of the same type of calculator had declined to less than $5. Yet business firms produced and sold many more calculators in 2000 than they did in 1972. Lower prices did not result in less production or in a decline in the number of calculators supplied."

15. What is the difference between substitutes and complements? Indicate two goods that are substitutes for each other. Indicate two goods that are complements.

16. Do business firms operating in competitive markets have a strong incentive to serve the interest of consumers? Are they motivated by a strong desire to help consumers? Are "good intentions" necessary if individuals are going to engage in actions that are helpful to others? Discuss.

*Asterisk denotes questions for which answers are given in Appendix B.

CHAPTER 4
Demand and Supply: Applications and Extensions

FOCUS

- How are the markets for products and resources related?
- What happens when prices are set by law above or below the market equilibrium level?
- How do rent controls affect the maintenance and quality of rental housing? How do minimum-wage rates influence the job opportunities of low-skilled workers?
- What are "black markets"? How does the lack of a well-structured legal environment affect their operation?
- How does a tax or subsidy affect a market? What determines the distribution of the tax burden (or subsidy benefit) between buyers and sellers?
- What is the Laffer curve? What does it indicate about the relationship between tax rates and tax revenues?

The division of labour, from which so many advantages are derived, is not originally the effect of any human wisdom, which foresees and intends that general opulence to which it gives occasion. It is the necessary, though very slow and gradual consequence of a certain propensity in human nature . . .; the propensity to truck, barter, and exchange one thing for another. **—Adam Smith[1]**

Nations stumble upon establishments, which are indeed the result of human action, but not the execution of any human design. **—Adam Ferguson[2]**

[1]Adam Smith, *An Inquiry into the Nature and Causes of the Wealth of Nations* (New York: Modern Library, 1937), 13.
[2]Adam Ferguson, *An Essay on the History of Civil Society* (Edinburgh: A. Millar and T. Caddel, London, 1767), 187.

Markets are everywhere. They exist in many different forms and degrees of sophistication. In elementary schools, children trade Baseball cards and Silly Bandz; in households, individuals trade chores ("I'll clean the bathroom, if you'll clean the kitchen"); and in the stock market, individuals who have never met exchange shares of corporate stock and other financial assets worth billions of dollars each business day. Even making an activity illegal does not eliminate the market for it. Instead, the market is merely pushed underground. The exchange of illegal drugs or tickets to a big game at illegal prices illustrates this point.

Trading with other individuals is a natural part of human behavior that exists regardless of legal and societal conditions. As Adam Smith put it more than 230 years ago, human beings have a natural propensity "to truck, barter, and exchange one thing for another" (see the quotation at the chapter opening). We all want to improve our standard of living, and trade with others helps us achieve this goal—by allowing us to get the goods and services we really want and giving us the opportunity to earn the income necessary to buy them. Further, as Adam Ferguson points out, markets are a result of human action, not human design.[3] They

arise because people can improve their lives by trading with others.

Market prices coordinate the actions of buyers and sellers, but sometimes the "price" of a good or service in a particular market is called something different. For example, in the labor market, the price is often called the "wage rate." In the loanable funds market, the price is generally referred to as the "interest rate." However, as Juliet observes in Shakespeare's *Romeo and Juliet*, "What's in a name? That which we call a rose by any other name would smell as sweet." The same is true for prices. When the price of something is referred to by another term, such as the wage or interest rate, it will still play the same role. Therefore, when these special terms are used, we put them along the vertical axes of supply and demand diagrams, just as we do "price"—because that's what they are.

In the previous chapter, we saw how the forces of supply and demand determine market prices and coordinate the actions of buyers and sellers in the absence of government intervention. In this chapter, we turn our attention to using the supply and demand model to understand more fully what happens when governments intervene in markets by implementing price controls, taxes, and subsidies.

4-1 THE LINK BETWEEN RESOURCE AND PRODUCT MARKETS

Understanding the interrelationship among markets is vitally important. A change in one market will also lead to changes in other markets. This section addresses the link between the resource and product markets.

The production process generally involves (1) the purchase of resources—like raw materials, labor services, tools, and machines; (2) transformation of the resources into products (goods and services); and (3) sale of the goods and services in a product market. Production is generally undertaken by business firms. Typically, business firms will demand resources, and households will supply them. Firms demand resources *because* they contribute to the production of goods and services. In turn, households supply them in order to earn income.

Just as in product markets, the demand curve in a **resource market** is typically downward-sloping and the supply curve upward-sloping. The inverse relationship between the amount of a resource demanded and its price exists because businesses will substitute away from a resource as its price rises. In contrast, there will be a direct relationship between the amount of a resource supplied and its price because a higher price means greater rewards to those who provide more. As in product markets, prices will coordinate the choices of buyers and sellers in resource markets, bringing the quantity demanded into balance with the quantity supplied.

The labor market is a large component of the broader resource market. Actually, there is not just one market for labor, but rather there are many labor markets, one for each

Resource market
The market for inputs used to produce goods and services.

---

[3]This theme was a focus of much of the work of Nobel Prize–winning economist Friedrich Hayek.

EXHIBIT 1

Resource Prices, Opportunity Cost, and Product Markets

When the supply of young workers falls, it pushes the wage rates of waiters and waitresses upward (a). In the product market (b), the higher wage rates will increase the opportunity costs of restaurants, reducing supply (shift from S_1 to S_2), thus leading to higher meal prices.

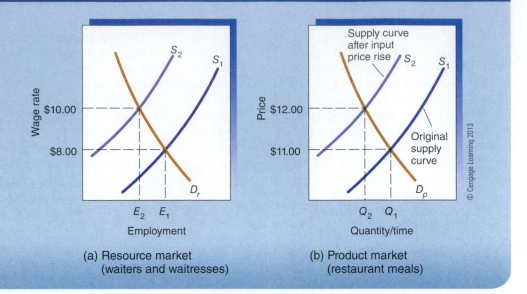

(a) Resource market
(waiters and waitresses)

(b) Product market
(restaurant meals)

different skill–experience–occupational category. Let's look at the labor market for wait-staff (waiters and waitresses). **Exhibit 1** shows how resource and product markets are linked. The supply of young workers in many occupations, including waitstaff, has declined in recent years in many areas of the United States. This lower supply has caused the wages (tip-inclusive wages) of waitstaff to increase (for example, from $8 to $10 in Exhibit 1a). The higher price of this resource increases the cost of producing restaurant meals. This higher cost, in turn, reduces the supply (shifting S_1 to S_2) of restaurant meals, pushing the price upward (Exhibit 1b). When the price of a resource increases, it will lead to higher production costs, lower supply, and higher prices for the goods and services produced with the resource.

Of course, lower resource prices have the opposite effect. Lower resource prices reduce costs and expand the supply of consumer goods made with the lower-priced resources (shifting the supply curve to the right). The increase in supply will lead to a lower price in the product market. *Thus, when the price of a resource—such as labor—changes, the prices of goods and services produced with that resource will change in the same direction.*

Changes in product markets will also influence resource markets. There is a close relationship between the demand for products and the demand for the resources required for their production. An increase in demand for a consumer good—automobiles, for example—will lead to higher auto prices, which will increase the profitability of producing automobiles and give automakers an incentive to expand output. But the expansion in automobile output will require additional resources, causing an increase in the demand for, and prices of, the resources required for their production (steel, rubber, plastics, and the labor services of autoworkers, for example). The higher prices of these resources will cause other industries to conserve on their use, freeing them up for more automobile production.

The process will work in reverse if demand for a product falls. A decrease in demand will not only reduce the price of the product but will also reduce the demand for and prices of the resources used to produce it. *Thus, when the demand for a product changes, the demand for (and prices of) the resources used to produce it will change in the same direction.*

Price controls

Government-mandated prices that are generally imposed in the form of maximum or minimum legal prices.

4-2 THE ECONOMICS OF PRICE CONTROLS

Buyers often complain that prices are too high, while sellers complain that they are too low. Unhappy with the prices established by market forces, various groups might try to persuade the government to intervene and impose **price controls**. Price controls force buyers or sellers to alter the prices of certain products. Price controls may be either price ceilings, which set a maximum legal price for a product, or price floors, which impose a minimum legal price. Imposing price controls may look like a simple, easy way for the government to help buyers at the expense of sellers (or vice versa). However, price controls reduce the gains from trade, and they generate secondary effects that often harm even the intended beneficiaries. Let's consider this issue in more detail.

4-2a THE IMPACT OF PRICE CEILINGS

Exhibit 2 shows the impact of imposing a **price ceiling** (P_1) for a product below its equilibrium level (P_0). At the lower price, the quantity supplied by producers is lower on the supply curve, at Q_S, while the quantity demanded by consumers is greater, at Q_D, on the demand curve. A **shortage** ($Q_D - Q_S$) of the good will result because the quantity demanded by consumers exceeds the quantity supplied by producers at the new controlled price. After the price ceiling is imposed, the quantity of the good exchanged declines from the equilibrium quantity to Q_S, and the gains from trade (consumer and producer surplus) fall as well.

Normally, a higher price would ration the good to the buyers most willing to pay for it. Because the price ceiling keeps this from happening, though, other means must be used to allocate the smaller quantity Q_S among consumers wanting to purchase Q_D. Predictably, nonprice factors will become more important in the rationing process. Sellers will ration their goods and services to eager buyers on the basis of factors other than their willingness to pay. For example, sellers will be more inclined to sell their products to their friends, to buyers who do them favors, and even buyers willing to make illegal "under-the-table" payments. (The accompanying Applications in Economics box, "The Imposition of Price Ceilings After Hurricanes," highlights this point.) Time might also be used as the rationing device, with those willing to wait in line the longest being the ones able to purchase the good. In addition, the below-equilibrium price reduces the incentive of sellers to expand the future supply of the good. At the lower price, suppliers will direct resources away from production of the good and into other, more profitable areas. As a result, the product shortage will worsen over time.

What other secondary effects can be expected? *In the real world, there are two ways that sellers can raise prices. First, they can raise their money price, holding quality constant. Or, second, they can hold the money price constant while reducing the*

Price ceiling
A legally established maximum price sellers can charge for a good or resource.

Shortage
A condition in which the amount of a good offered for sale by producers is less than the amount demanded by buyers at the existing price. An increase in price would eliminate the shortage.

EXHIBIT 2

The Impact of a Price Ceiling

When a price ceiling like P_1 pushes the price of a product (rental housing, for example) below the market equilibrium, a shortage will develop. Because prices are not allowed to direct the market to equilibrium, nonprice elements will become more important in rationing the good.

© Cengage Learning 2013

quality of the good. (The latter might also include reducing the size of the product, say, for example, a candy bar or a loaf of bread.) Faced with a price ceiling, sellers will use quality reductions as a way to raise their prices. Because of the government-created shortage, many consumers will buy the lower-quality good rather than do without it.

It is important to note that a shortage is not the same as scarcity. *Scarcity is inescapable.* Scarcity exists whenever people want more of a good than nature has provided. This means, of course, that almost everything of value is scarce. *Shortages, on the other hand, are a result of prices being set below their equilibrium values—a situation that is avoidable if prices are permitted to rise.* Removing the price ceiling will allow the price to rise back to its equilibrium level (P_0 rather than P_1 in Exhibit 2). This will stimulate additional production, discourage consumption, and increase the incentive of entrepreneurs to search for and develop substitute goods. This combination of forces will eliminate the shortage.

APPLICATIONS IN ECONOMICS

The Imposition of Price Ceilings after Hurricanes

Major hurricanes, such as Sandy (northeastern United States in 2012), Katrina (Gulf Coast in 2005), Andrew (south Florida in 1992), and Hugo (Charleston, South Carolina, in 1989), not only cause massive property damage and widespread power outages but also dramatically increase the local demand for items such as lumber, gasoline, ice, batteries, chain saws, and gasoline-powered generators. As a result, the prices of these items rise significantly in the wake of a hurricane. After Hurricane Hugo, for example, a bag of ice went up in price to as much as $10, the price of plywood rose to about $200 per sheet, chain saws soared to the $600 range, and gasoline sold for as much as $10.95 per gallon.

The higher prices play two important roles. First, they encourage suppliers to bring more of these items quickly to the disaster area. Second, they allocate the supplies to those deriving the greatest value from their use. The higher prices will begin to subside as additional quantities of critically needed supplies flow into the disaster area, but it is precisely these higher prices that encourage this response.

It is a natural reaction to think that the higher prices are unfair and that price controls should be imposed to prevent "price gouging." State and local officials have often imposed price controls for precisely these reasons. After Hurricane Hugo, the mayor of Charleston signed emergency legislation making it a crime to sell goods in the city at prices higher than their pre-hurricane levels. Similarly, Mississippi's attorney general announced a crackdown on price gouging after Hurricane Katrina and after Hurricane Sandy, Governor Chris Christie's administration filed lawsuits alleging price gouging against more than 70 businesses, including hotels and gas stations that had raised

AP Images/Eric Gay

prices; convictions are punishable by fines of $20,000 per transaction.

While price ceilings may be motivated by a desire to help consumers by keeping prices low, they exert secondary effects that retard the recovery process. At the lower mandated prices, consumer demand quickly outstrips the available supplies creating artificial shortages. The controls also slow the flow of goods into the area. Shipments that do arrive are greeted by long lines of consumers, many of whom end up without anything after waiting for hours.

The price controls result in serious misallocation of resources. Electric generators provide one of the best examples. The lack of electric power after a hurricane means that gasoline pumps, refrigerators, cash registers, ATMs, and other electrical equipment do not work. Grocery stores can't open and thousands of dollars' worth of food spoils. Although gas stations have gasoline in their underground storage tanks, it can't be pumped out. ATMs and banks can't operate without electricity, so people can't get to

(continued)

their money, which is critical because almost all transactions in post-hurricane environments are made with cash.

Hardware stores that sell gasoline-powered electric generators typically have only a few in stock, but after a hurricane suddenly hundreds of businesses and residents want to buy them. In the absence of price controls, the price of these generators would rise and individual homeowners would generally be outbid by businesses, which can put the generators to use operating stores, gas stations, and ATMs. It is these uses that would yield enough revenue to cover the high price of the generators because they facilitate the provision of other goods and services that people desperately want. Given the large sums such businesses would be willing to pay, some with generators at home would even find it attractive to sell or lease them to buyers willing to pay attractive prices.

Market prices would allocate generators and other urgently needed supplies to those most willing to pay for them. Price ceilings keep this from happening. In the absence of price rationing people keep their generators at home, and it is commonplace for hardware store owners with a few generators on hand to take one home for their family and then sell the others to their close friends, neighbors, and relatives to run televisions and hair dryers. Moreover, the incentive of people to take action and bring generators in from other areas is slowed. For example, John Shepperson of Kentucky took time away from his normal job to buy 19 generators, rent a truck, and drive it 600 miles to the Katrina-damaged area of Mississippi. He thought he would be able to sell the generators at high enough prices to cover his cost and earn a profit. Instead his generators were confiscated, Shepperson was arrested for price gouging, held by police for four days, and the generators kept in police custody. They never made it to consumers with urgent needs who desperately wanted to buy them.

The dramatic change in conditions that often accompany a hurricane highlights the role prices play. It also illustrates how the secondary effects accompanying price controls can magnify the damage generated by hurricanes.

©iStockphoto.com/sorendls

4-2b RENT CONTROL: A CLOSER LOOK AT A PRICE CEILING

Rent controls are a price ceiling intended to protect residents from high housing prices. Rent controls are currently in place in many U.S. cities, including New York City; Washington, D.C.; Newark, New Jersey; and San Jose, California. Most of these measures were enacted during either World War II or the 1970s, when inflation was high. Rent controls peaked in the mid-1980s. At that time, more than 200 cities, encompassing about 20 percent of the nation's population, imposed rent controls.

Because rent controls push the price of rental housing below the equilibrium level, the amount of rental housing demanded by consumers will exceed the amount landlords will make available. Initially, if the mandated price is only slightly below equilibrium, the impact of rent controls may be barely noticeable. Over time, however, the effects will worsen. Inevitably, rent controls that continue will lead to the following results.

1. Shortages and black markets will develop. Because the quantity of housing demanded will exceed the quantity supplied, some people who value rental housing highly will be unable to find it. Frustrated by the shortage, they will try to induce landlords to rent to them. Some will agree to prepay their rent, including a substantial damage deposit. Others might agree to rent or buy the landlord's furniture at exorbitant prices in order to get an apartment. Still others will make under-the-table (black market) payments to secure housing.

2. The future supply of rental housing will decline. The below-equilibrium price will discourage entrepreneurs from constructing new rental housing units, and private investment will flow elsewhere. In the city of Berkeley, rental units available to students at the University of California dropped by 31 percent in the first five years after the city adopted rent controls in 1978.[4] In contrast, removal of rent controls will often lead to a sharp

---

[4]William Tucker, *The Excluded Americans* (Washington, DC: Regnery Gateway, 1990), 162. For additional information on rent controls, see William Tucker, "Rent Control Drives Out Affordable Housing," *USA Today Magazine* (July 1998); Walter Block, "Rent Controls," in *Fortune Encyclopedia of Economics*, ed. David Henderson (New York: Warner Books, 1993). The latter publication can also be found online at http://www.econlib.org.

increase in rental housing construction, as builders seek to expand the supply that lagged behind as the result of the controls. This happened in both Boston and Santa Monica following repeal of controls in the late 1990s.

3. The quality of rental housing will deteriorate.

When apartment owners are not allowed to raise their prices, they will use quality reductions to achieve this objective. Normal maintenance and repair service will deteriorate. Tenant parking lots will be eliminated (or rented out). Eventually, the quality of the rental housing will reflect the controlled price. Cheaper housing will be of cheaper quality.

4. Nonprice methods of rationing will become more important.

Because price no longer rations rental housing, other forms of competition will develop. Landlords will rely more heavily on nonmonetary discriminating devices. They will favor friends, people of influence, and those whose lifestyles resemble their own. In contrast, applicants with many children or unconventional lifestyles, and perhaps racial minorities, will find fewer landlords who will rent to them. In New York City, where rent controls are in force, a magazine article suggested that "joining a church or synagogue" could help people make the connections they need to get an apartment. Can you imagine having to devote this amount of effort to finding an apartment? If your city enacts rent controls, you just might have to.

Rent controls lead to shortages, poor maintenance, and deterioration in the quality of rental housing.

5. Inefficient use of housing space will result.

The tenant in a rent-controlled apartment will think twice before moving. Why? Even though the tenant might want a larger or smaller space or an apartment closer to work, he or she will be less likely to move because it will be much more difficult to find a unit that's vacant. Turnover will be lower, and many people will find themselves in locations and in apartments not well suited to their needs.

Imposing rent control laws may sound like a simple way to deal with high housing prices. However, the secondary effects are so damaging that many cities have begun repealing them. In the words of Swedish economist Assar Lindbeck: "In many cases, rent control appears to be the most efficient technique presently known to destroy a city—except for bombing."[5] Though this may overstate the case, both economics and experience show that the controls adversely impact the quantity and quality of rental housing.

4-2c THE IMPACT OF PRICE FLOORS

Price floor
A legally established minimum price buyers must pay for a good or resource.

A **price floor** establishes a minimum price that can legally be charged. The government imposes price floors on some agricultural products, for example, in an effort to artificially increase the prices that farmers receive. When a price floor is imposed above the current market equilibrium price, it will alter the market's operation. **Exhibit 3** illustrates the

---

[5]Assar Lindbeck, *The Political Economy of the New Left* (New York: Harper & Row, 1972), 39.

© Cengage Learning 2013

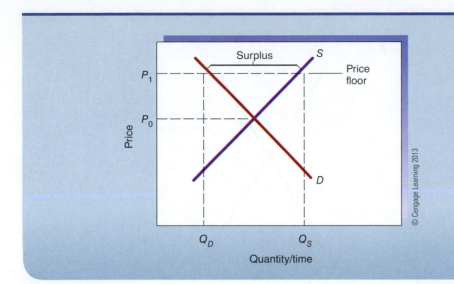

EXHIBIT 3

The Impact of a Price Floor

When a price floor such as P_1 keeps the price of a good or service above the market equilibrium, a surplus will result.

impact of imposing a price floor (P_1) for a product above its equilibrium level (P_0). At the higher price, the quantity supplied by producers increases along the supply curve to Q_S, while the quantity demanded by consumers decreases along the demand curve to Q_D. A **surplus** ($Q_S - Q_D$) of the good will result, as the quantity supplied by producers exceeds the quantity demanded by consumers at the new controlled price. Just like a price ceiling, a price floor reduces the quantity of the good exchanged and reduces the gains from trade.

As in the case of the price ceiling, nonprice factors will play a larger role in the rationing process. But because there is a surplus rather than a shortage, this time buyers will be in a position to be more selective. Buyers will purchase from sellers willing to offer them nonprice favors—better service, discounts on other products, or easier credit terms, for example. When it's difficult to alter the product's quality—in this case, improve it to make it more attractive for the price that must be charged—some producers will be unable to sell it.

It is important to note that a surplus doesn't mean the good is no longer scarce. People still want more of the good than is freely available from nature, even though they want less of it *at the controlled price* than sellers want to bring to the market. A decline in price would eliminate the surplus, but the item will be scarce in either case.

Surplus
A condition in which the amount of a good offered for sale by producers is greater than the amount that buyers will purchase at the existing price. A decline in price would eliminate the surplus.

4-2d MINIMUM WAGE: A CLOSER LOOK AT A PRICE FLOOR

In 1938, Congress passed the Fair Labor Standards Act, which mandated a national **minimum wage** of 25 cents per hour. During the past 70 years, the minimum wage has been increased many times. Most recently, in July 2009, the minimum wage was increased to $7.25 per hour. Numerous states, including California, Washington, Oregon, and Connecticut, have their own higher minimum-wage rates ranging to more than $9.00 per hour.

A minimum wage is a price floor. Because most employees in the United States earn wages in excess of the minimum, their employment opportunities are largely unaffected by the minimum wage law. However, low-skilled and inexperienced workers whose equilibrium wage rates are lower than the minimum wage will be affected.

Exhibit 4 shows the direct effect of a $7.25-per-hour minimum wage on the employment opportunities of a group of low-skilled workers. Without a minimum wage, the supply of and demand for these low-skilled workers would be in balance at some lower wage rate; here we use $5.00. Because the minimum wage makes low-skilled labor more

Minimum wage
Legislation requiring that workers be paid at least the stated minimum hourly rate of pay.

Employment and the Minimum Wage

If the market wage of a group of employees is $5.00 per hour, a $7.25-per-hour minimum wage will increase the earnings of workers able to retain their jobs, but reduce the employment opportunities of others as the number of jobs available shrinks from E_0 to E_1.

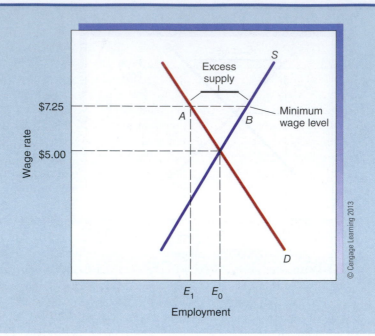

expensive, employers will substitute machines and more highly skilled workers for the now more expensive low-skilled employees. Fewer low-skilled workers will be hired when the minimum wage pushes their wages up. Graphically, this is reflected in the movement up along the demand curve in Exhibit 4 from the equilibrium point to the point associated with the higher, $7.25 wage rate (point *A*). The result will be a reduction in employment of low-skilled workers from E_0 to E_1.

On the supply side of the market, as the wages of low-skilled workers are pushed above equilibrium, there will be more unskilled workers looking for jobs. Graphically, this is reflected in the movement up along the supply curve in Exhibit 4 from the equilibrium point to the point associated with the higher, $7.25 wage rate (point *B*). At the $7.25 wage rate, the quantity of workers searching for jobs will exceed the quantity of jobs available, causing excess supply.

In a labor market, an excess supply will take the form of an abnormally high rate of unemployment. Thus, *economic analysis indicates that minimum-wage legislation will lead to high unemployment rates among low-skilled workers.* The exceedingly high unemployment rate of teenagers in the United States (a group with limited skills because they lack work experience) is consistent with this analysis. In April 2013, the unemployment rate of teenagers was 24.1 percent, compared to 6.1 percent for workers age 25 and older. The unemployment rate of teenagers is about four times the average rate for workers aged 25 and older. Of course, the higher unemployment rate of teenagers reflects their shifts back and forth between schooling and the labor force, but detailed studies indicate that the minimum wage is also a contributing factor.

It is important to remember that the market price—the wage rate—is only one dimension of the transaction. When a price floor pushes the wage rate above equilibrium, employers will have less incentive to offer nonwage benefits to employees because they will have no trouble hiring low-skilled workers. Predictably, a higher minimum wage will lead to a deterioration of the nonwage attributes of minimum-wage jobs, and so workers in these jobs will experience less convenient working hours, fewer training opportunities, and less continuous employment. Moreover, minimum wage legislation prohibits employers and employees from entering into agreements for mutually advantageous job opportunities that offer attractive work experiences at a wage below the minimum. As a result, employment opportunities such as internships that open doors and enhance future earnings are more difficult to arrange. In this regard, it is interesting that Congress, which utilizes hundreds of interns at a zero wage, exempts itself from minimum wage legislation.

The adverse impact of minimum wage laws on the work experience and training opportunities of youthful workers is particularly important. Low-paying, entry-level jobs often provide workers with experience that will help them move up the job ladder to higher-paying positions. Employment experience obtained at an early age, even on menial tasks, can help people acquire self-confidence, good work habits, and skills that make them more valuable to future employers. Mandated minimum wages will make it more difficult for youthful workers to acquire work experience and jobs with training opportunities.[6]

Workers who are able to maintain their employment at the higher minimum-wage rate—most likely the better qualified among those with low skill levels—gain from a minimum wage. However, some firms will respond to the higher minimum by reducing the weekly hours of the low-skill workers who remain employed. Thus, part of the increase in weekly earnings due to a higher hourly wage rate will be offset by a decrease in weekly hours worked.

How many fewer low-skilled workers are hired because of the minimum wage? Numerous studies have been conducted on the minimum wage's impact on employment levels. It is challenging, however, to isolate the effect of the minimum wage since other factors such as economic conditions also affect the number of workers employed. As a result, some studies find little or no effect of the minimum wage on employment levels. However, a recent review of more than 100 studies reported that 85 percent of them find that a higher minimum wage reduces employment. These studies indicate that a 10 percent increase in the minimum wage reduces the employment of low-skilled workers by 1 to 3 percent.[7] Minimum-wage supporters argue that the higher wages for low-skilled workers are worth this reduction in employment and job-training opportunities. The critics disagree, arguing that if permitted to work, the low-skill workers would gain experience and training, which would facilitate their movement up the job ladder to higher wage positions.

Proponents of minimum wage laws argue that they help the poor. Is this really true? According to the U.S. Department of Labor, most minimum wage earners are young, part-time workers and relatively few live below the poverty line. About one-half of minimum wage workers are between the ages of 16 to 24 years and approximately three-fifths hold a part-time job. Fewer than 20 percent of minimum wage workers are from families below the poverty line, and only about one out of every four is married. Only 15 percent are a sole earner providing support for a family with one or more children. Therefore, even if the adverse effects of a higher minimum wage on employment and training opportunities are small, a higher minimum wage does little to help the poor, making it a much less attractive antipoverty program than other alternatives.[8]

4-3 BLACK MARKETS AND THE IMPORTANCE OF THE LEGAL STRUCTURE

When price controls are imposed, exchanges at prices outside of the range set by the government are illegal. Governments may also make it entirely illegal to buy and sell certain products. This is the case with drugs like heroin and cocaine in the United States. Similarly, prostitution is illegal in all states except Nevada. However, controlling prices and making a good or service illegal doesn't eliminate market forces. When demand is strong and gains from trade can be had, markets will develop and exchanges will occur in spite of

---

[6] For evidence that the minimum wage limits training opportunities, see David Neumark and William Wascher, "Minimum Wages and Training Revisited," *Journal of Labor Economic* 19 (July 2001): 563–95.

[7] See David Neumark and William Wascher, "Minimum Wages and Employment," *Foundations and Trends in Microeconomics* 3, no. 1–2 (2007): 1–182.

[8] See David Neumark and William Wascher, "The Effects of Minimum Wages Throughout the Wage Distribution," Journal of Human Resources 39 (April 2004): 425–50; David Neumark and William Wascher, Minimum Wages. (Cambridge, MA: MIT Press, 2008); and Joseph J. Sabia and Richard V. Burkhauser, "Minimum Wages and Poverty: Will a $9.50 Federal Minimum Wage Really Help the Working Poor?" *Southern Economic Journal* 76 (January 2010): 592–623, for evidence on this point.

Black market
A market that operates outside the legal system in which either illegal goods are sold or legal goods are sold at illegal prices or terms.

©iStockphoto.com/Christa Brunt

Black markets like those for illegal drugs are characterized by less dependable product quality and the greater use of violence to settle disputes between buyers and sellers.

the restrictions. People will also engage in illegal exchanges in order to evade taxes. For example, the $5.85 per-pack cigarette tax in New York City has made cigarette smuggling into that city a thriving business.

Markets that operate outside the legal system are called **black markets**. How do black markets work? Can markets function without the protection of the law? As in other markets, supply and demand will determine prices in black markets, too. However, because black markets operate outside the official legal structure, enforcement of contracts and the dependability of quality will be less certain. Furthermore, participation in black markets involves greater risk, particularly for suppliers. Prices in these markets will have to be higher than they otherwise would be to compensate suppliers for the risks they are taking—the threat of arrest, possibility of a fine or prison sentence, and so on. Perhaps most important, in black markets there are no legal channels for the peaceful settlement of disputes. When a buyer or a seller fails to deliver, it is the other party who must try to enforce the agreement, usually through the use or threat of physical force.

Compared with normal markets, economic analysis indicates that black markets will be characterized by a higher incidence of defective products, higher profit rates (for those who do not get caught), and more violence. The incidence of phony tickets purchased from street dealers selling them at illegal prices and deaths caused by toxic, illicit drugs are reflections of the high presence of defective goods in these markets. The expensive clothes and automobiles of many drug dealers provide evidence of the high monetary profits present in black markets. Crime statistics indicate that violence is often used to settle disputes arising from black-market transactions. In urban areas, a high percentage of the violent crimes, including murder, are associated with illegal trades gone bad and competition among dealers in the illegal drug market.

The prohibition of alcohol in the United States from 1920 to 1933 provides additional evidence that violence, deception, and fraud plague markets that operate outside the law. When the production and sale of alcohol were illegal during the Prohibition era, gangsters dominated the alcohol trade, and the murder rate soared to record highs. There were also problems with product quality (tainted or highly toxic mixtures, for example) similar to the ones present in modern-day illegal-drug markets. When Prohibition was repealed and the market for alcoholic beverages began operating once again within the legal framework, these harmful secondary effects disappeared.

The operation of black markets highlights a point often taken for granted: *A legal system that provides for secure private-property rights, contract enforcement, and access to an unbiased court system for settling disputes is vitally important for the smooth operation of markets.* Markets will exist in any environment, but they can be counted on to function efficiently only when property rights are secure and contracts are impartially enforced.

4-4 THE IMPACT OF A TAX

Tax incidence
The way the burden of a tax is distributed among economic units (consumers, producers, employees, employers, and so on). The actual tax burden does not always fall on those who are statutorily assigned to pay the tax.

How do taxes affect market exchange? When governments tax goods, who bears the burden? Economists use the term **tax incidence** to indicate how the burden of a tax is *actually* shared between buyers (who pay more for what they purchase) and sellers (who receive less for what they sell). When a tax is imposed, the government can make either the buyer or the seller legally responsible for payment of the tax. The legal assignment is called the *statutory incidence* of the tax. However, the person who writes the check to the government— that is, the person statutorily responsible for the tax—is not always the one who bears the tax burden. The *actual incidence* of a tax may lie elsewhere. If, for example, a tax is placed statutorily on a seller, the seller might simply increase the price of the product. In this case, the buyers end up bearing some, or all, of the tax burden through the higher price.

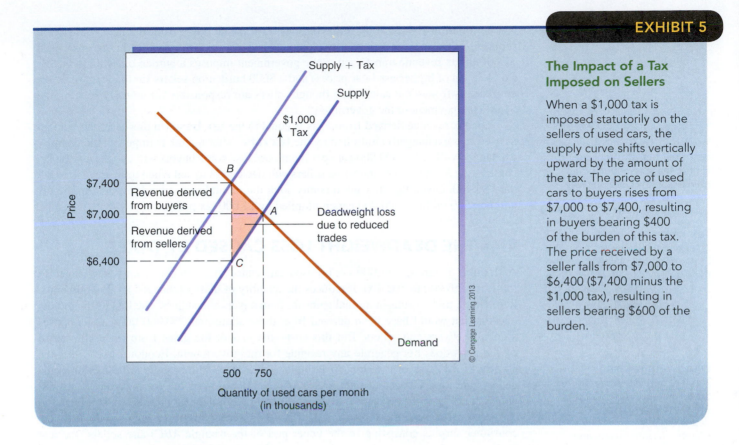

© Cengage Learning 2013

EXHIBIT 5

The Impact of a Tax Imposed on Sellers

When a $1,000 tax is imposed statutorily on the sellers of used cars, the supply curve shifts vertically upward by the amount of the tax. The price of used cars to buyers rises from $7,000 to $7,400, resulting in buyers bearing $400 of the burden of this tax. The price received by a seller falls from $7,000 to $6,400 ($7,400 minus the $1,000 tax), resulting in sellers bearing $600 of the burden.

To illustrate, **Exhibit 5** shows how a $1,000 tax placed on the sale of used cars would affect the market. (To simplify this example, let's assume all used cars are identical.) Here, the tax has statutorily been placed on the seller. When a tax is imposed on the seller, it shifts the supply curve upward by exactly the amount of the tax—$1,000, in this example. To understand why, remember that the height of the supply curve at a particular quantity shows the minimum price required to cause enough sellers to offer that quantity of cars for sale. Suppose you were a potential seller, willing to sell your car for any price over $6,000, but you would keep it unless you could pocket at least $6,000 from the sale. Because you now have to pay a tax of $1,000 when you sell your car, the minimum price you will accept *from the buyer* will rise to $7,000, so that after paying the tax, you will retain $6,000. Other potential sellers will be in a similar position. The tax will push the minimum price each seller is willing to accept upward by $1,000. Thus, the after-tax supply curve will shift vertically by this amount.

Sellers would prefer to pass the entire tax on to buyers by raising prices by the full amount of the tax, rather than paying any part of it themselves. However, as sellers begin to raise prices, customers respond by purchasing fewer units. At some point, to avoid losing additional sales, some sellers will find it more profitable to accept part of the tax burden themselves (in the form of a lower price net of tax), rather than to raise the price by the full amount of the tax. This process is shown in Exhibit 5.

Before the tax was imposed, used cars sold for a price of $7,000 (at the intersection of the original supply and demand curves shown by point *A*). After the $1,000 tax is imposed, the equilibrium price of used cars will rise to $7,400 (to point *B*, the intersection of the new supply curve including the tax, and the demand curve). Thus, despite the tax being statutorily imposed on sellers, the higher price shifts some of the tax burden to buyers. Buyers will now pay $400 more for used cars. Sellers now receive $7,400 from the sale of their used cars. However, after sending $1,000 in taxes to the government, they retain only $6,400. This is exactly $600 less than the seller would have received had the tax not been imposed. Because the distance between the supply curves is exactly $1,000, this net price can be found in Exhibit 5 by following the vertical line down from the new equilibrium (point *B*) to the original supply curve (point *C*) and over to the price axis. In this case, each $1,000 of tax revenue transferred to the government imposes a burden of $400 on buyers (in the form of higher used-car prices) and a $600 burden on sellers (in the form of lower net receipts from a car sale), even though sellers are responsible for actually sending the $1,000 tax payment to the government.

The tax revenue derived from a tax is equal to the **tax base** (in this case, the number of used cars exchanged) multiplied by the **tax rate**. After the tax is imposed, the quantity exchanged will fall to 500,000 cars per month because some buyers will choose not to purchase at the $7,400 price, and some sellers will decide not to sell when they are able to net only $6,400. Given the after-tax quantity sold, the monthly revenue derived from the tax will be $500 million (500,000 cars multiplied by $1,000 tax per car).

4-4a THE DEADWEIGHT LOSS CAUSED BY TAXES

As Exhibit 5 shows, a $1,000 tax on used cars causes the number of units exchanged to fall from 750,000 to 500,000. It reduces the quantity of units exchanged by 250,000 units. Remember, trade results in mutual gains for both buyers and sellers. The loss of the mutual benefits that would have been derived from these additional 250,000 units also imposes a cost on buyers and sellers. But this cost—the loss of the gains from trade eliminated by the tax—does not generate any revenue for the government. Economists call this the **deadweight loss** of taxation. In Exhibit 5, the size of the triangle *ABC* measures the deadweight loss. The deadweight loss is a burden imposed on buyers and sellers over and above the cost of the revenue transferred to the government. Sometimes it is referred to as the **excess burden of taxation**. It is composed of losses to both buyers (the lost consumer surplus consisting of the upper part of the triangle *ABC*) and sellers (the lost producer surplus consisting of the lower part of the triangle *ABC*).

The deadweight loss to sellers includes an indirect cost imposed on the people who supply resources to that industry (such as its suppliers and employees). The 1990 luxury-boat tax provides a vivid illustration of this point. Supporters of the luxury-boat tax assumed the tax burden would fall primarily on wealthy yacht buyers. The actual effects were quite different, though. Because of the tax, luxury-boat sales fell sharply and thousands of workers lost their jobs in the yacht-manufacturing industry. The deadweight loss triangle might seem like an abstract concept, but it wasn't so abstract to the employees in the yacht industry who lost their jobs! Their losses are part of what is reflected in the triangular area. Moreover, because luxury-boat sales declined so sharply, the tax generated only a meager amount of revenue. The large deadweight loss (or excess burden) combined with meager revenue for the government eventually led to the repeal of the tax.

4-4b ACTUAL VERSUS STATUTORY INCIDENCE

Economic analysis indicates that the actual burden of a tax—or more precisely, the split of the burden between buyers and sellers—does not depend on whether the tax is statutorily placed on the buyer or the seller. To see this, we must first look at how the market responds to a tax statutorily placed on the buyer. Continuing with the auto tax example, let's suppose that the government places the $1,000 tax on the buyer of the car, rather than the seller. After making a used-car purchase, the buyer must send a check to the government for $1,000. Imposing a tax on buyers will shift the demand curve downward by the amount of the tax, as shown in **Exhibit 6**. This is because the height of the demand curve represents the maximum price a buyer is willing to pay for the car. If a particular buyer is willing and able to pay only $5,000 for a car, the $1,000 tax would mean that the most the buyer would be willing to pay *to the seller* would be $4,000. This is because the total cost to the buyer is now the purchase price plus the tax.

As Exhibit 6 shows, the price of used cars falls from $7,000 (point *A*) to $6,400 (point *B*) when the tax is statutorily placed on the buyer. Even though the tax is placed on buyers, the

Tax base
The level or quantity of an economic activity that is taxed. Higher tax rates reduce the level of the tax base because they make the activity less attractive.

Tax rate
The per-unit amount of the tax or the percentage rate at which the economic activity is taxed.

Deadweight loss
The loss of gains from trade to buyers and sellers that occurs when a tax is imposed. The deadweight loss imposes a burden on both buyers and sellers over and above the actual payment of the tax.

Excess burden of taxation
Another term for deadweight loss. It reflects losses that occur when beneficial activities are forgone because they are taxed.

EXHIBIT 6

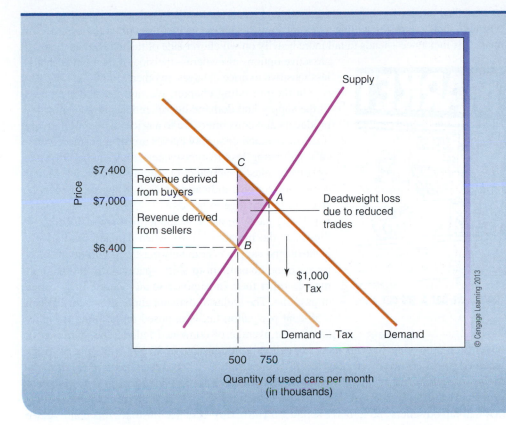

The Impact of a Tax Imposed on Buyers

When a $1,000 tax is imposed statutorily on the buyers of used cars, the demand curve shifts vertically downward by the amount of the tax. The price of used cars falls from $7,000 to $6,400, resulting in sellers bearing $600 of the burden. The buyer's total cost of purchasing the car rises from $7,000 to $7,400 ($6,400 plus the $1,000 tax), resulting in buyers bearing $400 of the burden of this tax. The incidence of this tax on used cars is the same regardless of whether it is statutorily imposed on buyers or sellers.

reduction in demand that results causes the price received by sellers to fall by $600. Thus, $600 of the tax is again borne by sellers, just as it was when the tax was placed statutorily on them. From the buyer's standpoint, a car now costs $7,400 ($6,400 paid to the seller plus $1,000 in tax to the government). Just as when the tax was imposed on the seller, the buyer now pays $400 more for a used car.

A comparison of Exhibits 5 and 6 makes it clear that the actual burden of the $1,000 tax is independent of its statutory incidence. In both cases, buyers pay a total price of $7,400 for the car (a $400 increase from the pretax level), and sellers receive $6,400 from the sale (a $600 decrease from the pretax level). Correspondingly, the revenue derived by the government, the number of sales eliminated by the tax, and the size of the deadweight loss are identical whether the law requires payment of the tax by the sellers or by the buyers. A similar phenomenon occurs with any tax. The 15.3 percent Social Security payroll tax, for example, is statutorily levied as 7.65 percent on the employee and 7.65 percent on the employer. The impact is to drive down the net pay received by employees and raise the employers' cost of hiring workers. Economic analysis tells us that the actual burden of this tax will probably differ from its legal assignment and that it will be the same regardless of how the tax is statutorily assigned. Because market prices (here, workers' gross wage) will adjust, the incidence of the tax will be identical regardless of whether the 15.3 percent is levied on employees or on employers or is divided between the two parties.

4-4c ELASTICITY AND THE INCIDENCE OF A TAX

If the actual incidence of a tax is independent of its statutory assignment, then what does determine the incidence? The answer: The incidence of a tax depends on the responsiveness of buyers and of sellers to a change in price. When buyers respond to even a small increase in price by leaving the market and buying other things, they will not be willing to accept a price that is much higher than it was prior to the tax. Similarly, if sellers respond to a small reduction

The actual burden of a tax is independent of whether it is imposed on buyers or sellers.

in what they receive by shifting their goods and resources to other markets, or by going out of business, they will not be willing to accept a much smaller payment, net of tax. The burden of a tax—its incidence—tends to fall more heavily on whichever side of the market has the least attractive options elsewhere—the side of the market that is less sensitive to price changes, in other words.

In the preceding chapter, we saw that the steepness of the supply and demand curves reflects how responsive producers and consumers are to a price change. Relatively inelastic demand or supply curves are steeper (more vertical), indicating less responsiveness to a change in price. Relatively elastic demand or supply curves are flatter (more horizontal), indicating a higher degree of responsiveness to a change in price.

Using gasoline as an example, part (a) of **Exhibit 7** illustrates the impact of a tax when demand is relatively inelastic and supply is relatively elastic. It will not be easy for gasoline consumers to shift—particularly in the short run—to other fuels in response to an increase in the price of gasoline. The inelastic demand curve shows this. When a 50-cent per-gallon tax is imposed on gasoline (roughly the current average of combined federal and state taxes), buyers end up paying 40 cents more per gallon ($3.00 instead of $2.60), while the net price received by sellers is only 10 cents less ($2.50 instead of $2.60). **When demand is relatively inelastic, or supply is relatively elastic, buyers will bear the larger share of the tax burden.**

Conversely, when demand is relatively elastic and supply is inelastic, more of the tax burden will fall on sellers and resource suppliers. The luxury-boat tax illustrates this point. As we mentioned earlier, Congress imposed a tax on the sale of luxury boats in 1990. Later, the tax

"THIS NEW TAX PLAN SOUNDS PRETTY GOOD... WE GET A 9% CUT AND BUSINESS PICKS UP THE BURDEN...."

By John Trever, Albuquerque Journal. Reprinted by permission.

EXHIBIT 7

How the Burden of a Tax Depends on the Elasticities of Demand and Supply

In part (a), when demand is relatively more inelastic than supply, buyers bear a larger share of the burden of the tax. In part (b), when supply is relatively more inelastic than demand, sellers bear a larger share of the tax burden.

(a) Tax on gasoline

(b) Tax on luxury boats

© Cengage Learning 2013

was repealed because of its adverse impact on sales and employment in the industry. There are many things wealthy potential yacht owners can spend their money on other than luxury boats *sold in the United States*. For one thing, they can buy a yacht someplace else, perhaps in Mexico, England, or the Bahamas. Or they can spend more time on the golf course, travel to exotic places, or purchase a nicer car or a vacation home. Because there are attractive substitutes, the demand for domestically produced luxury boats is relatively elastic compared with supply. Therefore, as Exhibit 7b illustrates, when a $25,000 tax is imposed on luxury boats, prices rise by only $5,000 (from $100,000 to $105,000), but output falls substantially (from 10,000 to 5,000 boats). The net price received by sellers falls by $20,000 (from $100,000 to $80,000 per boat). *When demand is relatively elastic, or supply is relatively inelastic, sellers (including resource suppliers) will bear the larger share of the tax burden.*

4-4d ELASTICITY AND THE DEADWEIGHT LOSS

We have seen that the elasticities of supply and demand determine how the burden of a tax is distributed between buyer and seller. They also influence the size of the deadweight loss caused by the tax because they determine the total reduction in the quantity exchanged. When either demand or supply is relatively inelastic, fewer trades will be eliminated by the tax, so the deadweight loss will be smaller. From a policy perspective, the excess burden of a tax system will therefore be lower if taxes are levied on goods and services for which either demand or supply is highly inelastic.

4-5 TAX RATES, TAX REVENUES, AND THE LAFFER CURVE

It is important to distinguish between the average and marginal rates of taxation. They can be very different, and both provide important information. The average tax rate is generally used to examine how different income groups are burdened by a tax, whereas the marginal tax rate is the key to understanding the negative economic effects created by a tax. Both can be computed with simple equations. The **average tax rate (ATR)** can be expressed as follows:

$$\text{ATR} = \frac{\text{Tax liability}}{\text{Taxable income}}$$

For example, if a person's tax liability was $3,000 on an income of $20,000, his or her average tax rate would be 15 percent ($3,000 divided by $20,000). The average tax rate is simply the percentage of income that is paid in taxes.

In the United States, the personal income tax provides the largest single source of government revenue. This tax is particularly important at the federal level. You may have heard that the federal income tax is "progressive." A **progressive tax** is defined as a tax in which the average tax rate rises with income. In other words, people with higher income pay a larger *percentage of their income* in taxes. Alternatively, taxes can be proportional or regressive. A **proportional tax** is defined as a tax in which the average tax rate remains the same across income levels. Under a proportional tax, everyone pays the same percentage of their income in taxes. Finally, a **regressive tax** is defined as a tax in which the average tax rate falls as income rises. If someone making $100,000 per year paid $30,000 in taxes (an ATR of 30 percent), while someone making $30,000 per year paid $15,000 in taxes (an ATR of 50 percent), the tax code would be regressive. Note that a regressive tax merely means that the *percentage* paid in taxes declines with income; the actual dollar amount of the tax bill might still be higher for those with larger incomes.

Although the average tax rate is useful in determining whether an income tax is progressive, proportional, or regressive, it is the marginal tax rate that is most relevant when individuals are making choices. It is the marginal tax rate that determines how much of an additional dollar of income must be paid in taxes (and thus, also, how much one gets to

Average tax rate (ATR)
Tax liability divided by taxable income. It is the percentage of income paid in taxes.

Progressive tax
A tax in which the average tax rate rises with income. People with higher incomes will pay a higher percentage of their income in taxes.

Proportional tax
A tax in which the average tax rate is the same at all income levels. Everyone pays the same percentage of income in taxes.

Regressive tax
A tax in which the average tax rate falls with income. People with higher incomes will pay a lower percentage of their income in taxes.

Marginal tax rate (MTR)
The additional tax liability a person faces divided by his or her additional taxable income. It is the percentage of an extra dollar of income earned that must be paid in taxes. It is the marginal tax rate that is relevant in personal decision-making.

keep). An individual's marginal tax rate can be very different from his or her average tax rate. The **marginal tax rate (MTR)** can be expressed as follows:

$$\text{MTR} = \frac{\text{Change in tax liability}}{\text{Change in taxable income}}$$

The MTR reveals both how much of one's *additional* income must be turned over to the tax collector and how much is retained by the individual taxpayer. For example, when the MTR is 25 percent, $25 of every $100 of additional earnings must be paid in taxes. The individual is permitted to keep only $75 of his or her additional income, in other words. The marginal tax rate is vitally important because it affects the incentive to earn additional income. The higher the marginal tax rate, the less incentive individuals have to earn more income. At high marginal rates, for example, many spouses will choose to stay home rather than take a job, and others will choose not to take on second jobs or extra work. **Exhibit 8** shows the calculation of both

EXHIBIT 8

Average and Marginal Tax Rates in the Income Tax Tables

This excerpt from the 2012 federal income tax table shows that in the 25 percent federal marginal income tax bracket, each $100 of additional taxable income a single taxpayer earns ($36,000 versus $36,100, for example) causes his or her tax liability to increase by $25 (from $5,036 to $5,061). Note that the average tax rate for a single taxpayer at $36,000 is about 14 percent ($5,036 divided by $36,000), even though the taxpayer's marginal rate is 25 percent.

2012 Tax Table–*Continued*

If line 43 (taxable income) is–		And you are–			
AT LEAST	BUT LESS THAN	SINGLE	MARRIED FILING JOINTLY	MARRIED FILING SEPARATELY	HEAD OF A HOUSEHOLD
			Your tax is–		
36,000					
36,000	36,050	5,036	4,534	5,036	4,784
36,050	36,100	5,049	4,541	5,049	4,791
36,100	36,150	5,061	4,549	5,061	4,799
36,150	36,200	5,074	4,556	5,074	4,806
36,200	36,250	5,086	4,564	5,086	4,814
36,250	36,300	5,099	4,571	5,099	4,821
36,300	36,350	5,111	4,579	5,111	4,829
36,350	36,400	5,124	4,586	5,124	4,836
36,400	36,450	5,136	4,594	5,136	4,844
36,450	36,500	5,149	4,601	5,149	4,851
36,500	36,550	5,161	4,609	5,161	4,859
36,550	36,600	5,174	4,616	5,174	4,866
36,600	36,650	5,186	4,624	5,186	4,874
36,650	36,700	5,199	4,631	5,199	4,881
36,700	36,750	5,211	4,639	5,211	4,889
36,750	36,800	5,224	4,646	5,224	4,896
36,800	36,850	5,236	4,654	5,236	4,904
36,850	36,900	5,249	4,661	5,249	4,911
36,900	36,950	5,261	4,669	5,261	4,919
36,950	37,000	5,274	4,676	5,274	4,926

$100 of additional income . . .

. . . results in $25 of additional tax liability.

the average and marginal tax rates within the framework of the 2012 federal income tax tables. In addition to the federal income tax, there are also state and local income taxes and payroll taxes. The taxpayer's marginal tax rate will reflect the combine impact of all taxes that reduce the take-home pay derived from additional earnings.

Governments generally levy taxes to raise revenue. The revenue derived from a tax is equal to the tax base multiplied by the tax rate. As we previously noted, taxes will reduce the level of the activity. When an activity is taxed more heavily, people will choose to do less of it. The higher the tax rate, the greater the shift away from the activity. If taxpayers can easily escape the tax by altering their behavior (perhaps by shifting to substitutes), the tax base will shrink significantly as rates are increased. This erosion in the tax base in response to higher rates means that an increase in tax rates will generally lead to a less-than-proportional increase in tax revenue.

Economist Arthur Laffer popularized the idea that, beyond some point, higher tax rates will shrink the tax base so much that tax revenue will eventually decline as tax rates are pushed to higher and higher levels. The curve illustrating the relationship between tax rates and tax revenues is called the **Laffer curve.** Exhibit 9 illustrates the concept of the Laffer curve as it applies to income taxes. Obviously, tax revenue would be zero if the income tax rate were zero. What isn't so obvious is that tax revenue would also be zero (or at least very close to zero) if the tax rate were 100 percent. Confronting a 100 percent tax rate, most individuals would go fishing or find something else to do rather than engage in taxable productive activity, since the 100 percent tax rate would eliminate all personal reward derived from earning taxable income. Why work when you have to give every penny of your earnings to the government?

As tax rates are reduced from 100 percent, the incentive to work and earn taxable income increases, income expands, and tax revenue rises. Similarly, as tax rates increase from zero, tax revenue expands. Clearly, at some rate greater than zero but less than 100 percent, tax revenue will be maximized (point *B* in Exhibit 9). This is not to imply that the tax rate that maximizes revenue is the ideal, or optimal, tax rate from the standpoint of the economy as a whole. Although it might be the tax rate that generates the most revenue for government, we must also consider the welfare reductions imposed on individuals by the deadweight loss created by the tax. As rates are increased and the maximum revenue point (*B*) is approached, relatively large tax rate increases will be necessary to expand tax revenue by even a small

Laffer curve
A curve illustrating the relationship between the tax rate and tax revenues. Tax revenues will be low at both very high and very low tax rates. When tax rates are quite high, lowering them can increase tax revenue.

EXHIBIT 9

Laffer Curve

Because taxing an activity affects the amount of it people will do, a change in tax rates will not lead to a proportional change in tax revenues. As the Laffer curve indicates, beyond some point (*B*), an increase in tax rates will cause tax revenues to fall. At high tax rates, revenue can be increased by lowering tax rates. The tax rate that maximizes tax revenue is higher than the ideal tax rate for the economy as a whole because of the large deadweight loss of taxation as tax rates increase toward point *B*.

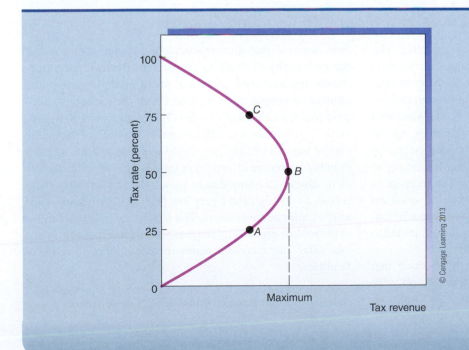

© Cengage Learning 2013

amount. In this range, the deadweight loss of taxation in the form of reductions in gains from trade will be exceedingly large relative to the additional tax revenue. Far from being ideal, the revenue maximizing tax rate will be highly inefficient.

The Laffer curve shows that it is important to distinguish between changes in tax rates and changes in tax revenues. Higher rates will not always lead to more revenue for the government. Similarly, lower rates will not always lead to less revenue. ***When tax rates are already high, a rate reduction may increase tax revenues. Correspondingly, increasing high tax rates may lead to less tax revenue.***

Evidence from the sharp reduction in marginal tax rates imposed on those with high incomes during the 1980s supports the Laffer curve. The top marginal rate was reduced from 70 percent at the beginning of the decade to 33 percent by the end of the decade. Even though the top rates were cut sharply, tax revenues and the share of the personal income tax paid by high-income earners actually rose as a result. During the decade, revenue collected from the top 1 percent of earners rose a whopping 51.4 percent (after adjusting for inflation). In 1980, 19 percent of the personal income tax was collected from the top 1 percent of earners. By 1990, at the lower tax rates, the top 1 percent of earners accounted for more than 25 percent of income tax revenues. The top 10 percent of earners paid just over 49 percent of total income taxes in 1980, but by 1990 the share paid by these earners had risen to 55 percent. Thus, the reduction in the exceedingly high rates increased the revenue collected from high-income taxpayers. Additional evidence on the impact of these tax changes in the 1980s is provided in Special Topic 1.

Many politicians advocate higher marginal tax rates on high-income earners in order to raise additional revenue and reduce the size of the federal budget deficit. When considering such proposals, it is important to keep in mind that higher marginal tax rates will lead to a smaller amount of taxable income produced by high earners. Predictably, such proposals will raise less revenue than their proponents envision as the tax base shrinks in response to the higher marginal tax rate.

APPLICATIONS IN ECONOMICS

The Laffer Curve and Mountain-Climbing Deaths

The Laffer curve can be used to illustrate many other relationships besides just tax rates and tax revenues. Economists J. R. Clark and Dwight Lee have used it to analyze the relationship between the safety of mountain climbing and mountain-climbing deaths on Mount McKinley, North America's highest peak. As the risk of dying from climbing Mount McKinley fell due to greater search-and-rescue efforts by national park personnel, the number of people seeking to "conquer the mountain" rose significantly. The increase in the number of climbers attempting to conquer the mountain offset the lower risk, leading to a Laffer curve-type relationship. In other words, greater search-and-rescue efforts led to a *higher* number of total deaths on the mountain.

Let's look at the problem numerically. Assume that if the probability of death from an attempted climb were 90 percent, only 100 people would attempt to climb the mountain each year, leading to an annual death rate of 90.

Now suppose that greater search-and-rescue efforts lower the probability of death to 50 percent. Because incentives matter, the increased safety will result in an increase in the number of people attempting to climb the mountain. Suppose that the number of climbers increases from 100 to 200. With 200 climbers and a 50 percent probability of death, the annual number of fatalities would increase to 100, 10 more than before rescue efforts were improved. The total number of mountain-climbing deaths is actually lowest when there is both a very high and a very low probability of death—just as the Laffer curve predicts. The number of deaths is largest in the middle probability ranges. Making a very risky mountain safer can therefore result in more rather than fewer fatalities.[1]

[1]See J. R. Clark and Dwight R. Lee, "Too Safe to Be Safe: Some Implications of Short- and Long-Run Rescue Laffer Curves," *Eastern Economic Journal* 23, no. 2 (Spring 1997): 127–37.

©iStockphoto.com/sorendls

4-6 THE IMPACT OF A SUBSIDY

The supply and demand framework can also be used to analyze the impact of a government **subsidy**. A subsidy is a payment to either the buyer or seller of a good or service, usually on a per-unit basis. When a subsidy is granted to buyers, proponents typically argue that the subsidy will make the purchase of the good more affordable. Correspondingly, subsidies to sellers are generally thought to improve the profitability of the producers in the industry. As we have seen in other cases, however, the effect of government programs often differ substantially from the stated intentions of their proponents. Because prices change when subsidies are imposed (just as when taxes are imposed), the benefit of a subsidy can be partially, or totally, shifted from buyer to seller, or vice versa.

Suppose that the government, in an effort to make the cost of college more affordable, granted full-time students a subsidy of $4,000 per year. What impact would this subsidy have on the price and quantity in the market for a college education? **Exhibit 10** provides insight on the answer to this question. Prior to the subsidy, the market price was determined by the intersection of the initial demand (D_1) and supply (S_1). Thus, the pre-subsidy equilibrium price for a year of college was $10,000. The subsidy to the student-buyers

Subsidy
A payment the government makes to either the buyer or the seller, usually on a per-unit basis, when a good or service is purchased or sold.

EXHIBIT 10

The Impact of a Subsidy Granted to Buyers

Here we illustrate how a $4,000 subsidy granted to full-time college students would impact the price and quantity of a year of college education. Prior to the subsidy, the equilibrium price of a year of college was $10,000 and Q_1 students attended college. The subsidy to students would cause demand to shift from D_1 to D_2, pushing the equilibrium price of a year of college to $12,000. Students would gain $2,000 in the form of a lower net cost of a year of college (the new net price after the subsidy is $8,000), but the suppliers would also gain $2,000 in the form of higher prices for their services. If the supply curve was more inelastic relative to the demand curve, the gains of the students would be smaller and those of the suppliers larger.

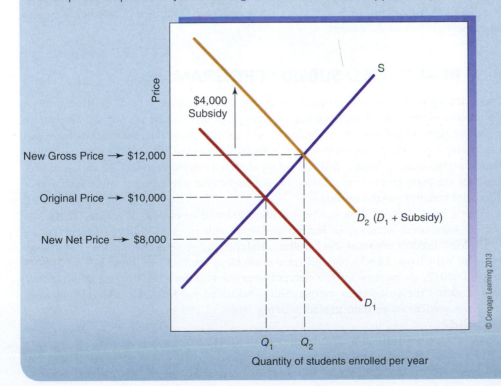

© Cengage Learning 2013

increases demand, causing the demand curve to shift upward by $4,000 from D_1 to D_2. A new equilibrium will occur at a higher price ($12,000 in our example) and larger output (Q_2 rather than Q_1). The net price to students will fall to $8,000, the $12,000 new market price minus the $4,000.

Interestingly, even though the students received an educational subsidy of $4,000, their net gain was only $2,000. The rest of the benefits went to the educational suppliers in the form of higher prices for their services.

As we previously discussed, the burden of a tax does not necessarily fall entirely or even primarily on the party writing out the check to the taxing authority. The same is true for subsidies. Parties other than the direct subsidy recipients may benefit substantially from the subsidies. Moreover, the direct recipients of the subsidy may gain less, and often substantially less, than their grant from the government.

4-6a ELASTICITY AND THE BENEFIT OF GOVERNMENT SUBSIDY PROGRAMS

What determines the allocation of the benefits derived from a subsidy? In the example of Exhibit 10, the benefit of the $4,000 subsidy granted to students was split evenly between buyers and sellers. However, the actual distribution of this benefit will depend on the elasticity of supply and demand—just as it does with a tax. Consider the case where the subsidy is granted to the buyers, causing the demand curve for the product to shift upward by the amount of the subsidy. If the supply curve is highly inelastic relative to demand, the increase in demand will lead primarily to higher prices and most of the benefits will be derived by the suppliers of the good or service. In contrast, if the supply curve is elastic and the demand curve inelastic, the increase in demand will lead to only a small increase in price and the primary beneficiaries of the subsidy will be consumers in the form of lower prices.

The greater share of the benefit of a subsidy will always be shifted toward the more inelastic side of the market. Thus, the more inelastic the supply, the larger the share of the benefit that will accrue to sellers. Conversely, the more inelastic the demand, the larger the share of the benefit that will accrue to buyers. Sometimes the subsidies will be granted to sellers rather than buyers. Nonetheless, the benefits will still flow primarily toward the more inelastic side of the market.

4-6b REAL-WORLD SUBSIDY PROGRAMS

The federal government now operates more than 2,000 separate subsidy programs, twice the number of the mid-1980s. Spending on these programs and the taxes that finance them are major items in the government budget. Some subsidy programs, such as Medicare and food stamps, provide payments to buyers. Others, such as the subsidies to the arts, public broadcasting, sports stadiums, and ethanol are directed toward suppliers. As we discussed, however, the party granted the subsidy may not be the one who captures the larger share of the actual benefit from the subsidy.

Let's take a closer look at the subsidies granted to college students. There has been a substantial increase in federal and state subsidies to college students since 1990. Measured in constant 2011 dollars, federal and state grants directly to college students rose from $2,933 per full-time equivalent student in 1990–1991 to $6,994 in 2011–2012, an increase of 138 percent over the two decades. Federal loans to college students increased even more rapidly. Adjusted for inflation, federal loans per full-time student more than tripled, soaring from $2,169 in 1990–1991 to $6,558 in 2011–2012.

As Exhibit 10 illustrated, subsidies in the form of grants and loans to students will increase the demand for college education and thereby push up its price. Indeed, this has been the case. Measured in constant 2011–2012 dollars, the average price of a year of college approximately doubled, increasing from $5,088 in 1989–1990 to $10,111 in 2011–2012. In 1989–1990, the price of a year of college was 9.8 percent of the median household income in the United States, but by 2011–2012, the figure had risen to 20.2 percent.[9]

Most students perceive that government aid in the form of grants and low-interest loans make it more economical for them to attend college. But there is another side to this issue: The subsidies are a driving force underlying the soaring cost of a college education, and rising student loan debt. Moreover, colleges themselves are major beneficiaries of the student subsidies. Thus, it is not surprising that college administrators are at the forefront of those lobbying for additional subsidies.

Subsidies for medical care have had a similar impact. The Medicare and Medicaid programs were introduced in the mid-1960s. Since the large subsidies accompanying these programs were initiated, prices of medical services have persistently increased at twice the rate of the general level of prices. Again, this suggests that the suppliers of these services derived a substantial share of the benefits in the form of higher prices for their services. Given that the supply of most medical services is highly inelastic, this is precisely what one would expect from an increase in the subsidies granted to buyers.

Both the educational and medical care subsidies are allocated to a subset of the population. For example, the Medicare program subsidizes the healthcare purchases of senior citizens, and the Medicaid program provides subsidies to low-income households. These subsidies increase the demand for health care and drive up the prices of medical service for all consumers, including those ineligible for either program. When only some of the buyers in a market are subsidized, groups that are ineligible for the subsidies will generally be harmed because they will have to pay higher prices than would be the case in the absence of the subsidies.

Ethanol, a bio-fuel alternative to gasoline made from corn, provides another example of a product that is heavily subsidized in the United States. Ethanol subsidies, which amount to approximately $1.75 per gallon, have a direct cost to taxpayers of approximately $6 billion per year. Ethanol is significantly more costly to produce than gasoline. In effect, the ethanol subsidies channel resources into production of a good that is valued less than its production cost. Ethanol's environmental benefits over gasoline are highly questionable. Why does the government subsidize ethanol? The ethanol subsidies increase the demand for corn, driving up its price. Corn farmers derive major benefits from the program, while the cost is spread thinly across taxpayers (who fund the subsidies) and consumers (who pay higher prices for the many products made from corn—from tortillas to soft drinks).

Like ethanol, many subsidy programs are driven by political considerations, the desire of politicians to favor various groups, particularly those that are well organized, in exchange for their votes and other forms of political support. Moreover, the subsidies often generate harmful secondary effects. Subsidized firms are encouraged to spend more time lobbying politicians and less time pleasing customers. They are also encouraged to undertake wasteful projects that fail to generate revenue sufficient to cover costs. In spite of the favoritism, subsidized enterprises often fail, leaving the taxpayer on the hook. Examples abound. Fisker Automotive, Solyndra, A123 Systems, Abound Solar, and SoloPower all received hundreds of millions in government grants and loans before failing and passing the bill for their failures on to taxpayers. As we proceed, we will consider the nature of favoritism and its relationship to the political process in more detail.

---

[9]The figures presented here are from Sandy Baum, et al., "Trends in Student Aid 2012," The College Board, Washington D.C., 2012, Table 3, and the U.S. Department of Education, National Center for Education Statistics, *Digest of Education Statistics*, Table 349. For additional details on the impact of subsidies to students on the cost of college, see Robert E. Martin and Andrew Gillen, "How College Pricing Undermines Financial Aid," The Center for College Affordability and Productivity, Washington, DC, March 2011.

LOOKING AHEAD

This chapter focused on how government-mandated price controls, taxes, subsidies, and prohibitions affect market outcomes. The next two chapters will apply the basic tools of economics to the political process more generally. In the chapters that follow, we will analyze how the political process works and explain why it sometimes works poorly.

KEY POINTS

- Resource markets and product markets are closely linked. A change in one will generally result in changes in the other.

- Legally imposed price ceilings result in shortages, and legally imposed price floors will cause surpluses. Both also cause other harmful secondary effects. Rent controls, for example, will lead to shortages, less investment, poor maintenance, and deterioration in the quality of rental housing.

- The minimum wage is a price floor for low-skilled labor. It increases the earnings of some low-skilled workers but also reduces employment and leads to fewer training opportunities and nonwage job benefits for many low-skilled workers.

- Because black markets operate outside the legal system, they are often characterized by deception, fraud, and the use of violence as a means of enforcing contracts. A legal system that provides secure private-property rights and unbiased enforcement of contracts enhances the operation of markets.

- The division of the actual tax burden between buyers and sellers is determined by the relative elasticities of demand and supply rather than on whom the tax is legally imposed.

- In addition to the cost of the tax revenue transferred to the government, taxes will reduce the level of the activity taxed, eliminate some gains from trade, and thereby impose an excess burden, or deadweight loss.

- As tax rates increase, the size of the tax base will shrink. Initially, rates and revenues will be directly related—revenues will expand as rates increase. However, as higher and higher rates are imposed, eventually an inverse relationship will develop—revenues will decline as rates are increased further. The Laffer curve illustrates this pattern.

- The division of the benefit from a subsidy is determined by the relative elasticities of demand and supply rather than to whom the subsidy is actually paid. For example, when the buyers of a good are subsidized, the subsidy will increase demand and lead to higher prices. If the supply is more elastic than the demand, the providers of the services will derive most of the benefits even though the subsidy was granted to the purchasers.

CRITICAL ANALYSIS QUESTIONS

1. *How will a substantial increase in demand for housing affect the wages and employment of carpenters, plumbers, and electricians?

2. Suppose that college students in your town persuaded the town council to enact a law setting the maximum price for rental housing at $400 per month. Will this help or hurt college students who rent housing? In your answer, address how this price ceiling will affect (a) the quality of rental housing; (b) the amount of rental housing available; (c) the incentive of landlords to maintain their properties; (d) the amount of racial, gender, and other types of discrimination in the local rental housing market; (e) the ease with which students will be able to find housing; and, finally, (f) whether a black market for housing would develop.

3. What is the difference between a price ceiling and a price floor? If a price ceiling for a good is set below the market equilibrium, what will happen to the quality and future availability of the good? Explain.

4. *To be meaningful, a price ceiling must be below the market price. Conversely, a meaningful price floor must be above the market price. What impact will a meaningful price ceiling have on the quantity exchanged? What impact will a meaningful price floor have on the quantity exchanged? Explain.

5. The tax on cigarettes in New York City is the highest in the nation—$5.85 per pack. Does this tax raise a lot of revenue for New York City? Why or why not? What are some of the secondary effects of this tax?

6. Analyze the impact of an increase in the minimum wage from the current level to $15 per hour. How would the following be affected?

    a. employment of people previously earning less than $15 per hour

    b. the unemployment rate of teenagers

    c. the availability of on-the-job training for low-skilled workers

    d. the demand for high-skilled workers who are good substitutes for low-skilled workers

7. What is a black market? What are some of the main differences in how black markets operate relative to legal markets?

8. How do you think the markets for organ donation and child adoption would be affected if they were made fully legal with a well-functioning price mechanism? What would be the advantages and disadvantages relative to the current system?

9. What is meant by the incidence of a tax? Explain why the statutory and actual incidence of a tax often differ.

10. What impact do government grants and loans to college students have on the cost of going to college? Are students the primary beneficiary of these subsidies? Discuss.

11. What is the nature of the deadweight loss accompanying taxes? Why is it often referred to as an "excess burden"?

12. *Suppose Congress were to pass legislation requiring that businesses employing workers with three or more children pay these employees at least $15 per hour. How would this legislation affect the employment level of low-skilled workers with three or more children? Do you think some workers with large families might attempt to conceal the fact? Why?

13. "We should impose a 20 percent luxury tax on expensive automobiles (those with a sales price of $50,000 or more) in order to collect more tax revenue from the wealthy." Will the burden of the proposed tax fall primarily on the wealthy? Why or why not?

14. *Should policy makers seek to set the tax on an economic activity at a rate that will maximize the revenue derived from the tax? Why or why not? Explain.

*Asterisk denotes questions for which answers are given in Appendix B.

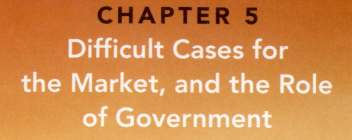

CHAPTER 5
Difficult Cases for the Market, and the Role of Government

FOCUS

- What is economic efficiency and how can it be used to evaluate markets?
- Why is it generally undesirable to pursue any goal to perfection?
- What is the role of government in a market economy?
- What are externalities? What are public goods?
- Why might markets fail to allocate goods and services efficiently?
- If the market has shortcomings, does this mean that government intervention will improve things?

The principal justification for public policy intervention lies in the frequent and numerous shortcomings of market outcomes.
—**Charles Wolf, Jr.**[1]

[1]Charles Wolf, Jr., *Markets or Government* (Cambridge, MA: MIT Press, 1988), 17.

As we previously discussed, market allocation and political decision-making are the two main alternatives for the organization of economic activity. Chapters 3 and 4 introduced you to how markets work and analyzed the impact of government intervention in the form of price controls, taxes, and subsidies. We noted that when property rights are well defined, and competition present, markets will tend to direct self-interested individuals into activities that promote the general welfare. But this will not always be the case. In this chapter, we turn our attention to potential problem areas when a conflict arises between personal self-interest and getting the most out of the available resources. We will also consider the implications of these problem areas with regard to the role of government. In the following chapter, we will analyze how the political process works and will compare it more directly with markets.

5-1 A CLOSER LOOK AT ECONOMIC EFFICIENCY

Economists use the standard of **economic efficiency** to assess the desirability of economic outcomes. We briefly introduced the concept in Chapter 3. We now want to explore it in more detail. The central idea of economic efficiency is straightforward. For any given level of cost, we want to obtain the largest possible benefit. Alternatively, we want to obtain any particular benefit for the least possible cost. Economic efficiency means getting the most value from the available resources—making the largest pie from the available set of ingredients, so to speak.

Economists acknowledge that individuals generally do not regard the efficiency of the entire economy as a primary goal for themselves. Rather, each person is interested in enlarging the size of his or her own slice. But if resources are used more efficiently, the overall size of the pie will be larger, and therefore, at least potentially, *everyone* could have a larger slice. For an outcome to be consistent with ideal economic efficiency, two conditions are necessary:

Rule 1. *Undertaking an economic action is efficient if it produces more benefits than costs.* To satisfy economic efficiency, all actions generating more benefits than costs must be undertaken. Failure to undertake all such actions implies that a potential gain has been forgone.

Rule 2. *Undertaking an economic action is inefficient if it produces more costs than benefits.* To satisfy economic efficiency, no action that generates more costs than benefits should be undertaken. When such counterproductive actions are taken, society is worse off because even better alternatives were forgone.

Economic efficiency results only when both of these conditions have been met. *Either failure to undertake an efficient action (Rule 1) or the undertaking of an inefficient action (Rule 2) will result in economic inefficiency.* To illustrate, consider **Exhibit 1**, which shows the benefits and costs associated with expanding the amount of any particular activity. We have avoided using a specific example here to ensure you understand the general idea of efficiency without linking it to a specific application. As we will show, the concept has wide-ranging applications, from the evaluation of government policy to how long you choose to brush your teeth in the morning.[2]

Economic efficiency
A situation that occurs when (1) all activities generating more benefit than cost are undertaken and (2) no activities are undertaken for which the cost exceeds the benefit.

---

[2]Note to students who may pursue advanced study in economics: Using the concept of efficiency to compare alternative policies typically requires that the analyst estimate costs and benefits that are difficult or impossible to measure. Costs and benefits are the values of opportunities forgone or accepted by individuals, *as evaluated by those individuals*. Then, these costs and benefits must be added up across all individuals and compared. But does a dollar's gain for one individual really compensate for a dollar's sacrifice by another? Some economists simply reject the validity of making such comparisons. They say that neither the estimates by the economic analyst of subjectively determined costs and benefits nor the adding up of these costs and benefits across individuals is meaningful. Their case may be valid, but most economists today nevertheless use the concept of efficiency as we present it. No other way to use economic analysis to compare policy alternatives has been found.

©iStockphoto.com/nicoolay

EXHIBIT 1

Economic Efficiency

As we use more time and resources to expand the level of an activity, the marginal benefits will generally decline and the marginal costs rise. From the viewpoint of efficiency, the activity should be expanded as long as the marginal benefits exceed the marginal costs. Therefore, quantity Q_2 is the economically efficient level of this activity. Q_1 is inefficient because some production that could generate more benefits than costs is not undertaken. Q_3 is also inefficient because some units are produced even though their costs exceed the benefits they create. Thus, either too much or too little of an activity will result in inefficiency.

© Cengage Learning 2013

In Exhibit 1, the marginal benefit curve shows the additional benefit associated with expanding the activity. The marginal cost curve shows the cost—including any opportunity costs—of spending additional time, effort, and resources on the activity. At Q_1, the height of the marginal benefit curve exceeds the height of the marginal cost curve. Thus, at that point, the additional benefits of expanding the activity past Q_1 exceed the additional costs. According to Rule 1 of economic efficiency, we should continue to expand the activity until we reach Q_2. Beyond Q_2 (at Q_3, for example), the height of the marginal benefit curve is less than the height of the marginal cost curve. The additional benefits of expanding the activity beyond Q_2 to Q_3 are smaller than the additional costs. According to Rule 2, at Q_3, we have gone too far and should cut back on the activity. Q_2 is the only point consistent with both rules of economic efficiency.

5-2 IF IT'S WORTH DOING, IT'S WORTH DOING IMPERFECTLY

Eliminating pollution. Earning straight As. Being completely organized. Cleaning your apartment until it sparkles. Making automobiles completely safe. Making airplanes fully secure against terrorist attacks. All of these are worthwhile goals, right? Well, they are until you consider the costs of actually achieving them. The heading for this section is, of course, a play on the old saying "If it's worth doing, it's worth doing to the best of your ability." Economics suggests, however, that this is not a sensible guideline. At some point, the gains from doing something even better will not be worth the cost. It will make more sense to stop short of perfection.

Exhibit 1 can also be used to illustrate this point. As more resources are dedicated to an activity, the marginal improvements (benefits) will become smaller and smaller, while the marginal costs will rise. The optimal time and effort put into the activity will be achieved at Q_2, and this will nearly always be well below one's best effort. Note that inefficiency results when either too little (for example, Q_1) or too much (for example, Q_3) time and effort are put into the activity.

Do you make decisions this way? Last time you cleaned your car or apartment, why did you decide to leave some things undone? Once the most important areas were clean, you likely began to skip over other areas (like on top of the refrigerator or under the bed), figuring that the benefits of cleaning these areas were simply not worth the cost. Very few people live in a perfectly organized and clean house, wash their hands enough to prevent all colds, brush their teeth long enough to prevent all cavities, or make their home as safe as Fort Knox. They recognize that the benefit of perfection in these, and many other areas, is simply not worth the cost.

Economics is about trade-offs; it is possible to pursue even worthy activities beyond the level that is consistent with economic efficiency. People seem to be more aware of this in their personal decision-making than when evaluating public policy. It is not uncommon to hear people say things like "We ought to eliminate all pollution" or "No price is too high to save a life."

If we want to get the most out of our resources, we need to think about both marginal benefits and marginal costs and recognize that there are alternative ways of pursuing objectives. Consequently, economists do not ask whether eliminating pollution or saving lives is worth the cost *in terms of dollars* per se, but whether it is worth the cost in terms of giving up other things that could have been done with those dollars—the opportunity cost. Spending an extra $10 billion on school safety requirements to save 50 lives isn't efficient if the funds could have been spent differently and saved the lives of 500 children. It is no more efficient for the government to pursue perfection than for individuals to do so. Regardless of sector, achievement of perfection is virtually never worth the cost.

Universal/Jersey Films/The Kobal Collection/Bennett, Tracy/Art Resources

In the movie, *"Along Came Polly"* (2004), Ben Stiller and Jennifer Aniston struggle to find the efficient (optimal) amount of organization in their lives. Aniston believes the eight minutes a day Stiller spends arranging decorative pillows on his bed (that nobody else sees) isn't worth the effort—he's over-organized. Meanwhile, Aniston can't find her car keys because of her inefficiently low level of organization. At the margin, Stiller would be better off organizing less, and Aniston would be better off organizing more.

5-3 THINKING ABOUT THE ECONOMIC ROLE OF GOVERNMENT

For centuries, philosophers, economists, and other scholars have debated the proper role of government. While the debate continues, there is substantial agreement that at least two functions of government are legitimate: (1) protecting individuals and their property against invasions by others and (2) providing goods that cannot easily be provided through private markets. These two functions correspond to what Nobel laureate James M. Buchanan conceptualizes as the protective and productive functions of government.

5-3a PROTECTIVE FUNCTION OF GOVERNMENT

The most fundamental function of government is the protection of individuals and their property against acts of aggression. As John Locke wrote more than three centuries ago, individuals are constantly threatened by "the invasions of others." Therefore, each individual "is willing to join in society with others, who are already united, or have a mind to unite, for the mutual preservation of their lives, liberties, and estates."[3] *The protective function of government involves the maintenance of a framework of security and order—an infrastructure of rules within which people can interact peacefully with one another.* Protection of person and property is crucial. It entails providing police protection and prosecuting aggressors who take things that do not belong to them. It also involves providing for a national defense designed to protect against foreign invasions. The legal

---

[3]John Locke, *Treatise of Civil Government*, 1690, ed. Charles Sherman (New York: Appleton-Century-Crofts, 1937), 82.

©Bettmann/Corbis

The English philosopher John Locke argued that people own themselves and, as a result of this self-ownership, they also own the fruits of their labor. Locke stressed that individuals are not subservient to governments. On the contrary, the role of governments is to protect the "natural rights" of individuals to their person and property. This view, also reflected in the "unalienable rights" section of the U.S. Declaration of Independence, is the basis for the protective function of government.

enforcement of contracts and rules against fraud are also central elements of the protective function. People and businesses that write bad checks, violate contracts, or knowingly supply others with false information, for example, are therefore subject to legal prosecution.

It is easy to see the economic importance of the protective function. When it is performed well, the property of citizens is secure, freedom of exchange is present, and contracts are legally enforceable. When people are assured that they will be able to enjoy the benefits of their efforts, they will be more productive. In contrast, when property rights are insecure and contracts unenforceable, productive behavior is undermined. Plunder, fraud, and economic chaos result. Governments set and enforce the "rules of the game" that enable markets to operate smoothly.

5-3b PRODUCTIVE FUNCTION OF GOVERNMENT

The nature of some goods makes them difficult to provide through markets. Sometimes it is difficult to establish a one-to-one link between the payment and receipt of a good. If this link cannot be established, the incentive of market producers to supply these goods is weak. In addition, high transaction costs—particularly, the cost of monitoring use and collecting fees—can sometimes make it difficult to supply a good through the market. When either of these conditions is present, it may be more efficient for the government to supply the good and impose taxes on its citizens to cover the cost.

One of the most important productive functions of government is providing a stable monetary and financial environment. If markets are going to work well, individuals have to know the value of what they are buying or selling. For market prices to convey this information, a stable monetary system is needed. This is especially true for the many market exchanges that involve a time dimension. Houses, cars, consumer durables, land, buildings, equipment, and many other items are often paid for over a period of months or even years. When the purchasing power of money fluctuates wildly, previously determined prices do not represent their intended values. Under these circumstances, exchanges involving long-term commitments are hampered, and the smooth operation of markets is undermined.

The government's tax, spending, and monetary policies exert a powerful influence on the stability of the overall economy. If properly conducted, these policies contribute to economic stability, full and efficient utilization of resources, and stable prices. However, improper stabilization policies can cause massive unemployment, rapidly rising prices, or both. For those pursuing a course in macroeconomics, these issues will be central to that analysis.

5-4 POTENTIAL SHORTCOMINGS OF THE MARKET

As we previously discussed, the invisible hand of market forces generally gives resource owners and business firms a strong incentive to use their resources efficiently and undertake projects that create value. Will this always be true? The answer to this question is "No." There are four major factors that can undermine the invisible hand and reduce the efficiency of markets: (1) lack of competition, (2) externalities, (3) public goods, and (4) poorly informed buyers or sellers. We will now consider each of these factors and explain why they may justify government intervention.

5-4a LACK OF COMPETITION

Competition is vital to the proper operation of the pricing mechanism. The existence of competing buyers and sellers reduces the power of both to rig or alter the market in their own favor. Although competition is beneficial from a social point of view, individually each of us would prefer to be loosened from its grip. Students do not like stiff competitors in their

© Cengage Learning 2013

EXHIBIT 2

Lack of Competition and Problems for the Market

If a group of sellers can restrict competition, the group may be able to gain by reducing supply (to S_2, for example) and raising the price (to P_2, for example) rather than charging the competitive market price of P_1. Under these circumstances, output will be less than the economically efficient level.

romantic lives, at exam time, or when they're trying to get into graduate school. Buyers on eBay hope for few competing bidders so they can purchase the items they're bidding on at lower prices. Similarly, sellers prefer fewer competing sellers so they can sell at higher prices.

Exhibit 2 illustrates how sellers can gain from restricting competition. In the absence of any restrictions on competition in the market, the price P_1 and output Q_1 associated with the competitive supply curve (S_1) will prevail. Here, Q_1 is the level of output consistent with economic efficiency. If a group of sellers is able to restrict competition, perhaps by forcing some firms out of the market and preventing new firms from entering, the group would be able to gain by raising the price of the product. This is illustrated by the price P_2 and output Q_2 associated with the restricted supply (S_2). Even though the output is smaller, the total revenue (price P_2 times quantity Q_2) derived by the sellers at the restricted output level is greater than at the competitive price P_1. Clearly, the sellers gain because, at the higher price, they are being paid more to produce less.

The restricted output level, however, is clearly less efficient. At the competitive output level Q_1, all units that were valued more than their cost are produced and sold. But this is not the case at Q_2. The additional units between Q_2 and Q_1 are valued more than their cost. Nonetheless, they will not be produced if suppliers are able to limit competition and restrict output. When competition is absent, there is a potential conflict between the interests of sellers and the efficient use of resources.

What can the government do to ensure that markets are competitive? The first guideline might be borrowed from the medical profession: Do no harm. A productive government will refrain from using its powers to impose licenses, discriminatory taxes, price controls, tariffs, quotas, and other entry and trade restraints that lessen the intensity of competition. In the vast majority of markets, sellers will find it difficult or impossible to limit the entry of rival firms (including rival producers from other countries). Thus, most suppliers will not be able to limit competition unless they get the government to impose various types of entry restrictions or mandates that provide them with an advantage relative to rivals. Predictably, private firms and interest groups will lobby for government action of this type. When governments succumb to these pressures and engage in actions that limit competition, however, economic inefficiency will result.

When entering a market is very costly and there are only a few existing sellers, it may be possible for these sellers by themselves to restrict competition. In an effort to deal with cases like this, the United States has enacted a series of "antitrust laws," most notably the Sherman Antitrust Act (1890) and the Clayton Act (1914), making it illegal for firms to collude or attempt to monopolize a market.

Virtually all economists favor competitive markets, but there is considerable debate about the impact of government action in this area. Many economists believe that, by and large, government policy in this area has been ineffective. Others stress that government policies have often been misused to actually limit competition, rather than promote it. Laws are often adopted that restrict entry into markets, protect existing producers from competitors, and limit price competition. For those taking a microeconomics course, noncompetitive markets and related policy alternatives will be analyzed in greater detail later.

5-4b EXTERNALITIES—A FAILURE TO ACCOUNT FOR ALL COSTS AND BENEFITS

Externalities
Spillover effects of an activity that influence the well-being of nonconsenting third parties.

When property rights are unclear or poorly enforced, the actions of an individual or group may "spill over" onto others and thereby affect their well-being without their consent. These spillover effects are called **externalities**. You are probably familiar with externalities. For example, when your neighbor's loud stereo makes it hard for you to study, you are experiencing an externality firsthand. Although your neighbors do not have a right to come in to your apartment and turn on your stereo, they do have a right to listen to their own stereo, and their listening may interfere with the quietness in your apartment. Their actions impose a cost on you, and they also raise an issue of property rights. Do your neighbors have a property right to play their stereo as loudly as they please? Or do you have a property right to quietness in your own apartment? When questions like these arise, how should the boundaries of property rights be determined, and what steps should be taken to ensure adequate enforcement? Although the volume of your neighbor's stereo may not be a major economic issue, it nonetheless illustrates the nature of the problems that arise when property rights are unclear and externalities are present.

External cost
Spillover effects that reduce the well-being of nonconsenting third parties.

External benefit
Spillover effects that generate benefits for nonconsenting third parties.

The spillover effects may either impose a cost or create a benefit for third parties—people not directly involved in the transaction, activity, or exchange. Economists use the term **external cost** to describe a situation in which the spillover effects harm third parties. If the spillover effects enhance the welfare of the third parties, an **external benefit** is present. We will analyze both external costs and external benefits and consider why both of them can lead to problems.

5-4c EXTERNAL COSTS

Economists worry about external costs because they may result in economic inefficiency. For example, resources may be used to produce goods that are valued less than their production costs, including the costs imposed on the nonconsenting third parties. Consider the production of paper. The firms in the market operate mills and purchase labor, trees, and other resources to produce the paper. But they also emit pollutants into the atmosphere that impose costs on residents living around the mills. The pollutants cause paint on buildings to deteriorate more rapidly. They make it difficult for some people to breathe normally, and perhaps cause other health hazards. If the residents living near a pulp mill can prove they have been harmed, they could take the mill to court and force the paper producer to cover the cost of their damages. But it might be difficult to prove that they were harmed and that the pulp mill is responsible for the damage. As you can see, the residents' property rights to clean air may be difficult to enforce, particularly if there are many parties emitting pollutants into the air.

If the residents are unable to enforce their property rights, the production of paper will result in an external cost that will not be registered through markets. **Exhibit 3** illustrates the implications of these external costs within the supply and demand framework. As the result of the external cost, the market supply curve S_1 will understate the true cost of producing paper. It reflects only the cost actually paid by the firms, and ignores the uncompensated costs imposed on the nearby residents. Under these circumstances, the firm will expand output to Q_1 (the intersection of the demand curve D and supply curve S_1) and the market price P_1 will emerge. Is this price and output consistent with economic efficiency? The answer is clearly "No." If all of the costs of producing the paper, including

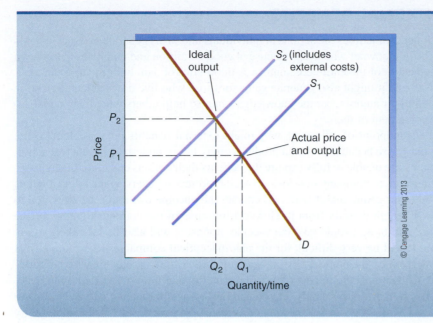

© Cengage Learning 2013

EXHIBIT 3

External Costs and Output That Is Greater Than the Efficient Level

When an activity such as paper production imposes external costs on nonconsenting third parties, these costs will not be registered by the market supply curve (S_1). As a result, output will be beyond the economically efficient level. The units between Q_2 and Q_1 will be produced, even though their cost exceeds the value they provide to consumers.

those imposed on third parties, were taken into account, the supply curve S_2 would result. From an efficiency standpoint, only the smaller quantity Q_2 should be produced. The units beyond Q_2 on out to Q_1 cost more than their value to consumers. People would be better off if the resources used to produce those units (beyond Q_2) were used to produce other things. Nonetheless, profit-maximizing firms will expand output into this range. Thus, when external costs are present, the market supply curve will understate production costs, and output will be expanded beyond the quantity consistent with economic efficiency. Moreover, resources for which property rights are poorly enforced will be overutilized and sometimes polluted. This is often the case with air and water when the property rights to these resources are poorly enforced.

What should be done about external costs? These costs arise because property rights are poorly defined or imperfectly enforced. Initially, therefore, it makes sense to think seriously about how property rights might be better defined and enforced. However, the nature of some goods will make the defining and enforcement of property rights extremely difficult. This will certainly be the case for resources like clean air and many fish species in the ocean. In cases that involve a relatively small number of people, the parties involved may be able to agree to rules and establish procedures that will minimize the external effects. For example, property owners around a small lake will generally be able to control access to the lake and prevent each other, as well as outsiders, from polluting or overfishing the lake.

However, in cases that involve large numbers of people, the transaction costs of arriving at an agreement will often be prohibitively high, so it is unrealistic to expect that private contracts among the parties will handle the situation satisfactorily. For example, this will be the case when a large number of automobiles and firms emit pollutants into the atmosphere. In these "large-number" cases, government regulations may be the best approach. At this point, we want you to see the nature of the problem when external costs are present. As we proceed, we will analyze a number of problems in this area in detail and will consider alternative approaches that might improve economic efficiency.

External costs resulting from poorly defined and enforced property rights underlie the problems of excessive air and water pollution.

5-4d EXTERNAL BENEFITS

As we mentioned, sometimes the actions of individuals and firms generate external benefits for others. The homeowner who keeps a house in good condition and maintains a neat lawn improves the beauty of the entire community. A flood-control dam built by upstream residents for their benefit might also generate gains for those who live downstream. Scientific theories benefit their authors, but the knowledge can also help others who did not contribute to the development of them.

From the standpoint of efficiency, why might external benefits be a problem? Here, inefficiency may arise because potential producers may fail to undertake productive activities because they are unable to fully capture the benefits their actions create for others. Suppose a pharmaceutical company develops a vaccine protecting users against a contagious virus or some other communal disease. Of course, the vaccine can easily be marketed to users who will benefit directly from it. However, because of the communal nature of the virus, as more and more people take the vaccine, nonusers will also be less likely to get the virus. But it will be very difficult for the pharmaceutical companies to capture any of the benefits derived by the nonusers. As a result, too little of the vaccine may be supplied.

Exhibit 4 illustrates the impact of external benefits like those generated by the vaccine within the framework of supply and demand. The market demand curve reflects the benefits derived by the users of the vaccine, while the supply curve reflects the opportunity cost of providing it. Market forces result in an equilibrium price of P_1 and output of Q_1. Is this outcome consistent with economic efficiency? Again, the answer is "No." The market demand curve D_1 will register only the benefits derived by the users. Those benefits that accrue to nonusers, who are now less likely to contract the flu, will not be taken into account by decision-makers. The producer of the vaccine makes it more likely that these people will not get sick, but it doesn't derive any benefit (sales revenue) from having done so. Thus, market demand D_1 understates the total benefits derived from the production and use of the vaccine. Demand D_2 provides a measure of these total benefits, including those that accrue to the nonusers. The units between Q_1 and Q_2 are valued more highly than what it costs to produce them. Nonetheless, they will not be supplied because the suppliers of the vaccine will be unable to capture the benefits that accrue to the nonusers. Thus, when external benefits are present, market forces may supply less than the amount consistent with economic efficiency.

EXHIBIT 4

External Benefits and Output That Is Less Than the Efficient Level

A vaccine that protects users against the flu will also help nonusers by making it less likely that they will catch it. But this benefit will not be registered by the market demand curve (D_1). In cases where external benefits like this are present, output will be less than the economically efficient level. Even though the units between Q_1 and Q_2 generate more benefits than costs, they will not be supplied because sellers are unable to capture the value of these external benefits.

© Cengage Learning 2013

While external benefits are a potential source of inefficiency, entrepreneurs have a strong incentive to figure out ways to capture more fully the gains their actions generate for others. In some cases, they are able to capture what would otherwise be external benefits by extending the scope of the firm. The accompanying Application in Economics, "Capturing External Benefits: The Case of Walt Disney World," provides an interesting and informative illustration of this point.

APPLICATIONS IN ECONOMICS

Capturing External Benefits: The Case of Walt Disney World

reuters/Charles W. Luzier/Landov

Sometimes projects that generate more benefits than cost are still unattractive because a substantial share of the benefits is external and therefore difficult to capture. If an entrepreneur could figure out a way to capture more of these benefits, an otherwise unprofitable project might be transformed into a profitable one. Sometimes this can be done by extending the scope of a project.

The development of golf courses is an example. Because of the beauty and openness of the courses, many people find it attractive to live nearby. Thus, constructing a golf course typically generates an external benefit—an increase in the value of the nearby property. In recent years, golf course developers have figured out how to capture this benefit. Now, they typically purchase a large tract of land around the planned course *before it is built*. This lets them resell the land at a higher price after the golf course has been completed and the sur-

rounding land has increased in value. By extending the scope of their activities to include real estate as well as golf course development, they are able to capture what would otherwise be external benefits.

Florida's Walt Disney World is an interesting case study in entrepreneurial ingenuity designed to capture external benefits more fully. When Walt Disney developed Disneyland in California, the market value of the land in the immediate area soared as a result of the increase in demand for services (food, lodging, gasoline, and so on). Because the land in the area was owned by others, the developers of Disneyland were unable to capture these external benefits. In addition, Disney felt as if some of the adult nightclubs that had opened around his existing Disneyland park were imposing external costs on him by detracting from the family image his park was trying to attain.

Because of his experience with these externalities, when Walt Disney World was developed outside of Orlando, Florida, in the mid-1960s, Walt Disney purchased far more land than was needed for the amusement park. This enabled him to capture the increased land value surrounding his development (when he resold the land for a higher price) and reduce the negative externalities imposed on him via his control of the surrounding property.

The purchases were made as secretly as possible to prevent speculators from driving up the land prices if Disney's actions were detected. Disney even created a handful of smaller companies, with names like the Latin-American Development and Managers Corporation and the Reedy Creek Ranch Corporation, to purchase the land. After his first major land purchase of 12,400 acres, Walt Disney was at a meeting at which he was offered an opportunity to purchase an additional 8,500 acres. Walt Disney's assistant was rumored to have said, "But Walt, we already own 12,000 acres, enough to build the park." Disney replied, "How would you like to own 8,000 acres around our existing Disneyland facility right now?" His assistant immediately responded, "Buy it!"

After another major acquisition of 1,250 acres, Disney began concentrating on buying smaller land parcels around his main property. By June 1965, Disney had purchased 27,400 acres, or about 43 square miles—an area 150 times larger than

(continued)

his existing Disneyland park, and about twice as big as Manhattan. In October 1965, when an Orlando newspaper finally broke the story that Disney was behind the land purchases, the remaining land prices around his property jumped from $183 an acre to $1,000 an acre overnight. But by then, except for several small parcels he was unable to acquire, Walt Disney had purchased all of the land he wanted.

Florida eventually gave Walt Disney permission to create an autonomous Reedy Creek Improvement District, outside the authority of any local government in Florida. In a very real sense, Walt Disney World is a jurisdiction of its own, separate from any other local government authority. Because of this, Walt Disney World can write its own zoning restrictions and building codes. It can also plan its own roadways, lakes, security, sidewalks, airports, and recreational areas. Walt Disney World is able to provide goods and services like these—that might normally be considered public goods—by charging general admission fees to its park. This helped Disney overcome the potential free-rider problems sometimes associated with producing these goods.

Just as Disney expected, the value of the land surrounding Walt Disney World soared as the demand for hotels, restaurants, and other businesses increased along with the development of the amusement park. Through the years, the resale of land near the park has been a major source of revenue for the company. To a large degree, the success of the Disney Corporation reflects Walt Disney's entrepreneurial ability to deal with externality and public-good problems.

5-4e PUBLIC GOODS AND WHY THEY POSE A PROBLEM FOR THE MARKET

Public goods

Goods for which rivalry among consumers is absent and exclusion of nonpaying customers is difficult.

What are public goods? **Public goods** have two distinguishing characteristics; they are (1) nonrival in consumption and (2) nonexcludable. Let's take a closer look at both of these characteristics.

Nonrivalry in consumption means that making the good available to one consumer does not reduce its availability to others. In fact, providing it to one person simultaneously makes it available to other consumers. A radio broadcast signal provides an example. The same signal can be shared by everyone within the listening range. Having additional listeners tune in does not detract from the availability of the signal. Clearly, most goods do not have this shared consumption characteristic, but are instead rival-in-consumption. For example, two individuals cannot simultaneously consume the same pair of jeans. Further, a pair of jeans purchased by one person does not make jeans more readily available to others.

The second characteristic of a public good—nonexcludability—means that it is impossible (or at least very costly) to exclude nonpaying customers from receiving the good. Suppose an antimissile system were being built around the city in which you live. How could some people in the city be protected by the system and others excluded? Most people will realize there is no way the system can protect their neighbors from incoming missiles without providing similar protection to other residents. Thus, the services of the antimissile system have the nonexcludability characteristic.

It is important to note that it is the characteristic of the good, not the sector in which it is produced, that determines whether it qualifies as a public good. There is a tendency to think that if a good is provided by the government, then it is a public good. This is not the case. Many of the goods provided by governments clearly do not have the characteristics of public goods. Medical services, education, mail delivery, trash collection, and electricity come to mind. Although these goods are often supplied by governments, they do not have either nonrivalry or nonexcludability characteristics. Thus, they are not public goods.

Free riders

A person who receives the benefit of a good without paying for it. Because it is often virtually impossible to restrict the consumption of public goods to those who pay, these goods are subject to free-rider problems.

Why are public goods difficult for markets to allocate efficiently? The nonexcludability characteristic provides the answer. Because those who do not pay cannot be excluded, sellers are generally unable to establish a one-to-one link between the payment and receipt of these goods. Realizing they cannot be excluded, potential consumers have little incentive to pay for these goods. Instead, they have an incentive to become **free riders**, people who receive the benefits of the good without helping to pay for its cost. But, when a large number of people become free riders and revenues thus are low, not very much of the good is supplied. This is precisely the problem: Markets will tend to undersupply public goods, even when the population in aggregate values them highly relative to their cost.

Suppose national defense were provided entirely through the market. Would you voluntarily help to pay for it? Your contribution would have little impact on the total supply of defense available to each of us, even if you made a large personal contribution. Many citizens, even though they might value defense highly, would become free riders, and few funds would be available to finance national defense.

For most goods, it is easy to establish a link between payment and receipt. If you do not pay for a gallon of ice cream, an automobile, a television set, a DVD player, and literally thousands of other items, suppliers will not provide them to you. Thus, there are very few public goods. National defense is the classic example of a public good. Radio and TV signals, software programs, flood-control projects, mosquito abatement programs, and perhaps some scientific theories also have public good characteristics. But beyond this short list, it is difficult to think of additional goods that qualify.

Just because a good is a public good does not necessarily mean that markets will fail to supply it. When the benefit of producing these goods is high, entrepreneurs will attempt to find innovative ways to gain by overcoming the free-rider problem. For example, radio and television broadcasts, which have both of the public good characteristics, are still produced well by the private sector. The free-rider problem is overcome through the use of advertising (which generates indirect revenue from listeners), rather than by directly charging listeners. Private entrepreneurs have developed things like scrambling devices (so nonpaying customers can't tune into broadcasts free of charge), copy protection on DVDs, and tie-in purchases (for example, tying the purchase of a software instruction manual to the purchase of the software itself) to overcome the free-rider problem. The marketing of computer software provides an interesting illustration. Because the same software program can be copied without reducing the amount available to others, and it is costly to prevent consumption by nonpayers, software clearly has public good characteristics. Nonetheless, Bill Gates became the richest man in the world by producing and marketing it!

In spite of the innovative efforts of entrepreneurs, however, the quantity of public goods supplied strictly through market allocation might still be smaller than the quantity consistent with economic efficiency. This creates a potential opportunity for government action to improve the efficiency of resource allocation.

5-4f POTENTIAL INFORMATION PROBLEMS

Like other goods, information is scarce. Thus, when making purchasing decisions, people are sometimes poorly informed about the price, quality, durability, and side effects of alternative products. Imperfect knowledge is not the fault of the market. In fact, the market provides consumers with a strong incentive to acquire information. If they mistakenly purchase a "lemon," they will suffer the consequences. Furthermore, sellers have a strong incentive to inform consumers about the benefits of their products, especially in comparison with competing products. However, circumstances will influence the incentive structure confronted by both buyers and sellers.

The consumer's information problem is minimal if the item is purchased regularly. Consider the purchase of soap. There is little cost associated with trying different brands. Because soap is a regularly purchased product, trial and error is an economical means of determining which brand is most suitable to one's needs. Regularly purchased items such as toothpaste, most food products, lawn service, and gasoline provide additional examples of **repeat-purchase items**. When purchasing items like these, the consumer can use past experience to acquire accurate information and make wise decisions.

Repeat-purchase items
An item purchased often by the same buyer.

Furthermore, the sellers of repeat-purchase items also have a strong incentive to supply consumers with accurate information about them because failing to do so will adversely affect future sales. Because future demand is directly related to the satisfaction level of current customers, sellers of repeat-purchase items will want to help their customers make satisfying long-run choices. This helps harmonize the interests of buyers and sellers.

But harmony will not always occur. Conflicting interests, inadequate information, and unhappy customers can arise when goods are either (1) difficult to evaluate on inspection and seldom repeatedly purchased from the same producer, or (2) potentially capable of serious and lasting harmful side effects that cannot be predicted by a typical consumer. Under these conditions, consumers might make decisions they will later regret.

When customers are unable to distinguish between high-quality and low-quality goods, business entrepreneurs have an incentive to cut costs by reducing quality. Businesses that follow this course may survive and even prosper. Consider the information problem when an automobile is purchased. Are consumers capable of properly evaluating the safety equipment? Most are not. Of course, some consumers will seek the opinion of experts, but this information will be costly and difficult to evaluate. In this case, it might be more efficient to have the government regulate automobile safety and require certain safety equipment.

Similar issues arise with regard to product effectiveness. Suppose a new wonder drug promises to reduce the probability a person will be stricken by cancer or heart disease. Even if the product is totally ineffective, many consumers will waste their money trying it. Verifying the effectiveness of the drug will be a complicated and lengthy process. Consequently, it may be better to have experts certify its effectiveness. The federal Food and Drug Administration was established to perform this function. However, letting the experts decide is also a less than ideal solution. The certification process is likely to be costly and lengthy. As a result, the introduction of products that are effective may be delayed for years, and they are likely to be more costly than they would be otherwise.

5-4g INFORMATION AS A PROFIT OPPORTUNITY

Consumers are willing to pay for information that will help them make better decisions. This presents a profit opportunity. Entrepreneurial publishers and other providers of information help consumers find what they seek by offering product evaluations by experts. For example, dozens of publications provide independent expert opinions about automobiles and computers at a low cost to potential purchasers. Laboratory test results and detailed product evaluations on a wide variety of goods are provided by *Consumer Reports* and other publications.

Franchise
A right or license granted to an individual to market a company's goods or services or use its brand name. The individual firms are independently owned but must meet certain conditions to continue to use the name.

Franchises are another way entrepreneurs have responded to the need of consumers for more and better information. A **franchise** is a right or license granted to an individual to market a company's goods or services (or use their brand name). Fast-food restaurants like McDonald's and Wendy's are typically organized as franchises. The individual restaurants are independently owned, but the owner pays for the right to use the company name and must offer specific products and services in a manner specified by the franchiser. Franchises help give consumers reliable information. The tourist traveling through an area for the first time with very little time to search out alternatives may find that eating at a franchised restaurant and sleeping at a franchised motel are the cheapest ways to avoid annoying and costly mistakes that might come from patronizing an unknown local establishment. The franchiser sets the standards for all firms in the chain and establishes procedures, including continuous inspections designed to maintain the standards. Franchisers have a strong incentive to maintain their reputation for quality, because if it declines, their ability to sell new franchises and to collect ongoing franchise fees is adversely affected. Even though the tourist may visit a particular establishment only once, the franchise turns that visit into a "repeat purchase" because the reputation of the entire national franchise operation is at stake.

Similarly, advertising a brand name nationally puts the brand's reputation at stake each time a purchase is made. How much would the Coca-Cola Company pay to avoid the sale of a dangerous bottle of Coke? Surely, it would be a large sum. Interbrand, a branding consulting agency that evaluates and ranks the top brand names in the world, estimated that Coca-Cola's brand name was worth $70 billion in 2010. The value of that brand name is a hostage to quality control. The firm would suffer enormous damage if it failed to maintain the quality of its product. For example, in 2000 and 2001, Firestone's brand name suffered an immense reduction in value after only a few Firestone tires were suspected of being defective. Firestone is still attempting to recover fully from its loss in brand name value.

Brand names (like Coca-Cola), franchises (like McDonald's or Best Western), consumer-ratings magazines (like Consumer Reports), and private-sector certification firms (like Underwriters Laboratories, Inc.) are ways the private sector helps buyers overcome potential information problems.

Enterprising entrepreneurs have found ways to assure buyers that products meet high standards of quality, even when the producer is small and not so well known. Consider the case of Best Western Motels.[4] Best Western owns no motels; however, building on the franchise idea, it publishes rules and standards with which motel owners must comply if they are to use the Best Western brand name and the reservation service that the company also operates. To protect its brand name, Best Western sends out inspectors to see that each Best Western Motel meets these standards. Every disappointed customer harms the reputation and reduces the value of the Best Western name, which reduces the willingness of motel owners to pay for use of the name. The standards are designed to keep customers satisfied. Even though each motel owner has only a relatively small operation, renting the Best Western name provides the small operator with the kind of international reputation formerly available only to large firms. In effect, Best Western acts as a regulator of all motels bearing its name. It profits by requiring efficient standards—those that produce maximum visitor satisfaction for every dollar spent by the motels utilizing the franchise name. As it does so, it helps eliminate problems in the market that result from imperfect information.

Underwriters Laboratories Inc. (UL) is another example of private-sector regulation aimed at overcoming potential information problems. UL is a private-sector corporation that has been testing and certifying products for more than 100 years based on its own set of quality standards. You have probably seen the UL mark on many of your household appliances. Sellers pay a fee to have UL evaluate their products for possible certification. The value of the UL brand depends on its careful evaluation of every product it certifies. If UL allows defective products to carry its mark, its brand value will diminish.

Information published by reliable sources, franchising, and brand names can help consumers make better-informed decisions. Although these options are effective, they will not always provide an ideal solution. Government regulation may sometimes be able to improve the situation, but this, too, has some predictable shortcomings. As with other things, there is no general solution to imperfect information problems.

5-5 MARKET AND GOVERNMENT FAILURE

Throughout this textbook, we stress that a sound legal system—one that protects individuals and their property and provides access to evenhanded courts for the enforcement of contracts and settlement of disputes—is vitally important for the smooth operation of markets. So, too, is a monetary regime that provides people with access to a sound currency—money that maintains its value through time. Beyond these functions, however, there is little justification for government action when there is reason to expect that markets will allocate resources efficiently.

However, as we have shown in this chapter, a lack of competition, externalities, public goods, and information problems often pose challenges and sometimes undermine the efficient operation of markets. Economists use the term **market failure** to describe the situation where there is reason to believe that markets will fail to achieve the conditions implied by idealized economic efficiency. Private entrepreneurs can profit, however, from solving these problems so markets can sometimes overcome these potential challenges on their own.

It is tempting to jump to the conclusion that if the market fails to achieve economic efficiency, then the government can intervene and improve the situation. Indeed, even professional economists often make this error. But we must not forget that government directed by political decision-making is merely an alternative form of economic organization. It is not a corrective device that can be counted on to make choices that will promote economic efficiency. There is government failure, as well as market failure. **Government failure** is present when political choices lead to outcomes that conflict with the

Market failure
A situation in which the structure of incentives is such that markets will encourage individuals to undertake activities that are inconsistent with economic efficiency.

Government failure
A situation in which the structure of incentives is such that the political process, including democratic political decision-making, will encourage individuals to undertake actions that conflict with economic efficiency.

---

[4]This section draws from Randall G. Holcombe and Lora P. Holcombe, "The Market for Regulation," *Journal of Institutional and Theoretical Economics* 142, no. 4 (1986): 684–96.

efficient allocation of resources. In order to evaluate the potential of political decision-making to improve on the shortcomings of the market and allocate resources efficiently, we need better knowledge about how the political process works. This will be the focal point of the next chapter.

LOOKING AHEAD
Political decision-making is complex, but the tools of economics can enhance our understanding of how it works. This is the subject matter of the next chapter.

KEY POINTS

- Economists use the standard of economic efficiency to assess the desirability of economic outcomes. Efficiency requires (1) that all actions generating more benefit than cost be undertaken and (2) that no actions generating more cost than benefit be undertaken.

- Although perfection is a noble goal, it is rarely worth achieving because additional time and resources devoted to an activity generally yield smaller and smaller benefits and cost more and more. Inefficiency can result when either too little or too much effort is put into an activity.

- Governments can enhance economic well-being by performing both protective and productive functions. The protective function involves (1) the protection of individuals and their property against aggression and (2) the provision of a legal system for the enforcement of contracts and settlement of disputes. The productive function of government can help people obtain goods that would be difficult to supply through markets.

- When markets fail to meet the conditions for ideal economic efficiency, the problem can generally be traced to one of four sources: absence of competition, externalities, public goods, or poor information.

- Externalities reflect a lack of fully defined and enforced property rights. When external costs are present, output can be too large—units are produced even though their costs exceed the benefits they generate. In contrast, external benefits can lead to an output that is too small—some units are not produced even though the benefits of doing so would exceed the cost.

- Public goods are goods for which (1) rivalry in consumption is absent and (2) it is difficult to exclude those who do not pay. Because of the difficulties involved in establishing a one-to-one link between payment and receipt of such goods, the market supply of public goods will often be less than the economically efficient quantity.

- Entrepreneurs in markets have an incentive to find solutions to each market problem, and new solutions are constantly being discovered. But problems remain that can potentially be improved through government action.

- Both markets and government can have problems in achieving the efficient allocation of resources. The term *market failure* describes the situation where markets will fail to achieve the conditions implied by idealized economic efficiency. But political action may also result in outcomes that are inefficient, a situation known as *government failure*.

CRITICAL ANALYSIS QUESTIONS

1. *Why is it important for producers to be able to prevent non-paying customers from receiving a good?

2. In response to the terrorist attacks of September 11, 2001, airline security screening increased dramatically. As a result, the travel time of airline passengers has increased substantially. Would it make economic sense to devote enough resources to completely prevent any such future attacks? Why or why not?

3. What are the distinguishing characteristics of "public goods"? Give two examples of a public good. Why are public goods difficult for markets to allocate efficiently?

4. Which of the following are public goods? Explain, using the definition of a public good.
   a. an antimissile system surrounding Washington, D.C.
   b. a fire department
   c. tennis courts
   d. Yellowstone National Park
   e. elementary schools

5. Explain in your own words what is meant by external costs and external benefits. Why may market outcomes be less than ideal when externalities are present?

6. English philosopher John Locke argued that the protection of each individual's person and property (acquired without the use of violence, theft, or fraud) was the primary function of government. Why is this protection important to the efficient operation of an economy?

7. "If it's worth doing, it's worth doing to the best of your ability." What is the economic explanation for why this statement is frequently said but rarely followed in practice? Explain.

8. "Unless quality and price are regulated by government, travelers would have no chance for a fair deal. Local people would be treated well, but the traveler would have no way to know, for example, who offers a good night's lodging at a fair price." Is this true or false? Explain.

9. *If sellers of toasters were able to organize themselves, reduce their output, and raise their prices, how would economic efficiency be affected? Explain.

10. What are external costs? When are they most likely to be present? When external costs are present, what is likely to be the relationship between the market output of a good and the output consistent with ideal economic efficiency?

11. *"Elementary education is obviously a public good. After all, it is provided by the government." Evaluate this statement.

12. What are the necessary conditions for economic efficiency? In what four situations might a market fail to achieve ideal economic efficiency?

13. What is market failure? If market failure is present, does this imply that government intervention will lead to a more efficient allocation of resources? Why or why not?

14. Apply the economic efficiency criterion to the role of government. When would a government intervention be considered economically efficient? When would a government intervention be considered economically inefficient?

*Asterisk denotes questions for which answers are given in Appendix B.

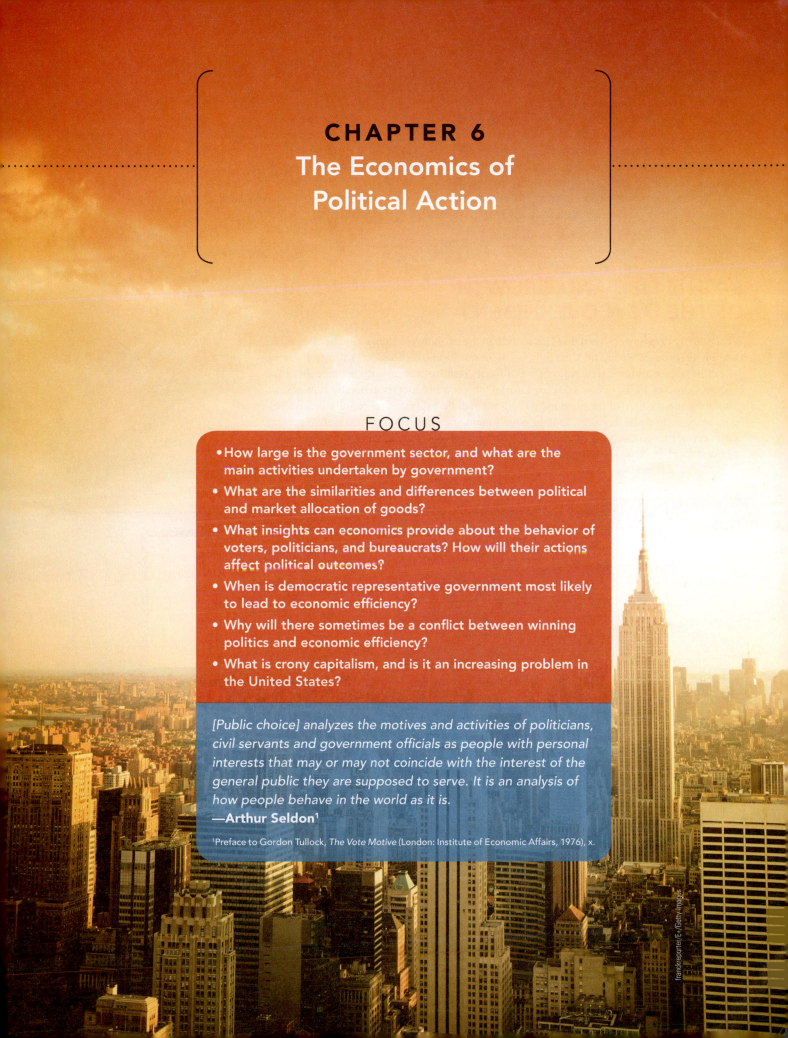

CHAPTER 6
The Economics of Political Action

FOCUS

- How large is the government sector, and what are the main activities undertaken by government?
- What are the similarities and differences between political and market allocation of goods?
- What insights can economics provide about the behavior of voters, politicians, and bureaucrats? How will their actions affect political outcomes?
- When is democratic representative government most likely to lead to economic efficiency?
- Why will there sometimes be a conflict between winning politics and economic efficiency?
- What is crony capitalism, and is it an increasing problem in the United States?

[Public choice] analyzes the motives and activities of politicians, civil servants and government officials as people with personal interests that may or may not coincide with the interest of the general public they are supposed to serve. It is an analysis of how people behave in the world as it is.
—Arthur Seldon[1]

[1]Preface to Gordon Tullock, *The Vote Motive* (London: Institute of Economic Affairs, 1976), x.

As we have previously discussed, the protection of property rights, evenhanded enforcement of contracts, and provision of a stable monetary environment are vital for the smooth and efficient operation of markets. Governments that perform these functions well will help their citizens prosper and achieve higher levels of income. Governments may also help allocate goods difficult for markets to handle. However, it is crucially important to recognize that government is simply an alternative form of economic organization. In most industrialized nations, the activities of governments are directed by the democratic political process. In this chapter, we will use the tools of economics to analyze how this process works.

6-1 THE SIZE AND GROWTH OF THE U.S. GOVERNMENT

What exactly does government do? Has its role in the economy shrunk or grown over time? Data on government spending shed light on these questions. As **Exhibit 1** illustrates, total government expenditures (federal, state, and local combined) were only 9.4 percent of the U.S. economy in 1930. (*Note:* GDP, or Gross Domestic Product, is generally how economists measure the size of the economy. The term will be explained more fully in a macroeconomics course.) In that year, federal government spending by itself was only 3 percent of the economy. At the time, this made the federal government about half the size of all state and local governments combined.

EXHIBIT 1

The Growth of Government Spending between 1930 and 2012

U.S. government expenditures as a share of the economy's gross domestic product have risen dramatically over the past eighty years. They are now almost 40 percent of the U.S. economy.

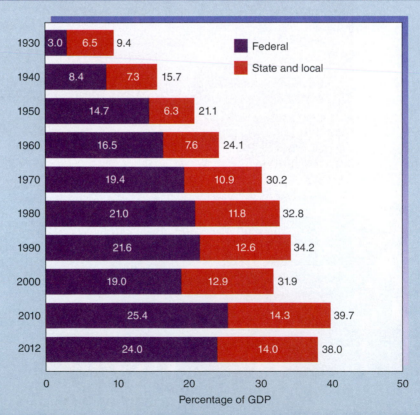

Year	Federal	State and local	Total
1930	3.0	6.5	9.4
1940	8.4	7.3	15.7
1950	14.7	6.3	21.1
1960	16.5	7.6	24.1
1970	19.4	10.9	30.2
1980	21.0	11.8	32.8
1990	21.6	12.6	34.2
2000	19.0	12.9	31.9
2010	25.4	14.3	39.7
2012	24.0	14.0	38.0

Percentage of GDP

Source: Bureau of Economic Analysis, http://www.bea.gov. Grants to state and local governments are included in federal expenditures. Individual data may not add to total due to rounding.

EXHIBIT 2

Government Spending by Category

The major categories of federal government spending are health care, Social Security, national defense, and income security (welfare transfers). The major categories of state and local government spending are education, health and welfare programs, and administration.

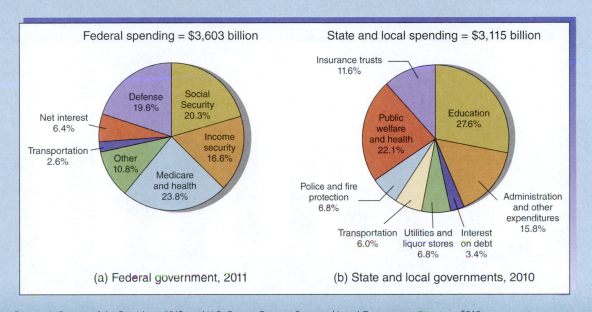

Federal spending = $3,603 billion

- Defense 19.6%
- Social Security 20.3%
- Net interest 6.4%
- Income security 16.6%
- Transportation 2.6%
- Other 10.8%
- Medicare and health 23.8%

State and local spending = $3,115 billion

- Insurance trusts 11.6%
- Education 27.6%
- Public welfare and health 22.1%
- Police and fire protection 6.8%
- Administration and other expenditures 15.8%
- Transportation 6.0%
- Utilities and liquor stores 6.8%
- Interest on debt 3.4%

(a) Federal government, 2011   (b) State and local governments, 2010

Source: Economic Report of the President, 2013, and U.S. Census Bureau, State and Local Government Finances, 2010

Between 1930 and 1980, the size of government grew very rapidly. By 1980, government expenditures had risen to 32.8 percent of the economy, *more than three times* the level of 1930. Moreover, the federal government grew to about twice the size of all state and local governments combined, despite the fact that they were growing rapidly, too. After remaining fairly constant between 1980 and 2000, the size of government increased dramatically between 2000 and 2010 to almost 40 percent of the U.S. economy, and it remained at 38 percent in 2012.

Exhibit 2 shows the major categories of government spending for both the federal government and state and local governments. The major categories of federal spending are health care, Social Security, national defense, and other income transfers. Education, administration, and public welfare and health constitute the largest areas of spending for state and local governments.

Transfer payments are transfers of income from some individuals (who pay taxes) to others (who receive government payments). Social Security, unemployment benefits, and welfare are examples of transfer payments. Direct income transfers now account for almost half of the total spending of the government. As **Exhibit 3** illustrates, government spending on income transfers has grown rapidly. In 1930, income transfers summed to only 1.1 percent of total income. By 1970, the figure had jumped to 8.3 percent; by 2010, it had risen to 18.0 percent of national income. In 2012 the figure had fallen slightly to 17.4 percent from its peak in 2010. Obviously, the government has become much more involved in tax-transfer activities during the past 80 years.

Given the size and growth of government, understanding how the political process works and how it is likely to affect the economy is vitally important. The remainder of this chapter will address this issue.

Transfer payments
Payments to individuals or institutions that are not linked to the current supply of a good or service by the recipient.

EXHIBIT 3

The Growth of Government Transfer Payments

The government taxes approximately 20 percent of national income away from some people and transfers it to others. Means-tested income transfers—those directed toward the poor—account for only about one-sixth of all income transfers. Government income-transfer activities have grown substantially over the past eighty years.

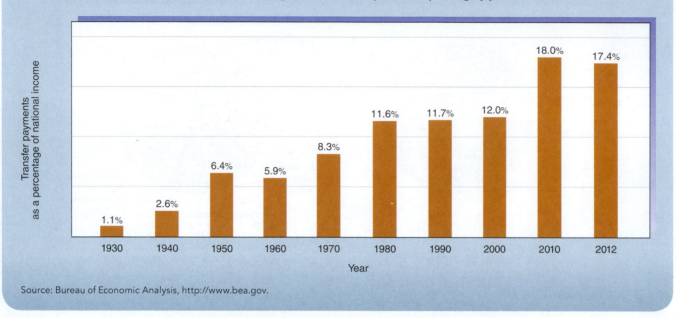

Source: Bureau of Economic Analysis, http://www.bea.gov.

6-2 SIMILARITIES AND DIFFERENCES BETWEEN POLITICAL AND MARKET ALLOCATION

This chapter will focus on the analysis of how the political process works. Let's begin by considering some of the major similarities and differences between the two sectors. Competition is present in the government sector, just as it is in the market sector. The nature of the competition and criteria for success differ, but intense competition is present in both. In the government sector, politicians compete for elective office. Bureau chiefs and agency heads compete for larger budgets. Government employees compete for promotions and higher pay rates. Perhaps most importantly, business, labor, and other special interest groups compete for program funding, favorable bureaucratic rulings, and other political favors that serve their narrow interests.

Scarcity and the opportunity cost of resource use are present in both sectors. If the government uses resources to achieve one goal, those resources are unavailable to achieve others. Thus, just as in the market sector, provision of goods through government is costly, and this is true even if the good is provided free of charge to certain consumers.

But there are also important differences between market and political allocation, and these differences shed light on how the two processes allocate resources. Let's consider four of the key differences.

First, public sector organization can break the linkage between payment and consumption of a good. In the market sector, goods are allocated to those who are willing to pay the price: there is a one-to-one relationship between a person's payment and receipt of a good. This is often not the case when decisions are made politically. Sometimes goods are allocated to people even if they have paid little or nothing to cover their cost. In other instances, however, individuals are required to pay dearly for a government program even though they derive few, if any, benefits from it.

Second, private-sector action is based on mutual agreement; public-sector action is based on majority rule. In the market sector, when two parties engage in trade, their actions are voluntary and motivated by the expectation of mutual gain. Corporations like Exxon and Microsoft, no matter how large or powerful, cannot take income from you or force you to buy their products. Mutual gain is the foundation for market exchange. In contrast, political action is based on majority rule, either through direct voting or through legislative procedures involving elected representatives. If a legislative majority decides on a particular policy, the minority must accept the policy and help pay for it, even if they strongly object. Political action, even when it is democratic, creates "losers" as well as "winners." Further, as we will explain, there is no assurance that the gains the winners derive from a project will exceed the losses imposed on the losers.

Third, when political choices are made legislatively, voters face a "bundle purchase" problem. They must choose among candidates who represent a bundle of positions on issues. On election day, the voter cannot choose the views of one politician on healthcare and agricultural subsidies for example, and simultaneously choose the views of a different politician on social security reform and national defense. This greatly limits the voter's power to make his or her preferences count on specific issues. The situation in markets is quite different. A buyer can purchase some groceries or clothing from one store, while choosing related items from different suppliers. There is seldom a bundle-purchase problem in markets.

Fourth, income and influence are distributed differently in the two sectors. People who supply more highly valued resources in the marketplace have larger incomes. The number of these dollar "votes" earned by a person in the marketplace will reflect his or her abilities, ambitions, skills, past savings, inheritance, good fortune, and willingness to produce for others, among other things. In contrast, in a democratic setting, one citizen, one vote is the rule. But there are ways other than voting to influence political outcomes. People can donate their money and time to help a campaign. They can also try to influence friends and neighbors, write letters to legislators, and speak in public on behalf of a candidate or cause. The greatest rewards of the political process go to those best able and most willing to use their time, persuasive skills, organizational abilities, and financial contributions to help politicians get votes. People who have more money and skills of this sort—and are willing to spend them in the political arena—can expect

OUTSTANDING ECONOMIST

JAMES BUCHANAN (1919–2013)

The 1986 winner of the Nobel Prize in Economics, James Buchanan might properly be called the "father of public choice economics." Rather than assuming that voters, elected political officials, and bureaucrats are "saints" seeking to promote the common good, Buchanan assumed that the key political players responded to the structure of incentives. His work illustrated that, like the market, the political process has deficiencies that often result in counterproductive government actions and misallocation of resources. As he put it, public choice analysis is "government without the romance." Buchanan's most famous work, *The Calculus of Consent* (1962), coauthored with Gordon Tullock, argues that unless constitutional rules are structured in a manner that will bring the self-interests of the political players into harmony with the wise use of resources, government action will often be counterproductive.[1] Given the continued growth of government, Buchanan's work is now perhaps more relevant than at any time in American history.

[1] J. M. Buchanan and G. Tullock, *The Calculus of Consent* (Ann Arbor: University of Michigan Press, 1962).

to benefit themselves and their favorite causes more handsomely. Thus, while the sources of success and influence differ between sectors, the allocation of income and influence is unequal in both.

6-3 POLITICAL DECISION-MAKING: AN OVERVIEW

Public-choice analysis
The study of decision-making as it affects the formation and operation of collective organizations, like governments. In general, the principles and methodology of economics are applied to political science topics.

When political decisions are made democratically, or in a representative democracy, as we assume in this chapter, the choices of individuals will influence outcomes in the government sector, just as they do in the market sector. **Public-choice analysis** is a branch of economics that applies the principles and methodology of economics to the operation of the political process. Public-choice analysis links the theory of *individual* behavior to political action, analyzes the implications of the theory, and tests them against events in the real world. Over the past 50 years, research in this area has greatly enhanced our understanding of how the political process works and the structure of the outcomes it generates.[2] Just as economists use self-interest and the structure of incentives to analyze markets, public-choice economists use them to analyze political choices and the operation of government. After all, the same people make decisions in both sectors. If self-interest and the structure of incentives influence market choices, there is good reason to expect that they will also influence choices in a political setting.

The collective decision-making process can be thought of as a complex interaction among voters, legislators, and bureaucrats. Voters elect a legislature, which levies taxes and allocates budgets and regulatory authority to various government agencies and bureaus. The bureaucrats in charge of these agencies utilize the funds to supply government services and income transfers, and to exercise regulatory authority as well. In a representative democracy, voter support determines who is elected to the legislature. A majority vote of the legislature is generally required for the passage of taxes, budget allocations, and regulatory legislation. Let's take a closer look at the incentive structure confronting the three primary political players—voters, legislators, and bureaucrats—and consider how they affect the operation of the political process.

6-3a INCENTIVES CONFRONTED BY THE VOTER

How do voters decide whom to support? Self-interest dictates that voters, like market consumers, will ask, "What can you do for me and my goals, and how much will it cost me?" The greater the voter's perceived net personal gain from a particular candidate's election, the more likely it is that the voter will favor that candidate. In contrast, the greater the perceived net economic cost imposed on the voter by the positions of a candidate, the less inclined the voter will be to support the candidate. Other things being equal, voters will tend to support those candidates who they believe will provide the most government services and transfer benefits to them and their favorite causes, net of costs.

How well will voters be informed about political issues and candidates? When decisions are made collectively, the choices of a single person will not be decisive. The probability that an individual vote will decide a city, state, or national election is virtually zero. Realizing that their votes will not affect the outcome, individual voters have little incentive to spend much effort seeking the information needed to cast an informed ballot. Economists refer to this lack of incentive as the **rational ignorance effect**.

Rational ignorance effect
Because it is highly unlikely that an individual vote will decide the outcome of an election, a rational individual has little or no incentive to search for and acquire the information needed to cast an informed vote.

As the result of the rational ignorance effect, most voters simply rely on information supplied to them freely by candidates (via political advertising) and the mass media, as

[2]The contributions of Kenneth Arrow, James Buchanan, Duncan Black, Anthony Downs, William Niskanen, Mancur Olson, Robert Tollison, and Gordon Tullock have been particularly important. Public choice is something of a cross between economics and political science. Thus, advanced courses are generally offered in both departments.

Voters, politicians, and bureaucrats are the primary decision-makers in the political arena.

well as conversations with friends and coworkers. Surveys, in fact, indicate that huge numbers of voters are unable even to identify their own congressional representatives, much less know where they stand on issues like Social Security reform, tariffs, and agricultural price supports. Given that voters gain little from casting a more informed vote, their meager knowledge of political candidates and issues is not surprising.

When people can put information to good use in serving their own goals, they will put forth more effort to acquire it. Consider the incentive of auto purchasers to make well-informed choices. They often shop at several dealerships, take different models for test drives, review consumer publications, and consult with various car experts as they make their purchasing decisions. Most important, if an auto buyer makes a bad choice, he or she will personally bear the consequences. In contrast, voters gain little or nothing if they cast a more informed vote. It is a virtual certainty that their vote will not decide the outcome of an election, and therefore there will be no adverse consequences of casting a poorly informed vote. Thus, it is actually *reasonable* to expect people to be far better informed when choosing a car than a senatorial, congressional, or other political candidate.

The fact that citizens recognize that their individual vote will not sway the outcome also helps explain why many do not vote. Even in a presidential election, only about half of all voting-age Americans take the time to register and vote. The turnout for state and local elections is generally still lower. Given the low probability that one's vote will be decisive, low voter turnout is an expected result.

6-3b INCENTIVES CONFRONTED BY THE POLITICIAN

What motivates political candidates and officeholders? Economics indicates that their actions and political positions will be heavily affected by the pursuit of votes. No doubt, many of them genuinely care about the "public interest" and the quality of government, but they need to be elected to achieve their objectives, whatever they might be. Moreover, if a candidate is going to be successful, their positive attributes must be brought to the attention of rationally ignorant voters focused on their families, jobs, various civic activities, and local sports teams (which are probably more entertaining). The successful candidate needs an expert staff, sophisticated polling techniques to uncover popular issues and positions, and high-quality advertising to shape his or her image favorably. This, of course, will be costly. It is not unusual for an incumbent candidate for the U.S. Senate to spend $15 million or more seeking to win an election. In other words, votes are the necessary objective of politicians, but money helps them get those votes. Predictably, the pursuit of campaign contributions then shapes the actions of politicians, too.

Are we implying that politicians are selfish, caring only for their pocketbooks and reelection chances? The answer is "No." Factors other than personal political gain, narrowly defined, may well influence their actions. Sometimes an elected official may feel so strongly about an issue that he or she will knowingly take a position that is politically unpopular and damaging to his or her future electoral prospects. None of this is inconsistent with the economic view of the political process. Over time, however, the politicians most likely to remain in office are the

Just as the general does not want his Camp Swampy budget cut, most heads of agencies want expanded budgets to help them do more and do it more comfortably.

ones who focus on how their actions will influence their reelection prospects. Just as profits are the lifeblood of the market entrepreneur, votes are the lifeblood of the politician.

Politicians face competition for elected office from other candidates. Like market suppliers, political suppliers have an incentive to find ways to gain an advantage over their competitors. Catering to the strongly held views of voters and contributors is one way of doing that. Enacting rules that put potential challengers at a disadvantage is another. When geographic political districts are redrawn, for example, politicians frequently manipulate the process to increase their chances of reelection—a process known as "gerrymandering." Incumbents can also attempt to use government resources for their reelection campaigns, an advantage challengers do not have. Campaign finance "reforms" that make it more difficult for a challenger to raise funds may also provide incumbents with an additional advantage.

6-3c INCENTIVES CONFRONTED BY THE GOVERNMENT BUREAUCRAT

Like other people, bureaucrats who staff government agencies, especially those who rise to decision-making levels, have narrowly focused interests. They usually want to see their own agency's goals furthered. Doing so, however, requires larger budgets or greater authority to regulate or both. In turn, larger budgets and more authority lead to more satisfaction, prestige, and career opportunities for the bureaucrats. Economic analysis suggests there is a strong tendency for government bureaucrats and employees to want to expand their budgets and their authority well beyond what would be economically efficient. Indeed, analysts recognize that bigger programs often have strong, organized political backing. In contrast "efficiency has no political constituency."

Legislative bodies are in charge of overseeing these bureaus, but the individual legislators themselves generally know little about the true costs of agency decisions, especially the costs to those regulated. This makes it even more likely that bureaucrats will be able to get funding and authority beyond what's economically efficient.

In summary, the political process, which begins with voter-driven elections and proceeds to legislative decisions and bureaucratic actions, brings about results that please some voters and displease others. The goals of the three major categories of participants—voters, politicians, and bureaucrats—frequently conflict with one another. Each group wants more of the government's limited supply of resources. Coalitions form and the members of each coalition hope to enhance their ability to get the government to do what they want. Sometimes this results in productive activities on the part of the government, and sometimes it does not.

6-4 WHEN THE POLITICAL PROCESS WORKS WELL

Under what conditions are voting and representative government most likely to result in productive actions? People have a tendency to believe that support by a majority makes a political action productive. However, if a project is truly productive, it will always be possible to allocate its costs such that *all* voters gain. This would mean that,

EXHIBIT 4

The Benefits Derived by Voters from a Hypothetical Road Construction Project

When taxes are levied in proportion to benefits received (tax plan B), any efficient project can pass unanimously (and any inefficient project will fail unanimously). When taxes are not levied in accordance with benefits received (tax plan A), efficient projects can fail to win a majority vote (or inefficient projects can pass in a majority vote).

	BENEFITS RECEIVED (1)	TAX PAYMENT	
VOTER		PLAN A (2)	PLAN B (3)
Adams	$20	$5	$12.50
Chan	12	5	7.50
Green	4	5	2.50
Lee	2	5	1.25
Diaz	2	5	1.25
Total	**$40**	**$25**	**$25.00**

© Cengage Learning 2013

even if voting rules required unanimity or near unanimity, all truly productive government projects would pass if the costs were allocated in the right manner. **Exhibit 4** helps illustrate this point. Column 1 presents hypothetical data on the distribution of benefits from a government road construction project. These benefits sum to $40, which exceeds the $25 cost of the road, so the project is productive. But if the project's $25 cost were allocated equally among the voters (plan A), Adams and Chan gain substantially, but Green, Lee, and Diaz lose. If the fate of the project is decided by majority vote, the project will be defeated by the "no" votes of Green, Lee, and Diaz. This productive government project fails to obtain a majority vote in this case because of the way that the costs have been allocated.

Because the project is indeed productive, there is an alternative way to allocate its costs so that Adams, Chan, Green, Lee, and Diaz all benefit. This can be accomplished by allocating the cost of the project among voters in proportion to the benefits that they receive (plan B). Under this arrangement, Adams would pay half ($12.50) of the $25 cost, because he receives half ($20) of the total benefits ($40). The other voters would all pay in proportion to the benefits they receive. Under this plan, all voters would gain from the proposal. Even though the proposal could not secure a majority when the costs were allocated equally among voters, it will be favored by all five voters when they are taxed in proportion to the benefits they receive (plan B).

This simple illustration highlights an extremely important point about voting and the efficiency of government action. *When voters pay in proportion to benefits received, all voters will gain if the government action is productive, and all will lose if it is unproductive.*[3] *When the benefits and costs derived by individual voters are closely related, the voting process will enact efficient projects while rejecting inefficient ones. When voters pay in proportion to the benefits they receive, there will tend to be harmony between good politics and sound economics.*

---

[3]The principle that productive projects generate the potential for political unanimity was initially articulated by Swedish economist Knut Wicksell in 1896. See Wicksell, "A New Principle of Just Taxation," in *Public Choice and Constitutional Economics*, James Gwartney and Richard Wagner (Greenwich, CT: JAI Press, Inc., 1988). Nobel laureate James Buchanan stated that Wicksell's work provided him with the insights that led to his large role in the development of modern public-choice theory.

Distribution of Benefits and Costs among Voters

It is useful to visualize four possible combinations for the distribution of benefits and costs among voters to consider how the alternative distributions affect the operation of representative governments. When the distribution of benefits and costs is both widespread among voters (type 1) or both concentrated among voters (type 3), representative government will tend to undertake projects that are productive and reject those that are unproductive. In contrast, when the benefits are concentrated and the costs are widespread (type 2), representative government is biased toward the adoption of inefficient projects. Finally, when benefits are widespread but the costs concentrated (type 4), the political process may reject projects that are productive.

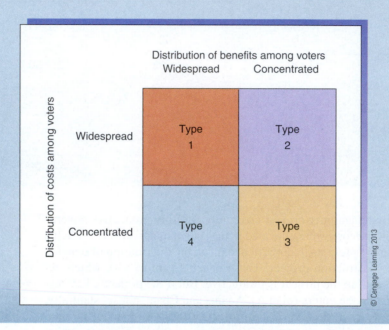

© Cengage Learning 2013

User charges

Payments users (consumers) are required to make if they want to receive certain services provided by the government.

How might the cost of a government service be linked to the benefits received? **User charges**, which require people who use a service more to pay a larger share of the cost, provide one way. User charges are most likely to be levied at the local level. Local services such as electricity, water, and garbage collection are generally financed with user charges. Sometimes the intensity of the use of a service and the amount paid for it can be linked by specifying that the revenue from a specific tax be used for a designated purpose. For example, many states finance road construction and maintenance with the revenue collected from taxes on gasoline and other motor fuels. The more an individual drives—getting more benefits from the roads—the more that individual pays.

Exhibit 5 provides a useful way to look at the possible linkage between the benefits and costs of government programs. The benefits from a government action may be either widespread among the general public or concentrated among a small subgroup (for example, farmers, students, business interests, senior citizens, or members of a labor union). Similarly, the costs may be either widespread or highly concentrated among voters. Thus, as the exhibit shows, there are four possible patterns of voter benefits and costs: (1) widespread benefits and widespread costs, (2) concentrated benefits and widespread costs, (3) concentrated benefits and concentrated costs, and (4) widespread benefits and concentrated costs.

When both the benefits and costs are widespread among voters (type 1 issue), essentially everyone benefits and everyone pays. Although the costs of type 1 measures may not be precisely proportional to the benefits individuals receive, there will be a rough relationship. When type 1 measures are productive, almost everyone gains more than they pay. There will be little opposition, and political representatives have a strong incentive to support such proposals. In contrast, when type 1 proposals generate costs in excess of benefits, almost everyone loses, and representatives will face pressure to oppose such issues. Thus, for type 1 projects, the political process works pretty well. Productive projects will tend to be accepted and unproductive ones rejected.

Similarly, there is reason to believe that the political process will work fairly well for type 3 measures—those for which both benefits and costs are concentrated on one or more small subgroups. In some cases, the concentrated beneficiaries may be the same group of people paying for the government to provide them a service. In other cases, the subgroup of beneficiaries may differ from the subgroup footing the bill. Even in this case, however, when the benefits exceed the costs, the concentrated group of beneficiaries will have an incentive to expend more resources lobbying for the measure than those harmed by it will expend opposing it. Thus, when the benefits and costs are both concentrated, there will be a tendency for productive projects to be adopted and unproductive ones to be rejected.

6-5 WHEN THE POLITICAL PROCESS WORKS POORLY

Although the political process yields reasonable results when there is a close relationship between the receipt of benefits and the payment of costs, the harmony between good politics and sound economics breaks down when the beneficiaries differ from those bearing the costs (type 2 and type 4 projects). Inefficiency may also arise from other sources when governments undertake economic activities. In this section, we consider four major reasons why the political allocation of resources will often result in inefficiency.

6-5a SPECIAL-INTEREST EFFECT

Trade restrictions that limit the import of steel and lumber from abroad; subsidies for sports stadiums, the arts, and various agricultural products; federal spending on an indoor rain forest in Iowa; a tattoo-removal program in San Luis Obispo County, California; special grants and loans to a business producing expensive electric sports cars: These seemingly diverse programs funded by tax dollars from the federal government have one thing in common—they reflect the attractiveness of special-interest issues to vote-seeking politicians. A **special-interest issue** is one that generates substantial personal benefits for a small number of constituents while the costs are spread widely across the bulk of citizens (type 2 projects). Individually, a few people gain a great deal, but many others lose a small amount. In aggregate, the losses may exceed the benefits.

How will a vote-seeking politician respond to special-interest issues? Because their personal stake is large, members of the interest group (and lobbyists representing their interests) will feel strongly about such issues. Many of the special-interest voters will vote for or against candidates strictly on the basis of whether they are supportive of their positions. In addition, interest groups are generally an attractive source of campaign resources, including financial contributions. In contrast, most other rationally ignorant voters will either not know or will care little about special-interest issues. Even if voters know about some of these programs, it will be difficult for them to punish their legislators because each politician represents a bundle of positions on many different issues. While politicians would gain little from support of the rationally ignorant and unorganized majority, organized interest groups are eager to provide cooperative politicians with vocal supporters, campaign workers, and, most important, financial contributions.

As a result, politicians have a strong incentive to support legislation that provides concentrated benefits to special-interest groups at the expense of disorganized groups (like the bulk of taxpayers and consumers). Consider the cotton subsidy program. This program, which dates back to the New Deal era, has provided cotton farmers with subsidies averaging approximately $2 billion per year since 1995. Moreover, because the subsidies are linked to production, the overwhelming bulk of these transfers go to well-off large farmers. Five percent of the recipients collect more than half of the subsidies, and 80 percent of this federal largess is bestowed on the largest 20 percent of growers. The top 1 percent of

Special-interest issue
An issue that generates substantial individual benefits to a small minority while imposing a small individual cost on many other citizens. In total, the net cost to the majority might either exceed or fall short of the net benefits to the special-interest group.

EXHIBIT 6

Trading Votes and Passing Counterproductive Legislation

All three projects are inefficient and would not pass majority vote individually. However, representatives from districts A, B, and C could trade votes (logrolling) or put together pork-barrel legislation that would result in all three projects passing.

	NET BENEFITS (+) OR COSTS (−) TO VOTERS IN DISTRICT			
VOTERS OF DISTRICT[a]	CONSTRUCTION OF POST OFFICE IN A	DREDGING HARBOR IN B	CONSTRUCTION OF MILITARY BASE IN C	TOTAL
A	+$10	−$ 3	−$ 3	+$ 4
B	−$ 3	+$10	−$ 3	+$ 4
C	−$ 3	−$ 3	+$10	+$ 4
D	−$ 3	−$ 3	−$ 3	−$ 9
E	−$ 3	−$ 3	−$ 3	−$ 9
Total	−$ 2	−$ 2	−$ 2	−$ 6

[a]We assume the districts are of equal size.

© Cengage Learning 2013

cotton farmers received an average subsidy of $175,000 in 2010. What explains the political popularity of this program? The special interest effect provides the answer. The subsidy recipients feel strongly about the program and congressional supporters can count on them for political contributions. In contrast, the taxpayers and consumers of cotton products are almost totally unaware of the cost the program imposes on them. Thus, there is a strong incentive for congressional representatives to support the interests of the cotton farmers even though the program promotes inefficient use of resources and redistributes income from the less well-off to those with higher incomes.

The cotton subsidy program is not unusual. Numerous government programs reflect this same pattern of incentives. Moreover, even when special interest programs are highly inefficient, politicians will often gain from supporting them. For another real-world illustration of how the special-interest effect works, see Applications in Economics, "Sweet Subsidies to Sugar Growers: A Case Study of the Special-Interest Effect."

The power of special interests is further strengthened by logrolling and pork-barrel legislation. **Logrolling** involves the practice of vote trading by politicians in order to get the necessary support to pass desired legislation. **Pork-barrel legislation** is the term used to describe the bundling of unrelated projects benefiting many interests into a single bill. Both logrolling and pork-barrel legislation will often make it possible for special-interest projects to gain legislative approval, even though each project is counterproductive and individually could not muster the needed votes.

Exhibit 6 provides a numeric illustration of the forces underlying logrolling and pork-barrel legislation. Here we analyze the operation of a five-member legislature considering three projects: construction of a post office in district A, dredging of a harbor in district B, and spending on a military base in district C. For each district, the net benefit or cost is shown—that is, the benefit to the district minus the tax cost imposed on it. The total cost of each of the three projects exceeds the benefits (as shown by the negative number in the total row at the bottom of the table); therefore, each is counterproductive. If the projects were voted on separately, each would lose by a 4-to-1 vote because only one district would gain, and the other four would lose. However, when the projects are bundled together through either logrolling (representatives A, B, and C could agree to trade votes) or pork-barrel legislation (all three programs put on the same bill), they can all pass, despite the fact that all are inefficient.[4] This can be seen by noting that the total combined net benefit is positive for representatives A, B, and C.

Logrolling
The exchange between politicians of political support on one issue for political support on another.

Pork-barrel legislation
A package of spending projects bundled into a single bill. It is often used as a device to obtain funding for a group of projects intensely desired by regional or interest groups that would be unlikely to pass if voted on separately.

---

[4]Logrolling and pork-barrel policies can sometimes lead to the adoption of productive measures. However, if a project is productive, there would always be a pattern of finance that would lead to its adoption even if logrolling and pork-barrel policies were absent. Thus, the tendency for logrolling and pork-barrel policies to result in the adoption of inefficient projects is the more significant point.

The political incentive to support special interest projects, including those that are counterproductive, is even stronger than the simple numeric example of Exhibit 6 implies. As the result of the rational ignorance effect, those harmed by pork-barrel and other special-interest policies will often be unaware of the adverse impact the projects exert on their welfare. Moreover, the power of special interests is further enhanced by **earmarking**, detailed directives written into spending bills that require budgeted funds to be spent in specific locations, or on specific projects or programs. In effect, earmarks let members of Congress direct federal spending to specific firms, districts, and states. These directives are often inserted into bills late in the legislative process by powerful committee members or through logrolling as a means of obtaining needed votes for legislative passage. Not surprisingly, firms and groups benefiting substantially from the earmarks are often those making large contributions to the political campaigns of the senators and representatives inserting the earmarks. In recent years, the national defense, transportation, energy, and homeland security bills have been "stuffed" with earmark spending.

Even the legislation enacted to address the fiscal cliff problem in January 2013 contained $12 billion in benefits for producers of windmill energy, $222 million in tax rebates for liquor makers, $78 million in write-offs for NASCAR track owners, a $62 million tax credit for StarKist's plant in American Samoa, and $410 million in tax benefits to Hollywood movie studios.

Earmarking
The direction of budgeted funds to specific projects, programs, and locations. The technique is costly but provides major benefits to business firms and other concentrated constituent groups, and to the districts where the spending takes place. The benefits are often targeted to those willing to make substantial campaign contributions.

APPLICATIONS IN ECONOMICS

Sweet Subsidies to Sugar Growers: A Case Study of the Special-Interest Effect

For many years, the price of sugar in the United States has been two or three times as high as the world price. Why? Because the U.S. government severely restricts the quantity of sugar imported. This keeps the domestic price of sugar high. As a result, the roughly 60,000 sugar growers in the United States gain about $1.9 billion. That's more than $30,000 per grower! Most of these benefits are reaped by large growers with incomes far above the national average. In contrast, these subsidies cost the average American household about $20 in the form of higher prices for products containing sugar. Even more important, the resources of Americans are wasted producing a good we are ill suited to produce and one that could be obtained at a substantially lower cost through trade. As a result, Americans are worse off.

Why does Congress support this program year after year? Given the sizable impact the restrictions have on the personal wealth of sugar growers, it is perfectly sensible for the growers, particularly the large ones, to use their wealth and political clout to help politicians who support their interests. This is precisely what they have done. During the 2010 and 2012 election cycles, the sugar lobby contributed more than $10 million to candidates and political action committees. One company alone, American Crystal Sugar, contributed $4.4 million. During the same period, the industry spent another $30 million lobbying for continuation of the subsidies, including $5.5 million by American Crystal Sugar.

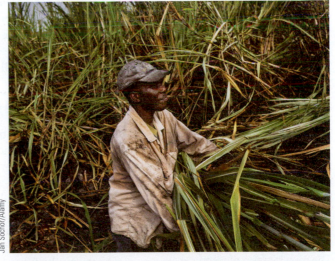

Jan Sochor/Alamy

In contrast, it makes no sense for the average voter to investigate this issue or give it any significant weight when deciding for whom to vote. In fact, most voters are unaware that this program is costing them money. Here, as in several other areas, politicians have a strong incentive to support policies favored by special interests, solicit those parties for political contributions, and use the funds to attract the support of other voters, most of whom know nothing about the sugar program. Even though the sugar program is counterproductive, it is still a political winner.

©iStockphoto.com/sorendls

Why don't representatives oppose measures that force their constituents to pay for projects that benefit others? There is some incentive to do so, but the constituents of any one elected representative would capture only a tiny portion of the benefits of tax savings from improved efficiency. The savings, after all, would be spread nationwide among all taxpayers. We would not expect the president of a corporation to devote any significant amount of the firm's resources toward projects that chiefly benefit other firms. Neither should we expect an elected representative to devote political resources to projects like defeating pork-barrel programs when the bulk of the benefits derived from spending reductions and tax savings will accrue to constituents in other districts. Instead, representatives have a strong incentive to fight for more spending for their constituents and not worry much about the spending pushed by other members of Congress.

When the benefits of a governmental action are spread far and wide among the unorganized, and the costs are highly concentrated (type 4 of Exhibit 5), special-interest groups—those who stand to bear the cost—are likely to oppose and lobby strongly against even an efficient project. Most other voters will be largely uninformed and uninterested. Once again, politicians will have an incentive to respond to the views of the concentrated interests. A proposal to reduce or eliminate a tariff (tax) on an imported good would be an example of this type of legislation. Although many thousands of consumers would benefit from the lower prices that result, the domestic firms that compete with the imported good would devote substantial resources toward lobbying to keep the tariff in place. Projects of this type will tend to be rejected even when they are productive, that is, when they would generate larger benefits than costs.

There is a tendency to believe that if a project or program can muster a political majority, it will be good for the society. The special interest effect illustrates that this is not necessarily the case. *Majority voting and representative democracy work poorly when concentrated interests can benefit at the expense of disorganized groups such as taxpayers and consumers. In the case of special-interest issues, there is a conflict between good politics—getting elected—and the efficient use of resources.* The special-interest effect helps explain the presence of numerous government programs that increase the size of government but reduce the overall size of the economic pie. As we discuss diverse topics throughout this text, counterproductive political action that has its foundation in the special-interest effect will arise again and again.

6-5b SHORTSIGHTEDNESS EFFECT

Current economic conditions will have a major impact on the choices of voters on election day. As a result, incumbent politicians will want to institute programs that will provide visible results prior to the next major election. Thus, legislators have a strong incentive to favor projects that yield highly visible current benefits at the expense of costs that will be difficult to identify and mostly observable in the future. In contrast, politicians will find projects unattractive when they generate visible costs now with the expectation of future gain. Economists refer to this bias inherent in the political process as the **shortsightedness effect**.

As the result of the shortsightedness effect, elected political officials will have a strong incentive to spend on programs designed to provide highly visible benefits before the next election, but they will be reluctant to levy the taxes for their finance. Borrowing provides politicians with an alternative to current taxes: it makes it possible for them to spend now and push the visible taxes into the future. Thus, the political process is biased toward debt finance. The experience of the United States during the past five decades illustrates this bias. During the past 53 years, the federal government of the United States has run 48 budget deficits but only five surpluses. During fiscal years 2009 through 2012, nearly 40 percent of federal expenditures were financed by borrowing. The federal debt has grown to levels not seen since World War II. Moreover, the experience of Greece and several other European countries indicates that elected political officials will sometimes continue with a borrow-and-spend political strategy until they drive their country into virtual economic collapse.

Shortsightedness effect
The misallocation of resources that results because public-sector action is biased (1) in favor of proposals yielding clearly defined current benefits in exchange for difficult-to-identify future costs and (2) against proposals with clearly identifiable current costs that yield less concrete and less obvious future benefits.

The shortsightedness effect also explains why vote-seeking politicians find it attractive to promise future benefits without levying the taxes that are sufficient for their finance. This has been the case with both the Social Security and Medicare programs. The unfunded liabilities of these two programs are now more than *five times* the size of the official outstanding federal debt. By the time the higher taxes (or benefit cuts) for these programs are confronted, the politicians who gained votes from the promised benefits will be long gone.

It is worth taking a moment to consider the differences between the public and private sectors in terms of how future benefits and costs are considered in current decisions. As we explained in Chapter 2, private-property rights provide a means by which the value of future benefits can be immediately captured (and costs must be borne) by a property owner. Owners who do not invest now to properly maintain their homes or cars, for example, will bear the consequences of the reduced value of those assets. Correspondingly, the value of a firm's stock will immediately rise (or fall), depending on the shareholders' perception of the expected future benefits and costs of an action taken by the company's executives today. In contrast, there is no such market indicator or incentive in the public sector, so decision-makers there naturally tend to place more weight on current benefits and costs and less weight on the future.

6-5c RENT-SEEKING

There are two ways individuals can acquire wealth: production and plunder. When individuals produce goods or services and exchange them for income, they not only enrich themselves, but they also enhance the wealth of the society. Sometimes the rules—or lack of rule enforcement—also allow people to get ahead by taking, or plundering, from others. This method not only fails to generate additional income—the gain of one is a loss to another—but it also consumes resources and thereby reduces the wealth of the society.

Rent-seeking is the term economists use to describe actions taken by individuals and groups seeking to use the political process to take the wealth of others.[5] Perhaps "favor seeking" would be a more descriptive term for this type of activity, which generally involves "investing" resources in lobbying and other activities designed to gain favors from the government. The incentive for individuals to spend time and effort in rent-seeking will be determined by how rewarding it is. Rent-seeking will be unattractive when constitutional constraints prevent politicians from taking the property of some and transferring it to others (or forcing some to pay for things desired by others).

However, when the government becomes heavily involved in income transfer activities and the granting of favors to some at the expense of others (instead of simply acting as a neutral force protecting property rights and enforcing contracts), people will spend more time rent seeking and less time producing. Rather than competing by offering consumers more for their money, rent-seekers compete by using resources to obtain more funds from taxpayers. Rent-seeking is a natural outgrowth of government activism. When the government is heavily involved in the granting of contracts, subsidies, tax credits, low-interest loans, regulatory favors, and other forms of government intervention, business firms, labor organizations, and other well-organized interests will compete for the government favors. The result

Rent-seeking
Actions by individuals and groups designed to restructure public policy in a manner that will either directly or indirectly redistribute more income to themselves or the projects they promote.

JUST BETWEEN YOU AND ME, IF I'M ELECTED, I PLAN TO TAKE MONEY AWAY FROM OTHER PEOPLE AND GIVE IT TO YOU FOLKS!

E-mail BobThaves@aol.com
©2000 ThavesDist. by NEA, Inc.
www.comics.com

2000 Thaves/Dist. by Universal Uclick

To get elected (or reelected), politicians have a strong incentive to provide spending programs to important interest groups to secure their support.

[5]See the classic work of Charles K. Rowley, Robert D. Tollison, and Gordon Tullock, *The Political Economy of Rent-Seeking* (Boston: Kluwer Academic Publishers, 1988) for additional details on rent-seeking.

will be a shift of resources away from productive activities and into rent-seeking. Economic efficiency will decrease and output and income levels will fall below their potential.

6-5d INEFFICIENCY OF GOVERNMENT OPERATIONS

Will government enterprises and agencies be operated efficiently? The incentive to keep cost low and provide customers with highly valued goods and services differs substantially between the market and government sectors. In the market sector, there is a strong incentive to produce efficiently because lower costs mean higher profits. The profit motive also provides private firms with a strong incentive to supply goods and services that are highly valued relative to their cost. Bankruptcy weeds out private sector firms that have high costs and serve their customers poorly.

In the public sector, the structure of incentives is much different. There is nothing like profit and loss that might be used to evaluate the performance of public sector managers and bureaus. Neither is there a mechanism like bankruptcy that can be counted on to eventually bring inefficient public sector operations to a halt. In fact, failure to achieve a targeted objective (for example, a lower crime rate or improvement in student achievement scores) is often used as an argument for *increased* public-sector funding of an agency or its programs. Furthermore, public-sector managers are seldom in a position to gain personally from measures that reduce costs. The opposite is often true, in fact. If an agency fails to spend its entire budget for a given year, not only does it have to return the extra money, but its budget for the next year is likely to be cut. Because of this, government agencies typically go on a spending spree near the end of a budget period if they discover they have failed to spend all the current year's allocated funds.

It is important to note that the argument of internal inefficiency is not based on the assumption that employees of a bureaucratic government are lazy or less capable. Many agency managers are highly capable, diligent, and focused strongly on their mission within the agency. Rather, the inefficiency stems from the incentives and opportunities that such managers and workers confront. Government enterprises do not have owners that are risking their wealth on the future success of the firm. No decision-maker in the firm can reap substantial economic gain if the firm produces more efficiently or incorporates a new product or service highly valued relative to its costs. In the public sector, there is no test like profit and loss that might be used to measure inefficiency, much less eliminate it. Given this incentive structure, inefficient use of resources is the predicted result.

The empirical evidence is consistent with this view. Economies dominated by government control, like those of the former Soviet bloc, Indonesia, Syria, and Nigeria (and many other African countries), have performed poorly. The level of output per unit of resource input in countries with numerous government enterprises is low. Similarly, when private firms are compared with government agencies providing the same goods or services (like garbage collection, hospitals, electric and water utilities, weather forecasting, and public transportation), studies indicate that private firms generally provide the services more economically.

6-6 POLITICAL FAVORITISM, CRONY CAPITALISM, AND GOVERNMENT FAILURE

Crony Capitalism
A situation where the institutions of markets are maintained, but the allocation of resources, and the profit and loss of businesses, are determined by political decision-making rather than consumer purchases and market forces. To a large degree, the activities of business firms are directed and controlled by government spending and regulation. In turn, many of the business firms will use contributions and other forms of political support to compete for government favors.

Public-choice analysis indicates that as government spending, subsidies, income transfers, loan guarantees, financial bailouts, targeted tax credits, and regulatory favors grow, businesses and other well-organized groups have a greater incentive to expend resources seeking to obtain the government favors. As a result, crony capitalism tends to expand relative to market allocation. **Crony capitalism** is the situation where the allocation of resources, and winners and losers in business, are determined by political favors rather than by consumer preferences translated through the market profit and loss system. Under crony capitalism, rather than providing equal treatment of individuals and businesses under the law, government uses spending, subsidies, and regulations to favor those most willing to provide political decision-makers with campaign contributions and other forms of political support. In essence, crony capitalism reflects the intermingling of government and business. The politicians use the favoritism to obtain political resources (e.g. contributions, support of organized interest groups) while the businesses use the government favors to enhance their profitability.

Is crony capitalism an emerging problem in the United States? There is reason to believe that it is. As Exhibit 1 shows, federal, state, and local government expenditures now sum to nearly 40 percent of income, up from 32 percent as recently as 2000. Transfers and subsidies accounted for 17.4 percent of national income in 2012, compared to 12.0 percent in 2000 (see Exhibit 3). Social Security and healthcare comprise the bulk of the transfers, but there were more than 2,000 federal subsidy programs in 2010, compared to 1,425 just a decade earlier.

A substantial portion of government spending is driven by what Clemson University economist Bruce Yandle calls the "bootleggers and Baptists" coalition.[6] During the era when many states and counties had bans on the sale of alcoholic beverages, the bootleggers and Baptists both supported the bans, the former because it increased the demand for their product and the latter for moral reasons. Like the bootleggers, opportunistic rent-seekers often frame their programs in a manner designed to attract support from naïve idealists. They argue their programs will enhance child safety, promote energy independence, save family farms, or some other widely supported goal. But when one looks below the surface, you note that the programs provide favoritism that generates handsome profits for the rent-seekers.

Let's consider some examples that illustrate special-interest politics, rent-seeking, and bootlegger–Baptist-type coalitions at work. The Consumer Product Safety Improvement Act of 2008 (CPSIA) and the role played by giant toy manufacturer Mattel in its passage provide an example. The bill imposed new lead testing requirements on manufacturers of products ranging from apparel to home furnishings and toys. Between 1998 and 2007, Mattel had 36 costly recalls, which both damaged its reputation and added to its legal expenses. By 2008, however, it had completed its own product-testing lab. Mattel played a central role in the writing of the CPSIA, and the act permitted Mattel to test its own products because, unsurprisingly, its lab met the specifications of the legislation it helped to formulate. The act also provided Mattel with a sizeable advantage relative to its smaller rivals, who had to submit their products for costly testing at independent laboratories. Equally important, the testing virtually eliminated the secondhand toy and children's clothing market. Clearly, Goodwill and other retailers of used toys and clothing with zippers, buttons, or other accessories with even a touch of paint could not afford to test these products and still make them available at economical prices. Literally, tens of millions of dollars of used toys and clothing were rendered useless and eliminated from the market. This made it possible for Mattel to charge higher prices than would have otherwise been the case. Like many other rent-seekers, Mattel used the bootlegger–Baptist strategy to achieve their goals. They argued that the requirement would protect children from suffering great harm and benefitted from the support of consumer lobby groups. Controversy over these claims helped to divert attention away from the cost that the program was sure to impose on taxpayers and consumers. There was no evidence that

General Electric, the nation's sixth largest corporation derives major benefits from ties to government, while Goodwill suffered greatly from restrictions imposed on the sale of items containing lead that were pushed by toy-maker Mattel.

AP Images/J. Scott Applewhite

Luis Acosta/AFP/Getty Images

[6]See Bruce Yandle, "Bootleggers and Baptists: The Education of a Regulatory Economist," *Regulation* 7, no. 3 (May/June 1983): 12–16; and "Bootleggers and Baptists in Retrospect," *Regulation* 22, no. 3 (1999): 5–7.

even one child had suffered health damage from lead paint on toys or clothing. Nonetheless, Mattel was able to reap huge benefits from the child safety legislation.[7]

General Electric, the nation's sixth-largest corporation, is heavily involved in crony capitalism activities. It derives major benefits from government subsidies for wind farms, wind turbine engines, high-speed rail, solar panels, and tax advantages for export products. Jeffrey Immelt, GE's CEO, is a close friend and major supporter of President Obama. In March of 2011, the president named Immelt chairman of his Council on Jobs and Competitiveness, and before that Immelt was on the President's Economic Recovery Advisory Board. He's a regular companion when President Obama travels abroad to promote American exports. In 2010, GE managed to rack up worldwide profits of $14.2 billion, $5.1 billion from its U.S. operations. Its U.S. corporate income tax bill was zero. In fact, GE received a tax benefit of $3.2 billion. This did not happen by chance. Over the past decade the company has pursued "an aggressive strategy that mixes fierce lobbying for tax breaks and innovative accounting that enables it to concentrate its profits offshore." The GE tax division, including lobbyists, had 975 employees in 2010. The team includes former officials from the Treasury, the IRS and virtually all the tax-writing committees in Congress. Over the last decade, GE has spent tens of millions of dollars pushing for tax savings and subsidies ranging from more generous depreciation schedules on jet engines to "green energy" credits for its wind turbines.[8]

It is interesting to consider the difference in the incentive structure confronted by business firms directed by markets compared to crony capitalists directed by political decision-making. In both cases, pursuit of profit will direct the actions of the firm. Market entrepreneurs have a strong incentive to serve the interests of consumers spending their own money. In order to be successful, market entrepreneurs must produce goods and services that consumers value more than the resources required for their production. When they do so, their actions are productive. In contrast, crony capitalists have a strong incentive to serve the interests of political decision-makers spending someone else's money. Crony capitalists succeed by providing political players with campaign contributions and other political resources in exchange for government contracts, subsidies, tax benefits, and other forms of political favoritism. Their activities will often be counterproductive.

While the cozy relationship between government contractors and political leaders is nothing new, the expanded role of the government provides reason for additional concern. Can political decision-makers really be evenhanded when they derive substantial political support from those benefiting from their spending, regulatory, and tax policies? The answer to this question exerts an impact on not only economic efficiency, but also the legitimacy of the democratic political process.

6-7 THE ECONOMIC WAY OF THINKING ABOUT MARKETS AND GOVERNMENT

When analyzing the operation of markets and government, it is vitally important to keep two points in mind. First, the government's protective role provides the foundation for the smooth operation of markets. A government that protects private property, enforces contracts evenhandedly, maintains monetary stability, and refrains from regulations that restrict entry into markets is central to the efficient operation of markets.

Second, both the market and the political process have shortcomings. In Chapter 5, we focused on the shortcomings of the market and explained why markets sometimes fail to achieve the efficient use of resources. This chapter provides a parallel analysis for the

---

[7]Timothy P. Carney, "Mattel Exempted from Toy Safety Law It Helped Write," *Washington Examiner*, September 4, 2009.

[8]See David Kocieniewski, "G.E.'s Strategies Let It Avoid Taxes Altogether," *New York Times*, March 24, 2011. Data from the Center for Responsive Politics indicate that General Electric spent $160 million on lobbying and political contributions during 2004–2010.

political process. The accompanying **Thumbnail Sketch** lists the major deficiencies of both sectors. It indicates the conditions that underlie both market and government failure.

There is a tendency to idealize democratic governance—to focus on the stated objectives of political officials rather than the actual effects of their policies. Public-choice analysis warns against this naïve view. It focuses on how the political process really works, even if that is not how we might like for it to work. Public-choice analysis also indicates that the presence of government failure will grow as government becomes larger and more intrusive. A larger government will mean more grants, contracts, subsidies, and regulatory favors. This will create more special interest spending, rent seeking, and crony capitalism. Public choice also highlights the importance of institutions, constitutional rules, and procedures that encourage productive political actions and restrain those that are counterproductive. Higher income levels and living standards can be achieved if institutions more consistent with economic progress are adopted. This will be a recurring theme throughout this book.

Thumbnail Sketch
What Weakens the Case for Market-Sector Allocation Versus Public-Sector Intervention, and Vice Versa?

These factors weaken the case for market-sector allocation:

1. lack of competition
2. externalities
3. public goods
4. poor information

These factors weaken the case for public-sector action:

1. the special-interest effect
2. the shortsightedness effect
3. rent-seeking
4. weak incentives for operational efficiency

©iStockphoto.com/baianliang

LOOKING AHEAD

Cases involving potential government intervention will be discussed repeatedly throughout this book. The tools presented in this chapter and the previous one will help us better understand both the potential and the limitations of public policy as a source for economic progress.

KEY POINTS

- In recent years, government spending has increased, and it is now nearly 40 percent of the U.S. economy.

- There are both similarities and differences between market and political allocation. Competition is present in both, but its nature differs between the two sectors. While the government can use its taxing power to break the link between payment and receipt of a good for an individual, it cannot do so for the economy as a whole. In the public sector, voters face a "bundle" purchase problem; they are unable to vote for some policies favored by one candidate and other policies favored by the candidate's opponent. Power and income are unequal in both sectors, but the factors influencing their distribution differ between the two.

- In a representative democracy, government is controlled by voters who elect politicians to set policy and hire bureaucrats to run government agencies. The incentives faced by all three classes of participants influence political outcomes.

- Voters have a strong incentive to support the candidate who offers them the greatest gain relative to their personal costs. Because collective decisions break the link between the choice of the individual and the outcome of the issue, voters are likely to be poorly informed on most political matters.

- Politicians have a strong incentive to follow a strategy that will enhance their chances of getting elected (and reelected). Political competition more or less forces them to focus on how their actions influence their support among voters and potential contributors.

- The distribution of the benefits and costs among voters influences how the political process works. When voters pay in proportion to the benefits they receive from a public-sector project, productive projects tend to be approved and counterproductive ones rejected. When the costs of a policy are distributed among

voters differently than are the benefits, democratic decision-making will tend to be less efficient.

- Government actions will often lead to economic inefficiency as the result of (1) the special-interest effect, (2) the shortsightedness effect, (3) rent-seeking, and (4) weak incentives to keep costs low within government enterprises and agencies. Thus, just as the market sometimes fails to allocate goods efficiently, so, too, will the political process.

- As the size and scope of government grow, public-choice analysis indicates that political activity involving the exchange of government favors for political support will become more widespread. More resources will be channeled into rent-seeking and inefficient government programs, particularly those favored by special interest groups.

CRITICAL ANALYSIS QUESTIONS

1. Are voters likely to be well informed on issues and the positions of candidates? Why or why not?

2. *"The government can afford to take a long view when it needs to, while a private firm has a short-term outlook. Corporate officers, for example, typically care about the next 3 to 6 months, not the next 50 to 100 years. Government, not private firms, should own things like forests, which take decades to develop." Evaluate this view.

3. "If there are problems with markets, government will generally be able to intervene and correct the situation." Is this statement true? Explain your response.

4. *"The political process sometimes leads to economic inefficiency because we elect the wrong people to political office. If the right people were elected, a democracy governed by majority rule would allocate resources efficiently." Evaluate this statement.

5. What is rent-seeking? When is it likely to be widespread? How does it influence economic efficiency? Explain.

6. "The average person is more likely to make a well-informed choice when purchasing a personal computer than when voting for a congressional candidate." Is this statement true? Why or why not?

7. "Government action is based on majority rule, whereas market action is based on mutual consent. The market allows for proportional representation of minorities, but minorities must yield to the views of the majority when activities are undertaken through government." In your own words, explain the meaning of this statement. Is the statement true? Why or why not?

8. *"Voters should simply ignore political candidates who play ball with special-interest groups and vote instead for candidates who will represent all the people when they are elected. Government will work far better when this happens." Evaluate this view.

9. If a project is efficient (its total benefits exceed its total costs), would it be possible to allocate the cost of the project in a manner that would provide net benefits to each voter? Why or why not? Explain. Will efficient projects necessarily be favored by a majority of voters? Explain.

10. *"When an economic function is turned over to the government, social cooperation replaces personal self-interest." Is this statement true? Why or why not?

11. What is the shortsightedness effect? How does it influence the attractiveness of government borrowing? Explain.

12. *"Public policy is necessary to protect the average citizen from the power of vested interest groups. In the absence of government intervention, regulated industries such as airlines, railroads, and trucking will charge excessive prices; products will be unsafe; and the rich will oppress the poor. Government curbs the power of special-interest groups." Evaluate this statement.

13. "Because government-operated firms do not have to make a profit, they can usually produce at a lower cost and charge a lower price than privately owned enterprises." Evaluate this view.

14. If a senator trades his or her vote on an issue for a $10,000 payment, would you consider this corruption? If a senator votes a certain way in "exchange" for a $10,000 contribution to his or her political campaign, would you consider this corruption? Is there a major difference between the two? Discuss.

15. The United States imposes highly restrictive sugar import quotas that result in a domestic price that is generally two or three times the world price. The quotas benefit sugar growers at the expense of consumers. Given that there are far more sugar consumers than growers, why aren't the quotas abolished? Has government action in this area improved the living standards of Americans? Why or why not?

16. The Federal Drug Administration will not approve new pharmaceutical products unless the developer can prove that its product is both safe and effective as a remedy for specified ailments. Do you think the "safe and effective" criterion would be a good one for Congress to adopt for the passage of new legislation? Why or why not? Do you think most government action would meet this criterion? Discuss.

*Asterisk denotes questions for which answers are given in Appendix B.

PART 3

Core Macroeconomics

Growth of output is the key to a higher living standard.

Macroeconomics is about growth of the economy and fluctuations in output, employment, and the general level of prices. Growth of output is extremely important because it makes higher levels of consumption and living standards possible. Fluctuations in output and prices can retard growth and generate economic hardship. What causes economic fluctuations? What can economic policy do to promote more stability? Why do some countries grow and achieve high levels of income while others remain poor? Part 3 will focus on these questions and related issues.

CHAPTER 7
Taking the Nation's Economic Pulse

FOCUS

- **What is GDP? How is GDP measured?**
- **When making comparisons over time, why is it important to adjust nominal GDP for the effects of changes in the price level?**
- **What do price indexes measure? How can they be used to estimate the rate of inflation and adjust for changes in the general level of prices?**
- **Is GDP a good measure of output? What are its strengths and weaknesses?**

It has been said that figures rule the world; maybe. I am quite sure that it is figures which show us whether it is being ruled well or badly. —**Johann Wolfgang Goethe, 1830**

Measurement is the making of distinction; precise measurement is making sharp distinctions. —**Enrico Fermi**[1]

[1]As quoted by Milton Friedman in *Economic Freedom: Toward a Theory of Measurement*, ed. Walter Block (Vancouver, British Columbia, Canada: The Fraser Institute, 1991), 11.

Our society likes to keep score. The sports pages supply us with the win–loss records that reveal how well the various teams are doing. We also keep score on the performance of our economy. The scoreboard for economic performance is the *national-income accounting system*. Just as a firm's accounting statement provides information on its performance, national-income accounts supply performance information for the entire economy.

Simon Kuznets, the winner of the 1971 Nobel Prize in economics, developed the basic concepts of national-income accounting during the 1920s and 1930s (see the Outstanding Economist feature). Through the years, these procedures have been modified and improved. In this chapter, we will explain how the flow of an economy's output (and income) is measured. We will also explain how changes in the quantity of goods and services produced are separated from changes that reflect merely inflation (higher prices). Finally, we will analyze the strengths and weaknesses of the measurement tools used to assess the performance of our national economy.

7-1 GDP—A MEASURE OF OUTPUT

The **gross domestic product (GDP)** is the market value of final goods and services produced within a country during a specific time period, usually a year. GDP is the most widely used measure of economic performance. The GDP figures are closely watched both by policy-makers and by those in the business and financial communities. In the United States, the numbers are prepared quarterly and released a few weeks following the end of each quarter.

GDP is a "flow" concept. By analogy, a water gauge measures the amount of water that flows through a pipe each hour. Similarly, GDP measures the market value of production that "flows" through the economy's factories and shops each year (or quarter).

Gross domestic product (GDP)
The market value of all final goods and services produced within a country during a specific period.

7-1a WHAT COUNTS TOWARD GDP?

First and foremost, GDP is a measure of output. Thus, it cannot be arrived at merely by summing the totals from the nation's cash registers during a period. The key phrases in the definition of GDP—"market value" of "final goods and services" "produced" "within a country" "during a specific time period"—reveal a great deal about what should be included in and excluded from the calculation of GDP. Let's take a closer look at this issue.

Only final goods and services count. If output is to be measured accurately, all goods and services produced during the year must be counted once and only once. Most goods go through several stages of production before they end up in the hands of their ultimate users. To avoid double-counting, one must take care to differentiate between **intermediate goods**—goods in intermediate stages of production—and **final market goods and services**—those purchased for final use rather than for resale or further processing.

Sales at intermediate stages of production are not themselves counted in GDP because the value of the intermediate goods is embodied within the final-user good. Adding the sales price of both the intermediate good and the final-user good would exaggerate GDP. For example, when a wholesale distributor sells steak to a restaurant, the final purchase price paid by the patron of the restaurant for the steak dinner will reflect the cost of the meat. Double-counting would result if we included both the sale price of the intermediate good (the steak sold by the wholesaler to the restaurant) and the final purchase price of the steak dinner.

Intermediate goods
Goods purchased for resale or for use in producing another good or service.

Final market goods and services
Goods and services purchased by their ultimate user.

OUTSTANDING ECONOMIST

Simon Kuznets (1901–1985) Simon Kuznets provided the methodology for modern national-income accounting and developed the first reliable national-income measures for the United States. Kuznets is often referred to as the "father of national-income accounting." A native Russian, he immigrated to the United States at the age of 21 and spent his academic career teaching at the University of Pennsylvania, Johns Hopkins University, and Harvard University.

Exhibit 1 will help clarify the accounting method for GDP. Before the final good, bread, is in the hands of the consumer, it will go through several intermediate stages of production. The farmer produces a pound of wheat and sells it to the miller for 30 cents. The miller grinds the wheat into flour and sells it to the baker for 65 cents. The miller's actions have *added* 35 cents to the value of the wheat. The baker combines the flour with other ingredients, makes a loaf of bread, and sells it to the grocer for 90 cents. The baker has *added* 25 cents to the value of the bread. The grocer stocks the bread on the grocery shelves and provides a convenient location for consumers to shop. The grocer sells the loaf of bread for $1, *adding* 10 cents to the value of the final product. Only the final market value of the product—the $1 for the loaf of bread—is included in GDP. This price reflects the value added at each stage of production. The 30 cents *added* by the farmer, the 35 cents by the miller, the 25 cents by the baker, and the 10 cents by the grocer sum to the $1 purchase price.

Only transactions involving production count. Remember, GDP is a measure of goods and services "produced." Financial transactions and income transfers are excluded because they merely move ownership from one party to another. They do not involve

EXHIBIT 1

GDP and the Stages of Production

Most goods go through several stages of production. This chart illustrates both the market value of a loaf of bread as it passes through the various stages of production (column 1) and the additional value added by each intermediate producer (column 2). GDP counts only the market value of the final product. Of course, the amount added by each intermediate producer (column 2) sums to the market value of the final product.

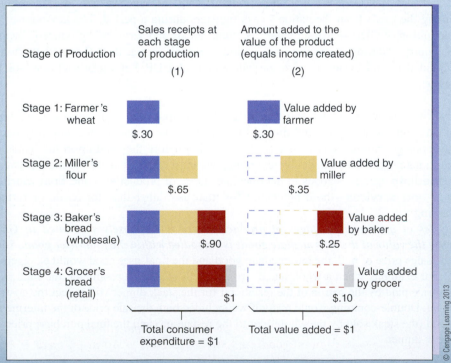

current production and are therefore not included in GDP. (*Note:* If a financial transaction involves a sales commission, the commission is included in GDP because it involves a service rendered during the current period.)

Thus, the purchases and sales of stocks, bonds, and U.S. securities are not included in GDP. Neither are private- and public-sector income transfers. If your aunt sends you $100 to help pay for your college expenses, your aunt has less wealth and you have more, but the transaction adds nothing to current production. Government income transfer payments, such as Social Security, welfare, and veterans payments, are also omitted. The recipients of these transfers are not producing goods in return for the transfers. Therefore, it would be inappropriate to add them to GDP.

Only production within the country is counted. GDP is a measure of "domestic product." Therefore, it counts only goods and services produced within the geographic borders of the country. When foreigners earn income within U.S. borders, it adds to the GDP of the United States. For example, the incomes of Canadian engineers and Mexican baseball players earned in the United States are included in the U.S. GDP. However, the earnings of Americans abroad—for example, an American college professor teaching in England—do not count toward the U.S. GDP because this income is not generated within the borders of the United States.

Only goods produced during the current period are counted. As the definition indicates, GDP is a measure of output "during the current period." Transactions involving the exchange of goods or assets produced during earlier periods are omitted because they do not reflect current production. For example, the purchases of "secondhand" goods, such as a used car or a home built five years ago, are not included in this year's GDP. Production of these goods was counted at the time they were produced and initially purchased. Resale of such items produced during earlier years merely changes the ownership of the goods or assets. It does not add to current production. Thus, these transactions should not be included in current GDP. (*Note:* As in the case of financial transactions, sales commissions earned by those helping to arrange the sale of used cars, homes, or other assets are included in GDP because they reflect services provided during the current period.)

7-1b DOLLARS ARE THE COMMON DENOMINATOR FOR GDP

In elementary school, each of us was taught the difficulties of adding apples and oranges. Yet, this is precisely the nature of aggregate output. Literally millions of different commodities and services are produced each year. How can the production of apples, oranges, shoes, movies, roast beef sandwiches, automobiles, dresses, legal services, education, heart transplants, haircuts, and many other items be added together? Answer: The "market value" of each is added to GDP.

The vastly different goods and services produced in our modern world have only one thing in common: Someone pays a price for them. Therefore, when measuring output, units of each good are weighted according to their market value—the purchase price of the good or service. If a consumer pays $25,000 for a new automobile and $25 for a nice meal, production of the automobile adds 1,000 times as much to output as production of the meal. Similarly, production of a television set that is purchased for $1,000 will add 1/25 as much to output as the new automobile and 40 times the amount of the meal.

Each good produced increases output by the amount the purchaser pays for the good. The total spending on all goods and services produced during the year is then summed, in dollar terms, to obtain the annual GDP.

7-2 GDP AS A MEASURE OF BOTH OUTPUT AND INCOME

There are two ways of looking at and measuring GDP. First, *the GDP of an economy can be reached by totaling the expenditures on goods and services produced during the year.* National-income accountants refer to this method as the *expenditure approach.* Alternatively, *GDP can be calculated by summing the income payments to the resource suppliers of the things used to produce those goods and services.* Production of goods and services is costly because the resources required for their production must be bid away from their alternative uses. These costs generate incomes for resource suppliers. Thus, this method of calculating GDP is referred to as the *resource cost–income approach.*

The prices used to weight the goods and services included in GDP reflect both the market value of the output and the income generated by the resources. From an accounting viewpoint, when a good is produced and sold, the total payments to the factors of production (including the producer's profit or loss) must be equal to the sales price generated by the good.[2] For example, consider a beauty salon operator who leases a building and equipment, purchases various cosmetic products, and combines these items with labor to provide hairdressing services for which customers pay $500 per day. The market value of the output, $500 per day, is added to GDP. The $500 figure is also equal to the income resource owners receive from the provision of the service.

The link between the market value of a good and the income (including the profit or loss) earned by resource suppliers occurs for each good or service produced. This same link is also present in the aggregate economy. In accounting terms, the idea can be illustrated as follows:

The dollar flow of expenditures on final goods = The dollar flow of income (and indirect cost) from final goods

GDP is a measure of the value of the goods and services that were purchased by households, investors, governments, and foreigners. These purchasers valued the goods and services more than the purchase price; otherwise they would not have purchased them. GDP is also a measure of aggregate income. Production of the goods involves human toil, wear and tear on machines, use of natural resources, risk, managerial responsibilities, and other of life's unpleasantries. Resource owners have to be compensated with income payments in order to induce them to supply these resources.

Thus, GDP is a measure of both (1) the market value of the output produced and (2) the income generated by those who produced the output. This highlights a very important point: Increases in output and growth of income are linked. An expansion in output—that is, the additional production of goods and services that people value—is the source of higher income levels.

Exhibit 2 summarizes the components of GDP for both the expenditure and resource cost–income approaches. Except for a few complicating elements that we will discuss in a moment, the revenues business firms derive from the sale of goods and services are paid directly to resource suppliers in the form of wages, self-employment income, rents, profits, and interest. We now turn to an examination of these components and the two alternative ways of deriving GDP.

7-2a DERIVING GDP BY THE EXPENDITURE APPROACH

When derived by the expenditure approach, GDP has four components: (1) personal consumption expenditures, (2) gross private domestic investment, (3) government consumption and gross investment, and (4) net exports to foreigners. The left side of **Exhibit 3** presents the values of these four components in 2012. Later, we will discuss the right side, which deals with the resource cost–income approach.

---

[2]In the national-income accounts, the terms profit and corporate profit are used in the accounting sense. Thus, they reflect both the competitive rate of return on assets (opportunity cost of capital) and the firm's economic profit and loss, which were discussed in Chapter 3.

EXHIBIT 2

Two Ways of Measuring GDP

EXPENDITURE APPROACH	RESOURCE COST–INCOME APPROACH
Personal consumption expenditures	Aggregate income
+	Compensation of employees (wages and salaries)
Gross private domestic investment	Income of self-employed proprietors
+	Rents
Government consumption and gross investment	Profits
+	Interest
Net exports of goods and services	+
=	Nonincome cost items
GDP	Indirect business taxes
	Depreciation
	+
	Net income of foreigners
	=
	GDP

© Cengage Learning 2013

There are two methods of calculating GDP. It can be calculated either by summing the expenditures on the "final-user" goods and services purchased by consumers, investors, governments, and foreigners (net exports) or by summing the income payments and direct cost items that accompany the production of goods and services.

EXHIBIT 3

Two Ways of Measuring GDP— 2012 Data (billions of dollars)

EXPENDITURE APPROACH		RESOURCE COST–INCOME APPROACH	
Personal Consumption	$11,120	Employee Compensation	$8,566
Durable goods	$1,219	Proprietors' Income	$1,202
Nondurable goods	$2,564	Rents	$463
Services	$7,337	Corporate Profits	$1,951
Gross Private Investment	$2,062	Interest Income	$504
Fixed Investment	$2,004	Indirect Business Taxes	$1,163
Inventories	$58	Depreciation (Capital Consumption)[a]	$2,079
Gov. Cons. and Gross Inv.	$3,063	Net Income of Foreigners	−$243
Federal	$1,214		
State and local	$1,849		
Net Exports	−$560		
Gross Domestic Product	$15,685	Gross Domestic Product	$15,685

[a]Includes $1,648 billion for the depreciation of privately owned capital, $364 billion for the depreciation of government-owned assets, and plus $67 billion for statistical discrepancy.

Source: U.S. Department of Commerce. These data are also online at http://www.bea.gov.

The left side shows the flow of expenditures and the right side the flow of income payments and indirect costs. Both procedures yield GDP.

Consumption purchases. **Personal consumption** purchases are the largest component of GDP; in 2012, they amounted to $11,120 billion. Most consumption expenditures are for nondurable goods or services. Food, clothing, recreation, medical and legal services, and fuel are included in this category. These items are used up or consumed in a relatively short time. Durable goods, such as appliances and automobiles, constitute approximately one-tenth of all consumer purchases. These products are consumed over a longer period of time, even though they are fully counted when they are purchased.

Gross private investment. The next item in the expenditure approach, **private investment**, is the production or construction of capital goods that provide a "flow" of future service. Unlike food or medical services, they are not immediately "used." Business plants and equipment are investment goods because they will help produce goods and services in the future. Similarly, a house is an investment good because it will also provide a stream of services long into the future. Increases in business inventories are also classified as investment because they will provide future consumer benefits.

Personal consumption
Household spending on consumer goods and services during the current period. Consumption is a flow concept.

Private investment
The flow of private-sector expenditures on durable assets (fixed investment) plus the addition to inventories (inventory investment) during a period. These expenditures enhance our ability to provide consumer benefits in the future.

Depreciation
The estimated amount of physical capital (for example, machines and buildings) that is worn out or used up producing goods during a period.

Gross investment includes expenditures for both (1) the replacement of machinery, equipment, and buildings worn out during the year and (2) net additions to the stock of capital assets. Net investment is simply gross investment minus an allowance for **depreciation** and obsolescence of machinery and other physical assets during the year.

Net investment is an important indicator of the economy's future productive capability. A substantial amount of net investment indicates that the capital stock of the economy is growing, thereby enhancing the economy's future productive potential (shifting the economy's production possibilities frontier outward). In contrast, a low rate of net investment, or even worse, a negative net investment, implies a stagnating or even contracting economy. Of course, the impact of investment on future income will also be affected by the productivity of investment—whether the funds invested are channeled into wealth-creating projects. Other things being the same, however, countries with a large net investment rate will tend to grow more rapidly than those with a low (or negative) rate of net investment. In 2012, gross private investment expenditures in the United States were $2,062 billion, 13.0 percent of GDP. Of course, a large portion ($1,648 billion) of this figure was for the replacement of private assets worn out during the year. Thus, net private investment was $414 billion, only 2.6 percent of GDP.

Inventory investment
Changes in the stock of unsold goods and raw materials held during a period.

Because GDP is designed to measure current production, allowance must be made for goods produced but not sold during the year—that is, for **inventory investment**, or changes during the year in the market value of unsold goods on shelves and in warehouses. If business firms have more goods on hand at the end of the year than they had at the beginning of the year, inventory investment will be positive. This inventory investment must be added to GDP. Conversely, a decline in inventories would indicate that the purchases of goods and services exceeded current production. In this case, inventory *disinvestment* would be a subtraction from GDP. In 2012, the United States invested $67 billion in additional inventories.

Government consumption and gross investment. In 2012, federal, state, and local government consumption and investment in the United States summed to $3,063 billion, approximately 20 percent of total GDP. The purchases of state and local governments exceeded those of the federal government by a wide margin. The government component includes both (1) expenditures on items like office supplies, law enforcement, and the operation of veterans hospitals, which are "consumed" during the current period, and (2) the purchase of long-lasting capital goods, like missiles, highways, and dams for flood control. (Remember, transfer payments are excluded from GDP because they do not involve current production.) As a result, the government's total expenditures are substantially higher than its total consumption and investment expenditures. Unlike the other components of GDP, government purchases are counted at their *cost* to taxpayers rather than their *value* to those receiving them. In cases in which the value of the item to citizens is low relative to the tax cost of providing it, the government expenditures will overstate the value derived from the item.

Net exports
Exports minus imports.

Exports
Goods and services produced domestically but sold to foreigners.

Imports
Goods and services produced by foreigners but purchased by domestic consumers, businesses, and governments.

Net exports. The final item in the expenditure approach is **net exports**, or total exports minus imports. **Exports** are domestically produced goods and services sold to foreigners. **Imports** are foreign-produced goods and services purchased domestically. Remember, GDP is a measure of domestic production—output produced within the borders of a nation. Therefore, when measuring GDP by the expenditure approach, we must (1) add exports (goods produced domestically that were sold to foreigners) and (2) subtract imports (goods produced abroad that were purchased by Americans). For national-income accounting purposes, we can combine these two factors into a single entry:

$$\text{Net exports} = \text{Total exports} - \text{Total imports}$$

Net exports may be either positive or negative. When we sell more to foreigners than we buy from them, net exports are positive. In recent years, however, net exports have been negative, indicating that we were buying more goods and services from foreigners than we were selling to them. In 2012, net exports were *minus* $560 billion.

These four major components—personal consumption, gross private investment, government consumption and investment, and net exports—sum to GDP. In 2012, this figure was equal to $15,685 billion.

7-2b DERIVING GDP BY THE RESOURCE COST–INCOME APPROACH

The right side of Exhibit 3 illustrates how, rather than summing the flow of expenditures on final goods and services, we could reach GDP by summing the flow of costs incurred and income generated. Labor services play a very important role in the production process. It is therefore not surprising that employee compensation, $8,566 billion in 2012, provides the largest source of income generated by the production of goods and services.

Self-employed proprietors undertake the risks of owning their own business and simultaneously provide their own labor services to their firm. Their earnings in 2012 contributed $1,202 billion to GDP, 7.7 percent of the total. Together, employees and self-employed proprietors accounted for approximately three-fifths of GDP.

Machines, buildings, land, and other physical assets also contribute to the production process. Rents, corporate profits, and interest are payments to people who provide either the physical resources or the financial resources required for the purchase of physical assets. Rents are returns to resource owners who permit others to use their assets during a time period. Corporate profits are earned by stockholders, who bear the risk of the business undertaking and provide the financial capital the firm needs to purchase resources. Interest is a payment to parties who extend loans to producers.

Not all cost components of GDP result in an income payment to a resource supplier. In order to get to GDP, we also need to account for three other factors: indirect business taxes, the cost of depreciation, and the net income of foreigners.

Indirect business taxes. Taxes imposed on the sale of a good that increase the cost of the good to consumers are called **indirect business taxes**. The sales tax is a clear example. When you make a $1.00 purchase in a state with a 5 percent sales tax, the purchase actually costs you $1.05. The $1.00 goes to the seller to pay wages, rent, interest, and managerial costs. The 5 cents goes to the government. Indirect business taxes boost the market price of goods when GDP is calculated by the expenditure approach. Similarly, when looked at from the factor-cost viewpoint, taxes are an indirect cost of supplying the goods to the final consumers.

Depreciation. As machines are used to produce goods, they wear out and become less valuable. Even though this decline in the value of capital assets is a cost of producing goods during the current period, it does not involve a direct payment to a resource owner. Thus, it must be estimated. Depreciation is an estimate, based on the expected life of the asset, of the decline in the asset's value during the year. In 2012, depreciation (sometimes called *capital consumption allowance*) of private- and public-sector capital amounted to $2,079 billion, approximately 13.3 percent of GDP.

Net income of foreigners. The sum of employee compensation, proprietors' income, rents, corporate profits, and interest yields **national income**, the income of Americans, whether earned domestically or abroad. If depreciation and indirect business taxes—the two indirect cost components—are added to national income, the result will be **gross national product (GNP)**, the output of Americans, whether generated in the United States or abroad. Put another way, GNP counts the income that Americans earn abroad, but it omits the income foreigners earn in the United States.

Indirect business taxes
Taxes that increase a business firm's costs of production and, therefore, the prices charged to consumers. Examples are sales, excise, and property taxes.

National income
The total income earned by a country's nationals (citizens) during a period. It is the sum of employee compensation, self-employment income, rents, interest, and corporate profits.

Gross national product (GNP)
The total market value of all final goods and services produced by the citizens of a country. It is equal to GDP minus the net income of foreigners.

Net income of foreigners
The income that foreigners earn by contributing labor and capital resources to the production of goods within the borders of a country minus the income the nationals of the country earn abroad.

Because GDP is a measure of domestic output, the net income earned by foreigners must be added when GDP is derived using the resource cost-income approach. The **net income of foreigners** is equal to the income foreigners earn in the United States minus the income that Americans earn abroad. If Americans earn more abroad than foreigners earn in the United States, the net income of foreigners will be negative. In recent years, this has been the case. The net income of foreigners is generally small. In 2012, it was *minus* $243 billion, less than 2 percent of GDP. As Exhibit 3 indicates, when this figure is added to the other components, GDP derived by the resource cost method summed to $15,685 billion in 2012, the same figure as for the expenditure approach.

7-2c THE RELATIVE SIZE OF GDP COMPONENTS

Exhibit 4 shows the relative size of each of the GDP components during 2009–2012. When the expenditure approach is used, personal consumption is by far the largest component of GDP. Consumption accounted for 71 percent of GDP during 2009–2012, compared with only 14 and 20 percent for private investment and government purchases, respectively. When GDP is measured using the resource cost–income approach, compensation to employees is the dominant component (55 percent of GDP). During 2009–2012, corporate profits and interest combined accounted for 15 percent of GDP.

EXHIBIT 4

The Major Components of GDP in the United States, 2009–2012

The relative sizes of the major components of GDP usually fluctuate within a fairly narrow range. The average proportion of each component during 2009–2012 is demonstrated here for both (a) the expenditure and (b) the resource cost–income approaches.

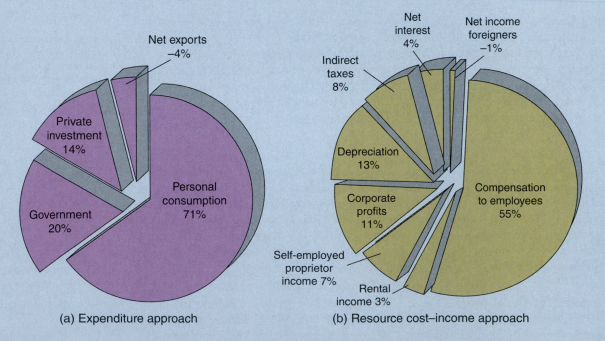

(a) Expenditure approach

(b) Resource cost–income approach

Numbers may not add up to 100 percent due to rounding.

Source: http://www.economagic.com.

7-3 ADJUSTING FOR PRICE CHANGES AND DERIVING REAL GDP

GDP was developed to help us better assess what is happening to output (and income) over time. This is important because expansion in the production of goods and services people value is the source of higher incomes and living standards. When comparing GDP across time periods, however, we confront a problem; the nominal value of GDP may increase as the result of either (1) an expansion in the quantity of goods produced or (2) higher prices. Because only the former will improve our living standards, it is very important to distinguish between the two.

When tracking the path of GDP and other income measures across time periods, economists use price indexes to adjust **nominal values** (or *money values*, as they are often called) for the effects of inflation—an increase in the general level of prices over time. When the term **real** accompanies GDP and income data (for example, *real GDP* or *real wages*), this means that the data have been adjusted for changes in the general level of prices through time. When comparing data at different points in time, it is nearly always the real changes that are of most interest.

What precisely is a price index, and how can it be used to adjust GDP and other figures for the effects of inflation? A price index measures the cost of purchasing a market basket (or "bundle") of goods at a point in time relative to the cost of purchasing the identical market basket during an earlier reference period. A base year (or period) is chosen and assigned a value of 100. As prices increase and the cost of purchasing the reference bundle of goods rises relative to the base year, the price index increases proportionally. Thus, a price index of 110 indicates that the general level of prices is 10 percent higher than during the base period. An index of 120 implies prices that are 20 percent higher than the base period, and so on. *Note:* See the Addendum at the end of this chapter for additional details on how price indexes are constructed.

Nominal values
Values expressed in current dollars.

Real values
Values that have been adjusted for the effects of inflation.

7-3a KEY PRICE INDEXES: THE CONSUMER PRICE INDEX AND THE GDP DEFLATOR

Price indexes indicate what is happening to the general level of prices. The most widely used are the consumer price index (CPI) and the GDP deflator. Because the construction of the CPI is simpler, we will begin with it.

The **consumer price index (CPI)** *is designed to measure the impact of price changes on the cost of the typical bundle of goods purchased by households.* A bundle of 211 items that constitute the "typical bundle" purchased by urban consumers during the 1982–1984 base period provides the foundation for the CPI. The quantity of each good reflects the quantity actually purchased by the typical household during the base period. Every month, the Bureau of Labor Statistics surveys approximately 26,400 stores representative of the urban United States to derive the average price for each of the food items, consumer goods and services, housing, and property taxes included in the index. The cost of purchasing this 211-item market basket at current prices is then compared with the cost of purchasing the same market basket at base-year prices. The result is a measure of current prices compared with 1982–1984 base-period prices. In 2012, the value of the CPI was 229.6 compared with 100 during the 1982–1984 base period. This indicates that the price level in 2012 was 129.6 percent higher than the price level of 1982–1984.

There is a major deficiency of the CPI for urban households: It makes no allowance for the tendency of households to substitute away from goods and services as they become relatively more expensive. For example, if the price of beef rises, then consumers will substitute toward pork, chicken, and other meat products that are now relatively less expensive. The CPI does not account for this spending shift because it maintains the quantities of the typical bundle constant over lengthy time frames. As a result, most economists believe that the regular CPI overstates the impact of the increase in the general level of prices.

Consumer price index (CPI)
An indicator of the general level of prices. It attempts to compare the cost of purchasing the market basket bought by a typical consumer during a specific period with the cost of purchasing the same market basket during an earlier period.

Chained consumer price index

A measure of the consumer price index that accounts for changes in the market basket of goods bought on a monthly basis rather than on a lagged basis as done with the traditional consumer price index. This change typically reduces the annual inflation rate by 0.2 to 0.3 percentage points.

GDP deflator

A price index that reveals the cost during the current period of purchasing the items included in GDP relative to the cost during a base year (currently 2005). Unlike the consumer price index (CPI), the GDP deflator also measures the prices of capital goods and other goods and services purchased by businesses and governments.

Inflation

An increase in the general level of prices of goods and services. The purchasing power of the monetary unit, such as the dollar, declines when inflation is present.

To adjust for this shortcoming, the Bureau of Labor Statistics also calculates an alternative version: the **chained consumer price index**. The chained CPI adjusts the quantities of the typical market basket each month to reflect the impact of the shifts away from the goods that have become relatively more expensive. As a result, the chained CPI is widely believed to provide a more accurate measure of changes in the general level of prices.

***The GDP deflator** is a broader price index than either of the CPI measures. It is designed to measure the change in the average price of the market basket of goods included in GDP.* In addition to consumer goods, the GDP deflator includes prices for capital goods and other goods and services purchased by businesses and governments. Therefore, in addition to consumer goods, the bundle used to construct the GDP deflator will include such items as large computers, airplanes, welding equipment, and office space. The overall bundle is intended to be representative of those items included in GDP. As in the case of the CPI, a base year (currently the year 2005) is chosen for the GDP deflator and assigned a value of 100. Values of the GDP deflator above 100 indicate that the general level of prices is higher than during the base period.

In the construction of the GDP deflator, the cost of purchasing the typical bundle of goods included in this year's GDP is always compared with the cost of purchasing that same bundle at last year's prices. Each year's percentage change in prices, based on the updated bundle, is then used to chain together the index. Like the chained CPI, the bundle of goods included in the GDP deflator is updated regularly to reflect the substitution away from goods that have become relatively more expensive. Because of this constant updating of the typical bundle, the GDP deflator is thought to yield a slightly more accurate measure of changes in the general level of prices than the regular CPI.

The annual inflation rate is simply the percentage change from one year to the next in the general level of prices. Both the CPI and the GDP deflator can be used to estimate the rate of **inflation**. When using either price index (PI),

$$\text{Inflation rate} = \frac{\text{This year's PI} - \text{Last year's PI}}{\text{Last year's PI}} \times 100$$

If the price index this year was 220, compared with 200 last year, for example, the inflation rate would equal 10 percent:

$$\frac{220 - 200}{200} \times 100 = 10$$

Exhibit 5 presents data during 2000–2012 for the CPI, chained CPI, and GDP deflator and uses each to estimate the annual rate of inflation. All three indexes were set at 100.0 in 2000 to facilitate comparability. The actual base period for each of the three indexes is 1982–1984 for the consumer price index, December 1999 for the chained CPI, and 2005 for the GDP deflator. Even though the three price indexes are based on different market baskets and procedures, their estimates for the annual rate of inflation are similar.

However, because of their more frequent updating of the typical market bundle and adjustment for the substitution away from goods with higher relative prices, the chained CPI and GDP deflator generally indicate that the annual rate of inflation is between 0.2 and 0.3 percentage points lower than the regular CPI. Over a more lengthy time frame, these relatively small annual differences add up. As Exhibit 5 indicates, between 2000 and 2012 the chained CPI and the GDP deflator price indexes rose to 129.2 and 130.1, respectively. But the regular CPI rose by a larger amount to 133.3 during this 12-year period. Despite different market baskets and procedures, their estimates for the annual rate of inflation are similar. The difference between the two alternative measures is usually only a few tenths of a percentage point.

The CPI and GDP deflator were designed for different purposes. Choosing between the two depends on what we are trying to measure. If we want to determine how rising prices affect the money income of consumers, the CPI would be most appropriate because it includes only consumer goods. However, if we want an economy-wide measure of inflation with which to adjust GDP data, the GDP deflator is clearly the appropriate index because it includes a broader set of goods and services.

EXHIBIT 5

The Consumer Price Index and GDP Deflator: 2000–2012

Year	CPI Index	CPI Inflation Rate (%)	Chained CPI Index	Chained CPI Inflation Rate (%)	GDP Deflator Index	GDP Deflator Inflation Rate (%)
2000	100.0	–	100.0		100.0	
2001	102.8	2.8	102.3	2.3	102.3	2.3
2002	104.5	1.6	103.5	1.2	103.9	1.6
2003	106.9	2.3	105.7	2.1	106.1	2.1
2004	109.7	2.7	108.3	2.5	109.1	2.8
2005	113.4	3.4	111.5	2.9	112.7	3.3
2006	117.1	3.2	114.7	2.9	116.4	3.2
2007	120.4	2.8	117.6	2.5	119.7	2.9
2008	125.0	3.8	122.0	3.7	122.4	2.2
2009	124.6	−0.4	121.4	−0.5	123.5	0.9
2010	126.6	1.6	123.2	1.4	125.1	1.3
2011	130.6	3.2	126.9	3.1	127.8	2.1
2012	133.3	2.1	129.2	1.8	130.1	1.8

Each of the three indexes were set at 100.0 in 2000 in order to facilitate comparability. The actual base period for each of the three indexes is 1982–1984 for the consumer price index, December 1999 for the chained CPI, and 2005 for the GDP deflator. As we indicate in the text, a value of 100 is assigned to each of the indexes during the base year.

7-3b USING THE GDP DEFLATOR TO DERIVE REAL GDP

We can use the GDP deflator together with **nominal GDP** to measure **real GDP**, which is GDP in dollars of constant purchasing power. If prices are rising, we simply deflate the nominal GDP during the latter period to account for the effects of inflation.

Exhibit 6 illustrates how real GDP is measured and why it is important to adjust for price changes. Between 2005 and 2012, the nominal GDP of the United States increased from $12,623 billion to $15,685 billion, an increase of 24.3 percent. However, a large portion of this increase in nominal GDP reflected inflation rather than an increase in real output. When making GDP comparisons across time periods, we generally do so in terms of

Nominal GDP
GDP expressed at current prices. It is often called money GDP.

Real GDP
GDP adjusted for changes in the price level.

EXHIBIT 6

	Nominal GDP (billions of dollars)	Price Index (GDP deflator, 2005 = 100)	Real GDP (billions of 2005 dollars)
2005	$12,623	100.0	$12,623
2012	15,685	115.4	13,592
Percentage Increase	24.3	15.4	7.7

Source: http://www.economagic.com.

Changes in Prices and Real GDP in the United States, 2005–2012

Between 2005 and 2012, nominal GDP increased by 24.3 percent. But when the 2012 GDP is deflated to account for price increases, we see that real GDP increased by only 7.7 percent.

the purchasing power of the dollar during the base year of the GDP deflator, currently 2005. The GDP deflator, the price index that measures changes in the cost of all goods included in GDP, increased from 100.0 in 2005 to 115.4 in 2012. This indicates that prices rose by 15.4 percent between 2005 and 2012. To determine the real GDP for 2012 in terms of 2005 dollars, we deflate the 2012 nominal GDP for the rise in prices:

$$\text{Real GDP}_{2012} = \text{Nominal GDP}_{2012} \times \frac{\text{GDP Deflator}_{2005}}{\text{GDP Deflator}_{2012}}$$

Because prices were rising, the latter ratio is less than 1. Measured in terms of 2005 dollars, the real GDP in 2012 was $13,592 billion, only 7.7 percent more than in 2005. So although money GDP (nominal GDP) expanded by 24.3 percent, real GDP increased by only 7.7 percent.

Data on both money GDP and price changes are essential for meaningful output comparisons between two time periods. By itself, a change in money GDP tells us nothing about what is happening to the rate of real production. For example, not even a doubling of money GDP would lead to an increase in real output if prices more than doubled during the time period. On the other hand, money income could remain constant while real GDP increased if there were a reduction in prices. Knowledge of both nominal GDP and the general level of prices is required for real income comparisons over time.

APPLICATIONS IN ECONOMICS

Converting Prior Data to Current Dollars: The Case of Gasoline

We have explained how the GDP deflator can be used to convert nominal GDP data to real GDP (measured in terms of the dollar's purchasing power during the base year of the GDP deflator). Sometimes, however, it makes more sense to convert income or other data during prior years to the purchasing power of the dollar during the current year. A price index can also be used to accomplish this task. To convert an earlier observation to current dollars, just multiply the observation by the price index during the current period and then divide it by the price index during the earlier period. If prices have risen in recent years, this will "inflate" the data for the earlier year and thereby bring them into line with the current purchasing power of the dollar.

Let's illustrate this point and at the same time analyze the changes in gasoline prices during the last several decades.

As gas prices rose sharply during 2007, the media reported that they had risen to an all-time high in the United States. In nominal terms, this was indeed the case, but what about the real price of gasoline?

The accompanying table presents data for the nominal price (column 1) of a gallon of unleaded regular gasoline for various years since 1973. The parallel data for the consumer price index (CPI) are presented in column 2. The nominal price of gasoline in 1973 was 39 cents. To convert this figure to the purchasing power of the dollar in February 2013, multiply the 39 cents by the ratio of the CPI in February 2013 divided by the CPI in 1973. This real price (shown in column 3), measured in terms of the 2013 price level, is equal to $2.04 (0.39 times the ratio of 232.2/44.4).

(Continued)

Both crude oil prices and gasoline prices rose sharply throughout the 1970s. By 1980, the nominal price of gasoline had risen to $1.25. This would make the real price of gasoline measured in 2013 dollars equal to $3.52 ($1.25 times the ratio of 232.2/82.4), almost has high as the price in 2013. What was the real price of gasoline in 1976, 1985, 1990, 1995, and 2005? As an exercise, derive these figures to make sure that you understand how to convert data from an earlier time period into the purchasing power of the dollar during the current year

Price of a Gallon of Regular Unleaded Gasoline

YEAR	NOMINAL PRICE (1)	CPI (1982–1984 = 100) (2)	REAL PRICE (3)
1973	$0.39	44.4	$2.04
1976	0.61	56.9	?
1980	1.25	82.4	3.52
1985	1.20	107.6	?
1990	1.16	130.7	?
1995	1.15	152.4	?
2000	1.51	172.2	2.04
2005	2.30	195.3	?
2010	2.79	218.1	2.97
2013 (February)	3.69	232.2	3.69

Source: U.S. Energy Information Administration, *Monthly Energy Review*. The data for regular unleaded gasoline were unavailable prior to 1976. Thus, the 1973 observation is for regular leaded gasoline, which was slightly cheaper during that period.

7-4 PROBLEMS WITH GDP AS A MEASURING ROD

Even real GDP is an imperfect measure of current output and income. Some productive activities are omitted because their value is difficult to determine. The introduction of new products complicates the use of GDP as a measuring rod. Also, when production involves harmful side effects that are not fully registered in the market prices, GDP will fail to measure the level of output accurately. Let's take a closer look at some of the limitations of GDP.

7-4a NONMARKET PRODUCTION

GDP does not count household production because it does not involve a market transaction. As a result, the household services of millions of people are excluded. If you mow the yard, repair your car, paint your house, pick up relatives from school, or perform similar productive household activities, your efforts add nothing to GDP because no market transaction is involved. Such nonmarket productive activities are sizable—10 percent to 15 percent of total GDP.

Excluding household production results in some oddities in national-income accounting. Suppose, for example, that a woman marries her gardener, and, after the marriage, the spouse-gardener works for love rather than for money. GDP will decline because the services of the spouse-gardener no longer involve a market transaction and therefore no longer contribute to GDP. In contrast, if a family member decides to enter the labor force and hires someone to perform services previously provided by household members, there will be a double-barreled impact on GDP. It will rise as a result of (1) the market earnings of the new labor-force entrant plus (2) the amount paid to the person hired to perform the services that were previously supplied within the household.

Most important, omitting household production makes income comparisons across lengthy time periods less meaningful. Compared with the situation today, 50 years ago Americans were far more likely to produce sizable amounts of their own food and clothing.

Only a small proportion of married women worked, and child care services were almost exclusively provided within the household. Today, people are also more likely to eat out at a restaurant than prepare their own food; hire a lawn service than mow their own lawn; and purchase an automatic dishwasher than do the dishes by hand. These and many other similar changes involve the substitution of a market transaction, which adds to GDP. Because the share of total production provided within the household has declined relative to production that involves market transactions, current GDP, even in real dollars, is overstated relative to the earlier period. Correspondingly, this factor causes an upward bias to the growth rate of real GDP.

7-4b UNDERGROUND ECONOMY

Underground economy
Unreported barter and cash transactions that take place outside recorded market channels. Some are otherwise legal activities undertaken to evade taxes. Others involve illegal activities, such as trafficking drugs and prostitution.

Some people attempt to conceal various economic activities in order to evade taxes or because the activities themselves are illegal. Economists call these activities, which are unreported and therefore difficult to measure, the **underground economy**.

Because cash transactions are hard for government authorities to trace, they are the lifeblood of the underground economy. This is why drug trafficking, smuggling, prostitution, and other illegal activities are generally conducted in cash. Not all underground economic activity is illegal. A large portion of the underground economy involves legal goods and services that go unreported so that people can try to evade taxes. The participants in this legal-if-reported portion of the underground economy are quite diverse. Taxicab drivers and wait staff may pocket fees and tips. Small-business owners may fail to ring up and report various cash sales. Craft and professional workers may fail to report cash income. Employees ranging from laborers to bartenders may work "off the books" and accept payment in cash in order to qualify for income-transfer benefits or evade taxes (or allow their employers to evade taxes).

Even though they are often productive, these unreported underground activities are not included in GDP. Estimates of the size of the underground economy in the United States range from 10 percent to 15 percent of total output. The available evidence indicates that the size of the underground economy is even larger in Western Europe (where tax rates are higher) and South America (where regulations often make it more costly to operate a business legally).

7-4c LEISURE AND HUMAN COSTS

GDP excludes leisure and the human cost associated with the production of goods and services. Only output matters; no allowance is made for how long or how hard people work to generate it. Simon Kuznets, the "inventor" of GDP, believed that these omissions substantially reduced the accuracy of GDP as a measure of economic well-being.

The average number of hours worked per week in the United States has declined through the years. The average nonagricultural production worker spent only 33.7 hours per week on the job in 2012, compared with more than 40 hours in 1947—a 15 percent reduction in weekly hours worked. Clearly, this reduction in the length of the workweek raised the American standard of living, even though it did not enhance GDP.

GDP also fails to take into account human costs. On average, jobs today are less physically strenuous and are generally performed in a safer, more comfortable environment than they were a generation ago.[3] To the extent that working conditions have improved through the years, GDP figures understate the growth of real income.

7-4d QUALITY VARIATION AND THE INTRODUCTION OF NEW GOODS

If GDP is going to measure accurately changes in real output, changes in the price level must be measured accurately. This is a difficult task in a dynamic world where new and improved products are constantly replacing old ones. Think about how much more functional

---

[3]For evidence on this point, see "Have a Nice Day," *2001 Annual Report, Federal Reserve Bank of Dallas* (available online at http://www.dallasfed.org).

today's computers are compared with yesterday's typewriters, for example. Even after adjusting for inflation, today's personal computer probably costs more than the typewriter of 1980. But there is also a huge difference between the quality of the two products. Thus, a portion of the higher price of improved products like computers is due to quality improvements rather than pure inflation. Although statisticians attempt to make some allowance for quality improvements and new products, they are generally thought to be inadequate. Most economists believe that price indexes, including the GDP deflator, overestimate the rate of inflation by approximately 1 percent *annually* because quality improvements aren't accounted for accurately. If so, annual changes in output are underestimated by a similar amount. Although 1 percent per year might seem small, errors of this size make a huge difference over long time periods.

7-4e HARMFUL SIDE EFFECTS AND ECONOMIC "BADS"

GDP makes no adjustment for harmful side effects that sometimes arise from production, consumption, and the destructive acts of man and nature. If they do not involve market transactions, economic "bads" are ignored in the calculation of GDP. Yet, in a modern industrial economy, production and consumption sometimes generate side effects that either detract from current consumption or reduce our future production possibilities. When property rights are defined imperfectly, air and water pollution are sometimes side effects of economic activity. For example, an industrial plant may pollute the air or water while producing goods. Automobiles may put harmful chemicals into the atmosphere while providing us with transportation. GDP makes no allowance for these negative side effects. In fact, expenditures on the cleanup of air and water pollution, should they be undertaken, will add to GDP.

Similarly, GDP makes no allowance for various acts of destruction. Consider the impact of the September 11, 2001, terrorist attacks. In addition to roughly 3,000 fatalities, property losses were estimated at approximately $20 billion, including the destruction of the World Trade Center, portions of the Pentagon, and the four commercial planes hijacked. But GDP makes no allowance for these losses. Therefore, none of this destruction influenced GDP. In fact, the cleanup cost, which continued for months, actually added to GDP. Of course, GDP was indirectly adversely affected by the attacks: some people and businesses weren't able to function for some time afterward, if ever. Air travel and tourism spending fell. Other responses to the attacks, like the increase in expenditures on security, national defense, and the reconstruction of the Pentagon, enhanced GDP. But the GDP numbers did not reflect the loss of property or life. The same is true for destruction accompanying hurricanes, earthquakes, and other acts of nature. Even if billions of dollars of assets are destroyed, there will be no adjustment made to the GDP numbers.

7-5 DIFFERENCES IN GDP OVER TIME

Per capita GDP is simply GDP divided by population. It is a measure of income per person or the average level of income. As real per capita GDP increases, so too does the average level of real income. **Exhibit 7** presents the data for per capita real GDP (measured in 2005 dollars) for the United States for various years since 1930. In 2012, per capita GDP was more than twice the figure of 1970 and six times the figure for 1930. What do these figures reveal? As we previously discussed, some of the measurement deficiencies of GDP will result in an overstatement of current real GDP relative to earlier periods. For example, current per capita GDP is biased upward because, compared with earlier periods, more output now takes place in the market sector and less in the household sector. Other biases, however, are in the opposite direction. Reductions in both time and physical demands of work as well as the introduction of improved products and new technologies provide examples of the latter. On balance, the direction of the overall bias is uncertain.

However, one thing is clear: GDP comparisons are less meaningful when there is a dramatic difference in the bundle of goods available. This is generally the case when comparisons are made across distant time periods. Consider the 1930s, compared with today. In the 1930s, there were no jet planes, television programs, automatic dishwashers,

EXHIBIT 7

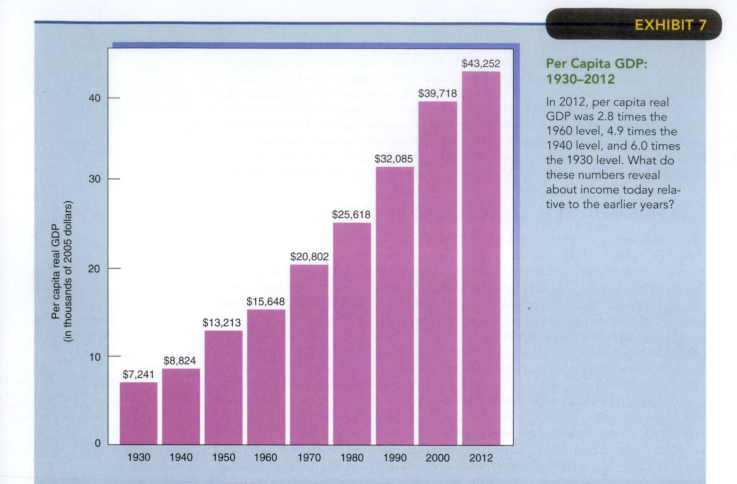

**Per Capita GDP:
1930–2012**

In 2012, per capita real GDP was 2.8 times the 1960 level, 4.9 times the 1940 level, and 6.0 times the 1930 level. What do these numbers reveal about income today relative to the earlier years?

Source: Derived from U.S. Department of Commerce data.

personal computers, or iPads. In 1930, even a millionaire could not have purchased the typical bundle consumed by the average American in 2012.[4] When the potential goods available differ substantially between time periods (or countries), comparative GDP statistics lose some of their precision.

Shortcomings aside, however, there is evidence that GDP per person is a broad indicator of general living standards. As per capita GDP in the United States has increased over time, the quality of most goods has increased while the amount of work time required for their purchase has declined. In many cases, the changes have been dramatic. (See the boxed feature, "The Time Cost of Goods: Today and Yesterday.") Like per capita GDP, these data indicate that our income levels and living standards have improved. Various quality-of-life variables paint a similar picture. For example, as per capita GDP has risen in the United States and other countries, life expectancy and leisure time have gone up, whereas illiteracy and infant mortality rates have gone down. This suggests that increases in per capita GDP and improvements in living standards are closely related.

---

[4]The following quotation from the late Mancur Olson, longtime professor of economics at the University of Maryland, illustrates this point:

   The price level has risen about eight times since 1932, so a $25,000 income then would be the "equivalent" of an income of $200,000 today—one could readily afford a Rolls-Royce, the best seats in the theater, and the care of the best physicians in the country. But the 1932 Rolls-Royce, for all its many virtues, does not embody some desirable technologies available today in the humblest Ford. Nor would the imposing dollar of 1932 buy a TV set or a home videocassette recorder. And if one got an infection, the best physicians in 1932 would not be able to prescribe an antibiotic.

APPLICATIONS IN ECONOMICS

The Time Cost of Goods: Today and Yesterday

Many of you have heard stories from your parents or grandparents about how low prices were when they were young. A bottle of soda cost only a nickel, and a brand-new car was less than $2,000. But their wages were also low, typically only a few dollars per day. In this chapter, you have learned that there is a difference between nominal and real values. Economists generally use the CPI or GDP deflator to adjust for changes in the general level of prices in order to compare real wages or income levels across time periods. There is, however, an alternative way of looking at this issue: You could estimate how long a person working at the average wage rate would have to work in order to earn enough to purchase various items at different points in time.

The productivity of the average worker in America has increased substantially through the years. This increased worker productivity is the key to higher real incomes and improved living standards. When people are able to produce more per hour of work, they will be able to achieve a higher standard of living.

Using average wage rates, W. Michael Cox and Richard Alm of the Federal Reserve Bank of Dallas have computed the time of work required for the typical worker to purchase many common items. Their analysis shows that Americans today are able to acquire most goods with much less work time than was previously the case. Some examples are shown in the accompanying table.

In 1908, a new automobile cost $850, which took the average worker 4,696 hours to earn. In 1955, a new automobile costing $3,030 took 1,638 hours of work, and by 2012, a new automobile cost a typical worker only 879 hours of work. The time cost of a new car today is less than 20 percent of the time cost in 1908. Furthermore, even today's most economical model is light-years away from the 1908 version with regard to power, performance, and dependability.

The prices of technology products, such as computers, calculators, and cellular phones, in particular, have fallen dramatically in recent years. Cellular phones and computers now cost only a small fraction of the time required for their purchase just a few years ago. In 1984, it took the average worker more than 10 weeks of work to purchase a personal computer; by 2012, the work time cost had fallen to 17 hours. In 1901, spending on food, clothing, and shelter consumed 76 percent of the typical worker's paycheck. Because of greater productivity and higher real earnings, today the average worker spends only 36 percent of earnings on these items.

As worker productivity grows, real incomes increase, and the time cost required to purchase products falls. This process generates higher living standards and brings goods that used to be luxuries, costing weeks' or months' worth of a worker's salary, within the reach of most Americans.

The Cost of Products to an Average-Wage Worker in Minutes or Hours of Work

Item	Old Cost	Cost in 2012
Eggs (1 dozen)	80 minutes in 1919	5 minutes
Sugar (5 lbs.)	72 minutes in 1919	9 minutes
Coffee (1 lb.)	55 minutes in 1919	13 minutes
Bread (1 lb.)	13 minutes in 1919	4 minutes
Mattress and box spring (twin)	161 hours in 1929	15 hours
Refrigerator	3,162 hours in 1916	30 hours
Clothes washer and dryer	256 hours in 1956	34 hours
Automobile	4,696 hours in 1908	879 hours
Coast-to-coast air flight	366 hours in 1930	16 hours
Calculator	31 hours in 1972	9 minutes
Microwave oven	97 hours in 1975	7 hours
Personal computer	435 hours in 1984	17 hours

Source: W. Michael Cox and Richard Alm, "Time Well Spent: The Declining Real Cost of Living in America," *1997 Annual Report, Federal Reserve Bank of Dallas*: 2–24. Also see Michael Cox, *Myths of Rich and Poor* (New York: Basic Books, 1999). Data updated by authors.

Continued

Is an automobile really more expensive now than it was in 1955? You might be surprised to learn that in 1955 it took a typical worker 1,638 hours of work time to purchase a car. Today, a vastly improved model can be purchased after only 879 hours of work.

7-6 THE GREAT CONTRIBUTION OF GDP

Although GDP is a broad indicator of income levels and living standards, this is not its major purpose. ***GDP was designed to measure the value of the goods and services produced during a time period. In spite of its limitations, real GDP is a reasonably precise measure of the rate of output and the year-to-year changes in that output.***

Adjusted for changes in prices, annual and quarterly GDP data provide the information required to track the economy's performance level. These data allow us to compare the current rate of output with that of the recent past. Without this information, it would be more difficult to evaluate current performance of the economy.

LOOKING AHEAD

GDP provides us with a measure of economic performance. In the next chapter, we will take a closer look at the path of real GDP in the United States and introduce other indicators of economic performance. Later, we will investigate the factors that underlie both the level of and fluctuations in real GDP.

KEY POINTS

- Gross domestic product (GDP) is a measure of the market value of final goods and services produced within the borders of a country during a specific time period, usually a year.

- Income transfers, purely financial transactions, and exchanges of goods and assets produced during earlier periods are not included in GDP because they do not involve current production.

- When derived by the expenditure approach, GDP has four major components: (1) personal consumption, (2) gross private investment,

(3) government consumption and gross investment, and (4) net exports.

- When derived by the resource cost–income approach, GDP equals (1) the direct income components (wages and salaries, self-employment income, rents, interest, and corporate profits) plus (2) indirect business taxes, depreciation, and the net income of foreigners.

- Price indexes measure changes in the general level of prices over time. They can be used to adjust nominal values for the effects of inflation. The most widely used price indexes are the GDP deflator and the consumer price index (CPI).

- The rate of inflation is the percentage change in the general level of prices from one year to the next. It is equal to PI_2 minus PI_1 divided by PI_1 multiplied by 100.

- In addition to the regular (or traditional) CPI, the Bureau of Labor Statistics also provides a chained CPI that adjusts the quantities of the index for movements away from goods with relative price increases. Because of their more frequent updating of the typical market bundle and adjustment for the substitution away from goods with higher relative prices, the chained CPI and GDP deflator generally provide a slightly lower estimate for the annual rate of inflation than the traditional CPI.

- The following formula can be used to convert the nominal GDP data of the current period (2) to real GDP measured in terms of the general level of prices of an earlier period (1):

$$\text{Real GDP}_2 = \text{Nominal GDP}_2 \times \frac{\text{GDP deflator}_1}{\text{GDP deflator}_2}$$

- Even real GDP is an imperfect measure of current production. It excludes household production and the underground economy, fails to take leisure and human costs into account, and adjusts imperfectly for quality changes.

- Real GDP is vitally important because it is a reasonably accurate measure of how well the economy is doing compared to the recent past. Per capita GDP is a broad indicator of income levels and living standards across time periods.

CRITICAL ANALYSIS QUESTIONS

1. *Indicate how each of the following activities will affect this year's GDP:
   a. the sale of a used economics textbook to the college bookstore
   b. Smith's $500 doctor bill for setting her son's broken arm
   c. family lawn services provided by Smith's 16-year-old child
   d. lawn services purchased by Smith from the neighbor's 16-year-old child who has a lawn-mowing business
   e. a $5,250 purchase of 100 shares of stock at $50 per share plus the sales commission of $250
   f. a multibillion-dollar discovery of natural gas in Oklahoma
   g. a hurricane that causes $10 billion of damage in Florida
   h. $60,000 of income earned by an American college professor teaching in England

2. If nominal GDP increased by 6 percent during a year, while the GDP deflator increased by 4 percent, by how much did real GDP change during the year?

3. *A large furniture retailer sells $100,000 of household furnishings from inventories built up last year. How does this sale influence GDP? How are the components of GDP affected?

4. Suppose a group of British investors finances the construction of a plant to manufacture skateboards in St. Louis, Missouri. How will the construction of the plant affect GDP? Suppose the plant generates $100,000 in corporate profits this year. Will these profits contribute to GDP? Why or why not?

5. *Why might even real GDP be a misleading index of changes in output between 1950 and 2013 in the United States?

6. What are price indexes designed to measure? Outline how they are constructed. When GDP and other income figures are compared across time periods, explain why it is important to adjust for changes in the general level of prices.

7. *In 1982, the average hourly earnings of private nonagricultural production workers were $7.87 per hour. By 2012, the

average hourly earnings had risen to $19.77. In 2012, the CPI was 229.6, compared with 96.5 in 1982. What were the real earnings of private nonagricultural production workers in 2012 measured in 1982 dollars?

8. The receipts and year of release of the five movies with the largest nominal box office revenues, along with the CPI data of each year are presented below. Assuming that the receipts for each of the movies were derived during their year of release, convert the receipts for each to real dollars for the year 2012 (2012 CPI 229.6). Which movie had the largest real box office receipts?

MOVIES	BOX OFFICE RECEIPTS (MILLIONS)	YEAR RELEASED	CPI IN YEAR RELEASED
Avatar	$760.5	2009	214.5
Titanic	600.8	1997	160.5
Star Wars	461.0	1977	60.6
Shrek 2	437.2	2004	188.9
E.T.: The Extra-Terrestrial	399.9	1982	96.5

9. *How much do each of the following contribute to GDP?
   a. Jones pays a repair shop $1,000 to rebuild the engine of her automobile.
   b. Jones spends $200 on parts and pays a mechanic $400 to rebuild the engine of her automobile.
   c. Jones spends $200 on parts and rebuilds the engine of her automobile herself.
   d. Jones sells her four-year-old automobile for $5,000 and buys Smith's two-year-old model for $10,000.
   e. Jones sells her four-year-old automobile for $5,000 and buys a new car for $20,000.

10. What is the difference between the consumer price index (CPI) and the GDP deflator? Which would be better to use if

you want to measure whether your hourly earnings this year were higher than they were last year? Why?

11. *Indicate whether the following statements are true or false:

   a. "For the economy as a whole, inventory investment can never be negative."

   b. "The net investment of an economy must always be positive."

   c. "An increase in GDP indicates that the standard of living of people has risen."

12. *How do the receipts and expenditures of a state-operated lottery affect GDP?

13. GDP does not count productive services, such as child care, food preparation, cleaning, and laundry, provided within the household. Why are these things excluded? Is GDP a sexist measure? Does it understate the productive contributions of women relative to men? Discuss.

14. *Indicate how each of the following will affect this year's GDP:

   a. You suffer $10,000 of damage when you wreck your automobile.

   b. You win $10,000 in a state lottery.

   c. You spend $5,100 in January for 100 shares of stock ($5,000 for the stock and $100 for the sales commission) and sell the stock in August for $8,200 ($8,000 for the stock and $200 for the sales commission).

   d. You pay $500 for this month's rental of your apartment.

   e. You are paid $300 for computer services provided to a client.

   f. You receive $300 from your parents.

   g. You get a raise from $8 to $10 per hour and simultaneously decide to reduce your hours worked from 20 to 16 per week.

   h. You earn $4,000 working in Spain as an English instructor.

15. The accompanying chart presents 2012 data from the national-income accounts of the United States.

COMPONENT	BILLIONS OF DOLLARS
Personal consumption	$11,119.6
Employee compensation	8,565.8
Rents	462.6
Gov't consumption & investment	3,062.8
Imports	2,744.0
Depreciation	2,078.9
Corporate profits	1,950.6
Interest income	504.3
Exports	2,184.0
Gross private investment	2,062.3
Indirect business taxes	1,163.2
Self-employment income	1,202.3
Net income of foreigners	–243.0

   a. Indicate the various components of GDP when it is derived by the expenditure approach. Calculate GDP using the expenditure approach.

   b. Indicate the various components of GDP when it is derived by the resource cost–income approach. Calculate GDP using the resource cost–income approach.

16. *Fill in the blanks in the following table:

YEAR	NOMINAL GDP (IN BILLIONS)	GDP DEFLATOR (2005 = 100)	REAL GDP (BILLIONS OF 2005 DOLLARS)
1960	$526.4	18.6	a. _____
1970	$1,038.3	24.3	b. _____
1980	$2,788.1	c. _____	$5,832.8
1990	d. _____	72.3	$8,033.9
2000	$9,951.5	e. _____	$11,231.9
2005	$12,638.4	100.0	f. _____
2012	$15,684.8	115.4	g. _____

*Asterisk denotes questions for which answers are given in Appendix B.

ADDENDUM

THE CONSTRUCTION OF A PRICE INDEX

Price indexes are designed to measure the magnitude of changes in the general level of prices through time. The price index during the current year (PI_2) is

$$PI_2 = \frac{\text{Cost of purchasing the typical bundle this year}}{\text{Cost of purchasing the same bundle during the base year}} \times 100$$

The typical (representative) bundle might be the bundle actually chosen during the earlier base year. Alternatively, it could be the bundle chosen this year. *In either case, the quantities of the various goods do not change from year to year; only the prices change.*

Let's suppose that the bundle used to calculate the index was the quantity of each good actually chosen during the base year. This is how the consumer price index is calculated. In this case, the cost of purchasing the base-year bundle this year would be the sum of the price of each good this year (P_2) multiplied by the quantity consumed during the base year (Q_1). The cost of purchasing the *same bundle* during the base year would be the sum of the price

©iStockphoto.com/sorendls

of each good during the base year (P_1) multiplied by the quantity of each good chosen during the base year (Q_1). Therefore, the mathematical formula for the price index during the current year (PI_2) could be written:

$$PI_2 \times \frac{\sum P_2 Q_1}{\sum P_1 Q_1} \times 100$$

If prices on average are higher during the current period than they were during the base year, then this expression will be greater than 100. This indicates that it is now more costly to purchase the representative bundle than it was during the base year. Correspondingly, if the general level of prices is currently lower today than during the base period, then PI_2 would be less than 100. Thus, the current price index indicates how the current level of prices compares with the level during the base period.

Let's consider a simple example that illustrates more fully how price indexes are constructed. Suppose that your typical daily consumption bundle is two hamburgers, one order of French fries, and three Coca-Colas. Initially, the price of a hamburger was $3, French fries $1, and Coca-Cola $1. The price index during this base period is assigned a value of 100. Your expenditures on the bundle during the base period (the denominator in the previous formula) were $10 ($6 for the two hamburgers, $1 for the French fries, and $3 for the three Coca-Colas).

Now consider the implications if prices in the current period are $3.50 for a hamburger, $1.75 for French fries, and 75 cents for a Coca-Cola. Now the cost of purchasing this bundle (numerator in the previous formula) is $11 ($7 for the two hamburgers, $1.75 for the French fries, and $2.25 for the three Coca-Colas). This would yield a price index of 110 ($11 divided by $10 multiplied by 100). The price index of 110 indicates that the general level of prices for the three-good bundle is now 10 percent higher than it was during the base period.

Of course, the number of goods and the quantities included in the consumer price index (CPI) and GDP deflator are far greater than the bundle we considered in this simple illustration. Nonetheless, the general idea is the same. The cost of purchasing the typical bundle in the current period is compared with the cost of purchasing the same bundle during a base year, which is assigned a value of 100. If the cost of purchasing the bundle is now higher than it was during the base period, then the value of this year's price index will be greater than 100. As the price index changes from year to year, it indicates the magnitude of the change in the general level of prices.

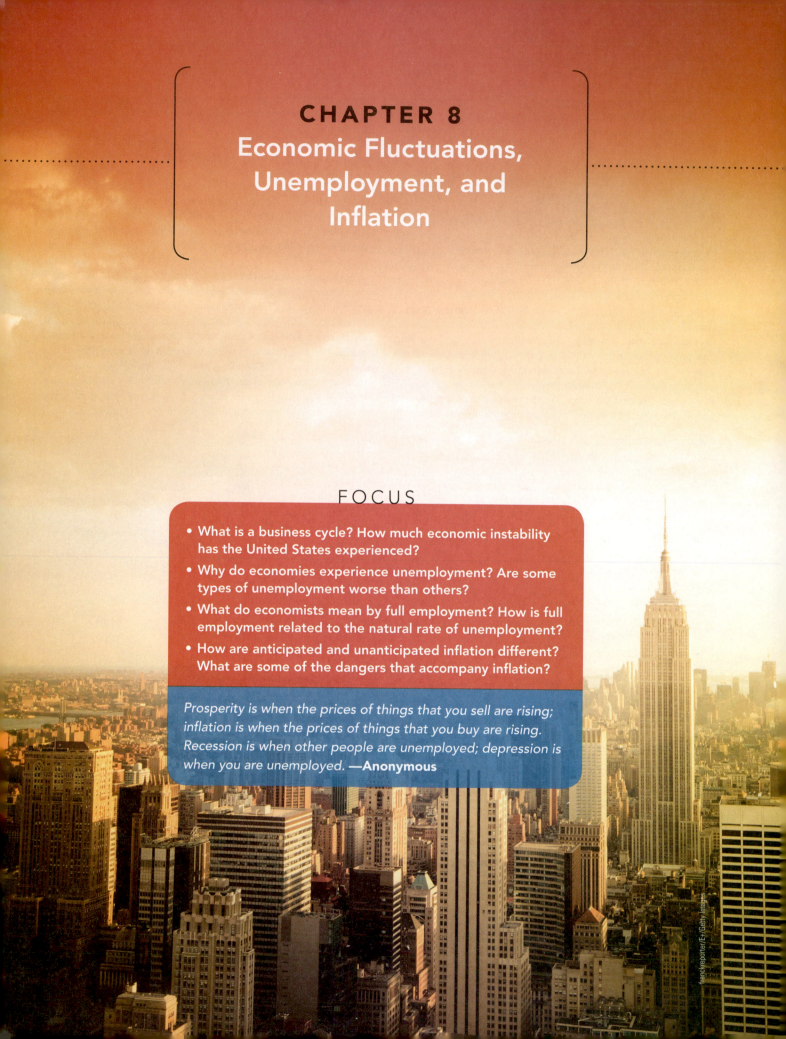

CHAPTER 8
Economic Fluctuations, Unemployment, and Inflation

FOCUS

- What is a business cycle? How much economic instability has the United States experienced?

- Why do economies experience unemployment? Are some types of unemployment worse than others?

- What do economists mean by full employment? How is full employment related to the natural rate of unemployment?

- How are anticipated and unanticipated inflation different? What are some of the dangers that accompany inflation?

Prosperity is when the prices of things that you sell are rising; inflation is when the prices of things that you buy are rising. Recession is when other people are unemployed; depression is when you are unemployed. —**Anonymous**

As we have already discussed, macroeconomics is about growth of income and fluctuations in that growth. The primary objectives of macroeconomic policy are to help promote rapid and stable growth, a high level of employment, and stability in the general level of prices. Most all economists are supportive of these goals, but there is considerable controversy about how they can best be achieved. As we proceed, we will analyze both economic growth and stability in detail and consider how these objectives can be attained.

The performance of the economy influences our job opportunities, income levels, and quality of life. Thus, key indicators of economic performance, such as growth of real GDP, the rate of unemployment, and the inflation rate, are closely watched by investors, politicians, and the media. This chapter will focus on how several key economic indicators are derived and explain how changes in these measures influence our lives.

8-1 SWINGS IN THE ECONOMIC PENDULUM

During the last hundred years, the annual growth rate of real GDP in the United States has averaged approximately 3 percent. But there have been considerable fluctuations in the year-to-year growth. During the Great Depression of the 1930s, economic growth plunged. Real GDP declined by 7.5 percent or more each year from 1930 to 1932. In 1933, it was almost 30 percent less than it was in 1929. The 1929 level of real GDP was not reached again until 1939. World War II was characterized by a rapid expansion of GDP, which was followed by a decline after the war. Real GDP did not reach its 1944 level again until 1953, although the output of consumer goods did increase significantly in the years immediately following the war.

Exhibit 1 presents the growth rate figures (four-quarter moving average) for real GDP for 1960–2013. Real GDP grew rapidly throughout most of the 1960s, during periods 1972–1973, 1976–1977, 1983–1988, most of the 1990s, and 2002–2007. Since 1960, however, there have also been eight periods (1960, 1970, 1974–1975, 1980, 1982, 1991, 2001, and 2008–2009) of falling real GDP. Although the economic ups and downs have continued, the fluctuations have been less severe in recent decades than during the first 50 years of the twentieth century. Figures on GDP and related data can be obtained from the Bureau of Economic Analysis on the Internet at http://www.bea.gov/.

8-1a A HYPOTHETICAL BUSINESS CYCLE

The United States and other industrial economies have been characterized by instability when it comes to the growth of real GDP. Inevitably, real GDP growth has been followed

EXHIBIT 1

Instability in the Growth of Real GDP, 1960–2013

Although real GDP in the United States fluctuates substantially, periods of positive growth outweigh the periods of declining real GDP. Since 1960, the U.S. growth rate of real GDP has averaged approximately 3 percent annually. Economists refer to periods of declining real GDP as recessions. The recessionary periods are shaded.

Source: *Economic Report of the President* (Washington, DC: Government Printing Office, various issues).

Business cycle

Fluctuations in the general level of economic activity as measured by variables such as the rate of unemployment and changes in real GDP.

Recession

A downturn in economic activity characterized by declining real GDP and rising unemployment. In an effort to be more precise, many economists define a recession as two consecutive quarters in which there is a decline in real GDP.

Depression

A prolonged and very severe recession.

by economic slowdowns. Economists refer to these swings in the rate of output as the **business cycle**. The business cycle is characterized by periods of growth in real output and other aggregate measures of economic activity followed by periods of decline.

Exhibit 2 shows a hypothetical business cycle. When most businesses are operating at capacity level and real GDP is growing rapidly, a *business peak*, or boom, is present. As business conditions slow, the economy begins the *contraction*, or recessionary, phase of the cycle. During the contraction, the sales of most businesses decline, real GDP grows at a slower rate or perhaps falls, and unemployment in the labor market increases.

The bottom of the contraction phase is referred to as the *recessionary trough*. After the downturn reaches bottom and economic conditions begin to improve, the economy enters the *expansion* phase of the cycle. Here business sales rise, GDP grows rapidly, and the rate of unemployment declines. Eventually, the expansion blossoms into another business peak. The peak, however, inevitably ends and turns into a contraction, beginning the cycle anew.

The term **recession** is widely used to describe conditions during the contraction and recessionary trough phases of the business cycle. This is a period during which real GDP declines. Often, a recession is defined as a decline in real GDP for two or more consecutive quarters.[1] When a recession is prolonged and has a sharp decline in economic activity, it is called a **depression**.

In one important respect, the term *business cycle* is misleading. The word *cycle* is often used to describe events of similar time length that occur regularly, like the seasons of the year, for example. As Exhibit 1 illustrates, this is not the case with the business cycle. The expansions and contractions last varying lengths of time, and the swings differ in terms of their magnitude. For example, the recessions of 1961, 1982, and 1990 were followed by eight years or more of uninterrupted growth of output. In contrast, the recession of 1980 was followed by an expansion that lasted only 12 months. The expansionary phase following the recessions of 1970 and 1974–1975 fell between these two extremes. Clearly, the duration of real-world expansions and contractions is varied and unpredictable.

How can we know where an economy is in the business cycle? Of course, changes in real GDP will tell us. However, these numbers are available only quarterly, and it usually takes four to six weeks after the quarter is over before reliable figures are released. Various measures that are available monthly or more often can provide clues. For example, auto sales, new housing starts, new factory orders, and even the stock market will generally

---

EXHIBIT 2

The Business Cycle

In the past, ups and downs have often characterized aggregate business activity. Despite these fluctuations, there has been an upward trend in real GDP in the United States and other industrial nations. During economic expansions, construction and investment are increasing. In contrast, recessions are characterized by plant closings and high unemployment.

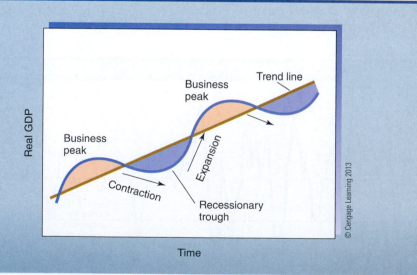

---

[1]See Geoffrey H. Moore, "Recessions," in *The Fortune Encyclopedia of Economics*, ed. David R. Henderson (New York: Time Warner, Inc., 1993), for additional information on recessions in the United States. This publication is also available online at http:/www.econlib.org/.

increase during an expansion and decline when the economy dips into a recession. As a result, these indicators are monitored carefully.

8-2 ECONOMIC FLUCTUATIONS AND THE LABOR MARKET

Fluctuations in real GDP influence the demand for labor and employment. In our modern world, people are busy with jobs, household work, school, and other activities. **Exhibit 3** illustrates how economists classify these activities in relation to the **civilian labor force**,

During economic expansions, construction and investment are increasing. In contrast, recessions are characterized by plant closings and high unemployment.

Civilian labor force
The number of people 16 years of age and older who are either employed or unemployed. To be classified as unemployed, a person must be looking for a job.

EXHIBIT 3

Population, Employment, and Unemployment, April 2013

The accompanying diagram illustrates the alternative participation-status categories for the adult population. Data are measured in millions, except those expressed as percentages.

Civilian population 16 and older

- **Not in the labor force**
  Household workers
  Students
  Retirees
  Disabled

- **Civilian labor force**
  - **Employed**
    Employees
    Self-employed workers
  - **Unemployed**
    New entrants
    Reentrants
    Lost last job
    Quit last job
    Laid off

	NUMBER OF PERSONS, APRIL 2013
Noninstitutional civilian population (age 16 and older)	245.2
Not in labor force	89.9
Total civilian labor force	155.2
Employed	143.6
Unemployed	11.7
Labor force participation rate	63.3%
Employment–population ratio	58.6%
Unemployment rate	7.5%

Source: http://www.bls.gov/.

defined as the number of people aged 16 years and older who are either employed or seeking employment. The noninstitutional civilian adult population is divided into two broad categories: (1) people not in the labor force and (2) people in the labor force. There are various reasons why people aren't in the labor force. Some are retired. Others are working in their own households or attending school. Still others are not working because they are ill or disabled. Although many of these people are quite busy, their activities lie outside the market labor force.

As Exhibit 3 shows, **unemployed** workers who are seeking work are included in the labor force along with employed workers. The **labor force participation rate** is the number of people in the civilian labor force (including both those who are employed and those who are unemployed) as a percentage of the civilian population 16 years of age and older. In April 2013 the population (16 years of age and older) of the United States was 245.2 million, 155.2 million of whom were in the labor force. Thus, the U.S. labor force participation rate was 63.3 percent (155.2 million divided by 245.2 million).

The labor force participation rate varies substantially across countries. For example, in 2011, the labor force participation rate was 64.1 percent in the United States, 66.8 percent in Canada, and 65.1 percent in Sweden. In contrast, the labor force participation rate was only 56.3 percent in France and 48.1 percent in Italy. The percentage of married women in the labor force is generally smaller in countries like Italy and France that have low labor force participation rates.

In the United States, one of the most interesting labor force developments in recent decades is the dramatic increase in the labor force participation rate of women. **Exhibit 4** illustrates this point. In 2012, 57.7 percent of women worked outside the home, up from 32.7 percent in 1948. Married women accounted for most of this increase. More than half of all married women now are in the labor force, compared to only 20 percent immediately following World War II. While the labor force participation of women rose, the rate for men fell. In 2012, the labor force participation rate of men was 70.2 percent, down from 83.3 percent in 1960 and 86.6 percent in 1948. Clearly, the composition of workforce participation within the family has changed substantially during the past six decades.

The **unemployment rate** is a key barometer of conditions in the aggregate labor market. Nonetheless, the term is often misunderstood. It is important to note that unemployment is different from not working. As we previously discussed, there are several reasons—including household work, school attendance, retirement, and illness or disability—why a person may be neither employed nor looking for a job. These people, though not employed, are not counted as unemployed.

Unemployed
The term used to describe a person not currently employed who is either (1) actively seeking employment or (2) waiting to begin or return to a job.

Labor force participation rate
The number of people in the civilian labor force 16 years of age or older who are either employed or actively seeking employment as a percentage of the total civilian population 16 years of age and over.

Unemployment rate
The percentage of unemployed people in the labor force. Mathematically, it is equal to the number of people unemployed divided by the number of people in the labor force.

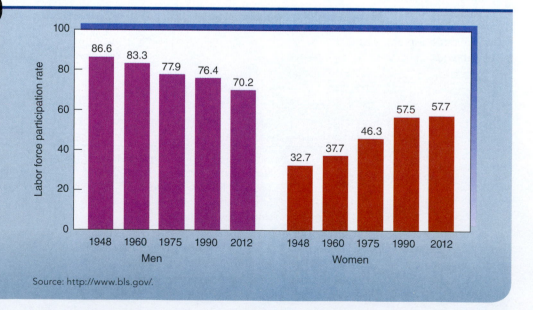

EXHIBIT 4

Labor Force Participation Rate of Men and Women, 1948–2012

As the chart illustrates, the labor force participation rate for women has been steadily increasing for several decades, while the rate for men has been declining.

Source: http://www.bls.gov/.

MEASURES OF ECONOMIC ACTIVITY

Deriving the Unemployment Rate

Each month, the Bureau of Labor Statistics (BLS) contacts a sample of 55,000 households that reflects the population characteristics of the United States. Specially trained interviewers pose identical questions designed to determine whether each of the approximately 110,000 adults in these households is employed, unemployed, or not in the labor force. People aged 16 years and older are considered employed if they (1) worked at all (even as little as 1 hour) for pay or profit during the survey week, (2) worked 15 hours or more without pay in a family-operated enterprise during the survey week, or (3) have a job at which they did not work during the survey week because of illness, vacation, industrial disputes, bad weather, time off, or personal reasons. People are considered unemployed if they (1) do not have a job, (2) are available for work, and (3) have actively looked for work during the past four weeks. Looking for work may involve any of the following activities: (1) registering at a public or private employment office, (2) meeting with prospective employers, (3) checking with friends or relatives, (4) placing or answering advertisements, (5) writing letters of application, or (6) being in a union or on a professional register. In addition, those not working are classified as unemployed if they are either waiting to start a new job within thirty days or waiting to be recalled from a layoff. The BLS uses its survey data to calculate the unemployment rate and other employment-related statistics each month. States use the BLS survey and employment figures from industries covered by unemployment insurance to construct state and area employment statistics. These labor market figures are published by the U.S. Department of Labor in the Monthly Labor Review and on the Internet at http://www.bls.gov/.

©iStockphoto.com/Sorendls

ZUMA Press, Inc./Alamy

It is important to note that only people employed or unemployed are counted as part of the labor force. Part-time as well as full-time workers are counted as employed members of the labor force. The rate of unemployment is the number of people unemployed expressed as a percentage of the labor force. In April 2013, the rate of unemployment in the United States was 7.5 percent (11.7 million out of a labor force of 155.2 million). (See the accompanying Measures of Economic Activity feature for information on how the Bureau of Labor Statistics derives the unemployment rate.)

In addition to the rate of unemployment, many economists also use the **employment/population ratio**—the number of people employed expressed as a percentage of the population 16 years old and older—to monitor labor market conditions. This ratio will tend to rise during an expansion and fall during a recession. Both the number of people employed and the population aged 16 and older are well defined and readily measurable. Their measurement does not require a subjective judgment as to whether a person is actually "available for work" or "actively seeking employment." Thus, some believe that the employment/population ratio is a more objective measure of job market conditions than the rate of unemployment. The accompanying **Thumbnail Sketch** shows the formulas that are used to calculate the major indicators of labor market conditions.

Exhibit 5 tracks both the employment–population ratio and the labor force participation rate during 1980–2013. Both figures trended upward during the 1980s and 1990s. The labor force participation rate rose from 64 percent in 1980 to 67 percent in 2000. During this same period, the employment–population ratio increased from 60 percent to 64 percent. Since 2000, however, the trend has reversed. By the first quarter of 2013, the labor force

Employment/population ratio

The number of people 16 years of age and over employed as civilians divided by the total civilian population 16 years of age and older. The ratio is expressed as a percentage.

Thumbnail Sketch
Formulas for Key Labor Market Indicators

1. Labor force = Employed + Unemployed
2. Labor force participation rate = Number in labor force/Population (aged 16 and older)
3. Unemployment rate = Number unemployed/Number in labor force
4. Employment/population ratio = Number employed/Population (aged 16 and older)

participation rate had fallen to 63.5 percent, its lowest level in more than three decades. The employment–population ratio has also fallen sharply, dipping to 58.6 percent during the first quarter of 2013. While most of the reductions in labor force participation and employment came during the 2008–2009 recession, both have increased only modestly since the recession ended in June 2009. Economic studies indicate a majority of the recent decline in the labor force participation rate is due to cyclical rather than demographic factors.[2]

EXHIBIT 5

Labor Force Participation Rate and Employment–Population Ratio, 1980–2013

Here we illustrate the path of the labor force participation rate and the employment–population ratio. Note how both ratios trended upward during 1980–2000, but they have been declining since 2000. Both fell sharply during the 2008–2009 recession, and their rebound has been weak during the recovery phase of this business cycle.

[2]Willem Van Zandweghe, "Interpreting the Recent Decline in Labor Force Participation." Federal Reserve Bank of Kansas City *Economic Review* (Quarter 1, 2012): 5–34; and Daniel Aaronson, Jonathan Davis, and Loujia Hu, "Explaining the Decline in the U.S. Labor Force Participation Rate," *Chicago Fed Letter*, no. 296 (March 2012): 1–4.

8-2a DYNAMIC CHANGE AND REASONS FOR UNEMPLOYMENT

In a dynamic world, where information is scarce and people are free to choose among jobs, some unemployment is inevitable. As new products are introduced and new technologies developed, some firms are expanding while others are contracting. Similarly, some firms will be starting operations, while others will be going out of business. This process results in the creation of new jobs and the disappearance of old ones. At the same time, some potential workers will be switching from school or other nonwork activities to the labor force, while others are retiring or taking a leave from the labor force. Furthermore, workers are mobile. At any point in time, some will voluntarily quit and search for better opportunities. Although some unemployment will always be present, there is a positive side to the unemployment–job search process: it makes it possible for individuals to better match their skills and preferences with the job requirements of employers. Better-matched employees and employers increase both productivity and earnings.

Unemployment may occur for reasons other than the loss of a job, however. For example, people often experience periods of unemployment as they enter and reenter the labor force. The Department of Labor lists five reasons why workers may experience unemployment. **Exhibit 6** shows the share of unemployed workers in each of these five categories in April 2013. Interestingly, 10.9 percent of the unemployed workers were first-time entrants into the labor force; 26.9 percent were reentering the labor force after exiting it to obtain additional schooling, do household work, or for other reasons. Therefore, 37.8 percent of the unemployed workers—over one-third—were unemployed because they were entering or reentering the labor force. About 1 out of every 14 unemployed workers (7.4 percent) quit their job. People laid off and waiting to return to their previous positions contributed 10.0 percent to the total. Workers dismissed from their job accounted for nearly one-half (44.8 percent) of the total number of unemployed workers.

Young workers often switch jobs and move between schooling and the labor force as they search for a career path that best fits their abilities and preferences. As the result of this job switching, the unemployment rate of younger workers is substantially higher than that of more established workers. As **Exhibit 7** shows, the unemployment rate of workers 20 to 24 years of age in April 2013 was about twice the rate for their counterparts aged 25 years and older. Further, the unemployment rate for teenagers was approximately four times the rate for those 25 years and older. The unemployment rates for men were higher than for women for all age groups.

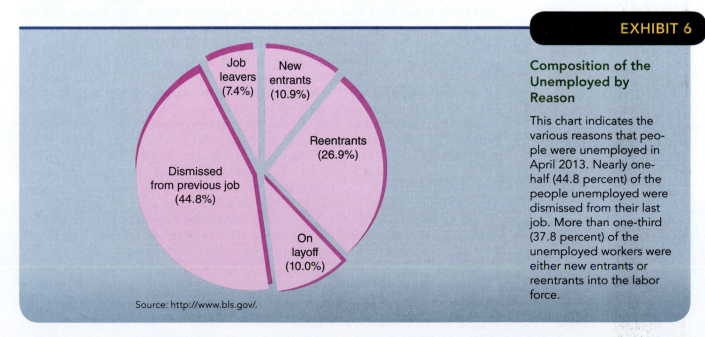

EXHIBIT 6

Composition of the Unemployed by Reason

This chart indicates the various reasons that people were unemployed in April 2013. Nearly one-half (44.8 percent) of the people unemployed were dismissed from their last job. More than one-third (37.8 percent) of the unemployed workers were either new entrants or reentrants into the labor force.

Job leavers (7.4%)
New entrants (10.9%)
Reentrants (26.9%)
Dismissed from previous job (44.8%)
On layoff (10.0%)

Source: http://www.bls.gov/.

EXHIBIT 7

The Unemployment Rate by Age and Gender, April 2013

Group	Civilian Rate of Unemployment April 2013 (Percentage)
Total, all workers	7.5
Men, Total	7.7
Ages 16–19	26.2
Ages 20–24	14.0
Ages 25 and older	6.3
Women, Total	7.3
Ages 16–19	22.1
Ages 20–24	12.3
Ages 25 and older	5.9

Source: http://www.bls.gov/.

8-3 THREE TYPES OF UNEMPLOYMENT

Although some unemployment is consistent with economic efficiency, this is not always the case. Abnormally high rates of unemployment generally reflect weak demand conditions for labor, counterproductive policies, and/or the inability or lack of incentive on the part of potential workers and potential employers to arrive at mutually advantageous agreements. To clarify matters, economists divide unemployment into three categories: frictional, structural, and cyclical. Let us take a closer look at each of these three classifications.

8-3a FRICTIONAL UNEMPLOYMENT

Frictional unemployment
Unemployment due to constant changes in the economy that prevent qualified unemployed workers from being immediately matched up with existing job openings. It results from imperfect information and search activities related to suitably matching employees with employers.

Unemployment that is caused by constant changes in the labor market is called **frictional unemployment**. It occurs because (1) employers are not fully aware of all available workers and their job qualifications and (2) available workers are not fully aware of the jobs being offered by employers. In other words, the main cause of frictional unemployment is imperfect information.

For example, an employer looking for a new worker seldom hires the first applicant who walks into the employment office. The employer wants to find the "best available" worker to fill the opening. It is costly to hire workers who perform poorly. It is sometimes even costly to terminate their employment. So, employers search—they expend time and resources screening applicants in an effort to find the best-qualified workers who are willing to accept their wage and employment conditions.

Similarly, job seekers search for their best option among the potential alternatives. They make telephone calls, search newspaper ads and Internet sites, submit to job interviews, use employment services, and so on. The pursuit of personal gain—landing jobs that are more attractive than the current options they face—motivates job seekers to engage in job search activities.

However, as a job seeker finds out about more and more potential job opportunities, it becomes less likely that additional searching will uncover a more attractive option. Therefore, the *marginal benefit* derived from a job search declines with the time spent searching for a job because it becomes less likely that it will lead to a better position. The *marginal cost* of a job search rises as a more lengthy search leads to the discovery of more attractive job opportunities, and rejecting such options will become more and more costly.

As the marginal benefit of the job search declines and the marginal costs rise, eventually a rational job seeker will conclude that additional search is no longer worth the cost. He or she will then accept the best alternative available at that point. However, this process will take time, and during this time the job seeker is contributing to the frictional unemployment of the economy.

It is important to note that, even though frictional unemployment is a side effect, the job search process typically leads to improved economic efficiency and a higher real income for employees (see the accompanying Myths of Economics feature).

Changes that affect the costs and benefits of a job search influence the level of unemployment. The Internet has had an interesting effect on the job search process. Increasingly, both employers and employees are using Internet sites as a means of communicating with each other. Employers provide information about job openings in various skill and occupational categories, and employees supply information about their education, skills, and experience. This electronic job search process reduces information costs and makes it possible for both employers and employees to consider quickly a wide range of alternatives. This will tend to reduce both search time and frictional unemployment.

On the other hand, a change that makes it cheaper to reject available opportunities and continue searching for jobs will increase the level of unemployment. For example, an increase in unemployment benefits would make it less costly to continue looking for a preferred job. As a result, job seekers will expand the length of their search time, and the unemployment rate will rise.

8-3b STRUCTURAL UNEMPLOYMENT

In the case of **structural unemployment**, changes in the basic characteristics of the economy prevent the "matching up" of available jobs with available workers. It is not always easy to distinguish between frictional and structural unemployment. In each case, job openings and potential workers searching for jobs are both present. The crucial difference between the two is that with frictional unemployment, workers possess the necessary skills

Structural unemployment
Unemployment due to the structural characteristics of the economy that make it difficult for job seekers to find employment and for employers to hire workers. Although job openings are available, they generally require skills many unemployed workers do not have.

MYTHS OF ECONOMICS

"Unemployment Would not Exist if the Economy Were Operating Efficiently."

Nobody likes unemployment. Certainly, an extended period of unemployment can be a very painful experience. Looking for a job, however, performs an important labor market function: It leads to improved matches between workers' skills and employers' job requirements.

Job searchers are "shopping"—they are searching for information about the job opportunity that best fits their skills, earning capabilities, and preferences. Similarly, employers shop when they are seeking labor services. They, too, acquire information about available workers that will help them select employees whose skills and preferences match the demands of the job.

This shopping results in some unemployment, but it also provides both employees and employers with information that will help them make better choices. If the resources of an economy are going to be used effectively, the skills of workers must be matched well with the jobs of employers. Waste will result if, for example, a person with high-level computer skills ends up working as a janitor while someone else with minimal computer skills is employed as a computer programmer. Moreover, as workers try to find jobs for which their skills are well suited, they achieve higher wage rates, and the economy is able to generate a larger output.

Perhaps thinking about the rental housing market will help you better understand why search time can be both beneficial and productive. Like the employment market, the rental housing market is characterized by imperfect information and dynamic change. New housing structures are built; older structures depreciate and are torn down. Families move from one community to another. In this dynamic world, it makes sense for renters to shop around from time to time to find the housing quality, price, and location that best fit their preferences and budgets. Similarly, landlords search among renters, seeking to rent their accommodations to those who value them most highly. As a result of this shopping, housing vacancies inevitably occur. But does this mean the housing market is inefficient? No. It is the result of imperfect information and the search for a more efficient match on the part of both landlords and renters.

Of course, some types of unemployment, particularly cyclical unemployment, are indicative of inefficiency. However, this is not the case with frictional unemployment. The job searching (as well as the frictional unemployment that accompanies it) helps both job seekers and employers make better choices, and it leads to a more efficient match of applicants with job openings than would otherwise be possible. It is perfectly consistent with economic efficiency.

©iStockphoto.com/sorendls

to fill the job openings; with structural unemployment, they do not. There are many causes of structural unemployment. The introduction of new products and production technologies can substantially alter the relative demand for workers with various skills. Changes of this type can affect the job opportunities of even highly skilled workers, particularly if their skills are not easily transferable to other industries and occupations. The "computer revolution" has dramatically changed the job opportunities of many workers. The alternatives available to workers with the skills required to operate and maintain high-tech equipment have improved substantially, while the prospects of those without such skills have, in some cases, deteriorated drastically.

Shifts in public-sector priorities can also cause structural unemployment. For example, environmental regulations designed to improve air quality led to a reduction in the demand for coal during the 1990s and 2000s. As a result, many coal miners in West Virginia, Kentucky, and other coal-mining states lost their jobs. Unfortunately, the skills of many of the job losers were ill suited for employment in expanding industries. Structural unemployment was the result.

Institutional factors can also make it difficult for some workers to find jobs. For example, minimum-wage legislation may push the wages of low-skilled workers above their productivity levels and thereby severely retard the job opportunities available to them. High unemployment benefits reduce the opportunity cost of unemployment and may also lead to higher levels of structural unemployment. See Applications in Economics for a suggested policy alternative that would reduce the adverse unintended consequences of the current unemployment benefit system.

8-3c CYCLICAL UNEMPLOYMENT

Cyclical unemployment
Unemployment due to recessionary business conditions and inadequate labor demand.

When there is a general downturn in business activity, **cyclical unemployment** arises. Because fewer goods are being produced, fewer workers are required to produce them. Employers lay off workers and cut back employment.

An unexpected fall in the general level of demand for goods and services will cause cyclical unemployment to rise. In a world of imperfect information, adjustments to unexpected declines in demand are often painful. When the demand for labor declines, workers will at first not know whether they are being laid off because their employer is experiencing lower demand or if the reduction in demand is widespread throughout the economy. Similarly, they will not immediately know whether their poor current employment opportunities are temporary or long term. If a reduction in demand is limited to only a few employers, the dismissed workers will generally be able to find jobs with other employers in a short period of time. The situation is different, however, when there is a general decline in demand. Many employers will lay off workers and few other employers will be hiring. Under these circumstances, workers' search efforts will be less fruitful, and the duration of their unemployment abnormally long. Unemployment of this type is referred to as cyclical unemployment. As we proceed, we will consider the causes of cyclical unemployment and analyze how it might be reduced.

APPLICATIONS IN ECONOMICS

Would Personal Savings Accounts Reduce the Rate of Unemployment?

Under the current unemployment insurance system, workers and their employers are required to pay taxes on wages and salaries, which are used to finance benefits for unemployed workers covered by the program. Typically, the benefits replace about 50 percent of a worker's prior pretax earnings for up to 26 weeks. During several recessions, Congress has extended the benefits for an additional 13 weeks. Moreover, during the recession and sluggish recovery from the 2008–2009 recession, the benefits were extended to up to 99 weeks. In many European countries, the unemployment benefits are even higher than in the United States, and people are sometimes permitted to continue drawing benefits for two or three years.

Unfortunately, unemployment programs have an unintended secondary effect: They increase the unemployment rate. The benefits make it less costly for an unemployed worker to turn down available jobs and continue searching while receiving the payments. They also reduce the incentive of the unemployed to switch occupations or move to another location in order to find employment. As a result, workers stay unemployed longer and the overall unemployment rate is higher than it would be otherwise. In fact, empirical evidence indicates that there is a spike in the number of unemployed workers obtaining employment just prior to and immediately after their unemployment benefits are exhausted. The persistently higher unemployment rates in Europe, where the benefits are more generous, also indicate that the program pushes the unemployment rate upward, perhaps by as much as 2 or 3 percentage points.

To deal with this problem, Lawrence Brunner and Stephen Colarelli have proposed that a system of personal savings accounts be substituted for the current system.[1] Instead of paying a payroll tax, employees and their employers would make equivalent payments into an unemployment personal savings account owned by the employee. Workers could then access the funds in their accounts during periods of unemployment. Upon retirement, any funds remaining in the account would be available to the worker, and, in case of death, unused funds would be passed along to the worker's heirs. Because this system would mean that workers would be using their own funds rather than the government's during periods of unemployment, the approach would eliminate the perverse incentive structure generated by the current system.

Question for Thought

1. Would the proposed reform increase the incentive to search for and accept employment rather than undergo lengthy periods of unemployment? Why or why not? Can you think of problems this system would create compared with the current system?

[1]Lawrence Brunner and Stephen M. Colarelli, "Individual Unemployment Accounts," *Independent Review* 8 (Spring 2004): 569–85.

8-4 EMPLOYMENT FLUCTUATIONS— THE HISTORICAL RECORD

Employment and output are closely linked over the business cycle. If we are going to produce more goods and services, we must either increase the number of workers or increase the output per worker. Although productivity, or output per worker, is the primary source of long-term economic growth, it changes slowly from year to year. Consequently, rapid increases in output, such as those that occur during a strong business expansion, generally require an increase in employment. As a result, output and employment tend to be positively related. Conversely, there is an inverse relationship between growth of output and the rate of unemployment.

The empirical evidence is consistent with this view. As **Exhibit 8** shows, the unemployment rate generally increases during a recession (indicated by shading), and declines during periods of expansion in output. During the recession of 1960–1961, the rate of unemployment rose to approximately 7 percent. In contrast, it declined throughout the economic boom of the 1960s, only to rise again during the recession of 1970. During the recession of 1974–1975, the unemployment rate jumped to more than 9 percent. Similarly, it soared to nearly 11 percent during the severe recession of 1982 and to 10 percent during the 2008–2009 recession. Conversely, it declined substantially during the expansions of 1983–1989, 1992–2000, and 2002–2006.

8-4a FULL EMPLOYMENT AND THE NATURAL RATE OF UNEMPLOYMENT

Full employment, a term widely used by economists and public officials alike, does not mean zero unemployment. As we have noted, in a world of imperfect information, both employees and employers will "shop" before they agree to accept a job or hire a new worker. Much of this shopping is efficient, because it leads to better matches between the skills of employees and the skills employers need. Some unemployment is therefore necessary for a

Full employment
The level of employment that results from the efficient use of the labor force taking into account the normal (natural) rate of unemployment due to information costs, dynamic changes, and the structural conditions of the economy. For the United States, full employment is thought to exist when approximately 95 percent of the labor force is employed.

The Unemployment Rate, 1960–2013

Here, we illustrate the rate of unemployment during the 1960–2013 period. As expected, the unemployment rate rose rapidly during each of the eight recessions. (The shaded years indicate recessions.) In contrast, soon after each recession ended, the unemployment rate began to decline as the economy moved to an expansionary phase of the business cycle. Also note that the actual rate of unemployment was substantially greater than the natural rate during and immediately following each recession.

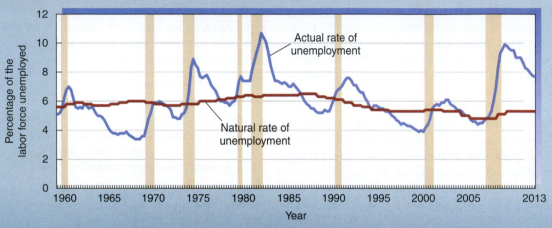

Source: http://www.bls.gov/; and Robert J. Gordon, *Macroeconomics* (Boston: Addison-Wesley, 2012).

Natural rate of unemployment

The "normal" unemployment rate due to frictional and structural conditions in labor markets. It is the unemployment rate that occurs when the economy is operating at a sustainable rate of output. The current natural rate of unemployment in the United States is thought to be approximately 5 percent.

dynamic labor market to operate efficiently. *Consequently, economists define full employment as the level of employment that results when the rate of unemployment is "normal," considering both frictional and structural factors.* In the United States, full employment is currently believed to be approximately 95 percent of the labor force.

Closely related to the concept of full employment is the **natural rate of unemployment**, the amount of unemployment reflected by job shopping and imperfect information. *The natural rate of unemployment is not a temporary high or low; it is a rate that is sustainable. Economists sometimes refer to it as the unemployment rate accompanying the economy's "maximum sustainable" rate of output.* When unemployment is at its natural rate, full employment is present, and the economy is achieving the highest rate of output that it can sustain.

The natural rate of unemployment, however, is not fixed. It is affected by the structure of the labor force and by changes in public policy. Over time, changes in the demographic composition of the labor force will influence the natural rate. The natural rate of unemployment increases when youthful workers expand as a proportion of the workforce. Because youthful workers change jobs and move in and out of the labor force often, they experience high rates of unemployment (see Exhibit 7). Therefore, the overall rate of unemployment is pushed upward as they become a larger share of the labor force. This is what happened during the 1960s and 1970s. In 1960, youthful workers (ages 16 to 24) constituted only 16 percent of the labor force. But as the postwar baby boom generation entered the labor market, youthful workers as a share of the labor force rose dramatically. By 1980, one out of every four workers was in the youthful-worker grouping. In contrast, prime-age workers (over age 25) declined from 84 percent of the U.S. workforce in 1960 to only 75 percent in 1980. As a result of these demographic changes, studies indicate that the natural rate of unemployment rose from approximately 5 percent in the late 1950s to more than 6 percent in the mid-1980s.

Since the late 1980s, the situation has reversed. The natural rate of unemployment has declined as the baby boomers moved into their prime working years and youthful workers shrank as a share of the labor force. Today, most researchers estimate that the natural rate is once again about 5 percent.

Public policy may also influence the natural rate of unemployment. When public policy makes it more costly to employ workers and/or less costly for people to remain unemployed, it increases the natural rate of unemployment. The economies of Spain, Italy, and France illustrate this point. During the past several decades, the labor markets of these three countries have been characterized by generous unemployment benefits, nationwide mandated wage rates, and regulations that make it expensive to dismiss workers. Regulations of this type reduce the flexibility of labor markets and make it more costly to hire and employ workers. Unsurprisingly, over the past several decades, the three European economies have persistently experienced higher unemployment rates than similar economies with freer labor markets. High unemployment rates over lengthy time periods are indicative of structural rather than cyclical factors.

The relationship between the *actual* unemployment rate and the *natural* unemployment rate for the United States over the last five decades can be observed in Exhibit 8. Note that the actual unemployment rate fluctuates around the natural rate in response to cyclical economic conditions. The actual rate generally rises above the natural rate during a recession and falls below the natural rate when the economy is in the midst of an economic boom. For example, the actual rate of unemployment was substantially above the natural rate during the recessions of 1974–1975, 1982, and 2008–2009. The reverse was true during the latter stages of the lengthy expansions of the 1960s, 1980s, 1990s, and 2002–2007. As we proceed, we will often compare the actual and natural rates of unemployment. In a very real sense, macroeconomics studies why the actual and natural rates differ and attempts to discern the factors that cause the natural rate to change over time.

8-5 ACTUAL AND POTENTIAL GDP

If an economy is going to realize its potential, full employment is essential. When the actual rate of unemployment exceeds the natural rate, the actual output of the economy will fall below its potential. Potential output does not represent the absolute maximum level of production that could, for example, be generated in wartime or other situations during which the level of aggregate demand is abnormally high. Rather, it is the rate that would be expected under more normal circumstances.

Potential output can therefore be thought of as the maximum *sustainable* output level consistent with the full employment of resources currently available in the economy. To estimate the economy's potential output level, we need to look at three factors: the size of the labor force, the quality (productivity) of labor, and the natural rate of unemployment. Because these factors cannot be estimated with certainty, some variation exists in the estimated values of the potential rate of output.

Exhibit 9 shows the relationship between the actual and potential output of the United States since 1960. The relationship between actual and potential GDP reflects the business cycle. Note the similarity of the actual real GDP data of Exhibit 9 and the hypothetical data of an idealized business cycle of Exhibit 2. Although the actual data of Exhibit 9 are irregular compared to the hypothetical data, periods of expansion and economic boom followed by contraction and recession are clearly observable. During the boom phase, actual output expands rapidly and may temporarily exceed the economy's long-run potential. In contrast, recessions are characterized by an actual real GDP that is less than its potential. As we proceed, we will focus on how we can achieve maximum potential output while minimizing economic instability.

Potential output
The level of output that can be achieved and sustained in the future, given the size of the labor force, its expected productivity, and the natural rate of unemployment consistent with the efficient operation of the labor market. Actual output can differ from the economy's potential output.

8-6 THE EFFECTS OF INFLATION

Inflation is a sustained increase in the general level of prices. When inflation is on the rise, it costs more to purchase a typical bundle of goods and services. Of course, even when the general level of prices is stable, some prices will be rising and others will be falling. During a period of inflation, however, the impact of the rising prices will outweigh the impact of

The Actual and Potential GDP

Here, we illustrate both the actual and potential GDP. Note the gap between the actual and potential GDP during recessions.

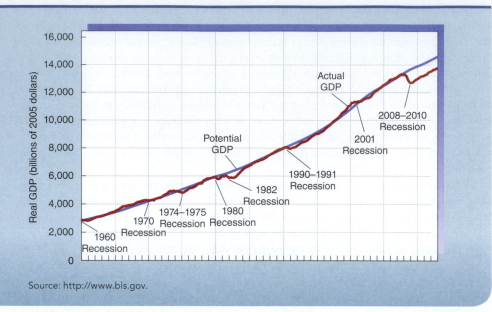

Source: http://www.bls.gov.

falling prices. Because of the higher prices (on average), a dollar will purchase less than it did previously. Inflation, therefore, can also be defined as a decline in the value (the purchasing power) of money.

How do we determine whether prices are generally rising or falling? Essentially, we answered that question in the preceding chapter when we indicated how a price index is constructed. When the general level of prices is rising, the price index will also rise. In turn, the annual rate of inflation is merely the year-to-year change in an index of the general level of prices. The consumer price index (CPI) and the GDP deflator are the price indexes most widely used to measure the inflation rate in the United States. As discussed earlier, these two measures of the rate of inflation tend to follow a similar path.

It's important to note that inflation affects the prices of things we sell as well as the prices of goods we buy. Both resource and product prices are influenced by inflation. Before we become too upset about inflation "robbing us of the purchasing power of our paychecks," we need to realize that inflation influences the size of those paychecks. For example, the weekly earnings of employees would not have risen at a sharp annual rate of 7 percent during the 1970s if the rate of inflation hadn't increased rapidly during the period, too. Wages are also a price. Inflation raises both prices and wages.

How rapidly has the general level of prices risen in the United States? Using the annual rate of change in the CPI, **Exhibit 10** shows the U.S. inflation rate since the mid-1950s. During the 1950s and into the mid-1960s, the annual inflation rate was generally low. The average inflation rate during the 1956–1965 period, for example, was just 1.6 percent. Beginning in the latter half of the 1960s, however, inflation began to accelerate upward, jumping to 12 percent or more during 1974, 1979, and 1980. During the 1973–1981 period, the inflation rate averaged 9.2 percent. Price increases moderated again in the mid-1980s, and the inflation rate averaged 2.9 percent during the period 1983–2013. Additional details on inflation and related measures can be obtained on the Internet at http://www.bls.gov/.

The rate of inflation varies widely among countries. **Exhibit 11** provides data on the annual inflation rates during 2006–2012 for Canada, Germany, Switzerland, and the United States—four countries with low rates of inflation. The annual inflation rates of these countries were less than 4 percent during this period; moreover, the year-to-year variations in inflation were relatively small—typically no more than 1 or 2 percent.

Exhibit 11 also presents parallel inflation rate data for four high-inflation countries: Bolivia, Iceland, Russia, and Venezuela. In contrast with the low-inflation countries, the inflation rate of the high-inflation countries was not only higher, but it also varied substantially more from one year to another. For example, consider the data for Venezuela. The

EXHIBIT 10

The Inflation Rate, 1956–2013

Here, we present the annual rate of inflation since 1956. Between 1956 and 1965, prices increased at an annual rate of only 1.6 percent. In contrast, the inflation rate averaged 9.2 percent during the 1973–1981 era, reaching double-digit rates in several years. Since 1982, the rate of inflation has been lower (the average annual rate was 2.9 percent during the period 1983–2013) and more stable.

inflation rate in Venezuela rose from 13.7 in 2006 to 31.4 in 2008. It receded to 21.1 by 2012. The other countries in the high-inflation group also experienced wide fluctuations in their annual rates of inflation. The data of Exhibit 11 reflect a general pattern. *High rates of inflation are almost always associated with substantial year-to-year swings in the inflation rate.*

8-6a UNANTICIPATED AND ANTICIPATED INFLATION

Before we examine the effects of inflation, it is important that we distinguish between unanticipated and anticipated inflation. **Unanticipated inflation** is an increase in the price level that comes as a surprise, at least to most individuals. For example, suppose that, based on the recent past, most people anticipate an inflation rate of 3 percent. If the actual inflation rate turns out to be 10 percent, it will catch people off guard. When the inflation rate is high and variable, it will be virtually impossible for people to anticipate it accurately.

Unanticipated inflation
An increase in the general level of prices that was not expected by most decision-makers.

EXHIBIT 11

Variations in the Annual Inflation Rates of Selected Countries, 2006–2012

Country	2006	2007	2008	2009	2010	2011	2012
Low inflation (%)							
Canada	2.0	2.1	2.4	0.3	1.8	2.9	1.5
Germany	1.8	2.3	2.6	0.3	1.1	2.1	2.0
Switzerland	1.1	0.7	2.4	−0.5	0.7	0.2	−0.7
United States	3.2	2.9	3.8	−0.4	1.6	3.2	2.1
High inflation (%)							
Boliva	6.6	4.8	7.8	5.6	6.1	5.8	3.3
Iceland	6.7	5.1	12.7	12.0	5.4	4.0	5.2
Russia	9.7	9.0	14.1	11.7	6.9	8.4	5.0
Venezuela	13.7	18.7	31.4	28.6	29.1	27.2	21.1

Source: International Monetary Fund, http://www.imf.org.

Anticipated inflation
An increase in the general level of prices that was expected by most decision-makers.

Anticipated inflation, on the other hand, is a change in the price level that is widely expected. Decision-makers are generally able to anticipate slow, steady rates of inflation—like those in Canada, Germany, Switzerland, and the United States during the period 2006–2012—with a high degree of accuracy. When the general level of prices is more stable, this will exert a positive impact on real output and the level of prosperity. The experience of the United States illustrates this point. During the 1983–2012 period, U.S. inflation was low and relatively stable. This period was characterized by strong growth and only 34 months of recession. In contrast, when the inflation rate was high and variable during the 1970s, the United States experienced two recessions (1974–1975 and 1979–1980) and sluggish growth of real GDP.

8-6b WHY DOES INFLATION ADVERSELY AFFECT THE ECONOMY?

People will not be able to predict high and variable rates of inflation. There are three major reasons why such rates will adversely affect GDP and the overall health of the economy.

1. High and variable inflation reduces investment.
Unanticipated inflation alters the outcomes of long-term projects, such as the purchase of a machine or an investment in a business; it will increase the risks and retard the level of such productive activities. For example, when the price level rises 15 percent one year and 40 percent the next year and then increases again by 20 percent the following year, no one knows what to expect. Unanticipated changes of even 5 percent or 10 percent in the rate of inflation can often turn an otherwise profitable project into a personal economic disaster. Given the uncertainty that it creates, many decision makers will simply forgo capital investments and other transactions involving long-term commitments when the rate of inflation is highly variable and therefore unpredictable. As a result, mutually advantageous gains from trade will be lost and the efficiency of markets reduced.

2. Inflation distorts the information delivered by prices.
Prices communicate important information concerning the relative scarcity of goods and resources. Some prices can be easily and regularly changed. But this will not be true for others, particularly those set by long-term contracts. For example, time delays will occur before the prices accompanying rental lease agreements, items sold in catalogs, mortgage interest rates, and collective bargaining contracts can be changed. Because some prices will respond quickly to inflation whereas others will change more slowly, an unanticipated change in the rate of inflation will change *relative prices* as well as the *general price level*. The distorted relative prices will be a less reliable indicator of relative scarcity. As a result of these unreliable price signals, producers and resource suppliers will often make choices that they will later regret, and the allocation of resources will be less efficient than it would have been if the general level of prices had been more stable.

3. High and variable inflation results in less productive use of resources.
Failing to anticipate accurately the inflation rate can have a substantial effect on one's wealth. Because of this, when the inflation rate is high, people will spend more of their time and money trying to predict and cope with the future rate of inflation. These are resources that could have been used to produce goods and services demanded by the marketplace. For example, managers will spend more time coping with frequent price changes and less time improving production methods and products. Speculative market practices will occur as people try to outguess one another about the future direction of prices. As a result, funds will flow into speculative-type investments instead of more productive ones that increase output.

8-6c WHAT CAUSES INFLATION?

We need to acquire some additional tools of analysis before we can answer in detail the question of what causes inflation. However, at this point we can list two particular causes.

First, economists emphasize the link between aggregate demand and supply. If aggregate demand rises more rapidly than supply, prices will rise. Second, nearly all economists believe that a rapid expansion in a nation's stock of money causes inflation. The old saying is that prices will rise because "there is too much money chasing too few goods." The hyperinflation experienced by Zimbabwe, Russia, and several other countries of the former Soviet Union during various periods since 1990 has been primarily the result of monetary expansion. Once we develop additional knowledge about the operation of our economy, we will consider this issue in more detail.

LOOKING AHEAD

In this chapter, we looked at business cycles and how they affect employment, and how inflation, both anticipated and unanticipated, affects output. In the next chapter, we will begin to develop a macroeconomic model that will help us better understand the factors that influence these indicators of economic performance.

KEY POINTS

- During the past century, real GDP in the United States has grown at an average annual rate of approximately 3 percent. Cyclical movements in real GDP have accompanied this growth of output.

- The four phases of the business cycle are *expansion*, *peak (or boom)*, *contraction*, and *recession*. A recession is often defined as two back-to-back quarters of declining real GDP. If a recession is quite severe, it is called a depression.

- There are three types of unemployment: (1) frictional unemployment, (2) structural unemployment, and (3) cyclical unemployment. In a world of imperfect information and dynamic change, some unemployment is inevitable.

- Full employment is the employment level consistent with the economy's natural rate of unemployment. Both full employment

and the natural rate of unemployment are associated with the economy's maximum sustainable rate of output.

- Potential output is the maximum *sustainable* output level consistent with the economy's resource base and current institutional arrangements.

- Inflation is an increase in the general level of prices. It is important to distinguish between anticipated and unanticipated inflation. Unanticipated changes in the rate of inflation often alter the intended terms of long-term agreements and cause people to regret choices they have previously made.

- Inflation, particularly unanticipated inflation, has harmful effects. These include (1) adverse impact on investment and other time-dimension contracts, (2) distortion of relative prices, and (3) the shift of productive resources into activities designed to prevent inflation from eroding one's wealth.

CRITICAL ANALYSIS QUESTIONS

1. List the major phases of the business cycle and indicate how real GDP, employment, and unemployment change during these phases. Are the time periods of business cycles and the duration of the various phases relatively similar and therefore highly predictable?

2. *Explain why even an efficiently functioning economic system will have some unemployed resources.

3. *Classify each of the following as employed, unemployed, or not in the labor force:

   a. Brown is not working; she applied for a job at Walmart last week and is awaiting the result of her application.
   b. Martinez is vacationing in Florida during a layoff at a

   General Motors plant due to a model changeover, but he expects to be recalled in a couple of weeks.
   c. Green was laid off as a carpenter when a construction project was completed. He is looking for work but has been unable to find anything except a $10-per-hour job, which he turned down.
   d. West works 70 hours per week as a homemaker for her family of nine.
   e. Carson, a 17-year-old, works six hours per week as a delivery person for the local newspaper.
   f. Chang works three hours in the mornings at a clinic and for the last two weeks has spent the afternoons looking for a full-time job.

4. What is full employment? When full employment is present, will the rate of unemployment be zero? Explain.

5. Is the natural rate of unemployment fixed? Why or why not? How are full employment and the natural rate of unemployment related? Is the actual rate of unemployment currently greater or less than the natural rate of unemployment? Why?

6. *How are the following related to one another?

  a. the actual rate of unemployment
  b. the natural rate of unemployment
  c. cyclical unemployment
  d. potential GDP

7. *Use the following data to calculate (a) the labor force participation rate, (b) unemployment rate, and (c) the employment/population ratio:

Population (aged 16 and over)	10,000
Labor force	6,000
Not currently working	4,500
Employed full-time	4,000
Employed part-time	1,500
Unemployed	500

8. *People are classified as unemployed if they are not currently working at a job and if they made an effort to find a job during the past four weeks. Does this mean that there were no jobs available? Does it mean that there were no jobs available for which the unemployed workers were qualified? What does it mean?

9. What impact will high and variable rates of inflation have on the economy? How will they influence the risk accompanying long-term contracts and related business decisions?

10. The nominal salary paid to the president of the United States along with data for the consumer price index (CPI) are given for various years below.

Year	Presidential Salary	CPI (2000 = 100)
1920	$75,000	11.6
1940	75,000	8.1
1960	100,000	17.2
1980	200,000	47.9
2000	400,000	100.0

  a. Calculate the president's real salary measured in the purchasing power of the dollar in 2000.
  b. In which year was the real presidential salary the highest?
  c. The president's nominal salary was constant between 1920 and 1940. What happened to the real salary? Can you explain why?

11. "When employees are dismissed from employment for reasons other than poor performance, unemployment benefits should replace 100 percent of their prior earnings while they are searching for a new job." Do you think this proposal is a good one? Why or why not? If instituted, would the policy influence how quickly laid-off workers would find new jobs? What impact would the policy have on the unemployment rate?

12. Suppose that the consumer price index at year-end 2011 was 150 and by year-end 2012 had risen to 160. What will be the inflation rate during 2012?

13. *"My money wage rose by 6 percent last year, but inflation completely erased these gains. How can I get ahead when inflation continues to wipe out my increases in earnings?" What's wrong with this way of thinking?

14. Data for nominal GDP and the GDP deflator (2005 = 100) in 2009 and 2010 for six major industrial countries are presented in the accompanying Table A.

  a. Use the data provided to calculate the 2009 and 2010 real GDP of each country measured in 2005 prices. Place the figures in the blanks provided.
  b. Use the data for the GDP deflator to calculate the inflation rate of each country. Put your answers in the blanks provided.
  c. Which country had the highest growth rate of real GDP? Which had the lowest?
  d. Which countries had the highest and the lowest inflation rates?
  e. Which one of the countries had the most inflation during this period?

15. The following Table B presents the 2011 population, employment, and unemployment data among working age persons for several countries.

  a. Calculate the number of people in the labor force for each country.
  b. Calculate the labor force participation rate for each country, and put the figures in the blanks provided. Which country had the highest labor force participation rate? Which country had the lowest?
  c. Calculate the unemployment rate for each country, and put the figures in the blanks provided. Which country had the highest unemployment rate? Which had the lowest?

*Asterisk denotes questions for which answers are given in Appendix B.

TABLE A

Country	Nominal GDP (billions of local currency units) 2011	2012	GDP Deflator (2005 = 100) 2011	2012	Real GDP (in 2005 currency units) 2011	2012	Inflation Rate 2012
United States	15,075.7	15,684.8	113.4	115.4	———	———	———
Canada	1,718.7	1,817.6	115.2	119.7	———	———	———
Japan	470,623.2	475,867.9	92.4	91.6	———	———	———
Italy	1,579.2	1,566.3	110.9	112.7	———	———	———
Australia	1,444.6	1,488.3	128.1	127.4	———	———	———
United Kingdom	1,515.8	1,541.5	115.5	117.1	———	———	———

Source: International Monetary Fund, http://www.imf.org

TABLE B

Country	Population (in millions)	Number Employed (in millions)	Number Unemployed	Rate of Labor Force Participation (percentage)	Rate of Unemployment (percentage)
United States	239.6	139.9	13.7	———	———
Canada	27.6	17.2	1.2	———	———
Japan	110.9	62.3	2.7	———	———
Germany	71.0	39.5	2.5	———	———
France	49.9	25.5	2.6	———	———
Australia	18.1	11.4	0.6	———	———
Italy	51.6	22.7	2.1	———	———

Source: www.bls.gov. Data are based on persons aged 15 and older for Australia, Japan, Germany, and Italy. Data are based on persons aged 16 and older for United States, Canada, and France.

CHAPTER 9
An Introduction to Basic Macroeconomic Markets

FOCUS

- What is the circular flow of income? What are the major markets that coordinate macroeconomic activities?

- Why is the aggregate demand for goods and services inversely related to the price level?

- Why is an increase in the price level likely to expand output in the short run, but not in the long run?

- What determines the equilibrium level of GDP of an economy? When equilibrium is present, how will the actual rate of unemployment compare with the natural rate?

- What is the difference between the real interest rate and the money interest rate? Does inflation help borrowers relative to lenders?

- What determines the exchange rate? What is the relationship between the inflow of capital and the trade deficit?

Macroeconomics is interesting . . . because it is challenging to reduce the complicated details of the economy to manageable essentials. Those essentials lie in the interactions among the goods, labor, and assets [loanable funds] markets of the economy. —**Rudiger Dornbusch and Stanley Fischer**[1]

[1]Rudiger Dornbusch and Stanley Fischer, *Macroeconomics* (New York: McGraw-Hill, 1978).

Macroeconomics is primarily about economic growth and fluctuations in output, employment, and the general level of prices. As previously noted, the real GDP of the United States has grown at an average annual rate of about 3 percent during the past century. This growth has improved the living standards of Americans, but it has been uneven. In some years, the economy has grown by more than 3 percent. In others, it has grown by much less. In still other years, it has actually declined. The United States has also experienced fluctuations in employment and the rate of inflation. The experience of other countries has been similar. All countries experience short-term fluctuations in output and employment, and varying degrees of inflation.

It is one thing to describe these fluctuations and another to understand their causes. In this chapter, we will develop a simple macroeconomic model that explains the factors underlying output, employment, and the general level of prices. In subsequent chapters, we will use this model to analyze economic fluctuations and what might be done about them.

9-1 UNDERSTANDING MACROECONOMICS: OUR GAME PLAN

A model is like a road map: It illustrates relationships. The simple model developed in this chapter will help us better understand macroeconomic relationships. It will also help us analyze the impact of macroeconomic policy.

Macroeconomic policy is usually divided into two components: fiscal policy and monetary policy. **Fiscal policy** relates to the government's taxation and spending policies to achieve macroeconomic goals. In the United States, fiscal policy is conducted by Congress and the president. It is thus a reflection of the political process. **Monetary policy** encompasses actions that alter the **money supply**—the amount of cash in our billfolds and deposits in our checking accounts. The direction of monetary policy is determined by a nation's central bank, the Federal Reserve System in the United States. Ideally, both monetary and fiscal policy are used to promote business stability, high employment, the growth of output, and a stable price level.

Initially, as we develop our basic macroeconomic model, we will assume that monetary and fiscal policies are unchanged—that Congress and the president aren't making fiscal policy changes and that the Federal Reserve is keeping the money supply constant. Of course, changes in government expenditures, taxes, and the money supply are potentially important. We will investigate their impact in detail in subsequent chapters.

9-2 FOUR KEY MARKETS: RESOURCES, GOODS AND SERVICES, LOANABLE FUNDS, AND FOREIGN EXCHANGE

Businesses generally purchase resources from households and use them to produce goods and services. In turn, households generally use a substantial portion of the income they earn from the sale of their productive services to purchase goods and services supplied by businesses. *Thus, there is a circular flow of output and income between these two key sectors, businesses and households. This circular flow of income is coordinated by four key macroeconomic markets: (1) goods and services, (2) resources, (3) loanable funds, and (4) foreign exchange.*

Exhibit 1 illustrates both the circular flow of income between the household and business sectors and the interrelationships among the key macroeconomic markets. This is a very important exhibit and really much less complicated than it might first appear. It essentially depicts the macroeconomic model explained in this chapter and used to analyze the economy. It will help you see more clearly the various spending flows and interrelationships among the key markets—where the money comes from and where it goes.

Fiscal policy
The use of government taxation and expenditure policies for the purpose of achieving macroeconomic goals.

Monetary policy
The deliberate control of the money supply, and, in some cases, credit conditions, for the purpose of achieving macroeconomic goals.

Money supply
The supply of currency, checking account funds, and traveler's checks. These items are counted as money because they are used as the means of payment for purchases.

EXHIBIT 1

Four Key Markets and the Circular Flow of Income

The circular-flow diagram is a visual model of the economy. The circular flow of income is coordinated by four key markets. First, the resource market (bottom loop) coordinates businesses demanding resources and households supplying them in exchange for income. Second, the loanable funds market (lower center) brings the net saving of households plus the net inflow of foreign capital into balance with the borrowing by businesses and governments. Third, the foreign exchange market (top right) brings the purchases (imports) from foreigners into balance with sales (exports plus net inflow of capital) to them. Finally, the goods and services market (top loop) coordinates the demand (consumption, investment, government purchases, and net exports) with the supply of domestically produced goods and services (real GDP).

© Cengage Learning 2013

Resource market

A highly aggregated market encompassing all resources (labor, physical capital, land, and entrepreneurship) contributing to the production of current output. The labor market is the largest component of this market.

Goods and services market

A highly aggregated market encompassing the flow of all final-user goods and services. The market counts all items that enter into GDP. Thus, real output in this market is equal to real GDP.

The bottom loop of this circular-flow diagram depicts the **resource market**, a highly aggregated market that includes the markets for labor services, natural resources, and physical capital. In the resource market, business firms demand resources because they need them to produce goods and services. Households supply labor and other resources in exchange for income. The forces of demand and supply determine prices in the resource market. The payments made to households and the suppliers of other resources sum to national income. Some of that income is taxed and used to finance the expenditures of governments. A portion is generally saved, but most of us use the bulk of our income to buy goods and services.

The **goods and services market** constitutes the top loop of the circular-flow diagram. In this market, sometimes called the *product market*, businesses supply goods and services in exchange for sales revenue. This market counts all items in the economy's GDP. As the arrows flowing into the goods and services market (top loop) show, there are four major sources of expenditures in this market: (1) household expenditures on consumption (and new housing), (2) business investment, (3) government purchases, and (4) net exports. The expenditures of households, business investors, governments, and foreigners (net exports) compose the aggregate (total) demand for domestic output. As you can see, the goods and services market is a highly diverse market. It includes items such as cheeseburgers, pizza, hairstyling, movie tickets, clothing, television sets, and DVD players—goods purchased primarily by consumers. It also includes investment goods such as tools, manufacturing equipment, and office buildings, generally purchased by business firms. Finally, things like highways, fire protection, and national defense, which are usually purchased by governments, are also part of the goods and services market.

Two other key markets help direct the flow of income between households and businesses. One is the **loanable funds market**. The loanable funds market is the market in which money is borrowed and loaned. It matches people who want to borrow money with those who want to lend it. If you borrow money to go to college or buy a car, you are participating in the loanable funds market.

The net **saving** of the household sector supplies funds to the loanable funds market. The demand for funds arises from businesses to finance investment projects and from government to finance budget deficits. In an open economy like the United States, people also borrow from and lend money to foreigners. Notice the net inflow of capital from foreign economies into the loanable funds market in Exhibit 1. If the funds borrowed from foreigners exceed the loans made to them, there will be a net inflow of funds. This will increase the supply of funds that can be loaned to borrowers. However, if foreigners borrow more money than they supply, there will be a net outflow of funds. The price in the loanable funds market is the interest rate. Like prices in other markets, the interest rate will tend to bring the quantity demanded (funds borrowed by businesses and governments) into balance with the quantity supplied (the net saving of households plus the net inflow of capital from foreigners). When the borrowed funds are spent on investment goods and government purchases, they return to the circular flow.

The other key market is the **foreign exchange market**. The foreign exchange market determines the rate—or price—at which two countries' currencies are exchanged. Firms generally want to be paid in their local currency. International transactions, therefore, generally require one of the trading partners to convert its domestic currency to that of the other partner. Exchanges like this take place in the foreign exchange market. For example, if an American firm purchases glassware from a Mexican supplier, the firm would typically exchange dollars for pesos and then use the pesos to pay for the glassware. This generates demand for pesos. Conversely, when foreigners buy U.S. products, it generates demand for U.S. dollars. The **exchange rate**—the price of one currency relative to another—brings the purchases from foreigners into balance with the sales to them because rates of exchange are also subject to the laws of supply and demand.

Look closely at the right side of Exhibit 1 to determine what happens to the flow of income received by households. A major portion of household income is used to purchase consumer goods from domestic producers. These expenditures flow directly into the goods and services market. However, there are three types of "leakages" that can occur: Households will use some of their income to purchase imports; some of the income will be taxed away by the government; and some of it will be saved. Imports, net taxes, and net saving are leakages from the circular flow of income.

However, these income leakages don't just evaporate into thin air. They tend to be channeled into the loanable funds and foreign exchange markets and back into the circular flow. The loanable funds market will tend to direct the net saving of households toward business investment and government purchases. The foreign exchange market will tend to direct import expenditures toward either spending by foreigners on exports or supplying funds to the loanable funds market. As we proceed, we will investigate in more detail how the loanable funds and foreign exchange markets influence the leakages from and injections to the circular flow of income.

As we noted in Chapter 7, there are two ways of measuring gross domestic product (GDP), the aggregate domestic output of an economy. First, GDP can be measured by adding up the spending of consumers, investors, governments, and foreigners (net exports) on goods and services produced during the year. This method is equivalent to measuring the flow of output as it moves through the top loop—the goods and services market—of the circular-flow diagram. Alternatively, GDP can be measured by summing the income payments, both direct and indirect, received by the resource suppliers who produced the goods and services. This method uses the bottom loop—the resource market—to measure the flow of output.

Loanable funds market
A general term used to describe the market that coordinates the borrowing and lending decisions of business firms and households. Commercial banks, savings and loan associations, the stock and bond markets, and insurance companies are important financial institutions in this market.

Saving
The portion of after-tax income that is not spent on consumption. Saving is a "flow" concept.

Foreign exchange market
The market in which the currencies of different countries are bought and sold.

Exchange rate
The price of one unit of foreign currency in terms of the domestic currency. For example, if it takes $1.50 to purchase an English pound, the dollar–pound exchange rate is 1.50.

9-3 AGGREGATE DEMAND FOR GOODS AND SERVICES

What goes on in the aggregate goods and services market is central to the health of an economy. Indeed, if we could keep our eye on just one market in an economy, we would choose the goods and services market. It is important to note that the "quantity" and "price" in this highly aggregated, or combined, market differ from their counterparts in markets for specific goods. In the aggregate market for goods and services, the "quantity" (graphed on the *x*-axis) refers to the output of the entire economy—its GDP, in other words. The "price" (graphed on the *y*-axis) refers to the price level in the entire economy, which is measured by a general price index (such as the GDP deflator or consumer price index).

Demand and supply can help us understand highly aggregated markets just as they do markets for specific goods (say, for mp3 players or Starbucks coffee). Because demand in the goods and services market aggregates, or combines together, the purchases of all consumers, investors, governments, and foreigners, it is called "aggregate demand." The **aggregate demand curve** shows the various quantities of *domestically produced* goods and services purchasers are willing to buy at different price levels. As **Exhibit 2** illustrates, the aggregate demand curve (*AD*) slopes downward to the right, indicating an inverse relationship between the amount of goods and services demanded and the price level.

Aggregate demand curve
A downward-sloping curve showing the relationship between the price level and the quantity of domestically produced goods and services all households, business firms, governments, and foreigners (net exports) are willing to purchase.

9-3a WHY DOES THE AGGREGATE DEMAND CURVE SLOPE DOWNWARD?

The reason the aggregate demand curve slopes downward is different from the reason the demand curve for a single product does. The inverse relationship between price and the amount demanded of a specific commodity—television sets, for example—reflects the fact that consumers will buy the good in lieu of substitute goods when its price goes down. This

---

EXHIBIT 2

The Aggregate Demand Curve

The quantity of goods and services purchased will increase (to Y_2) as the price level declines (to P_2). Other things being constant, the lower price level will increase the wealth of people holding money, lead to lower interest rates, and make domestically produced goods cheaper relative to foreign goods. All these factors will tend to increase the quantity of goods and services purchased at the lower price level.

Reduction in price level will increase quantity of goods and services demanded.

© Cengage Learning 2013

is because the good becomes less expensive relative to others. In contrast, a price reduction in the aggregate goods and services market indicates that the level of prices in the entire economy has declined. When this happens, the prices of *all* goods are lower. When the prices of all goods produced domestically fall by the same proportion, there will be no incentive for *domestic* buyers to substitute one good for another.

Nonetheless, there will still be an inverse relationship between price and quantity in the goods and services market. There are three major reasons a lower price level will lead to an increase in the aggregate quantity of goods and services demanded by purchasers.

1. A lower price level will increase the purchasing power of money.
As the level of prices declines, the purchasing power of money increases. For example, suppose that you have $2,000 in your bank account. Consider how a 20 percent reduction in the level of prices will influence your wealth and spending. At the lower price level, your $2,000 will buy more goods and services. In fact, your $2,000 will buy as much as $2,500 would have purchased at the previous higher price level. Other people will be in the same position you are. They will be wealthier and able to buy more. (*Note:* Remember we are assuming that the supply of money is fixed—that the Federal Reserve is keeping the money supply constant.) Because of this increase in wealth, people will purchase more goods and services.

2. The interest-rate effect: A lower price level will reduce the demand for money and lower the real interest rate, which will stimulate additional purchases.
When the average price of everything is lower, consumers and businesses will need less money to conduct their normal activities. Households will be able to get by just fine with a smaller money balance because, at the lower price level, they will be spending a smaller amount on food, clothing, and other items they regularly purchase. Similarly, businesses will need less money to pay employee wages, taxes, and other business expenses. At the lower price level, both consumers and businesses will attempt to reduce their money balances and shift more funds to interest-earning assets like bonds and savings deposits. This will channel more funds into the loanable funds market, placing downward pressure on interest rates.

What impact will a lower interest rate have on the demand for goods and services? A reduction in the interest rate will make it cheaper to purchase goods and services on credit. Both households and businesses will demand more goods and services as a result. Households can be expected to increase their purchases of interest-sensitive consumption goods, like automobiles and consumer durables. Similarly, firms will invest more in business expansion and new construction. This effect through the interest rate also contributes to the downward slope of the aggregate demand curve.

3. Other things being constant, a lower price level will make domestically produced goods less expensive relative to foreign goods.
As a result, if prices fall in the United States, for example, imports will decline as Americans find that many domestically produced goods are now cheaper than are products produced abroad. At the lower price level, Americans will tend to purchase fewer Japanese automobiles, Korean textiles, Italian shoes, and other imports because these items are now more expensive relative to domestically produced goods. At the same time, foreigners will increase their purchases of American-made goods that are now relatively cheaper. Therefore, net exports (exports minus imports) will tend to rise.[2] The increase in net exports at the lower U.S. price level will directly increase the quantity demanded of domestically produced goods. This international-substitution effect is a third reason the aggregate demand curve slopes downward.

---

[2]An increase in exports and a decline in imports will place some upward pressure on the foreign exchange value of the currency. However, the lower interest rates (point 2 above) will result in an outflow of capital, which will place downward pressure on the foreign exchange value of the currency. Most economists believe that this latter effect will dominate. If it does, a depreciation in the nation's currency will stimulate net exports, which will also increase the quantity demanded of goods and services.

Thumbnail Sketch

Why Is The Aggregate Quantity Demanded Inversely Related to the Price Level?

A decrease in the price level will raise the aggregate quantity demanded because:

1. The real wealth of people holding money will increase when prices fall; this will encourage additional consumption.

2. A fall in the demand for money at the lower price level will reduce interest rates, which will encourage current investment and consumption.

3. Net exports will expand (because the prices of domestic goods will have fallen relative to foreign goods).

©iStockphoto.com/baianliang

9-3b THE DOWNWARD-SLOPING AGGREGATE DEMAND CURVE: A SUMMARY

The above **Thumbnail Sketch** summarizes the reasons why a lower price level increases the quantity demanded of domestically produced goods and services. A lower price level will (1) increase the purchasing power of money, (2) lower interest rates, and (3) reduce the price of domestically produced goods relative to goods produced abroad. Each of these factors will tend to increase the quantity demanded in the goods and services market.

If the price level were to rise, the effects would be just the opposite. At a higher price level, (1) the wealth of people holding money would be less; (2) the demand for money would be greater, which would lead to higher interest rates; and (3) domestic goods would be more expensive relative to those produced abroad. Each of these factors would tend to reduce the quantity demanded of domestically produced goods.

9-4 AGGREGATE SUPPLY OF GOODS AND SERVICES

Aggregate supply curve
The curve showing the relationship between a nation's price level and the quantity of goods supplied by its producers. In the short run, it is an upward-sloping curve, but in the long run the aggregate supply curve is vertical.

In light of our discussion of aggregate demand, it shouldn't surprise you that the general shape of the **aggregate supply curve** differs from the shape of the supply curve for a single good. As we already noted, when the price level rises, the prices of all goods rise, rather than the price of one good relative to other goods. Thus, the general shape of the aggregate supply (*AS*) curve is not a reflection of changes in the relative prices of goods.

When we examine aggregate supply, it is particularly important to distinguish between the short run and the long run. In the short run, some prices, particularly those in labor markets, are set by prior contracts and agreements. Households and businesses are unable to adjust these prices when unexpected changes occur, including unexpected changes in the price level. In contrast, the long run is a time period long enough that people are able to modify their behavior in response to price changes. We now consider both the short-run and long-run aggregate supply curves.

9-4a AGGREGATE SUPPLY IN THE SHORT RUN

The short-run aggregate supply (SRAS) curve shows the various quantities of goods and services domestic firms will supply in response to changing demand conditions that alter the level of prices in the goods and services market. As Exhibit 3 part (a) shows, the *SRAS* curve in the goods and services market slopes upward to the right. The upward slope

EXHIBIT 3

The Aggregate Supply Curve

The short-run aggregate supply (SRAS) curve shows the relationship between the price level and the quantity supplied of goods and services by domestic producers (part a). In the short run, firms will generally expand output as the price level increases; the higher prices will improve their profit margins because many of their cost components will be temporarily fixed as the result of prior long-term commitments. However, once people have had time to adjust their prior long-term commitments, resource markets (and costs) will adjust to the higher level of prices, and firms will no longer have an incentive to supply a larger output at the higher price level. The vertical long-run aggregate supply (LRAS) curve in part (b) illustrates this point. The economy's full-employment rate of output—YF, the maximum output rate that is sustainable—is determined by the supply of resources, level of technology, and structure of institutions, factors that are insensitive to changes in the price level.

(a) Short-run aggregate supply

(b) Long-run aggregate supply

© Cengage Learning 2013

reflects the fact that, in the short run, an unanticipated increase in the price level will, on average, improve the profitability of firms. They will respond with an expansion in output.

The *SRAS* curve is based on a specific expected price level, P_{100} in the case of Exhibit 3, and rate of inflation that generates that price level. When the expected price level is actually achieved, the profitability rate of firms, on average, will be normal, and they will supply output Y_0.

Consider how firms would respond if strong demand led to an unexpected increase in the price level (to P_{105}, for example). Important components of producers' costs are determined by long-term contracts. These components include interest rates on their loans, collective bargaining agreements with their employees, lease agreements on buildings and machines, and other contracts with resource suppliers. The prices incorporated into these long-term contracts at the time of the agreement are based on the expectation of price level (P_{100}) for the current period and tend to be temporarily fixed. So, in the short run, the higher prices enhance producers' profitability because the prices for which they can sell their products rise, but some of their costs (like labor) don't. When this happens, firms will happily respond by expanding their output (to Y_1). Their profits will be higher if they do.[3]

---

[3]Other factors may also contribute to the positive relationship between the price level and output in the short run. In response to a general increase in demand, some firms may expand output without much of an increase in price because they believe that their current strong sales are only temporary and that a price increase would drive some of their regular customers to rival suppliers. Other firms may expand output because they mistakenly believe that the demand for their product has increased relative to other products. In the long run, higher costs relative to product prices will make it impossible to sustain such expansions in output.

Conversely, an unexpected reduction in the price level to P_{95} will have the opposite effect. It will decrease product prices relative to costs and thereby reduce profitability. In response, firms will reduce output to Y_2. Thus, as Exhibit 3(a) illustrates, there is a direct relationship between the amount producers will supply and the price level in the goods and services market in the short run.

9-4b AGGREGATE SUPPLY IN THE LONG RUN

Things are different, though, when it comes to aggregate supply in the long run. In the long run, a higher price level won't change the relationship between product and resource prices. Once people have time to adjust their prior commitments fully, competitive forces will restore the usual relationship between product prices and costs. Profit rates will return to normal, and firms will not have any additional incentive to pump out extra goods and services. *The long-run aggregate supply (LRAS) curve shows the relationship between the price level and quantity of output after decision-makers have had time to adjust their prior commitments, or take steps to counterbalance them, when the price level changes.* Therefore, as Exhibit 3 part (b) illustrates, the *LRAS* curve is vertical.

In the long run, once people have had time to adjust their choices, an increase in demand and higher price level will not expand the quantity supplied. The forces that generate the increase in quantity supplied in the short run will not be present in the long run. Costs that are temporarily fixed as the result of contractual agreements will rise once the long-term contracts expire and are renegotiated. When this happens, resource prices will increase in the same proportion as product prices. A proportional increase in costs and product prices will leave the incentive to produce unchanged. Consider how a firm with a selling price of $50 and per-unit costs of $50 will be affected when both the price it can sell its product for and the resources used to make it double. After the price increase, the firm's sales price per unit will be $100, but so, too, will its per-unit costs. Thus, neither the firm's profit rate nor its incentive to produce more of the good has changed. Therefore, in the long run, an increase in the price level will fail to exert a lasting impact on aggregate output.

As we discussed in Chapter 2, at a point in time, the production possibilities of a nation are constrained by the supply of resources, level of technology, and institutional arrangements that influence the efficiency of resource use. The long-run aggregate supply curve is an alternative way to visualize the economy's production possibilities. Rather than showing the output of physical units like the production possibilities curve does, the long-run aggregate supply curve shows the real dollar value of the units produced. The vertical long-run supply curve indicates that a change in the price level doesn't loosen the constraints limiting our production possibilities. For example, a doubling of prices will not improve technology. Neither will it expand the availability of productive resources, nor improve the efficiency of our economic institutions.

Thus, there is no reason a higher price level would increase our ability to produce goods and services in the long run. This is precisely what the vertical *LRAS* curve implies. The temporary hike in aggregate supply—shown by the upward slope of the *SRAS* curve—is purely a short-run phenomenon. It can't last. The accompanying **Thumbnail Sketch** summarizes the factors that underlie both the short-run and long-run aggregate supply curves.

9-5 EQUILIBRIUM IN THE GOODS AND SERVICES MARKET

Equilibrium
A balance of forces permitting the simultaneous fulfillment of plans by buyers and sellers.

We are now ready to combine our analysis of aggregate demand and aggregate supply to see how they determine the price level and rate of output in the economy. When a market is in **equilibrium**, the forces exerted by buyers and sellers balance one another. Buyers are willing to purchase all the units that sellers are willing to supply *at the current price level*. Because the equilibrium price clears the market—all units produced are sold—some refer to it as the "market-clearing price."

Thumbnail Sketch

Why Is the Short-Run Aggregate Quantity Supplied Directly Related to the Price Level?

As the general level of sales prices for products increases, profit margins will improve because some costs of production are temporarily fixed by long-term contracts.

Why is the long-run aggregate supply curve vertical?

1. Once people have had time to adjust fully to a new price level, the normal relationship between product prices and resource costs will be restored.
2. The sustainable potential output of an economy is determined by its quantity of resources, level of technology, and the efficiency of its institutional structures—not by the price level.

9-5a EQUILIBRIUM IN THE SHORT RUN

As **Exhibit 4** illustrates, short-run equilibrium is present in the goods and services market at the price level P, at which the aggregate quantity demanded is equal to the aggregate quantity supplied. This occurs at the output rate Y, where the *AD* and *SRAS* curves intersect. At the price level P, the amount that buyers want to purchase is just equal to the quantity that sellers are willing to supply.

If a price level lower than P were present, the aggregate quantity demanded would exceed the aggregate quantity supplied. Purchasers would want to buy more goods and services than producers would be willing to produce. This excess demand would place upward pressure on prices, causing the price level to rise toward P. In contrast, at a price level greater than P, the aggregate quantity supplied would exceed the aggregate quantity

EXHIBIT 4

Short-Run Equilibrium in the Goods and Services Market

Short-run equilibrium in the goods and services market occurs at the price level P, where the *AD* and *SRAS* curves intersect. If the price level were lower than P, excess demand in goods and services markets would push prices upward. Conversely, if the price level were higher than P, excess supply would result in falling prices.

demanded. Producers would be unable to sell all the goods they produce. This would result in downward pressure (toward *P*) on prices. Only at the price level *P* will there be a balance of forces between the amount of goods demanded by consumers, investors, governments, and foreigners and the amount supplied by domestic firms.

9-5b EQUILIBRIUM IN THE LONG RUN

In the short run, the goods and services market will gravitate toward a price level that brings quantity demanded and quantity supplied in the economy into balance. *However, a second condition is required for long-run equilibrium: decision-makers who agreed to long-term contracts influencing current prices and costs must have correctly anticipated the current price level at the time they arrived at the agreements.* If this is not the case, buyers and sellers will want to modify the agreements when their long-term contracts expire. In turn, their modifications will affect costs, profit margins, and output.

Exhibit 5 illustrates a long-run equilibrium in the goods and services market. As in Exhibit 3, the subscripts attached to the *SRAS* and *AD* curves indicate the price level (the price index) that decision-makers anticipated at the time they made their decisions about their long-term contracts. In this case, when buyers and sellers made their purchasing and production choices, they anticipated that the price level during the period would be P_{100}. As the intersection of the *AD* and *SRAS* curves reveals, P_{100} was actually attained. In long-run equilibrium, aggregate demand (*AD*) intersects with *SRAS* along the economy's vertical *LRAS*.

When the price level expectations about the long-term contracts turn out to be correct, then the current resource prices and real interest rates will tend to persist into the future. Profit rates will be normal. The choices of buyers and sellers will harmonize, and neither will have reason to modify their previous contractual agreements when they come up for renegotiation. Thus, the current rate of output (*YF*) is sustainable in the future. This also corresponds to full employment in the economy. Long-run equilibrium is present, and it will persist into the future until changes in other factors alter *AD* or *SRAS*.

EXHIBIT 5

Long-Run Equilibrium in the Goods and Services Market

When the goods and services market is in long-run equilibrium, two conditions must be present. First, the quantity demanded must equal the quantity supplied at the current price level. Second, the price level anticipated by decision makers must equal the actual price level. The subscripts on the *SRAS* and *AD* curves indicate that buyers and sellers alike anticipated the price level P_{100}, where the 100 represents an index of prices during an earlier base year. When the anticipated price level is actually attained, current output (*Y_r*) will equal the economy's potential GDP, and full employment will be present.

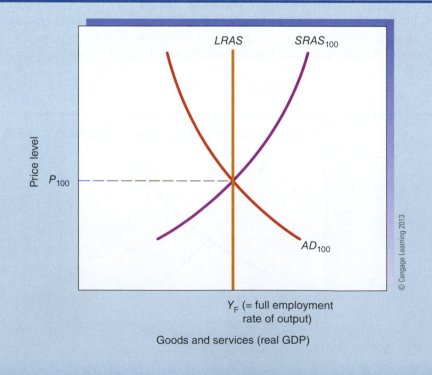

9-5c LONG-RUN EQUILIBRIUM, POTENTIAL OUTPUT, AND FULL EMPLOYMENT

As we discussed in Chapter 8, potential GDP is equal to the economy's *maximum sustainable output* consistent with its resource base, current technology, and institutional structure. Potential GDP is neither a temporary high nor an abnormal low. When long-run equilibrium is present, the actual output achieved is equal to the economy's potential GDP.

The long-run equilibrium output rate (Y_F in Exhibit 5) also corresponds with the full employment of resources. When full-employment output is present, the job search time of unemployed workers will be normal, given the characteristics of the labor force and the institutional structure of the economy. Only frictional and structural unemployment will be present; cyclical unemployment will be absent.

When an economy is in long-run equilibrium, the actual rate of unemployment will be equal to the natural rate. Remember, the natural rate of unemployment reflects the normal job search process of employees and employers, given the structure of the economy and the laws and regulations that affect the operation of markets. It is a rate that is neither abnormally high nor abnormally low; it can be sustained into the future. If long-run equilibrium is present, unemployment will be at its natural rate.

Let's summarize what we've learned: In long-run equilibrium, (1) output will be equal to its potential, (2) full employment will be achieved, and (3) the actual rate of unemployment will be equivalent to the natural rate of unemployment. It is this long-run maximum sustainable output that economists are referring to when they speak of "full-employment output" or "potential GDP."

9-5d WHAT HAPPENS WHEN THE ECONOMY'S OUTPUT DIFFERS FROM ITS LONG-RUN POTENTIAL?

Scenario 1: output is greater than long-run potential What happens when changes in the price level catch buyers and sellers by surprise? When the actual price level differs from the level forecast by buyers and sellers, some decision-makers will enter into agreements that they will later regret—agreements that they will want to change as soon as they have an opportunity to do so.

Consider the situation when the price level increases more than was anticipated. Failing to foresee the strong demand and higher product prices, many resource suppliers will have agreed to long-term contracts that are not as attractive as they initially thought they would be. For example, many union officials and employees will have made commitments to money wages that are now unattractive, given the strong demand and higher general level of prices. Other resource suppliers will find themselves in a similar position. In the short run, the atypically low resource costs relative to product prices make profit margins abnormally high. In this case, firms will pump out more output to boost their profits. Employment expands and unemployment falls below its natural rate.

An economic boom is present, but the abnormally large output and high level of employment are not sustainable. The "mistakes," based on a failure to predict the strength of current demand, will be recognized and corrected when contracts expire. Real wages (and other resource prices) will increase and eventually reflect the higher price level and rate of inflation. Profit margins will return to normal. When these adjustments are completed, the temporarily large output rate and high employment level will decline and return to normal.

How can output, even temporarily, be pushed beyond the economy's potential GDP? Remember, potential GDP is a sustainable rate of output; it can be maintained. Motivated by strong demand and high profitability, firms can expand output through intensive supervision, more overtime work, a reduction in downtime for maintenance, and similar measures. However, this intense pace cannot be maintained over lengthy periods. The situation is much like that of students who stay up later, watch less television, and spend less time on social and leisure activities in order to increase their study time prior to a major exam. They are able to increase their "productivity" temporarily, but the intense schedule cannot be maintained. Similarly, business firms can temporarily push output beyond long-run potential. But, given the constraints of the current resource base, the higher output rate cannot be sustained. Markets will adjust and output will recede to its long-run potential.

Scenario 2: output is less than long-run potential   What will happen if product prices either decline or increase less rapidly than anticipated? Given the lower than expected price level, many employers will find themselves committed to wages and other resource prices that are extremely high relative to the prices they can get for their products. Profit margins will be squeezed, causing producers to reduce output and lay off employees. Unemployment will rise above its *natural rate*, and current output will fall short of the economy's potential GDP. Recessionary conditions will be present.

But the weak demand for resources and abnormally high unemployment will place downward pressure on resource prices and, as long-term contracts are eventually renegotiated, resource prices will fall. In turn, this will reduce costs, and eventually the lower cost will make it possible for firms to once again earn normal returns. As this happens, the economy will be directed back to its long-run equilibrium output and employment rates. Clearly, this adjustment process will take time, several quarters or perhaps even a year or two.

Again, let's summarize what we've learned: An unexpected change in the price level (rate of inflation) will alter the rate of output in the short run. An unexpected *increase* in the price level will stimulate output and employment during the next year or two, whereas an unexpected *decrease* in the price level will cause output and employment to fall.

As we have said, in addition to the aggregate goods and services market, the resource market, loanable funds market, and foreign exchange market help coordinate the circular flow of income between households and businesses. All four of these markets are interrelated—changes in one will have repercussions in the others. We will now turn to an analysis of the resource, loanable funds, and foreign exchange markets and how they work in tandem with the goods and services market.

9-6 RESOURCE MARKET

The expected rate of inflation influences the prices incorporated into long-term contracts, like collective bargaining agreements. If the actual price level differs from what was expected, output will differ from long-run equilibrium.

The resource market is the place where labor services, raw materials, machines, and other factors of production are bought and sold. Within the framework of our circular-flow analysis, households supply resources (like their labor) in exchange for income. Business firms demand resources to produce goods and services, as Exhibit 1 showed. By far, labor is the largest component of the resource market. In the United States, labor costs make up approximately 70 percent of production costs. Because of the labor market's size and importance, we will focus considerable attention on it.

An increase in the price of labor and other resources will increase the cost of production and make it less profitable for firms to employ resources. As a result, businesses will demand less labor and other resources as the prices of those resources increase. Thus, the demand curve in the resource market will have the usual downward slope to the right. Although working and supplying resources generate income, they also require a person to give up other things—like leisure. Higher resource prices—like higher wages—will make it more attractive for people to give up some leisure and supply labor and other resources instead. Therefore, the quantity supplied of labor and other resources expands as resource prices increase.

Todd McInturf/Rapport Press/Newscom

EXHIBIT 6

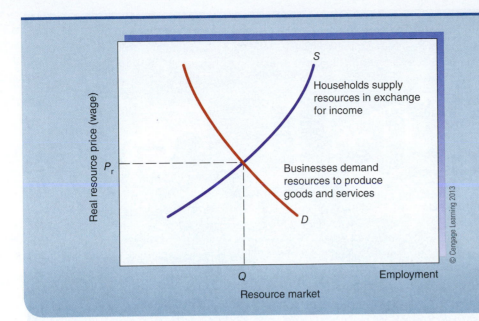

Resource market

Equilibrium in the Resource Market

In general, as resource prices increase, the amount demanded by producers declines and the amount supplied by resource owners expands. In equilibrium, resource price brings the amount demanded into balance with the amount supplied in the aggregate-resource market. The labor market is a major component of the resource market.

As **Exhibit 6** illustrates, there will be a tendency to move toward a price level that will bring the amount of resources demanded by business firms into balance with the amount supplied by resource owners, just as goods and services are brought into balance between consumers and producers. At this price (P_r), the choices of both buyers and sellers in the aggregate resource market harmonize—they are consistent with each other. If either excess demand or excess supply were present, the market would move back toward equilibrium.

The markets for resources and products are closely related. The demand for resources is directly linked to the demand for goods and services. An increase in demand in the goods and services market will generate additional demand for resources. Similarly, a reduction in aggregate demand in the goods and services market will reduce the demand for resources.

Changes in resource markets will also exert an effect on the goods and services market. The cost of producing goods and services is influenced directly by the price of resources. Other things constant, an increase in resource prices will increase costs and squeeze profit margins, causing the supply curve (*SRAS*) in the product market to shift to the left. If inputs are costing firms more, higher product prices will be required to provide firms with the same incentive to supply any given level of output. Conversely, a reduction in resource prices will lower costs and improve profit margins in the goods and services market. An increase in aggregate supply (a shift to the right in *SRAS*) will result. As we analyze the macroeconomy, the interrelations between these two markets will arise again and again.

9-7 LOANABLE FUNDS MARKET

As we have said, the loanable funds market is the market in which borrowers demand funds and lenders supply them. The price in this market is the interest rate. To keep things simple, we will assume that there is a single interest rate. In reality, of course, borrowers and lenders make deals at many different interest rates. Those interest rates depend on what a person or firm is buying, the length of time they want to borrow the money for, and the level of risk involved. Banks, insurance companies, and brokerage firms often act as intermediaries between lenders and borrowers in the loanable funds market.

Essentially, borrowers are exchanging future income to get purchasing power now. Most of us are impatient; we want things now rather than in the future. *From the viewpoint of borrowers, interest is the price they have to pay to get money now. From the lender's viewpoint, interest is the reward they get for waiting, for reducing their current spending so they can loan funds to someone else.*

Banks, savings and loan associations, and brokerage firms help coordinate saving and borrowing in the loanable funds market.

Peter Scholey/Alamy

As part (a) of **Exhibit 7** illustrates, more funds will be borrowed at lower interest rates. A lower interest rate will make it cheaper for households to purchase consumption goods and for businesses to undertake investment projects. They will borrow more at

EXHIBIT 7

Interest Rates and the Loanable Funds Market

The interest rate in the loanable funds market will bring the quantity of funds demanded by borrowers into balance with the quantity supplied by lenders (part a). As part (b) illustrates, inflation will influence the nominal interest rate. Suppose that when people expect the general level of prices to be stable (zero inflation) in the future, a 6 percent interest rate brings quantity demanded into balance with quantity supplied. Under these conditions, the money interest rate and real interest rate will be equal. When people expect prices to rise at a 5 percent rate, however, the money rate of interest (i) will rise to 11 percent even though the real interest rate (r) remains constant at 6 percent.

(a) Interest rate determination

(b) Inflation and nominal interest rate

© Cengage Learning 2013

lower rates. As a result, the demand curve for loanable funds slopes downward to the right. Conversely, higher interest rates make it more attractive to save (and lend funds). Thus, the supply curve for loanable funds slopes upward to the right, indicating that there is a direct relationship between the interest rate and the quantity of funds supplied by lenders. The interest rate will coordinate the actions of borrowers and lenders. It will tend to move toward an equilibrium rate (in the case of Exhibit 7(a), 6 percent). This is the rate at which the quantity of funds supplied by lenders just equals the quantity demanded by borrowers.

It is important to think of the interest rate in two ways. First, there is the **money interest rate**, the percentage of the amount borrowed that must be paid to the lender in addition to the repayment of the principal. Money interest rates are those typically quoted in newspapers and business publications. Second, there is the **real interest rate**, which reflects the actual burden to borrowers and the payoff to lenders after accounting for the impact of inflation.

The rate of inflation expected by borrowers and lenders will influence the attractiveness of various interest rates. Perhaps an example will illustrate this point and highlight the distinction between the money interest rate and the real interest rate. Suppose that a borrower and lender—both anticipating that the general level of prices will be stable—agree to a 6 percent interest rate for a one-year loan of $1,000. After a year, the borrower must pay the lender $1,060—the $1,000 principal plus the 6 percent interest. Now, suppose during the year prices rise 5 percent as the result of inflation. Because of this, the $1,060 repayment after a year commands only about 1 percent more purchasing power than the original $1,000 did when it was loaned. The lender receives only a 1 percent return for making the purchasing power available to the borrower. In this case, the real interest return to the lender (and real cost to the borrower) is just 1 percent. Lenders are unlikely to continue making funds available at such bargain rates. They are going to begin charging higher rates.

When inflation is persistent, people will come to anticipate it. Once borrowers and lenders expect a rate of inflation—5 percent, for example—they will build that rate into their loanable funds agreements. Lenders will demand (and borrowers will agree to pay) a higher money interest rate to compensate for the impact of inflation. This premium for the expected decline in purchasing power of the dollar is called the **inflationary premium**. It is equal to the expected rate of inflation. The relationship between the real interest rate and money interest rate is

Real interest rate = Money interest rate − Inflationary premium

Part (b) of Exhibit 7 illustrates how people's expectations about inflation influence money interest rates. Here, we consider a situation in which a 6 percent market rate of interest would emerge when borrowers and lenders anticipate stable prices. Because the expected rate of inflation is zero, there will be no inflationary premium and, under these conditions, the money interest rate will be equal to the real interest rate. Now consider how a persistent inflation rate of 5 percent will influence the choices of both borrowers and lenders. Compared with the situation in which the inflation rate was zero and the interest rate 6 percent, an 11 percent interest rate will now be required to provide lenders with the same incentive to loan funds. Similarly, an 11 percent interest rate will provide borrowers with the same incentive to demand funds. When people expect a 5 percent rate of inflation, both the supply and demand curves will shift vertically by this amount to compensate for the expected rate of inflation. As a result, the money rate of interest will increase to 11 percent: 5 percent of that is the inflationary premium; 6 percent is the real return that lenders earn.

Of course, the expected rate of inflation and inflationary premium cannot be directly observed. Therefore, neither can the real interest rate. Nonetheless, it is easy to see why the money interest rate can be misleading. It doesn't reflect the real cost of borrowing money. (Remember: *real* always means adjusted for inflation.) What people expect inflation to be and what it actually ends up being can be different. Even though this is problematic, the

Money interest rate
The percentage of the amount borrowed that must be paid to the lender in addition to the repayment of the principal. The money interest rate overstates the real cost of borrowing during an inflationary period. When inflation is anticipated, an inflationary premium will be incorporated into this rate. The money interest rate is often called the nominal interest rate.

Real interest rate
The interest rate adjusted for expected inflation: It indicates the real cost to the borrower (and yield to the lender) in terms of goods and services.

Inflationary premium
A component of the money interest rate that reflects compensation to the lender for the expected decrease, due to inflation, in the purchasing power of the principal and interest during the course of the loan. It is determined by the expected rate of future inflation.

money interest rate will nonetheless vary directly with what people expect inflation to be. If they expect inflation will be higher, the inflationary premium will be higher, too, as will the money rate of interest. Only the *real* interest rate reflects the true cost of borrowing and the true return of lending money.

9-7a DOES INFLATION HELP BORROWERS?

When inflation occurs, borrowers will be able to repay their loans with dollars that have less purchasing power. Thus, it looks like inflation will systematically favor borrowers relative to lenders. But this is incorrect. When inflation is present and decision-makers come to expect it, the money (or nominal) interest rate will be pushed upward by the expected rate of inflation. If the inflation rate is forecast accurately, then the inflationary premium built into the nominal interest rate will fully compensate lenders for the reduction in the purchasing power of the dollar as the loan is repaid.

Of course, borrowers and lenders may not always forecast the future rate of inflation accurately. If the actual rate of inflation is higher than was expected, then borrowers will tend to gain relative to lenders. For example, suppose borrowers and lenders expect a 3 percent future rate of inflation and therefore agree to an 8 percent interest rate on a loan—5 percent representing the real interest rate and 3 percent the inflationary premium. If the actual rate of inflation turns out to be higher than 3 percent—6 percent, for example—then the real amount paid by the borrower and received by the lender will decline. When the actual rate of inflation is greater than is anticipated, borrowers gain at the expense of lenders.

But the converse is true when the actual rate of inflation is less than expected. Suppose that after the borrower and lender agree to the 8 percent loan, the price level remains stable. In this case, the borrower ends up paying an 8 percent real interest rate rather than the 5 percent that was expected. When the actual rate of inflation is less than anticipated, lenders gain at the expense of borrowers.

Systematic forecasting errors are unlikely to happen on a regular basis. Sometimes the inflation rate will be higher than decision-makers anticipated, but in other instances it will be lower. However, there is no reason to expect that decision-makers will consistently either overestimate or underestimate the expected rate of inflation. Therefore, there is no reason why inflation will help either borrowers or lenders in a systematic manner.

9-7b INTEREST RATES AND MACROECONOMIC MARKETS

The circular-flow diagram (Exhibit 1) illustrates both the inflow and outflow to the loanable funds market. The net saving of households and net capital inflow from foreigners provide the inflow—the supply of funds—into the loanable funds market. Borrowing by businesses and governments generates the demand for loanable funds.

Businesses and governments often borrow money by issuing bonds on which they pay interest. Issuing bonds is simply a method of demanding loanable funds. In turn, the purchasers of bonds are supplying loanable funds. There is an inverse relationship between bond prices and interest rates. When interest rates rise, the market value of bonds previously issued will fall. Conversely, lower interest rates will push the market value of bonds previously issued upward. (For a detailed explanation of this point, see the Applications in Economics box on bonds and interest rates).

In an open economy like that of the United States, domestic residents are also able to borrow from and lend to foreigners. When foreigners supply more loanable funds to the domestic market than Americans supply to foreigners, there will be a net inflow of foreign capital that will supplement domestic saving. Conversely, if Americans are net lenders, there will be a net outflow of capital from the domestic market. The real interest rate in the loanable funds market will move toward the rate that will bring the quantity of funds demanded into equality with the quantity supplied, *including the net inflow or outflow of capital.*

EXHIBIT 8

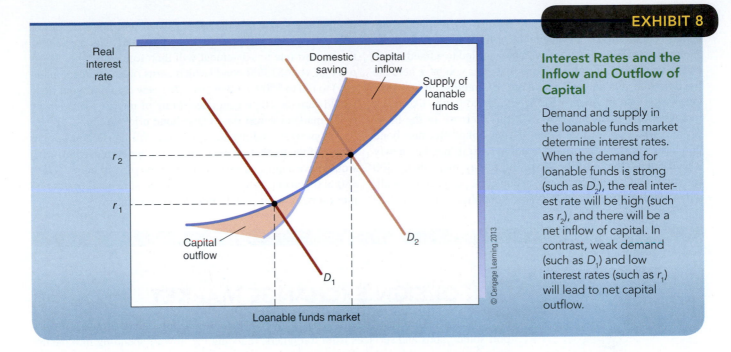

Interest Rates and the Inflow and Outflow of Capital

Demand and supply in the loanable funds market determine interest rates. When the demand for loanable funds is strong (such as D_2), the real interest rate will be high (such as r_2), and there will be a net inflow of capital. In contrast, weak demand (such as D_1) and low interest rates (such as r_1) will lead to net capital outflow.

© Cengage Learning 2013

In today's global financial markets, the flow of capital to the domestic loanable funds market will be directly related to the real interest rate. As **Exhibit 8** shows, when domestic demand is weak (D_1, for example) and the real interest rate low (r_1), capital will flow outward toward other markets where the rate of return is expected to be higher. In contrast, strong domestic demand (D_2, for example) for loanable funds and high real interest rates will lead to an inflow of capital.

Like the resource market, the loanable funds market is interrelated with the goods and services market. We saw that the interest rate generally falls when the price level falls, which helps explain why the *AD* curve slopes downward to the right. In addition, the real interest rate may change for other reasons. When it does, it will affect the aggregate demand schedule. The real interest rate influences how households allocate their income between saving and current consumption. An increase in the interest rate will discourage current consumption by making it more attractive to save and more expensive to borrow. This will reduce aggregate demand. Lower interest rates will have the opposite effect. As we proceed, we will analyze in more detail the interrelationship between the loanable funds market and the goods and services market.

APPLICATIONS IN ECONOMICS

Bonds, Interest Rates, and Bond Prices

Bonds are simply IOUs issued by firms and governments. Issuing bonds is a method of borrowing in the loanable funds market. The entity issuing the bond promises to pay interest at a fixed rate on the amount borrowed (called principal) while the loan is outstanding and to repay the principal on a specified date in the future (for example, five or ten years after the bond is issued). The date when the principal comes due is called the bond's *maturity* date. Each year until that time, the issuing entity usually makes regular interest payments (for example, quarterly or semiannually) to bondholders.

Even though interest rates may change over time, *the bondholder will receive the fixed interest rate specified on the face of the bond.* Although bonds are issued for lengthy periods of time—the U.S. Treasury issues bonds for up to 30 years—they can be sold to another party at any time prior to their maturity. Each day, most of the bonds sold in the bond market are ones that have been issued previously.

When overall interest rates rise, the prices of these previously issued bonds will fall. Suppose you bought a newly issued $1,000 bond that pays 8 percent per year in perpetuity

(Continued)

© iStockphoto.com/sorendls

(forever). (*Note*: Bonds that pay interest in perpetuity are called "consols" and are available in the United Kingdom.) As long as you own the bond, you are entitled to a fixed return of $80 per year. Let's also assume that after you have held the bond for one year and collected your $80 interest for that year, the market rate of interest for newly issued bonds like yours increases to 10 percent. How will this increase in the interest rate affect the market price of your bond? Because bond purchasers can now earn 10 percent interest if they buy newly issued bonds, they will be unwilling to pay more than $800 for your bond, which pays only $80 interest per year. After all, why would anyone pay $1,000 for a bond that yields only $80

interest per year when the same $1,000 will now purchase a bond that yields $100 (10 percent) per year? The increase in the interest rate to 10 percent will therefore cause the *market price* of your $1,000 bond (which earns only 8 percent annually) to fall to $800. At that price, the new owner of your bond would earn the 10 percent market rate of interest. This is why rising market interest rates cause bond prices to fall.

Conversely, falling interest rates will cause bond prices to rise. If the market interest rate had fallen to 6 percent, what would have happened to the market value of your bond? (*Hint:* $80 is 6 percent of $1,333.) As you can see, bond prices and interest rates are inversely linked to each other.

9-8 FOREIGN EXCHANGE MARKET

Look back at Exhibit 1 and note the various transactions with foreigners. Households import some goods and services from foreigners, reducing the flow of spending into the domestic product market. But foreigners buy some of the goods produced by the domestic firms, and these exports add to the flow of spending into the domestic product market. In addition, there is an inflow of money from foreigners into the loanable funds market and an outflow of money to foreigners. As we just discussed, the size and direction of this net flow of money depend on the real interest rate.

Exhibit 9 illustrates how the foreign exchange market tends to bring purchases from foreigners into balance with the sales to them. The dollar price of foreign currency is measured along the vertical axis. A fall in the dollar price of foreign currency—shown by a movement down the vertical axis—means a dollar will buy more units of various foreign currencies. This will make it cheaper for Americans to purchase things from foreigners. Thus, we say that the dollar has **appreciated**, meaning that it will now buy more foreign goods than it previously could. As the dollar price for foreign exchange falls (movement down the vertical axis), Americans buy more from foreigners and therefore demand a larger quantity of foreign currency in order to make the purchases. The demand curve for foreign currency therefore slopes downward to the right.

In contrast, an increase in the dollar price of foreign currency—shown by movement up the vertical axis—means that more dollars are needed to purchase a unit of foreign currency. This makes foreign purchases more expensive for Americans. Thus, we say the dollar has **depreciated**. As the dollar depreciates, a unit of foreign currency will purchase a larger quantity of dollars. This depreciation in the dollar makes American goods less expensive for foreigners. As the dollar depreciates (movement up the vertical axis), foreigners buy more from Americans and supply more foreign currency in exchange for dollars. The supply curve for foreign currency therefore slopes upward to the right.

The forces of supply and demand in the foreign exchange market will move the exchange rate toward the equilibrium price (P_1 in Exhibit 9). In equilibrium, the quantity demanded of foreign currency will just equal the quantity supplied. Imports plus the outflow of capital for investment abroad to foreign countries will equal exports plus the inflow of capital from the investments of foreigners in the United States.[4] Mathematically, when the exchange market is in equilibrium, the following relationship exists:

$$\text{Imports} + \text{Capital outflow} = \text{Exports} + \text{Capital inflow} \qquad (9\text{-}1)$$

Appreciation
An increase in the value of a currency relative to foreign currencies. An appreciation increases the purchasing power of the currency over foreign goods.

Depreciation
A reduction in the value of a currency relative to foreign currencies. A depreciation reduces the purchasing power of the currency over foreign goods.

---

[4]There are two other small items, gifts to and from foreigners and net income from investments abroad, that also influence the demand for and supply of foreign exchange. Because these factors are so small, however, their omission will not alter the general analysis presented here.

EXHIBIT 9

Foreign Exchange Market

Americans demand foreign currencies to pay for goods and services they import and investments they make abroad. Foreigners supply foreign currency in exchange for U.S. dollars in order to purchase American exports and make investments in the United States. The exchange rate will bring the quantity demanded into balance with the quantity supplied. This will also bring imports plus capital outflow into equality with exports plus capital inflow.

© Cengage Learning 2013

This relationship can be rewritten as

$$\textbf{Imports} - \textbf{Exports} = \textbf{Capital inflow} - \textbf{Capital outflow} \qquad (9\text{-}2)$$

The right side of Equation 9-2 is also called *net capital inflow*. Because it is a net figure, it can be either positive (indicating an inflow of capital) or negative (indicating an outflow of capital).

The left side of the equation (imports minus exports) indicates the nation's balance of trade. On the one hand, when imports exceed exports, this is referred to as a **trade deficit**. On the other hand, when exports exceed imports, this is referred to as a **trade surplus**. There is an interesting relationship between the flow of trade and the flow of capital: When a trade deficit is present, there must be an inflow of capital. The reverse is also true: An inflow of capital implies a trade deficit. Conversely, when a trade surplus (exports are greater than imports) is present, there must also be an outflow of capital.

When the exchange rate is determined by market forces, trade deficits will be closely linked with an inflow of capital. In contrast, trade surpluses will be closely linked with an outflow of capital.

Exhibit 10 shows the relationship between the inflow of capital and trade deficits in the United States in recent decades, measured as a share of GDP. Notice how large capital inflows (shown in part a) are closely associated with correspondingly large trade deficits (shown in part b). In the late 1970s and early 1980s, the net inflow of capital was relatively small; so too was the trade deficit. Between 1983 and 1987, the net inflow of capital soared, reaching more than 3 percent of GDP during the latter part of the period. Again, the trade deficit increased by a similar amount. Between 1988 and 1992, the inflow of capital slowed to a trickle and the trade deficit shrank to about 0.5 percent of GDP. During the last decade, however, the inflow of capital soared once again, reaching

Trade deficit
The situation when a country's imports of goods and services are greater than its exports.

Trade surplus
The situation when a country's exports of goods and services are greater than its imports.

EXHIBIT 10

Net Capital Inflow and the Trade Deficit

When a country's exchange rate is determined by market forces, the size of the net inflow of capital and trade deficit will be closely linked, as the figures here show. Notice that when the United States has experienced an increase in net capital inflow, its trade deficit has increased by a similar magnitude.

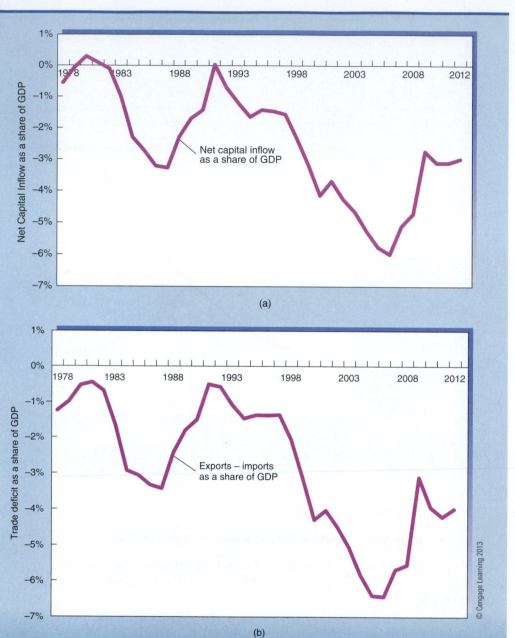

6 percent of GDP; the trade deficit increased hugely, too. Clearly, these two factors are closely related; this is to be expected when a country's exchange rate is determined by market forces.

Are trade deficits bad? Trade deficits imply that a nation is borrowing financial capital from foreigners. Thus, this question is a little like asking if it is bad to borrow. The answer depends on how the funds are used. If the borrowing (inflow of capital) is channeled into productive investments, it will increase the productivity of Americans and lead to higher future income. When an economy provides an attractive investment environment, an inflow of capital and a trade deficit are likely to occur. Trade deficits arising from this source are not bad. However, if borrowing from foreigners is used unproductively or to increase current consumption, it will reduce future income. In recent years, a large portion of the capital inflow to the United States has been used to finance federal budget deficits. This borrowing has made it possible for the federal government to spend at record high levels without having to levy equivalent taxes. As a result, current consumption has been higher, and investment lower, than would otherwise have been the case. Borrowing of this type reduces the rate of capital formation and thereby slows the growth of future income. A family with financial problems cannot solve them by borrowing more in order to maintain its current level of consumption. Neither can a nation.

9-9 LONG-RUN EQUILIBRIUM

We have now discussed all four basic macroeconomic markets: goods and services, resources, loanable funds, and foreign exchange. Like the legs of a chair, these four macroeconomic markets are dependent upon each other. When an economy is in long-run equilibrium, the interrelationships among these four markets will be in harmony. The relationship among resource prices, interest rates, exchange rates, and product prices will be such that, on average, firms will be just able to cover their costs of production, including a competitive return on their investment. In other words, the typical producer's return to capital must equal the interest rate, that is, the opportunity cost of capital. Higher returns would induce producers to expand output, whereas lower returns would cause them to cut back on production. These market adjustments will move an economy toward long-run equilibrium.

LOOKING AHEAD In this chapter, we focused on macroequilibrium. We introduced the four basic macroeconomic markets and analyzed the implications of their equilibriums. However, we live in a world of dynamic change and unexpected events that are constantly disrupting equilibrium. The following chapter will consider what happens when various factors disrupt equilibrium and analyze how these changing conditions influence economic performance.

KEY POINTS

- The circular flow of income and expenditures shows how money flows through the four basic markets that make up the macroeconomy. Those four markets are the (a) goods and services market, (b) resource market, (c) loanable funds market, and (d) foreign exchange market.

- The aggregate demand curve shows the various quantities of domestically produced goods and services that purchasers are willing to buy at different price levels. It slopes downward to the right because the quantity purchased by consumers, investors, governments, and foreigners (net exports) will be larger at lower price levels.

- The aggregate supply (AS) curve shows the various quantities of goods and services that domestic suppliers will produce at different price levels. The short-run aggregate supply (SRAS) curve will slope upward to the right because higher product prices will improve profit margins when important cost components like labor are temporarily fixed in the short run.

- In the long run, output is constrained by the economy's resource base, current technology, and efficiency of its existing institutions. A higher price level does not loosen these constraints. Thus, the long-run aggregate supply (LRAS) curve is vertical.

- Two conditions are necessary for long-run equilibrium in the goods and services market: (a) the quantity demanded must equal the quantity supplied, and (b) the *actual* price level must equal the price level decision makers *anticipated* when they entered into their long-term agreements. When long-run equilibrium is present, output will be at its maximum sustainable level.

- The aggregate demand—aggregate supply model reveals the determinants of the price level and real output. In the short run, price and output will move toward the intersection of the aggregate demand (AD) and short-run aggregate supply (SRAS) curves. In the long run, price and output will gravitate to the levels represented by the intersection of the AD, SRAS, and LRAS curves.

- When the economy is in long-run equilibrium, potential output will be achieved and full employment will be present (the actual rate of unemployment will equal the natural rate).

- It is important to distinguish between real interest rates and money interest rates. The real interest rate reflects the real burden to borrowers and the payoff to lenders after inflation. It is equal to the money rate of interest minus the inflationary premium. The inflationary premium depends on the expected rate of inflation.

- When the exchange rate is determined by market forces, trade deficits will be closely linked with an inflow of capital. Conversely, trade surpluses will be closely linked with an outflow of capital.

- Macroeconomic equilibrium requires that equilibrium be achieved in all four key macroeconomic markets and that they be in harmony with one another.

CRITICAL ANALYSIS QUESTIONS

1. In your own words, explain why aggregate demand is inversely related to the price level. Why does the explanation for the inverse relationship between price and quantity demanded for the aggregate demand curve differ from that of a demand curve for a specific good?

2. What is the relationship between an economy's production possibilities curve and its long-run aggregate supply curve? Why is the long-run aggregate supply curve vertical?

3. Why does the short-run aggregate supply curve slope upward to the right? If the prices of both resources and goods and services increased proportionally (by the same percentage), would business firms be willing to expand output? Why or why not?

4. *If the price level in the current period is higher than buyers and sellers anticipated, what will tend to happen to real wages and the level of employment? How will the profit margins of businesses be affected? How will the actual rate of unemployment compare with the natural rate of unemployment? Will the current rate of output be sustainable in the future? Why or why not?

5. What is the current money interest rate on ten-year government bonds? Is this also the real interest rate? Why or why not?

6. *If the real interest rate in the loanable funds market increases, what will happen to the net inflow of foreign capital? Explain.

7. Explain why it's possible to temporarily achieve output levels beyond the economy's long-run potential. Why can't the high rates of output be sustained?

8. If the price level in the current period is lower than buyers and sellers anticipated, how will output and employment be affected? What is likely to happen to the rate of unemployment?

9. Suppose you purchase a $5,000 bond that pays 7 percent interest annually and matures in five years. If the inflation rate in recent years has been steady at 3 percent annually, what is the estimated real rate of interest? If the inflation rate during the next five years is 6 percent, what will happen to your real rate of return?

10. *How are the following related to each other?
    a. the long-run equilibrium rate of output
    b. the potential real GDP of the economy
    c. the output rate at which the actual and natural rates of unemployment are equal

11. Does inflation transfer wealth from lenders to borrowers? Why or why not?

12. *If a bond pays $1,000 per year in perpetuity (each year in the future), what will the market price of the bond be when the long-term interest rate is 10 percent? What would it be if the interest rate were 5 percent?

13. How are bond prices related to interest rates? Why are they related?

14. How is a nation's trade balance related to its net inflow of foreign capital? If a nation is running a trade deficit, is this bad? Why or why not?

15. *The following chart indicates the aggregate demand (AD) and short-run aggregate supply ($SRAS$) schedules of decision-makers for the current period. Both buyers and sellers previously anticipated that the price level during the current period would be P_{105}.
    a. Indicate the quantity of GDP that will be produced during this period.
    b. Will it be a long-run equilibrium level of GDP? Why or why not?
    c. What will the relationship between the actual and natural rates of unemployment be during the period? Explain your answer.

AD_{105}	PRICE LEVEL	$SRAS_{105}$
6,900	90	4,500
6,600	95	4,800
6,300	100	5,100
6,000	105	5,400
5,700	110	5,700
5,400	115	6,000

16. Consider an economy with the following aggregate demand (AD) and short-run aggregate supply ($SRAS$) schedules. Decision-makers have previously made decisions anticipating that the price level during the current period will be P_{105}.
    a. Indicate the quantity of GDP that will be produced during the period.
    b. Is it a long-run equilibrium level of GDP? Why or why not?
    c. How will the unemployment rate during the current period compare with the natural rate of unemployment?
    d. Will the current rate of GDP be sustainable into the future? Why or why not?

AD_{105}	PRICE LEVEL	$SRAS_{105}$
6,300	90	4,500
6,000	95	4,800
5,700	100	5,100
5,400	105	5,400
5,100	110	5,700
4,800	115	6,000

*Asterisk denotes questions for which answers are given in Appendix B.

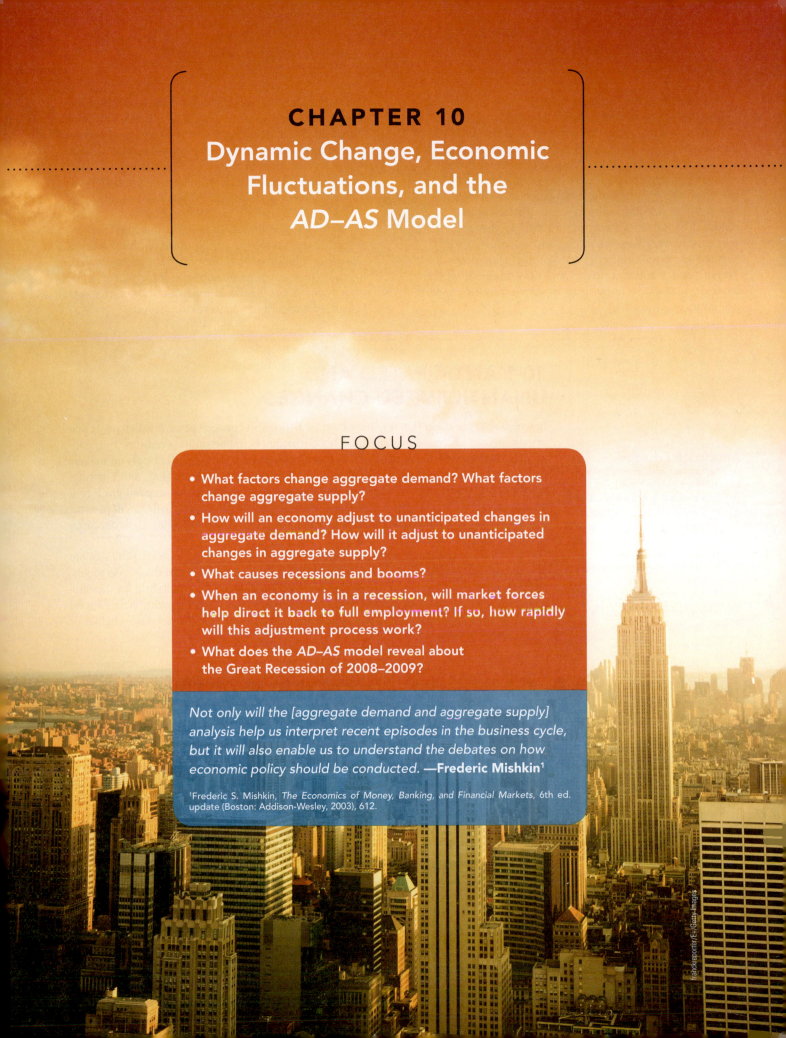

CHAPTER 10
Dynamic Change, Economic Fluctuations, and the *AD–AS* Model

FOCUS

- What factors change aggregate demand? What factors change aggregate supply?

- How will an economy adjust to unanticipated changes in aggregate demand? How will it adjust to unanticipated changes in aggregate supply?

- What causes recessions and booms?

- When an economy is in a recession, will market forces help direct it back to full employment? If so, how rapidly will this adjustment process work?

- What does the *AD–AS* model reveal about the Great Recession of 2008–2009?

Not only will the [aggregate demand and aggregate supply] analysis help us interpret recent episodes in the business cycle, but it will also enable us to understand the debates on how economic policy should be conducted. —**Frederic Mishkin**[1]

[1]Frederic S. Mishkin, *The Economics of Money, Banking, and Financial Markets*, 6th ed. update (Boston: Addison-Wesley, 2003), 612.

Franckreporter/E+/Getty Images

In Chapter 9, we focused on the equilibrium conditions in the four basic macroeconomic markets. Equilibrium is important, but we live in a dynamic world that continually wars against it. Unexpected changes are constantly occurring. New products and technologies are developed; consumers and investors become more optimistic (or pessimistic) about the future; weather affects crop yields; international tensions disrupt or threaten to disrupt the supply of a key resource, and so on. Consequently, equilibrium is continually disrupted. Thus, if we want to understand how the real world works, we need to know how macroeconomic markets adjust to change.

In this chapter, we focus on what happens when the macroequilibrium of an economy is disrupted. The linkage between these disruptions and the ups and downs of the business cycle is also investigated. If economic change throws an economy into a recession, will market forces direct it back to full employment? If so, how quickly will this occur? This chapter will examine these questions and related issues.

We will continue to assume that the government's tax, spending, and monetary policies don't change. The impact of changes in these policy variables will be examined in subsequent chapters. For now, our focus is on the basic macroeconomic markets and how they respond to various disruptions.

©iStockphoto.com/nicoolay

10-1 ANTICIPATED AND UNANTICIPATED CHANGES

In Chapter 8, we stated that it is important to distinguish between price-level changes that are anticipated and those that are not. This distinction is important in several areas of economics. **Anticipated changes** are foreseen by economic participants. Decision makers have time to adjust to them before they occur. For example, suppose that, under normal weather conditions, a new drought-resistant hybrid seed is expected to expand grain production in the Midwest by 10 percent next year. As a result, buyers and sellers will plan for a larger supply of grain and lower grain prices in the future. They will adjust their decision-making behavior accordingly.

In contrast, **unanticipated changes** catch people by surprise. New products are introduced, technological discoveries alter production costs, droughts reduce crop yields, and demand expands for some goods and contracts for others. It is impossible for decision makers to foresee many of these changes. As we will explain in a moment, there is good reason to expect that the path of the adjustment process will be influenced by whether or not a change is anticipated.

Anticipated change
A change that is foreseen by decision-makers in time for them to make adjustments.

Unanticipated change
A change that decision makers could not reasonably foresee. The choices they made prior to the change did not take it into account.

10-2 FACTORS THAT SHIFT AGGREGATE DEMAND

The aggregate demand curve isolates the effect of the price level on the quantity demanded of goods and services. As we discussed in the previous chapter, a reduction in the price level will (1) increase the wealth of people holding a fixed quantity of money, (2) reduce the real rate of interest, and (3) make domestically produced goods cheaper than those produced abroad. All three of these factors will lead to an increase in the quantity of goods and services demanded at the lower price level.

The price level, however, is not the only factor that influences the demand for goods and services. When we constructed the aggregate demand curve, we assumed that several other factors affecting the choices of buyers in the goods and services market were constant. Changes in these "other factors" will shift the entire aggregate demand schedule, altering the amount purchased at each price level. Let us take a closer look at the major factors that alter aggregate demand, causing a shift in the *AD* curve.

1. Changes in real wealth. Ownership of stocks and housing constitutes a large share of the wealth of Americans. Between 2002 and 2006, stock prices in the United States increased by more than 60 percent. During the same period, housing

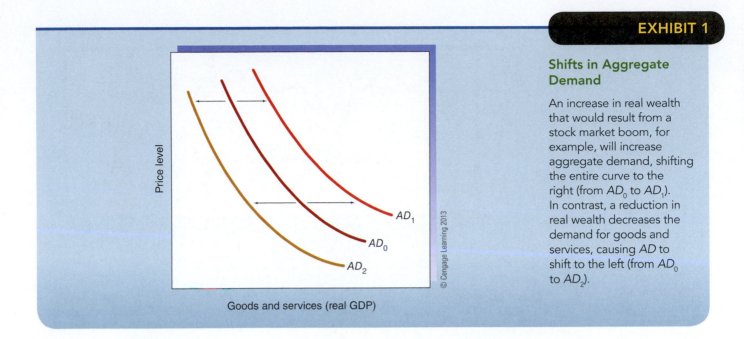

EXHIBIT 1

Shifts in Aggregate Demand

An increase in real wealth that would result from a stock market boom, for example, will increase aggregate demand, shifting the entire curve to the right (from AD_0 to AD_1). In contrast, a reduction in real wealth decreases the demand for goods and services, causing *AD* to shift to the left (from AD_0 to AD_2).

prices increased by nearly 90 percent. This huge increase in both stock and housing prices increased the wealth of Americans. In contrast, stock prices plummeted by more than 50 percent during the sixteen months following October 2007, and housing prices fell by more than 30 percent between the fourth quarter of 2006 and the fourth quarter of 2008. These price declines reduced the wealth of Americans.

How will changes in the wealth of households affect the demand for goods and services? If the real wealth of households increases, perhaps as the result of higher prices in stock, housing, and/or real estate markets, people will demand more goods and services. As Exhibit 1 illustrates, this increase in wealth will shift the entire *AD* curve to the right (from AD_0 to AD_1). More goods and services are purchased at each price level. Conversely, a reduction in wealth will reduce the demand for goods and services, shifting the *AD* curve to the left (to AD_2).

2. Changes in the real interest rate. As we discussed in Chapter 9, the major macroeconomic markets are closely related. A change in the real interest rate in the loanable funds market will influence the choices of consumers and investors in the goods and services market. A lower real interest rate makes it cheaper for consumers to buy major appliances, automobiles, and houses now rather than in the future. Simultaneously, a lower interest rate will also stimulate business spending on capital goods (investment). If a firm must borrow, the real interest rate will contribute directly to the cost of a project. Even if the firm uses its own funds, it sacrifices interest that could have been earned by loaning the funds to someone else. Therefore, a lower interest rate reduces the opportunity cost of a project, regardless of whether it is financed with internal funds or by borrowing.

Because a fall in the real interest rate makes both consumer and investment goods cheaper, both households and investors will increase their current expenditures in response. In turn, their additional expenditures will increase aggregate demand, shifting the entire *AD* curve to the right. In contrast, a higher real interest rate makes current consumption and investment goods more expensive, which leads to a reduction in aggregate demand, shifting the *AD* curve to the left.

3. Changes in the expectations of businesses and households about the future direction of the economy. What people think will happen in the future influences current purchasing decisions. Optimism about the future direction of the economy will stimulate current investment. Business decision-makers know that an

EXHIBIT 2

Consumer Sentiment Index, 1978–2012

The consumer sentiment index developed by the University of Michigan is shown here. It is designed to measure whether consumers are becoming more optimistic or more pessimistic about the economy. Note how the index has turned down sharply prior to and during the early stages of recent recessions (shaded areas).

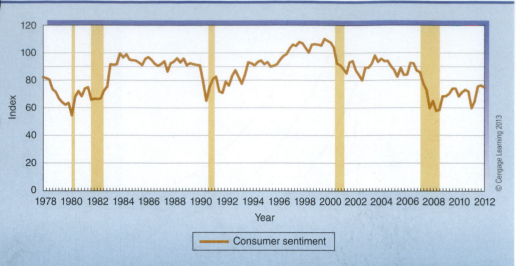

expanding economy will mean strong sales and improved profit margins. Investment today may be necessary if business firms are going to benefit fully from these opportunities. Similarly, consumers are more likely to buy big-ticket items, such as automobiles and houses, when they expect an expanding economy to provide them with both job security and rising income in the future. Increased optimism encourages additional current expenditures by both investors and consumers, increasing aggregate demand.

Of course, pessimism about the future of the economy exerts just the opposite effect. When investors and consumers expect an economic downturn (a recession), they will cut back on their current spending to avoid overextending themselves. This pessimism leads to a decline in aggregate demand, shifting the *AD* curve to the left.

The University of Michigan conducts a monthly survey of consumers and uses the information to develop a **consumer sentiment index**. Exhibit 2 presents this index for the 1978–2012 period. An increase in the consumer sentiment index indicates that consumers are more optimistic about the future. A decline indicates increased consumer pessimism. Notice how the index fell sharply prior to and during the early stages of the recessions that occurred in this period. The reduction was particularly sharp prior to and during the most recent recession. The index fell to 57.7 in the fourth quarter of 2008, near its all-time low. The index rebounded during 2009–2012, but remained below the levels typically achieved during an expansionary phase of the business cycle.

Consumer sentiment index

A measure of the optimism of consumers based on their responses to a set of questions about their current and expected future personal economic situation. Conducted by the University of Michigan, it is based on a representative sample of U.S. households.

4. Change in the expected rate of inflation.
When consumers and investors believe that the rate of inflation will go up in the future, they have an incentive to spend more during the current period. This expectation of higher inflation will stimulate current aggregate demand, shifting the *AD* curve to the right.

In contrast, if people expect inflation to decline in the future, this will discourage current spending. When prices are expected to decline (or at least increase less rapidly), people will have an incentive to wait before they buy things. This expectation of lower inflation will cause current aggregate demand to fall, shifting the *AD* curve to the left.

5. Changes in income abroad.
Changes in the income of a nation's trading partners will influence the demand for its exports. If the income of a nation's trading partners increases rapidly, the demand for its exports will expand. This will stimulate its aggregate demand. For example, rapid growth of income in Europe, Canada, and Mexico increases the demand of consumers in these areas for U.S.-produced goods. This will cause U.S. exports to expand, increasing aggregate demand (shifting the *AD* curve to the right).

Thumbnail Sketch
What Factors Affect Aggregate Demand?[1]

These factors *increase* aggregate demand (*AD*):

1. An increase in real wealth
2. A decrease in the real rate of interest
3. Optimism about future economic conditions
4. A rise in the expected rate of inflation
5. Higher real incomes abroad
6. A depreciation in the foreign exchange value of a nation's currency

These factors *decrease* aggregate demand (*AD*):

1. Lower real wealth
2. An increase in the real rate of interest
3. Pessimism about future economic conditions
4. A fall in the expected rate of inflation
5. Lower real incomes abroad
6. An appreciation in the foreign exchange value of a nation's currency

[1]The impact of macroeconomic policy is considered later.

©iStockphoto.com/baianliang

Conversely, when a nation's trading partners are experiencing recessionary conditions, citizens in these countries reduce their purchases, including their purchases of foreign-produced goods. Thus, a decline in the income of a nation's trading partners will reduce its exports and the aggregate demand for its products.

6. Changes in exchange rates. As we previously discussed, changes in exchange rates influence the relative price of both imports and exports. If the dollar appreciates, imported goods will be cheaper for Americans to buy, and goods exported from the United States will be more expensive for foreigners to purchase. As a result, U.S. imports will rise and exports will fall. This decline in net exports (exports minus imports) will reduce aggregate demand (shifting the *AD* curve to the left).

If the dollar depreciates, the effect will be just the opposite. When the value of the dollar falls, foreign-produced goods become more expensive for U.S. consumers, whereas U.S.-produced goods become cheaper for foreigners. This is precisely what happened during the 2003–2007 period, when the dollar depreciated by about 15 percent relative to the euro and several other major currencies. When the dollar depreciates, imports will tend to fall and exports rise. In turn, this increase in net exports will stimulate aggregate demand in the United States (shifting the *AD* curve to the right).[2]

The accompanying **Thumbnail Sketch** summarizes the major factors that change aggregate demand and shift the *AD* curve. Other factors include the government's spending, taxing, and monetary policies. In subsequent chapters, we will analyze the impact of fiscal and monetary policy on aggregate demand and economic performance. We now turn to the analysis of the factors that alter aggregate supply. Then we will be in a position to consider how macroeconomic markets adjust and whether these adjustments will help keep output and employment high.

10-3 SHIFTS IN AGGREGATE SUPPLY

What factors will cause the aggregate supply curve to shift? The answer to this question will differ depending on whether the change in supply is long run and sustainable or short run and only temporary. A long-run change in aggregate supply indicates that it will be possible to achieve and sustain a larger rate of output. For example, the discovery of a

---

[2]Later, when discussing international finance, we will analyze the determinants of the exchange rate and consider in more detail how changes in exchange rates affect both trade and macroeconomic markets.

lower-cost source of energy would cause a long-run change in aggregate supply. If this happened, both long-run aggregate supply (*LRAS*) and short-run aggregate supply (*SRAS*) would change.

In contrast, changes that temporarily alter the production capacity of an economy will shift the *SRAS* curve, but not the *LRAS* curve. A drought in California would be an example of such a short-run change. The drought will hurt in the short run, but it will eventually end, and output will return to the long-run normal rate. Changes that are temporary in nature shift only the *SRAS* curve. Let's consider the factors that change long-run and short-run aggregate supply in more detail.

10-3a CHANGES IN LONG-RUN AGGREGATE SUPPLY

Productivity
The average output produced per worker during a specific time period. It is usually measured in terms of output per hour worked.

Remember, the long-run aggregate supply curve shows the maximum rate of sustainable output of an economy, given its current (1) resource base, (2) level of technology, and (3) institutional arrangements that affect its **productivity** and the efficient use of its resources. Changes in any of these three determinants of output will cause the *LRAS* curve to shift.

As part (a) of **Exhibit 3** illustrates, changes that increase the economy's production capacity will shift the *LRAS* curve to the right. Over time, net investment will expand the supply of physical capital, natural resources, and labor (human resources). Physical capital investment expands the supply of buildings, machines, and other physical assets. Education and training improve the quality of the labor force and thereby expand the availability of human capital. Because investment in physical and human capital enhances output both now and in the future, it increases both long-run and short-run aggregate supply, causing both curves to shift to the right. However, things can work the other way around, too. Reductions in physical and human capital over time could cause the current and long-term production capacity of an economy to fall, shifting the *SRAS* and *LRAS* curves to the left.

Improvements in technology—the discovery of economical new products or less costly ways of producing goods and services—also permit us to squeeze a larger output from a given resource supply. The enormous improvement in our living standards during the last 250 years is largely the result of the discovery and adoption of technologically superior ways of transforming resources into goods and services. The development of the internal combustion engine, electricity, and nuclear power has vastly altered our energy sources (and consumption). The railroad, automobile, and airplane dramatically changed both the

---

EXHIBIT 3

Shifts in Aggregate Supply

Factors like an increase in the stock of capital or an improvement in technology will expand the economy's potential output and shift the *LRAS* curve to the right as shown in part (a). Factors like favorable weather or falling resource prices (say, a temporary drop in the price of a major import like oil) will shift the SRAS curve to the right, as shown in part (b).

(a) Increase in *LRAS*

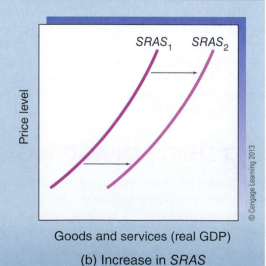

(b) Increase in *SRAS*

© Cengage Learning 2013

speed and cost of transportation. More recently, high-tech products like personal computers, checkout scanners, iPhones, and the Internet have cut the cost of doing business and expanded our production capacity. Technological improvements of this type enhance productivity and thereby shift both *LRAS* and *SRAS* curves to the right.

Finally, institutional changes can affect productivity and efficiency and change both short- and long-run aggregate supply. Depending on how well a government's institutional, or policy, changes are designed, they can increase aggregate supply by enhancing economic efficiency and productivity or decrease it by encouraging waste and making production more costly.

The long-run growth of real GDP in the United States has been about 3 percent per year. In other words, we have been able to expand our productivity steadily over the years. Hence, the *LRAS* and *SRAS* curves have gradually drifted to the right at about a 3 percent annual rate, sometimes a little faster and sometimes a little slower.

10-3b CHANGES IN SHORT-RUN AGGREGATE SUPPLY

Changes can sometimes influence current output without altering the economy's long-run capacity. When this is the case, the *SRAS* curve will shift even though the *LRAS* curve remains unchanged. What types of changes would do this?

1. Changes in resource prices. When we derived the *SRAS* schedule in Chapter 9, we held resource prices constant. But a change in resource prices will alter *SRAS*, although not necessarily *LRAS*. A reduction in resource prices will lower production costs and therefore shift the *SRAS* curve to the right, as illustrated in part (b) of Exhibit 3. However, unless the lower cost of resources reflects a long-term increase in their supply, *LRAS* won't change. Conversely, an increase in the price of resources used in production will increase firms' costs, shifting the *SRAS* curve to the left. But unless the higher prices are the result of a long-term reduction in the size of the economy's resource base, they will not reduce *LRAS*.[3]

2. Changes in the expected rate of inflation. As we learned, a change in the expected rate of inflation will affect aggregate demand (*AD*) in the goods and services market. It will also alter short-run aggregate supply (*SRAS*). If sellers in the goods and services market expect the future rate of inflation to increase, they will be less motivated to sell their products at lower prices in the current period. After all, goods that they do not sell today will be available for sale in the future at what they anticipate will be even higher prices because of inflation. But they will have produced them earlier at lower costs. Therefore, an increase in the expected rate of inflation will reduce the *current* supply of goods, thereby shifting the *SRAS* curve to the left. Of course, a reduction in the expected rate of inflation will have just the opposite effect. When sellers scale back their expectations of future price increases, their incentive to sell in the current period rises. Why should they wait to sell what they've produced now, if prices aren't going to go up very much in the future? Thus, a reduction in the expected rate of inflation will increase short-run aggregate supply, shifting the *SRAS* curve to the right.

3. Supply shocks. **Supply shocks** can also alter current output without directly affecting the productive capacity of the economy. Supply shocks are surprise occurrences that

Supply shock
An unexpected event that temporarily increases or decreases aggregate supply.

---

[3]The definition of long-run aggregate supply helps clarify why a change in resource prices will affect short-run aggregate supply but not long-run aggregate supply. When an economy is operating on its *LRAS* curve, the relationship between resource prices (costs) and product prices will reflect normal competitive market conditions. Because both profit and unemployment rates are at their normal levels, there is no tendency for resource prices to change relative to product prices when current output is equal to the economy's long-run potential. Therefore, when an economy is operating on its *LRAS* schedule, any change in resource prices will be matched by a proportional change in product prices, leaving the incentive to supply resources (and output) unchanged.

Thumbnail Sketch

What Factors Affect Long-Run and Short-Run Aggregate Supply?[1]

These factors *increase* long-run aggregate supply (*LRAS*):

1. An increase in the supply of resources
2. Technology and productivity improvements
3. Institutional changes that improve the efficiency of resource use

These factors *decrease* long-run aggregate supply (*LRAS*):

1. A decrease in the supply of resources
2. Technology and productivity deteriorations
3. Institutional changes that reduce the efficiency of resource use

These factors *increase* short-run aggregate supply (*SRAS*):

1. A fall in resource prices (production costs)
2. A fall in the expected rate of inflation
3. Favorable supply shocks, such as good weather or lower prices of important imported resources

These factors *decrease* short-run aggregate supply (*SRAS*):

1. A rise in resource prices (production costs)
2. A rise in the expected rate of inflation
3. Unfavorable supply shocks, such as bad weather or higher prices of important imported resources

[1]The impact of macroeconomic policy will be considered later.

©iStockphoto.com/baianliang

©iStockphoto.com/raisbeckfoto

The world price of oil increased sharply in 2007–2008 and again in 2010–2011. For oil importing countries like the United States, the higher oil price will raise the costs of transportation and production, reducing aggregate supply.

temporarily increase or decrease current output. For example, adverse weather conditions, a natural disaster, or a temporary rise in the price of imported resources (for example, oil in the case of the United States) will reduce current supply, even though they do not alter the economy's long-term production capacity. They lower short-run aggregate supply (shift the *SRAS* curve to the left) without directly affecting *LRAS*, in other words. In contrast, favorable weather conditions or a temporary fall in the world price of major resources imported by a country will expand current output, even though the economy's long-run capacity remains unchanged.

The accompanying **Thumbnail Sketch** summarizes the major factors that influence both long-run and short-run aggregate supply. Of course, macroeconomic policy can also influence aggregate supply. Like aggregate demand, we will study the impact macroeconomic policies have on aggregate supply in subsequent chapters.

10-4 STEADY ECONOMIC GROWTH AND ANTICIPATED CHANGES IN LONG-RUN AGGREGATE SUPPLY

As we've said, changes that people anticipate affect the economy differently from changes they don't. When a change takes place slowly and predictably, decision makers will make choices based on their anticipation of the event. These changes do not generally disrupt equilibrium in markets. With time, net investment and improvements in technology and institutional efficiency will lead to increases in the sustainable rate of output and shift the economy's *LRAS* curve to the right.

EXHIBIT 4

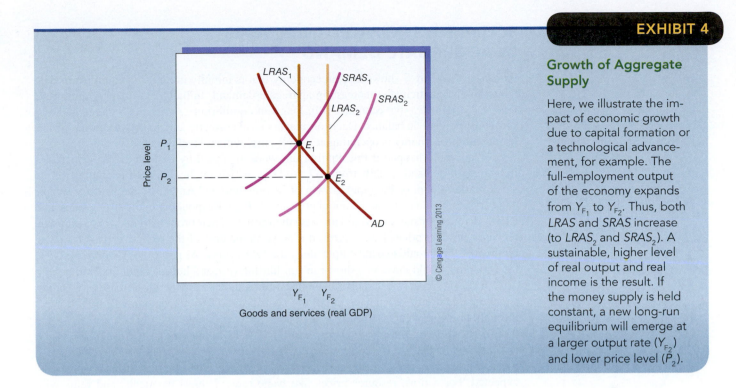

Growth of Aggregate Supply

Here, we illustrate the impact of economic growth due to capital formation or a technological advancement, for example. The full-employment output of the economy expands from Y_{F_1} to Y_{F_2}. Thus, both *LRAS* and *SRAS* increase (to *LRAS*$_2$ and *SRAS*$_2$). A sustainable, higher level of real output and real income is the result. If the money supply is held constant, a new long-run equilibrium will emerge at a larger output rate (Y_{F_2}) and lower price level (P_2).

Exhibit 4 illustrates the impact of economic growth on the goods and services market. Initially, the economy is in long-run equilibrium at price level P_1 and output Y_{F_1}. The growth expands the economy's potential output, shifting both the *LRAS* and *SRAS* curves to the right (to *LRAS*$_2$ and *SRAS*$_2$). Because these changes are gradual, decision makers have time to anticipate the changing market conditions and adjust their behavior accordingly.

When economic growth expands the economy's production possibilities, a higher rate of real output can be achieved and sustained. The larger output can be attained even while unemployment remains at its natural rate. If the money supply is held constant, the increase in aggregate supply will lead to a lower price level (P_2).

During the past 50 years, real output has expanded significantly in the United States and other countries. However, contrary to the presentation of Exhibit 4, the price level has generally not declined. This is because monetary policy-makers have expanded the supply of money. As we will see later, an increase in the money supply stimulates aggregate demand, shifting *AD* to the right and pushing the price level upward.

10-5 UNANTICIPATED CHANGES AND MARKET ADJUSTMENTS

In contrast to anticipated changes, unanticipated changes in aggregate demand and aggregate supply will disrupt long-run equilibrium in the goods and services market. If a change isn't anticipated, initially, it may be unclear to decision-makers whether the change—an increase in sales, for example—reflects a random occurrence or a real change in demand conditions. Businesses will also take some time to differentiate between temporary fluctuations and more permanent changes. Even after decision-makers are convinced that market conditions have changed, it will take some time for them to make new decisions and carry them out. Moreover, in some cases, long-term contracts will delay the adjustment process.

Equilibrium may be disrupted by unexpected changes in either aggregate demand or aggregate supply. We will begin with the analysis of changes in aggregate demand.

10-5a UNANTICIPATED INCREASES IN AGGREGATE DEMAND

Part (a) of **Exhibit 5** shows how an economy that is initially in long-run equilibrium will adjust to an unanticipated increase in aggregate demand. Initially, at output Y_F and price level P_{100} (point E_1), the economy is in long-run equilibrium. Aggregate demand and aggregate supply are in balance. Decision-makers have correctly anticipated the current price level, and the economy is operating at its full-employment level of output.

What would happen if this equilibrium were disrupted by an unanticipated increase in aggregate demand (a shift from AD_1 to AD_2), which might result for example from a stock market boom or the rapid growth of income abroad? An excess demand for goods and services would result at the initial price level (P_{100}). Responding to the strong sales and excess demand, businesses would increase their prices. Their profit margins would improve (because product prices have increased relative to the cost of the resources used to make them), and they would expand output along the *SRAS* curve. As part (a) of Exhibit 5 shows, the economy would move to a short-run equilibrium (e_2), at a larger output (Y_2) and higher price level (P_{105}). (*Note:* A short-run equilibrium is indicated with a lowercase *e*, whereas a capital *E* is used to designate a long-run equilibrium. This convention will be followed throughout the text.)

In the short run, the economy's output will deviate from full-employment capacity when prices in the goods and services market deviate from the price level people anticipated. This will happen when unusually strong demand pushes prices up more than was expected. For a time, resource prices like wage rates, interest payments, and rents will remain at the initial price level (P_{100}), lagging behind the prices producers can get for their products. The higher price level will temporarily improve firms' profit margins, which will motivate them to expand both output and employment in the short run. As a result, the un-

---

EXHIBIT 5

An Unanticipated Increase in Aggregate Demand

In response to an unanticipated increase in aggregate demand for goods and services that shifts AD_1 to AD_2 (shown in part a), prices will rise to P_{105} in the short run and output will increase temporarily to Y_2, exceeding full-employment capacity. However, over time, prices in resource markets, including the labor market, will rise as the result of the strong demand.

The higher resource prices will mean higher production costs, which will reduce aggregate supply to $SRAS_2$ (as shown in part b). In the long run, a new equilibrium will emerge at a higher price level (P_{110}) and an output consistent with the economy's sustainable capacity. Thus, the increase in aggregate demand will expand output only temporarily.

(a) Short-run effects of increase in *AD*

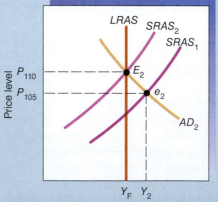

(b) Long-run effects of increase in *AD*

employment rate will drop below its natural rate, and the economy's output will temporarily exceed its long-run potential.

This isn't the end of the story, though. ***The increase in GDP above the economy's long-run potential will last only until temporarily fixed resource prices (and interest rates) can be adjusted upward by people in light of the new stronger demand conditions.*** The strong demand accompanying the high level of output (rates beyond Y_F) will put upward pressure on prices in the resource and loanable funds markets. As part (b) of Exhibit 5 shows, eventually the rising resource prices and costs will shift the short-run aggregate supply curve to the left (to $SRAS_2$). Given sufficient time, wages, other resource prices, and interest rates will completely adjust. When this happens, a new long-run equilibrium (E_2) will be established at a higher price level (P_{110}). Correspondingly, profit margins will return to their normal levels, output will recede to the economy's long-run potential, and unemployment will return to its natural rate.

Notice that because an increase in aggregate demand doesn't change the economy's production capacity, it cannot permanently expand output (beyond Y_F). The increase in demand temporarily expands output, but in the long term, it only increases the price level.

10-5b UNANTICIPATED REDUCTIONS IN AGGREGATE DEMAND

How would the goods and services market adjust to an unanticipated reduction in aggregate demand? For example, suppose decision makers become more pessimistic about the future or an unexpected decline in income abroad reduces demand for their products.

Exhibit 6 will help us analyze what happens during an unanticipated reduction in aggregate demand. In part (a) of Exhibit 6, the economy is in long-run equilibrium (E_1) at output Y_F and the price level P_{100}. The reduction in demand will shift aggregate demand

---

EXHIBIT 6

An Unanticipated Reduction in Aggregate Demand

The short-run impact of an unanticipated fall in aggregate demand, shifting AD_1 to AD_2, will be a decline in output to Y_2 and a lower price level of P_{95} (as shown in part a). Temporarily, profit margins will decline, output will fall, and unemployment will rise above its natural rate. In the long run, weak demand and excess supply in the resource market will lead to lower wages and resource prices. This will lower production costs, leading to an expansion in short-run aggregate supply, shifting it to $SRAS_2$ (as shown in part b). However, this method of restoring equilibrium (E_2) may be both painful and quite lengthy.

(a) Short-run effects of decline in *AD*

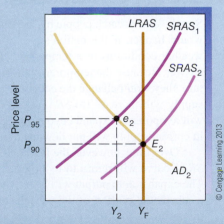

(b) Long-run effects of decline in *AD*

© Cengage Learning 2013

The United States experienced a sharp reduction in housing prices in 2007–2011. What impact will this have on aggregate demand?

from AD_1 to AD_2, disrupting the initial equilibrium. As a result of the fall in demand, businesses will be unable to sell Y_F units of output at the initial price level of P_{100}. In the short run, business firms will reduce their output (to Y_2) and cut their prices (to P_{95}) in response to the weak demand conditions. Because many business costs are temporarily fixed, profit margins will fall. Predictably, firms will cut back on output and lay off workers, causing the unemployment rate to rise. The actual rate of unemployment will rise above the economy's natural rate of unemployment. Weak demand and excess supply will be widespread in resource markets. Many firms will have excess production capacity, and the demand for investment funds will be weak. These forces will place downward pressure on both resource prices and interest rates.

If resource prices quickly adjust downward in response to weak demand, then the decline in output to Y_2 will be brief. Lower resource prices will reduce costs and increase aggregate supply, shifting the $SRAS_1$ curve to $SRAS_2$, as part (b) shows. The result will be a new long-run equilibrium (E_2) at the economy's full-employment output rate (Y_F) and a lower price level (P_{90}). Lower interest rates will also help keep the economy on track. Given the excess production capacity of many firms, weak demand for capital goods (investment) will reduce the demand for loanable funds, which will put downward pressure on interest rates. The lower rates will stimulate current spending, which will help offset the lower demand and direct the economy back to full employment.

Resource prices and interest rates, however, may not adjust quickly. Long-term contracts and uncertainty about whether the weak demand is only temporary will slow down the adjustment process. Moreover, workers and unions may be reluctant to accept lower wages. If resource prices are downwardly inflexible, as many economists believe, the adjustment process may be lengthy and painful. Pessimism on the part of both investors and consumers may also complicate the adjustment process. This has been the case in recent recessions. As Exhibit 2 shows, consumer confidence remained at a low level for 12 to 18 months after the 1990–1991 and 2001 recessions were over and even longer in the aftermath of the 2008–2009 recession. This pessimism acted as a drag on the growth of aggregate demand, and, as a result, the initial recovery from these recessions was sluggish.

10-5c UNANTICIPATED INCREASES IN SHORT-RUN AGGREGATE SUPPLY

Supply shocks catch people by surprise. That is, in part, why they're called "shocks." What would happen if the nation's output expanded because of a favorable shock, like good weather conditions or a temporary fall in the world price of oil? **Exhibit 7** provides the answer. Because the temporarily favorable supply conditions can't be counted on in the future, they won't change the economy's long-term production capacity. Short-run aggregate supply will increase (to $SRAS_2$), but $LRAS$ will remain unchanged. Output (and income) will temporarily expand beyond the economy's full-employment constraints. This increase in current supply will put downward pressure on the price level.

Over time, however, the favorable conditions will come to an end. As this happens, the $SRAS$ curve will return to its original position, and long-run equilibrium will be restored. The expansion in output will be only temporary. Knowing this, many households will save a substantial portion of the extra income they earn during the expansion for a time when things aren't so prosperous.

What would happen if the favorable conditions increasing supply reflected long-term factors? For example, suppose the discovery and development of a huge natural gas field in the United States lowered energy prices and these price reductions were expected to be long-term rather than temporary. In this instance, both the $LRAS$ and the $SRAS$ would

EXHIBIT 7

An Unanticipated, Temporary Increase in Aggregate Supply

Here, we show the impact of an unantici-pated, but temporary, increase in aggregate supply that might result from a bumper crop caused by favorable weather, for example. The increase in aggregate supply, shifting it to $SRAS_2$, will lead to a lower price level of P_{95} and an increase in current GDP to Y_2. Because the favorable supply conditions cannot be counted on in the future, the economy's long-run aggregate supply will not increase.

Goods and services (real GDP)

© Cengage Learning 2013

increase (shift to the right). This case would parallel the analysis of Exhibit 4. A new long-run equilibrium at a higher output would result.

10-5d UNANTICIPATED REDUCTIONS IN SHORT-RUN AGGREGATE SUPPLY

In recent decades, the U.S. economy has been jolted by several unfavorable supply-side factors. During the summer of 1988, the worst drought to hit the country in fifty years made for an extremely poor harvest in the U.S. agricultural belt. In 1973, 1979, 1990, and 2000–2001, the United States, which imports more than half of the oil it consumes, was hit with sharply higher oil prices due to instability in the Middle East. In 2007–2008, the world price of crude oil soared to more than $140 per barrel and the average nominal price of gasoline soared to more than $4 per gallon. The higher oil prices raised the transporta-tion costs of virtually everything as well as the production costs of numerous items, such as plastics, fertilizer, and asphalt.

How do unfavorable supply shocks like this affect macroeconomic markets? As Exhibit 8 (part a) illustrates, an unfavorable supply shock, such as might result from adverse weather or a higher world price of oil, will reduce supply (from S_1 to S_2) in the domestic resource market. Resource prices will rise to P'_r. In turn, the higher resource prices will reduce short-run aggregate supply (the shift from $SRAS_1$ to $SRAS_2$ in part b) in the goods and services market. Because supply shocks of this type are generally unantici-pated, initially they will reduce output and put upward pressure on prices in the goods and services market.

If an unfavorable supply shock is expected to be temporary, as will generally be the case, long-run aggregate supply will be unaffected. For example, unfavorable weather con-ditions for a year or two do not represent a permanent change in the climate. As normal weather returns, supply and prices in the resource market will return to normal, and the economy will return to long-run equilibrium at output Y_F.

The Effects of an Adverse Supply Shock

Suppose that there's an unanticipated fall in the economy's supply of resources, perhaps because of a crop failure or sharp increase in the price of a major imported resource like oil. Resource prices will rise from P_r to P'_r, as shown in part (a). The higher resource prices will shift the SRAS curve to the left, as shown in part (b). In the short run, the price level will rise to P_{110}, and output will decline to Y_2. What happens in the long run depends on whether the reduction in the supply of resources is temporary or permanent. If it is temporary, resource prices will fall in the future, permitting the economy to return to its initial equilibrium (E_1). Conversely, if it is permanent, the production capacity of the economy will shrink, shifting LRAS to the left, and e_2 will become the new long-run equilibrium.

(a) Resource market

(b) Goods and services (real GDP)

© Cengage Learning 2013

When an adverse supply-side factor is more permanent, the long-run supply curve will also shift to the left. For example, an oil price increase that is expected to continue for several years will reduce long-run as well as short-run aggregate supply. Under these circumstances, the economy will have to adjust to a lower level of output. Whether the decline in aggregate supply is temporary or permanent, other things being constant, the price level will rise. Similarly, output will decline, at least temporarily.

10-6 THE PRICE LEVEL, INFLATION, AND THE *AD–AS* MODEL

In the basic *AD–AS* model, the level of prices is measured on the y-axis in both the goods and services and resource markets. This approach makes it easier to visualize relative price changes. If prices change in one of the markets, goods and services for example, this indicates that prices in that market have changed *relative* to those in other markets. It is important to note, however, that this structure implicitly incorporates the assumption that the actual and expected rates of inflation are initially zero.

As we have previously discussed, when persistent inflation is present, it will be anticipated by both buyers and sellers. Moreover, the anticipated inflation will be incorporated into the price agreements of long-term contracts, including those affecting important components of costs. When the actual and anticipated rates of inflation are equal, persistent price increases will be present in both goods and services and resource markets, even though the relative prices between the two markets are unchanged.

However, once decision-makers anticipate a given rate of inflation and build it into long-term contracts, an actual rate of inflation that is less than expected is essentially the equivalent of a reduction in the price level when price stability (zero inflation) is anticipated. For example, consider the situation in which 5 percent inflation has been present over a lengthy time period and therefore the 5 percent rate has been built into long-term contracts, including those in resource markets. If weak demand causes the inflation rate to fall to, say, 2 percent, the adjustments will be the same as those for a reduction in product prices when zero inflation is anticipated (see Exhibit 6). In both cases, prices in the goods and services market will fall relative to resource prices. In the short run, profit margins will be squeezed, and firms will cut back on output. Workers will be laid off, and the economy may well fall into a recession.

Similarly, the impact of an inflation rate that is greater than was anticipated will be like that of an increase in the price level when price stability is anticipated. Both will increase product prices relative to resource prices, which will enhance profits and thereby induce firms to expand output and employment.

10-7 UNANTICIPATED CHANGES, RECESSIONS, AND BOOMS

The *AD–AS* model indicates that unanticipated changes will disrupt macroequilibrium and result in economic instability. On the one hand, unanticipated reductions in either aggregate demand or short-run aggregate supply can throw an economy into a recession. On the other hand, unanticipated increases in aggregate demand or short-run aggregate supply can generate an unsustainable economic boom—a temporarily high level of output and employment that cannot be maintained.

However, the model also suggests that changes in resource prices and interest rates will tend to direct an economy back toward full employment following a disruption. Let's take a closer look at these two forces that underlie the self-corrective mechanism of macroeconomic markets.

1. Changes in real resource prices will help direct an economy toward equilibrium. Price adjustments in the resource market will help keep an economy on an even keel. When an economy is in a recession and its output is less than its full-employment potential, the demand for resources will be weak. Underutilized assets and unemployment of resources will be widespread. However, the weak demand will place downward pressure on resource prices. As real resource prices fall, costs will decline, and this will help restore profit margins and strengthen the incentive of producers to expand output. Thus, the lower resource prices will help direct a recessionary economy back toward full employment.

In contrast, when a booming economy is operating beyond its full-employment capacity—when unemployment is less than the natural unemployment rate—strong demand will push up the real price of labor (wages) and other resources. In turn, the higher resource prices will increase costs and reduce profit margins. As costs increase, firms will cut back their output, directing the economy toward its full-employment potential.

2. Changes in real interest rates help stabilize aggregate demand and redirect economic fluctuations. Real interest rates tend to reflect business conditions. During an economic downturn, businesses borrow less money for new investment projects. The demand for loanable funds is weak, and real interest rates generally fall. In turn, the lower interest rates lead to higher consumption and make investment projects cheaper, motivating businesses to undertake them. This helps offset the decline in aggregate demand and redirect output toward the full-employment level.

Conversely, during an economic boom, businesses borrow more money to invest in projects that will help them meet the stronger demand for their goods and services. The demand for loanable funds will strengthen, putting upward pressure on real interest rates. In turn, the higher interest rates will make it more expensive to purchase consumer durables and undertake investment projects. This helps restrain aggregate demand and redirect output toward the full-employment level.

Interest rate adjustments will also help offset potential economic disturbances arising from shifts in expectations about future business conditions. Suppose consumers and business operators suddenly become more pessimistic and, as a result, reduce their current level of spending. This will lower consumer spending and increase saving. Demand in the loanable funds market will be weak. Thus, the supply of loanable funds will increase relative to the demand. However, this will lead to lower real interest rates, which will help keep the economy on track by offsetting spending reductions caused by the increased pessimism.

Just the opposite will happen if consumers and businesses suddenly became more optimistic. If they suddenly decide to spend more of their current income, this will reduce the supply of loanable funds relative to the demand, causing real interest rates to rise. The higher rates will then make current spending less attractive and will help stabilize aggregate demand.[4]

The implications of the *AD–AS* model with regard to economic instability might be summarized in the following manner:

Various shocks (unanticipated changes in *AD* or *AS*) can disrupt full-employment equilibrium and lead either to recessionary unemployment or to an inflationary boom. In the short run, long-term contracts and misperceptions about the current price level can lead to output levels that differ from long-run equilibrium. With time, however, changes in real resource prices and interest rates will act as a stabilizing force and direct a market economy back to its full employment potential.

But the *AD–AS* model does not indicate how quickly the market adjustment process will work. This is an area in which the views of economists often differ. Some believe that, if not undermined by harmful policies, market forces will direct the economy back to full employment within a relatively short time frame, and therefore recessions will generally last only a few quarters. Other economists argue that the self-corrective mechanism of markets works slowly, and therefore without appropriate macroeconomic policy changes, recessions will be long and painful. As we proceed, we will present each of these views in detail and examine their policy implications.

10-7a EXPANSIONS AND RECESSIONS: THE HISTORICAL RECORD

Exhibit 9 shows the time intervals of the expansions and recessions experienced by the U.S. economy since 1950. There have been ten business cycles, periods of expansion followed by a recession, during this period of six decades. The expansions have generally been lengthier than the recessions. The ten full expansions since 1950 have averaged approximately sixty months in length, and three of those expansions have lasted seven years or more. In contrast, the average length of the recessions has been about 11 months. The recession that began in December 2007 lasted 18 months, making it the longest in more than 70 years.

10-7b USING THE *AD–AS* MODEL TO THINK ABOUT THE BUSINESS CYCLE AND THE GREAT RECESSION OF 2008–2009

The 1930s were a period of extremely high unemployment and depressed economic conditions. The unemployment rate rose to nearly 25 percent of the labor force in 1932 and 1933.

---

[4] The foreign exchange market may also help stabilize the business cycle. When an economy dips into a recession, investment prospects will deteriorate, leading to a reduction in the inflow of capital from abroad. In turn, the decline in capital inflow will lead to depreciation in the foreign exchange rate, which will stimulate net exports and aggregate demand and thereby help to redirect the economy back toward full employment. Just the opposite will occur during the expansionary phase of the business cycle. However, these adjustments are not likely to be very important in countries like the United States where the international trade sector is a relatively small share of the economy. Thus, we focus on the importance of the interest rate and resource price adjustments as the primary forces that will direct a market economy toward full employment.

EXHIBIT 9

PERIOD OF EXPANSION	LENGTH (IN MONTHS)	PERIOD OF RECESSION	LENGTH (IN MONTHS)
Oct '49 to July '53	44	July '53 to May '54	10
May '54 to August '57	39	August '57 to April '58	9
April '58 to April '60	24	April '60 to February '61	10
February '61 to Dec '69	105	Dec '69 to November '70	10
Nov '70 to Nov '73	36	Nov '73 to March '75	16
March '75 to January '80	58	January '80 to July '80	6
July '80 to July '81	12	July '81 to November '82	16
Nov '82 to July '90	92	July '90 to March '91	9
March '91 to March '01	120	March '01 to November '01	8
November '01 to November '07	73	December '07 to June '09	18
July '09 to ?[a]	47		

Expansions and Recessions, 1950–2012

The accompanying table indicates the periods of both economic expansions (rising GDP) and recessions (falling GDP) since 1950. As the table indicates, the length of both varies substantially, but the expansions have clearly been longer.

[a]To date, this expansion has continued through May 2013.

Source: http://www.nber.org.

Between 1931 and 1940, the rate of unemployment exceeded 14 percent during each year. These extreme conditions explain why this period is referred to as the Great Depression.

While the length and severity of the 2008–2009 downturn was not comparable to the Great Depression, it was the longest recession since the 1930s. Because of its length and severity, some refer to it as the Great Recession.

Why did the United States experience a strong expansion during 2003–2007, and why did the boom turn to a bust in 2008? The *AD–AS* model provides considerable insight on this issue. Between 2002 and mid-year 2006, there was a sharp increase in housing prices. Nationwide, the average home price increased by 89 percent during this period. At the same time, stock prices were also increasing rapidly. Just as the *AD–AS* model indicates, this huge increase in stock and housing prices increased wealth, stimulated aggregate demand, and generated an economic boom.

But the situation began to change during the second half of 2006. Housing prices reversed and began to fall. Mortgage default rates and housing foreclosures started to rise. The construction industry contracted sharply. As housing wealth fell, people became more pessimistic, causing a further reduction in aggregate demand. Then, during 2007 and the first half of 2008, the world price of crude oil soared to $140 per barrel, pushing the price of gasoline to $4 per gallon, twice the price of a year earlier. By 2008, stock prices were plummeting, further reducing wealth and aggregate demand. All of these adverse forces combine to reduce both aggregate demand and supply, and just as the *AD–AS* model indicates, they generated a sharp decline in real output and employment.

Exhibit 10 provides additional perspective on both the business cycle and the 2008–2009 recession; it shows data on the change in both real housing and stock prices during the first two years of expansions and contractions since 1969. Note how both housing and stock prices have risen during the expansionary phase of the business cycle. Prior to the most recent recession, the average real home price rose by 7 percent during the first two years of the expansionary phase. Similarly, real stock prices rose by an average of 35 percent during the expansions. These higher asset prices increase wealth and stimulate aggregate demand. This will lead to increases in output and employment during this phase of the cycle.

But just the opposite happens during the contraction. During the past seven recessions, the average real home price fell by 12 percent, and the average real stock price fell by 38 percent. When housing and stock prices fall, household wealth will decline, causing a reduction in aggregate demand. In turn, the reductions in wealth and demand will both contribute to the initial downturn and complicate the recovery process.

Changes in the Real Price of Stock Shares and Housing (Single-Family Homes) during Business Cycles since 1969

The change in stock and housing prices during the first two years of expansions and recessions are presented here. Both generally rise during expansions and fall during recessions. Note that the housing price reduction accompanying the 2008 recession was substantially greater than during earlier recessions. This was a major reason for the severity of the recession. Similarly, note how housing prices continued to decline during the recovery and expansion from the 2008 recession. This was unprecedented in recent decades and contributed to the weakness of the recovery.

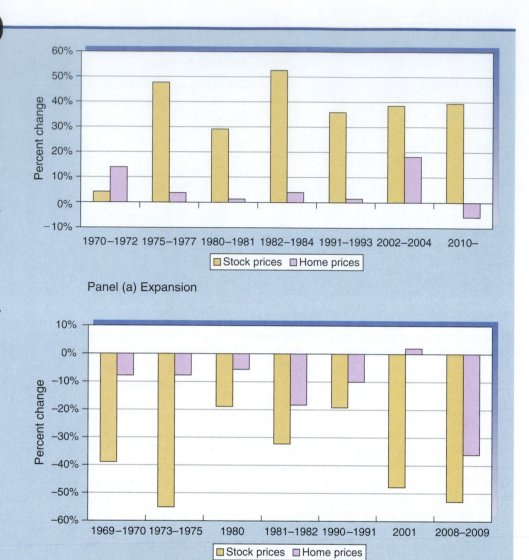

Panel (a) Expansion

Panel (b) Recession

Source: The stock prices are based on Standard and Poor's monthly opening prices. The housing prices prior to 1976 are based on National Association of Realtors median existing home sale prices. The sale prices for 1976 to 1986 are from the Office of Federal Housing Enterprise Oversight. The housing price data since 1987 are from the Case-Shiller quarterly housing price index. All prices were adjusted for inflation using the consumer price index (CPI).

The rise and fall of stock prices prior to and following the 2008–2009 recession were not substantially different than for the earlier business cycles. But, this was not the case for housing prices. As Exhibit 10 shows, the increase in housing prices during the expansion prior to the 2008 recession and the subsequent decline that began more than a year before the recession were far greater than those of earlier business cycles. Housing prices fell by 35 percent during the 2008–2009 recession, nearly three times the average decline of the prior recessions. Clearly, the housing price boom and bust was a central factor underlying the 2008–2009 recession. Finally, notice what happened to housing prices during the first two years of the recovery and expansion from the most recent recession: They fell another 5 percent. This decline in housing prices during the expansionary phase is unprecedented in recent decades. No doubt, this factor contributed to the weakness of the most recent recovery. As we proceed, we will investigate this issue in more detail.

LOOKING AHEAD

The *AD–AS* model enhances our understanding of macroeconomic markets and potential sources of economic fluctuations. It also provides a constructive framework with which to address key unanswered questions. Can fiscal and monetary policy promote economic stability? Can they help direct an economy out of a recession? If so, how might this be achieved? Have macroeconomic policies sometimes been the source of economic instability? The next four chapters will focus on these questions and related issues.

KEY POINTS

- It is important to distinguish between changes that are anticipated and unanticipated because the impact on the economy will differ between the two.

- An increase in aggregate demand involves a shift of the entire *AD* curve to the right. Major factors causing an increase in aggregate demand (other than government policies) are (1) an increase in real wealth, (2) a lower real interest rate, (3) increased optimism on the part of businesses and consumers, (4) an increase in the expected rate of inflation, (5) higher real income abroad, and (6) a depreciation in the exchange rate. Conversely, if these factors change in the opposite direction, a decrease in aggregate demand will result.

- It is important to distinguish between long-run and short-run aggregate supply. The following factors will increase long-run aggregate supply (*LRAS*): (1) increases in the supply of labor and capital resources, (2) improvements in technology and productivity, and (3) institutional changes improving the efficiency of resource use. Changes in resource prices, the expected rate of inflation, and supply shocks will cause shifts in short-run aggregate supply (*SRAS*).

- An increase in output due to economic growth (an increase in the economy's production capacity) will increase both short-run and long-run aggregate supply, permitting the economy to achieve and sustain a larger output level.

- Unanticipated changes in either aggregate demand or aggregate supply will disrupt long-run equilibrium and cause current output to differ from the economy's long-run potential.

- Unanticipated increases in aggregate demand and favorable supply shocks can cause economic booms that push output beyond the economy's long-run potential and unemployment below its natural rate. However, as decision-makers adjust to the strong demand, resource prices and interest rates will rise, and output will recede to long-run capacity.

- Unanticipated reductions in aggregate demand and adverse supply shocks can lead to below-capacity output and abnormally high rates of unemployment. Eventually, lower resource prices (and lower real interest rates) will direct the economy back to long-run equilibrium. This adjustment process will take time, and it may be quite lengthy if wages and prices are downwardly inflexible.

- Changes in resource prices and interest rates will help keep an economy on track. During a recession, resource prices and interest rates will decline, and this will help direct the economy back toward full employment. However, there is considerable debate about how rapidly this adjustment process works.

- During the past six decades, economic expansions have been far lengthier than recessions. However, the depth and severity of the recession that started in December 2007 has once again placed the issue of economic instability and recovery from a recession at the forefront of macroeconomics.

CRITICAL ANALYSIS QUESTIONS

1. *Explain how and why each of the following factors would influence current aggregate demand in the United States:
   a. increased fear of recession
   b. increased fear of inflation
   c. rapid growth of real income in Canada and Western Europe
   d. a reduction in the real interest rate
   e. a higher price level (Be careful.)

2. *Indicate how each of the following would influence U.S. aggregate supply in the short run:
   a. an increase in real wage rates
   b. a severe freeze that destroys half the orange trees in Florida
   c. an increase in the expected rate of inflation in the future
   d. an increase in the world price of oil, a major import
   e. abundant rainfall during the growing season in agricultural states

3. What impact would a change that shifts an economy's production possibilities curve outward have on the long-run aggregate supply curve? How have improvements in computer technology affected production possibilities and the long-run aggregate supply curve? Explain.

4. When an economy dips into a recession, consumers will often be relatively pessimistic about the future for an extended period of time. How will this pessimism affect the speed and strength of the recovery? Feel free to use the data of Exhibit 2 in your response to this question.

5. What is the difference between an anticipated and an unanticipated increase in aggregate demand? Provide an example of each. Which is more likely to result in a temporary spurt in the growth of real output?

6. Assume that both union and management representatives agree to wage increases because they expect prices to rise 10 percent during the next year. Explain why the unemployment rate will probably increase if the actual rate of inflation next year is only 3 percent.

7. During 2007, there was a substantial reduction in housing prices, and the world price of crude oil rose sharply. How did these two changes influence aggregate demand and aggregate supply in the United States? Use the *AD–AS* model to indicate the expected impact of these changes on output and the price level.

8. *When actual output exceeds an economy's full-employment output, how will the self-correcting mechanism direct the economy to long-run equilibrium? Why can't the above-normal output be maintained?

9. How will (a) an unexpected 3 percent fall in the price level in the goods and services market differ from (b) 1 percent inflation when 4 percent inflation had been expected? What impact would (a) and (b) have on the real price of resources, profit margins, output, and employment? Explain.

10. Suppose that an unexpectedly rapid growth in real income abroad leads to a sharp increase in the demand for U.S. exports. What impact will this change have on the price level, output, and employment in the short run in the United States? In the long run?

11. Construct the *AD, SRAS,* and *LRAS* curves for an economy experiencing (a) full employment, (b) an economic boom, and (c) a recession.

12. Consider an economy with the following aggregate demand (*AD*) and aggregate supply (*AS*) schedules. These schedules reflect the fact that, prior to the period we're examining, decision makers entered into contracts and made choices anticipating that the price level would be P_{105}.

AD_{105} (IN TRILLIONS)	PRICE LEVEL	$SRAS_{105}$ (IN TRILLIONS)
$5.1	95	$3.5
4.9	100	3.8
4.7	105	4.2
4.5	110	4.5
4.3	115	4.8

a. Indicate the quantity of GDP that will be produced and the price level that will emerge during this period.

b. Is the economy in long-run equilibrium? Why or why not?

c. How will the unemployment rate during the current period compare with this economy's natural rate of unemployment?

d. What will tend to happen to resource prices in the future? How will this affect the equilibrium rate of output?

e. Will the rate of GDP produced during this period be sustainable into the future? Why or why not?

13. (a) Housing prices rose sharply between 2002 and mid-year 2006. Use the *AD–AS* model to illustrate the impact of the housing price increases on output and employment. (b) During 2007 and 2008, housing prices fell sharply. Use the *AD–AS* model to illustrate the impact of these price declines on output and employment.

*Asterisk denotes questions for which answers are given in Appendix B.

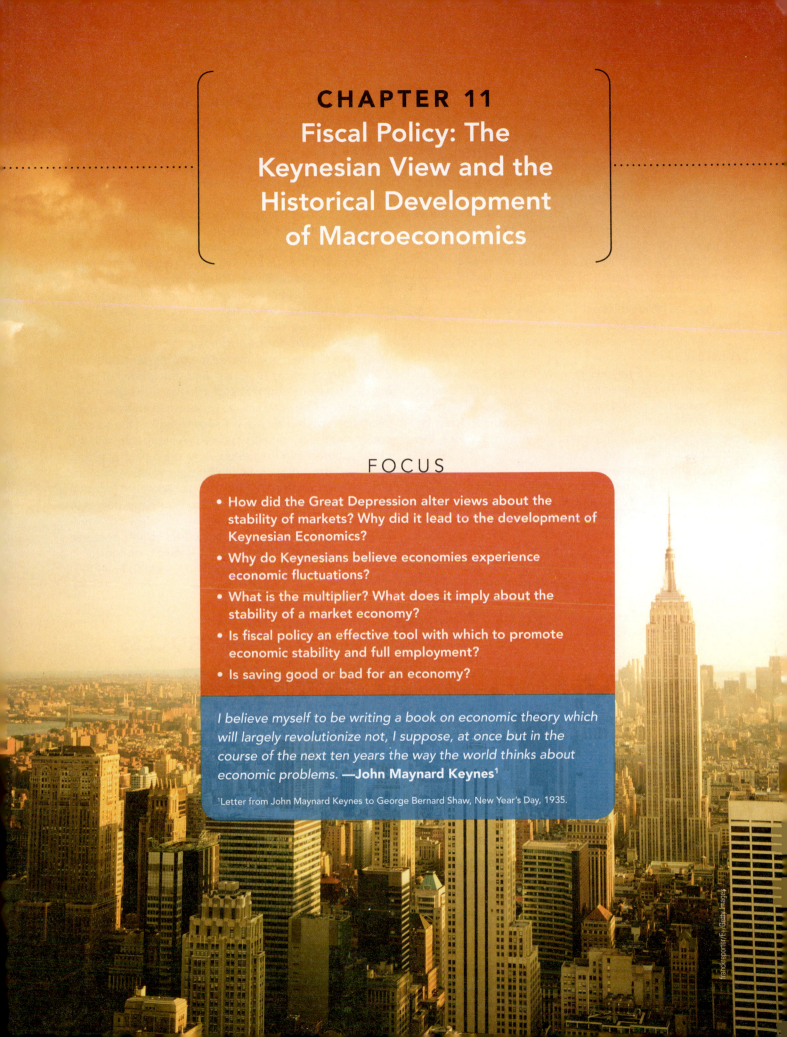

CHAPTER 11
Fiscal Policy: The Keynesian View and the Historical Development of Macroeconomics

FOCUS

- How did the Great Depression alter views about the stability of markets? Why did it lead to the development of Keynesian Economics?
- Why do Keynesians believe economies experience economic fluctuations?
- What is the multiplier? What does it imply about the stability of a market economy?
- Is fiscal policy an effective tool with which to promote economic stability and full employment?
- Is saving good or bad for an economy?

I believe myself to be writing a book on economic theory which will largely revolutionize not, I suppose, at once but in the course of the next ten years the way the world thinks about economic problems. —**John Maynard Keynes**[1]

[1]Letter from John Maynard Keynes to George Bernard Shaw, New Year's Day, 1935.

The Great Depression exerted a huge impact on modern macroeconomics. The national income accounts that we use to measure gross domestic product are an outgrowth of this era. Several of the basic concepts of macroeconomics and much of the terminology used today were initially introduced during the 1930s. The Great Depression also led to the development of a theory that provided both an explanation for the prolonged unemployment of the 1930s and a recipe for how to generate a recovery. This theory, developed by the English economist John Maynard Keynes (pronounced "canes"), dominated macroeconomics to such a large extent that the theories he developed were soon known as Keynesian economics.

Keynesian analysis indicated that fiscal policy could be used to maintain a high level of output and employment. The Keynesian view reached a pinnacle in the 1960s. The cover of the December 31, 1965, issue of *TIME* magazine posed the question, "Are we all Keynesians now?" In the midst of strong growth boosted by expansionary fiscal policy, particularly tax reductions, the answer was clearly, "Yes."

But the response proved to be premature. The 1970s were characterized by both high unemployment and inflation. As we will soon illustrate, the Keynesian model provided an explanation for either unemployment or inflation, but it did not account for the simultaneous occurrence of both. The Keynesian theory was designed to explain economic instability and prolonged depressed conditions. Thus, it should not be surprising that its popularity waned even more during the stability of 1982–2007. However, the severity of the plunge in output and employment in 2008 has generated renewed interest and a reexamination of Keynesian economics.

Perhaps surprising to some, active use of fiscal policy is a relatively recent phenomenon. Prior to the 1960s, policy-makers focused primarily on how to balance the government's budget, and they generally did so except during times of war or severe recession. Given the limited experience with active use of fiscal policy, the presence of alternative theories and areas of continued debate should not be surprising.

This chapter, and the next, will present both the primary fiscal policy theories and the views of their critics. There are also areas of widespread agreement, and these will be noted as we proceed. In areas in which disagreements remain, we will seek to explain the sources underlying the continuing debate. We will begin with the presentation of the Keynesian view, primarily because it provides historical perspective on the evolution of modern macroeconomics. The following chapter will focus on alternative theories that have arisen over the past four decades. Taken together, these two chapters provide a balanced presentation of current views on the potential and limitations of fiscal policy as a stabilization tool.

©iStockphoto.com/nicoolay

11-1 THE GREAT DEPRESSION AND THE MACROADJUSTMENT PROCESS

The 1930s dramatically altered views about the stability of a market economy. Prior to the Great Depression, most economists thought that markets would adjust and direct an economy back to its long-run potential rather quickly. Prolonged recessionary conditions were thought to be impossible. The Great Depression changed all of that.

For those who are familiar only with the relative stability of recent decades, the depth and length of the economic decline during the 1930s are difficult to comprehend: between 1929 and 1933, real GDP in the United States fell by more than 30 percent. In 1933, nearly 25 percent—one-quarter—of the U.S. labor force was unemployed. The depressed conditions continued throughout the decade. In 1939, a decade after the plunge began, the rate of unemployment was still 17 percent, and real per capita income was approximately the same as it was in 1929. Other industrial countries experienced similar conditions during the 1930s.

11-1a THE GREAT DEPRESSION AND KEYNESIAN ECONOMICS

Keynesian economics provided a reasonable explanation for the prolonged depressed conditions of the 1930s. Keynes believed that spending motivated firms to supply goods and services. He argued that if total spending fell—as it might, for example, if consumers and investors became pessimistic about the future—then firms would respond by cutting back production. Less spending would thus lead to less output.[2]

Keynes rejected the view that lower wages and interest rates would get the economy back on track and eliminate abnormally high rates of unemployment. He argued that wages and prices are highly inflexible, particularly in a downward direction. Even when demand is weak, Keynes and his followers believed powerful trade unions and large corporations would be able to maintain their wages and prices at a high level. Further, even if wages did decline, this would reduce incomes and exert a negative impact on aggregate demand.

Keynes also rejected the potential effectiveness of interest rate cuts to get the economy back on track. He argued that when excess capacity is widespread and people are extremely pessimistic about the future, lower interest rates will fail to stimulate additional investment. Moreover, when nominal interest rates fall to extremely low levels—rates near zero, for example—significant additional reductions capable of stimulating the economy would be impossible. Keynes believed that all of these conditions were present during the Great Depression. Under these circumstances, he did not believe that market forces would direct the economy back to full employment.

The Keynesian model was an outgrowth of the Great Depression. It provided an explanation for the widespread and prolonged unemployment of the 1930s.

11-1b OUTPUT, EMPLOYMENT, AND KEYNESIAN ECONOMICS

Keynes also introduced a different concept of equilibrium and a different mechanism for its achievement. In the Keynesian view, equilibrium takes place when total spending in the economy is equal to current output. When this is the case, business firms will just be able to sell the quantity of goods and services they are currently producing. Their inventories will be neither rising nor falling, and therefore they will have no reason to either expand or contract output.

Keynesians believe that changes in output rather than changes in prices direct the economy toward equilibrium. An increase in total spending demand would generate expanding sales and reduce the inventories of firms. Businesses would respond with an expansion in output, and the higher level of output would be maintained as long as spending remained at the higher level.

On the other hand, a decline in total spending would lead to a reduction in sales and rising inventories. If total spending fell below the full-employment level of output, business firms would cut back on employment and reduce their output to the level of spending, and, most significantly, the lower level of output and employment would persist as long as the level of spending was unchanged. Therefore, if total spending is deficient—if it is less than full-employment output—high rates of unemployment will be present, output will continue below the economy's potential, and these conditions will persist as long as the spending on goods and services remains weak.

This is exactly what Keynes believed was happening during the 1930s. Consumers were unwilling to spend much because reductions in stock prices and the value of other assets had reduced their wealth and incomes, and they were extremely pessimistic about the future. Businesses responded with reductions in output because there was little demand for their products. Moreover, investment came to a complete standstill because underutilized resources and capacity were abundantly available.

---

[2]See the classic book by John Maynard Keynes, *The General Theory of Employment, Interest, and Money* (London: Macmillan, 1936), for the presentation of this theory.

11-1c THE MULTIPLIER AND ECONOMIC INSTABILITY

Keynes also argued that market forces could not be counted on to maintain spending levels consistent with full employment because even minor disturbances will often be amplified into major disruptions. The **multiplier principle** can be used to explain his argument. The multiplier principle *builds on the point that one individual's expenditure becomes the income of another*. Predictably, income recipients will spend a portion of their additional earnings on consumption. In turn, their consumption expenditures will generate additional income for others who will also spend a portion of it.

Perhaps an example will illuminate the multiplier concept. Suppose an entrepreneur undertakes a $1 million investment project. The project will increase spending directly by $1 million. This is not the entire story, however. The investment project will require plumbers, carpenters, masons, lumber, cement, and many other resources. The project will generate $1 million of income for the suppliers of these resources. What will they do with this income? After setting aside (saving) a portion of it, the resource suppliers will spend a fraction of the additional income. They will buy food, clothing, recreation, medical care, and thousands of other items. How will this spending influence the incomes of those who supply these products and services? Their incomes will increase, also. These people will save a portion of it and will spend some of it on current consumption. This consumption spending will result in still more additional income generated and received by the suppliers of the additional goods and services.

The term *multiplier* is also used to indicate the number by which the initial investment would be multiplied to obtain the total increase in the economy's income. If the $1 million investment resulted in $4 million of additional income, the **expenditure multiplier** would be 4. The total increase in income would be four times the amount of the initial increase in spending. Similarly, if total income increased by $3 million, the multiplier would be 3.

The size of the multiplier depends on the proportion of the additional income that households choose to spend on consumption.[3] Keynes referred to this fraction as the **marginal propensity to consume (MPC)**. Mathematically,

$$\text{MPC} = \frac{\text{Additional consumption}}{\text{Additional income}}$$

For example, if your income increases by $100 and you increase your current consumption expenditures by $75 as a result, your marginal propensity to consume is 75/100, which is 3/4 or 0.75.

Exhibit 1 illustrates why the size of the multiplier is dependent upon the MPC. Continuing with the previous example, we consider the impact of the $1 million investment project when the MPC is equal to 3/4. Initially, a $1 million investment will result in $1 million of additional income in round 1 for those undertaking the project. Because the MPC is 3/4, consumption will increase by $750,000 (the other $250,000 will flow into saving) and turn into other people's income in round 2. The recipients of the round 2 income of $750,000 will spend 3/4 of it on current consumption. Hence, their spending will increase income by $562,500 in round 3. Exhibit 1 indicates the additions to income through other rounds. In total, income will increase by $4 million, given an MPC of 3/4. The multiplier is 4.

If the MPC had been greater, income recipients would have spent a larger share of their additional income on current consumption during each round. Thus, the additional income generated in each round would have been greater, increasing the size of the multiplier.

Multiplier principle
The concept that an increase in spending on a project will generate income for the resource suppliers, who will then increase their consumption spending. In turn, their additional consumption will generate income for others and lead to still more consumption. As this process goes through successive rounds, total income will expand by a multiple of the initial increase in spending.

Expenditure multiplier
The ratio of the change in equilibrium output to the independent change in investment, consumption, or government spending that brings about the change. Numerically, the multiplier is equal to 1 *divided by* (1 − MPC) when the price level is constant.

Marginal propensity to consume (MPC)
Additional current consumption divided by additional current disposable income.

---

[3]For the purposes of simplicity when calculating the size of the multiplier, we will assume that all additions to income are either (1) spent on domestically produced goods or (2) saved. This assumption means that we are ignoring the impact of taxes and spending on imports as income expands via the multiplier process.

The Multiplier Principle

Expenditure Stage	Additional Income (Dollars)		Additional Consumption (Dollars)	Marginal Propensity to Consume
Round 1	1,000,00	→	750,000	3/4
Round 2	750,000	→	562,500	3/4
Round 3	562,500	→	421,875	3/4
Round 4	421,875	→	316,406	3/4
Round 5	316,406	→	237,305	3/4
Round 6	237,305	→	177,979	3/4
Round 7	177,979	→	133,484	3/4
Round 8	133,484	→	100,113	3/4
Round 9	100,113	→	75,085	3/4
Round 10	75,085	→	56,314	3/4
All Others	225,253	→	168,939	3/4
Total	4,000,00		3,000,00	3/4

© Cengage Learning 2013

There is a precise relationship between the MPC and the multiplier, in other words. The expenditure multiplier, *M*, is

$$M = \frac{1}{1 - MPC}$$

The multiplier concept also works in reverse—reductions in spending will also be magnified and generate even larger reductions in income. Thus, even modest reductions in investment or consumption, perhaps due to increased pessimism about the future, might throw an economy into a recession. Keynesians argue that the multiplier concept indicates that market economies are extremely fragile and that they have a tendency to fluctuate back and forth between excessive and deficient demand.

11-1d ADDING REALISM TO THE MULTIPLIER

When considering the multiplier, it is important to understand the chain reactions that underlie the concept. Exhibit 1 implicitly assumes that the additional spending will always

OUTSTANDING ECONOMIST

JOHN MAYNARD KEYNES (1883–1946)

Keynes might properly be referred to as the "father of macroeconomics." The son of a prominent nineteenth-century economist (John Neville Keynes), he earned a degree in mathematics from King's College, Cambridge, where he would later return and spend most of his career as an economist. His *General Theory of Employment, Interest, and Money*, published in 1936, revolutionized the way that economists think about macroeconomics. This work, written in the midst of the Great Depression, provided both a plausible explanation for the massive unemployment and a strategy for ending it. Keynes married an idea with a moment in time.

Although Keynes's work was groundbreaking, it was also controversial. Keynes argued that governments should run budget deficits during a recession to stimulate demand and direct the economy back to full employment. But this idea challenged the entrenched views of both policy-makers and economists. Nonetheless, his ideas soon triumphed and dominated the thinking of macroeconomists for three decades following his untimely death due to a heart attack in 1946. Most observers would rate Keynes as the most influential economist of the twentieth century.

bring previously idle workers into the labor force. For example, the analysis implies that the electricians, plumbers, masons, and others involved in the initial construction project would not have been working if the project had not been undertaken. When unemployment is exceedingly high, as it was during the Great Depression, this may be largely the case. However, during more normal times when there are fewer unemployed resources, much of the additional spending will merely bid resources away from other activities. Under these circumstances, there will be upward pressure on prices, and the additions to income will be smaller, perhaps substantially smaller, than the multiplier analysis implies.

It is also important to consider how the initial addition to spending is derived. If the increase in spending is financed by borrowing, there will be upward pressure on real interest rates, which will reduce spending in other areas. Correspondingly, if the additional spending were the result of a government project financed by taxes, the higher taxes would reduce spending in other areas, at least partially offsetting the impact of the multiplier.[4] These factors indicate that during normal times, the demand stimulus effects of a spending project will be substantially weaker than the multiplier analysis suggests.

11-1e KEYNES AND ECONOMIC INSTABILITY: A SUMMARY

The central message of Keynes can be summarized as follows: Businesses will produce only the quantity of goods and services they believe consumers, investors, governments, and foreigners will plan to buy. If these planned aggregate expenditures are less than the economy's full-employment output, output will fall short of its potential. Moreover, reductions in spending will often be amplified by the multiplier and tend to feed on themselves. Downturns will breed pessimism among both consumers and investors, which will lead to lower prices for assets such as stocks and houses, causing total spending and output to plummet downward by even larger amounts. When total expenditures (aggregate demand) on goods and services are deficient, market economies do not have an automatic mechanism that will return the economy to full employment. Prolonged unemployment will persist. Against the backdrop of the Great Depression, this was a compelling argument.

While the Keynesian view indicates that market economies will tend to swing back and forth between recessions caused by weak demand and economic booms caused by excessive demand, there is a positive side to Keynesian analysis. There is a remedy for the fluctuations: Fiscal policy can be used to control aggregate demand and smooth the ups and downs of the business cycle. We now turn to this topic.

11-2 THE KEYNESIAN VIEW OF FISCAL POLICY

As we noted in Chapter 9, fiscal policy involves the use of the government's spending, taxing, and borrowing policies. Until now, we have assumed that the government's fiscal policy remained unchanged. We are now ready to relax this assumption and investigate the effect of fiscal policy on output, prices, and employment. We want to isolate the impact of changes in fiscal policy from changes in monetary policy. Thus, we will continue to assume that the monetary authorities are holding the supply of money constant. We will relax this assumption and investigate the impact of monetary policy in subsequent chapters.

The federal budget is the primary tool of fiscal policy. When the supply of money is constant, government expenditures must be financed with either (1) taxes or revenues derived from other sources or (2) borrowing. If the government's revenue from taxes and other sources is equal to its total expenditure, a **balanced budget** is present. The budget need not be in balance, however. A **budget deficit** occurs when total government

Balanced budget
A situation in which current government revenue from taxes, fees, and other sources is just equal to current government expenditures.

Budget deficit
A situation in which total government spending exceeds total government revenue during a specific time period, usually one year.

---

[4]The multiplier analysis is often abused by proponents of government spending projects. For example, proponents of tax-subsidized sports stadiums and industrial development projects often use the multiplier to argue that spending on such projects will generate a huge increase in income and employment for the local economy, while ignoring the offsetting spending reductions as the result of the higher taxes.

spending exceeds total government revenue from all sources. When this happens, the government must borrow funds to finance the excess of its spending relative to revenue. It borrows by issuing interest-bearing bonds that become part of what we call the national debt, the total amount of outstanding government bonds. Conversely, a **budget surplus** is present when the government's revenues exceed its total expenditures. The surplus allows the government to reduce its outstanding debt.

Budget surplus
A situation in which total government spending is less than total government revenue during a time period, usually a year.

While budget conditions are often used to gauge the direction of fiscal policy, it is important to recognize that changes in the size of the deficit or surplus can originate from two different sources. *First, changes in the size of the deficit or surplus may merely reflect the state of the economy.* During a recession, tax revenues generally fall and expenditures on transfer programs increase because of the weak economic conditions. This will shift the budget toward a deficit—even with no changes in fiscal policy. Just the opposite will happen during the expansionary phase of the business cycle. The rapid growth of income during an expansion will increase tax revenues and reduce income transfers, causing the budget to shift toward a surplus (or smaller deficit), even if there has not been any change in fiscal policy. *Second, changes in the deficit or surplus may reflect* **discretionary fiscal policy**. Discretionary fiscal policy requires passage of tax and/or spending legislation by Congress and the president that alter the size of the budget deficit (or surplus). When we speak of "changes in fiscal policy," we are referring to this latter type of action—a deliberate change in tax laws or government spending levels (or both) that affect the budget deficit or surplus.

Discretionary fiscal policy
A change, in laws or appropriation levels, that alters government revenues and/or expenditures.

11-3 FISCAL POLICY AND THE GOOD NEWS OF KEYNESIAN ECONOMICS

Keynesians argue that the federal budget should be used to promote a level of total spending (aggregate demand) consistent with the full-employment rate of output. How might policymakers use the budget to stimulate aggregate demand? First, an increase in government purchases of goods and services will directly increase aggregate demand. As the government spends more on highways, flood-control projects, education, and national defense, for example, these expenditures will increase demand in the goods and services market. Second, changes in tax policy will also influence aggregate demand. For example, a reduction in personal taxes will increase the current disposable income of households. As their after-tax income rises, people will spend more on consumption. In turn, this increase in consumption will stimulate aggregate demand. Similarly, a reduction in business taxes increases after-tax profitability, which will stimulate both business investment and aggregate demand.

When an economy is operating below its potential capacity, Keynesians believe the government should institute **expansionary fiscal policy**. In other words, the government should increase its purchases of goods and services or cut taxes or both. Of course, this policy will increase the government's budget deficit. To finance the enlarged budget deficit, the government will have to borrow from either private domestic sources or foreigners.[5]

Expansionary fiscal policy
An increase in government expenditures and/or a reduction in tax rates, such that the expected size of the budget deficit expands.

Exhibit 2 illustrates the case for expansionary fiscal policy when an economy is experiencing abnormally high unemployment caused by deficient aggregate demand. Initially, the economy is operating at e_1. Output is below potential capacity, Y_F, and unemployment exceeds its natural rate. As we discussed in Chapter 10, if there is no change in policy, abnormally high unemployment and excess supply in the resource market will eventually reduce real wages and other resource prices, which will lower costs and direct the economy toward a full-employment equilibrium like E_3. In addition, weak demand for

---

[5]Alternatively, the government could borrow from its central bank—the Federal Reserve Bank in the United States. However, as we will see in the following chapter, this method of financing a budget deficit would expand the money supply. Because we want to differentiate between fiscal and monetary effects, we must hold the supply of money constant. So for now, we assume that government deficits must be financed by borrowing from private sources.

EXHIBIT 2

Expansionary Fiscal Policy to Promote Full Employment

Here, we illustrate an economy operating in the short run at Y_1, below its potential capacity of Y_F. There are two routes to a long-run, full-employment equilibrium. First, policy-makers could wait for lower wages and resource prices to reduce costs, increase supply to $SRAS_3$, and restore equilibrium at E_3. Most Keynesians believe this market-adjustment method will be slow and uncertain. Alternatively, expansionary fiscal policy could stimulate aggregate demand (shift it to AD_2) and guide the economy to E_2.

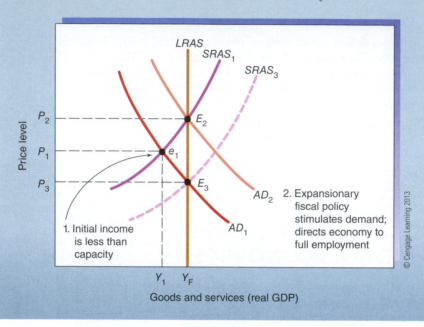

© Cengage Learning 2013

According to the Keynesian view, increases in government spending on infrastructure during a recession will stimulate aggregate demand and thereby help promote recovery.

AP Images/Bill Waugh

investment goods will place downward pressure on interest rates, which will stimulate aggregate demand and also help to direct the economy back to full employment. However, these adjustments may work slowly.

Rather than depending on the economy's self-corrective mechanism, Keynesians favor a shift to a more expansionary fiscal policy—an increase in government spending or a reduction in taxes, or some combination of the two. In other words, they advocate a deliberate increase in the budget deficit in order to stimulate aggregate demand.

Furthermore, they argue that the multiplier process will magnify the initial increase in spending. Suppose that the government holds taxes constant and increases its spending on highways and school construction by $20 billion. The additional spending will generate $20 billion in income for those undertaking the construction projects. As these individuals use a portion of this income to buy consumer goods, the multiplier process indicates that their spending will trigger more income and spending by others. Thus, Keynesians expect that the total increase in aggregate demand will be substantially greater than the initial $20 billion increase in government purchases.

When an economy is operating below its potential capacity, the Keynesian prescription calls

EXHIBIT 3

Restrictive Fiscal Policy to Combat Inflation

Strong demand such as AD_1 will temporarily lead to an output rate beyond the economy's long-run potential (Y_F). If the high level of demand persists, it will lead to a long-run equilibrium (E_3) at a higher price level.

However, restrictive fiscal policy could restrain demand to AD_2 (or better still, prevent demand from expanding to AD_1 in the first place) and thereby guide the economy to a noninflationary equilibrium (E_2).

for expansionary fiscal policy—a deliberate change in expenditures and/or taxes that will increase the size of the government's budget deficit. An appropriate dose of expansionary fiscal policy, if timed properly, will stimulate aggregate demand (shift the curve to AD_2 in Exhibit 2) and guide the economy to full-employment equilibrium (E_2).

Moreover, Keynesians argue that economic recovery will be a struggle for market economies because the downturn will tend to feed on itself. As incomes decline during a recession, consumers will cut their spending, which will reduce the demand for goods and services and lead businesses to cut back on both output and employment. Pessimism will spread throughout the economy and output will plunge downward. But government can break the pattern by stepping in with expansionary fiscal policy. If the government increases its spending and reduces taxes, this will enhance private-sector incomes, stimulate consumption, and thereby boost aggregate demand and help keep the economy on a positive growth path.

The Keynesian view also provides a fiscal policy remedy for inflation. Suppose that an economy is experiencing an inflationary economic boom as the result of excessive aggregate demand. As **Exhibit 3** illustrates, in the absence of a change in policy, the strong demand (AD_1) will push up wages and other resource prices. In time, the higher resource prices will increase costs, reduce aggregate supply (from $SRAS_1$ to $SRAS_3$), and lead to a higher price level (P_3). Keynesians argue, however, that **restrictive fiscal policy** can be used to reduce aggregate demand (shift it to AD_2) and guide the economy to a noninflationary equilibrium (E_2). A reduced level of government purchases will diminish aggregate demand directly. Alternatively, higher taxes on households and businesses could be used to dampen consumption and private investment. The restrictive fiscal policy—a spending reduction and/or an increase in taxes—will shift the government budget toward a surplus (or smaller deficit). *Keynesians believe that a shift toward a more restrictive fiscal policy is the proper prescription with which to combat inflation generated by excessive aggregate demand.*

The Keynesian theory challenges the view that a responsible government should constrain spending within the bounds of its revenues. *Rather than balancing the budget*

Restrictive fiscal policy
A reduction in government expenditures and/or an increase in tax rates such that the expected size of the budget deficit declines (or the budget surplus increases).

Countercyclical policy
A policy that tends to move the economy in an opposite direction from the forces of the business cycle. Such a policy would stimulate demand during the contraction phase of the business cycle and restrain demand during the expansion phase.

annually, Keynesians stressed the importance of **countercyclical policy,** *that is, policy designed to "counter" or offset fluctuations in aggregate demand.* On the one hand, when an economy is threatened by a recession, the government should shift to a more expansionary fiscal policy, increasing spending or reducing taxes in a manner that will increase the size of the budget deficit. On the other hand, fiscal policy should become more restrictive—the budget should be shifted toward a smaller deficit or larger surplus—in response to a threat of inflation. According to the Keynesian view, fluctuations in aggregate demand are the major source of economic disturbances. Moreover, wise use of fiscal policy can help stabilize and maintain demand at or near the full-employment rate of output.

11-3a FISCAL POLICY CHANGES AND PROBLEMS OF TIMING

In the 1960s, Keynesian economists were highly optimistic that fiscal policy could be instituted in a manner that would smooth the ups and downs of the business cycle. Over time, the earlier optimism has been tempered. If discretionary fiscal policy changes are going to reduce economic instability, they must be timed correctly. Fiscal stimulus must be felt during recessions and restraint during inflationary booms. But proper timing of fiscal policy is not an easy task. There are three major reasons why this is true.

First, a change in fiscal policy will require legislative action. But the political process moves slowly. This is particularly true in a country like the United States that has a number of checks and balances built into its political system. Congressional committees must meet, hear testimony, and draft legislation. Key legislators may choose to delay action in an attempt to amend the legislation so that it benefits their own constituents and supporters. Passage will require the approval of the House of Representatives, the Senate, and the president. Predictably, this process will take a significant amount of time.

Second, a change in policy will not immediately impact the macroeconomy. Even after a policy change is adopted, another six to twelve months will generally pass before it will have much impact on the economy. If government expenditures are going to be increased, time will be required for competitive bids to be submitted and government contracts granted. Contractors might not be able to begin work right away. Although a tax cut might exert some stimulus more quickly, typically several months will pass before the primary effects of the cut are felt throughout the economy.

Third, because of these delays, if fiscal policy is going to exert a stabilizing influence, policy-makers need to know what economic conditions are going to be like twelve to eighteen months in the future. However, this is a big problem because our ability to forecast when the economy is about to dip into a recession or experience an economic boom is extremely limited. Therefore, in a world of dynamic change and unpredictable events, macroeconomic policy making is a little bit like lobbing a ball at a target that often moves in unforeseen directions.

Given these time lags and forecasting limitations, policy-making errors will occur. Sometimes fiscal policy changes will end up adding stimulus during periods of strong demand and restraint during periods of recession. Changes of this type would add to rather than reduce economic instability.

Thus, a discretionary change in fiscal policy is like a double-edged sword—it has the potential to do harm as well as good. If timed correctly, it will reduce economic instability. But, when timed incorrectly, a fiscal policy change can also be a source of instability.

11-3b AUTOMATIC STABILIZERS

Automatic stabilizers
Built-in features that tend automatically to promote a budget deficit during a recession and a budget surplus during an inflationary boom, even without a change in policy.

Fortunately, a few fiscal programs tend automatically to apply demand stimulus during a recession and demand restraint during an economic boom. Programs of this type are called **automatic stabilizers**. They are automatic in that, without any new legislative action, they tend to increase the budget deficit (or reduce the surplus) during a recession and increase the surplus (or reduce the deficit) during an economic boom.

The major advantage of automatic stabilizers is that they institute countercyclical fiscal policy without the delays associated with legislative action. They minimize the problem of proper timing, in other words. On the one hand, when unemployment is rising and business conditions are slow, these stabilizers automatically reduce tax revenues collected and increase government spending, giving the economy a shot in the arm. On the other hand, automatic stabilizers help apply the brakes to an economic boom, increasing tax revenues and decreasing government spending. Three of these built-in stabilizers deserve specific mention: unemployment compensation, the corporate profit tax, and the progressive income tax.

Unemployment compensation   When an economy begins to dip into a recession, the government will pay out more money in unemployment benefits as the number of laid-off and unemployed workers expands. Simultaneously, the receipts from the employment tax that finance the unemployment compensation system will decline because fewer workers are paying into the system. Therefore, this program will automatically run a deficit during a business slowdown. In contrast, during an economic boom, the tax receipts from the program will increase because more people are now working, and the amount paid out in benefits will decline because fewer people are unemployed. Thus, the program will automatically tend to run a surplus during good times. So without any change in policy, the unemployment compensation program has the desired countercyclical effect on aggregate demand.[6]

The corporate profit tax   The corporate profit tax is a highly important automatic stabilizer because corporate profits are highly sensitive to cyclical conditions. During a recession, corporate profits decline sharply, and so, too, do corporate tax payments. In turn, the decline in tax revenues will enlarge the size of the budget deficit. In contrast, when the economy is expanding, corporate profits typically increase much more rapidly than wages, income, or consumption. This increase in corporate profits will result in a rapid increase in the "tax take" from the business sector during the expansion phase of the business cycle. Thus, corporate tax payments will go up during an expansion and fall rapidly during a contraction, even though no new legislative action has been instituted.

The progressive income tax   When incomes grow rapidly, the average personal income tax liability of individuals and families increases. With rising incomes, more people will find their income above the "no tax due" cutoff. Others will jump up into higher tax brackets. Therefore, during an economic expansion, personal income tax revenues increase more rapidly than income, because income will grow at a more incremental pace. Other things constant, the budget moves toward a surplus (or smaller deficit), even though the economy's tax rate structure is unchanged. Conversely, when incomes decline, many individuals will be taxed at lower rates or not at all. Income tax revenues will fall more rapidly than income, automatically enlarging the size of the budget deficit during a recession.

During the 1960s, it was widely believed that discretionary fiscal policy could be instituted in a manner that would help promote economic stability. Both Keynesian and non-Keynesian economists now recognize that proper timing of fiscal policy is more difficult than was previously thought. Automatic stabilizers minimize the problem of appropriate timing and thereby exert an important stabilizing impact on the economy. However, the timing dif-

---

[6]Although unemployment compensation has the desired countercyclical effect on demand, it also reduces the opportunity cost of remaining unemployed. As a result of this incentive effect, higher unemployment benefits and longer periods of eligibility will lead to more lengthy spells of unemployment and higher unemployment rates. Historically, in the United States unemployed workers have been permitted to draw benefits for 26 weeks, and this was extended to 39 weeks a few times during serious recessions. However, during the 2008–2009 recession and recovery, the benefits were extended to up to 99 weeks. Research in this area indicates that these benefit extensions added approximately three quarters of a percentage point to the unemployment rates of recent years (Daniel Aaronson, Bhashkar Mazumder, and Shani Schechter, "What Is Behind the Rise in Long-Term Unemployment?," Federal Reserve Bank of Chicago *Economic Perspectives*, Second Quarter 2010, pp. 28–51).

ficulties mean that the potential of discretionary fiscal policy is substantially more limited. Discretionary changes may have their greatest relevance during severe and lengthy recessions such as the one that began in December of 2007. As we proceed, we will consider the potential of fiscal stimulus to promote the recovery of a highly depressed economy in detail.

11-3c SAVING, SPENDING, DEBT, AND THE IMPACT OF FISCAL POLICY

Currently, consumption spending comprises approximately 70 percent of GDP. Household saving is merely after-tax income not spent on consumption. Historically, Keynesian economists have persistently stressed the importance of consumption spending and warned of the dangers accompanying excessive saving. Keynesians argue that when a large number of households try to increase their saving and reduce their consumption, total saving may not increase. Instead, the reduction in consumption may reduce the overall demand for goods and services, causing businesses to reduce output and lay off workers. In turn, as output and income fall, saving may decline rather than increase. This is often referred to as the **paradox of thrift**.

Paradox of thrift
The idea that when many households simultaneously try to increase their saving, actual saving may fail to increase because the reduction in consumption and aggregate demand will reduce income and employment.

Within the framework of the *AD–AS* model, the increase in saving by households would increase the supply of loanable funds and reduce interest rates, which would tend to offset the reduction in consumer demand. Keynesians do not believe this will be the case. Perhaps a simple example will help to explain their concerns and the underlying logic of the paradox of thrift. Suppose a family decides to eat out less often and save an additional $200 per month. Keynesians argue that their actions will reduce the incomes of restaurants by $200 per month, and as a result of this reduction in net income, the savings of the restaurant owners will fall by this amount. Thus, the family saves $200 more per month, but the restaurant owners save $200 less, so there is no net change in saving. If numerous families cut back on their consumption spending in an effort to increase their saving, the results would be the same. According to the Keynesian view, there would be no increase in saving, but consumption, aggregate demand, and output would decline.[7]

Eventually, the deficient demand, excess capacity, and weak investment would place downward pressure on both interest rates and resource prices, but this might well be a painful process. Keynesians fear that this will be the case, and that is why they have persistently stressed the implications of the paradox of thrift and the potential dangers of excessive saving.

However, there is also a paradox of excessive consumption and deficient saving, which is often overlooked. You cannot have a strong, healthy economy if all or most households face financial troubles because they are spending just about everything they earn (or can borrow) on consumption. When families and individuals are heavily indebted and have little or no savings, they are in a very poor position to deal with irregular expenses like repairs, health issues, or other financial setbacks that are a part of life.

Is saving good or bad for the economy? Straight thinking on this question is important. Although an abrupt increase in saving may exert an adverse impact on the economy in the short run, saving provides the source of investment capital that allows businesses to expand production and the economy to grow. Other things remaining constant, countries that persistently save and invest more will grow more rapidly. Moreover, when households save on a regular basis, live within their means, and avoid excessive debt, they will be better able to deal with unexpected expenses, sustain a steady consumption rate, and achieve greater financial security.

There is evidence that Americans have saved too little and drifted into excessive debt. As **Exhibit 4** shows, household debt as a share of income has increased significantly during the past quarter of a century. From 1960 to 1985, household debt fluctuated between

---

[7]For additional details on both the paradox of thrift and the Keynesian perspective, see Interview with Steve Fazzari of Washington University, "On Keynesian Economics," January 12, 2009, EcoTalk.org, at http://www.econtalk.org/archives/2009/01/fazzari_on_keyn.html.

EXHIBIT 4

Household Debt as a Share of After-Tax Income: 1960–2012

The household debt to income ratio has increased steadily since the mid-1980s and is now approximately twice the level of that of the 1960s and 1970s. This heavy indebtedness makes it more difficult for households to deal with unexpected expenses and achieve financial security.

Source: http://www.economagic.com.

55 percent and 70 percent of after-tax income. However, beginning in the mid-1980s, the household debt to income ratio started to increase, soaring to a peak of 130 percent in 2007.

The high level of debt made it more difficult for households to deal with the 2008–2009 recession. It also reduced the effectiveness of Keynesian fiscal policy. As the recession set in during the first half of 2008, the Bush administration responded with a Keynesian tax cut. Households were sent a check for $600 for each adult and another $300 for each child. It was hoped that this would induce households to increase their spending and ignite economic recovery. But this did not happen. Given their high level of indebtedness, households were in no mood to spend more and take on still additional debt. Instead, as Exhibit 4 shows, they increased their saving and reduced their indebtedness.

The Obama Administration also applied the Keynesian prescription. In February 2009, the new administration adopted an $800 billion spending package financed by borrowing. As in the case of the Bush strategy, it was hoped that the additional spending would increase household income and trigger a multiplier effect of additional consumption. The federal budget deficit, first under president Bush and then under president Obama, soared to 10 percent of GDP, the highest levels since World War II. According to Keynesian analysis, the large budget deficits would stimulate aggregate demand and ignite recovery. Nonetheless, the growth of real GDP was slow and the unemployment rate was still above 9 percent during the early summer of 2011. *Why weren't the Keynesian responses to the 2008–2009 recession more effective? The high levels of household debt probably dampened their impact, but there are also other explanations and the following chapter will consider several of them.*

LOOKING AHEAD

The Keynesian view has its critics. There are alternative theories about the potency of fiscal policy. The following chapter will present these alternative views, along with other hotly debated topics concerning the potential and limitations of fiscal policy.

KEY POINTS

- During the Great Depression, John Maynard Keynes developed a model that implied a market economy could remain below full employment for lengthy periods of time.

- In the Keynesian model, equilibrium occurs when the spending on consumption, investment, government purchases, and net exports is equal to total output. Firms will produce only the quantity of goods and services they believe consumers, investors, governments, and foreigners plan to buy. If this spending level is less than full-employment output, firms will not alter their production levels and the less than full-employment rate of output will persist. Keynes believed this was the situation during the Great Depression.

- According to the Keynesian view, fluctuations in total spending (aggregate demand) are the major source of economic instability. Keynesians believe that market economies have a tendency to fluctuate between economic booms driven by excessive demand and recessions resulting from insufficient demand. The multiplier concept magnifies these fluctuations.

- When an economy is operating below full-employment capacity, increases in aggregate expenditures lead to an expansion in both output and employment. Once capacity is reached, further expansions in expenditures lead only to higher prices. The Keynesian model highlights the importance of maintaining demand at a level consistent with full employment and price stability.

- When an economy is in a recession, Keynesians do not believe that reductions in either resource prices or interest rates will promote recovery. As a result, market economies are likely to experience recessions that are both severe and lengthy.

- The federal budget is the primary tool of fiscal policy. Rather than balancing the budget annually, Keynesians believe that fiscal policy should reflect business cycle conditions. During a recession, fiscal policy should become more expansionary (a larger deficit should be run). During an inflationary boom, fiscal policy should become more restrictive (shift toward a budget surplus).

- Changes in fiscal policy must be timed properly if they are going to exert a stabilizing influence on an economy. The ability of policy-makers to time fiscal policy changes in a counter-cyclical manner is reduced by (1) the inability of the political process to act rapidly, (2) the time lag between when a policy change is instituted and when it affects the economy, and (3) the inability to forecast accurately the future direction of the economy.

- Automatic stabilizers help promote stability because they are able to add demand stimulus during a recession and restraint during an economic boom without legislative action.

- Although an abrupt increase in saving may exert an adverse impact on the economy in the short run, saving provides the financing for investment that powers long-term growth. Moreover, a healthy economy is dependent on households saving regularly and avoiding excessive debt.

CRITICAL ANALYSIS QUESTIONS

1. What determines the equilibrium rate of output in the Keynesian model? Why did Keynes think the Great Depression lasted so long and the unemployment rate remained so high throughout the 1930s?

2. What do Keynesians think cause fluctuations in output? What must be done to maintain full-employment capacity?

3. *What is the multiplier principle? What determines the size of the multiplier? Does the multiplier make it more or less difficult to stabilize the economy? Explain.

4. What is a budget deficit? How are budget deficits financed? Why do Keynesians believe that budget deficits will increase aggregate demand?

5. From a stabilization standpoint, why is proper timing of a change in fiscal policy important? Is it easy to time fiscal policy changes properly? Why or why not?

6. *According to the Keynesian view, what fiscal policy actions should be taken if the unemployment rate is high and current GDP is well below potential output?

7. Are discretionary changes in fiscal policy likely to be instituted in a manner that will help smooth theups and downs of the business cycle? Why or why not?

8. What are automatic stabilizers? Explain their major advantage.

9. "An increase in aggregate demand will tend to increase real output by a larger amount when unemployment is widespread than when the economy is operating at or near full employment." Is this statement true? Explain.

10. When output and employment slowed in early 2008, the Bush Administration and the Democratic Congress passed legislation sending households a check for $600 for each adult (and $300 per child). These checks were financed by borrowing. Would a Keynesian favor this action? Why or why not?

11. If uncertainty about the future causes households to increase their saving and reduce their consumption spending during a recession, how will this affect the economy? Explain. If households save little and spend most of their income on current consumption, how will this affect the economy? Explain.

*Asterisk denotes questions for which answers are given in Appendix B.

CHAPTER 12
Fiscal Policy, Incentives, and Secondary Effects

FOCUS

- How do the crowding-out and new classical models of fiscal policy modify the Keynesian analysis?
- Is discretionary fiscal policy an effective stabilization tool? Why or why not?
- Are there supply-side effects of fiscal policy?
- Will increases in government spending financed by borrowing help promote recovery from a recession?
- Is the United States headed for a debt crisis?

The main difference between Keynes and modern economics is the focus on incentives. Keynes studied the relation between macroeconomic aggregates, without any consideration for the underlying incentives that lead to the formation of these aggregates. By contrast, modern economists base all their analysis on incentives. —**Luigi Zingales**[1]

[1]Luigi Zingales, Booth School of Business at the University of Chicago, March 10, 2009. Online debate sponsored by *The Economist*, http://www.economist.com/debate/days/view/276/print.

As we discussed in the previous chapter, Keynesian analysis indicates that fiscal policy provides a potential tool through which aggregate demand can be controlled and maintained at a level consistent with full employment and price stability. During the 1970s, however, the economic instability, along with high rates of both unemployment and inflation, illustrated some of the difficulties involved in the effective use of fiscal policy as a stabilization tool. Moreover, in recent decades, economists have become more aware of secondary effects that reduce the potency of fiscal policy. More attention has also been paid to the incentive effects accompanying fiscal changes. The chapter-opening quote by Luigi Zingales highlights these points. This chapter focuses on these topics and investigates how they affect the operation of fiscal policy and its potential to improve the performance of a market economy. The chapter will also address the current debate among economists about the effectiveness of "fiscal stimulus" as a tool with which to promote recovery from a severe recession and the potential dangers resulting from high levels of government debt.

12-1 FISCAL POLICY, BORROWING, AND THE CROWDING-OUT EFFECT

Keynesian analysis indicates that expansionary fiscal policy will exert a powerful impact on aggregate demand, output, and employment. Other economists disagree. When the government runs a budget deficit, the funds will have to come from somewhere. If we rule out money creation (monetary policy), the government will have to finance its deficit by borrowing from either domestic or foreign lenders. But the additional government borrowing will increase the demand for loanable funds, which will push real interest rates upward. In turn, the higher real interest rates will reduce private investment and consumption, thereby dampening the stimulus effects of expansionary fiscal policy. Economists refer to this squeezing out of private spending by a deficit-induced increase in the real interest rate as the **crowding-out effect**.

Suppose the government increases its spending or reduces taxes and, as a result, runs a budget deficit of $100 billion. As **Exhibit 1** shows, the government's additional borrowing will increase demand in the loanable funds market and place upward pressure on real interest rates. How will the higher interest rates influence private spending? Consumers will reduce their purchases of interest rate–sensitive goods, such as automobiles and consumer durables. A higher interest rate will also increase the opportunity cost of investment projects. Businesses will postpone spending on plant expansions, heavy equipment, and capital improvements. Residential-housing construction and sales will also be hurt. Thus, the higher real interest rates caused by the larger deficit will retard private spending. If it were not for the reduction in private spending, aggregate demand would increase to AD_2 (the dotted curve of part a), but given the reduction in private spending, aggregate demand remains unchanged at AD_1.

The crowding-out effect implies that the demand stimulus effects of budget deficits will be weak because borrowing to finance the deficits will increase interest rates and thereby crowd out private spending on investment and consumption. This reduction in private spending will partially, if not entirely, offset the additional spending financed by the deficit. Thus, the net impact of expansionary fiscal policy on aggregate demand, output, and employment will be small.

Furthermore, as private investment is crowded out by the higher interest rates, the output of capital goods will decline. As a result, the future stock of capital (for example, heavy equipment, other machines, and buildings) available to future workers will be smaller than it would have been otherwise. In other words, deficits will have an adverse effect on capital formation and tend to retard the growth of productivity and income.

Keynesians respond that even if crowding out occurs when the economy is at or near full employment, it will be less important during a recession, particularly a serious one. During the severe recession of 2008–2009, short-term interest rates fell to nearly zero even

Crowding-out effect
A reduction in private spending as a result of higher interest rates generated by budget deficits that are financed by borrowing in the private loanable funds market.

EXHIBIT 1

The Crowding-Out Model—Higher Interest Rates Crowd Out Private Spending

The crowding-out effect indicates that budget deficits will lead to higher interest rates, which will reduce private investment and consumption, offsetting the demand stimulus of expansionary fiscal policy. If the government borrows an additional $100 billion to finance a budget deficit, the demand for loanable funds will increase by this amount (shift from D_1 to D_2 in frame b), leading to higher real interest rates. If it were not for the higher real interest rates, aggregate demand would increase to AD_2 (dotted curve of part a). However, at the higher interest rates, private investment and consumption will decline. As a result, aggregate demand will remain unchanged at AD_1. The crowding-out effect indicates that expansionary fiscal policy will have little or no impact on aggregate demand.

(a) Goods and services (real GDP)

(b) Loanable funds

© Cengage Learning 2013

though the federal government was running huge deficits.[2] Under circumstances like these, the immediate crowding-out effect is likely to be small, and therefore, the budget deficits will stimulate output and employment just as the Keynesian analysis implies. The proponents of crowding out counter that while this may be true during the recession, the deficits will mean more borrowing and less private spending as the economy begins to recover. As a result, the recovery will be weaker than would have been the case if government borrowing had been more restrained.

The implications of the crowding-out analysis are symmetrical. Restrictive fiscal policy will "crowd in" private spending. If the government collects greater tax revenues and/or reduces spending, the budget will shift toward a surplus (or smaller deficit). As a result, the government's demand for loanable funds will decrease, placing downward pressure on the real interest rate. The lower real interest rate will stimulate additional private investment and consumption. So the fiscal policy restraint will be partially, if not entirely, offset by an expansion in private spending. *As the result of this crowding in, restrictive fiscal policy will be largely ineffective as a weapon against inflation.*

12-1a DO GLOBAL FINANCIAL MARKETS MINIMIZE THE CROWDING-OUT EFFECT?

Today, financial capital can rapidly move in and out of countries. Suppose the budget deficit of the United States increases and additional borrowing by the U.S. Treasury pushes real interest rates upward, just as the crowding-out theory implies. Think about how investors will respond to this situation. The higher real interest yields on bonds and other financial

---

[2]Expansionary monetary policy also contributed to the low short-term interest rates of 2008–2009. The impact of monetary policy on interest rates, output, and employment will be discussed in Chapter 14.

A Visual Presentation of the Crowding-Out Effect in an Open Economy

The implications of the crowding-out effect in an open economy are illustrated here. As was shown in the previous exhibit, government borrowing to finance a budget deficit will place upward pressure on real interest rates. This will retard private investment and aggregate demand. In an open economy, the higher interest rates will also increase the inflow of capital from abroad, which will cause the dollar to appreciate and net exports to decline. Thus, in an open economy, the higher interest rates will trigger reductions in both private investment and net exports, which will weaken the expansionary impact of a budget deficit.

© Cengage Learning 2013

assets will attract funds from abroad. In turn, this inflow of financial capital will increase the supply of loanable funds and thereby moderate the rise in real interest rates in the United States.[3]

At first glance, the crowding-out effect would appear to be weakened because the inflow of funds from abroad will moderate the upward pressure on domestic interest rates. Closer inspection, though, reveals that this will not be the case. Foreigners cannot buy more U.S. bonds and financial assets without "buying" more dollars in the foreign exchange market. Thus, additional bond purchases will increase the demand for U.S. dollars (and the supply of foreign currencies) in the foreign exchange market—the market that coordinates exchanges of the various national currencies. As foreigners demand more dollars to buy financial investments in the United States, this will increase the demand for the dollar, causing it to appreciate. In turn, the appreciation of the dollar will make imports cheaper for Americans. Simultaneously, it will make U.S. exports more expensive for foreigners. Predictably, the United States will import more and export less. Thus, net exports will decline (or net imports increase), causing a reduction in aggregate demand. Therefore, while the inflow of capital from abroad will moderate the increase in the interest rate and the crowding out of private domestic investment, it will also reduce net exports and thereby retard aggregate demand.

Exhibit 2 summarizes the crowding-out view of budget deficits in an open economy. The additional government borrowing triggered by the budget deficits will cause interest rates to rise, and this will lead to two secondary effects that will dampen the stimulus impact of the deficits. First, the higher interest rates will reduce private investment, which will directly restrain aggregate demand. Second, the higher interest returns will also attract an inflow of foreign capital, which will moderate the increase in interest rates, but it will also cause the dollar to appreciate. In turn, the appreciation of the dollar will reduce both net

---

[3]For students who are unsure about the demand for and supply of loanable funds, this would be a good time to review the topic within the framework of our basic macro model outlined by Exhibit 1 in Chapter 9. As this exhibit indicates, household saving and the inflow of financial capital from abroad supply loanable funds. In turn, private investment and borrowing by the government to finance budget deficits generate the demand for these funds.

exports and aggregate demand. *According to the crowding-out theory, these two factors will largely, if not entirely, offset the stimulus effects of a larger budget deficit.*

12-2 FISCAL POLICY, FUTURE TAXES, AND THE NEW CLASSICAL MODEL

Thus far, we have implicitly assumed that the current consumption and saving decisions of taxpayers are unaffected by budget deficits. This may not be the case. The 1995 Nobel laureate Robert Lucas (University of Chicago), Thomas Sargent (New York University), and Robert Barro (Harvard University) have been leaders among a group of economists arguing that budget deficits imply higher future taxes and that taxpayers will reduce their current consumption just as they would have if the taxes had been collected during the current period. Because this position has its foundation in classical economics, these economists and their followers are referred to as **new classical economists**.

In the Keynesian model, a tax cut financed by borrowing will increase the current income of households, and they respond by increasing their consumption. New classical economists argue that this analysis is incorrect because it ignores the impact of the higher future tax liability implied by the budget deficit and the interest payments required to service the additional debt. Rather than increasing their consumption in response to a larger budget deficit, new classical economists believe that households will save all or most of their increase in disposable income so that they will be able to pay the higher future taxes implied by the additional government debt. Thus, new classical economists do not believe that budget deficits will stimulate additional consumption and aggregate demand.

The new classical economists stress that debt financing simply substitutes higher future taxes for lower current taxes. Thus, budget deficits affect the timing of the taxes but not their magnitude. A mere change in the timing of taxes will not alter the wealth of households. Therefore, there is no reason to believe that current consumption will change when current taxes are cut and government debt and future taxes are increased by an equivalent amount. This view that taxes and debt financing are essentially equivalent is known as **Ricardian equivalence**, after the nineteenth-century economist, David Ricardo, who initially developed the idea.[4]

Perhaps an illustration will help explain the underlying logic of the new classical view. Suppose you knew that your taxes were going to be cut by $1,000 this year, but that next year they were going to be increased by $1,000 plus the interest on that figure. Would this year's $1,000 tax cut cause you to increase your consumption spending? New classical economists argue that it would not. They believe that most people would recognize that their wealth is unchanged and would therefore save most of this year's tax cut to be better able to pay next year's higher taxes. Correspondingly, new classical economists argue that when debt is substituted for taxes, people will recognize that the additional debt means higher future taxes and that therefore they will save more in order to pay them.

Exhibit 3 illustrates the implications of the new classical view on the potency of fiscal policy. Suppose that the fiscal authorities issue $100 billion of additional debt in order to cut taxes by an equal amount. The government borrowing increases the demand for loanable funds (D_1 shifts to D_2 in part b) by $100 billion. If taxpayers didn't think that higher future taxes would result from the debt, they would expand their consumption in response to the lower taxes and the increase in their current

New classical economists
Economists who believe that there are strong forces pushing a market economy toward full-employment equilibrium and that macroeconomic policy is an ineffective tool with which to reduce economic instability.

Ricardian equivalence
The view that a tax reduction financed with government debt will exert no effect on current consumption and aggregate demand because people will fully recognize the higher future taxes implied by the additional debt.

---

[4]See Robert J. Barro, "The Ricardian Approach to Budget Deficits," *Journal of Economic Perspectives* (Spring 1989): 37–44; and John J. Seater, "Ricardian Equivalence," *Journal of Economic Literature* (March 1993): 142–90.

EXHIBIT 3

The New Classical View—Higher Expected Future Taxes Crowd Out Private Spending

New classical economists emphasize that budget deficits merely substitute future taxes for current taxes. If households did not anticipate the higher future taxes, aggregate demand would increase to AD_2. However, demand remains unchanged at AD_1 when households fully anticipate the future increase in taxes (part a). Simultaneously, the additional saving to meet the higher future taxes will increase the supply of loanable funds to S_2 and allow the government to borrow the funds to finance its deficit without pushing up the real interest rate (part b). In this model, fiscal policy exerts no effect. The real interest rate, real GDP, and level of employment all remain unchanged.

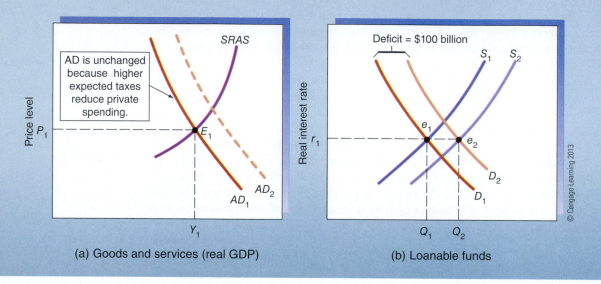

(a) Goods and services (real GDP)

(b) Loanable funds

disposable income. Under these circumstances, aggregate demand in the goods and services market would expand to AD_2 (part a). In the new classical model, though, this will not be the case. Realizing that the $100 billion in additional debt will mean higher future taxes, taxpayers will maintain their initial level of consumption spending and use the tax cut to increase their savings in order to generate the additional income required to pay the higher future taxes. Because consumption is unchanged, aggregate demand also remains constant (at AD_1). At the same time, the additional saving (to pay the implied increase in future taxes) allows the government to finance its deficit without an increase in the real interest rate.

According to the new classical view, changes in fiscal policy have little effect on the economy. Debt financing and larger budget deficits will not stimulate aggregate demand. Neither will they affect output and employment. Similarly, the real interest rate is unaffected by deficits because people will save more in order to pay the higher future taxes. In the new classical model, fiscal policy is completely impotent.

In Chapter 1, we indicated that failure to consider the secondary effects is one of the most common errors in economics. Once the secondary effects are considered, both the crowding-out and new classical models indicate that spending increases financed by borrowing will provide little if any net stimulus to the economy. Put another way, both the crowding-out and new classical theories indicate that budget deficits and expansionary fiscal policy will be far less potent than the Keynesian analysis implies. Nonetheless, politicians continue to argue that their favorite spending programs will create jobs and improve economic performance. Are they right? The accompanying box feature "Is Job Creation a Good Reason to Support a Government Spending Program?" provides insight on this issue.

APPLICATIONS IN ECONOMICS

Is Job Creation a Good Reason to Support a Government Spending Program?

Jobs are typically used to produce goods and services that we value. But we must not forget that it is the value of the goods produced that is important; the jobs are merely a means to that end. If people do not keep their eyes on this basic fact, they may be misled to support projects that destroy wealth rather than create it.

Politicians are fond of talking about the jobs created by their spending programs. Suppose the government spends $50 billion employing one million workers to build a high-speed train linking Los Angeles and Las Vegas. Supporters of projects like this often argue that they should be undertaken because they will create a huge number of jobs. Is this a sound argument? When thinking about the answer to this question, consider the following two points.

First, the government will have to use either taxes or borrowing to finance the project. Taxes of $50 billion will reduce consumer spending and private savings by this amount, and this will diminish employment in other sectors by a magnitude similar to the employment created by the spending on the project. Alternatively, if the project is financed by debt,

the additional borrowing will lead to higher interest rates and future taxes to cover interest payments. This will also divert funds away from other projects, both private and public. Thus, the net impact will be primarily a reshuffling of jobs rather than job creation.

Second, what really matters is the value of what is produced, not jobs. If jobs were the key to high incomes, we could easily create as many as we wanted. For example, the government could pay attractive wages hiring the unemployed to dig holes one day and fill them up the next. The program would create jobs, but as a nation we would also be poorer because such jobs would not generate goods and services that people value. Job creation, either real or imagined, is not a sound reason to support a program. Instead, the proper test is opportunity cost: The value of what is produced relative to the value of what is given up. If people value the output generated by the government-spending program more than the production it crowds out, it will increase our incomes and living standards. If the opposite is the case, then the additional spending will make us worse off.

12-3 POLITICAL INCENTIVES AND THE EFFECTIVE USE OF DISCRETIONARY FISCAL POLICY

As we discussed in the last chapter, inability to forecast the future direction of the economy and the time lag between when a fiscal change is needed and when it can be instituted and begin to exert an impact on the economy make it difficult to use discretionary fiscal policy in a stabilizing manner. In addition to these practical problems, the political incentive structure also makes appropriate timing of fiscal changes less likely.

As our analysis of public choice stressed, politicians—at least those who survive for very long—will be attracted to policies that will help them win the next election. Predictably, legislators will be delighted to spend money on programs that benefit their constituents but reluctant to raise taxes because they impose a visible cost on voters. The political incentive structure encourages legislation that increases spending and reduces taxes when the economy is weak. But there is very little incentive to reduce spending and increase taxes when the economy is strong. As a result, deficits will be far more common than surpluses. Thus, discretionary fiscal policy is unlikely to be instituted in a countercyclical manner.

12-4 IS DISCRETIONARY FISCAL POLICY AN EFFECTIVE STABILIZATION TOOL?

In recent decades, the effectiveness of fiscal policy as a stabilization tool has been hotly debated and widely analyzed by macroeconomists. A synthesis view has emerged. Most macroeconomists—both Keynesian and non-Keynesian—are now largely in agreement on the following three issues.

1. Proper timing of discretionary fiscal policy is both difficult to achieve and crucially important. Given our limited ability to forecast ups and downs in the business cycle, the delays that inevitably accompany fiscal changes, and the structure of political incentives, the effectiveness of discretionary fiscal policy as a stabilization tool is limited. Put simply, persistent fiscal changes are unlikely to be instituted in a manner that will smooth the ups and downs of the business cycle. Therefore, most macroeconomists now place less emphasis on the use of discretionary fiscal policy as a stabilization tool.[5]

2. Automatic stabilizers reduce fluctuations in aggregate demand and help keep the economy on track. Because they are not dependent upon legislative action, automatic stabilizers are able consistently to shift the budget toward a deficit during a recession and toward a surplus during an economic boom. Thus, they add needed stimulus during a recession and act as a restraining force during an inflationary boom. Although some economists question their potency, nearly all agree that they exert a stabilizing influence.

3. Fiscal policy is much less potent than the early Keynesian view implied. Both the crowding-out and new classical models indicate that there are secondary effects of budget deficits that will substantially, if not entirely, offset their impact on aggregate demand. In the crowding-out model, higher real interest rates and a decline in net exports offset the expansionary effects of budget deficits. In the new classical model, higher future taxes lead to the same result. Both models indicate that fiscal policy will have little, if any, effect on current aggregate demand, employment, and real output during normal economic times.

12-5 THE SUPPLY-SIDE EFFECTS OF FISCAL POLICY

So far, we have focused on the potential impact of fiscal policy on aggregate demand. However, when fiscal changes alter tax rates, they influence the incentive of people to work, invest, and use resources efficiently. Thus, tax changes may also influence aggregate supply. Prior to 1980, macroeconomists generally ignored the supply-side effects of changes in tax rates, thinking they were of little importance. **Supply-side economists** challenged this view. The supply-side argument was central to the tax rate reductions of the 1980s, the capital gains rate reductions of 1997, and the tax legislation of 2002.

From a supply-side viewpoint, the marginal tax rate is crucially important. As we discussed in Chapter 4, the marginal tax rate determines the breakdown of a person's additional income between tax payments on the one hand and personal income on the other. Lower marginal tax rates mean that individuals get to keep a larger share of their additional earnings. For example, reducing the marginal tax rate from 40 percent to 30 percent allows individuals to keep 70 cents of each additional dollar they earn,

Supply-side economists
Economists who believe that changes in marginal tax rates exert important effects on aggregate supply.

---

[5]As the following statement from Keynes indicates, he did not believe that spending on government projects would be an effective countercyclical tool:

Organized public works, at home and abroad, may be the right cure for a chronic tendency to a deficiency of effective demand. But they are not capable of sufficiently rapid organization (and above all cannot be reversed or undone at a later date), to be the most serviceable instrument for the prevention of the trade cycle.

John Maynard Keynes in *Collected Works, vol. XXVII*, 122.

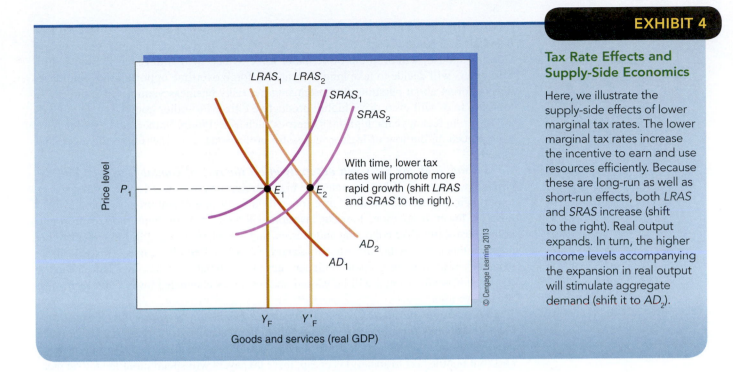

EXHIBIT 4

Tax Rate Effects and Supply-Side Economics

Here, we illustrate the supply-side effects of lower marginal tax rates. The lower marginal tax rates increase the incentive to earn and use resources efficiently. Because these are long-run as well as short-run effects, both *LRAS* and *SRAS* increase (shift to the right). Real output expands. In turn, the higher income levels accompanying the expansion in real output will stimulate aggregate demand (shift it to *AD₂*).

instead of only 60 cents. In turn, the lower tax rates and accompanying increase in take-home pay provide them with a greater incentive to earn. Supply-side economists believe that these incentive effects will bring more resources into productive activities. Most significantly, they argue that high marginal rates—for example, rates of 50 percent or more—substantially reduce the incentive of people to work, invest, and use resources productively.

The supply-side effects of a tax change are fundamentally different from the demand-side effects. On the demand side, lower taxes increase the after-tax incomes of consumers and thereby stimulate consumption and aggregate demand. *On the supply side, lower tax rates increase the incentive of people to work, supply resources, and use them more efficiently and thereby increase aggregate supply.*

Exhibit 4 graphically depicts the impact of a supply-side tax cut, one that reduces marginal tax rates. The lower marginal tax rates increase aggregate supply because the new incentive structure encourages taxpayers to earn more and use resources more efficiently. If taxpayers think the cut will be permanent, both long- and short-run aggregate supply (*LRAS* and *SRAS*) will increase. Real output and income will expand. As real income expands, aggregate demand will also increase (shift to *AD₂*). If the lower marginal rates are financed by a budget deficit, though, aggregate demand may increase by a larger amount than aggregate supply, putting upward pressure on the price level.

Supply-side economics should not be viewed as a short-run countercyclical tool. It will take time for people to react to the tax cuts and move their resources out of investments designed to lower their taxes and into higher-return, production-oriented activities. The full positive effects of lower marginal tax rates will not be observed until both labor and capital markets have time to adjust fully to the new incentive structure. *Supply-side economics is a long-run, growth-oriented strategy, not a short-run stabilization tool.*

12-5a WHY DO HIGH TAX RATES RETARD OUTPUT?

There are three major reasons why high tax rates are likely to retard the growth of output. *First, as we have explained, high marginal tax rates discourage work effort and productivity.* When marginal tax rates soar to 55 or 60 percent, people get to keep less than half of what they earn, so they tend to work less. Some (for example, those with a working spouse) will drop out of the labor force. Others will simply work fewer hours. Still others will decide to take longer vacations, forgo overtime opportunities, retire earlier, or forget about pursuing that promising but risky business venture. In some cases, high tax rates will even drive highly productive citizens to other countries where taxes are lower. In recent years, high-tax countries such as Belgium, France, and Sweden have experienced an outflow of highly successful professionals, business entrepreneurs, and athletes.

Second, high tax rates will adversely affect the rate of capital formation and the efficiency of its use. When tax rates are high, foreign investors will look for other places to put their money, and domestic investors will look for investment projects abroad where taxes are lower. In addition, domestic investors will direct more of their time and effort into hobby businesses (like collecting antiques, raising horses, or giving golf lessons) that may not earn much money but are enjoyable and have tax-shelter advantages. This will divert resources away from projects with higher rates of return but fewer tax-avoidance benefits. As a result, scarce capital will be wasted and resources channeled away from their most productive uses.

Third, high marginal tax rates encourage people to substitute less-desired tax-deductible goods for more-desired nondeductible goods. High marginal tax rates make tax-deductible expenditures cheap for people in high tax brackets. Because the personal cost (but not the cost to society) is cheap, these taxpayers will spend more money on pleasurable, tax-deductible items, like plush offices, professional conferences held in favorite vacation spots, and various other fringe benefits (for example, a company-paid luxury automobile or business entertainment). Because purchasing tax-deductible goods lowers their tax bill, people will often buy them even though they do not value them as much as it costs to produce them.

12-5b HOW IMPORTANT ARE THE SUPPLY-SIDE EFFECTS?

There is considerable debate among economists about the strength of the supply-side incentive effects. Critics of supply-side economics argue that the tax cuts of the 1980s reduced real federal tax revenues and led to large budget deficits, without having much impact on economic growth. This suggests that the supply-side effects are not very strong. Defenders of the supply-side position respond by noting that rate reductions in both the 1960s and the 1980s resulted in impressive growth and lengthy economic expansions. They also stress that the supply-side response in top income brackets—where lower rates have the largest incentive effects—is particularly strong.[6] See the boxed feature "Have Supply-Side Economists Found a Way to Soak the Rich?."

Supply-side critics also point out that most elasticity estimates indicate that a 10 percent change in after-tax wages increases the quantity of labor supplied by only 1 or 2 percent. This suggests that changes in tax rates exert only a modest impact on the amount of labor supplied. Supply-side advocates, however, argue that these estimates reflect only the adjustments that occur over relatively short time periods. In the long run, they claim that tax cuts increase the labor supply by much more. Recent work by Nobel laureate Edward Prescott of Arizona State University supports this view. Prescott used marginal tax differences between France and the United States to estimate the labor supply response in the long run. Prescott found that the elasticity of

---

[6]The incentive effects are greater in the upper brackets because a similar percentage rate reduction will have a greater impact on take-home pay in this area. For example, if a 70 percent marginal tax rate is cut to 50 percent, take-home pay per additional dollar of earnings will increase from 30 cents to 50 cents, a 67 percent increase in the incentive to earn. Conversely, if a 14 percent marginal rate is reduced to 10 percent, take-home pay per dollar of additional earnings will increase from 86 cents to 90 cents, only a 5 percent increase in the incentive to earn.

APPLICATIONS IN ECONOMICS

Have Supply-Side Economists Found a Way to Soak the Rich?

Under a progressive rate structure, marginal tax rates rise with income level. The highest marginal tax rates are imposed on those with the largest incomes. The supply-side view stresses that high marginal rates have such a negative effect on the incentive to earn (and the taxable income base) that reducing these high rates can actually increase the revenues collected from high-income taxpayers. The Laffer curve analysis presented in Chapter 4 highlights this point. The Laffer curve indicates that as tax rates are increased from zero, rate increases will increase the revenue derived from the tax. Eventually, however, higher and higher rates will lead to a maximum revenue point, and rate increases beyond this level will actually reduce the revenue collected. Thus, when tax rates are exceedingly high, more revenue could be collected from these high-income taxpayers if their rates were reduced.

Since 1960, the personal income tax rate imposed on high-income earners has varied considerably. What effect have the rate changes had on the revenue collected from them? **Exhibit 5**

EXHIBIT 5

How Have Changes in Marginal Tax Rates Affected the Share of Taxes Paid by the Rich?

The accompanying graph shows the share of the personal income taxes paid by the top one-half percent of earners from 1960 to 2010. During this period, there were four major reductions in marginal tax rates. First, the Kennedy–Johnson tax cut reduced the top rate from 91 percent in 1963 to 70 percent in 1965. During the Reagan years, the top rate was reduced from 70 percent in 1980 to 50 percent in 1982 and to approximately 30 percent in 1986. In 1997, the capital gains tax rate was sliced from 28 to 20 percent. Interestingly, the share of the tax bill paid by these "super-rich" earners increased after each of these tax cuts. These findings suggest that, at least for this group of high-income recipients, strong supply-side effects accompanied the rate cuts. Perhaps surprising to some, these high-income taxpayers paid a larger portion of the tax bill when the top marginal rate was less than 40 percent (1986–2010) than when it was 70 percent or more.

Source: http://www.irs.gov.

presents data on the share of the personal income tax collected from the top one-half percent of income recipients. When the top marginal tax rate was sliced from 91 percent to 70 percent by the Kennedy–Johnson tax cut of 1964, the share of the personal income tax paid by these high earners rose from 16 percent to 18 percent. In contrast, as inflation pushed more and more tax-payers into higher brackets during the 1970s, the share paid by the top one-half percent declined. When the tax cuts of the 1980s once again reduced the top rates, the share paid by the top one-half percent climbed to more than 20 percent of the total. When the top marginal rate was increased in 1991 and again in 1993, there was little change in the share of taxes paid by the top group. Beginning in 1997, the tax rate on income from capital gains was cut from 28 percent to 20 percent. This rate reduction was accompanied by a substantial increase in revenues derived from the capital gains taxes and personal income taxes collected from high-income taxpayers.[1]

Throughout the 1986–2012 period, the top marginal personal income tax rate in the United States was less than 40 percent. During 2004–2012 the top rate was 35 percent, down from 39.6 percent in 2000. In contrast, prior to 1981, the top marginal rate was 70 percent or more. Nonetheless, as Exhibit 5 illustrates, the share of federal income tax revenue collected from high earners was larger during the more recent period. In fact, the top one-half percent of earners has paid more than 22 percent of the personal income tax each year since 1997. In 2010, the top one-half percent of earners paid 26 percent of all federal personal income tax. Clearly, these recent figures are well above the 14 percent to 19 percent collected from these taxpayers in the 1960s and 1970s, when much higher marginal rates were imposed on the rich.[2]

These data suggest that if you want to collect a lot of revenue from the rich, you better not push the tax rate on their marginal income too high. This sounds counterintuitive. Is it really true? We will have additional evidence on this issue in the near future. In 2013, the top federal income tax rate will rise to 39.6 percent. When the 3.8 percent Medicare tax is added, the top marginal rate will be pushed to 43.4 percent. Further, the capital gains tax rate will rise from 15 percent in 2012 to 23.8 percent in 2013. Thus, the 2013 top federal marginal tax rates will rise to their highest level since 1986.

Will the higher 2013 rates lead to an increase in revenue collected from those with high incomes? Supply-side economists doubt this will be the case. Nonetheless, it will make an interesting economic experiment.

[1]High earners also respond to high marginal tax rates imposed by states. A recent study estimated that between 1998 and 2007, more than 1,100 people per day moved from the nine highest income-tax states such as California, New Jersey, New York, and Ohio to the nine states without a personal income tax, including Florida, Nevada, New Hampshire, and Texas. See Arthur Laffer and Stephen Moore, "Soak the Rich, Lose the Rich; Americans Know How to Use the Moving Van to Escape High Taxes," *Wall Street Journal*, May 18, 2009.

[2]For additional evidence on the impact of tax rates on both output and revenue, see Lawrence Lindsey, *The Growth Experiment: How the New Tax Policy Is Transforming the U.S. Economy* (New York: Basic Books, 1990). For additional information on supply-side economics, see James Gwartney, "Supply-side Economics" in *The Encyclopaedia of Economics,* ed. David Henderson (Indianapolis: Liberty Fund, 2007: available online). For a critical analysis of supply-side economics, see Joel B. Slemrod, ed., *Does Atlas Shrug?: The Economic Consequences of Taxing the Rich* (New York: Russell Sage Foundation, 2000).

labor supply in the long run was substantially greater than in the short run. He estimates that France's higher marginal tax rates reduce the hours of labor supplied by French adults by nearly 30 percent annually compared to their American counterparts.[7]

The supply-side view has exerted considerable impact on tax policy throughout the world. Since 1980, there has been a dramatic shift away from high marginal tax rates. Sixty-two countries imposed a personal income tax with a top marginal rate of 50 percent or more in 1980, but only ten countries levied such high rates in 2011. Almost all countries with a personal income tax have lower rates today than in the early 1980s.

12-6 FISCAL POLICY AND RECOVERY FROM RECESSIONS

As we previously discussed, time lags, inability to forecast the future direction of the economy, and the political process all reduce the likelihood that discretionary fiscal policy

[7]Prescott concludes, "I find it remarkable that virtually all of the large difference in labor supply between France and the United States is due to differences in tax systems. I expected institutional constraints on the operation of labor markets and the nature of the unemployment benefit system to be more important. I was surprised that the welfare gain from reducing the intratemporal tax wedge is so large." See Edward C. Prescott, "Richard T. Ely Lecture: Prosperity and Depression," *American Economic Review*, Papers and Proceedings 92, no. 2 (May 2002): 9.

will be used effectively to reduce the ups and downs of the business cycle. However, debate continues on the potential of expansionary fiscal policy to promote recovery from a serious recession like that of 2008–2009. Let's consider two of the key issues of this continuing debate.

12-6a WILL FISCAL STIMULUS SPEED RECOVERY?

Will increases in government spending financed by borrowing speed recovery from a severe recession? Keynesians clearly believe that the answer to this question is "yes." The Keynesian view stresses that private sector spending will decline during a severe recession and that the government needs to expand its spending in order to reignite the private sector. During a severe recession like that of 2008–2009, interest rates may essentially fall to zero, and even these low rates may fail to stimulate much private investment. Under these conditions, crowding out of private spending will be minimal. Moreover, unemployed and underemployed resources will be widespread, and, as a result, the additional government spending will have a substantial multiplier effect. Thus, Keynesians argue that expansionary fiscal policy will stimulate aggregate demand and help promote recovery from serious recessions.

In contrast, critics of Keynesian economics argue that the side effects of the increased spending and expanded debt will exert an adverse impact on both the recovery process and long-term growth. They raise three major points in support of their view. First, they argue that the increased borrowing and expansion of government debt will mean higher future interest payments and tax rates, and this will retard long-term growth. Even if the government is able to borrow at low interest rates during a downturn, as has been the case for the most recent recession, some combination of higher interest rates and higher taxes will be required for the future financing and refinancing of the larger debt. The higher interest rates will increase costs and squeeze out private spending, particularly spending on investment. At the same time, the higher taxes will reduce the incentive of both households and businesses to earn, invest, and engage in productive activities. All of these factors will weaken the recovery from recession, reduce capital formation, and lead to a slower rate of future growth.

Second, government spending is driven by political rather than economic considerations. The political process does not have anything like profit and loss that will direct resources into productive projects and away from unproductive ones. Political favoritism will become more important, and efficient allocation of resources less. Predictably, counterproductive use of resources will result.

Third, an increase in politically directed spending will lead to more rent-seeking. Incentives matter. When the government is spending a lot on special projects, subsidies, grants, and income transfers, businesses and other organized groups will spend more on lobbying, political contributions, and other efforts designed to attract the government funds. Resources will be channeled toward wasteful rent-seeking and away from productive activities that provide consumers with goods and services that are more highly valued than their cost. Predictably, the result will be favoritism, cronyism, and even political corruption. Ironically, most of the wasteful rent-seeking activity will add to GDP as it is currently measured. For example, if business executives, lawyers, and even economists are spending more of their time schmoozing government officials, preparing grant proposals, designing politically attractive projects, and so on, such expenditures will enhance GDP. So, too, will inefficient government projects. For example, if the government spends $50 billion on the construction of a railroad from Los Angeles to Las Vegas, the project will add $50 billion to GDP even if the railroad never even covers its operating cost in the future. As a result, GDP will overstate the value of the goods and services produced.

12-6b TAX CUTS VERSUS SPENDING INCREASES

When seeking to promote recovery from a recession, would it be better to reduce taxes or increase government spending? Keynesian economists tend to favor spending increases.

They often argue that increases in government spending will expand GDP by more than tax reductions, because 100 percent of the increase in government purchases will be pumped into the economy, whereas part of the tax reduction will be saved or spent abroad. As a result, Keynesians believe that the multiplier effect of an increase in government spending will be greater than that of a tax cut.[8]

But the rapidity of the effects is also a consideration, and tax cuts can generally begin to impact the economy more rapidly than increases in government spending. Reductions in tax rates can increase both the disposable income and the incentive to earn almost immediately. Even if a substantial portion of an increase in after-tax income is not spent quickly, there will be an immediate positive impact on the financial position of households. In contrast, government-spending projects are often a lengthy process spread over several years. For example, the Congressional Budget Office estimated that only 15 percent of the spending funded by the stimulus package passed in February 2009 occurred during the initial year, while nearly half (48 percent) was not spent until 2011 and beyond. As President Obama noted during the summer of 2011, many of the "shovel-ready" projects were not quite as shovel ready as the administration initially thought.

Compared to an increase in government spending, a tax cut is less likely to change the composition of labor demand and increase structural unemployment. New government spending programs often change the structure of aggregate demand. As a result of this structural change, increases in government spending often exert an adverse transitional impact on the rate of unemployment.

When considering the impact of a tax cut, it is important to differentiate between one-time tax rebates and reductions in tax rates. Sending government checks to most all households, as was done by the stimulus packages of both Presidents Bush and Obama, increase disposable income, but they do not provide additional incentive for people to earn, invest, and employ others. As supply-side analysis indicates, a tax cut of this type is unlikely to exert much impact on long-term productive activity.

Similarly, the impact of a temporary tax cut will be much weaker than a permanent one. A temporary tax cut provides a short-term windfall increase in current income, but it does not exert much impact on either long-term income or the incentive to earn. Moreover, compared to a permanent tax reduction, a temporary tax cut generates uncertainty. As a result, market participants, unsure about whether and how policies might change, often choose to cancel or delay long-term business ventures. Thus, temporary tax rebates and even rate reductions are largely ineffective as a tool for the promotion of recovery and long-term growth.

12-7 U.S. FISCAL POLICY: 1990–2013

Changes in government expenditures and shifts in the federal budget are indicative of the direction of fiscal policy. Increases in government spending financed by borrowing will shift the budget toward a deficit. This combination is indicative of a more expansionary fiscal policy. In contrast, reductions in government spending and shifts in the federal budget toward surplus are indicative of a move toward a more restrictive fiscal policy.

Exhibit 6 provides data on federal spending during 1990–2013. As Exhibit 6 (upper frame) shows, real federal spending was relatively constant during the 1990s. Measured in constant 2005 dollars, real federal spending in 2000 was $2.14 trillion, compared to

---

[8]The empirical evidence on the size of the tax and spending multipliers is mixed. Estimates of the multipliers range from approximately 1 to 3, and some have found the multiplier effects of a tax cut to be stronger than those for an increase in government spending, whereas others have found the reverse. See Valerie A. Ramey, "Identifying Government Spending Shocks: It's All in the Timing," University of California, San Diego, Working Paper, June 2008; Christina D. Romer and David H. Romer, "The Macroeconomic Effects of Tax Changes: Estimates Based on a New Measure of Fiscal Shocks," University of California, Berkeley Working Paper, March 2007; and John F. Cogan, Tobias Cwik, John B. Taylor, and Volker Wieland, "New Keynesian versus Old Keynesian Government Spending Multipliers," NBER Working Paper No. 14782, March 2009.

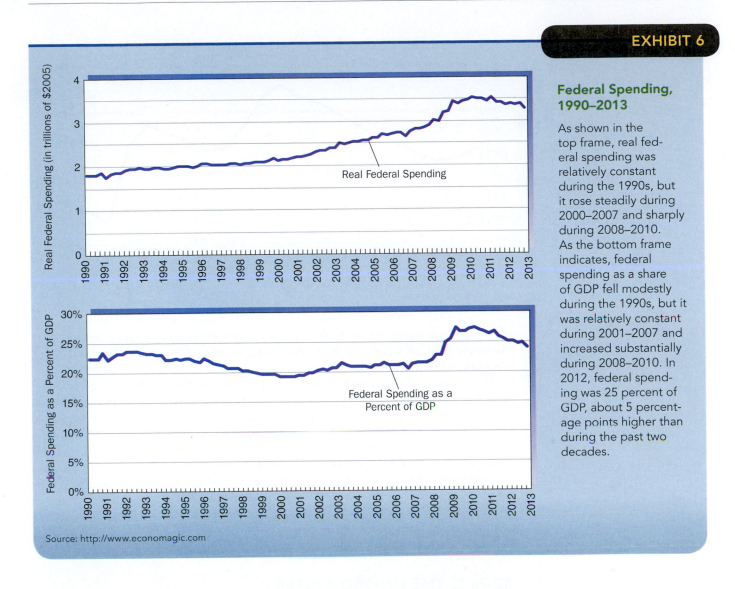

Federal Spending, 1990–2013

As shown in the top frame, real federal spending was relatively constant during the 1990s, but it rose steadily during 2000–2007 and sharply during 2008–2010. As the bottom frame indicates, federal spending as a share of GDP fell modestly during the 1990s, but it was relatively constant during 2001–2007 and increased substantially during 2008–2010. In 2012, federal spending was 25 percent of GDP, about 5 percentage points higher than during the past two decades.

EXHIBIT 6

Source: http://www.economagic.com

$1.81 trillion in 1990. Thus, real federal spending increased by only 18 percent during the 1990s. By 2010, real federal spending had soared to $3.51 trillion, more than 60 percent higher than a decade earlier. Measured as a share of GDP federal spending fell from 22.5 percent in 1990 to 19.1 percent in 2000 (lower frame). However, by 2010 federal spending had risen to 26.9 percent of GDP, substantially higher than the figure at the beginning of the decade. Thus, both real government spending and federal spending as a share of GDP grew far more rapidly during 2000–2010 than during the 1990s. The 2010 figures were elevated by the recession. In 2011 and 2012, federal spending declined in real terms and as a share of GDP. Nonetheless, federal spending as a share of GDP was 24.8 percent in 2012, well above the 19.1 figure for 2000.

As **Exhibit 7** shows, the federal budget moved from deficit to surplus during the 1990s, but it shifted in the opposite direction during 2000–2010. Measured as a share of GDP, the budget deficit was in the 3 percent to 5 percent range in the early part of the 1990s, but it fell steadily throughout the remainder of the decade. By 2000, a federal budget surplus of 2.4 percent was present. But the situation changed dramatically during the following decade. The combination of the 2001 recession and sluggish recovery, increases in defense spending, and the Bush administration's tax cut quickly moved the budget from surplus to deficit. During 2003–2007, deficits between 1.2 percent and 3.5 percent of GDP were present. As the economy dipped into a recession in 2008, the shortfall soared to 9 percent during 2009–2010. Thus, both government expenditures and the federal budget indicate that fiscal policy was relatively restrictive during the 1990s, but it shifted toward expansion

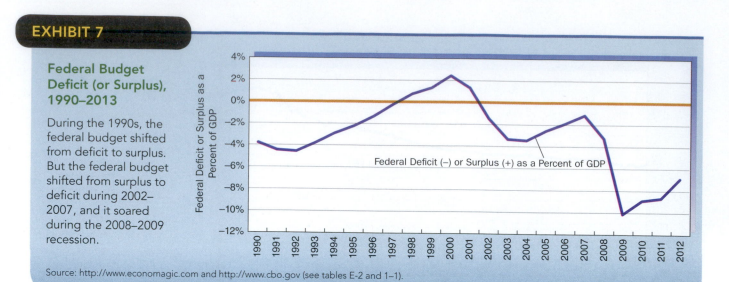

EXHIBIT 7

Federal Budget Deficit (or Surplus), 1990–2013

During the 1990s, the federal budget shifted from deficit to surplus. But the federal budget shifted from surplus to deficit during 2002–2007, and it soared during the 2008–2009 recession.

Source: http://www.economagic.com and http://www.cbo.gov (see tables E-2 and 1–1).

during the most recent decade. Moreover, it was highly expansionary during and following the recession of 2008–2009. While the deficit as a share of GDP shrank during 2011–2012, it remained at historic high levels.

Clearly, the fiscal policy response to the recession of 2008–2009 has been precisely what Keynesian analysis would recommend. The administrations of both Presidents Bush and Obama increased government spending and enlarged the budget deficit. Under the Bush administration, a $168 billion stimulus package was passed in early 2008. Most of these funds went for checks of $600 per adult and $300 per child sent to households with incomes of less than $150,000. Later in the year, the Troubled Asset Relief Program (TARP) authorized another $700 billion to bail out troubled financial institutions. When the Obama administration took over in 2009, still another stimulus package of $787 billion was passed. As Exhibits 6 and 7 show, these programs pushed federal spending to 26 percent of GDP and the budget deficit to 10 percent of the economy in 2009. During 2009–2011, about 35 percent of the federal budget was financed through borrowing.

12-7a IS THE UNITED STATES ON THE PATH TO A DEBT CRISIS?

The large budget deficits of recent years have pushed the federal debt to exceedingly high levels. **Exhibit 8** illustrates the path of three alternative debt measures as a share of GDP since 1990. Total federal debt rose to more than 100 percent in 2012, the highest level since the end of World War II. This figure, often referred to as the national debt, includes bonds held in federal trust funds such as that for Social Security as well as those held by the Federal Reserve System. In essence, these bonds represent Treasury borrowing from other parts of the federal government. Note that the ratio of federal debt to GDP fell during the 1990s, but it has risen sharply during the past decade. The second measure, privately held debt, or net federal debt as it is sometimes called, is comprised of funds the federal government has borrowed from private investors. Even if this debt is not paid off, it will still impose an interest cost on the federal taxpayer. Like the national debt, the privately held debt shrank during the 1990s, but it has increased sharply in recent years. Finally, Exhibit 8 presents data on federal borrowing from foreigners. While the interest payments on domestically held bonds will be paid to Americans, the interest on bonds held by foreigners will be paid to investors in other countries. The federal borrowing from foreigners was less than 15 percent throughout the 1990s, and it was approximately 10 percent in 2000. Since then, the federal government's borrowing from foreigners has increased sharply, soaring to 35 percent of GDP in 2012.

Are the current high levels of government debt dangerous? When thinking about this question, it is important to recognize two different factors underlying the political

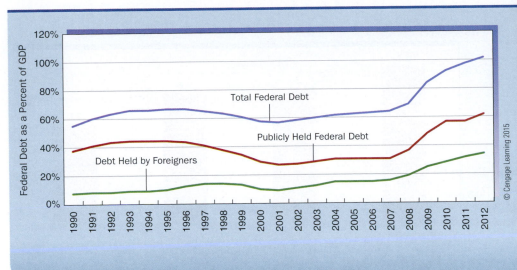

© Cengage Learning 2015

EXHIBIT 8

Alternative Measures of Federal Debt: 1990–2012.

The total federal debt, publicly-held debt, and the debt held by foreigners measured as a share of GDP are shown here. Note how each of these measures soared during 2008–2012. The foreign held debt as a share of GDP more than tripled between 2001 and 2012.

attractiveness of debt financing: (1) its potential use as a countercyclical stabilization tool and (2) its use to shift the cost of government, particularly the visible costs, from current to future generations. Until now, we have focused almost exclusively on the first factor, but economics provides several important insights on the second—the use of borrowing to benefit current citizens at the expense of future generations. Consider the following three factors.

First, as public-choice analysis indicates, democratically elected politicians will find debt financing attractive. The shortsightedness effect indicates that policies that provide voters with highly visible benefits at the expense of future costs that are difficult to identify will be political winners. Debt financing of current spending fits that pattern perfectly. Current spending can provide voters with highly visible goods, services, and transfer payments, while borrowing to finance this spending can push the most visible cost into the future. Thus, politicians have a strong incentive to follow this strategy. The evidence is consistent with this view. Before 1960, it was widely believed that governments, like households, should balance their budgets. But Keynesian economics changed this orthodoxy. In the post-1960 Keynesian era, budget deficits became the norm. During the 53 years since 1960, there have been 49 deficits and four surpluses.

Second, unfunded promises are another form of debt finance, and the future tax burden of these programs is certain to increase in the years immediately ahead. Like government bonds, unfunded promises for future Social Security, health care, and government employee pension benefits imply higher future taxes. Because the large baby-boom generation is now moving into the retirement phase of life, the tax burden accompanying these programs will rise sharply during the next two decades.

Third, the political incentive structure explains why countries might get caught in a vicious circle of debt financing, higher taxes, and sluggish growth. As a country's debt and unfunded promises increase, the bills will eventually come due and taxes will have to be raised to meet the obligations. But the higher taxes will slow economic growth, which will make it more difficult to raise the revenues to fund the debt and promised benefits. In turn, this will generate pressure for still more borrowing.

Several European countries—including Greece, Italy, Spain, and Portugal—are currently confronting this vicious circle. Their debt levels and promised benefits to their citizenry have pushed spending levels beyond their

Increases in government spending, budget deficits, expansion in government debt, and higher taxes to pay the required interest payments can lead to a lengthy economic decline. The recent experience of Greece illustrates this point.

EXHIBIT 9

Economic Growth and Government Debt as a Share of GDP, 1970–2009

Countries with high government debt to GDP ratios tend to grow more slowly than those with less debt.

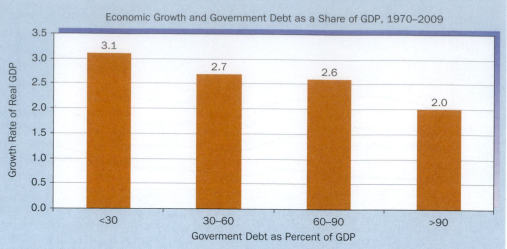

Economic Growth and Government Debt as a Share of GDP, 1970–2009

Source: Thomas Herndon Michael Ash, Robert Pollin, "Does High Public Debt Consistently Stifle Economic Growth? A Critique of Reinhart and Rogoff," Political Economy Research Institute, University of Massachusetts, Working Paper 322, April 2013, Table 5.

tax capacities. Further, as they increase taxes, growth slows and, as a result, the higher taxes generate little additional revenue. As **Exhibit 9** shows, countries with higher levels of debt grow less rapidly. Since 1970, countries with a debt to GDP ratio of 90 percent or more have grown at an annual rate of only 2 percent, a full percentage point less than countries with debt of less than 30 percent of GDP.

Can countries escape from this vicious circle? Clearly the answer is "yes." The experiences of both Ireland and Canada illustrate this point. In the 1980s, Ireland's debt to GDP ratio soared to more than 100 percent, leading to a decline in its bond rating and higher interest rates on its outstanding debt. Against this background, the Irish government slashed its expenditures and reduced its budget deficit. Canada confronted a similar experience in the late 1990s. Following the spending cuts, both countries were able to achieve strong growth and reduce their debt as a share of the economy.

However, the experience of other countries has not been so positive. Greece has been unable to escape the vicious circle of debt, high taxes, and stagnation. It continues to struggle to meet the conditions of its bailouts from the European Union. The economies of Italy, Spain, and Portugal are currently experiencing recession and high levels of unemployment largely because of their inability to control the growth of government spending and debt. Japan has experienced two decades of sluggish growth and growing debt as a share of GDP.

As of 2013, the U.S. budget deficit had declined to 7 percent of GDP. If the expansion continues, government projections indicate the deficit will continue to fall, and the rising federal debt/GDP ratio will eventually peak and begin to decline. But the future demographics are highly unfavorable, and there is no assurance the weak expansion will continue. Thus, the current situation is one of uncertainty for both the United States and several other economies with high levels of government debt.

LOOKING AHEAD

Fiscal policy is not the only macroeconomic policy tool. Monetary policy also influences the economy. We are now ready to integrate the monetary system into our analysis. Chapter 13 will focus on the operation of the banking system and the factors that determine the supply of money. In Chapter 14, we will analyze the impact of monetary policy on real output, interest rates, and the price level.

KEY POINTS

- The crowding-out model indicates that expansionary fiscal policy will lead to higher real interest rates and less private spending, particularly for investment. In an open economy, the higher interest rates will also lead to the following secondary effects: an inflow of capital, an appreciation of the dollar, and a reduction in net exports. The crowding-out theory implies that these secondary effects will largely offset the demand stimulus of expansionary fiscal policy.

- The new classical model stresses that financing government spending with debt rather than taxes changes the timing, but not the level, of taxes. According to this view, people will expect higher future taxes, which will lead to more saving and less private spending. This will tend to offset the expansionary effects of a deficit.

- Keynesian and non-Keynesian economists are now largely in agreement on the following three issues: (1) Proper timing of discretionary fiscal policy is both difficult to achieve and crucially important, (2) automatic stabilizers reduce the fluctuation of aggregate demand and help promote economic stability, and (3) fiscal policy is much less potent than early Keynesians thought.

- When fiscal policy changes marginal tax rates, it influences aggregate supply by altering the attractiveness of productive activity relative to leisure and tax avoidance.

Other things being constant, lower marginal tax rates will increase aggregate supply. Supply-side economics should be viewed as a long-run strategy, not a countercyclical tool.

- Keynesian economists believe that increases in government spending financed by borrowing will increase aggregate demand and help promote recovery from a serious recession like that of 2008–2009. Non-Keynesian economists argue that Keynesian policies will lead to higher future interest rates and taxes, inefficient use of resources, and wasteful rent-seeking that will both retard recovery and slow future economic growth.

- Tax cuts can generally begin to exert an impact on the economy more rapidly than spending increases. Further, rate reductions and permanent rate changes will exert a larger impact than tax rebates and temporary tax cuts.

- Political decision-makers have responded to the 2008–2009 recession with large increases in both government spending and budget deficits. The deficits have pushed federal debt to levels unseen since World War II. Potential danger accompanies high debt levels because higher taxes will be necessary to finance interest payments and the higher taxes will slow economic growth. In turn, the slower economic growth will reduce government revenues, making it more difficult to control future deficits and debt.

CRITICAL ANALYSIS QUESTIONS

1. Suppose that you are a member of the Council of Economic Advisers. The president has asked you to prepare a statement on the question, "What is the proper fiscal policy for the next twelve months?" Prepare such a statement, indicating (a) the current state of the economy (that is, the unemployment rate, growth in real income, and rate of inflation) and (b) your fiscal policy suggestions. Should the budget be in balance? Explain the reasoning behind your suggestions.

2. *What is the crowding-out effect? How does it modify the implications of the basic Keynesian model with 1. Suppose that you are a member of the Council of Economic Advisers. The president has asked you to prepare a statement on the question, "What is the proper fiscal policy for the next twelve months?" Prepare such a statement, indicating (a) the current state of the economy (that is, the unemployment rate, growth in real income, and rate of inflation) and (b) your fiscal policy suggestions. Should the budget be in balance? Explain the reasoning behind your suggestions.

3. *What is the crowding-out effect? How does it modify the implications of the basic Keynesian model with regard to fis-

cal policy? How does the new classical theory of fiscal policy differ from the crowding-out model?

4. Suppose that the government provides each taxpayer with a $1,000 tax rebate financed by issuing additional Treasury bonds. Outline alternative views that predict how this fiscal action will influence interest rates, aggregate demand, output, and employment.

5. Will increases in government spending financed by borrowing help promote a strong recovery from a severe recession? Why or why not?

6. Outline the supply-side view of fiscal policy. How does this view differ from the various demand-side theories? Would a supply-side economist be more likely to favor a $1,000 rebate to all taxpayers or an equivalent reduction in marginal tax rates? Why?

7. Are changes in discretionary fiscal policy likely to be instituted in a manner that will reduce the ups and downs of the business cycle? Why or why not?

8. "Bill Clinton reduced government spending and shifted the federal budget toward surplus, while Presidents Bush and Obama adopted the Keynesian policies of spending growth financed by borrowing. If we want to return to prosperity, we need to discard the Bush-Obama policies and return to those of President Clinton." Explain why you either agree or disagree with this view.

9. If the government becomes more heavily involved in subsidizing some businesses and sectors of the economy while levying higher taxes on others, how will this influence the quantity of rent seeking? How will this affect long-term growth? Explain your response.

10. Does fiscal policy have a strong impact on aggregate demand? Did the shift of the federal budget from deficit to surplus during the 1990s weaken aggregate demand? Did the government spending increases and large budget deficits of 2008–2011 strengthen aggregate demand? Discuss.

11. *How do persistently large budget deficits affect capital formation and the long-run rate of economic growth? Do the proponents of the Keynesian, crowding-out, and new classical theories agree on the answer to this question? Discuss.

12. What is the current rate of unemployment? How rapidly has real GDP grown during the past three years? What do these figures indicate about the validity of the Keynesian view? Explain.

13. Marginal tax rates were cut substantially during the 1980s, and although rates were increased in the early 1990s, the marginal rates applicable in the highest income brackets were still well below the top rates of the 1960s and 1970s. How did the lower rates of the 1980s and 1990s affect the share of taxes paid by high-income taxpayers? Were the lower rates of the 1980s and 1990s good or bad for the economy? Discuss.

14. *If the impact on tax revenues is the same, does it make any difference whether the government cuts taxes by (a) reducing marginal tax rates or (b) increasing the personal exemption allowance? Explain.

15. The "cash for clunkers" program of 2009 provided a subsidy of about $4,000 to those willing to buy a new car and have their old one destroyed. How did this policy affect the demand for new cars during the five months of the program? How did it affect the demand for new cars after it expired? How did it affect the price and availability of used cars? Do you think it would be a good idea to adopt a permanent program like this? Why or why not?

16. *The American Wind Energy Association argues for additional government support because wind-generated electricity creates more employment per kilowatt-hour than the alternatives: 27 percent more jobs than coal and 66 percent more than natural gas. Is this a sound economic argument for increased use of wind power? If the jobs created pay similar wages, what does the statement imply about the cost of generating energy with wind power relative to coal and natural gas?

*Asterisk denotes questions for which answers are given in Appendix B.

CHAPTER 13
Money and the Banking System

FOCUS

- What is money? How is the money supply defined?
- What is a fractional reserve banking system? How does it influence the ability of banks to create money?
- What are the major functions of the Federal Reserve System?
- What are the major tools with which the Federal Reserve controls the supply of money?
- How did the financial crisis of 2008–2009 affect Federal Reserve policy?

Money is whatever is generally accepted in exchange for goods and services—accepted not as an object to be consumed but as an object that represents a temporary abode of purchasing power to be used for buying still other goods and services.
—Milton Friedman[1]

[1]Milton Friedman, *Money Mischief: Episodes in Monetary History* (New York: Harcourt Brace Jovanovich, 1992), 16.

The simple macroeconomic model we have developed so far has four major markets: (1) the goods and services market, (2) the resources market, (3) the loanable funds market, and (4) the foreign exchange market. When people make exchanges in any of these markets, they generally use money. Money is used to purchase all types of goods, services, physical assets like houses, and financial assets like stocks and bonds. This chapter focuses on the nature of money, how the banking system works, and how the central bank—the Federal Reserve System in the United States—controls the supply of money.

13-1 WHAT IS MONEY?

As the chapter-opening quote from Milton Friedman indicates, money is the item commonly used to pay for goods, services, assets, and outstanding debts. Most modern money is merely paper or electronic digits indicating funds in a bank account. Paradoxically, money has little or no intrinsic value. Nonetheless, most of us would like to have more of it. Why? Because money is an asset that performs three basic functions: It serves as a medium of exchange, it provides a means of storing value for future use, and it is used as an accounting unit.

13-1a MONEY AS A MEDIUM OF EXCHANGE

Medium of exchange
An asset that is used to buy and sell goods or services.

Money is one of the most important inventions in human history because of its role as a **medium of exchange**. Money simplifies and reduces the costs of transactions. Think what it would be like to live in a barter economy—one without money, in which goods were traded for goods. If you wanted to buy a pair of jeans, for example, you would first have to find someone willing to trade you the jeans for your labor services or something else you were willing to supply. Without money, transaction costs would be exceedingly high and gains from trade vastly reduced. But money frees us from cumbersome barter procedures and "oils the wheels" of trade. As a result, each of us can specialize in the supply of those things that we do best and easily buy the many goods and services we want.

At various times in the past, societies have used gold, silver, beads, seashells, and other commodities as mediums of exchange. It is costly to use a valuable commodity as money. Here's why. Precious metals, like gold, would be cumbersome to carry around for use as payment. In fact, it might even be dangerous to do so. Moreover, think about how much it costs to create a thousand dollar bill: just a cent or two, perhaps. But if gold bars, for example, were used instead of bills as money, it would take a lot of resources to produce enough of them to facilitate today's current volume of trade. Further, if a precious metal was used as money, people would employ scarce resources producing "money," and as a result, fewer resources would be available to produce desired goods and services.

13-1b MONEY AS A STORE OF VALUE

Money is also a financial asset—a method of storing value for use in the future. Put another way, it provides readily available purchasing power for dealing with an uncertain future. Thus, most people hold some of their wealth in the form of money. Moreover, it is the most **liquid** of all assets. It can be easily and quickly transformed into other goods at a low transaction cost, usually without an appreciable loss in value.

Liquid asset
An asset that can be easily and quickly converted to money without loss of value.

Store of value
An asset that will allow people to transfer purchasing power from one period to the next.

However, there are some disadvantages of using money as a **store of value**. The value of a unit of money—a dollar, for example—is measured in terms of what it will buy. Its value, therefore, is inversely related to the price level in the economy. When inflation rises, the purchasing power of money declines—as does its usefulness as a store of value. This imposes a cost on people holding money.

Bettmann/Corbis

Money is the item commonly used to buy and sell things. During the Second World War, prisoners of war used cigarettes as money in POW camps.

Other assets, like land, houses, stocks, or bonds, also serve as a store of value, but they aren't as liquid as money. It will take time to locate an acceptable buyer for a house, a plot of land, or an office building. Stocks and bonds are quite liquid—they can usually be sold quickly for only a small commission—but they are not readily acceptable as a direct means of payment.

13-1c MONEY AS A UNIT OF ACCOUNT

Money also serves as a **unit of account**. Just as we use yards or meters to measure distance, we use units of money—the dollar in the United States—to measure the exchange value and cost of goods, services, assets, and resources. The value (and cost) of movie tickets, personal computers, labor services, automobiles, houses, and numerous other items is measured in units of money. Money serves as a common denominator for the expression of both costs and benefits. If consumers are going to spend their income wisely, they must be able to compare the costs of a vast array of goods and services. Prices measured in units of money help them make such comparisons. Similarly, sound business decisions require cost and revenue comparisons. Resource prices and accounting procedures measured in money units facilitate this task.

Unit of account
A unit of measurement used by people to post prices and keep track of revenues and costs.

13-2 HOW THE SUPPLY OF MONEY AFFECTS ITS VALUE

Money in most modern nations is **fiat money**—money with no intrinsic value. Why is fiat money valuable? Governments often designate it as "legal tender," meaning it must be accepted as payment for debt. But the main thing that makes money valuable is the same thing that generates value for other commodities: demand relative to supply. People demand money because it reduces the cost of exchange. When the supply of money is limited relative to the demand, money will become more valuable. Conversely, when the supply of money expands relative to demand, it will become less valuable.

Fiat money
Money that has neither intrinsic value nor the backing of a commodity with intrinsic value; paper currency is an example.

If the purchasing power of money is to remain stable over time, its supply must be limited. When the supply of money grows more rapidly than the output of goods and services, prices will rise. In layman's terms, "too much money is chasing too few goods."

When government authorities rapidly expand the supply of money, it becomes less valuable in exchange and is virtually useless as a store of value. The rapid growth in the supply of money in Germany following World War I provides a dramatic illustration of this point. During the period 1922–1923, the supply of German marks increased by 250 percent in some months. The German government was printing money almost as fast as the printing presses would run. Because money became substantially more plentiful in relation to goods and services, it quickly lost its value. As a result, an egg cost 80 billion marks and a loaf of bread 200 billion. Workers picked up their wages in suitcases. Shops closed at the lunch hour to change price tags. The value of money had eroded. More recently, several countries including Poland, Russia, Ukraine, and Zimbabwe have followed this same pattern. These countries expanded the supply of money rapidly to pay for government expenditures and, as a result, experienced very high rates of inflation. Thus, while fiat money is economical to produce, this feature also makes it easier for governments to use money creation to finance expenditures, expand the money supply rapidly, and thereby erode its purchasing power.

13-3 HOW IS THE MONEY SUPPLY MEASURED?

How is the money supply defined and measured? There is not a single answer to this question. Economists and policy makers have developed several alternative measures. We will briefly describe the two most widely used measures.

13-3a THE M1 MONEY SUPPLY

M1 (money supply)
The sum of (1) currency in circulation (including coins), (2) checkable deposits maintained in depository institutions, and (3) traveler's checks.

Currency
Medium of exchange made of metal or paper.

Demand deposits
Non–interest-earning checking deposits that can be either withdrawn or made payable on demand to a third party. Like currency, these deposits are widely used as a means of payment.

Other checkable deposits
Interest-earning deposits that are also available for checking.

Above all else, money is a medium of exchange. The narrowest definition of the money supply, **M1**, focuses on this function. Based on its role as a medium of exchange, it is clear that **currency**—coins and paper bills—falls into this definition. But currency isn't the only form of money readily used for exchange. If you want to buy something from a store, many will let you pay with either a check or debit card that will transfer funds from your bank account to theirs. Therefore, checkable bank deposits that can easily be used as a means of payment should be included in the M1 money supply measure.

There are two kinds of checkable deposits. First, there are **demand deposits**, non–interest-earning deposits with banking institutions that are available for withdrawal ("on demand") at any time without restrictions. Demand deposits are usually withdrawn either by writing a check or by using a debit card tied to your account. Second, there are **other checkable deposits** that earn interest but carry some restrictions on their transferability. Interest-earning checkable deposits generally either limit the number of checks depositors can write each month or require the depositor to maintain a substantial minimum balance ($1,000, for example).

Like currency and demand deposits, interest-earning checkable deposits are available for use as a medium of exchange. Traveler's checks are also a means of payment. They can be freely converted to cash at parity (equal value). *Thus, the M1 money supply comprises (1) currency in circulation, (2) checkable deposits (both demand deposits and interest-earning checkable deposits), and (3) traveler's checks.*

As Exhibit 1 shows, the total M1 money supply in the United States was $2,524 billion in April 2013. Demand and other checkable deposits accounted for more than one-half of the M1 money supply. This large share reflects the fact that most of the nation's business is conducted with checks and electronic payment transfers.

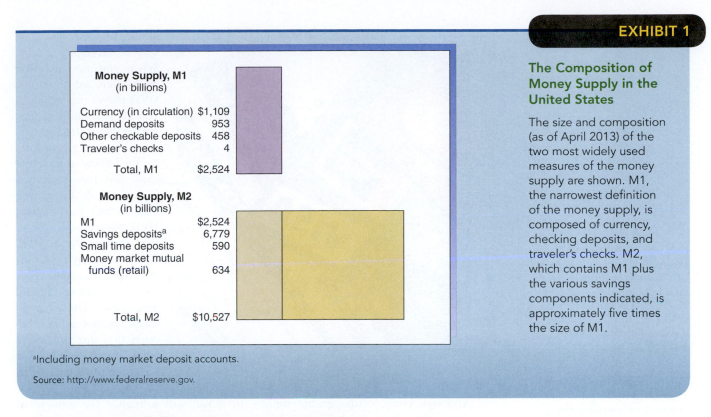

Source: http://www.federalreserve.gov.

aIncluding money market deposit accounts.

EXHIBIT 1

The Composition of Money Supply in the United States

The size and composition (as of April 2013) of the two most widely used measures of the money supply are shown. M1, the narrowest definition of the money supply, is composed of currency, checking deposits, and traveler's checks. M2, which contains M1 plus the various savings components indicated, is approximately five times the size of M1.

13-3b THE BROADER M2 MONEY SUPPLY

In modern economies, several financial assets can be easily converted into checking deposits or currency; therefore, the line between money and "near monies" is often blurred. Broader definitions of the money supply include various assets that can be easily converted to checking account funds and cash. The most common broad definition of the money supply is **M2**. It includes all the items included in M1 plus (1) savings deposits, (2) time deposits of less than $100,000 at all **depository institutions**, and (3) money market mutual funds.

Although the non-M1 components of the M2 money supply are not generally used as a means of making payment, they can be easily and quickly converted to currency or checking deposits for such use. For example, if you maintain funds in a savings account, you can easily transfer the funds to your checking account. **Money market mutual funds** are interest-earning accounts offered by banks and brokerage firms that pool depositors' funds and invest them in highly liquid short-term securities. Because these securities can be quickly converted to cash, depositors are permitted to write checks against these accounts.

Many economists—particularly those who stress the store-of-value function of money—prefer the broader M2 definition of the money supply to the narrower M1 concept. As Exhibit 1 shows, in April 2013 the M2 money supply was $10,527 billion, about four times the M1 money supply. Other definitions of the money supply have been developed for specialized purposes, but the M1 and M2 definitions are the most important and most widely used.

13-3c CREDIT CARDS VERSUS MONEY

It is important to distinguish between money and credit. Money is a financial asset that provides the holder with future purchasing power. **Credit** is a liability acquired when one borrows funds. This distinction sheds light on a question students frequently ask: "Because credit cards are often used to make purchases, why aren't credit card expenditures part of the money supply?" In contrast with money, credit cards do not have purchasing power. They

M2 (money supply)
Equal to M1 plus (1) savings deposits, (2) time deposits (accounts of less than $100,000) held in depository institutions, and (3) money market mutual fund shares.

Depository institutions
Businesses that accept checking and savings deposits and use a portion of them to extend loans and make investments. Banks, savings and loan associations, and credit unions are examples.

Money market mutual funds
Interest-earning accounts that pool depositors' funds and invest them in highly liquid short-term securities. Because these securities can be quickly converted to cash, depositors are permitted to write checks (which reduce their share holdings) against their accounts.

Credit
Funds acquired by borrowing.

©iStockphoto.com/Sinopics

Money is an asset; it is part of the wealth of the people who hold it. In contrast, credit card purchases create a liability. They are merely a convenient method of arranging a short-term loan.

Federal reserve system
The central bank of the United States; it carries out banking regulatory policies and is responsible for the conduct of monetary policy.

Central bank
An institution that regulates the banking system and controls the money supply.

Savings and loan associations
Financial institutions that accept deposits in exchange for shares that pay dividends. Historically, these funds were channeled into residential mortgage loans, but today they offer essentially the same services as a commercial bank.

Credit unions
Financial cooperative organizations of individuals with a common affiliation (such as an employer or a labor union). They accept deposits, including checkable deposits, pay interest (or dividends) on them out of earnings, and lend funds primarily to members.

Commercial banks
Financial institutions that offer a wide range of services (for example, checking accounts, savings accounts, and loans) to their customers. Commercial banks are owned by stockholders and seek to operate at a profit.

are merely a convenient way of arranging a loan. When you use your Visa or MasterCard to buy a DVD player, for example, you are not really paying for the player. Instead, you are taking out a loan from the institution issuing your card, and that institution is paying for the player. You haven't paid for the DVD player until you've paid your credit card bill down far enough to cover its cost. The same goes for your other credit card purchases. Thus, credit cards are not money because they don't represent purchasing power. Instead, the outstanding balance on your credit card is a liability, money you owe to the company that issued the card.

Although credit cards are not money, their use will influence the amount of money people will want to hold. Credit cards make it possible for people to buy things throughout the month and then pay for them in a single transaction at the end of the month. This makes it possible for people to conduct their regular business affairs with less money than would otherwise be needed. Thus, widespread use of credit cards will tend to reduce the average quantity of money people hold.

13-4 THE BUSINESS OF BANKING

We must understand a few things about the business of banking before we can explain the factors that influence the supply of money. The banking industry in the United States operates under the jurisdiction of the **Federal Reserve System**, the nation's **central bank**. We will discuss the Federal Reserve System in detail later in this chapter.

The banking system is an important component of the loanable funds market. Like other private businesses, banks are profit-seeking operations. Banks provide services (for example, the safekeeping of funds and checking account services) and pay interest to attract both checking and savings depositors. They help bring together people who want to save for the future and those who want to borrow in order to undertake investment projects. The primary source of revenue for banks is the income they derive from their loans and investments.

When deciding whether to extend a loan for a project, bankers have a strong incentive to take into account the project's expected profitability and the borrower's creditworthiness. If the borrowed funds are channeled into an unprofitable project, the borrower may not be able to repay the loan. This will hurt the bank's profitability. The efficient allocation of investment funds by banks is an important source of economic growth. Profitable business projects increase the value of resources and promote economic growth; unprofitable projects have the opposite effect and tie up resources better used elsewhere. Thus, an efficiently operating loanable funds market is an important source of growth and prosperity, and the banking system plays a central role in the operation of this market.

In the United States, the banking system consists of **savings and loan institutions**, **credit unions**, and **commercial banks**. All of these institutions now accept both checking and savings deposits and extend a wide variety of loans to their customers. They are all under the jurisdiction of the Federal Reserve System, which applies similar regulations and offers similar services to each. ***Therefore, when we speak of the banking industry, we are referring not only to commercial banks but also to savings and loan associations and credit unions.***

The major functions of banks can be discerned by examining their balance sheets. The major liabilities of banks are transaction (checking), savings, and time deposits. *From the viewpoint of a bank*, these are liabilities because they represent an obligation of the bank to its depositors. Outstanding interest-earning loans constitute the major class of banking assets. In addition, most banks own sizable amounts of interest-earning securities—bonds issued by either governments or private corporations. Banks use the deposits of their customers to finance their loans and investments.

It's important to note that banks maintain only a small fraction of their assets in **bank reserves**—vault cash plus reserve deposits with the Federal Reserve—in reserve against their checking and saving deposits. Savings cannot always be withdrawn immediately, and they are generally more stable than checking deposits. Therefore, banks are required to maintain reserves only against their checking deposits. We will now take a closer look at the historical development and operation of a fractional reserve banking system.

13-4a FRACTIONAL RESERVE BANKING

Economists often draw an analogy between our current banking system and the goldsmiths of a long-ago era. In the past, gold was used as the means of making payments. It was money. People would store their money with a goldsmith for safekeeping, just as many of us open a checking account for safety reasons. Gold owners received a certificate granting them the right to withdraw their gold any time they wished. If they wanted to buy something, they would go to the goldsmith, withdraw gold, and use it as a means of making a payment. Thus, the money supply was equal to the amount of gold in circulation plus the gold deposited with goldsmiths.

It was inconvenient to make a trip to the goldsmith every time one wanted to buy something. Because the certificates were redeemable in gold, they began to circulate as a means of payment. The depositors were pleased with this arrangement because it eliminated the need for a trip to the goldsmith every time something was purchased. As long as they had confidence in the goldsmith, sellers were glad to accept the certificates as payment.

As gold certificates began to circulate, the daily withdrawals and deposits with goldsmiths declined even more. Goldsmiths earned money by lending out gold. They made nothing on the gold just sitting in their vaults. Think what would happen if the local goldsmiths kept 20 percent of the total gold deposited with them in order to meet the day-to-day requests to redeem gold certificates and loaned out the remaining 80 percent to merchants, traders, and other citizens. One hundred percent of the gold certificates would then circulate as money, along with that portion of gold that had been loaned out—80 percent of total deposits, in other words. As a result, the *total* money supply circulating in the economy— gold certificates plus actual gold—would expand to 1.8 times the amount of gold deposited with the goldsmiths. By issuing loans and retaining only a fraction of the total gold in their vaults, the goldsmiths actually increased the money supply.

In principle, our modern banking system is very similar to goldsmithing. The United States has a **fractional reserve banking** system. Banks are required to maintain only a fraction of their deposits in the form of vault cash and other reserves. These are called **required reserves**. Just as the early goldsmiths did not have enough gold to pay all their depositors simultaneously, our banks also do not have enough reserves to pay all depositors at once. To make money, the early goldsmiths expanded the money supply by issuing loans. So, too, do present-day bankers.

There are important differences between modern banking and early goldsmithing, though. Today, the actions of individual banks are regulated by a central bank. The central

Bank reserves
Vault cash plus deposits of banks with Federal Reserve banks.

Fractional reserve banking
A system that permits banks to hold reserves of less than 100 percent against their deposits.

Required reserves
The minimum amount of reserves that a bank is required by law to keep on hand to back up its deposits. If reserve requirements were 15 percent, banks would be required to keep $150,000 in reserves against each $1 million of deposits.

bank is supposed to follow policies designed to promote a healthy economy. It also acts as a lender of last resort. If the customers of a bank all attempted to withdraw their deposits simultaneously, the central bank would intervene and supply the bank with enough funds to meet the demand.

13-4b BANK RUNS, BANK FAILURES, AND DEPOSIT INSURANCE

Compared to other businesses, banks are more vulnerable to failure because their liabilities to depositors are current but most of their assets are illiquid. This means that if a significant share of depositors lose confidence and withdraw their funds from a bank, it will quickly lead to problems. In turn, when a bank fails, it affects not only the bank's owners and employees but its depositors as well. If many banks fail, the affects can spread and undermine the operation of an economy.

The U.S. economy has had its share of banking problems. Between 1922 and 1933, more than 10,000 banks (one-third of the total) failed. Most of these failures were the result of "bank runs"—panic withdrawals when people lost confidence in the banking system. Remember, under a fractional reserve system, banks do not have a sufficient amount of reserves to redeem the funds of all (or even most) depositors if they should seek to withdraw their funds at the same time.

Federal Deposit Insurance Corporation (FDIC)
A federally chartered corporation that insures the deposits held by commercial banks, savings and loans, and credit unions.

The bank failures of the 1920s and 1930s led to the establishment of the **Federal Deposit Insurance Corporation (FDIC)** in 1934. The FDIC guarantees the deposits of banking customers up to some limit—currently $250,000 per account. Even if the bank should fail, depositors will be able to get their money (up to the $250,000 limit). Member banks pay an insurance premium to the FDIC for each dollar deposited with them, and the FDIC uses these premiums to reimburse depositors when a bank fails.

The FDIC protected depositors, restored confidence, and led to the virtual elimination of bank runs. But there is a down side to the system: It reduces the incentive of depositors to monitor banks and move their funds toward those with a strong portfolio of high-quality investments and loans. As a result, it is easier for banks to undertake riskier investments that are also a source of bank failure. There are still bank failures; 51 failed in 2012. But bank failures are far less common now, and they are almost always the result of bad investments rather than bank runs.

13-5 HOW BANKS CREATE MONEY BY EXTENDING LOANS

Let us consider a banking system without a central bank, one in which only currency acts as a reserve against deposits. Initially, we will assume that all banks are required by law to maintain 20 percent or more of their deposits as cash in their vaults. This proportion of the percentage of reserves that must be maintained against checkable transaction deposits is called the **required reserve ratio**. The required reserve ratio in our example is 20 percent.

Required reserve ratio
The ratio of reserves relative to a specified liability category (for example, checkable deposits) that banks are required to maintain.

Excess reserves
Actual reserves that exceed the legal requirement.

Now suppose that you find $1,000 that your long-deceased uncle had apparently hidden in the basement of his house. You take the bills to the First National Bank and open a checking account. How much will the $1,000 in your newly opened account expand the economy's money supply? First National is now required to keep $200 of the $1,000 in vault cash—20 percent of your deposit. So after placing $200 in the bank vault, First National has $800 of **excess reserves**—reserves over and above the amount the law requires it to retain. Given its current excess reserves, First National can now extend an $800 loan. Suppose it loans $800 to a local citizen to help pay for a car. At the time the loan is extended, the money supply will increase by $800 as the bank adds the funds to the checking account of the borrower. No one else has less money. You still have your $1,000 checking account, and the borrower has $800 for the car.

When the borrower buys the car, the seller accepts a check and deposits the $800 in a bank, Citizen's State Bank. What happens when the check clears? The temporary excess reserves of the First National Bank will be eliminated when it pays $800 to the Citizen's State Bank. But when Citizen's State Bank receives $800 in currency, it will now have excess reserves. It must keep 20 percent of it, or $160, as required reserves, but the remaining $640 can be loaned out. Because Citizen's State, like other banks, wants to earn income, it will be quite happy to "extend a helping hand" to someone who wants to borrow that money. When the second bank loans out its excess reserves, the deposits of the person borrowing the money will increase by $640. Another $640 has now been added to the money supply. You still have your $1,000, the automobile seller has an additional $800, and the new borrower has just received an additional $640. Because you found the $1,000 and deposited it in the bank, the money supply has increased by $1,440 ($800 + $640).

Of course, the process can continue. **Exhibit 2** shows what happens when the money creation process continues through several more stages. When the reserve requirement is 20 percent, the money supply can expand to a maximum of $5,000, the initial $1,000 plus an additional $4,000 in demand deposits that can be created by extending new loans.

The multiple by which new reserves increase the stock of money is called the **deposit expansion multiplier**. It is determined by the ratio of required reserves to deposits. In fact, the **potential deposit expansion multiplier** is merely the reciprocal of the required reserve ratio (r). Mathematically, the potential deposit expansion multiplier is equal to $1/r$. In our example, the required reserves are 20 percent or one-fifth of the total deposits. So the potential deposit expansion multiplier is 5. If only 10 percent reserves were required, the potential deposit expansion multiplier would be 10, the reciprocal of one-tenth. *The lower the percentage of reserves required, the larger the potential expansion in the money supply generated by creation of new reserves. However, the fractional reserve requirement does place a ceiling on the expansion in the money supply resulting from the creation of new reserves.*

Deposit expansion multiplier
The multiple by which an increase in reserves will increase the money supply. It is inversely related to the required reserve ratio.

Potential deposit expansion multiplier
The maximum potential increase in the money supply as a ratio of the new reserves injected into the banking system. It is equal to the inverse of the required reserve ratio.

EXHIBIT 2

Creating Money from New Reserves

When banks are required to maintain 20 percent reserves against demand deposits, the creation of $1,000 of new reserves will potentially increase the supply of money by $5,000.

BANK	NEW CASH DEPOSITS: ACTUAL RESERVES	NEW REQUIRED RESERVES	POTENTIAL DEMAND DEPOSITS CREATED BY EXTENDING NEW LOANS
Initial deposit (Bank A)	$1,000.00	$ 200.00	$ 800.00
Second stage (Bank B)	800.00	160.00	640.00
Third stage (Bank C)	640.00	128.00	512.00
Fourth stage (Bank D)	512.00	102.40	409.60
Fifth stage (Bank E)	409.60	81.92	327.68
Sixth stage (Bank F)	327.68	65.54	262.14
Seventh stage (Bank G)	262.14	52.43	209.71
All others (other banks)	1,048.58	209.71	838.87
Total	5,000.00	1,000.00	4,000.00

© Cengage Learning 2013

13-5a THE ACTUAL DEPOSIT MULTIPLIER

Will the introduction of new currency reserves fully expand the money supply by the amount of the multiplier? The answer is "No." The actual deposit multiplier will generally be less than its potential for two reasons.

First, the deposit expansion multiplier will be reduced if some people decide to hold the currency rather than deposit it in a bank. For example, suppose the person who borrowed the $800 in the preceding example spends only $700 and stashes the remaining $100 away for a possible emergency. Only $700 can then end up as a deposit in the second stage and contribute to the excess reserves that underlie the expansion of the money supply. The potential of new loans in the second stage and in all subsequent stages will be reduced proportionally. When currency remains in circulation outside of banks, it reduces the size of the deposit expansion multiplier.

Second, the actual deposit multiplier will be less than its maximum potential if banks fail to use all the new excess reserves to extend loans. Banks are in business to make profit, and they will generally be able to increase their net income by extending loans and undertaking investments, rather than holding excess reserves. In the past, this has certainly been the case, and therefore, historically, the excess reserves of banks have been small. However, in the midst of the uncertainty of the financial crisis of 2008, the excess reserves of banks skyrocketed. Moreover, in October 2008 the Federal Reserve acquired the authority to pay interest on bank reserves. This interest rate can be used to affect the excess reserves of banks and the size of the money deposit multiplier. We now turn to an examination of the Federal Reserve and the tools it has to control the money supply of the United States.

13-6 THE FEDERAL RESERVE SYSTEM

Most countries have a central banking authority that controls the money supply and conducts monetary policy. As we previously noted, the central bank of the United States is the Federal Reserve System. The European Central Bank is the central bank for countries using the euro as their currency. In the United Kingdom, the central bank is the Bank of England; in Canada, it is the Bank of Canada; in Japan, it is the Bank of Japan. Central banks are responsible for the conduct of monetary policy.

13-6a STRUCTURE OF THE FED

The Federal Reserve (and most other central banks) is supposed to regulate the money supply and provide a monetary climate that is in the best interest of the entire economy. Congress has instructed the Federal Reserve, or the Fed, as it is often called, to conduct monetary policy in a manner that promotes both full employment and price stability. Unlike commercial banks, the Federal Reserve is not a profit-making institution. The earnings of the Fed, over and above its expenses, belong to the U.S. Treasury.

Exhibit 3 illustrates the structure of the Fed. There are three major centers of decision making within the Federal Reserve: (1) the Board of Governors, (2) the district and regional banks, and (3) the Federal Open Market Committee.

The Board of Governors The Board of Governors is the decision-making hub of the Fed. This powerful board consists of seven members, each appointed to a staggered 14-year term by the nation's president with the advice and consent of the U.S. Senate. The president designates one of the seven members as chair for a four-year term. The Fed chairman directs the Federal Reserve staff, presides over board meetings, and testifies frequently before Congress. Because of the importance of monetary policy and the power of the position, the Fed chair is often said to be the second most influential person—next to the president—in the United States. In 2006, Ben Bernanke was appointed Fed chair. Bernanke succeeded Alan Greenspan, who retired after serving as Fed Chair for nearly two decades.

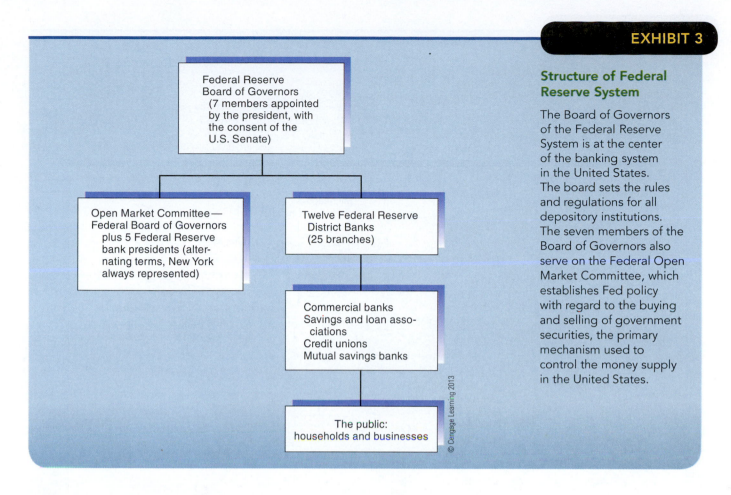

© Cengage Learning 2013

EXHIBIT 3

Structure of Federal Reserve System

The Board of Governors of the Federal Reserve System is at the center of the banking system in the United States. The board sets the rules and regulations for all depository institutions. The seven members of the Board of Governors also serve on the Federal Open Market Committee, which establishes Fed policy with regard to the buying and selling of government securities, the primary mechanism used to control the money supply in the United States.

The Board of Governors establishes the rules and regulations that apply to all depository institutions. It sets the reserve requirements and regulates the composition of the asset holdings of depository institutions. The board is the rule maker, and often the umpire, of the banking industry.

The Federal Reserve District Banks There are 12 Federal Reserve District Banks with 25 regional branches spread throughout the nation. **Exhibit 4** shows the regions covered by each of the twelve district banks. These district and regional banks operate under the supervision of the Board of Governors. Federal Reserve banks are bankers' banks; they provide banking services for commercial banks. Private citizens and corporations do not bank with the Fed.

The district banks are primarily responsible for the monitoring of the commercial banks in their region. They audit the books of depository institutions regularly to ensure their compliance with reserve requirements and other regulations of the Fed. The district banks also play an important role in the clearing of checks throughout the banking system. Most depository institutions, regardless of their Fed membership status, maintain deposits with Federal Reserve Banks. As a result, the clearing of checks through the Federal Reserve System becomes merely an accounting transaction.

The Federal Open Market Committee The **Federal Open Market Committee (FOMC)** is a powerful committee that determines the Fed's policy with respect to the purchase and sale of government bonds and other financial assets. As we shall soon see, this is the primary tool used by the Fed to control the money supply in the United States. The seven members of the Board of Governors, plus the twelve presidents of the Federal Reserve district banks, participate in the FOMC meetings, but at any point in time, only twelve of the nineteen members will get to vote. The twelve voting members of this important policy-making arm of the Fed are (1) the seven members of the Board of Governors, (2) the president of the New

Federal Open Market Committee (FOMC)
A committee of the Federal Reserve system that establishes Fed policy with regard to the buying and selling of government securities—the primary mechanism used to control the money supply. It is composed of the seven members of the Board of Governors and the twelve district bank presidents of the Fed.

EXHIBIT 4

The 12 Federal Reserve Districts

The map shows the 12 Federal Reserve districts and the city in which the district bank is located. These district banks monitor the commercial banks in their region and assist them with the clearing of checks.

If you look at any dollar bill, it will identify the Federal Reserve district bank that initially issued the currency. The Board of Governors of the Fed is located in Washington, D.C.

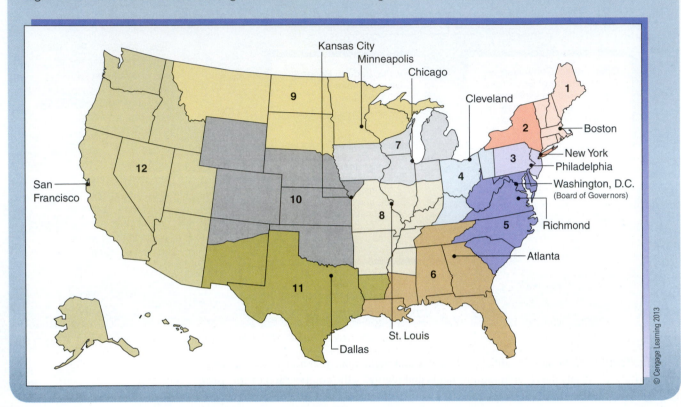

York district bank, and (3) four (of the remaining eleven) additional presidents of the Fed's district banks, who rotate as voting members. The FOMC meets every four to six weeks in the huge conference room of the Federal Reserve Building in Washington, D.C.

The independence of the Fed Like the Supreme Court, the structure of the Federal Reserve provides it with considerable independence from both Congress and the executive branch of government. Several factors contribute to this independence. The lengthy terms—fourteen years—protect the seven members of the Fed's Board of Governors from political pressures. Because their terms are staggered—a new governor is appointed only every two years—even two-term presidents are well into their second term before they are able to appoint a majority of the Fed's governing board. The Fed's earnings on its financial assets, mostly government bonds, provide it with substantially more funding than is needed to cover its operating costs. Thus, it is not dependent upon Congress for funding allocations. The Fed does not even have to undergo audits from the General Accounting Office, a government agency that audits the books of most government operations. This independence of the Fed is designed to reduce the likelihood that political pressures will adversely affect its ability to follow a stable, noninflationary monetary policy.

Does the independence of a central bank affect policy? There is considerable variation in the independence of central banks. Like the Fed, the European Central bank and the central banks of Japan, England, and Canada also have considerable independence from the other branches of their governments. In other instances, however, central banks are directly beholden to political officials. Studies indicate that central banks that are strongly influenced by political considerations are more likely to follow inflationary policies. Politicians in countries with high budget deficits have often pressured their central banks to expand the money supply in order to finance government spending. When they do so, the result is rapid growth in the money supply and inflation.

13-6b HOW THE FED CONTROLS THE MONEY SUPPLY

The Fed has four major tools it can use to control the money supply: (1) the establishment of reserve requirements for banks, (2) buying and selling U.S. government securities and other financial assets in the open market, (3) the volume of loans extended to banks and other institutions, and (4) the interest rate it pays banks on funds held as reserves. We will analyze in detail how each of these tools can be used to regulate the amount of money in circulation.

Reserve requirements The Federal Reserve System requires banking institutions (including credit unions and savings and loan associations) to maintain reserves against the checking deposits of their customers. The reserves of banking institutions are composed of (1) currency held by the bank (vault cash) and (2) deposits of the bank with the Federal Reserve System. A bank can always obtain additional currency by drawing on its deposits with the Federal Reserve. So, both the bank's cash on hand and its deposits with the Fed can be used to meet the demands of depositors. Both therefore count as reserves.

Exhibit 5 indicates the required reserve ratio—the percentage of each deposit category that banks are required to keep in reserve (either as vault cash or deposits with the Fed). As of December 2012, the reserve requirement for checking accounts was set at 3 percent for amounts above $12.4 million up to $79.5 million and 10 percent for amounts in excess of $79.5 million. Currently, banks are not required to keep reserves against their savings and time deposits or against the first $12.4 million of their checking deposits.

Why are commercial banks required to maintain assets in the form of reserves? One reason is to prevent imprudent bankers from overextending loans and thereby placing themselves in a poor position to deal with any sudden increase in withdrawals by depositors. The quantity of reserves needed to meet such emergencies is not left totally to the judgment of individual bankers. The Fed imposes the reserve level.

The Fed's control over reserve requirements, however, is important for another reason. By altering reserve requirements, the Fed can alter the funds banks have available to extend loans and undertake other investments. In turn, the volume of these loans and investments will alter the money supply.

If the Fed wanted to increase the supply of money, it would reduce the reserve requirements. The lower reserve requirements would increase the excess reserves of banks, placing them in a position to extend more loans and thereby increase the money supply. During normal times, the profit-seeking banks will use the newly created excess reserves to extend additional credit throughout the economy. As they do so, their actions will expand the money supply.

EXHIBIT 5

The Required Reserve Ratio of Banking Institutions

Banking institutions are required to maintain 3 percent reserves against checking account deposits of over $12.4 million and up to $79.5 million and 10 percent reserves for transaction deposits over $79.5 million (in effect December 2012).

CHECKING ACCOUNTS[a]		
0–$12.4 MILLION	$12.4–$79.5 MILLION	>$79.5 MILLION
0%	3%	10%

[a]The dividing points are adjusted each year to reflect changes in total checking account deposits in all banking institutions.

Source: http://www.federalreserve.gov.

An increase in the reserve requirements will have the opposite effect. The higher reserve requirements increase the funds that banks must maintain in reserve against the checking deposits of their customers. In order to meet the higher reserve requirements, many banks will reduce their outstanding loans and investments. As the volume of loans (and other forms of credit) extended by banks declines, so, too, will the money supply. ***Thus, an increase in the reserve requirements will reduce the supply of money.***

Banks can maintain reserves in excess of the level required by the Fed. However, they are in business to make money, and it will generally be more profitable for them to hold interest-earning assets like loans and bonds rather than excess reserves. Before 2008, most banks shaved their excess reserves to low levels, and, as a result, the excess reserves for the banking system as a whole were minimal. This changed dramatically during the economic crisis of 2008–2009. We will consider this change in more detail as we proceed.

In recent years, the Fed has seldom used its regulatory power over reserve requirements to alter the supply of money. Why? Several factors combine to provide the explanation. First, changes in reserve requirements can be disruptive to banking operations. An increase in the required reserve ratio may force many banks to sell securities quickly or call in loans, even if there has been no change in the level of their deposits. Second, reserve requirement changes are a blunt instrument—small changes in reserve requirements can sometimes lead to large changes in the money supply. Moreover, the magnitude and timing of a change in the money supply resulting from a change in reserve requirements are difficult to predict with precision. For these reasons, the Fed has usually preferred to use other monetary tools.

Open market operations
The buying and selling of U.S. government securities and other financial assets in the open market by the Federal Reserve.

Open market operations   The most common tool used by the Fed to alter the money supply is **open market operations**—the buying and selling of U.S. securities and other financial assets on the open market. As we indicated earlier, Fed policy in this area is conducted by the Federal Open Market Committee (FOMC). This committee meets every few weeks to map out the Fed's policy.

For six decades following World War II, the Fed purchased and sold only U.S. government securities in its conduct of open market operations. However, since December 2007, the Fed has been buying and selling a broader range of financial assets, including corporate bonds, commercial paper, and mortgage-backed securities. If the Fed wants to expand the money supply, it simply purchases more of these financial assets. It pays for them merely by writing a check on itself. Unlike you and me, the Fed does not have to check to see if it has adequate funds in its account. ***When the Fed buys things, it injects "new money" into the economy in the form of additional currency in circulation and deposits with commercial banks. In essence, the Fed creates money out of nothing.***

Consider the following case. Suppose the Fed purchases $10,000 of U.S. securities from Maria Valdez. The Fed receives the securities, and Valdez receives a check for $10,000. If she merely cashes the check drawn on the Federal Reserve, the amount of currency in circulation would expand by $10,000, increasing the money supply by that amount. If, as is more likely to be the case, she deposits the funds in her checking account at the First National Bank, her checking account will increase by $10,000, and new excess reserves will be created. The First National Bank is required to increase its reserve holdings by only a fraction of Valdez's $10,000 deposit. Assuming that the bank is required to keep 10 percent in reserves, it can now extend new loans of up to $9,000 while maintaining its initial reserve position. As the money deposit multiplier indicates, the extension of the new loans will contribute to a further expansion in the money supply. Part of the new loans will eventually be deposited in other banks, and these banks will also be able to extend additional loans. As the process continues, the money supply expands by a multiple of the securities purchased by the Fed.

Open market operations can also be used to reduce the money supply. ***If the Fed wants to reduce the money supply, it sells some of its current holdings of government securities or other assets.*** When the Fed sells assets, a buyer like Maria Valdez will pay for them with a check drawn on a commercial bank. As the check clears, both the buyer's checking deposits and the reserves of the bank on which the check was written will decline. Thus, the action will reduce the money supply both directly (by reducing checking deposits) and indirectly (by reducing the quantity of reserves available to the banking system).

Extension of loans by the Fed When banking institutions borrow from the Federal Reserve, they must pay interest on the loans. Historically, member banks have borrowed from the Fed primarily to meet temporary shortages of reserves. The interest rate that banks pay on these short-term loans from the Federal Reserve is called the **discount rate**. These loans through the discount window are for brief time periods, a few days or weeks, in order to provide a bank a little time to adjust its loan and investment portfolios and bring its reserves in line with the requirements. Essentially, these discount rate loans are a temporary bridge extended to banks with a short-term liquidity problem, and typically they are repaid in a matter of days or a few months at the most. Other things being constant, an increase in the discount rate will reduce borrowing from the Fed and thereby exert a restrictive impact on the money supply. Conversely, a lower discount rate will make it cheaper for banks to borrow from the Fed and exert an expansionary impact on the supply of money.

The discount rate is closely related to the interest rate in the **federal funds market**. The federal funds market is a private loanable funds market in which banks with excess reserves extend short-term loans (sometimes for as little as a day) to other banks trying to meet their reserve requirements. The interest rate in the federal funds market fluctuates with the demand for loanable funds. In recent years, the Fed has linked the discount rate to the federal funds rate, typically setting the discount interest rate a fraction of a percent higher than the Fed's target federal funds rate.

Announcements following the regular meetings of the Fed's Board of Governors often focus on the Fed's target for the federal funds rate. If the Fed wants to lower the federal funds interest rate, it will purchase government securities or other financial assets and thereby inject additional reserves into the banking system. This will expand the supply of money and reduce the federal funds rate. Conversely, if the Fed wants to increase the federal funds rate, it will sell some of its asset holdings and thereby drain reserves from the system. In turn, the reduction in the reserves will lower the money supply and place upward pressure on the federal funds rate.

Before 2008, the Fed extended only short-term discount rate loans, and they were extended only to member banks. As the Fed responded to the severe downturn of 2008, there was a dramatic change in its loan extension policy. The Fed began making longer-term loans as well as loans to nonbank financial institutions such as insurance companies and brokerage firms. Like the discount rate loans, these new types of loans inject additional reserves into the banking system and thereby exert an expansionary impact on the money supply.

Discount rate
The interest rate the Federal Reserve charges banking institutions for short-term loans.

Federal funds market
A loanable funds market in which banks seeking additional reserves borrow short-term funds (generally for seven days or less) from banks with excess reserves. The interest rate in this market is called the federal funds rate.

Interest rate the Fed pays banks on reserves Beginning in October 2008, the Fed began paying commercial banks interest on their reserves. As of June 2011, the Fed was paying commercial banks an interest rate equal to the target federal funds rate on both required and excess reserves. However, the Fed can set the interest rate on these reserves at whatever level it chooses. This provides it with another tool with which to conduct monetary policy.

If the Fed wants the banks to expand the money supply by extending more loans, it will set the interest rate paid on excess reserves at a very low level, possibly even zero. This will encourage banks to reduce their excess reserves, extend more loans, and thereby expand the supply of money. On the other hand, if the Fed wants to reduce the money supply, it can increase the interest rate paid on excess reserves and thereby provide commercial banks with a stronger incentive to hold excess reserves rather than extend more loans. This will reduce the money expansion multiplier and thereby reduce the money supply.

Controlling the money supply—a summary Exhibit 6 summarizes the monetary tools of the Federal Reserve. If the Fed wants to increase the money supply, it can decrease reserve requirements, purchase additional financial assets, extend additional loans, and/or lower the interest rate it pays banks on excess reserves. On the other hand, if the Fed wants to reduce the money supply, it can increase the reserve requirements, sell some of its asset holdings, extend fewer loans, and/or pay banks a higher interest rate on their excess reserves. Because the Fed typically seeks only small changes in the money stock (or its rate of increase), at any point in time, it typically uses only one of these tools, usually open market operations, to accomplish a desired objective.

EXHIBIT 6

Summary of Monetary Tools of the Federal Reserve	FEDERAL RESERVE POLICY	EXPANSIONARY MONETARY POLICY	RESTRICTIVE MONETARY POLICY
	1. Reserve requirements	*Reduce reserve requirements* because this will create additional excess reserves and induce banks to extend more loans, which will expand the money supply.	*Raise reserve requirements* because this will reduce the excess reserves of banks and induce them to make fewer loans, which will contract the money supply.
	2. Open market operations	*Purchase additional U.S. securities and other assets*, which will increase the money supply and also expand the reserves available to banks.	*Sell U.S. securities and other assets*, which will decrease the money supply and also contract the reserves available to banks.
	3. Extension of loans	*Extend more loans* because this will increase bank reserves, encouraging banks to make more loans and expand the money supply.	*Extend fewer loans* because this will decrease bank reserves, discourage bank loans, and reduce the money supply.
	4. Interest paid on excess bank reserves	*Reduce the interest paid on excess reserves* because this will induce banks to hold less reserves and extend more loans, which will expand the money supply.	*Increase the interest paid on excess reserves* because this will induce banks to hold more reserves and extend fewer loans, which will contract the money supply.

© Cengage Learning 2013

13-6c RECENT FED POLICY, THE MONETARY BASE, AND THE MONEY SUPPLY

Federal Reserve policy changed dramatically during the financial crisis of 2008. The Fed moved to both (1) assist troubled institutions, the collapse of which might have endangered the stability of financial markets and (2) inject additional reserves into the banking system in order to combat the sharp economic downturn.

Exhibit 7 illustrates the recent dramatic changes in Fed policy. Historically, the Fed's asset holdings have increased gradually and were primarily U.S. Treasury securities. As the top panel shows, the Fed's assets soared from $923 billion in the second quarter of 2008 to $2.1 trillion in the second quarter of 2009. Thus, Fed assets more than doubled in just 12 months. Increases in the Fed's asset holdings reflect expansionary monetary policy and they are often referred to as "quantitative easing." The surge of Fed asset holdings that began in the second half of 2008 is now known as QE1.

After a short lull, the Fed resumed its expansionary stance during the fourth quarter of 2010 and continued it through the second quarter of 2011. During this period Fed assets expanded by approximately another one-half trillion dollars, reaching $2.9 trillion mid-year 2011. Commentators often refer to this phase as QE2. In late 2012, the Fed announced QE3 and its plans to purchase $85 billion of Treasury and mortgage-backed securities each month. Execution of this plan resulted in another surge in asset holdings.

Exhibit 7 (bottom panel) shows the dramatic changes in the composition of Fed assets over the past few years. During QE1, Fed holdings of U.S. Treasury securities actually declined, but its purchases of mortgage-backed securities and loans skyrocketed. The huge increase in loans included extension of Fed credit to nonbanking institutions such as brokerage firms and insurance companies. During QE2, the situation was the opposite: U.S. Treasury securities soared while mortgage-backed securities and loan holdings fell. By mid-year 2011, Fed holdings of Treasury securities were $1.6 trillion, more than twice the year-end 2007 level. During QE3, there was a substantial increase in Fed holdings of Treasury and mortgage-backed securities, while loans returned to their historic low levels.

EXHIBIT 7

Federal Reserve Assets, 2000–2013

In response to the 2008–2009 recession, the Fed's asset holdings skyrocketed (top panel). During the initial phase of the reponse (QE1), the Fed sharply increased its purchases of mortgage-backed securities and extension of loans, including those to nonbanking institutions such as brokerage firms and insurance companies (bottom panel). Later, the Fed vastly increased its holdings of Treasury securities and continued to expand its total assets in 2010–2013 (QE2 and QE3).

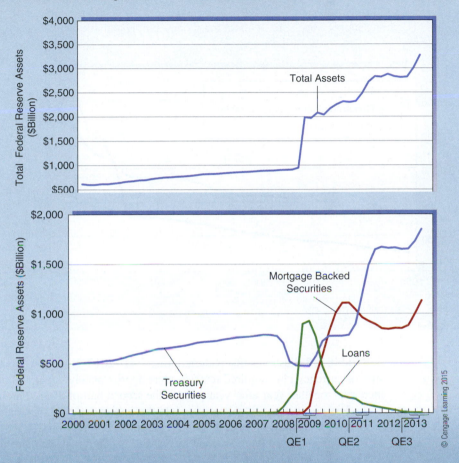

© Cengage Learning 2015

The Fed's huge increase in purchase of assets and extension of loans has dramatically increased the monetary base. The **monetary base** is equal to the currency in circulation plus the reserves of commercial banks (vault cash and reserve deposits with the Fed). The monetary base is important because it provides the foundation for the money supply. The currency in circulation contributes directly to the money supply, while the bank reserves provide the underpinnings for checking deposits.

Historically, as the Fed increased its assets, thereby injecting additional reserves into the economy and expanding the monetary base, the money supply increased by a multiple of the additional reserves just as the deposit expansion multiplier implies. Some of the additional reserves would flow into currency and some into bank reserves. In turn, banks would use their additional reserves to extend loans and undertake investments, which, along with the currency expansion, would expand the money supply. Excess reserves would be shaved to near zero because neither vault cash nor deposits with the Fed earn interest. Under these conditions, the (1) monetary base and (2) currency plus required reserves were virtually equal, and they moved up in lockstep together.

Monetary base
The sum of currency in circulation plus bank reserves (vault cash and reserves with the Fed). It reflects the purchases of financial assets and extension of loans by the Fed.

EXHIBIT 8

The Monetary Base, the M1 Money Supply, and Excess Reserves, 1990–2013

The monetary base provides the foundation for the money supply. It reflects the Fed's purchase of financial assets and its extension of loans. Before mid-year 2008, the monetary base grew gradually year after year and excess reserves were negligible. Thus, the monetary base and the sum of currency plus required reserves were virtually equal. While the M1 money supply was substantially greater than the monetary base, the two expanded together. But, since the second half of 2008, the Fed has injected a massive amount of reserves into the banking system and both the monetary base and excess reserves soared. If offsetting action is not taken, how will this dramatic increase in the monetary base affect the money supply in the future?

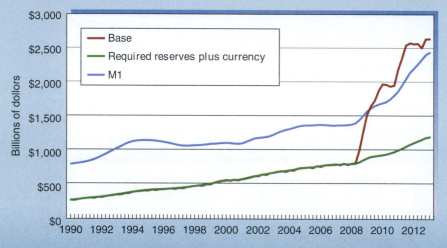

Source: http://www.economagic.com (All figures are in billions.)

Exhibit 8 illustrates this pattern during 1990–2013. Note how the monetary base and sum of currency plus required reserves were approximately equal and how they gradually increased together year after year prior to the second half of 2008. Throughout this period, as the Fed injected additional reserves into the system and thereby expanded the monetary base, the M1 money supply increased by a similar proportion. As the available reserves expanded, banks used them to extend loans and undertake investments until the excess reserves were negligible.

But all of this changed dramatically starting in the second half of 2008 as the Fed increased its security holdings and outstanding loans. As Exhibit 8 shows, the monetary base (currency plus bank reserves) soared between mid-year 2008 and mid-year 2009. By the first quarter of 2013, the monetary base was more than triple the 2008 level.

How did this more than tripling of the monetary base affect the money supply? The M1 money supply expanded at an average annual rate of 11 percent during 2009–2012, while the M2 measure grew at a 6 percent annual rate during the same period. By the first quarter of 2013, the M1 and M2 levels were, respectively, 72 percent and 35 percent greater than in 2008. Although these money supply increases are substantial, they are far less than their potential. The money supply has grown much less rapidly than the monetary base because the banks are holding vast excess reserves rather than using them to extend loans and undertake investments.

As Exhibit 8 shows, the excess reserves of banks have been more than $1 trillion since 2009. As of the first quarter of 2013, they stood at $1.6 trillion. Why aren't the banks using the excess reserves to make loans and investments? Given the weak economy, the demand for loans, particularly low-risk loans, is weak. Further, the Fed has pushed short-term interest rates down to virtually zero. Therefore, the yields available on Treasury bills and other low-risk investments are extremely low.

Let's summarize how the Fed has responded to the financial crisis of 2008. During the first year following the crisis, the Fed purchased more than a trillion dollars of mortgage-backed securities and vastly expanded its loans to banks and other financial institutions. During 2010–2012, it expanded its holdings of Treasury securities and continued to increase the monetary base. Most of this huge injection of reserves was held on the balance sheet of banks in the form of excess reserves. Thus, the M1 and M2 money supply figures increased far less than the monetary base. As the economy begins to recover, however, the huge overhang of excess reserves means that the money supply could soar if banks begin using them to extend loans and undertake investments. This would lead to inflation, and some fear that this will be the case.

If this begins to happen, Fed policy-makers hope to respond in a manner that will control the money supply growth and potential threat of inflation without throwing the economy back into recession. Will they be able to do so? What impact have the Fed policies had on the economy? What are the implications for the future? We will analyze these complex questions in the next two chapters.

13-6d THE FED AND THE TREASURY

Many students tend to confuse the Federal Reserve with the U.S. Treasury, probably because both sound like monetary agencies. However, the Treasury is a budgetary agency. If the federal government is running a budget deficit, the Treasury will issue U.S. securities as a method of financing the deficit. Newly issued U.S. securities are almost always sold to domestic or foreign investors (or government trust funds). Bonds issued by the Treasury to finance a budget deficit are seldom purchased directly by the Federal Reserve. In any case, the Treasury is primarily interested in obtaining funds so that it can pay Uncle Sam's bills. Except for nominal amounts, mostly coins, the Treasury does not issue money. Borrowing—the public sale of new U.S. securities—is the primary method used by the Treasury to cover any excess of expenditures in relation to revenues from taxes and other sources.

While the Treasury is concerned with how the federal government will pay its bills, the Fed is concerned primarily with the availability of money and credit for the entire economy. The Fed does not issue U.S. securities. It merely purchases and sells them as a means of controlling the economy's money supply. Unlike the Treasury, the Fed can purchase government bonds by writing a check on itself without having deposits, gold, or anything else to back it up. In doing so, the Fed creates money out of thin air. The Treasury does not have this power. The Fed does not have an obligation to meet the financial responsibilities of the U.S. government. That is the domain of the Treasury. Although the two agencies cooperate with each other, they are distinctly different institutions established for different purposes (see the accompanying **Thumbnail Sketch**).

Thumbnail Sketch

What Are the Differences between the U.S. Treasury and the Federal Reserve Banking System?

The U.S. Treasury

1. Is concerned with the finances of the federal government
2. Issues bonds and sells them to investors to finance the budget deficits of the federal government
3. Does not determine the money supply

The Federal Reserve

1. Is concerned with the monetary climate of the economy
2. Does not issue bonds
3. Controls the money supply and often uses the buying and selling of bonds issued by the U.S. Treasury to do so

It is important to recognize that the buying and selling of bonds by the Treasury and by the Fed have different effects on the supply of money. The key point here is that the Treasury and the Fed handle revenues collected from the selling of bonds in different ways. When the Treasury issues and sells bonds, it does so in order to generate additional funds to cover the spending of the federal government. The people who buy the bonds from the Treasury have less money, but when the federal government spends the funds, the recipients of the spending will have more money. Thus, Treasury borrowing and spending do not change the supply of money.

In contrast, when the Fed sells bonds, in effect, it takes the revenues and holds them, keeping them out of circulation. Because this money is out of circulation and can no longer be used for the purchase of goods and services, the money supply shrinks. However, if the Fed later wishes to increase the money supply, it can buy bonds, which will increase the availability of bank reserves and the money supply.

13-7 AMBIGUITIES IN THE MEANING AND MEASUREMENT OF THE MONEY SUPPLY

In the past, economists have generally used the *growth rate* of the money supply (either M1 or M2) to gauge the direction of monetary policy. A rapid growth rate of the money supply was indicative of expansionary monetary policy—a policy that was adding stimulus to the economy. Conversely, slow growth, or a decline, in the money stock implied a more restrictive monetary policy. However, financial innovations and structural changes can alter the nature of money across time. Let's consider four changes during the past several decades that have altered the nature of money and the reliability of money supply growth figures as a gauge of monetary policy.

1. Introduction of interest-earning checking accounts.
Throughout most of the 1970s, M1 consisted almost entirely of currency and demand deposits. At the time, regulations virtually prohibited banks from offering their customers interest-earning checking accounts. Increased competition from mutual funds led to the repeal of the regulatory restraints in 1980, and this repeal was followed by rapid growth of interest-earning checking deposits. In turn, the growth of these deposits pushed up the growth rate of the M1 money supply. The growth of M1 during the 1980s, however, was misleading. To a degree, it reflected a change in the nature of the M1 money supply. Interest-earning checking accounts are less costly to hold than currency and demand deposits. In essence, interest-earning checking accounts are partly medium-of-exchange money and partly savings. As a result, the M1 money supply of the 1980s is not precisely comparable with the figures for earlier years.

2. Shift from interest-earning checking deposits to money market mutual funds.
Beginning in 1994, a number of banks began to encourage customers to move deposits from interest-earning checking accounts into money market deposit accounts. Each of these accounts provides customers with similar services. However, because interest-earning checking deposits are included in M1 but money market deposits are not, this shift reduced the size of the M1 money supply figures. As with the introduction of interest-earning checking during the 1980s, these shifts distorted the M1 money supply statistics and reduced their comparability across time periods.

3. Widespread use of the U.S. dollar outside of the United States.
The U.S. dollar is widely used in other countries. To a degree, this has been true for a long time. However, in recent years, many countries have relaxed legal restraints that limited the domestic use of foreign currencies (and the maintenance of foreign currency bank accounts). The number of countries in which it is legal for citizens to maintain a foreign currency bank account

from 42 in 1985 to more than 100.[2] As noted earlier, the currency component of the M1 money supply was $1,109 billion in April 2013. According to a recent study by the Federal Reserve, more than one-half and perhaps as much as two-thirds of this currency is held overseas. The movement of these funds abroad (and our inability to measure them with any degree of precision) reduces the reliability of the M1 money supply figures and their growth as an indicator of monetary policy. (*Note:* There is also some impact on M2. However, because the currency component is a much smaller proportion of M2 than M1, the distortion of M2 is less severe.)

4. Substitution of electronic payments for checks and cash. Increasingly, money is becoming electronic. More and more consumer purchases are being handled with debit cards, credit cards, and electronic transfers rather than by check or cash. Many people have their "paycheck" deposited directly into their bank account and make regular payments like those for utilities, mortgage and auto loans, and investment accounts with automatic transfers. With the touch of a few computer keys, you can also shop on the Internet and use your deposits to pay for magazines, financial advice, and numerous consumer goods. Currently, less than half of consumer purchases are paid for with either check or cash, compared to 80 percent just a decade ago. These changes in payment methods make it possible for both individuals and businesses to hold smaller money balances (cash and checking deposits) than would otherwise be the case. They also reduce the comparability across time periods of the money supply data, particularly the M1 figures.

Because of these dynamic changes in the nature of money, economists now place less emphasis on the growth rate of the money supply figures as a monetary policy indicator. Most now rely on a combination of factors to evaluate the direction and appropriateness of monetary policy. We will follow this procedure as we consider the impact of monetary policy in subsequent chapters.

---

[2]See James Gwaney, Robert Lawson, and Joshua Hall, *Economic Freedom of the World: 2012 Annual Report* (Vancouver, British Columbia: Fraser Institute, 2012).

LOOKING AHEAD

In this chapter, we focused on the banking industry and the mechanics of monetary policy. The following chapter will analyze how monetary policy affects output, growth, and the general level of prices.

KEY POINTS

- Money is a financial asset that is widely accepted as a medium of exchange. It is a means of storing purchasing power for the future and is used as a unit of account. Without money, exchange would be both costly and tedious. Money derives its value from its scarcity (supply) relative to its usefulness (demand).

- There are two primary measures of the money supply. The narrowest definition of money supply (M1) includes only (1) currency in the hands of the public, (2) checkable deposits (both demand and interest earning) held in depository institutions, and (3) traveler's checks. The broader M2 money supply includes M1 plus (1) savings deposits, (2) time deposits (of less than $100,000), and (3) money market mutual fund shares.

- Banking is a business. Commercial banks, savings and loan associations, and credit unions provide similar services and they are all part of the banking industry.

- Banks provide their depositors with the safekeeping of money, clearing services on checkable deposits, and interest payments on time (and some checking) deposits. They earn most of their income by extending loans and investing in interest-earning securities.

- Under a fractional reserve banking system, banks are required to maintain only a fraction of their deposits in the form of reserves (vault cash or deposits with the Fed). Excess reserves may be invested or loaned to customers. When banks extend loans, they create additional deposits and thereby expand the money supply.

- The Federal Reserve System was established to provide a stable monetary framework for the entire economy. The Fed is a banker's bank. The structure of the Fed is designed to insulate it from political pressures so it will have greater freedom to follow policies more consistent with economic stability.

- The Fed has four major tools with which to control the money supply: (1) the establishment of reserve requirements, (2) open market operations, (3) the extension of loans, and (4) setting the interest rate paid to banks on their reserves. If the Fed wanted to increase the money supply, it could decrease the reserves banks are required to hold, buy government bonds and other financial assets in the open market, extend more loans, or reduce the interest rate it pays banks on their excess reserves. Open market operations—the buying or selling of bonds and other assets—have been the primary tool used by the Fed to alter the money supply.

- The monetary base provides the foundation for the money supply. The Fed alters the monetary base through its purchases of assets and extension of loans. The monetary base increased sharply starting in the second half of 2008, as the Fed shifted toward a more expansionary monetary policy to combat the severe downturn.

- The Federal Reserve and the U.S. Treasury are distinct agencies. The Fed is concerned primarily with the money supply and the establishment of a stable monetary climate, whereas the Treasury focuses on budgetary matters—tax revenues, government expenditures, and the financing of government debt.

- Historically, the rate of change of the money supply has been used to judge the direction and intensity of monetary policy. However, recent financial innovations and structural changes (for example, the widespread use of U.S. currency in other countries) have blurred the meaning of money and reduced the reliability of the money growth figures as a monetary policy indicator.

CRITICAL ANALYSIS QUESTIONS

1. *What is meant by the statement "This asset is illiquid"? List some things you own and rank them from most liquid to most illiquid.

2. What determines whether a financial asset is included in the M1 money supply? Why are interest-earning checkable deposits included in M1, whereas interest-earning savings accounts and Treasury bills are not?

3. *What makes money valuable? Does money perform an economic service? Explain. Could money perform its function better if there were twice as much of it? Why or why not?

4. "People are poor because they don't have very much money. Yet, central bankers keep money scarce. If people had more money, poverty could be eliminated." Evaluate this view. Do you think it reflects sound economics?

5. Why are banks able to maintain reserves that are only a fraction of the demand and saving deposits of their customers? Is your money safe in a bank? Why or why not?

6. *Suppose you withdraw $100 from your checking account. How does this transaction affect (a) the supply of money, (b) the reserves of your bank, and (c) the excess reserves of your bank?

7. The excess reserves of the banking system were quite large during mid-year 2013. If the banks use these excess reserves to extend additional loans, what will happen to the money supply? Explain. Is this a potential problem? Why or why not?

8. *How will the following actions affect the money supply?
   a. a reduction in the discount rate
   b. an increase in the reserve requirements
   c. purchase by the Fed of $100 million in U.S. securities from a commercial bank

   d. sale by the U.S. Treasury of $100 million in newly issued bonds to a commercial bank
   e. an increase in the discount rate
   f. sale by the Fed of $200 million in U.S. securities to a private investor

9. What's wrong with this way of thinking? "When the government runs a budget deficit, it simply pays its bills by printing more money. As the newly printed money works its way through the economy, it waters down the value of paper money already in circulation. Thus, it takes more money to buy things. Budget deficits are the major cause of inflation."

10. *If the Federal Reserve does not take any offsetting action, what would happen to the supply of money if the general public decided to increase its holdings of currency and decrease its checking deposits by an equal amount?

11. What is the federal funds interest rate? If the Fed wants to use open market operations to lower the federal funds rate, what action should it take? Explain.

12. *If the Fed wants to expand the money supply, why is it more likely to do so by purchasing bonds and other financial assets rather than by lowering reserve requirements?

13. Are the following statements true or false?
   a. "You can never have too much money."
   b. "When you deposit currency in a commercial bank, cash goes out of circulation and the money supply declines."
   c. "If the Fed would create more money, Americans would achieve a higher standard of living."

14. Why is the actual money deposit multiplier generally less than the potential multiplier?

15. How would the following influence the growth rates of the M1 and M2 money supply figures over time?

    a. an increase in the quantity of U.S. currency held overseas

    b. a shift of funds from interest-earning checking deposits to money market mutual funds

    c. a reduction in the holdings of currency by the general public because debit cards have become more popular and widely accepted

    d. the shift of funds from money market mutual funds into stock and bond mutual funds because the fees to invest in the latter have declined

16. *Suppose that the Federal Reserve purchases a bond for $100,000 from Donald Truck, who deposits the proceeds in the Manufacturer's National Bank.

    a. What will be the impact of this transaction on the supply of money?

    b. If the reserve requirement ratio is 20 percent, what is the maximum amount of additional loans that the Manufacturer's Bank will be able to extend as the result of Truck's deposit?

    c. Given the 20 percent reserve requirement, what is the maximum increase in the quantity of checkable deposits that could result throughout the entire banking system because of the Fed's action?

    d. Would you expect this to happen? Why or why not? Explain.

17. Suppose that the reserve requirement is 10 percent and the balance sheet of the People's National Bank looks like the accompanying example.

    a. What are the required reserves of People's National Bank? Does the bank have any excess reserves?

    b. What is the maximum loan that the bank could extend?

    c. Indicate how the bank's balance sheet would be altered if it extended this loan.

    d. Suppose that the required reserves were 20 percent. If this were the case, would the bank be in a position to extend any additional loans? Explain.

ASSETS		LIABILITIES	
Vault cash	$ 20,000	Checking deposits	$200,000
Deposits at Fed	30,000		
Securities	45,000	Net worth	15,000
Loans	120,000		

18. *Suppose that the reserve requirements are 10 percent and that the Federal Reserve purchases $2 billion in securities from a brokerage firm on a given day.

    a. How will this transaction affect the M1 money supply?

    b. If the brokerage firm that sold the bonds to the Fed deposits the proceeds of the sale into its account with Nation's Bank, what is the maximum amount of additional loans that Nation's Bank will be able to extend as a result of this deposit?

    c. If additional loans are extended throughout the banking system and the proceeds are always redeposited back into a checking account, by how much will the M1 money supply increase if banks use all their additional reserves to extend new loans?

*Asterisk denotes questions for which answers are given in Appendix B.

CHAPTER 14
Modern Macroeconomics and Monetary Policy

FOCUS

- How does monetary policy affect interest rates, output, and employment?
- Can monetary policy stimulate real GDP in the short run? Can it do so in the long run?
- How does monetary policy affect economic stability? How does it affect inflation?
- What are the proper goals of monetary policy?
- How did the Fed respond to the Crisis of 2008? What will be the future impact of this policy?

The conventional wisdom once held that money doesn't matter. Now there is wide agreement that monetary policy can significantly affect real economic activity in the short run, though only price level in the long run.
—Daniel L. Thornton and David C. Wheelock[1]

[1]Daniel L. Thornton and David C. Wheelock, "Editor's Introduction," *Federal Reserve Bank of St. Louis: Review* (May/June 1995): vii.

In the preceding chapter, we noted that many consider the chair of the Federal Reserve System to be the second most important person—next to the president—in the United States. Why is this so? Along with other members of the Fed's Board of Governors and Federal Open Market Committee, the Fed chairman is in charge of monetary policy. When monetary policy keeps prices stable—that is, when it keeps the inflation rate at a persistently low level—markets operate more smoothly. Conversely, the consequences of monetary instability and high rates of inflation are often disastrous. This makes the conduct of monetary policy extremely important.

Until now, within the framework of the aggregate demand–aggregate supply model, we assumed that the supply of money was constant. We now relax this assumption. The previous chapter outlined the tools the Fed has to alter the supply of money. This chapter focuses on how monetary policy works—how changes in the supply of money affect interest rates, output, and prices.

14-1 IMPACT OF MONETARY POLICY: A BRIEF HISTORICAL BACKGROUND

Like the modern view of fiscal policy, the modern view of monetary policy has evolved over the years. In the aftermath of the Great Depression and Keynesian revolution, there was great debate about the importance of monetary policy. During the 1950s and 1960s, many economists argued that monetary policy could be used to control inflation but that it was often ineffective as a means of stimulating aggregate demand. It was popular to draw an analogy between monetary policy and the workings of a string. Like a string, monetary policy could be used to "pull" (hold back) price increases and thereby control inflation. However, just as one cannot "push" with a string, many leading economists did not believe that monetary policy could be used to push (stimulate) aggregate demand.

Beginning in the late 1950s, this view was hotly contested by Nobel laureate Milton Friedman and other economists, who later became known as monetarists. The monetarists argued that changes in the money supply had a powerful influence on the economy's output in the short run, but in the long run, monetary policy affected only the general level of prices. Furthermore, monetarists argued that erratic monetary policy was the primary *source* of both economic instability and inflation. Milton Friedman summarized the monetarists' position in his 1967 presidential address to the American Economic Association when he stated,

> *Every major contraction in this country has been either produced by monetary disorder or greatly exacerbated by monetary disorder. Every major inflation episode has been produced by monetary expansion.*[2]

A modern view of monetary policy emerged from this debate. While minor disagreements remain, most economists now agree that monetary policy exerts an impact on output, employment, inflation, and economic stability.[3] We now turn to the presentation of this modern consensus view.

14-2 THE DEMAND AND SUPPLY OF MONEY

Why do individuals and businesses want to hold cash and bank deposit money rather than bonds, stocks, automobiles, buildings, and consumer durables? As you think about this question, don't confuse (1) the desire to hold money balances with (2) the desire for more

---

[2]Milton Friedman, "The Role of Monetary Policy," *American Economic Review* (March 1968): 12.

[3]The evolution of the views of Paul Samuelson, who might properly be regarded as the father of American Keynesian economics, illustrates the change in the Keynesian view with regard to the relative importance of monetary and fiscal policy. Commenting on the twelfth edition of his classic text in 1985, Samuelson stated, "In the early editions of the book, fiscal policy was top banana. In later editions that emphasis changed to equality. In this edition we've taken a stand that monetary policy is most important."

wealth (or income). Of course, all of us would like to have more wealth, but we may be perfectly satisfied with our holdings of money in relation to our holdings of other goods, *given our current level of wealth.* When we say people want to hold more (or less) money, we mean that they want to restructure their wealth toward larger (smaller) money balances.

People hold money for several reasons. At the most basic level, we hold money so that we can buy things. Households hold money balances so that they can pay for the weekly groceries, the monthly utilities and house payments, gasoline for the car, lunch for the kids, and other items purchased regularly. Businesses demand money so they can pay their workers, buy supplies, and conduct other transactions. People also hold money for unexpected expenses like an accident or a medical emergency. Economists call this the *precautionary motive* for holding money. In addition, money is a means of storing value—a convenient way to set aside purchasing power for future use.

Higher interest rates make it more costly to hold money, however. Consider the cost of holding $1,000 in currency and demand deposits (which do not earn interest) rather than in interest-earning bonds, for example. If the interest rate is 10 percent, it will cost you $100 per year to hold an additional $1,000 of non–interest-earning money. In contrast, if the interest rate is 1 percent, the annual cost of holding the $1,000 money balance will be only $10. Even if you put the $1,000 in an interest-earning checking account, you could probably earn more interest if you purchased a U.S. Treasury Security or some other less liquid form of savings with the funds. Thus, the opportunity cost of holding money is directly related to the nominal interest rate.

A curve that outlines the relationship between the interest rate (measured on the *y*-axis) and the quantity of money (measured on the *x*-axis) is called the **demand for money.** As part (a) of **Exhibit 1** shows, there is an inverse relationship between the interest rate and the quantity of money demanded. This inverse relationship reflects the fact that higher interest rates make it more costly to hold money instead of interest-earning assets like savings deposits and Treasury Securities. Therefore, as interest rates rise, individuals and businesses will try to manage their affairs with smaller money balances.

The demand for money balances will generally increase with the nominal value of transactions. If wages and prices increase, people will need more money in their wallets (or checking accounts) to make their regular daily, weekly, and monthly purchases. Businesses will also require more money to pay their bills. Similarly, if prices remain constant but the quantity of goods bought and sold in the economy increases, larger money balances will

Demand for money

A curve that indicates the relationship between the interest rate and the quantity of money people want to hold. Because higher interest rates increase the opportunity cost of holding money, the quantity of money demanded will be inversely related to the interest rate.

OUTSTANDING ECONOMIST

MILTON FRIEDMAN (1912–2006)

Milton Friedman, the 1976 recipient of the Nobel Prize, is widely regarded as the most influential spokesman for a free market economy in the twentieth century. More than anyone else, Friedman developed the modern view of monetary policy. At a time when the role of money was largely ignored by the dominant Keynesian perspective, Friedman almost single-handedly convinced the economics profession that monetary policy exerted a strong impact on the economy. His *Monetary History of the United States* (1963) with Anna Schwartz presented powerful evidence that monetary policy not only mattered but it was also the major source of economic instability. The chapter on the Great Contraction illustrated that the Great Depression was primarily, if not exclusively, the result of a perverse monetary policy rather than a defect of market economies. Even his critics eventually concluded that, by and large, his views about the importance of monetary policy were correct.

Friedman's popular books *Capitalism and Freedom* (1962) and *Free to Choose* (1980), coauthored with his wife, Rose, are classic treatises in support of economic freedom. He had an uncanny ability to connect with both the general public and the brightest in his field. After retiring from the University of Chicago, he went on to spend nearly three decades on the faculty of Stanford University. Most people would rate Friedman and John Maynard Keynes as the most influential economists of the twentieth century.

EXHIBIT 1

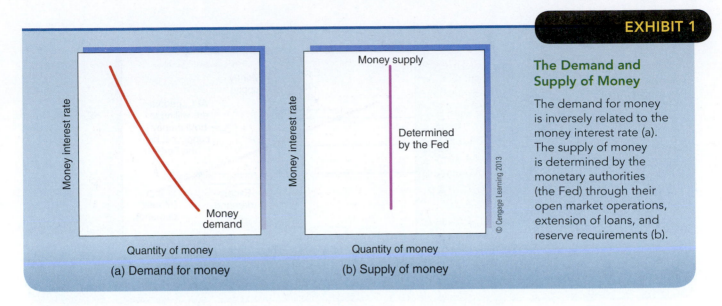

(a) Demand for money   (b) Supply of money

The Demand and Supply of Money

The demand for money is inversely related to the money interest rate (a). The supply of money is determined by the monetary authorities (the Fed) through their open market operations, extension of loans, and reserve requirements (b).

be needed to conduct those transactions. In other words, as nominal GDP increases, as the result of *either* higher prices or the growth of real output, the demand for money balances will also increase. When this happens, the entire demand curve for money will shift to the right. Conversely, a decline in nominal GDP will decrease the demand for money, shifting the curve to the left.

Changes in institutional factors can also affect the demand for money. For example, the greater availability and widespread use of credit and debit cards in recent years has made it easier for households to manage their affairs with less money. The increased availability of short-term loans has had a similar effect. Both of these factors have gradually reduced the demand for money (shifting the entire curve to the left).

As we discussed in the previous chapter, monetary policy is conducted by the monetary authorities—the Federal Reserve in the case of the United States. The Fed can use reserve requirements, the extension of loans, and especially open market operations to regulate the supply of money. Changes in the interest rate do not alter the Fed's ability to determine the supply of money. Therefore, as Exhibit 1 (part b) shows, the money supply schedule is vertical. The vertical supply curve reflects that the quantity of money is determined by Fed policy, and the Fed's ability to set the money supply is unaffected by the interest rate.

14-2a THE EQUILIBRIUM BETWEEN MONEY DEMAND AND MONEY SUPPLY

Exhibit 2 brings money demand and money supply together and shows how they determine the equilibrium rate of interest. The money interest rate will move toward i_e when the quantity of money demanded by households and businesses is just equal to the quantity supplied by the Fed. At the equilibrium interest rate, people are willing to hold the stock of money the Fed has supplied to the economy.

At a preceding equilibrium interest rate, i_2, for example, people will not want to hold as much money as the Fed has supplied. Accordingly, they will try to reduce their money balances. A number of people (and businesses) will do so by using some of their money balances to buy bonds. This increase in the demand for bonds will drive bond prices up and interest rates down. (*Remember:* Higher bond prices imply lower interest rates.) As a result, the money interest rate will move toward the i_e equilibrium. In contrast, at a below-equilibrium money interest rate, i_3, for example, an excess demand for money will be present. People would like to hold a larger quantity of money than the Fed has supplied. In this case, people will sell some of the bonds they own to get more money. In turn, the sale of their bonds will reduce bond prices and put upward pressure on interest rates. This will cause the interest rate to once again move toward i_e.

Money Supply, Money Demand, and Equilibrium

The money interest rate will tend to gravitate toward equilibrium, i_e, where the quantity of money demanded by households and businesses will equal the quantity of money supplied by the Fed.

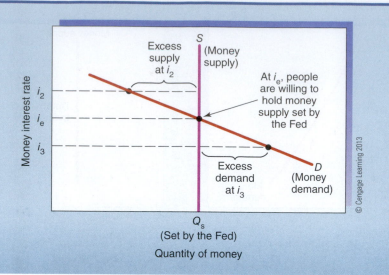

Excess supply at i_2

S (Money supply)

At i_e, people are willing to hold money supply set by the Fed

i_2

i_e

i_3

Excess demand at i_3

D (Money demand)

Money interest rate

Q_s (Set by the Fed)

Quantity of money

© Cengage Learning 2013

14-3 HOW DOES MONETARY POLICY AFFECT THE ECONOMY?

How will a change in the money supply affect the economy? As we previously discussed, the Fed typically uses open market operations to control the supply of money. If the Fed wants to shift to a more **expansionary monetary policy**, it will generally buy bonds issued by the U.S. Treasury or a financial institution. The Fed will pay for the bonds by writing a check on itself, thereby creating money out of thin air; and as the check clears, it will also make additional reserves available to the banks.

Exhibit 3 shows the impact on the economy. Let's first consider the situation in which the money interest rate (i_1 in the money balances market) is equal to the real interest rate (r_1 in the loanable funds market). This indicates that the expected rate of inflation is zero. When the Fed purchases bonds in order to increase the money supply (shifting S_1 to S_2 in part a), it bids up bond prices and injects additional reserves into the banking system. Profit-seeking banks will generally use the additional reserves to extend more loans and increase their investments. This combination of factors—higher bond prices and excess reserves—will increase the supply of loanable funds (shift from S_1 to S_2 in part b). In the short run, this will cause the real interest rate to fall to r_2.

How will the Fed's bond purchases, the creation of additional bank reserves, and a lower real interest rate influence the demand for goods and services? As part (c) of Exhibit 3 shows, aggregate demand will increase (shift from AD_1 to AD_2). Economists stress the importance of three factors that contribute to this increase in aggregate demand.

1. The lower real interest rate will make current investment and consumption cheaper. At the lower interest rate, entrepreneurs will undertake some investment projects they otherwise wouldn't have. Spending by firms on structures and equipment will increase. Likewise, consumers will decide to expand their purchases of automobiles and consumer durables, which can now be bought with smaller monthly payments.

2. The lower interest rate will tend to cause financial capital to move abroad, the foreign exchange rate of the dollar to depreciate, and net exports to expand. Here's how: As domestic interest rates fall, both domestic and foreign investors will shift some of their financial investments to countries where interest rates are higher and they can get better returns on their investments. As investors shift funds abroad, they will supply dollars and demand foreign currency to

Expansionary monetary policy

A shift in monetary policy designed to stimulate aggregate demand. Injection of additional bank reserves, lower short-term interest rates, and acceleration in the growth rate of the money supply are indicators of a more expansionary monetary policy.

EXHIBIT 3

(a) Money balances

(b) Loanable funds

(c) Goods and services (real GDP)

Lower r increases AD

© Cengage Learning 2013

The Transmission of Monetary Policy

When the Fed shifts to a more expansionary monetary policy, it will generally buy additional bonds. This will supply the banking system with additional reserves. Both the Fed's bond purchases and the banks' use of the additional reserves to extend new loans will increase the supply of loanable funds (shift it from S_1 to S_2, part b) and put downward pressure on the real rate of interest. As the real interest rate falls (to r_2), aggregate demand increases (to AD_2 in part c). Because the effects of the monetary expansion were unanticipated, the expansion in AD leads to both an increase in current output (to Y_2) and higher prices (inflation) in the short run. The increase in output, however, will only be temporary.

purchase the new foreign assets. This will cause the dollar to depreciate in the foreign exchange market. In turn, the depreciation in the exchange-rate value of the dollar will make imports more expensive for Americans and U.S. exports cheaper for foreigners. As a result, U.S. imports will decline and exports will expand. This increase in net exports will also stimulate the nation's aggregate demand as foreigners buy more U.S. goods and services.

3. The lower interest rate will tend to increase asset prices—for example, the prices of stocks and houses—which will also increase aggregate demand. Here's how this works: The lower interest rates will increase the value of the stream of income or services derived from assets. As a result, the prices of stocks, bonds, houses, and other assets will rise. In turn, the rising prices of these assets will increase the wealth of households, inducing them to consume more and thereby stimulate aggregate demand. Further, the higher prices of housing and other physical assets will make their production more profitable and motivate entrepreneurs to expand their investment spending on them. This, too, will add to aggregate demand. In summary, when the Fed purchases bonds and expands the availability of bank reserves the real interest rate will decline. The lower interest rate will lead to an increase in investment and consumption, a depreciation in the foreign exchange value of the dollar, and higher asset prices.

In turn, these factors will stimulate aggregate demand, output, and employment. This sequence is sometimes referred to as the interest rate transmission mechanism of monetary policy.[4]

14-3a THE EFFECTS OF AN UNANTICIPATED EXPANSIONARY MONETARY POLICY

As we have previously discussed, modern macroeconomic analysis emphasizes whether a change is anticipated or unanticipated. If people do not anticipate the increase in aggregate demand accompanying an expansionary monetary policy, the prices of products will rise more quickly than the costs of producing them in the short run. As a result, the profit margins of businesses will improve, and they will respond by expanding their output (as the increase in real output from Y_1 to Y_2 in part c of Exhibit 3 shows).

Exhibit 4 (part a) shows the potential of expansionary monetary policy to direct a recessionary economy to full employment. Consider an economy initially at output Y_1,

---

EXHIBIT 4

The Effects of Expansionary Monetary Policy

If the impact of an increase in aggregate demand accompanying an expansionary monetary policy is felt when the economy is operating below capacity, the policy will help direct the economy to a long-run full-employment equilibrium (E_2 in part a). In this case, the increase in output from Y_1 to Y_F will be long term. In contrast, if the stimulus on aggregate demand is imposed on an economy already at full employment (part b), it will lead to excess demand and higher product prices. Output will temporarily increase (to Y_2). However, in the long run, the strong demand will push up resource prices, shifting short-run aggregate supply to $SRAS_2$. The price level will rise to P_3, and output will recede (to Y_F) from its temporary high.

(a) Output is initially at less than full employment

© Cengage Learning 2013

(b) Output is initially at full employment

---

[4]There is also a more direct route through which expansionary monetary policy may stimulate aggregate demand. When the Fed expands the supply of money, it will create an "excess supply of money" *at the initial money interest rate*. People may respond by directly increasing their purchases of goods and services in an effort to reduce their money balances to desired levels. Obviously, this will increase aggregate demand. This direct path is most relevant when the government expands the supply of money by paying its bills with newly created currency. Because the money supply of the United States is generally expanded via open market operations and control of short-term interest rates, we have focused on the transmission of monetary policy through the interest rate. The implications of both the direct and indirect paths are identical—both indicate that expansionary monetary policy will stimulate aggregate demand.

which is below full-employment capacity (Y_F). Expansionary monetary policy will lower interest rates and increase aggregate demand (to AD_2). Real output will then expand (to Y_F). In essence, the expansionary monetary policy provides an alternative to the economy's self-corrective mechanism. If demand is unchanged, reductions in real interest rates and resource prices will eventually direct the economy back to full employment, but many economists believe that expansionary monetary policy can speed up this process.

How will an expansion of the money supply by the Fed influence the price level and output if the economy is already at full employment? Although this is not a desirable strategy, it is interesting to analyze the outcome. As part (b) of Exhibit 4 shows, an unanticipated shift to a more expansionary monetary policy will increase aggregate demand, causing the prices of products to rise relative to the costs of making them. Keep in mind that important production components, like labor, lease agreements, and insurance premiums are generally temporarily fixed by long-term contracts. When this is the case, real output will initially increase to Y_2, which is beyond the economy's long-run capacity of Y_F. However, the high rate of output (Y_2) will not be sustainable. Eventually, the long-term contracts based on the previously weaker demand (AD_1) will end, and the new agreements will reflect the new stronger demand. As a result, the temporarily fixed resource prices will rise pushing costs up, which will shift *SRAS* upward and to the left. Eventually, a new long-run equilibrium (E_2) will be established at a higher price level (P_3). Output will fall to Y_F. Thus, when an economy is already at full employment, an unexpected shift to a more expansionary monetary policy will temporarily increase output, but in the long run, it only leads to higher prices.

14-3b THE EFFECTS OF AN UNANTICIPATED RESTRICTIVE MONETARY POLICY

Suppose that the Fed moves toward a more **restrictive monetary policy** by selling bonds to the general public. The sale of bonds will reduce both the supply of money and the reserves of banks as people take money out of their accounts to buy the bonds. Exhibit 5 shows the impact of the more restrictive monetary policy on the loanable funds and goods and services markets. The Fed's sale of bonds increases their supply and pushes bond prices downward. It also drains reserves from the banking system as people buy the bonds

Restrictive monetary policy
A shift in monetary policy designed to reduce aggregate demand and put downward pressure on the general level of prices (or the rate of inflation). A reduction in bank reserves, higher short-term interest rates, and a reduction in the growth rate of the money supply are indicators of a more restrictive monetary policy.

EXHIBIT 5

The Short-Run Effects of a More Restrictive Monetary Policy

When the Fed shifts to a more restrictive policy, it sells bonds, which reduces the reserves available to banks, decreases the supply of loanable funds, and puts upward pressure on interest rates (a). The higher interest rates decrease aggregate demand (shift it to AD_2 in b). When the reduction in aggregate demand is unanticipated, real output will decline (to Y_2) and downward pressure on prices will result.

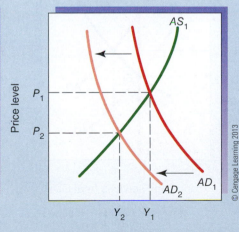

(a) Loanable funds market

(b) Goods and services (real GDP)

(reducing the ability of banks to extend loans). As a result, the supply of loanable funds will fall, causing the real interest rate to rise (from r_1 to r_2 in part a of Exhibit 5). In turn, the higher real interest rate will reduce spending on both investment goods and consumer durables because they'll be more costly to finance. The higher rate will also cause an in-flow of capital from abroad and lead to the appreciation in the exchange rate of the dollar. The dollar appreciation will encourage U.S. citizens to buy imported products (which will become cheaper for them) and discourage foreigners from buying U.S. exports (because they will be more costly for them). This will then lead to lower net U.S. exports (and lower aggregate demand in the United States). The higher interest rates will also reduce housing and other asset prices, discouraging new construction and investment. All of these factors will tend to reduce aggregate demand (shift it from AD_1 to AD_2 in part b of Exhibit 5).

The unexpected decline in the demand for goods and services will put downward pressure on prices, squeeze profit margins, and reduce output. As part (b) of Exhibit 5 shows, the price level will decline (to P_2), and output will fall (to Y_2) as a result of the restrictive monetary policy.

The appropriateness of a restrictive policy depends on the state of the economy. Exhibit 6 illustrates this point. When there is upward pressure on prices because of strong demand, restrictive policy is an effective weapon against inflation. Suppose that, as illustrated by part (a) of Exhibit 6, an economy is temporarily operating at e_1 and Y_1—beyond its full employment real GDP of Y_F. Strong aggregate demand is putting upward pressure on prices. In this case, a restrictive policy will help keep the price level constant and offset the inflationary forces. If a proper "dose" of a restrictive policy is administered at the right time, it will lower aggregate demand (to AD_2) and direct the economy to a noninflationary, long-run equilibrium at P_2 and Y_F (that is, E_2).

As part (b) of Exhibit 6 shows, however, an unanticipated shift to restrictive policy will be damaging to an economy operating at full-employment equilibrium. If the output of an economy is at full employment (or worse still, at less than full employment), a restrictive policy will reduce aggregate demand (shift it to AD_2), and output will decline from Y_F to Y_2. Under these circumstances, the restrictive policy will cause output to fall below the economy's full-employment capacity and throw the economy into a recession.

EXHIBIT 6

The Effects of a Restrictive Monetary Policy

The stabilization effects of restrictive monetary policy depend on the state of the economy when the policy exerts its primary impact. Restrictive monetary policy will reduce aggregate demand. If the restraint takes effect when aggregate demand is strong and the economy is overheated, it will limit or even prevent the occurrence of an inflationary boom (a). In contrast, if the restraint in aggregate demand takes effect when the economy is at full employment, it will disrupt the long-run equilibrium, reduce output, and result in a recession (b).

(a) Restrictive policy to control inflation

(b) Restrictive policy that causes a recession

© Cengage Learning 2013

14-3c SHIFTS IN MONETARY POLICY AND ECONOMIC STABILITY

As with fiscal policy, monetary policy must be properly timed if it is going to exert a stabilizing impact on the economy. Exhibits 4 and 6 highlight this point. When an economy is operating below its long-run capacity, expansionary monetary policy can increase aggregate demand and push the output of the economy to its sustainable potential (part a of Exhibit 4). Similarly, if properly timed, restrictive monetary policy can help control (or prevent) inflation (part a of Exhibit 6).

If it is timed improperly, however, monetary policy can be destabilizing. Expansionary monetary policy will cause inflation if the effects of the policy are felt when the economy is already at or beyond its capacity (part b of Exhibit 4). Similarly, if the effects of a restrictive policy come when an economy is operating at its potential GDP, a recession is the likely outcome (part b of Exhibit 6). Worse still, the impact of a restrictive policy can be disastrous if imposed on an economy that's already in a recession.

14-4 MONETARY POLICY IN THE LONG RUN

14-4a THE QUANTITY THEORY OF MONEY

Since the middle of the eighteenth century, economists have argued that excessive money growth leads to inflation. A century ago, Englishman Alfred Marshall and American Irving Fisher formalized the **quantity theory of money** in support of this view. *The quantity theory of money predicts that an increase in the supply of money will cause a proportional increase in the price level.*

The quantity theory of money can be more easily understood once we recognize that there are two ways of viewing GDP. As the *AD–AS* model shows, nominal GDP is the sum of the price, P, times the output, Y, of each final-product good purchased during the period. In aggregate, P represents the economy's price level, while Y indicates real income or real GDP. There is also a second way of visualizing GDP. When the existing money stock, M, is multiplied by the number of times, V, that money is used to buy final products, this, too, yields the economy's nominal GDP. Therefore,

$$PY = \text{GDP} = MV$$

The **velocity of money** (V) is simply the average number of times a dollar is used to purchase a final product or service during a year. Velocity is equal to nominal GDP divided by the size of the money stock. For example, in 2012, GDP was equal to $15,685 billion, whereas the M1 money supply was $2,310 billion. Therefore, the velocity of the M1 money stock was 6.8 ($15,685 billion divided by $2,310 billion). The velocity of the M2 money stock can be derived in a similar manner. In 2012, the M2 money stock was $10,006 billion. Thus, the velocity of M2 was 1.6 ($15,685 billion divided by $10,006 billion).

The concept of velocity is closely related to the demand for money. When decision-makers conduct a specific amount of business with a smaller amount of money, their demand for money balances is reduced. Each dollar, though, is being used more often, so the velocity of the money has increased. Thus, for a given GDP level, when the demand for money declines, the velocity of money increases. Correspondingly, an increase in the demand for money is a reflection of a reduction in velocity.

When considering the behavior of prices, output, money, and velocity over time, we can write the quantity theory equation in terms of growth rates:

Rate of inflation + Growth rate of real output = Growth rate of the money supply + Growth rate of velocity

Quantity theory of money
A theory that hypothesizes that a change in the money supply will cause a proportional change in the price level because velocity and real output are unaffected by the quantity of money.

Velocity of money
The average number of times a dollar is used to purchase final goods and services during a year. It is equal to GDP divided by the stock of money.

Equation of exchange
$MV = PY$, where M is the money supply, V is the velocity of money, P is the price level, and Y is the output of goods and services produced in an economy.

Economists call the $MV = PY$ relationship the **equation of exchange** because it reflects both the monetary and real sides of each final-product exchange. The quantity theory of money, though, assumes that Y and V are determined by factors other than the amount of money in circulation. Classical economists believed that real output, Y, was determined by factors like technology, the size of the economy's resource base, and the skill of its labor force. These factors were thought to be unrelated to changes in the money supply. Likewise, the velocity of money, V, was thought to be determined primarily by institutional factors, like the organization of banking and credit, the frequency of income payments, transportation speed, and the communication system. These factors will generally change slowly.

Thus, classical economists thought that, for all practical purposes, both Y and V were constant (or changed only by small amounts) over periods of two, three, or four years. If both Y and V are constant, then the $MV = PY$ relationship indicates that an increase in the money supply (M) will lead to a proportional increase in the price level (P). Correspondingly, an increase in the growth rate of the money supply can be expected to cause a similar increase in the rate of inflation. Thus, the quantity theory of money highlights the linkage between monetary growth and inflation.

14-4b LONG-RUN IMPACT OF MONETARY POLICY: THE MODERN VIEW

Now let's consider the long-run impact of expansionary monetary policy within the framework of our basic macroeconomic model. We will begin with a simple case. Suppose real GDP is growing at a 3 percent annual rate and that the monetary authorities (the Fed in the case of the United States) are expanding the money supply by 3 percent each year. In addition, let's assume that the velocity of money is constant. This would imply that the 3 percent annual increase in output, or GDP, would lead to a 3 percent annual increase in the demand for money. In this case, the 3 percent monetary growth would be consistent with stable prices (zero inflation). Initially, we will assume that the economy's real interest rate is 4 percent. Because the inflation rate is zero, the nominal rate of interest is also equal to 4 percent. **Exhibits 7 and 8** illustrate an economy initially (period 1) characterized by these conditions.

What will happen if the monetary authorities permanently increase the growth rate of the money supply from 3 percent to 8 percent annually (see part a of Exhibit 7, beginning in period 2)? In the short run, the expansionary monetary policy will reduce the real interest rate and stimulate aggregate demand (shift it to AD_2 in part b of Exhibit 7), just as we previously explained (in Exhibits 3 and 4). For a time, real output will exceed the economy's potential. However, many resource suppliers will want to modify their long-term agreements as soon as they can in light of the strong demand conditions. Over time, more and more resource suppliers (including workers represented by union officials) will have the opportunity to alter their prior contracts. As this happens, wages and other resource prices will increase. As they do, costs will rise and profit margins will fall back to normal levels. The higher costs will reduce aggregate supply (shift it to AS_2). As the rapid monetary growth continues in subsequent periods (periods 3, 4, and so on), both AD and AS will shift upward. As shown in Exhibit 7b, the price level will rise to P_{105}, P_{110}, and so on to still higher levels as the money supply continues to grow more rapidly than the monetary growth rate consistent with stable prices. The continuation of the expansionary monetary policy leads to a higher and higher price level—that is, a sustained inflation.

Suppose an inflation rate of 5 percent eventually emerges from the more rapid growth rate of the money supply (8 percent rather than 3 percent). In the long run, more and more people will make decisions based on the persistent 5 percent inflation because it will be what they come to expect. In the resource market, both buyers and sellers will eventually include the 5 percent expected inflation rate into long-term contracts like collective bargaining agreements. Once this happens, resource prices and costs will rise as rapidly as prices in the goods and services market. When the 5 percent long-run rate of inflation is fully anticipated, it will fail to either reduce real wages or improve profit margins. Output will recede to its long-run potential, and unemployment will return to its natural rate.

EXHIBIT 7

The Long-Run Effects of a More Rapid Expansion in the Money Supply on the Goods and Services Market

Here, we illustrate the long-run impact of an increase in the annual growth rate of the money supply from 3 to 8 percent. Initially, prices are stable (P_{100}) when the money supply is expanding by 3 percent annually. The acceleration in the growth rate of the money supply increases aggregate demand (shifts it to AD_2). At first, real output may expand beyond the economy's potential (Y_F). However, abnormally low unemployment and strong demand conditions will create upward pressure on wages and other resource prices, shifting aggregate supply to AS_2. Output will return to its long-run potential and the price level will increase to P_{105} (E_2). If the more rapid monetary growth continues in subsequent periods, AD and AS will continue to shift upward, leading to still higher prices (E_3 and periods beyond). The net result of the process is sustained inflation.

(a) Growth rate of the money supply

(b) Impact in the goods and services market

© Cengage Learning 2013

EXHIBIT 8

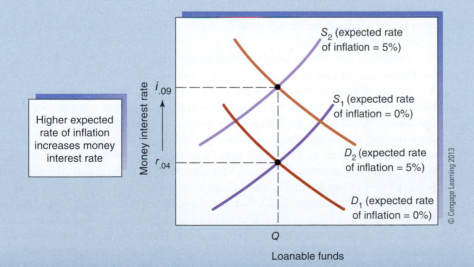

Higher expected rate of inflation increases money interest rate

© Cengage Learning 2013

The Long-Run Effects of More Rapid Expansion in the Money Supply on the Loanable Funds Market

When prices are stable, supply and demand in the loanable funds market are in balance at a real and nominal interest rate of 4 percent. If a more rapid monetary expansion leads to a long-term 5 percent inflation rate, borrowers and lenders will build the higher inflation rate into their decision-making. As a result, the nominal interest rate (i) will rise to 9 percent—the 4 percent real rate plus a 5 percent inflationary premium.

Exhibit 8 shows the long-run adjustments in the loanable funds market once borrowers and lenders expect the 5 percent inflation rate. When lenders expect a 5 percent annual increase in the price level, a 9 percent interest rate will be necessary to provide them with as much incentive to supply loanable funds as a 4 percent rate did *when stable prices were expected.* Thus, the supply of loanable funds will shift vertically by the 5 percent expected rate of inflation. Simultaneously, borrowers who were willing to pay 4 percent interest on their loans when stable prices were expected will be willing to pay 9 percent when they expect prices to increase by 5 percent annually. The demand for loanable funds will therefore also increase (shift vertically) by the expected inflation rate. Once borrowers and lenders anticipate the higher (5 percent) inflation rate, the equilibrium money interest rate will rise to 9 percent. Of course, the real interest rate is equal to the money interest rate (9 percent) minus the expected rate of inflation (5 percent). In the long run, a 4 percent real interest rate will emerge with inflation, just as it did with stable prices. Therefore, in the long run, expansionary monetary policy will not reduce real interest rates. Nominal interest rates will rise and reflect the higher expected rate of inflation, but real interest rates will be unchanged.

Real-world observations support the linkage between monetary expansion and high nominal interest rates. During the 1970s, the monetary policy of the United States was highly expansionary, and it led to both inflation and high nominal interest rates. On the other hand, interest rates were lower during the 1960s and 1990–2008, when monetary policy was less expansionary and the inflation rate lower. The picture is the same internationally. The highest interest rates in the world are found in countries experiencing hyperinflation due to very rapid money supply growth: Argentina and Brazil in the 1980s, Russia and Turkey during the 1990s, and Venezuela during the most recent decade, for example. Conversely, the lowest interest rates are found in countries like Switzerland that have followed monetary policies that have kept the inflation rate low.

14-4c MONEY AND INFLATION

Modern analysis highlights the difference between the short- and long-run effects of monetary policy. In the short run, shifts in monetary policy exert an impact on real output and employment. A shift to a more restrictive policy will tend to reduce real output and employment, while a shift to a more expansionary monetary policy will tend to increase them.

However, if the more expansionary policy persists, the long-run impact will be inflation and higher nominal interest rates, without any positive impact on real output and employment. The more rapid the sustained growth rate of the money supply (relative to real output), the higher the expected rate of inflation. Thus, modern analysis indicates that the long-run implications of the earlier quantity theory of money are correct: Money growth and inflation are closely linked.

The empirical evidence is highly consistent with this view. **Exhibit 9** presents data on the annual growth rate of the money supply (adjusted for the growth rate of the nation's output) and the rate of inflation for 87 countries for which data were available for the 1990–2010 period. Countries with single-digit rates of money growth—for example, Central African Republic, India, Japan, South Korea, Switzerland, and the United States—also experienced single-digit rates of inflation. Similarly, countries with rates of money growth in the 10 percent to 25 percent range experienced rates of inflation in this same range. The data for Colombia, Indonesia, Hungary, Paraguay, Peru, and Nigeria illustrate this point. Countries like Romania, Turkey, and Venezuela, with money growth rates in the 30 percent to 50 percent range, had inflation rates within this same range. Finally, look at the data for Brazil and Democratic Republic of Congo. The average annual rate of money growth of these countries exceeded 75 percent during 1990–2010. So, too, did their rates of inflation.

When looked at over a lengthy time period, the link between money growth and inflation is one of the most consistent relationships in all of economics. Inflation is a monetary phenomenon. Persistently low rates of money growth lead to low rates of inflation. Similarly, high rates of money growth lead to high rates of inflation.

Money and Inflation—An International Comparison, 1990–2010

The relationship between the average annual growth rate of the money supply and the rate of inflation is shown here for the 1990–2010 period.

Clearly, there is a close relationship between the two. Higher rates of money growth lead to higher rates of inflation.

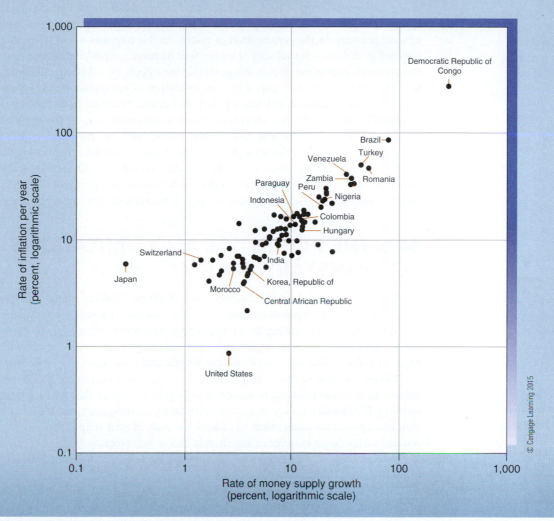

14-4d TIME LAGS, MONETARY SHIFTS, AND ECONOMIC STABILITY

While analyzing how monetary policy works, we glossed over a crucially important issue: the time lag between a change in monetary policy and when the change begins to exert an impact on interest rates, aggregate demand, and eventually output and the price level. While the Fed can shift policy rapidly, it will take time for the change to impact the economy. Economists estimate that it will generally take 6 to 18 months for a shift in monetary policy to exert a major impact on aggregate demand and real output. An even longer time lag—12 to 30 months—often passes before there is a significant impact on the price level and inflation rate.

The transmission of monetary policy sheds light on why it takes time for monetary policy to work. When the Fed shifts toward monetary expansion and injects additional reserves into the banking system, short-term interest rates will fall. But this reduces the opportunity cost of holding money balances. At the lower interest rate, households and businesses are willing to hold a larger quantity of money, and therefore, the velocity of money will decline.

As a result, the initial effects of the expansionary monetary policy will often be weak. For a time, total spending (aggregate demand) may not change much because the reduction in velocity is, at least partially, offsetting the increase in the supply of money. If the reduction in the interest rate is substantial and persistent, the weak impact of the monetary expansion may be lengthy. Of course, if the more expansionary monetary policy persists, it will eventually lead to increasing aggregate demand and rising interest rates. A combination of the lower real interest rates and more readily available credit will eventually stimulate aggregate demand and real output. This will lead to rising nominal interest rates and some upward pressure on the general level of prices. As this happens—and 18 to 36 months may pass before it does—the velocity of money will increase, amplifying the demand stimulus of the monetary expansion. It is at this point that the effects on inflation will be the strongest.

The same forces will also affect the operation of restrictive monetary policy. When the Fed shifts to a more restrictive policy and drains reserves from the banking system, the federal funds and other short-term interest rates will rise. At the higher rates, however, people will want to hold less money, and the velocity of money will increase. For a time, the increase in velocity will at least partially offset the reduction in the supply of money and weaken the initial restrictive effects of the policy. Of course, if the restrictive policy persists, higher interest rates will eventually reduce aggregate demand, but several quarters may pass before the restrictive policy exerts a strong impact on the economy.

14-5 THE POTENTIAL AND LIMITATIONS OF MONETARY POLICY

What can be achieved with monetary policy? When thinking about this question, it is important to keep two points in mind. First, expansionary monetary policy cannot promote long-term growth. Increasing the money supply will not create more output. Second, shifts in monetary policy exert an impact on output and the general level of prices with a time lag. Moreover, these time lags are of variable length, and sometimes they will be quite long.

Given our limited forecasting ability, these time lags will make it difficult for policy-makers to institute changes in monetary policy in a manner that will promote economic stability. If monetary policy-makers are constantly shifting back and forth between expansion and restriction in an effort to control the path of real output and employment, their actions will become a source of uncertainty and policy errors are sure to result. Put another way, monetary policy that veers to one direction and then to the other is likely to generate instability rather than reduce it.

In the long run, the impact of monetary policy will be primarily on the general level of prices. Thus, control of inflation is the responsibility of monetary policy-makers. Equally important, price stability provides the foundation for the smooth operation of a market economy. When monetary policy keeps the inflation rate at a low and therefore easily predictable rate, it lays the foundation for long-term healthy growth. In fact, price stability is so important that it is one of our 12 Keys to Prosperity.

The high standard of living that Americans enjoy is the result of gains from specialization, division of labor, and mass production processes. Price stability and the smooth operation of the pricing system will help individuals more fully realize the potential gains

KEYS TO ECONOMIC PROSPERITY

Price Stability

Maintenance of price stability is the essence of sound monetary policy; price stability provides the foundation for both economic stability and the efficient operation of markets.

The Federal Reserve is responsible for the conduct of monetary policy. If it achieves approximate price stability, it has done all it can do to create an environment for growth and prosperity.

from these sources. In contrast, high and variable rates of inflation create uncertainty, distort relative prices, and reduce the efficiency of a market economy.

While shifts to a more expansionary monetary policy can promote real output and employment in the short run, they cannot do so in the long run. Moreover, constant shifts in monetary policy will result in policy errors and generate uncertainty. If investors and other business decision makers can count on monetary policy-makers to maintain price stability, a potential source of uncertainty is reduced. This will encourage investment and other business activities and thereby promote a high level of employment and strong economic growth.

How can Fed policy best achieve price stability? Some believe the Fed should establish an inflation target, between zero and 2 percent, for example, and promise to keep the rate of inflation within that range. If the rate of inflation rose above the 2 percent upper limit, the Fed would shift toward a more restrictive monetary policy. On the other hand, if the inflation rate fell below the zero limit, monetary policy would be shifted toward expansion. Others favor Fed targeting of nominal GDP growth. Suppose the Fed promised to use monetary policy to keep the annual growth rate of nominal GDP as close as possible to 5 percent. If nominal GDP growth was greater than 5 percent, the Fed would shift toward restriction. When nominal GDP growth fell below the 5 percent target, the Fed would be more expansionary. The long-term annual real growth of the U.S. economy has averaged a little more than 3 percent. Thus, 5 percent growth of nominal GDP would keep the inflation rate low—in the 2 percent range.

Those who favor either an inflation or nominal GDP target typically buttress their case with two additional points. First, the monetary authorities should focus on a long run preannounced strategy such as the targeting of either of these variables. This would reduce uncertainty by providing people with assurance regarding the future direction of monetary policy. Second, it is a mistake for monetary policy-makers to target real variables such as real GDP, employment, or unemployment. Monetary policy cannot control real variables, at least not for long, and when it seeks to do so, it will nearly always result in more rather than less instability. When the monetary authorities persistently achieve price stability, they have done all they can do to establish the environment for long-run prosperity. For additional perspective on the linkage between monetary policy and economic instability, see Applications in Economics: "What Causes the Ups and Downs of the Business Cycle: The Austrian View."

APPLICATIONS IN ECONOMICS

What Causes the Ups and Downs of the Business Cycle: The Austrian View

In macroeconomics there are several schools of thought, including Keynesian, monetarist, and Austrian. In the wake of the recent financial crisis, the Austrian theory of the business cycle has gained substantial attention because it provides a plausible explanation for recent events, particularly in the housing market.

Like monetarists, Austrian economists argue that the boom–bust cycle is the result of improper monetary policy undertaken by the Fed. But the two differ with regard to the explanation. The core of the Austrian view is that the market interest rate is one of the most important prices in the economy and when the central bank manipulates this rate, it distorts the signals sent to borrowers and lenders.

In the Austrian view, the interest rate is a key determinant of the time structure of capital and the length of the production process. When interest rates are low, the time structure of production lengthens as longer-term investments become more profitable. On the other hand, when interest rates are high, the time structure of production shortens as the higher interest rates make longer-term investments less attractive. Undertaking a five-year process of building a new factory, for example, might be profitable at a lower interest rate, but not a higher one.

Normally, changes in the market interest rate correspond to changes in the time preferences of consumers. When households cut back on current consumption and save more for their retirement, for example, they are sending a signal to producers that they want fewer goods today in exchange for more goods in the future. The increase in saving (the supply of loanable funds) will result in lower real interest rates. In turn, the lower interest rates will provide entrepreneurs with the incentive to undertake longer-term investments that will expand the supply of consumer goods in the future.

However, when expansionary monetary policy pushes interest rates to artificially low levels, entrepreneurs will undertake additional investments, but there is no increase in saving that will provide the income for the purchase of the larger future output. Because of the low interest rates, people will try to increase both investment and consumption at the same time. Moreover, the lower interest rates will induce entrepreneurs to undertake longer-term investments like houses, shopping malls, and office buildings that will expand the availability of goods and services in the more distant future. For a time, the artificially low interest rates will generate an economic boom. Output will increase rapidly and the unemployment rate will decline to a low level.

But the boom will not be sustainable. Given the economy's resource constraint, the strong demand for both consumption and investment goods will eventually lead to inflation. The monetary authorities may respond to the inflation with monetary restriction and higher interest rates, which will bring the boom to a halt. However, even if the monetary authorities continue with an expansionary, low–interest rate policy, many of the investment projects will end up being unprofitable because the low saving rate will mean that future consumer income will be insufficient to purchase the larger output when it is brought to the market. As a result, capital will be misallocated into unprofitable projects. Recently constructed assets such as houses and office buildings will sit empty and production inventories will pile up. Austrians refer to this as *malinvestment*. Once the bust comes, excess capacity will be present in many industries, sectors, and regions. Falling prices will occur in areas of excessive investment, and it will sometimes take years to eliminate this excess capacity—for the malinvestment to be "cleansed" from the system.

It is interesting to think about the recent economic turbulence within the framework of the Austrian business cycle theory. Beginning in early 2002, the Fed pushed interest rates to historic low levels and kept them there throughout 2002–2004. In turn, the low interest rates encouraged long-term investments, particularly in the housing industry. Housing prices soared, construction expanded, and the U.S. economy grew rapidly during 2002–2004. By 2005, however, the inflation rate was on the rise, and the Fed shifted to a more restrictive policy. As interest rates rose, the housing boom turned to a bust. Housing prices leveled off in mid-year 2006, and they soon began to fall. Many homeowners had insufficient saving to support their housing investments, and both default and foreclosures were soon soaring. By 2008, many of the lenders who funded the mortgages were also in financial trouble. Just as the Austrian theory predicts, the result was excessive investment in housing, unsold inventories, and empty structures.

In many ways, the differences between the ideas of John Maynard Keynes and Friedrich Hayek of the Austrian school represent central debates within the economics profession as a whole. For additional information on this issue, see Special Topic 4, "Great Debates of Economics: Keynes versus Hayek." Economists are even having a little fun with the debate. A YouTube rap video titled "Fear the Boom and Bust" (http://www.youtube.com/watch?v=d0nERTFo-Sk) with actors depicting Keynes and Hayek arguing about the recent financial crisis and other key issues has attracted more than 2 million views! Have a look at it. We think you will enjoy it.

14-6 RECENT MONETARY POLICY OF THE UNITED STATES

Exhibit 10 presents data on two important indicators of monetary policy: the federal funds interest rate (left frame) and the annual rate of change in the M2 money supply (right frame). Low (and declining) short-term interest rates coupled with more rapid growth of the M2 money supply is indicative of a more expansionary monetary policy. On the other hand, rising short-term rates and slow growth of M2 imply a more restrictive monetary policy.

It is interesting to follow the path of monetary policy during the 1990s. The Fed focused on the maintenance of a low stable rate of inflation, and it largely achieved this goal. The federal funds interest rate fluctuated but was always greater than 4 percent. The annual growth rate of the M2 money supply moved within a narrow range between 3 percent and 7 percent. The inflation rate was low (between 2 percent and 4 percent) during the decade. The 1990s were a period of rapid economic growth. This illustrates that when the Fed achieves price stability, it creates the environment for strong growth and high employment.

14-6a FED POLICY, HOUSING PRICES, AND THE CRISIS OF 2008

During 2002–2004, Fed policy shifted toward expansion. As Exhibit 10 (left frame) shows, monetary policy pushed short-term interest rates to historic lows during this time frame. The federal funds rate was less than 2 percent throughout the three-year period. The M2 money supply grew rapidly—approximately 7 percent annually during 2002–2004, providing further evidence that monetary policy was expansionary.

Between January 2002 and mid-year 2006, housing prices increased by 87 percent. This run-up in housing prices was fueled by several factors. Government regulations

---

EXHIBIT 10

Indicators of Monetary Policy, 1990–2013

The federal funds interest rate (left panel) and growth rate of the M2 money supply (right panel) are monetary policy indicators. Note that the federal funds rate was 2 percent or less during 2002–2004 and the M2 growth rate was above 5 percent during 2001–2003. In contrast, the federal funds rate rose and the M2 growth rate fell during 2005–2006. This pattern of monetary expansion followed by restriction was a contributing factor to the housing boom and bust. The Fed shifted again (toward expansion) in 2007–2009 as the economy plunged into recession. In 2010–2012 the federal funds rate remained near zero and the M2 money supply grew rapidly.

Source: http://www.economagic.com.

were imposed on banks; and two huge government-sponsored mortgage lenders, Fannie Mae and Freddie Mac, made credit for housing finance both abundantly available and easily accessible. Beginning in the late 1990s, there was a substantial increase in the volume of mortgage loans extended, with little or no down payment to parties borrowing large amounts relative to their income. Moreover, these loans were often bundled together into a relatively new type of asset, mortgage-backed securities, that were sold throughout the world. These securities were marketed and widely held by both commercial and investment banks with only small amounts of reserves and capital relative to their mortgage holdings.

But monetary policy also contributed to the boom and bust in housing prices. The historically low interest rates of 2002–2004 increased the demand for housing and provided fuel for the soaring housing prices of the era. However, just as our analysis predicts, the expansionary monetary policy eventually generated upward pressure on the general level of prices. By 2005, the inflation rate had risen to 5 percent, and the Fed shifted to a more restrictive policy. Short-term interest rates were pushed upward and the growth of the M2 money supply slowed (see Exhibit 10). In turn, the higher interest rates increased borrowing costs, weakening the demand for housing. By the second half of 2006, housing prices were leveling off and beginning to fall, mortgage defaults were increasing, and housing foreclosures rising. All of this was well before the recession began in December 2007.

The housing bust eventually spread to the rest of the economy and generated trouble for lending institutions holding large quantities of the mortgage-backed securities that tumbled in value as mortgage default rates rose. Other factors added to the Crisis of 2008. The world price of crude oil nearly tripled between the beginning of 2007 and July 2008, pushing the price of gasoline above $4 per gallon in the United States. Stock prices fell by more than 50 percent during the 17 months following October 2007. The importance of the combination of factors underpinning the 2008 crisis is subject to debate, but inappropriate monetary policy clearly played a role. (See Special Topic 5, "The Crisis of 2008: Causes and Lessons for the Future," for additional information on this topic.)

14-6b FED POLICY DURING AND FOLLOWING THE FINANCIAL CRISIS

As the economy plunged into recession during the first half of 2008, the Fed injected a huge quantity of reserves into the banking system. In the 12 months beginning in July 2008, the Fed doubled both its asset holdings and the monetary base. As Exhibit 10 shows, this policy pushed the federal funds and other short-term interest rates to near zero and the M2 money supply expanded at an annual rate of 9 percent, well above the average of the two previous decades. The Fed often referred to this policy as "quantitative easing." Because the highly expansionary monetary policy initiated during the second half of 2008 was the first round of a series of easing policies, it is now known as QE1.

While the Fed injected a huge quantity of reserves into the banking system, the money supply increased much more slowly than the monetary base. The demand for new loans was weak, therefore banks were extending few new loans. Instead, their excess reserves soared.

Even though the recession ended in June 2009, growth was slow and the unemployment rate remained high in the second half of 2009 and throughout 2010. Beginning in the fourth quarter of 2010, the Fed announced another round of quantitative easing, QE2. The monetary base increased by another $600 billion between December 2010 and June 2011 (see Chapter 13, Exhibit 8). In the 12 months that followed the initiation of QE2, the annual growth rate of M2 again jumped to more than 9 percent (see Exhibit 10). As the economic sluggishness continued, the Fed announced a third round of quantitative easing during the last quarter of 2012. This time, it pledged to purchase $85 billion in Treasury and mortgage-backed securities each month.

EXHIBIT 11

The Velocity of the M1 and M2 Money Supply, 1990–2013

The path of the M1 and M2 velocity is shown here. Note how the velocity of M1 increased for more than a decade prior to 2007 but plunged during the second half of 2008. After fluctuating within a relatively narrow range during 1990–2007, the velocity of M2 also fell sharply in 2008. The Fed's low interest rate policy contributed to these sharp reductions in velocity, and this secondary effect weakened the potency of expansionary monetary policy in the aftermath of the 2008 crisis.

Source: http://www.economagic.com

Why hasn't the expansionary monetary policy exerted a stronger impact on the economy? Why hasn't it led to inflation as some thought would be the case? The collapse in the velocity of money provides insight on both of these issues. As the analysis of the demand for money indicates, there will be an inverse relationship between the nominal interest rate and the amount of money people are willing to hold (see Exhibit 1). When interest rates decline to low levels, people will hold a larger quantity of money and the velocity of money will fall. This is precisely what happened as the Fed pushed interest rates to near zero in response to the crisis.

Exhibit 11 tracks the velocity of both M1 and M2 during 1990–2013. Before 2007, the velocity of M1 trended upward while the velocity of M2 fluctuated within a narrow range. But look what happened in 2008. The velocity of both M1 and M2 plunged. When interest rates are near zero, there is little incentive for households and businesses to shift away from money balances and into the loanable funds market (bonds, certificates of deposit, and similar savings instruments). A substantial share of the general public simply held a large portion of the expanded money supply and the velocity of money declined. Of course, some shifted funds into stocks, real estate, and other riskier assets in an effort to earn more than a negligible return. As we previously discussed, the lower interest rates will push the prices of these assets upward, create a wealth effect, and thereby stimulate aggregate demand. In this regard, the Fed policy worked. Stock prices rose substantially from their March 2009 low; by 2013, they were twice their recessionary low. Similarly, the earlier decline in housing prices reversed direction, and by 2012–2013 they were on an upward path.

But the low interest rate policy has also reduced the current income and wealth of people who maintain all or most of their savings in money market accounts, savings deposits, bonds, and similar saving instruments. In this regard, senior citizens have been particularly hard hit because many of them expected to supplement their Social Security income with

EXHIBIT 12

Annual Growth Rate in Nominal GDP, 1990–2013

The growth rate of nominal GDP reflects the combination of changes in the money supply and its velocity. During 1990–2007,the annual growth of nominal GDP averaged 5.4 percent and was generally in the 4 percent to 6 percent range. After plunging in 2008–2009, nominal GDP grew about 4 percent annually during 2010–2012. This modest growth rate suggests that monetary policy was not excessively expansionary in the aftermath of the 2008 recession.

Source: http://www.economagic.com

earnings from these sources. Even though the Fed's low interest rate policy increased the value of stocks and bonds, it has also created a wealth effect in the opposite direction that acts as a drag on both consumption and aggregate demand. As a result, the stimulus effects are far more modest than the growth of bank reserves and money supply figures imply.

The growth of nominal GDP reflects the combination of the change in the money supply and the change in velocity. Exhibit 12 presents data on the growth of nominal GDP since 1990. The average growth of nominal GDP averaged 5.4 percent during 1990–2008, and it generally fluctuated within the 4 percent to 6 percent range. During the recession of 2001, nominal GDP growth dipped to 3 percent, but it soon returned to the 4 percent to 6 percent range. However, as the 2008 recession set in, nominal GDP actually declined in 2009. During 2010–2012, it has grown at an annual rate of approximately 4 percent. Thus, while the historically low interest rates, massive increase in Fed assets, and substantial growth of the money supply are indicative of highly expansionary policy, the generally normal increase in nominal GDP during 2010–2013 is inconsistent with the view that Fed policy has been excessively expansionary.

Nonetheless, the Fed now confronts a dilemma. As the economy recovers, if the Fed does not shift toward restrictive policy soon enough, the vast quantity of excess reserves, rising interest rates, and reversal of the downward trend in money velocity could lead to future inflation that would be exceedingly difficult to control. On the other hand, if the Fed moves toward restraint too soon, it could stifle the recovery and throw the economy back into another recession.

Monetary policy has been on a stop–go path for almost a decade now. As the experience of the 1970s indicates, once you are on this course, it is not easy to get back to economic stability. It will be interesting to see how it works out, but the unpredictability of the time lags and the Fed's past record provide reasons for concern.

LOOKING AHEAD

The next chapter will focus on macroeconomic stabilization policy and factors that influence its effectiveness. We will also consider current conditions, the broader historical record, and their implications for the future of the U.S. economy.

KEY POINTS

- The quantity of money people want to hold is inversely related to the money interest rate. Higher interest rates make it more costly to hold money instead of interest-earning assets like bonds. The supply of money is vertical because it is determined by the Fed. The money interest rate will gravitate toward the rate at which the quantity of money people want to hold is just equal to the quantity supplied by the Fed.

- The impact of a shift in monetary policy is generally transmitted through interest rates, exchange rates, and asset prices.

- When instituting a more expansionary monetary policy, the Fed generally increases the reserves available to banks and pushes interest rates downward. In the short run, an *unanticipated* shift to a more expansionary policy will stimulate aggregate demand and thereby increase output and employment.

- When instituting a more restrictive monetary policy, the Fed drains reserves from the banking system and pushes interest rates upward. In the short run, an unanticipated shift to a more restrictive monetary policy will increase real interest rates and reduce aggregate demand, output, and employment.

- The quantity theory of money postulates that the velocity of money is constant (or approximately so) and that real output is independent of monetary factors. When these assumptions hold, an increase in the stock of money will lead to a proportional increase in the price level.

- While monetary policy can influence real output in the short run, in the long run, expansionary monetary policy will merely lead to inflation.

- Shifts in monetary policy exert an impact on output and employment only after time lags that are variable and sometimes lengthy. These variable time lags reduce the likelihood that monetary policy-makers will be able to make regular changes in monetary policy in a stabilizing manner. Historically, erratic monetary policy has often been a source of economic instability.

- Monetary policy consistent with price stability is a key ingredient of effective stabilization policy. If monetary policy-makers achieve price stability, they have done all they can do to promote growth and prosperity.

- The Fed's low interest rate policy of 2002–2004, followed by its shift to a more restrictive policy in 2005–2006, contributed to the boom and bust of housing prices that provided the foundation for the Crisis of 2008.

- In response to the recession of 2008, the Fed pushed short-term interest rates to near zero and rapidly expanded the money supply. However, the velocity of money declined sharply and partially offset the monetary expansion. The growth of nominal GDP during 2010–2012 suggests Fed policy was not overly expansionary. However, the Fed now faces a dilemma: A shift toward restrictive policy may lead to a recession, but staying with the monetary expansion for too long could result in high rates of inflation.

CRITICAL ANALYSIS QUESTIONS

1. Why do people hold money? How will an increase in the interest rate influence the amount of money that people will want to hold?

2. *How would each of the following influence the quantity of money you would want to hold?
   a. an increase in the interest rate earned on checking deposits
   b. an increase in the expected rate of inflation
   c. an increase in income
   d. an increase in the differential interest rate between money market mutual funds and checking deposits

3. *What is the opportunity cost of the following?
   a. purchasing a $100,000 house
   b. holding the house for one year
   c. obtaining $1,000
   d. holding the $1,000 in your checking account for one year

4. Historically, shifts toward a more expansionary monetary policy have often been associated with increases in real output. Is this surprising? Why or why not? Can an expansion in the money supply increase real output and employment? Why or why not?

5. What impact will an unanticipated increase in the money supply have on the real interest rate, real output, and employment in the short run? How will expansionary monetary policy affect these factors in the long run? Explain.

6. How rapidly has the money supply (M1) grown during the past twelve months? How rapidly has M2 grown? Do you think the monetary authorities should increase or decrease the growth rate of the money supply during the next year? Why? (The data necessary to answer this question are available at the Web site of the Federal Reserve Bank of St. Louis, http://www.stls.frb.org.)

7. If the Fed shifts to a more restrictive monetary policy, it will generally sell some of its current holdings of bonds in the open market. How will this action influence each of the following? Briefly explain each of your answers.

   a. the reserves available to banks
   b. real interest rates
   c. household spending on consumer durables
   d. the exchange rate value of the dollar
   e. net exports
   f. the prices of stocks and real assets like apartment or office buildings
   g. real GDP

8. Has monetary policy exerted a stabilizing impact on the U.S. economy during the past decade? Why or why not?

9. Is stability in the general level of prices through time important? Why or why not? Should price stability be the goal of monetary policy? Should monetary policy-makers try to shift monetary policy in a manner that will smooth the ups and downs of the business cycle? Explain your responses.

10. *Many economists believe that there is a "long and variable time lag" between the time a change in monetary policy is instituted and the time its primary impact on output, employment, and prices is felt. If true, how does this long and variable time lag affect the ability of policy-makers to use monetary policy as a stabilization tool?

11. *"Historically, when interest rates are high, the inflation rate is high. High interest rates are a major cause of inflation." Evaluate this statement.

12. According to economists of the Austrian school, what is the major cause of the business cycle? Would economists of the Keynesian school agree? Discuss.

13. What is the quantity theory of money? Is the theory valid?

14. Did monetary policy contribute to the economic crisis of 2008? Why or why not? How did monetary policy makers respond to this crisis? Has their response created an environment for future stability and growth? Explain.

15. What impact did the near zero interest rates of 2009–2012 have on the incentive of people to hold money balances? How did the low interest rates affect the wealth of people who had savings deposits, money market mutual funds, and CDs as their primary instruments of savings? What impact would these two factors have on the expansionary effects of the Fed's monetary policy? Explain.

*Asterisk denotes questions for which answers are given in Appendix B.

CHAPTER 15
Stabilization Policy, Output, and Employment

FOCUS

- Can monetary and fiscal policy reduce the ups and downs of the business cycle? Why or why not?

- How are expectations formed? Do expectations influence how macroeconomic policy works?

- What is the Phillips curve? Why were the early views about the Phillips curve wrong?

- Have important areas of agreement emerged from the experience and debate on stabilization policy of the past 50 years? Are there points of continuing disagreement?

- Why has the recovery from the 2008–2009 recession been so weak? How will this recession affect the future of the U.S. economy?

Unfortunately, policy-makers cannot act as if the economy is an automobile that can quickly be steered back and forth. Rather, the procedure of changing aggregate demand is much closer to that of a captain navigating a giant supertanker. Even if he gives a signal for a hard turn, it takes a mile before he can see a change, and ten miles before the ship makes the turn.
—Robert J. Gordon[1]

[1]Robert J. Gordon, *Macroeconomics* (Boston: Little, Brown, 1978), 334.

In previous chapters, we analyzed the impact of both fiscal and monetary policy on output, employment, and prices. We also noted that the initial impact of a policy change is often different than the impact over a more lengthy time period. We now want to take a more comprehensive look at stabilization policy. Can active management of fiscal and/or monetary policy reduce economic instability? This chapter will consider the record and examine both the potential and limitations of stabilization policy in more detail.

15-1 ECONOMIC FLUCTUATIONS: THE PAST 100 YEARS

Wide fluctuations in the general level of business activity—income, employment, and the price level—make personal economic planning extremely difficult. Such changes can cause even well devised investment plans to go awry. The tragic stories of unemployed workers begging for food and newly impoverished investors jumping out of windows during the Great Depression vividly portray the enormous personal and social costs of economic instability and the uncertainty that it generates.

Historically, there have been substantial fluctuations in real output. **Exhibit 1** illustrates the growth record of real GDP in the United States during the past century. Prior to World War II, double-digit swings in real GDP during a single year were not uncommon. Real GDP rose by more than 10 percent annually during World War I, during an economic boom in 1922, during a mid-1930s recovery, and again during World War II. In contrast,

EXHIBIT 1

Economic Instability: The Record of the Past Century

Prior to the conclusion of World War II, the United States experienced double-digit increases in real GDP in 1918, 1922, 1935–1936, and 1941–1943. In contrast, real output fell by 5 percent or more in 1920–1921, 1930–1932, 1938, and 1946. However, as illustrated here, fluctuations in real GDP have been considerably more moderate since 1950. Most economists believe that more appropriate macroeconomic policy—particularly monetary policy—deserves much of the credit for the increased stability of recent decades.

Source: Historical Statistics of the United States, 224 and Bureau of Economic Analysis, http://www.bea.gov.

output fell at an annual rate of 5 percent or more during the 1920–1921 recession, in the depression years of 1930–1932 and 1938, and again following World War II. Since 1950, economic ups and downs have been much more moderate. Nevertheless, periods of recession and economic boom are still observable.

15-2 CAN DISCRETIONARY POLICY PROMOTE ECONOMIC STABILITY?

There is widespread agreement about the goals of macroeconomic policy. Economists of almost all persuasions favor the goals of steady growth, price stability, and full employment (unemployment at the natural rate). However, there are disagreements about how to achieve these objectives. Most of these disagreements focus on the potential and limitations of discretionary macro policy as a stabilization tool.

If monetary and fiscal policies could inject stimulus during economic slowdowns and apply restraint during inflationary booms, this would help reduce the ups and downs of the business cycle. Some macroeconomists, sometimes called **activists**, believe that this is possible. The activists believe that policy-makers will be able to manage demand and respond to various disruptions and changing economic conditions in a manner that will promote economic stability. Other economists, called **nonactivists**, argue that the discretionary use of monetary and fiscal policy in response to changing economic conditions is likely to do more harm than good. The nonactivists note that erratic use of macro policy has been a major source of economic instability in the past. Thus, they believe that the economy would be more stable if policy-makers merely followed a steady course rather than constantly responding to turns in the economic road.

Both activists and nonactivists recognize that conducting macro policy in a stabilizing manner is not an easy task. Let's take a closer look at some of the complicating factors and available tools that might help improve the effectiveness of stabilization policy.

15-2a THE TIME LAG PROBLEM

If monetary and fiscal policies are going to exert a stabilizing impact, proper timing is crucially important. Three different types of time lags complicate the achievement of proper timing.

First, there is the **recognition lag**, the time period between a change in economic conditions and recognition of the change by policy-makers. It generally takes a few months to gather and tabulate reliable information on the recent performance of the economy in order to determine whether it has dipped into a recession or whether the inflation rate has accelerated, and so forth.

Second, even after the need for a policy change is recognized, there is generally an additional time period before the policy change is instituted. Economists refer to this delay as **administrative lag**. In the case of monetary policy, the administrative lag is generally quite short. The Federal Open Market Committee meets every few weeks and is in a position to institute a change in monetary policy quickly. This is a major advantage of monetary policy. For discretionary fiscal policy, the administrative lag is usually more lengthy. Congressional committees must meet. Legislation must be proposed and debated. Congress must act, and the president must consent. Each of these steps typically takes several months. These delays are a major disadvantage that limits the use of discretionary fiscal policy as a stabilization tool.

Finally, there is the **impact lag**, the time period between the implementation of a macro policy change and when the change exerts its primary impact on the economy. Although the impact of a change in tax rates is generally felt quickly, the expansionary effects of an increase in government spending are usually less rapid. It will take time for contractors to submit competitive bids and new contracts to be arranged and signed. Several months may pass before work on a new project actually begins. As we discussed in the previous chapter, the impact lag for monetary policy is variable and often lengthy. Six to eighteen months may pass before a shift in monetary policy exerts much impact on demand, output, and employment. Moreover, the time lag before there is a significant impact on the general level of prices and the rate of inflation is likely to be even longer.

Activists
Economists who believe that discretionary changes in monetary and fiscal policy can reduce the degree of instability in output and employment.

Nonactivists
Economists who believe that discretionary macro policy adjustments in response to cyclical conditions are likely to increase, rather than reduce, instability. Nonactivists favor steady and predictable policies regardless of business conditions.

Recognition lag
The time period after a policy change is needed from a stabilization standpoint but before the need is recognized by policy-makers.

Administrative lag
The time period after the need for a policy change is recognized but before the policy is actually implemented.

Impact lag
The time period after a policy change is implemented but before the change begins to exert its primary effects.

15-3 FORECASTING TOOLS AND MACRO POLICY

If a shift in policy is going to exert the desired effect at the proper time, policy-makers cannot wait until a problem develops before they act. They need to know what economic conditions will be like six to fifteen months in the future. Policy-makers need to know if a recession or an economic boom is around the corner. How can they find out? Forecasting tools can provide them with some information. Let's consider some of the forecasting devices available to policy-makers.

15-3a INDEX OF LEADING INDICATORS

Index of leading indicators

An index of economic variables that historically has tended to turn down prior to the beginning of a recession and turn up prior to the beginning of a business expansion.

The **index of leading indicators** is the single most widely used and closely watched forecasting tool. The index is a composite statistic based on ten key variables that generally turn down prior to a recession and turn up before the beginning of a business expansion (see the Measures of Economic Activity, "Index of Leading Indicators"). The index is published monthly, and a decline for three consecutive months is considered a warning that the economy is about to dip into a recession.

Exhibit 2 illustrates the path of the index during the 1959–2013 period. The index has correctly forecast each of the eight recessions since 1959. On five occasions, the downturn occurred eight to ten months prior to a recession, providing policy-makers with sufficient

EXHIBIT 2

Index of Leading Indicators

The shaded periods represent recessions. The index of leading indicators forecast each of the eight recessions during the 1959–2013 period. As the arrows show, however, the time lag between when the index turned down and when the economy fell into a recession varied. In addition, on four occasions (1962, 1966, 1984, and 1995), the index forecast a recession that did not occur.

[a]The arrows indicate the number of months that the downturn in the index preceded a recession. An asterisk (*) indicates a false signal of a recession.

Source: http://www.conference-board.org.

MEASURES OF ECONOMIC ACTIVITY

The Index of Leading Indicators

History indicates that no single indicator is able to forecast accurately the future direction of the economy. However, several economic variables do tend to reach a high or low prior to the peak of a business expansion or the trough of an economic recession. Such variables are called leading economic indicators.

To provide more reliable information on the future direction of the economy, economists have devised an index of ten such indicators:

1. Length of the average workweek in hours
2. Initial weekly claims for unemployment compensation
3. New orders placed with manufacturers
4. Percentage of companies receiving slower deliveries from suppliers
5. Contracts and orders for new plants and equipment
6. Permits for new housing starts
7. Interest rate spread, ten-year Treasury bonds less federal funds rate
8. Index of consumer expectations
9. Change in the index of stock prices (500 common stocks)
10. Change in the money supply (M2)

The variables included in the index were chosen both because of their tendency to lead (or predict) turns in the business cycle and because they are available frequently and promptly. In some cases, it is easy to see why a change in an economic indicator precedes a change in general economic activity. Consider the indicator of "new orders placed with manufacturers" (measured in constant dollars). An expansion in the volume of orders is generally followed by an expansion in manufacturing output. Similarly, manufacturers will tend to scale back their future production when a decline in new orders signals the probability of weak future demand for their products. The index of leading indicators can be found in *Business Cycle Indicators*, published by the Conference Board, a nonprofit business and research organization and online at http://www.conference-board.org.

lead time to modify policy, particularly monetary policy. In all but one instance, the downturn in the index preceded the recession by an even longer period. For example, it turned down 18 months prior to the 1990–1991 recession.

A downturn in the index, however, is not always an accurate indicator of the future. On four occasions (1962, 1966, 1984, and 1995), a decline in the index of leading indicators forecast a recession that did not materialize. This has given rise to the quip that the index has accurately forecast twelve of the last eight recessions.

Consider the path of the index of leading indicators prior to and during the recession that started in December 2007. The index turned down eight months before the start of the recession and declined steadily until it reached a low in March 2009. The index rose three consecutive months in April, May, and June of 2009, thereby forecasting the recovery that actually started in June of that year.

15-3b COMPUTER FORECASTING MODELS

Economists have developed highly complex econometric (statistical) models to improve the accuracy of macroeconomic forecasts. In essence, these models use past data on economic interrelationships to project how currently observed changes will influence the future path of key economic variables, such as real GDP, employment, and the price level. The most elaborate models use hundreds of variables and equations to simulate the future direction of various sectors and the economy's overall output and employment. Powerful high-speed computers are employed to forecast the future direction of the economy and analyze the effects of policy alternatives.

To date, the record of computer forecasting models is mixed. When economic conditions are relatively stable (for example, when the growth of real GDP and the rate of inflation follow a steady trend), the models have generally provided accurate forecasts for both aggregate economic variables and important subcomponents of the economy.

Unfortunately, however, they have generally missed the major turns in the economic road. For example, none of the major computer models predicted the recessions of either 1990 or 2001. Neither did they forecast the severity of the downturn in 2008.

15-3c MARKET SIGNALS AS FORECASTING TOOLS

Many policy-makers have favorite indicators—such as the consumer confidence index or the number of first-time applicants for unemployment benefits—that they believe are particularly good forecasting tools. Information supplied by certain markets can also sound an early warning that a change in policy is needed. For example, because they fluctuate daily and are determined in auction markets, changes in commodity prices often foretell future changes in the general price level. An increase in a broad index of commodity prices implies that money is plentiful (relative to demand). This suggests that the Fed should shift toward a more restrictive policy in order to offset future inflation. In contrast, falling commodity prices indicate that deflation is a potential future danger, in which case the Fed might want to shift toward a more expansionary policy.

Changes in exchange rates are also a source of information about the relative scarcity of money and fear of inflation. A decline in the exchange rate value of the dollar relative to other currencies suggests a fear of higher inflation and a reluctance to hold dollars. This would signal the need to shift to a more restrictive policy. Conversely, an increase in the exchange rate value of the dollar would indicate that the Fed has some leeway to shift to a more expansionary monetary policy. Most policy-makers view market signals like commodity prices and exchange rates as supplements to, rather than substitutes for, other forecasting devices.

15-3d IS ACCURATE FORECASTING FEASIBLE?

Many economists maintain that accurate forecasts of turns in the economy are beyond the reach of economics. Two major factors underlie this view. First, turns in the economic road often reflect economic shocks and unforeseen events—for example, discovery of a new resource or technology, abnormal weather, or political upheaval in an important oil-exporting nation. There is no reason to believe that economists or anyone else will be able to predict these changes accurately and consistently. Thus, while economic theory helps to predict the implications of unforeseen events, it cannot foretell what those events will be and when they might occur. Second, the critics of forecasting models argue that the future will differ from the past because people will often make different choices as the result of what they learned from previous events. Therefore, forecasting models based on past relationships—including elaborate computer models—will never be able to generate consistently accurate predictions.

One thing is for sure: Forecasting the future direction of the economy is an imperfect science, and it is likely to remain so in the foreseeable future. But this is not the only deterrent to effective stabilization policy. Policy-makers must also deal with expectations. A policy shift may exert a very different impact, depending on whether it is widely expected or catches people by surprise. Expectations may also influence the length of time lags and potency of alternative policy measures. Given the importance of expectations, we need to analyze how they are formed.

15-4 HOW ARE EXPECTATIONS FORMED?

There are two general theories about how expectations are formed: adaptive and rational expectations.

Under the simplest theory, the **adaptive-expectations hypothesis**, it is assumed that decision-makers rely on what has happened in the recent past as the best indicator of what will happen in the future. For example, individuals would expect the price level to be stable next year if stable prices had been present during the past two or three years.

Adaptive-expectations hypothesis
The hypothesis that economic decision-makers base their future expectations on actual outcomes observed during recent periods. For example, according to this view, the rate of inflation actually experienced during the past two or three years would be the major determinant of the rate of inflation expected for the next year.

Similarly, if prices had risen at an annual rate of 4 or 5 percent during the past several years, then people would expect similar increases next year. Of course, as conditions change, people will alter their expectations. However, under the adaptive expectations theory, there will always be a time lag before people will alter their expectations in response to changing conditions.

The **rational-expectations hypothesis** is more complex. Under this theory, people form their expectations about the future on the basis of all available information, including knowledge about policy changes and how they affect the economy. According to this view, rather than merely assuming that the future will be like the immediate past, people also consider the expected effects of changes in policy. Based on their understanding of economic policy, for example, people may alter their expectations regarding the future rate of inflation when the government runs a larger deficit or expands the supply of money more rapidly.

Perhaps an example will help clarify the difference between the two theories. Suppose that prices had increased at an annual rate of 3 percent during each of the past three years. In addition, assume that decision-makers believe there is a relationship between the growth rate of the money supply and rising prices. They note that the money stock has expanded at a 12 percent annual rate during the last nine months, up from the 4 percent rate of the past several years. According to the rational-expectations hypothesis, people will integrate the shift to the more expansionary monetary policy into their forecast of the future inflation rate. For example, they might project an increase in the inflation rate, perhaps to the 6 to 10 percent range. In other words, based on the more expansionary monetary policy, people will begin to anticipate the higher rate of inflation even before it actually occurs. In contrast, under the adaptive-expectations hypothesis, the more expansionary monetary policy would exert no impact on the expectations of people, at least not until there was an increase in the rate of inflation.

The rational-expectations hypothesis does not assume that forecasts will always be correct. We live in a world of uncertainty. Even rational decision-makers will err. But they will not continue to make the same errors.

There are two major differences between the two theories: (1) how quickly people adjust to a change and (2) the likelihood of systematic forecasting errors. If the adaptive-expectations theory is correct, people will adjust more slowly. When a more expansionary policy leads to inflation, for example, there will be a significant time lag, perhaps two or three years, before people come to expect the inflation and incorporate it into their decision making. In contrast, the rational-expectations theory implies that people will begin to anticipate more inflation as soon as they observe a move toward a more expansionary policy—perhaps even before there is an actual increase in the rate of inflation. Therefore, the time lag between a shift in policy and a change in expectations will be shorter under rational than under adaptive expectations.

Second, systematic errors will occur under adaptive but not under rational expectations. For example, with adaptive expectations, when the inflation rate is rising, decision-makers will systematically tend to underestimate the future rate of inflation. In contrast, when the rate of inflation is falling, individuals will tend systematically to overestimate its

Rational-expectations hypothesis

The hypothesis that economic decision-makers weigh all available evidence, including information concerning the probable effects of current and future economic policy, when they form their expectations about future economic events (like the probable future inflation rate).

OUTSTANDING ECONOMIST

ROBERT LUCAS (1937–)

The 1995 Nobel laureate Robert Lucas is generally given credit for the introduction of the rational-expectations theory into macroeconomics. Lucas's technical work in this area has substantially altered the way economists think about macroeconomic policy. He is a longtime professor of economics at the University of Chicago.

future rate. The errors will be random under rational expectations. With rational expectations, people will be as likely to overestimate as to underestimate the inflationary impact of a shift to a more expansionary policy.

15-5 MACRO POLICY IMPLICATIONS OF ADAPTIVE AND RATIONAL EXPECTATIONS

When it comes to setting macro policy, does it make any difference how quickly people alter their expectations and whether errors are random or systematic? The *AD–AS* model can be used to address this question. Suppose that there is a shift to a more expansionary macro policy—an increase in the money growth rate, for example. As Exhibit 3 illustrates, the policy shift will stimulate aggregate demand and place upward pressure on the price level (or the inflation rate in the dynamic case). Under adaptive expectations (part a), people will initially fail to anticipate the higher prices. Therefore, as we have previously discussed, output will temporarily increase to Y_2, beyond the economy's long-run potential. Correspondingly, employment will expand and unemployment will recede below the economy's natural rate. When the effects of expansionary policy are unanticipated, both output and employment increase in the short run.

However, the output rate beyond the economy's capacity will be unsustainable even with adaptive expectations. As the expansionary policies persist and the rate of inflation increases, people will eventually begin to anticipate the higher rate of inflation. Once this happens, resource prices will rise as rapidly as product prices, and output will return to

---

EXHIBIT 3

Expectations and the Short-Run Effects of Demand Stimulus

Because under adaptive expectations people do not anticipate inflation until after it occurs, a shift to a more expansionary policy will increase aggregate demand and lead to a temporary increase in real GDP from Y_F to Y_2, (part a). In contrast, under rational expectations, people quickly anticipate the inflationary impact

of demand–stimulus policies and therefore resource prices and production costs rise as rapidly as prices. In this case, both *AD* and *SRAS* shift upward, leading to an increase in the general level of prices (inflation), but there is no change in real output, even in the short run (part b).

(a) Expansionary policy under adaptive expectations

(b) Expansionary policy under rational expectations

its long-run potential (Y_F). As a result, the high level of output and employment will only be temporary.

Part (b) of Exhibit 3 illustrates the impact of expansionary macroeconomic policy under rational expectations. Remember, with rational expectations, decision-makers will quickly begin to anticipate the probable effects of the more expansionary policy—stronger demand and a rising rate of inflation, for example—and alter their choices accordingly. Agreements specifying future wage rates and resource prices will quickly make allowance for an expected increase in the price level. When buyers and sellers in the resource market anticipate fully and adjust rapidly to the effects of the demand–stimulus policies, wage rates and resource prices will rise as rapidly as product prices. Hence, the short-run aggregate supply curve will shift upward (to $SRAS_2$) as rapidly as the aggregate demand curve. Under these circumstances, an expansionary policy that leads to an increase in aggregate demand will generate only a higher general level of prices (the move from E_1 to E_2 in part b of Exhibit 3). There will be no real output increase even in the short run. Thus, the rational-expectations hypothesis implies that when decision-makers quickly anticipate the inflationary side effects of an expansionary policy, the policy will fail to expand output even temporarily.

The policy implications of the two theories differ in the short run but not in the long run. In the short run, demand–stimulus policies will expand output and employment under adaptive expectations but not under rational expectations. In the long run, however, the implications of the two theories are identical. Like rational expectations, the adaptive-expectations theory indicates that decision-makers will eventually anticipate the inflationary effects of the more expansionary policy. Once this happens, output will recede to the economy's long-run potential. Therefore, both theories imply that the long-run effects of a more expansionary macro policy will be inflation rather than sustainable increases in output. Both also imply that price stability and full-employment output are complementary when considered over lengthy time frames.

15-6 THE PHILLIPS CURVE: THE VIEW OF THE 1960s VERSUS TODAY

In the late 1950s, British economist A. W. Phillips examined the historical data on the relationship between wage inflation and unemployment in the United Kingdom.[2] As a result, a curve indicating the relationship between the rate of inflation and the rate of unemployment is known as the **Phillips curve**. Exhibit 4 uses a graphic from the 1969 *Economic Report of the President* to illustrate the idea of the Phillips curve. When the unemployment rate was plotted against the rate of inflation in the United States during 1954–1968, the points mapped out a curve indicating that there was an inverse relationship between the rate of inflation and the rate of unemployment. When inflation was high, the unemployment rate tended to be low. Correspondingly, when the inflation rate was low, the unemployment rate tended to be high.

In the 1960s, most macroeconomists ignored the potential impact of expectations. Instead, they believed that there was a direct trade-off between inflation and unemployment—that a lower rate of unemployment could be achieved if we were willing to tolerate a little more inflation.[3] This view provided the foundation for the inflationary policies of the 1970s. As John Maynard Keynes once noted, ideas have consequences, both when they are right and when they are wrong.

Phillips curve
A curve that illustrates the relationship between the rate of inflation and the rate of unemployment.

---

[2]A. W. Phillips, "The Relationship between Unemployment and the Rate of Change of Money Wages in the United Kingdom, 1861–1957," *Economica* 25 (1958): 238–99.

[3]For example, Nobel prize winners Paul Samuelson and Robert Solow told the American Economic Association in 1959, "In order to achieve the nonperfectionist's goal of high enough output to give us no more than 3 percent unemployment, the price index might have to rise by as much as 4 to 5 percent per year. That much price rise [inflation] would seem to be the necessary cost of high employment and production in the years immediately ahead." See Paul A. Samuelson and Robert Solow, "Our Menu of Policy Changes," *American Economic Review* (May 1960).

EXHIBIT 4

Early View of the Phillips Curve

The Phillips curve shows the relationship between inflation and unemployment. The dots on this diagram from the 1969 Economic *Report of the President* represent the inflation rate and unemployment rate for each year between 1954 and 1968. Note that the chart suggests that higher rates of inflation are associated with lower rates of unemployment. Because they failed to recognize the importance of expectations, many economists and policy-makers in the 1960s and 1970s thought this relationship was stable. Thus, they believed that expansionary (inflationary) policies could permanently reduce the rate of unemployment. As the record of the 1970s shows, this view is fallacious.

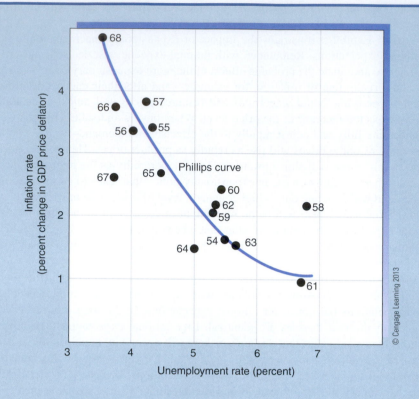

© Cengage Learning 2013

Beginning in the latter part of the 1960s, both monetary and fiscal policy became more expansionary. The inflation rate rose to the 3 percent to 6 percent range, but as the higher rates of inflation persisted, the unemployment rate also began to rise. As macroeconomic policy became even more expansionary, the unemployment rate dipped briefly, but it soon returned to exceedingly high levels. By the end of the 1970s, the U.S. economy was characterized by high rates of both inflation and unemployment. The inflation rate in 1979 was 11.3 percent, and in 1980 it jumped to 13.5 percent, about 10 percentage points higher than the rates of the late 1960s. But even these high rates of inflation failed to reduce the unemployment rate. In 1980, the rate of unemployment stood at 7.1 percent, well above the 4.9 percent registered during the recessionary year of 1970.

What went wrong? Given what we know today about expectations, this is now an easy question to answer. As both the adaptive- and rational-expectations theories indicate, the alleged trade-off between inflation and unemployment will dissipate once people anticipate a higher rate of inflation. Put another way, the Phillips curve is not fixed. When the inflation rate increases, people will come to anticipate the higher rate of inflation, and this will cause the Phillips curve to shift upward and to the right. The adaptive-expectations theory implies that there will be a time lag—perhaps one to three years—before people are able to anticipate and adjust fully to a higher rate of inflation. But once the higher inflation rate is anticipated, it will not lead to an expansion in either output or employment. The rational-expectations theory indicates that the adjustment period will be brief. In fact, with rational expectations, there may not be any trade-off between inflation and unemployment, even in the short run.

Integration of expectations into the Phillips curve analysis indicates that there is no sustainable trade-off between inflation and unemployment. Expectations undermine the simple Phillips curve analysis of the 1960s.[4]

15-6a EXPECTATIONS AND THE MODERN VIEW OF THE PHILLIPS CURVE

If accurately anticipated by decision-makers, even high rates of inflation—rates of 10 or 15 percent, for example—will fail to reduce unemployment below its natural rate.[5] Of course, people won't always correctly anticipate the rate of inflation, particularly if there is an abrupt change in the rate. Within the expectations framework, it is the difference between the actual and expected inflation rate that will influence output and employment. On the one hand, when inflation is greater than anticipated, profit margins will improve, output will expand, and unemployment will fall below its natural rate. On the other hand, when the actual rate of inflation is less than the expected rate, profits will be abnormally low, output will recede, and unemployment will rise above its natural rate.

Exhibit 5 recasts the Phillips curve within the expectations framework. When people underestimate the actual rate of inflation, abnormally low unemployment will occur. Conversely, when decision-makers expect a higher rate of inflation than what actually occurs—when they overestimate the inflation rate—unemployment will rise above its natural rate. When the actual and expected inflation rates are equal, the economy's output will be at its potential and unemployment at its natural rate.

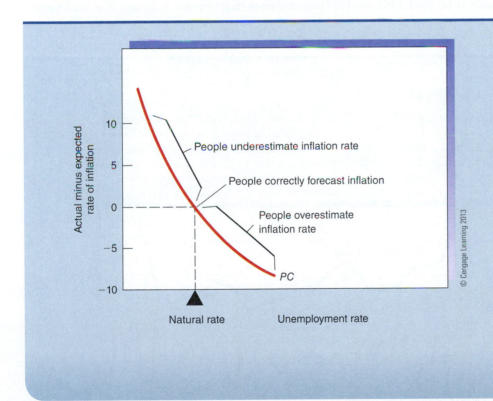

EXHIBIT 5

Modern Expectational Phillips Curve

It is the difference between the actual and expected rates of inflation that influences the unemployment rate, not the size of the inflation rate, as the earlier, naive Phillips curve analysis implied. When inflation is greater than anticipated (people underestimate it), unemployment will fall below the natural rate. In contrast, when inflation is less than people anticipate (people overestimate it) unemployment will rise above the natural rate. If decision-makers correctly anticipate the inflation rate, the natural rate of unemployment will result.

---

[4]Even during the 1960s, there were some critics of the inflation–unemployment trade-off view. See Edmund S. Phelps, "Phillips Curves, Expectations of Inflation and Optimal Employment over Time," *Economica* 3 (1967): 254–81; and Milton Friedman, "The Role of Monetary Policy," *American Economic Review* (May 1968): 1–17.
[5]Empirically, higher rates of inflation are generally associated with greater variability in the inflation rate. Erratic variability increases economic uncertainty. It is likely to inhibit business activity, reduce the volume of mutually advantageous exchange, and cause the level of employment to fall. Thus, higher, more variable inflation rates may well increase the rate of unemployment.

When the inflation rate is steady, when it is neither rising nor falling, people will come to anticipate the rate accurately. The steady rate will be built into long-term contracts, like collective bargaining agreements, building leases, and bank loans. Under these conditions, profit margins will be normal, and output will move toward the economy's long-run potential. Correspondingly, the actual rate of unemployment will move toward its natural rate—its minimum sustainable rate. In fact, the natural rate of unemployment is sometimes defined as the unemployment rate present when the inflation rate is neither rising nor falling. In contrast with the early Phillips curve view, the modern view indicates that if policy-makers want to keep the unemployment rate low, they should follow policies consistent with a low and steady rate of inflation—one that people will be able to forecast accurately.

Exhibit 6 presents data on the *change* in the inflation rate (the four-quarter moving average) over the past several decades. The exhibit illustrates the impact of both abrupt changes and low steady rates of inflation. When the change in the inflation rate spikes upward, it means there has been a sharp increase in the rate of inflation during the last 12 months. Conversely, a downward spike means that the inflation rate has fallen sharply. Predictably, these abrupt changes will be difficult for people to forecast accurately. Therefore, the actual rate of inflation is likely to rise above the expected rate when the inflation rate increases abruptly and fall below it when there is an abrupt downturn in the inflation rate.

Thus, one would expect the unemployment rate to fall when there is a sharp upturn in the inflation rate and rise when there is a sharp downturn. As Exhibit 6 shows, this has been the case. Notice how the substantial increases in the rate of inflation during 1973 and 1976–1978 and even the more moderate increases of the 1980s were associated with downturns in the rate of unemployment. In contrast, the sharp reductions in the rate of inflation during 1974, 1980–1981, and 1989 preceded substantial increases in the rate of unemployment.

EXHIBIT 6

Unemployment and Changes in the Rate of Inflation

Here, we show the relationship between changes in the inflation rate (four-quarter moving average) and the rate of unemployment. Abrupt changes in the inflation rate will be difficult for people to anticipate correctly. Notice how the sharp falls in the inflation rate during 1974, 1980–1981, and 1988–1989 preceded recessions and substantial increases in the unemployment rate. Also notice that the steadier (and lower) inflation rates during 1990–2004 were associated with lower and more stable rates of unemployment.

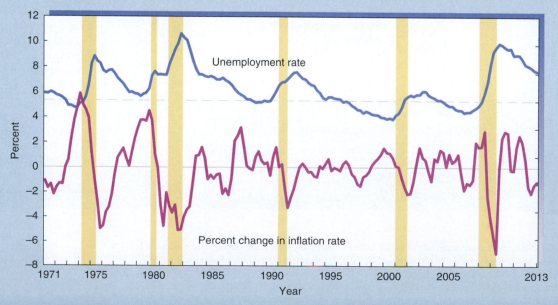

Source: http://www.economagic.com.

The economic crisis of 2008–2009 was a little different. In that case, a sharp decline in the inflation rate was associated with a substantial increase in the unemployment rate during the same time period.

Exhibit 6 also shows that when the inflation rate is steadier, the unemployment rate tends to be lower and more stable. Note how, compared to the 1970s, the inflation rate was lower and the swings in the rate were more moderate during 1985–2005. Correspondingly, the rate of unemployment was also lower and more stable during the latter period of greater price stability.

15-6b WHAT HAVE WE LEARNED ABOUT MACRO POLICY?

Macroeconomics is relatively new. Prior to the Great Depression, research on measurement of national income and sources of economic fluctuations was sparse. It was not until the 1960s that policy-makers developed much interest in the possible use of fiscal policy as a stabilization tool. Moreover, 50 years ago, neither economists nor policy-makers thought that monetary policy exerted much impact on anything other than the general level of prices. While awareness of the potential effects of fiscal and monetary policy increased during 1960–1980, there was little appreciation of the time lags, importance of expectations, and difficulties involved in the effective use of these tools to promote stability.

Macroeconomics has come a long way during the past half century. Real-world experience, research, and developments in economic theory have vastly expanded our knowledge of both the potential and limitations of fiscal and monetary policy. Substantial agreement has emerged on a number of key points. Debate continues on several others. Let's consider both.

15-6c AREAS OF AGREEMENT

1. It is difficult to time changes in monetary and fiscal policy correctly.
If it is going to exert a stabilizing impact, a macro policy change must exert stimulus during downturns and restraint during inflationary booms. Automatic stabilizers can help achieve these objectives, but *effective use of discretionary policy is problematic.* Given our limited forecasting abilities and the time lags accompanying changes in monetary and fiscal policy, persistent shifts in policy are likely to be destabilizing. Put another way, steady policies will lead to more stability than constant policy changes in response to business cycle conditions.

2. Expansionary policies that generate strong demand and inflation will not reduce the rate of unemployment below the natural rate—at least not for long.
Both the integration of expectations into macroeconomic analysis and the experience of the 1970s illustrate that there is no sustainable trade-off between inflation and unemployment. Once people come to expect inflation, the inflation–unemployment trade-off will dissipate. Moreover, excessively expansionary monetary and fiscal policy will lead to high and variable inflation rates that will generate uncertainty and instability, and thereby retard long-run economic growth.

15-6d AREAS OF CONTINUED DEBATE

While general agreement has emerged in some areas, debate continues in others. These unresolved questions add to the excitement of economics. We will mention three key areas of continued debate among macroeconomists.

1. Does fiscal policy exert much impact on aggregate demand?
While most economists do not believe that discretionary fiscal policy can be constantly adjusted in a manner that will promote stability, nonetheless, many believe that budget deficits provide demand stimulus, particularly during a severe recession. Others argue that the secondary effects of higher interest rates and future taxes undermine the potency of fiscal policy.

2. During a severe recession, will an increase in government spending be more effective than a reduction in taxes as a tool to promote recovery? Most Keynesian economists favor increases in government spending because they fear that a large share of a tax reduction will be saved and therefore not add much stimulus to aggregate demand. Non-Keynesians argue that the demand stimulus effects of spending increases will often be timed poorly and that they will generally be driven by special interest politics and therefore likely to flow into projects that are economically inefficient. Moreover, supply-side economists argue that reductions in tax rates will enhance the incentive to work, invest, and employ others, which will help promote recovery.

3. Is economic instability the result of the natural tendencies of a market economy or the errors of policy-makers? Many economists, particularly Keynesians, believe that market economies are inherently unstable. This view stresses that economic expansions breed optimism, rising asset prices, and strong aggregate demand, which culminate in inflation and an unsustainable economic boom. Similarly, a downturn will tend to feed on itself, leading to pessimism, falling asset prices, and reductions in aggregate demand, which, if not counteracted by macro policy, will end in chronic and prolonged recessions.

Other economists, particularly monetarists, argue that economic fluctuations are largely the result of stop–go monetary policy. They believe that the severe episodes of both inflation and depression have been the result of monetary disturbances. Those who stress policy errors cite the unstable and highly expansionary monetary policy of the 1970s as the primary reason for the inflation and instability of that era. They also point to the 30 percent decline in the money supply between 1929 and 1933 and another decline during 1937–1938 as the primary cause of the Great Depression. (For more information on this topic, see Special Topic 6, "Lessons from the Great Depression.")

The crisis of 2008 illustrates the continuing debate. Those who stress the inherent instability of markets point to the excessive leverage of major banks, the fear, and the sharp reduction in demand that engulfed the economy during the latter half of 2008 as support for their view. On the other hand, those who stress the role of policy errors argue that the primary cause of the crisis was housing regulations that undermined sound lending practices and the instability of Fed policy during 2002–2006. Of course, the two theories are not mutually exclusive. Both the nature of markets and policy errors may be important sources of economic instability.

Economists continue to debate the sources of economic instability and the effectiveness of macroeconomic policy. Two of the 20th century's greatest economists, John Maynard Keynes (left) and Frederich Hayek (right), represent polar views. Keynes believed that fiscal policy could reduce economic instability; Hayek believed the opposite.

15-6e CURRENT POLICY AND IMPLICATIONS FOR THE FUTURE

In some ways, the recession of 2008–2009 was generated by "the perfect storm," a combination of improper monetary policy, perverse regulation, a long-term increase in household indebtedness, and excessive leverage by financial institutions. (See Special Topic 5, "The Crisis of 2008: Causes and Lessons for the Future," for a detailed analysis of this issue.)

The policy response to this recession will almost surely exert a long-term impact on macroeconomics. More than any in American history, this recession provides an experiment on the potency of Keynesian fiscal policy and activist monetary policy. The budget deficits during fiscal years 2009–2011 were approximately 9 percent of GDP, by far the largest since World War II. The Fed doubled its asset holdings during the last six months of 2008, and by mid-year 2013, they were more than three times the level of June 2008. In total, this quantitative easing injected $2.4 trillion of additional reserves into the banking system. Thus, both fiscal and monetary policy were highly expansionary during and following the recession of 2008–2009.

How did the economy respond to the fiscal and monetary stimulus? It is revealing to compare and contrast the recessions of 1981–1982 and 2008–2009. These were the two most severe recessions since the Great Depression. Both were long, the former lasted 16 months and the latter 18 months. The unemployment rate soared to more than 10 percent during both recessions. Interestingly, the policy responses were dramatically different. In contrast with the government spending increases and expansionary monetary policy of the most recent recession, tax rates were sharply reduced and monetary policy was restrictive during the 1981–1982 recession. Exhibit 7 presents data on the path of unemployment and growth of real GDP during the two years prior to and three and one-half years following the two recessions. During the 1981–1982 recession, unemployment

EXHIBIT 7

Unemployment and Real GDP Growth Rates: A Comparison of the 1981–1982 and 2008–2009 Recessions

The 1981–1982 and 2008–2009 recessions were the most severe of the post–World War II era. The unemployment rate and growth of real GDP for the two years before and after the end of these recessions are shown here. The unemployment rate rose to 10.8 percent during the 1981–1982 recession and to 10 percent during the 2008–2009 recession (left frame). Two years after the end of the earlier recession, the unemployment rate had receded to pre-recession levels, but it remained high (9 percent) after two years of recovery from the most recent recession. Similarly, the growth of real GDP was far more rapid during the earlier recession than the later recession (right frame).

Source: www.economagic.com.

soared to 10.8 percent, up from 7.2 percent at the beginning of the downturn. In the most recent recession, the unemployment rate jumped to 10 percent, up from 5 percent prior to the onset of the decline. Two years after the end of the 1981–1982 recession, the economy had recovered nicely and the unemployment rate was lower than at the beginning of the recession. But this was not the case for the most recent recession. Two years after it ended, the unemployment rate was still 9 percent, far above the rate prior to the downturn and only a percentage point less than its peak level during the recession. Even three and half years later, the unemployment rate was 7.8 percent, almost 3 percentage points higher than when the downturn began.

As Exhibit 7 right frame shows, the growth of real GDP during the recovery paints a similar picture. During the first six quarters of the recovery from the 1981–1982 recession, real GDP grew at an annual rate of between 5 percent and 9 percent. The average annual real growth rate during these six quarters was 6.7 percent. In contrast, the growth rate of real GDP averaged 2.2 percent during the first six quarters of recovery from the 2008–2009 recession, a third the figure of the 1981–1982 recession. During the initial three and a half years of the recovery phase, real GDP growth averaged 5.4 percent for the earlier recession but only 2.1 percent in the most recent downturn. Clearly, the recovery phase from the more recent recession was substantially weaker than for that of the earlier one. In fact, the recovery phase from the current recession is the weakest of any since the Great Depression.

The stagnation of private investment is a major reason for the weakness of the recovery. Exhibit 8 provides data for net private business investment for 1960–2011. Net private business investment was negative in 2009, indicating that the new investment was not even enough to cover the depreciation of existing assets. In 2010 and 2011, net investment was still only slightly above 1 percent of GDP, well below any year prior to the current recession. Net private business investment is crucially important because it provides the tools, equipment, and capital assets for workers in the future. When private business investment grows rapidly, it will enhance the productivity of workers. The low level of net investment of the current recession will mean both lower productivity and wages in the years immediately ahead.

EXHIBIT 8

Net Private Business Investment as a Percent of GDP, 1960–2011

Domestic business investment during and following the recession of 2008–2009 fell to the lowest levels since the Great Depression. This will adversely affect the supply of capital (equipment and tools) available to American workers in the years immediately ahead. As a result, the growth of productivity and income during the next decade are likely to be slow.

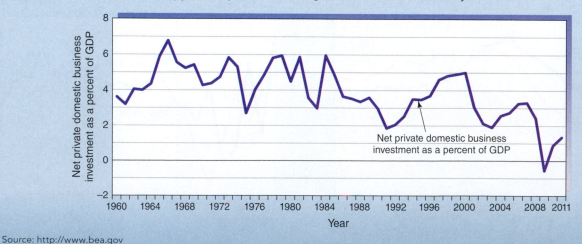

Source: http://www.bea.gov

EXHIBIT 9

Long-Term Unemployment 1960–2013

The long-term unemployment rate (percent unemployed six months or more as a share of the labor force) soared to 4 percent in 2010–2011. This was substantially higher than at any time in the post–World War II era. Many economists believe that the extension of unemployment benefits for up to 99 weeks was an important contributor to these high long-term unemployment rates.

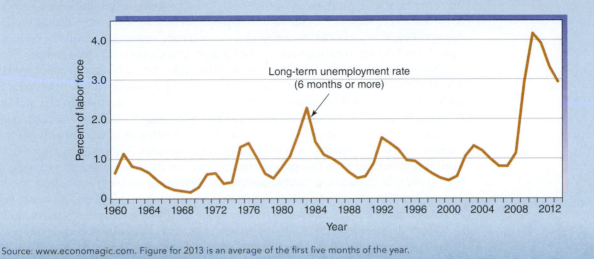

Source: www.economagic.com. Figure for 2013 is an average of the first five months of the year.

Exhibit 9 provides data on the long-term unemployment rate, the share of the labor force unemployed for more than 26 weeks, over the last 50 years. In 2010–2011, the long-term unemployment rate hovered around 4 percent, twice the rate of most earlier recessions. The long-term rate reached 2.3 percent during the severe 1982 recession, but other than that, it never reached 2 percent during any of the post–World War II recessions.

Why was the long-term unemployment rate so high during and following the most recent recession? Extension of unemployment benefits for up to 99 weeks was a large item included in the various "stimulus packages" of 2008–2011. This extension was longer than in any past recession. Think about how payments that replaced 50 percent to 60 percent of the after-tax earnings from your previous job would affect your incentive to find and accept a job quickly. Predictably, this reduction in the opportunity cost of unemployment would result in more lengthy spells of unemployment and a higher unemployment rate, particularly the long-term rate. Many workers close to retirement would be able to use these benefits to bridge the gap from employment into the retirement phase of life. Studies indicate that the extension of the benefits added approximately three-fourths of a percentage point to the unemployment rate.[6] Thus, while the extensions of the benefits to nearly two years may have reduced the hardships accompanying unemployment, they also resulted in higher unemployment rates than would otherwise have occurred. Moreover, when workers are unemployed for lengthy spells, their skills deteriorate, and as a result, their future earnings will be lower. This, too, will adversely affect the growth of future income in the United States.

15-6f WHY HAS THE FISCAL AND MONETARY STIMULUS FAILED TO PROMOTE A STRONGER RECOVERY?

Given the huge fiscal and monetary stimulus, why has the recovery from the 2008–2009 recession been so weak? Several factors contributed to the weakness. Let's consider a number of the most important fiscal and monetary factors.

[6] For evidence on this point, see Daniel Aaronson, Bhashkar Mazumder, and Shani Schechter, "What Is Behind the Rise in Long-Term Unemployment?," Federal Reserve Bank of Chicago *Economic Perspectives*, Second Quarter 2010, 28–51.

First, the fiscal stimulus spending programs were largely temporary. Both the Bush and Obama administrations tried to stimulate the economy by sending onetime checks to most Americans. Windfall income transfers of this type do not provide the recipients with either a job or income they can count on in the future. Neither do they provide additional incentive to work, invest, and earn. Both economic theory and past research indicate that such tax reductions exert little impact on either aggregate demand or output. Moreover, the nature of the hastily designed spending programs suffered from the same deficiency. Teachers, healthcare workers, and others employed on stimulus funds recognized the uncertainty of future funding from this source. Workers on "shovel-ready" projects knew they were a one-time occurrence. Even recipients of the extended unemployment benefits knew they would eventually run out. People are reluctant to purchase a car or house, undertake a business venture, or make other long-term commitments on the basis of such temporary income sources.

Second, politically directed stimulus spending will result in numerous counterproductive projects. It is naïve to think otherwise. The political process does not have anything like profit and loss that will consistently direct resources toward productive projects and away from counterproductive ones. Instead, as public choice analysis indicates, special-interest lobbying, campaign contributions, and other forms of political favoritism will direct the stimulus spending. Predictably, a huge share of the stimulus funds will be channeled toward special interest spending projects like ethanol subsidies, wind and solar energy, and high-speed rail. These energy and transportation sources are more expensive than the alternatives. In effect, the spending directs resources toward high cost and away from low-cost methods of production. Such counterproductive spending undermines the recovery process.

Third, the large federal deficits and growth of the federal debt to more than 100 percent of GDP generated uncertainty and fear of another financial collapse. Moreover, the high level of debt was even more troublesome because the situation was sure to get worse as the unfunded liabilities of the Social Security and Medicare programs generated still more spending as the baby boomers retired in the years immediately ahead. Against this background, political decision-makers still refused to accept reality and develop a strategy to control federal spending and the ballooning debt. As we have previously stressed, the political process is myopic. Thus, the failure of political decision-makers to take corrective action was not particularly surprising. Nonetheless, it was still a source of both concern and uncertainty.

Finally, there was also uncertainty generated by what economic historian Robert Higgs calls regime change, the situation in which people are reluctant to undertake business ventures and investments because the government is constantly changing the rules.[7] Higgs argues that uncertainty generated by the numerous policy changes that altered the structure of the economy during the New Deal era prolonged the Great Depression. President Roosevelt is often lauded for bold actions during the Great Depression, but the facts indicate they were largely ineffective. Investment came to a standstill and the unemployment rate was nearly 20 percent six years after the New Deal policies were initiated. (For additional information on this era, see Special Topic 6, "Lessons from the Great Depression.")

Something similar to regime change happened during and following the recent recession. Consider the following events of 2008–2011: The Bush stimulus and bank bailout (the Troubled Asset Relief Program); the $800 billion Obama stimulus program; a huge increase in government spending; adoption of a healthcare bill leading to more political direction of one-sixth of the economy; the cash-for-clunkers program; the temporary $8,000 tax credit for first-time home buyers; the largest budget deficits since World War II; growth of the debt to historic peacetime levels; the failure to pass a federal budget during 2009–2012; the delay of the tax legislation for 2011–2012 until just three weeks prior to the beginning of the tax year; the vast expansion in regulation of energy; the change in unionization rules; and even the prohibition of a new production line by a large manufacturer (Boeing) in a right-to-work state.

The constant changing of the rules, regulations, taxes, and subsidies embodied in these programs and many others created an environment of uncertainty and business responded

---

[7]Robert Higgs, "Regime Uncertainty: Why the Great Depression Lasted So Long and Why Prosperity Resumed After the War," *The Independent Review* 1, no. 4 (Spring 1997).

in a predictable manner: delay of investments and new business ventures until you have more information about the direction of future policy. Viewed from this perspective, the collapse of private investment (see Exhibit 8) is not that surprising.[8] During difficult times, politicians are under pressure to "do something." Unfortunately, there is no assurance that what they do will be helpful.

Turning to monetary policy, why wasn't the Fed's huge injection of reserves and near-zero interest rate policy more effective? First, the huge increase in reserve money generated uncertainty about future inflation and the Fed's commitment to price stability. As the Phillips curve analysis indicates, it is the actual rate of inflation relative to the expected rate that determines the impact of expansionary monetary policy on output and employment. If people expect a higher rate of inflation than actually occurs, output and employment will be adversely affected. As the Fed injected a huge quantity of reserves into the banking system, many expected the inflation rate to increase sharply. The soaring gold prices of 2009–2011 are consistent with this view. But the actual rate of inflation during 2009–2012 was modest. Thus, the actual inflation rate may well have been less than the expected rate, contributing to output and employment levels below their long-run potential.

Second, during normal times, if the Fed pushed interest rates downward, one would expect this to lead to an increase in investment, consumption, and asset prices. However, fiscal and regulatory policies were a source of uncertainty that retarded private investment. At the same time, the heavy indebtedness of households dampened the impact of the low interest rates on consumption. Household debt rose steadily relative to personal income during 1985–2007. By 2008, the household debt-to-income ratio was far higher than during prior decades (see Exhibit 4, Chapter 11). Moreover, the falling housing prices of recent years made households well aware of the imprudence of their high debt levels, and they responded with efforts to reduce their indebtedness. Thus, their spending was not very responsive to the Fed's low interest rate policy.

Third, while the Fed's low interest rate policy places upward pressure on asset prices, it also reduces both the velocity of money and the wealth of people relying on savings deposits, money market mutual funds, certificates of deposits, and similar saving instruments. Both of these factors would reduce current spending and wealth, and thereby offset, at least partially, the stimulus effects of the lower interest rates.

Finally, the Fed's low interest rate policy has enabled Congress and the president to vastly expand the spending and debt of the federal government. When the federal government can borrow at interest rates of just one or two percent, it will be able to continue increasing its spending without experiencing large increases in current interest expense. But the interest charges accompanying the vast expansion in federal debt will soar once interest rates rise, as they are sure to do, as the recovery matures. Predictably, this will weaken both the recovery process and future growth.

The experience of Canada provides insight on how to deal with it. Like the United States today, Canada confronted rising government expenditures, large budget deficits, and a government debt of more than 100 percent of its GDP in the mid-1990s. Canada responded with broad reductions in government spending, reform of welfare and entitlement programs, and a shift from budget deficits to surpluses. The result was more rapid economic growth, expansion in employment, and a reduction in the rate of unemployment.

While reflecting on the current troubles of the U.S economy, we must not forget that 1983–2012 was the most stable period in American history. During this 30-year period, there were only three downturns, and the economy experienced only 35 months of recession. As **Exhibit 10** illustrates, this stability is unprecedented. From 1910 to 1959, the U.S. economy was in recession 32.8 percent of the time. Between 1960 and 1982, recession was present 22.8 percent of the time. But, during 1983–2012, the economy was in recession only 9.4 percent of the time. The economic ups and downs of the past 50 years have been less severe than during earlier periods. Inspection of Exhibit 1 also illustrates this point.

---

[8]For evidence that an increase in uncertainty adversely affected the growth of GDP and employment during 2008–2011, see Scott R. Baker, Nicholas Bloom, and Steven J. Davis, "Measuring Economic Policy Uncertainty," Chicago Booth School of Business Working Number 13-02, January 1, 2013.

EXHIBIT 10

Reduction in the Incidence of Recession

The U.S. economy was in recession 32.8 percent of the time during the 1910–1959 period and 22.8 percent of the time between 1960 and 1982, but only 9.4 percent of the time during 1983–2012.

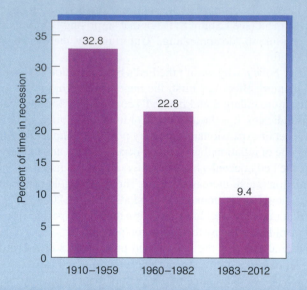

Source: R. E. Lipsey and D. Preston, Source Book of Statistics Relating to Construction (1966); and National Bureau of Economic Research, http://www.nber.org.

LOOKING AHEAD

As we have stressed, macroeconomics is about economic growth and fluctuations. While recent chapters have focused on fluctuations, the next three chapters will address economic growth. They will explain why income levels and growth rates differ across countries and analyze what policy-makers can do to create an environment conducive for growth and prosperity.

KEY POINTS

- Historically, the United States has experienced substantial swings in real output. Prior to World War II, year-to-year changes in real GDP of 5 to 10 percent were experienced on several occasions. In recent decades, the fluctuations in real GDP have been more moderate.

- If stimulus could be injected during periods of recession and restraint during inflationary booms, macro policy could moderate the ups and downs of the business cycle. Proper timing, however, is difficult to achieve because it takes time to recognize and institute a policy change, and the effects of the change are not immediate.

- In order to time a change properly, policy-makers need to know where the economy will be six to eighteen months in the future. Forecasting devices such as the index of leading indicators will be helpful, but forecasting is a highly imperfect science.

- There are two major theories as to how expectations are formed. According to the adaptive-expectations hypothesis, individuals form their expectations about the future on the basis of data from the recent past. The rational-expectations hypothesis assumes that people use all pertinent information, including data on the conduct of current policy, when forming their expectations about the future.

- With adaptive expectations, an unanticipated shift to a more expansionary policy will temporarily stimulate output and employment. In contrast, with rational expectations, expansionary policy may fail to increase output, and, if achieved, any increase in output will be brief. However, both expectations theories indicate that sustained expansionary policies will lead to inflation without permanently increasing output and employment.

- The Phillips curve outlines the relationship between inflation and unemployment. In the 1960s, it was widely believed that higher rates of inflation could be used to reduce the unemployment rate. This view provided the foundation for the expansionary policies of the 1970s and the inflation they generated. Integration of expectations into macro analysis makes it clear that the early view of the Phillips curve is fallacious.

- Policy-makers responded to the recession of 2008–2009 with increases in government spending, large budget deficits, and expansionary monetary policy. Nonetheless, the recovery to date has been weak. Temporary spending programs, counterproductive projects, uncertainty generated by constant policy changes, a high level of federal debt, and doubts about the Fed's commitment to price stability contributed to the sluggishness of the recovery.

CRITICAL ANALYSIS QUESTIONS

1. The chair of the Council of Economic Advisers has requested that you write a short paper explaining how economic policy can be used to stabilize the economy and achieve a high level of economic growth during the next five years. Be sure to make specific proposals. Indicate why your recommendations will work. You may submit your paper to your instructor.

2. *How does economic instability during the past sixty years compare with instability prior to World War II? Is there any evidence that stabilization policy has either increased or decreased economic stability during recent decades?

3. State in your own words the adaptive-expectations hypothesis. How does the theory of rational expectations differ from that of adaptive expectations?

4. What is the index of leading indicators? Why is it useful to macro policy-makers?

5. *How would you expect the actual unemployment rate to compare with the natural unemployment rate in the following cases?

   a. Prices are stable and have been stable for the last four years.
   b. The current inflation rate is 3 percent, and this rate was widely anticipated more than a year ago.
   c. Expansionary policies lead to an abrupt increase in the inflation rate from 3 percent to 7 percent.
   d. There is an abrupt reduction in the inflation rate from 7 percent to 2 percent.

6. Compare and contrast the impact of an unexpected shift to a more expansionary monetary policy under rational and adaptive expectations. Are the implications of the two theories different in the short run? Are the long-run implications different? Explain.

7. What are some of the practical problems that limit the effective use of discretionary monetary and fiscal policy as stabilization tools?

8. During difficult times, politicians are under strong pressure to take action. One recently stated, "We are going to keep trying things until we fine something that works." Do you believe this is a good strategy? Why or why not?

9. How does the long-term unemployment rate present during 2009–2012 compare with the long-term rate accompanying prior recessions? Why do you think this was the case?

10. Prior to the mid-1970s, many economists thought that inflation would lead to a lower rate of unemployment. Why? How does the modern view of the Phillips curve differ from the earlier view?

11. *Answer the following questions:

    a. What is the most important thing the Fed can do to promote economic stability?
    b. Can expansionary monetary policy reduce interest rates and stimulate a higher growth rate of real output in the long run?
    c. If monetary policy is too expansionary, how will nominal interest rates and the general level of prices be affected?

12. Keynesian economists argue that economic conditions in recent years would have been much worse if it had not been for the increases in government spending and the large budget deficits. They also argue that the recovery would have been more robust if the spending increases and budget deficits had been larger. Indicate why you either agree or disagree with this perspective.

*Asterisk denotes questions for which answers are given in Appendix B.

CHAPTER 16
Creating an Environment for Growth and Prosperity

FOCUS

- How does the growth of income during the past 200 years compare with growth prior to 1800?
- How does sustained economic growth change income levels and the lives of people?
- What are the major sources of economic growth?
- What institutions and policies will promote growth and prosperity?
- Is foreign aid an effective tool for the reduction of poverty?

Certain fundamental principles—formulating sound monetary and fiscal policies, removing domestic price controls, opening the economy to international market forces, ensuring property rights and private property, creating competition, and reforming and limiting the role of government—are essential for a healthy market economy.
—Economic Report of the President, 1991

R obert Lucas, the 1995 Nobel laureate, has stated, "Once you start thinking about economic growth, it is hard to think about anything else."[1] Why do Lucas and many other economists place so much emphasis on economic growth? Growth of real output is necessary for the growth of real income. Without growth, higher income levels and living standards cannot be achieved.

What are the sources of economic growth? Why do some countries grow and achieve high levels of income while others stagnate? The Keys to Prosperity series has already addressed several dimensions of this issue, but we now want to consider it more directly, and in a more comprehensive manner.

16-1 HISTORICAL PERSPECTIVE ON THE ECONOMIC GROWTH OF THE PAST TWO CENTURIES

Prior to 1800, most of the world's population struggled 50, 60, and 70 hours per week in order to obtain food and other basic necessities of life. It was a constant struggle for survival and many lost the battle. Moreover, this had been the case for thousands of years. The late Angus Maddison, an economist for the Organisation for Economic Co-operation and Development, is widely recognized as the leading authority on historical income and life expectancy data. **Exhibit 1** presents Maddison's estimates for the past thousand years. As Exhibit 1 part a shows, measured in 1990 dollars, the GDP per person of the world was $667 in 1820, compared to $450, in 1000. Thus, over 800 years, per person income levels

EXHIBIT 1

GDP Per Capita and Life Expectancy, 1000–2003

As frame (a) shows, the world GDP per person changed very little during the 800 years between 1000 and 1820. During the past 200 years, however, the GDP per person of the world has risen by a factor of nearly 10, and the increase in the West has been almost twenty-fold. As frame (b) illustrates, the figures for life expectancy follow a similar pattern.

(a) GDP per capita

(b) Life Expectancy

Source: Angus Maddison, *Contours of the World Economy, 1–2030 AD: Essays in Macro-Economic History* (Oxford: Oxford University Press, 2007).

---

[1] Robert E. Lucas Jr., "On the Mechanics of Economic Development," *Journal of Monetary Economics* 22, no. 1 (1988): 3–42.

increased by about 50 percent. The West (Western Europe and its offshoots of the United States, Canada, Australia, and New Zealand) did a little better, as income in this region approximately tripled from $426 in 1000 to $1,202 in 1820. But even the figures for the West imply that it took around 500 years for income to double.[2]

Now, take a good look at what has happened since 1820. During the past 200 years, there has been a virtual explosion of economic growth. By 2003, the world's income per person had risen to $6,516, ten times the level of 1820. In the West, income per person soared to $23,710 in 2003, nearly 20 times the figure for 1820. Thus, after experiencing centuries of income levels at or near subsistence, real per capita income has skyrocketed during the past 200 years.

The life expectancy data follow a similar pattern. As Exhibit 1 part (b) shows, life expectancy at birth for the world rose from 24 years to 26 years between 1000 and 1820, but it then increased to 31 years in 1900 before soaring to 64 years in 2003. In the West, life expectancy rose from 24 years to 36 years between 1000 and 1820, and by 2003 it had skyrocketed to 76 years.

16-2 ECONOMIC GROWTH, PRODUCTION POSSIBILITIES, AND THE QUALITY OF LIFE

Economic growth expands the productive capacity of an economy. As **Exhibit 2** shows, an expansion in output can be illustrated within the production possibilities framework. For example, if a country experiences economic growth between 2015 and 2025, this means the country will be able to produce a larger quantity of both consumer and capital goods in 2025 than was true in 2015. This growth will shift the economy's production possibilities curve outward (from *AA* to *BB*).

When a nation's real GDP is increasing more rapidly than its population, **per capita GDP**—that is, GDP per person—will also expand. Growth of per capita GDP means more goods and services per person. In most cases, this will mean that the typical person has a higher standard of living—a better diet, improved health and access to medical services,

Per capita GDP
Income per person. Increases in income per person are vital for the achievement of higher living standards.

EXHIBIT 2

Economic Growth and Production Possibilities

Economic growth expands the sustainable output level of an economy. This can be illustrated by an outward shift in the production possibilities curve.

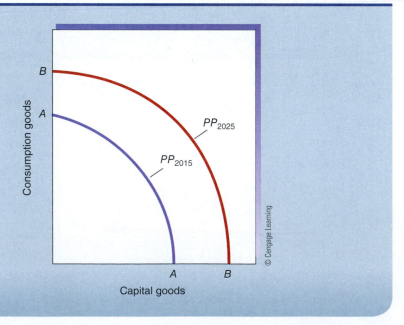

---

[2]Angus Maddison, *Contours of the World Economy, 1–2030 AD: Essays in Macro-Economic History* (Oxford: Oxford University Press, 2007).

and greater educational opportunity. Studies have also shown that as per capita income increases, people place more emphasis on clean air and water and generally take more time for recreation and leisure. Thus, a higher per capita income means not only more material goods but also better health, a cleaner environment, more leisure time, and the availability of a wider range of goods and services that most would consider an improvement in the quality of life.

16-2a THE IMPACT OF SUSTAINED ECONOMIC GROWTH

There is a tendency to think that a 1 or 2 percent difference in growth is of little consequence. When sustained over a lengthy period, however, seemingly small differences in growth can have a huge impact.

The **rule of 70** provides a simple tool that can help us understand the importance of sustained growth. This rule makes it easy to figure how many years it will take for income to double at various rates of growth. If you divide 70 by a country's average growth rate, it will approximate the number of years required for the income level to double.[3] For example, at an average annual growth rate of 5 percent, it would take 14 years (70 divided by 5) for the income level to double. At a 1 percent growth rate, it would take 70 years for income to double. (*Note:* The rule of 70 also applies to the rate of return on savings and investments. Clearly, over a long period, small differences in rates of return can make a big difference in the accumulated value of your savings or investment.)

Exhibit 3 illustrates the impact of differences in growth rates over 30 years. Consider four countries with the same initial level of per capita income, $10,000. The exhibit indicates what their incomes will be 30 years later at four different growth rates: 4 percent,

Rule of 70
If a variable grows at a rate of x percent per year, 70/x will approximate the number of years required for the variable to double.

EXHIBIT 3

The Impact of Growth Rate Differences over a 30-Year Period

Here, we consider the impact of growth over a 30-year period on four economies with the same initial income level, $10,000. If a country grows 4 percent annually, 30 years later its income will be $32,434, more than 3.2 times the initial figure. In contrast, if a country grows at a 2 percent annual rate, 30 years later its income will be only a little more than half that of the economy that grew more rapidly. The income of a country growing at a 1 percent rate will be even lower, $13,478.

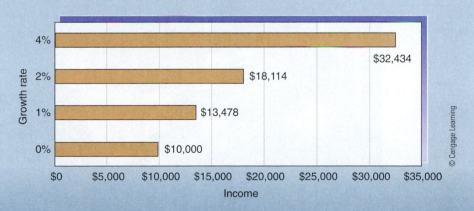

© Cengage Learning

---

[3]Sometimes this rule is called the rule of 72, rather than 70. Whereas 70 yields more accurate estimates for growth rates of less than 5 percent, 72 yields slightly more accurate estimates when the annual rate of growth exceeds 5 percent.

2 percent, 1 percent, and 0 percent. After 30 years, the country growing at an annual rate of 4 percent will have an income of $32,434. The income of the country growing at a 2 percent rate will be only $18,114. A country with a 1 percent rate of growth will achieve only an income of $13,478 after 30 years, while the income of the country with a 0 percent growth rate will still be $10,000. Thus, even though the four countries all had the same initial income, 30 years later the income level of the one with the 4 percent growth rate will be far greater than that of the others. Clearly, differences in sustained growth rates over a few decades will substantially alter the relative incomes of countries.

16-3 SOURCES OF ECONOMIC GROWTH AND HIGH INCOMES

Why do some countries grow and achieve high income levels whereas others remain poor and less developed? Gains from trade, entrepreneurial discovery, and investment are the major sources of economic growth. Let's take a closer look at each.

16-3a GAINS FROM TRADE

As we have stressed throughout this textbook, trade is mutually advantageous. Trade moves goods, services, and resources from people who value them less to people who value them more. It also helps trading partners achieve larger outputs and income levels as the result of division of labor, specialization, and adoption of methods of mass production. For example, goods ranging from pencils to automobiles to cell phones can be produced more economically when they are supplied by firms producing them in the millions to sell to the world marketplace rather than selling only thousands domestically.

It is easy to recognize that our living standard would be meager if we could not trade with others, as we all acquire numerous goods through trade that would be costly or virtually impossible for us to produce for ourselves. When individuals and businesses are permitted to trade over a broader market area, they will be able to produce a larger output and consume

Henry Ford developed the automobile assembly line shown here. His mass production methods resulted in substantially lower per unit cost. Mass production methods and expansion in the size of the market help us get more from the available resources and achieve higher income levels.

AP Images/Ford Motor Co.

a more diverse bundle of goods. Conversely, obstacles that restrict trade, either domestic or international, will reduce output, income, and the general living standard of the populace.

16-3b ENTREPRENEURSHIP, TECHNOLOGY, AND THE DISCOVERY OF BETTER WAYS OF DOING THINGS

The discovery of new products and new production methods provide a driving force for economic growth. Sometimes these discoveries reflect **technological advancement**. In other instances, they are the result of innovation; the practical application, extension, and dissemination of new ideas, processes, and technologies. During the past two centuries, the substitution of power-driven machines for human labor; the development of miracle grains, fertilizer, and new sources of energy; and improvements in transportation and communication have vastly improved living standards. Innovations and advancements in technology continue to affect the availability of goods and services. Just think of the new products introduced during the last 50 years: high-definition televisions, computers, electronic mail, microwave ovens, video cameras, cell phones, iPads, heart-bypass surgery, hip replacements, LASIK eye surgery, auto air conditioners, and so on. These products and others have made it possible for us to live longer, keep our homes and workplaces comfortable regardless of the outside temperature, communicate with both the written and spoken word with people throughout the world, and enjoy entertainment well beyond what was available to even kings and queens of another era.

New and improved products have replaced older ones and often rendered them obsolete. The automobile replaced the horse and buggy; the computer word processor replaced the typewriter; the phonograph was replaced by the cassette tape player, which was later largely replaced by CD and now by portable media players like the iPod. Joseph Schumpeter, a great Austrian economist, referred to this discovery and replacement process as "creative destruction."

But new and improved products do not just happen. They must be discovered. This highlights the role of the entrepreneur, the decision-maker willing to take risks and try out new ideas.[4] Some of the new ideas will be good ones, but many will not. The majority of new businesses fail within the first few years, and relatively few turn into major successes like Microsoft, eBay, or FedEx did.

In order to be successful, an entrepreneur must be good at discovering how to apply scientific knowledge in a practical manner. For example, Henry Ford played only a minor

Technological advancement
The introduction of new techniques or methods that increase output per unit of input.

Entrepreneurial discovery of improved products and lower-cost production methods is a driving force of economic growth. For example, when it was initially developed, the phonograph made recorded music available to millions of listeners. But it was eventually replaced by the CD player and still later by the iPod. Economists refer to this replacement of a product by a new and superior one as "creative destruction."

©Sippakorn/Shutterstock.com

©iStockphoto.com/Andres balcazar

© Shai_Halud /Shutterstock.com

---

[4]The modern understanding of the importance of entrepreneurship as a source of economic growth is founded on the work of Joseph Schumpeter and Israel Kirzner. See Joseph A. Schumpeter, *Capitalism, Socialism, and Democracy* (New York: Harper, 1942); Israel M. Kirzner, *Competition and Entrepreneurship* (Chicago: University of Chicago Press, 1973); and "Entrepreneurial Discovery and the Competitive Market Process: An Austrian Approach," *Journal of Economic Literature* 35, no. 1 (1997): 60–85.

role in the invention and development of the automobile. Nonetheless, through his innovative assembly line production techniques, he lowered the production cost of automobiles, making cars affordable to more people.

Before a new idea is tried, it is difficult to tell if it is a good one. From the standpoint of economic growth, it is vitally important that entrepreneurs have a strong incentive to try out new ideas, but it is also important that wasteful projects that reduce the value of resources be brought to a halt. In a market economy, profits and losses achieve these objectives. New ideas that increase the value of resources—by creating enough value to consumers to offset the opportunity cost of production—generate economic profits for the entrepreneurs who discover them. In contrast, ideas that drain resources away from other more valuable uses and turn them into something not as valuable to consumers result in losses, which will provide entrepreneurs with a strong incentive to discontinue such projects. Thus, the market process promotes both the discovery of better ways of doing things and the termination of projects that reduce the value of resources. In this manner, the profit and loss system helps to direct (and quickly redirect) resources toward projects that promote economic growth.

16-3c INVESTMENT IN PHYSICAL AND HUMAN CAPITAL

Investment in both physical capital (machines) and human capital (knowledge and skills) can expand the productive capacity of a worker. For example, farmers working with modern tractors and plows can cultivate many more acres than could their great grandparents, who probably worked with hoes. Similarly, a cabinetmaker, skilled after years of training and experience, can build cabinets far more rapidly and efficiently than can a beginner. In turn, people who produce more goods and services valued by others will tend to have higher incomes.

Other things constant, countries using a larger share of their resources to produce tools, machines, and factories will tend to grow more rapidly. Correspondingly, allocation of more resources to education and training will also enhance economic growth. It is important, however, to recognize that investment is not a "free lunch." When more resources are used to produce machines, factories, and schooling, fewer resources are available to produce current-consumption goods.

While investment is a source of growth, high investment rates do not guarantee rapid growth. The experiences of the centrally planned economies of the former Soviet bloc countries illustrate this point. These economies had both very high rates of capital formation and rapid improvements in schooling levels. Despite their high rates of investment, however, their performance was unimpressive. Slow growth and poor living standards eventually led to their collapse.

Exhibit 4 summarizes the three major sources of economic growth and high levels of income. It also summarizes how and why each of the three factors contributes to the growth and income of an economy.

EXHIBIT 4

Major Sources of Economic Growth and High Levels of Income

The major sources of growth and high income levels are gains from trade, entrepreneurial discovery, and investment in physical and human capital.

SOURCE OF GROWTH	EXPLANATION
1. Gains from trade	Specialization, division of labor, and economies of scale lead to larger outputs.
2. Entrepreneurship	Innovation, technological improvements, and discovery of better ways of doing things make larger outputs and higher income levels possible.
3. Investment in physical capital, work experience, and human capital	Machines, structures, and tools (physical capital) and education, and training (human capital) make larger outputs possible.

© Cengage Learning

OUTSTANDING ECONOMIST

DOUGLASS C. NORTH (1920–)

The 1993 recipient of the Nobel Prize in Economics, Douglass C. North is best known for his application of both economic theory and statistical analysis to topics in the field of economic history. A professor at Washington University in St. Louis and Senior Fellow at Stanford's Hoover Institution, North's work has shown that the development of both patent laws and the corporation as a legal entity were important sources of economic growth during the seventeenth and eighteenth centuries. His analysis of the link between institutional change and economic progress has played an important role in the development of modern growth theory.

Recognition of trade, entrepreneurial discovery, and investment as the cornerstones of economic growth and the achievement of higher income levels also sheds light on why per capita income was so low throughout most of world history. Prior to some time around 1800, most people were involved in agricultural activities where they produced most of what they consumed. The costs of both transportation and communications were high, and there was very little trade. Moreover, the trade that did occur was generally among those residing in the same village or within a close proximity. Given this limited amount of trade, the gains from specialization, economies of scale, technological improvements, innovation, and even investment were stifled. Against this background, low and stagnating income levels are an expected result.

16-3d THE INSTITUTIONAL ENVIRONMENT

Institutions and policies influence the volume of trade, entrepreneurial discovery, and investment. How important are the legal, business, political, trade, and social rules and regulations that make up a country's institutional environment? What institutions and policies promise to enhance the performance of an economy? During the last several decades, considerable research has focused on these questions. Building on the work of Peter Bauer and Douglass C. North, modern growth analysis stresses the importance of institutions and policies for the development and efficient use of resources. Daron Acemoglu of MIT, Robert Barro of Harvard University, and Barry Weingast of Stanford University are among the leading contributors to the recent literature in this area.[5] This institutional approach stresses that when nations foster a sound economic environment, people will trade, invest, and engage in entrepreneurial activities in a manner that will stimulate economic growth and make high levels of income possible. In many ways, the modern institutional approach to growth reflects the view of Adam Smith, who also stressed the importance of policies and institutions.

Institutions

The legal, regulatory, and social constraints that affect the security of property rights and enforcement of contracts. They exert a major impact on the incentive to engage in productive activities, innovate, and realize gains from trade, particularly when the trading partners do not know each other.

16-4 WHAT INSTITUTIONS AND POLICIES WILL PROMOTE GROWTH?

The growth process reflects a combination of factors, and they are often interrelated. Much as the performance of an athletic team reflects the joint output of the team members, economic growth is jointly determined. And just as one or two weak players can substantially

[5]For background on this literature, see Peter T. Bauer, *Dissent on Development: Studies and Debates in Development Economics* (Cambridge, MA: Harvard University Press, 1972); Douglass C. North, *Institutions, Institutional Change, and Economic Performance* (Cambridge: Cambridge University Press, 1990); Robert Barro and Xavier Sala-i-Martin, *Economic Growth* (New York: McGraw-Hill, 1995); and Daron Acemoglu, Simon Johnson, and James A. Robinson, "Institutions as a Fundamental Cause of Long-Run Growth," in *Handbook of Economic Growth*, vol.1, Philippe Aghion and Steven Durlauf, eds. (Amsterdam: Elsevier, 2005), 385–472.

reduce overall team performance, weakness in one or two key areas can substantially harm the overall performance of an economy.

The role of government is vitally important for the achievement of economic growth and high levels of income. If an economy is going to achieve its full potential, institutions and policies must encourage productive activities and discourage counterproductive ones.

Let's take a closer look at the role of government and six key factors that are central to the growth process.

KEYS TO ECONOMIC PROSPERITY

Role of Government

Governments promote economic progress when they protect individuals and their property, enforce contracts impartially, provide access to money of stable value, avoid high taxes and excessive regulation, and foster competitive markets and free international trade.

©iStockphoto.com/malerapaso

16-4a LEGAL SYSTEM: SECURE PROPERTY RIGHTS, RULE OF LAW, AND EVEN-HANDED ENFORCEMENT OF CONTRACTS

As we discussed in Chapter 2, private ownership rights legally protect people against those who would use violence, theft, or fraud to take things that do not belong to them. The important thing about private ownership is the incentive structure that it creates. When labor services, other resources, goods, and assets are privately owned, people will have a strong incentive to engage in productive activities, actions that increase the value of resources. With well-defined and enforced private ownership rights, people get ahead by helping and cooperating with others. Employers, for example, have to provide prospective employees and other resource suppliers with at least as good a deal as they can get elsewhere. Similarly, if they are going to succeed, business owners will have to provide potential customers with goods and services that they value highly (relative to cost). Entrepreneurs will have a strong incentive to innovate and discover new and better products and production methods. Investors will have a potent incentive to search for and undertake productive projects. The bottom line: When property is owned privately, people are permitted to keep what they earn; this provides them with a powerful stimulus to develop and use resources wisely, innovate and discover better ways of doing things, and invest and conserve for the future.

Throughout history, people have searched for, and established, alternatives to private ownership they thought would be more humanitarian or more productive. These experiences have ranged from unsuccessful to disastrous. To date, there is no record of an institutional arrangement that provides individuals with as much freedom and incentive to use resources productively and efficiently as does private ownership.[6]

In contrast, when private ownership rights are insecure or highly restricted, the incentive of entrepreneurs to engage in productive activity is eroded. Citizens will spend more time trying to take the property of others through political and legal plunder and less time producing and developing resources. When a citizen or investor's assets are at risk of being

---

[6]For evidence that a legal system that protects property rights, enforces contracts, and relies on rule-of-law principles for the settlement of disputes among parties promotes economic growth, see Stephen Knack and Philip Keefer, "Institutions and Economic Performance: Cross-Country Tests Using Alternative Institutional Measures," *Economics and Politics* 7 (1995): 207–27.

taken by others because property rights are not enforced, the incentive to invest in building the productive capital assets that help to generate prosperity is diminished. As a result, growth will be retarded, and income will fall well short of its potential.

The security of property rights is often undermined by political instability, civil unrest, and war. Historically, some governments have confiscated the physical and financial assets of their citizens, imposed punitive taxes on them, and used regulations to punish those out of favor with the current political regime. Countries with a history like this will find it difficult to restore confidence and reestablish the security of property rights.

Unfortunately, the political climate of many poor, **less-developed countries** is highly unstable. In some cases, prejudice, injustice, and highly unequal wealth status create a fertile environment for political upheaval. In other instances, political corruption and a history of favoritism to a ruling class provide the seeds for unrest. In recent years, political instability has contributed to the dismal economic performance of several nations, including the Democratic Republic of the Congo, Haiti, Iraq, Syria, and Venezuela.

> **Less-developed countries**
> Countries with low per capita incomes, low levels of education, widespread illiteracy, and widespread use of production methods that are largely obsolete in high-income countries. They are sometimes referred to as developing countries.

16-4b COMPETITIVE MARKETS

Competition is a disciplining force for both buyers and sellers. In a competitive environment, producers must provide goods at a low cost and serve the interests of consumers; if they don't, other suppliers will. Firms that develop improved products and figure out how to produce them at a low cost will succeed. Sellers that are unwilling or unable to provide consumers with quality goods at competitive prices will be driven from the market. This process leads to improved products and production methods and directs resources toward projects that create more value. Government policies that restrict these competitive forces, like business subsidies, price controls, and entry barriers and restraints stifle competition and thus hinder economic progress.

When property rights are clearly defined and enforced, competitive markets direct entrepreneurs toward projects that are both profitable and wealth enhancing. Rising incomes and higher living standards are a natural result.

16-4c STABLE MONEY AND PRICES

A stable monetary environment provides the foundation for the efficient operation of a market economy. In contrast, monetary and price instability makes both the price level and relative prices unpredictable, generates uncertainty, and undermines the security of contractual exchanges. When prices increase 20 percent one year, 50 percent the next year, 15 percent the year after that, and so on, the ability of individuals and businesses to develop sensible long-term plans and investment decisions is undermined. Many investors and business decision-makers will move their activities to countries with a more stable environment. Foreigners will invest elsewhere, and citizens will often go to great lengths to get their savings (potential funds for investment) out of the country. Without monetary stability, potential gains from capital investment and other exchanges involving time commitments will be eroded and the people of the country will fail to realize their full potential.

Moreover, monetary shifts from expansion to restriction will generate economic instability. They will jerk the economy back and forth between booms and busts. This pattern of monetary policy will also create uncertainty, retard private investment, and reduce the rate of economic growth.

16-4d MINIMAL REGULATION

Many countries impose regulations that limit entry into various businesses and occupations. In those countries, if you want to start a business or provide a service, you have to acquire a license, fill out forms, get permission from different bureaus, show that you are qualified, indicate that you have sufficient financing, and meet various other regulatory tests. Some officials may refuse your application unless you are willing to pay a bribe or contribute to their political coffers. Often, well-established and politically influential businesses that you would be competing against can successfully oppose your application. The World Bank reports that, given the regulations in place in 2012, legally opening a business takes 105 days in Haiti, 119 days in Brazil, and 144 days in Venezuela. By way of comparison, opening this same business would take only three days in Hong Kong or Singapore and six days in the United States.[7]

Proponents often argue that regulations will keep the unqualified out of a market, prohibit unfair competition, raise wages, reduce prices, or restrict the layoff of workers. Unfortunately, even when regulations reflect good intentions, they often generate harmful unintended consequences. For example, restrictions that make it more difficult to lay off an employee will reduce the incentive of employers to hire workers. Regulations designed to keep out unwanted rivals will limit competition and lead to higher prices. Fixing prices below the market level will lead to shortages and deterioration in the quality of a product or service, but fixing prices above market levels will lead to surpluses. The list of unintended side effects of regulations goes on and on.

Many worry that without government regulation of food, safety and other items, people will be harmed by bad products or employers providing unsafe working conditions. However, under a legal system with sound enforcement of liability, individuals and businesses are accountable for their actions that harm others. Those harmed will be in a position to collect for damages in a court of law. Moreover, competition is the great regulator. When competition is present, business firms that offer shoddy products, fail to keep their promises, or seek to mislead consumers will soon be exposed by rivals. Unethical business practices may lead to some temporary returns, but this is not a recipe for long-term success. Regulation is a poor substitute for well-defined property rights, a sound legal system, and the natural regulatory process of competitive markets.

16-4e THE AVOIDANCE OF HIGH TAX RATES

High marginal tax rates take a large share of the rewards generated by productive activities, making it less attractive for people to work and undertake profitable business projects. In less-developed economies, high taxes often drive business activity into the underground economy, or black markets, where the legal structure is less certain and property rights less secure. In developed economies, the high rates often reduce the supply of labor and other productive resources. Some potential workers will drop out of the labor force to work at home where their labor is not taxed. Others will simply work fewer hours, retire earlier, or take jobs with longer vacations or a more preferred location. People who are not permitted to keep much of what they earn tend not to earn very much.

High taxes also retard capital formation and reduce the efficiency of resource use. They will both repel foreign investment and cause domestic investors to search for investment projects abroad where taxes and production costs are lower. In turn, the lower level of investment will mean slower growth of worker productivity and earnings. High tax rates will also encourage people to purchase items that are tax deductible even though they are not valued as much as nondeductible goods of similar price. Worse yet, high tax rates can drive a nation's most productive citizens abroad where taxes are lower. All of these things will retard a country's economic growth.

16-4f TRADE OPENNESS

Like domestic trade, international trade is mutually beneficial. The residents of a country can gain by specializing in the production of goods and services they can produce at a relatively low cost and trade for those that would be costly to produce domestically. Thus,

---

[7] World Bank, *Doing Business 2013.*

trade makes it possible for each country to use more of its resources producing goods and services it can supply at a low cost. Together, trading partners are able to produce more goods and services and purchase a wider variety of them at cheaper prices. Trade openness and the competition that flows from it will also keep domestic producers on their toes— they will be less likely to gouge consumers with high prices, for example.

In contrast, policies that restrict international trade stifle this process and retard economic progress. Obviously, tariffs (taxes on imported goods) and quotas fall into this category because they limit the ability of domestic citizens to trade with people in other countries. So, too, do trade restrictions that impede international exchanges involving financial and real assets. When a nation's financial markets are integrated with the world, the nation will be able to attract worldwide savings at the lowest possible price (or interest rate). Similarly, its citizens will have access to the most attractive investment opportunities, regardless of where those opportunities are located.

As a result, domestic businesses will be able to acquire financial capital at a lower cost, and domestic investors will be able to earn more attractive returns than would otherwise be the case. The international trade section of this book will analyze these issues in more detail.

The accompanying **Thumbnail Sketch** summarizes the key elements of an institutional and policy environment conducive to growth and prosperity. It also indicates what governments can do to help their citizens achieve higher income levels.

16-4g OTHER FACTORS THAT MAY INFLUENCE GROWTH AND INCOME

Through the years, economists have developed several theories about why some countries grow and achieve high income levels while others remain poor. Some of these theories have validity; others are either incorrect or incomplete. In this section, we will consider noninstitutional factors that are often thought to influence growth.

1. Growth of the population. Thomas Malthus developed one of the earliest theories of economic growth, or more accurately a theory about why growth could not be sustained. Malthus argued that as per person income increased much above the subsistence level, it would trigger a population boom that would soon drive income back to the lowest level necessary to sustain life. Because population would grow exponentially while the resources required to expand production would only grow linearly, a rapid growth of

Thumbnail Sketch
Institutions, Policies, and Economic Growth

The following institutions and policies provide the foundation for growth and the achievement of high levels of income:

1. Legal system: Private ownership, rule of law, and even-handed enforcement of contracts
2. Competitive markets: Freedom of entry into businesses and occupations
3. Monetary and price stability: Low and predictable rates of inflation
4. Minimal regulation: Avoid regulations that restrict entry and interfere with voluntary exchange
5. Low taxes: Keep tax rates, particularly marginal tax rates, low
6. Trade openness: Avoid tariffs, quotas, and other regulations that restrict residents from trading with people in other countries

population would soon eliminate income levels above subsistence.[8] This bleak picture of existence at or near subsistence has caused some to refer to economics as the "dismal science."

Exhibit 1 highlights why Malthus's theory seemed reasonable at the end of the eighteenth century. Prior to 1800, there was very little economic growth. As Exhibit 1 illustrates, both per capita income and life expectancy in 1800 were not much different than in 1000. Fortunately, the past 200 years indicate that Malthus was wrong. Today, the world population is sixfold that of the era of Malthus. Even though the amount of land used for agriculture has fallen, global food production per person is at an all-time high. Malthus's theory failed to incorporate the role of technological improvements, innovation, and the discovery of better ways of doing things. Put another way, his theory ignored that people have brains and two hands, as well as mouths: They are not just consumers; they are also producers, entrepreneurs, and innovators. Today, some of the most densely populated areas of the world, places like Hong Kong, Singapore, and Japan, also have some of the world's highest per capita incomes.

2. Natural resources.   There is a tendency to think that the wealth of nations is largely dependent upon natural resources. Resources clearly give some nations an advantage. For example, oil-rich countries like Saudi Arabia, Bahrain, and the United Arab Emirates have substantially higher per capita incomes than other similar countries with few natural resources. But it is equally clear that resource endowments are not the primary source of cross-country differences in growth and income. Some of the highest-income countries in the world have few natural resources. Other than their harbor, neither Hong Kong nor Singapore has significant natural resources. Likewise, Japan has few natural resources, and it imports almost all of its industrial energy supply. Nonetheless, the growth rates of all three have been among the most rapid in the world since 1960. Conversely, many resource-rich countries such as Nigeria, Venezuela, and Russia have both low income levels and poor records of economic growth.

These observations highlight the importance of institutions. Countries that follow sound policies are able to import the resources required for growth and prosperity. Without sound institutions and policies, however, resource-rich countries are generally unable to sustain strong growth and achieve high levels of income. Moreover, abundant resources can often undermine the incentive to adopt sound institutions. Historically, resource riches have often led to conflict, instability, authoritarian political regimes, and even war. This has given rise to what some refer to as the "resource curse," the view that abundant resources often lead to the evolution of corrupt governments and weak institutions that undermine the productive use of resources.

3. Foreign aid.   Proponents of foreign aid ranging from scholars like Jeffrey Sachs's to celebrities such as the Irish rock star Bono argue that foreign aid can be used to provide physical and educational infrastructure that will help direct poor countries toward economic growth and human development. According to this view, assistance from high-income developed countries to low-income less-developed countries can provide the latter with the start-up capital needed to ignite the growth process. Given their low incomes, poor countries may be unable to save enough to finance major investment projects like roads and power-generating plants. Further, many believe that projects like these provide the foundation for economic growth. Thus, if the world's wealthy countries provide aid, it could be channeled into investment that would trigger growth and development.

While the theory sounds reasonable, the record of foreign aid has been dramatically different. The law of unintended consequences helps explain why. By its nature, aid is driven by political rather than economic considerations. It often props up political leaders opposed to constructive reforms and, in some cases, ends up in their personal bank accounts. There are also harmful side effects on the development of

---

[8]Thomas Malthus, *An Essay on the Principle of Population* (London: J. Johnson, 1798).

APPLICATIONS IN ECONOMICS

Poverty, Foreign Aid, and the Quality of Institutions in Africa

More foreign aid has been directed toward Africa than any region of the world. During 1980–2005, the per capita foreign aid to sub-Saharan Africa was 2.8 times the amount directed to Latin America and 6.4 times the figure for Asia. Omitting South Africa and oil-rich Nigeria, foreign aid summed to 12 percent of GDP of sub-Saharan Africa during the past two decades.

The results can only be described as disappointing. Using the latest data available from the World Bank, Exhibit 5 shows the extreme and moderate poverty rates for sub-Saharan Africa and the rest of the developing world during 1980–2005. The extreme poverty rate is equal to the percentage of the population with an income level of less than $1.25 per day measured in 2005 dollars, while the moderate rate is the percentage with

an income of less than $2 per day. (*Note:* High-income countries such as Japan, Australia, and those of Western Europe and North America are omitted in these calculations.) In sub-Saharan Africa, the extreme poverty rate fell from 60.8 percent in 1980 to 57.0 percent in 2000, and 51.1 percent in 2005. During the same time period, the extreme poverty rate in other less developed countries fell from 58.1 percent to 20.9 percent. Thus, over the 25-year time frame, the extreme poverty rate fell by only 10 percentage points in sub-Saharan Africa, compared to 27 percentage points among less developed countries in other regions.

The pattern for the moderate poverty rate was similar. In sub-Saharan Africa, the moderate poverty rate fell from 77.3 percent in 1980 to 72.2 percent in 2005. In contrast, in the

---

EXHIBIT 5

Poverty Rates in Africa and the Rest of the World, 1980–2005

As part a shows, the extreme poverty rate in sub-Saharan Africa was 51 percent in 2005, compared to 21 percent in the rest of the world. While the extreme poverty rate outside of Africa fell by 37 percentage points between 1980 and 2005, the rate fell by only 10 percentage points in Africa during this 25-year period. As part b shows, the moderate poverty rate followed a similar pattern. (*Note:* the high-income countries of North America and Europe, along with Australia, New Zealand, and Japan, are excluded from these figures.)

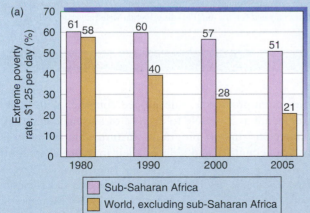

(a) Extreme Poverty Rate for sub-Saharan Africa and the Rest of the Developing World

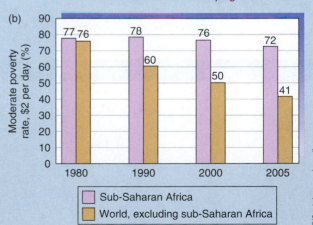

(b) Moderate Poverty Rate for sub-Saharan Africa and the Rest of the Developing World

Source: Joseph Connors, *Global Poverty: The Role of Economic Freedom, Democracy and Foreign Aid* (PhD diss., Florida State University, 2011). This poverty rate data by country are from the World Bank, World Development Indicators, 2009 (Washington, DC: World Bank).

Note: The extreme and moderate poverty rates are the percentage of the population living on less than $1.25 and $2 per day, respectively. These numbers are normalized across countries using the purchasing power parity method.

rest of the less-developed world, the moderate poverty rate plunged from 75.5 percent in 1980 to 41.4 percent in 2005. While both the extreme and moderate poverty rates of sub-Saharan Africa and other less developed countries were similar in 1980, the poverty rates in the sub-Saharan countries were much higher in 2005. Moreover, the number of Africans living in extreme poverty increased by more than 100 million in the last decade alone.

Why hasn't foreign aid been more effective in Africa? Malaria and human immunodeficiency virus provide part of the explanation, and foreign assistance has funded valuable medical resources for treatment in both of these areas. But counterproductive institutions and policies are a major factor underlying the generally poor results. Almost all foreign aid is either granted to, or channeled through, governments. During 1980–2005, foreign aid covered between 60 and 70 percent of government expenditures in sub-Saharan African countries. This aid often made it possible for governments, including

The one-dollar-per-day poverty rate in Africa is approximately three times that of the rest of the world.

ones that were highly corrupt, to remain in power even though their policies were characterized by uncertain protection of property rights, biased law enforcement, trade restrictions, and regulations that restrict entry into markets and impose heavy costs on business.

The *Economic Freedom of the World* project provides ratings for the legal structure, security of property rights, openness of international trade, and regulation of business for 144 countries. Most sub-Saharan African countries rank in the bottom group in all of these areas.[1]

Think for a moment about how high trade restrictions impact Africa. The countries of sub-Saharan Africa are approximately the geographic size of the typical U.S. state. Before resources and products can cross these national boundaries, they are subject to both taxes and customs clearance delays that often last two or three weeks. This is a costly, time-consuming, and onerous ordeal that exerts a corrupting influence on both business and government. Most important, it is a major deterrent to gains from specialization, economies of scale, entrepreneurship, and investment. If trade restrictions of this type were present among the states, the United States would also be poor.

The trade restrictions alone would be enough to undermine prosperity, but when coupled with legal systems that fail to enforce contracts and protect property rights, and regulations that restrict entry and drive up the cost of doing business, the results are catastrophic. The United Nations Millennium Development Goals project has substantially increased the level of aid to Africa in recent years. Without major changes in institutions and policies, however, past experience indicates that this aid will be largely ineffective. Foreign aid, even in large doses, will not reduce poverty, at least not by much, unless institutions and policies consistent with economic growth are present.

[1]James Gwartney, Robert Lawson, and Joshua Hall, *Economic Freedom of the World: 2012 Annual Report* (Vancouver, British Columbia: Fraser Institute, 2012). For a detailed analysis of the impact of both economic freedom and foreign aid on poverty, see Joseph Connors, *Global Poverty: The Role of Economic Freedom, Democracy and Foreign Aid* (PhD diss., Florida State University, 2011).

markets. High-income countries often provide less-developed countries with agricultural products and actually use the aid as a vehicle to dispose of surplus commodities resulting from their agricultural price support programs. In turn, this aid has often disrupted markets in less-developed countries and reduced their long-term capabilities of producing food products.

Studies indicate that foreign assistance has been largely ineffective and sometimes disastrously so.[9] At the same time, the poor countries that registered the most impressive

[9]For additional information on the impact of foreign aid on economic growth, see G. Raghuram Rajan and Arvind Subramanian. "Aid and Growth: What Does the Cross-Country Evidence Really Show?" *The Review of Economics and Statistics* 90, no. 4 (November 2008): 643–65; Simeon Djankov, Jose G. Montalvo, and Marta Reynal-Querol, "Does Foreign Aid Help?" *Cato Journal* 26, no. 1 (2006): 1–28; and William Easterly, *The White Man's Burden: Why the West's Efforts to Aid the Rest Have Done So Much Ill and So Little Good* (New York: Penguin, 2006).

growth during 1960–1990—like Hong Kong and Singapore—received little foreign aid. Instead, they followed policies supportive of market allocation and had respect for private property. In contrast, the countries that received the most aid recorded unimpressive growth and now have the world's lowest per capita income levels. In most cases, they are also characterized by institutions and policies—for example, investment controls, trade restrictions, and corrupt legal and political systems that undermine economic progress. Unless widespread institutional change is undertaken, the residents of these countries face a very bleak future. (See the Applications in Economics: "Poverty, Foreign Aid, and the Quality of Institutions in Africa.")

4. Climate and location. Jeffery Sachs of Columbia University has been at the forefront of those arguing that tropical climate conditions and location far away from the world's major markets adversely affect growth and income. According to this view, the hot and humid tropical climatic conditions erode the energy level of workers and increase the risk of disabling and life-threatening diseases such as malaria. Furthermore, this view argues the lengthy travel distance to the world's major markets of Western Europe, North America, and Japan make tropical countries unattractive as a location for productive facilities.[10]

The income levels of tropical countries, with a few exceptions, are generally lower than incomes in more temperate climates. But it is also true that the institutions and policies of most tropical countries are less consistent with the principles outlined in this chapter that foster gains from trade, entrepreneurship, and investment. Thus, most economists believe that the generally poorer performance of tropical countries is largely a reflection of their poor institutional quality rather than their climate and location.[11]

16-4h INSTITUTIONS, POLICIES, AND PROSPERITY

The shape and structure of incentives are central to the achievement of growth and high income levels. Unless countries adopt institutions and policies supportive of trade, entrepreneurial discovery, and private investment, they will be unable to sustain long-term growth and achieve high income levels. As the work of the noted economist, William Baumol, highlights, the rules of the game make a huge difference; they determine what individuals do with their time, talents, and energy.[12] Baumol notes that the institutional environment may encourage productive, unproductive, or even destructive activities. When institutions and policies provide secure property rights, a fair and balanced judicial system, monetary stability, and effective limits on the transfer of

---

[10]For additional information on the impact of climate and location on growth and income, see Jeffrey Sachs, "Tropical Underdevelopment," NBER Working Paper No. 8119 (February 2001); John Gallup, Jeffrey Sachs, and Andrew Mellinger, "Geography and Environment," NBER Working Paper No. w6849 (December 1998); and Jared Diamond, *Guns, Germs, and Steel: The Fates of Human Societies* (New York: W. W. Norton & Company, 1997).

[11]For literature on the importance of institutions relative to climate and location, see Daron Acemoglu, Simon Johnson, and James A. Robinson, "The Colonial Origins of Comparative Development: An Empirical Investigation," *American Economic Review* 91 (December 2001): 1369–1401; Robert E. Hall and Charles I. Jones, "Why Do Some Countries Produce So Much More Output per Worker than Others?" *Quarterly Journal of Economics* 114 (February 1999): 83–116; Mancur Olson, "Big Bills Left on the Sidewalk: Why Some Nations Are Rich, and Others Poor," *Journal of Economic Perspectives* 10 (Spring 1996): 3–24; Dani Rodrik, Arvind Subramanian, and Francesco Trebbi, "Institutions Rule: The Primacy of Institutions over Geography and Integration in Economic Development," *Journal of Economic Growth* 9 (June 2004): 131–65; and Jeffrey D. Sachs, "Institutions Don't Rule: Direct Effects of Geography on Per Capita Income," NBER Working Paper no. 9490 (February 2003).

[12]See William Baumol, "Entrepreneurship: Productive, Unproductive and Destructive," *Journal of Political Economy* 98 (October 1990): 893–921; and William J. Baumol, *Entrepreneurship, Management, and the Structure of Payoffs* (Cambridge, MA: MIT Press, 1993).

wealth through taxation and regulation, creative individuals are more likely to engage in product development, investment, and other productive activities. However, if the legal and regulatory environment fails to protect property rights and is often used to favor some at the expense of others, the same individuals are instead more likely to engage in attempts to manipulate the political and legal process in order to plunder wealth from others. Rent seeking, lobbying, bribes, and other forms of plunder replace productive activities.

For example, when entrepreneurs know that market forces will be used to allocate goods, a steel entrepreneur will react to more intense competition by trying to find a better way of producing steel (productive entrepreneurship). But when political bailouts are more probable, the steel producer will be more likely to lobby for subsidies, tariff protection, or regulatory favors (unproductive entrepreneurship). In turn, institutions that encourage productive activities and discourage counterproductive ones will lead to more growth and higher incomes.

LOOKING AHEAD

This chapter focused on the general characteristics of key institutions and policies that economic analysis indicates will help promote growth. The following chapter will present evidence on cross-country differences in income levels and growth rates and provide empirical evidence on the sources of those differences.

KEY POINTS

- The economic growth of the past two centuries has been unprecedented. While the per person income of the world increased by only about 50 percent during the 800 years from 1000 to 1800, it has increased by tenfold during the past 200 years. The growth of per person income in the West since 1800 has been even more impressive.

- Economic growth increases the production possibilities of an economy. The growth of per capita real GDP means more goods and services per person, which typically leads to higher living standards and improvements in life expectancy, literacy, and health.

- Even seemingly small differences in growth rates sustained over two or three decades will substantially alter relative incomes. For example, if Country A and Country B have the same initial income but the growth rate of A is 2 percentage points greater than that of B, after 35 years the income level of Country A will be twice that of B.

- Economic growth is a complex process. Economists stress the importance of three major sources of economic progress: (1) gains from trade and expansion in the size of the market,

(2) discovery of new technologies and innovative applications, and (3) investment in physical and human capital.

- The institutional and policy environment exerts a major impact on growth and income. The following institutions and policies provide the foundation for efficient use of resources, economic growth, and the achievement of high levels of income:

  1. a legal system that protects property rights and enforces contracts in an even-handed manner
  2. competitive markets
  3. monetary and price stability
  4. minimal regulation
  5. avoidance of high tax rates
  6. openness to international trade

- While population growth, natural resources, foreign aid, and climatic conditions can influence growth and income, without sound institutions and policies, these factors will fail to generate long-term sustained growth and prosperity.

CRITICAL ANALYSIS QUESTIONS

1. How does economic growth influence the living standards of people? Does it really make much difference whether an economy grows at 2 percent or 4 percent annually? Discuss.

2. Indicate in your own words why trade, entrepreneurial discovery, and investment are important sources of economic growth and achievement of high income levels.

3. *"Without aid from industrial nations, poor countries are caught in a poverty trap. Because they are poor, they are unable to save and invest; and, lacking investment, they remain poor." Evaluate this view.

4. What happened to economic growth between 1000 and 1800? How did the situation change after 1800? Why were these two periods so dramatically different? Discuss.

5. Why is competition important for the efficient use of resources? What must a firm do in order to compete effectively? Competitive forces often result in firms being driven out of business. How does this "business failure" influence the growth of income?

6. "Regulatory policies that restrict trade and voluntary agreements between parties will retard economic progress." Indicate why you either agree or disagree with this statement.

7. What must an entrepreneur do in order to introduce a new innovative product? What determines whether the new product will be a success or failure? How important is innovation as a source of economic growth? Discuss.

8. *"Because government-operated firms do not have to make a profit, they can usually produce at a lower cost and charge a lower price than privately owned enterprises." Evaluate this view.

9. How does money of stable value influence the volume of trade? When the inflation rate is volatile, how is the volume of trade affected? How will this influence the income levels of people?

10. What impact do natural resources have on economic growth? Will it be possible for a country with few natural resources to grow rapidly? Why or why not?

11. Why did Thomas Malthus believe that per person income could never rise much above the subsistence level? Given the era of his writings, was Malthus's view on this topic surprising? Why or why not?

12. *The diversity of goods available to consumers today is much greater than in the past. How does this influence consumer welfare? Do the GDP growth figures capture the impact of the increased diversity? Why or why not?

13. *When the government is heavily involved in the regulation of markets, how will this influence the gains from trade? How will it influence the degree of rent-seeking by business and labor groups and the campaign contributions available to politicians?

14. Suppose that you have just been appointed to a high-level position in the economic analysis unit of the State Department. The secretary of state has asked you to prepare a memo describing the key policies and economic arrangements that less-developed countries should follow in order to achieve rapid growth and high income levels. Briefly describe your response. Be sure to indicate why each factor you mention is important if a nation is going to attain a high level of economic progress.

*Asterisk denotes questions for which answers are given in Appendix B.

CHAPTER 17
Institutions, Policies, and Cross-Country Differences in Income and Growth

FOCUS

- How large are the income differences across countries?
- How do growth rates vary across countries? Are the rich countries getting richer while the poor are getting poorer?
- How does the quality of institutions and policies differ across countries?
- What impact do sound institutions and policies have on growth and income?

History is overwhelmingly a story of economies that failed to produce a set of economic rules of the game (with enforcement) that induce sustained economic growth. The central issue of economic history and of economic development is to account for the evolution of political and economic institutions that create an economic environment that induces increasing productivity.[1]
—Douglass C. North, 1993 Nobel Laureate

[1]Douglass C. North, "Institutions," *Journal of Economic Perspectives* 5 (Winter 1991): 98.

franckreporter/E+/Getty Images

In the last chapter, we explained why the institutions and policies of a country exert a major impact on economic growth. This chapter will investigate this issue empirically. We will begin by looking at the cross-country differences in income levels and growth rates. Then we will turn to the measurement of institutional quality, consider how institutions differ across countries, and analyze how these differences influence economic performance. The chapter concludes with a discussion of the relationship between political decision-making and economic institutions and policies.

17-1 HOW LARGE ARE THE INCOME DIFFERENCES ACROSS COUNTRIES?

When different currencies are used, how can incomes be measured across countries? One possibility would be to use the exchange rate to convert the income figures to a common currency. For example, if the income per person in France was 20,000 euros and the exchange rate was 1.4 dollars to the euro, you could multiply the French income in euros by 1.4 to convert it into dollars. In this case, the average French income would be $28,000. However, the exchange rate is influenced by international exchanges of assets like stocks and bonds, and it reflects only goods and services that are traded internationally. Thus, it may not be a good measure of cross-country differences in the cost of purchasing the typical bundle consumed by people in different countries.

Economists generally prefer to use the **purchasing power parity (PPP) method** when comparing incomes across countries. This procedure is very similar to the use of the consumer price index (CPI) to adjust for differences in the general level of prices across time periods. The cost in domestic currency of purchasing a specific bundle of goods and services that is typically consumed is derived. This bundle would include items like housing, food, electricity, gasoline, automobiles, and other items that are consumed in almost every country. The cost of purchasing this bundle is then used to derive the general level of prices (and the purchasing power of the domestic currency) in each country. Finally, this price index is used to convert the incomes in different countries to a common currency. Most economists believe that the PPP method results in income comparisons that more accurately reflect real income differences across countries and time periods.

Exhibit 1 shows per person GDP for 2011 for various high-, middle-, and low-income countries. The figures were derived by the PPP method. Take a close look at these income

Purchasing power parity method (PPP)

Method in which the relative purchasing power of each currency is determined by comparing the amount of each currency required to purchase a common bundle of goods and services in the domestic market. This information is then used to convert the GDP of each nation to a common monetary unit like the U.S. dollar.

EXHIBIT 1

The 2011 per Person GDP Levels of Various High-, Middle-, and Low-Income Countries (measured in 2005 PPP U.S. dollars)

HIGH-INCOME COUNTRIES		MIDDLE-INCOME COUNTRIES		LOW-INCOME COUNTRIES	
Singapore	53,591	Poland	17,938	China	7,418
Norway	46,971	Hungary	17,294	Ukraine	6,365
Hong Kong	44,640	Chile	15,251	Egypt	5,547
United States	42,486	Russia	14,714	Bolivia	4,503
Switzerland	39,385	Malaysia	14,174	Indonesia	4,094
Netherlands	37,118	Botswana	13,021	Philippines	3,638
Canada	35,715	Mexico	12,814	India	3,223
Ireland	35,439	Venezuela	11,258	Nigeria	2,237
Australia	34,853	Brazil	10,279	Bangladesh	1,569
Germany	34,573	South Africa	9,678	Uganda	1,188
United Kingdom	32,809	Peru	9,037	Malawi	789
Japan	30,660	Thailand	7,635	Niger	642

Source: World Bank, *World Development Indicators Online*, accessed June 2013.

data. The three countries with the highest income per person are Singapore ($53,591), Norway ($46,971), and Hong Kong ($44,640). The United States was fourth at $42,486. Switzerland, Netherlands, Canada, and Ireland all had income levels above $35,000. Incomes in the middle group ranged from Poland's $17,938 to Thailand's $7,635. The per person income in Hungary, Chile, Russia, and Malaysia was clustered in the $14,000 to $17,500 range. In the lower group, the income levels of China, Ukraine, and Egypt ranged between $5,500 and $7,500. The income levels of Indonesia, Philippines, India, and Nigeria were even lower. The per person incomes in the four highest-income countries were more than 50 times those of Malawi and Niger.

Some caution is necessary regarding the precision of the income figures of Exhibit 1, particularly the size of the differences between high- and low-income countries. Remember, GDP excludes most productive activities within the household sector because they do not involve a market exchange. Household production will nearly always be a larger share of total output in low- than high-income countries. For example, families in a low-income country like Nigeria or even Mexico are more likely than their U.S. counterparts to make their own clothing, raise and prepare their own food, provide their own child care services, and even build their own homes. These productive labor services, originating in the household sector, are excluded from GDP. Because of this omission, the per person GDP figures will tend to understate the income levels of less-developed countries (LDCs) relative to their richer counterparts.

However, given the size of the income differences between the high- and low-income countries of Exhibit 1, it is clear that the differences are still huge even after taking the omission of household production into account. Data on other quality-of-life factors are highly consistent with this view. For example, the residents of countries with higher per person incomes nearly always live longer and have lower illiteracy and infant mortality rates than those living in countries with lower incomes.

17-2 HOW DO GROWTH RATES VARY ACROSS COUNTRIES?

Which countries are growing most rapidly? Which are falling behind? Exhibit 2 presents data on the growth of per person GDP for (a) high-growth economies, (b) high-income industrial nations, and (c) the economies with the worst growth records. The left side of Exhibit 2 indicates the ten fastest-growing countries in the world during 1990–2010. All of these countries achieved an average annual growth rate of 3.8 percent or more over this lengthy time frame. China, Vietnam, India, Taiwan, and Sri Lanka head the list. All of the high-growth countries were classified as LDCs a quarter of a century ago.[2] One-third of the world's population live in the two most populated countries, China and India. Both of these countries are included in the high-growth list. Remember, a 4 percent annual growth rate means that per person GDP doubles approximately every 17 years. Clearly, per person incomes in the high-growth economies have increased sharply during the last couple of decades, and living standards improved dramatically.

Among the high income industrial economies, Australia and Norway grew the most rapidly. The per capita growth rates of the top eight were tightly clustered between 1.0 percent and 1.8 percent. The growth rates of Japan and Italy were only slightly lower.

Unfortunately, LDCs dominate not only the high-growth list but also the group with the worst economic record (see the right side of Exhibit 2). The income levels of this latter group have not only failed to grow, they have regressed. The per capita incomes of ten LDCs declined at an annual rate of 0.8 percent or more during 1990–2011.

The growth picture of LDCs is clearly one of diversity. The ten fastest-growing countries in the world since 1990, including two with a third of the world's population (China and India), were all LDCs. Income per person in these countries has grown more than twice

---

[2]Since 1980, the income level of Hong Kong has risen so much that it is no longer classified as less developed.

EXHIBIT 2

The Growth of Per Person GDP for High-Growth, High-Income Industrial, and Low-Growth Countries, 1990–2011

High Growth	Growth of Per Person GDP, 1990–2011 (%)	High-Income Industrial	Growth of Per Person GDP, 1990–2011 (%)	Low Growth	Growth of Per Person GDP, 1990–2011 (%)
China	9.5%	Australia	1.8%	Kyrgyz Republic	−0.8%
Vietnam	5.9%	Norway	1.8%	Central African Republic	−0.8%
India	4.8%	Netherlands	1.7%	Cote d'Ivoire	−0.9%
Tawain	4.4%	United Kingdom	1.6%	Madagascar	−0.9%
Sri Lanka	4.3%	Germany	1.4%	Ukraine	−1.1%
Korea, Rep.	4.3%	United States	1.4%	Georgia	−1.1%
Panama	4.0%	Canada	1.4%	Burundi	−1.2%
Dominican Republic	4.0%	France	1.0%	Tajikistan	−1.7%
Chile	3.8%	Japan	0.7%	Moldova	−2.0%
Poland	3.8%	Italy	0.6%	Congo, Dem. Rep.	−3.0%

Source: World Bank, *World Development Indicators Online*, accessed June 2013.

as fast as in the high-income industrial countries. These countries have not only closed the gap, but in a few cases, they now have higher income levels than many of their historically wealthier counterparts. At the same time, other LDCs are doing very poorly and falling further and further behind. Later in this chapter, we will return to this topic and consider the reasons underlying the differential growth rates among the poor countries of the world.

17-3 ECONOMIC FREEDOM AS A MEASURE OF SOUND INSTITUTIONS

In the last chapter, we discussed the major sources of economic growth: gains from trade, entrepreneurial discovery, and investment. Realization of gains from these sources is largely dependent upon institutions and policies supportive of voluntary exchange, market allocation, freedom to compete, and protection of people and their property from aggressors. These ingredients comprise the foundation of **economic freedom**.

Economic freedom reflects the concept of self-ownership: the idea that individuals have a right to choose—to decide how they will use their time and talents, but they do not have a right to the time, talents, and resources of others. Thus, individuals do not have a right to take things from others or demand that others provide things for them. Economic freedom is present when adults are free to consume, produce, and trade with others as long as their actions do not harm the person or property of another party. Use of violence, theft, fraud, and physical invasions are not permissible, but otherwise, individuals who are economically free are free to choose and compete as they see fit.

Economic freedom is complex and multidimensional. Therefore, it is difficult to measure. In the mid-1980s, the Fraser Institute of Vancouver, Canada, began work on a special project designed to measure the consistency of a nation's institutions and policies with economic freedom. Several leading scholars, including Nobel laureates Milton Friedman, Gary Becker, and Douglass C. North, participated in the endeavor. This eventually led to the development of the *Economic Freedom of the World* (EFW) index that is now published annually by a worldwide network of more than seventy institutes.

The EFW index uses 42 separate components to measure the consistency of a nation's institutions and policies with personal choice, freedom of exchange, open markets, and

Economic freedom
Method of organizing economic activity characterized by (1) personal choice, (2) voluntary exchange coordinated by markets, (3) freedom to enter and compete in markets, and (4) protection of people and their property from aggression by others.

Hong Kong is a modern economic miracle. Its real income per person in 2009 was more than eight times its 1960 figure. It is one of the freest economies in the world.

protection of private property. The World Bank, International Monetary Fund (IMF), and similar widely recognized organizations form the primary data source for the components of the EFW index. The data for each of the components are placed on a zero to ten scale and used to derive a summary rating, as well as ratings in five major areas.[3] In order to achieve a high EFW rating, a country must provide secure protection of privately owned property, even-handed enforcement of contracts, and a stable monetary environment. It also must keep taxes low, refrain from creating barriers to both domestic and international trade, and rely more fully on markets rather than governments to allocate goods and resources. In many respects, the EFW index reflects the institutional and policy factors that Chapter 16 indicates are important sources of economic growth.

The EFW data for some countries go back to 1970, and the ratings are available for 113 countries throughout the 1990–2010 period. **Exhibit 3** presents data on the ten highest- and ten lowest-rated economies, as well as the ratings of ten other large countries over the two decades. In order to rank in the top group, a country would have to maintain persistently high ratings. Thus, the countries in the top group might be thought of as those that persistently maintained institutions and policies supportive of economic freedom.

Hong Kong, Singapore, New Zealand, and the United States headed the list of the most persistently free economies during 1990–2010. At the other end of the spectrum,

EXHIBIT 3

The Economic Freedom Rating for the Top-, Middle-, and Lowest-Rated Countries, Average for 1990–2010.

	TOP-RATED COUNTRIES			MIDDLE-RATED COUNTRIES			LOWEST-RATED COUNTRIES	
1	Hong Kong	8.9	13	Japan	7.7	104	Nigeria	4.9
2	Singapore	8.7	15	Germany	7.7	105	Venezuela	4.8
3	New Zealand	8.4	19	Chile	7.5	106	Congo, Rep. Of	4.8
4	United States	8.3	29	France	7.2	107	Syria	4.7
5	Switzerland	8.3	39	South Korea	6.9	108	Burundi	4.6
6	United Kingdom	8.2	51	Indonesia	6.6	109	Algeria	4.5
7	Canada	8.2	53	Mexico	6.5	110	Zimbabwe	4.5
8	Australia	8.0	65	Argentina	6.1	111	Guinea-Bissau	4.4
9	Ireland	8.0	90	Brazil	5.6	112	Congo, Dem. R.	3.9
10	Netherlands	7.9	94	China	5.5	113	Myanmar	3.6

Source: James Gwartney, Robert Lawson, and Joshua Hall. *Economic Freedom of the World, 2012 Annual Report* (Vancouver, British Columbia: Fraser Institute, 2012).

[3]The five areas are (1) size of government; (2) legal system and protection of property rights; (3) access to sound money; (4) freedom to trade with foreigners; and (5) regulation of credit, labor, and business. To the fullest extent possible, the components of the index are based on objective variables such as government consumption as a share of total consumption, standard deviation of the inflation rate, and mean tariff rate. When it was necessary to use survey data to measure important elements of economic freedom, as was often the case in the legal and regulatory areas, data from outside sources were used in order to minimize value judgments. For additional details, see James Gwartney, Robert Lawson, and Joshua Hall, *Economic Freedom of the World: 2012 Annual Report* (Vancouver, British Columbia: Fraser Institute, 2012) and the Web site http://www.freetheworld.com.

Myanmar, Democratic Republic of the Congo, Guinea-Bissau, Zimbabwe, Algeria, and Burundi had the least free economies. Among the large economies, Germany, Chile, Japan, and France were more toward the economically free end of the spectrum, whereas Brazil, China, and Argentina were in the less free range.

17-4 INSTITUTIONS, POLICIES, AND ECONOMIC PERFORMANCE

If institutions and policies are important, the freer economies should outperform those that are less free. When considering the impact of institutions, it is important to focus on long-term growth and income rather than short-term growth, which may reflect mostly the ups and downs of business cycle conditions. Thus, our focus will be on the relationship between institutional quality and economic performance over a lengthy time period. We now turn to an examination of this issue.

The 113 countries with economic freedom ratings throughout 1990–2010 were divided into **quartiles**. The 28 countries with the highest average economic freedom rating over the period comprise the top quartile, the 28 with the next highest average ratings make up the next quartile, and so on. **Exhibit 4** presents data on the per person income levels of the quartiles, ranged from the least free to the most free. Clearly, the economies with institutions and policies more consistent with economic freedom had substantially higher income levels. The per person income of countries in the freest quartile were more than twice those of the second freest quartile. Correspondingly, the income levels of countries in the second quartile were twice those of the third quartile, which were substantially greater than those of the least economically free quartile. The per person incomes of countries in the freest quartile were more than seven times the income levels of countries in the least free quartile. Clearly, there is a strong positive relationship between economic freedom and income levels.

Exhibit 5 uses the quartile analysis to illustrate the relationship between economic freedom and growth. In the freest quartile of economies, per person income grew at an average annual rate of 3.6 percent during the two-decade period, compared to 2.8 for the second freest quartile and 2.4 percent for the third quartile. Countries in the least free group grew at an annual rate of only 1.6 percent. Thus, the income per person of countries in the top quartile grew more than twice the average rate of those in the bottom quartile.

The growth figures of Exhibit 5 were adjusted for initial income level, but not for other factors such as location relative to major markets, access to ocean coastline, years of

Quartile
A quarter (25 percent) of a group. The quartiles are often arrayed on the basis of an indicator like income or degree of economic freedom.

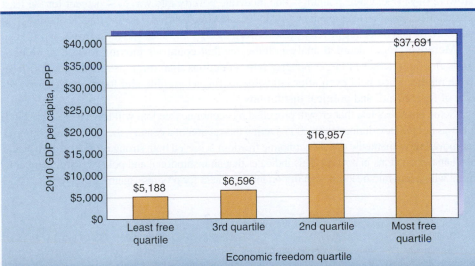

EXHIBIT 4

Economic Freedom and Income

The 2010 income per person of countries ordered by economic freedom rating is shown here by quartiles. Note the strong positive linkage. The income per person in countries in the freest quartile was about seven times the figure for the least free group.

Source: James Gwartney, Robert Lawson, and Joshua Hall, *Economic Freedom of the World, 2012 Annual Report* (Vancouver, British Columbia: Fraser Institute, 2012).

EXHIBIT 5

Economic Freedom and Growth

The relation between the economic freedom of a country and its growth rate during 1990–2010 is shown here. Countries in the most economically free quartile grew at an annual rate of 3.6 percent compared to 1.6 percent growth for the least free quartile.

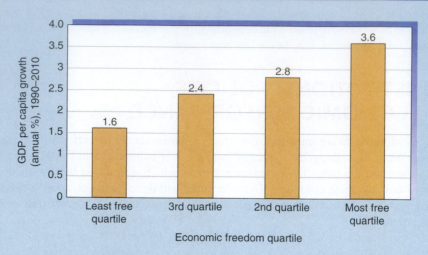

Source: James Gwartney, Robert Lawson, and Joshua Hall, *Economic Freedom of the World*, 2012 *Annual Report* (Vancouver, British Columbia: Fraser Institute, 2012).

Note: The data for growth were adjusted to control for the initial level of income.

schooling, and degree of democracy. However, more comprehensive analysis indicates that even after these factors are taken into consideration, countries with more economic freedom achieve higher income levels and grow more rapidly.[4]

The data of Exhibits 4 and 5 are for average income and growth rate. What about the poorest segment of the population? What impact does economic freedom have on the poverty rate? The World Bank provides data on extreme and moderate poverty rates. The extreme poverty rate is the percentage of the population with an income of less than $1.25 per day, while the moderate poverty rate is the share of the population with an income of less than $2 per day. As we indicated in the last chapter, both the extreme and moderate poverty rates have declined substantially since 1980.

Exhibit 6 provides data for both the extreme and moderate poverty rates according to economic freedom quartiles arranged from lowest to highest. Clearly, the poverty rates were much lower in the freer economies. The extreme poverty rate in 2005 (the latest year for which these data are available) was 41.5 percent for the least free economies, but only 2.7 percent in those that were most free. Correspondingly, the moderate poverty rate was 57.4 percent for the least free quartile, compared to only 3.6 percent in the most free quartile. The two middle quartiles had both extreme and moderate poverty rates between those of the least and most free economies.

Moreover, more detailed analysis indicates that countries moving toward more economic freedom achieved larger poverty rate reductions than did those that were less free. These relationships held even after adjustments for geographic and locational factors, receipt of foreign aid, and political institutions.[5]

Some observers fear that growth propelled by economic freedom will leave the poor behind. This was not the case during 1980–2005. During this quarter of a century, the developing countries that moved most markedly toward economic freedom achieved both strong economic growth and substantial reductions in poverty. This indicates that an institutional and policy environment consistent with economic freedom is an important ingredient for progress against poverty.

---

[4]For additional details on how economic freedom affects income levels and growth rates, see Niclas Berggren, "The Benefits of Economic Freedom: A Survey," *Independent Review* 8 (Fall 2003): 193–211; John W. Dawson, "Institutions, Investment, and Growth: New Cross-Country and Panel Data Evidence," *Economic Inquiry* 36 (October 1998): 603–19; and James Gwartney, "Institutions, Economic Freedom, and Cross-Country Differences in Performance," *Southern Economic Journal* 75, no. 4 (April 2009): 937–56.

[5]Joseph Connors, *Global Poverty: The Role of Economic Freedom, Democracy, and Foreign Aid* (PhD diss., Florida State University, 2011).

EXHIBIT 6

(a) Economic freedom quartile

(b) Economic freedom quartile

Economic Freedom and the Poverty Rate

The 2005 extreme and moderate poverty rates are shown here according to the economic freedom quartiles arrayed from least to most free. Clearly, both the extreme and the moderate poverty rates are lower in the more free economies.

Source: Joseph Connors, *Global Poverty: The Role of Economic Freedom, Democracy, and Foreign Aid* (PhD diss., Florida State University, 2011). The poverty rate data by country are from the World Bank, *World Development Indicators, 2009* (Washington, DC: World Bank).

Note: The extreme and moderate poverty rates are the percentage of the population living on less than $1.25 and $2 per day, respectively. These numbers are measured in constant 2005 dollars and normalized across countries using the purchasing power parity method.

17-5 ECONOMIC FREEDOM, INSTITUTIONS, AND INVESTMENT

As we discussed in the previous chapter, investment is an important source of economic growth. Other things constant, countries that invest more will tend to grow more rapidly, and, with time, achieve higher levels of income. The quality of institutions and policies will influence the flow of investment funds toward or away from a country. Private investors will be attracted to economies in which markets are open, the regulatory burden is minimal, and the legal system protects property rights and provides for evenhanded enforcement of exchange agreements. In contrast, when regulations limit entry and restrict voluntary exchange, taxes are high, protection of property rights is uncertain, and political favoritism rampant, investors will take their funds elsewhere.

Exhibit 7 illustrates the impact of institutions and policies on private investment and its productivity during 1980–2005. The data are separated into three economic freedom-rating categories (greater than 7.0, 5.0–7.0, and less than 5.0) during this quarter of a century. As Exhibit 7(a) shows, private investment as a share of GDP increased sharply with the level of economic freedom. On average, private investment constituted 18.7 percent of GDP for countries with an EFW rating of 7.0 or more compared to 15.6 percent for the middle group and only 11.2 percent for the least free group. Thus, the private investment rate of the economically free group was 67 percent higher than for the least free group.

EXHIBIT 7

Economic Freedom and the Level and Productivity of Private Investment

Here, data are presented for both the level and productivity of private investment for countries with an average EFW rating during 1980–2005 of greater than 7.0, between 5.0 and 7.0, and less than 5.0. As frame (a) shows, private investment as a share of GDP was substantially higher in the more free countries. Frame (b) presents data on the impact of a percentage point increase in investment as a share of GDP on the annual rate of economic growth during 1980–2005. Note the productivity of investment in the freest economies was more than three times the level for the least free countries. These figures are after adjustment for the impact of initial income level, changes in human capital, tropical location, and share of the population residing near an ocean coastline.

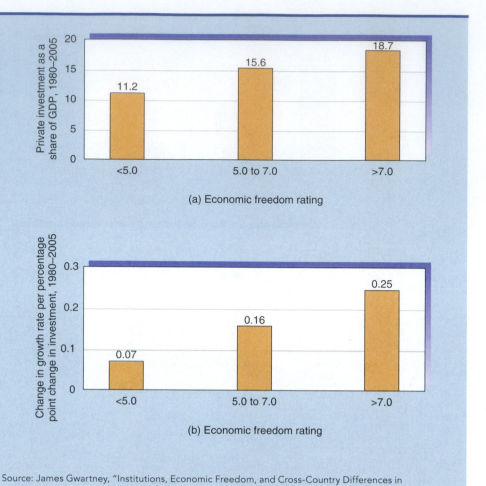

(a) Economic freedom rating

(b) Economic freedom rating

Source: James Gwartney, "Institutions, Economic Freedom, and Cross-Country Differences in Performance," *Southern Economic Journal* 75 (April 2009): 937–56.

Exhibit 7(b) illustrates the impact on long-term growth of a one percentage point increase in private investment as a share of GDP for the three different levels of economic freedom. In countries with EFW ratings of 7.0 or more, a one percentage point increase in private investment as a share of GDP was associated with a 0.25 percent increase in growth during the 1980–2005 period. For countries with EFW ratings between 5.0 and 7.0, a percentage point increase in investment as a share of GDP enhanced growth by only 0.16 percent, and when EFW was less than 5.0, a percentage point increase in the investment/GDP ratio increased growth by only 0.07 percent. Thus, the productivity of investment—the impact of a unit change on growth—was more than three times higher in the more free economies than for the group with the least economic freedom. These figures are after adjustment was made for initial income level, changes in human capital, tropical location, share of the population residing near an ocean coastline and government investment as a share of GDP.[6] The model was also tested for less-developed countries only, and the pattern of results was similar.

The investment figures add clarity to the relationship between sound institutions and economic performance. Countries with institutions more consistent with economic free-

---

[6]For a more detailed analysis of how economic freedom influences economic performance through investment, See James Gwartney, Randall Holcombe, and Robert Lawson, "Institutions and the Impact of Investment on Growth," *Kyklos* 59 (May 2006): 255–76.

dom generally attract more investment and direct the investment into higher productivity projects than countries that are less free. In turn, the additional investment and higher productivity boosts the growth rate of the more economically free economies. As a result, freer economies achieve higher income levels and make more progress against poverty than do those that are less free.

17-6 ORIGINS OF INSTITUTIONS

In an important recent book, *Why Nations Fail*, economists Daron Acemoglu of the Massachusetts Institute of Technology, and James Robinson of Harvard University argue that institutions determine the fate of nations. Successful nations adopt institutions and policies that limit the power of political leaders, provide secure property rights, and permit open markets—all of which encourage trade, innovation, and entrepreneurship. In contrast, nations fail when their institutions and policies are "extractive," when they allow the politically powerful to take resources and income from others.[7]

Why do some nations have good institutions and others bad? Acemoglu and Robinson believe history provides a big part of the answer. They argue that a country's history during the colonial era exerted a major impact on the evolution of its institutions. Researchers have found that countries with colonial settlers who planned on staying were likely to develop sound institutions and policies. Because of their long-term commitment, they sought to protect individual property rights and limit the power of government. In contrast, colonizers settling in harsh climates and with short-term interests in the extraction of mineral resources were more likely to choose institutions that provided few limitations on the power of government. They were not very interested in individual rights, protection of property, and evenhanded application and enforcement of the law. Even after independence, the colonial institutional influences remained and continued to exert an impact on institutions and policies.

According to this view, countries like the United States, Canada, Australia, and New Zealand developed sound institutions and policies because their colonizing Europeans planned on staying. They had long-range plans and sought to protect their investments, gains from trade, and returns on new discoveries. Conversely, protective institutions were largely absent in Africa and Latin America, where the European colonizers were primarily interested in resource extraction.

Is institutional change possible? History can help answer that. What happened 50 or 100 years ago continues to shape the institutions and policies of various countries. While no country can entirely escape its past, there are at least three reasons to believe that the opportunity for constructive institutional change is now greater than in the past. First, the colonial era is over. Countries that were previously colonized by European powers are now in a position to make their own institutional and policy choices. Second, the collapse of communism has also expanded the opportunity for institutional change. Much like former colonies, the institutional choices of countries under Soviet domination were also limited. Third, and perhaps most important, substantial reductions in transportation and communication costs have increased the importance of institutions and policies. Lower transportation and communication costs mean that, to a greater extent than in the past, entrepreneurs can choose where to locate a productive facility. This increases the potential gains from trade, including

---

[7]Daron Acemoglu and James A. Robinson, *Why Nations Fail* (New York: Crown, 2012). For additional information on the importance of institutions as a source of economic success, see Robert E. Hall and Charles I. Jones, "Why Do Some Countries Produce So Much More Output per Worker than Others?" *Quarterly Journal of Economics* 114 (February 1999): 83–116; and Daron Acemoglu, Simon Johnson, and James A. Robinson, "The Colonial Origins of Comparative Development: An Empirical Investigation," *American Economic Review* 91 (December 2001): 1369–401.

those accompanying the importation of investment and technology from abroad. It also increases the incentive for countries to adopt sound institutions and policies.

17-6a RECENT INSTITUTIONAL CHANGE AND ECONOMIC PERFORMANCE

There is evidence that a number of countries have made substantial changes in their institutions and policies in recent decades. Beginning in the 1960s, both Hong Kong and Singapore began to liberalize their economies and, by the 1970s, both were among the world's freest economies. Their growth rates have been impressive. In 1960, the per capita incomes of both Hong Kong and Singapore were well below those of Latin American countries like Brazil, Argentina, and Venezuela. The figures are now dramatically different. In 2011, the per person incomes of Hong Kong and Singapore were more than three times those of the Latin American countries. Singapore and Hong Kong now rank first and third in the world in per capita income (see Exhibit 1).

Other economies have undertaken major reforms during the last three decades. The EFW can be used along with data on institutional reform from the International Monetary Fund to identify the major reformers.[8] **Exhibit 8** provides information on both institutional change and its impact. Countries that have achieved and sustained an increase of two points or more in their EFW rating following adoption of reforms are included in this exhibit. China and Chile began instituting key reforms in the 1970s. At the time, both were among the least free economies in the world, but the reform process increased their EFW ratings substantially. In turn, their growth rates have been impressive since 1980. China was the world's fastest-growing economy during 1980–2011 and Chile's 3.3 percent annual growth rate was well above average during that period. Chile now has the highest per capita income level in South America.

Eight other economies undertook major reforms beginning in the 1980s. Four of these countries (Bangladesh, Botswana, Ghana, and Mauritius) began the reform process with very low incomes, while the other four (Iceland, Ireland, New Zealand, and United Kingdom) started from higher income levels. Since 1990, the per capita income of the 1980s reformers has grown at an average annual rate of 2.5 percent. The growth rates of Ireland, Bangladesh, and Mauritius have been particularly impressive. During 1995–2011, the eight countries achieved an annual growth rate of 2.8 percent.

During the 1990s, 12 additional countries instituted major reforms that increased their EFW rating by two or more points. Except for Hungary and Israel, all of the 1990 reformers had very low incomes prior to the institution of reforms. This is a diverse group, including countries from Asia, Latin America, Africa, and Eastern Europe. The average growth record of the twelve was 3.2 percent during 2011. The growth achievements of Estonia, India, and Poland were particularly impressive.

Finally, Exhibit 8 also contains information on countries with reductions in EFW of one-half point or more between 1995–2005. Since the mid-1980s, the overall EFW ratings have been increasing, primarily as a result of a more stable monetary policy, lower tax rates, and trade liberalization. Thus, reductions in EFW ratings have been far less common than increases. There were only three countries—the Democratic Republic of the Congo, Venezuela, and Zimbabwe—with rating reductions of half a point or more. Monetary instability, confiscation of property, and violation of rule of law principles played a role in the declining economic freedom rating of these countries. As Exhibit 8 shows, the rating reductions were accompanied by poor economic performance. Both the Democratic Republic of the Congo and Zimbabwe had negative growth rates during 1995–2011. While Venezuela achieved a positive growth of 0.8 percent during 1995–2011, all of this growth occurred during 2005–2011, and it was driven by the rising world price of oil of that period.

---

[8]See International Monetary Fund, "Building Institutions," *IMF World Economic Outlook* (September 2005).

EXHIBIT 8

The Growth Rates and Income Levels of Countries with Major Changes in Institutions and Policies since 1975

	Beginning Year of Change	Sustained EFW Increase	2005 EFW Rating	Growth 1980–2011(%)	Growth 1990–2011(%)	Growth 1995–2011(%)	Per Capita GDP, 2011 ($ U.S.)
Countries Beginning Reform during the 1970s							
Chile	1976	3.8	7.8	3.3	3.8	2.9	15,251
China	1978	2.1	6.3	8.9	9.5	9.1	7,418
Average		**3.0**	**7.1**	**6.1**	**6.6**	**6.0**	**11,335**
Countries Beginning Reform during the 1980s							
Bangladesh	1987	2.2	6.0		3.6	4.1	1,569
Botswana	1985	2.3	7.2		3.0	3.6	13,021
Ghana	1985	3.6	6.2		2.9	3.4	1,652
Iceland	1988	3.0	7.8		1.3	1.9	33,514
Ireland	1987	1.6	7.9		3.2	2.9	35,439
Mauritius	1985	2.5	7.5		3.6	3.5	12,733
New Zealand	1985	2.3	8.5		1.1	1.1	24,429
United Kingdom	1980	1.9	8.1		1.6	1.7	32,809
Average		**2.4**	**7.4**		**2.5**	**2.8**	**19,396**
Countries Beginning Reform during the 1990s							
Costa Rica	1991	2.1	7.4			2.5	10,735
El Salvador	1994	3.0	7.6			1.7	6,032
Estonia	1995	2.3	8.0			5.3	18,130
Hungary	1995	2.3	7.5			2.5	17,294
India	1990	2.1	6.6			5.3	3,223
Israel	1991	3.7	7.1			1.7	26,719
Nicaragua	1994	4.2	6.5			2.2	3,366
Peru	1993	4.0	7.2			3.4	9,037
Poland	1990	2.9	6.9			4.4	17,938
Tanzania	1995	2.9	6.3			3.3	1,336
Uganda	1995	3.6	6.5			3.6	1,188
Zambia	1996	3.4	6.7			2.1	1,431
Average		**3.0**	**7.0**			**3.2**	**9,702**
Countries that Regressed							
Congo, Republic	1995	−0.5	4.0		−3.0	−0.5	329
Venezuela	2000	−0.9	4.9		0.8	0.6	11,258
Zimbabwe	1998	−2.6	2.9		−2.7	−3.4	500
Average					**−1.6**	**−1.1**	**4,029**

Source: James Gwartney and Robert Lawson, *Economic Freedom of the World: 2012 Annual Report*, International Monetary Fund, *World Economic Outlook*, September 2005, Chapter 3, "Building Institutions", and World Bank, *World Development Indicators Online.* The International Monetary Fund data are the source of the year in which the reforms were initiated.

Sustained growth of per capita income of 2 percent or more over a lengthy time period is relatively uncommon. As Exhibit 2 shows, none of the high-income industrial economies grew at annual rates of 2 percent or more during 1990–2011. Interestingly, seven of the ten countries that made major moves toward reform during the 1970s and 1980s achieved an annual growth rate of more than 2 percent during 1995–2011. While their rates varied substantially, all of the countries moving toward reform achieved a positive growth of income per person. This is strong evidence that changes in institutional quality exert an impact on growth and income.

17-7 THE DECLINING ECONOMIC FREEDOM OF THE UNITED STATES

The United States ranked as the world's third freest economy, behind only Hong Kong and Singapore, throughout most of 1980–2000. The situation changed substantially during the past decade. As **Exhibit 9** shows, the summary EFW rating of the United States fell from 8.65 in 2000 to 7.70 in 2010, a reduction of almost one full unit. By 2010, the U.S. ranking had fallen to 16th, down from the third place position it occupied in 2000. Several factors contributed to the decline in the U.S. rating. Government spending on both consumption and transfer payments were higher in 2010 than a decade earlier, pushing the ratings for these components down. The rating in the legal system and protection of property rights area also declined substantially during the past decade. Non-tariff barriers rose, reflecting an increasing cost of meeting heightened security standards and clearing customs. A decline in the share of credit allocated to the private sector and increased regulations and administrative costs imposed on business also contributed to the decline in the U.S. rating.

While a one-point decline does not sound like much, the summary EFW ratings fall within a narrow range between three and nine. Research on the impact of a one-unit reduction in the EFW rating indicates that it is associated with approximately a one percentage point decline in long run economic growth. In this regard, it is interesting to note that the growth of real per capita GDP in the United States averaged 2.3 percent in the 1980s and 2.2 percent during the 1990s, but it fell to an annual rate of only 0.7 percent during 2000–2010. If the United States continues to follow policies restrictive of economic freedom, it can expect to grow at a slower rate in the years ahead.

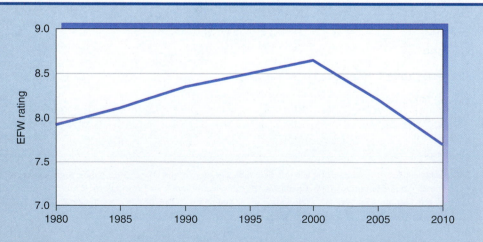

EXHIBIT 9

Economic Freedom of the United States, 1980–2010

While the EFW rating of the United States increased from 7.92 in 1980 to 8.62 in 2000, it has declined substantially during the past decade. By 2010, the rating fell to 7.70, its lowest level in more than three decades. Unless this trend is reversed, future growth of the U.S. economy is likely to be sluggish.

Source: James Gwartney, Robert Lawson, and Joshua Hall, *Economic Freedom of the World: 2012 Annual Report* (Vancouver, British Columbia: Fraser Institute).

APPLICATIONS IN ECONOMICS

China: Institutions, Markets, and Growth

Since 1980, China has been the world's fastest-growing economy. How can this be? Isn't China a centrally planned socialist economy? It certainly was for three decades following World War II. However, even though the Communist Party of China remains in charge, the Chinese economy has experienced remarkable change during the past three decades.

Following the 1978 Communist Party Congress, China began introducing institutional reforms that have dramatically changed the structure of the economy. Today, there are essentially two Chinese economies: (1) agriculture, small businesses, and "special economic zones" and (2) state enterprises. The activities in the first category take place within a now relatively free economy, whereas those in the second continue to be owned and operated by various levels of government.

China's liberalization started with the agricultural sector. Following the 1978 Communist Party Congress, collective farms were dismantled and replaced with what the Chinese refer to as a contract responsibility system. Under this system, families are now permitted to lease land from the government for periods of up to 50 years. Except for a modest production quota supplied to the government, farmers are permitted to keep what they produce and/or sell it at market prices. Even though the legal ownership of land remains with the state, the system of long-term leases provides a farmer with something akin to a private property right, particularly as renewal of the leases has now become virtually automatic. Currently, more than 85 percent of the grain output (rice, wheat, and barley) is produced privately and sold at market-determined prices.

Success in China's agriculture led to reforms in other sectors. Restrictions on the operation of small-scale service and retail businesses were relaxed in the 1980s. The number of self-employed household businesses and single proprietorships increased from 140,000 in 1978 to 2.6 million in 1981. Private restaurants, stores, and repair shops sprang up and began to compete with state-operated enterprises. By the mid-1980s, Chinese cities were teeming with sidewalk vendors, restaurants, small retail businesses, and hundreds of thousands of individuals providing personal services. Moreover, townships and villages were permitted to both directly operate businesses and authorize local entrepreneurs to do likewise. These enterprises purchased resources and labor services and sold their products at market determined prices. They were directed by profits and losses, much like firms in a market economy.

China also established so-called special economic zones. Approximately 30 percent of the people in the Chinese labor force now work in these areas. Regulations are more liberal and taxes lower in the zones. People are permitted to establish businesses, engage in trade with foreigners, maintain bank accounts in foreign currencies, and undertake investment without having to obtain government approval. During recent decades, the zones attracted a large amount of investment from abroad, which has contributed to the growth of the Chinese investment rate. Economic activity in these regions has also made a sizable contribution to the growth of the trade sector.

The Chinese economy has become much more open to international trade in recent decades. In 1980, international trade (the average of imports plus exports) as a share of GDP was 10 percent of the Chinese economy. But this changed rapidly during the 1980s and 1990s. In recent years, the trade sector has comprised 30 percent or more of the Chinese economy. By way of comparison, international trade is about 15 percent of the U.S. economy. Even though China is more populous, measured as a share of GDP, China's trade sector is more than double the size of the trade sector of the United States. No doubt, the increased openness and rapid expansion of the trade sector have been major factors contributing to the impressive growth of the Chinese economy

China's economic freedom ranking is still relatively low. In 2010, it ranked 100th among the 144 countries of the EFW report. But the movements toward economic liberalization have boosted its EFW rating substantially. China's EFW rating in 2010 was 6.16 up from 5.75 in 2000, and 3.74 in 1980. Moreover, the degree of economic freedom in the special economic zones, which now cover a large share of the economy, is substantially greater than for the country as a whole.

The liberal reforms have surely contributed to China's rapid growth.[1] However, it is possible that some of the growth has been exaggerated. This was the case for the former Soviet Union and the countries of Eastern Europe during the 1970s and 1980s. Because centrally planned economies do not rely on market prices to allocate goods and services, output in the planned sector is generally measured by the physical quantities of goods produced and the value of inputs used. These factors might not reliably reflect the value of what is actually produced. Also, the movement of the labor force away from the rural agriculture sector toward an urbanized market economy tends to overstate the growth of real GDP. Output in the former is often omitted from GDP because it does not involve a market transaction, while the latter is generally included. This will also tend to exaggerate the growth of GDP. Thus, while China's growth is clearly impressive, the figures should be interpreted with a degree of caution.

[1]For a detailed account on the liberal reforms and their impact on the growth of China, see Ronald Coase and Ning Wang, *How China Became Capitalist* (New York: Palgrave Macmillan, 2012).

©iStockphoto.com/sorendls

17-8 RICH AND POOR NATIONS REVISITED

Observing income differences between the wealthy and poor nations, some have argued that the rich are consistently getting richer while the poor are getting poorer. Is this true? Look back at Exhibit 2 as you think about this question. Interestingly, as Exhibit 2 shows, countries with a low per capita income in 1990 dominate the list of both countries that have grown most rapidly and those that have regressed and experienced falling incomes since 1990.

How can this pattern be explained? When you think about it, the rapid growth of LDCs with a low initial income should not be surprising. When low-income countries establish sound institutions and policies, they actually have an advantage. The low-income economies can copy or emulate ideas and technologies that have been successful in the high-income countries. Further, in a world of diminishing returns, the rate of return on investment in low-income economies with sound institutions will generally be higher than in capital-rich, more advanced economies. Thus, foreign investors will be attracted, and high investment rates will promote more rapid growth. To a degree, the rapid growth in recent decades of economies such as China, South Korea, Botswana, India, Singapore, and Hong Kong reflects these advantages. These countries would not have grown as rapidly if their initial incomes had been higher, and they had not been in a position to attract investment and emulate technologies, business procedures, and other ideas from more advanced economies. It is also important to note that the high-growth economies of Exhibit 2 had either persistently high economic freedom ratings (Hong Kong and Singapore) or a major improvement in their EFW rating (China, Botswana, Ireland, and India are examples).

However, if a low-income country is going to benefit from borrowing technologies from more advanced economies and an influx of investment capital, it must have sound institutions. Access to modern technology is of little value when the institutional and policy environment undermine the potential attractiveness of entrepreneurial activity. This has been the case in many LDCs. The ten economies with the worst growth records shown in Exhibit 2 are all among the world's least free economies. Disastrous institutional conditions explain the persistence of both low incomes and poor growth. Many low-income economies continue to perform poorly and even regress because their institutions and policies stifle gains from trade, entrepreneurship, and investment.

17-9 ECONOMIC RULES AND POLITICAL DECISION-MAKING

A country's economic rules make a huge difference in its economic growth. When the institutions and policies of a country encourage market exchanges, reward the discovery of better ways of doing things, and protect people and their property, investment will be attracted to the nation, and people will engage in productive activities. Rapid growth and movement up the income ladder will result. In contrast, if the rules make unproductive and destructive activities profitable, people will pursue such activities and potentially productive resources will be squandered.

Economic institutions reflect the political process. A legal system that provides for the protection of individuals and their property and the unbiased enforcement of contracts is particularly important for growth and prosperity.

Tim Graham/Alamy

Economics indicates the types of institutions and policies that will lead to wealth creation, growth, and prosperity. However, institutions and policies are an outgrowth of the political process. Unfortunately, there is no assurance that political decision-making will lead to sound policies.

Authoritarian political regimes will typically reflect the interests of those holding power and their desire to maintain their control. If more rapid growth will help an authoritarian government remain in power, it will be an incentive to move toward sounder policies. In recent decades, Chile, Singapore, South Korea, and Taiwan moved toward economic liberalization even though their political regimes were authoritarian. China's Communist government has also moved in this direction since 1978 even while maintaining a firm grip on the political machinery of the country. But growth may not always be advantageous to those in political control. In addition, history teaches that power corrupts. Even if an authoritarian government adopts some sensible economic policies, there is no assurance that they will persist.

Won't **democracy** ensure that a government will undertake productive policies? Think about the difference between markets and political democracy as you ponder this question. The two are quite different. Market exchange is based on agreement and mutual gain. When markets are open and property rights are well defined, market activities will persist only when they are mutually advantageous. Most important, the agreement of the market participants provides strong evidence that the activity is productive. In contrast, the majority rules criteria of democracy generate "losers" as well as "winners." And there is no assurance that the gains of the winners will be greater than the costs imposed on the losers. This is particularly true when the primary beneficiaries of the decisions differ from those who are paying the costs related to those decisions.

As public choice analysis highlights, there are several circumstances under which there is good reason to expect that the costs imposed on the minority will be greater than, and often substantially greater than, the benefits derived by the political majority. Majoritarian democracy tends to be shortsighted. It is biased toward the adoption of programs that provide immediate, highly visible benefits at the expense of future costs that are difficult to identify. Furthermore, special interests will exert disproportional power at the expense of the ordinary citizen. Political incentives will lead politicians to "trade" favors to interest groups in exchange for political contributions that will help them win the next election. When the government becomes heavily involved in activities that provide favors to some at the expense of others, people will be encouraged to divert resources away from productive activities and toward lobbying, campaign contributions, and other forms of political favor seeking. All of these shortcomings tend to corrupt the political process and lead even democratic governments to adopt counterproductive policies.

Aren't our elected political leaders acting with good intentions and trying to do what is right? No doubt, many of them are. But, as we discussed in Chapter 1, good intentions will not guarantee desirable outcomes. Neither will they provide protection from unsound policies. The doctors of the eighteenth century had good intentions. They thought that leeches would draw various diseases out of the bloodstream and lead to recovery. But their good intentions did not protect their patients from the adverse consequences of unsound practices. Neither will good intentions protect ordinary citizens from unsound governmental policies.

Could political institutions be designed in a manner that would make political action more reflective of mutual agreement and provide better protection of economic rights? Clearly, the answer is "yes." Such a design would include (1) checks on the powers of both the executive and simple legislative majorities; (2) constitutional protection of economic rights like ownership of property, freedom to trade and compete, and use of alternative currencies; and (3) political decentralization so that citizens

Democracy
A form of political organization in which adult citizens are free to participate in the political process (vote, lobby, and choose among candidates), elections are free and open, and majority voting, either directly or by elected representatives, decides outcomes.

can more easily escape from governmental units that fail to provide an attractive economic environment.[9]

However, merely because it is possible to design a political system reasonably consistent with growth and prosperity does not mean it will happen. Just because we have knowledge about what works does not mean sound policies will flow from the political process. As the chapter-opening quote from Professor North indicates, history is a story about countries that fail to adopt and enforce a set of economic rules that generate sustained economic growth. Achievement and maintenance of political power often conflict with sound economics.

The ingredients of sound institutions and policies in the decades ahead are the same as they have been in decades past: well-defined property rights, rule of law, monetary and price stability, open markets, low taxes, control of government spending, and neutral treatment of both people and enterprises. (See the Keys to Prosperity list in the inside front cover of this book.) Countries that adopt sound institutions and follow policies reflective of these factors will grow and prosper. Those that fail to do so will stagnate and regress. The future of the United States and other countries throughout the world in the twenty-first century will be shaped by their actions in this vitally important area.

LOOKING AHEAD

As we have already discussed, international trade is an important source of growth and prosperity. The following chapter will provide a more detailed analysis of this issue.

---

[9]The framers of the U.S. Constitution recognized the danger of unlimited government. They sought to limit federal actions to those areas of widespread agreement through the establishment of two legislative bodies based on different criteria; separation of powers among the executive, legislative, and judicial branches; and the listing of the specifi c powers of the central government (the enumerated powers of Article I, Section 8). All other powers were left to the states and the people (Tenth Amendment). Thus, decentralization of government was also an integral part of the structural design. The U.S. Constitution also provides some protection for both trade and private ownership. Taxes on exports and state legislation "impairing the obligation of contracts" (Article I, Section 10) were prohibited. The Fifth Amendment specifi es that private property shall not be "taken for public use without just compensation." With the passage of time, however, the economic protections built into the U.S. Constitution have been eroded by court decisions. This is particularly true for the enumerated powers section.

KEY POINTS

- PPP comparisons indicate that the per person income in wealthy countries such as Singapore, Norway, Hong Kong, and the United States is about 50 times the income level of the world's poorest countries. While these figures may result in some overstatement because GDP excludes production within the household sector, it is clear that the income differences between high- and low-income countries are huge.

- The world's fastest-growing economies were all low-income, less-developed countries (LDCs) a couple of decades ago. China and India, with a third of the world's population, are included in the fast-growing group of LDCs. But there is also a large number of LDCs that have experienced falling incomes in recent decades.

- The Economic Freedom of the World (EFW) index is designed to measure the consistency of a nation's institutions and policies with personal choice, voluntary exchange, open markets, and protection of property rights. In order to score high on this index, countries must rely on markets, refrain from regulations that restrain trade, keep taxes low, and provide access to sound money and a legal system that protects privately owned property and enforces contracts in an evenhanded manner.

- Countries with institutions and policies more consistent with economic freedom have grown more rapidly, attained higher income levels, and achieved lower poverty rates than those that are less free. The 2010 per capita income in the persistently free quartile of countries was more than seven times the figure for the least free quartile.

- Both the level and productivity of investment is higher in countries with institutions and policies more consistent with economic freedom than in those that are less free. This is a contributing factor to the more rapid growth and higher income levels of the freer economies.

- Countries that have substantially improved the quality of their institutions in recent decades have registered impressive growth rates. Ireland, Bangladesh, Chile, Estonia, and even China are examples. In contrast, countries such as Zimbabwe and Venezuela that have moved toward policies that conflict with economic freedom have performed poorly.

- Economic institutions and policies will reflect political choices. The political environment often conflicts with the adoption of sound economic policy. Even democratic politics will sometimes lead to the adoption of policies that reduce growth and prosperity.

CRITICAL ANALYSIS QUESTIONS

1. Name five countries with a high income per capita. Why do you think the income is so high in these countries? How many of your high-income countries also ranked among the fastest-growing countries in the world since 1990?

2. Name five of the fastest-growing economies in the world since 1990. Why do you think these economies have grown so rapidly?

3. "The rich countries are getting richer, while the poor are getting poorer." Evaluate this statement.

4. What conditions must be present for a country to achieve a high score on the *Economic Freedom of the World* (EFW) index?

5. Indicate five of the world's economies that are most free. How do the income levels and growth rates of freer economies compare with those that are less free?

6. *What are the major sources of economic growth? Why do some countries grow and achieve high-income levels while others stagnate in poverty? What do you think can be done to change this situation?

7. Has the United States become more or less economically free during the past decade? What impact will this have on the future economic growth of the United States?

8. *If there were no high-income developed countries like those of Western Europe, North America, and Japan, would less-developed countries like Hong Kong, Singapore, South Korea, China, and India have been able to grow so rapidly in recent decades? Explain.

9. Do we count on majority rule to protect civil liberties such as the right to free speech, freedom of the press, the right to assembly, and religious freedom? Should we count on majority rule to protect economic rights like the freedom to trade, the freedom to compete in the business or occupation of one's choice, and the protection against the taking of one's property by others, including the government? Discuss both of these questions.

10. *Does a country have to be democratic in order to achieve economic freedom? If a country is democratic, will it necessarily be economically free? Why or why not?

11. Why are income levels in the United States so high? Is the United States prosperous because it is democratic? Discuss.

12. *Firms can choose where to establish a production facility. What are some of the major factors that will influence whether a firm will invest and produce in a country?

13. *Even though workers in low-wage countries often seek to immigrate to higher-wage countries, the flow of investment toward many low-wage countries is small. Why is this so?

14. *Why will political decentralization make it more difficult for governments to levy taxes and spend the revenues on things that provide citizens with little value relative to cost?

*Asterisk denotes questions for which answers are given in Appendix B.

ADDENDUM

THE MOST RECENT ECONOMIC FREEDOM RATINGS

Institutions and policies generally change slowly, and it takes time for changes to exert much impact on income. Thus, we have generally focused on the quality of institutions and policies over a lengthy time frame such as 1990–2010. However, the recent data are also of interest. The map and the following chart provide the 2011 economic freedom ratings for the 152 countries now included in the Economic Freedom of the World Project.

Economic Freedom Index

9.0–8.0	Most Free
7.9–7.5	
7.4–7.0	
6.9–6.5	
6.4–6.0	
5.9–5.5	
Less than 5.5	Least Free
	Indicates data unavailable to rate these countries

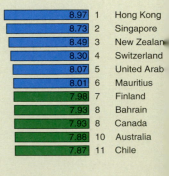

8.97	1	Hong Kong
8.73	2	Singapore
8.49	3	New Zealan
8.30	4	Switzerland
8.07	5	United Arab
8.01	6	Mauritius
7.98	7	Finland
7.93	8	Bahrain
7.93	8	Canada
7.88	10	Australia
7.87	11	Chile

7.85	12	United Kingdom
7.81	13	Jordan
7.78	14	Denmark
7.77	15	Taiwan
7.76	16	Estonia
7.73	17	United States
7.72	18	Cyprus
7.68	19	Germany
7.66	20	Ireland
7.65	21	Malta
7.64	22	Peru

7.62	23	Armenia
7.62	23	Qatar
7.61	25	Georgia
7.61	25	Lithuania
7.59	27	Austria
7.59	27	Hungary
7.58	29	Sweden
7.57	30	Netherlands
7.56	31	Norway
7.53	32	Spain
7.50	33	Japan
7.50	33	Korea, South

© Cengage Learning.

7.49	35	Luxembourg
7.46	36	Rwanda
7.46	36	Slovak Rep
7.41	38	Lebanon
7.40	39	Bahamas
7.38	40	France
7.37	41	Iceland
7.36	42	Belgium
7.35	43	Uruguay
7.34	44	Portugal
7.32	45	Romania
7.31	46	Latvia
7.31	46	Oman
7.27	48	Albania
7.26	49	Bulgaria
7.26	49	Israel
7.26	49	Montenegro
7.25	52	Botswana
7.25	52	Czech Rep.
7.23	54	Nicaragua
7.22	55	Kuwait
7.21	56	Guatemala
7.21	56	Honduras
7.21	56	Philippines
7.20	59	Poland
7.14	60	Saudi Arabia
7.13	61	Dominican Rep.
7.12	62	Jamaica
7.11	63	Costa Rica
7.10	64	Fiji
7.10	64	Uganda
7.10	64	Zambia
7.08	67	Panama
7.06	68	Malaysia
7.06	68	Mongolia
7.06	68	Turkey
7.05	71	Brunei Darussalam
7.05	71	Macedonia
7.03	73	El Salvador
7.02	74	Cambodia
7.01	75	Croatia
6.98	76	Gambia, The
6.96	77	Barbados
6.96	77	Pap. New Guinea
6.95	79	Trinidad & Tob.
6.90	80	Indonesia
6.87	81	Tunisia
6.86	82	Moldova
6.85	83	Italy
6.84	84	Kazakhstan
6.83	85	Greece
6.82	86	Belize
6.81	87	Kenya
6.80	88	South Africa
6.78	89	Paraguay
6.71	90	Ghana
6.67	91	Bosnia and Herzegovina
6.66	92	Sri Lanka
6.65	93	Tanzania
6.64	94	Mexico

6.64	94	Thailand
6.61	96	Colombia
6.59	97	Slovenia
6.56	98	Haiti
6.56	98	Morocco
6.56	98	Swaziland
6.55	101	Russia
6.51	102	Brazil
6.51	102	Kyrgyz Republic
6.46	104	Serbia
6.42	105	Mauritania
6.39	106	Namibia
6.37	107	Madagascar
6.36	108	Bolivia
6.36	108	Egypt
6.35	110	Lesotho
6.34	111	Guyana
6.34	111	India
6.34	111	Pakistan
6.33	114	Bangladesh
6.32	115	Sierra Leone
6.31	116	Yemen, Rep.
6.30	117	Azerbaijan
6.30	117	Malawi
6.30	117	Timor-Leste
6.29	120	Suriname
6.24	121	Cape Verde
6.23	122	Vietnam
6.22	123	China
6.21	124	Nigeria
6.19	125	Nepal
6.16	126	Ukraine
6.05	127	Iran
6.01	128	Tajikistan
5.97	129	Senegal
5.95	130	Benin
5.95	130	Mali
5.94	132	Burkina Faso
5.94	132	Cameroon
5.85	134	Ecuador
5.76	135	Cote d'Ivoire
5.73	136	Gabon
5.69	137	Argentina
5.68	138	Guinea-Bissau
5.63	139	Mozambique
5.60	140	Niger
5.57	141	Togo
5.47	142	Ethiopia
5.32	143	Algeria
5.28	144	Congo, Dem. R.
5.26	145	Burundi
5.26	145	Central Afr. Rep.
5.17	147	Angola
4.98	148	Chad
4.59	149	Zimbabwe
4.57	150	Congo, Rep. Of
4.08	151	Myanmar
3.93	152	Venezuela

PART 4

International Economics

The world is becoming a global village.

The volume of international trade has grown dramatically in recent decades. Although the same general principles apply to both domestic and international trade, the latter also involves the exchange of one currency for another. Thus, this part will analyze the impact of both international trade and the operation of the foreign exchange market.

CHAPTER 18
Gaining from International Trade

FOCUS

- How has the volume of international trade changed in recent decades?
- Under what conditions can a nation gain from international trade?
- What effects do trade restrictions have on an economy?
- How have open economies performed relative to those that are more closed?
- What accounts for the political popularity of trade restraints?
- Do trade restrictions create jobs? Does trade with low-wage countries depress wage rates in high-wage countries like the United States?

The evidence is overwhelmingly persuasive that the massive increase in world competition—a consequence of broadening trade flows—has fostered markedly higher standards of living for almost all countries who have participated in cross-border trade. I include most especially the United States.
—Alan Greenspan[1]

[1]Alan Greenspan, speech before the Alliance for the Commonwealth Conference on International Business (Boston, Massachusetts, June 2, 1999).

We live in a shrinking world. Spurred by cost reductions in transportation and communications, the volume of international trade has grown rapidly in recent decades. The breakfast of many Americans includes bananas from Honduras, coffee from Brazil, or hot chocolate made from Nigerian cocoa beans. Many Americans listen to music on iPods assembled in China, fuel their automobiles with gasoline refined from crude oil from Venezuela or Canada, and watch television on a set produced in Japan. Similarly, many Americans work for companies that sell a substantial number of their products to foreigners. Why do people engage in international trade? The expectation of gain provides the answer. If both parties did not expect to gain, they would not agee to the exchange.

18-1 THE TRADE SECTOR OF THE UNITED STATES

As Exhibit 1 illustrates, the size of the trade sector of the United States has grown rapidly during the last several decades. In 1960, total exports of goods and services accounted for 5.1 percent of the U.S. economy, whereas imports summed to 4.3 percent. By 1980, both exports and imports were approximately 10 percent of the economy. In 2012, exports accounted for 13.9 percent of total output, while imports summed to 17.5 percent. Thus, U.S. international trade (exports + imports) in goods and services has risen by 50 percent as a share of the economy since 1980 and more than tripled since 1960.

Who are the major trading partners of Americans? Exhibit 2 shows the share of U.S. trade (exports + imports) with each of its ten leading trading partners. These ten countries account for approximately two-thirds of the total volume of U.S. trade. Canada, China, Mexico, and Japan are the four largest trading partners of Americans. Nearly half of all

---

EXHIBIT 1

The Growth of the Trade Sector in the United States: 1960–2012

During the past several decades, international trade has persistently risen as a share of GDP. Imports of goods and services as a share of GDP rose from 4 percent in 1960 to 10 percent in 1980 and 17 percent in 2012. Similarly, exports increased from 5 percent of GDP in 1960 to 10 percent in 1980 and almost 14 percent in 2012.

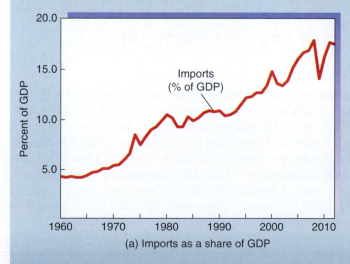

(a) Imports as a share of GDP

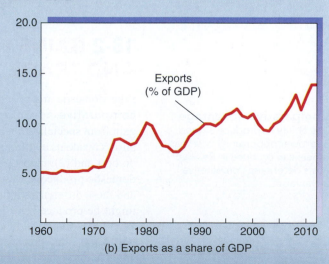

(b) Exports as a share of GDP

Source: http://www.economagic.com. The figures are based on data for imports, exports, and GDP.

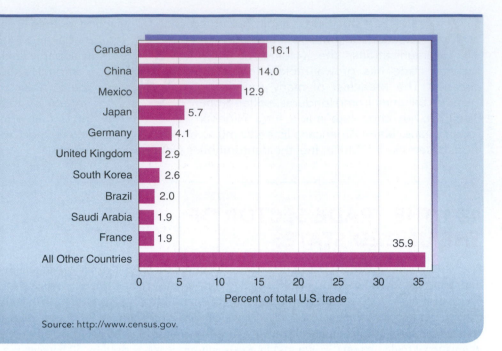

The 2012 Leading Trading Partners of the United States

Canada, China, Mexico, and Japan are the leading trading partners of the United States. Approximately one-half of all U.S. trade involves imports from or exports to these four countries.

Source: http://www.census.gov.

U.S. trade is with these four countries. The United States also conducts a substantial volume of trade with the nations of the European Union, particularly Germany, the United Kingdom, and France.

What are the leading imports and exports of the United States? Capital goods like automobiles, computers, semiconductors, telecommunications equipment, and industrial machines are bought and sold in worldwide markets. The United States both imports and exports substantial quantities of these goods. Civilian aircraft, electrical equipment, chemicals, and plastics are also among the leading products the United States exports. Crude oil, textiles, toys, sporting goods, and pharmaceuticals are major products it imports.

Clearly, the impact of international trade differs across industries. The majority of the television sets, diamonds, shoes, DVD players, and motorcycles consumed in the United States are imported. In contrast, a large proportion of the aircraft, power-generating equipment, scientific instruments, construction equipment, and fertilizers produced in the United States are exported to foreigners.

18-2 GAINS FROM SPECIALIZATION AND TRADE

Comparative advantage
The ability to produce a good at a lower opportunity cost than others can produce it. Relative costs determine comparative advantage.

Like domestic trade, international trade promotes growth and prosperity. The law of **comparative advantage** explains why a group of individuals, regions, or nations can gain from specialization and exchange. International trade leads to mutual gains because it allows residents of different countries to (1) specialize in the production of those things they do best and (2) import goods foreign producers are willing to supply at a lower cost than domestic producers. Resources and labor-force skills differ substantially across countries, and these differences influence costs. A good that is quite costly to produce in one country might be produced at a lower cost in another. For example, the warm, moist climates of Brazil, Colombia, and Guatemala make it more economical to produce coffee. Countries with temperate climates and an abundance of fertile land, such as Canada and Australia, are able to produce products such as wheat, feed grains, and beef at a low cost. In contrast, land is scarce in Japan, a nation with a highly skilled labor force. The Japanese, therefore, specialize in manufacturing, using their comparative advantage to produce cameras, automobiles, and electronic products for export. With international trade, the residents of different countries can gain by specializing in the production of goods they can produce economically. They can then sell those goods in the world market and use the proceeds to import other goods that are expensive to produce domestically.

Because the law of comparative advantage is often misunderstood, we will take the time to illustrate the principle in some detail. To keep things simple, let's consider a case involving only two countries, the United States and Japan, and two products, food and clothing. Furthermore, let's assume that labor is the only resource used to produce these products. In addition, because we want to illustrate that gains from trade are nearly always possible, we are going to assume that Japan has an **absolute advantage**—that the Japanese workers are more efficient than the Americans—at producing both food and clothing. Exhibit 3 illustrates this situation. Perhaps due to their prior experience or higher skill levels, Japanese workers can produce three units of food per day, compared with only two units per day for U.S. workers. Similarly, Japanese workers are able to produce nine units of clothing per day, compared with one unit of clothing per day for U.S. workers.

Can two countries gain from trade if one of them can produce both goods with fewer resources? The answer is "Yes." As long as the *relative* production costs of the two goods differ between Japan and the United States, gains from trade will be possible. Consider what would happen if the United States shifted three workers from the clothing industry to the food industry. This reallocation of labor would allow the United States to expand its food output by six units (two units per worker), while clothing output would decline by three units (one unit per worker). Suppose Japan reallocates labor in the opposite direction. When Japan moves one worker from the food industry to the clothing industry, Japanese clothing production expands by nine units, while food output declines by three units. The exhibit shows that this reallocation of labor *within* the two countries has increased their joint output by three units of food and six units of clothing.

The source of this increase in output is straightforward: Aggregate output expands because the reallocation of labor permits each country to specialize more fully in the production of the goods it can produce at a *relatively* low cost. Our old friend, the opportunity-cost concept, reveals the low-cost producer of each good. If Japanese workers produce one additional unit of food, they sacrifice the production of three units of clothing. Therefore,

Absolute advantage
A situation in which a nation, as the result of its previous experience and/or natural endowments, can produce more of a good (with the same amount of resources) than another nation can.

EXHIBIT 3

Gains from Specialization and Trade

Columns 1 and 2 indicate the daily output of either food or clothing of each worker in the United States and Japan. If the United States moves three workers from the clothing industry to the food industry, it can produce six more units of food and three fewer units of clothing. Similarly, if Japan moves one worker from food to clothing, clothing output will increase by nine units, while food output will decline by three units. With this reallocation of labor, the United States and Japan are able to increase their aggregate output of both food (three additional units) and clothing (six additional units).

Country	Output per Worker Day		Potential Change in Output[a]	
	Food (1)	Clothing (2)	Food (3)	Clothing (4)
United States	2	1	+6	−3
Japan	3	9	−3	+9
Change in Total Output			+3	+6

© Cengage Learning 2013

[a]Change in output if the United States shifts three workers from the clothing to the food industry and if Japan shifts one worker from the food to the clothing industry.

in Japan the opportunity cost of one unit of food is three units of clothing. Conversely, one unit of food in the United States can be produced at an opportunity cost of only a half-unit of clothing. American workers are therefore the low-opportunity-cost producers of food, even though they cannot produce as much food per day as the Japanese workers. Simultaneously, Japan is the low-opportunity-cost producer of clothing. The opportunity cost of producing a unit of clothing in Japan is only a third of a unit of food, compared with two units of food in the United States. The reallocation of labor illustrated in Exhibit 3 expanded joint output because it moved resources in both countries toward areas where they had a comparative advantage.

To reiterate: As long as the relative costs of producing the two goods differ in the two countries, gains from specialization and trade will be possible. Both countries will find it cheaper to trade for goods they can produce only at a high opportunity cost. For example, both countries will gain if the United States trades food to Japan for clothing at a trading ratio greater than one unit of food to one half-unit of clothing (the U.S. opportunity cost of food) but less than one unit of food to three units of clothing (the Japanese opportunity cost of food). Any trading ratio between these two extremes will permit the United States to acquire clothing more cheaply than it could be produced within the country and simultaneously permit Japan to acquire food more cheaply than it could be produced domestically.

18-2a HOW TRADE EXPANDS CONSUMPTION POSSIBILITIES

Because trade permits nations to expand their joint output, it also allows each nation to expand its consumption possibilities. The production possibilities concept can be used to illustrate this point. Suppose that there were 200 million workers in the United States and 50 million in Japan. Given these figures and the productivity of workers indicated in Exhibit 3, **Exhibit 4** presents the production possibilities curves for the two countries. If the United States used all of its 200 million workers in the food industry, it could produce 400 million units of food per day—two units per worker—and zero units of clothing (*N*).

EXHIBIT 4

The Production Possibilities of the United States and Japan before Specialization and Trade

Here, we illustrate the daily production possibilities of a U.S. labor force with 200 million workers and a Japanese labor force with 50 million workers, given the cost of producing food and clothing presented in

Exhibit 3. In the absence of trade, consumption possibilities will be restricted to points such as *US*₁ in the United States and *J*₁ in Japan along the production possibilities curve of each country.

(a) United States

(b) Japan

Alternatively, if the United States used all its workers to produce clothing, daily output would be 200 million units of clothing and no food (*M*). Intermediate output combinations along the production possibilities line (*MN*) between these two extreme points also could be achievable. For example, the United States could produce 150 million units of clothing and 100 million units of food (*US*₁).

Part (b) of Exhibit 4 illustrates the production possibilities of the 50 million Japanese workers. Japan could produce 450 million units of clothing and no food (*R*), 150 million units of food and no clothing (*S*), or various intermediate combinations, like 225 million units of clothing and 75 million units of food (*J*₁). The slope of the production possibilities constraint reflects the opportunity cost of food relative to clothing. Because Japan is the high-opportunity-cost producer of food, its production possibilities constraint is steeper than the constraint for the United States.

In the absence of trade, the consumption of each country is constrained by its own production possibilities. Trade, however, expands the consumption possibilities of both. As we previously said, both countries can gain from specialization if the United States trades food to Japan at a price greater than one unit of food equals one half-unit of clothing but less than one unit of food equals three units of clothing. Suppose that they agree on an intermediate price of one unit of food equals one unit of clothing. As part (a) of **Exhibit 5** shows, when the United States specializes in the production of food (where it has a comparative advantage) and trades food for clothing (at the price ratio where one unit of food equals one unit of clothing), it can consume along the line *ON*. If the United States insisted on self-sufficiency, it would be restricted to consumption possibilities like *US*₁ (100 million units of food and 150 million units of clothing) along its production possibilities constraint of *MN*. With trade, however, the United States can achieve a combination like *US*₂

EXHIBIT 5

Consumption Possibilities with Trade

The consumption possibilities of a country can be expanded with specialization and trade. If the United States can trade one unit of clothing for one unit of food, it can specialize in the production of food and consume along the *ON* line (rather than its original production possibilities constraint, *MN*). Similarly, when Japan is able to trade one unit of clothing for one unit of food, it can specialize in the production of clothing and consume any combination along the line *RT*. For example, with specialization and trade, the United States can increase its consumption from *US*₁ to *US*₂, gaining 50 million units of clothing and 100 million units of food. Simultaneously, Japan can increase consumption from *J*₁ to *J*₂, a gain of 125 million units of food and 25 million units of clothing.

(a) United States

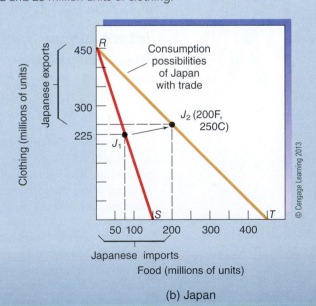

(b) Japan

© Cengage Learning 2013

(200 million units of food and 200 million units of clothing) along the line *ON*. Trade permits the United States to expand its consumption of both goods.

Simultaneously, Japan is able to expand its consumption of both goods when it is able to trade clothing for food at the one-to-one price ratio. As part (b) of Exhibit 5 illustrates, Japan can specialize in the production of clothing and consume along the constraint *RT* when it can trade one unit of clothing for one unit of food. Without trade, consumption in Japan would be limited to points like J_1 (75 million units of food and 225 million units of clothing) along the line *RS*. With trade, however, it is able to consume combinations like J_2 (200 million units of food and 250 million units of clothing) along the constraint *RT*.

Look what happens when Japan specializes in clothing and the United States specializes in food. Japan can produce 450 million units of clothing, export 200 million to the United States (for 200 million units of food), and still have 250 million units of clothing remaining for domestic consumption. Simultaneously, the United States can produce 400 million units of food, export 200 million to Japan (for 200 million units of clothing), and still have 200 million units of food left for domestic consumption.

The implications of the law of comparative advantage are clear: Trade between nations will lead to an expansion in total output and mutual gain for each trading partner when each country specializes in the production of goods it can produce at a relatively low cost and uses the proceeds to buy goods that it could produce only at a high cost.

18-2b **SOME REAL-WORLD CONSIDERATIONS**

To keep things simple, we ignored the potential importance of transportation costs, which, of course, reduce the potential gains from trade. Sometimes transportation and other transaction costs, both real and artificially imposed, exceed the potential for mutual gain. In this case, exchange does not occur.

We also assumed that the cost of producing each good was constant in each country. This is seldom the case. Beyond some level of production, the opportunity cost of producing a good will often increase as a country produces more and more of it. Rising marginal costs as the output of a good expands will limit the degree to which a country will specialize in the production of a good. This situation would be depicted by a production possibilities curve that was convex, or bowed out from the origin. In a case like this, there will still be gains from trade, but generally such a situation won't lead to one country completely specializing in the production of the good.

KEYS TO ECONOMIC PROSPERITY

International Trade

When people are permitted to engage freely in international trade, they are able to achieve higher income levels and living standards than would otherwise be possible.

©iStockphoto.com/malerapaso

Like trade within a country, trade between people living in different nations is mutually beneficial. As we just explained, the trading partners will be able to produce a larger joint output and consume a larger, more diverse bundle of goods when they each specialize in areas where they have a comparative advantage. Open markets also lead to gains from other sources. We will briefly discuss three of them.

1. More gains from large-scale production. International trade makes it possible for both domestic producers and consumers to derive larger gains from the lower per-unit costs that often accompany large-scale production, marketing, and distribution activities. When economies of scale are important in an industry, successful domestic firms will be able to produce larger outputs and achieve lower unit costs than they would if they were unable to sell their products internationally. This is particularly important for firms located in small countries. For example, textile manufacturers in Malaysia, Taiwan, and South Korea would face much higher per-unit costs if they could not sell abroad because the domestic markets of these countries are too small to support large-scale production. There simply aren't enough buyers. However, if the firms can access the world market, where there are many more buyers, they can operate on a large scale and compete quite effectively.

Domestic consumers also benefit because international trade often makes it possible for them to acquire goods at lower prices from large-scale producers in other countries. The aircraft industry vividly illustrates this point. Given the huge design and engineering costs it takes to produce a single jet, no firm would be able to produce them economically if it weren't able to sell them abroad. Because of international trade, however, consumers around the world are able to purchase planes economically from large-scale producers like Boeing, which is based in the United States.

International trade generates gains from specialization. economics of scale, and more competitive markets. As a result, trading partners are able to achieve higher living standards.

2. Gains from more competitive markets.
International trade promotes competition and encourages production efficiency and innovation. Competition from abroad keeps domestic producers on their toes and gives them a strong incentive to improve the quality of their products.

International trade also allows technologies and innovative ideas developed in one country to be disseminated to others. In many cases, local entrepreneurs will emulate production procedures and products that have been successful in other places and even further improve or adapt them for local markets. Dynamic competition of this type is an important source of growth and prosperity, particularly for less-developed countries (LDCs).

3. More pressure to adopt sound institutions.
Not only do firms in open economies face more intense competition, so, too, do their governments. The gains from trade and the prosperity that results from free trade motivate political officials to establish sound institutions and adopt constructive policies. If they do not, both labor and capital will move toward more favorable environments. For example, neither domestic nor foreign investors will want to put their funds in countries characterized by hostile business conditions, monetary instability, legal uncertainty, high taxes, and inferior public services. When labor and capital are free to move elsewhere, implementing government policies that penalize success and undermine productive activities becomes more costly. This aspect of free trade is generally overlooked, but it may well be one of its most beneficial attributes.[2]

18-3 SUPPLY, DEMAND, AND INTERNATIONAL TRADE

Like other things, international trade can be analyzed within the supply and demand framework. An analysis of supply and demand in international markets can show us how trade influences prices and output in domestic markets.

Consider the market for a good that U.S. producers are able to supply at a low cost. Using soybeans as an example, **Exhibit 6** illustrates the relationship between the domestic and world markets. The price of soybeans is determined by the forces of supply and demand in the world market. In an open economy, domestic producers are free to sell and domestic consumers are free to buy the product at the world market price (P_w). At this price, U.S. producers will supply Q_p, and U.S. consumers will purchase Q_c. Reflecting their low cost (comparative advantage), U.S. soybean producers will export $Q_p - Q_c$ units at the world market price.

---

[2]For evidence that trade openness helps improve the institutional quality of a country, see International Monetary Fund, "Building Institutions," *IMF World Economic Outlook* (September 2005).

EXHIBIT 6

Producer Benefits from Exports

The price of soybeans and other internationally traded commodities is determined by the forces of supply and demand in the world market (b). If U.S. soybean producers are prohibited from selling to foreigners, the domestic price will be P_n (a). Free trade permits the U.S. soybean producers to sell Q_p units at the higher world price (P_w). The quantity $Q_p - Q_c$ is the amount U.S. producers export. Compared with the no-trade situation, the producers' gain from the higher price ($P_w b c P_n$) exceeds the cost imposed on domestic consumers ($P_w a c P_n$) by the triangle abc.

(a) U.S. market for soybeans

(b) World market for soybeans

© Cengage Learning 2013

Let's compare this open-economy outcome with the outcome that would occur in the absence of trade. If U.S. producers were not allowed to export soybeans, the domestic price would be determined by the domestic supply (S_d) and demand (D_d) only. A lower "no-trade" price (P_n) would emerge.

Who are the winners and losers as the result of free trade in soybeans? Clearly, soybean producers gain. Free trade allows domestic producers to sell a larger quantity (Q_p rather than Q_n). As a result, the net revenues of soybean producers will rise by $P_w b c P_n$. In contrast, domestic consumers of soybeans will have to pay a higher price under free trade. Soybean consumers will lose (1) because they have to pay P_w rather than P_n for the Q_c units they purchase, and (2) because they lose the consumer surplus on the $Q_n - Q_c$ units now purchased at the higher price. Thus, free trade imposes a net cost of $P_w a c P_n$ on consumers. As you can see in Exhibit 6, however, the gains of soybean producers outweigh the losses to the consumers by the triangle abc. In other words, free trade leads to a net welfare gain.

This exporting example makes it seem like free trade benefits producers relative to consumers, but this ignores the secondary effects: If foreigners do not sell goods to Americans, they will not have the purchasing power necessary to purchase goods from Americans. U.S. imports—the purchase of goods from low-cost foreign producers—provide foreigners with the dollar purchasing power necessary to buy U.S. exports. In turn, the lower prices in the import-competitive markets will benefit the U.S. consumers who appeared at first glance to be harmed by the higher prices (compared with the no-trade situation) in export markets.

Using shoes as an example, Exhibit 7 illustrates the situation when the United States is a net importer. In the absence of trade, the price of shoes in the domestic market would be P_n, the intersection of the domestic supply and demand curves. However, the world price of shoes is P_w. In an open economy, many U.S. consumers would take advantage of the low

(a) U.S. market for shoes

(b) World market for shoes

EXHIBIT 7

Consumer Benefits from Imports

In the absence of trade, the domestic price of shoes would be P_n. Because many foreign producers have a comparative advantage in the production of shoes, international trade leads to lower prices. At the world price P_w, U.S. consumers will demand Q_c units, of which $Q_c - Q_p$ are imported. Compared with the no-trade situation, consumers gain $P_n abP_w$, while domestic producers lose $P_n acP_w$. A net gain of abc results.

shoe prices available from foreign producers. At the lower world price, U.S. consumers would purchase Q_c units of shoes, importing $Q_c - Q_p$ from foreign producers.

Compared with the no-trade situation, free trade in shoes results in lower prices and greater domestic consumption. The lower prices lead to a net consumer gain of $P_n abP_w$. Domestic producers lose $P_n acP_w$ in the form of lower sales prices and reductions in output. However, the net gain of the shoe consumers exceeds the net loss of producers by abc.

International competition will direct resources toward producers who have a comparative advantage. If domestic producers have a comparative advantage in the production of a good—if they are a low opportunity cost producer, they will be able to compete effectively in the world market and profit from the export of goods to foreigners. In turn, the exports will generate the purchasing power necessary to buy goods that foreigners can supply more economically.

18-4 THE ECONOMICS OF TRADE RESTRICTIONS

Despite the potential benefits of free trade, almost all nations have erected trade barriers. Tariffs, quotas, and exchange rate controls are the most commonly used trade-restricting devices. Let's consider how various types of trade restrictions affect the economy.

18-4a THE ECONOMICS OF TARIFFS

A **tariff** is a tax on imports from foreign countries. As **Exhibit 8** shows, average tariff rates of between 30 percent and 50 percent of product value were often levied on products imported to the United States prior to 1945. The notorious Smoot-Hawley Tariff Act of 1930 pushed the average tariff rate upward to 60 percent. Many economists believe that this legislation contributed significantly to the length and severity of the Great Depression. During the past 70 years, however, tariff rates in the United States have declined substantially. In 2010, the average tariff rate on imported goods was only 3.5 percent.

Exhibit 9 shows the impact of a tariff on automobiles. In the absence of a tariff, the world market price of P_w would prevail in the domestic market. At that price, U.S. consumers

Tariff
A tax levied on goods imported into a country.

EXHIBIT 8

How High Are U.S. Tariffs?

Tariff rates in the United States spiked up sharply in the early 1930s, then declined during the period from 1935 to 1950. After rising slightly during the late 1950s, they have trended downward since 1960. In 2010, the average tariff rate on merchandise imports was 3.5 percent.

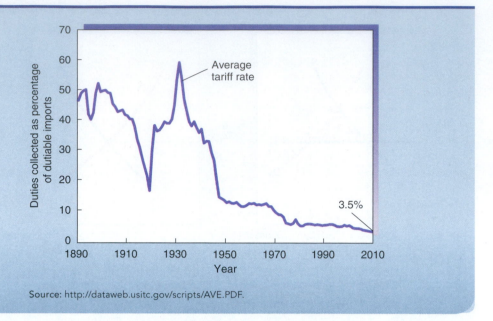

Source: http://dataweb.usitc.gov/scripts/AVE.PDF.

EXHIBIT 9

The Impact of a Tariff

Here, we illustrate the impact of a tariff on automobiles. In the absence of the tariff, the world price of automobiles is P_w. U.S. consumers purchase Q_1 units (Q_{d1} from domestic producers plus $Q_1 - Q_{d1}$ from foreign producers). The tariff makes it more costly for Americans to purchase automobiles from foreigners. Imports decline and the domestic price increases. Higher prices reduce consumer surplus by the areas $S + U + T + V$. Producers gain the *area S*, and the tariff generates T tax revenues for the government. The areas U and V are deadweight losses.

© Cengage Learning 2013

purchase Q_1 units. Domestic producers supply Q_{d1}, while foreigners supply $Q_1 - Q_{d1}$ units to the U.S. market. When the United States levies a tariff, t, on automobiles, Americans can no longer buy cars at the world price. U.S. consumers now have to pay $P_w + t$ to purchase an automobile from foreigners. At that price, domestic consumers demand Q_2 units (Q_{d2} supplied by domestic producers and $Q_2 - Q_{d2}$ supplied by foreigners). The tariff results in a higher domestic price and lower level of domestic consumption.

The tariff benefits domestic producers and the government at the expense of consumers. Because domestic producers don't have to pay the tariff, they will expand their output in response to the higher (protected) market price. In effect, the tariff acts as a subsidy to domestic producers. Domestic producers gain the area S (Exhibit 9) in the form of additional net revenues. The tariff raises revenues equal to the area T for the government. The areas U and V represent costs imposed on consumers and resource suppliers that do not benefit the government. Simply put, U and V represent *deadweight losses*: consumer and producer surpluses that could have been gained if the tariff hadn't been imposed.

As a result of the tariff, resources that could have been used to produce other U.S. goods more efficiently (compared with producing them abroad) are diverted to automobile production. Ultimately, we end up producing fewer products in areas where we have a comparative advantage and more products in areas where we are a high-cost producer. Because of this, potential gains from specialization and trade will go unrealized. In addition, most nations, including the United States, impose higher tariffs on some goods than others. This encourages producers in specific industries to lobby for higher tariffs on goods they produce. This diverts resources away from production and toward plunder, which also reduces the overall size of the economic pie.

18-4b THE ECONOMICS OF QUOTAS

An **import quota**, like a tariff, is designed to restrict foreign goods and protect domestic industries from foreign competition. A quota places a ceiling on the amount of a product that can be imported during a given period (typically a year). The United States imposes quotas on several products, including brooms, shoes, sugar, dairy products, and peanuts. For example, since 1953, the United States has imposed an annual peanut quota that in 2011 limited imports to 105.8 million pounds, about three-tenths of a pound per American.

Using peanuts as an example, **Exhibit 10** illustrates the impact of a quota. If there were no trade restraints, the domestic price of peanuts would be equal to the world market price (P_w).

Import quota

A specific limit or maximum quantity (or value) of a good permitted to be imported into a country during a given period.

The Impact of a Quota

Here, we illustrate the impact of a quota, such as the one the United States imposes on peanuts. The world market price of peanuts is P_w. If there were no trade restraints, the domestic price would also be P_w, and the domestic consumption would be Q_1. Domestic producers would supply Q_{d1} units, while $Q_1 - Q_{d1}$ would be imported. A quota limiting imports to $Q_2 - Q_{d2}$ would push up the domestic price to P_2. At the higher price, the amount supplied by domestic producers increases to Q_{d2}. Consumers lose the sum of the area $S + U + T + V$, while domestic producers gain the area S. In contrast with tariffs, quotas generate no revenue for the government. The area T goes to foreign producers, who are granted permission to sell in the U.S. market.

© Cengage Learning 2013

Under those circumstances, Americans would purchase Q_1 units. At the price P_w, domestic producers would supply Q_{d1}, and the amount $Q_1 - Q_{d1}$ would be imported from foreign producers.

Now consider what happens when a quota limits imports to $Q_2 - Q_{d2}$, a quantity well below the free-trade level of imports. Because the quota reduces the foreign supply of peanuts to the domestic market, the price of the quota-protected product increases (to P_2). At the higher price, U.S. consumers will reduce their purchases to Q_2, and domestic producers will happily expand their production to Q_{d2}. With regard to the welfare of consumers, the impact of a quota is similar to that of a tariff. Consumers lose the area $S + U + T + V$ in the form of higher prices and the loss of consumer surplus. Similarly, domestic producers gain the area S, while the areas U and V represent deadweight losses in the form of reductions in consumer surplus, gains that buyers would have derived in the absence of the quota.

While the adverse impact of a quota on consumer welfare is similar to that of a tariff, there is a big difference with regard to the area T. Under a tariff, the U.S. government would collect revenues equal to T, representing the tariff rate multiplied by the number of units imported. With a quota, however, these revenues will go to foreign producers, who are granted licenses (quotas) to sell various amounts in the U.S. market. Clearly, this right to sell at a premium price (because the domestic price exceeds the world market price) is extremely valuable. Thus, foreign producers will compete for the permits. They will hire lobbyists, make political contributions, and engage in other rent-seeking activities in an effort to secure the right to sell at a premium price in the U.S. market.

In many ways, quotas are more harmful than tariffs. With a quota, foreign producers are prohibited from selling additional units regardless of how much lower their costs are relative to those of domestic producers. In contrast to a tariff, a quota brings in no revenue for the government. Whereas a tariff transfers revenue from U.S. consumers to the Treasury, quotas transfer these revenues to foreign producers. Rewarding domestic producers with higher prices and foreign producers with valuable import permits will create *two* interest groups with a strong incentive to lobby for a quota. As a result, lifting the quota will often be more difficult than lowering a tariff would be.

In addition to tariffs and quotas, governments sometimes use regulations and political pressure to restrain foreign competition. For example, the United States prohibits foreign airlines from competing in the domestic air travel market. Japanese regulations make it illegal for domestic automobile dealers to sell both foreign and domestically produced vehicles; this makes it more difficult for foreign manufacturers to establish the dealer networks they need to penetrate the Japanese market effectively. Like tariffs and quotas, regulatory barriers such as these reduce the supply to domestic markets and the gains from potential trades. Overall output is reduced, and domestic producers benefit at the expense of domestic consumers.

18-4c EXCHANGE RATE CONTROLS AS A TRADE RESTRICTION

Some countries fix the exchange rate value of their currency above the market rate and impose restrictions on exchange rate transactions.[3] At the official (artificially high) exchange rate, the country's export goods will be extremely expensive to foreigners. As a result, foreigners will purchase goods elsewhere, and the country's exports will be small. In turn, the low level of exports will make it extremely difficult for domestic residents to obtain the foreign currency they need to purchase imports. Exchange rate controls both reduce the volume of trade and lead to black-market currency exchanges. Indeed, a large black-market premium indicates that the country's exchange rate policy is substantially limiting the ability of its citizens to trade with foreigners. While exchange rate controls have declined in popularity, they are still an important trade barrier in countries such as Myanmar, Venezuela, and Nigeria.

---

[3]The most common exchange rate restriction is that individuals are required to obtain approval from the government before they engage in transactions involving foreign currency.

18-5 WHY DO NATIONS ADOPT TRADE RESTRICTIONS?

As social philosopher Henry George noted over a century ago, trade restraints act like blockades. Why would political officials want to erect blockades against their own people? As we consider this question, we will take a look at three arguments often raised by the proponents of trade restrictions: the national-defense, infant-industry, and antidumping arguments. Finally, we will look at the politics of trade restrictions and analyze how the nature of the restraints influences their political popularity.

18-5a THE NATIONAL-DEFENSE ARGUMENT

According to the national-defense argument, certain industries—aircraft, petroleum, and weapons, for example—are vital to a nation's defense. Therefore, these industries and their inputs should be protected from foreign competitors so that a domestic supply of necessary materials would be available in case of an international conflict. Would we want to be entirely dependent upon Arabian or Russian petroleum? Would complete dependence on French aircraft be wise? Many Americans would answer "no," even if it meant imposing trade restrictions that would lead to higher prices on products they buy.

Although the national-defense argument has some validity, it is often abused. Relatively few industries are truly vital to our national defense. If a resource is important for national defense, often it would make more sense to stockpile the resource during peacetime rather than follow protectionist policies to preserve a domestic industry. Furthermore, fostering an economy robust enough to produce the mass quantity of goods necessary to sustain a war effort in the first place is, itself, part of a strong defense.

18-5b THE INFANT-INDUSTRY ARGUMENT

Infant-industry advocates believe that new domestic industries should be protected from foreign competition for a period of time so that they will have a chance to develop. As the new industry matures, it will be able to stand on its own feet and compete effectively with foreign producers, at which time the protection can be removed.

The infant-industry argument has a long and often notorious history. Alexander Hamilton used it to argue for the protection of early U.S. manufacturing. The major problem with the argument is that the protection, once granted, will be difficult to remove. For example, a century ago, this argument was used to gain tariff protection for the newly emerging steel industry in the United States. Over time, the steel industry developed and became very powerful, both politically and economically. Despite its maturity, the tariffs remained. To this day, legislation continues to provide the steel industry with various protections that limit competition from abroad.

18-5c THE ANTIDUMPING ARGUMENT

Dumping involves the sale of goods by a foreign firm at a price below cost or below the price charged in the firm's home-base market. Dumping is illegal and if a domestic industry is harmed, current law provides relief in the form of antidumping duties (tariffs imposed against violators). Proponents of the antidumping argument argue that foreign producers will temporarily cut prices, drive domestic firms out of the market, and then use their monopoly position to gouge consumers. However, there is reason to question the effectiveness of this strategy. After all, the high prices would soon attract competitors, including other foreign suppliers.

> Protective tariffs are as much applications of force as are blockading squadrons, and their objective is the same—to prevent trade. The difference between the two is that blockading squadrons are a means whereby nations seek to prevent their enemies from trading; protective tariffs are a means whereby nations attempt to prevent their own people from trading.
> —Henry George[4]

Dumping
Selling a good in a foreign country at a lower price than it's sold for in the domestic market.

---

[4]Henry George, *Protection or Free Trade* (Washington, DC: U.S. Government Printing Office, 1886), 37.

Antidumping cases nearly always involve considerable ambiguity. The prices charged in the home market generally vary, and the production costs of the firms charged with dumping are not directly observable. This makes it difficult to tell whether a dumping violation has really occurred. Furthermore, aggressive price competition is an integral part of the competitive process. When demand is weak and inventories are large, firms will often temporarily slash prices below per unit production cost in order to reduce excessively large inventories. Domestic firms are permitted to engage in this practice, and consumers benefit from it. Why shouldn't foreign firms be allowed to do the same?

One thing is for sure: Antidumping legislation gives politicians another way to channel highly visible benefits to powerful business and labor interests—another open invitation for rent seeking. The dumping charges are adjudicated by political officials in the International Trade Commission and the Department of Commerce. Consequently, it's naive to believe that political considerations won't be an important element underlying the charges that are levied and how they are resolved. Unsurprisingly, the number of claimants bringing charges of dumping has increased substantially over the past few decades.

APPLICATIONS IN ECONOMICS

Do More Open Economies Perform Better?

Economic theory indicates that more open economies will perform better than those with sizable trade restrictions. Is this really true? In order to address this question, a measure of trade openness—the freedom of individuals to engage in voluntary exchange across national boundaries—is needed. Economist Charles Skipton developed a trade openness index (TOI) for 81 countries during the 1980–2002 period.[1] To achieve a high rating on the zero-to-ten TOI scale (with ten indicating more openness to free trade), a country had to maintain low tariff rates, a freely convertible currency (no exchange rate controls), and refrain from imposing quotas and other regulations reducing the size of its trade sector.

Exhibit 11 shows the countries with the ten highest and ten lowest trade openness ratings. The ratings reflect the *average* degree of openness for the entire 1980–2002 period. This is important because the gains from increased openness can only be realized over time. Expanding the openness of trade is a long-term growth strategy, not a short-term "quick fix." Hong Kong, Singapore, Bahrain, Belgium, and Malaysia head the list of the most open of the 81 economies. By way of comparison, the United States ranked sixteenth. At the other end of the spectrum, the TOI indicates that Bangladesh, Iran, Burundi, Sierra Leone, and Algeria were the least open economies during the period.

As Exhibit 11 shows, the 2005 average GDP per person of $28,251 of the ten most open economies was nearly ten times the comparable figure for the ten least open economies. Moreover, the more open economies also grew more rapidly. During 1980–2005, real GDP per person in the ten most open economies expanded at an annual rate of 3.1 percent, compared with 1.4 percent in the ten least open economies. Of course, the data of Exhibit 11 do not take into account other cross-country differences that theory indicates will influence growth. However, Skipton found that even after the differences in countries' inflation rates, legal structures, and similar factors were taken into account, trade openness continued to have a strong positive impact on both per capita GDP and growth rates.[2]

[1]Charles Skipton, *The Measurement of Trade Openness* (PhD diss., Florida State University, 2003).

[2]For additional information on the relationship between international trade and economic growth, see Jeffrey A. Frankel and David Romer, "Does Trade Cause Growth?" *American Economic Review* (June 1999): 379–99; and Jeffrey D. Sachs and Andrew Warner, "Economic Reform and the Process of Global Integration," *Brookings Papers on Economic Activity*, no. 1 (1995): 1–95.

franckreporter/E+/Getty Images

franckreporter/E+/Getty Images

EXHIBIT 11

Trade Openness, Income, and Growth

	TOI	GDP PER CAPITA (2005 DOLLARS)	GROWTH RATE, 1980–2005
Ten Most Open Economies			
Hong Kong	10.0	$30,989	3.9
Singapore	9.9	26,390	4.3
Bahrain	8.6	19,112	1.0
Belgium	8.6	28,575	1.7
Malaysia	8.6	9,681	3.6
Luxembourg	8.5	53,583	3.7
Netherlands	8.4	29,078	1.6
Taiwan	8.4	20,868	5.1
Ireland	8.1	34,256	4.5
Australia	7.9	29,981	1.9
Average	**8.7**	**$28,251**	**3.1**
Ten Least Open Economies			
India	4.3	$3,072	4.0
Tanzania	4.1	662	2.3
Egypt	4.1	3,858	2.5
Pakistan	3.9	2,109	2.4
Syria	3.8	3,388	0.6
Algeria	3.4	6,283	0.5
Sierra Leone	3.4	717	–1.1
Burundi	3.0	622	1.0
Iran	2.9	7,089	1.1
Bangladesh	2.5	1,827	2.2
Average	**3.5**	**$2,963**	**1.4**

Source: The trade openness index data are from Charles Skipton, *The Measurement of Trade Openness* (PhD diss., Florida State University, 2003), Table 4.6. The initial calculations were through 1999, but they were updated through 2002 by Skipton. The per capita GDP and growth rates are from the World Bank, *World Development Indicators*, CD-ROM, 2007. The per capita income figures were derived by the purchasing power parity method.

18-5d SPECIAL INTERESTS AND THE POLITICS OF TRADE RESTRICTIONS

Regardless of the arguments made by the proponents of trade restrictions, their political attractiveness is primarily the result of their special interest nature. Murray Weidenbaum, former chairman of the President's Council of Economic Advisors, put it this way: "Protectionism is a politician's delight because it delivers visible benefits to the protected parties while imposing the costs as a hidden tax on the public."[5] As we discussed in Chapter 6, special interest issues are often a source of economic inefficiency.

---

[5]Murray L. Weidenbaum, personal correspondence with the authors. Weidenbaum is a former chairman of the President's Council of Economic Advisers and former director of the Center for the Study of American Business of Washington University.

The politics of trade restrictions are straightforward and play out over and over again. Well-organized business and labor interests gain substantially from restrictions that limit competition from abroad. Because their personal gain is large, they will feel strongly about the issue and generally vote for or against candidates on the basis of their positions on trade restrictions. Most important, the special-interest groups will be an attractive source of political contributions. When it comes to consumers, however, even if the total cost of the restrictions is quite large, it will be spread thinly among them; most consumers will be unaware that they are paying slightly higher prices for various goods because of the restrictions.

As you can see, courting special-interest groups helps politicians solicit campaign contributions and generate votes on the one hand. On the other hand, little political gain can be derived from poorly organized and largely uninformed consumers. Given this incentive structure, the adoption of trade restrictions is not surprising.

The U.S. tariff code itself is a reflection of the politics of trade restrictions. It is both lengthy (the schedule fills 3,151 pages) and highly complex. This makes it difficult for even a well-educated citizen to figure out how it works. High tariffs are imposed on some products (for example, apparel, tobacco, and footwear), whereas low tariffs are imposed on others. Highly restrictive quotas limit the import of a few commodities, most notably agricultural products. Even though this complex system of targeted trade restrictions is costly to administer, it is no accident. It reflects the rent seeking of special-interest groups and the political contributions and other side payments the system generates for politicians.

18-6 TRADE BARRIERS AND POPULAR TRADE FALLACIES

Fallacies abound in the area of international trade. Why? Failure to consider the secondary effects of international trade is part of the answer. Key elements of international trade are closely linked; you cannot change one element without changing the other. For example, you cannot reduce imports without simultaneously reducing the demand for exports. The political incentive structure is also a contributing factor. As business, labor, and political leaders seek to gain from trade restrictions, they will often use half-truths and wrong-headed ideas to achieve their political objectives. Two of the most popular trade fallacies involve the effects of imports on employment and the impact of trade with low-wage countries. Let's take a closer look at both.

18-6a TRADE FALLACY 1: TRADE RESTRICTIONS THAT LIMIT IMPORTS SAVE JOBS AND EXPAND EMPLOYMENT

Like most fallacies, this one has just enough truth to give it some credibility. When tariffs, quotas, and other trade barriers limit imports, they are likely to foster employment in the industries shielded from competition. But this is only half of the story: Simultaneously, jobs in other domestic sectors will be destroyed. Here's how: When trade barriers reduce the amount of goods Americans buy from foreigners, sales to foreigners will also fall. This is because our imports provide foreigners with the dollars they need to buy our exports. Because foreigners cut back on the items they would normally buy from us, other U.S. sectors will suffer job losses because they're selling less.

Furthermore, when trade restrictions are imposed on a resource domestic producers use as an input, they will have to pay a higher price for it than their foreign rivals. This will increase their costs and make it more difficult for them to compete internationally. As a result, they will have to lay off some of their employees. The import quotas imposed on steel during 2002–2003 vividly illustrate this point. The quotas helped the domestic steel industry, but they virtually wiped out the domestic industry producing steel barrels, a product the United States had exported prior to the quota being imposed. The quota also increased costs and reduced the competitiveness of industries that were major users of steel, like the automobile- and appliance-manufacturing industries. Employment in those industries fell as well. The same phenomenon occurred after the United States imposed sugar quotas. The import quotas pushed domestic sugar prices to two or three times the world price. As a result, several large candy makers relocated abroad so that they could buy sugar at the lower world price. Again, the jobs lost in U.S. industries using sugar were an offset to any employment gains of the domestic sugar producers.

On balance, there is no reason to expect that trade restrictions will either create or destroy jobs. Instead, they will reshuffle them. The restrictions artificially direct workers and other resources toward the production of things that we do poorly, as shown by our inability to compete effectively in the world market. Simultaneously, employment will decline in areas where American firms would be able to compete successfully in the world market if it were not for the side effects of the restrictions. In other words, more Americans will be employed producing things we do poorly and fewer will be employed producing things we do well. As a result, our overall income level will be lower than it would have been otherwise.

18-6b TRADE FALLACY 2: FREE TRADE WITH LOW-WAGE COUNTRIES LIKE MEXICO AND CHINA WILL REDUCE THE WAGES OF AMERICANS

Many Americans believe that without trade restrictions, their wages will fall to the wage levels of workers in poor countries. How can Americans compete with workers in countries like Mexico and China who are willing to work for $1 or less per hour? This fallacy stems from a misunderstanding of both the source of high wages and the law of comparative advantage. Workers in the United States generally are well educated, possess high skill levels, and work with large amounts of capital equipment. These factors contribute to their high productivity, which is the source of their high wages. Similarly, in countries like Mexico and China, wages are low precisely because productivity is low. Workers are generally less skilled in these countries, and there is less capital equipment to make them more productive.

The key thing to remember, though, is that gains from trade emanate from comparative advantage, not absolute advantage (see Exhibits 3, 4, and 5). The United States cannot produce *everything* more cheaply than Mexico or China merely because U.S. employees are more productive and work with more capital. Neither can Mexico and China produce *everything* more cheaply merely because their wage rates are low compared with the United Sates.

As long as there are differences between countries when it comes to their comparative advantages, gains from trade will be possible, no matter what the wages of the employees in the two countries are. Trade reflects relative advantage, not wage levels. We can illustrate this point using trade between individuals. No one argues that trade between doctors and lawn service workers, for example, will cause the wages of doctors to fall. Because of their different skills and costs of providing alternative goods, both high-wage doctors and low-wage lawn-care workers can gain from trade. The same is also true for trade between rich and poor nations.

If foreigners have a comparative advantage and can sell us a product for less than we ourselves can produce it, we can gain by buying it. This will give us more resources to invest in and produce other things. Perhaps an extreme example will illustrate this point. Suppose a foreign producer is willing to supply us automobiles free of charge (perhaps because its employees were willing to work for nothing). Would it make sense to impose tariffs or quotas to keep the automobiles from coming into the country? Of course not. Resources that were previously used to produce automobiles would then be freed up to produce other goods, and the real income and availability of goods would expand. It makes no more sense to erect trade barriers to keep out cheap foreign goods than it would to keep out the free autos.

18-7 INSTITUTIONS AND THE CHANGING NATURE OF GLOBAL TRADE

Since World War II, liberalized trade policies and lower transportation and communication costs have propelled the growth of international trade. The growth of trade has also resulted in a changing institutional environment. In the aftermath of World War II, the major industrial nations of the world established the **General Agreement on Tariffs and Trade (GATT)**.

General Agreement on Tariffs and Trade (GATT)
An organization formed after World War II to set the rules for the conduct of international trade and reduce trade barriers among nations.

EXHIBIT 12

U.S. Trade with Canada and Mexico, 1980–2012

Measured as a share of GDP, U.S. trade with both Canada and Mexico has increased sharply following the passage of NAFTA. The trade share with Mexico continues to rise.

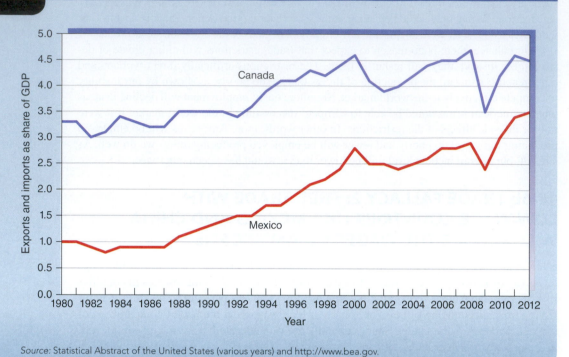

Source: Statistical Abstract of the United States (various years) and http://www.bea.gov.

World Trade Organization (WTO)
The new name given to GATT in 1994; the WTO is currently responsible for monitoring and enforcing multilateral trade agreements among its 159 member countries.

For almost five decades, GATT played a central role in reducing tariffs and relaxing quotas. The average tariff rates of GATT members fell from approximately 40 percent in 1947 to about 3.0 percent in 2010, for example.

Following 1993, GATT was given a new name: the **World Trade Organization (WTO)**. This organization of 159 countries is now responsible for monitoring and enforcing the trade agreements developed through GATT. The WTO gives member nations a forum for development of trade rules and the settlement of disputes among members.

Many countries have also entered into special trade agreements, particularly with regional neighbors. The 1994 North American Free Trade Agreement (NAFTA) established by the United States, Canada, and Mexico is an example. As a result of NAFTA, the tariffs of most goods moving among the three countries have been eliminated. As **Exhibit 12** shows, U.S. trade with both Mexico and Canada grew rapidly following the adoption of NAFTA. Measured as a share of GDP, trade with Mexico jumped from 1.4 percent in 1990 to 3.5 percent in 2012. During the same period, trade with Canada rose from 3.5 percent of GDP to 4.5 percent. This growth of trade, particularly with Mexico, however, has not been without controversy. Business and labor groups often blame employment contractions and plant closings on competition with Mexican firms. The news media generally give such stories ample exposure. However, there is no evidence that increased trade with Mexico has adversely affected the U.S. economy. The growth rate of the United States was strong and the unemployment rate relatively low during the period following the passage of NAFTA. The dire predictions about the "jobs going to Mexico" were not realized.

Since the end of World War II, the United States and most other high-income countries have been leaders among those pursuing and promoting more liberal trade policies. In contrast, India, China, and most of the less-developed economies of Africa and Latin America imposed sizable trade restraints that they were reluctant to relax. However, this pattern has changed during the past three decades. Observing the success of open economies like Hong Kong and Singapore, many less-developed countries (LDCs) unilaterally reduced many of their trade restrictions. On average, the tariff rates of LDCs are now less than half their levels of the early 1980s. Recognizing that trade is an important source of higher income levels, many leaders of LDCs are now among the leading advocates of trade liberalization. By contrast, the United

States, Japan, and the European Union nations have agricultural price support and subsidy programs that would be difficult to maintain in a free trade environment. These programs are now major stumbling blocks that retarding trade liberalization. Furthermore, protectionist proponents—particularly those in high-income countries like the United States—have successfully lobbied to impose labor and environmental regulations that block trade liberalization. Meanwhile, the Internet and other technological changes continue to reduce transport and communications costs and thereby encourage the movement of goods, ideas, and people across national boundaries. All of this promises to enliven trade issues in the years ahead.

LOOKING AHEAD

There are many similarities between domestic trade and trade across national boundaries, but there is also a major difference: International trade generally involves the exchange of one currency for another in the foreign exchange market. For students studying macroeconomics, we will now turn to this issue.

KEY POINTS

- The volume of international trade has grown rapidly in recent decades. In the United States, international trade (imports plus exports) summed to 31 percent of GDP in 2012, compared with 12 percent in 1980 and 6 percent in 1960.

- Comparative advantage rather than absolute advantage is the source of gains from trade. As long as relative production costs of goods differ, trading partners will be able to gain from trade. Specialization and trade make it possible for trading partners to produce a larger joint output and expand their consumption possibilities.

- Imports increase the domestic supply and lead to lower prices for consumers. Exports reduce the domestic supply and push prices upward, but this means the exporters can sell their products at higher prices. The net effect of international trade is an expansion in total output and higher income levels for both trading partners.

- Import restrictions, such as tariffs and quotas, reduce the supply of foreign goods to domestic markets. This results in higher prices. Essentially, the restrictions are a subsidy to producers (and workers) in protected industries at the expense of (1) consumers and (2) producers (and workers) in export industries. Jobs protected by import restrictions are offset by jobs destroyed in export-related industries.

- Trade restrictions generally provide concentrated benefits to the producers in industries they're designed to protect. The costs are spread thinly among consumers in the form of higher prices. Even though the impact of trade restrictions on the economy as a whole is harmful, they generate benefits for interest groups that politicians can then tap for campaign contributions and other side payments.

- Persistently open economies have grown more rapidly and have achieved higher per capita income levels than economies more closed to international trade.

CRITICAL ANALYSIS QUESTIONS

1. Why do American households and businesses buy things from foreigners? What are the characteristics of the items we buy from foreigners? What are the characteristics of the things we sell to foreigners?

2. *"Trade restrictions limiting the sale of cheap foreign goods in the United States are necessary to protect the prosperity of Americans." Evaluate this statement made by an American political leader.

3. Suppose as the result of the Civil War that the United States had been divided into two countries and that, through the years, high trade barriers had grown up between the two. How might the standard of living in the "divided" United States have been affected? Explain.

4. *Can both of the following statements be true? Why or why not?
   a. "Tariffs and import quotas promote economic inefficiency and reduce the real income of a nation. Economic analysis suggests that nations can gain by eliminating trade restrictions."
   b. "Economic analysis suggests that there is good reason to expect that trade restrictions will exist in the real world."

5. "Imports destroy jobs; exports create them. The average American is hurt by imports and helped by exports." Do you agree or disagree with this statement? Explain.

6. *"An increased scarcity of a product benefits producers and harms consumers. In effect, tariffs and other trade restrictions

increase the domestic scarcity of products by reducing the supply from abroad. Such policies benefit domestic producers of the restricted product at the expense of domestic consumers." Evaluate this statement.

7. Suppose that a very high tariff was placed on steel imported into the United States. How would that affect employment in the U.S. auto industry? (*Hint:* Think about how higher steel prices will impact the cost of producing automobiles.)

8. "Getting more Americans to realize that it pays to make things in the United States is the heart of the competitiveness issue." (This is a quote from an American business magazine.)

   a. Would Americans be better off if more of them paid higher prices in order to "buy American" rather than purchase from foreigners? Would U.S. employment be higher? Explain.

   b. Would Californians be better off if they bought goods produced only in California? Would the employment in California be higher? Explain.

9. How do tariffs and quotas differ? Can you think of any reason why foreign producers might prefer a quota rather than a tariff? Explain your answer.

10. *It is often alleged that Japanese producers receive subsidies from their government permitting them to sell their products at a low price in the U.S. market. Do you think we should erect trade barriers to keep out cheap Japanese goods if the source of their low price is a government subsidy? Why or why not?

11. The European Union has virtually eliminated trade restrictions among its members, and most members now use a common currency. What impact have these changes had on European economies?

12. *Does international trade cost Americans jobs? Does interstate trade cost your state jobs? What is the major effect of international and interstate trade?

13. "The United States is suffering from an excess of imports. Cheap foreign products are driving American firms out of business and leaving the U.S. economy in shambles." Evaluate this view.

14. The United States uses an import quota to maintain the domestic price of sugar well above the world price. Analyze the impact of the quota. Use supply and demand analysis to illustrate your answer. To whom do the gains and losses of this policy accrue? How does the quota affect the efficiency of resource allocation in the United States? Why do you think Congress is supportive of this policy?

15. As U.S. trade with low-wage countries like Mexico increases, will wages in the United States be pushed down? Why or why not? Are low-wage workers in the United States hurt when there is more trade with Mexico? Discuss.

16. *"Tariffs not only reduce the volume of imports, they also reduce the volume of exports." Is this statement true or false? Explain your answer.

17. "Physical obstacles like bad roads and stormy weather increase transaction costs and thereby reduce the volume of trade. Tariffs, quotas, exchange rate controls, and other human-made trade restrictions have similar effects." Evaluate this statement. Is it true? Why or why not?

*Asterisk denotes questions for which answers are given in Appendix B.

CHAPTER 19
International Finance and the Foreign Exchange Market

FOCUS

- What determines the exchange rate value of the dollar relative to other currencies? Why do exchange rates change?

- What are the alternative types of exchange rate systems? Which types work well and which will lead to financial problems?

- What information is included in the balance-of-payments accounts of a nation? Will the balance-of-payments accounts of a country always be in balance?

- Is a balance-of-trade deficit bad?

Currencies, like tomatoes and football tickets, have a price at which they are bought and sold. An exchange rate is the price of one currency in terms of another.
—Gary Smith[1]

[1]Gary Smith, *Macro Economics* (New York: W. H. Freeman, 1985), 514.

Trade across national boundaries is complicated by the fact that nations generally use different currencies to buy and sell goods in their respective domestic markets. The British use pounds; the Japanese, yen; the Mexicans, pesos; 18 European countries, the euro; and so on. Therefore, when a good or service is purchased from a seller in another country, it is generally necessary for someone to convert one currency to another.

As we previously discussed, the forces of supply and demand will determine the exchange rate value of currencies in the absence of government intervention. This chapter focuses more directly on the foreign exchange market. We will consider how exchange rates both exert an impact on and are influenced by the flow of trade and the flow of capital across national boundaries. We will also analyze alternative exchange rate regimes and consider some of the recent changes in the structure of currency markets around the world.

19-1 FOREIGN EXCHANGE MARKET

Foreign exchange market
The market in which the currencies of different countries are bought and sold.

When trading parties live in different countries, an exchange will often involve a currency transaction. Currency transactions take place in the **foreign exchange market**, the market where currencies of different countries are bought and sold. Suppose that you own a sporting goods shop in the United States and are preparing to place an order for athletic shoes. You can purchase them from either a domestic or foreign manufacturer. If you decide to purchase the shoes from a British firm, either you will have to change dollars into pounds at a bank and send them to the British producer or the British manufacturer will have to go to a bank and change your dollar check into pounds. In either case, purchasing the British shoes will involve an exchange of dollars for pounds.

Suppose the British producer has offered to supply the shoes for 30 pounds per pair. How can you determine whether this price is high or low? To compare the price of the British-supplied shoes with the price of those produced domestically, you must know the **exchange rate** between the dollar and the pound. *The exchange rate is one of the most important prices because it enables consumers in one country to translate the prices of foreign goods into units of their own currency. Specifically, the dollar price of a foreign good is determined by multiplying the foreign product price by the exchange rate (the dollar price per unit of the foreign currency).* For example, if it takes $1.80 to obtain 1 pound, then the British shoes priced at 30 pounds would cost $54 (30 times the $1.80 price of the pound).

Exchange rate
The domestic price of one unit of foreign currency. For example, if it takes $1.80 to purchase one English pound, the dollar–pound exchange rate is 1.80.

Suppose the exchange rate is $1.80 = 1 pound and that you decide to buy 200 pairs of athletic shoes from the British manufacturer at 30 pounds ($54) per pair. You will need 6,000 pounds in order to pay the British manufacturer. If you contact an American bank that handles foreign exchange transactions and write the bank a check for $10,800 (the $1.80 exchange rate multiplied by 6,000), it will supply the 6,000 pounds. The bank will typically charge a small fee for handling the transaction.

Where does the American bank get the pounds? The bank obtains the pounds from British importers who want dollars to buy things from Americans. Note that the U.S. demand for foreign currencies (such as the pound) is generated by the demand of Americans for things purchased from foreigners. In contrast, the supply of foreign currencies in exchange for dollars reflects the demand of foreigners for things bought from Americans.

Exhibit 1 presents data on the exchange rate—the cents required to purchase a European euro, Japanese yen, British pound, and Canadian dollar—from 1990 to 2013. Under the flexible rate system present in most industrial countries, the exchange rate between currencies changes from day to day and even from hour to hour. The exchange rate figures for years prior to 2013 are the average for the year. The 2013 figures are for exchange rates as of May 31, 2013.

Appreciation
An increase in the value of the domestic currency relative to foreign currencies. An appreciation makes foreign goods cheaper for domestic residents.

An **appreciation** in the value of a nation's currency means that fewer units of the currency are now required to purchase one unit of a foreign currency. For example, as Exhibit 1 shows, it took 151.85 cents to purchase a British pound in 2013, down from

EXHIBIT 1

Foreign Exchange Rates, 1990–2013

Year	Euro	Japanese Yen	British Pound	Canadian Dollar	Index of Exchange Rate Value of the Dollar[a] (26 Currencies)
1990	—	0.690	178.41	85.7	71.4
1992	—	0.789	176.63	82.7	76.9
1994	—	0.979	153.19	73.2	90.9
1996	—	0.919	156.07	73.3	97.5
1998	—	0.763	165.73	67.4	115.9
2000	92.3	0.928	151.56	67.3	119.6
2001	89.5	0.823	143.96	64.6	126.1
2002	94.5	0.799	150.25	63.7	126.8
2003	113.2	0.863	163.47	71.4	119.3
2004	124.4	0.925	183.30	76.8	113.8
2005	124.5	0.908	182.04	82.5	110.8
2006	125.6	0.860	184.34	88.2	108.7
2007	137.1	0.849	200.20	93.2	103.6
2008	147.3	0.967	185.45	93.8	99.9
2009	139.4	1.067	156.61	87.6	105.7
2010	132.6	1.139	154.52	97.1	101.8
2011	139.3	1.255	160.43	101.1	97.2
2012	128.6	1.253	158.53	100.1	99.8
2013	129.9	0.992	151.85	96.7	101.9

[a]2013 figures are as of May 31, 2013.
Source: http://research.stlouisfed.org/fred2/

185.45 cents in 2008. Thus, the dollar appreciated against the pound during this period. As the result of this appreciation, goods purchased from British suppliers became less expensive to Americans.[2] At the same time, the prices of American goods to British consumers moved in the opposite direction. An appreciation of the U.S. dollar relative to the British pound is the same thing as a depreciation in the British pound relative to the dollar.

When a **depreciation** occurs, it will take more units of the domestic currency to purchase a unit of foreign currency. During the 2002–2008 period, the dollar depreciated against all of the major currencies (see Exhibit 1). In 2008, it took 185.45 cents to purchase a British pound, up from 143.96 in 2001. Similarly, it took 147.3 cents to purchase a euro in 2008, up from only 89.5 in 2001. The number of cents required to purchase a Canadian dollar and a Japanese yen also increased during this time frame. As the number of cents required to purchase a unit of foreign currency increases, the dollar depreciates, and foreign goods become more expensive for Americans.

Exhibit 1 also provides an index of the foreign exchange value of the dollar against 26 major currencies. This broad index provides evidence on what is happening to the dollar's general exchange rate value.[3] An increase in the index implies an appreciation in the dollar, whereas a decline is indicative of a depreciation. Between 1996 and 2002, the dollar appreciated by approximately 30 percent against these twenty-six currencies. Between 2002 and 2013, however, the index indicates that the dollar depreciated by approximately

Depreciation
A reduction in the value of the domestic currency relative to foreign currencies. A depreciation makes foreign goods more expensive for domestic residents.

[2]Because an appreciation means a lower price of foreign currencies, some may think it looks like a depreciation. Just remember that a lower price of the foreign currency means that one's domestic currency will buy more units of the foreign currency and thus more goods and services from foreigners.

[3]In the construction of this index, the exchange rate of each currency relative to the dollar is weighted according to the proportion of U.S. trade with the country. For example, the index weights the U.S. dollar–Japanese yen exchange rate more heavily than the U.S. dollar–Swiss franc exchange rate because the volume of U.S. trade with Japan exceeds the volume of trade with Switzerland.

Flexible exchange rates
Exchange rates that are determined by the market forces of supply and demand. They are sometimes called floating exchange rates.

20 percent (down to 101.9 from 126.8) relative to this broad bundle of currencies. Frequently, people will use the terms "*strong*" and "*weak*" when referring to the exchange rate value of a currency. A currency is said to be strong when it has been appreciating in value, whereas a weak currency is one that has been depreciating on the foreign exchange market.

A pure **flexible exchange rate** system is one in which market forces alone determine the foreign exchange value of the currency. The exchange rate system in effect since 1973 might best be described as a managed flexible rate regime. It is flexible because all the major industrial countries allow the exchange rate value of their currencies to float. But the system is also "managed" because the major industrial nations have from time to time attempted to alter supply and demand in the foreign exchange market by buying and selling various currencies. Compared with the total size of this market, however, these transactions have generally been small. Thus, the exchange rate value of major currencies like the U.S. dollar, British pound, Japanese yen, and the European euro is determined primarily by market forces. Several countries link their currency to major currencies like the U.S. dollar or European euro. As we proceed, we will investigate alternative methods of linking currencies and analyze the operation of different regimes.

19-2 DETERMINANTS OF THE EXCHANGE RATE

To simplify our explanation of how the exchange rate is determined, let's assume that the United States and Great Britain are the only two countries in the world. When Americans buy and sell with each other, they use dollars. Therefore, American sellers will want to be paid in dollars. Similarly, when the British buy and sell with each other, they use pounds. As a result, British sellers will want to be paid in pounds.

In our two-country world, the demand for pounds in the exchange rate market originates from the purchases by Americans of British goods, services, and assets (both real and financial). For example, when U.S. residents purchase men's suits from a British manufacturer; travel in the United Kingdom; or purchase the stocks, bonds, or physical assets of British business firms, they demand pounds from (and supply dollars to) the foreign exchange market to pay for these items.

Correspondingly, the supply of foreign exchange (pounds in our two-country case) originates from sales by Americans to foreigners. When Americans sell goods, services, or assets to the British, for example, the British buyers will supply pounds (and demand dollars) in the exchange rate market in order to acquire the dollars to pay for the items purchased from Americans.[4]

Exhibit 2 illustrates the supply and demand curves of Americans for foreign exchange—British pounds in our two-country case. The demand for pounds is downward sloping because a lower dollar price of the pound—meaning a dollar will buy more pounds—makes British goods cheaper for American importers. The goods produced by one country are generally good substitutes for the goods of another country. This means that when foreign (British) goods become cheaper, Americans will increase their expenditures on imports (and therefore the quantity of pounds demanded will increase). Thus, as the dollar price of the pound declines, Americans will both buy more of the lower-priced (in dollars) British goods and demand more pounds, which are required for the purchases.

Similarly, the supply curve for pounds is dependent upon the sales by Americans to the British (i.e., the purchase of American goods by the British). An increase in the dollar price of the pound means that a pound will purchase more dollars and more goods priced in dollars. Thus, the price (in pounds) of American goods, services, and assets to British

---

[4]We analyze the foreign exchange market in terms of the demand for and supply of foreign currencies. Alternatively, this analysis could be done in terms of the supply of and demand for dollars. Because one currency is traded for another, the same actions that generate a demand for foreign exchange simultaneously generate a supply of dollars. Correspondingly, the same exchanges that create a supply of foreign currencies simultaneously generate a demand for dollars in the foreign exchange market.

EXHIBIT 2

Equilibrium in the Foreign Exchange Market

The dollar price of the pound is measured on the vertical axis. The horizontal axis indicates the flow of pounds to the foreign exchange market. The equilibrium exchange rate is $1.80 = 1 pound. At the equilibrium price, the quantity of pounds demanded just equals the quantity supplied. On the one hand, a higher dollar price per pound ($2.00 = 1 pound) will lead to an excess supply of pounds, causing the dollar price of the pound to fall. On the other hand, a lower dollar price per pound ($1.60 = 1 pound) will result in an excess demand for pounds, causing the pound to appreciate.

purchasers declines as the dollar price of the pound increases. As this happens, the British will purchase more from Americans and therefore supply more pounds to the foreign exchange market. Thus, the supply curve for pounds will slope upward to the right.

As Exhibit 2 shows, equilibrium is present at the dollar price of the pound that brings the quantity demanded and quantity supplied of pounds into balance, $1.80 in this case. *The market-clearing price of $1.80 per pound not only equalizes demand and supply in the foreign exchange market but also equalizes (1) the value of U.S. purchases of items supplied by the British with (2) the value of items sold by U.S. residents to the British.* Demand and supply in the currency market are simply the mirror images of these two factors.

What would happen if the price of the pound were above equilibrium—$2.00 = 1 pound, for example? At the higher dollar price of the pound, British goods would be more expensive for Americans. Americans would cut back on their purchases of shoes, glassware, textile products, financial assets, and other items supplied by the British, and the quantity of pounds demanded by Americans would therefore decline. Simultaneously, the higher dollar price of the pound would make U.S. exports cheaper for the British. For example, an $18,000 American automobile would cost British consumers 10,000 pounds when 1 pound trades for $1.80, but it would cost only 9,000 pounds when 1 pound exchanges for $2.00. If the dollar price of the pound were $2.00, the British would supply more pounds to the foreign exchange market than Americans would demand. As you can see in Exhibit 2, this excess supply of pounds would cause the dollar price of the pound to decline until equilibrium is restored at the $1.80 = 1 pound price.

At a below-equilibrium price, such as $1.60 = 1 pound, an opposite set of forces would be present. The lower dollar price of the pound would make British goods cheaper for Americans and American goods more expensive for the British. At the $1.60 price for a pound, the purchases of Americans from the British would exceed their sales to them, leading to an excess demand for pounds. In turn, the excess demand would cause the dollar price of the pound to rise until equilibrium was restored at $1.80 = 1$ pound.

The implications of the analysis are general. In our multicountry and multicurrency world, the demand for foreign currencies in exchange for dollars reflects the purchases by Americans of goods, services, and assets from foreigners. The supply of foreign currencies in exchange for dollars reflects the sales by Americans of goods, services, and assets to foreigners. The equilibrium exchange rate will bring the quantity of foreign exchange demanded by Americans into balance with the quantity supplied by foreigners. It will also bring the purchases by Americans from foreigners into balance with the sales by Americans to foreigners.

19-3 WHY DO EXCHANGE RATES CHANGE?

When exchange rates are free to fluctuate, the market value of a nation's currency will appreciate and depreciate in response to changing market conditions. Any change that alters the quantity of goods, services, or assets bought from foreigners relative to the quantity sold to them will alter the exchange rate. Let's consider the major factors that will alter the foreign exchange value of a nation's currency.

19-3a CHANGES IN INCOME

An increase in domestic income will encourage the nation's residents to spend a portion of their additional income on imports. When the income of a nation grows rapidly, the nation's imports tend to rise rapidly as well. As **Exhibit 3** illustrates, an increase in imports also increases the demand for foreign exchange (the pound in our two-country case). As the demand for pounds increases, the dollar price of the pound rises (from $1.80 to $2.00). This depreciation of the dollar reduces the incentive of Americans to import British goods and services, while increasing the incentive of the British to purchase U.S. exports. These two forces will restore equilibrium in the foreign exchange market at a new, higher dollar price of the pound.

Just the opposite takes place when the income of a trading partner (Great Britain in our example) increases. Rapid growth of income abroad will lead to an increase in U.S.

EXHIBIT 3

The Growth of U.S. Income and Imports

Other things constant, if incomes grow in the United States, U.S. imports will grow. The increase in the imports will increase the demand for pounds, causing the dollar price of the pound to rise (from $1.80 to $2.00).

© Cengage Learning 2013

exports, causing the supply of foreign exchange (and demand for dollars) to increase. This will cause the dollar to appreciate—the dollar price of the pound will fall, in other words.

What will happen if both countries are growing? Other things constant, it is the relative growth rate that matters. A country that grows more rapidly than its trading partners will increase its imports relative to its exports, which will cause the exchange rate value of its currency to fall. Conversely, sluggish growth of a country's income relative to its trading partners will lead to a decline in imports relative to exports, which will cause the exchange rate value of its currency to rise. Granted, it seems paradoxical that sluggish growth relative to one's trading partners will cause a country's currency to appreciate, but that's in fact what happens.

19-3b DIFFERENCES IN RATES OF INFLATION

Other things constant, domestic inflation will cause the value of a nation's currency to depreciate, whereas deflation will cause its currency to appreciate. Suppose prices in the United States rise by 50 percent while our trading partners are experiencing stable prices. The domestic inflation will cause U.S. consumers to increase their demand for imported goods (and foreign currency). In turn, the inflated domestic prices will cause foreigners to reduce their purchases of U.S. goods, thereby reducing the supply of foreign currency to the exchange market. As **Exhibit 4** illustrates, the exchange rate will adjust to this set of circumstances. In our two-country example, the dollar will depreciate relative to the pound.

Exchange rate adjustments permit nations with even high rates of inflation to engage in trade with countries experiencing relatively stable prices.[5] A depreciation in a nation's currency in the foreign exchange market compensates for the nation's inflation rate. For example, if inflation increases the price level in the United States by 50 percent and the value of the dollar in exchange for the pound depreciates (such that the value of the foreign currency increases 50 percent), then the prices of American goods measured in pounds are unchanged to British consumers. Thus, when the exchange rate value of the dollar changes

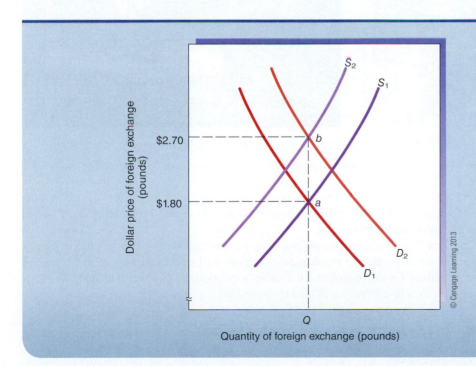

EXHIBIT 4

Inflation with Flexible Exchange Rates

If prices were stable in Britain while the price level increased 50 percent in the United States, the U.S. demand for British products (and pounds) would increase, whereas U.S. exports to Britain would decline, causing the supply of pounds to fall. These forces would cause the dollar to depreciate relative to the pound.

© Cengage Learning 2013

[5]However, high rates of inflation are likely to cause greater variability in the foreign exchange value of a currency across time periods. In turn, this increased variability of the exchange rate will generate uncertainty and reduce the volume of international trade—particularly transactions involving a time dimension. Thus, exchange rate instability is generally harmful to the health of an economy.

American consumer purchases an auto from a Japanese manufacturer.

American vacationer buys a ticket on British Airways.

Foreign student pays tuition to Harvard.

Foreign investor purchases a bond from a U.S. corporation.

How will each of these transactions influence the demand for and supply of foreign currencies in exchange for the dollar?

from $1.80 = 1 pound to $2.70 = 1 pound, the depreciation in the dollar restores the original prices of U.S. goods to British consumers even though the price level in the United States has increased by 50 percent.

On the one hand, when domestic prices are increasing more rapidly than those of one's trading partners, the value of the domestic currency will tend to depreciate in the foreign exchange market. On the other hand, if a nation's inflation rate is lower than that of its trading partners, then its currency will tend to appreciate.

19-3c CHANGES IN INTEREST RATES

Financial investments will be quite sensitive to changes in real interest rates—that is, interest rates adjusted for the expected rate of inflation. International loanable funds will tend to move toward areas where the expected real rate of return (after compensation for differences in risk) is highest. *Thus, increases in real interest rates relative to a nation's trading partners will tend to cause that nation's currency to appreciate.* For example, if real interest rates rise in the United States relative to Britain, British citizens will demand dollars (and supply their currency, pounds) in the foreign exchange market to purchase the high-yield American assets. The increase in demand for the dollar and supply of pounds will then cause the dollar to appreciate relative to the British pound.

In contrast, when real interest rates in other countries increase relative to rates in the United States, short-term financial investors will move to take advantage of the higher yields abroad. As investment funds move from the United States to other countries, there will be an increase in the demand for foreign currencies and an increase in the supply of dollars in the foreign exchange market. A depreciation in the dollar relative to the currencies of the countries with the higher real interest rates will be the result.

19-3d CHANGES IN THE BUSINESS AND INVESTMENT CLIMATE

The inflow and outflow of capital will also be influenced by the quality of the business and investment environment. The monetary, legal, regulatory, and tax climates are particularly important here. Countries that follow a monetary policy consistent with price stability, protect property rights, keep taxes low, and treat people impartially will tend to attract capital. In turn, the inflow of capital will strengthen the demand for the domestic currency and thereby cause it to appreciate. In contrast, when investors are concerned about the stability of the monetary climate, fairness of the legal system, high taxes, and excessive regulation, many will choose to do business elsewhere. As they do so, an outflow of capital and depreciation in the foreign exchange value of the domestic currency will result. Thus, other things constant, the foreign exchange value of a nation's currency will tend to appreciate when its policy environment is improving, while it will tend to depreciate if investors believe that the policy climate is deteriorating.

The accompanying **Thumbnail Sketch** summarizes the major forces that cause a nation's currency to appreciate or depreciate when exchange rates are determined by market forces.

19-4 INTERNATIONAL FINANCE AND ALTERNATIVE EXCHANGE RATE REGIMES

There are three major types of exchange rate regimes: (1) flexible rates; (2) fixed rate, unified currency; and (3) pegged exchange rates. So far, we have focused on the operation of a flexible rate regime. We now consider the other two.

Thumbnail Sketch

What Factors Cause a Nation's Currency to Appreciate or Depreciate?

These Factors Will Cause a Nation's Currency to Appreciate:

1. Slow growth of income (relative to one's trading partners) that causes imports to lag behind exports
2. A rate of inflation that is lower than that of one's trading partners
3. Domestic real interest rates that are higher than real interest rates abroad
4. A shift toward sound policies that attract an inflow of capital

These Factors Will Cause a Nation's Currency to Depreciate:

1. Rapid growth of income (relative to one's trading partners) that stimulates imports relative to exports
2. A rate of inflation that is higher than that of one's trading partners
3. Domestic real interest rates that are lower than real interest rates abroad
4. Movement toward unsound policies that cause an outflow of capital

19-4a FIXED RATE, UNIFIED CURRENCY SYSTEM

Obviously, the 50 states of the United States have a unified currency, the dollar. In addition, the U.S. dollar has been the official currency of Panama for more than a century. Ecuador adopted the U.S. dollar as its official currency in 2000, and El Salvador did so in 2001. The currency of Hong Kong is also closely linked to the U.S. dollar. Hong Kong has a **currency board** that has the power to create currency only in exchange for a specific quantity of U.S. dollars (7.7 HK dollars = 1 U.S. dollar).[6] Countries that adopt the currency board approach do not conduct monetary policy. Instead, they merely accept the monetary policy of the nation to which their currency is tied—the U.S. policy in the case of Hong Kong. Thus, the United States, Panama, Ecuador, El Salvador, and Hong Kong have a unified currency regime.

Eighteen countries of the European Union—Austria, Belgium, Cyprus, Estonia, Finland, France, Germany, Greece, Ireland, Italy, Latvia, Luxembourg, Malta, Netherlands, Portugal, Slovakia, Slovenia, and Spain—have also established a unified currency regime. The official currency in each of these countries is the euro. Several other European countries, including Bulgaria, Lithuania, Bosnia, and Herzegovina use a currency board to link their domestic currency to the euro. Thus, the euro is a unified currency in all of these countries. In turn, the foreign exchange value of the euro relative to other currencies, such as the dollar, the British pound, and the Japanese yen, is determined by market forces (flexible exchange rates).

The distinguishing characteristic of a fixed rate, unified currency regime is the presence of only one central bank with the power to expand and contract the supply of money. For the dollar, that central bank is the Federal Reserve System; for the euro, it is the European Central Bank. Those linking their currency at a fixed rate to the dollar or the euro do not conduct monetary policy; they merely accept the monetary policy of the central bank for their currency. For example, the former central banks of the countries now using the euro no longer have the power to create money. In essence, they are now branches of the European Central Bank, much like the regional and district Federal Reserve banks are branches of the Fed. Similarly, currency boards do not create additional currency. They merely agree to exchange their domestic currency for the currency to which it is linked at a fixed rate.

A pure gold standard system, in which each country agrees to exchange units of its domestic currency for gold at a designated price and fully backs its domestic money supply with gold, is also a fixed rate, unified system. In this case, the world supply of gold (rather than a central bank) determines the total supply of money. If a country's purchases from foreigners exceeded its sales to them, its supply of gold would fall, which would reduce the domestic supply of money. This would put downward pressure on the domestic price level and bring the payments to and receipts from foreigners back into balance. Things would change in the opposite direction if a country were selling more to foreigners than it was purchasing from them. In this case, the excess of sales relative to purchases would lead to an inflow of gold, expansion in the domestic money supply, and higher domestic prices. International financial arrangements approximated those of a gold standard during the period between the U.S. Civil War and the establishment of the Federal Reserve System in 1913.

Between 1944 and 1971, most of the world operated under a system of **fixed exchange rates**, where each nation fixed the price of its currency relative to others. In essence, this was a quasi-unified system. It was unified in the sense that the value of one currency was fixed relative to others over lengthy time periods. But it was not a fully unified system because each country continued to exercise control over its monetary policy. Nations maintained

---

Currency board
An entity that (1) issues a currency with a fixed designated value relative to a widely accepted currency (for example, the U.S. dollar), (2) promises to continue to redeem the issued currency at the fixed rate, and (3) maintains bonds and other liquid assets denominated in the other currency that provide 100 percent backing for all currency issued.

Fixed exchange rate
An exchange rate that is set at a determined amount by government policy.

---

[6]A currency board like that of Hong Kong does two things. First, it issues domestic currency at a fixed rate in exchange for a designated foreign currency. Second, the foreign currency is then invested in bonds denominated in that currency. This means that the money issued by the currency board is backed 100 percent by the foreign currency. Therefore, the holders of the money issued by the currency board know that it will always have sufficient funds to exchange the domestic currency for the foreign one at the fixed rate. In essence, the country with a currency board accepts the monetary policy of the nation to which its currency is tied.

reserves with the **International Monetary Fund (IMF)**, which could be drawn on when payments to foreigners exceeded receipts from them. This provided each with some leeway in the conduct of monetary policy. However, countries running persistent payment deficits would eventually deplete their reserves. This constrained the country's monetary independence and provided its policy-makers with an incentive to keep its monetary policy approximately in line with that of its trading partners. Under this fixed exchange rate regime, nations often imposed tariffs, quotas, and other trade barriers in an effort to keep their payments and receipts in balance at the fixed rate. Various restrictions on the convertibility of currencies were also common. These problems eventually led to the demise of the system.

19-4b PEGGED EXCHANGE RATE REGIME

A **pegged exchange rate system** is one in which a country commits itself to the maintenance of a specific exchange rate (or exchange-rate range) relative to another currency (like the U.S. dollar) or a bundle of currencies. In contrast with the currency board approach, however, countries adopting the pegged exchange rate continue to conduct monetary policy. Thus, an excess of purchases from foreigners relative to sales to them does not automatically force the country to reduce its domestic money supply.

However, maintaining the pegged rate will restrict the independence of monetary policy. A country can either (1) follow an independent monetary policy and allow its exchange rate to fluctuate or (2) tie its monetary policy to maintain the fixed exchange rate. It cannot, however, maintain the convertibility of its currency at the fixed exchange rate while following a monetary policy more expansionary than the country to which its currency is tied. Attempts to do so will lead to a financial crisis—a situation in which falling foreign currency reserves eventually force the country to forgo the pegged exchange rate.

This is precisely what happened in Mexico during 1989–1994. Mexico promised to exchange the peso for the dollar at a pegged rate, but it also expanded its domestic money supply much more rapidly than the United States. In the early 1990s, this led to a higher rate of inflation in Mexico than in the United States. Responding to the different inflation rates, more and more people shifted away from the Mexican peso and toward the dollar. By December 1994, Mexico's foreign exchange reserves were virtually depleted. As a result, it could no longer maintain the fixed exchange rate with the dollar. Mexico devalued its currency, triggering a crisis that affected several other countries following similar policies.

In 1997–1998, much the same thing happened in Brazil, Thailand, and Indonesia. Like Mexico, these countries sought to maintain fixed exchange rates (or rates within a narrow band), while following monetary and fiscal policies that were inconsistent with the fixed rate. As their reserves declined, they were forced to abandon their exchange rate pegs. This was extremely disruptive to these economies. Imports suddenly became much more expensive and therefore less affordable. Businesses (including banks) that had borrowed money in dollars (or some other foreign currency) were unable to repay their loans as the result of the sharp decline in the exchange rate value of the domestic currency. In turn, these disruptions led to severe economic declines.

Both economic theory and real-world experience indicate that either a purely flexible exchange rate regime or a fixed rate, unified regime with a single central bank will work reasonably well. In contrast, a pegged exchange rate regime is something like a time bomb. Pushed by political considerations, monetary policy makers in most countries are unable to follow a course consistent with the maintenance of pegged rates. Failure to do so, however, eventually leads to abandonment of the peg and a financial crisis.

19-5 BALANCE OF PAYMENTS

Just as countries calculate their gross domestic product (GDP) so that they have a general idea of their domestic level of production, most countries also calculate their balance of international payments in order to keep track of transactions across national boundaries. The

International Monetary Fund (IMF)

An international banking organization, currently with more than 185 member nations, designed to oversee the operation of the international monetary system. Although it does not control the world supply of money, it does hold currency reserves for member nations and makes currency loans to national central banks.

Pegged exchange rate system

A commitment to use monetary and fiscal policy to maintain the exchange rate value of the domestic currency at a fixed rate or within a narrow band relative to another currency (or bundle of currencies).

Balance of payments
A summary of all economic transactions between a country and all other countries for a specific time period, usually a year. The balance-of-payments account reflects all payments and liabilities to foreigners (debits) and all payments and obligations received from foreigners (credits).

balance of payments summarizes the transactions of the country's citizens, businesses, and governments with foreigners. Balance-of-payments accounts are kept according to the principles of basic bookkeeping. Any transaction that creates a demand for foreign currency (and a supply of the domestic currency) in the foreign exchange market is recorded as a debit, or minus, item. Imports are an example of a debit item. Transactions that create a supply of foreign currency (and demand for the domestic currency) on the foreign exchange market are recorded as a credit, or plus, item. Exports are an example of a credit item. ***Because the foreign exchange market will bring quantity demanded and quantity supplied into balance, it will also bring the total debits and total credits into balance.***

Exhibit 5 summarizes the balance-of-payments accounts of the United States for 2012. As the exhibit shows, the transactions can be grouped into one of three separate categories: the current account, capital account, or the official reserve account. Let's take a look at each of these major categories.

EXHIBIT 5

U.S. Balance of Payments, 2012 (in billions of dollars)

		DEBITS	CREDITS	BALANCE
CURRENT ACCOUNT				
1	U.S. merchandise exports		1,564.1	
2	U.S. merchandise imports	–2,299.4		
3	Balance of merchandise trade (1 + 2)			–735.3
4	U.S. service exports		630.4	
5	U.S. service imports	–434.6		
6	Balance on service trade (4 + 5)			195.8
7	Balance on goods and services (3 + 6)			–539.5
8	Income receipts of Americans from abroad		742.0	
9	Income receipts of Foreigners in the United States	–543.4		
10	Net income receipts			198.6
11	Net unilateral transfers			–134.1
12	Balance on current account (7 + 10 + 11)			–475.0
CAPITAL ACCOUNT				
13	Foreign investment in the United States (capital inflow)		11.3	
14	U.S. investment abroad (capital outflow)	–62.7		
15	Net Other Currency Transactions[a]		157.2	
16	Balance on capital account (13 + 14 + 15)			105.8
OFFICIAL RESERVE TRANSACTIONS				
17	U.S. official reserve assets	–4.5		
18	Foreign official assets in the U.S.		373.7	
19	Balance, Official Reserve Account (17 + 18)			369.2
20	Total (12 + 16 + 19)			0.0

Source: http://www.bea.gov.

[a]Statistical discrepancy is included in this figure.

19-5a CURRENT-ACCOUNT TRANSACTIONS

Current-account transactions involve only current exchanges of goods and services and current income flows (and gifts). They do not involve changes in the ownership of either real or financial assets. **Current-account** transactions are dominated by the trade in goods and services. The export and import of merchandise goods are the largest components in the current account. When U.S. producers export their products, foreigners will supply their currency in exchange for dollars in order to pay for the U.S.-produced goods. Because U.S. exports generate a supply of foreign exchange and demand for dollars in the foreign exchange market, they are a credit (plus) item. In contrast, when Americans import goods, they will demand foreign currencies and supply dollars in the foreign exchange market. Thus, imports are a debit (minus) item.

In 2012, the United States exported $1,564.1 billion of merchandise goods compared with imports of $2,299.4 billion. The difference between the value of a country's merchandise exports and the value of its merchandise imports is known as the **balance of merchandise trade** (or *balance of trade*). If the value of a country's merchandise exports falls short of the value of its merchandise imports, it is said to have a balance-of-trade deficit. In contrast, the situation in which a nation exports more than it imports is referred to as a trade surplus. In 2012, the United States ran a merchandise-trade deficit of $735.3 billion (line 3 of Exhibit 5).

The export and import of services are also sizable. Service trade involves the exchange of items like insurance, transportation, banking services, and items supplied to foreign tourists. Like the export of merchandise goods, service exports generate a supply of foreign exchange and demand for dollars. For example, a Mexican business that is insured by an American company will supply pesos and demand dollars to pay its premiums for the service. Thus, service exports are recorded as credits in the balance-of-payments accounts of exporting nations. Conversely, the import of services from foreigners generates a demand for foreign currency and a supply of dollars in the exchange market. Therefore, service imports are a debit item.

As Exhibit 5 illustrates, in 2012, U.S. service exports were $630.4 billion, compared with service imports of $434.6 billion. Thus, the United States ran a $195.8 billion surplus on its service trade transactions (line 6 of Exhibit 5). When we add the balance of service exports and imports to the balance of merchandise trade, we obtain the **balance on goods and services**. In 2012, the United States ran a $539.5 billion deficit (the sum of the $735.3 billion merchandise-trade deficit and the $195.8 billion service surplus) in the goods and services account.

Two other relatively small items are also included in current-account transactions: (1) net income from investments and (2) unilateral transfers. Americans have made substantial investments in stocks, bonds, and real assets in other countries. As these investments abroad generate income, dollars will flow from foreigners to Americans. This flow of income to Americans will supply foreign currency (and create a demand for dollars) in the foreign exchange market. Thus, the net income to Americans is entered as a credit in the U.S. current account. Correspondingly, foreigners earn income from their investments in the United States. This net income to foreigners is recorded as a debit in the U.S. current account because the supply of dollars to the foreign exchange market creates a demand for foreign exchange.

As Exhibit 5 shows, in 2012, Americans earned $742.0 billion from investments abroad, whereas foreigners earned $543.4 billion from their investments in the United States. On balance, Americans earned $198.6 billion more on their investments abroad than foreigners earned on their investments in the United States. This $198.6 billion net inflow of investment income reduced the size of the deficit on current-account transactions.

Gifts to foreigners, like U.S. aid to a foreign government or private gifts from U.S. residents to their relatives abroad, generate a demand for foreign currencies and supply of dollars in the foreign exchange market. Thus, they are a debit item. Correspondingly, gifts to Americans from foreigners are a credit item. Because the U.S.

Current account
The record of all transactions with foreign nations that involve the exchange of merchandise goods and services, current income derived from investments, and unilateral gifts.

Balance of merchandise trade
The difference between the value of merchandise exports and the value of merchandise imports for a nation. It is also called simply the *balance of trade* or *net exports*. The balance of merchandise trade is only one component of a nation's total balance of payments and its current account.

Balance on goods and services
The exports of goods (merchandise) and services of a nation minus its imports of goods and services.

government and private U.S. citizens gave $134.1 billion more to foreigners than we received from them, this net unilateral transfer was entered as a debit item on the current account in 2012.

19-5b BALANCE ON CURRENT ACCOUNT

Balance on current account
The import–export balance of goods and services, plus net investment income earned abroad, plus net private and government transfers. If the value of the nation's export-type items exceeds (is less than) the value of the nation's import-type items plus net unilateral transfers to foreigners, a current-account surplus (deficit) is present.

The difference between (1) the value of a country's current exports (both goods and services) and earnings from its investments abroad and (2) the value of its current imports (again, both goods and services) and the earnings of foreigners on their domestic assets (plus net unilateral transfers to foreigners) is known as the **balance on current account**. The current-account balance provides a summary of all current-account transactions. As with the balance of trade, when the value of the current-account debit items (import-type transactions) exceeds the value of the credit items (export-type transactions), we say that the country is running a current-account deficit. Alternatively, if the credit items are greater than the debit items, the country is running a current-account surplus. In 2012, the United States ran a current-account deficit of $475.0 billion.

Because trade in goods and services dominates current-account transactions, the trade- and current-account balances are closely related. Countries with large trade deficits (surpluses) almost always run substantial current-account deficits (surpluses).

19-5c CAPITAL-ACCOUNT TRANSACTIONS

Capital account
The record of transactions with foreigners that involve either (1) the exchange of ownership rights to real or financial assets or (2) the extension of loans.

In contrast with current-account transactions, **capital-account** transactions focus on changes in the ownership of real and financial assets. These transactions are composed of (1) direct investments by Americans in real assets abroad (or by foreigners in the United States) and (2) loans to and from foreigners. When foreigners make investments in the United States—for example, by purchasing stocks, bonds, or real assets from Americans—their actions will supply foreign currency and generate a demand for dollars in the foreign exchange market. Thus, these capital inflow transactions are a credit.

Conversely, capital outflow transactions are recorded as debits. For example, if a U.S. investor purchases a shoe factory in Mexico, the Mexican seller will want to be paid in pesos. The U.S. investor will supply dollars (and demand pesos) on the foreign exchange market. Because U.S. citizens will demand foreign currency (and supply dollars) when they invest in stocks, bonds, and real assets abroad, these transactions enter into the balance-of-payments accounts as a debit. In 2012, foreign investments in the United States (capital inflow) summed to 11.3 billion, while U.S. investments abroad (capital outflow) totaled $62.7 billion. In 2012, there was also a net capital inflow of $157.2 billion from other currency transactions including financial derivatives and changes in U.S. currency abroad. Because the capital inflow exceeded the outflow, the United States ran a $105.8 billion capital-account surplus in 2012.

19-5d OFFICIAL RESERVE ACCOUNT

Official reserve account
The record of transactions among central banks.

As we noted earlier, the current exchange rate regime is not a pure flexible rate system. Countries with pegged exchange rates will often engage in official reserve transactions in an effort to maintain their pegged rate. These transactions are debited and credited in a country's **official reserve account**. Even countries with flexible exchange rates may engage in official reserve transactions in order to influence their exchange rate. When a nation's currency is appreciating rapidly, a country may try to slow the appreciation by purchasing foreign financial assets. Conversely, when a currency is depreciating, the country may attempt to halt the depreciation by using some of its foreign currency reserves to purchase the domestic currency in the foreign exchange market. Because of the credibility and widespread use of the U.S. dollar, these official reserve transactions often involve assets denominated in dollars, particularly bonds issued by the U.S. Treasury.

The official reserve transactions are usually small relative to the size of the foreign exchange market, but they were sizable in 2012. As the financial market turmoil continued after the 2008–2009 recession, foreign central banks purchased $373.7 billion of dollar assets, mostly Treasury bonds. The U.S. purchases of foreign reserves were small, only $4.5 billion. Thus, the United States ran a surplus of $369.2 billion on official reserve transactions in 2012. (*Note:* the transactions in the capital and official reserve accounts are sometimes labeled Financial Account transactions.)

What impact do these purchases of U.S. Treasury bonds by foreign central banks have on the U.S. economy? Their impact is much like that of other capital inflows. These foreign purchases, like other capital inflows, will increase the demand for the dollar in the foreign exchange market, causing the foreign exchange value of the dollar to be higher than would otherwise be the case. They will also lead to lower domestic interest rates. Domestic interest rates will fall because the capital inflow will raise the supply of loanable funds. There is a positive side to these official reserve purchases of the dollar. If foreign central banks did not have confidence in both the economy and the monetary policy of the United States, they would not want to purchase and hold U.S. financial assets.

19-5e THE BALANCE OF PAYMENTS MUST BALANCE

The sum of the debit and credit items of the balance-of-payments accounts must balance. Thus, the following identity must hold:

Current-Account Balance + Capital-Account Balance + Official Reserve-Account Balance = 0

However, the specific components of the accounts need not balance. For example, the debit and credit items of the current account need not be equal. Specific components may run either a surplus or a deficit. Nevertheless, because the balance of payments as a whole must balance, a deficit in one area implies an offsetting surplus in other areas. Similarly, even though market forces will bring about an overall balance, there is no reason to expect that the trade flows between any two countries will be in balance. See the accompanying Myths of Economics box feature on this topic.

If a nation is experiencing a current-account deficit, it must experience an offsetting surplus on the sum of its capital-account and official reserve-account balances. This has been the case for the United States in recent years.

In 2012, the United States ran a $475.0 billion current-account deficit and a $105.8 billion capital-account surplus. The difference between these two figures—a $369.2 billion deficit—was exactly offset by a $369.2 billion surplus in the official reserve account. Thus, the deficits and surpluses of the current-, capital-, and official reserve accounts summed to zero as is shown in Exhibit 5 (line 20).

Under a pure flexible rate system, official reserve transactions would be zero. Under these conditions, a capital-account surplus (inflow of capital) would mean that the current account must have a deficit. Similarly, a capital-account deficit (outflow of capital) would mean that the current account must have a surplus.

With flexible exchange rates, changes in the net inflow of capital will influence the current-account balance. If a nation is experiencing an increase in net foreign investment, perhaps as the result of attractive investment opportunities, this increase in the capital-account surplus (inflow of capital) will enlarge the current-account deficit. In contrast, capital flight (outflow of capital) will move the current account toward a surplus.

19-6 EXCHANGE RATES, CURRENT ACCOUNT BALANCE, AND CAPITAL INFLOW

Exhibit 6 presents data on the foreign exchange value of the dollar, current-account balance, and inflow of capital for the United States since 1978. (*Note:* While the data in the

EXHIBIT 6

The Exchange Rate, Current-Account Balance, and Net Foreign Investment

Here, we show the relationship between the exchange rate, the current-account deficit, and net foreign investment (capital inflow). The shaded areas represent recessions.

(a) Exchange-rate value of the dollar (compared with 26 currencies)

(b) Current-account balance as a share of GDP

(c) Net capital inflow as a share of GDP

Note: Data are given in billions of dollars.

Source: http://research.stlouisfed.org/fred2/

MYTHS IN ECONOMICS

"If Other Countries Are Treating Us Fairly, Our Exports to Them Should Be Approximately Equal to Our Imports from Them."

Politicians like to bash countries like Japan and China that export much more to us than they import from us. Some have even called for trade restraints to limit imports from these countries until our exports to and imports from them are brought into balance. This view is based on a misconception about bilateral trade balances. Flexible exchange rates will bring total purchases from foreigners into balance with total sales to them. However, there is no reason to expect that imports and exports with any specific country will be in balance.

Consider the trade "deficits" and "surpluses" of a doctor who likes to golf. The doctor can be expected to run a trade deficit with sporting goods stores, golf caddies, and course operators. Why? These suppliers sell items that the golfer–doctor purchases in sizable quantities. The doctor, on the other hand, probably sells few items the sporting goods store purchases. Similarly, the doctor can be expected to run trade surpluses with medical insurers, elderly patients, and those with chronic illnesses. These trading partners are major purchasers of the services provided by the doctor, although the doctor might purchase very little from them.

The same principles are at work across nations. A nation will tend to run trade deficits with countries that are low-cost suppliers of items it imports and trade surpluses with countries that buy a lot of the things it exports. Japan is a major importer of resources like oil and a major exporter of high-tech manufacturing goods. Americans import a lot of the latter, but they export very little of the former. Similarly, China is a low-cost producer of labor-intensive items like toys and textile products, items that are costly for a high-wage country like the United States to produce domestically. On the other hand, the United States is a low-cost producer of high-tech products and grains like wheat and corn that are purchased only in small quantities by poor countries like China. The bottom line is this: Japan and China are low-cost producers of many items that we import, and the United States is not a major exporter of items imported intensively by Japan and China. Thus, our bilateral trade deficits with them are perfectly understandable.

In recent years, the United States has run trade surpluses with Netherlands, Australia, Belgium, Luxembourg, Brazil, and the United Kingdom. Do these bilateral trade surpluses indicate that the United States treats these countries unfairly? Of course not. The surpluses merely reflect that these countries import substantial amounts of items supplied economically by U.S. producers and export only small amounts of items imported intensively by Americans. It may be good politics to bash those with whom we run bilateral trade deficits, but the argument is nonetheless based on a fallacious view of trade balances between countries.

francxreporter/E+/Getty Images

middle frame are for the current-account balance, the trade balance figures would be virtually identical because trade in goods and services is the dominant component of the current account.) The link between the inflow of capital and the current-account deficit is clearly visible. As the middle and lower panels illustrate, the two are mirror images. When the inflow of capital increases, the current-account (trade) balance shifts toward a deficit. Correspondingly, when net capital inflow shrinks, so, too, does the current-account deficit. This is the expected outcome under a flexible rate system. With flexible rates, the overall payments to and receipts from foreigners must balance. Thus, a deficit in one area is not an isolated event. If a nation runs a current-account (trade) deficit, it must also run a capital-account (plus official reserve account) surplus of equal magnitude.

Prior to 1981, net capital inflow in the United States was relatively small, and so too was the current-account deficit. However, as the U.S. economy grew briskly following the 1982 recession, net capital inflow (bottom panel) in the United States increased sharply. Simultaneously, the U.S. dollar appreciated and the current-account deficit widened. As the U.S. economy slowed during the late 1980s and the recession of the early 1990s, net capital inflow fell to a trickle, and the current account actually registered a small surplus in 1991. But as the U.S. economy recovered from the 1990 recession and grew rapidly during the 1990s, once again net capital inflow increased substantially, the U.S. dollar appreciated, and the current account moved toward a large deficit.

As during the expansions of the 1980s and 1990s, there was also an inflow of capital and a substantial increase in the U.S. current-account deficit during the expansion that began in 2002. However, there was also an important difference. While the dollar appreciated during the two earlier recoveries, it depreciated during the most recent expansion. Furthermore, more than half of the inflow of capital reflects dollar purchases by foreign central banks. In many cases, these purchases were motivated by foreigners' desire to slow the depreciation of the dollar (and the appreciation of their domestic currency). As we noted in Exhibit 1, during 2002–2013, the dollar depreciated by 20 percent against an index of 26 currencies, and the depreciations relative to the euro and Canadian dollar were even greater. Had it not been for the sizable purchases of U.S. Treasury bonds by foreign central banks in recent years, the depreciation of the dollar would surely have been larger.

As Exhibit 6 shows, trade (and current account) deficits are closely linked to the inflow of capital. When foreigners are making more "investments" in a country than the residents of the country are making abroad, a capital account surplus will occur. In turn, the capital account surplus generally leads to a trade (and current account) deficit. In essence, trade (and current-account) deficits are the flip side of capital inflows.

Whether an inflow of capital is good or bad depends on the source of the inflow and how the funds are used. When the inflow of capital occurs because the investment environment of the country is attractive and foreigners are providing the funds for productive investments, this is a positive development. The investments will increase the machines, tools, and other capital assets available to domestic workers, which will increase both their future productivity and earnings. Clearly, trade and current account deficits arising from this source will exert a positive impact on both the country's current and future income.

However, if the inflow of capital is used to increase current consumption or for the finance of unproductive projects, it will reduce future income. In recent years, a substantial portion of the capital inflow to the United States has been used to finance federal budget deficits. This borrowing has made it possible for Americans to consume more today, but the interest expenses will mean less consumption in the future. Moreover, political decision-makers have channeled a large share of these borrowed funds into counterproductive projects and subsidies for favored businesses and interest groups. Use of capital inflow in this manner will reduce the future income of Americans. In addition, as the recent financial troubles of Greece illustrate, when this process is taken to a high level, it can lead to indebtedness to foreigners that will even endanger the creditworthiness of a government.

When considering the significance of the U.S. trade deficit, one should keep two points in mind. First, no legal entity is responsible for the trade deficit. It reflects an aggregation of the voluntary choices of businesses and individuals.[7] Thus, it is not like a business loss or even the budget deficit of a government. Second, to a large degree, the inflow of capital reflects the confidence of investors in both the U.S. economy and the policies of the United States. If either should become less attractive in the future, the situation would change. For example, if the United States continued to run large deficits that push the federal debt to high levels, the confidence of both domestic and foreign investors would diminish. This would lead to a decline in the capital inflow and a reduction in the trade deficit. As the experience of Greece indicates, this is not an attractive way to shift the trade balance toward a surplus.

---

[7]As the late Herbert Stein, a former chair of the President's Council of Economic Advisers, once put it: "The trade deficit does not belong to any individual or institution. It is a pure-statistical aggregate, like the number of eggs laid in the U.S. or the number of bald-headed men living here." See Herbert Stein, "Leave the Trade Deficit Alone," *The Wall Street Journal* (March 11, 1987).

KEY POINTS

- Because countries generally use different currencies, international trade usually involves the conversion of one currency to another. The currencies of different countries are bought and sold in the foreign exchange market. The exchange rate is the price of one national currency in terms of another.

- The dollar demand for foreign exchange arises from the purchase (import) of goods, services, and assets by Americans from foreigners. The supply of foreign currency in exchange for dollars arises from the sale (export) of goods, services, and assets by Americans to foreigners. The equilibrium exchange rate will bring these two forces into balance.

- With flexible exchange rates, the following will cause a nation's currency to appreciate: (1) rapid growth of income abroad (and/or slow domestic growth), (2) low inflation (relative to one's trading partners), (3) rising domestic real interest rates (and/or falling rates abroad), and (4) improvement in the business and investment environment. The reverse of these conditions will cause a nation's currency to depreciate.

- There are three major types of exchange rate regimes: (1) flexible rates; (2) fixed rate, unified currency; and (3) pegged exchange rates. Both flexible rate and fixed rate, unified currency systems work quite well. Pegged rate systems, however, often lead to problems because they require that the nation follow a monetary policy consistent with maintaining the pegged rate. Political pressure often makes this difficult to do.

- The balance-of-payments accounts provide a summary of transactions with foreigners. There are three major balance-of-payments components: (1) the current account, (2) capital account, and (3) the official reserve account. The balances of these three components must sum to zero, but the individual components of the accounts need not be in balance.

- Under a pure flexible rate system, there will be no official reserve-account transactions. Under these circumstances, the current and capital accounts must sum to zero. This implies that an inflow of capital will shift the current account toward a deficit, while an outflow of capital will move the current account toward a surplus.

- Trade deficits are not necessarily bad. Countries that grow rapidly and follow policies that investors find attractive will tend to experience an inflow of capital and a trade deficit. However, if the inflow of capital is used to finance a higher level of current consumption or channeled into unproductive projects, future income will be adversely affected

- There is no reason to expect that bilateral trade between countries will balance. A country will tend to run a bilateral trade deficit with countries that are low-cost producers of items that it imports in large quantities.

CRITICAL ANALYSIS QUESTIONS

1. If the dollar depreciates relative to the Japanese yen, how will this affect the dollar price of a Japanese camera produced by Nikon, for example? How will this change influence the quantity of Nikon cameras purchased by Americans?

2. How will the purchases of items from foreigners compare with the sales of items to foreigners when the foreign exchange market is in equilibrium? Explain.

3. Will a flexible exchange rate bring the imports of goods and services into balance with the exports of goods and services? Why or why not?

4. *The accompanying chart indicates an actual newspaper quotation of the exchange rate of various currencies. On February 2, did the dollar appreciate or depreciate against the British pound? How did it fare against the Canadian dollar?

U.S. DOLLAR EQUIVALENT

	FEBRUARY 1	FEBRUARY 2
British pound	1.755	1.746
Canadian dollar	0.6765	0.6775

5. *Suppose the exchange rate between the United States and Mexico freely fluctuates in the open market. Indicate whether each of the following would cause the dollar to appreciate or depreciate relative to the peso.

   a. an increase in the quantity of drilling equipment purchased in the United States by Pemex, the Mexican oil company, as a result of a Mexican oil discovery

   b. an increase in the U.S. purchase of crude oil from Mexico as a result of the development of Mexican oil fields

   c. higher real interest rates in Mexico, inducing U.S. citizens to move some of their financial investments from U.S. to Mexican banks

   d. lower real interest rates in the United States, inducing Mexican investors to borrow dollars and then exchange them for pesos

   e. inflation in the United States and stable prices in Mexico

   f. an increase in the inflation rate from 2 percent to 10 percent in both the United States and Mexico

   g. an economic boom in Mexico, inducing Mexicans to buy more U.S.-made automobiles, trucks, electric appliances, and manufacturing equipment

   h. attractive investment opportunities in Mexico, inducing U.S. investors to buy stock in Mexican firms

6. Explain why the current-account balance and capital-account balance must sum to zero under a pure flexible rate system.

7. Rapidly growing strong economies often experience trade deficits, whereas economies with sluggish growth often have trade surpluses. Can you explain this puzzle?

8. *In recent years, a substantial share of the domestic capital formation in the United States has been financed by foreign investors. Is this dependence on foreign capital dangerous? What would happen if the inflow of foreign capital came to a halt?

9. *Suppose that the United States were running a current-account deficit. How would each of the following changes influence the size of the current-account deficit?

   a. a recession in the United States

   b. a decline in the attractiveness of investment opportunities in the United States

   c. an improvement in investment opportunities abroad

10. If taxes imposed on personal and corporate income increased substantially in the United States and the monetary policy of the United States was less stable and more inflationary than other countries, how would these policies affect the trade deficit? Why?

11. If foreigners have confidence in the U.S. economy and therefore move to expand their investments in the United States, how will the U.S. current-account balance be affected? How will the exchange-rate value of the dollar be affected?

12. Is a trade surplus indicative of a strong, healthy economy? Why or why not?

13. *"Changes in exchange rates will automatically direct a country to a current-account balance under a flexible exchange rate system." Is this statement true or false?

14. *Several members of Congress have been highly critical of Japan and China because U.S. imports from these countries have persistently been substantially greater than our exports to them.

   a. Under a flexible exchange rate system, is there any reason to expect that the imports from a given country will tend to equal the exports to that country?

   b. Can you think of any reason why the United States might persistently run a trade deficit with these countries?

15. *In recent years, the central banks of both Japan and China have purchased large amounts of U.S. Treasury bonds. These purchases increase the exchange rate value of the dollar relative to the Japanese yen and Chinese yuan. Are these purchases harmful to the U.S. economy? Why or why not?

*Asterisk denotes questions for which answers are given in Appendix B.

PART 5
Core Microeconomics

Microeconomics focuses on the choices of consumers, the operation of firms, the structure of markets, and the choices of resource suppliers and employers.

Consumers are the ultimate judge of both products and business firms. Their choices determine which survive and which fail. The competitive process is highly dynamic. Numerous businesses come and go. Each year, newly incorporated businesses account for approximately 10 percent of the total. However, about 60 percent of the new businesses will fail within the first six years. Microeconomics analyzes the dynamic interaction among consumers, business firms, and resource suppliers, and how it affects the quality of our lives.

CHAPTER 20
Consumer Choice and Elasticity

FOCUS

- What are the fundamental postulates underlying consumer choice?
- How does the law of diminishing marginal utility help explain the law of demand?
- How do the demand curves of individuals translate into a market demand curve?
- What is demand elasticity? What does it measure? Why is it important?

The most famous law in economics, and the one economists are most sure of, is the law of demand. On this law is built almost the whole edifice of economics. —**David R. Henderson**[1]

A thing is worth whatever a buyer will pay for it.
—**Publilius Syrus, first century B.C.**[2]

[1]David R. Henderson, "Demand," in *The Concise Encyclopedia of Economics*, ed. David R. Henderson (http://www.econlib.org/library/CEE.html).

[2]Quoted in Michael Jackman, ed., *Macmillan Book of Business and Economic Quotations* (New York: Macmillan, 1984), 150.

The statement of David Henderson highlights the central position of the law of demand in economics. As Publilius Syrus noted more than 2,000 years ago, demand reflects the willingness of individuals to pay for what is offered in the marketplace. In this section, we begin our examination of microeconomic markets for specific products with an analysis of the demand side of markets. In essence, we will be going "behind" the market demand curve to see how it is made up of individual consumer demands and what factors determine the choices of individual consumers.[3]

20-1 FUNDAMENTALS OF CONSUMER CHOICE

Each of us must decide how to allocate our limited income among the many possible things we would like to buy. The prices of goods, *relative to each other,* are important determining factors. If your favorite cereal doubled in price, would you switch to a different brand? Would your decision be different if all cereals, not just yours, doubled in price? Your choice *between* brands of cereal will be affected only by the change in relative prices. If the prices of all cereals rose by a proportional amount, you might quit purchasing cereal, but this would not give you a strong reason to switch to a different brand. Relative prices measure opportunity cost. If cereal is $5 per box when movie tickets are $10, you must give up two boxes of cereal to purchase one movie ticket.

Several fundamental principles underlie the choices of consumers. Let's take a closer look at the key factors influencing consumer behavior.

1. Limited income necessitates choice. Because of scarcity, we all have limited incomes. The limited nature of our income requires us to make choices about which goods we will and will not buy. When more of one good or service is bought, we must buy less of some other goods if we are to stay within our budget.

2. Consumers make decisions purposefully. The goals that underpin consumer choice can usually be met in alternative ways. If two products cost the same, a consumer will choose to buy the one expected to have the higher benefit. Conversely, if two products yield equal benefits, the consumer will choose to buy the less expensive one. Fundamentally, economics assumes that consumers are rational—that they are able to weigh the costs and benefits of alternative choices.

3. One good can be substituted for another. Consumers can achieve *utility*—that is, satisfaction—from many different alternatives. Either a hamburger or a taco might satisfy your hunger, whereas going either to a movie or to a football game might satisfy your desire for entertainment. With $600, you might either buy a new TV set or take a short vacation. No single good is so precious that some of it will not be given up in exchange for a large enough quantity of other goods. Even seemingly unrelated goods are sometimes substituted one for another. For example, high water prices in Southern California have led residents there to substitute cactus gardens and reduced flow showerheads for water.

4. Consumers must make decisions without perfect information, but knowledge and past experience will help. In Chapter 1, we noted that information is costly to acquire. Asking family and friends, searching through magazines such as *Consumer Reports,* and contacting your local Better Business Bureau are all ways of gathering information about products and potential sellers. The time and effort consumers spend acquiring information will be directly related to the value derived from it. Predictably, consumers will spend more time and money to inform themselves when they are

---

[3]You may want to review the section on demand in Chapter 3 before proceeding with this chapter.

© Tatiana Volgutova/Shutterstock.com

Consumers will seek to spend their income in a manner that will provide them with the maximum value (total utility).

buying "big ticket" items such as automobiles or air-conditioning systems than when they are buying pencils or paper towels.

While no one has perfect foresight, your own experiences—and those of others—will help you make better-informed choices. You have a pretty good idea of what to expect when you buy a cup of coffee and a bagel at your favorite restaurant. Your expectations might not always be fulfilled precisely the same way every time (for example, the coffee may be weak or the bagel too crispy), but even then, you will gain valuable information that will help you project the outcome of future choices more accurately.

5. The law of diminishing marginal utility applies: As the rate of consumption increases, the marginal utility gained from consuming additional units of a good will decline. Utility is a term economists use to describe the subjective personal benefits that result from taking an action. The **law of diminishing marginal utility** states that the **marginal (or additional) utility** derived from consuming successive units of a product will eventually decline as the rate of consumption increases. For example, the law says that even though you might like ice cream, your marginal satisfaction from additional ice cream will eventually decline as you eat more and more of it. Ice cream at lunchtime might be great. An additional helping for dinner might also be good. However, after you have had it for lunch and dinner, another serving as a midnight snack will be less attractive. When the law of diminishing marginal utility sets in, the additional utility derived from still more units of ice cream declines.

The law of diminishing marginal utility explains why, even if you really like a certain product, you will not spend your entire budget on it. As you increase your consumption of any good, the utility you derive from each additional unit will become smaller and smaller, eventually becoming less than the price. At that point, you will not want to purchase any more units of the good.

Law of diminishing marginal utility
The basic economic principle that as the consumption of a product increases, the marginal utility derived from consuming more of it (per unit of time) will eventually decline.

Marginal utility
The additional utility, or satisfaction, derived from consuming an additional unit of a good.

20-2 MARGINAL UTILITY, CONSUMER CHOICE, AND THE DEMAND CURVE OF AN INDIVIDUAL

The law of diminishing marginal utility helps us understand the law of demand and the shape of the demand curve. The height of an individual's demand curve at any specific unit is equal to the maximum price the consumer would be willing to pay for that unit—its **marginal benefit** to the consumer—given the number of units he or she has already purchased. Although marginal benefit is measured in dollars, the dollar amount reflects the opportunity cost of the unit in terms of other goods forgone. If a consumer is willing to pay, at most, $5 for an additional unit of the product, this indicates a willingness to give up, at most, $5 worth of other goods. *Because a consumer's willingness to pay for a unit of a good is directly related to the utility derived from consuming the unit, the law of diminishing marginal utility implies that a consumer's marginal benefit, and thus the height of the demand curve, falls as the quantity consumed increases.*

Exhibit 1 shows this relationship for a hypothetical consumer Jones, relative to her weekly consumption of pizza. Because of the law of diminishing marginal utility, each additional pizza consumed per week will generate less marginal utility for Jones than did the previous pizza. For this reason, Jones's maximum willingness to pay—her marginal benefit—will fall as the quantity consumed increases. In addition, the steepness of Jones's demand curve, or its responsiveness to a change in price—its elasticity—is a reflection of how rapidly Jones's marginal utility diminishes with additional consumption. An individual's demand curve for a good whose marginal value declines more rapidly, will be steeper.

Given what we now know about a consumer's maximum willingness to pay for additional units of a good, we are in a position to discuss how many units the consumer will choose to purchase at various prices. *At any given price, consumers will purchase all units of a good for which their maximum willingness to pay—their marginal benefit—is greater than the price.* They will stop at the point at which the marginal benefit of the next unit would be less than the price. Although there are some problems related to dividing up certain kinds of goods (for example, it is hard to purchase half a car), we can generally say that a consumer will purchase all units of a good up to the point at which the marginal benefit from it equals the price of the good ($MB = P$).

Marginal benefit
The maximum price a consumer will be willing to pay for an additional unit of a product. It is the dollar value of the consumer's marginal utility from the additional unit, and therefore it falls as consumption increases.

EXHIBIT 1

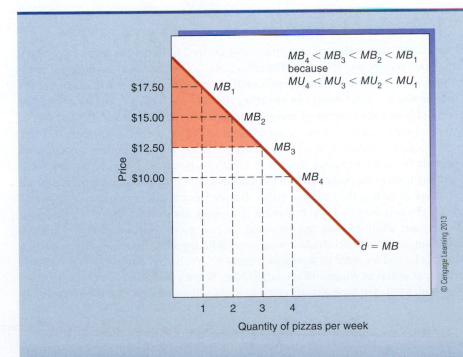

Diminishing Marginal Utility and the Individual's Demand Curve

An individual's demand curve, Jones's demand for personal pizzas in this case, reflects the law of diminishing marginal utility. Because marginal utility (*MU*) falls with increased consumption, so does the consumer's maximum willingness to pay—marginal benefit (*MB*). A consumer will purchase until *MB* = Price, so at a price of $12.50 per pizza, Jones would purchase three pizzas and receive a consumer surplus shown by the shaded triangle.

Returning to Exhibit 1, if the price of pizza were $12.50, Jones would purchase three pizzas per week.[4] Remember from Chapter 3 that consumer surplus is defined as the difference between the maximum price the consumer is willing to pay and the price actually paid, summed over all units consumed. Because the height of the demand curve reflects Jones's maximum willingness to pay for pizza, the shaded triangle that lies above the price shows the total consumer surplus derived from her consumption of the three pizzas. When a consumer has purchased all units to the point at which $MB = P$, total consumer surplus is maximized.

Within this framework, how would a consumer respond to a decrease in the price of a good? The consumer will increase purchases to the point at which marginal benefit diminishes to the level of the new lower price. If marginal utility declines rapidly with consumption, the consumer will expand his or her purchases only slightly. If marginal utility declines less rapidly, it will take a larger expansion in purchases to reach this point. The law of diminishing marginal utility underlies a person's demand curve for a product. The shape and steepness of the curve, for example, depend on his or her marginal utility.

20-2a CONSUMER EQUILIBRIUM WITH MANY GOODS

The last time you were at the mall, you probably saw something that you liked, perhaps a nice shirt. After all, there are many things we would like—many different alternatives that would give us utility. Next, you looked at the price tag: "Fifty dollars, wow! That's too much." What you were really saying was, "I like the shirt, but not as much as the $50 worth of other goods that I would have to give up for it." Consumer choice is a constant comparison of value relative to price. Consider another example: Perhaps you prefer expensive steak to a hamburger. Even if you do, your happiness may often be better served if you buy the hamburger and then spend the savings on something else.

The idea that consumers choose among products by comparing their relative marginal utility (MU) to price (P) can be expressed more precisely. A consumer with a limited amount of income to spend on a group of products is not likely to do the following math, but will act as though he or she had, and will end up consuming a bundle of goods and services such that

$$\frac{MU_A}{P_A} = \frac{MU_B}{P_B} = \cdots = \frac{MU_n}{P_n}$$

In this formula, MU represents the marginal utility derived from the last unit of a product, and P represents the price of the good. The subscripts $_{A, B,\ldots,n}$ indicate the different products available to the consumer. *This formula implies that the consumer will maximize his or her satisfaction (or total utility) by ensuring that the last dollar spent on each good purchased yields an equal degree of marginal utility.* Alternatively stated, the last unit of each item purchased should provide the same marginal utility *per dollar spent on it*. Thus, if the price of a gallon of ice cream is twice as high as the price of a smoothie, the ice cream should provide twice the marginal benefits to justify its purchase. Thus, a consumer will purchase these items to the point at which the marginal utility of the last gallon of ice cream is exactly twice as high as the marginal utility derived from the last smoothie.

Perhaps the best way to grasp this point is to think about what happens when your ratios of marginal utility to price are not equal for two goods. Suppose that you are at a local restaurant eating buffalo chicken wings and drinking Coke. For simplicity, assume that a large Coke and an order of wings each costs $2. With your $10 budget, you decide to purchase four orders of wings and one large Coke. When you finish your Coke, there are still lots of wings left. You have already eaten so many wings, though, that those remaining

---

[4]Jones would certainly purchase the first and second pizzas because $MB > P$. For the third pizza, $MB = P$, so Jones would be indifferent to buying the unit or not purchasing it. For a good that is easily divisible, say, pounds of roast beef, the consumer could continue purchasing up to 2.9999 pounds at a deli counter. Thus, economists are comfortable with simply concluding that the consumer will purchase this final unit, implying that Jones will purchase three pizzas.

do not look as attractive. You could get more utility with fewer wings and another Coke, but it is too late. You have not spent your $10 in a way that gets you the most for your money. Instead of satisfying the preceding condition, you find that the marginal utility of wings is lower than the marginal utility of a Coke, and because they both have the same price ($2), this implies that

$$\frac{MU_{\text{WINGS}}}{P_{\text{WINGS}}} < \frac{MU_{\text{COKE}}}{P_{\text{COKE}}}$$

If you had purchased fewer wings and more Coke, your total utility would have been higher. Consuming the added Coke would have lowered its marginal utility, decreasing the value of the right side of the equation. Simultaneously, spending less on wings would have raised the marginal utility of wings, increasing the value of the left side of the equation. You will maximize your utility—and get the most "bang for the buck" from your budget—when you make these values (the ratios) equal.

The equation can also be used to illustrate the law of demand. Beginning with a situation in which the two sides were equal, suppose that the price of wings increased. It would lower the value of *MU/P* for wings below the *MU/P* for Coke. In response, you would reallocate your budget, purchasing fewer of the more costly wings and more Coke. Thus, we have the law of demand—as the price of wings rises, you will purchase less of them. When people try to spend their money in a way that gives them the greatest amount of satisfaction, the consumer decision-making theory outlined here is difficult to question. In the next section, we will take the theory a little further.

20-2b PRICE CHANGES AND CONSUMER CHOICE

The demand curve or schedule shows the amount of a product that consumers are willing to buy at alternative prices during a specific time period. The law of demand states that the amount of a product bought is inversely related to its price. We have seen how the law of demand can be derived from fundamental principles of consumer behavior. Now, we go further and distinguish two different phenomena underlying a consumer's response to a price change. First, as the price of a product declines, the lower opportunity cost will induce consumers to buy more of it—even if they have to give up some other products, whose price had not fallen. This tendency to substitute a product that has become cheaper for goods that are now relatively more expensive is called the **substitution effect** of a price change.

Second, if a consumer's money income is unchanged, a reduction in the price of a product they consume will increase his or her real income—the amount of goods and services he or she is able to purchase with that fixed amount of money income. If your rent were to decline by $100 per month, for example, that would allow you to buy more of many other goods. This increase in your real income has the same effect as if the rent had remained the same but your income had risen by $100 per month. As a result, this second way in which a price change affects consumption is called the **income effect**. Typically, consumers will respond to the income effect by buying more of the cheaper product and other products as well because they can better afford to do so. Substitution and income effects generally work in the same direction: They both cause consumers to purchase more of a good as its price falls and less of a good as its price rises.[5]

20-2c TIME COSTS AND CONSUMER CHOICE

You may have heard the saying that "time is money." It is certainly true that time has value and that this value can sometimes be measured in dollars. As we have learned, the monetary price of a good is not always a complete measure of its cost to the consumer. Consuming

Substitution effect
That part of an increase (decrease) in amount consumed that is the result of a good being cheaper (more expensive) in relation to other goods because of a reduction (increase) in price.

Income effect
That part of an increase (decrease) in amount consumed that is the result of the consumer's real income being expanded (contracted) by a reduction (rise) in the price of a good.

---

[5]The substitution effect will always work in this direction. The income effect, however, may work in the reverse direction for some types of goods known as inferior goods. These will be addressed later in this chapter.

most goods requires not only money but also time; and time, like money, is scarce to the consumer. So a lower time cost, like a lower money price, will make a product more attractive. For example, one study showed that patients in a dentist's office are willing to pay more than $5 per minute saved to shorten their time spent in waiting rooms.[6] Similarly, fast food and air travel are demanded mainly for the time savings they offer.

Time costs, unlike money prices for goods, differ among individuals. They are higher for people with higher wage rates, for example. Other things being equal, high-wage consumers choose more time-saving commodities than do people with lower time costs and wages. For example, high-wage consumers are overrepresented among airplane and taxicab passengers but underrepresented among television watchers, chess players, and long-distance bus travelers.

Failure to account for time costs can lead to bad decisions. For example, which is cheaper for consumers: (1) waiting in line three hours to purchase a $25 concert ticket or (2) buying the same ticket for $40 without standing in line? A consumer whose time is worth more than $5 per hour will find that $40 without the wait in line is less costly. As you can see, time costs matter. For example, when government-imposed price ceilings (discussed in Chapter 4) create shortages, rationing by waiting occurs. For many consumers, the benefit of the lower price due to the ceiling will be largely, if not entirely, offset by their increased time cost of having to wait in line.

20-2d MARKET DEMAND REFLECTS THE DEMAND OF INDIVIDUAL CONSUMERS

The market demand schedule is the relationship between the market price of a good and the amount demanded by all the individuals in the market area. Because individual consumers purchase less at higher prices, the amount demanded in a market area as a total is also inversely related to price.

Exhibit 2 shows the relationship between individual demand and market demand for a hypothetical two-person market. The individual demand curves for both Jones and Smith are shown. Jones and Smith each consume three pizzas per week at a price of $12.50. The

EXHIBIT 2

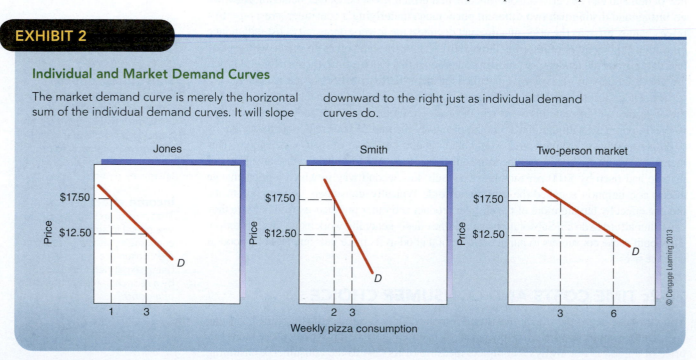

Individual and Market Demand Curves

The market demand curve is merely the horizontal sum of the individual demand curves. It will slope downward to the right just as individual demand curves do.

Jones

Smith

Two-person market

Price

Weekly pizza consumption

© Cengage Learning 2013

[6]Rexford E. Santerre and Stephen P. Neun, *Health Economics: Theories, Insights and Industry Studies* (Orlando, FL: Harcourt, 2000), 113.

amount demanded in the two-person market is six pizzas. If the price rises to $17.50 per pizza, the amount demanded in the market will fall to three pizzas, one demanded by Jones and two by Smith. *The market demand is simply the horizontal sum of the individual demand curves of consumers—in this case, Smith and Jones.*

In the real world, there can be millions of consumers in a market. But the relationship between the demand curves of individuals and the market demand curve will still be just like the one shown in Exhibit 2. At any given price, the amount purchased in the market will be the sum of the amounts purchased by each consumer in the market. Furthermore, the total amount demanded in the market will decline as price increases because individual consumers will purchase fewer units at the higher prices. The market demand curve reflects the collective choices of the individual consumers.

20-3 ELASTICITY OF DEMAND

Although it is important to recognize that consumers will buy less of a product as its price increases, it is also often important to know whether the increase will lead to a large or small reduction in the amount purchased. Economists have designed a tool called the price elasticity of demand to measure this sensitivity of amount purchased in response to a change in price. The equation for the **price elasticity of demand** is as follows:

$$\text{Price elasticity of demand} = \frac{\text{Percentage change in quantity demanded}}{\text{Percentage change in price}} = \frac{\%\Delta Q}{\%\Delta P}$$

This ratio is often called the *elasticity coefficient*. To express it more briefly, we use the notation %ΔQ to represent percentage change in quantity and %ΔP to represent percentage change in price. (The Greek letter delta [Δ] means "change in.") The law of demand states that an increase in a product's price lowers the quantity of it purchased, whereas a decrease in price raises it. *Because a change in price causes the quantity demanded to change in the opposite direction, the price elasticity coefficient is always negative, although economists often ignore the sign and use the absolute value of the coefficient.*

To see how the concept of elasticity works, suppose that the price of the Ford Explorer rises 10 percent, while other prices remain the same. Ford could expect Explorer sales to fall substantially—perhaps 30 percent—as sport-utility vehicle (SUV) buyers respond by switching to other SUVs whose prices have not changed. This strong response by buyers means that the demand for the Explorer is elastic.

Now consider a different situation. Suppose that, because of a new tax, the price of not only the Explorer *but of all new SUVs* rises 10 percent. In this case, consumers' options are much more limited. They can't simply switch to a cheaper close substitute as they could when the price of the Explorer alone rose. They might either simply pay the extra money for a new SUV or settle for a used SUV instead. Because of this, the 10 percent rise in the price of all new SUVs will lead to a smaller consumer response, perhaps a 5 percent decline in sales of new SUVs.

To calculate the elasticity coefficient for the Explorer in the initial example, we begin with the 30 percent decline in quantity demanded and divide it by the 10 percent increase in the price. Thus, the elasticity of demand for the Explorer would be

$$\frac{\%\Delta Q}{\%\Delta P} = \frac{-30\%}{+10\%} = -3$$

(or 3.0 if we ignore the minus sign). This means that the percentage change in quantity demanded is three times the percentage change in price.

To calculate the demand elasticity for *all* SUVs (our second example), we see that the percentage change in quantity, 5 percent, divided by the percentage change in price, 10 percent, gives us −1/2, or −0.5. When it comes to the price elasticity of demand for all SUVs, the percentage change in quantity demanded (using our hypothetical numbers) is

Price elasticity of demand
The percentage change in the quantity of a product demanded divided by the percentage change in the price that caused the change in quantity. The price elasticity of demand indicates how responsive consumers are to a change in a product's price.

only half the percentage change in price, not three times the percentage change in price as it was with the Explorer.

Often, we will have to derive the percentage change in quantity and price. If you know the quantities that will be purchased at two different prices, you can then derive the percentage change in both the price and the quantity. For example, suppose that a price change from P_0 to P_1 causes a change in quantity demanded from Q_0 to Q_1. The change in quantity demanded would therefore be $Q_0 - Q_1$. To calculate the percentage change in quantity, we divide the actual change by the midpoint (or average) of the two quantities.[7] Although it is often easy to find the midpoint without a formula (halfway between $4 and $6 is $5), it can also be found as $(Q_0 + Q_1)/2$. Finally, because 0.05 is simply 5 percent, we multiply by 100. Thus, we can express the percentage change in quantity demanded as

$$\frac{(Q_0 - Q_1)}{[(Q_0 + Q_1)/2]} \times 100$$

Similarly, when the change in price is $P_0 - P_1$, the *percentage* change in price is

$$\frac{(P_0 - P_1)}{[(P_0 + P_1)/2]} \times 100$$

Dividing the resulting percentage change in quantity by the percentage change in price gives us the elasticity.

Using substitution, it is possible to derive a version of the elasticity formula that incorporates these two percentage calculations. Because each term is multiplied by 100 and the denominator of each term contains a 2, these factors cancel out of the final expression. After simplification this version is

$$\frac{[(Q_0 - Q_1)/(Q_0 + Q_1)]}{[(P_0 - P_1)/(P_0 + P_1)]}$$

A numerical example will help you understand this. Suppose that Trina's Cakes can sell fifty specialty cakes per week at $7 each, or it can sell seventy specialty cakes per week at $6 each. The percentage difference in quantity is the difference in the quantity demanded $(50 - 70 = -20)$ divided by the midpoint (60) times 100. The result is a -33.33 percent change in quantity $(-20 \div 60 \times 100 = -33.33)$.

Now that we've calculated the percentage change in quantity demanded of cakes, let's calculate the percentage change in the price. The percentage change in price is the difference in the two prices ($7 - $6 = $1) divided by the midpoint price ($6.50) times 100, or a 15.38 percent change in price $(1 \div 6.5 \times 100 = 15.38)$. Dividing the percentage change in quantity by the percentage change in price $(-33.33 \div 15.38)$ gives an elasticity coefficient of -2.17. Alternatively, we could have expressed this directly as

$$\frac{[(50 - 70)/(50 + 70)]}{[(7 - 6)/(7 + 6)]} = \frac{(-20/120)}{(1/13)} = \frac{(-1/6)}{(1/13)} = \frac{-13}{6} = -2.17$$

The same result is obtained either way. The elasticity of 2.17 (ignoring the sign) indicates that the percentage change in quantity is just over twice the percentage change in price.

The elasticity coefficient lets us make a precise distinction between elasticity and inelasticity. When the elasticity coefficient is greater than 1 (ignoring the sign), as it was for the demand for Trina's Cakes, demand is elastic. When it is less than 1, demand is inelastic. Demand is said to be of *unitary elasticity* if the price elasticity is exactly 1.

---

[7]This formula uses the average of the starting point and the ending point of the change so that it will give the same result whether we start from the lower or the higher price. This arc elasticity formula is not the only way to calculate elasticity, but it is the most frequently used.

20-3a GRAPHIC REPRESENTATION OF PRICE ELASTICITY OF DEMAND

Exhibit 3 presents demand curves of varying elasticity. A demand curve that is completely vertical is said to be *perfectly inelastic*, shown in part (a) of Exhibit 3. In the real world, such demand does not exist because the substitutes for a good become more attractive as the price of that good rises. Moreover, because of the income effect, we should expect that a higher price will always reduce the quantity demanded, other things remaining the same.

EXHIBIT 3

Price Elasticity of Demand

(a) Perfectly inelastic: Despite an increase in a product's price, consumers still purchase the same amount of it. Substitution and income effects prevent this from happening in the real world, though.

(b) Relatively inelastic: A percentage increase in a product's price results in a smaller percentage reduction in its sales. The demand for cigarettes has been estimated to be highly inelastic.

(c) Unit elastic: The percentage change in quantity demanded of a product is equal to the percentage change in its price. A curve with a decreasing slope results. Sales revenue (price times quantity sold) is constant.

(d) Relatively elastic: A percentage increase in a product's price leads to a larger percentage reduction in purchases of it. When good substitutes are available for a product (as in the case of apples), the amount of it purchased will be highly sensitive to price changes.

(e) Perfectly elastic: Consumers will buy all of Farmer Jones's wheat at the market price, but none will be sold above the market price.

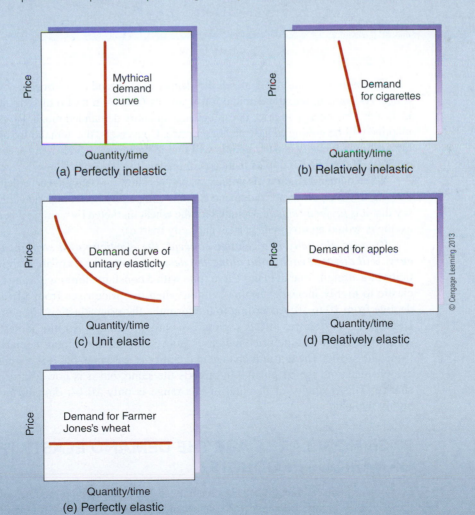

© Cengage Learning 2013

EXHIBIT 4

Slope of the Demand Curve versus Price Elasticity

With this straight-line (constant slope) demand curve, demand is more elastic in the high price range. The formula for elasticity shows that, when price rises from $1 to $2 and quantity falls from 110 to 100, demand is inelastic. A price rise of the same magnitude (but of a smaller percentage), from $10 to $11, leads to a decline in quantity of the same size (but of a larger percentage), so that elasticity is much greater. (Price elasticities are negative, but economists often ignore the sign and look only at the absolute value.)

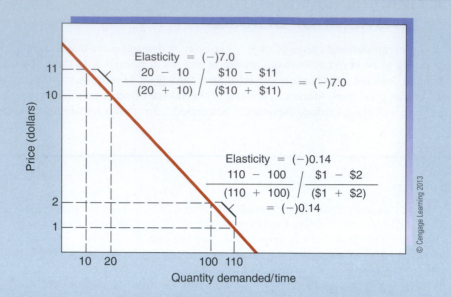

$$\text{Elasticity} = (-)7.0$$
$$\frac{20 - 10}{(20 + 10)} \bigg/ \frac{\$10 - \$11}{(\$10 + \$11)} = (-)7.0$$

$$\text{Elasticity} = (-)0.14$$
$$\frac{110 - 100}{(110 + 100)} \bigg/ \frac{\$1 - \$2}{(\$1 + \$2)}$$
$$= (-)0.14$$

© Cengage Learning 2013

The more inelastic the demand, the steeper the demand curve *over any specific price range.* As you can see, the demand for cigarettes (shown in part b of Exhibit 3) is highly inelastic; a big change in price doesn't change quantity demanded much. People who crave nicotine will be willing to pay the higher price. Conversely, the demand for apples (shown in part d) is relatively elastic. People will find it easy to switch to oranges or bananas, for example, if the price of apples increases dramatically.

When demand elasticity is unitary, as part (c) shows, a demand curve that is convex to the origin will result. When a demand curve is completely horizontal, an economist would say that it is *perfectly elastic.* Demand for the wheat marketed by a single wheat farmer, for example, would approximate perfect elasticity (part e).

Because elasticity is a relative concept, the elasticity of a straight-line demand curve will differ at each point along the demand curve. As Exhibit 4 shows, the elasticity of a straight-line demand curve (one with a constant slope) will range from highly elastic to highly inelastic. In this exhibit, when the price rises from $10 to $11, sales decline from 20 to 10. According to the formula, the price elasticity of demand is −7.0. Demand is very elastic in this region. In contrast, demand is quite inelastic in the $1 to $2 price range. As the price increases from $1 to $2, the amount demanded declines from 110 to 100. The ten-unit change in quantity is the same, but it is a smaller *percentage* change. And the $1 change in price is the same, but it is now a larger *percentage* change. The elasticity of demand in this range is only −0.14; demand in this case is highly inelastic.

20-3b HOW LARGE ARE THE DEMAND ELASTICITIES OF VARIOUS PRODUCTS?

Economists have estimated the price elasticity of demand for many products. As Exhibit 5 shows, the elasticity of demand varies substantially among products. The demand is highly inelastic for several products—salt, toothpicks, matches, coffee, and gasoline (short-run)—in

EXHIBIT 5

Estimated Price Elasticity of Demand for Selected Products

INELASTIC

Salt	– 0.1
Matches	– 0.1
Toothpicks	– 0.1
Airline travel, short run	– 0.1
Gasoline, short run	– 0.2
Gasoline, long run	– 0.7
Residential natural gas, short run	– 0.1
Residential natural gas, long run	– 0.5
Coffee	– 0.25
Fish (cod), consumed at home	– 0.5
Tobacco products, short run	– 0.45
Legal services, short run	– 0.4
Physician services	– 0.6
Dental services	– 0.7
Taxi, short run	– 0.6
Automobiles, long run	– 0.2
Cigarette consumption, long run, Canada	– 0.3

APPROXIMATELY UNITARY ELASTICITY

Movies	– 0.9
Housing, owner occupied, long run	– 1.2
Shellfish, consumed at home	– 0.9
Oysters, consumed at home	– 1.1
Private education	– 1.1
Tires, short run	– 0.9
Tires, long run	– 1.2
Radio and television receivers	– 1.2

ELASTIC

Restaurant meals	– 2.3
Foreign travel, long run	– 4.0
Airline travel, long run	– 2.4
Fresh green peas	– 2.8
Automobiles, short run	– 1.2–1.5
Chevrolet automobiles	– 4.0
Fresh tomatoes	– 4.6
Hospital care in California	– 4.8

Sources: Hendrick S. Houthakker and Lester D. Taylor, *Consumer Demand in the United States, 1929–1970* (Cambridge, MA: Harvard University Press, 1966, 1970); Douglas R. Bohi, *Analyzing Demand Behavior* (Baltimore: Johns Hopkins University Press, 1981); Hsaing-tai Cheng and Oral Capps Jr., "Demand for Fish," *American Journal of Agricultural Economics* 70, no. 3 (1988): 533–42; Rexford E. Santerre and Stephen P. Neun, *Health Economics: Theories, Insights and Industry Studies* (Orlando, FL: Harcourt, 2000); Martin Gaynor and William Vogt, "Competition among Hospitals," *The RAND Journal of Economics* (Winter 2003): 764–85; and Nikolay Gospodinov and Ian Irvine, "A 'Long March' Perspective on Tobacco use in Canada," *Canadian Journal of Economics* 38, no. 2 (2005): 366–93.

their normal price range. In contrast, the demand curves for fresh tomatoes, Chevrolet automobiles, and fresh green peas are highly elastic. The demand for movies, housing, private education, radios, and television sets is near 1.0 (unitary).

20-3c WHY DO THE PRICE ELASTICITIES OF DEMAND VARY?

The primary determinants of a product's price elasticity of demand are the availability of good substitutes and to the share of the typical consumer's total budget expended on a product. Let's consider each of these factors.

Availability of Substitutes   *The most important determinant of the price elasticity of demand is the availability of substitutes. When good substitutes for a product are available, a price increase induces many consumers to switch to other products. Demand is elastic.* For example, if the price of apples increases consumers might substitute oranges or bananas.

When good substitutes for a product are unavailable, the demand for it will tend to be inelastic. Medical services are an example. When we are sick, most of us find witch doctors, faith healers, palm readers, and aspirin to be highly imperfect substitutes for the services of a physician. Not surprisingly, the demand for physician services is inelastic.

The availability of substitutes increases as the product class becomes more specific, thus increasing price elasticity. For example, as Exhibit 5 shows, the price elasticity of Chevrolets, a narrow product class, exceeds that of the broad class of automobiles in general. If the price of Chevrolets alone rises, many substitute cars are available. But if the prices of all automobiles rise together, consumers have fewer good substitutes.

Product's Share of the Consumer's Total Budget If the expenditures on a product are quite small relative to the consumer's budget, the income effect will be small even if there is a substantial increase in the price of the product. This will make demand less elastic. Compared to one's total budget, expenditures on some commodities are minor. Matches, toothpicks, and salt are good examples. Most consumers spend less than a couple of dollars per year on each of these items. A doubling of their price would exert little influence on a family's budget. Therefore, even if the price of such a product were to rise sharply, consumers would still not find it worthwhile to spend much time and effort looking for substitutes.

Exhibit 6 provides a graphic illustration of both elastic and inelastic demand curves. In part (a), the demand curve for fast-food hamburgers is elastic because there are good substitutes—for example, tacos, burritos, salads, chicken, and other sandwiches. Therefore, when the price of the hamburgers increases from $4.00 to $6.00, the quantity purchased declines sharply from 100 million to only 25 million. The calculated price elasticity equals –3.0. The fact that the absolute value of the coefficient is greater than 1 confirms that the demand for hamburgers is elastic over the price range shown.

Part (b) of Exhibit 6 shows the demand curve for cigarettes. Because most smokers do not find other products to be a good substitute, the demand for cigarettes is highly inelastic. As the price of cigarettes increases from $4.00 to $6.00, the number of packs purchased falls by only a small amount (from 100 million to 90 million). The price elasticity coefficient is –0.26, substantially less in absolute value than 1, confirming that the demand for cigarettes is inelastic. (*Exercise:* Use the price elasticity formula to verify the values of these elasticity coefficients.)

EXHIBIT 6

Inelastic and Elastic Demand

As the price of fast-food hamburgers (a) rose from $4 to $6, the quantity purchased fell sharply from 100 million to 25 million. The percentage reduction in quantity is larger than the percentage increase in price. Thus, the demand for the hamburgers is

elastic. In contrast, an increase in the price of cigarettes from $4 to $6 leads to only a small reduction in the number of packs purchased (b). Because the percentage reduction in quantity is smaller than the percentage increase in price, demand is inelastic.

(a) Half-pound hamburgers per week (in millions)

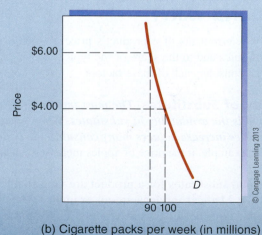

(b) Cigarette packs per week (in millions)

© Cengage Learning 2013

20-3d TIME AND DEMAND ELASTICITY

As changing market conditions raise or lower the price of a product, both consumers and producers will respond. However, the response will not be instantaneous, and it is likely to become larger over time. *In general, when the price of a product increases, consumers will reduce their consumption by a larger amount in the long run than in the short run. Thus, the demand for most products will be more elastic in the long run than in the short run. This relationship between elasticity and the length of the adjustment period is sometimes referred to as the second law of demand.*

The first law of demand says that buyers will respond predictably to a price change, purchasing more when the price is lower than when the price is higher, if other things remain the same. The second law of demand says that the response of buyers will be greater after they have had time to adjust more fully to a price change.

20-4 HOW DEMAND ELASTICITY AND PRICE CHANGES AFFECT TOTAL EXPENDITURES (OR REVENUES) ON A PRODUCT

By looking at demand elasticity, we can determine changes in total consumer spending on a product when its price changes. We can do this in three different ways: by looking at (1) changes in an individual's total spending, using the demand elasticity from his or her demand curve for the product; (2) changes in the total combined spending of all consumers, using the elasticity from the total market demand curve; or (3) changes in total consumer spending on the product, using the demand curve facing the firm that produces it. This third method allows us to look at elasticity based not on what consumers spend, but on what the producer receives from selling the product.

Total expenditures (or revenues) simply amount to the price of the product times the number of units of it purchased (or sold). Because total expenditures are equal to the price times the quantity, and because the price and the quantity move in opposite directions, the net effect of a price change on the total spending on a product depends on whether the (percentage) price change or the (percentage) quantity change is greater.

CHANGE IN TOTAL EXPENDITURES	=	PRICE	×	QUANTITY
?	=	↑	×	↓
?	=	↓	×	↑

When demand is inelastic, the price elasticity coefficient is less than 1. This means that the percentage change in price is greater than the percentage change in quantity. *Therefore, when demand is inelastic, the change in the price will dominate and, as a result, the price and total expenditures will change in the same direction.* In other words, when the price of an inelastic product (say, cigarettes) increases, spending on it will increase, too—and vice versa. Conversely, when demand is elastic, the change in quantity will be greater than the change in the price. *As a result, the impact of the change in quantity will dominate, and therefore the price and expenditures will move in opposite directions.* In other words, when the price of a product with an elastic demand (say, fast-food hamburgers) increases, spending on it will decrease.

When demand elasticity is unitary, the change in quantity demanded will be equal in magnitude to the change in price. With regard to their impact on total expenditures, these two effects will exactly offset each other. *Thus, when price elasticity of demand is equal to 1, total expenditures will remain unchanged as price changes.*

EXHIBIT 7

Demand Elasticity and How Changes in Price Affect Total Consumer Expenditures or a Firm's Total Revenue

PRICE ELASTICITY OF DEMAND	NUMERICAL ELASTICITY COEFFICIENT (IN ABSOLUTE VALUE)	IMPACT OF RAISING PRICE ON TOTAL CONSUMER EXPENDITURES OR A FIRM'S TOTAL REVENUE	IMPACT OF LOWERING PRICE ON TOTAL CONSUMER EXPENDITURES OR A FIRM'S TOTAL REVENUE
Elastic	1 to ∞	decrease	increase
Unit Elastic	1	unchanged	unchanged
Inelastic	0 to 1	increase	decrease

© Cengage Learning 2013

Exhibit 7 summarizes the relationship between changes in the price of a product and changes in total spending on it when demand is elastic, inelastic, and unit elastic. The demand curves shown in Exhibit 6 can also be used to show the link between elasticity and changes in total spending. When the price of cigarettes (part b), increases from $4.00 to $6.00, the price elasticity of demand is 0.26, indicating that demand is inelastic. This increase in cigarette prices leads to an increase in spending on the product from $400 million ($4.00 × 100 million units) to $540 million ($6.00 × 90 million units). If the change had occurred in the opposite direction, with the price falling from $6.00 to $4.00, total expenditures would have declined.

The price elasticity of demand for fast-food hamburgers when the price increases from $4.00 to $6.00 (part a of Exhibit 6) is 3.0, indicating that demand is elastic. In this case, price and expenditures will move in opposite direction. The increase in the price of hamburgers lowers total consumer spending on the product from $400 million ($4.00 × 100 million hamburgers) to $150 million ($6.00 × 25 million hamburgers). If the price change had been in the opposite direction, with the price falling from $6.00 to $4.00, total expenditures would have risen.

When a firm increases the price of its product, its revenues may rise, fall, or remain the same. If the demand for the firm's product is inelastic, the higher price will expand the firm's total revenue. However, if the demand for the firm's product is elastic, a price increase will lead to substantially lower sales and a decline in total revenue. In the case of unitary elasticity, the price increase will leave total revenue unchanged.

Beyond the price elasticity of demand, two other elasticity relationships are important. We therefore end this chapter with a brief discussion of income elasticity of demand and price elasticity of supply.

Income elasticity
The percentage change in the quantity of a product demanded divided by the percentage change in consumer income that caused the change in quantity demanded. It measures the responsiveness of the demand for a good to a consumer's change in income.

Normal good
A good that has a positive income elasticity, so that as consumer income rises, demand for the good rises, too.

20-5 INCOME ELASTICITY

Increases in consumer income will increase the demand (the quantity demanded at each price) for most goods. Income elasticity tells us how responsive the demand for a product is to income changes. **Income elasticity** is defined as

$$\text{Income elasticity} = \frac{\text{Percentage change in quantity demanded}}{\text{Percentage change in income}}$$

As Exhibit 8 shows, although the income elasticity coefficients for products vary from one good to another, they are normally positive. In fact, the term **normal good** refers to any good with a positive income elasticity of demand. Some normal goods have lower income elasticities than others, however. In general, goods that people

Estimated Income Elasticity of Demand for Selected Products

LOW-INCOME ELASTICITY		HIGH-INCOME ELASTICITY	
Margarine	−0.20	Private education	2.46
Fuel	0.38	New cars	2.45
Electricity	0.20	Recreation and amusements	1.57
Fish (haddock)	0.46	Alcohol	1.54
Food	0.51		
Tobacco	0.64		
Hospital care	0.69		

Sources: Hendrick S. Houthakker and Lester D. Taylor, *Consumer Demand in the United States, 1929–1970* (Cambridge, MA: Harvard University Press, 1966); L. Taylor, "The Demand for Electricity: A Survey," *Bell Journal of Economics* 6, no. 1 (1975): 74–110; F. W. Bell, "The Pope and the Price of Fish," *American Economic Review* 58, no. 5 (1968): 1346–50; and Rexford E. Santerre and Stephen P. Neun, *Health Economics: Theories, Insights and Industry Studies* (Orlando, FL: Harcourt, 2000).

regard as "necessities" will have low income elasticities (between 0 and 1). Significant quantities are purchased even at low incomes, and, as income increases, spending on these items will increase by less than a proportional amount. It is understandable that items such as fuel, electricity, bread, tobacco, economy clothing, and potatoes have a low income elasticity.

Goods that consumers regard as "luxuries" generally have a high (greater than 1) income elasticity. For example, private education, new automobiles, swimming pools, and vacation travel are all highly income-elastic. As the consumer's income increases, the demand for these goods expands even more rapidly, and therefore spending on these items increases as a proportion of income.

A few commodities, such as margarine, low-quality meat cuts, and bus travel, actually have a negative income elasticity. Economists refer to goods with a negative income elasticity as **inferior goods**. As income expands, the demand for inferior goods will decline. Conversely, as income declines, the demand for inferior goods will increase.

Inferior good
A good that has a negative income elasticity, so that as consumer income rises, the demand for the good falls.

20-6 PRICE ELASTICITY OF SUPPLY

The **price elasticity of supply** is the percentage change in quantity supplied, divided by the percentage change in the price causing the supply response. Because this measures the responsiveness of sellers to a change in price, it is analogous to the price elasticity of demand. However, the price elasticity of supply will be positive because the quantity producers are willing to supply is directly related to price. As in demand elasticity, time plays a role. In the next two chapters, we will discuss more fully the factors that determine supply elasticity. For now, it is important simply to recognize the concept of supply elasticity and the fact that suppliers (like buyers) will be more responsive to a price change when they have had more time to adjust to it.

Price elasticity of supply
The percentage change in quantity supplied, divided by the percentage change in the price that caused the change in quantity supplied.

LOOKING AHEAD Market demand indicates how strongly consumers desire a good or service. In the following chapter, we will turn to a firm's costs of production—costs that arise because resources are demanded for alternative uses. These two topics—consumer demand and the cost of production—are central to understanding how markets work and the conditions necessary for the efficient allocation of resources.

KEY POINTS

- Consumers will try to allocate their limited incomes among a multitude of goods in a way that maximizes their utility. The role of relative prices, information, and preferences, as well as the law of diminishing marginal utility, help explain the choices consumers make and the downward slope of a person's demand curve for products.

- The market demand curve for a product is the horizontal sum of the demand curve of the individuals for the product.

- The price elasticity of demand measures the responsiveness of the quantity of a product purchased to a change in its price.

- The availability of substitutes is the primary determinant of the price elasticity of demand for a product. When there are good substitutes available, and the item is a sizable component of the consumer's budget, its demand will tend to be elastic. When only poor substitutes are available, demand will tend to be inelastic.

- Typically, the price elasticity of a product will increase as consumers have had more time to adjust to a change in its price. This direct relationship between the size of the elasticity coefficient and the length of the adjustment period is often referred to as the *second law of demand*.

- The concept of elasticity helps us determine how a change in price will affect total consumer expenditures on a product or a firm's total revenues derived from it. When the demand for a product is elastic, a price change will cause total spending on it to change in the opposite direction. When demand for a product is inelastic, a change in price will cause total spending on it to change in the same direction.

- The concept of elasticity can also be applied to consumer income (which is called the income elasticity of demand) and supply (which is called the price elasticity of supply).

CRITICAL ANALYSIS QUESTIONS

1. Suppose that, in an attempt to raise more revenue, Nowhere State University (NSU) increases its tuition. Will this necessarily result in more revenue? Under what conditions will revenue (a) rise, (b) fall, or (c) remain the same? Explain this, focusing on the relationship between the increased revenue from students who enroll at NSU despite the higher tuition and the lost revenue from lower enrollment. If the true price elasticity were –1.2, what would you suggest the university do to expand revenue?

2. *A bus ticket between two cities costs $150 and the trip will take 25 hours, whereas an airplane ticket costs $450 and takes five hours. Kathy values her time at $12 per hour, and Rachel values her time at $18 per hour. Will Kathy take the bus or the plane? Which will Rachel take? Explain.

3. *Recent research confirms that the demand for cigarettes is not only inelastic, but it also indicates that smokers with incomes in the lower half of all incomes respond to a given price increase by reducing their purchases by amounts that are more than four times as large as the purchase reductions made by smokers in the upper half of all incomes. How can the income and substitution effects of a price change help explain this finding?

4. A consumer is currently purchasing three pairs of jeans and five T-shirts per year. The price of jeans is $30, and T-shirts cost $10. At the current rate of consumption, the marginal utility of jeans is 60, and the marginal utility of T-shirts is 30. Is this consumer maximizing his or her utility? Would you suggest that he buy more jeans and fewer T-shirts, or more T-shirts and fewer jeans?

5. When residential electricity in the state of Washington cost about half as much as in nearby Montana, the average household in Washington used about 1,200 kilowatt-hours per month, whereas Montanans used about half that much per household. Do these data provide us with two points on the average household's demand curve for residential electricity in this region? Why or why not?

6. *People who are wealthy are widely believed to have more leisure time than people who are poor. However, even though we are a good deal wealthier today than our great-grandparents were 100 years ago, we appear to live more hectic lives and have less free time. Can you explain why?

7. What are the major determinants of a product's price elasticity of demand? Studies indicate that the demand for Florida oranges, Bayer aspirin, watermelons, and airfares to Europe are elastic. Why?

8. Most systems of medical insurance substantially lower the out-of-pocket costs consumers have to pay for additional units of physician services and hospitalization. Some reduce these costs to zero. How does this method of payment affect the consumption levels of medical services? Might this method of organization result in "too much" consumption of medical services? Discuss.

9. Are the following statements true or false? Explain your answers.

   a. A 10 percent reduction in price that leads to a 5 percent increase in the amount purchased indicates a price elasticity of more than 1.

b. A 10 percent reduction in price that leads to a 2 percent increase in total expenditures (or total revenue) indicates a price elasticity of more than 1.

c. If the percentage change in price is less than the resultant percentage change in quantity demanded, demand is inelastic.

10. *Respond to the following questions: If you really like pizza, should you try to consume as much pizza as possible? If you want to succeed, should you try to make the highest possible grade in your economics class?

11. *Sue loves ice cream but cannot stand frozen-yogurt desserts. In contrast, Carole likes both foods and can hardly tell the difference between the two. Who will have the more elastic demand for yogurt?

12. *Jill's Sausage Dog Stand projects the following demand for Jill's sausage dogs:

PRICE ($)	QUANTITY PURCHASED (per day)
2	50
4	40
6	20

a. Calculate the price elasticity of demand between $2 and $4. Is demand in this range elastic or inelastic?

b. Calculate the price elasticity of demand between $4 and $6. Is demand in this range elastic or inelastic?

13. Suppose John, the owner-manager of a local hotel projects the following demand for his rooms:

PRICE ($)	QUANTITY PURCHASED (per Night)
90	100
110	90
130	70

a. Calculate the price elasticity of demand between $90 and $110.

b. Is the price elasticity of demand between $90 and $110 elastic, unit elastic, or inelastic?

c. Will John's total revenue rise if he increases the price from $90 to $110?

d. Calculate the price elasticity of demand between $110 and $130.

e. Is the price elasticity of demand between $110 and $130 elastic, unit elastic, or inelastic?

f. Will John's total revenue rise if he increases the price from $110 to $130?

*Asterisk denotes questions for which answers are given in Appendix B.

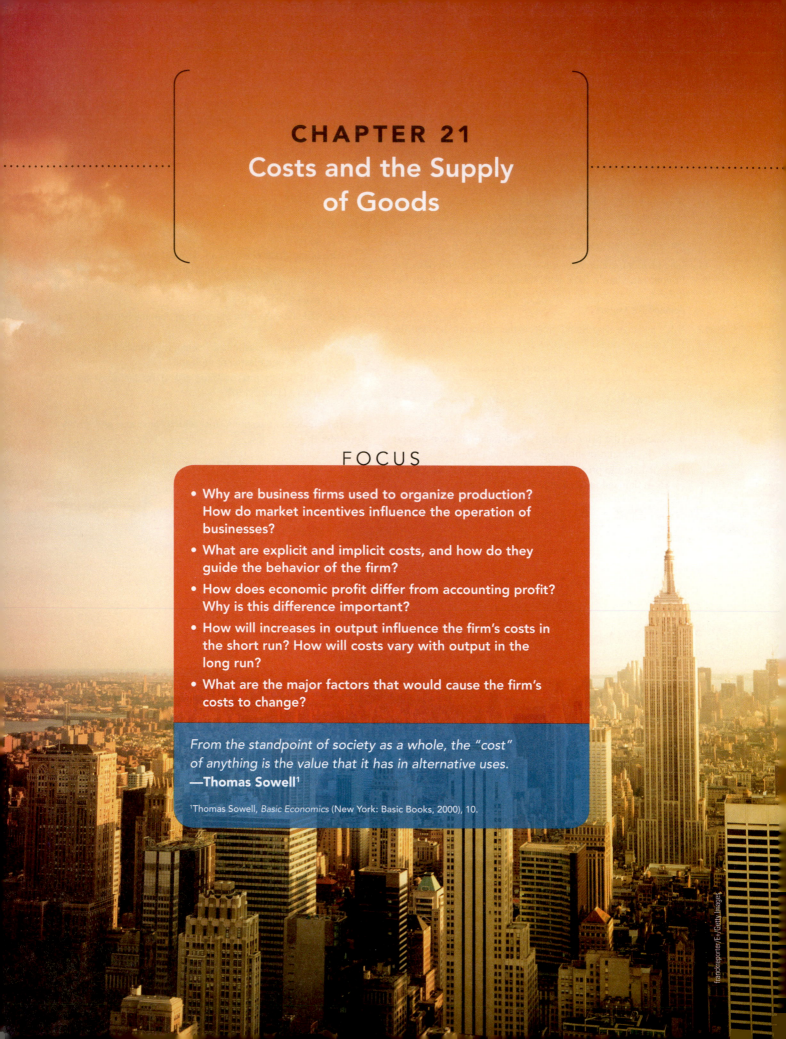

CHAPTER 21
Costs and the Supply of Goods

FOCUS

- Why are business firms used to organize production? How do market incentives influence the operation of businesses?

- What are explicit and implicit costs, and how do they guide the behavior of the firm?

- How does economic profit differ from accounting profit? Why is this difference important?

- How will increases in output influence the firm's costs in the short run? How will costs vary with output in the long run?

- What are the major factors that would cause the firm's costs to change?

From the standpoint of society as a whole, the "cost" of anything is the value that it has in alternative uses.
—**Thomas Sowell**[1]

[1]Thomas Sowell, *Basic Economics* (New York: Basic Books, 2000), 10.

Demand and supply interact to determine the market price of a product. In the preceding chapter, we showed that the demand for a product reflects the strength of consumer desire for that product. In this chapter, we will focus on the cost of production. The resources needed to produce one good could be used to produce other goods instead. As Thomas Sowell says in the quotation that begins this chapter, the cost to society of anything is the value that it has in alternative uses. The market price for resources makes that cost clear to producers as they must bid resources away from alternative uses. The maker of soccer balls, for example, must compete against producers of other goods whe. the machines, raw materials, and labor produce the balls.

Costs carry an important message: T producers the value of the resources if le their alternative uses. If the per-unit cos producing a good exceeds its price, produ ers will suffer losses, reduce output, and some may go out of business. Only when a producer can generate enough value for consumers to allow the price to exceed production costs, will the firm be profitable and survive. This chapter lays the foundation for a detailed investigation of the links between costs, business output, and market supply.

21-1 THE ORGANIZATION OF THE BUSINESS FIRM

The business firm is an entity designed to organize raw materials, labor, and machines with the goal of producing goods and/or services. Firms (1) purchase productive resources from households and other firms, (2) transform them into a different commodity, and (3) sell the transformed product or service to consumers. In market economies, business firms choose their own price, output level, and methods of production. They not only reap the benefits of sales revenues, but they also must pay the costs of the resources they use.

21-1a INCENTIVES, COOPERATION, AND THE NATURE OF THE FIRM

In privately owned firms, owners risk their wealth on the success of the business. If the firm is successful and earns profits, these financial gains go to the owners. Conversely, if the firm suffers losses, the owners must bear the consequences.

The property right of owners to the residual income of the firm plays a very important role: It provides owners with a strong incentive to organize and operate their business in a manner that will maximize the value of their output to consumers while keeping the cost of producing output low. The wealth of these **residual claimants** is directly influenced by the success or failure of the firm. Thus, they have both the authority and a strong incentive to see that resources under their direction are used efficiently and directed toward production of goods that are valued more highly than their costs.

There are two ways of organizing productive activity: contracting and **team production**. In principle, all production could be accomplished solely through contracting. For example, a builder might have a house built by contracting with one person to pour the concrete, another to construct the wooden part of the house, a third to install the roofing, a fourth to do the electrical wiring, and so on. No employees would have to be involved in such a project. More commonly, though, goods and services are produced with some combination of contracting and the use of team production.

Team production involves the employment of workers operating under the supervision of the owner, or the owner's representative—a manager. While team production can often reduce transaction costs, it leads to another set of problems. Team members—the employees working for the firm—must be monitored and given incentives to avoid **shirking**, or working at less than the expected rate of productivity. Taking long work breaks, paying more attention to their own convenience than to work results, and wasting time when diligence is called for are examples of shirking. Hired managers, even including those at the top, must be monitored and given incentives to avoid shirking.

Residual claimants
Individuals who personally receive the excess, if any, of revenues over costs. Residual claimants gain if the firm's costs are reduced or revenues increase.

Team production
A production process in which employees work together under the supervision of the owner or the owner's representative.

Shirking
Working at less than the expected rate of productivity, which reduces output. Shirking is more likely when workers are not monitored, so that the cost of lower output falls on others.

Imperfect monitoring and imperfect incentives are always a problem with team production. It is part of a larger class of what economists call **principal–agent problems**. If you have ever taken a car to an auto mechanic, you have confronted this problem. The mechanic wants to get the job done quickly and make as much money as possible. The car owner not only wants to get the job done quickly also, but wants the problem fixed in a lasting way, at the lowest possible cost. Because the mechanic typically knows far more about the job than the customer, it is hard for the customer to monitor the mechanic's work. Therefore, the mechanic (the agent) may not act in the best interest of the customer (the principal).

The owner of a firm is in a similar situation. It is often difficult to monitor the performance of individual employees and motivate them to work together productively. If it is going to keep costs low and the value of output high, a firm must discover and adopt an incentive structure that motivates executives, managers, and workers to cooperate productively and discourages shirking. An effective incentive structure will align the costs and benefits faced by employees making decisions with those of the firm as a whole. Ultimately, it is the job of the owners, as residual claimants, to develop an effective incentive structure that will minimize the principal–agent problem.

21-1b THREE TYPES OF BUSINESS FIRMS

Business firms can be organized in one of three primary ways: as a proprietorship, a partnership, or a corporation. The structure chosen determines how the owners share the risks and liabilities of the firm and how they participate in making decisions.

A **proprietorship** is a business firm owned by a single individual who is fully liable for the debts of the firm. In addition to assuming the responsibilities of ownership, the proprietor often works directly for the firm, providing managerial and other labor services. Many small businesses, including restaurants, barbershops, and farms, are business proprietorships. As **Exhibit 1** shows, proprietorships account for 72 percent of the business firms in the United States. Because most proprietorships are small, however, they account for only 4 percent of all business revenues.

A **partnership** consists of two or more people who are co-owners of a business firm. The partners share risks and responsibilities in an agreed-upon manner. There is no difference between a proprietorship and a partnership in terms of owner liability. In both cases, the owners are fully liable for all business debts incurred by the firm. Many law, medical,

Proprietorship
A business firm owned by an individual who possesses the ownership right to the firm's profits and is personally liable for the firm's debts.

Partnership
A business firm owned by two or more individuals who possess ownership rights to the firm's profits and are personally liable for the debts of the firm.

EXHIBIT 1

How Business Firms Are Organized

Nearly three out of every four firms are proprietorships, but only 4 percent of all business revenue is generated by proprietorships. Corporations account for about one out of every five firms but generate 82 percent of all revenues.

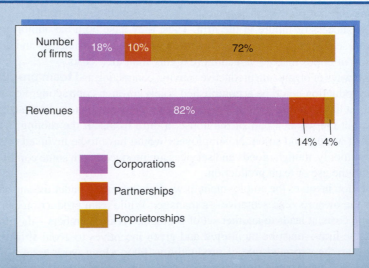

Source: *Statistics of Income Tax Stats Integrated Business Data*, Internal Revenue Service, Table 1. (Data are for 2008.)

and accounting firms are organized along partnership lines. However, this form of business structure accounts for only 10 percent of the total number of firms and 14 percent of all business revenues.

The business firms that are **corporations** account for 82 percent of total business revenue, even though they constitute only 18 percent of all firms. What accounts for the attractiveness of this business structure? From its start, by an act of the British Parliament in 1862, the corporation, or "joint stock company," as it is also called, grew in importance for two main reasons. First, although the stockholders of the corporation are the legal owners, their liability is limited to the value of their shares of the corporation. If a corporation owes you money, you cannot directly sue the stockholders. Of course, you can sue the corporation. However, if a corporation goes bankrupt, you and others to whom the firm owes money may simply be out of luck. This limited liability makes it possible for corporations to attract investment funds from a large number of "owners" who do not participate in the day-to-day management of the firm.

Second, ownership can easily be transferred under the corporate structure. The shares, or ownership rights, of an owner who dies can be sold by the heirs to another owner without disrupting the business firm. Because of this, the corporation is an ongoing concern. Similarly, stockholders who become unhappy with the way a corporation is run can bail out simply by selling their stock.

While there are advantages to the corporate form of business organization, large corporations with many stockholders—millions in some cases—are also more likely to suffer from principal–agent problems. The stockholders elect a board of directors, which in turn appoints the company's high-level managers. Internal corporate policies and competition for control of the firm by outsiders can be used to reduce these principal–agent problems.

Another disadvantage of the corporate form of business organization is higher taxation. While the incomes of sole proprietors and partnerships are taxed as ordinary personal income, the income of corporations is taxed twice—once as corporate income and again as personal income when it accrues to the owners in the form of dividends or capital gains. Since 1977, an increasing number of states allow a hybrid form of business organization called the *limited liability company* (LLC), which combines the advantages of limited liability of a corporation but the tax advantages of a sole proprietorship or partnership.

21-2 HOW WELL DOES THE CORPORATE STRUCTURE WORK?

Do corporations serve the interests of consumers? Are corporate managers in a position to serve themselves at the expense of their customers and stockholders? When thinking about these questions, keep three points in mind.

First, in a market economy, firms must compete for investment funds and for customers. Investors are free to buy and sell the shares of corporations. Similarly, consumers are free to choose among firms, including both corporate and noncorporate businesses. This competitive process greatly limits the ability of managers to benefit personally at the expense of either customers or stockholders. If a business firm is not managed in a manner that serves the interests of both its shareholders and customers, they will choose other options. Moreover, investor-driven changes in a company's stock price and consumer-driven changes in sales revenue provide channels through which managerial performance can be judged, and managers can be held accountable, by shareholders and the board of directors.

Second, the compensation of managers can be structured in a manner that will bring their interests into harmony with those of the shareholder-owners. This is generally the case. The salary increases and bonuses of most high-level managers are directly related to the firm's profitability and the price of its shares. In recent years, salaries have constituted only about 10 percent of the compensation of chief executive officers (CEOs). The other 90 percent has been in the form of bonuses, often stock awards and stock options (the right to buy shares at a certain price) related to company performance.

Corporation
A business firm owned by shareholders who possess ownership rights to the firm's profits, but whose liability is limited to the amount of their investment in the firm.

Corporate managers have a strong incentive to serve the interests of customers and stockholders because of the following: competition for investment funds and consumer sales, the linkage of their compensation to company performance, and the threat of takeover if the company is run poorly.

Third, the threat of corporate takeover helps keep current managers from straying too far from a profit-maximization strategy. Managers who do not serve the interests of their shareholders leave the firm vulnerable to a takeover, a move by an outside person or group to gain control of the firm. Poor management will cause market value of the firm's stock to decline, making it an attractive prospect for takeover specialists shopping for a poorly run business, the value of which could be substantially increased by a new and better management team.

The prevalence of the corporate form of business organization provides strong evidence that it is an effective form of business organization in many sectors of the economy. Rival forms of business organization, including proprietorships, partnerships, consumer cooperatives, employee ownership, and mutually owned companies, can and do compete in the marketplace for investment funds and customers. Nonetheless, the corporate structure is the dominant form of business organization (see Exhibit 1). If the corporation was not generally a cost-efficient and consumer-sensitive form of organization, this would not be the case.

21-3 THE ECONOMIC ROLE OF COSTS

Consumers would like to have more economic goods, but resources to produce them are scarce. How much of each desired good should be produced? In a market economy, consumer demand and production costs are central to performing this balancing function. *The demand for a product represents the voice of consumers instructing firms to produce the good. Conversely, a firm's costs represent the desire of consumers not to sacrifice goods that could be produced if the same resources were employed elsewhere.* A profit-seeking firm will try to produce only those units of output for which buyers are willing to pay full cost. Proper measurement and interpretation of costs by the firm are critical to both the firm's profitability and its efficient use of resources.

21-3a CALCULATING ECONOMIC COSTS AND PROFITS

Profit directs the actions of business firms. Profit is simply the firm's total revenue minus its total costs. But to calculate profit correctly, costs must be measured properly. Most people think of costs as amounts paid for raw materials, labor, machines, and similar inputs. However, this concept of cost, which stems from accounting procedures, excludes some important components.

The key to understanding the economist's concept of profit is to remember the idea of *opportunity cost*—the highest valued alternative forgone by the resource owner when the resource is used. These costs may be either explicit or implicit. **Explicit costs** result when the firm makes a monetary payment to resource owners. Money wages, interest, and rental payments are a measure of what the firm gives up to employ the services of labor and capital resources. These are relatively easy to track. But firms also incur **implicit costs**—those associated with the use of resources owned by the firm. For example, the owners of small proprietorships often work for their own businesses, for little or no pay. These businesses incur an implicit cost—an opportunity cost—associated with the use of this resource (the owners' labor services). The highest valued alternative forgone in this case is the maximum amount of money the owners could have earned doing something else. The **total cost** of production is the sum of these explicit and implicit costs incurred by the employment of all resources involved in the production process.

Accounting statements also generally omit the implicit cost of equity capital—the cost of funds supplied by the firm's owners. If a firm borrows financial capital from a bank or other private source, it will have to pay interest. Accountants properly record this interest expense as a cost. In contrast, when the firm acquires financial capital by issuing shares of stock, accountants don't record this as an expense. Essentially, this is because the stockholders *are* the firm's owners. Either way, acquiring capital has an opportunity cost. Banks will demand interest payments, and shareholders will expect a return from their investment in the form of dividend payments or rising share value.

Economists use the normal return on financial capital as a basis for determining the implicit **opportunity cost of equity capital**. If the normal rate of return on financial capital is 10 percent, for example, investors will not continue to supply equity capital unless they can earn this normal return. Thus, it is an opportunity cost of equity capital.

21-3b HOW DO ECONOMIC AND ACCOUNTING PROFIT DIFFER?

Economic profit is total revenues minus total costs, including both the explicit and implicit cost components. Economic profit will be positive only if the earnings of the business exceed the opportunity cost of all the resources used by the firm, *including the opportunity cost of assets owned by the firm and any unpaid labor services supplied by the owner.* In contrast, economic losses result when the earnings of the firm are insufficient to cover explicit and implicit costs. That is why the **normal profit rate** is zero economic profit, yielding just the competitive rate of return on the capital (and labor) of owners. A higher rate would draw more competitors and their investors into the market; a lower rate would cause competitors and their investors to exit the market.

Remember, zero economic profits do not imply that the firm is about to go out of business. On the contrary, they indicate that the owners are receiving exactly the normal profit rate, or the competitive market rate of return on their investment.

Whenever accounting procedures omit implicit costs, like those associated with owner-provided labor services or equity capital, the firm's opportunity costs of production will be understated. This understatement of cost leads to an overstatement of profits. Therefore, the **accounting profits** of a firm are generally greater than the firm's economic profits (see the Applications in Economics feature on accounting costs). For most large corporations, though, omitting the implicit costs of services provided by an owner isn't an issue. In this case, the accounting profits approximate the returns to the firm's equity capital. High accounting profits (measured as a rate of return on a firm's assets), relative to those of other firms, suggest that a firm is earning an economic profit. Correspondingly, a low rate of accounting profit implies economic losses. Either positive or negative economic profits, of course, call for a change in output. Such a change, however, will take time.

Explicit costs
Payments by a firm to purchase the services of productive resources.

Implicit costs
The opportunity costs associated with a firm's use of resources that it owns. These costs do not involve a direct money payment. Examples include wage income and interest forgone by the owner of a firm who also provides labor services and equity capital to the firm.

Total cost
The costs, both explicit and implicit, of all the resources used by the firm. Total cost includes a normal rate of return for the firm's equity capital.

Opportunity cost of equity capital
The rate of return that must be earned by investors to induce them to supply financial capital to the firm.

Economic profit
The difference between the firm's total revenues and its total costs, including both the explicit and implicit cost components.

Normal profit rate
Zero economic profit, providing just the competitive rate of return on the capital (and labor) of owners. An above-normal profit will draw more entry into the market, whereas a below-normal profit will lead to an exit of investors and capital.

Accounting profits
The sales revenues minus the expenses of a firm over a designated time period, usually one year. Accounting profits typically make allowances for changes in the firm's inventories and depreciation of its assets. No allowance is made, however, for the opportunity cost of the equity capital of the firm's owners, or other implicit costs.

APPLICATIONS IN ECONOMICS

Economic and Accounting Costs: A Hypothetical Example

The revenue–cost statement for a corner grocery store owned and operated by Emily Blake is presented here.

TOTAL REVENUE	
Sales (groceries)	$170,000
Costs (explicit)	
Groceries, wholesale	$76,000
Utilities	4,000
Taxes	6,000
Advertising	2,000
Labor services (employees)	12,000
Total (explicit) costs	$100,000
Net (accounting) profit	$70,000
Additional (implicit) costs	
Interest (personal investment)	$7,000
Rent (Emily's building)	18,000
Salary (Emily's labor)	50,000
Total (implicit) costs	$75,000
TOTAL EXPLICIT AND IMPLICIT COSTS	$175,000
ECONOMIC PROFIT (TOTAL REVENUE MINUS EXPLICIT AND IMPLICIT COSTS)	–$5,000

Emily works full-time as the manager, chief cashier, and janitor. She has $140,000 worth of refrigeration and other equipment invested in the store. Last year, her total sales were $170,000, and suppliers and employees were paid $100,000. Emily's revenues therefore exceeded explicit costs by $70,000. This is what was recorded on the accounting statements as profit.

But did Emily really make a profit last year? Let's look at her opportunity costs and see: If Emily didn't have $140,000 of her own money invested in equipment, she could be earning 5 percent interest on the money in the bank, which would add up to $7,000 each year. Similarly, if the building she owns weren't being used as a grocery store, it could be rented to someone else for $1,500 per month. Rental income forgone is therefore $18,000 per year. In addition, because Emily is tied up working in the grocery store, a $50,000 managerial position she could hold at another local grocery store is forgone. Considering the interest, rental, and salary income that Emily had to forgo to operate the grocery store last year, her implicit costs were $75,000. This makes her total costs—both explicit and implicit—$175,000. (Recall that explicit costs were $100,000.) That's $5,000 *less* than her actual revenues of $170,000. As a result, Emily incurred an economic loss of $5,000, despite the accounting profit of $70,000 recorded on the store's books.

franckreporter/E+/Getty Images

21-4 SHORT-RUN AND LONG-RUN TIME PERIODS

Time plays an important role in the production process. All of a firm's resources can be expanded (or contracted) over time, but for specialized equipment, expanding (and contracting) availability quickly is likely to be very expensive or even impossible. Economists often speak of the **short run** as a time period so short that the firm is unable to alter its present plant size. In the short run, the firm is typically stuck with its existing plant and heavy equipment. These assets are "fixed" for a given time period, in other words. The firm can alter output, however, by applying larger or smaller amounts of "variable" resources, like labor and raw materials. In this way, the existing plant capacity can be used more or less intensively in the short run.

How long is the short run? *The short run is that period of time during which at least one factor of production, usually the size of the firm's plant, cannot be changed.* The length varies across industries and firms. A trucking firm might be able to hire more drivers and buy or rent more trucks and double its hauling capacity in a few months. In other industries, particularly those that use assembly lines and mass-production techniques, increasing production capacity may take several years.

The **long run** is a time period long enough for existing firms to alter the size of their plants and for new firms to enter (or exit) the market. *All of the firm's resources are variable in the long run.* In the long run, firms can expand their output by increasing the sizes of their plants—perhaps by adding on to them or by constructing entirely new facilities.

An example may help you understand the distinction between the short- and long-run time periods: If a tablet computer manufacturer hired 200 additional workers and ordered

Short run (in production)
A time period so short that a firm is unable to vary some of its factors of production. The firm's plant size typically cannot be altered in the short run.

Long run (in production)
A time period long enough to allow the firm to vary all of its factors of production.

more raw materials in order to squeeze more production out of its existing plant, it would be making a short-run adjustment. In contrast, if the manufacturer built an additional plant (or expanded the size of its current facility) and installed additional heavy equipment, it would be making a long-run adjustment.

21-5 CATEGORIES OF COSTS

In the short run, we can break a firm's costs into two categories—fixed and variable. Each category of costs behaves differently. Seeing that behavior graphically will help us understand how the profit-maximizing level of the firm's output is determined. It will also be important to distinguish between a firm's total costs and its per-unit costs, which we call "average" costs.

Each of the firm's fixed costs, and their sum, called **total fixed cost** (*TFC*), will remain unchanged when output rises or falls in the short run. For example, a firm's insurance premiums; its property taxes; and, most significantly, the opportunity cost of using its fixed assets will be present whether the firm produces a large or small amount of output. These costs will not vary with output. They can be avoided only if the firm goes out of business.

What will happen to **average fixed cost** (*AFC*), which is fixed cost *per unit*, as output expands? Remember that the firm's fixed cost will be the same whether output is 1, or 100, or 1,000. The *AFC* is simply fixed cost divided by output. As output increases, *AFC* declines because the fixed cost will be spread over more and more units (see part a of **Exhibit 2**).

Some costs vary with output. For example, additional output can usually be produced by hiring more workers and buying more raw materials. The sum of those and other costs that rise as output increases is the firm's **total variable cost** (*TVC*). At any given level of output, the firm's **average variable cost** (*AVC*), which is variable cost *per unit*, is the total variable cost divided by output.

A firm's total cost (*TC*) is the sum of the fixed and variable costs. At zero output a firm has no variable costs, thus total cost will be equal to total fixed cost. As output expands from zero, variable costs begin to increase, causing total cost to rise with output even though fixed costs are remaining unchanged. **Average total cost** (*ATC*), sometimes referred to as unit cost, can be found by dividing total cost by the total number of units produced. *ATC* is also equal to the sum of the average fixed and average variable costs. One way to look at ATC is that it is the amount of revenue needed per unit of output to cover total cost.

The economic way of thinking focuses on what happens "at the margin." How much does it cost to produce an additional unit? **Marginal cost** (*MC*) is the change in

Total fixed cost
The sum of the costs that do not vary with output. They will be incurred as long as a firm continues in business and the assets have alternative uses.

Average fixed cost
Total fixed cost divided by the number of units produced. It always declines as output increases.

Total variable cost
The sum of those costs that rise as output increases. Examples of variable costs are wages paid to workers and payments for raw materials.

Average variable cost
The total variable cost divided by the number of units produced.

Average total cost
Total cost divided by the number of units produced. It is sometimes called per-unit cost.

Marginal cost
The change in total cost required to produce an additional unit of output.

EXHIBIT 2

(a) Average fixed cost

(b) Marginal cost

(c) Average total cost

© Cengage Learning 2013

The General Characteristics of Short-Run Cost Curves

Average fixed costs (a) will be high for small rates of output, but they will always decline as output expands. Marginal cost (b) will rise sharply as the plant approaches its production capacity, q. As graph (c) shows, ATC will be a U-shaped curve because AFC will be high for small rates of output, and MC will be high as the plant's production capacity is approached.

total cost that results from the production of one additional unit. The profit-conscious decision-maker recognizes *MC* as the addition to cost that must be covered by additional revenue if producing the marginal unit is to be profitable. In the short run, as illustrated by part (b) of Exhibit 2, *MC* will generally decline at first if output is increased, reach a minimum, and then increase. The rising *MC* simply reflects the fact that it becomes increasingly difficult to squeeze additional output from a plant as the facility's maximum capacity (the dotted line of part b of Exhibit 2) is approached. The accompanying **Thumbnail Sketch** summarizes how the firm's various costs are related to one another.

21-6 OUTPUT AND COSTS IN THE SHORT RUN

As a firm changes its rate of output in the short run, how will its unit cost be affected? In the short run, the firm can vary its output by using its fixed plant size more (or less) intensively. Exhibit 2 shows two ways that this can result in high unit costs. First, when the output rate of a plant is small relative to its capacity, the facility is being underutilized, causing *AFC* to be high and *ATC* to be high, too. It will be costly to operate a large plant, with its high fixed costs, substantially below its production capacity. Alternatively, overutilization can also cause high unit costs. An overutilized plant will mean congestion—time spent by workers waiting for machines and similar costly delays. Requiring output beyond the least-cost, or designed, output level of a plant will lead to high *MC* and therefore to high *ATC*.

Thus, the ATC curve will be U-shaped, as pictured in part (c) of Exhibit 2. ATC will be high for both an underutilized plant and an overutilized plant. It will be high for an underutilized plant because average fixed cost will be high. It will be high for an overutilized plant because marginal cost will be high.

Thumbnail Sketch
Compact Glossary on Cost

Term	Symbol	Equation	Definition
Fixed cost			Cost that is independent of the output level
Variable cost			Cost that varies with the output level
Total fixed cost	TFC		Cost of the fixed inputs (equals sum of quantity times unit price for each fixed input)
Total variable cost	TVC		Cost of the variable inputs (equals sum of quantity times unit price for each variable input)
Total cost	TC	$TC = TFC + TVC$	Cost of all inputs (equals fixed costs plus variable costs)
Marginal cost	MC	$MC = \Delta TC \div \Delta q$	Change in total cost resulting from a one-unit rise in output (q) [equals the change in total cost divided by the change in output]
Average fixed cost	AFC	$AFC = TFC \div q$	Total fixed cost per unit of output (equals total fixed cost divided by total output)
Average variable cost	AVC	$AVC = TVC \div q$	Total variable cost per unit of output (equals total variable cost divided by total output)
Average total cost	ATC	$ATC = AFC + AVC$	Total cost per unit of output (equals average fixed cost plus average variable cost)

21-6a DIMINISHING RETURNS AND PRODUCTION IN THE SHORT RUN

Our analysis of the changes in unit cost as the output rate rises reflects a long-established economic law. This **law of diminishing returns** states that, as more and more units of a variable factor are applied to a fixed amount of other resources, output will eventually increase by smaller and smaller amounts. Therefore, the impact on output of additional units of the variable factor will diminish. The cost per unit of adding the variable factor may be the same, but the added output per dollar spent falls. The impact on cost per unit of output is clear: When the returns to the variable factor are rising, marginal costs (the additions to total variable cost needed to add a unit of output) are falling. Similarly, when the returns to the variable factor are falling, marginal cost is rising.

The law of diminishing returns is as famous in economics as the law of gravity is in physics. It is based on common sense and real-life observation. Have you ever noticed that as you apply a single resource more intensively, the resource eventually tends to accomplish less and less? Consider a wheat farmer who applies fertilizer (a variable resource) more and more intensively to an acre of land (a fixed factor). At some point, the application of additional 100-pound units of fertilizer will expand the wheat yield by successively smaller amounts.

Essentially, the law of diminishing returns is a constraint imposed by nature. If it were not valid, it would be possible to raise all the world's food in a flowerpot. We would be able to increase output simply by applying another unit of labor and fertilizer to the world's most fertile flowerpot! In the real world, of course, this is not the case; the law of diminishing returns is valid, reflecting a constraint we all must face.

Exhibit 3 illustrates the law of diminishing returns numerically. Column 1 indicates the quantity of the variable resource, labor in this example, which is combined with a specified amount of the fixed resource. Column 2 shows the **total product** that will result as the utilization rate of labor increases. Column 3 provides data on the **marginal product**, the change in total output associated with each additional unit of labor. Without the application of labor, output will be zero. As additional units of labor are applied, total product (output) rises. As the first three units of labor are applied, total product increases by successively larger amounts (8, then 12, then 14). Beginning with the fourth unit, however, diminishing returns

Law of diminishing returns
The postulate that as more and more units of a variable resource are combined with a fixed amount of other resources, using additional units of the variable resource will eventually increase output only at a decreasing rate. Once diminishing returns are reached, it will take successively larger amounts of the variable factor to expand output by one unit.

Total product
The total output of a good that is associated with each alternative utilization rate of a variable input.

Marginal product
The increase in the total product resulting from a unit increase in the employment of a variable input. Mathematically, it is the ratio of the change in total product to the change in the quantity of the variable input.

EXHIBIT 3

The Law of Diminishing Returns (Hypothetical Data)

(1) Units of the Variable Resource, Labor (per day)	(2) Total Product (output)	(3) Marginal Product	(4) Average Product
0	0		—
1	8	8	8.0
2	20	12	10.0
3	34	14	11.3
4	46	12	11.5
5	56	10	11.2
6	64	8	10.7
7	70	6	10.0
8	74	4	9.3
9	75	1	8.3
10	73	−2	7.3

© Cengage Learning 2013

are confronted. When the fourth unit of labor is added, marginal product—the change in the total product—declines to 12 (down from 14, when the third unit was applied). As additional units of labor are applied, marginal product continues to decline. It is increasingly difficult to squeeze a larger total product from the fixed resources (for example, plant size and equipment). Eventually, marginal product becomes negative (beginning with the tenth unit).

Column 4 of Exhibit 3 provides data for the **average product** of labor, which is simply the total product divided by the units of labor applied. Note that the average product increases as long as the marginal product is greater than the average product. Whenever the marginal unit's contribution is greater than the average, it must cause the average to rise. (A good analogy would be your grade point average. If the grade you get in this course is higher than your overall grade point average, your grade in this class will increase your overall average.) Here, marginal product rises through the first four units. The marginal product of the fifth unit of labor, though, is 10, less than the average product for the first four units of labor (11.5). Therefore, beginning with the fifth unit, the average product declines as additional labor is applied. When marginal productivity is below the average, it brings down the average product.

Using the data from Exhibit 3, **Exhibit 4** illustrates the law of diminishing returns graphically. Initially, the total product curve (part a) increases quite rapidly. As diminishing marginal returns are confronted (beginning with the fourth unit of labor), total product increases more slowly. Eventually, a maximum output (75) is reached with the application of the ninth unit of labor. The marginal product curve (part b) reflects the total product curve. Geometrically, marginal product is the slope—the rate of increase—of the total product

Average product
The total product (output) divided by the number of units of the variable input required to produce that output level.

EXHIBIT 4

The Law of Diminishing Returns

As units of variable input (labor) are added to a fixed input, total product will increase, first at an increasing rate and then at a declining rate (a). This will cause both marginal and average product curves (b) to rise at first and then decline. Note that the marginal product curve intersects the average product curve at its maximum (when four units of labor are used). The smooth curves indicate that labor can be increased by amounts of less than a single unit.

(a) Total product curve

(b) Average and marginal product curve

© Cengage Learning 2013

curve. That slope, the marginal product, reaches its maximum here with the application of three units of labor. Beyond three units, diminishing returns are present. Eventually, at ten units of labor, the marginal product becomes negative. When marginal product becomes negative, total product is necessarily declining. The average product curve rises as long as the marginal product curve is above it, because each added unit of labor is raising the average. The average product reaches its maximum at four units of labor. Beyond that, each additional unit of labor brings down the average product, and the curve slopes downward.

21-6b DIMINISHING RETURNS AND THE SHAPE OF THE COST CURVES

What impact will diminishing returns have on a firm's costs? Once a firm confronts diminishing returns, larger and larger additions of the variable factor are required to expand output by one unit. This will cause marginal cost (MC) to rise. As MC continues to increase, eventually it will exceed average total cost. Until that point, MC is below ATC, bringing ATC down. When MC is greater than ATC, the additional units cost more than the average, and ATC must increase. Think about what happens when you get a grade on an exam above your current class average. Your class average goes up. What happens if a unit of above-average cost is added to output? Average total cost rises. The firm's *MC* curve therefore crosses the *ATC* curve at the *ATC*'s lowest point. For output rates beyond the minimum *ATC,* the rising *MC* causes *ATC* to increase.

Exhibit 5 numerically illustrates the effect of the law of diminishing returns on a firm's short-run cost curve. Here, we assume that Royal Roller Blades, Inc., combines units of a variable input with a fixed factor to produce units of output (pairs of inline skates). Columns 2, 3, and 4 indicate how the total cost schedules vary as output is expanded. Total fixed costs (*TFC*), representing the opportunity cost of the fixed factors of production, are $50 per day at all levels of output. For the first four units of output, total variable costs (*TVC*) increase at a decreasing rate—by $15 with the production of the first unit, $10 with the production of the second unit, $9 with the third, and so on. Why? In this range, there are increasing returns to the variable input. Beginning with the fifth unit of output, however, diminishing marginal returns are present. From this point on, *TVC* and *TC* increase by successively larger amounts as output is expanded.

EXHIBIT 5

The Numerical Short-Run Cost Schedules of Royal Roller Blades, Inc.

	TOTAL COST DATA (PER DAY)			AVERAGE/MARGINAL COST DATA (PER DAY)			
(1) OUTPUT PER DAY	(2) TFC	(3) TVC	(4) TC (2) + (3)	(5) AFC (2) ÷ (1)	(6) AVC (3) ÷ (1)	(7) ATC (4) ÷ (1)	(8) MC Δ(4) ÷ Δ(1)
0	$50	$0	$50	—	—	—	—
1	50	15	65	$50.00	$15.00	$65.00	$15
2	50	25	75	25.00	12.50	37.50	10
3	50	34	84	16.67	11.33	28.00	9
4	50	42	92	12.50	10.50	23.00	8
5	50	52	102	10.00	10.40	20.40	10
6	50	64	114	8.33	10.67	19.00	12
7	50	79	129	7.14	11.29	18.43	15
8	50	98	148	6.25	12.25	18.50	19
9	50	122	172	5.56	13.56	19.11	24
10	50	152	202	5.00	15.20	20.20	30
11	50	202	252	4.55	18.36	22.91	50

EXHIBIT 6

Costs in the Short Run

Using data from Exhibit 5, this exhibit shows the general shape of the firm's short-run total cost curves (a), and average and marginal cost curves (b). Note that when output is small (for example, two units), *ATC* will be high because the *AFC* is so high. Similarly, when output is large (for example, eleven units), per-unit cost (*ATC*) will be high because additional units will be extremely costly to produce at this point. Thus, the short-run *ATC* curve will be U-shaped.

(a) Total cost data

(b) Average and marginal cost data

Columns 5 through 8 of Exhibit 5 are the average and marginal cost schedules. For small output rates, the *ATC* of producing roller blades is high, primarily because of the high *AFC*. Initially, *MC* is less than *ATC,* so *ATC* is falling. When diminishing returns set in for output rates beginning with five units, however, *MC* rises. Beginning with the sixth unit of output, *MC* exceeds *AVC,* causing *AVC* to rise. Beginning with the eighth unit of output, *MC* exceeds *ATC,* causing it also to rise. *ATC* thus reaches its minimum at seven units of output. Look carefully at the data of Exhibit 5 to be sure that you fully understand the relationships among the various cost curves. Do you understand how columns 4 to 8 are derived from columns 1 to 3?

Using the numeric data of Exhibit 5, **Exhibit 6** graphically illustrates the total, the average, and the marginal cost curves. Note that the *MC* curve intersects both the *AVC* and *ATC* curves at their minimum points (part b). As *MC,* driven up by diminishing returns, continues to rise above *ATC,* unit costs rise higher and higher as output increases beyond seven units.

In sum, the firm's short-run cost curves reflect the law of diminishing marginal returns. Assuming that the price of the variable resource is constant, *MC* declines so long as the marginal product of the variable input is rising. This results because, in this range, smaller and smaller additions of the variable input are required to produce each extra unit of output. The situation is reversed, however, when diminishing returns are confronted. Once diminishing returns set in, more and more units of the variable factor are required to generate each additional unit of output. *MC* will rise because the marginal product of the variable resource is declining. Eventually, *MC* exceeds *AVC* and *ATC,* causing these costs also to rise. A U-shaped, short-run average total cost curve results.

21-7 OUTPUT AND COSTS IN THE LONG RUN

The short-run analysis relates costs to output *for a specific size of plant.* Firms, though, are not committed forever to their existing plants. In the long run, all resources used by the firm are variable, thus there are no long-run fixed costs.

EXHIBIT 7

EXHIBIT 7

Long-Run Average Total Cost

The short-run average total cost curves are shown for three alternative plant sizes. If these three were the only possible plant sizes, the long-run average total cost curve would be *ABCD*.

How will the firm's choice of plant size affect per-unit production costs? **Exhibit 7** illustrates the short-run *ATC* curves for three different plant sizes, ranging from small to large. If these three plant sizes were the only possible choices, which one should the firm choose as it plans for the future? The answer depends on the rate of output the firm expects to produce from the plant. The smallest plant would have the lowest cost if an output rate of less than q_1 were produced. The medium-size plant would provide the least cost method of producing output rates between q_1 and q_2. For any output level greater than q_2, the largest plant would be the most cost efficient.

*The long-run **ATC** curve shows the minimum average cost of producing each output level when the firm is free to choose among all possible plant sizes. It can best be thought of as a planning curve because it reflects the expected per-unit cost of producing alternative rates of output while plants are still in the blueprint stage.*

Exhibit 7 illustrates the long-run *ATC* curve when only three plant sizes are possible, and the planning curve *ABCD* is thus mapped out. Of course, given sufficient time, firms can usually choose among many plants of various sizes. **Exhibit 8** presents the long-run planning curve under these circumstances. It is a smooth curve, with each short-run *ATC* curve tangent to it.

It is important to keep in mind that no single plant size could produce the alternative output rates at the costs indicated by the planning curve *LRATC* in Exhibit 8. Any of the planning curve options are, of course, available to the firm before a plant size is chosen and the plant is built.

EXHIBIT 8

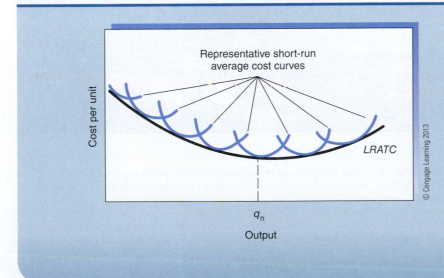

Representative short-run average cost curves

LRATC

The Planning Curve (LRATC)

When many different plant sizes are possible, the long-run average total cost curve (*LRATC*) can be mapped out. When firms are able to plan large volumes of output, using mass-production methods will generally lead to lower per-unit costs. This helps explain why the *LRATC* has a downward-sloping portion.

But it can *operate* in the short run only *after* a plant size has been chosen and put in place. The *LRATC* curve outlines the *possibilities* available in the planning stage. It shows the expected output and average total costs of production for the firm depending on the plant size it chooses.

21-7a ECONOMIES AND DISECONOMIES OF SCALE

Do larger firms have lower minimum unit costs than smaller ones?[2] There are three major reasons why planning a larger volume of output generally reduces, at least initially, unit costs: (1) economies accompanying the use of mass-production methods, (2) higher productivity as a result of specialization and "learning by doing," and (3) economies in promotion and purchasing.[3] Let's consider each of these factors.

Mass-production techniques usually are economical only when large volumes of output are planned, because they tend to involve large development and setup costs. Once the production methods are established, though, marginal costs are low. For example, the use of molds, dies, and assembly line production methods reduce the per-unit cost of automobiles only when the planned volume of output is in the millions. High-volume methods, although cheaper to use for high rates of output and high volumes, will typically require high fixed costs and therefore cause unit costs to be far higher for low volumes of production.

Large-scale operation also allows the specialized use of labor and machines. In a giant auto plant, hundreds of different jobs must be done, and many of them require a training period for each worker. In a small plant, a single worker might do ten or twenty of these jobs, so each worker would have a much longer, more costly training period. Even then, the worker doing so many tasks might never fully develop the same level of

Mass-production methods can often reduce average costs for firms planning higher output volumes.

REUTERS/SUKREE SUKPLANG/LANDOV

---

[2]Throughout this section, we assume that firms with larger plants necessarily plan a larger volume of output than do their smaller counterparts. Reality approximates these conditions. Firms choose large plants because they are planning to produce a large volume.

[3]Note the distinction between rate and volume of output. Rate of output is the number of units produced during a specific period (for example, the next six months). Volume is the total number of units produced during all time periods. For example, Boeing might produce two 787 airplanes per month (rate of output) while planning to produce a volume of two hundred 787s during the expected life of the model. Increasing the rate (reducing the time period during which a given output is produced) tends to raise costs, whereas increasing the volume (total amount produced) tends to lower costs per unit.

proficiency of the more specialized worker. Baseball players improve by playing base-ball, and pianists by playing the piano. Similarly, the employees of a firm improve their skills as they experience "learning by doing" in their jobs. Even better, concentration on a narrower range of tasks can help workers discover or develop cost-reducing tech-niques. The result of greater size and specialization is often more output per unit of labor.

Large firms are also able to achieve lower costs by spreading fixed costs (like the costs of advertising, developing specialized equipment, and searching out and negotiating bet-ter input prices, for example) over many more units. For example, both McDonald's and General Motors are able to spread these costs over a large number of stores and volume of sales. The cost advantages of scale come in many forms.

Economic theory explains why, at least initially, larger firms have lower unit costs than comparable smaller firms. Declining unit costs mean that **economies of scale** are present over the initial range of outputs. The long-run *ATC* curve is falling.

What about *dis*economies of scale? As output continues to expand, is there reason to believe that larger firms will eventually have higher average total costs than smaller ones? The underlying causes of diseconomies of scale are less obvious, but they do oc-cur. As a firm gets bigger and bigger, beyond some point bureaucratic inefficiencies *may* result. Inflexible procedures tend to replace managerial genius. Innovation requires clear-ance from more levels of management and becomes more difficult and costly. Motivating the workforce, carrying out managerial directives, and monitoring results of plans are also more complex when the firm is larger, and principal–agent problems grow as the number of employees increases and more levels of communication and monitoring are needed.

Circumstances vary, so diseconomies of scale set in at smaller firm sizes for some kinds of firms than for others. For example, firms in the fast-food industry can be very large and remain efficient; economies of scale apparently outweigh the diseconomies, even for giants like McDonald's. But in the fine-dining segment of the restaurant industry, the best restaurants seem to be small. Customers demand individual attention, and a constantly changing, innovative menu that takes advantage of the continually changing array of lo-cally available fresh ingredients—with consistently high quality as the only constant—is important. There are few truly gourmet restaurant chains because disec-onomies seem to set in at a much smaller size at these firms. The bottom line for diseconomies of scale is this: For some firms, bureaucratic inef-ficiencies, principal–agent problems, difficulties with innovation, and similar problems that increase with firm size cause long-run average total costs to rise beyond some output level. However, there is consid-erable variation among industries and even among firms in the same industry concerning the precise output level at which diseconomies of scale begin to occur.

It is important to note that scale economies and diseconomies stem from sources different from those of increasing and diminishing returns. Economies and diseconomies of scale are long-run concepts. They relate to conditions of production when all factors are variable. In contrast, increasing and diminishing returns are short-run concepts, ap-plicable only when the firm has at least one fixed factor of production.

21-7b ALTERNATIVE SHAPES OF THE *LRATC*

Exhibit 9 outlines three different long-run average total cost (*LRATC*) curves, each describing real-world conditions in differing industries. For a firm described by the cost curve in part (a), both economies and dis-economies of scale are present. Higher per-unit costs will result if the firm chooses a plant size other than the one that minimizes the cost of producing output *q*. If each firm in an industry faces the same cost con-ditions, we can generalize and say that all plants larger or smaller than this ideal size will experience higher unit costs. A very narrow range

Economies of scale
Reductions in the firm's per–unit costs associated with the use of large plants to produce a large volume of output.

The consistently high quality of gourmet restaurants like 18 Seaboard in Raleigh, North Carolina, can seldom be dupli-cated by chain restaurants, in part because a gourmet chef must make decisions daily about which locally available fresh ingredients will be used and how they will be used to produce a constantly innova-tive menu, delivered by an attentive and dedicated staff. Thus, diseconomies of scale limit the size of firms like 18 Seaboard.

Rick Stroup/18 Seaboard

EXHIBIT 9

Three Different Types of Long-Run Average Total Cost Curves

For one type of *LRATC* curve, economies of scale are present for output levels less than q, but immediately beyond q, diseconomies of scale occur (a). In another instance, economies of scale are important until some minimum output level (q_1) is attained. Once the minimum level has been attained, there is a wide range of output levels (q_1 to q_2) consistent with the minimum *LRATC* for the industry (b). In the third situation, economies of scale exist for all relevant output levels (c). As we will see later, this type of *LRATC* curve has important implications for how industries are structured.

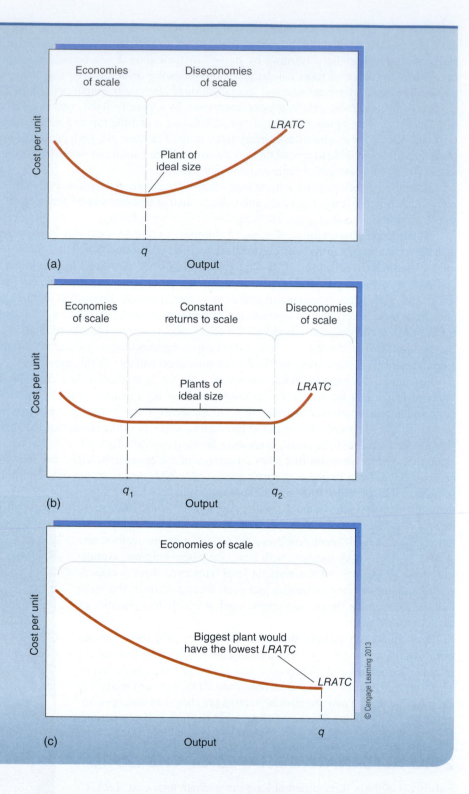

(a)

(b)

(c)

© Cengage Learning 2013

Constant returns to scale
Unit costs that are constant as the scale of the firm is altered. Neither economics nor diseconomies of scale are present.

of plant sizes would be expected in industries with the *LRATC* depicted by part (a). Some agricultural products and retail lines approximate these conditions.

Part (b) demonstrates the general shape of the *LRATC* that economists believe is present in most industries. Initially, economies of scale exist, but once a minimum efficient scale is reached, wide variation in firm size is possible. Firms smaller than the minimum efficient size would have higher per-unit costs, but firms larger than that would not gain a cost advantage. **Constant returns to scale** are present for a broad range of output rates (between q_1 and q_2), in other words. This situation is consistent with real-world conditions in many industries. For example, small firms can be as efficient as larger ones in the apparel, lumber, and publishing industries, as well as in several retail industries.

In part (c) of Exhibit 9, economies of scale exist for all relevant output levels. The larger the firm size, the lower the per-unit cost. The *LRATC* for local telephone service can approximate the curve shown here.

21-8 WHAT FACTORS CAUSE COST CURVES TO SHIFT?

When we drew the general shapes of a firm's cost curves in both the long run and short run, we assumed that certain other factors—resource prices, taxes, regulations, and technology—remained constant as the firm altered its rate of output. Let's now consider how changes in these factors affect the firm's costs.

21-8a PRICES OF RESOURCES

If the price of resources used should rise, the firm's cost curves will shift upward, as **Exhibit 10** shows. Higher resource prices will increase the cost of producing each alternative output level. For example, what happens to the cost of producing automobiles when the price of steel rises? The cost of producing automobiles also rises. Conversely, lower resource prices will reduce costs and shift the cost curves downward at each level of output.

21-8b TAXES

Taxes are a component of a firm's cost. Suppose that an excise tax of 20 cents were levied on the seller for each gallon of gasoline sold. What would happen to the seller's costs? They would increase, just as they did in Exhibit 10. The firm's average total and marginal cost curves would shift upward by the amount of the tax. If the tax were an annual business license fee instead, it would raise the average cost, but not the variable cost. Can you explain why?

21-8c REGULATIONS

The government often imposes health, safety, environmental, and production regulations on business firms. Federal regulations under the Americans with Disabilities Act compel

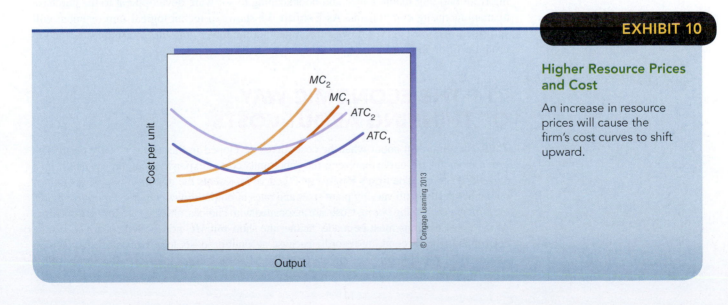

EXHIBIT 10

Higher Resource Prices and Cost

An increase in resource prices will cause the firm's cost curves to shift upward.

© Cengage Learning 2013

Egg Production Costs and Technological Change

Suppose an egg producer discovers (or develops) a "super" mineral water that makes it possible to get more eggs from the same number of chickens. Because of this technological improvement, various output levels of eggs can now be produced with less feed, space, water, and labor. Costs will be reduced. The egg producer's ATC and MC curves will shift downward.

© Cengage Learning 2013

many firms to make their facilities accessible to people in wheelchairs, and the Patient Protection and Affordable Care Act (PPACA) requires certain firms to provide health benefits to full-time workers. Other regulations force firms to build certain features into their products. Strong bumpers and air bags in automobiles are examples. Although regulations provide benefits, they are also costly. Just processing the paperwork that must be submitted to regulators is costly, and so are the compulsory changes themselves. Like tax increases, increases in regulatory compliance costs will shift cost curves upward. In some cases, only fixed costs will be affected; in other instances, variable costs will be altered as well. In both cases, the firm's ATC will be higher.

21-8d TECHNOLOGY

Improvements in technology often make it possible to produce a specific amount of output with fewer resources. Computers and robotics have lowered costs in many industries. The Internet has made it easy to find and outsource many business-to-business services, ranging from building maintenance and bookkeeping to software development to the purchase of manufacturing components. As Exhibit 11 shows, a technological improvement will shift the firm's cost curves downward, reflecting the lower amount of resources needed to produce different levels of output.

21-9 THE ECONOMIC WAY OF THINKING ABOUT COSTS

Think for a moment about what the cost curves developed in this chapter really mean. The firm's short-run MC curve represents the opportunity cost of expanding output, *given the firm's current plant size*. The firm's long-run ATC curve represents the opportunity cost per unit of output associated with varying plant sizes and rates of output, *given that the alternative plants are still on the drawing board*. Costs are associated with choices, and they are forward-looking. At the time decisions must be made, neither the short-run MC nor the long-run ATC can be determined from accounting records, because accounting costs look backward. Accounting figures yield valuable information about historical costs, but, as the following section illustrates, they must be interpreted carefully when they are used to forecast future costs.

21-9a WHAT ARE SUNK COSTS?

Sunk costs are the historical costs of past decisions that cannot be reversed. Sunk costs give managers hindsight when it comes to making current decisions, but the specific costs themselves are no longer relevant. When past choices cannot be reversed—no refund is available, for example—money that has been spent is gone for good. Today's choices must be based on the costs and benefits expected under *current and future* market conditions, if mistakes are to be avoided (see the accompanying Myths of Economics feature).

To minimize costs, business decision-makers need to realize that sunk costs are, indeed, *sunk*. A simple example will emphasize this point. Suppose that the firm in Exhibit 5 pays $100,000 to purchase and install a roller blade–producing machine. The machine is expected to last ten years. The company's books record the cost of the machine as $10,000 each year under the heading of depreciation. The machine can be used only to make roller blades, though. Because dismantling and reinstallation costs are high, it cannot be leased or sold to another firm. Also, it has no scrap value. In other words, there are no alternative uses for the machine. The machine's annual production of roller blades will generate $50,000 of revenues for the firm when it is employed with raw materials and other factors of production that cost $46,000. Thus, the net revenue generated by the machine is $4,000.

Should the firm continue to use the machine? Its depreciation figures suggest that the machine is costing the firm $10,000 annually, compared to the $4,000 net revenue it generates. Put another way, accounting costs indicate that the machine is reducing the firm's profit by $6,000 annually. The machine's depreciation cost, however, is a sunk cost. It was incurred when the machine was purchased and installed, which is over and done with now. The *current* opportunity cost of the machine is therefore precisely zero. Because using the machine generates $4,000 of additional net revenue, the firm can gain by continuing with its operation. Of course, if market conditions are not expected to improve, the firm will not

Sunk costs
Costs that have already been incurred as a result of past decisions. They are sometimes referred to as historical costs.

MYTHS OF ECONOMICS

"A Good Business Decision-Maker Will Never Sell a Product for Less Than Its Production Costs."

This statement contains a grain of truth. A profit-seeking entrepreneur will not undertake a project knowing the costs can't be covered. However, the statement fails to emphasize (1) the time dimension of the production process and (2) the uncertainty associated with business decisions. The production process takes time. Raw materials must be purchased, employees hired, and plants equipped. Retailers must contract with suppliers. As these decisions are made, costs result. Many of the firm's costs of production are incurred long before its product is ready for marketing.

Even a good business decision-maker is not always able to predict the future because market conditions can change quickly and unexpectedly. At the time the product is ready for sale, buyers might be unwilling to pay a price that will cover the seller's past costs of production. These past costs, however, are now sunk costs and no longer relevant. Decisions must now be made on the basis of the firm's current costs of delivering value to buyers, and the revenues to be gained by doing so.

Should a grocer refuse to sell oranges that are about to spoil because their wholesale cost cannot be covered? The grocer's current opportunity cost of selling the oranges at this point is nearly zero. The alternative would be to throw them in the garbage next week. Almost any price, even one far below past costs, will be better than letting the oranges spoil.

Consider another example. Suppose a couple that owns a house plans to relocate temporarily. Should they refuse to rent the house they're moving out of for $500 (if this is the best offer available) because their monthly house payment is $800? Of course not. The house payment will go on, regardless of whether they rent the house. If the homeowners can cover their opportunity costs (perhaps the expected wear and tear plus a $60 monthly fee for a property management service), they will gain by renting rather than leaving the house vacant.

Past mistakes provide useful lessons for the future, but they cannot be reversed. Bygones are bygones, even if they resulted in business loss. There is no need to fret over spilt milk, burnt toast, or yesterday's business losses.

franckreporter/E+/Getty Images

purchase a similar machine or replace the machine when it wears out, but this should not influence its decision whether to continue operating the one it already has.

21-9b HOW WILL COST INFLUENCE SUPPLY?

Costs underpin the firm's supply decisions. A strictly profit-maximizing firm will compare the expected revenues derived from a decision or a course of action with the expected costs. If the anticipated revenues exceed costs, then the course of action will be chosen because it is expected to expand profits (or reduce losses).

For short-run supply decisions, the marginal cost of producing additional units is the relevant cost to consider. To maximize profits, the decision-maker should compare the expected marginal costs with the expected additional revenue from larger sales. If the latter exceeds the former, output (the quantity supplied) should be expanded.

While marginal costs are central in the short run, average total costs are the relevant cost consideration in the long run. Before entering an industry (or purchasing capital assets for expansion or replacement), a profit-maximizing decision-maker will compare the expected market price with the expected long-run average total cost. Profit-seeking potential entrants will supply the product if, and only if, they expect the market price to exceed their long-run average total cost. Similarly, existing firms will continue to supply a product in the long run only if they expect that the market price will enable them at least to cover their long-run average total cost.

LOOKING AHEAD

This chapter focused on the relationship between output and cost in both the short and long runs. The next three chapters will use these general principles to analyze the price and output decisions of firms under alternative market conditions.

KEY POINTS

- The business firm is used to organize productive resources and transform them into goods and services. There are three major types of business structure—proprietorships, partnerships, and corporations.

- The principal–agent problem tends to reduce efficiency within the firm. Monitoring and the structure of incentives can be used to minimize inefficiencies arising from this source.

- The demand for a product indicates the intensity of consumers' desires for the item. The (opportunity) cost of producing the item indicates the intensity of consumers' desires for other goods that could have been produced instead, with the same resources.

- In economics, total cost includes not only explicit payments for resources employed by the firm, but also the implicit costs associated with the use of productive resources owned by the firm (like the opportunity cost of the firm's equity capital or owner-provided services) that could be used elsewhere.

- Because accounting methods omit the cost of equity capital (and sometimes other implicit costs), they tend to understate the opportunity cost of producing a good and overstate the firm's economic profit.

- Economic profit (or loss) results when a firm's sales revenues exceed (or are less than) its total costs, both explicit and implicit.

- Firms that are earning the market (or "normal") rate of return on their assets will therefore make zero economic profit.

- The firm's short-run average total cost (*ATC*) curve will tend to be U-shaped.

- The law of diminishing returns explains why a firm's short-run marginal and average total costs will eventually rise. When diminishing marginal returns are present, successively larger amounts of the variable input will be required to increase output by one more unit. As this happens, marginal cost will rise.

- The long-run *ATC* (*LRATC*) reflects the costs of production for plants of various sizes. When economies of scale are present, *LRATC* will decline. When constant returns to scale are experienced, *LRATC* will be constant. When diseconomies of scale are present, *LRATC* will rise.

- Changes in (1) resource prices, (2) taxes, (3) regulations, and (4) technology will cause the cost curves of firms to shift.

- Sunk costs are costs that have already been incurred and cannot be recovered. Sunk costs give managers hindsight when it comes to making current decisions, but the specific costs themselves are no longer directly relevant for current and future decisions.

CRITICAL ANALYSIS QUESTIONS

1. The owners of a firm are residual income claimants. How does their property right to the residual income affect their incentive to (a) produce efficiently and keep cost low and (b) supply goods that consumers value highly relative to cost? Why is this important?

2. Which of the following statements do you think reflect sound economic thinking? Explain your answer.
   a. "I paid $400 for this economics course. Therefore, I'm going to attend the lectures even if they are useless and boring."
   b. "Because we own rather than rent, and the house is paid for, housing doesn't cost us anything."
   c. "I own 100 shares of stock that I can't afford to sell until the price goes up enough for me to get back at least my original investment."
   d. "Private education is costly to produce, whereas public schooling is free."

3. Suppose a firm produces bicycles. Will the firm's accounting statement reflect the opportunity cost of the bicycles? Why or why not? What costs would an accounting statement reveal? Should current decisions be based on accounting costs? Explain.

4. What is the principal–agent problem? When will the principal–agent problem be most severe? Why might there be a principal–agent problem between the stockholder owners and the managers of a large corporation?

5. *"If a firm maximizes profit, it must minimize the cost of producing the profit-maximizing output." Is this statement true or false? Explain your answer.

6. What are some of the advantages of the corporate business structure of ownership for large business firms? What are some of the disadvantages? Is the corporate form of business ownership cost efficient? In a market economy, how would you tell whether the corporate structural form was efficient?

7. Explain the factors that cause a firm's short-run average total costs initially to decline but eventually to increase as the rate of output rises.

8. Which of the following are relevant to a firm's decision to increase output: (a) short-run average total cost, (b) short-run marginal cost, (c) long-run average total cost? Justify your answer.

9. Economics students often confuse (a) diminishing returns related to the variable factors of production and (b) diseconomies of scale. Explain the difference between the two, and give one example of each.

10. "Firms that make a profit have increased the value of the resources they used; their actions created wealth. In contrast, the actions of firms that make losses reduce wealth. The discovery and undertaking of profit-making opportunities are key ingredients of economic progress." Evaluate the statement.

11. *Is profit maximization consistent with the self-interest of corporate owners? Is it consistent with the self-interest of corporate managers? Is there a conflict between the self-interests of owners and those of managers?

12. *What is the opportunity cost of (a) borrowed funds and (b) equity capital? Under current tax law, firms can record as an expense the opportunity cost of borrowed funds, but not equity capital. How does this tax law affect the amount of debt the firm wants to incur, compared with the amount of money it raises by selling equity?

13. Why do economists consider normal returns to capital to be a cost? How does economic profit differ from normal profit?

14. *Draw a U-shaped, short-run ATC curve for a firm. Construct the accompanying MC and AVC curves.

15. What is shirking? If the managers of a firm are attempting to maximize its profits, will they have an incentive to limit shirking? How might they go about doing so?

16. What are implicit costs? Do implicit costs contribute to the opportunity cost of production? Should an implicit cost be counted as cost? Give three examples of implicit costs. Does the firm's accounting statement take implicit costs into account? Why or why not?

17. *Consider a machine purchased one year ago for $12,000. The machine is being depreciated $4,000 per year over a three-year period. Its current market value is $5,000, and the expected market value of the machine one year from now is $3,000. If the interest rate is 10 percent, what is the expected cost of holding the machine during the next year?

18. *Investors seeking to take over a firm often bid a positive price for the business even though it is currently experiencing losses. Why would anyone ever bid a positive price for a firm operating at a loss?

19. Fill in the blanks in the accompanying table shown at the bottom of page and answer the following questions:
   a. What happens to total product when marginal product is negative?
   b. What happens to average product when marginal product is greater than average product?
   c. What happens to average product when marginal product is less than average product?
   d. At what point does marginal product begin to decrease?
   e. At what point does marginal cost begin to increase?
   f. Summarize the relationship between marginal product and marginal cost.
   g. What happens to marginal costs when total product begins to fall?
   h. What is happening to average variable costs when they equal marginal costs?
   i. Marginal costs equal average variable costs between what output levels?
   j. What is happening to average total costs when they equal marginal costs?
   k. Marginal costs equal average total costs between what output levels?

*Asterisk denotes questions for which answers are given in Appendix B.

Units of Variable Input	Total Product	Marginal Product	Average Product	Price of Input	Total Variable Cost	Average Variable Cost	Total Fixed Cost	Total Cost	Average Total Cost	Marginal Cost
0	0	___	___	$1	___	___	$2	___	___	___
1	6	___	___	$1	___	___	$2	___	___	___
2	15	___	___	$1	___	___	$2	___	___	___
3	27	___	___	$1	___	___	$2	___	___	___
4	37	___	___	$1	___	___	$2	___	___	___
5	45	___	___	$1	___	___	$2	___	___	___
6	50	___	___	$1	___	___	$2	___	___	___
7	52	___	___	$1	___	___	$2	___	___	___
8	50	___	___	$1	___	___	$2	___	___	___

CHAPTER 22
Price Takers and the Competitive Process

FOCUS

- How do firms that are price takers differ from those that are price searchers?
- What determines the output of a price taker?
- How do price takers respond to changes in price in the short run? In the long run?
- How does time influence the elasticity of supply?
- What must firms do in order to make profits? How do profits and losses influence the supply and market price of a product?
- Does competition provide an incentive for producers to supply goods that consumers want at a low cost?

Competition means decentralized planning by many separate persons. —**Friedrich A. von Hayek**[1]

[I]t is competition that drives down costs and prices, induces firms to produce the goods consumers want, and spurs innovation and the expansion of new markets…
—**President's Council of Economic Advisers**[2]

[1]Friedrich A. von Hayek, "The Use of Knowledge in Society," *American Economic Review* 35 (September 1945): 521.

[2]President's Council of Economic Advisers, *Economic Report of the President, 1996* (Washington, DC: U.S. Government Printing Office, 1996), 155.

In the previous chapter, we focused on cost conditions of business firms. In this chapter and the next two, we will take a closer look at the price and output decisions of the firm, and how they are influenced by costs and market conditions. The importance of profits, losses, and competition will be addressed. As we proceed, we will also analyze how the structure of a market—for example, the number of firms, the control they have over price, and the ease of entry into the market—influences both the decision making of firms and the operation of markets.

22-1 PRICE TAKERS AND PRICE SEARCHERS

Price takers
Sellers who must take the market price in order to sell their product. Because each price taker's output is small relative to the total market, price takers can sell all their output at the market price, but they are unable to sell any of their output at a price higher than the market price.

This chapter will focus on markets in which the firms are **price takers**: They simply take the price that is determined in the market. *In a price-taker market, the firms all produce identical products (for example, wheat, eggs, or regular unleaded gasoline), and each seller is small relative to the total market. Thus, the output of any single firm has no effect on the market price. Each firm can sell all its output at the market price but cannot sell any of its output at a higher price.* When a firm is a price taker, there is no pricing decision to be made. Price takers try to choose the output level that will maximize profit, given their costs and the price determined by the market.

In the real world, most firms are not price takers. They are usually able to increase their prices, at least a little, without losing all their customers. For example, if Nike increased the price of its athletic shoes by 10 percent, the number of shoes sold would decline, but

APPLICATIONS IN ECONOMICS

Netherlands Flower Auctions Illustrate Competitive Markets[1]

The FloraHolland and Bloemenveiling Aalsmeer flower auctions in the Netherlands, each run by a growers' cooperative, operate as highly competitive markets with a large number of both buyers and sellers. FloraHolland itself has 98 percent of the Netherlands' trade, and the Netherlands has 60 percent of the world's trade. Thousands of growers from the Netherlands and around the world sell their products in these auctions. Each business day, several thousand buyers representing wholesale florists around the world, participate in the auction. Many bid by computer from outside the Netherlands. These auctions sell more than 17 million flowers each day from their locations in the Netherlands. This high volume is made possible by the speed of the Dutch auction system. Under this system, each lot of flowers is displayed and a "clock" runs backward from the highest to the lowest price per unit. The buyer pushes a button indicating his or her willingness to purchase when the clock reaches an acceptable per-unit price. The purchaser is the first buyer to push the button. There are 39 such clocks operated by these two firms. Flowers and plants auctioned in the morning will be available in shops around the world within 24 hours. Competition is

increasing, as large flower markets of this kind develop all over the world. Very large retailers like Walmart have also begun buying flowers directly from growers in the tropics.

[1]Information in this feature came in part from "Petal Power," *Economist* 383, no. 8528 (May 12, 2007): 73; and "Dutch Flower Auctions," *Economist* (downloaded June 3, 2009), from http://www.Economist.com.

it would not fall to zero. Firms like Nike are not price takers. They are **price searchers**: They choose the price that they will charge for their product, but the quantity that they are able to sell is very much related to that price. To maximize their profits, price searchers must not only decide how much to produce but also what price to charge. Price-taker markets and price-searcher markets have differing methods of competition, differing ease of entry for competitors, and perhaps differing scale economies, too. We will examine markets in which the firms are price searchers in the next two chapters.

If most real-world firms are price searchers, why is it important to analyze price-taker markets? There are several reasons. First, even though most firms are not price takers, there are a number of important markets, particularly in agriculture, in which the firms do essentially take the price determined in the market. Second, the price-taker model helps clarify the relationship between the decision making of individual firms and the market supply. Finally, and perhaps most important, the study of markets in which firms are price takers enhances our knowledge of **competition as a dynamic process,** *including its operation in markets other than those that are price takers*.

Historically, the term **pure competition** has been used to refer to markets in which firms are price takers. However, the expression "price-taker market" is more descriptive. Furthermore, this label avoids the implication that competitive forces are necessarily less pure or less intense in price-searcher markets. Often, this is not the case. When **barriers to entry** are low, the competitive process is just as important in price-searcher markets as it is when the firms are price takers.

Nonetheless, it should be noted that price-taker markets and purely competitive markets are really alternative names for the same thing. So when you hear people talk about pure competition or purely competitive markets, they mean markets with characteristics like those analyzed in this chapter.

22-2 WHAT ARE THE CHARACTERISTICS OF PRICE-TAKER MARKETS?

Consider the situation of Andy, a Texas cattle rancher. In the financial pages of the local newspaper, he finds that the current market price of quality steers is 94 cents per pound. Even if his ranch is quite large, there is little that Andy can do to change the market price of beef cattle. After all, there are tens of thousands of farmers who raise cattle. Thus, Andy supplies only a small portion of the total cattle market. The amount that he sells will exert little or no effect on the market price of cattle. Andy is a price taker.

The firms in a market will be price takers when the following four conditions are met:

1. All the firms in the market are producing an identical product (for example beef, or eggs of a given grade).
2. A large number of firms exist in the market.

Price searchers

Firms that face a downward-sloping demand curve for their product. The amount the firm is able to sell is inversely related to the price it charges.

Competition as a dynamic process

Rivalry or competitiveness between or among parties (for example, producers or input suppliers) to deliver a better deal to buyers in terms of quality, price, and product information.

Pure competition

A market structure characterized by a large number of small firms producing an identical product in an industry (market area) that permits complete freedom of entry and exit. Also called price-taker markets.

Barriers to entry

Obstacles that limit the freedom of potential rivals to enter and compete in an industry or market.

Producers in the wheat-farming and beef cattle markets are price takers. If they are going to sell their output, they must do so at the price determined by the market. Because individual producers are small relative to the total market, they can sell as many units as they like at the market price.

The Price Taker's Demand Curve

The market forces of supply and demand determine price (b). Price takers have no control over price. Thus, the demand for the product of the firm is perfectly elastic (a).

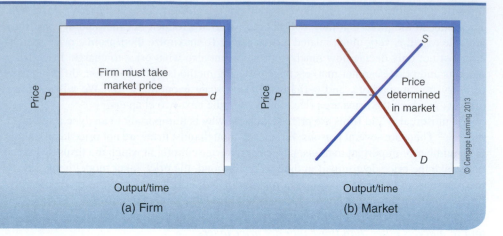

(a) Firm

(b) Market

3. Each firm supplies only a very small portion of the total amount supplied to the market.
4. No barriers limit the entry or exit of firms in the market.

Exhibit 1 illustrates the relationship between the market forces (part b) and the demand curve facing the price-taking firm (part a). If the firm sets a price above the market level, consumers will simply buy from other sellers. Why pay the higher price when the identical good is abundantly available elsewhere at the lower market price? For example, if the market price of wheat were $5.00 per bushel, a farmer would be unable to find buyers for wheat if he tried to sell his at $5.50 per bushel. A firm would gain nothing by setting its price below the market level, because any small firm in the market can already sell as much as it wants at the market price. A price reduction would only reduce revenue and profit. A firm that is a price taker thus faces a perfectly elastic demand for its product. (In Exhibit 1, note that a lowercase *d* is used to denote the demand curve faced by the *firm,* whereas an uppercase *D* indicates the *market* demand curve.)

22-3 HOW DOES THE PRICE TAKER MAXIMIZE PROFIT?

The firm's output decision is based on maximizing profit, which requires comparing revenue with cost. A firm will continue to expand output as long as the additional revenues from the production and sales of the additional units exceed their marginal costs, thereby increasing profit. In the preceding chapter, we discovered that the law of diminishing returns assures that a firm's short-run marginal costs will eventually increase as the firm expands its output. As the firm continues to add additional variable resources to its fixed plant facilities, marginal productivity falls, and marginal costs rise, and eventually increase to the point where it is no longer profitable to further expand output.

What about the benefits or additional revenues from output expansion? **Marginal revenue (*MR*)** is the change in the firm's total revenue per unit of output. It is the additional revenue derived from the sale of an additional unit of output. Mathematically,

Marginal revenue (*MR*)
The incremental change in total revenue derived from the sale of one additional unit of a product.

$$MR = \frac{\textbf{Change in total revenue}}{\textbf{Change in output}}$$

Because the price taker sells all units at the same price, its marginal revenue will be equal to the market price. That is, producing and selling one more unit of output

EXHIBIT 2

Profit Maximization When the Firm Is a Price Taker

The price taker will maximize profits by producing the output level q, where P = MC.

increases the firm's revenue by exactly the amount of the current market price. The firm's marginal revenue curve is a horizontal line at the market price. For a price-taker firm the marginal revenue curve is also the demand curve faced by the price-taker firm shown in Exhibit 1.

To maximize profits, in the short run, the price taker will expand its output until marginal cost just equals marginal revenue (price). **Exhibit 2** illustrates this decision. The firm will continue to expand output as long as the marginal revenue curve (*MR*) lies above the marginal cost (*MC*) curve. The profit of the price taker is maximized at the output rate at which $P = MR = MC$. In Exhibit 2, this occurs at output *q*. The firm will not expand output beyond *q* because those units would add more to the firm's costs than to its revenue, thus reducing profit.

Using Exhibit 2 it is also possible to illustrate the firm's total revenue, total cost, and profit as areas in the diagram. The total revenue of the firm would be the sales price of each unit, *P*, multiplied by output sold, *q*. Total revenue is represented by the area *P0qB*. The firm's total cost, in contrast, can be found by multiplying the average total cost (*ATC*) by the output level. Total cost is represented by the area *C0qA*. Because the firm's total revenues exceed its total costs, it is making short-run economic profit shown by the area of excess revenue over cost (the shaded area *PCAB*).

In the real world, of course, decisions are not made by entrepreneurs who spend time drawing demand and marginal cost curves. However, business firms do attempt to maximize their profits, producing units only when it is profitable to do so. Experimentation, trial and error, and strong competitive forces will eventually lead firms to seek out the level of output consistent with this rule for profit maximization.

22-3a PROFIT MAXIMIZING—A NUMERIC EXAMPLE

Exhibit 3 uses numeric data to illustrate profit-maximizing decision-making for a firm that is a price taker. As column 6 of Exhibit 3 shows, the firm maximizes profit at an output of fifteen units.

There are two ways to look at this profit-maximizing output rate. First, profit is equal to the difference between total revenue and total cost. Thus, profit will be maximized at the output rate where this difference (*TR* minus *TC*) is greatest. For output rates less than eleven units the firm would actually experience losses. But at fifteen units of output, an $11 profit is earned ($75 total revenue minus $64 total cost). A look at the profit figures of column 6 shows that it's impossible to earn a profit larger than $11 at any other rate of output.

EXHIBIT 3

Profit Maximization for a Price Taker: A Numeric Illustration

(1) OUTPUT (PER DAY)	(2) TOTAL REVENUE (TR)	(3) TOTAL COST (TC)	(4) MARGINAL REVENUE (MR)	(5) MARGINAL COST (MC)	(6) PROFIT (TR – TC)
0	$0.00	$25.00	$0.00	$0.00	$–25.00
1	5.00	29.80	5.00	4.80	–24.80
2	10.00	33.75	5.00	3.95	–23.75
3	15.00	37.25	5.00	3.50	–22.25
4	20.00	40.25	5.00	3.00	–20.25
5	25.00	42.75	5.00	2.50	–17.75
6	30.00	44.75	5.00	2.00	–14.75
7	35.00	46.50	5.00	1.75	–11.50
8	40.00	48.00	5.00	1.50	–8.00
9	45.00	49.25	5.00	1.25	–4.25
10	50.00	50.25	5.00	1.00	–0.25
11	55.00	51.50	5.00	1.25	3.50
12	60.00	53.25	5.00	1.75	6.75
13	65.00	55.75	5.00	2.50	9.25
14	70.00	59.25	5.00	3.50	10.75
15	75.00	64.00	5.00	4.75	11.00
16	80.00	70.00	5.00	6.00	10.00
17	85.00	77.25	5.00	7.25	7.75
18	90.00	85.50	5.00	8.25	4.50
19	95.00	95.00	5.00	9.50	0.00
20	100.00	108.00	5.00	13.00	–8.00
21	105.00	125.00	5.00	17.00	–20.00

In **Exhibit 4,** part (a) presents the total revenue and total cost approach in graph form. (However, the curves are drawn smoothly, as though output could be increased by tiny amounts, not just in whole-unit increments like those shown in Exhibit 3.) Profits will be greatest when the total revenue line lies above the total cost curve by the largest vertical amount, at 15 units of output.

You can also use the marginal approach to determine the profit-maximizing rate of output for the firm. Remember, as long as price (marginal revenue) exceeds marginal cost, production and sale of additional units will add to the firm's profit (or reduce its losses). A look at columns 4 and 5 of Exhibit 3 reveals that *MR* is greater than *MC* for the first 15 units of output. Producing these units will expand the firm's profit. In contrast, producing any unit beyond fifteen adds more to cost than to revenue. Profit will therefore decline when output is expanded beyond fifteen units. Given the firm's cost and revenue schedule, profits are maximized by producing fifteen, and only fifteen, units per day.

Part (b) of Exhibit 4 graphically illustrates the marginal approach. Note here that the output rate at which the marginal cost and marginal revenue curves intersect (15 units) coincides with the output rate in part (a) at which the total revenue curve exceeds the total cost curve by the largest amount. Beyond that output rate, *MR* is less than *MC,* so profit will decline.

22-3b LOSSES AND WHEN TO GO OUT OF BUSINESS

Suppose that changes in the bigger marketplace cause the price to drop below a firm's average total cost at all possible output levels. How will a profit-maximizing firm respond to this situation? The answer to this question depends both on the firm's revenues relative to its *variable* cost and on its expectations about the future. The firm's owner has three options: (1) continue to operate in the short run, (2) shut down temporarily, or (3) go out of business.

(a) Total revenue/total cost approach

(b) Marginal revenue/marginal cost approach

© Cengage Learning 2013

EXHIBIT 4

The Firm's Profit-Maximizing Output Level—Total and Marginal Approaches

Using the data of Exhibit 3, we can find the profit-maximizing output of a price taker using either the total approach or the marginal approach. Using the total approach, we find that profits are maximized when the firm's total revenues exceed its total costs by the greatest amount (a). Using the marginal approach, we find that profits are maximized by comparing marginal revenue and marginal costs (b).

If the firm anticipates that the lower market price is temporary, it may want to continue operating in the short run as long as it can cover its variable cost.[3] **Exhibit 5** illustrates why. The firm shown in this exhibit would minimize its loss at output level q, where $P = MR = MC$. But at q, total revenues ($0qBP_1$) are less than total costs ($0qAC$). The firm faces short-run economic losses. Even if it shuts down completely, it will still incur fixed costs, *unless the firm goes out of business.* If it anticipates that the market price will increase enough to allow the firm to cover its average total costs in the future, it may not want to terminate operations and sell its assets. It may choose to produce q units in the short run, even though it will incur losses. At price P_1, producing output q is more advantageous than shutting down, because the firm is able to cover its variable costs and have revenue remaining to pay some of its fixed costs. If it were to shut down but not sell out, the firm would lose the entire amount of its fixed cost.

---

[3]Keep in mind the opportunity-cost concept. The firm's fixed costs are opportunity costs that do not vary with the level of output. They can be avoided if, and only if, the firm goes out of business. To specify fixed costs, we need to know (1) how much the firm's fixed assets would bring if they were sold or rented to others and (2) any other costs, such as operating license fees and debts, that could be avoided if the firm declared bankruptcy and/or went out of business. Because fixed costs can be avoided if the firm goes out of business, the firm will foresee greater losses from operating even in the short run if it does not expect conditions to improve.

Operating with Short-Run Losses

A firm making losses will operate in the short run if it (1) can cover its variable costs now and (2) expects price to be high enough in the future to cover all its costs.

Shutdown

A temporary halt in the operation of a firm. Because the firm anticipates operating in the future, it does not sell its assets and go out of business. The firm's variable cost is eliminated by the shutdown, but its fixed costs continue.

Going out of business

The sale of a firm's assets and its permanent exit from the market. By going out of business, a firm is able to avoid its fixed costs, which would continue during a shutdown.

A Temporary Shutdown A firm will temporarily shut down if it cannot cover its variable cost but does not want to go out of business because it expects to be able to operate profitably in the future. Ski resorts, for example, generally close for several months each summer and reopen during the winter. During these short-run shutdowns, the ski resort still pays its fixed costs, such as its rent, taxes, and insurance. The ski resort avoids only variable costs during the winter months.

What if the market price drops below the firm's average variable cost (for example, to P_2)? When this happens, not only is the firm not covering its fixed costs, it's not fully covering its variable costs either. In other words, if the firm operates, it will lose even more money. Under these circumstances, a temporary **shutdown** is preferable to short-run operation. Even if the firm's owner expects the market price to increase later, enabling the firm to survive and prosper in the future, shutting down in the short run will minimize its losses. The firm will still have to pay its fixed costs, but it won't be taking an additional loss on each unit it produces. Temporary shutdowns are actually regularly planned in some markets. For example, many ski resorts, golf courses, hotels, and restaurants in vacation areas plan to shut down in slow seasons, operating only when tourists or other seasonal purchasers provide enough demand. The price-taker model predicts that these firms will operate only when they expect to cover at least their variable costs.

The firm's third option is **going out of business** immediately. If the firm is sold, even the losses resulting from its fixed costs can be avoided. When market conditions are not expected to change for the better, going out of business is the preferred option.

22-4 THE FIRM'S SHORT-RUN SUPPLY CURVE

The price taker that intends to stay in business will maximize profits (or minimize losses) when it produces the output level at which $P = MR = MC$ *and variable costs are covered. Therefore, the portion of the firm's short-run marginal cost curve that lies above its average variable cost is the short-run supply curve of the firm.*

EXHIBIT 6

The Short-Run Supply Curve for the Firm and the Market

As price increases, firms will expand output along their *MC* curve. Thus, the firm's *MC* curve is also its supply curve (a). When resource prices are constant, the short-run market supply (a) is merely the sum of the supply produced by all the firms in the market (b).

© Cengage Learning 2013

(a) Representative firm

(b) Market

Exhibit 6 illustrates that, as the market price increases, the firm will expand output along its *MC* curve. If the market price were less than P_1, the firm would shut down immediately and produce zero output. If the market price is P_1, a price equal to the firm's minimum average variable cost, the firm may supply output q_1 in the short run. Economic losses will result, but the firm would incur similar losses if it shut down completely. As the market price increases to P_2, the firm will happily expand output along its *MC* curve to q_2. At P_2, price is equal to average total costs. At this point, the firm is making a "normal rate of return," or zero economic profits. Higher prices will result in a still larger short-run output. For example, when the price rises to P_3, the firm will supply q_3 units. At this price, economic profits will result. As long as price exceeds average variable cost, higher prices will cause the firm to expand output along its *MC* curve, which therefore becomes the firm's short-run supply curve.

22-5 THE SHORT-RUN MARKET SUPPLY CURVE

The short-run market supply curve shows the total quantity supplied at alternative market prices. *When the firms are price takers, the short-run market supply curve is the horizontal summation of the marginal cost curves (ΣMC) above the level of average variable cost for all of the firms in the market. Because individual firms will supply a larger amount at a higher price, the short-run market supply curve will slope upward to the right.*

Exhibit 6 illustrates this relationship. As the price of the product rises from P_1 to P_2 to P_3, the individual firms expand their output along their marginal cost curves. Because the individual firms supply a larger output as the market price increases, the total amount supplied to the market also expands.

22-6 PRICE AND OUTPUT IN PRICE-TAKER MARKETS

The short-run market supply curve, together with the demand curve for the industry's product, will determine the market price. At the short-run equilibrium market price, each firm will have expanded output until marginal costs are equal to the market price, and they may be earning either economic profits or losses.

EXHIBIT 7

Long-Run Equilibrium in a Price-Taker Market

The two conditions necessary for long-run equilibrium in a price-taker market are depicted here. First, quantity supplied and quantity demanded must be equal in the market (b). Second, the firms in the industry must earn zero economic profit (the "normal rate of return") at the established market price (a).

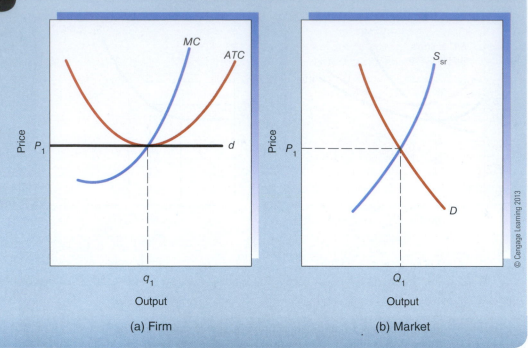

(a) Firm

(b) Market

© Cengage Learning 2013

22-6a LONG-RUN EQUILIBRIUM

In the long run, existing firms will have the opportunity to expand (or contract) the sizes of their plants, and firms will also be able to enter and exit the industry. As these long-run adjustments are made, output in the whole industry may either expand or contract. If economic profit is present, new firms will enter the industry to capture some of those profits. Current producers will have an incentive to expand the scale of their operations to capture some of the additional profits, too. This increase in supply will put downward pressure on prices. In contrast, if firms in the industry are suffering economic losses, they will leave the market. This decrease in supply will put upward pressure on prices. This process of entry and exit will continue until the profit rate in the industry has returned to a normal level ("zero economic profit") consistent with the profit rates in other competitive industries. Therefore, as **Exhibit 7** shows, when a price-taker market is in long-run equilibrium, the quantity supplied and the quantity demanded will be equal at the market price

APPLICATIONS IN ECONOMICS

Experimental Economics and the Significance of Competition

In fields like physics and chemistry, scientists use controlled laboratory experiments to test and verify the basic principles on which their science is built. Historically, it was thought that experiments of this type were not an option for economists. But this changed during the middle part of the twentieth century and over the past 50 years, economists have conducted numerous experiments investigating key elements of economic theory.

Vernon Smith, currently at Chapman University, won the 2002 Nobel Prize in Economics for his path-breaking work in

experimental economics. In one of his early experiments, Smith brought individuals into a laboratory setting and arbitrarily assigned them roles as buyers and sellers in a game-like activity. Each buyer was assigned a maximum value representing the maximum price he or she would be willing to pay for a hypothetical commodity. If the buyer could purchase the commodity at a price less than their maximum value, they would receive a cash payment equal to the difference between the two. Each buyer gained financially by purchasing at lower prices—just

franckreporter/E+/Getty Images

as buyers do in real markets. The sellers were treated similarly. All sellers were assigned a minimum value representing their cost, and if they were able to sell the commodity for more than this minimum, they would receive a cash payment for the difference. Buyers and sellers were free to make verbal offers and enter into exchanges at any mutually agreeable price.

The competitive price-taker model predicts that all mutually advantageous trades among buyers and sellers will be undertaken and that, as trades occur, the price will tend to converge toward a single price—the market price. Smith and other experimental researchers confirmed that this was indeed the case. After the experiments, participants often describe the experience as disorganized and chaotic. Thus, many are startled when shown that their actions (trades) achieved the maximum income for the group and that a sealed envelope, given to them prior to the experiment, approximated both the price of most trades and the maximum joint gains achieved by the group. The competitive model presented in this chapter provided the foundation for these predictions.

Prior to the work in experimental economics, many economists thought this model was relevant only under highly restrictive conditions. Experimental researchers, however, have found that outcomes approximating those of the competitive price-taker model generally emerge even when the

strict assumptions of the model are not fully met. For example, even if the number of sellers is relatively small, say ten to fifteen, outcomes similar to those predicted by the price-taker model generally occur.

At first, Smith himself was surprised that efficient outcomes were achieved under a wide variety of conditions, but after numerous experiments, he stated that

> *In many experimental markets, poorly informed, error-prone, and uncomprehending human agents interact through the trading rules to produce social algorithms which demonstrably approximate the wealth maximizing outcomes traditionally thought to require complete information and cognitively rational actors.*[1]

In addition to analyzing the exchange process, experimental research has addressed numerous other topics, including the impact of alternative auction rules, the likelihood of a stock market or real estate bubble, and the provision of public goods. Experimental economics is one of the most exciting and fruitful areas of current economic research.

[1]Vernon L. Smith, "Economics in the Laboratory," *Journal of Economic Perspectives* 8, no. 1 (Winter 1994): 118.

(part b) and each firm in the industry will be earning normal (zero) economic profit (that is, its minimum *ATC* will just equal the market price [part a]).

In price-taker markets, a single price will emerge and all of the potential gains from trade between the buyer-consumers and seller-suppliers will be realized. Does the price-taker model really work in the real world? As the Applications in Economics feature on experimental economics and the significance of competition indicates, the general implications of the price-taker model are approximated even when the restrictive assumptions of the model are not fully met.

When long-run equilibrium is present, firms will have no incentive to alter either their output levels or their plant sizes. Neither will there be incentive for net investment to flow into or away from the industry. Thus, the market price and output will persist into the future. This is why it is referred to as a long-run equilibrium.

22-6b HOW WILL THE MARKET RESPOND TO AN INCREASE IN DEMAND?

Suppose that a price-taker market is in long-run equilibrium. What will happen if there is an increase in demand? **Exhibit 8** shows us. When the market demand increases from D_1 to D_2, the market price will rise from P_1 to P_2. The higher price will induce firms to expand output (from q_1 to q_2 in part a of the exhibit) along their *MC* curves. In the short run, producers will make economic profits. The profits will attract new firms to the industry and cause the existing firms to expand the scale of their plants. Hence, the market supply will increase (shift from S_1 to S_2) and eventually eliminate the short-run profits. If the prices of resources supplied to the industry are unchanged, the market supply will continue to expand (shift to the right) until the price of returns to its initial level (P_1), even though output has expanded to Q_3.

EXHIBIT 8

Market Response to Increased Demand

When demand increases from D_1 to D_2, the market price rises from P_1 to P_2, inducing firms to expand output (b). Firms make short-run profits (a), which draw new competitors into the industry. The supply then expands (shifts from S_1 to S_2). If cost conditions are unchanged, the expansion in supply will continue until the market price declines to its initial level of P_1.

(a) Firm

2. . . . causing the price to rise to P_2, leading to profits.

MC

ATC

Price

P_2

P_1

d_2

d_1

q_1 q_2

Output

(b) Market

3. Profits lead to new entry and increase in market supply.

Short-run price

S_1 / S_2

4. A new equilibrium is reached, at a higher output and the original price.

Price

P_2

P_1

S_{lr}

1. Demand rises from D_1 to D_2, . . .

D_1 D_2

Q_1 Q_2 Q_3

Output

© Cengage Learning 2013

22-6c HOW WILL THE MARKET RESPOND TO A DECREASE IN DEMAND?

Economic profits attract new firms to an industry. In contrast, economic losses encourage firms to move out of the industry and into other areas where the profitability potential is more favorable. Economic losses mean firms are earning less than a normal market rate of return. The opportunity cost of continuing in the industry exceeds the gain.

Exhibit 9 shows market forces reacting to economic losses. Initially, assume that an equilibrium price exists in the industry. The firms are able to cover their average costs of production. Now suppose that consumer incomes fall, lowering the product's demand and its market price. At the new, lower price, firms in the industry will not be able to cover their costs of production. In the short run, they will reduce output along their MC curves. The lower output by the individual firms results in a lower quantity supplied in the market.

In the face of short-run losses, some firms will leave the industry, causing the industry supply to decline, indicated by the shift from S_1 to S_2. Firms will continue to exit until the price rises enough that the firms remaining in the industry can once again earn a normal rate of return, or zero economic profit. At that point, a new long-run equilibrium is established. For a real-world example of how a market adjusts to changing demand and cost conditions, see the Applications in Economics feature on coffee production in a price takers' market.

22-6d THE LONG-RUN MARKET SUPPLY CURVE

The *long-run market supply curve* shows how the quantity supplied in an industry varies with the market price, given enough time for firms to adjust the sizes of their plants (or other fixed factors) and to enter or exit the industry. Because the curve is constructed from points of long-run equilibrium, at each point the market price is equal to the minimum average total

EXHIBIT 9

The Impact of a Fall in Demand

Lower market demand will cause the price to fall and short-run losses to occur. The losses will cause some firms to go out of business and others to reduce their output. In the long run, the market supply will

fall, causing the market price to rise. The supply will continue to decline and price will continue to rise until the short-run losses have been eliminated

3. . . . causing firms to reduce output or to exit, decreasing the market supply until . . .

4. . . . equilibrium is reached at a lower output and the original price.

2. . . . causing the price to fall to P_2, leading to losses . . .

Initial equilibrium

Short-run price

1. Demand falls from D_1 to D_2, . . .

(a) Firm

(b) Market

© Cengage Learning 2013

cost for firms in the industry. Therefore, the shape of the curve depends on what happens to the cost of production as the *industry's* output is altered; there are three possibilities.

Long-run supply in constant-cost industries If resource prices remain unchanged, the long-run market supply curve will be horizontal, or perfectly elastic. In terms of economics, this describes a **constant-cost industry**. Exhibits 8 and 9 both depict constant-cost industries. As Exhibit 8 shows, in these industries an increase in market demand for the product results in only a temporary increase in the price of the product. With time, the higher price and profits will stimulate expansion and additional production, which will push the market price back down precisely to its initial level (and profitability back to its normal rate).

Similarly, Exhibit 9 illustrates the impact of a decline in demand in a constant-cost industry. Here, market price falls inducing losses and the exit of firms. Assuming resource prices and production costs are unaffected by the change in market output, the reduction in demand lowers the price in the short run, but it returns to its original level in the long run. Thus, in a constant-cost industry, the *long-run market supply curve* (S_{lr}) is perfectly elastic.

Long-run supply in increasing-cost industries In most industries, an increase in *industry* output will lead to higher resource prices and per-unit production costs for all the firms in the industry. Economists refer to such industries as **increasing-cost industries**. Exhibit 10 depicts an increasing-cost industry. The rising resource costs cause the firms' average and marginal cost curves to shift upward (to ATC_2 and MC_2) as the industry expands. For an increasing-cost industry, the market price necessary to result in zero economic profit (long-run equilibrium) will have to be higher as the industry gets larger (now P_2). The long-run market supply curve for the product will therefore slope upward to the right.

Constant-cost industry
An industry for which factor prices and costs of production remain constant as market output is expanded. The long-run market supply curve is therefore horizontal in these industries.

Increasing-cost industry
An industry for which costs of production rise as output is expanded. In these industries, even in the long run, higher market prices will be needed to induce firms to expand total output. As a result, the long-run market supply curve in these industries will slope upward to the right.

EXHIBIT 10

Increasing Costs and Long-Run Supply

(a) Firm

4. . . . profits disappear for the firm and a new equilibrium results at a higher price and output, . . .

MC_2

MC_1

ATC_2

ATC_1

Price

P_2

P_1

d_2

d_1

q_1

Output/time

(b) Market

3. . . . causing added output from current and new producers, increasing the market supply, lowering price, and raising cost until . . .

2. . . . causing the price to rise temporarily to P_3 leading to profits, . . .

S_1

S_2

S_{lr}

Price

P_3

P_2

P_1

5. . . . reflected in a new, long-run market equilibrium.

D_1

D_2

1. Demand rises from D_1 to D_2, . . .

Q_1 Q_2

Output/time

© Cengage Learning 2013

Decreasing-cost industry

An industry for which costs of production decline as the industry expands. The market supply is therefore inversely related to price. Such industries are atypical.

Long-run supply in decreasing-cost industries Sometimes, resource prices will decline when an industry expands, causing the cost curves to shift downward as new firms enter the industry. For example, as the electronics industry expands, suppliers of certain components may be able to adopt large-scale production techniques that will lead to lower component prices. In such **decreasing-cost industries**, the long-run (but not the short-run) market supply curve will slope downward to the right. Decreasing-cost industries are rare.

22-6e SUPPLY ELASTICITY AND THE ROLE OF TIME

The short- and long-run supply curve distinction offers a convenient two-stage analysis, but in the real world there are many intermediate production "runs." The delivery rates for some factor inputs that could not be easily increased in a one-week time period can be increased over a two-week period. It might take two weeks, for example, to hire reliable workers who need no special skills. Expanding other factors might take a month, and still others, six months. More precisely, the cost penalty for quicker availability is greater for some productive resources than others. In any case, a faster expansion usually means that greater cost penalties are encountered in order to obtain the earlier availability of the resources needed to expand production.

As a result, the supply curve for products is typically more inelastic the shorter the time frame of the response to a price change. Exhibit 11 illustrates this point. When the price of a product increases from P_1 to P_2, the immediate supply response of the firms is small, reflecting the high cost of hasty expansion. After one week, firms are willing to expand output only from Q_1 to Q_2. After one month, cost reductions made possible by the longer production-planning period allow firms to offer Q_3 units at the price P_2. After three months, the rate of output expands to Q_4. In the long run, when it is possible to adjust all inputs to the desired utilization levels (after a six-month time period, for example), firms are willing to supply Q_5 units of output at the market price of P_2.

In central areas of large cities, the supply of parking spaces can be expanded only by using higher-cost space and higher-cost techniques, such as taller parking garages that use a large portion of the building for access ramps. As a result, the unit cost of parking spaces increases as the total number is expanded. Thus, provision of parking space is an increasing-cost industry.

Tetra Images/Alamy

22-7 THE ROLE OF PROFITS AND LOSSES

Profit is a reward that business owners will earn if they produce a good that consumers value more (as measured by their willingness to pay) than the alternative goods that could have been produced with those same resources (as measured by the cost of bidding the resources away from their alternative uses). In contrast, losses are a penalty imposed on businesses that reduce the value produced from resources. Losses are a signal that the other goods that could have been produced with those same resources were of greater value than what is currently being produced. Losses and bankruptcies are the market's way of providing signals and incentives to bring such wasteful activities to a halt, releasing those resources for use in other more highly valued uses.

The price-taker model also highlights the role of profits and losses in directing the actions of entrepreneurs and resource suppliers in an economy. When consumer demand for a product increases, higher economic profits result in the entry of new firms to satisfy this increased demand. Additional resources flow into the production of the now more

EXHIBIT 11

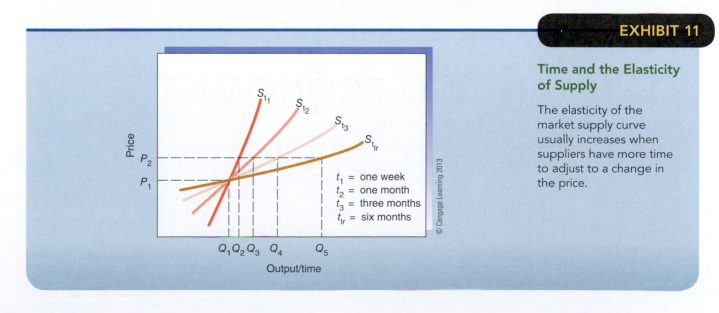

t_1 = one week
t_2 = one month
t_3 = three months
t_{lr} = six months

© Cengage Learning 2013

Time and the Elasticity of Supply

The elasticity of the market supply curve usually increases when suppliers have more time to adjust to a change in the price.

highly valued good and away from other industries. In contrast, when consumer demand for a product decreases, economic losses result in firms going out of business and reallocation of resources toward other industries where they are now more valuable. It is the profit and loss mechanism, driven by consumer demand and the costs of production that steers the allocation of resources in a market economy.

We live in a world of changing tastes and technology, imperfect knowledge, and uncertainty. Entrepreneurs can never be certain in advance if their ideas will be successful in the marketplace, and business decision-makers cannot be sure of future market prices or costs. Economics Nobel laureate Friedrich von Hayek (see the accompanying Outstanding Economist Box) viewed the competitive market system itself as a discovery process that helps to identify and determine what the prices of goods and costs of resources are, as well as which products are more highly valued than their costs (and which are not). Just like a football game is a process that allows us to discover which team is better, the market is a process that helps us to discover the best uses for our resources. Without the process taking place, the answers would not be known. The answers are, rather, a result of discoveries that occur as the process unfolds.

Nonetheless, the reward–penalty structure of a market economy is clear. *Firms that anticipate correctly the products and services for which future demand will be most urgent (relative to production costs) and produce and market them efficiently will make economic profits. Those that are inefficient and allocate resources incorrectly to areas of weak demand (relative to costs) will be penalized with losses.*

The firms most adept at giving consumers value for their money thrive and expand. Those less successful in doing so tend to shrink or even to disappear from the market. Free entry and the competitive process will protect the consumer from arbitrarily high prices. When profits are present, profit-seeking entrepreneurs will put more resources into these markets, supply will expand, and eventually the price will be driven down to the unit cost.

22-8 COMPETITION PROMOTES PROSPERITY

KEYS TO ECONOMIC PROSPERITY

Competition

Competition motivates businesses to produce efficiently, cater to the views of consumers, and search for innovative improvements.

©iStockphoto.com/malerapaso

OUTSTANDING ECONOMIST

FRIEDRICH A. VON HAYEK (1899–1992)

The writings of this 1974 Nobel Prize recipient spanned seven decades. Friedrich von Hayek's analysis on knowledge and markets greatly enhanced the understanding of how the competitive market process works. Hayek also made important contributions in the areas of monetary theory, law and economics, business cycles, and capital theory. He is also well known for the idea that market exchanges create an "extended order" in which perfect strangers who never meet nonetheless cooperate with one another to achieve their individual goals. Hayek stressed the role of the competitive market process as a procedure that helps us discover the best use of resources, the costs of production, and the prices of goods and services.

Apic/Hulton Archive/Getty Images

©iStockphoto.com/sorendls

The price-taker model highlights the importance of the competitive process. Competition puts pressure on producers to operate efficiently and use resources wisely. Holding quality constant, lower costs will mean more profit. Therefore, pursuit of profit will encourage each firm to minimize its cost of production—to use the set of resources least valued in other uses to produce the desired output. Firms that fail to keep costs low will be driven from the market.

Similarly, firms in competitive markets have a strong incentive to discover and produce goods and services that consumers value highly relative to cost. Thus, resources will be drawn to those uses where they are most productive, as judged by the consumers' willingness to pay. The ability of firms freely to expand or contract their businesses and enter or exit markets means that resources will not be trapped unproductively in a particular industry when they're valued more highly elsewhere.

If firms are going to be successful in competitive markets, they must also be innovative and forward-looking. The production techniques and product offerings that lead to success today will not necessarily pass the competitive market test tomorrow. Producers who survive in a competitive environment cannot become complacent. On the contrary, they must be willing to experiment and quick to adopt improved methods.

In competitive markets, business firms must serve the interests of consumers. As Adam Smith noted more than 200 years ago, competition harnesses personal self-interest and channels it into activities that enhance our living standards. Smith stated that

> *It is not from the benevolence of the butcher, the brewer, or the baker, that we expect our dinner, but from their regard to their own self-interest. We address ourselves, not to their humanity but to their self-love, and never talk to them of our own necessities, but of their advantages.*[4]

Sellers profit when they supply products valued more highly than the resources needed to make them. But their actions also help the rest of us get more value from those resources than we would otherwise. As Smith properly noticed, personal self-interest is a powerful source of economic progress when it is directed by the competitive market process.

LOOKING AHEAD

Consumers often seek variety in product design, style, durability, service, and location. Differentiating products gives firms some control over the prices they can charge. In the next two chapters, we will examine markets in which the firms are price searchers. We will also consider the impact entry barriers have on markets and pricing.

[4]Adam Smith, *An Inquiry into the Nature and Causes of the Wealth of Nations* (1776; Cannan's ed., Chicago: University of Chicago Press, 1976), 18.

KEY POINTS

- A firm facing a perfectly elastic demand for its product is a price taker. A firm that can raise its price without losing all of its customers (and that must lower its price in order to sell more units) is a price searcher.

- To maximize profit, a price taker will expand its output as long as the sale of additional units adds more to revenues than to costs. Therefore, the profit-maximizing price taker will produce the output level at which marginal revenue (and price) equals marginal cost.

- A firm that experiences losses but that anticipates being able to cover its costs in the long run will operate in the short run if it can cover its average variable costs. Conversely, the firm will shut down if it cannot cover its average variable costs. A firm that does not anticipate being able to cover its average total cost even in the long run will minimize losses by immediately going out of business.

- The price taker's short-run marginal cost curve (above its average variable cost) is its supply curve. The short-run market supply curve is the horizontal summation of the marginal cost curves (above *AVC*) of the firms in the industry.

- When the market price exceeds the firm's average total cost, it will earn an economic profit. When entry barriers are absent, profits will attract new firms into the industry and stimulate the existing firms to expand. This increasing market supply continues and puts downward pressure on the price until it reaches the level of average total cost, eliminating the economic profit.

- When the market price is less than the firm's average total cost, the resulting losses imply that the resources could be used elsewhere to produce more value. Losses will cause firms to leave the industry or to reduce the scale of their operations. This declining market supply continues and puts upward pressure on price until the firms remaining in the market are once again able to earn normal returns (zero economic profit).

- As the output of an industry expands in response to rising demand, "fixed" resources like the size of the firm's plant will make it costly for firms to expand output quickly. The diminishing

returns and rising marginal costs of firms explain why the short-run market supply curve slopes upward to the right.

- Normally, as industry output expands, rising factor prices push the costs of each firm upward, causing the long-run market supply curve to slope upward to the right also. However, in the long run, firms can alter the size of their plants and other resources that are fixed in the short run. As a result, the market supply curve is generally more elastic in the long run than the short run.

- Firms earn economic profit by producing goods that can be sold for more than the cost of the resources required to produce them. Profit is a reward people get for increasing the value of resources. Conversely, losses are a penalty imposed on those who use resources in a way that reduces their value.

- Competition motivates producers to operate efficiently, heed the views of consumers, and discover better products and lower-cost production methods. In competitive markets, self-interested producers will be directed toward wealth-creating activities that generate economic progress.

CRITICAL ANALYSIS QUESTIONS

1. Farmers are often heard to complain about the high costs of machinery, labor, and fertilizer, suggesting that these costs drive down their profits. Does it follow that if, for example, the price of fertilizer fell by 10 percent, farming (a highly competitive industry with low barriers to entry) would be more profitable? Explain.

2. *If the firms in a price-taker market are making short-run profits, what will happen to the market price in the long run? Explain.

3. "In a price-taker market, if a business operator produces efficiently—that is, if the cost of producing the good is minimized—the operator will be able to make at least a normal profit." True or false? Explain.

4. Suppose the government of a large city levies a 5 percent sales tax on hotel rooms. How will the tax affect (a) prices of hotel rooms, (b) the profits of hotel owners, and (c) gross expenditures (including the tax) on hotel rooms?

5. If coffee suppliers are price takers, how will an unanticipated increase in demand for their product affect each of the following, in a market that was initially in long-run equilibrium?
   a. the short-run market price of the product
   b. industry output in the short run
   c. profitability in the short run
   d. the long-run market price in the industry
   e. industry output in the long run
   f. profitability in the long run

6. *Suppose that the development of a new drought-resistant hybrid seed corn leads to a 50 percent increase in the average yield per acre without increasing the cost to the farmers who use the new technology. If the producers in the corn

production industry were price takers, what would happen to the following?
   a. the price of corn
   b. the profitability of corn farmers who quickly adopt the new technology
   c. the profitability of corn farmers who are slow to adopt the new technology
   d. the price of soybeans, a substitute product for corn

7. "When the firms in the industry are just able to cover their cost of production, economic profit is zero. Therefore, if demand falls, causing prices to go down even a little bit, all of the firms in the industry will be driven out of business." True or false? Explain.

8. Why does the short-run market supply curve for a product slope upward to the right? Why does the long-run market supply curve generally slope upward to the right? Why is the long-run market supply curve generally more elastic than the short-run supply curve?

9. *How does competition among firms affect the incentive of each firm to (a) operate efficiently (produce at a low per-unit cost) and (b) produce goods that consumers value? What happens to firms that fail to do these two things?

10. Will firms in a price-taker market be able to earn profits in the long run? Why or why not? What determines profitability? Discuss.

11. *During 2011, drought conditions throughout much of Europe substantially reduced the size of the corn, wheat, and soybean crops, three commodities for which demand is inelastic. Use the price-taker model to determine how the drought affected (a) prices of the three commodities, (b) revenue from the three crops, and (c) the profitability of those farming the three crops.

12. Why is competition in a market important? Is there a positive or negative effect on the economy when strong competitive pressures drive various firms out of business? Discuss.

13. Do business firms in competitive markets have a strong incentive to serve the interests of consumers? Are they motivated by a strong desire to help consumers? Are "good intentions" necessary if individuals are going to engage in actions that are helpful to others? Discuss.

14. A combination of high crude oil prices and government subsidies for ethanol have led to a sharp increase in the demand for corn in recent years. How will this increase in demand for corn influence (a) the price of corn; (b) the quantity of corn supplied; (c) the cost of producing soybeans and wheat, crops that are often produced on land suitable for production of corn; (d) the price of cereals, tortillas, and other products produced from corn; and (e) the price of beef, chicken, and pork, meats produced from animals that are generally fed large quantities of corn? Explain each of your answers.

15. *The accompanying table presents the expected cost and revenue data for the Tucker Tomato Farm. The Tuckers produce tomatoes in a greenhouse and sell them wholesale in a price-taker market.

   a. Fill in the firm's marginal cost, average variable cost, average total cost, and profit schedules.

   b. If the Tuckers are profit maximizers, how many tomatoes should they produce when the market price is $500 per ton? Indicate their profits.

   c. Indicate the firm's output level and maximum profit if the market price of tomatoes increases to $550 per ton.

   d. How many units would the Tucker Tomato Farm produce if the price of tomatoes fell to $450 per ton? What would be the firm's profits? Should the firm stay in business? Explain.

Cost and Revenue Schedules for Tucker Tomato Farm, Inc.

OUTPUT (TONS PER MONTH)	TOTAL COST	PRICE PER TON	MARGINAL COST	AVERAGE VARIABLE COST	AVERAGE TOTAL COST	PROFITS (MONTHLY)
0	$1,000	$500	—	—	—	—
1	1,200	500	—	—	—	—
2	1,350	500	—	—	—	—
3	1,550	500	—	—	—	—
4	1,900	500	—	—	—	—
5	2,300	500	—	—	—	—
6	2,750	500	—	—	—	—
7	3,250	500	—	—	—	—
8	3,800	500	—	—	—	—
9	4,400	500	—	—	—	—
10	5,150	500	—	—	—	—

16. In the accompanying table, you are given information about two firms that compete in a price-taker market. Assume that fixed costs for each firm are $20.

   a. Complete the table.

   b. What is the lowest price at which firm A will produce?

   c. How many units of output will it produce at that price? (Assume that it cannot produce fractional units.)

   d. What is the lowest price at which firm B will produce?

   e. How many units of output will it produce?

   f. How many units will firm A produce if the market price is $20?

   g. How many units will firm B produce at the $20 price? (Assume that it cannot produce fractional units.)

   h. If each firm's total fixed costs are $20 and the price of output is $20, which firm would earn a higher net profit or incur a smaller loss?

   i. How much would that net profit or loss be?

*Asterisk denotes questions for which answers are given in Appendix B.

	FIRM A				FIRM B		
QUANTITY	TOTAL VARIABLE COST	MARGINAL COST	AVERAGE VARIABLE COST	QUANTITY	TOTAL VARIABLE COST	MARGINAL COST	AVERAGE VARIABLE COST
1	$24	—	—	1	$8	—	—
2	30	—	—	2	10	—	—
3	38	—	—	3	16	—	—
4	48	—	—	4	24	—	—
5	62	—	—	5	36	—	—
6	82	—	—	6	56	—	—
7	110	—	—	7	86	—	—

CHAPTER 23
Price-Searcher Markets with Low Entry Barriers

FOCUS

- What are the characteristics of competitive price-searcher markets? How are price and output determined in such markets?

- How will profit and loss influence the choices of price searchers?

- Why do some economists criticize price-searcher behavior when entry barriers are low, while others like the results?

- Is price discrimination bad?

- Why is the role of the entrepreneur left out of economic models? How do the actions of entrepreneurs influence innovation and development of improved products?

- Does successful innovation by some businesses lead to the failure of others? Is this bad?

[T]he price to the price searcher is not determined for him as if by some impersonal market mechanism. Instead he must search out the optimal (wealth-maximizing) price. And, not knowing the demand schedule exactly, he will have to resort to retrial-and-error search processes.
—Armen A. Alchian and William R. Allen[1]

[1]Armen A. Alchian and William R. Allen, *University Economics*, 2nd ed. (Belmont, CA: Wadsworth Publishing, 1967), 113.

As we noted in the previous chapter, price-taker firms decide what output to produce, but they do not have a pricing decision to make. They must take the market-determined price for their output, and they operate in a market with low entry barriers. In this chapter, we will focus on markets in which entry barriers are also low, but firms can instead decide the price they charge. These firms differ in that they face a downward sloping demand curve. If they increase their price they will sell fewer units, and if they reduce their price they will sell more units. This is in contrast to a price-taker firm whose horizontal demand curve means they lose all their sales if they raise price.

23-1 COMPETITIVE PRICE-SEARCHER MARKETS

Markets that are characterized by (1) low entry barriers and (2) firms that face a downward-sloping demand curve are called **competitive price-searcher markets**.[2] The low entry barriers ensure that these markets are competitive, and the firm's downward-sloping demand curve means that the sellers in these markets have to search for the price and output combination that will maximize their profits.

In contrast with price-taker markets, in which the firms produce identical products, price searchers produce **differentiated products**. For example, a hamburger from Burger King is not identical to one from McDonald's or Five Guys. The products supplied by the alternative sellers may differ in their design, dependability, location, packaging, and a multitude of other factors. This product differentiation explains why the firms confront a downward-sloping demand curve. Because some consumers are willing to pay more to get the specific product they like best, the firm will lose some but not all its customers to rivals if it raises its price.

Rival firms, however, supply products that are quite similar. Because good substitutes are readily available from other suppliers, the demand curve faced by the firms in competitive price-searcher markets will be downward sloping, but highly elastic.

Given the low entry barriers, new entrants will be attracted if an activity is profitable. Thus, sellers in competitive price-searcher markets face competition from both firms already in the market and potential new firms that might be attracted.

Sometimes economists use the term **monopolistic competition** to describe markets quite similar to those of the competitive price-searcher model, but because there is nothing "monopolistic" about these markets, we believe that this term is misleading. Competitive price searcher is much more descriptive of the conditions in these markets. However, students should be aware that the expression "monopolistic competition" is often used to describe markets like those analyzed in this chapter.

For the price searcher, demand is not simply a given. Price searchers must try to estimate how buyers will respond to the various prices that might be charged. In essence, the firm must try to figure out what the demand curve for its product looks like. The firm, by changing product quality, style, location, and service (among many other factors), and by advertising, can also alter the demand for its products. It can increase demand by drawing customers from rivals if it can convince consumers that its products provide more value. In the real world, most firms occupy the complex and risky territory of the price searcher.

23-1a PRICE AND OUTPUT IN COMPETITIVE PRICE-SEARCHER MARKETS

How does a price searcher decide what price to charge and what level of output to produce? For the price searcher, reducing price in order to expand output and sales has two

Competitive price-searcher market
A market in which the firms have a downward-sloping demand curve, and entry into and exit from the market are relatively easy.

Differentiated products
Products distinguished from similar products by characteristics like quality, design, location, and method of promotion.

Monopolistic competition
A term often used by economists to describe markets characterized by a large number of sellers that supply differentiated products to a market with low barriers to entry. Essentially, it is an alternative term for a competitive price-searcher market.

---

[2]It is important to distinguish between the demand curve faced by the firm and the market demand curve. The competitive price-searcher model focuses on the *firm's* demand curve.

In the highly competitive market for custom-fitted golf clubs, firms use competitive weapons such as style, swingweight, variable length and club-shaft flexibility, advertising, and celebrity endorsements. Firms in this market are price searchers.

conflicting influences on total revenue, illustrated by areas in **Exhibit 1**. First, the increase in sales (from q_1 to q_2) due to the lower price will, by itself, add to the revenue of the price searcher as revenue is obtained on the additional units sold. Second, the price reduction, because it applies to all units sold—*including those that could otherwise have been sold at a higher price* (P_1, rather than the lower price, P_2) reduces the revenue received on the original q_1 units of output.

A numerical example will help to illustrate. Suppose a firm could sell three units at $5 for total revenue of $15, or at a reduced price of $4 it could sell 4 units for a total revenue of $16. When the firm lowers price to $4 to sell the fourth unit, this additional unit sold adds $4 to revenue. But there is an offsetting factor: The three units that could have been sold at $5 now only sell for $4, so the firm loses $1 in revenue on each of those original three units. Thus, the net addition to the firm's revenue (the marginal revenue from the sale of the fourth unit) is only $1, as the loss of $3 is deducted from the gain of $4. This can also be seen in the firm's total revenue, which was $15 at an output of three units (sold at $5) and only $16 at an output of four units (sold at $4).

As price is lowered, these two conflicting forces will result in marginal revenue (a change in total revenue) that is less than the selling price of the additional units. The price searcher's marginal revenue will always be less than price because the prices of units that could have been sold for more will be reduced as price is lowered in order to expand sales. Therefore, as Exhibit 1 shows, the price searcher's marginal revenue curve will always lie below the firm's demand curve.[3] (Remember, the lowercase *d* is used when the reference is to the *firm's* demand curve.)

EXHIBIT 1

Marginal Revenue of a Price Searcher

When a firm faces a downward-sloping demand curve, a price reduction that increases sales will exert two conflicting influences on total revenue. First, total revenue will rise because of an increase in the number of units sold (from q_1 to q_2). However, revenue losses from the lower price (P_2) on units that could have been sold at a higher price (P_1) will at least partially offset the additional revenues from increased sales. Therefore, the marginal revenue curve will lie inside the firm's demand curve.

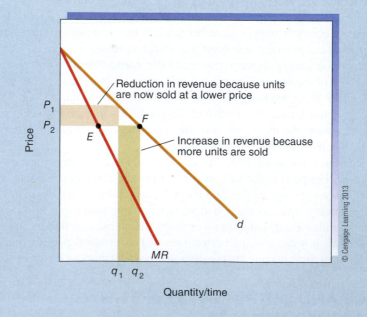

---

[3]For a straight-line demand curve, the marginal revenue curve will bisect any line from the *y*-axis to the demand curve, drawn parallel to the *x*-axis. For example, in Exhibit 1, the *MR* curve will divide the line P_2F into two equal parts, P_2E and EF.

© Cengage Learning 2013

EXHIBIT 2

The Price Searcher's Price and Output

A price searcher maximizes its profits by producing output q, for which $MR = MC$, and charging price P. The firm is making economic profits. What impact will these profits have if this is a typical firm?.

All firms maximize profits by producing all units for which marginal revenue is greater than marginal cost. Therefore, a price searcher will continue to lower price and expand output until marginal revenue is equal to marginal cost.

Exhibit 2 illustrates the profit-maximizing price and output. The price searcher will maximize profit by producing the level of output q, where marginal revenue is equal to marginal cost ($MC = MR$). For any output level less than q (for example, R), a price reduction and resulting sales expansion will add more to revenues than to costs, increasing profit. In contrast, all units beyond q (for example, S), add more to costs than to revenues, reducing profit. Profits will therefore be maximized by producing the output level q. The price the firm should charge is simply the price that will result in exactly q units being sold, which is a price of P. This price can be found by going up to the demand curve (to point A) at the profit maximizing level of output.

The firm in Exhibit 2 is making an economic profit in the short run. Total revenues PAq0 exceed the firm's total costs CBq0 at the profit-maximizing output level q. Given low barriers to entry in these markets, in the long run economic profits will result in other firms entering the market. These new rivals will draw customers away from existing firms and thereby reduce their demand. This entry of new firms into the market will continue until competition among rivals shifts the demand curve in far enough to eliminate the economic profit earned by the firms in the industry.

As Exhibit 3 illustrates, when long-run equilibrium is present in a competitive price-searcher market, the price will equal per-unit cost. Firms will produce at the $MR = MC$ output level, but they will be unable to earn economic profits because competitive pressures will force the price down to the per-unit cost level.

If losses are present in a specific market, with time, some of the firms in the market will go out of business. As firms leave, some of their previous customers will buy from other firms. The demand curve facing the remaining firms in the industry will then shift outward until the economic losses are eliminated and the long-run, zero-profit equilibrium illustrated by Exhibit 3 is restored.

Consider the role of profits and losses in competitive price-searcher markets. Profits will attract both new firms and additional investment capital into the market. In turn, the increased availability of the product (and similar products) will drive down the price until the profits are eliminated. Conversely, economic losses will cause competitors to exit the market and investment capital to move elsewhere. This will reduce the supply of the product and eventually make it possible for the firms remaining in the market to charge a price sufficient to cover their unit costs. *Thus, firms in competitive price-searcher markets can make either economic profits or losses in the short run. But, after long-run adjustments occur, only a normal profit (that is, zero economic profit) will be possible because entry barriers are low and competition is strong.*

Competitive Price-Searcher and Long-Run Normal Profit

Because firms are free to enter and exit the market, competition will eventually drive down prices to the level of average total cost for price searchers.

Competition drives price down to P = ATC

MC

ATC

Price

P

d

MR

© Cengage Learning 2013

q

Quantity/time

Contestable market

A market in which the costs of entry and exit are low, so a firm risks little by entering. Efficient production and zero economic profits should prevail in a contestable market.

23-2 CONTESTABLE MARKETS AND THE COMPETITIVE PROCESS

If firms can easily enter a market with little risk of suffering a substantial loss if they later exit the market, competition is likely to be intense, even if there are only a few firms operating within it. Markets in which firms can enter and exit with minimal risk are known as **contestable markets**.[4] Even if entering a contestable market requires a substantial amount of capital, this won't be a major deterrent if the funds can largely be recovered should the firm need to exit. This will be the case when the assets necessary to compete in a market can be either leased for short time periods or resold at something near their original purchase price.

When airport landing rights and facilities are available, an airline route is a classic example of a contestable market. Consider the case of the airline route between Salt Lake City, Utah, and Albuquerque, New Mexico. For many years, only Delta Airlines provided nonstop service on this route, because there is relatively little traffic. Furthermore, there would seem to be high barriers to entry, because it takes multimillion-dollar airplanes to compete, as well as a workforce, facilities for reservations, ticketing, baggage handling, and so on. Given that Delta was the only supplier on the route, one might have expected the price to be high and service relatively poor. However, if firms can easily rent facility space at airports, then the barriers to entry are much lower than the equipment costs suggest. The nonstop Salt Lake City–Albuquerque market, for example, can be entered by other airlines simply by shifting aircraft, personnel, and equipment from other routes and locations. Moreover, airlines often rent or lease their planes. This reduces both the amount of initial capital needed to enter a market and the risk of losing it should the venture fail. Indeed, recently US Airways has offered some service now in competition to Delta on the route. All along, several other airlines have served customers with connecting service, which requires a stop and perhaps a plane change at another city before completing the route connecting Albuquerque and Salt Lake City.

In a contestable market, potential competition, as well as actual entry, will discipline sellers. When entry and exit are not expensive, even a firm alone in a market faces the serious prospect of competition. Two important conditions will be present in contestable markets: (1) Prices above the level necessary to achieve zero economic profits will not be sustained, and (2) the costs of production will be kept to a minimum. This is because production inefficiencies and prices that are above costs present a profitable opportunity

---

[4]The classic article on this topic is William J. Baumol's "Contestable Markets: An Uprising in the Theory of Industry Structure," *American Economic Review* 72 (March 1982): 1–15.

Airliners are extremely expensive, so their cost might be a barrier to entry. But airplanes can also be leased and are highly mobile among markets, as are pilots, flight attendants, and office workers. These highly mobile resources allow firms to enter and exit a given transportation market with relative ease. Such a market is contestable.

©iStockphoto.com/Bim

for new entrants. Predictably, profit-seeking rivals will enter and drive the price down to the level of per-unit costs.

The contestable market model has important policy implications. If policy-makers are concerned that a market is not sufficiently competitive, they should take a close look at its entry barriers and what might be done to make it contestable. Much of economists' enthusiasm for deregulation can be traced to the fact that regulation often impedes market entry. Many economists believe that deregulating markets to make entry easier can lead to lower prices and better performance than other alternatives, including directly regulating prices.

23-3 EVALUATING COMPETITIVE PRICE-SEARCHER MARKETS

Because the long-run equilibrium conditions in price-taker markets are generally consistent with ideal economic efficiency, it is useful to compare and contrast them with long-run conditions in competitive price-searcher markets.

First, let us consider the similarities. Because of the low entry barriers, both price takers and competitive price searchers will have a strong incentive to serve the interests of consumers. Neither will be able to earn long-run economic profits. In the long run, competition will drive prices down to the level of average total cost in both price-taker and competitive price-searcher markets. Furthermore, entrepreneurs in both price-taker and price-searcher markets have a strong incentive to manage and operate their businesses efficiently. In both cases, operational inefficiency will lead to higher costs, losses, and forced exit from the market. Similarly, price takers and competitive price searchers alike will be motivated to develop and adopt new, cost-reducing procedures and techniques because lower costs will lead to higher short-run profits (or at least smaller losses).

The responses to changing demand conditions in price-taker and competitive price-searcher markets are also similar. In both cases, any increase in market demand that was not already expected leads to higher prices, short-run profits, expanded output, and the entry of new firms. With the entry of new producers and the expanded output of existing firms, the market supply will increase, putting downward pressure on the price. Profits drive this process until the market price falls to the level of average total cost, squeezing out all economic profit. Correspondingly, lower demand will lead to lower prices and short-run losses, causing output to fall and some firms to exit. As the market supply declines, prices will rise until the short-run losses are eliminated and the firms remaining in the market can again cover their costs. Thus, profits and losses direct the output decisions and market supply in both price-taker and competitive price-searcher markets.

What are some of the differences between the two market structures? As **Exhibit 4** shows, the price taker confronts a horizontal demand curve, while the demand curve of the price-searcher firm is downward sloping. This is important: It means that the marginal revenue of the price-searcher will be less than, not equal to, the price charged for the product sold. So, when the price searcher expands output until $MR = MC$, the price will still exceed the marginal cost (part b). In contrast, the price charged by a profit-maximizing price taker will equal the marginal cost (part a). In addition, when a price searcher is in long-run equilibrium, the firm's output rate will be less than the rate that minimizes average total cost. The price searcher would have a lower per-unit cost ($0.97 rather than $1.00) if a larger output were produced, but MR would be even less.

Some argue that the slightly higher prices (and unit costs) in competitive price-searcher markets indicate that these markets allocate goods and services inefficiently. However, it is important to recognize that the higher prices reflect the fact that it is costly to provide the greater product variety and diversity found in competitive price-searcher markets. But a broader range of choices also provides benefits. The greater variety makes it possible for a wider range of consumers to obtain the quality, style, and accompanying service that best fit their preferences and specific situation.

Are the higher prices accompanying the greater diversity worth the cost? This question can't be answered with certainty, but in some cases it is clear that consumers are willing to pay for it. For example, many consumers patronize small, conveniently located stores, even though they know that the same items are available at lower prices at large supermarkets.

EXHIBIT 4

Comparing Price-Taker and Price-Searcher Markets

Here, we illustrate the long-run equilibrium conditions of a price taker and a price searcher when entry barriers are low. In both cases, the price is equal to the average total cost, and economic profit is zero. However, because the price searcher confronts a downward-sloping demand curve for its product, its profit-maximizing price exceeds marginal cost, and output is not large enough to minimize average total cost when the market is in long-run equilibrium. For identical cost conditions, the price of the product in a price-searcher market will be slightly higher than in a price-taker market. Some argue that this higher price is indicative of inefficiency, whereas others believe that it merely reflects the higher cost accompanying greater variety and convenience.

(a) Price taker

(b) Price searcher

© Cengage Learning 2013

The two market structures also differ with regard to advertising: Price searchers often advertise, but price takers do not. Like variety, advertising is costly, and in the long run, consumers cover this cost in the form of higher prices. Do advertised products provide enough information and variety to justify the higher cost from the consumer's viewpoint? We cannot know for certain. However, we do know that producers are always free to use low-priced, more uniform, and less-advertised products to lure buyers away from firms that advertise and provide variety at a higher price. Some firms do, and sometimes the strategy works; yet many consumers choose to buy advertised goods and pay the higher prices. This result suggests that many customers do find that advertised products and greater variety are worth the added cost.

23-4 A SPECIAL CASE: PRICE DISCRIMINATION

So far, we have assumed that all sellers of a product will charge each customer the same price. Sometimes, though, price searchers can increase their revenues (and profits) by charging different prices to different groups of consumers. Businesses like hotels, restaurants, and drugstores often charge senior citizens less than other customers. Students and children are often given discounts at movie theaters and athletic events. Bars offer "ladies' night" discounts on drinks for women. Colleges often give financial aid (reduced tuition) to students from low-income families, or scholarships to students with good grades. These practices are called **price discrimination**. *To gain from such a practice, price searchers must be able to do two things: (1) identify and separate at least two groups with differing elasticities of demand and (2) prevent those who buy at the low price from reselling to the customers charged higher prices.*

Let us take a closer look at how sellers may gain from price discrimination. Suppose that a seller has two groups of customers: one with an inelastic demand for its product and the other with an elastic demand. An increase in the price charged the first group will increase the total revenue derived from that group. At the same time, a reduction in price will increase revenues derived from the latter. Thus, a seller may be able to increase total revenue and profit by charging the first group a higher price than the second.

The pricing of airline tickets illustrates the potential of price discrimination. The airline industry has found that the demand of business fliers is substantially less elastic than the demand of vacationers, students, and other travelers. Thus, airlines often charge higher fares to people who are unwilling to stay over a weekend, who spend only a day or two at their destination, and who make reservations a short time before their flight. These

Price discrimination
A practice whereby a seller charges different consumers different prices for the same product or service.

Andrew Holbrooke/The Image Works

Students from low-income families are likely to be more sensitive to tuition charges than those from high-income families. Colleges often make scholarships and other forms of financial aid more readily available to low-income students. This price discrimination makes it possible for them to generate larger revenues from tuition than would otherwise be the case.

high fares fall primarily on business travelers, who are less sensitive to price. In contrast, discount fares are offered to fliers willing to make reservations well in advance, travel during off-peak hours, and stay at their destinations over a weekend before returning home. Such travelers are likely to be vacationers and students, who are highly sensitive to price.

Exhibit 5 illustrates the logic of this policy. Part a shows what would happen if a single price were charged to all customers. Given the demand, the profit-maximizing firm expands output to 100, where *MR* equals *MC*. The profit-maximizing price on coast-to-coast flights is $400, which generates $40,000 of revenue per flight. Because the marginal cost per passenger is $100, this provid es the airline with net operating revenue of $30,000 with which to cover other costs.

However, as part b shows, although the market demand schedule is unchanged, the airline can do even better if it uses price discrimination. When it charges business travelers $500, most of these passengers continue to use the airline, because their demand is highly inelastic. Conversely, a $100 price cut generates substantial additional ticket sales from price-sensitive vacationers, students, and others whose demands are more elastic. Therefore, with price discrimination, the airline can sell sixty tickets (primarily to business travelers) at $500 and sixty additional tickets to others at $300. Total revenue jumps to $48,000 and leaves the airline with $36,000 ($48,000 minus 120 times the $100 marginal cost per passenger) of revenue in excess of variable cost. Compared with the single-price outcome (part a), the price discrimination strategy expands profit by $6,000.

When sellers can segment their market (at a low cost) into groups with differing price elasticities of demand, price discrimination can increase profits. For *each group*, the seller will maximize profit by equating marginal cost and marginal revenue. This rule will lead to higher prices for groups with a less elastic demand and lower prices for those with a more elastic demand. Compared with the single-price situation, price discrimination increases profitability because a higher price increases the net revenue from groups with an inelastic

---

EXHIBIT 5

Price Discrimination

As part (a) illustrates, a $400 ticket price will maximize profits on coast-to-coast flights if an airline charges a single price. However, the airline can do still better if it raises the price to $500 for passengers with a highly inelastic demand (business travelers) and reduces the price to $300 for travelers with a more elastic demand (for example, students and vacationers). When sellers can segment their market, they can gain by (1) charging a higher price to consumers with a less elastic demand and (2) offering discounts to customers whose demand is more elastic.

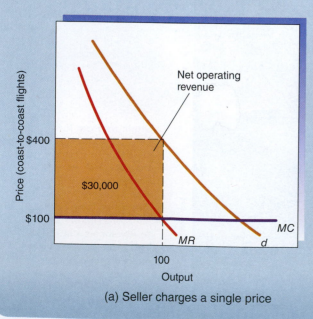

(a) Seller charges a single price

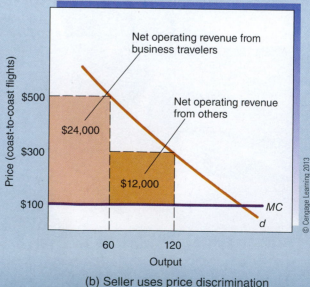

(b) Seller uses price discrimination

demand, while a lower price increases the net revenue from price-sensitive customers. With price discrimination, the number of units sold also increases (compare part a with part b) because the discounts provided to price-sensitive groups increase the quantity sold more than the higher prices charged the less-price-sensitive groups reduce sales.

Of course, this will work only if the two groups can't trade with each other. Movie theaters sell children's tickets to kids, and the tickets cannot be used by adults. Notice, though, that they don't try to sell popcorn at lower prices to children because popcorn could be too easily resold to adults.

How do buyers fare when a seller can price discriminate? Some buyers pay more than they would if a single, intermediate price were offered. They purchase fewer units, and they are worse off. In contrast, those for whom the price-discrimination process lowers the price are better off. Of course, with some products, such as airline transportation, a single buyer might be better off with some purchases and worse off with others.

On balance, however, we can expect that output will be greater with price discrimination than it would be with a single price. The market is not as understocked as it would have been in the absence of the price discrimination. So from an allocative efficiency standpoint, price discrimination gets high marks; it allows more trades, reducing the inefficiency due to price being set above marginal cost. Some of the gains that would accrue to consumers with an inelastic demand are transferred to the price searcher as increased revenue, but additional gains from trade are created by the increased output of goods that would be lost if price discrimination were absent.

In some markets, there is an additional gain from price discrimination: Production may occur that would be lost entirely if only a single price could be charged. With price discrimination, some otherwise unprofitable firms may be able to generate enough additional revenue to operate successfully in the marketplace. For example, some small towns might not provide enough revenue at a single price to enable a local physician to cover his or her opportunity costs. However, if the physician is able to discriminate on the basis of income, charging higher-income patients more than normal rates and lower-income patients less, the resulting revenues from practicing in the small town may enable the physician to stay in the community. In this case, all residents of the town may be better off because of the price discrimination, since it makes it possible for them to access a local physician. After all, even those being charged the highest prices are not disadvantaged if the price discrimination keeps the physician in town. They are just as able to seek physician services elsewhere as they would have been in the absence of the price-discriminating local doctor. With or without price discrimination, access to competing sellers (or buyers) protects market participants from unfair treatment.

In summary, if potential customers can be segmented into groups with different elasticities of demand and resale can be prevented, sellers can often gain by charging higher prices to those with the less elastic demand (and lower prices to those with a more elastic demand). Price discrimination can also increase the total gains from trade and thereby reduce allocative inefficiency. Sometimes it even allows production where none would have otherwise occurred.

23-5 ENTREPRENEURSHIP AND ECONOMIC PROGRESS

KEYS TO ECONOMIC PROSPERITY

Entrepreneurship

Entrepreneurial discovery and the development of improved products and production processes provide a central element of economic progress.

©iStockphoto.com/malerapaso

Scientific models simplify conditions in order to help us understand complex relationships. Economic models like the price-taker and price-searcher models are no exception. But these models are not rich enough to fully capture all aspects of the dynamic process of competition. Competitive markets provide entrepreneurs with a strong incentive to innovate and discover better ways of doing things. However, if we are going to get the most from the available resources, they must be directed toward the activities that create the most value. This target, however, is an ever-shifting one. Discovery of new products, technologies, and organizational structures creates opportunities for some and diminishes them for others. To a large degree, market economies are successful because they provide entrepreneurs with a strong incentive to search for and act on opportunities to move resources toward higher valued uses in a world of constant change.[5]

Entrepreneurs must make choices about how much output and what kind of output to produce and what price to charge. They also must figure out the type of business structure, scale of operation, and combination of jointly supplied goods and services that will keep per-unit costs low. The entry of firms into an industry earning short-run economic profit also reflects the decisions and behavior of entrepreneurs searching for profit opportunities. Moreover, all of these choices must be made with imperfect information under conditions of uncertainty. While the assumptions and operational elements of the price-taker and price searcher models incorporate these elements, they do not reflect the central role of entrepreneurial decision-making. Therefore, the picture is incomplete.

The role of the entrepreneur cannot be fully captured by the profit maximization assumption of a model. Better ways of doing things do not just happen; they must be discovered and developed by entrepreneurs. Further, the actions of entrepreneurs often cause entirely new markets to appear, and others to disappear. A hypothetical newspaper ad to hire an entrepreneur might read something like this:

Entrepreneur
Diverse Skills Required

WANTED

Must be (1) alert to new business opportunities and new problems before they become obvious; (2) willing to back judgments with hard work and creative effort before others recognize the correctness of judgments; (3) able to make correct decisions and convince others of their validity, so as to attract additional financial backing; and (4) able to recognize own inevitable mistakes and to back away from incorrect decisions without wasting additional resources. Exciting, exhausting, high-risk position. Pay will be very good for success and very poor for failure.

Entrepreneurship is a process in which individual entrepreneurs discover previously unnoticed profit opportunities and act on them. In this framework profit opportunities always exist in the marketplace, but they must be discovered. The rate of discovery will depend on the reward. In economies where it is attractive to discover better ways of do-

---

[5]For a more complete overview of entrepreneurship and references on the topic, see Mark Crosson, "Entrepreneurship," in *The New Palgrave: A Dictionary of Economics*, ed. John Eatwell et al. (New York: Stockton Press, 1987), 151–53; and Russell "Entrepreneurship," in *The Concise Encyclopedia of Economics*, 2nd ed., ed. David R. Henderson (Indianapolis: Liberty Fund, 2007).

ing things, the discovery rate of wealth creating opportunities will be higher and human progress more rapid.

Entrepreneurship and discovery can happen within existing business firms (often called "intrapreneurship") or from new entrants into the marketplace. Research shows that large existing corporations are more likely to make marginal improvements on existing products, while breakthrough ideas are more likely to come from new start-up firms.

An entrepreneur is someone who finds new combinations of resources and creates products and production methods that did not previously exist. Sifting through these many combinations is a complex task fraught with uncertainty because the number of ways of combining resources is almost limitless. A growing, vibrant economy will be characterized by the constant introduction of new products and services. Think of the new products that have been introduced during the last fifty years: microwave ovens, personal computers, cellular telephones, DVD players, video games, better coronary artery bypass techniques, and online social networks come to mind. Innovations like these have had an enormous impact on our lives.

But no one knows what the next innovative breakthrough will be or who will discover and develop it. Even smart professors, business leaders, and government officials are unable to pre-evaluate business ideas and differentiate between those that will succeed and the ones destined for failure. For example, Fred Smith, the founder of Federal Express Corporation, developed the business plan for FedEx as a class project while he was a student at Yale University. His business professor gave him a "C" because he thought the idea was infeasible. (See Applications in Economics Box on "Five Entrepreneurs Who Have Changed Our Lives.") Not even entrepreneurs themselves can know for certain in advance whether their business idea will be profitable. The only real test is to try it out within the framework of the competitive market process.

23-5a DYNAMIC COMPETITION, INNOVATION, AND BUSINESS FAILURES

Business failures are often painful for the parties directly involved. From the standpoint of the entire economy, however, business failures and the shrinkage of other firms play an important role: They weed out less efficient, high-cost producers and production, and release resources to be employed more productively elsewhere. The assets and workers of firms that shrink or fail become available for use by others, supplying goods that are more highly valued by consumers, relative to their costs. Without this release of resources, the expansion of both profitable firms and the entire economy would be slowed. Viewed from this perspective, business failures are often the flip side of consumers shifting their spending toward firms offering improved products and/or lower prices.

While business failures occur for a variety of reasons, including poor management and misjudgment of market conditions, innovative actions by rivals is also a major contributing factor. When a firm introduces a new, improved product or comes up with a lower-cost method of supplying a good, it will attract buyers away from other firms. Entrepreneurship is inherently a disruptive force in an economy because the introduction of new products leads to the obsolescence of others, a process known as "creative destruction." Examples abound. The digital camera has virtually eliminated the use and production of film. The introduction of digital music has resulted in the closure of stores selling CDs like Tower Records and Music Den. The innovations of on-demand movies, Netflix, and Redbox have driven traditional movie rental stores like Blockbuster and Movie Gallery (which ran Hollywood Video) into bankruptcy.

Even giant firms can be brought down by innovative rivals. During the 1990s, Microsoft's dominance of the computer industry was overwhelming. Between January 1990 and January 2000, Microsoft's stock price rose by about 8,000 percent. Apple lagged far behind Microsoft in both market share and brand name recognition. But things soon began to change. Apple introduced the iPod in 1996, which revolutionized how consumers purchased and listened to music, and gained substantial brand name recognition among consumers, especially younger consumers. In 2007, Apple introduced the iPhone, again changing the game, but this time in the market for cell phones. The innovative behavior of Apple continued, in 2008 the MacBook Air was introduced, and in 2010 the iPad again unleashed a wave of creative destruction, altering the way consumers receive news, read books, and play games. During the first decade of this century, the stock value of Microsoft fell by more than 40 percent, while that of Apple soared. By 2010, the market value of Apple surpassed that of the previously dominant Microsoft.

In a competitive economy, numerous businesses come and go. Each year, newly incorporated businesses account for about 10 percent of the total, but about 60 percent of them will fail within six years. Even during good economic times, approximately 1 percent of businesses file for bankruptcy each year, and many others close their doors or sell their assets to other, more successful (or at least more optimistic) operators.

From an economic standpoint then, business failure has a positive side; it gets rid of bad or outdated ideas, freeing up resources to be used in other endeavors. A vibrant economy will have both a large number of new business start-ups and a large number of business failures. However, as more ideas are tried, it will be more likely that we will stumble on to that one-in-a-million new innovation that will substantially improve our lives.

Let's summarize the importance of entrepreneurship. Discovery of new products and better ways of doing things is an important source of economic growth and improved living standards. These discoveries often come from unexpected sources and there is no way to tell in advance which will succeed and which will fail. Thus, it is vitally important that new ideas can be tested. Many will fail, but a few will succeed and transform our lives. This discovery process is too complex to be captured, at least not fully, by models, but it is nonetheless a central ingredient of a healthy, growing economy.

APPLICATIONS IN ECONOMICS

Five Entrepreneurs Who Have Changed Our Lives

Compared with movie stars and athletes, business entrepreneurs seldom command quite as much respect in our society. Often, their contributions are either overlooked or misunderstood. Everyone knows that highly successful entrepreneurs make a lot of money. But their innovative ideas and product improvements enhance the lives of others. If they did not, people would not buy their products and services. Entrepreneurs are a major source of economic progress and higher living standards. Their impact on our lives is far greater than most realize. Let's take a closer look at the impact of five leading entrepreneurs.

Fred Smith

AP Images

In 2012, FedEx had 300,000 employees and generated $42.7 billion in revenues. Fred Smith was the founder of the path-breaking firm. The idea behind FedEx came to him when he was in college in the 1960s, with his observation that computers were going to become a major part of people's lives. More important, he predicted a logical consequence: If computers were going to replace people for many tasks, the computers would have to be in good working order every day. If something went wrong, it would need to be fixed immediately. This would create a strong demand for a delivery system capable of getting parts and materials whenever and wherever they were needed.

Beginning in 1973, FedEx created a giant network of airplane and truck transportation capable of providing overnight delivery around the world. Smith's chief innovation was the development of a transportation system with a "central switch" or "central junction." For FedEx, that was Memphis, Tennessee. When one looks at moving an item from Detroit to Minneapolis via Memphis, it seems inefficient, says Smith. "But when you take all of the transactions on the network together, it's tremendously efficient."

Smith developed the idea and described the system in a paper for a business strategy course while studying in the M.B.A. program at Yale. Perhaps because it seemed far-fetched at the time, he reports that the professor gave him a "gentleman's C." In the following decade, however, Smith founded Federal Express and created the express delivery system outlined in his paper. FedEx has revolutionized the express mail and package

franckreporter/E+/Getty Images

delivery system. It has forced competitors, from the U.S. Postal Service to United Parcel Service, to become more efficient and to make major changes in their operations. Smith can take great pride in the fact that the market gave him a much higher grade than his old M.B.A. professor.

Oprah Winfrey

Oprah Winfrey is a billionaire, a successful entrepreneur, and a one-person conglomerate. Winfrey overcame personal difficulties to achieve her success. Her parents never married, and her childhood was spent traveling among temporary homes with family members in Mississippi, Nashville, and Milwaukee. She attended Tennessee State University in Nashville but left early to take a job at a local radio station.

In 1984, she started as a talk-show host in Chicago, but her program was soon the top talk show in the country. It has held that rating for nearly two decades and is now broadcast in more than 100 countries. Always inspirational, she decided in the mid-1990s that her show, which was often about dysfunctional relationships, was too negative. She began to make it more upbeat and also began to develop "lifestyle" products that were attractive and uplifting. As a child, Winfrey loved to read, so she formed Oprah's Book Club, which created many bestsellers. She has her own magazine, *O, the Oprah Magazine*. She was a cofounder of the Oxygen Network, a cable television network, and in January 2011 she launched a new network called OWN. Winfrey is an astute business executive, with her own company, Harpo, Inc. (that's Oprah spelled backward). Few entrepreneurs have changed more lives than Oprah has. She changed television by winning an international audience through candid and heartfelt discussion and she has expanded her influence through many other businesses. Most important perhaps, she has encouraged women to advance both emotionally and intellectually.

Peter Thiel

Many of you have probably never heard of this entrepreneur, but if you have ever used PayPal or Facebook, you have benefited from his entrepreneurial skills. Thiel was a cofounder of PayPal in 1998, and served as its CEO. He sold it to eBay in 2002 for $1.5 billion, personally netting $60 million. In 2004, Thiel invested $500,000 in Facebook. His net worth is reported to be $1.6 billion in March of 2013. As with many entrepreneurs, he has not had a perfect record in his still-young investment career. In 2005 he opened a hedge fund, Clarium Capital but the assets of that fund, once as high as $7.8 billion in mid-2008, have since fallen to just $681 million.

Thiel has many and varied talents and interests, from human rights, philosophy, and technology to film. He co-produced a film, *Thank You for Smoking*. As a student at Stanford, he founded *The Stanford Review* newspaper. Earlier in life he was a chess champion, ranking seventh in the U.S. under-13 age bracket.

His creativity even carries over to his charitable giving. In 2008, he pledged $500,000 to the new Seasteading Institute, to support their mission "to establish permanent, autonomous ocean communities to enable experimentation and innovation with diverse social, political, and legal systems." In 2010 he established a "Thiel Fellowship" that would award $100,000 to each of 20 people less than 20 years of age who promised to quit college and create their own entrepreneurial ventures. If the awardees have a fraction of the creativity of this imaginative entrepreneur, the future world will be an exciting place to live.

Sergey Brin and Larry Page

For years, Internet users struggled to find billions of bits of information scattered across the World Wide Web. Two Stanford computer science graduate students—Sergey Brin and Larry Page—dramatically simplified that process. Brin and

Page were in their early twenties when they dropped out of graduate school. Using their credit cards and those of their parents and friends, they formed Google, Inc., in a garage in Menlo Park, California. ("Googol" is the number 1 followed by 100 zeros.)

Google's computers are constantly searching the Web, downloading a huge number of files into the company's data-bases, and updating them regularly. The sophisticated programs sort and quickly bring the most important and reliable information to the top of users' screens. Information seekers love it. The keywords they type in for their searches also target the advertising that generates the firm's revenue. Unlike, say, a newspaper, which delivers the same ads to every reader, Google links advertising to the user's particular interests according to the topic being searched. Users see fewer ads, but advertisers get more targeted exposure of their messages.

In 2004, Google's stock went public. Even the stock offering was innovative—a "Dutch auction," whereby anyone, including individual investors, could bid on the shares. The bidder specified a price as high or low as he or she wanted and the number of shares to be purchased at that price. Following the auction, the stock opened on the market at just over $100 per share. While there have been ups and downs in the price, the stock was trading in the $900 per share range during the summer of 2013. The two founders of Google have not yet earned their doctorates, but they *have* earned a fortune. They did it by designing a system that benefits millions of people every day.

franckreporter/E+/Getty Images

LOOKING AHEAD

In this chapter, we have analyzed the choices facing price searchers and their behavior when barriers to entry are low. The following chapter will analyze the performance of price-searcher markets when the barriers to entry are relatively high.

KEY POINTS

- Firms in price-searcher markets with low barriers to entry face a downward-sloping demand curve. They are free to set the prices for the products that they sell but face strong competitive pressure from existing and potential rivals.

- Firms in price searcher markets with low entry barriers use product quality, style, convenience of location, advertising, and price as competitive weapons. Because each firm competes with rivals offering similar products, each confronts a highly elastic demand curve for its products.

- A profit-maximizing price searcher will expand output as long as marginal revenue exceeds marginal cost, lowering its price in the process, until $MR = MC$. The price charged by the profit-maximizing price searcher will be greater than its marginal cost.

- Firms in competitive price-searcher markets can experience either profits or losses in the short run. Profits will attract rival firms into the market until supply increases and the profit-maximizing price falls to the level of per-unit price. Losses will cause firms to exit the market until the price increases enough that the remaining firms can once again cover their per-unit costs. Because of the low entry barriers, the firms in competitive price-searcher markets will earn only normal returns (zero economic profit) in long-run equilibrium.

- Competition can come from potential as well as actual rivals. If entry and exit can be arranged at low cost, and if there are no legal barriers to entry, the theory of contestable markets indicates that competitive results will be approximated, even if there are only a few firms actually in the market.

- Competitive price-searcher markets provide more variety but may raise costs relative to price-taker markets because (1) price exceeds marginal cost at the profit-maximizing output level, (2) long-run average cost is not minimized, and (3) advertising is costly. When barriers to entry are low, however, price searchers have an incentive to (1) produce efficiently; (2) undertake production if, and only if, their actions are expected to increase the value of the resources used; and (3) be innovative in offering new product options.

- When a price searcher can (1) identify groups of customers that have different price elasticities of demand and (2) prevent customers from retrading the product, price discrimination may emerge. Sellers may be able to gain by charging higher prices to groups with a less elastic demand and lower prices to those with a more elastic demand. The practice generally leads to a larger output and more gains from trade than would otherwise occur.

- Entrepreneurs discover previously unnoticed profit opportunities and act on them. By discovering and developing new products that are highly valued relative to cost, entrepreneurs promote economic progress. The profit and loss system provides entrepreneurs with quick and persuasive feedback on the merit of their idea.

- Entrepreneurship is an inherently disruptive force in an economy as new products often cause the failure of old ones. But this creative destruction is an important source of improved products, lower costs production methods, and higher living standards.

CRITICAL ANALYSIS QUESTIONS

1. Price searchers can set the prices of their products. Does this mean that they will charge the highest possible price for their products? Why or why not?

2. Because price searchers can set their prices, does this mean that their prices are unaffected by market conditions? In price-searcher markets with low barriers to entry, will the firms be able to make economic profit in the long run? Why or why not?

3. *What determines the *variety* of styles, designs, and sizes of different products? Why do you think there are only a few different varieties of toothpicks but lots of different types of napkins on the market?

4. What do competitive price searchers have to do to make economic profit?

5. What must an entrepreneur do in order to introduce a new innovative product? What determines whether the new product will be a success or failure?

6. Is quality and style competition as important as price competition? Would you like to live in a country where government regulation restricted the use of quality and style competition? Why or why not? Do you think you would get more or less for your consumer dollar under restrictions like these? Discuss.

7. Suppose that a price searcher is currently charging a price that maximizes the firm's total revenue. Will this price also maximize the firm's profit? Why or why not? Explain.

8. *a. What determines whether corporations, individual proprietorships, employee-owned firms, consumer cooperatives, or some other form of business structure will dominate in a market?

   b. What determines whether small firms, medium-size firms, or large firms will dominate in a market?

9. Would our standard of living be higher if the government "bailed out" troubled businesses? If a firm goes out of business, what happens to the firm's assets, workers, and customers? Are business failures bad for the economy? Why or why not?

10. *Suppose that a group of investors wants to start a business operated out of a popular Utah ski area. The group is considering either building a new hotel complex or starting a new local airline serving that market. Each new business would require about the same amount of capital and personnel hiring. The group believes each endeavor has the same profit potential. Which is the safer (less likely to result in a substantial capital loss) investment? Why? Is there an offsetting advantage to the other investment?

11. Is price discrimination harmful to the economy? How does price discrimination affect the total amount of gains from exchange? Explain. Why do colleges often charge students different prices based on their family income?

12. *"When competition is intense, only the big firms survive. The little guy has no chance." True or false? Explain.

13. What is the primary requirement for a market to be competitive? Is competition necessary for markets to work well? Why or why not? How does competition influence the following: (a) the cost efficiency of producers, (b) the quality of products, and (c) the discovery and development of new products? Explain your answers.

14. *What keeps McDonald's, Walmart, General Motors, or any other business firm from raising prices, selling shoddy products, and providing lousy service?

15. "The superiority of the competitive market is the positive stimuli it provides for constantly improving efficiency, innovating, and offering consumers diversity of choice." This quotation is from Alfred Kahn, the architect of transportation deregulation during the 1970s. Evaluate the statement. Is it true? Discuss.

16. The accompanying graph shows the short-run demand and cost situation for a price searcher in a market with low barriers to entry.

    a. What level of output will maximize the firm's profit level?
    b. What price will the firm charge?
    c. How much revenue will the firm receive in this situation? How much is total cost? Total profit?
    d. How will the situation change over time?

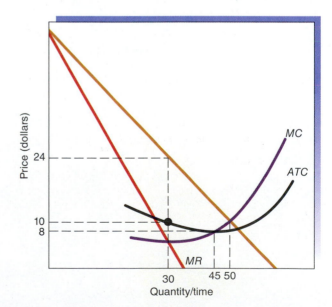

17. Rod N. Reel owns a dealership that sells fishing boats in an open, price-searcher market. To develop his pricing strategy, Rod hired an economist to estimate his demand curve. Columns (1) and (2) of the chart on the next page provide the data for the expected weekly quantity demanded for Rod's fishing boats at alternative prices. Rod's marginal (and average) cost of supplying each boat is constant at $5,000 per boat no matter how many boats he sells per week in this range. This cost includes all opportunity costs and represents the economic cost per boat.

   a. Find Rod's economic profits at each alternative price by calculating the difference between total revenue and total cost.

   b. Find Rod's marginal revenue and marginal cost from the sale of each additional boat.

   c. If Rod wants to maximize his profits, what price should he charge per boat?

   d. How many boats will Rod sell per week at the profit-maximizing price?

   e. What will Rod's profits be per week at this price and sales volume?

   f. At the price and sales level where profits are maximized, has Rod sold all boats that have higher marginal revenue than marginal cost?

   g. If Rod's profits are typical of all firms in the boat sales business, what might be expected to happen in the future? Will more boat dealers open in the area, or will some of the existing ones go out of business? What will happen to the profitability of the boat dealers in the future once the entry/exit has occurred?

   h. Challenge Question: Recall the relationship between elasticity of demand, price changes, and their impact on total revenues. As Rod lowers his price from $9,000 to $5,000, his total revenues keep increasing. Is demand in this price range elastic, inelastic, or unit elastic? When Rod lowers his price from $5,000 to $4,000, his total revenues stay the same. Is demand in this price range elastic, inelastic, or unit elastic? Can you guess what might happen at prices below $4,000? Explain.

*Asterisk denotes questions for which answers are given in Appendix B.

Price of Fishing Boats (1)	Number of Fishing Boats Sold per Week (2)	Total Revenue per Week (3)	Total Cost per Week (4)	Economic Profit per Week (5)	Marginal Revenue (6)	Marginal Cost (7)
$9,000	0	—	—	—	n/a	n/a
8,000	1	—	—	—	—	—
7,000	2	—	—	—	—	—
6,000	3	—	—	—	—	—
5,000	4	—	—	—	—	—
4,000	5	—	—	—	—	—

Price-Searcher Markets with High Entry Barriers

FOCUS

- What are the major barriers to entry that limit competitiveness in some markets?

- What is a monopoly? Does it guarantee the ability to make a profit?

- What is an oligopoly? When are oligopolists likely to collude? Why is it impossible to construct a general theory of output and price for an oligopolist?

- Will competition keep large firms in check in markets that have high barriers to entry? What problems may arise in such markets?

- What policy alternatives might improve the operation of markets with high barriers to entry?

"When the monopolist raises prices above the competitive level in order to reap his monopoly profits, customers buy less of the product, less is produced, and society as a whole is worse off. In short, monopoly reduces society's income."

"... [C]ompetition is a tough weed, not a delicate flower."

—George Stigler[1]

[1]Both quotes are from George J. Stigler, "Monopoly," in *The Concise Encyclopedia of Economics*, 2nd ed., David R. Henderson, editor, (Indianapolis, Ind.: Liberty Fund, Inc., 2007), available online at http://www.econlib.org/library/Enc/Monopoly.html.

In the previous two chapters, we analyzed the way firms behave in markets with low barriers to entry. In those markets, short-run economic profits lead to the entry of new firms and expansion in supply that drive profits down to a normal level (zero economic profit). We now turn to the analysis of firm behavior when entry barriers are high and there are few, if any, rival firms offering the same or similar products. This chapter focuses on factors that make entry into a market more difficult, and how this can reduce the ability of markets to keep firms in check. We will also consider policy alternatives that might improve the efficiency of these markets.

24-1 WHY ARE ENTRY BARRIERS SOMETIMES HIGH?

What makes it difficult for potential competitors to enter a market? Under certain conditions, four factors can be important: economies of scale, government licensing, patents, and control over an essential resource. Let's consider each.

24-1a ECONOMIES OF SCALE

When the fixed costs in an industry are large, bigger firms can generally achieve lower average total per-unit costs than can smaller ones. As our discussion of contestable markets indicated in the last chapter, however, economies of scale and high fixed costs are not a significant barrier to entry when the assets needed to enter the market can be leased, transferred to another location, or resold later without a major loss of value.

In some markets, however, this will not be the case. Airline routes may be contestable, but airplane manufacturing is not, because much of the equipment used to produce airplanes is of little use in the production of other things. Once it is in place, most of the equipment cannot be shifted to other uses. The cost of the equipment is a sunk cost. Under these circumstances, if necessary, the incumbent firm will continue operating for a lengthy period of time as long as it can cover its variable (operating) costs. Potential new entrants will recognize that this incentive structure will make it extremely difficult to displace the current incumbent. Thus, they will be reluctant to attempt entry, even if the current incumbent is earning economic profit. A dominant firm will tend to emerge in the industry, and if the market is not contestable, the cost advantages resulting from its size will protect it from potential rivals.

24-1b GOVERNMENT LICENSING AND OTHER LEGAL BARRIERS TO ENTRY

Government imposed legal barriers are the oldest and most prevalent method of protecting a business firm from potential competitors. Kings once granted exclusive business rights to favored citizens or groups. Tariffs that raise the price of imported goods and quotas that limit the quantity of imports have reduced the competitiveness of various markets for centuries. To compete in certain parts of the communications industry in the United States (for example, to operate a radio or television station), one must obtain a government license. Similarly, local governments often grant exclusive licenses for the local operation of cable television systems. Each of these measures reduces competition and protects the profits of favored firms, and often in effect provides a local monopoly franchise.

Licensing can also limit entry and reduce competitiveness even without the monopoly franchise feature. States and cities often require the operators of liquor stores, hairstyling shops, taxicabs, funeral homes, and many other businesses to obtain a license. Sometimes, these licenses cost little and are designed to ensure certain minimum standards. Often, however, they are costly to obtain and a major deterrent to the entry of potential rivals.

Licensing
A requirement that one obtain permission from the government in order to perform certain business activities or work in various occupations.

24-1c PATENTS

Most countries have patent laws to give inventors a property right to their inventions. A patent grants the owner the exclusive legal right to the commercial use of a newly invented product or process for a limited period of time—twenty years in the United States. Others are not allowed to copy the product or procedure without the permission of the patent holder. For example, when a pharmaceutical company is granted a patent for a newly developed drug, other potential suppliers must obtain permission from the patent holder before producing and selling the product during the life of the patent. Others might be able to supply the drug more economically. During that time period though, if they want to do so while the patent is in effect, they will have to purchase the production and marketing rights from the originating firm.

Both costs and benefits for consumers come with a patent system. The entry barrier created by the grant of a patent generally leads to higher consumer prices for several years, for products that have already been developed. On the positive side, however, patents increase the potential returns to inventive activity, thus encouraging scientific research and technological improvements. As we noted in the previous chapter, entrepreneurial discovery will occur at a faster rate when it is more profitable. A study at the Federal Trade Commission estimated the average cost of developing and testing a new pharmaceutical drug at more than $1 billion.[2] Without the profit potential accompanying patents, the incentive to engage in research and develop new products would be reduced.

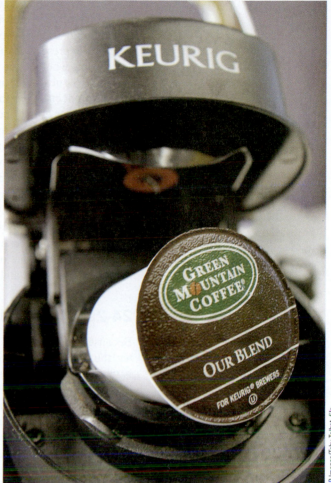

AP Images/Toby Talbot, file

24-1d CONTROL OVER AN ESSENTIAL RESOURCE

Control over a resource essential to produce a product may also insulate a firm from direct competitors. An example often cited is the Aluminum Company of America, which before World War II controlled the known supply of bauxite conveniently available to American firms. Without this critical raw material, potential competitors could not produce aluminum. Over time, however, other supplies of bauxite were discovered, and the Aluminum Company of America lost its advantage. Resource monopolies are seldom complete or long lasting. Profit opportunities provide potential competitors with an incentive to search for mineral deposits, new technologies, and substitute resources. Over time, they are usually found.

Barriers to entry like the different ones we've just described are often temporary, but they do exist. Let's see what happens when, at least temporarily, there is a barrier to entry high enough to limit the market to only one seller.

Both the Keurig coffee maker and the pods (K-Cups) were protected by patents, so companies like Starbucks and Dunkin' Donuts had to pay licensing fees to sell coffee in the patented K-Cups. In 2012 patents on the K-Cups expired, so other companies can now produce and sell K-Cups that are compatible with the Keurig machine. The increased competition will result in lower prices for consumers.

24-2 CHARACTERISTICS OF A MONOPOLY

The word *monopoly*, derived from two Greek words, means "single seller." We will define **monopoly** as a market characterized by (1) high barriers to entry and (2) a single seller of a well-defined product for which there are no good substitutes. Even this definition is ambiguous, because "high barriers" and "good substitutes" are both relative terms. Are the barriers to entry into the automobile or steel industries high? Many observers would argue

Monopoly
A market structure characterized by (1) a single seller of a well-defined product for which there are no good substitutes and (2) high barriers to the entry of any other firms into the market for that product.

[2]See Christopher P. Adams and Van V. Brantner, "Estimating the Cost of New Drug Development: Is It Really $802 Million?" *Health Affairs* 25, no. 2 (March/April 2006): 421–28.

that they are. After all, it takes a great deal of capital to operate at the least-cost scale of output in both of these industries. However, there are no *physical* or *legal* restraints that prevent an entrepreneur from producing automobiles or steel. If price is well above cost and profit potential is present, it should not be too difficult to find the necessary investment capital. Thus, some would argue that entry barriers into these industries are not particularly high.

"Good substitute" is also a subjective term. There is always some substitutability among products, even those produced by a single seller. Is a letter a good substitute for a telephone or e-mail message? For some purposes—correspondence between law firms, for example—a letter delivered by mail is a very good substitute. In other cases, when the speed of communication and immediacy of response are important, the telephone and e-mail are far superior forms of communication.

Monopoly, then, is a matter of degree. Only a small fraction of all markets are served by just one seller. In a few markets, governments have allocated specific markets to a single seller. In many communities, this is the case with cable television and providers of electricity. The monopoly model we discuss next will illuminate the operation of these markets. It will also help us understand markets in which there are just a few sellers and little active rivalry. When there are only two or three producers in a market, firms may seek to collude rather than compete, and thus, together, they may behave much like a monopoly.

24-2a PRICE AND OUTPUT UNDER MONOPOLY

Because a monopolist is a price searcher like the firms we examined in the previous chapter, the graphical analysis is similar. The main difference is that because the monopolist is the only seller in the market, the demand curve facing the firm (d) is the entire market demand curve (D), and the firm's output (q) is the entire market output (Q). *Like other price searchers, the monopolist will expand its output until marginal revenue equals marginal cost. This profit-maximizing output rate can be sold at the price indicated on the firm's demand curve.*

Exhibit 1 graphically illustrates how a monopolist derives the profit-maximizing output rate.[3] Output will be expanded to Q, where *MR 5 MC.* The monopolist will

EXHIBIT 1

The Short-Run Price and Output of a Monopolist

The monopolist will reduce its price and expand its output as long as MR exceeds MC. Output Q will result. When the price exceeds the average total cost at any output level, a profit will be earned.

© Cengage Learning 2013

---

[3]In this chapter, we assume that firms are unable to use price discrimination to increase their revenues. If they could, the analysis of price discrimination from the previous chapter would be relevant to their decision-making.

Profit Maximization for a Monopolist

Rate of Output (Per Day) (1)	Price (Per Unit) (2)	Total Revenue (1) × (2) (3)	Total Cost (Per Day) (4)	Profit (3) − (4) (5)	Marginal Cost (6)	Marginal Revenue (7)
0	—	—	$50.00	$−50.00	—	—
1	$25.00	$25.00	60.00	−35.00	$10.00	$25.00
2	24.00	48.00	69.00	−21.00	9.00	23.00
3	23.00	69.00	77.00	−8.00	8.00	21.00
4	22.00	88.00	84.00	4.00	7.00	19.00
5	21.00	105.00	90.50	14.50	6.50	17.00
6	19.75	118.50	96.75	21.75	6.25	13.50
7	18.50	129.50	102.75	26.75	6.00	11.00
8	17.25	138.00	108.50	29.50	5.75	8.50
9	16.00	144.00	114.75	29.25	6.25	6.00
10	14.75	147.50	121.25	26.25	6.50	3.50
11	13.50	148.50	128.00	20.50	6.75	1.00
12	12.25	147.00	135.00	12.00	7.00	−1.50
13	11.00	143.00	142.25	.75	7.25	−4.00

© Cengage Learning 2013

set a price of P to sell exactly the desired profit-maximizing level of output Q (the height of the demand curve at Q). Thus, output rate Q and price P will maximize the firm's profit.

The profits earned by the monopolist are also shown in Exhibit 1. At output Q and price P, the firm's total revenue is equal to $PAQ0$, the price times the number of units sold. The firm's total cost would be $CBQ0$, the average per-unit cost multiplied by the number of units sold. The firm's profits are total revenue less total cost, the shaded area of Exhibit 1 ($PABC$).

Exhibit 2 provides a numeric illustration of decision-making by a profit-maximizing monopolist. At low output rates, marginal revenue exceeds marginal cost. The monopolist will expand output as long as MR is greater than MC. Thus, an output rate of eight units per day will be chosen. (*Note:* If tiny portions of a unit could be produced and sold, then production would increase to where $MR = MC$.) Given the demand for the product, the monopolist can sell eight units at a price of $17.25 each. Total revenue will be $138, compared with a total cost of $108.50. The monopolist will make a profit of $29.50. The profit rate will be smaller at all other output rates. For example, if the monopolist reduces the price to $16 in order to sell nine units per day, revenue will increase by $6. However, the marginal cost of producing the ninth unit is $6.25. Because the cost of producing the ninth unit is greater than the revenue it brings in, profits will decline.

When high barriers to entry are present, they will insulate the monopolist from competition from new entrants producing a similar product. Thus, in markets with high entry barriers, short-run monopoly profits will not be competed away through the process of entry.

Protected by high entry barriers, a monopolist may be able to continue earning a profit, even in the long run. Does this mean that monopolists can charge as high a price as they want? Monopolists are often accused of price gouging. In evaluating this charge, however, it is important to recognize that, like other sellers, monopolists will seek to maximize *profit*, not *price*. Consumers will buy less as the price increases. Thus, a higher price is not always better for a monopolist. Exhibit 2 illustrates this point. What would happen to the profit of the monopolist if the price were increased from $17.25 to $18.50? At the higher price, only seven units would be sold, and total revenue would equal $129.50. The cost of producing seven units would be $102.75. Thus, when the

How a Monopolist Can Lose Money

Even a monopolist will lose money if its average total cost curve lies everywhere above the demand curve.

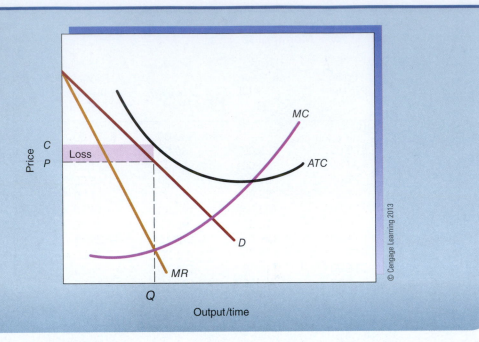

© Cengage Learning 2013

price is $18.50 and output seven units, profit is only $26.75—less than it would be at the lower price ($17.25) and larger output (eight units). The highest price is not usually the best price for the monopolist.

Will a monopolist always earn a profit? The ability of a monopolist to cover cost and make a profit is limited by the demand for the product that it produces. In some cases, a monopolist—even one protected by high barriers to entry—may be unable to sell its product for a profit. For example, there are thousands of clever, patented items that are never produced because demand–cost conditions are not favorable. **Exhibit 3** illustrates this possibility. Here, the monopolist's average total cost curve is above its demand curve at every level of output. Even when operating at the *MR = MC* rate of output, economic losses (shaded area) will occur. While output *Q* could be sold at price *P*, this price and quantity yield too little revenue to cover cost for the monopolist. This model explains why many small towns lack even a single bookstore, gourmet coffee shop, or any number of other specialty stores, even though if one opened up it would be the only one in town. Under these circumstances, not even a monopolist would want to operate—at least not for long.

24-3 THE CHARACTERISTICS OF AN OLIGOPOLY

In the United States, the domestic output in certain industries, such as the automobile, cigarette, and aircraft industries, is produced by five or fewer dominant firms. These industries are characterized by **oligopoly.** *Oligopoly* means "few sellers." *The distinguishing characteristics of an oligopolistic market are (1) a small number of rival firms, (2) interdependence among the sellers because each is large relative to the size of the market, (3) substantial economies of scale, and (4) high entry barriers to the market.*

Oligopoly
A market situation in which a small number of sellers constitutes the entire industry. It is competition among the few.

24-3a INTERDEPENDENCE AMONG OLIGOPOLISTIC FIRMS

Because the number of sellers in an oligopolistic industry is small, the supply decisions of any one firm will significantly influence the demand, price, and profit of rival firms. This adds to the complexity of the firm's decision-making. A firm that is deciding what price to charge, output to produce, or quality of product to offer must consider not only the currently available substitutes but also the potential reactions of rival producers. The business decisions of each firm depend on the policies it expects its major rivals to follow because those will influence the demand for all the rivals' products.

24-3b SUBSTANTIAL ECONOMIES OF SCALE

In an oligopolistic industry, large-scale production (relative to the total market) is generally required to achieve minimum per-unit cost. Economies of scale are present, so a small number of large-scale firms can produce enough of the product to meet the entire market demand. Using the automobile industry in the recent past as an example, Exhibit 4 illustrates the importance of economies of scale as a source of oligopoly. It has been estimated that each firm must produce approximately 1 million automobiles annually before its per-unit cost of production is minimized. However, when the selling price of automobiles is barely sufficient to cover costs, the total quantity demanded from these producers is only 6 million. To minimize costs, then, each firm must produce at least one-sixth (1 million of the 6 million) of the output demanded. If this is true, the industry can support no more than five or six domestic firms of cost-efficient size.

24-3c SIGNIFICANT BARRIERS TO ENTRY

As with monopoly, barriers to entry limit the ability of new firms to compete effectively in oligopolistic industries. Except where a market is contestable, economies of scale are probably the most significant entry barrier protecting firms in an oligopolistic industry. A potential competitor may be unable to start out small and gradually grow to the optimal size, because it must gain a large share of the market before it can minimize its per-unit cost. The manufacture of refrigerators, diesel engines, and automobiles seems to fall into this category. Other factors, including patent rights, control over an essential resource, and government-imposed entry restraints, can also prevent new competitors from entering profitable oligopolistic industries.

24-3d IDENTICAL OR DIFFERENTIATED PRODUCTS

The products of sellers in an oligopolistic industry may be either similar or differentiated. On the one hand, when firms produce identical products, like milk or gasoline, there is less opportunity for nonprice competition. On the other hand, when rival firms

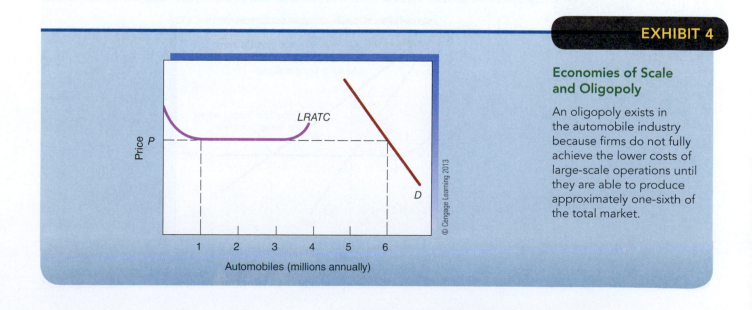

EXHIBIT 4

Economies of Scale and Oligopoly

An oligopoly exists in the automobile industry because firms do not fully achieve the lower costs of large-scale operations until they are able to produce approximately one-sixth of the total market.

produce differentiated products they are more likely to use style, quality, and advertising as competitive weapons. Each firm attempts to convince buyers that other products are poor substitutes.

24-4 PRICE AND OUTPUT UNDER OLIGOPOLY

Unlike the other firms we have examined, an oligopolist cannot determine the product price that will deliver maximum profit simply by estimating only its own costs and the *existing* market demand. The demand facing an oligopolistic firm depends also on the pricing behavior of its rivals. Suppose, for example, that Ford is considering how to price a new hybrid car model when it comes on the market next year. The number of cars it can sell at each price will depend not only on buyer preferences but also on the prices (and quality) of substitutes available from Toyota, General Motors, and other rival firms. What pricing strategy will each rival use if Ford puts a low price on its new model? How will each rival firm react to a higher Ford price?

Economic models cannot predict these complex interactions among rivals without making some strong, simplifying assumptions about how each firm reacts when another firm makes a change in price or quality. These simplifying assumptions will not be realistic for the general case, and therefore we cannot precisely predict the price and output that will emerge in an oligopoly. We can, however, zero in on a potential range of prices and the factors that will determine whether prices in the industry will be high or low relative to costs of production.

Consider a typical oligopolistic industry in which seven or eight rival firms produce the entire market output because substantial economies of scale are present. The firms produce nearly identical products and have similar costs of production. Exhibit 5 depicts the market demand conditions and long-run costs of production of the individual firms for such an industry.

What price will prevail? We can answer this question for two extreme cases. First, suppose that each firm sets its price independently of the other firms. There is no **collusion** (no agreement among the firms to limit output and keep the price high), so each competitive firm is free to seek additional customers and profits by offering buyers a slightly better deal than its rivals. Under these conditions, the market price would be driven down to P_c. Firms would be just able to cover their per-unit costs of production. If a single firm raised its price, its customers would switch to rival firms, which would now expand to accommodate the new customers. It would be self-defeating for any one firm to raise its price if the other firms didn't also raise theirs.

Collusion
Agreement among firms to avoid various competitive practices, particularly price reductions. It may involve either formal agreements or merely tacit recognition that competitive practices will be self-defeating in the long run. Tacit collusion is difficult to detect. In the United States, antitrust laws prohibit collusion and conspiracies to restrain trade.

EXHIBIT 5

Price and Output in an Oligopoly

If oligopolists were to act independently and compete with one another, price cutting would drive price down to P_c. In contrast, perfect cooperation among firms would lead to a higher price of P_m and a smaller output (Q_m rather than Q_c). The shaded area shows profit if firms collude. Demand here is the market demand.

© Cengage Learning 2013

What happens if the current price is greater than P_c, perhaps because the market has not yet adjusted fully to a recent reduction in resource prices that lowered production costs? As a result, price is above per-unit cost, and the firms are making economic profit. However, any *individual firm* that reduces its price slightly, by 1 or 2 percent, for example, will gain numerous customers if the other firms maintain the higher price. The price-cutting firm will attract some new buyers to the market, but more importantly, it will also lure many buyers away from rival firms charging higher prices. Thus, if the rival sellers act independently, each will have a strong incentive to reduce price in order to increase sales and gain a large share of the total market. Price will be driven down to P_c, and the economic profit will be eliminated.

However, oligopolists don't always compete with one another. They have a strong incentive to collude—to raise prices and restrict output in order to maximize their joint profits. The collusion may be either formal or informal. Formal collusion might even involve the formation of a **cartel**, like the Organization of the Petroleum Exporting Countries (OPEC). Under federal antitrust laws, both formal and informal collusive agreements to restrict output and raise prices are illegal in the United States. Nonetheless, let's see what would happen if oligopolists followed this course.

Exhibit 5 shows the marginal revenue curve that would accompany the market demand D for the product. Under perfect cooperation, the oligopolists would refuse to produce units for which marginal revenue to the group was less than marginal cost. Thus, they would restrict joint output to Q_m, where $MR = MC$. The market price would rise to P_m. With collusion, substantial joint profits (the shaded area of Exhibit 5) can be attained. If the collusion were perfect, the outcome would be identical to the one that would occur under monopoly.

Real-world outcomes are likely to be between the two polar case extremes of price competition and perfect collusion. Oligopolists generally recognize their interdependence and try to avoid vigorous price competition because they know it will drive down the price to the level of per-unit costs. But there are also obstacles to collusion, which is why prices in oligopolistic industries are unlikely to rise to the monopoly level. *As a result, oligopoly prices are typically above per-unit cost but below those a monopolist would charge.*

24-4a THE INCENTIVE TO COLLUDE . . . AND TO CHEAT

Rival oligopolists can profit as a group by colluding to restrict output and raise price. To achieve the higher price, however, they must reduce total market output. Returning to Exhibit 5, from a competitive outcome of Q_c and P_c, output must be restricted toward the monopoly level of Q_m to achieve a higher price near P_m. This raises a point of conflict: None of the oligopolists want to reduce their output independently, especially at a higher price! Although the firms have an incentive to collude in order to achieve higher prices, each of them also has an incentive to cheat on the agreement by producing and selling more units than would maximize profit for the industry as a whole.

Exhibit 6 explains why this is the case. An undetected price cut by a single firm will have a larger percentage impact on its sales than a similar price cut would have on total industry sales. For example, if all firms lowered price by 10 percent total industry sales might only rise by 10 percent, but if one firm lowers price by 10 percent its sales might rise by 30 percent. Both price cuts attract additional customers who normally wouldn't buy at the higher price, but a price cut by one firm also attracts current customers away from the other firms. Therefore, the demand facing each *individual firm* will be considerably more elastic than the market demand curve. As Exhibit 6 shows, the price P_i that maximizes the industry's profits will be higher than the price P_F that is best for a single oligopolist when the others stay with the higher price. If a firm can use secret rebates or other ways to undercut the price set by the collusive agreement while the other sellers maintain the higher price, it can expand its sales (beyond the level agreed upon by the cartel). This will more than make up for the reduction in per-unit profit margin from the price cut.

Cartel
An organization of sellers designed to coordinate supply decisions so that the joint profits of the members will be maximized. A cartel will seek to create a monopoly in the market.

EXHIBIT 6

Gaining from Cheating

The industry demand (D_i) and marginal revenue (MR_i) curves show that the joint profits of oligopolists would be maximized at Q_i, where $MR_i = MC$. Price P_i would be best for the industry as a whole (a). However, as part (b) shows, the demand curve (d_F) facing each firm (under the assumption that no other firms cheat) will be much more elastic than D_i.

Given the greater elasticity of its demand curve, an individual firm will have an incentive to cut its price to P_F and expand output to q_F, where $MR_F = MC$. In other words, an individual oligopolist can gain by secretly cutting its price and cheating on the collusive agreement—until the other firms find out and react by cutting their price.

(a) Industry

(b) Individual firm

© Cengage Learning 2013

In oligopolistic industries, there are two conflicting tendencies. *An oligopolistic firm has a strong incentive to cooperate with its rivals so that joint profit can be maximized. But it also has a strong incentive to cheat—to expand output secretly in order to increase its profit. Oligopolistic agreements, therefore, tend to be unstable.*

24-4b OBSTACLES TO COLLUSION

There are certain situations in which it is more difficult for oligopolists to collude. Five major obstacles limit collusive behavior.

1. As the number of firms in an oligopolistic market increases, the likelihood of effective collusion declines.

Other things being constant, an increase in the number of firms in an industry will make it more difficult for the oligopolists to communicate, negotiate, and enforce agreements among themselves. Opinions about the best collusive price arrangement are likely to differ because marginal costs, unused plant capacity, and estimates of market demand elasticity will often differ among the firms. As the number of firms expands, conflict arising from these and other sources will increase and make it more difficult to maintain collusive agreements.

2. When it is difficult to detect and eliminate price cuts, collusion is less attractive.

Unless firms have a way of policing the pricing and output activitiesof rivals, effective collusion will be unlikely as firms will cheat on the agreement. The history of the oil cartel OPEC highlights this point. Cheating by members on production and sales quota agreements is not easy to monitor by the others, and it has been a persistent problem for the cartel.

Some forms of price cutting are difficult for the rival firms to identify. For example, a firm might freely provide better credit terms, faster delivery, and other related services that improve the package offered to the buyer. In an industry supplying differentiated products, oligopolists can hold money prices constant and still use improvements in quality and style to provide consumers with more value. "Price cuts" like this cannot be easily and quickly duplicated by rivals. As a result, collusive agreements on price are largely ineffective when quality and style are important competitive weapons. The bottom line is this: When cheating (price cutting) is profitable and difficult for rivals to detect and police, collusive agreements—both formal and informal—will be difficult to maintain.

3. Low entry barriers are an obstacle to collusion.

Without barriers to entry oligopolists will be unable to sustain long-run economic profits because the profits will attract new competitors into the market. High prices will also make it more attractive for potential rivals to develop substitutes, which will reduce the demand for the product provided by the oligopolists. Of course, these factors will not work instantaneously, but over time they will reduce the ability to charge abnormally high prices and earn economic profits.

Again, the experience of OPEC illustrates this point. When OPEC attempts to cut production and push up world oil prices, the non-OPEC producers develop new oil fields and expand their output from existing sources. The higher prices also encourage energy conservation and greater use of alternative energy sources, such as coal, natural gas, and nuclear energy, and make it more profitable for firms across many other industries to introduce substitutes like more fuel-efficient, hybrid-electric cars. These innovations from rival sellers who can enter and compete with OPEC for customers cause the demand for oil to decrease and make it difficult for OPEC to collude successfully.

4. Unstable demand conditions are an obstacle to collusion.

Honest differences of opinion among oligopolists about what is best for the industry always exist, but unstable demand increases the likelihood of conflict. One firm might want to expand because it anticipates a sharp increase in future demand, whereas a more pessimistic rival may want to hold the line on existing industrial capacity. The larger the differences in expectations about future demand, the greater the potential for conflict among oligopolistic firms. When demand is more stable, successful collusion will be more likely.

Vladimir Weiss/Bloomberg/Getty Images

Collusive agreements among oligopolists and cartels like OPEC are difficult to maintain because any individual cartel member would be better off if it could cheat on the agreement and charge a slightly lower price, so long as other members do not.

5. Vigorous antitrust action increases the cost of collusion. Under existing antitrust laws in many nations, collusive behavior is prohibited by law. Secretive illegal agreements do, of course, happen. Simple informal cooperation might be conducted without having explicit discussions or collusive agreements. However, unlike formal (legal) collusive agreements, these informal agreements are not easily enforceable. Thus, vigorous antitrust action can discourage firms from making illegal agreements. As the threat of getting caught increases, participants will be less likely to attempt collusive behavior.

24-4c UNCERTAINTY AND OLIGOPOLY

Market power
The ability of a firm that is not a pure monopolist to earn persistently large profits, indicating that it has some monopoly power. Because the firm has few (or weak) competitors, it has a degree of freedom from vigorous competition.

Game theory
A tool used to analyze the strategic choices made by competitors in a conflict situation like the decisions made by firms in an oligopoly.

Uncertainty and imprecision characterize the theory of oligopoly. We know that firms will gain if they successfully restrict output and raise prices. However, collusion is fraught with conflicts and difficulties. In some industries, these difficulties are so great that the **market power** of the oligopolists is relatively small. In other industries, oligopolistic cooperation, although not perfect, can raise prices significantly, indicating a higher degree of market power. The use of **game theory** to analyze the costs and benefits of collusive behavior, under varying degrees of cooperation and conflict, has become an important part of economics. (See the accompanying Applications in Economics feature on this topic.) Although this developing field of economics does not yield precise predictions on oligopoly pricing and output, it does suggest the conditions that make it more likely that an oligopolist will be kept in check by competitive pressures.

APPLICATIONS IN ECONOMICS

Oligopolistic Decision-Making, Game Theory, and the Prisoner's Dilemma

In an oligopoly, a few firms compete in the same market, and the actions of each influence the demand faced by the others. One firm can gain customers at the expense of the others by cutting its price or increasing its advertising. The firms that fail to follow suit will lose customers. But if the other firms react competitively by doing the same, then all the firms lose. Thus, each firm finds itself on the horns of a dilemma—something like the classic "prisoner's dilemma."

Economists have increasingly used game theory like the prisoner's dilemma to analyze strategic choices made by competitors, particularly those in an oligopoly. To understand the prisoner's dilemma, consider the following hypothetical case. Al and Bob are taken prisoner and hauled into the local police station to be questioned separately. They are suspected of being the two men who robbed a local merchant, and each is told that if he makes the job of the police easier by confessing immediately, he will get only a six-month sentence. But each is also told that if he says nothing while the other confesses, then the one who did not confess immediately will get a twelve-month sentence. If neither confesses, both will be held for three months while the investigation continues. Al and Bob will not be allowed to communicate with each other. Will they confess?

To analyze such a situation, the game theorist begins by laying out the alternative outcomes and showing how they are related to choices made by the players of the game, as we do in **Exhibit 7**. For each man individually, in this version of the dilemma, the box reveals that the best choice depends on what the other

does. If Al confesses, then Bob can save six months of jail time by also confessing. The same holds for Al, if he thinks Bob will confess. But if neither confesses, both serve only three months in jail. The proper strategy for each prisoner depends heavily on his estimate of the likelihood that the other will confess. The problem becomes more complex if we consider prisoners who face a series of such decisions over time and each prisoner learns what the other has done before making his or her next choice.

Firms in an oligopoly must make decisions somewhat like those of the prisoners: Should a firm cut its price in order to attract more customers—luring some of them away from its competitors—or should it keep its price high and risk losing customers to competitors who cut *their* prices? If all firms keep the price high, then as a group they will reap more profit.

If all of them cut prices, then as a group they will reap less profit. But the firm that fails to cut price when the others do will lose many customers. The decision about whether or not to advertise has similar characteristics.

For example, consider the pricing policies or advertising strategies of large automakers, like Ford, Toyota, and General Motors. Suppose the profit rate of each would be 15 percent if all the major automobile producers raised their prices by a similar amount. In contrast, each would earn a profit rate of only 10 percent if intense competition led to lower prices. Industry profits are highest when all firms decide to charge high prices. However, if one automaker cuts prices, it will be able to steal customers away from its rivals and increase its profit rate to 20 percent.

EXHIBIT 7

The Prisoner's Dilemma

Al and Bob must each decide, without communicating with each other, whether to confess. Al knows that if Bob does not confess, then he can either confess and spend six months in jail, or not confess and spend three months. But if Bob does confess, then Al's failure to confess will cost him an additional six months in jail. Bob is in a similar situation, facing the same options under the same assumptions about whether Al confesses. Each man has an incentive to confess if he thinks the other one will, but an incentive not to confess if he thinks the other will also remain silent.

		Al's Choice	
		Confess	Not Confess
Bob's Choice	Confess	6 months each	Al: 12 months Bob: 6 months
	Not Confess	Al: 6 months Bob: 12 months	3 months each

© Cengage Learning 2013

Thus, if the firm thinks its rivals will continue to charge the higher prices, it will be tempted to cut its price. If the other firms follow a similar course, however, the strategy will backfire and the profit rate of all the firms in the industry will be less than the level it would have achieved had they all charged the higher prices.

Although our simplified analysis highlights the interdependence among the firms and the importance of probability estimates concerning the strategy of rivals, the real world is much more complex. The choices of the rival firms will be repeated over and over again, although often in modified forms. A prior strategy will be modified in light of previous reactions on the part of rivals. How attractive a strategy will be depends on its likelihood of being detected by rivals and the speed with which they will respond. In addition, the strategies of oligopolistic firms will be influenced by market conditions and the threat of foreign competition—factors that change with the passage of time. As you can see, additional assumptions will need to be made to account for these and other complex factors.

Economists have used game theory extensively to show how results change when the "rules of the game" change for the firms in an oligopolistic market, as well as for auction-bidding markets and other business decision-making situations. When the rules of the game are carefully defined and enforced, as they are in economic experiments held in laboratories, game theory has yielded interesting and important testable conclusions. Successful collusion, for example, is more likely to occur if the parties face the game repeatedly together. But in open markets in the real world, empirical work using game theory has been less successful. The use of models is always difficult when the problem to be solved is complex and when human expectations about the changing strategic choices of other human beings must be taken into account. There is no question, however, that game theory can be useful for scholars and business practitioners alike, by helping them frame the issues involved in strategic decision-making.[1]

[1]For a further explanation of game theory and the prisoner's dilemma, see Avinash Dixit and Barry Nalebuff, "Game Theory," in *The Concise Encyclopedia of Economics*, ed. David R. Henderson (Indianapolis, IN: Liberty Fund, Inc., 2002), http://www.econlib.org/library/CEE.html.

24-5 MARKET POWER AND PROFIT— THE EARLY BIRD CATCHES THE WORM

Our analysis of both monopoly and oligopoly indicates that because entry barriers into these markets are often high, firms can sometimes earn economic profits over lengthy periods of time. Does that mean that buying stock in one of these companies is a better investment?

The answer is no because the price of a share of stock in such a corporation would long ago have risen to reflect the firm's expected future profitability. Many of the present stockholders paid high prices for their stock because they expected these firms to continue to be highly profitable. In other words, these shareholders paid for any above-normal economic profits generated by the firm's market power at the time they purchased their ownership shares.

24-6 DEFECTS OF MARKETS WITH HIGH ENTRY BARRIERS

From Adam Smith's time to the present, economists have generally considered monopoly to be a problem. The attitude toward markets with few sellers and high entry barriers has been only slightly more tolerant. Generally, economists offer three major criticisms. We will outline each of them.

1. When entry barriers are high and there are few, if any, alternative suppliers, the discipline of market forces is weakened. In contrast, when alternatives are present, consumers are in a position to direct the behavior of suppliers. If you do not like the food at a local restaurant, you eat elsewhere. If you think prices are high and the selection poor at a particular grocery store, you go to a different one. But consider your alternatives if you do not like the local cable television service. You can voice a complaint to the company or your legislative representative, but the only exit option might be to stop your cable service, perhaps to rely instead on satellite dish service. Cable and satellite service are imperfect substitutes, each with its own disadvantages. When consumers do not have good exit options, they must either take what the seller offers or do without. Consequently, their ability to keep sellers in check is greatly reduced.

2. Reduced competition results in allocative inefficiency. The formal condition for allocative efficiency requires that all units are produced that are valued more highly than what it costs to produce them. When barriers to entry are low, profit-seeking producers of each good expand their output until its price is driven down to the level of per-unit costs. Because price equals cost, all units of the good that consumers value higher than the cost of production will be produced and sold. With high barriers to entry, however, price may exceed per-unit costs, even over the long run. Therefore some units might not be produced, even though consumers value them more than their costs. These are the units valued by consumers more than cost, but less than the higher monopoly price.

3. Government grants of monopoly power will encourage rent seeking; resources will be wasted by firms attempting to secure and maintain grants of market protection. Special favors granted by the government will lead to costly activities for those who seek such favors. As we noted in Chapter 6, economists refer to such activities as rent seeking. When licenses or other entry barriers erected by the government enhance the profitability and provide protection from the rigors of market competition, people will expend scarce resources to secure and maintain these political favors. From an efficiency standpoint, these rent-seeking costs related to getting and keeping monopoly power add to the welfare losses resulting from the allocative inefficiencies we previously mentioned.

Suppose the government issues a license providing a single seller the exclusive right to sell liquor in a specific market. If this grant of monopoly power permits the licensee to earn monopoly profit, potential suppliers will compete, each trying to convince government officials that it should be the one firm granted the license. The potential monopolists will lobby government officials, make political contributions, hire representatives to do consulting studies, and undertake other actions designed to obtain the monopoly grant. Each firm may be willing to spend up to the present value of the future expected monopoly profits trying to obtain the monopoly license. With several potential suppliers, the total rent-seeking expenditures of all firms combined may even exceed the economic profit expected from the monopoly enterprise.

The resources devoted to rent seeking have an opportunity cost (for example, a cable company could have instead used the money to provide better service to customers), and thus are wasteful from a societal point of view. Therefore, the total losses to society from monopolies created through government favors can far exceed the losses caused by allocative inefficiency.

24-7 POLICY ALTERNATIVES WHEN ENTRY BARRIERS ARE HIGH

What government policies might be used to counteract the problems that result from high barriers to entry? Economists suggest four policy options:

1. Control the structure of the industry to ensure the presence of rival firms.
2. Reduce artificial barriers that limit competition.
3. Regulate the price and output of firms in the market.
4. Supply the market with goods produced by a government firm.

Each of these policies has been used to either reduce entry barriers or counteract their negative results. We will briefly consider each of them and analyze both their potential and limitations as tools that can be used to improve the efficiency of resource use.

24-7a ANTITRUST POLICY AND CONTROLLING THE STRUCTURE OF AN INDUSTRY

The major problems associated with high barriers to entry and monopoly power are not present when rival sellers are present and compete. The United States, to a greater degree than most Western countries, has adopted antitrust laws designed to prevent monopoly and promote competition. Antitrust legislation began in 1890 with the passage of the Sherman Antitrust Act. Additional legislation, including the Clayton Act and the Federal Trade Commission Act of 1914, has buttressed policy in this area.

Antitrust laws give the U.S. Department of Justice the power to prosecute firms engaging in collusive behavior or other actions designed to create a monopoly or cartel. They also give the government the power to break up an existing monopoly and prevent mergers that significantly reduce competition. The Federal Trade Commission (FTC) is allowed to bring charges under the Sherman Act. Private firms can also bring suits charging antitrust violations by a rival under the Sherman and Clayton acts and collect up to three times any actual damages caused by the rival firm. Each year, far more cases are brought by private firms against their competitors than by the two federal agencies. Rival firms can also ask the two agencies to bring antitrust cases against successful competitors who may have, or threaten to gain, monopoly power.

Economists do not fully agree on the usefulness of antitrust action to increase the number of rival firms in an industry. Those who support such policies believe that only by preserving numerous competitors in a market can we be confident that monopoly has been controlled. Opponents point to the danger of protecting high-cost firms at the expense of both consumers and the more aggressive and successful firm(s) in the market. Protection of less efficient firms from successful competitors, they say, is all too common in the actual practice of antitrust policy.

There is one situation in which the application of antitrust action would clearly be inappropriate. When substantial economies of scale are present, unit cost will be minimized only if the entire industry output is produced by a single firm, a case known as **natural monopoly**. Here, breaking up the one large firm in order to increase the number of rivals in the industry would lead to higher per-unit costs. Because of their

Natural monopoly
A market situation in which the average costs of production continually decline with increased output. In a natural monopoly, the average costs of production will be lowest when a single, large firm produces the entire output demanded by the marketplace.

higher costs, the prices charged by the smaller firms might even exceed those of the lower-cost natural monopoly. Therefore, using antitrust laws to expand the number of firms is not an attractive option when economies of scale in an industry produce a natural monopoly.

24-7b REDUCE ARTIFICIAL BARRIERS TO TRADE

When government-imposed restrictions are the source of the monopoly power, the appropriate policy action is obvious: Remove the government restraints. But this is easier said than done. The restraints are generally in place because of the political influence of special-interest groups—the producers currently in the industry—who have a vested interest in restricting competition and keeping prices high. The politicians who supply these restrictions get political support from current producers in return, and removing them would be a costly political move. Thus, political considerations often make it difficult to remove government-imposed barriers to entry, such as licensing restrictions and tariff and quota restrictions on imported goods.

The interest groups behind government-imposed barriers to entry are highly concentrated and generally well organized politically. In contrast, the consumers who would benefit from more competitive markets are poorly organized, and the costs imposed on them by the restraints are nearly always thinly spread among them. As we discussed in Chapter 6, the political process often works to the advantage of the concentrated interests. As a result, even when lower barriers are needed to increase the competitiveness of an industry, political factors often prevent them.

24-7c REGULATE THE PRICE

Can government regulation improve the allocative efficiency of a monopoly or an oligopoly? **Exhibit 8** illustrates why ideal government price regulation, in the case of a monopolist, could theoretically improve resource allocation. The firm illustrated here is a natural monopoly. Its *LRATC* falls over the entire relevant range of output. Antitrust action dividing the firm into several smaller rivals will not help consumers because the unit costs of the smaller firms will be higher than if the output were produced by the monopolist. The profit maximizing monopolist will set price at P_0 and produce output Q_0, where

EXHIBIT 8

Regulating a Monopolist

If unregulated, a profit-maximizing monopolist with the costs indicated here will produce Q_0 units and charge P_0. If a regulatory agency forced the monopolist to reduce price to P_1, then the monopolist would expand output to Q_1. Ideally, we would like output to be expanded to Q_2, where $P = MC$, but regulatory agencies usually do not attempt to keep prices as low as P_2. Can you explain why?

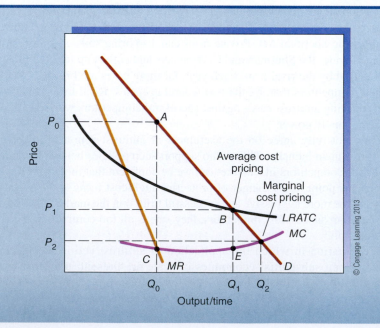

$MR = MC$. Consumers, however, would value additional units of output beyond Q_0 more than the cost of producing them violating the conditions for allocative efficiency. Let's consider the potential of two regulatory options and also analyze some of their real-world limitations.

Average cost pricing If a regulatory agency forces the firm in Exhibit 8 to reduce the price to P_1, at which point the *LRATC* curve intersects the market (and firm) demand curve, then the firm will expand output to Q_1. Because it cannot charge a price above P_1, the firm cannot increase its revenues by selling a smaller output at a higher price. Once the price ceiling is instituted, the firm can increase its revenues by P_1, and by only P_1, for each unit it sells. The regulated firm's *MR* is constant at P_1 for all units sold until output is increased to Q_1. Because the firm's *MC* is less than P_1 (and therefore less than *MR*), the profit-maximizing regulated firm shown here will expand output from Q_0 to Q_1. The benefits from the consumption of these units (ABQ_1Q_0) clearly exceed their costs (CEQ_1Q_0). Social welfare has improved as a result of the regulatory action (we will ignore the impact on the distribution of income). At this output level, revenues are sufficient to cover costs. The firm is making zero economic profit (or "normal" accounting profit).

Marginal cost pricing Even at the Q_1 output level, marginal cost is still less than price. Additional welfare gains could be achieved if output were increased to Q_2. However, if a regulatory agency forced the monopolist to reduce the price to P_2 (so the price would equal the marginal cost at the output level Q_2), economic losses would result. Even a monopolist, unless it is subsidized, wouldn't produce the product at P_2 or any price below P_1. But how large should a subsidy be? No one has the knowledge to set this subsidy, partly because prices, technologies, and the value of output change daily. Also, who has the incentive to fight the pressures on both sides for higher (or lower) subsidies? Marginal cost pricing is seldom practical.

24-7d PROBLEMS WITH REGULATION

Although regulating a monopoly might seem like a way to improve the efficiency of markets, both economic analysis and the history of regulation suggest that it has serious shortcomings. In practice, three factors tend to reduce the effectiveness of regulation and the probability that regulators will act on behalf of all citizens to control monopolies. Let's look at each of these factors.

1. Lack of information. When we discussed ideal regulation, we assumed that we knew what the firm's *ATC, MC,* and demand curves looked like. In reality, of course, regulators do not. Even the firms themselves will have difficulty knowing their costs, and especially their demand curves, with any precision. Furthermore, both supply and demand will vary over time and by location. The market for electricity is an excellent example. Because electricity cannot be stored for later use, the highly variable supply-and-demand conditions in that market cause the opportunity cost of power to change dramatically from one day, or even one hour, to the next. There is simply no way to have government-determined prices that are flexible and correct enough to avoid causing major shortages and surpluses of the good through time. In the summer of 2001, for example, sharply changing cost conditions for California utilities coupled with inflexible, regulated retail power rates combined to produce widespread power outages.

Because it is virtually impossible to estimate demand and marginal costs, regulatory agencies usually gauge profits (or the rate of return) to determine whether the regulated price is too high or too low. The regulatory agency seeks to impose a "fair" or "normal" rate of return on the firm. If the firm is making economic profits (that is, an abnormally high rate of return), the regulated price must be higher than P_1 in Exhibit 8, and therefore it should be reduced. Alternatively, if the firm is incurring losses (less than the fair, or normal, rate of return), this indicates that the regulated price is less than P_1 and that the firm should be permitted to charge a higher price.

The actual existence of profits, though, is not easily identifiable. Accounting profit, or the rate of return, is not the same as economic profit, which includes opportunity cost. Also, regulated firms have a strong incentive to adopt reporting techniques and accounting methods that conceal profits. Because of this, a regulatory agency will find it difficult or impossible to identify and impose a price consistent with allocative efficiency.

2. Cost shifting. Regulation changes incentives, so it can affect costs. If demand is sufficient, the owners of the regulated firm can expect the long-run rate of profit to be essentially fixed, regardless of whether efficient management reduces costs or inefficient management allows costs to increase. If costs decrease, the "fair return" rule imposed by the regulatory agency will force a price reduction; if costs increase, the "fair return" rule will allow a price increase. Compared to the managers of unregulated firms, managers of a regulated monopoly have more freedom to pursue personal objectives and less incentive to seek lower costs. Predictably, they will often fly first class, entertain lavishly at company expense, grant unwarranted wage increases, and so on. Production inefficiency and higher costs will result, but consumers are in a weak position to shift away from the good supplied by the monopolist.

3. Special-interest influence. The difficulties of government regulation discussed so far are practical limitations a regulatory agency confronts. Unfortunately, the political element of government regulation exacerbates the problem. Regulated firms have a strong incentive to see that "friendly," "reasonable" people serve as regulators, and they will invest political and economic resources toward this end. Just as rent-seeking activities designed to gain monopoly privileges in the first place can be expected, so, too, can activities to influence regulators' decisions. Few consumers will invest the time and resources required to understand regulatory policy and make the political contributions needed to counteract the influence peddling. Over time, regulatory commissions are therefore likely to reflect the views and interests of the business and labor interests they regulate (see the accompanying Applications in Economics box, "Government Regulation and the High Cost of Dying," for evidence on this point).

APPLICATIONS IN ECONOMICS

Government Regulation and the High Cost of Dying

Thanks to a vast array of licensing requirements and other regulations that restrict competition in the funeral industry, the price of a traditional funeral in the United States generally runs between $10,000 and $15,000.

When the entrepreneurial monks of St. Joseph Abbey in Louisiana tried to help lower these costs by opening a woodworking shop where they could produce and sell basic handmade wooden caskets for thousands of dollars less than the average price of a casket, the Louisiana State Board of Embalmers and Funeral Directors prohibited their sale of caskets. This state-operated licensing board restricts unwanted competition through regulations mandating that only licensed funeral directors are permitted to sell caskets—and only through state-licensed funeral homes. To comply, the monks would have had to build a funeral parlor with room for 30 people, a display room for at least six caskets, an arrangement room, and an embalming room, and they would have

to hire a full-time licensed funeral director just to sell their simple wooden caskets.

In just about every state, regulations such as these protect existing funeral homes from competition and result in significantly higher prices for consumers. In Minnesota, entrepreneur Verlin Stoll faces similar hurdles in trying to offer low-cost funerals such as regulations that require him to build a $30,000 embalming room, even though he outsources his embalming services and specializes in cremations and other types of funerals that do not require embalming.

While these types of regulations clearly limit competition and result in higher prices for consumers, politicians can often gain from their passage. Responding to lobbyists (the Louisiana Funeral Directors Association, for example) and well-organized interest groups, legislators often support anti-competitive regulations and sell them to the public under the guise that they are trying to protect the public health or consumers from shoddy products. In the end, however, these types of regulations allow existing funeral homes to act as a cartel and keep out lower-cost competitors.

Similar barriers restricting competition exist in many industries. So-called 'certificate of need' laws, for example, require new firms to prove to a state board that their entry will not adversely affect or compete with other existing firms in industries such as nursing homes, hospitals, limousines, and moving companies. In Nevada, entrepreneur Maurice Underwood is in court fighting to overturn a state law preventing him from opening a low-cost moving company unless he can prove his business would not "unreasonably and adversely" affect other companies by creating additional competition.

Even hair braiders can't escape these onerous anti-competitive regulations. After moving to Utah from Africa, Jestina Clayton attempted to provide African hair-braiding services but was thwarted by Utah's cosmetology board because she didn't have a cosmetology license that requires 2,000 hours (50 weeks) of cosmetology classes (and African hair braiding isn't even taught in those classes). After a complaint from a licensed competitor, the cosmetology board told Jestina that she would have to pay $18,000 to get permission from the board and obtain a license and face a fine of $2,000 per day if she continued to braid hair without a license. Similarly, in Mississippi, Melony Armstrong wanted to provide African hair-braiding services but was told by the licensing board that she would have to take more than 3,000 hours of classes.

Fortunately, some of these regulations are being overturned. The Louisiana monks took the Louisiana State Board of Embalmers and Funeral Directors to court and won their case. Minnesota entrepreneur Verlin Stoll is attempting to follow a similar path in court, and in Pennsylvania a federal

Photo courtesy Institute for Justice

judge recently struck down 11 parts of the state's funeral director law. African hair braiders Melony Armstrong and Jestina Clayton both won their cases in court as well.[1]

[1]See Eric Boehm, "Grave Robbers: Anti-Competitive Regulations for the Dead," (Irvington, NY: Foundation for Economic Education, May 7, 2013), http://www.fee.org/the_freeman/detail/grave-robbers-anti-competitive-regulations-for-the-dead; Institute for Justice, "Federal Judge Strikes Down Utah's Hairbraiding Licensing Scheme,"(August 9, 2012) http://www.ij.org/utah-hairbraiding-release-8-9-2012; *The Daily Reckoning.*

In summary, regulation not only has the potential to improve resource allocation in markets with few competitors, but it also generates adverse side effects. Both economic reasoning and decades of experience indicate that regulation is not a magic cure. Real-world cases of regulation, such as in electricity markets, provide evidence consistent with the idea that there is no single best solution.

24-7e SUPPLY MARKET WITH GOVERNMENT PRODUCTION

Government-operated firms—like the U.S. Postal Service and many local public utilities—present an alternative to both private monopoly and regulation. Here, too, however, economic thinking and experience indicate that these firms will fail to counteract fully the problems that stem from high barriers to entry. The same perverse managerial incentives that regulated firms experience—incentives to ignore efficiency and pursue personal or professional objectives at the firm's expense—also tend to plague government-operated firms. In addition, the rational ignorance effect comes into play here. Individual voters have little incentive to acquire information about the operation of government firms because, unlike the case of a personal investment, the individual's choices will not decide which investment will be purchased with the voter's money. Predictably, the "owners" of a government-operated firm (voters) will be uninformed about how well the firm is run, how it might be run better, or if another firm has a better plan. This is especially true when there are no direct competitors against which the firm's performance might be compared.

The operation of enterprises by the government does not create an environment that rewards managers or investors for efficient management and reductions in cost. Unlike in the private sector, no small group of investors can increase their wealth by taking over the firm and improving its management. Even more than with monopoly or oligopoly in the private sector, customers of the socialized monopoly cannot easily switch their business to other sellers. Voter-taxpayers who do not even consume the product often have to pay taxes to support its provision. When the government operates a business there is typically less investor scrutiny, less reward for efficiency, and less penalty for inefficiency or the production of inferior goods. Higher costs and lower-valued outputs are predictable results.

Government ownership, like unregulated monopoly and government regulation, is a less-than-ideal solution. Even those who denounce private sector monopoly seldom point to a government-operated monopoly as an example of how an industry should be run.

24-7f PULLING IT TOGETHER

The policy alternatives available when high barriers to entry are present are less than satisfying. Most are just not very attractive. Economies of scale often make antitrust actions impractical. When larger firms have lower per-unit costs, restructuring the industry to increase the number of firms will be both costly and difficult to maintain. Furthermore, antitrust policy opens the door for firms to use it against successful rivals that have simply given consumers a better deal and captured a large part of the market in the process. Policy actions to stop or to punish such progress are counterproductive for customers and for economic efficiency. Lifting government restrictions such as licensing requirements, quotas, and tariffs that limit competition is perhaps the surest way to improve the performance of markets with few suppliers. But the nature of the political process, particularly its tendency to cater to the views of well-organized interest groups at the expense of the unorganized majority of consumer/voters, often undermines the feasibility of this option.

Price regulation is also a less-than-ideal solution. Regulators do not possess the information necessary to impose an efficient outcome, and as part of the political process, they will be susceptible to manipulation by special interests. When firms are operated by the government, political objectives will be pursued at the expense of consumer interests and economic efficiency. Thus, government operation of firms also has its problems. In short, when economies of scale lead to a tendency toward monopoly, there is no ideal solution.

24-8 THE COMPETITIVE PROCESS IN THE REAL WORLD

When workers can work at remote locations, via the Internet and by contract if they wish, they have more options, and firms who can hire them—even small firms—no longer need large-scale production to achieve some of the economies of specialization previously available only to large firms. Both workers and firms can have some of the benefits of being in a large urban market even if they operate far from such markets.

JIMMY CHIN/National Geographic Creative

How competitive are markets today? As George Stigler points out in the second of his chapter-opening quotations, "Competition is a tough weed, not a delicate flower." Firms in markets that appear to be unrelated often compete with one another. For example, sellers of swimming pools compete with airlines, hotels, casinos, and automobile rental companies for the vacation and leisure time expenditures of consumers.

Over the past few decades, direct competition in almost all markets has increased. Lower transportation and communication costs have played an important role here. Lower transport costs make it more feasible for consumers to consider products offered by faraway suppliers. They also make it possible for producers to compete over a much larger geographic area, which often leads to lower per-unit costs and larger gains from economies of scale. Further, the Internet provides even those living in small towns with quick and easy access to worldwide markets. This widening of markets reduces the market power of both buyers and sellers and, at the same time, reduces potential problems related to economies of scale.

Technological change is also a powerful force for competitive markets. Innovation and nonprice competition on product quality, design, convenience, and other factors are used constantly by firms seeking greater market share and profitability. For a firm, innovation is the key to (temporary) profits. Successful innovation can give the innovating firm some degree of relief from competition while other firms struggle to catch up. Technical improvements, like newer and better computers or ways to make and sell them, cheaper and better inventory control methods, and innovative cell phones, have all made fortunes for the firms developing the information technology behind them. But the advantage is always temporary. Over time, each technical and business innovation becomes available to all firms, and the consumers of all products win, even as the profits of the innovating firms wane.

The competitiveness of markets is complex and difficult to measure directly. However, given the importance of quality competition, broader markets, and technological discoveries, most economists believe that the U.S. economy is more competitive today than it was, say, 50 or 75 years ago. Moreover, profit levels are considerably lower than many people think. A national sample poll of adults conducted by Opinion Research Corporation of Princeton, New Jersey, found that the average person thought profits constituted 29 percent of every dollar of sales in manufacturing. In reality, the after-tax accounting profits of manufacturing corporations are about 4 cents to 5 cents per dollar of sales. These figures also suggest that the U.S. economy, including the manufacturing sector, is relatively competitive.

LOOKING AHEAD

The last several chapters have focused on product markets. Of course, resources are required to produce products. The following chapters will focus on resource markets and the employment decisions of both business firms and resource suppliers.

KEY POINTS

- The four major sources of barriers to entry are economies of scale, government licensing, patents, and control of an essential resource.

- A monopoly is present when there is a single seller of a well-defined product for which there are no good substitutes and the entry barriers into the market are high. Although there are only a few markets in which the entire output is supplied by a single seller, the monopoly model also helps us better understand the operation of markets dominated by a small number of firms.

- Like other price searchers, a profit-maximizing monopolist will lower the price and expand its output as long as marginal revenue exceeds marginal cost. At the maximum-profit output, *MR* will equal *MC*. The monopolist will charge the price on its demand curve consistent with that output.

- If a monopolist is earning a profit, high barriers to entry will shield the firm from direct competition, thereby enabling it to earn long-run

economic profits. But sometimes demand and cost conditions will be such that even a monopolist will be unable to earn economic profit.

- An oligopolistic market is characterized by (1) a small number of rival firms, (2) interdependence among the sellers, (3) substantial economies of scale, and (4) high entry barriers into the market.

- There is no general theory for the determination of a unique price and output in an oligopolistic market. If rival oligopolists acted totally independently of their competitors, they would drive the price down to the per-unit cost of production. Alternatively, if they colluded perfectly, the price would rise to the level a monopolist would charge. The actual outcome under oligopoly will generally fall between these two extremes.

- Oligopolists have a strong incentive to collude and raise their prices. However, each firm will be able to gain if it (alone) can cut its price (or improve the quality of its product) because the demand curve confronted by the firm is more elastic than the industry demand curve. This introduces a conflict that makes it difficult to maintain collusive agreements, even where no law prohibits them.

- Oligopolistic firms are less likely to collude successfully against the interests of consumers if (1) there are more rival firms in the market, (2) it is costly to prohibit competitors from offering secret price cuts (or quality improvements) to customers, (3) entry barriers are low, (4) market demand conditions tend to be unstable, and/or (5) the threat of antitrust action is present.

- Economists criticize high barriers to market entry because (1) the ability of consumers to discipline producers is weakened, (2) the unregulated monopolist or oligopoly group can often gain by restricting

output and raising price, and (3) legal barriers to entry encourage firms to engage in wasteful rent-seeking activities.

- When entry barriers are high and competition among rival firms weak, the major policy alternatives are (1) antitrust action designed to maintain or increase the number of firms in the industry, (2) relaxation of regulations that limit entry and trade, (3) price regulation, and (4) provision of output by government firms. When feasible, option (2) is the most attractive alternative. Under most circumstances, all the other options have shortcomings.

- Competitive forces are present and growing, even in markets with high barriers to entry. Quality competition, the widening of markets, and technological change are all-important elements of the competitive process.

CRITICAL ANALYSIS QUESTIONS

1. "Barriers to entry are crucial to the existence of long-run profits, but they cannot guarantee the existence of profits." Evaluate.

2. "Monopoly is good for producers but bad for consumers. The gains of the former offset the losses of the latter. On balance, there is no reason to think that monopoly is bad for the economy." Is this statement true? Why or why not?

3. *Do monopolists charge the highest prices for which they can sell their products? Do they maximize their average profit per sale? Are monopolistic firms always profitable? Why or why not?

4. Compare the price and output policy of a purely competitive industry with the policy that would be established by a profit-maximizing monopolist or cartel. Who benefits and who is hurt? Construct the appropriate graphs to illustrate your answer.

5. Does economic theory indicate that an ideal regulatory agency that forces a monopolist to charge a price equal to either marginal or average total cost will improve economic efficiency? Explain. Does economic theory suggest that a regulatory agency will in fact regulate in a manner consistent with economic efficiency? What are some of the factors that complicate the regulatory function?

6. Is a monopolist subject to any competitive pressures? Explain. Would an unregulated monopolist have an incentive to operate and produce efficiently? Why or why not?

7. How will high entry barriers into a market influence

   a. the long-run profitability of the firms,

   c. the cost efficiency of the firms in the industry,

   c. the likelihood that some inefficient (high-cost) firms will survive, and

   d. the incentive of entrepreneurs to develop substitutes for the product supplied by the firms? Are competitive

pressures present in markets with high barriers to entry? Discuss.

8. *Why is oligopolistic collusion more difficult when there is product variation than when the products of all firms are identical?

9. In large cities, taxi fares are often set above the market equilibrium rate. Sometimes, the number of licenses is limited in order to maintain the above-market price. Other times, licenses are automatically granted to anyone wanting to operate a taxi. When taxi fares are set above market equilibrium, compare and contrast resource allocation under the restricted license system (assume the licenses are tradable) and the free-entry system. In which case will it be easier for customers to get a taxi? In which case will the amount of capital required to enter the taxi business be greater?

10. We have a theory to explain the equilibrium price and output for monopoly, but not for oligopoly. Why? How can game theory help us understand the decisions made by oligopolists?

11. *Historically, the real costs of transporting both goods and people have declined substantially. What impact do lower transportation costs have on the market power of individual producers? Do you think the U.S. economy is more or less competitive today than it was 100 years ago? Explain.

12. *"My uncle just bought 1,000 shares of Apple, one of the largest and most profitable companies in the United States. Given Apple's high profit rate, he will make a bundle from this purchase." Evaluate this statement. Is it necessarily true? Explain.

13. Gouge-em Cable Company is the only cable television service company licensed to operate in Backwater County. Most of its costs are access fees and maintenance expenses. These fixed costs total $640,000 monthly. The marginal cost of adding another subscriber to its system is constant at $2 per month. Gouge-em's demand curve can be determined from the data in the accompanying table.

SUBSCRIPTION PRICE	NUMBER OF SUBSCRIBERS (PER MONTH)
$25	20,000
20	40,000
15	60,000
10	80,000
5	100,000
1	150,000

a. What price will Gouge-em charge for its cable services? What are its profits at this price?

b. Now suppose the Backwater County Public Utility Commission has the data and believes that cable subscription rates in the county are too expensive and that

Gouge-em's profits are unfairly high. What regulated price will it set so that Gouge-em makes only a normal rate of return on its investment?

14. Suppose that you produce and sell children's tables in a local market. Past experience enables you to estimate your demand and marginal cost schedules. This information is presented in the accompanying table.

a. Fill in the missing revenue and cost schedules.

b. Assuming you are currently charging $55 per table set, what should you do if you want to maximize profits?

c. Given your demand and cost estimates, what price should you charge if you want to maximize your weekly profit? What output should you produce? What is your maximum weekly profit?

PRICE	QUANTITY DEMANDED (PER WEEK)	MARGINAL COST	TOTAL REVENUE	MARGINAL REVENUE	FIXED COST	TOTAL COST
$60	1	$50	—	—	$40	—
55	2	20	—	—	—	—
50	3	24	—	—	—	—
45	4	29	—	—	—	—
40	5	35	—	—	—	—
35	6	45	—	—	—	—

15. The accompanying diagram shows demand and long-run cost conditions in an industry.

a. Explain why the industry is likely to be monopolized.

b. Indicate the price that a profit-maximizing monopolist would charge and label it *P*.

c. Indicate the monopolist's output level and label it *Q*.

d. Indicate the maximum profits of the monopolist.

e. Will the profits attract competitors to the industry? Why or why not? Explain.

*Asterisk denotes questions for which answers are given in Appendix B

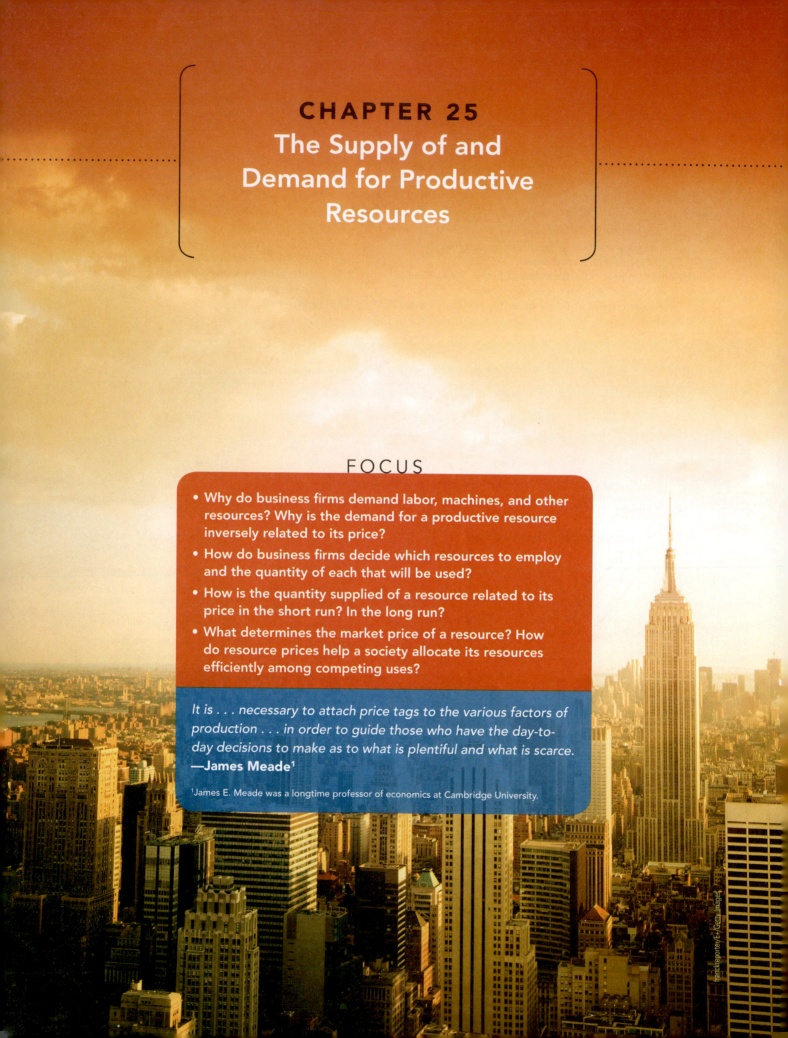

CHAPTER 25
The Supply of and Demand for Productive Resources

FOCUS

- Why do business firms demand labor, machines, and other resources? Why is the demand for a productive resource inversely related to its price?

- How do business firms decide which resources to employ and the quantity of each that will be used?

- How is the quantity supplied of a resource related to its price in the short run? In the long run?

- What determines the market price of a resource? How do resource prices help a society allocate its resources efficiently among competing uses?

It is . . . necessary to attach price tags to the various factors of production . . . in order to guide those who have the day-to-day decisions to make as to what is plentiful and what is scarce.
—**James Meade**[1]

[1]James E. Meade was a longtime professor of economics at Cambridge University.

Recent chapters have focused on product markets, markets in which consumers purchase goods and services supplied by business firms. Our analysis now shifts to **resource markets**, markets in which firms hire productive resources like machines and workers and use them to produce goods and services. (*Note:* Because resources are often referred to as *factors or inputs*, these markets are also known as *factor markets* or *input markets*.)

As in product markets, the forces of supply and demand combine to determine prices in resource markets. The buyers and sellers in resource markets are just the reverse of what they are in product markets. In resource markets, business firms are the purchasers; they demand resources used to produce goods and services. Households are the sellers; they (and firms they own) supply resources in exchange for income. The income from supplying productive resources, like the wages received from the sale of labor services, is the major source of income for most of us. Prices in resource markets coordinate the choices of buyers and sellers and bring the amount of each resource demanded into harmony with the amount supplied. Resource prices also help to channel factors of production into the areas where they are most productive. This enables us to have higher incomes and a larger supply of consumer goods than would otherwise be the case.

As the circular flow diagram of **Exhibit 1** illustrates, there is a close relationship between product and resource markets. Households earn income by selling factors of production—for example, the services of their labor and capital—to business firms. Their offers to sell form the supply curve in resource markets (bottom loop). The income that households get from the sale of resources gives them the buying power they need to purchase goods and services in product markets. These expenditures by households generate revenue and motivate firms to produce goods and services (top loop). In turn, firms demand resources because they contribute to the production of goods and services that can be sold in product markets.

EXHIBIT 1

The Market for Resources

Until now, we have focused on product markets, in which households demand goods and services that are supplied by firms (upper loop). We now turn to resource markets, in which firms demand factors of production—human capital (like the skills and knowledge of workers) and physical capital (like machines, buildings, and land). Factors of production are supplied by households in exchange for income (bottom loop). In resource markets, firms are buyers and households are sellers—just the reverse of the case for product markets.

25-1 HUMAN AND NONHUMAN RESOURCES

Resource markets
Markets in which business firms demand factors of production (for example, labor, capital, and natural resources) from household suppliers. The resources are then used to produce goods and services. These markets are sometimes called factor markets or input markets.

Nonhuman resources
The durable, nonhuman inputs used to produce both current and future output. Machines, buildings, land, and raw materials are examples. Investment can increase the supply of nonhuman resources. Economists often use the term *physical capital* when referring to nonhuman resources.

Human resources
The abilities, skills, and health of human beings that contribute to the production of both current and future output. Investment in training and education can increase the supply of human resources.

Investment in human capital
Expenditures on training, education, skill development, and health designed to increase human capital and people's productivity.

Derived demand
The demand for a resource; it stems from the demand for the final good the resource helps produce.

Broadly speaking, there are two different types of productive inputs, nonhuman and human. **Nonhuman resources** can be further broken down into physical capital, land, and natural resources. *Physical capital* consists of human-made resources, like tools, machines, and buildings that are used to produce other things.

Investment involves the use of resources in a manner that will increase future production capacity. The use of resources to produce machines, upgrade the quality of land, or discover natural resources provide examples of investments in nonhuman resources. Of course, investments involve a cost because the resources used to expand future production capacity could have been used to produce consumption goods directly. Why take the roundabout path? Investment and the indirect method often expand total output. The investment will be attractive if the value of the future output exceeds the cost of the reduction in current output.

Human resources consist of the skills and knowledge of workers. Investments in education, training, health, and experience can enhance the skills, abilities, and ingenuity of individuals and thereby increase their productivity. Economists refer to activities like these as **investment in human capital**. Like physical capital, human capital also depreciates—people's skills, for example, can decline with age or lack of use. Education and training will add to the stock of human capital whereas depreciation detracts from it.

Decisions to invest in human capital are no different than other investment decisions we make. Consider your decision about going to college. As you know, an investment in a college education requires you to sacrifice some current earnings as well as pay for direct expenses, like tuition and books. However, you are making the investment anyway because you expect it to lead to a better job and other benefits later. A rational person will attend college only if the expected future benefits outweigh the current costs.

In competitive markets, the price of resources, like the price of products, is determined by supply and demand. We will begin our analysis of resource markets by focusing on the demand for resources, both human and nonhuman.

25-2 THE DEMAND FOR RESOURCES

Profit-seeking producers employ laborers, machines, raw materials, and other resources because they help produce goods and services. The demand for a resource exists because there is a demand for goods that the resource helps to produce. *The demand for each resource is thus a **derived demand**; it is derived from the demand of consumers for products.*

For example, the demand for inputs like carpenters, plumbers, lumber, and glass windows is derived from the demand of consumers for houses and other consumer products these resources help to make. Most resources contribute to the production of numerous goods. For example, glass is used to produce windows, lightbulbs, and mirrors, among

OUTSTANDING ECONOMIST

GARY BECKER (1930–)

This 1992 Nobel Prize recipient is best known for his role in the development of human capital theory and his innovative application of that theory to areas as diverse as employment discrimination, family development, and crime. In his widely acclaimed book *Human Capital*,* Becker developed the theoretical foundation for human investment decisions in education, on-the-job training, migration, and health. Becker is a past president of the American Economic Association and a longtime professor at the University of Chicago.

*Gary Becker, *Human Capital* (New York: Columbia University Press, 1964).

EXHIBIT 2

The Demand Curve for a Resource

As the price of a resource increases, producers that use the resource intensely will (1) turn to substitute resources and (2) face higher costs, which will lead to higher product prices and lower output. At the lower rate of output, producers will use less of the resource that increased in price. Both of these factors contribute to the inverse relationship between the price and amount demanded of a resource.

other things. The total demand for a resource is the sum of the derived demands for each of its uses.

The demand curve for a resource shows the amount of the resource that will be used at different prices. As **Exhibit 2** shows, there is an inverse relationship between the price of a resource and the quantity of it demanded. As the price of a resource increases there are two reasons why less will be demanded: (1) Producers will turn to substitute resources, and (2) consumers will buy less of goods that become more expensive as the result of higher resource costs. Let us take a closer look at each of these factors.

25-2a SUBSTITUTION IN PRODUCTION

Firms use the combination of resources that minimizes costs. When the price of one resource goes up, firms switch to other lower-cost substitute resources. If the price of oak lumber increases, furniture manufacturers will begin to use other types of wood (like maple) or metals and plastics more intensely. Sometimes, producers will alter the style and dimensions of a product, or even relocate the business, in order to use less of a more expensive resource. The degree to which firms will be able to cut back on a more expensive resource will depend on the availability of substitute resources. *Other things constant, the demand for a resource will be more elastic the more (and better) substitute resources are available for it.*

25-2b SUBSTITUTION IN CONSUMPTION

An increase in the price of a resource will lead to higher costs of production and thus higher prices for the products it helps to produce. Faced with these higher product prices, *consumers* will turn to substitute products and cut back on their purchases of the now more expensive products. In turn, fewer resources will be required to produce the smaller amount of the product demanded by consumers at the now higher price (including less of the resource that rose in price).

Other things constant, the more elastic the demand for a product is, the more elastic the demand for the resources used to make it. This relationship stems from the derived nature of resource demand. An increase in the price of a product for which consumer demand is highly elastic will cause a sharp fall in the sales of the good. As a result, there will be a relatively sharp fall in the demand for the resources used to produce it.

Time and the Demand Elasticity of Resources

The demand for a resource will be more elastic (1) the easier it is for firms to switch to substitute inputs and (2) the more elastic the consumer demand for the products the resource helps produce. As the graph here shows, demand for a resource in the long run (D_{lr}) is nearly always more elastic than demand in the short run (D_{sr}).

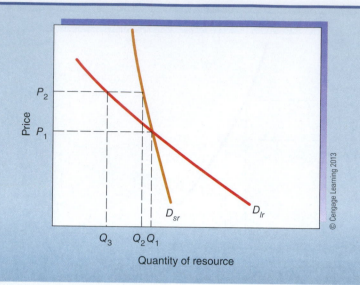

© Cengage Learning 2013

25-2c HOW TIME CHANGES THE DEMAND FOR RESOURCES

The elasticity of resource demand is also influenced by time. It takes time for both producers and consumers to make the adjustments described above after a resource price has changed. Producers may have to alter their plant and equipment, while consumers also need time to identify and utilize other substitutes. Thus, the demand for a resource generally becomes more elastic with the passage of time.

Exhibit 3 shows how time affects the elasticity of resource demand. The slope of the long-run demand curve (D_{lr}) is less steep, showing it is more elastic, than the slope of the short-run demand curve (D_{sr}). An increase in price from P_1 to P_2 will lead to only a small reduction in the quantity of the resource used (from Q_1 to Q_2) in the short run. Given more time, however, the increase in price to P_2 causes a much larger reduction in the quantity demanded (to Q_3).

25-2d SHIFTS IN THE DEMAND FOR A RESOURCE

Like the demand curve for a product, the entire demand curve for a resource may shift. There are three major reasons why.

1. A change in the demand for a product will cause a similar change in the demand for the resources used to produce it.

Because the demand for a resource is a derived demand, an increase in the demand for a consumer good simultaneously increases the demand for resources needed to make it. For example, the demand for personal computers and other computerized equipment has increased substantially over the past couple of decades. In turn, this stronger demand for the equipment generated an increase in demand for computer chips required for its production. Of course, a reduction in the demand for a product will have the opposite impact. Lower demand for the product will lead to a reduction in demand for the resources required for its production.

2. Changes in the productivity of a resource will alter demand—the higher the productivity of a resource, the greater will be the demand for it.

As the productivity of a resource increases, so does its value to potential users. Improvements in the quality of a resource—in the case of workers, their skill levels—will increase the productivity of the resource and therefore the demand for it. For example,

The demand for resources is a derived demand. A more complex tax code would increase the demand for (and thus the wages of) accountants, whereas a simpler tax code would have the opposite impact.

as workers gain valuable new knowledge and/or upgrade their skills, they enhance their productivity and essentially move into a different skill category—one in which demand is greater.

The productivity of a resource will also depend on the amount of other resources used with it in the production process. In general, additional capital will tend to increase the productivity of labor. For example, someone with a dump truck can haul more material than can the same person with a shovel. The quantity and quality of the tools with which employees work will significantly affect their productivity. Technological advances in robotics and computing have substantially increased the productivity of a wide range of occupations including journalists, book authors, autoworkers, coal miners, and forensic scientists. The link between technological advances and worker productivity helps explain why improvements in technology generally do not simply displace workers and thereby exert a large negative impact on employment, even in the occupations most directly affected. Of course, when firms substitute new technology for labor services, the demand for labor will fall. However, the new technology both makes the labor more productive and lowers the cost of production and prices for consumers, which in turn increase the demand for labor. These positive impacts of technology on the employment of labor will partially, and sometimes more than completely, offset any negative effects.

The productivity–demand link sheds light on why wage rates in the United States, Canada, Western Europe, and Japan are higher than in most other areas of the world. Given the skill level of workers, the technology, and the capital equipment with which they work, individuals in these countries produce more goods and services per hour of labor than workers in most other countries. In turn, the demand for their labor (relative to supply) is greater because of their high productivity. Essentially, the workers' greater productivity leads to their higher wage rates.

3. A change in the price of a related resource will affect the demand for the original resource.
A rise in the price of a resource will cause the demand for substitute resources to expand. For example, when the price of lumber increases, the demand for bricks will increase as homebuilders switch to building more brick homes and fewer wood homes. Conversely, an increase in the price of a resource that is a *complement* to a given resource will decrease the demand for the given resource. For example, higher lumber prices will tend to lower the demand for nails.

25-3 MARGINAL PRODUCTIVITY AND THE FIRM'S HIRING DECISION

How does a producer decide whether to employ additional units of a resource? As with other decisions, the marginal benefit relative to the marginal cost provides the answer. In resource markets, firms are mostly price takers, which means they can hire as many units of the resource as they wish without affecting the market price of the resource. Thus, the marginal cost of hiring one more worker is simply the worker's wage, while the marginal cost of purchasing a machine is its price. These represent the increase in the firm's costs from employing one more unit of each resource. But what about the marginal benefit of the resource to the firm? It is measured by the increase in the firm's revenue from employing one more unit of the resource. This is called the resource's **marginal revenue product (MRP)**. A profit-maximizing firm will only hire an additional unit of the resource if it generates more revenue for the firm than the cost of employing it. If the marginal revenue product of employing an additional unit of a resource is less than the cost, the firm will not employ it.

Suppose a retail store was considering hiring a security guard for $25 per hour to help reduce shoplifting. If the security guard could prevent $20 worth of shoplifting per hour, should the profit-maximizing firm hire the guard? Because the marginal cost of employing the security guard (the wage of $25) is higher than the guard's marginal revenue product (the $20 reduction in shoplifting per hour), the wise decision is for the firm not to hire the security guard. Hiring the guard will lower the firm's profit by $5 per hour. The guard should be employed only if the reduction in shoplifting exceeds the guard's wage cost. In most situations, the direct impact of hiring an additional resource on a firm's revenue is not as clear, so let's take a closer look at the firm's decision and how marginal revenue product is determined.

25-3a USING A VARIABLE RESOURCE WITH A FIXED RESOURCE

When an additional unit of the resource is used relative to a fixed amount of other resources, the firm's output will increase by an amount equal to the resource's **marginal product (MP)**. Because this is measured in units of physical output, it is sometimes referred to as marginal physical product. How much additional revenue can the firm derive from the employment of the resource? Recall that **marginal revenue (MR)** is the increase in the firm's revenue that results from the sale of each additional unit of output. Thus, a resource's marginal revenue product is equal to the marginal product of the resource multiplied by the marginal revenue of the good or service produced. *Because of the law of diminishing returns, the marginal product of a resource will fall as employment of the resource expands. As a result, the marginal revenue product of a resource will also decline as its employment expands.*

The relationship between the marginal revenue a firm gets from selling an additional unit of output and the price for which it is sold is different for *price-taker* firms than for *price searchers*, however. Because a price-taker firm sells all units produced at the same price, the price taker's marginal revenue will be equal to the market price of the product. The price searcher, however, must reduce the price of all units in order to expand the number of units sold. Consequently, the price searcher's marginal revenue will be less than the sales price of the units. The marginal product of a resource multiplied by the selling price of the product is called the resource's **value marginal product (VMP)**. *For a price-taker firm, the* **MRP** *of a resource is equal to its* **VMP** *because price and marginal revenue are equal. For a price-searcher firm, however, the* **MRP** *of a resource will be lower than its* **VMP** *because marginal revenue is less than price.*

Using these measures, Exhibit 4 illustrates how a firm decides how much of a resource to employ. Compute-Accounting, Inc., uses computer equipment and data entry operators to supply clients with monthly accounting statements. The firm is a price taker:

Marginal revenue product (MRP)
The change in the total revenue of a firm that results from the employment of one additional unit of a resource. The marginal revenue product of an input is equal to its marginal product multiplied by the marginal revenue of the good or service produced.

Marginal product (MP)
The change in total output that results from the employment of one additional unit of a resource.

Marginal revenue (MR)
The change in a firm's total revenue that results from the production and sale of one additional unit of output.

Value marginal product (VMP)
The marginal product of a resource multiplied by the selling price of the product it helps produce. For a price-taker firm, marginal revenue product (MRP) will be equal to the value marginal product (VMP).

The Short-Run Demand Schedule of a Firm

Compute-Accounting, Inc., uses computer technology and data-entry operators to provide accounting services in a competitive market. For each accounting statement processed, the firm receives a $200 fee (column 4). Given the firm's current fixed capital, column 2 shows how total output changes as additional data entry operators are hired. The marginal revenue product (MRP)

schedule (column 6) indicates how hiring an additional operator affects the total revenue of the firm. Because a profit-maximizing firm will hire an additional employee if, and only if, the employee adds more to revenues than to costs, the marginal revenue product curve is the firm's short-run demand curve for the resource (see Exhibit 5).

UNITS OF VARIABLE FACTOR (DATA-ENTRY OPERATORS) (1)	TOTAL OUTPUT (ACCOUNTING STATEMENTS PROCESSED PER WEEK) (2)	MARGINAL PRODUCT (CHANGE IN COLUMN 2 DIVIDED BY CHANGE IN COLUMN 1) (3)	SALES PRICE PER STATEMENT (4)	TOTAL REVENUE (2) × (4) (5)	MRP (3) × (4) (6)
0	0.0	—	$200	$0	—
1	5.0	5.0	200	1,000	1,000
2	9.0	4.0	200	1,800	800
3	12.0	3.0	200	2,400	600
4	14.0	2.0	200	2,800	400
5	15.5	1.5	200	3,100	300
6	16.5	1.0	200	3,300	200
7	17.0	0.5	200	3,400	100

It sells its service in a competitive market for $200 per statement. Given the fixed quantity of computer equipment owned by Compute-Accounting, column 2 shows how much total output (quantity of accounting statements) the firm can produce with different numbers of data entry operators. One data entry operator can process five statements per week. When two operators are employed, nine statements can be completed. Column 2 indicates how total output is expected to change as additional data entry operators are employed. Column 3 presents the marginal product schedule for data entry operators. Column 6, the *MRP* schedule, shows how the employment of each additional operator affects total revenue. Both the marginal product and the *MRP* of workers decline as additional operators are employed due to the law of diminishing returns.

How does Compute-Accounting is a price taker, the marginal revenue product and the value marginal product of labor are equal. Thus, the marginal revenue product of labor (column 6) can be calculated by multiplying the marginal product (column 3) times the sales price of an accounting statement (column 4).

How does Compute-Accounting decide how many operators to employ? It analyzes the benefits relative to the costs. As additional operators are employed, the output of processed statements (column 2) will increase, which will expand total revenue (column 5). Employing additional operators, though, will also add to production costs because the operators must be paid. Applying the profit-maximization rule, Compute-Accounting will hire additional operators as long as their employment adds more to revenues than to costs. This will be the case as long as the *MRP* (column 6) of the data entry operators exceeds their wage rate. At a weekly wage of $1,000, Compute-Accounting would hire only one operator. If the weekly wage dropped to $800, two operators would be hired. At still lower wage rates, additional operators would be hired.

*Profit-maximizing firms, both price takers and price searchers, will expand their employment of each variable resource until the **MRP** of the resource (the firm's additional revenue generated by the resource) is just equal to the price of the resource (the firm's marginal cost of employing the resource).*

EXHIBIT 5

The Firm's Demand Curve for a Resource

The firm's demand curve for a resource will reflect the marginal revenue product (MRP) of the resource. In the short run, it will slope downward because the marginal product of the resource will fall as more of it is used with a fixed amount of other resources. The location of the MRP curve will depend on (1) the price of the product, (2) the productivity of the resource, and (3) the quantity of other factors working with the resource.

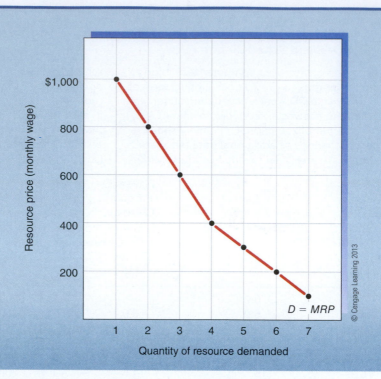

© Cengage Learning 2013

25-3b *MRP* AND THE FIRM'S DEMAND CURVE FOR A RESOURCE

Using the data in Exhibit 4, we can construct Compute-Accounting's demand curve for data entry operators. Recall that the height of a demand curve shows the maximum price (in this case, the wage) the buyer (the firm) would be willing to pay for the unit. Because the marginal revenue product of the first data entry operator is $1,000, the firm would be willing to hire this worker only up to a maximum price of $1,000. Because of this relationship, as **Exhibit 5** shows, a firm's short-run demand curve for a resource is precisely the *MRP* curve for the resource.[2] Using this demand curve yields the identical solutions as the table. Underlying the downward-sloping demand curve is the law of diminishing returns causing *MP*, and thus *MRP*, to fall as more workers are hired.

The location of the firm's *MRP* curve depends on (1) the price of the product, (2) the productivity of the resource, and (3) the amount of other resources with which the resource is working. Changes in any one of these three factors will cause the *MRP* curve to shift. For example, if Compute-Accounting purchased additional computer equipment making it possible for the operators to complete more statements each week, the *MRP* curve for labor would increase (shift outward). This increase in the quantity of the other resources working with labor would increase labor's productivity.

25-3c MULTIPLE RESOURCES AND HOW MUCH TO USE OF EACH

So far, we have analyzed the firm's hiring decision assuming that it used one variable resource (labor) and one fixed resource. Production, though, usually involves the use of many resources. How should these resources be combined to produce the product? We can answer this question by considering either the conditions for profit maximization or the conditions for cost minimization.

---

[2]Strictly speaking, this is true only for a variable resource that is employed with a fixed amount of another factor.

25-3d MAXIMIZING PROFITS WHEN MULTIPLE RESOURCES ARE USED

The same decision-making considerations apply when the firm employs several factors of production. The profit-maximizing firm will expand its use of a resource as long as the *MRP* of the resource exceeds its employment cost. If we assume that resources are perfectly divisible, the profit-maximizing decision rule implies that, in equilibrium, the *MRP* of each resource will be equal to the price of the resource. Therefore, the following conditions will exist for the profit-maximizing firm:

MRP of skilled labor = Price (wage rate) of skilled labor

MRP of unskilled labor = Price (wage rate) of unskilled labor

MRP of machine A = Price (explicit or implicit rental price) of machine A and so on, for all other factors

25-3e COST MINIMIZATION WHEN MULTIPLE RESOURCES ARE USED

To maximize its profits, the firm must produce the profit-maximizing output at the least possible cost. If the firm is minimizing costs, the marginal dollar expenditure for each resource will have the same impact on output as an additional dollar expenditure on other resources used to produce the product. Factors of production will be employed such that the marginal product *per last dollar spent* on each factor is the same for all factors.

To see why, consider a situation in which a $100 expenditure on labor caused output to rise by ten units, whereas an additional $100 expenditure on machines generated only a five-unit expansion in output. In this case, the firm could employ $100 less in machines, spend the $100 on labor instead, and produce five more units of output for the same total cost. By substituting labor for machines, it will reduce its *per-unit* cost.

If the marginal dollar spent on one resource increases output by a larger amount than a dollar expenditure on other resources, substituting the one with the high marginal product per dollar for the low one will always reduce costs. Substitution will continue to reduce unit costs (and increase profit) until the marginal product per dollar expenditure on each resource is equalized. This will occur because as additional units of a resource are hired, their marginal product will fall. Thus, the proportional relationship between the price of each resource and its marginal product will eventually be achieved.

Therefore, the following condition exists when per unit costs are minimized:

$$\frac{MP \text{ of skilled labor}}{\text{Price of skilled labor}} = \frac{MP \text{ of unskilled labor}}{\text{Price of unskilled labor}} = \frac{MP \text{ of machine A}}{\text{Price (rental value) of machine A}}$$

This relationship explains why workers with different skill levels earn different wages. If skilled workers are twice as productive as unskilled workers, their wage rates will tend to be twice those of unskilled workers. For example, suppose that a construction firm hiring workers to hang doors is choosing among skilled and unskilled workers. If skilled door hangers can complete four doors per hour, while unskilled workers can hang only two doors per hour, a cost-minimizing firm would hire only skilled workers—as long as their wages are less than twice the wages of unskilled workers. In contrast, only unskilled workers would be hired if the wages of skilled workers are more than twice that of unskilled workers. Because of competition, wages across skill categories will tend to mirror productivity differences.

It is important to note that low wages do not necessarily mean low cost. In other words, it is not always cheaper to hire the lowest-wage workers. It is not just wages, but rather wages *relative to productivity* that matter. If the wages of skilled workers are twice those of unskilled workers, it will still be cheaper to hire additional skilled workers if their marginal productivity (output per hour) is more than twice that of the unskilled workers.

Do employers in the real world really think in terms of equating the marginal product/price ratio (*MP/P*) for each factor of production? Probably not. Their thought process is likely going to be something more like this: "Can we reduce costs by using more of one resource and less of another?" However, regardless of how managers think about the problem, when a firm maximizes its profits and minimizes its costs, its marginal product/price ratio will be equal for all factors of production. The outcome will be *the same as if* the firm followed the cost-minimization, decision-making rule presented here.

Summing up, resources will only be employed if they generate enough revenue to cover the cost of their employment. Resources that are more productive will be able to command higher prices (or wage rates) because they generate more revenue for the firm. The marginal-productivity theory underlies the demand for resources. Of course, resource prices will also be influenced by supply. We now turn to that topic.

25-4 THE SUPPLY OF RESOURCES

Just as benefits and costs direct the choices of employers, so too will they guide the actions of resource suppliers. Resource owners will supply their services to an employer only if they perceive that the benefits of doing so exceed their costs (the value of the other things they could do with their time or resources). Because of this, employers must offer resource owners at least as good a deal as they can get elsewhere. For example, if an employer does not offer a potential employee pay, benefits, and working conditions as good as, or better than, others, the employer will be unable to hire that worker.

Resource owners will supply their services to those who offer them the best employment alternative. Other things constant, as the price of a specific resource increases, the incentive of potential suppliers to provide the resource increases.

An increase in the price of a resource will lure resource suppliers into the market. A decrease will cause them to shift into other activities. Therefore, as **Exhibit 6** illustrates, the supply curve for a specific resource will slope upward to the right.[3]

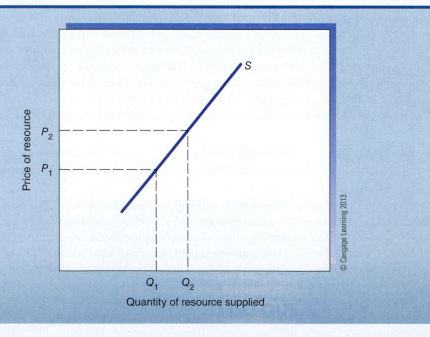

EXHIBIT 6

The Supply of a Resource

As the price of a resource increases, individuals have a greater incentive to supply it. Therefore, a direct relationship will exist between the price of a resource and the quantity supplied.

© Cengage Learning 2013

---

[3]Although the supply for nonhuman resources will always slope upward, the supply of labor at very high wage rates can become backward bending. As wages rise, individuals will substitute toward more work, but simultaneously the higher income will cause them to desire more leisure. At very high wage rates, the income effect might dominate, causing a negative relationship between wage rates and quantity of labor supplied in this range. For example, at a wage of $10,000 per hour, many individuals would probably supply fewer hours of work than at $500 per hour!

25-4a SHORT-RUN VERSUS LONG-RUN RESOURCE SUPPLY

Like demand, supply in resource markets can be different in the short run than in the long run. If the wage rate for certified public accountants (CPAs) rose, for example, we would expect more workers supplying their services as CPAs. But where do these additional CPAs come from? In the short run, the additional supply must come from those who are already qualified as CPAs but are currently doing other things. The higher wages might induce some college accounting professors and some stay-at-home spouses with accounting credentials to move into employment as CPAs. In the short run, however, there isn't enough time to alter the availability of a resource through investment in human and physical capital. In contrast, in the long run, resource suppliers have time to adjust their investment choices in response to a change in resource prices. With time, the higher wages and easier employment opportunities for CPAs will cause more students to major in accounting and other people to pursue the coursework needed to become a CPA. Higher resource prices will increase the quantity supplied in both the short run and the long run, but the response will be greater in the long run. Therefore, as **Exhibit 7** shows, the long-run supply of a resource will be more elastic than the short-run supply.

25-4b SHORT-RUN SUPPLY

The short-run supply response to a change in price is determined by how easily the resource can be transferred from one use to another—that is, **resource mobility**. The supply of resources with high mobility will be relatively elastic even in the short run. Conversely, resources that have few alternative uses (or are not easily transferable) are said to be immobile. The short-run supply of immobile resources will be highly inelastic.

Consider the mobility of labor. Within a skill category (for example, plumber, store manager, accountant, or secretary), labor will be highly mobile within the same geographic area. Movements between geographic areas and from one skill category to another are more costly to accomplish, though. Labor will thus be less mobile for movements of this variety. In addition, because it is easier for a highly skilled person to perform effectively in a lower-skill position than vice versa, short-run mobility will tend

Resource mobility
The ease with which factors of production are able to move among alternative uses. Resources that can easily be transferred to a different use or location are said to be highly mobile. Resources with few alternative uses are immobile.

EXHIBIT 7

Time and the Elasticity of Supply for Resources

If the wage rate for CPAs rises, for example, to P_2, we would expect more workers to supply CPA services. Because it takes time to be trained as a CPA, though, the quantity of CPA services supplied in the short run (S_{sr}) won't increase by much—just to Q_2. The supply of CPA services is therefore relatively inelastic in the short run. In the long run, though, it is more elastic and the quantity supplied increases to Q_3.

The supply curve for truck drivers will be considerably more elastic than the supply curve for doctors. Can you explain why?

to decline as the skill level of the occupation rises. Thus, the short-run supply curve in high-skill occupations like architect, mechanical engineer, and medical surgeon is usually quite inelastic.

What about the mobility of land? Land is highly mobile among uses when location doesn't matter. For example, the same land can often be used to raise corn, wheat, soybeans, or oats. As a result, the supply of land allocated to the production of each of these commodities will be highly responsive to changes in their relative prices. Undeveloped land on the outskirts of cities is particularly mobile among uses. It can be used for agriculture, but it can also quickly be subdivided and used for a housing development or a shopping center. Because land is totally immobile physically, you might think its supply is unresponsive to changes in price when it comes to how desirable it is (or isn't) due to its location. You can't move it to make it more desirable and get a better price, obviously. You can, however, expand its usable space by constructing multiple-story buildings, for instance. As the demand for a given location increases, higher and higher multilevel construction will be justified. This is why tall buildings are generally located in city centers, for example—because the demand for space is highest in these locations.

25-4c LONG-RUN SUPPLY

In the long run, the supply of resources can change substantially. Machines wear out, human skills depreciate, and even the fertility of land declines with use and erosion. These factors reduce the supply of resources. In contrast, investment can replace and expand the supply of productive resources, including machines, buildings, and durable assets. Correspondingly, investments in training and education can develop and improve the skills of future labor force participants. Thus, the supply of both physical and human resources in the long run is determined primarily by investment and depreciation.

As the price of a resource increases, more and more people will make the investments necessary to supply it. This will be true for human as well as physical resources. For example, higher salaries for engineers stimulate engineering degree enrollments. According to a study by Jaewoo Ryoo and Sherwin Rosen, a 1-percent increase in starting engineering salaries causes enrollment in engineering degree programs to rise by 2.5 to 4.5 percent.[4]

The long run, of course, is not a specified length of time. Investment can increase the availability of some resources fairly quickly. For example, it does not take very long to train additional truck drivers. However, it takes a long time to train physicians, dentists, lawyers, and pharmacists. Higher earnings in these occupations may have only a small impact on their current availability. Additional investment will flow into these areas, but it will typically be several years before there is a substantial increase in the quantity supplied.

---

[4]Jaewoo Ryoo and Sherwin Rosen, "The Engineering Labor Market," *Journal of Political Economy* 112, no. S1 (February 2004): S110-S140.

25-5 SUPPLY, DEMAND, AND RESOURCE PRICES

In a market economy, resource prices will be determined by the forces of supply and demand and will bring the choices of buyers and sellers into line with each other. **Exhibit 8** illustrates how the forces of supply and demand push the market wage rates of engineers toward equilibrium, where quantity demanded and quantity supplied are equal. Equilibrium is achieved when the price (wage rate) for engineering services is P_1. Given the market conditions illustrated by Exhibit 8, an excess supply is present if the price of engineering services exceeds P_1. Some engineers will be unable to find jobs at the above-equilibrium wage. This excess supply of engineers will cause the wage rate for engineers to fall. This will cause some of the engineers to look for jobs in other fields, and quantity supplied will fall, pushing the market toward equilibrium. In contrast, if the resource price is less than P_1, excess demand is present. Employers are unable to hire the amount of engineering services they want at a below-equilibrium resource price. Rather than doing without the resource, employers will attempt to hire engineers away from other firms by bidding the price up to P_1 and thereby eliminating the excess demand.

How will a resource market adjust to an unexpected change in market conditions? Suppose there is a sharp increase in the demand for houses, apartments, and office buildings. The increase in demand for these products will also increase the demand for resources required for their construction. Thus, the demand for resources like steel, lumber, brick, and the labor services of carpenters, architects, and construction engineers will increase. **Exhibit 9** shows the increase in demand for new houses and buildings (part a) and the accompanying increase in demand for construction engineers. The market demand for the services of construction engineers increases from D_1 to D_2 (part b), and initially there is a sharp rise in their wages (price increases from P_1 to P_2). The higher wages will motivate additional people to get the education and training necessary to become construction engineers. Over time, the entry of the newly trained construction engineers will increase the elasticity of the resource supply curve. As these new construction engineers eventually enter the occupation, the supply curve will become more elastic (S_{lr} rather than S_{sr}), which will place downward pressure on wages in the occupation (the move from b to c). Therefore, as part (b) of Exhibit 9 illustrates, the long-run price increase (to P_3) will be less than the short-run increase (to P_2).

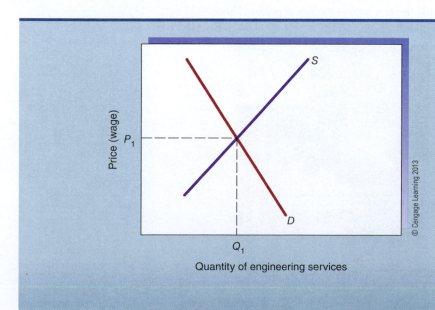

EXHIBIT 8

Equilibrium in a Resource Market

The market demand for a resource, such as engineering services, is a downward-sloping curve, reflecting the declining *MRP* of the resource. The market supply curve slopes upward because higher resource prices (wage rates) will motivate people to supply more of the resource. Market price will move toward equilibrium (P_1), where the quantity demanded and the quantity supplied are in balance.

EXHIBIT 9

Adjusting to Dynamic Change

An increase in the demand for housing and commercial buildings (part a) will lead to an increase in demand for the services of construction engineers (part b) and other resources used in the construction industry. Initially, the increase in the resource price will be substantial, jumping from P_1 to P_2 (point a versus point b in the graph). The increase will be particularly sharp if the supply of the resource is highly inelastic in the short run. The higher resource price will attract additional human capital investment, and, with time, the resource supply curve will become more elastic, which will moderate the price (or wage) increase to P_3 (point c).

(a) Product market—new houses and commercial buildings

(b) Resource market—services of construction engineers

© Cengage Learning 2013

The market adjustment to an unexpected reduction in demand for a resource is the same. The price falls farther in the short run than in the long run. At the lower price, some resource suppliers will use their talents in other areas, and the incentive for potential new suppliers to offer the resource will be less. With time, the quantity of the resource supplied will decline, moderating the reduction in its price. Those with the poorest alternatives (that is, lowest opportunity cost) will continue to provide the resource at the lower prices. Those with better alternatives will look for other opportunities.

Photodisc (RF)/Jupiter Images

©wavebreakmedia/Shutterstock.com

Workers in occupations like nursing that require substantial skill and education will generally earn higher wages than will those in occupations requiring little training or experience.

25-5a THE COORDINATING FUNCTION OF RESOURCE PRICES

Our analysis indicates that prices in resource markets play a vitally important role. These prices coordinate the actions of the firms demanding factors of production and the households supplying them. *Resource prices provide users with both information about the scarcity of the resources they're using and the incentive to conserve them in production. They also provide suppliers with an incentive to learn skills and provide resources—particularly those that are intensely demanded by users.* Without the use of resource markets and the price incentives they provide, efficient use and wise conservation of resources would be extremely difficult to achieve.[5]

LOOKING AHEAD

The analysis of this chapter can be applied to a broad range of economic issues. The next chapter will focus on the labor market and earnings differences among workers. Later, we will focus on the capital market and the allocation of resources over time. The operation of these two markets plays an important role in determining the distribution of income, a topic that will also be analyzed in detail in a subsequent chapter.

---

[5]Analysis of energy consumption under central planning illustrates this point. The centrally planned economies both used more energy per unit of output and their energy consumption was less responsive to changes in price than was true for economies that used markets to allocate energy. For evidence on these points, see Mikhail S. Bernstam, *The Wealth of Nations and the Environment* (London: Institute of Economic Affairs, 1991).

KEY POINTS

- Productive assets and services are bought and sold in resource markets. There are two broad classes of productive resources: (1) nonhuman capital and (2) human capital.

- The demand for resources is derived from the demand for products that the resources help produce. The quantity of a resource demanded is inversely related to its price because of substitutions made by both producers and consumers.

- The demand curve for a resource, like the demand for a product, can shift. The major factors that increase the demand for a resource are (1) an increase in demand for products that use the resource, (2) an increase in the productivity of the resource, and (3) an increase in the price of substitute resources.

- Profit-maximizing firms will hire additional units of a resource up to the point at which the marginal revenue product (*MRP*) of the resource equals its price. With multiple inputs, firms will expand their use of each until the marginal product divided by the price (*MP/P*) is equal across all inputs. When real-world decision makers minimize per-unit costs, the outcome will be as if they had followed these mathematical procedures, even though they may not consciously do so.

- The amount of a resource supplied will be directly related to its price. The supply of a resource will be more elastic in the long run than in the short run. In the long run, investment can increase the supply of both physical and human resources.

- The prices of resources are determined by supply and demand. Changes in the market prices of resources will influence the decisions of both users and suppliers. Higher resource prices give users a greater incentive to turn to substitutes and suppliers a greater incentive to provide more of the resource.

- Resource prices coordinate the actions of resource owners and business firms demanding their services. Changes in resource prices in response to changing market conditions are essential for the efficient allocation of resources in a dynamic world.

CRITICAL ANALYSIS QUESTIONS

1. "The demand for resources is a derived demand." What is meant by that statement? Why is the employment of a resource inversely related to its price?

2. How does a firm decide whether or not to employ an additional unit of a resource? What determines the combination of skilled and unskilled workers employed by a firm?

3. *Use the information in Exhibit 4 of this chapter to answer the following:

   a. How many employees (operators) would Compute-Accounting hire at a weekly wage of $250 if it were attempting to maximize profits?

b. What would the firm's maximum profit be if its fixed costs were $1,500 per week?

c. Suppose there were a decline in demand for accounting services, reducing the market price per monthly statement to $150. At this demand level, how many employees would Compute-Accounting hire at $250 per week in the short run? Would Compute-Accounting be able to stay in business at the lower market price? Explain.

4. *Are productivity gains the major source of higher wages? If so, how does one account for the rising real wages of barbers, who, by and large, have used the same techniques for a half-century? (*Hint:* Do not forget opportunity cost and supply.)

5. Are the following statements both correct? Are they inconsistent with each other? Explain.

a. "Firms will hire a resource only if they can make money by doing so."

b. "In a market economy, each resource will tend to be paid according to its marginal product. Highly productive resources will command high prices, whereas less productive resources will command lower prices."

6. *Many school districts pay teachers on the basis of their highest degree earned and number of years of service (seniority). They often find it quite easy to fill the slots for English and history teachers, but very difficult to find the required number of math and science teachers. Can you explain why?

7. Suppose that you were the manager of a large retail store that was currently experiencing a shoplifting problem. Every hour, approximately $15 worth of merchandise was being stolen from your store. Suppose that a security guard would completely eliminate the shoplifting in your store. If you were interested in maximizing your profits, should you hire a security guard if the wage rate of security guards was $20 per hour? Why or why not? What does this imply about the relationship between average shoplifting per hour in the economy and the wage rates of security guards?

8. *A dressmaker uses labor and capital (sewing machines) to produce dresses in a competitive market. Suppose the last unit of labor hired cost $1,000 per month and increased output by 100 dresses. The last unit of capital hired (rented) cost $500 per month and increased output by 80 dresses. Is the dressmaker minimizing costs? If not, what changes need to be made?

9. A firm is considering moving from the United States to Mexico. The firm pays its U.S. workers $12 per hour. Current U.S. workers have a marginal product of forty, whereas the Mexican workers have a marginal product of ten. How low would the Mexican wage have to be for the firm to reduce its wage cost per unit of output by moving to Mexico?

10. "The earnings of engineers, doctors, and lawyers are high because lots of education is necessary to practice in these fields." Evaluate this statement.

11. Other things constant, what impact will a highly elastic demand for a product have on the elasticity of demand for the resources used to produce the product? Explain.

12. *The following chart provides information on a firm that hires labor competitively and sells its product in a competitive market.

Units of Labor	Total Output	Marginal Product	Product Price	Total Revenue	MRP
1	14	—	$5	—	—
2	26	—	$5	—	—
3	37	—	$5	—	—
4	46	—	$5	—	—
5	53	—	$5	—	—
6	58	—	$5	—	—

a. Fill in the missing columns.

b. How many units of labor would be employed if the market wage rate were $40? Why?

c. What would happen to employment if the wage rate rose to $50? Explain.

13. Leisure Times, Inc., employs skilled workers and capital to install hot tubs. The capital includes the tools and equipment workers use to construct and install the tubs. The installation services are sold in a competitive market for $1,200 per hot tub. Leisure Times is able to hire workers for $2,200 per month, including the cost of wages, fringe benefits, and employment taxes. As additional workers are hired, the increase in the number of hot tubs installed is indicated in the table.

Number of Workers Employed	Number of Hot Tubs Installed (per Month)
1	5
2	12
3	18
4	23
5	27
6	30
7	32
8	33
9	34

a. Indicate the marginal product and *MRP* schedules of the workers.

b. What quantity of workers should Leisure Times employ to maximize its profit?

c. If a construction boom pushes the wages of skilled workers up to $2,500 per month, how many workers would Leisure Times employ to maximize its profit?

d. Suppose that strong demand for hot tubs pushes the price of installation services up to $1,500 per month. How would this affect employment of the skilled workers if the wage rate of the workers remained at $2,500 per month?

14. A recent flyer on a university campus stated that consumers should boycott sugar due to the low wages earned by laborers on sugar cane farms in Florida. Using the notion of derived demand, what impact would a boycott on sugar have on the wages of the farm laborers in the short run? In the long run?

*Asterisk denotes questions for which answers are given in Appendix B.

CHAPTER 26
Earnings, Productivity, and the Job Market

FOCUS

- Why do some people earn more than others?
- Are earnings differences according to race and gender the result of employment discrimination?
- Why are wages higher in the United States than in India or China?
- What is the source of higher wages? How does the growth of productivity affect wages?
- Does automation destroy jobs?

How can I be overpaid? The boss wouldn't pay me that amount if I wasn't worth it. —**Jackie Gleason**[1]

[1]This statement was made in response to a question about the amount he was being paid for the popular television show *The Honeymooners*, which ran during the 1950s and 1960s.

The earnings of U.S. workers are among the highest in the world. However, they vary widely. An unskilled laborer may earn $12 per hour, or even less. Lawyers and physicians often earn $250 per hour, or more. Dentists and even economists might receive

$200 per hour. How can these variations in earnings be explained? Why are the earnings of Americans so high? How have earnings changed in recent years, and what are the factors underlying these changes? This chapter will address these topics and related issues.

26-1 WHY DO EARNINGS DIFFER?

The earnings of individuals in the same occupation or with the same amount of education often differ substantially. So do the earnings of people in the same family. For example, one researcher found that the average annual earnings differential between brothers was $37,505, compared with $40,855 for men paired randomly.[2] The earnings of people with the same intelligence, level of training, or amount of experience also typically differ.

Several factors combine to determine a person's earning power. Some seem to be the result of good or bad luck. Others are clearly the result of conscious decisions people make. In the previous chapter, we analyzed how the market forces of supply and demand operate to determine resource prices. Wages are a resource price, and therefore the supply and demand model can be used to examine earnings differentials among workers.

For simplicity, we have proceeded as if employees earned only money payments. In reality, most workers receive a compensation package that includes **fringe benefits** as well as money wages. The fringe benefit component typically includes medical insurance, life insurance, pension benefits, and paid vacation days. When we use the terms *wages* and *earnings* in the following discussions, we are referring to the total compensation package that includes both wages and fringe benefits.

The **real earnings** of all employees in a competitive market economy would be equal if (1) all individuals were identical in preferences, skills, and background; (2) all jobs were equally attractive; and (3) workers were perfectly mobile among jobs. Given these conditions, if higher real wages existed in an area of the economy, the supply of workers in that area would expand until the wage differential was eliminated. Similarly, low wages in an area would cause workers to exit until wages there returned to normal. Of course, that's not the way things work in the real world. We all know that earnings differences are a fact of life. There are three reasons for this, and we'll discuss each one.

26-1a EARNINGS DIFFERENTIALS DUE TO NONIDENTICAL WORKERS

Workers differ in several important respects that affect both the supply of and demand for their services. In turn, these factors affect their wage rates. Let's consider these differences.

1. Worker productivity and specialized skills.
The demand for employees who are highly productive is greater than the demand for those who are less productive. People who can operate a machine more skillfully, hit a baseball more consistently, or sell life insurance policies with greater regularity are more valuable to employers. Compared with their less skillful counterparts, these employees contribute more to the firm's revenue. Put another way, the marginal revenue product (*MRP*) of the more productive employees is higher than the *MRP* of less productive ones. In competitive labor markets, workers earn a wage equal to their marginal revenue product. As a result, the labor services of more productive workers will command higher wages in the marketplace.

Worker productivity is the result of a combination of factors, including native ability, parental training, hard work, and investment in human capital. The link between higher

Fringe benefits
Benefits other than normal money wages that are supplied to employees in exchange for their labor services. Higher fringe benefits come at the expense of lower money wages.

Real earnings
Earnings adjusted for differences in the general level of prices across time periods or geographic areas. When real earnings are equal, the same bundle of goods and services can be purchased with the earnings.

---

[2]Christopher Jencks, *Inequality* (New York: Basic Books, 1972), 220. The salary figures are in 2012 dollars.

Demand, Supply, and Wage Rates for Skilled and Unskilled Workers

The productivity—and therefore marginal product (*MP*)—of skilled workers is greater than that of unskilled workers. As a result, as part (a) illustrates, the demand for skilled workers (D_s) will exceed the demand for unskilled workers (D_u). Education and training generally enhance skills. Because upgrading one's skills through investments in human capital is costly, the supply of skilled workers (S_s) is smaller than

the supply of unskilled workers at any given wage (part b). As part (c) illustrates, the wages of skilled workers are high relative to those of unskilled workers due to the strong demand and small supply of skilled workers relative to unskilled workers. (*Note*: The quantity of skilled labor employed may be far smaller, far larger, or, by accident, equal to the quantity of unskilled labor hired.)

(a) Demand for skilled and unskilled labor

(b) Supply of skilled and unskilled labor

(c) Wages of skilled and unskilled labor

© Cengage Learning 2013

productivity and higher earnings motivates people to invest in themselves in order to upgrade their knowledge and skills. If additional worker productivity didn't lead to higher earnings, people would have little incentive to incur the costs of skill development, including paying to go to college or get additional training.

Exhibit 1 shows the demand, supply, and wage rates for skilled versus unskilled workers. The productivity of skilled workers exceeds that of unskilled workers, and so does the demand for them. The vertical distance between the demand curve for skilled workers (D_s) and the demand curve for unskilled workers (D_u), shown in part (a), reflects the higher marginal product (*MP*) of skilled workers. Because human capital investments (education, training, and so on) are costly, the supply of skilled workers (S_s) will be smaller than the supply of unskilled workers (S_u). This is shown in part (b). The vertical distance between the two supply curves is the wage differential employers will need to pay skilled workers for the costs they incurred to acquire their skills.

Wages are determined by demand relative to supply (part c). Because the demand for skilled workers is large whereas their supply is small, the equilibrium wage of skilled workers will be high ($40 per hour). In contrast, because the supply of unskilled workers is large relative to the demand, their wage rates will be substantially lower ($10 per hour).

The skills that one person gains from a year of education, vocational school, or on-the-job training might be better or worse than those of someone else. Therefore, we should not expect a rigid relationship to exist between years of education (or training) and skill level. On average, however, there is a strong positive relationship between investment in education and earnings.

Exhibit 2 presents annual earnings data according to educational level for year-round, full-time workers in 2011. Notice that the earnings of both men and women increased consistently with additional schooling. High school graduates earned about 40 percent more than their counterparts with less than a high school education. Male college graduates working full-time, year-round earned $80,508, compared with $46,038 for men with only

Education and Earnings

The accompanying graph presents data for the mean annual earnings of year-round, full-time workers based on their gender and education. Note that the earnings of both men and women increased with additional education. Even though the data are for full-time workers, the earnings of women were only about two-thirds those of men with similar education.

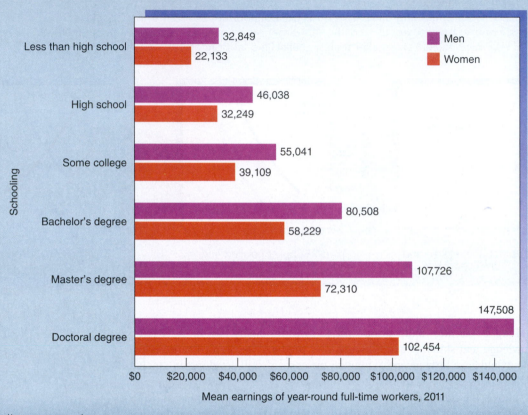

Mean earnings of year-round full-time workers, 2011

Source: http://www.census.gov/

a high school education. In the case of women, college graduates earned $58,229, compared with $32,249 for those who only graduated from high school. The earnings of both men and women continued to increase as they earned masters and doctoral degrees.

In addition to education, a person's intelligence, native ability, and motivation also affect his or her productivity and earnings. Research shows, however, that much of the extra income earned by high-wage earners is, in fact, the result of the knowledge and skills they acquired by making an investment in additional education. (See the accompanying Applications in Economics feature, "A College Degree as a Job Market Signal.") Other studies show that on-the-job training enhances the earnings of workers.

An investment in human capital and development of specialized skills can protect high-wage workers from the competition of others willing to offer their services at a lower price. Few people could develop the specialized skills of Steven Spielberg, LeBron James, or Oprah Winfrey. Similarly, the supply of heart surgeons, trial lawyers, engineers, business entrepreneurs, and many other specialized workers is limited in occupations in which specific skills, knowledge, and human capital investments contribute to job performance.

What about the large salaries received by CEOs of major corporations? Decisions made by CEOs can have a huge financial impact on their companies' profitability. Because of this, a good CEO can be particularly valuable when a company is in trouble, is facing new competitors, or is confronting a changing technological or regulatory environment. A CEO who turns losses into profits is worth millions to the stockholders of a major corporation.

The annual earnings of star athletes, entertainers, and television personalities often run into the millions of dollars. What is the marginal revenue product of a superstar entertainer like Cameron Diaz? How many more people will go see a movie starring Diaz rather than another actress less known or less talented? If an additional 2 million or 3 million people spend $10 to attend a movie, this will generate $20 million or $30 million of additional revenue. It is easy to see how hiring a "box office" star will generate a lot more money for a movie company. In turn, competitive labor markets will ensure that big stars get paid their marginal revenue product.

Economic studies have found that the marginal revenue product of many sports and entertainment superstars is pretty much in line with their salaries.[3] However, there may be another factor at work here. The earnings in some markets resemble tournaments. In tournaments, only the top-ranked person receives the big payoff, whereas those who finish second receive much less. This type of compensation is called **tournament pay**.[4] This name refers to reward systems structured like golf tournaments, in which a slight difference in productivity (perhaps one or two shots) is associated with a difference in pay of several hundred thousand dollars.

The tournament pay environment creates a strong incentive for potential superstars to expend considerable effort to become a top performer. As a result, many people spend long hours developing skills that will increase their chances of becoming a "star" in athletics, entertainment, professions, and business. The tournament system also encourages those who are unwilling to make such sacrifices to follow another path. Is this good or bad? Economics does not answer that question; it merely explains how these markets work.

2. Worker preferences. An important source of earnings differentials that is sometimes overlooked is worker preferences. People have different objectives in life. Some want to make a great deal of money. Many are willing to work two jobs or very long hours, undergo agonizing training and many years of education, or sacrifice social and family life to make money. Others might be "workaholics" because they enjoy their jobs. Still others might be satisfied with just enough money to get by, preferring to spend more time with their family, the Boy Scouts, watching television, on vacation, with a hobby, or at the local tavern.

Economics doesn't dictate that one set of worker preferences is more desirable than another any more than it suggests that people should eat more spinach and less pastrami. It does, however, show that worker preferences in the areas of money, work, and skill development will contribute to differences in earnings. Other things being constant, people who are more highly motivated by monetary objectives will be more likely to do the things necessary to command higher wage rates.

3. Race and gender. Discrimination on the basis of race or gender also contributes to earnings differences among people. **Employment discrimination** can directly limit the earnings opportunities of minority workers and women. Employment discrimination occurs when minority or female employees are treated differently from similarly productive white

What is the marginal revenue product of entertainment stars like Cameron Diaz? Do the earnings of star entertainers, athletes, and even business executives reflect the tournament pay nature of markets in these areas?

Tournament pay
A form of compensation in which the top performer (or performers) receives much higher rewards than do other competitors, even if the others perform at only a slightly lower level.

Employment discrimination
Unequal treatment of people on the basis of their race, gender, or religion, restricting their employment and earnings opportunities compared with others of similar productivity. Employment discrimination may stem from the prejudices of employers, customers, fellow employees, or all three.

---

[3]Paul M. Sommers and Noel Quinton, "Pay and Performance in Major League Baseball: The Case of the First Family of Free Agents," *Journal of Human Resources* (Summer 1982): 426–35.

[4]Edward Lazear and Sherwin Rosen, "Rank Order Tournaments as an Optimum Labor Contract," *Journal of Political Economy* 89 (October 1981): 841–64; and Robert Frank and Phillip Cook, *The Winner-Take-All Society* (New York: The Free Press, 1995).

APPLICATIONS IN ECONOMICS

A College Degree as a Job Market Signal: Why You Should Take More Math

"Why should I take this difficult course?" "When will I ever use this?" Students often complain about taking courses not directly related to their future career. This complaint often reflects an incomplete understanding of exactly why college graduates do better in the job market than those without a college degree. A college degree increases a person's earnings because of both human capital (knowledge that will directly increase job productivity) and signaling ("signs" to employers about a person's attitude and motivational characteristics), as well as his or her general analytical skills.

Suppose that an employer is looking for an employee who is a very good analytical problem solver. Without a way to observe this ability directly, the employer will likely look for indicators that signal this attribute. For example, even if a job doesn't directly require calculus, people with a good calculus grade are likely to possess better problem-solving skills than those with a poor grade (or those who dodged the subject). Thus, employers may favor job applicants with good calculus grades, even if calculus isn't directly used on the job.

In other words, even if a college degree added nothing to the knowledge or skills required to do a particular job, it could still help employers identify people with abilities that are difficult to observe. Similarly, students who are admitted to and graduate from elite universities like Harvard and Yale are likely to have superior abilities relative to those attending lower-ranked schools. Because of this signaling device, even mediocre graduates from top universities often have better entry-level job market prospects than do exceptional students from lesser-known schools. The signaling function also explains why students who choose majors considered "hard" (like engineering, economics, or finance) generally do better in the job market than those choosing "easy" majors (like physical education, marketing, or social work).

"When will I ever use this stuff?" "When will a good grade in challenging courses like math and economics matter?" The answer to these questions is "Soon!" They will matter most when you're searching for a job at the beginning stages of your career—when it's still difficult for employers to judge your true abilities.

or male employees. Of course, the earnings of minorities or women can differ from those of men, respectively, for reasons other than employment discrimination. Nonemployment discrimination—including access to high-quality education or specialized training, for example—can limit the opportunities of minority groups and women to acquire the human capital that would enhance their productivity and earnings. Other factors, like the limited opportunities that can result from growing up in a low-income or a single-parent family, can also influence skill development and educational achievement. In a later section in this chapter, we will analyze the impact of employment discrimination in more detail.

26-1b EARNINGS DIFFERENTIALS DUE TO NONIDENTICAL JOBS

Nonpecuniary job characteristics
Working conditions, prestige, variety, location, employee freedom and responsibilities, and other nonwage characteristics of a job that influence how employees evaluate the job.

Compensating wage differentials
Wage differences that compensate workers for risk, unpleasant working conditions, and other undesirable nonpecuniary aspects of a job.

When people evaluate employment alternatives, they consider working conditions as well as wage rates. Is a job dangerous? Does it offer the opportunity to acquire the experience and training that will enhance future earnings? Is the work strenuous and nerve wracking? Are the working hours, job location, and means of transportation convenient? These factors are what economists call **nonpecuniary job characteristics**. People will accept jobs with undesirable working conditions if the wages are high enough, compared to potential job alternatives with better working conditions. Because the higher wages, in essence, compensate workers for the unpleasant nonpecuniary attributes of a job, economists refer to wage differences stemming from this source as **compensating wage differentials**.

Examples abound of higher wages that compensate various workers for less-attractive working conditions. Because of the dangers involved, aerial window washers (those who hang from windows 20 stories up) earn higher wages than other window washers. Sales jobs involving a great deal of out-of-town travel typically pay more than similar jobs that aren't so inconvenient. Because the jobs are both physically demanding and sometimes dangerous, the wages of coal miners and oil rig workers are generally higher than those in other occupations available to low-skilled workers. Compensating factors even influence the earnings of economists. When economists work for colleges or universities, they generally enjoy a more independent and intellectually stimulating work environment than when they are employed in the business sector. Unsurprisingly, the earnings of academic economists are typically lower than those of business economists. However, it is important to remember that the academic economists with the lower earnings have chosen this job over business-sector employment. Thus, the lower earnings do not imply that they are worse off.

26-1c EARNINGS DIFFERENTIALS DUE TO THE IMMOBILITY OF LABOR

It is costly to move to a new location or train for a new occupation in order to get a job. As a result, labor, like other resources, isn't perfectly mobile. Some wage differentials therefore result because wages have not yet adjusted fully to changes in market conditions.

For example, as we've learned, when strong demand leads to wage increases, more and more people will train for the occupation in high demand. Eventually, supply will increase and moderate the wage increases. But this process will take time. Just the opposite will happen when demand falls. When the demand for workers in a given occupation or skill category falls, wages are likely to fall sharply in the short run. With time, some workers will move into other occupations, which eventually moderates the reduction in wages. But this will also take time. Some of the wage differences reflect the fact that this adjustment process doesn't happen instantly.

Institutional barriers can also limit the mobility of labor. Licensing requirements, for example, limit the mobility of labor into many occupations—medicine, taxicab driving, architecture, and mortuary science among them. Because minimum wages raise the cost to employers of hiring workers, they may retard the ability of low-skilled workers to obtain employment in certain sectors of the economy. These restrictions on labor mobility will also influence the size of wage differentials. Labor unions often promote policies designed to increase the demand for union labor and reduce the labor supply in unionized job categories. Their actions, though, often limit the ability of nonunionized workers (and firms) to enter and compete in the unionized sectors of the economy. To the extent that unions are successful, they hamper the mobility of nonunionized workers and create higher wages for those who are unionized. For more on this topic, see the Special Topic: Do Labor Unions Increase the Wages of Workers? later in this book.

26-1d SOURCES OF WAGE DIFFERENTIALS: A SUMMARY

As the accompanying **Thumbnail Sketch** shows, wage differentials stem from many sources, which can be categorized in three main ways: differences in workers, differences in jobs, and immobility of resources. Many of the wage differentials in these categories play an important allocative role, compensating people for (1) human capital investments that increase their productivity or (2) unfavorable working conditions. Other wage differentials reflect, at least partially, locational preferences or the desires of individuals for higher money income rather than nonmonetary benefits. Still other differentials, like those related to discrimination and occupational restrictions, are unrelated to worker productivity or preferences and do not promote efficient production.

We have focused on why real earnings will differ. In addition to the factors contributing to differences in real earnings, nominal earnings will also vary because of cost of living differences. In a large, geographically diverse country like the United States, the cost of living varies substantially across cities, regions, and communities. In cities like New York

Thumbnail Sketch
What Are the Sources of Earnings Differentials?

Differences in Workers

1. Productivity and specialized skills that reflect native ability, parental training, and investment in human capital (education)
2. Worker preferences (the trade-off that workers are willing to make between money earnings and other factors)
3. Race and gender discrimination

Differences in Jobs

1. Location of job
2. Working conditions (such as job safety and comfort in the workplace)
3. Opportunity for training and skill-enhancing work experience

Immobility of Resources

1. Temporary disequilibrium resulting from market changes
2. Institutional restrictions (for example, occupational licensing and union-imposed restraints)

and San Francisco, the level of prices can be 50 percent or even 100 percent higher than in other parts of the country. Put another way, the quantity of goods and services that can be purchased with $50,000 of earnings is substantially less in New York City than in rural Georgia or Kansas. Therefore, differences in nominal wages will also reflect cost-of-living differences among geographic locations.

APPLICATIONS IN ECONOMICS

America's Millionaires[1]

The number of millionaires has expanded substantially in recent decades. In 1995, there were only 3 million households with a net worth (assets minus liabilities) of $1 million or more in 2004 dollars. By 2010, the figure had grown to 8.9 million or 7 percent of the total (1 out of every 14).

Who are these millionaires? In terms of age, millionaires are typically in their late 50s. They tend to be older than the general population because it takes time to accumulate wealth of this magnitude. In addition, older workers have higher earnings, enabling them to increase wealth more rapidly.

- Not surprisingly, millionaires tend to be well educated. About 80 percent have a college degree. In fact, nearly two-fifths have a graduate degree. Those with more education have higher earnings, which is an important source for acquiring wealth.
- Millionaires are disproportionately self-employed entrepreneurs. While less than one-fifth of the workforce is self-employed, two-thirds of the millionaires fall into this category. To a degree, the income and wealth of millionaires are rewards that compensate them for assuming the greater financial risks that accompany self-employment and business ownership than those that accompany working for a salary.
- The vast majority of millionaires achieved their status through saving and investment. They save on average 20 percent of their income. Most of them are first-generation rich. Less than 20 percent received more than 10 percent of their wealth through an inheritance.

[1]Based on Thomas J. Stanley and William D. Danko, *The Millionaire Next Door: The Surprising Secrets of America's Wealthy* (New York: Longstreet Press, 1996); and Spectrem Group, "Number of Millionaire Households Reaches Nearly 9 Million But Remains Below 2007 Peak of 9.2 Million Households," Press Release, March 14, 2013.

26-2 THE ECONOMICS OF EMPLOYMENT DISCRIMINATION

How does employment discrimination affect the job opportunities available to women and minorities? Do employers gain from discrimination? Economics sheds light on both these questions. There are two outlets for labor market discrimination: wage rates and employment exclusion.

Exhibit 3 illustrates the impact of wage discrimination. When nonminority workers are preferred to minority workers (or male to female workers), the demand for the latter groups falls and, as a result, their wages will be lower. Essentially, there are two labor markets—one market for the favored group and another for the group against which the discrimination is directed. The demand for the favored group, such as white workers, is higher, but the less expensive labor of minority workers is a substitute productive resource. Both white and minority employees are employed, but the white workers are paid a higher wage rate.

Exclusionary practices are another form of employment discrimination. Either in response to outside pressure or because of their own views, employers might primarily hire white workers and other men for certain types of jobs. When minority and female workers are excluded from a large number of occupations, they are crowded into a smaller number of remaining jobs and occupations. If entry restraints prevent people from becoming supervisors, plumbers, electricians, and airline pilots, they will be pushed elsewhere. As a result, the supply of labor in the unrestricted occupations increases, causing wage rates in these occupations to fall. In turn, the exclusionary practices reduce supply and push wages up in occupations and industries dominated by white men.

Discrimination is costly to employers when they merely reflect their own prejudices. *If employers can hire equally productive minority employees (or women) at a lower wage than whites (or men), then the profit motive gives them a strong incentive to do so. Hiring the higher-wage whites when similar minority employees are available will increase the costs of firms that discriminate.* Employers who hire employees regardless of their race or gender will have lower costs and higher profits than rival firms that try to fill positions with (mostly) white men. Thus, competitive forces tend to reduce the profitability of firms that discriminate.

Discriminatory hiring practices can stem from factors other than employer prejudice, however. If either the firm's employees or its customers have a preference for or against various groups, this may lead to discriminatory hiring, even if the employer is totally unbiased. When discrimination is customer based, a worker from a favored group will be able to bring in more revenue for the firm. For example, adult nightclubs that hire attractive young women as dancers will generate more revenue than those that hire dancers from all age and gender groups. Similarly, Chinese restaurants that hire all (or almost all) Chinese servers are

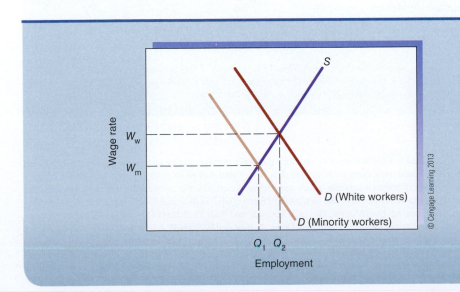

EXHIBIT 3

The Impact of Direct Wage Discrimination

If there is employment discrimination against minorities or women, then the demand for their services will decline, and their wage rate will fall from W_w to W_m.

© Cengage Learning 2013

likely to do better than if the ethnic and racial composition of their employees mirrors that of the labor force. Historically, customer-based discrimination has often gone unchallenged. This appears to be changing. In a highly publicized case, the Hooters restaurant chain was charged with discriminating against male servers. Although the Equal Employment Opportunity Commission dropped its four-year investigation, Hooters agreed to pay $3.75 million in damages and begin hiring male servers as the result of privately filed lawsuits.

26-2a HOW MUCH IMPACT DOES EMPLOYMENT DISCRIMINATION HAVE ON EARNINGS?

If we want to isolate the impact of employment discrimination, we must (1) adjust for differences between groups in education, experience, and other productivity-related factors and (2) then make comparisons between similarly qualified groups of employees who differ only with regard to race (or gender).

How do the earnings of minority workers compare with those of similarly productive white workers? Exhibit 4 presents the actual wages of various minority groups relative to whites and the "productivity-adjusted" minority/white wage ratio. The adjusted ratio is an estimate of how the wages of minority workers would compare with those of whites if the two groups had the same productivity characteristics (schooling, work experience, marital status, regional location, and union and industry status). During 2009–2012, the actual wages of black men were 76 percent of the wages of white men. When the workforce characteristics of black men were taken into account, however, the adjusted hourly earnings of black men rose to 85 percent of the earnings of white men. This implies that productivity related factors accounted for approximately one-third of the wage differential between the two groups. A 16 percent differential, which may well be the result of employment discrimination, remained after adjustment for the productivity characteristics.[5]

EXHIBIT 4

The Actual and Productivity-Adjusted Wages of Minorities Compared to Whites: 2009–2012

	MEN		WOMEN	
	ACTUAL	ADJUSTED	ACTUAL	ADJUSTED
White	100	100	100	100
African American	76	85	86	90
American Indian	79	93	83	94
Asian Americana	103	95	106	98
Mexican American	64	86	71	92
Other Hispanic	74	88	81	90

Source: These data were supplied by David Macpherson. They were derived from the 2009–2012 *Current Population Surveys*. The four-year time period was used to increase the sample size for the various groups. The data were adjusted for years of schooling, work experience, region, part-time status, citizenship status, industry, sector of employment, union status, and marital status.

---

[5]The figures presented in Exhibit 4 do not control for the lower average quality of schooling received by African Americans. Other researchers using more refined data have found that productivity factors account for a larger share of the earnings differential between whites and African Americans. For evidence on this point, see Francine D. Blau and Lawrence M. Kahn, "Race and Gender Pay Differentials," in *Research Frontiers in Industrial Relations and Human Resources*, ed. David Lewin, Olivia S. Mitchell, and Peter D. Scherer (Madison, WI: Industrial Relations Research Association, 1992), 381–416; and Derek A. Neal and William R. Johnson, "The Role of Premarket Factors in Black-White Wage Differences," *Journal of Political Economy* (October 1996): 869–95. For a detailed explanation of how the adjusted ratios of Exhibit 4 were derived and information on the significance of productivity factors and employment discrimination on the basis of gender, see David A. Macpherson and Barry T. Hirsch, "Wages and Gender Composition: Why Do Women's Jobs Pay Less?," *Journal of Labor Economics* (July 1995).

Mexican Americans constitute the second-largest minority group in the United States. Even though the actual wages of Mexican American men were only 64 percent of the wages of white men, their "adjusted" earnings were 86 percent of those for whites. Thus, the productivity-related factors accounted for three-fifths of the earnings difference between white and Mexican American men. This figure was not adjusted for the ability to speak English. Adjustment for this factor would almost certainly further narrow the differential. Interestingly, adjustment for productivity factors reduces the wages of Asian Americans relative to whites. Asian Americans typically have more education and tend to live in large cities where nominal earnings and the cost of living are higher. As a result, the "adjusted" earnings of Asian Americans are lower than their actual earnings figures.

Turning to the data for women, the productivity-adjusted wage rates of minority women relative to white women are between 90 percent to 98 percent for each of the groups included in Exhibit 4. This implies that employment discrimination on the basis of race adds between 2 percent to 10 percent to earnings differentials that may reflect discrimination on the basis of gender. For an analysis of earnings differences according to gender, see the Special Topic 11: Earnings Differences Between Men and Women? in the final section of this book.

26-3 THE LINK BETWEEN PRODUCTIVITY AND EARNINGS

In a competitive market setting, productivity—that is, output per worker—and earnings are closely linked. When workers are more productive, the demand for their services will be higher, and therefore they will be able to command higher wages. ***High productivity provides the underlying source of high wages. When the output per hour of workers is high, the real wages of the workers will also be high.***

In turn, the link between productivity and earnings provides individuals with a strong incentive to develop their talents and utilize their resources in ways that are helpful to others. As the value of the services provided to others increases, so too will the amount they are willing to pay for those services. If you want to earn a lot of money, you had better figure out how to provide services that are highly valued by others.

Productivity differences are an important source of differences in earnings among individuals. They are also an important source of earnings differences across countries. For example, the earnings per worker are vastly greater in the United States than they are in India or China because the output of U.S. workers is much greater than the output of their counterparts in those countries. The average worker in the United States is better educated, works with more productive machines, and benefits from more efficient economic organization than the average worker in India or China. Thus, the value of the output produced by the average U.S. worker is eight to ten times that produced by the average worker in India or China. American workers earn more because they produce more. If they did not produce more, they would not be able to earn more.

KEYS TO ECONOMIC PROSPERITY

Productivity and Earnings

In a market economy, productivity and earnings are closely linked. High productivity is the source of high earnings. To earn a large income, one must provide others with goods and services they value highly.

©iStockphoto.com/malerapaso

Chad Ehlers/Alamy

Labor-saving equipment can improve productivity. But profit-maximizing firms will adopt automated production methods and high-tech equipment only when they reduce costs. Cost-effective automation releases labor and other resources so that they can be used to expand production in other areas. In turn, the higher worker productivity and expansion in production makes higher income levels and living standards possible.

Automation
A production technique that reduces the amount of labor required to produce a good or service. It is beneficial to adopt the new labor-saving technology only if it reduces the cost of production.

Productivity differences also affect earnings across time. Today, American workers are substantially more productive than they were 50 years ago.[6] The output of goods and services per hour of U.S. workers in 2012 was approximately three times the level of the mid-1950s. Similarly, average real earnings (total compensation) per hour in 2009 were more than double those of fifty years ago. Earnings rose because productivity increased. If productivity had not increased, the increase in earnings would not have been possible.

Increased physical capital, improvements in the skill level of the labor force, and advances in technology drive productivity and earnings growth. For several decades, both the educational level of American workers and the capital equipment per worker have steadily increased. Technological advances have also enhanced productivity and contributed to the growth of output and income. Some people argue that technology and **automation** adversely affect workers (see the accompanying Myths in Economics feature). In fact, just the opposite is true. *Once you recognize that higher output is the source of higher earnings, the gains from capital formation and improvements in technology are apparent: Better machines and technological improvements make larger outputs possible. In turn, more productive workers will have higher earnings.*

Equipment and technology can improve productivity. But profit-maximizing firms will invest in new equipment and advanced technology only when they reduce costs. Cost-effective investments enhance output. In turn, the increased output per worker makes higher income levels and living standards possible.

26-3a PRODUCTIVITY, WAGES, AND THE COMPUTER REVOLUTION

What has been happening to the growth of productivity, and how has this influenced the wages of workers? **Exhibit 5** presents data on the change in both productivity (output per hour) and real hourly compensation of the United States for the periods 1948–1973, 1974–1995, and 1996–2012. Predictably, productivity growth and increases in real compensation per hour have moved together. During the period 1948–1973, both productivity and real hourly compensation grew at a rapid rate—approximately 3 percent annually. In contrast, both sagged

---

[6]For more on productivity growth, see Kevin J. Stiroh, "What Drives Productivity Growth?," *Economic Policy Review* (Federal Reserve Bank of New York) (March 2001): 37–59.

MYTHS IN ECONOMICS

"Automation Is the Major Cause of Unemployment. If We Keep Allowing Machines to Replace People, We Are Going to Run Out of Jobs."

Machines are substituted for people if, and only if, the machines reduce costs of production. Why did the automatic elevator replace human elevator operators or the power shovel virtually eliminate human ditch diggers? Because each is a cheaper method of accomplishing a task.

When automation and technological improvements reduce the cost of producing a good, they allow us to obtain each unit of the product with fewer resources. If the demand for the product is inelastic, consumers will spend less on the good and therefore have more of their income available for spending on other things. Consider the following example. Suppose that someone develops a new toothpaste that really prevents cavities and sells it for half the price of other brands. If the demand for toothpaste is inelastic, at the lower price consumers will spend less on this product than they did before. Furthermore, the decline in cavities will lower the demand for and spending on dental services. Will the lower toothpaste and dental care expenditures reduce employment? Less spending on dental care will mean that households now have more income to spend on other goods and services. As a result, they will spend more on clothes, recreation, vacations, personal computers, education, and other items. This additional spending, which would not have taken place without lower dental costs, will generate additional demand and employment in these sectors. Employment will decline in the dental care sector, but it will increase in other sectors. Jobs will be reshuffled, but there's no reason to expect that total employment will decline.

What would happen to employment if a technological improvement reduced production costs and the demand for the product were elastic? Under these circumstances, a cost-saving invention can lead to higher employment, even in the industry affected by the invention. This was essentially what happened in the automobile industry when Henry Ford's mass-production techniques reduced the cost (and price) of cars. When the price of automobiles fell 50 percent, consumers bought three times as many cars. Even though the worker hours per car fell by 25 percent between 1920 and 1930, employment in the industry increased by approximately 50 percent during the decade.

More recently, the same thing happened in the computer-manufacturing industry. As technological improvements reduced the cost of producing various types of computer equipment, the lower costs and lower prices for computer products generated such a large increase in sales that employment in the computer-manufacturing sector actually increased.

Of course, technological advances can diminish the earnings of individual people or groups. Home appliances, like automatic washers and dryers, dishwashers, and microwave ovens, have reduced the job opportunities of maids. Voice recognition technology has lowered the demand for telephone operators. In the future, online courses and videotaped lectures may reduce the earnings and opportunities of college professors. It is understandable why groups directly affected in this manner often fear and oppose automation.

Focusing on the loss of specific jobs, however, can be misleading. Clearly, running out of jobs is not a problem. Jobs represent obstacles—tasks that must be accomplished to loosen the bonds of scarcity. As long as our ability to produce goods and services falls short of our consumption desires, there will be jobs. A society running out of jobs would be in an enviable position: It would be nearing the impossible goal—victory over scarcity!

©iStockphoto.com/sorendls

badly during the period 1974–1995. Productivity growth averaged only 1.5 percent annually, and hourly real compensation rose at an annual rate of only 0.7 percent over the two decades (1974–1995). Although the reasons for slow productivity growth during this period are not entirely clear, most economists believe that slower improvement in the educational quality of the workforce, environmental regulations, and the inflation of the 1970s were contributing factors.

Beginning in the mid-1990s, both productivity and real compensation rebounded. Productivity per hour grew at an annual rate of 2.4 percent during 1996–2012, nearly twice the rate of 1974–1995. In turn, hourly compensation rose at an annual rate of 1.3 percent during 1996–2012, up from the 0.7 percent rate of the earlier period. Since the mid-1970s, hourly compensation has lagged behind productivity growth. Why has this been the case? The answer to this question is not entirely clear. However, improvements in working conditions provide part of the answer. The hourly compensation measure does not account for movements toward less strenuous work, a more comfortable work environment, and

EXHIBIT 5

Productivity and Employee Compensation in the United States, 1948–2012

As shown in the graph, worker productivity and compensation per hour are closely linked. Between 1974 and 1995, the growth of both productivity and real compensation per hour slowed substantially compared with the growth figures achieved during the 1948–1973 period. However, worker productivity and real hourly compensation rebounded during the 1996–2012 period.

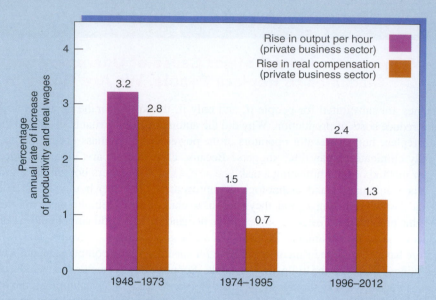

Source: Bureau of Labor Statistics, http://www.bls.gov/.

greater job safety, all of which have improved steadily in recent decades. Consideration of these factors would tend to boost the growth of overall worker compensation.

What accounts for the rebound in the growth of productivity of the past 15 years? Most economists believe that the recent acceleration in productivity growth is largely the result of the computer revolution and related technological innovations.[7] Information technology and investment in computer equipment soared during the 1990s, and this substantially enhanced productivity in many occupations. Research indicates that nearly two-fifths of the productivity growth during 1995–2000 and about one-quarter of the growth during 2000–2006 was the result of higher levels of investment in computer equipment and information technology.[8]

Some believe that the pace of technological change has quickened and new technologies now spread throughout the economy more rapidly. There is evidence that this has been the case since the early 1980s. While automation and rapid improvements in technology do not destroy jobs, they do result in changing work requirements, more job switching, and less career stability. Earlier generations of workers could typically expect to have a long-term career with one firm. This is now less true. Today's workers switch employers more often than their parents did. In 1983, the average full-time male worker aged 22 to 59 expected to remain with his current employer for an additional 18.0 years. By 2001, this figure had fallen to 13.7 years. A similar pattern was present for women.[9]

Is the computer revolution going to continue, or have we already witnessed its major impact? Will the speedup of technological change continue at a rapid rate, or perhaps even accelerate, in the decades immediately ahead? It is too early to determine the precise answers to these questions. But one thing is for sure: The answers will exert a powerful impact on our future lives.

---

[7]For a discussion of the new-economy perspective, see Kevin J. Stiroh, "Is There a New Economy?," *Challenge* (July/August 1999): 82–101.

[8]Dale W. Jorgenson, Mun S. Ho, and Kevin J. Stiroh, "A Retrospective Look at the U.S. Productivity Growth Resurgence," *Journal of Economic Perspectives* 22 (Winter 2008): 3–24.

[9]Leora Friedberg, Michael Owyang, and Tara Sinclair, "Searching for Better Prospects: Endogenizing Falling Job Tenure and Pension Coverage," *Topics in Economic Analysis and Policy* 6, no.1 (2006): 1–40.

LOOKING AHEAD

As we have learned, productivity and earnings are influenced by both human capital and physical capital investments. This chapter focused on the labor market. The following chapter will analyze investment choices and the operation of the capital market.

KEY POINTS

- The real earnings of individuals would be equal if (1) all individuals were identical in preferences, skills, and background; (2) all jobs were equally attractive; and (3) workers were perfectly mobile among jobs. Earnings differences among individuals result from the absence of these conditions.

- Wage differences play an important allocative role. They generally compensate people for (1) investments in education and training that enhance productivity and the development of highly specialized skills and (2) unfavorable working conditions and/or job locations. Wage differences can also result from differences in workers' preferences, employment discrimination, and institutional factors that restrict worker mobility.

- Employment discrimination reduces the wages of people being discriminated against by either lowering the demand for their services or restricting their entry into various job categories. Productivity differences also contribute to earnings differentials between groups. Research indicates that the earnings of African American and Mexican American men are, respectively, approximately 84 percent and 86 percent those of white men of similar productivity.

- Productivity is the ultimate source of high wages and earnings. Workers in the United States (and other high-income industrial countries) earn high wages because their output per hour is high as the result of (1) greater worker knowledge and skills (human capital) and (2) the use of modern machinery (physical capital).

- Automated methods of production will be adopted only if they reduce costs. Although automation might reduce employment in a specific industry, it also releases resources that can be employed in other areas. Improved technology permits us to achieve larger output and income levels than would otherwise be possible.

- The growth of productivity in the United States during 1996–2012 was more rapid than during the two prior decades. The computer revolution and lower cost of information technology equipment was a major contributor to the more rapid productivity growth of recent years.

CRITICAL ANALYSIS QUESTIONS

1. Why do some people earn higher wages than others? Why are wages in some occupations higher than in others? How do wage differentials influence the allocation of resources? Explain.

2. *Why are real wages in the United States higher than in other countries? Is the labor force itself responsible for the higher wages of American workers? Explain.

3. Indicate the major sources of earnings differences between (a) a lawyer and a minister; (b) an accountant and an elementary school teacher; (c) a business executive and a social worker; (d) a country lawyer and a Wall Street lawyer; (e) an experienced, skilled craftsperson and a 20-year-old high school dropout; and (f) an upper-story and a ground-floor window washer?

4. a. If minority employees are discriminated against, how will this affect their earnings? Use supply and demand analysis to explain your answer.

   b. If the average earnings differ between two groups of employees (for example, whites and blacks), does this mean that the group with the lower earnings is experiencing employment discrimination? Why or why not?

5. Is there a relationship between the growth of productivity and changes in wage rates? Can higher earnings be achieved without higher productivity? Why or why not? Discuss.

6. *"Jobs are the key to economic progress. Unless we create more jobs, our standard of living will fall." Is this statement true or false? Explain.

7. "If Jones has a skill that is highly valued, she will be able to achieve high market earnings. In contrast, Smith may work just as hard or even harder and still earn only a low income."

   a. Does hard work necessarily lead to a high income?
   b. Why are the incomes of some workers high and others low?
   c. Do you think the market system of wage determination is fair? Why or why not?
   d. Can you think of a more equitable system? If so, explain why it is more equitable.

8. People who have invested heavily in human capital (for example, lawyers, doctors, and even college professors) generally have higher wages, but they also generally work more hours than other workers. Can you explain why?

9. *"If individuals had identical abilities and opportunities, earnings would be equal." Is this statement true or false?

10. Other things being constant, how will the following influence the hourly earnings of employees? Explain your answer.

   a. The employee must work the midnight to 8:00 A.M. shift.

   b. The job involves split shifts (work three hours, off two hours, work three additional hours, and so on).

   c. The employer provides low-cost child care services on the premises.

   d. The job is widely viewed as prestigious.

   e. The job requires employees to move often from city to city.

   f. The job requires substantial amounts of out-of-town travel.

11. *Consider two occupations (A and B) in which people have the same skills and abilities. When employed, workers in the two occupations work the same number of hours per day. In occupation A, employment is stable throughout the year, whereas employment in B is characterized by seasonal layoffs. In which occupation will the hourly wage rate be highest? Why? In which occupation will the annual wage be highest? Why?

12. "Technological change eliminates thousands of jobs every year. Unless something is done to slow the growth of technology, ordinary workers will face a bleak future of low wages and high unemployment." Explain why you either agree or disagree with this statement.

13. If an individual is motivated primarily by the desire to make money, will he or she have an incentive to be helpful to others? Will he or she have an incentive to develop skills that others value highly? Why or why not?

*Asterisk denotes questions for which answers are given in Appendix B.

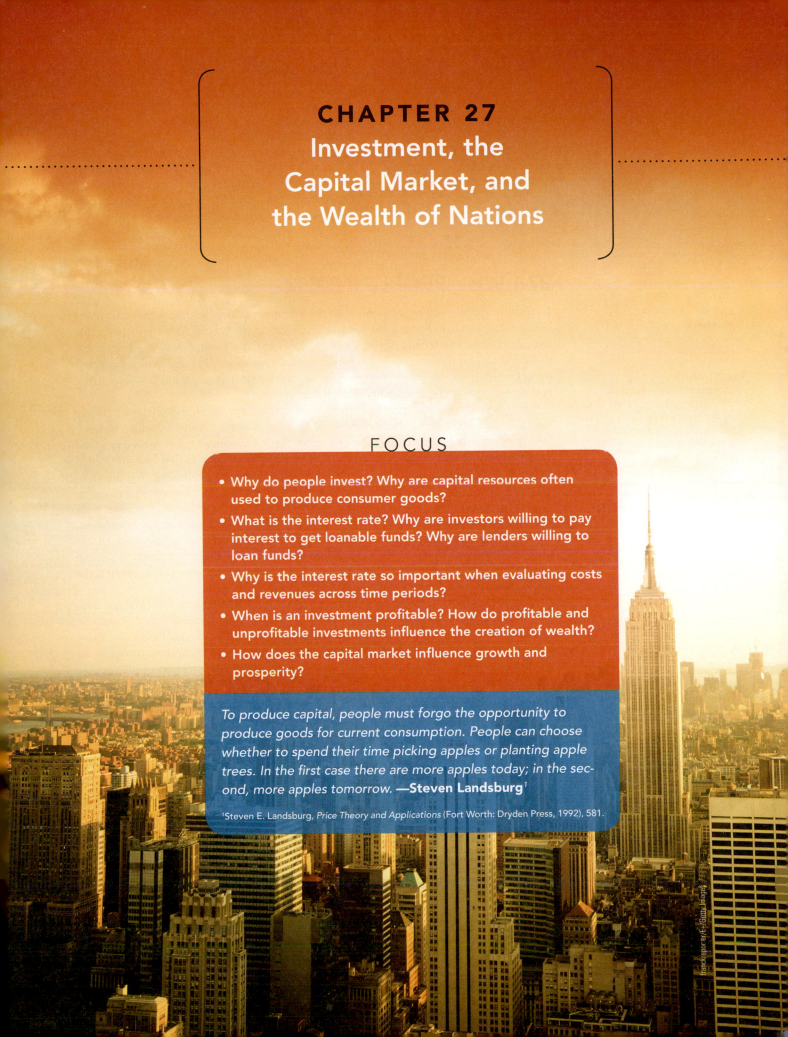

CHAPTER 27
Investment, the Capital Market, and the Wealth of Nations

FOCUS

- Why do people invest? Why are capital resources often used to produce consumer goods?

- What is the interest rate? Why are investors willing to pay interest to get loanable funds? Why are lenders willing to loan funds?

- Why is the interest rate so important when evaluating costs and revenues across time periods?

- When is an investment profitable? How do profitable and unprofitable investments influence the creation of wealth?

- How does the capital market influence growth and prosperity?

To produce capital, people must forgo the opportunity to produce goods for current consumption. People can choose whether to spend their time picking apples or planting apple trees. In the first case there are more apples today; in the second, more apples tomorrow. —**Steven Landsburg**[1]

[1]Steven E. Landsburg, *Price Theory and Applications* (Fort Worth: Dryden Press, 1992), 581.

As we noted in the previous chapter, there is a close relationship between productivity and earnings. In turn, productivity is influenced by investment choices. Consider choices about whether to construct an apartment building, purchase a new computer, or go to law school. The returns derived from investments like these are usually spread over years or even decades. Some costs, such as maintenance expenses, can also be incurred over time. How can people compare the benefits and costs of an activity when both are spread across lengthy periods of time? Why is the method of allocating investment in an economy a vitally important determinant of economic progress? This chapter will help you answer these questions.

27-1 WHY PEOPLE INVEST

Capital
Resources that enhance our ability to produce output in the future.

Investment
The purchase, construction, or development of capital resources, including both nonhuman capital and human capital. Investments increase the supply of capital.

Saving
Current income that is not spent on consumption goods. Saving makes it possible for resources to be devoted to investments (like the making of tractors or other equipment used in production).

Capital is a term used by economists to describe long-lasting resources that are valued because they can help us produce goods and services in the future. As we previously discussed, there are two broad categories of capital: (1) *physical capital* (buildings, machines, tools, and natural resources) and (2) *human capital* (the knowledge and skills of people). **Investment** is the purchase, construction, or development of a capital resource. Thus, investment expands the availability of capital resources.

Saving is income not spent on current consumption. Investment and saving are closely linked. In fact, the two words describe different aspects of the capital formation process. *Saving refers to the nonconsumption of income, while investment refers to the use of the unconsumed income to produce a capital resource.* Sometimes saving and investment are conducted by the same person, like when a farmer saves current income (refrains from spending it on consumption goods) in order to purchase a new tractor (an investment good).

It is important to recognize that saving is required for investment. Someone must save—refrain from consumption—in order to provide the resources for investment. When investors finance a project with their own funds, they are also saving (refraining from current consumption). Investors, however, do not always use their own funds to finance investments. Sometimes they will borrow funds from others. When this is the case, it is the lender rather than the investor who is doing the saving.

Consumption is the goal of economic activity. Why would anyone want to delay consumption in order to undertake an investment? Sometimes more consumption goods can be produced by first using resources to produce capital resources and then using these resources to produce the desired consumer goods. Using capital to produce consumption goods makes sense, but only if it allows us to produce more consumption goods than we otherwise could.

For example, suppose that Robinson Crusoe can catch fish by either (1) combining his labor with natural resources (direct production) or (2) constructing a net and eventually combining his labor with this capital resource (indirect production). Let's assume that Crusoe can catch two fish per day by hand-fishing, but three fish per day if he constructs and uses a net that will last for 310 days. Now suppose it will take Crusoe 55 days to build the net. The opportunity cost of constructing the net will be 110 fish (two fish per day not caught for each of the 55 days he spends building the net). As the accompanying chart shows, if Crusoe invests in the capital resource (the net), his output during the next year (including the 55 days required to build the net) would be 930 fish (three per day for 310 days). Alternatively, hand-fishing during the year would lead to an output of only 730 fish (two fish per day for 365 days).

NUMBER OF FISH CAUGHT

	WITHOUT NET	WITH NET
Per day	2	3
Annually	730	930

In other words, Crusoe's investment will enhance his net productivity by 200 fish annually. In the short term, however, investing in the net will require a sacrifice. During the 55 days it takes to construct the net, Crusoe's production of consumption goods will decline.

How can Crusoe or any other investor know if the value of the larger future output is worth the short-term cost? Most of us have a preference for goods now rather than later. For example, if you are typical, you would prefer a sleek new sports car now rather than the same car ten years from now. On average, individuals possess a **positive rate of time preference**. That is, other things being the same, people subjectively value goods obtained sooner more highly than goods obtained later.

When only Crusoe is involved, the attractiveness of the investment in the fishing net depends on his rate of time preference. If he places a high value on a couple of fish per day during the next 55 days, as indeed he may if he is on the verge of starvation, the cost of the investment may well exceed the value of the larger future output. If Crusoe could find someone who would loan him fish while he built the net, however, he could consume the borrowed fish now while building the net and pay later with the extra fish made possible by the net. If such a loan is available, the attractiveness of the investment (building the net instead of hand-fishing now) will be influenced by the price of borrowing fish. Is the cost of borrowing fish in order to maintain his consumption while he constructs the net worth the extra cost? To answer this question, Crusoe must consider the cost of paying for earlier availability—he must consider, in effect, the interest rate.

27-2 INTEREST RATES

The interest rate links the future to the present. It allows individuals to evaluate the value today—the present value—of future income and costs. In essence, it is the market price of earlier availability. From the viewpoint of a potential borrower, the interest rate is the premium that must be paid in order to acquire goods sooner and pay later. From the lender's viewpoint, it is a reward for waiting—a payment for supplying others with current purchasing power in terms of greater purchasing power in the future.

In a modern economy, people often borrow funds to finance current investments and consumption. Because of this, the interest rate is often defined as the price of loanable funds. But we should remember that it is the earlier availability of goods and services purchased, not the money itself, that is desired by the borrower.

27-2a HOW INTEREST RATES ARE DETERMINED

Interest rates are determined by the demand for and supply of loanable funds. Investors demand funds in order to finance capital assets they believe will increase output and generate profit. Simultaneously, consumers demand loanable funds because they have a positive rate of time preference: They prefer earlier availability.

The demand of investors for loanable funds stems from the productivity of capital. Investors are willing to borrow in order to finance the use of capital in production because they expect that expanding future output will provide them with more than enough resources to repay the amount borrowed—the principal—and interest on the loan. Our example of Robinson Crusoe illustrates this point. Remember, Crusoe could increase his output by 200 fish this year if he could take off 55 days from hand-fishing in order to build a net. But doing so would reduce Crusoe's fish production by 2 fish per day while he was constructing the net. Suppose a fishing crew from a neighboring island visited Crusoe and offered to lend him 110 fish so he could undertake the capital investment project (building the net). If Crusoe could borrow the 110 fish (the principal) in exchange for, say, 165 fish one year later (110 fish to repay the principal and 55 as interest on the loan), the investment project would be highly profitable. Crusoe could repay the funds borrowed, plus the 50 percent interest rate, and still have 145 additional fish (the 200 additional fish caught minus the 55 fish paid in interest).

Investors can gain by borrowing funds to undertake investment projects only when the capital assets they purchase permit them to expand output (or reduce costs) by enough to make the interest payments and still have more output than they would have without the investment.

As Exhibit 1 illustrates, the interest rate brings the choices of investors and consumers wanting to borrow funds into harmony with the choices of lenders willing to supply funds. Higher interest rates make it more costly for investors to undertake capital spending projects and for consumers to buy now rather than later. Both investors and consumers will therefore curtail their borrowing as the interest rate rises. Investors will borrow less because some investment projects that would be profitable at a low interest rate will be unprofitable at higher rates. Some consumers will reduce their current consumption rather than pay the high interest premium when the interest rate increases. Therefore, the amount of funds demanded by borrowers is inversely related to the interest rate.

The interest rate also rewards people (lenders) willing to reduce their current consumption in order to provide loanable funds to others. If some people are going to borrow in order to undertake an investment project (or consume more than their current income), others must curtail their current consumption by an equal amount. In essence, the interest rate provides lenders with the incentive to reduce their current consumption so that borrowers can either invest or consume beyond their present income. Higher interest rates give people willing to save (willing to supply loanable funds) the ability to purchase more goods in the future in exchange for sacrificing current consumption. Even though people have a positive rate of time preference, they will give up current consumption to supply funds to the loanable funds market if the price is right. Higher interest rates will induce people to save more. Therefore, as the interest rate rises, the quantity of funds supplied to the loanable funds market will increase.

As Exhibit 1 illustrates, the interest rate will bring the quantity of funds demanded into balance with the quantity supplied. *At the equilibrium interest rate, the quantity of funds borrowers demand for investment and consumption will just equal the quantity of funds lenders save,* so the interest rate brings the choices of borrowers and lenders into harmony.

EXHIBIT 1

Determining the Interest Rate

The demand for loanable funds stems from the consumer's desire for earlier availability and the productivity of capital. As the interest rate rises, current goods become more expensive in comparison with future goods. Therefore, borrowers will demand fewer loanable funds. In contrast, higher interest rates will stimulate lenders to supply additional funds to the market.

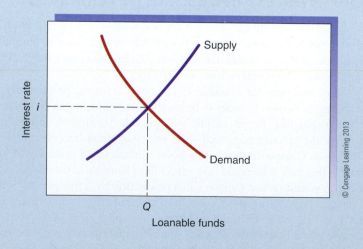

© Cengage Learning 2013

27-2b THE MONEY RATE VERSUS THE REAL RATE OF INTEREST

We have emphasized that the interest rate is a premium paid by borrowers for earlier availability and a reward received by lenders for delaying consumption of *goods and services*. However, during a period of inflation—a general increase in prices—the nominal interest rate, or **money rate of interest**, is a misleading indicator of really how much borrowers are paying and lenders are receiving. Inflation reduces the purchasing power of money. Rising prices mean that when the borrower repays the loan principal in the future, the money received by the lender will not be able to purchase as many goods and services as when the funds were initially loaned.

When inflation is common, lenders will recognize they are being repaid with dollars of less purchasing power. Unless they are compensated for the anticipated inflation by an upward adjustment in the interest rate, they will supply fewer funds to the loanable funds market. At the same time, when borrowers anticipate inflation, they will want to purchase goods and services now before they become even more expensive in the future. Thus, they are willing to pay an **inflationary premium**, an additional amount of interest that reflects the expected rate of future price increases. For example, if borrowers and lenders were willing to agree on a 4 percent interest rate when both anticipated price stability, they would have the same incentive to agree to a 9 percent interest rate when both anticipated a 5 percent rate of inflation.

Therefore, when people anticipate inflation, the money interest rate will rise and it will overstate the "true" cost of borrowing and the yield from lending. This true cost is the **real rate of interest**, which is equal to the money rate of interest minus the inflationary premium. It reflects the real burden to borrowers and the payoff to lenders in terms of their being able to buy goods and services.

Our analysis indicates that high rates of inflation will lead to a high money rate of interest. The real world is consistent with this view. Money interest rates rose to historical highs in the United States as inflation soared to double-digit rates during the 1970s. Inflation rates have been much lower since the mid-1980s and, so too, have nominal interest rates. Cross-country comparisons also illustrate the link between inflation and high interest rates. The world's lowest money interest rates are found in nations such as Germany, Switzerland, and Japan, all with low rates of inflation. In contrast, the highest money interest rates have been present in Russia, Venezuela, Zimbabwe, and other countries with high rates of inflation.

27-2c INTEREST RATES AND RISK

So far, we've assumed there is only a single interest rate present in the loanable funds market. In the real world, of course, there are many interest rates. They include the mortgage rate, the prime interest rate (the rate charged to business firms with strong credit ratings), the consumer loan rate, and the credit card rate, to name but a few.

Interest rates in the loanable funds market will differ mainly because of differences in the risks associated with the loans. It is riskier, for example, to loan money to an unemployed worker than to a well-established business with substantial assets. Similarly, unsecured credit card loans are riskier than loans secured with an asset such as a house or a plot of land. Moreover, as recent experience vividly illustrates, a mortgage loan for the purchase of a house is far riskier when the down payment of the borrower is small. The risk also increases with the duration of the loan. The longer the time period of the loan, the more likely it is that the borrower's ability to repay the loan will deteriorate or market conditions change in a highly unfavorable manner.

As **Exhibit 2** shows, the money rate of interest on a loan has three components. The pure-interest component is the real price one must pay for earlier availability. The inflationary-premium component reflects the expectation that the loan will be repaid with dollars of less purchasing power as the result of inflation. The risk-premium component reflects the probability of default—the risk imposed on the lender by the possibility that the borrower may be unable to repay the loan.

Money rate of interest
The rate of interest in monetary terms that borrowers pay for borrowed funds. During periods when borrowers and lenders expect inflation, the money rate of interest exceeds the real rate of interest.

Inflationary premium
A component of the money interest rate that reflects compensation to the lender for the expected decrease, due to inflation, in the purchasing power of the principal and interest during the course of the loan. It is determined by the expected rate of future inflation.

Real rate of interest
The money rate of interest minus the expected rate of inflation. The real rate of interest indicates the interest premium in terms of real goods and services that one must pay for earlier availability.

EXHIBIT 2

The Three Components of Money Interest

The money interest rate reflects three components: pure interest, inflationary premium, and risk premium. When decision makers expect a high rate of inflation while the loan is outstanding, the inflationary premium will be substantial. Similarly, the risk premium will be large when the probability of default by the borrower is high.

Risk premium

Inflationary premium

Pure interest

27-3 THE PRESENT VALUE OF FUTURE INCOME AND COSTS

If you deposited $100 today in a savings account earning 6 percent interest, you would have $106 one year from now. To put it another way, to have $106 one year from now requires that you invest $100 today. *The interest rate allows us to make this conversion from present to future dollars. The interest rate connects the value of dollars (and capital assets) today with the value of dollars (expected income and receipts) in the future. It is used to "discount" the value of a dollar received in the future so that its present worth can be determined today.*

Present value (PV)
The current worth of future income after it is discounted to reflect the fact that revenues in the future are valued less highly than revenues now.

The **present value (PV)** of a payment received one year from now can be expressed as follows:

$$PV = \frac{\text{Receipt One Year from Now}}{1 + \text{Interest Rate}}$$

If the interest rate is 6 percent, the current value of $100 to be received one year from now is

$$PV = \frac{100}{1.06} = \$94.34$$

If you put $94.34 in a savings account yielding 6 percent interest, during the year the account would earn $5.66 interest (6 percent of $94.34) and grow to $100 one year from now. Thus, the present value of $100 to be received a year from now is $94.34.

Discounting
The procedure used to calculate the present value of future income, which is inversely related to both the interest rate and the amount of time that passes before the funds are received.

Economists use the term **discounting** to describe this procedure of reducing the value of a dollar to be received in the future to its present worth. Clearly, the value of a dollar in the future is inversely related to the interest rate. For example, if the interest rate is 10 percent, the present value of $100 received one year from now would be only $90.91 ($100 divided by 1.10). At still higher interest rates, the present value of $100 a year from now would be even lower.

The present value of $100 received two years from now is

$$PV = \frac{100}{(1 + \text{Interest Rate})^2}$$

If the interest rate is 6 percent, $100 received two years from now would be equal to $89 today ($100 divided by 1.06^2). In other words, $89 invested today would yield $100 two years from now.

The present-value procedure can be used to determine the current value of any future income (or cost) stream. If R represents receipts received at the end of various years in the future (indicated by the subscripts) and i represents the interest rate, the present value of the future income stream is

$$PV = \frac{R_1}{(1 + i)} + \frac{R_2}{(1 + i)^2} + \cdots + \frac{R_n}{(1 + i)^n}$$

Exhibit 3 shows the present value of $100 received at various times in the future at several different discount rates. The chart clearly illustrates two points. First, the present value of income received in the future declines with the interest rate. The present value of the $100 received one year from now, when discounted at a 4 percent interest rate, is $96.15, compared with $98.04 when a 2 percent discount rate is used. Second, the present value of the $100 also declines as the date of its receipt is set farther into the future. If the discount rate is 6 percent, the present value of $100 received one year from now is $94.34, compared with $89 if the $100 is received two years from now. If the $100 is received five years from now, its current worth is only $74.73. *So the present value of a future dollar payment is inversely related both to the interest rate and to how far in the future the payment will be received.*

To see in a more personal way the importance of interest and the value of saving, consider what you could gain by saving just $1,000 per year ($83.33 per month) for ten years in a tax-free individual retirement account. If you begin at age 25 and continue only until age 35 (putting nothing into the account after that), and the account returns 8 percent annually, it will be worth $168,627 when you reach age 65. In contrast, if you wait until age 35 and then save $1,000 per year for thirty years (not ten years of savings as before) with the same 8 percent annual return, by age 65 your account will be worth only $125,228. Ten years of saving, starting with age 25, yields far more than 30 years of saving at the same amount each year but waiting until age 35 to start. Which savings plan is more attractive to you?

The Present Value of $100 to Be Received in the Future

PRESENT VALUE OF $100 TO BE RECEIVED
A DESIGNATED NUMBER OF YEARS
IN THE FUTURE AT ALTERNATIVE DISCOUNT RATES

YEARS IN THE FUTURE	2 PERCENT	4 PERCENT	6 PERCENT	8 PERCENT	12 PERCENT	20 PERCENT
1	98.04	96.15	94.34	92.59	89.29	83.33
2	96.12	92.46	89.00	85.73	79.72	69.44
3	94.23	88.90	83.96	79.38	71.18	57.87
4	92.39	85.48	79.21	73.50	63.55	48.23
5	90.57	82.19	74.73	68.06	56.74	40.19
6	88.80	79.03	70.50	63.02	50.66	33.49
7	87.06	75.99	66.51	58.35	45.23	27.08
8	85.35	73.07	62.74	54.03	40.39	23.26
9	83.68	70.26	59.19	50.02	36.06	19.38
10	82.03	67.56	55.84	46.32	32.20	16.15
15	74.30	55.53	41.73	31.52	18.27	6.49
20	67.30	45.64	31.18	21.45	10.37	2.61
30	55.21	30.83	17.41	9.94	3.34	0.42
50	37.15	14.07	5.43	2.13	0.35	0.01

The columns indicate the present value of $100 to be received a designated number of years in the future at different discount (interest) rates. For example, at a discount rate of 2 percent, the present value of $100 to be received five years from now is $90.57. Note that the present value of the $100 declines as either the interest rate or the number of years in the future increases.of years in the future increases.

© Cengage Learning 2013

27-4 PRESENT VALUE, PROFITABILITY, AND INVESTMENT

Investment involves an up-front cost of acquiring a machine, skill, or other asset expected to generate additional output and revenue in the future. How can an investor know if the expected future revenues will be sufficient to cover the costs? The discounting procedure helps provide the answer. It permits the investor to place both the costs and the expected future revenues of an investment project into present-value terms. If the present value of the revenue derived from the investment exceeds the present value of the cost, it makes sense to undertake the investment. If the revenues and costs of such an investment turn out as expected, the investor will earn a profit, and the project will create wealth.

In contrast, if the cost of the project exceeds the discounted value of the future receipts, losses will be incurred. The losses reflect that the project diminished the value of the resources. Investments like these are counterproductive.

Let's pencil in the figures for a hypothetical investment option and determine whether it is a good investment. Suppose a truck rental firm is contemplating the purchase of a new $100,000 truck. Past experience indicates that after figuring in the truck's operational and maintenance expenses, the firm can rent it out for a net revenue of $30,000 annually (received at the end of each year). The firm will be able to do this every year for four years—the expected life of the vehicle.[2] Because the firm can borrow and lend funds at an interest rate of 8 percent, we will discount the future expected income at an 8 percent rate. Exhibit 4 illustrates the calculation. Column 4 shows how much $30,000, available at year-end for each of the next four years, is worth today. In total, the present value of the expected rental receipts is $99,360—less than the purchase price of the truck. Therefore, the project should not be undertaken.

If the interest rate in our example had been 6 percent, the results would have been different. The present value of the future rental income would have been $103,950.[3] It pays to purchase a capital good whenever the present value of the income generated by it exceeds its purchase price. At the lower interest rate, the investment project would have been productive (and profitable).

EXHIBIT 4

The Discounted Present Value of $100,000 of Truck Rental for Four Years (Interest Rate = 8 Percent)

Year (1)	Expected Future Income Received at Year-End (2)	Discounted Value per Dollar (8 Percent Rate) (3)	Present Value of Income (4)
1	$30,000	$0.926	$27,780
2	30,000	0.857	25,710
3	30,000	0.794	23,820
4	30,000	0.735	22,050
Total			$99,360

© Cengage Learning 2013

---

[2]For the sake of simplicity, we assume that the truck has no scrap value at the end of four years.
[3]The derivation of this figure is shown in the following tabulation:

Year	Expected Future Income (Dollars)	Discounted Value Per Dollar (6% rate)	Present Value of Income (Dollars)
1	30,000	0.943	28,290
2	30,000	0.890	26,700
3	30,000	0.840	25,200
4	30,000	0.792	23,760
Total			103,950

27-4a EXPECTED FUTURE EARNINGS, THE INTEREST RATE, AND ASSET VALUES

The present value of the expected revenue from a project minus the cost of an investment will tell us whether the project should be undertaken. Once *an investment project has been completed*, its market value will be directly linked to the present value of the expected future net earnings from the asset. If the present value of the expected net earnings rises (or falls), so too will the value of the asset.

The value of an asset is equal to the present value of the expected net revenues that can be earned by the asset. If the asset is expected to generate a constant annual net income each year in the future, its value would be equal to

$$\text{Asset Value} = \frac{\textbf{Annual Net Income from the Asset}}{\textbf{Interest Rate}}$$

What is the market value of a tract of land if it is expected to generate $1,000 of net rental income each year indefinitely into the future? If the market interest rate is 10 percent, investors would be willing to pay $10,000 for the land ($1,000 divided by 0.10). When purchased at this price, the land would provide an investor with the 10 percent market rate of return. Similarly, if an asset generates $2,500 of net earnings annually and the market interest rate is 10 percent, the asset would be worth $25,000 ($2,500 divided by 0.10). There is a direct relationship between the expected future earnings generated by an asset and the asset's market value. *As the present value of the future earnings of an asset increases, so too does the market value of the asset.*

The interest rate will also influence the market value of assets. Lower interest rates will increase the present value of the future income and therefore the market value of the asset generating the income stream. For example, if the interest rate was 5 percent, the market value of the land tract (or other asset) expected to generate $1,000 each year in the future would be $20,000 ($1,000 divided by .05). Thus, the market value of assets is directly linked to the future income stream generated by the asset and inversely linked to the interest rate.

The direct link between expected future earnings and the price of an asset provides asset owners with a strong incentive to make sure the assets are being used wisely. Some entrepreneurial investors are particularly good at (1) identifying a business that is poorly operated, (2) purchasing the business at a depressed price, (3) improving the operational efficiency of the firm, and then (4) reselling the business at a handsome profit. Suppose that a poorly run business currently has net earnings of $1 million per year. What is the market value of the business? If the firm is expected to continue earning $1 million per year, the market value of the firm would be $10 million if the interest rate is 10 percent. Suppose that an alert entrepreneur buys the business for $10 million and improves the operational efficiency of the firm. As the result of these changes, the annual net earnings of the firm increase to $2 million per year. Now how much is the firm worth? If the $2 million annual earnings are expected to continue into the future, the net present value of the firm would rise to $20 million. Thus, the entrepreneur would be able to sell the firm for a very substantial profit.

As this example illustrates, business managers and asset owners have a strong incentive to use the resources under their control efficiently. If they fail to do so, the value of the assets will decline, and the business will be vulnerable to a takeover by those capable of using the resources more efficiently and thereby improving the firm's profitability.

27-4b INVESTORS AND CORPORATE INVESTMENTS

In modern market economies, investment choices are often made by corporate officers, under the scrutiny of corporate boards of directors. Nevertheless, individual investors (buyers and sellers of stock) influence that process through the stock market. Stock market investors who believe that a corporation is currently making decisions likely to increase its future profits will buy more of the corporation's stock, driving up its price. Similarly, stockholders who believe that the corporation's current investment decisions will reduce future profits have an incentive to "bail out" by selling their stock holdings, reducing the market value of the stock. Either way, the price of a corporation's shares gives corporate officers fast feedback on what investors think of their decisions.

Often corporate officers own stock themselves and the value of their pay package generally depends on the stock price. Also, the members of the corporate board (which hires and fires the officers) are typically large shareholders. Thus, the corporate officers have a strong incentive to act on the feedback from the stock market. The choices of consumers of the firm's products are the ultimate judge of its future profitability. However, the choices of investors and their fund managers provide early information today about the expected future success of business ventures.

27-5 INVESTING IN HUMAN CAPITAL

Investments in human capital (like the decision to go to college, for example) are the same as other investment decisions. Just like physical capital, discounting can also help us gauge whether or not to make a human capital investment.

Exhibit 5 shows the human capital decision confronting Juanita, an 18-year-old high school graduate thinking about pursuing a bachelor's degree in business administration. Just as an investment in a truck involves a cost in order to generate a future income, so does a degree in business administration. If Juanita does not go to college, she will be able to begin work immediately, starting at annual earnings of E_1. But if she goes to college, she will incur direct costs (C_d) in the form of tuition, books, transportation, and related expenses. She will also bear the opportunity cost (C_o) of lower earnings while she's in college. However, studying business

EXHIBIT 5

Investing in Human Capital

Juanita, an 18-year-old who has just finished high school, is trying to decide whether or not to go to college and get a business degree. If Juanita goes to college and majors in business administration, she will incur the direct cost (C_d) of the college education—tuition, books, transportation, and so on—plus the opportunity cost (C_o) of earnings she forgoes while in college. However, with a business degree, she can expect to earn an additional amount of income (B) during her career. If the discounted present value of the additional future earnings exceeds the discounted value of the direct and indirect costs of a college education, the business degree will be a profitable investment for Juanita.

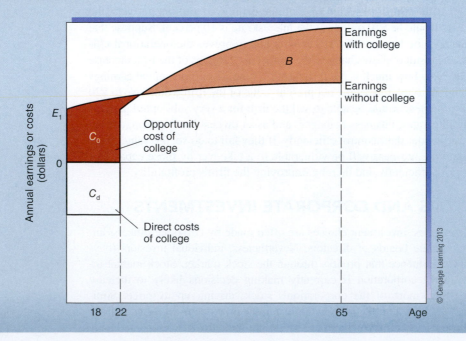

© Cengage Learning 2013

APPLICATIONS IN ECONOMICS

Does It Pay to Go to an Elite University?

Early research on this question found that students who attend highly selective schools like those of the Ivy League have higher subsequent earnings than similar students going to less selective colleges. This was true even after accounting for factors like the students' SAT score, the average SAT score of the school attended, race, gender, high school GPA, income of parents, and student athlete status. But there remained one question: Did the students attending the more selective schools earn more because they received a better education or because they were more ambitious and highly motivated?

A recent study by Princeton University economists Stacy Dale and Alan Krueger sheds light on this question.[1] In addition to controlling for the typical set of student characteristics, Dale and Krueger were able to make earnings comparisons between students (1) who were accepted by a more selective college but decided to attend a less selective one and (2) those who actually attended a more selective college. This technique enabled them to account more fully for the potential impact of motivation and ambition on earnings. Further, the earnings data used by Dale and Krueger were from actual Social Security records rather than the less accurate self-reported earnings.

Dale and Krueger found that students attending a more selective college such as Yale University did not earn more than similar students attending a less selective school such as Penn State University. However, minorities and students with poorly educated parents were exceptions. The latter groups

Sandra Baker/Alamy

did have higher earnings if they attended a more selective school. This is consistent with the view that going to more selective schools provides these groups with important contacts and connections that they would not otherwise be able to obtain.

The Dale and Krueger study also reports two other intriguing results. First, earnings were higher for those who applied to more selective schools. This suggests that ambition and a willingness to work hard are more important determinants of earnings than the selectivity of the school one actually attends. Second, students who attended schools with higher tuition did not earn more income than similar students who attended less expensive schools. Thus, students may want to think twice before attending an expensive school, particularly if they are borrowing money to do so.

[1]Stacy Dale and Alan B. Krueger. "Estimating the Return to College Selectivity over the Career Using Administrative Earning Data," Princeton University Industrial Relations Section Working Paper Number 563, February 2011.

franckreporter/E+/Getty Images

will expand Juanita's knowledge and skills, and enable her to earn more money later (see the areas in the exhibit labeled "Earnings with college" versus "Earnings without college"). Will the higher future income be worth the cost? To answer this question, Juanita must project the additional income she would earn by getting a business degree, discount each year's additional income, and compare the total with the discounted value of the cost of getting the degree—including the opportunity cost of the earnings she forgoes while attending college. If the discounted present value of Juanita's additional future income exceeds the discounted present value of the cost, acquiring the degree is a worthwhile investment. Of course, other nonmonetary considerations might also affect Juanita's decision, but the return on the investment is an important factor.

27-6 UNCERTAINTY, ENTREPRENEURSHIP, AND PROFIT

Firms and individual investors can sometimes earn persistent economic profits—returns in excess of the opportunity cost of funds—if they can restrict entry into various industries and occupations. Economic profits, however, can also be earned in competitive markets with no entry restrictions. *In competitive markets, there are two sources of economic profit: uncertainty and entrepreneurship.*

First, let's talk about how uncertainty enables people to earn an economic profit. Investment opportunities put people in a position to earn a handsome return, but they also expose them to additional uncertainty. We live in a world of uncertainty, imperfect information, and dynamic change. Unanticipated changes create winners and losers. If people didn't care about the uncertainty related to different investment projects, they wouldn't demand higher returns for higher risk projects. Most people, though, dislike uncertainty; they would prefer to know they'll collect $1,000 rather than take a 50-50 chance of collecting either nothing or $2,000. To accept the uncertainty accompanying riskier investments, they will demand a premium—an economic profit. For example, compared to government bonds, the returns on stocks are considerably more uncertain. This uncertainty of return is one reason why stocks have historically yielded a higher average return than bonds.

Entrepreneurship is a second source of economic profit. As we previously discussed, at any given time, there are an infinite number of potential investment projects from which to choose. Investing in some of them will increase the value of resources and lead to handsome returns. Successful entrepreneurship involves the identification of previously unnoticed profit opportunities. To finance their investments, would-be entrepreneurs usually have to use their own money and the money of co-venturers, in addition to whatever they can borrow. Entrepreneurs with successful track records will find it easier to get capital for their investment projects. Thus, over time, capital markets will allocate more control over investment dollars to those entrepreneurs with the most successful investment records.

The introduction of new products often makes older ones obsolete. Examples abound: The personal computer replaced the typewriter, digital music players replaced the phonograph, and digital cameras are replacing film models. Joseph Schumpeter referred to outcomes of this type as "creative destruction." How does creative destruction influence the living standards of people like you?

OUTSTANDING ECONOMIST

JOSEPH SCHUMPETER (1883–1950)

Born in Austria, Joseph Schumpeter was a longtime professor of economics at Harvard University. Generally recognized as one of the top five economists of the twentieth century, Schumpeter is perhaps best known for his views on entrepreneurship and the future of capitalism. He believed that the discovery and introduction of new and better products and organizational methods were constantly making the old ways of doing things obsolete. He referred to this process as "creative destruction" and argued that it was the primary fuel of economic progress.

The great Harvard economist Joseph Schumpeter believed that entrepreneurial discovery of new, improved ways of doing things drove economic progress and improved living standards. As Schumpeter put it, "The fundamental impulse that sets the capitalist engine in motion comes from the new consumer's goods, the new methods of production or transportation, and new markets, and the new forms of industrial organization that capitalist enterprise creates."[4]

27-6a RETURNS TO PHYSICAL AND HUMAN CAPITAL

Income reflects the returns from both human and physical capital. The earnings of employees and self-employed workers are mostly returns to human capital, while interest, corporate profits, and rental income are primarily returns to physical capital.[5] **Exhibit 6**

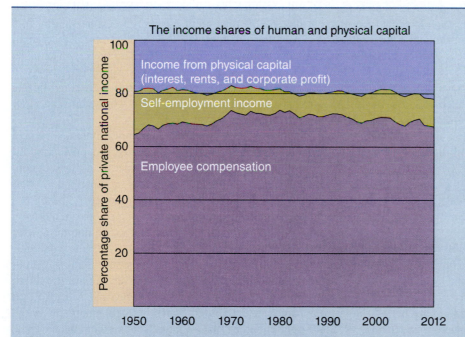

The income shares of human and physical capital

Source: http://www.bea.gov/.

Note: Private national income is the sum of employee compensation, self employment income, interest, rents, and corporate profits.

EXHIBIT 6

The Income Shares of Human and Physical Capital, 1950–2012

The shares of national income derived from human capital (employee compensation and self-employment income) and physical capital (interest, corporate profits, and rents) are shown here. Over the past several decades, approximately 80 percent of national income was earned by the owners of human capital, while the share of physical capital owners summed to around 20 percent. Note that the share going to physical capital rose to 23 percent during 2011 and 2012, while the share of human capital fell to 77 percent. At this point, it is uncertain whether this recent larger earnings share of physical capital is a temporary fluctuation or reflective of a longer-term trend.

presents data on these measures of human and physical capital earnings as a share of national income for the United States since 1950. Throughout this lengthy period, the earnings share of human capital was approximately 80 percent of national income while the share of physical capital summed to around 20 percent. Moreover, these income shares fluctuated within a relatively narrow range. During 2011–2012, however, the share going to physical capital rose to an atypical high of 23 percent, while the share allocated to human capital shrank to only 77 percent. In the years immediately ahead, it will be interesting to see if the recent high earnings share of physical capital is maintained or if the recent figures are merely a temporary aberration.

27-7 WHY IS THE CAPITAL MARKET SO IMPORTANT?

KEYS TO ECONOMIC PROSPERITY

Innovation and the Capital Market

If the potential gains from innovative ideas and human ingenuity are going to be fully realized, it must be relatively easy for individuals to try their innovative and potentially ingenious ideas, but difficult to continue if the idea is a bad one.

©iStockphoto.com/malerapaso

If a nation is going to reach its full potential, it must have a mechanism that will attract savings and channel them into the investments that are most likely to create wealth. In a market economy, the capital market performs this function. Private investors, such as small business owners, corporate stockholders, and venture capitalists, place their own funds at risk in the capital market. Investors will sometimes make mistakes; sometimes they will undertake projects that prove to be unprofitable. However, if investors were unwilling to take such chances, many new ideas would go untested and many worthwhile but risky projects would not be undertaken.

In a world of uncertainty, mistaken investments are a necessary price that must be paid for fruitful innovations in new technologies and products. Such counterproductive projects, however, must be recognized and brought to a halt in a timely manner. In a market economy, the capital market performs this function. If a firm continues to experience losses, eventually investors will terminate the project and stop wasting their money.

New products, improved technologies, and lower cost production methods are a driving force that propels economic growth and higher living standards. But we do not know what they will be and who will discover and implement them during the next two or three decades. Based on the past, however, we can be pretty sure that many of the most successful new products and technologies will come from start-up businesses that are not even in existence today.

Measured on the basis of market capitalization, Apple, Google, and Microsoft all ranked among the ten largest companies in the United States in 2013. Interestingly, all three were founded after 1975 and went public in 1980 or later. None of them were ranked higher than 123rd on the *Fortune* 500 in 1995. Thus, in the relatively short span these companies grew from midgets to giants. As they did so, they were a powerful driving force for economic growth. This linkage between innovation and growth highlights why it is vitally important that entrepreneurs are both able to try out their new ideas but are forced to bring them to a halt if they do not generate revenues sufficient to cover cost.

Given the pace of change and the diversity of entrepreneurial talent, the knowledge required for sound decision-making about the allocation of capital is far beyond the scope

---

[4]Joseph A. Schumpeter, *Capitalism, Socialism, and Democracy* (New York: Harper Torchbooks, 1950), 83.

[5]As used here, rent is income derived by owners who lease (rent) assets like buildings and equipment to another party for a period of time.

©iStockphoto.com/kadmy

The capital market will channel the savings of individuals into the finance of investment goods like trucks and earth-moving equipment. Does it make any difference whether these investment projects are profitable? Why or why not?

of any single leader, industrial planning committee, or government agency. Without a private capital market, there is no mechanism that can be counted on to consistently channel investment funds into wealth-creating projects.

When investment funds are allocated by the government, rather than by the market, an entirely different set of factors comes into play. Political influence rather than market returns will decide which projects will be undertaken. Businesses will use contributions, lobbying, and other resources to curry favor with key political officials. In turn, the politicians will use subsidies, tax breaks, and "bailouts" to help those most willing to provide them with political support. Clearly, this system of crony capitalism will encourage rent-seeking and favor large firms with more lobbying clout at the expense of new start-up businesses. It will protect inefficient firms and slow the innovation and discovery process.

Profits and losses direct investors toward productive projects and away from those that are counterproductive. The political process does not have anything similar to profit and loss that can be counted on to direct funds toward wealth creation. As a result, inefficient allocation of capital is a predictable outcome.

The experiences of Eastern Europe and the former Soviet Union illustrate this point. For four decades (1950–1990), the investment rates in these countries were among the highest in the world. Central planners allocated approximately one-third of the national output into capital investment. Even these high rates of investment, however, did little to improve living standards because political rather than economic considerations determined which projects would be funded. Resources were often wasted on impractical projects and high visibility ("prestige") investments favored by important political leaders. Misdirection of investment and failure to keep up with dynamic change eventually led to the collapse of these systems.

Historically, the government of the United States has played a minor role in the allocation of capital. But this has changed in recent years. Beginning in the latter half of the 1990s, federal regulations and subsidies played a major role in directing capital toward the housing industry. Regulations imposed on the banking industry and the policies of two large government-sponsored corporations, Fannie Mae and Freddie Mac, expanded the availability of credit and promoted mortgage loans with little or no down payment. The policies were designed to increase the affordability of housing and promote home ownership among those with low and moderate incomes. These policies played a central role in the creation of a housing boom, followed by a bust and the 2008 financial crisis. (*Note:* For a detailed analysis of this issue, see Special Topic 5: The Crisis of 2008: Causes and Lessons for the Future.

Further, the government has become much more involved in the allocation of capital in other ways. During 2008–2012, approximately half of the saving flowing into the loanable funds market was consumed by federal borrowing to finance the budget deficit. In the energy area, the government has provided huge subsidies to high-cost energy sources such as ethanol, wind, and solar, while regulations have reduced the supply of lower-cost petroleum and natural gas. During the financial crisis, the government provided emergency loans to several companies, including large banks, the American Insurance Group, General Motors, and Chrysler. The operation of the capital market is undermined when investors are permitted to keep the revenues from profitable activities but bailed out by the government—that is, taxpayers—when they make unwise choices and experience losses. Under these circumstances, investors will have less incentive to evaluate risks and act prudently, and they will have more incentive to cater to political officials who can provide them with bailouts, subsidies, tax breaks, and other forms of favoritism.

Has the nature of the capital market in the United States been permanently altered? Will political considerations and centralized government decision-making play a much larger role in future allocation of capital? At this point, it is too early to know the answer to these questions. But one thing is for sure: How they are answered will exert a dramatic impact on America's future.

LOOKING AHEAD

As the preceding two chapters have stressed, investment in physical and human capital will influence the wealth and income of both individuals and nations. Differences among individuals with regard to these factors will also contribute to income inequality. The next chapter will focus on this topic.

KEY POINTS

- We can often produce more consumption goods by first using our resources to produce physical and human capital resources and then using these capital resources to produce the desired consumption goods. Because resources used to produce capital goods will be unavailable for the direct production of consumption goods, saving is necessary for investment.

- The interest rate is the price of earlier availability. It is the premium that borrowers must pay to lenders to acquire goods now rather than later.

- The demand for loanable funds reflects the productivity of capital resources and the positive rate of time preference. The market interest rate will bring the quantity of funds demanded by borrowers into balance with the quantity supplied by lenders.

- During inflationary times, the money rate of interest incorporates an inflationary premium reflecting the expected future increase in the price level. When inflation is expected, the money rate of interest exceeds the real rate of interest.

- The money rate of interest on a specific loan reflects three basic factors—the pure interest rate, an inflationary premium, and a risk premium that is directly related to the probability of default by the borrower.

- The interest rate allows individuals to put a current value on future revenues and costs. The discounting procedure can be used to calculate the present value of an expected net income stream from a potential investment project. If the present value of the expected revenues exceeds the present value of the expected costs—and if things turn out as anticipated—the project will be profitable.

- The present value of expected future net earnings will determine the market value of existing assets. An increase in the expected future earnings of an asset will increase its market value.

- Economic profit plays a central role in allocating capital and determining which investment projects will be undertaken. In a competitive environment, economic profit reflects uncertainty and entrepreneurship—the ability to recognize and undertake profitable projects that have gone unnoticed by others.

- To grow and prosper, a nation must have a mechanism that will attract savings and channel them into investments that create wealth. The capital market performs this function in a market economy.

CRITICAL ANALYSIS QUESTIONS

1. *How would the following changes influence the rate of interest in the United States?

   a. an increase in the positive time preference of lenders
   b. an increase in the positive time preference of borrowers
   c. an increase in domestic inflation
   d. increased uncertainty about a nuclear war
   e. improved investment opportunities in Europe

2. What is capital investment? Why do business firms often use machinery and other capital assets to produce goods and services?

3. How are human and physical capital investment decisions similar? How do they differ? What determines the profitability of a physical capital investment? Do human capital investors make profits? If so, what is the source of the profit? Explain.

4. *A lender made the following statement to a borrower: "You are borrowing $1,000, which is to be repaid in twelve monthly installments of $100 each. Your total interest charge is $200, which means your interest rate is 20 percent." Is the effective interest rate on the loan really 20 percent? Explain.

5. In a market economy, investors have a strong incentive to undertake profitable investments. What makes an investment profitable? Do profitable investments create wealth? Why or why not? Do all investments create wealth? Discuss.

6. *Over long periods of time, the rate of return of an average investment in the stock market has exceeded the return on high-quality bonds. Is the higher return on stocks surprising? Why or why not?

7. The interest rates charged on outstanding credit card balances are generally higher than the interest rate that banks charge customers with a good credit rating. Why do you think the credit card rate is so high? Should the government impose an interest rate ceiling of, say, 10 percent? If it did, who would be hurt and who would be helped? Discuss.

8. *If the money rate of interest on a low-risk government bond is 10 percent and the inflation rate for the last several years has been steady at 4 percent, what is the estimated real rate of interest?

9. Suppose you are contemplating the purchase of a commercial lawn mower at a cost of $10,000. The expected lifetime of the machine is three years. You can lease the asset to a local business for $4,000 annually (payable at the end of each year) for three years. The lessee is responsible for the upkeep and maintenance of the machine during the three-year period. If you can borrow (and lend) money at an interest rate of 8 percent, will the investment be a profitable undertaking? Is the project profitable at an interest rate of 12 percent? Provide calculations in support of your answer.

10. *Alicia's philosophy of life is summed up by the proverb "A penny saved is a penny earned." She plans and saves for the future. In contrast, Mike's view is "Life is uncertain; eat dessert first." Mike wants as much as possible now.

   a. Who has the highest rate of time preference?
   b. Do people like Alicia benefit from the presence of people like Mike?
   c. Do people like Mike benefit from the presence of people like Alicia? Explain.

11. *Some countries with very low incomes per capita are unable to save very much. Are people in these countries helped or hurt by people in high-income countries with much higher rates of saving?

12. *According to a news item, the owner of a lottery ticket paying $3 million over twenty years is offering to sell the ticket for $1.2 million cash now. "Who knows?" the ticket owner explained. "We might not even be here in 20 years, and I do not want to leave it to the dinosaurs."

   a. If the ticket pays $150,000 per year at the end of each year for the next twenty years, what is the present value of the ticket when the appropriate rate for discounting the future income is thought to be 10 percent?
   b. If the discount rate is in the 10 percent range, is the sale price of $1.2 million reasonable?
   c. Can you think of any disadvantages of buying the lottery earnings rather than a bond?

13. Suppose you are moving into a new apartment you expect to rent for five years. The owner of the apartment offers to provide you with a used refrigerator for free and promises to maintain and repair the refrigerator during the next five years. You also have the option of buying a new energy-efficient refrigerator (with a five-year free maintenance agreement) for $700. The new refrigerator will reduce your electric bill by $150 per year and will have a market value of $200 after five years. If necessary, you can borrow money from the bank at an 8 percent rate of interest. Which option should you choose?

14. *Suppose that you are considering whether to enroll in a summer computer-training program that costs $2,500. If you take the program, you will have to give up $1,500 of earnings from your summer job. You figure that the program will increase your earnings by $500 per year for each of the next ten years. Beyond that, it is not expected to affect your earnings. If you take the program, you will have to borrow the funds at an 8 percent rate of interest. From a strictly monetary viewpoint, should you enroll in the program?

15. "In a world of uncertainty, it is important that entrepreneurs be able to introduce new products and try out innovative ideas. But it is also important that unproductive projects be brought to a halt." Evaluate this statement.

16. *Will political officials be more likely to channel funds into wealth-creating projects than private investors and entrepreneurs? Why or why not? Discuss.

*Asterisk denotes questions for which answers appear in Appendix B.

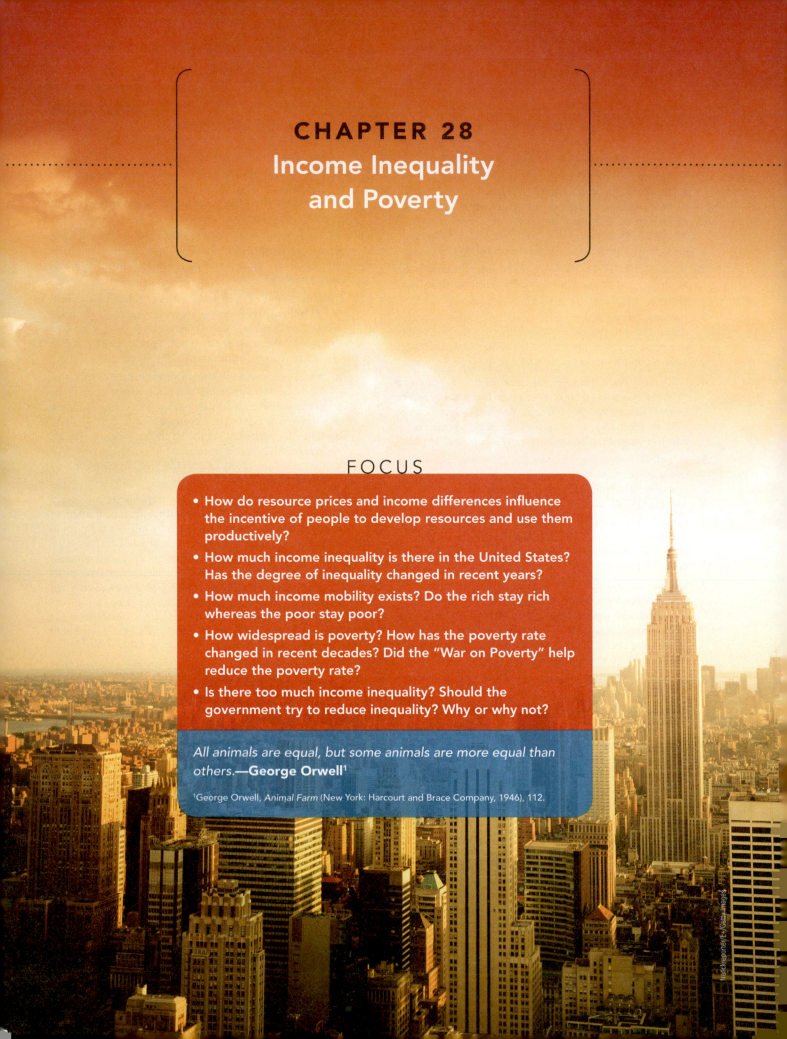

CHAPTER 28
Income Inequality and Poverty

FOCUS

- How do resource prices and income differences influence the incentive of people to develop resources and use them productively?

- How much income inequality is there in the United States? Has the degree of inequality changed in recent years?

- How much income mobility exists? Do the rich stay rich whereas the poor stay poor?

- How widespread is poverty? How has the poverty rate changed in recent decades? Did the "War on Poverty" help reduce the poverty rate?

- Is there too much income inequality? Should the government try to reduce inequality? Why or why not?

All animals are equal, but some animals are more equal than others.—**George Orwell**[1]

[1]George Orwell, *Animal Farm* (New York: Harcourt and Brace Company, 1946), 112.

Differences in resource prices and the productivity of individuals will cause incomes to vary. Of course, economic inequality is present in all societies. Neither politics nor central planning will eliminate it. Nonetheless, most of us are troubled by the extremes of inequality—the extravagant luxury of some and the grinding poverty of others. How much inequality is there in the United States? Do wealthy families continually enjoy high incomes? What effect have income-transfer programs had on the welfare of the poor? This chapter focuses on these questions and related issues.

28-1 HOW MUCH INCOME INEQUALITY EXISTS IN THE UNITED STATES?

Money income is only one component of economic well-being. Factors such as leisure, noncash-transfer benefits, the nonmonetary advantages and disadvantages of a job, and the expected stability of future income also affect people's economic welfare. Money income is quite important, however, because it makes it possible to buy market goods and services. It is also easy to measure and is therefore widely used as a yardstick of economic well-being and degree of inequality.

Exhibit 1 presents data on money income in the United States. First, the left panel shows the share of *before-tax* annual money income by quintile—that is, by each fifth of the total population of families—ranked from the lowest to the highest. If there were total income equality, each quintile (20 percent) of families would generate 20 percent of the aggregate income. Given the differences in education, skills, ability, work effort, age, family size, and other factors among families, clearly we would not expect this to be the case. Some families will be able to generate more income than others. It is, however, informative to look at the shares of income by quintile.

During the last four decades, the share of income earned by the top quintile has steadily risen, whereas that earned by the bottom group has fallen.[2] In 1970, the top

EXHIBIT 1

Share of Money Income by Quintile during Selected Years, 1970–2009

Source: http://www.census.gov. The data for the left panel are for family income and the data for the right panel are for household income. The after-tax income data for 2010 are unavailable.

---

[2]A reduction in the share of income earned by the bottom quintile income group does not imply that their income level fell. It merely indicates that their income did not grow as rapidly as that of other groups, particularly the top quintile. The inflation-adjusted income of the bottom quintile of earners has increased in recent decades.

quintile earned 40.9 percent of the aggregate money income, while the share earned by the lowest quintile was 5.4 percent. By 2010, the share of before-tax money income of the top group had risen to 47.8 percent, whereas that earned by the bottom 20 percent of families had fallen to 3.8 percent. Thus, in 2010, the top quintile of families earned approximately twelve times as much before-tax money income as the bottom quintile of families.

Low-income families are the primary beneficiaries of noncash-transfer programs that provide people with food (food stamps), health care, and housing. Correspondingly, under a system of progressive taxation, which the United States has, taxes take a larger share of income as one's earnings increase. As a result, we would expect *after-tax* and *transfer* incomes to be more equal than before-tax incomes. Using household data, the right panel of Exhibit 1 shows that this is indeed the case. After taxes and transfers, the bottom quintile of households received 4.6 percent of the total income in 2009 (compared with 3.5 percent of the before-tax income), and the top quintile of households received 44.4 percent (compared with 49.5 percent before taxes). Notice that taxes and transfers increased the income share of the bottom three quintiles. As you can see, taxes and transfers do, in fact, reduce income inequality. (*Note:* Household income is used here because after-tax and family transfer-income data are unavailable. In addition to families, households include individuals living by themselves and unrelated people living together.)

A market economy does not have a central distributing agency that carves up the economic pie and allocates slices to various individuals. Rather, each individual produces his or her own slice of the pie. If one person's income grows, it does not mean that another's must shrink. The distribution of income is actually a result of many individual efforts and decisions. We now turn to the consideration of the factors that underlie the distribution of income in the United States.

28-1a THE FACTORS AFFECTING INCOME DISTRIBUTION

How meaningful are the data of Exhibit 1? If all families (and households) were similar except with regard to the amount of income they earned, the use of annual income data as an index of inequality would be quite reasonable. However, the fact is that the aggregate data lump together (1) small and large families, (2) prime-age earners and elderly retirees, (3) multi-earner families and families without any current earners, and (4) husband–wife families and single-parent families.

Consider just one factor: the impact of age and the pattern of lifetime income. Typically, the annual income of young people is low, particularly if they are going to school or are getting training. Many people under 25 years of age studying to be lawyers, doctors, engineers, and economists will have low annual incomes during this phase of their lives. But this does not mean that they are poor—at least not in the usual sense. After completing their formal education and acquiring work experience, these people move into their prime working years. At this point, their annual incomes are generally quite high, particularly in families in which both spouses are employed outside the home. Remember, however, that this is also a time when families are purchasing homes and providing for their children, which is costly. Consequently, the economic well-being of these people as measured by their earnings may well be overstated. In other words, although these people are earning more at this stage in their lives, they also have more responsibilities. Finally, people reach the retirement phase, characterized by less work, more leisure, and smaller family sizes. Even families that are quite well off tend to experience incomes well below average during the retirement phase. *Given the life cycle of income, lumping together families of different ages (phases of their life-cycle earnings) results in substantial inequality in the annual income figures. This would be so even if the incomes of families over a lifetime were approximately equal.*

Exhibit 2 highlights major differences between high- and low-income families that underlie the distributional data of Exhibit 1. The typical high-income family

EXHIBIT 2

Differing Characteristics of High- and Low-Income Families, 2011

	Bottom 20 Percent of Income Recipients	Top 20 Percent of Income Recipients
EDUCATION OF HOUSEHOLDER		
Percent with less than high school	27	2
Percent with college degree or more	11	63
AGE OF HOUSEHOLDER (PERCENT DISTRIBUTION)		
Under 35	33	12
35–64	48	78
65 and older	19	10
FAMILY STATUS		
Married couple family (percentage of total)	44	92
Single parent family (percentage of total)	56	8
PERSONS PER FAMILY	3	3.4
EARNERS PER FAMILY	0.7	2.1
Percent of married-couple families in which wife works full-time	11	62
PERCENT OF TOTAL WORK HOURS SUPPLIED BY GROUP	6	33

Source: http://www.census.gov and author calculations from the March 2012 Current Population Survey.

(top 20 percent) is headed by a well-educated person in the prime working-age phase of life. His or her income is supplemented by the earnings of other family members, particularly working spouses. In contrast, people with little education, nonworking retirees, younger workers (under age 35), and single-parent families are substantially overrepresented among low-income families (the bottom 20 percent of income recipients). In 2011, 27 percent of the householders in the lowest income quintile failed to complete high school, compared with only 2 percent for the highest income quintile. Although only 11 percent of the household heads in the bottom quintile completed college, 63 percent of the householders in the top group did so. Seventy-eight percent of the high-income families had household heads in the prime working-age category (age thirty-five to sixty-four), compared with only 48 percent of the low-income families. Only one parent was present in 56 percent of the low-income families, whereas 92 percent of the high-income group were dual-parent families. High-income families are also larger than low-income families, which might surprise you. In 2011, there were 3.4 people per family in the top income quintile, compared to only 3.0 people per family in the bottom quintile.

Moreover, there was a striking difference between low- and high-income families in the percentage of hours each group worked. No doubt, much of this difference reflected factors like family size, the age of the wage earners, whether both spouses worked, and whether two spouses were present in the home. In high-income families, the average number of workers per family was 2.1, compared with 0.7 for low-income families. Among married-couple families, a wife working full time was present only 11 percent of the time in low-income families, compared with 62 percent of the time in high-income families. As we would expect, couples who decide not to have the wife work full-time pay for this choice by falling down the income distribution ladder.

In terms of their work effort, the top 20 percent of income recipients contributed 33 percent of the total number of hours worked in the economy, whereas the bottom

20 percent contributed only 6 percent of the total work time. In other words, high-income families worked 5.5 times as many hours as low-income families. As we noted earlier, they also earned approximately twelve times as much before-tax income. Clearly, differences in the amount of time worked were a major factor contributing to the income inequality of Exhibit 1. Less work time generally means more time for leisure. See Application in Economics: "The Increasing Leisure Time of Americans" for information on recent changes in this factor.

In summary, Exhibit 2 sheds a great deal of light on the distributional data presented in Exhibit 1. *Those with high incomes are far more likely to be well-educated, dual-parent families with both parents working outside the home in their prime earning years. In contrast, those with low incomes are often single-parent families headed by a poorly educated adult who is either youthful or elderly.* The household heads of those families with little income are often either out of the labor force or working only part-time. Given these factors, it is not surprising that the top 20 percent of recipients have substantially higher incomes, both before and after taxes, than the bottom quintile.

APPLICATIONS IN ECONOMICS

The Increasing Leisure Time of Americans

In the United States, men spend approximately 54 hours per week commuting to and from a job and performing work activities either in the marketplace or at home. The comparable figure for women is 47 hours per week. The rest of their time is available for leisure activities.

Leisure time is a valuable commodity. It is the time that you are not working at a job or at home performing tasks such as washing clothes and cutting the grass. Your leisure time is the time that you have simply to do things that you enjoy. It includes activities like watching TV, playing video games, visiting friends, going to bars, and attending sporting events.

Like an increase in market income, an increase in leisure makes us better off. The amount of leisure time available to the average American has increased substantially in recent decades. After adjusting for demographic changes, Mark Aguiar and Erik Hurst find that leisure rose, between 1965 and 2003, on average by 7.9 hours per week for men and 6 hours per week for women.[1] This increase in leisure time is roughly equal to ten and eight extra weeks of vacation from work for men and women, respectively.

The source of the increased leisure time differs for men and women. Men now have more leisure because they have reduced their market work time more than they have increased their hours working at home. For women, the reverse is true. Women have more leisure because they have reduced their time devoted to housework more than they increased their time spent in market labor.

The increase in leisure has not been evenly spread out across education groups. In 1965, the amount of leisure was quite similar across various levels of education for both men and women. However, this situation has changed significantly during the last four decades. The average hours of leisure rose by 10.2 hours for men with a high school degree or less but by only 5.5 hours for men with more than a high school degree. This same pattern was also present for women. Women with a high school degree or less increased their leisure time by 9 hours per week compared with only 5.7 hours for those with schooling beyond the high school level. Given their higher hourly earnings, the opportunity cost of leisure time is greater for those with more education. Thus, it is not surprising that individuals with more education had smaller increases in leisure time than those with less schooling.

Interestingly, the increase in leisure inequality across education groups is the mirror image of the change in market income inequality. In recent decades, the market earnings of those with more education have increased more rapidly than have those with less schooling. However, just the opposite has been the case for the increase in leisure time. Thus, the increase in time worked (and reduction in leisure) has contributed to the growing income gap between college graduates and those with only a high school education that has been observed in recent decades.

[1]Mark Aguiar and Erik Hurst, "Measuring Trends in Leisure: The Allocation of Time over Five Decades," *Quarterly Journal of Economics* 122 (August 2007): 969–1006.

franckreporter/E+/Getty Images

28-1b WHY HAS INCOME INEQUALITY INCREASED?

Exhibit 1 indicates that there has been an increase in income inequality in the United States during the last couple of decades. Why has the gap between the rich and the poor been growing? Research in this area shows that at least four factors have contributed to the rise in income inequality.

1. The increasing proportion of single-parent and dual-earner families.

The nature of the family and the allocation of work responsibilities within the family have changed dramatically in recent decades. In 2012, nearly one-third (32 percent) of all families with children were headed by a single parent, double the figure of the mid-1960s. At the same time, the labor force participation rate of married women increased from 40 percent in 1970 to 60 percent in 2012.

As a result, today we have more single-parent families and more dual-earner families. Both of these changes tend to promote income inequality. Consider two hypothetical families, the Smiths and the Browns. In 1970, both were middle-income families with two children and one parent working earning $60,000 (in 2014 dollars). Now consider their 2014 counterparts. The Smiths of 2014 are divorced, and one of them, probably Mrs. Smith, is trying to work part-time and take care of the two children. The probability is very high that the single-parent Smith family of 2014 will be in the low-income rather than the middle-income category. The Smiths may well be in the bottom quintile of the income distribution. In contrast, the Browns of 2014 both work outside the home, and each earns $60,000 annually. Given their dual incomes, the Browns are now a high-income rather than a middle-income family. Along with many other dual-income families (see Exhibit 2), the Browns' 2014 family income will probably place them in the top quintile of income recipients.

Even if there were no changes in earnings between skilled and less-skilled workers, the recent changes within the family would increase the income inequality among families and households. Today, more single-parent families like the Smiths fall into the low-income quintile, whereas more dual-earner families like the Browns fall into the high-income quintile. The gap between the earnings of these two groups has therefore increased the overall income inequality in the United States.

2. Earnings differentials between skilled and less-skilled workers.

In 1970, workers with little education who were willing to work hard, often in a hot and sweaty environment, received high wages. This is less true today. In 1974, the annual earnings of men who graduated from college were only 27 percent higher than the earnings of male high school graduates—hardly a huge payoff for the time and cost of a college degree. Since 1974, however, things have changed dramatically. By the mid-1980s, the earnings premium of male college graduates relative to male high school grads rose to the 50–60 percent range, approximately twice the premium of 1974. By 2011, the income premium of male college graduates relative to high school graduates rose to 84 percent. Similarly, during the last two decades, the earnings of women college graduates have increased sharply relative to women with only a high school education.

Why have the earnings of people with more education (and skill) risen relative to those with less education (and skill)? As the Applications in Economics feature indicates, an increase in the time worked of those with more education has played a role. Structural factors have also contributed. Deregulation of the transportation industry and the declining power of unions may have reduced the number of high-wage, blue-collar jobs available to workers with little education. International competition has also played a role because, increasingly, American workers must compete in a global economy. Furthermore, innovations and cost reductions in both communications and transportation have made it easier for firms to hire workers in different locations. Firms producing goods that require substantial amounts of less-skilled labor can easily move to places like Korea, Taiwan, and Mexico, where less-skilled labor is cheaper. In contrast, the United States is more attractive than most other countries to firms requiring substantial amounts of high-skilled, well-educated workers. Globalization has, therefore, reduced the demand for American workers with few skills and little education but increased the demand for high-skilled workers with college degrees. This has made for a wider earnings gap among workers in high-income countries like the United States. However, it is worth noting that this process enhances income levels in low-income countries and thereby reduces *worldwide* income inequality.

3. The increasing number of markets characterized by a few people at the top with very high earnings. As we discussed in the chapter on wage differentials, the market compensation of star entertainers and athletes, the most talented professionals, and top business executives is often like that of winner-take-all tournaments. At any point in time, a few people at the top have huge earnings, whereas most others in these areas have modest or even low incomes. As transportation and communication costs have declined, markets have increasingly become national and even global, rather than local. This not only increases the incomes of a few people at the top, but it also increases the degree of income inequality.

4. Sharply lower marginal tax rates than in the 1970s. Prior to 1981, high-income Americans confronted top marginal tax rates of up to 70 percent. This encouraged high-income earners to structure their business affairs and invest in ways that sheltered much of their income from the Internal Revenue Service. As we indicated in Chapter 4, the taxable incomes of the top 10 percent of earners expanded sharply when the top marginal tax rates were reduced to the 30 percent range during the 1980s. Some of this increase in income reflected greater work effort due to the increased incentive to earn. Much of it, however, merely reflected the fact that people were engaging in fewer activities to shelter their earnings from taxes. The flip side of fewer tax shelter activities accompanying lower marginal tax rates led to an increase in the visible income of the rich. As more of the income of the rich is observable, money income statistics such as those of Exhibit 1 will register an increase in income inequality.

28-2 INCOME MOBILITY AND INEQUALITY IN ECONOMIC STATUS

Income mobility
Movement of individuals and families either up or down income-distribution rankings when comparisons are made at two different points in time. When substantial income mobility is present, a person's current position in the rankings will not be a very good indicator of what his or her position will be a few years in the future.

Statistics on the distribution of annual income do not reflect **income mobility**—movements up and down the income ladder. Therefore, they may be misleading. Consider two countries with identical distributions of annual income. In both cases, the annual income of the top quintile of income recipients is ten times greater than the bottom quintile. Now, suppose that in the first country—we will refer to it as Static—the same people are at the top of the income distribution year after year. Similarly, the poor people of Static remain poor year after year. Static is characterized by an absence of income mobility. In contrast, earners in the second country, which we will call Dynamic, are constantly changing places. Indeed, during every five-year period, each family spends one year in the upper-income quintile, one year in each of the three middle-income quintiles, and one year in the bottom-income quintile. In Dynamic, no one is rich for more than one year (out of each five), and no one is poor for more than a year. Obviously, the nature of economic inequality in Static is vastly different from that in Dynamic. You would not know it, though, by looking at their identical annual income distributions.

The contrast between Static and Dynamic highlights an important point: Income mobility is an important facet of economic inequality. Until recently, detailed data on income mobility were sparse. This is now beginning to change.[3] **Exhibit 3** presents data on the mobility of individual income between 1987 and 2007 in the United States of

---

[3]For a review of the literature on income mobility, see Isabel V. Sawhill and Daniel P. McMurrer, *Income Mobility in the United States* (Washington, DC: Urban Institute, 1996); and Gary S. Fields and Efe A. Ok, "The Measurement of Income Mobility: An Introduction to the Literature" in *Handbook of Income Inequality Measurement*, ed. Jacques Silber (Boston: Kluwer Academic, 1999). For recent research on income mobility, see Pew Charitable Trust 's Economic Mobility Project: http://www.economicmobility.org.

EXHIBIT 3

Income Mobility—Income Ranking, 1987 and 2007

PERCENT DISTRIBUTION by INCOME STATUS OF INDIVIDUAL IN 1987	PERCENT DISTRIBUTION BY INCOME STATUS OF INDIVIDUAL IN 2007				
	HIGHEST QUINTILE	NEXT-HIGHEST QUINTILE	MIDDLE QUINTILE	NEXT-LOWEST QUINTILE	LOWEST QUINTILE
Highest quintile	48.4	23.3	13.5	7.5	7.3
Next-highest quintile	24.4	29.1	20.7	15.0	10.7
Middle quintile	14.0	25.2	26.0	19.8	15.0
Next-lowest quintile	7.8	15.5	23.4	28.5	24.7
Lowest quintile	5.4	6.9	16.4	29.2	42.3

Source: Gerald Auten, Geoffrey Gee, and Nicholas Turner, "Income Inequality, Mobility, and Turnover at the Top in the US, 1987–2010," *American Economic Review* (May 2013): 168–72.

those aged 35–40 in 1987. The data compare the relative income positions of the *same individuals* at two different points in time. Based on their 1987 income, each family was placed into income quintiles ranked from highest to lowest. Later, the 2007 real-income level of the *same individuals* was used once again to group the income of each by quintiles.

The first row of Exhibit 3 shows the relative income position in 2007 of people in the top quintile of income recipients in 1987. Approximately one-half (48 percent) of those with incomes in the top quintile in 1987 were able to maintain this lofty position 20 years later. Slightly more than one-half (52 percent) of the top income group in 1987 had fallen to a lower income quintile by 2007. However, only about 15 percent of the high-income individuals fell to one of the bottom two quintiles of the 2007 income distribution. This suggests that once families are able to achieve high-income status, they rarely fall back to a very low level of income.

The bottom row of Exhibit 3 tracks the experience of those in the lowest income quintile in 1987. Slightly more than two-fifths (42.3 percent) of the individuals in the lowest income quintile remained there in 2007. More than one-quarter (28.7 percent) moved up to one of the top three income quintiles in 2007. Among those in the next-to-lowest income quintile in 1987, nearly one-half (46.7 percent) had moved up to one of the three higher income groupings by 2007.

The income mobility data reveal something concealed by the annual figures: There is considerable movement up and down the economic ladder. Relative income positions often change over time. A sizable portion of those with a high relative income during one year subsequently find themselves in a lower income position. At the same time, many of those with low relative incomes during a given year move up to higher income quintiles in subsequent years. What about intergenerational income mobility? Individuals whose parents' income was in the bottom or top quintile are more likely to remain there as adults. Forty percent of children who started in the highest income quintile remained in the top quintile as an adult.[4] Likewise, 43 percent of children who initially were in the bottom quintile stayed there. Those who started in the middle quintile, however, were almost evenly distributed across the quintiles as adults.

Many economists argue that differences in household expenditures are a more accurate indicator of economic well-being than are the annual income figures. On the one hand, if your income or earnings prospects in the future are good, you're likely to spend

---

[4]See Economic Mobility Project, The Pew Charitable Trusts, "Pursuing the American Dream: Economic Mobility Across Generations," July 2012. For additional information about intergenerational income mobility, see Sandra E. Black and Paul J. Devereux, "Recent Developments in Intergenerational Mobility," in *Handbook of Labor Economics, Volume 4B*, eds., Orley Ashenfelter and David Card (Amsterdam: Elsevier, 2011), pp. 1487–541..

Generational Mobility: There is a positive correlation between the earnings of fathers and sons. If a father has lifetime earnings 20 percent above the average of his generation, a son can expect to earn about 10 percent more. If a grandfather had earnings 20 percent above the average, his grandson can expect to have earnings about 5 percent above the average.

Clarissa Leahy/Riser/Getty Images

more than your current income. On the other hand, if your future income is expected to be lower, you're likely to save more, causing spending to be less than your current income. To a large degree, current expenditures reflect long-term economic status.

What do expenditures reveal about the degree of inequality in the United States? The expenditure statistics indicate that the degree of inequality is significantly smaller than the corresponding figure for annual income. For example, in 2012, the household expenditures of the bottom 20 percent of households were approximately 9 percent of the total. This is substantially greater than their income share both before and after taxes. Correspondingly, the expenditures of the top 20 percent of households constituted approximately 38 percent of the total, well below their income share. Moreover, the share of household expenditures by quintile has been relatively constant during the last four decades. This suggests that the increase in inequality as measured by the annual income data is a reflection of dynamic change, temporary fluctuations in annual income, and measurement issues rather than a true increase in economic inequality.

28-3 POVERTY IN THE UNITED STATES

Poverty threshold income level

The level of money income below which a family is considered to be poor. It differs according to family characteristics (e.g., number of family members) and is adjusted when consumer prices change.

In an affluent country like the United States, income inequality and poverty are related issues. Poverty could be defined in strictly relative terms—the bottom one-fifth of all income recipients, for example. However, this definition would not be very helpful because it would mean that the poverty rate would never change, as 20 percent of the population would always be classified as poor.

The official definition of poverty in the United States is based on the perceived minimum income necessary to provide food, clothing, shelter, and basic necessities for a family to survive. This **poverty threshold income level** varies with family size and composition, and it is adjusted annually for changes in prices. The official poverty threshold is based only on money income. (See the Measures of Economic Activity feature for additional details on how the poverty rate is measured.)

Who are the poor? **Exhibit 4** presents data on both the number of poor families and the poverty rate for 1959, 1976, and 2011. In 2011, 9.5 million families, 11.8 percent of the total, were classified as poor. As Exhibit 4 shows, there has been a substantial change in the composition of the poverty population during the last several decades. In 1959,

	1959	1976	2011
NUMBER OF POOR FAMILIES			
(IN MILLIONS)	8.3	5.3	9.5
PERCENT OF POOR FAMILIES HEADED BY A:			
Female	23	48	52
Black	26	30	26
Elderly person			
(age 65 and older)	22	14	7
Person who worked at least			
some during the year	70	55	44
POVERTY RATE			
All families	18.5	10.1	11.8
Married couple families	15.8	7.2	6.2
Female-headed families	42.6	32.5	31.2
All individuals	22.4	11.7	15.0
Whites	18.1	9.1	12.8
Blacks	55.1	31.1	27.6
Children (younger than age 18)	27.3	16.0	21.9

The Changing Composition of the Poor and Poverty Rates, Selected Groups: 1959, 1976, and 2011

Source: U.S. Department of Commerce, Characteristics of the Population below the Poverty Level: 1982, Table 5; and http://www.census.gov/.

elderly people and the working poor formed the core of the poverty population. Twenty-two percent of the poor families were headed by an elderly person in 1959 versus only 7 percent in 2011. In 1959, 70 percent of the heads of poor families worked at least part of the year, but in 2011, only 44 percent of them worked during the year.

In recent decades, the proportion of families headed by women in the United States has increased whereas the proportion of husband–wife families has declined. Because the poverty rate of families headed by women is several times higher than the rate for husband–wife families (31.2 percent compared with 6.2 percent in 2011), an increase in family instability tends to push the poverty rate upward. It also tends to increase the number of households headed by women among poor families. In 2011, 52 percent of the poor families were headed by a woman, compared with only 23 percent in 1959.

Rather than calculating the poverty rate of families, one could measure the poverty rate of individuals. The poverty rate of individuals is, in fact, somewhat higher than the poverty rate of families. In 2011, 15.0 percent of people in the United States were classified as poor, compared with 11.8 percent for families. The poverty rate of black individuals in 2011 was 27.6 percent, compared with 12.8 percent for white individuals. Nonetheless, more than two-thirds of the people in poverty were white. Perhaps the most tragic consequence of poverty is its impact on children. Moreover, the poverty rate among children has been increasing. In 2011, 22 percent of the children in the United States lived in poverty, up from 16 percent in 1976.

28-3a TRANSFER PAYMENTS AND THE POVERTY RATE

In the mid-1960s, it was widely believed that an increase in income transfers directed toward the poor would substantially reduce, if not eliminate, the incidence of poverty. The 1964 *Economic Report of the President* argued that poverty could be virtually eliminated if the federal government increased its expenditures on transfer programs by approximately 2 percent of aggregate income. Following the declaration of the "War on Poverty" by President Lyndon Johnson's administration, transfer expenditures increased rapidly. Measured in 1982–1984 dollars, **means-tested income transfers**—those limited to people with incomes below a certain cutoff point—tripled, expanding from $24 billion in 1965

Means-tested income transfers
Transfers that are limited to people or families with an income below a certain cutoff point. Eligibility is thus dependent upon low-income status.

MEASURES OF ECONOMIC ACTIVITY

How Is the Poverty Rate Calculated?

Families and individuals are classified as poor or nonpoor based on the poverty threshold income level originally developed by the Social Security Administration (SSA) in 1964. Consumption survey data showed that low- and median-income families of three or more people spent approximately one-third of their income on food. Because of this, the SSA established the poverty threshold income level at three times the cost of an economical, nutritionally adequate food plan. A slightly larger multiple was used for smaller families and individuals living alone. The poverty threshold figure varies according to family size because the food costs vary by family size and composition. It is adjusted annually to account for rising prices. The following chart illustrates how the poverty threshold for a family of four has increased as prices have risen from 1959 to 2013.

1959	$2,973
1970	3,968
1980	8,414
1990	13,359
2000	17,603
2013	23,550

Even though the poverty threshold income level is adjusted for prices, it is actually an absolute measure of economic status. As real income increases, the poverty threshold declines relative to the income of the general populace.

The official poverty rate is the number of people or families living in households with a money income below the poverty threshold as a percentage of the total. Only money income is considered. Income received in the form of noncash benefits, like food stamps, medical care, and housing subsidies, is completely ignored in the calculation of the official poverty rate. Because of this omission, the official rate tends to overstate the degree of poverty. To remedy this deficiency, the Bureau of the Census has developed several alternative measures of poverty that count the estimated value of noncash benefits as income. In addition to the official poverty rate, the bureau now publishes annual data for the "adjusted" poverty rates that include a valuation for various noncash benefits. Of course, including these benefits reduces the poverty rate. For example, the official poverty rate for families was 11.8 percent in 2011, but the adjusted poverty rate that included the value of the noncash food, housing, and medical benefits was only 8.1 percent.

The poverty rate is calculated each year based on a survey of about 60,000 households designed to reflect the population of the United States. The major source for comprehensive data on this topic is the Bureau of the Census annual publication, *Income, Poverty, and Health Insurance Coverage in the United States.*

franckreporter/E+/Getty Images

to $70 billion in 1975. After 1975, transfer expenditures continued to expand, but the rate of increase was slower. Measured as a share of aggregate income, means-tested transfers jumped from 1.5 percent in 1965 to 5.3 percent in 2002.[5]

Did the expansion in government income transfers reduce the poverty rate as the 1964 *Economic Report of the President* anticipated? **Exhibit 5** shows the poverty rate from 1947 through 2011. Interestingly, the poverty rate declined substantially during the period prior to the War on Poverty. It fell from 32 percent in 1947 to 13.9 percent in 1965. The downward trend continued for a few more years, reaching 10 percent in 1968. However, shortly after the War on Poverty was initiated, the downward trend in the poverty rate came to a halt. Since 1968, the poverty rate has fluctuated within a narrow band around the 10 percent level. In 2011, it was 11.8 percent—slightly higher than 1968. When noncash benefits like Medicaid and food stamps are counted as income, the poverty rate is lower, but the overall pattern is still much the same. The largely unchanged poverty rate during the last four decades is particularly remarkable when you consider that over this same time span, real income per person in the United States has approximately doubled.

Why wasn't the War on Poverty more effective? One reason is that means-tested income transfers generate two major side effects that reduce their effectiveness. *First, transfer*

---

[5]U.S. House of Representatives, Committee on Ways and Means, *Green Book, 2004: Background Material and Data on Programs within the Jurisdiction of the Committee on Ways and Means*, 18th ed. (Washington, DC: GPO, March 2004), appendix K.

programs that significantly reduce the hardship of poverty also reduce the opportunity cost of choices that often lead to poverty. This factor is sometimes called the **Samaritan's dilemma.** To the extent that antipoverty programs reduce the negative effects of, for example, births by unmarried mothers, abandonment of children by fathers, dependency on drugs or alcohol, or dropping out of school, they inadvertently encourage people to make choices that result in these conditions. Of course, this is not the intent of the transfers, but nonetheless it is one of their side effects. In the short run, these secondary effects are probably not very important. Over the longer term, however, their negative consequences can be substantial.

Second, income-linked transfers reduce the incentive of low-income individuals to help themselves. When the size of transfers is linked to income, larger transfers tend to increase the **implicit marginal tax rate** imposed on the poor. The implicit marginal tax rate is the amount of additional (marginal) earnings that must be paid explicitly in taxes or—in the case of the poor—implicitly in the form of lower income supplements. The marginal tax rate determines the fraction of an additional dollar earned that an individual is permitted to keep, so it is an important determinant of the incentive to earn. Participants in the food stamp program, for example, have their food stamp benefits reduced by $30 for every $100 of income they earn. Consequently, every $100 of additional income leads to only a $70 increase in well-being (spendable net income) after the reduction in food stamp benefits is taken into account. When a person qualifies for several programs like food stamps, Medicaid, and housing benefits, the problem is compounded, and the combined implicit marginal tax rate can frequently exceed 50 or 60 percent. In some cases, the rate may exceed 100 percent. Under these circumstances, if recipients work, the money they make would actually reduce their spendable income. Because high implicit marginal tax rates reduce the incentive of poor families to work and earn, transfers often merely replace income that otherwise would have been earned. When this is the case, they add little or nothing to the *net* income of the poor. (See the Applications in Economics: "Implicit Marginal Tax Rates and the Incentive to Earn: A Real-World Example.")

Samaritan's dilemma
The dilemma that occurs when assisting low-income citizens with transfers reduces the opportunity cost of choices that lead to poverty. Providing income transfers to the poor and discouraging behavior that leads to poverty are conflicting goals.

Implicit marginal tax rate
The amount of additional (marginal) earnings that must be paid explicitly in taxes or implicitly in the form of reduced income supplements. The marginal tax rate establishes the fraction of an additional dollar earned that an individual is permitted to keep, so it is an important determinant of the incentive to work and earn.

EXHIBIT 5

The Poverty Rate, 1947–2011

The official poverty rate of families fell sharply during the 1950s and 1960s, but it has remained near 10 percent since 1968. The shaded area of the bars shows the additional decline in the poverty rate when noncash benefits are counted as income. When the value of these noncash transfer benefits is added, the poverty rate ranges from 7 percent to 8 percent. This statistic remained unchanged throughout most of the 1968–2011 period.

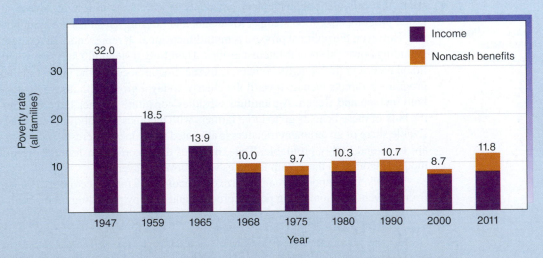

Source: U.S. Department of Commerce, *Characteristics of the Population below the Poverty Level: 1982*, table 5, and http://www.census.gov/.

28-3b ESTIMATING THE COSTS OF REDISTRIBUTION

The U.S. government has numerous income-transfer programs, including many that are unrelated to helping the poor. In 2012, income-transfers and subsidy programs intended to help various groups purchase food, housing, and health care summed to 15 percent of aggregate income.[6] As we discussed in Chapter 6, politicians will often be able to gain by proposing programs that provide concentrated benefits to readily identifiable groups (for example, farmers, senior citizens, or unemployed workers) while imposing a small personal cost on disparate groups like taxpayers and consumers in general. Because of this, the presence and size of transfer programs are not surprising.

Income transfers are also costly in terms of the economy's overall output level. The higher marginal tax rates needed to finance transfers and subsidies mean that taxpayers get to keep less of what they earn. Furthermore, recipients often qualify for larger transfers if their income is lower, which causes them to earn even less. Thus, transfer programs typically weaken the incentive of both taxpayer-donors and the subsidy recipients to work and earn. As a result, the cost of the transfers will be greater than the amount of income transferred. A study by economists Sam Allgood and Arthur Snow sought to measure the loss of output due to the lower supply of labor associated with higher marginal tax rates accompanying income transfers.[7] Allgood and Snow estimated that it costs between $1.26 and $3.22 in terms of lost output for every additional dollar redistributed from the top 60 percent of income recipients to the bottom 40 percent.

Helping transfer recipients achieve long-term well-being is also more difficult than it first appears. Competition for the transfers and subsidies will often erode much of the recipient's gain. See the Application in Economics: "Why Transfer Programs Will Not Help Their Intended Beneficiaries Very Much" for additional details about why this is the case.

28-4 INCOME INEQUALITY: SOME CONCLUDING THOUGHTS

Is there too much inequality in the United States? Should transfer programs be expanded or contracted? These are normative questions that positive economics cannot definitively answer. Economics can help identify and quantify the cost (in terms of lost output) and the expected effectiveness of alternative programs, but it can't make a judgment about whether that cost or amount is good or bad. Many people, including a good number of economists, would like to see income inequality reduced. This is a stated objective of many government programs. The progressive income tax system, the **Earned Income Tax Credit** (a tax credit that provides supplementary payments to workers with low incomes), and means-tested programs like food stamps, Medicaid, and housing subsidies are examples.

However, the political process is multidimensional. It represents a diverse set of forces, including powerful special-interest groups. Therefore, it shouldn't surprise you that the political record in this area, like others, is mixed. Social Security, the largest income-transfer program, redirects income toward the elderly, today a group with above-average levels of both income and wealth. Agriculture subsidies constitute another large transfer program; the bulk of these benefits go to large farmers with incomes well above the average. Another sizable share of government transfers is allocated to business interests, including many that are large and highly profitable. Thus, many of the income transfers are from those with modest incomes to those with incomes well above the average.

Finally, it is important to recognize that income in a market economy is not like manna from heaven. It is something people produce and earn by providing others with goods and

Earned Income Tax Credit
A feature of the personal income tax system that provides supplementary payments to workers with low incomes.

---

[6]http://www.bea.gov.
[7]See Sam Allgood and Arthur Snow, "The Marginal Cost of Raising Tax Revenue and Redistributing Income," *Journal of Political Economy* (December 1998). This study builds on earlier work by Edgar K. Browning and William Johnson, "The Trade-Off between Equality and Efficiency," *Journal of Political Economy* (April 1984), and Charles L. Ballard, "The Marginal Efficiency Cost of Redistribution," *American Economic Review* (December 1988).

APPLICATIONS IN ECONOMICS

Implicit Marginal Tax Rates and the Incentive to Earn: A Real-World Example

High marginal tax rates reduce the incentive of people to earn and develop their skills. As low-income households increase their earnings, they will qualify for fewer and fewer benefits from food stamps, school lunch subsidies, Medicaid, and other means-tested transfer programs. As a result, the implicit marginal tax rates confronted by low-income households are often extremely high.

Exhibit 6 shows the implicit marginal tax rates facing a low-income mother with one child in West Virginia. Because state welfare programs vary, these numbers would be somewhat different for individuals living in other states (and households of different sizes and characteristics). But the pattern of the implicit marginal tax rates shown here is not atypical.

The exhibit shows the total transfer benefits the mother would receive and taxes she would owe at different levels of earned income. Her spendable income is calculated as her work earnings plus her benefits, minus her taxes. When she does not hold a job, and thus has zero earned income, she receives $8,976 in transfer benefits, which equals her spendable income. If she were to accept a part-time job earning $10,000 per year, her benefits would be reduced to $6,503 and she would now owe $765 in taxes, resulting in spendable income of $15,738.

Note how the implicit marginal tax rate rises with earnings. The combination of taxes and reductions in transfer benefits takes more than 40 percent of the increase in earnings

in the $5,000–$15,000 range. Here, the West Virginia mother gets to keep less than 60 percent of every dollar she earns. The implicit marginal tax rate peaks in the $15,000–$20,000 interval. In this range, the implicit marginal tax rate is 74 percent. Thus, additional earnings from employment in this range increase her spendable income by only 26 cents for every dollar earned. If you got to keep only 26 cents of every dollar you earned, how would this affect your incentive to work and develop your skills?

These numbers do not include the costs associated with her holding employment (such as transportation, clothing, and child care). If these work-related expenses summed to only 15 percent of earnings, this would mean that the combination of taxes, loss of transfers, and work-related expenses would take approximately 90 percent of her additional earnings in the $15,000–$20,000 range. Moreover, these numbers tend to understate the true work disincentives because other in-kind benefit programs, such as Medicaid and housing assistance, are not included in the calculations because they are difficult to quantify. However, they are also removed as earned income rises, compounding the work disincentives faced by transfer recipients. Clearly, high marginal tax rates like those of Exhibit 6 help explain why the transfer programs accompanying the War on Poverty were not very effective: The transfers reduced the incentive of those with low incomes to develop their skills and increase their earnings.

franckreporter/E+/Getty Images

EXHIBIT 6

Earned Income from Work	Transfer Benefits	Income and Employment Taxes	Spendable Income	Implicit Marginal Tax Rate
$0	$8,976	$ 0	$ 8,976	
5,000	8,225	383	12,842	22.7%
10,000	6,503	765	15,738	42.1
15,000	4,955	1,420	18,535	44.1
20,000	1,914	2,072	19,842	73.9
25,000	1,115	2,697	23,419	28.5

The Effect of Transfer Benefits and Taxes on the Incentive of a West Virginia Mother with One Child to Earn Income (July 2007)

Source: Based on Anthony C. Gregory and J. Sebastian Leguizamon, "Quit Punishing the Working Poor: Reduce Work Disincentives in the Welfare System," in *Unleashing Capitalism: Why Prosperity Stops at the West Virginia Border and How to Fix It*, ed. Russell S. Sobel (Morgantown, WV: Public Policy Foundation of West Virginia, 2007).
Note: Transfer benefits include TANF, Earned Income Tax Credit, food stamps; taxes include Social Security, Medicare, and federal and state income taxes.

services they are willing to pay for. The allocation of income reflects the choices of individuals with differing preferences, talents, educational levels, entrepreneurial skills, rate of saving, and so on. Wage differentials, profits, losses, and interest rates coordinate the choices of these vastly different individuals and bring them into harmony with one another. Income inequality is a natural outgrowth of this process. Indeed, policies that modify the process can generate perverse, counterproductive incentives.

When it comes to issues of fairness, some people argue that the process—the system, in other words—that generates the outcomes is more important than the actual result. Do all people in the economy have an opportunity to acquire education and training? Are people from all segments of society free to compete in business and labor markets? Do incomes reflect their choices, voluntary exchanges, and productive efforts? These questions are about opportunity, economic freedom, and how income is acquired. Many people believe that these things, rather than the income-distribution patterns that result from them, are the key elements of economic fairness.

Perhaps the following example will illustrate the difference between the process and pattern view. Suppose a million people purchase a $10 lottery ticket, and the proceeds are used to finance a $10 million jackpot for one person. This activity will clearly increase income inequality. But is it unfair? Those who adhere to the process view would stress that the outcome merely reflects the voluntary choices of participants who were well aware of the rules of the game prior to their purchasing a ticket. According to this view, it is the process rather than the outcome that is the primary determinant of fairness.

Economics provides insight into both the allocative role and sources of differences in income. It also indicates that it will be costly, in terms of lost output, to redistribute income through taxes and transfers. Of course, this does not reveal whether there is too much inequality or whether the government should play a larger or smaller role in the allocation of income. It does, however, enable us to address these normative issues in a more thoughtful way.

APPLICATIONS IN ECONOMICS

Why Transfer Programs Will Not Help Their Intended Beneficiaries Very Much

As the data of this chapter show, the achievements of antipoverty transfer programs fell far short of the initial expectations. Indeed, the economic way of thinking would lead a person to believe that it's difficult to transfer income to a group of recipients in a way that will significantly improve their long-term well-being. The unintended consequences that alter people's incentives explain why this is true.

Governments must establish criteria to determine who should get the transfers, subsidies, and other political favors and who should not. Without these criteria, benefit programs would exhaust their budgets. Typically, governments require potential recipients to do something, own something, buy something, or be something in order to qualify for the transfer. However, as people take the steps necessary to qualify, they erode much of the benefit.

Consider the case in which the recipients have to do something (for example, fill out forms, take an exam, submit a detailed proposal, lobby government officials, endure delays, or contribute to selected political campaigns) in order to obtain the transfer. These actions are costly and will reduce the recipient's net gain. In some cases, almost all of the gain may be eroded. Perhaps a simple example will help illustrate this important point. Suppose the U.S. government decided to give away a $50 bill between 9 A.M. and 5 P.M. each weekday to anyone willing to show up at one of six teller windows at the U.S. Department

of Treasury. Certainly, a line would emerge. How much time would people be willing to wait in the line? A person whose time was worth $5 per hour would be willing to spend up to 10 hours waiting in line for the $50. But it might take longer than 10 hours if there were enough other people, whose time was worth less, say $3 or $4 per hour. And everyone would find that the waiting consumed much of the value of the $50 transfer. If the government's objective is to make the recipients $50 richer, it will fail. In fact, some of those waiting in line for the $50 bill will gain very little. For example, if the wait were 10 hours, the net benefit of a person with an opportunity cost of $4.90 would be only $1. So it is with real-world transfers. When you consider the cost of what has to be done for someone to qualify for the transfer, the net gain of the recipient is often small.

In other cases, the government will require recipients to own something (for example, land with an acreage allotment to grow wheat, a license to operate a taxicab, or a permit to sell in a restricted market) in order to qualify for a transfer or subsidy. Recipients will gain when programs like this are initiated or unexpectedly expanded. But once programs of this type are established, people will bid up the price of the asset needed to acquire the subsidy. The higher price of the asset, such as the taxicab license or the land with a wheat allotment, will capture the value of the expected future subsidy. Once this happens, the rate of return in the business or occupation (for example, farming or operating a taxicab) will be driven down to the normal level. The current recipients don't benefit from the subsidy program continuing at the expected benefit level. Essentially, they paid for the expected benefit of the subsidy when they purchased the asset needed to get it.

Interestingly, even though they don't benefit, current recipients will fight to keep the program going if it is threatened. Repealing (or reducing) the subsidies will be harmful because it will reduce the value of the asset they currently hold. This explains why eliminating farm subsidies, for example, is difficult even though the subsidies do not make farming more profitable for the current operators. Economist Gordon Tullock refers to this as the *transitional gains trap*, because once programs like these get started, they will be difficult to eliminate even though current recipients aren't benefiting from them.[1]

Sometimes, recipients are required to purchase a good or service in order to qualify for a subsidy. For example, the Medicare and Medicaid programs subsidize health care purchases made by senior citizens and the poor. Several states provide educational subsidies for college tuition or the purchase of textbooks. As we discussed in Chapter 4, subsidizing the purchase of a good will increase its demand and lead to higher prices. As a result, some of the benefits of such subsidies will accrue to the suppliers rather than the purchasers. Again, the subsidized recipients will not gain as much as it might appear.

Finally, sometimes the government requires that recipients be something in order to qualify for the subsidy. Programs of this type are often intended to help protect people against the adverse effects of certain events such as unemployment or catastrophic storms. Unfortunately, the programs also encourage choices that increase the adverse effects of such events. For example, consider the impact of subsidized insurance premiums for those living in hurricane-prone areas. These subsidies reduce the owners' personal cost of rebuilding their properties after a hurricane. But the lower personal costs also encourage people to build in hurricane-prone areas. As more of them do so, the overall cost of damage from hurricanes increases. The secondary effects of unemployment insurance are much the same. The benefits paid to the unemployed will reduce the opportunity cost of continuing a job search while unemployed. As a result, periods of unemployment will be longer and the rate of unemployment higher than would have otherwise been the case.

The ability of transfers to improve the well-being of a designated group is far more limited than is generally recognized. Transfer programs alter incentives and generate unintended consequences that erode some, if not most, of the benefits derived by the recipients. Thus, the net gains of the intended beneficiaries are often much less than they appear to be.

[1]See Gordon Tullock, "The Transitional Gains Trap," *Bell Journal of Economics* 6 (Autumn 1975): 671–78.

LOOKING AHEAD

Income transfers are the focal point of many current policy issues, including Social Security and health care. The special topics in the final section of the book analyze this issue and other topics.

KEY POINTS

- In 2010, the bottom 20 percent of families earned 3.8 percent of aggregate income; the top 20 percent of families earned approximately twelve times that amount (47.8 percent). After taxes and transfers are taken into account, the top quintile of households earn nearly ten times the income of the bottom quintile.

- A substantial percentage of the inequality in annual income reflects differences in age, education, family size, marital status, number of earners in the family, and time worked. Young inexperienced workers, students, single-parent families, and retirees are overrepresented among those with low current incomes.

- Income inequality has risen during the last four decades. The following four factors contributed to this increase: (1) an increase in the proportion of both single-parent and dual-earner families, (2) an increase in earnings differentials on the basis of skill and education, (3) more "winner-take-all" markets, and (4) increases in the reported income of those in the top tax brackets due to lower marginal tax rates.

- The tracking of household income over time indicates that there is considerable movement of individuals both up and down the income spectrum. The data on the distribution of income at a particular point in time can be misleading because they do not reflect this movement up and down the income ladder.

- Nearly one-eighth of American families were officially classified as poor in 2011. Those living in poverty were generally younger, less educated, less likely to be working, and more likely to be living in families headed by a woman than those who were not poor. There is considerable movement both into and out of poverty. A relatively small proportion of families constitute the long-term poor.

- During the last several decades, income transfers—including means-tested transfers—have expanded rapidly both in real dollars and as a share of personal income. As a weapon against poverty, transfers have been largely ineffective. Even though per capita income more than doubled between 1965 and 2011, there was little reduction in the overall poverty rate during this period.

- Income transfers large enough to improve the economic status of the poor will (1) encourage behavior that increases the risk of poverty and/or (2) create high implicit marginal tax rates that reduce the recipient's incentive to earn.

- Positive economics cannot determine how much inequality should be present. The nature of the income-generating process as well as the pattern of income distribution is relevant to the issue of fairness.

CRITICAL ANALYSIS QUESTIONS

1. Do you think the current distribution of income in the United States is too unequal? Why or why not? What criteria do you think should be used to judge the fairness of the distribution of income? Is the final outcome more important than the process that generates the income?

2. *Is annual money income a good measure of economic status? Is a family with an $80,000 annual income able to purchase twice the quantity of goods and services as a family with $40,000 of annual income? Is the standard of living of the $80,000 family twice as high as that of the $40,000 family? Discuss.

3. What is income mobility? If there is substantial income mobility in a society, how does this influence the importance of income distribution data?

4. *Consider a table such as Exhibit 3 in which the family income of parents is grouped by quintiles down the first column, and that of their offspring is grouped by quintiles across the other columns. If there were no intergenerational mobility in this country, what pattern of numbers would appear in the table? If the nation had attained complete equality of opportunity, what pattern of numbers would emerge? Explain.

5. Do individuals have a property right to income they acquire from market transactions? Is it a proper function of government to tax some people in order to provide benefits to others? Why or why not? Discuss.

6. *Because income transfers to the poor typically increase the implicit marginal tax rate they confront, does a $1,000 transfer payment necessarily increase the income of poor recipients by $1,000? Why or why not?

7. *Sue is a single parent with two children. She is considering a part-time job that pays $800 per month. She is currently drawing monthly cash benefits of $300, food stamp benefits of $100, and Medicaid benefits valued at $80. If she accepts the job, she will be liable for employment taxes of $56 per month and lose all transfer benefits. What is Sue's implicit marginal tax rate for this job?

8. What groups are overrepresented among those with relatively low incomes? Do the poor in the United States generally stay poor? Why or why not?

9. Some people argue that taxes exert little effect on people's incentive to earn income. Suppose you were required to pay a tax rate of 50 percent on all money income you earn while in school. Would this affect your employment? How might you minimize the personal effects of this tax?

10. Large income transfers are targeted toward the elderly, farmers, and the unemployed, regardless of their economic condition. Why do you think this is so? Do you think there would be less income inequality if the government levied higher taxes in order to make larger income transfers? Why or why not?

11. The outcome of a state lottery game is certainly a very unequal distribution of the prize income. Some players are made very rich, whereas others lose their money. Using this example, discuss whether the fairness of the process or the fairness of the outcome is more important, and how they differ.

12. "Means-tested transfer payments reduce the current poverty rate. However, they also create an incentive structure that discourages self-sufficiency and self-improvement. Thus, they tend to increase the future poverty rate. Welfare programs essentially purchase a lower poverty rate today in exchange for a higher poverty rate in the future." Evaluate this statement.

13. Was the poverty rate increasing or decreasing prior to the War on Poverty initiated by the Johnson administration? As income-transfer programs accompanying the War on Poverty increased beginning in the latter half of the 1960s, what happened to the poverty rate?

14. Suppose one family has $100,000 whereas another has only $20,000. Is this outcome fair? What is your initial reaction? Compare and contrast your views depending on the following:
   a. The family with the higher income has both a husband and wife working, whereas the other family has chosen for the wife to remain home with the children rather than work in the labor force.
   b. The family with the higher income is headed by a person who completed a college degree, whereas the other family is headed by someone who dropped out of high school.
   c. The family with the higher income derived most of its income from the farm subsidy program.
   d. The family with the higher income received it as an inheritance from parents who just died.

*Asterisk denotes questions for which answers are given in Appendix B.

PART 6
Applying the Basics: Special Topics in Economics

Economics is about how the real world works.

Economics has a lot to say about current issues and real-world events. How are government spending, taxes, and borrowing affecting the future prosperity of Americans? Does the current Social Security system face problems, and what might be done to minimize them? Are stocks a good investment for a young person? What caused the economic crisis of 2008, and what are the important lessons we need to learn from it? What might be done to improve the quality of health care? How can we best protect the environment? This section focuses on these topics and several other current issues.

SPECIAL TOPIC 1
Government Spending and Taxation

FOCUS

- How has government spending per person changed historically in the United States?
- How has the composition of government spending changed in recent decades?
- Do taxes measure the cost of government?
- Do the rich pay their fair share of taxes? Do they pay less now than they did a couple of decades ago?
- How does the size of government in the United States compare with other countries?
- How has the share of the population paying taxes and receiving various types of transfer benefits changed in recent years? How is this likely to influence the fiscal future of the United States?

[A] wise and frugal government, which shall restrain men from injuring one another, shall leave them otherwise free to regulate their own pursuits of industry and improvement, and shall not take from the mouth of labor the bread it has earned. This is the sum of good government. . . . —**Thomas Jefferson**[1]

I'm proud to be paying taxes in the United States. The only thing is—I could be just as proud for half the money. —**Comedian Arthur Godfrey**

[1]Thomas Jefferson, First Inaugural Address (March 4, 1801).

franckreporter/E+/Getty Images

In Chapters 5 and 6, we analyzed the economic role of government and the operation of the political process. We learned that whereas the political process and markets are alternative ways of organizing the economy, a sound legal system, secure property rights, and stable monetary regime are vitally important for the efficient operation of markets. We also noted that there may be advantages of using government to provide certain classes of goods that are difficult to supply efficiently through markets. However, as public-choice analysis indicates, the political process is not a corrective device. Even democratic representative government will often lead to the adoption of counterproductive programs. This feature will take a closer look at government in the United States and will provide additional details with regard to its spending, taxing, and borrowing.

ST01-1 GOVERNMENT EXPENDITURES

As we noted in Chapter 6, total government spending (federal, state, and local) sums to almost 40 percent of the U.S. economy. The size of government has grown substantially over the past 80 years. Measured as a share of GDP, total government spending rose from less than 10 percent in 1930 to a little more than 30 percent in 1980 and nearly 40 percent in 2012. Approximately three-fifths of the spending by government now takes place at the federal level. Federal expenditures on just four things—(1) income transfers (including Social Security and other income-security programs), (2) health care, (3) national defense, and (4) net interest on the national debt—accounted for 87 percent of federal spending in 2011. (See Chapter 6, Exhibit 2.) This means that expenditures on everything else— the federal courts, national parks, highways, education, job training, agriculture, energy, natural resources, federal law enforcement, and numerous other programs—were less than 14 percent of the federal budget. Major spending categories at the state and local level include education, public welfare and health, transportation and highways, utilities, and law enforcement.

ST01-2 FEDERAL SPENDING PER PERSON, 1792–2012

Article 1, Section 8, of the U.S. Constitution outlined a limited set of functions that the federal government was authorized to perform. These included the authority to raise up an army and navy, establish a system of weights and measures, issue patents and copyrights, operate the post office, and regulate the value of money that it issued. Beyond this, the federal government was not authorized to do much else. The founders of the United States were skeptical of governmental powers, and they sought to limit those powers, particularly those at the federal level. (See the quotation by Thomas Jefferson at the beginning of this feature.)

During the United States' first 125 years, the constitutional limitations worked pretty much as planned; the economic role of the federal government was quite limited, and its expenditures were modest. In the nineteenth century, except during times of war, most government expenditures were undertaken at the state and local level. The federal government spent funds on national defense and transportation (roads and canals) but not much else.

Exhibit 1 presents data on real federal spending per person (measured in terms of the purchasing power of the dollar in 2010). Just before the Civil War, real federal expenditures were $60 per person, not much different than the $50 figure of 1800. Federal spending per person rose sharply during the Civil War, but it soon receded and remained in a range between $125 and $200 throughout the 1870–1916 period. Thus, before World War I, federal expenditures per person were low and the growth of government was modest.

Beginning with the World War I spending of 1917, however, the situation changed dramatically. Federal spending remained well above the prewar levels during the 1920s

EXHIBIT 1

Real Federal Expenditure per Capita: 1792–2012

Real federal spending per person (measured in 2010 dollars) was generally less than $50 before the Civil War, and it ranged from $125 to $200 throughout the 1870–1916 period. However, beginning with the spending buildup for World War I in 1917, real federal spending per person soared, reaching $11,051 in 2012—almost 80 times the level of 1916.

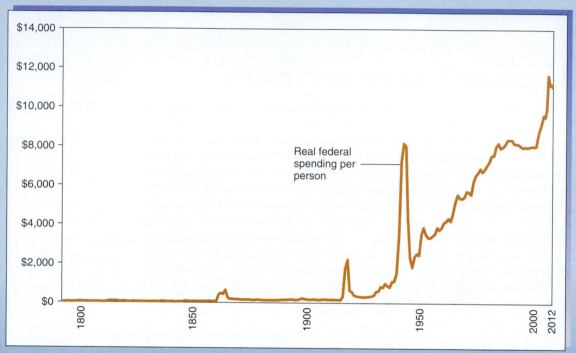

Source: U.S. Census Bureau, *Historical Statistics of the United States* (Washington, DC: U.S. Dept. of Commerce, U.S. Bureau of the Census, 1975); and *Economic Report of the President* (Washington, DC: U.S. Government Printing Office, 2013).

and rose rapidly during the 1930s. It soared during World War II, and after receding at the end of the war, federal spending continued to grow rapidly throughout the 1950–1990 period. After a brief reduction during the 1990s, per capita real federal spending is once again on the upswing. Whereas per capita federal spending fell by 4.6 percent during the 1990s, it increased by 40 percent during 2000–2010. In 2012, it amounted to $11,051, roughly 80 times the $142 figure of 1916. The additional government expenditures came with a cost. On average, Americans paid more federal taxes in one week during 2012 than during the entire year in 1916. Based on current budget projections, the federal tax burden will continue to grow.

Not only has federal spending grown rapidly, but also there has been a dramatic shift in the composition of that spending. Since 1960, spending on defense has fallen as both a share of the budget and as a share of the economy, whereas expenditures on health care, transfer payments, and subsidies have soared.

As Exhibit 2 illustrates, defense expenditures constituted more than half (52.2 percent) of federal spending in 1960. By 2000, defense spending was only 16.5 percent of the federal budget. Largely because of the wars in Iraq and Afghanistan, defense spending has expanded during the past decade, reaching 24.8 percent of the federal budget in 2012. Government expenditures on income transfers (including Social Security and other transfer programs) and health care (primarily Medicare and Medicaid) have soared during the past half century. As Exhibit 2 shows, income transfers and health care expenditures rose from 21.5 percent of the federal budget in 1960 to 57.2 percent in 2012.

EXHIBIT 2

The Changing Composition of Federal Spending

In 2012, national defense expenditures accounted for 24.8 percent of the federal budget, down from 52.2 percent in 1960. In contrast, spending on income transfers and health care rose from 21.5 percent of the federal budget in 1960 to 57.2 percent in 2012.

(a) Defense expenditures

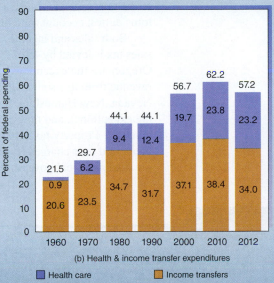

(b) Health & income transfer expenditures

■ Health care   ■ Income transfers

Source: *Economic Report of the President* (Washington, DC: U.S. Government Printing Office, 2013).

Thus, there has been a dramatic change in the composition of federal spending during the last five decades. In contrast with earlier times, national defense is no longer the primary focus of the federal government. In essence, the federal government has become an entity that taxes working-age Americans in order to provide income transfers and health care benefits primarily for senior citizens. Furthermore, spending on the elderly is almost certain to increase as the baby-boomers move into the retirement phase of life during the next two decades.

ST01-3 TAXES AND THE FINANCE OF GOVERNMENT

Government expenditures must be financed through taxes, user charges, or borrowing.[2] Borrowing is simply another name for future taxes that will have to be levied to pay the interest on the borrowed funds. Thus, it affects the timing but not the level of taxes. In the United States, taxes are by far the largest source of government revenue. The power to tax sets governments apart from private businesses. Of course, a private business can put whatever price tag it wishes on its products, but no private business can force you to buy its goods. With its power to tax, a government can force citizens to pay, whether or not they receive something of value in return. As government expenditures have increased, so, too, have taxes. Taxes now take approximately one-third of the income generated by Americans.

---

[2]In addition to user charges, taxes, and borrowing, the operations of government might be financed by printing money. But this is also a type of tax (it is sometimes called an "inflation tax") on those who hold money balances.

ST01-3a TYPES OF TAXES

Exhibit 3 indicates the major revenue sources for the (1) federal and (2) state and local levels of government. At the federal level, the personal income tax accounts for more than 45 percent of all revenue. Although income from all sources is covered by the income tax, only earnings derived from wages and salaries are subject to the payroll tax. Payroll taxes on the earnings of employees and self-employed workers finance the Social Security and Medicare programs. The payroll tax accounts for about 35 percent of federal revenue. The remaining sources of revenue, including the corporate income tax, excise taxes, and customs duties, account for a little less than 20 percent of federal revenue.

Both sales and income taxes are important sources of revenue for state governments. A sales tax is levied by 45 of the 50 states (Alaska, Delaware, Montana, New Hampshire, and Oregon are the exceptions). State and local governments derive about 18 percent of their revenue from this source. Personal income taxes are imposed by 41 states (Alaska, Florida, Nevada, New Hampshire, South Dakota, Tennessee, Texas, Washington, and Wyoming are the exceptions), and they provide approximately 11 percent of state and local government revenue.[3] Property taxes (levied mostly at the local level), grants from the federal government, and user charges (prices for government services) also provide substantial revenues for state and local governments.

EXHIBIT 3

Sources of Government Revenue

The major sources of government revenue are shown here. More than 45 percent of federal revenues are derived from the personal income tax. The share of federal revenue derived from the payroll tax is only slightly less. The major revenue sources of state and local governments are sales and excise taxes, personal income taxes, user charges, grants from the federal government, and property taxes.

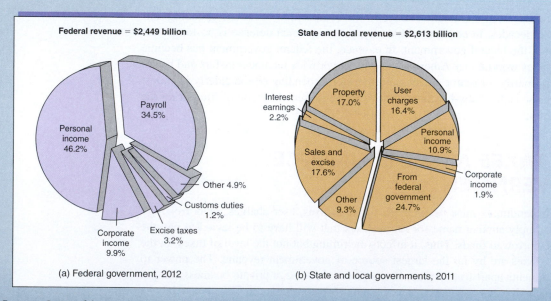

(a) Federal government, 2012

(b) State and local governments, 2011

Source: *Economic Report of the President* (Washington, DC: Government Printing Office, 2013) and U.S. Census Bureau, *State and Local Government Finances*, 2011.

---

[3]New Hampshire and Tennessee have limited income taxes that only tax income derived from dividend and interest (so wage income is not subject to the personal income tax).

ST01-4 TAXES AND THE COST OF GOVERNMENT

There are no free lunches. Regardless of how they are financed, activities undertaken by the government are costly. When governments purchase resources and other goods and services to provide missiles, education, highways, health care, and other goods, the resources used by the government will be unavailable to produce goods and services in the private sector. As a result, private-sector output will be lower. This reduction in private-sector output is an opportunity cost of government. Furthermore, this cost will be present whether government activities are financed by taxes or borrowing.

Moreover, a tax dollar extracted from an individual or a business ends up costing the private economy much more than just one dollar. There are two main reasons why this is the case. *First, the collection of taxes is costly*. The administration, enforcement, and compliance of tax legislation require a sizable volume of resources, including the labor services of many highly skilled experts. The IRS itself employs more than 100,000 people. In addition, an army of bookkeepers, tax accountants, and lawyers is involved in the collection process. According to the Office of Management and Budget, each year individuals and businesses spend more than 6.6 billion hours (the equivalent of 3.3 million full-time year-round workers) keeping records, filling out forms, and learning the tax rules and other elements of the tax-compliance process.[4] More than half of U.S. families now retain tax-preparation firms like H&R Block and Jackson Hewitt to help them file the required forms and comply with the complex rules. Businesses spend roughly $5 billion each year in tax-consulting fees to the four largest accounting firms, to say nothing of the fees paid to other accounting, law, and consulting firms. In total, the resources involved amount to between 3 percent and 4 percent of national income (or 12 to 15 percent of the revenues collected). If these resources were not tied up with the tax-collection process, they could be employed producing goods and services for consumption.

Second, taxes impose an additional burden on the economy because they eliminate some productive exchanges (and cause people to undertake some counterproductive activities). As we noted in Chapter 4, economists refer to this as an *excess burden* (or *deadweight loss*) because it imposes a burden over and above the tax revenue transferred to the government. It results because taxes distort incentives. When buyers pay more and sellers receive less due to the payment of a tax, trade and the production of output become less attractive and decline. Individuals will spend less time on productive (but taxed) market activities and more time on tax avoidance and untaxed activities such as leisure. Research indicates that these deadweight losses add between 9 percent and 16 percent to the cost of taxation.[5] This means that $1 in taxes paid to the government imposes a cost of somewhere between $1.20 and $1.30 on the economy. Thus, the cost of a $100-million government program financed with taxes is really somewhere between $120 million and $130 million. As a result, the government's supply of goods and services generally costs the economy a good bit more than either the size of the tax bill or the level of government spending implies.

When considering the cost of taxation, it is also important to recognize that all taxes are paid by people. Politicians often speak of imposing taxes on "business" as if part of the tax burden could be transferred from individuals to a nonperson (business). This is not the case. Business taxes, like all other taxes, are paid by individuals. A corporation or business firm might write the check to the government, but it merely collects the money from someone else—from its customers in the form of higher prices, its employees in the form of lower wages, or its stockholders in the form of lower dividends—and transfers the money to the government.

---

[4]Office of Management and Budget, *Information Collection Budget of the United States Government,* and Tax Foundation *Special Brief,* by Arthur Hall (March 1996).

[5]The classic article on this topic is Edgar K. Browning, "The Marginal Cost of Public Funds," *Journal of Political Economy* 84, no. 2 (April 1976): 283–98.

ST01-5 HOW HAS THE STRUCTURE OF THE PERSONAL INCOME TAX CHANGED?

The personal income tax is the largest single source of revenue for the federal government. The rate structure of the income tax is progressive; taxpayers with larger incomes face higher tax rates. During the past half century, the structure of the rates has been modified several times. In the early 1960s, there were 24 marginal tax brackets ranging from a low of 20 percent to a high of 91 percent. The Kennedy–Johnson tax cut reduced the lowest marginal rate to 14 percent and the top rate to 70 percent. The rate reductions during the Reagan years cut the top marginal rate initially to 50 percent in 1981 and later to approximately 30 percent during the period 1986–1988. During the 1990s, the top rate was increased to 39.6 percent, but the tax reductions during the administration of George W. Bush rolled back the top rate to 35 percent. The top rate was increased back to 39.6 percent beginning in 2013.

Thus, since the late 1980s, Americans with the highest incomes have paid sharply lower top marginal tax rates—rates in the 30 to 40 percent range, compared to top rates of 91 percent in the early 1960s and 70 percent before 1981. These reductions in the top rate make it tempting to jump to the conclusion that high-income Americans are now getting a free ride—that they now shoulder a smaller share of the personal income tax burden than in the past. But such a conclusion would be fallacious.

Exhibit 4 presents the Internal Revenue Service data on the share of the personal income tax paid by various classes of high-income taxpayers, as well as those in the bottom half of the income distribution, for the years 1963, 1980, 1990, and 2010. These data show that the share of the personal income tax paid by high-income Americans has increased substantially since 1963, and the increase has been particularly sharp since 1980. For example, the top 1 percent of earners paid 37.4 percent of the personal income tax in 2010, up from 19.1 percent in 1980 and 18.3 percent in 1963. The top 10 percent of income recipients paid 70.6 percent of the personal income tax in 2010, compared to 49.3 percent in 1980 and 47 percent in 1963. At the same time, the share of the personal income tax paid by the bottom half of the income recipients has steadily fallen from 10.4 percent of the total in 1963 to 7.1 percent in 1980 and 2.4 percent in 2010.

EXHIBIT 4

Share of Federal Income Taxes Paid by Various Groups, 1963–2010

Even though marginal tax rates have been reduced substantially during the past three decades, upper-income Americans pay a much larger share of the federal income tax today than was previously the case. In 2010, the richest 1 percent of Americans paid 37.4 percent of the federal income tax, up from 18.3 percent in 1963 and 19.1 percent in 1980. The 5 percent of Americans with the highest incomes paid more than half of the personal income tax, whereas the entire bottom half of the income distribution (the bottom 50 percent) paid only 2.4 percent of the total.

| | SHARE OF TOTAL FEDERAL PERSONAL INCOME TAX PAID | | | |
INCOME GROUP	1963	1980	1990	2010
Top 1%	18.3%	19.1%	25.1%	37.4%
Top 5%	35.6%	36.8%	43.6%	59.0%
Top 10%	47.0%	49.3%	55.4%	70.6%
Top 25%	68.8%	73.0%	77.0%	87.1%
Top 50%	89.6%	93.0%	94.2%	97.6%
Bottom 50%	10.4%	7.1%	5.8%	2.4%

Source: Internal Revenue Service (also available online at the Tax Foundation's Web site: www.taxfoundation.org/).

What is going on here? How can one explain the fact that high-income Americans are now paying more of the personal income tax even though their rates are now sharply lower than those in effect before 1981? Two major factors provide the answer. First, when marginal rates are cut by a similar percentage, the "incentive effects" are much greater in the top tax brackets. For example, when the top rate was cut from 91 percent to 70 percent during the Kennedy–Johnson years, high-income taxpayers in this bracket got to keep $30 out of every $100 of additional earnings after the tax cut, compared to only $9 before the rates were reduced. Thus, their incentive to earn additional income increased by a whopping 233 percent (30 minus 9 divided by 9)! Conversely, the rate reduction in the lowest tax bracket from 20 percent to 14 percent meant that the low-income taxpayers in this bracket now got to keep $86 of each additional hundred dollars that they earned compared to $80 before the tax cut. Their incentive to earn increased by a modest 7.5 percent (86 minus 80 divided by 80). Because the rate reductions increased the incentive to earn by much larger amounts in the top tax (and therefore highest-income) brackets, the income base on which high-income Americans were taxed expanded substantially as their rates were reduced. As a result, the tax revenues collected from them declined only modestly. In the very highest brackets, the rate reductions actually increased the revenues collected from high-income Americans. (See Laffer curve analysis of Chapter 4.) In contrast, the incentive effects were much weaker in the lower tax brackets and, as a result, rate reductions led to approximately proportional reductions in revenues collected from low- and middle-income taxpayers. This combination of incentive effects shifts the share of taxes paid toward those with higher incomes, the pattern observed in Exhibit 4.

Second, both the standard deduction and personal exemption have been increased substantially during the last couple of decades. This means that Americans are now able to earn more income before they face any tax liability. In 2010, for example, 48 percent of those filing an income tax return either had zero tax liability or actually received funds from the IRS as the result of the **Earned Income Tax Credit**. This change in the structure of the personal income tax explains why people in the bottom half of income now pay such a small percentage of the personal income tax: 2.4 percent in 2010 compared to 10.4 percent in 1963.[6]

ST01-6 INCOME LEVELS AND OVERALL TAX PAYMENTS

In addition to the personal income tax, the federal government also derives sizable revenues from payroll, corporate income, and excise taxes. How is the overall burden of federal taxes allocated among the various income groups? **Exhibit 5** presents Congressional Budget Office estimates for the average amount of federal taxes paid in 2009 according to income. On average, the top quintile (20 percent) of earners are estimated to pay 23.2 percent of their income in federal taxes. The average federal tax rate for the quintile with the next-highest level of income falls to 15.1 percent, and the average tax rate continues to fall as income declines. The average tax rate of the bottom quintile is 1.0 percent, less than one-twentieth the average rate for the top quintile of earners. Clearly, the federal tax system is highly progressive, meaning that it takes a larger share of the income of those with higher incomes than from those with lower income levels.

Earned Income Tax Credit

A provision of the tax code that provides a credit or rebate to people with low earnings (income from work activities). The credit is eventually phased out if the recipient's earnings increase.

---

[6]The data of Exhibit 4 consider only the tax liability of taxpayers. They do not reflect the payments from IRS to taxpayers as the result of the Earned Income Tax Credit, which was established in the mid-1980s. If these payments to taxpayers were taken into consideration, the net taxes paid by the bottom half of income recipients would have been less than 1 percent. Thus, the data of Exhibit 4 actually understate the reduction in the net share of taxes paid by the bottom half of income recipients during the last two decades.

EXHIBIT 5

Total Federal Taxes as a Share of Income, 2009

Federal taxes are highly progressive. In 2009, federal taxes took 23.2 percent of the income generated by the top quintile (20 percent) of earners, compared to 11.1 percent from the middle-income quintile and 1.0 percent from the lowest quintile of earners.

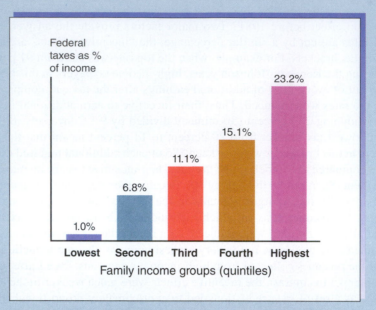

Source: Congressional Budget Office, Average Federal Tax Rates (http://www.cbo.gov/publication/43373). Total federal taxes include income, payroll, and excise taxes.

ST01-7 SIZE OF GOVERNMENT: A CROSS-COUNTRY COMPARISON

There is substantial variation in the size of government across countries. As **Exhibit 6** illustrates, the relative size of government in most other high-income industrial countries is greater than that of the United States. In 2011, government spending summed to more than 50 percent of the economies of Denmark, France, Belgium, Greece, and Austria. Government spending as a share of the economy in Japan and Canada was similar to that of the United States, about 41 percent. Interestingly, the size of government was substantially smaller in South Korea, Singapore, Thailand, and Hong Kong—four Asian nations that have achieved rapid growth and substantial increases in living standards during the last four decades.

ST01-8 HOW DOES THE SIZE OF GOVERNMENT AFFECT ECONOMIC GROWTH?

Throughout this text, we have analyzed how governments influence the efficiency of resource use and the growth of income. It is clear that a legal environment that protects people and their property and provides for the impartial enforcement of contracts is vitally important. So, too, is a monetary and regulatory environment that provides the foundation for the smooth operation of markets. As we discussed in Chapter 5, there are also a few goods—economists call them *public goods*—that may be difficult to provide through markets. National defense, roads, and flood-control projects provide examples. Because they generate joint benefits and it is difficult to limit their availability to paying customers, sometimes they can be provided more efficiently through government. But public goods are rare, and the market can often devise reasonably efficient methods of dealing with them. If resources are going to be allocated efficiently, government spending on provision of public goods will generally be only a small share of the economy.

As governments expand beyond these core functions, however, the beneficial effects wane and eventually become negative as government moves into areas ill suited for political action

EXHIBIT 6

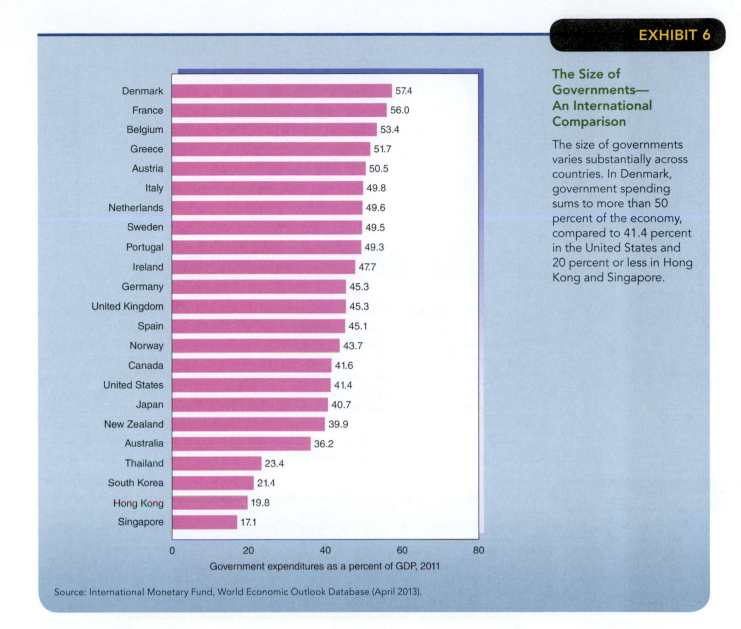

The Size of Governments— An International Comparison

The size of governments varies substantially across countries. In Denmark, government spending sums to more than 50 percent of the economy, compared to 41.4 percent in the United States and 20 percent or less in Hong Kong and Singapore.

Government expenditures as a percent of GDP, 2011

Source: International Monetary Fund, World Economic Outlook Database (April 2013).

and in which the political process works poorly. Thus, expansion of government activities beyond a certain point will eventually exert a negative impact on the economy. **Exhibit 7** illustrates the implications with regard to the expected relationship between the size of government and economic growth, *assuming that governments undertake activities based on their rate of return.* As the size of government, measured on the horizontal axis, expands from zero (complete anarchy), initially the growth rate of the economy—measured on the vertical axis— increases. The *A* to *B* range of the curve illustrates this situation. As government continues to grow as a share of the economy, expenditures are channeled into less-productive (and later counterproductive) activities, causing the rate of economic growth to diminish and eventually to decline. The range of the curve beyond *B* illustrates this point.[7] Thus, our analysis indicates that there is a set of activities and size of government that will maximize economic growth. Expansion of government beyond (and outside of) these functions will retard growth.

How large is the growth-maximizing size of government? Do large governments actually retard economic growth? These are complex questions, but they have been addressed

---

[7]In the real world, governments may not undertake activities based on their rate of return and comparative advantage. Many governments that are small relative to the size of the economy fail to focus on the core activities that are likely to enhance economic growth. Thus, one would expect that the relationship between size of government and economic growth will be a loose one.

EXHIBIT 7

Economic Growth Curve and Government Size

If a government undertakes activities in the order of their productivity, its expenditures will promote economic growth (the growth rate will move from A to B). Additional expenditures, however, will eventually retard growth (the growth rate will move along the curve to the right of B).

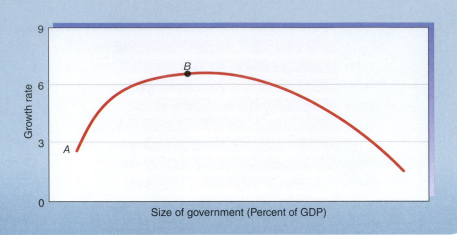

by several researchers. **Exhibit 8** sheds light on these issues. This exhibit presents data on the relationship between size of government (*x*-axis) and economic growth (*y*-axis) for the twenty-three long-standing members of the Organisation for Economic Co-operation and Development (OECD). The exhibit contains five dots (observations) for each of the 23 countries—one for each of the five decades during the period 1960–2009. Thus, there are 115 total dots. Each dot represents a country's total government spending as a share of GDP *at the beginning of the decade* and its accompanying growth of real GDP *during that decade*. Government expenditures ranged from a low of about 15 percent of GDP in some countries to a high of more than 60 percent in others. As the plotted line in the exhibit shows, there is an observable negative relationship between size of government and long-term real GDP growth.

EXHIBIT 8

Government Spending and Economic Growth Among the Twenty-Three OECD Countries: 1960–2009

Here we show the relationship between size of government and the growth of real GDP for the 23 longtime OECD members during each decade since 1960. The data indicate that a 10 percent increase in government expenditures as a share of GDP reduces the annual rate of growth by approximately 1 percent. The data also imply that the size of government in these countries is beyond the range that maximizes economic growth.

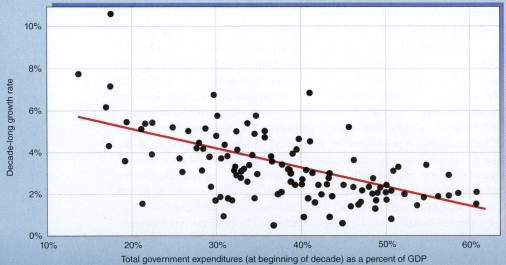

Source: OECD, OECD *Economic Outlook* (various issues), and the World Bank, *World Development Indicators* (various issues).

Countries with higher levels of government spending grew less rapidly. The line drawn through the points of Exhibit 9 indicates that a 10-percentage-point increase in government expenditures as a share of GDP leads to approximately a 1-percentage-point reduction in economic growth.[8]

Time series data for specific countries have also been used to investigate the link between size of government and growth. Edgar Peden estimates that for the United States, the "maximum productivity growth occurs when government expenditures represent about 20% of GDP." Gerald Scully estimates that the growth-maximizing size of government (combined federal, state, and local) is between 21.5 percent and 22.9 percent of the economy. Although the methodology of these studies differs, they do have one thing in common: They indicate that in the ranges observed, high levels of government spending tend to retard economic growth.[9] They also indicate that the size and scope of most governments around the world are larger than the size that would maximize the income growth of their citizens. Moreover, the estimates imply that the recent expansion in the size of the government sector in the United States is likely to reduce the growth of income in the years immediately ahead.

ST01-9 EXPENDITURES, TAXES, DEBT FINANCE, AND DEMOCRACY

Exhibit 9 presents data on the percent of persons age 18 and older with and without a personal income tax liability. During the quarter of a century before 2000, the share of

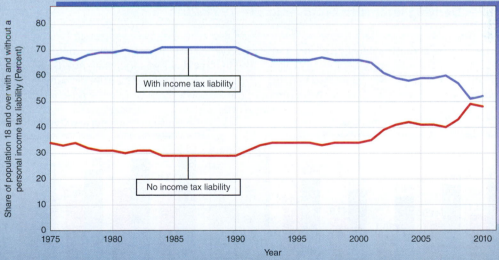

EXHIBIT 9

Share of Population 18 and Older with and without a Personal Income Tax Liability

The percent of the population age 18 and older with and without a personal income tax liability is shown here. Note how the share paying income taxes fluctuated between 66 percent and 71 percent throughout 1975–2000. Over the same period, the share with no income tax liability was about one-third of the adult population. Since 2003, however, 60 percent or less have had an income tax liability. In 2010, 52 percent of Americans had an income tax liability, while 48 percent did not.

Source: Internal Revenue Service and *Economic Report of the President* (various issues). The number of persons with an income tax liability was derived by summing (1) the joint returns with a tax liability times two and (2) the number of individual returns with a tax liability. This figure was then divided by the population age 18 and older to derive the percentage of the 18 and older population with a tax liability.

[8]For additional information on the relationship between size of government and growth, see James Gwartney, Robert Lawson, and Randall Holcombe, "The Scope of Government and the Wealth of Nations," *The Cato Journal* (Fall 1998): 163–90.

[9]See Edgar Peden, "Productivity in the United States and Its Relationship to Government Activity: An Analysis of 57 Years, 1929–1986," *Public Choice* 69 (1991): 153–73; and Gerald Scully, *What Is the Optimal Size of Government in the United States?* (Dallas, TX: National Center for Policy Analysis, 1994).

Americans paying income taxes fluctuated within a narrow range between 66 percent and 71 percent. However, the share paying income taxes has declined sharply during the past decade. Since 2003, 60 percent or less has had an income tax liability. In 2010, only 52 percent of Americans paid any federal income tax.

On the other hand, the percent of the population paying no income tax has risen sharply. Throughout 1975–2000, approximately one-third of Americans had no income tax liability. But the legislation passed under the administration of George W. Bush increased the "no tax" income threshold and doubled the child tax credit. These changes eliminated the income tax liability of many Americans. By 2010, nearly half of the population (48 percent) paid no income taxes. While many without an income tax liability are responsible for payroll taxes, the payroll tax is directed toward only two programs: Social Security and Medicare. Thus, payroll taxes do not contribute to the finance of government in other areas.

While the share of people paying taxes has declined sharply since 2000, the share benefiting from transfers has been rising. However, a little more than half of American families derive income from transfer programs. As **Exhibit 10** shows, the percent of families receiving transfers from at least one program fell from 54.1 in 1991 to 49.5 percent in 2000, but the figure has risen during the past decade, reaching 55.7 percent in 2011. When income from government employment is included, approximately two-thirds of all families benefit from government spending. In 2011, 64.3 percent of families derived income from either transfer programs or government employment. If the people employed by businesses with government contracts and those receiving subsidies (for example, the producers of ethanol, sugar and several other agricultural products, and wind and solar energy) were also included, the share of Americans heavily dependent on government would be even larger.

One might think that the large share of Americans receiving transfers is driven by the Medicare and Social Security retirement programs. In order to shed light on this issue, the

---

EXHIBIT 10

Share of Families Deriving Income from Government, 1991–2011

More than half of American families derive income from transfer programs. The percent of families receiving transfers from at least one program fell from 54.1 in 1991 to 49.5 percent in 2000, but by 2011 the figure had risen to 55.7 percent. When income from government employment is also included, 64.3 percent of American families now derive income from the government. When only families with individuals younger than age 62 are included, the percentage receiving transfers is somewhat lower, but the pattern over the past two decades is the same.

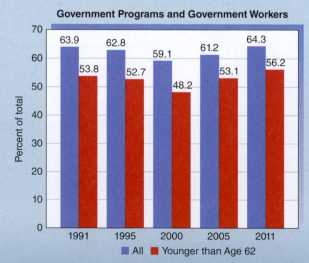

Source: These figures were derived from the Current Population Survey data. The following income transfers were included: Medicare, Medicaid, food stamps, unemployment compensation, school lunch program, housing subsidies, Social Security, and welfare.

share receiving transfers for families with only individuals younger than the age of 62 was derived. The pattern for this group was essentially the same as for all families. In 1991, 43.1 percent of the younger family group were recipients of transfer payments. While this figure declined to 36.1 percent in 2000, by 2011 it rebounded to 45.6 percent. When government employees are included, more than one-half of the families with individuals younger than 62 derived income from the government.

What are the implications of these patterns of tax payments and government spending? People who are not paying taxes have little reason to resist increases in government spending because they are not paying for them. In fact, they have every incentive to pressure politicians for more government services and transfers because someone else will be covering their cost. Similarly, people who are dependent on government spending for a sizable share of their income will be more supportive of government spending than those who derive their income from private-sector activities.

Debt financing is also related to the observed pattern of taxing and spending. Borrowing makes it possible for politicians to provide voters with current benefits without having to impose a parallel visible cost in the form of higher taxes. This enables elected officials to increase the number of people dependent on government spending without having to increase current taxes.

To a large degree, the modern democratic political process has become a game in which politicians seek to use the fiscal powers of government to assemble a political majority. Is this a dangerous trend that may undermine democracy and lead to fiscal collapse? Eighteenth-century Scottish philosopher Alexander Tytler warned of this possibility:

A democracy cannot exist as a permanent form of government. It can only exist until the voters discover that they can vote themselves largesse from the public treasury. From that moment on, the majority always votes for the candidates promising the most benefits from the public treasury with the result that a democracy always collapses over loose fiscal policy.[10]

Is Tytler correct? Are the spending, taxing, and debt financing policies of the United States taking the country down a dangerous path? We do not know the answer to this question, but there are some troubling signs.

Measured as a share of GDP, total government expenditures are now about 7 percentage points higher than during the 1990s. During 2009 and 2010, the federal government financed approximately 40 percent of its expenditures by borrowing. The huge deficits of recent years have pushed the federal debt to nearly 100 percent of GDP, a level not seen since the aftermath of World War II. Moreover, the unfunded future benefits promised to senior citizens under the Social Security and Medicare programs are another form of debt, and these liabilities are more than two times the size of the official national debt. As the baby boomers move into the retirement phase of life during the next decade, if Social Security and Medicare are not reformed, then spending on these programs will far outstrip the revenues for their finance.

Several members of the European Union (EU), including Greece, Portugal, Italy, and Spain, now confront exceedingly high debt levels and prior commitments to voters that make it difficult for them to reduce government spending. To date, other EU countries with marginally stronger government finances have been willing to provide emergency loans and other assistance. But this is not a long-run solution. The United States appears to be headed down the same path. There are steps that could be taken, but special interest politics and the myopic nature of the political process may make them untenable. We are in the midst of an interesting, though unattractive, experiment in political economy as Western democracies face troubled fiscal waters in the years immediately ahead.

---

[10]Some attribute this statement to Lord Thomas Macaulay. The author cannot be verified with certainty. For additional information on this topic, see Loren Collins, "The Truth About Tytler" at www.lorencollins.net/tytler.html.

KEY POINTS

- During the first 125 years of U.S. history, federal expenditures per person were small and grew at a relatively slow rate. But the size and nature of government has changed dramatically during the past 100 years. Today, the real (adjusted for inflation) spending per person of the federal government is roughly 80 times the level of 1916.

- During the last five decades, the composition of federal spending has shifted away from national defense and toward spending on income transfers and health care.

- As the size of government has grown, taxes have increased. Taxes impose a burden on the economy over and above the revenue transferred to the government because of (1) the administration and compliance costs and (2) the deadweight losses that accompany taxation.

- Overall, the federal tax system of the United States is highly progressive. Taxes as a percentage of income are approximately twenty times greater for the top quintile (20 percent) of families than for the bottom quintile.

- The size of government of the United States is smaller than that of the major Western European countries but is larger than for a number of high-growth Asian economies.

- When governments focus on the core activities of providing (1) a legal and enforcement structure that protects people and their property from aggression by others and (2) a limited set of public goods, they promote economic growth. However, when governments grow beyond this size, expanding into activities for which they are ill suited, they deter growth.

- More than half of American families derive benefits from various transfer programs, while the share of the population paying federal income tax has declined substantially during the past decade. Moreover, large budget deficits have pushed the debt to GDP ratio to levels not seen since the aftermath of World War II. These factors, along with upward pressure on expenditures for Social Security and Medicare as the baby-boomers retire, will make it very difficult to control federal finances. Thus, the United States confronts a troublesome fiscal future in the years immediately ahead.

CRITICAL ANALYSIS QUESTIONS

1. *How do taxes influence the efficiency of resource use? How much does it cost for the government to raise an additional dollar (or $1 billion) of tax revenue?

2. During the past five decades, there has been a shift in the composition of the federal budget toward more spending on income transfers and health care and a smaller share for national defense. Does economics indicate that this change will help Americans achieve higher living standards? Discuss.

3. Because the structure of the personal income tax is progressive, a larger share of income is taxed at higher rates as real income increases. Therefore, economic growth automatically results in higher taxes unless offsetting legislative action is taken. Do you think this is an attractive feature of the current tax system? Why or why not?

4. Compared with the situation before 1981, the marginal tax rates imposed on individuals and families with high incomes are now lower. What was the top marginal personal income tax rate in 1980? What is the top rate now? Are you in favor of or opposed to the lower marginal rates? Why?

5. *As the result of changes during the last two decades, the bottom half of income recipients now pay little or no personal income tax. Rather than paying taxes, many of them now receive payments back from the IRS as the result of the Earned Income Tax Credit and Child Tax Credit programs. Do you think the increase in the number of people who pay no taxes will affect the efficiency of the political process? Why or why not?

6. How have the size and functions of government changed during the last two centuries? Did the framers of the U.S. Constitution seek to limit the size of the federal government? If so, how?

7. Can democracy survive if a majority of the citizenry pay little or nothing in taxes while benefiting directly from a higher level of government spending? Why or why not? Discuss.

*Asterisk denotes questions for which answers are given in Appendix B.

SPECIAL TOPIC 2
The Economics of Social Security

FOCUS

- Why will the Social Security program confront problems in the near future?

- Will the Social Security Trust Fund make it easier to pay the promised benefits to future retirees?

- Does Social Security transfer income from the rich to the poor? How does it impact the economic status of blacks, Hispanics, and those with fewer years of life expectancy?

- Does the Social Security system need to be modernized?

Over the next 30 years, the retirement of the baby-boom generation will pose new challenges for the Social Security program, the federal government, and the U.S. economy.
—Dan Crippen[1]

[1]Dan Crippen, Statement of Congressional Budget Office Director, before the Special Committee on Aging, United States Senate, December 10, 2001

The Social Security program in the United States is officially known as Old Age and Survivors Insurance (OASI). It is designed to provide the elderly with a flow of income during retirement. In spite of its official title, Social Security is not based on principles of insurance. Private insurance and pension programs invest the current payments of customers in buildings, farms, or other real assets. Alternatively, they buy stocks and bonds that finance the development of real assets. These real assets generate income that allows the pension fund (or insurance company) to fulfill its future obligations to its customers.

Social Security does not follow this savings-and-investment model. Instead, it taxes current workers and uses the revenues to finance benefits for existing retirees. There is no buildup of productive assets that the federal government can use to fund the future benefits promised today's workers. When current workers retire, their promised Social Security benefits will have to come from taxes levied on future generations. *In essence, Social Security is an intergenerational income-transfer program.* The system is based on "pay as you go" rather than on the savings-and-investment principle.

The Social Security retirement program is financed by a flat-rate payroll tax of 10.6 percent applicable to employee earnings up to a cutoff level. In 2013, the earnings cutoff was $113,700. Thus, employees earning $113,700 or more paid $12,052 in Social Security taxes to finance the OASI retirement program.[2] The income cutoff is adjusted upward each year by the growth rate of nominal wages. Whereas the payroll tax is divided equally between employee and employer, it is clearly part of the employees' compensation package, and most economists believe that the burden of this tax falls primarily on the employee. The formula used to determine retirement benefits favors those with lower earnings during their working years. However, as we will discuss later, the redistributive effects toward those with lower incomes are more apparent than real.

When the program began in 1935, not many people lived past age 65, and the nation had lots of workers and few eligible retirees. As **Exhibit 1** illustrates, there were 16.5 workers for every Social Security beneficiary in 1950. That ratio has declined sharply through the years. As a result, higher and

EXHIBIT 1

Workers per Social Security Beneficiary

In 1950, there were 16.5 workers per Social Security beneficiary. By 2010, the figure had fallen to just 2.9. By 2030, there will be only 2.2 workers per retiree. As the worker–beneficiary ratio falls under a pay-as-you-go system, either taxes must be increased or benefits must be reduced (or both).

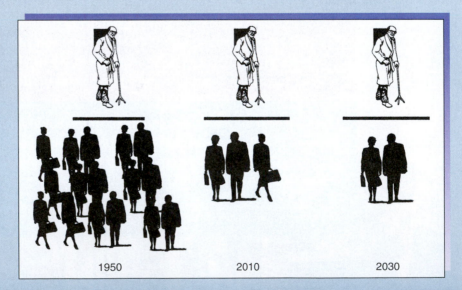

1950   2010   2030

Source: 2013 Annual Report of the Board of Trustees of the Federal Old Age and Survivors Insurance and Disability Insurance Trust Funds (Washington, DC: Government Printing Office, 2013), p. 55.

---

[2]Additional payroll taxes are levied for the finance of disability programs (1.8 percent) and Medicare (2.9 percent). Thus, the total payroll tax sums to 15.3 percent, but only revenues from the 10.6 percent rate are used for the finance of benefits to retirees and surviving dependents. (*Note:* The earnings cutoff does not apply to the Medicare portion of the payroll tax.)

higher taxes per worker have been required just to maintain a constant level of benefits. There are currently 2.9 workers per Social Security retiree. By 2030, however, that figure will decline to only 2.2.

When there were many workers per beneficiary, it was possible to provide retirees with generous benefits while maintaining a relatively low rate of taxation. Many of those who retired in the 1960s and 1970s received real benefits of three or four times the amount they paid into the system, far better than they could have done had they invested the funds privately. The era of high returns, however, is now over. The program has matured, and the number of workers per beneficiary has declined. Payroll taxes have risen greatly over the decades, and still higher taxes will be necessary merely to fund currently promised benefits.

Studies indicate that those now age 40 and younger can expect to earn a real rate of return of about 2 percent on their Social Security tax dollars, substantially less than what they could earn from personal investments. Thus, Social Security has been a good deal for current and past retirees. It is not, however, a very good deal for today's middle-aged and younger workers.

ST02-1 WHY IS SOCIAL SECURITY HEADED FOR PROBLEMS?

The flow of funds into and out of a pay-as-you-go retirement system is sensitive to demographic conditions. The Social Security system enjoyed a period of highly favorable demographics between 1990 and 2010. The U.S. birthrate was low during the Great Depression and World War II. As this relatively small generation moved into the retirement phase of life during 1990–2010, the number of Social Security beneficiaries grew slowly. At the same time, the large baby-boom generation born following World War II was working and pushing the revenues flowing into the system upward. Thus, the payments to Social Security recipients increased at a modest rate, while the tax revenues grew rapidly during the two decades following 1990.

However, as **Exhibit 2** shows, the situation is going to change dramatically in the years immediately ahead. The retirement of the large baby-boom generation, along with rising life expectancies, will lead to a rapid increase in senior citizens during the next two decades. The number of people age 65 years and older will soar from 40 million in 2010 to 71 million in 2030. As a result, the number of workers per Social Security retiree will fall from today's 2.9 to only 2.2 in 2030.

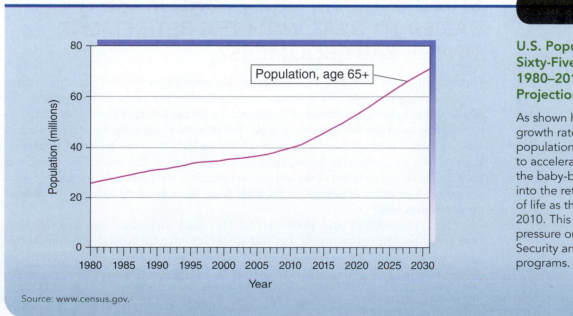

EXHIBIT 2

U.S. Population Age Sixty-Five and Older, 1980–2010, and Projections to 2030

As shown here, the growth rate of the elderly population will continue to accelerate rapidly as the baby-boomers move into the retirement phase of life as they have since 2010. This will place strong pressure on both the Social Security and Medicare programs.

Source: www.census.gov.

The Forthcoming Deficit between Payroll Tax Revenues and Benefit Expenditures

Given current payroll taxes and retirement benefit levels, the system will run larger and larger deficits during the 2010–2030 period and beyond.

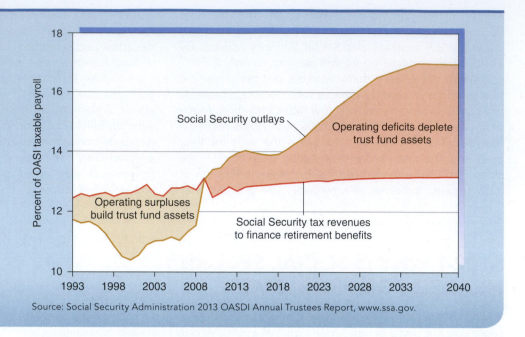

Source: Social Security Administration 2013 OASDI Annual Trustees Report, www.ssa.gov.

Exhibit 3 illustrates the impact of these demographic changes on the pay-as-you-go Social Security system. Between 1984 and 2009, the funds flowing into the system (pushed up by the large baby-boom generation) exceeded the expenditures on benefits to retirees (pulled down by the small Great Depression/World War II generation). But the retirement of the baby-boomers that began in 2010 will push the future expenditures of the system upward at a rapid rate. The deficit of revenues from the payroll tax relative to retirement benefits will grow larger and larger as the number of beneficiaries relative to workers continues to grow in the decades ahead.

What happened to the 1984–2009 surpluses of Social Security receipts relative to expenditures? Congress spent the surpluses, and the U.S. Treasury issued a special type of IOU, nonmarketable bonds, into the Social Security Trust Fund (SSTF). The future deficits of the system will draw down these bonds and are projected to deplete them by 2033.

ST02-2 WILL THE TRUST FUND MAKE IT EASIER TO DEAL WITH THE RETIREMENT OF THE BABY-BOOMERS?

Perhaps surprising to some, the answer to this question is "No." Unlike the bonds, stocks, and physical assets of a private pension fund or insurance company, the SSTF bonds will not generate a stream of future income for the federal government. Congress has already spent the funds, so there is no "pot of money" set aside for the payment of future benefits. Instead, the trust fund bonds are an IOU from one government agency, the Treasury, to another, the Social Security Administration. The federal government is both the payee and recipient of the interest and principal represented by the SSTF bonds. *No matter how many bonds are in the trust fund, their net asset value to the federal government is zero!*

Thus, the number of IOUs in the trust fund is largely irrelevant.[3] The size of the trust fund could be doubled or tripled, but that would not give the federal government any

---

[3]Of course, the SSTF bonds represent funds borrowed by the Treasury from the Social Security system. This increases the legitimacy of claims on these funds by future Social Security recipients. It also indicates that the trust fund is similar to what is called *budget authority*, which provides the legal permission for the government to spend funds on an item.

additional funds for the payment of benefits. Correspondingly, the trust fund could be abolished and the government would not be relieved of any of its existing obligations or commitments. In order to redeem the bonds and thereby provide the Social Security system with funds to cover future deficits, the federal government will have to raise taxes, cut other expenditures, or borrow from the public. Neither the presence nor the absence of the trust fund will alter these options.

As we indicated in Chapter 6, politicians have an incentive both to spend on programs providing highly visible benefits and conceal the burden of taxes. The Social Security Trust Fund has helped them do this. During the last two decades, the government has spent the entire surplus and even borrowed beyond these amounts. Moreover, as Congress and several presidents were spending the surpluses on current programs, most political leaders projected the view that funds were being set aside for the future retirement of the baby-boomers. Given the structure of political incentives, this art of deception should not be surprising.

ST02-3 THE REAL PROBLEM CREATED BY THE CURRENT SYSTEM

The payroll tax revenues flowing into the Social Security system are now less than the benefits paid out to current retirees, and this deficit will become larger and larger throughout the next two decades. Under current law, revenues will be sufficient to pay only about three-quarters of promised benefits by 2030, and less in later years. If benefits are reduced, then current beneficiaries and people near retirement will—quite understandably—feel that a commitment made to them has been broken.

There are only four ways to cover future shortfalls: (1) cut benefits, (2) increase taxes, (3) cut spending in other areas, or (4) borrow. None of these options is attractive, and, regardless of how the gap is filled, there is likely to be an adverse impact on the economy. Moreover, not even robust economic growth will eliminate the future shortfall. Retirement benefits are indexed to average growth in nominal wages. If higher productivity enables *real* (inflation-adjusted) wages to rise quickly, so will future Social Security benefits. For example, if inflation is zero and real wages start growing at 2 percent a year instead of their previous level of 1 percent, then the formula used to calculate Social Security benefits will also begin to push those benefits up more rapidly. Higher economic growth may temporarily improve Social Security's finances, but under current law the improvement will not last.[4]

ST02-4 DOES SOCIAL SECURITY HELP THE POOR?

Social Security has gained many supporters because of the belief that it redistributes wealth from the rich to the poor. The system is financed with a flat tax rate up to the cutoff limit, but the formula used to calculate benefits disproportionately favors workers with low lifetime earnings.[5] However, other aspects of the system tend to favor those with

---

[4]See Garth Davis, "Faster Economic Growth Will Not Solve the Social Security Crisis," Heritage Center for Data Analysis (February 3, 2000).

[5]Retirement benefits are based on the best 35 years of earnings from a worker's career. Benefits are calculated by taking 90 percent of the first $9,492 a year of earnings, 32 percent of earnings between $9,492 and $57,216, and just 15 percent of earnings above $57,216 up to the earnings cutoff of $113,700. Therefore, as base earnings rise, benefits fall as a percentage of average earnings (and payroll taxes paid) during one's lifetime. For example, the retirement benefits of people with base annual earnings of $10,000 sum to 87 percent of their average working year earnings. In contrast, the retirement benefits of those with base earnings of $60,000 are only 40 percent of their average pre-retirement earnings. These figures are based on the formula for 2013. The figures are adjusted each year for the growth of nominal wages.

higher incomes. First, workers with more education and high earnings tend to live longer than those with less education and lower earnings. As **Exhibit 4** shows, the age-adjusted mortality rate of people with less than a high school education is 8 to 10 percent higher than the average for all Americans. As years of schooling increase, mortality rates fall. The age-adjusted mortality rate of college graduates is 21 percent below the average for all Americans, whereas the rate for people with advanced degrees is 32 percent below the average. Given the strong correlation between education and earnings, the age-adjusted mortality figures indicate that, on average, Americans with higher earnings live longer than their counterparts with less education and lower earnings. As a result, high-wage workers will, on average, draw Social Security benefits for a longer period of time than will low-wage workers. Correspondingly, low-wage workers are far more likely to pay thousands of dollars in Social Security taxes and then die before, or soon after, becoming eligible for retirement benefits.

Second, low-wage workers generally begin full-time work at a younger age. Many work full time and pay Social Security taxes for years, while future high-wage workers are still in college and graduate school. Low-wage workers generally pay more into the system earlier and therefore forgo more interest than do high-wage workers.

Third, labor participation tends to fall as spousal earnings increase. As a result, couples with a high-wage worker are more likely to gain from Social Security's spousal benefit provision, which provides the nonworking spouse with benefits equal to 50 percent of those the working spouse receives.

Two recent studies taking these and other related factors into consideration suggest that Social Security may actually transfer wealth from low-wage to high-wage workers. A research project using data from the Social Security Administration and the Health and Retirement Study found that when Social Security benefits are assessed for family units rather than for individuals, the progressivity of the system disappears. Another study adjusted for differences in mortality rates, patterns of lifetime income, and other factors. It found that if a 2 percent real interest rate (discount rate) is used to evaluate the pattern of taxes paid and benefits received, the redistributive effects of Social Security

EXHIBIT 4

Mortality Rates by Level of Education

As shown here, the age-adjusted mortality rates are lower for those with more education. Because of the close link between education and income, people with higher incomes tend to live longer and, therefore, draw Social Security benefits for a lengthier time period than those with less education and income.

Age-adjusted mortality rate

+8%   +10%   +9%   +9%

U.S. average

−4%

−8%

−21%

−32%

| 0–4 | 5–7 | 8 | 1–3 | 4 | 1–3 | 4 | |
| — Elementary — | — High school — | — College — | Graduate school |

——————— Highest grade completed ———————

Source: Center for Data Analysis, Heritage Foundation.

are essentially neutral. However, at a more realistic 4 percent real interest rate, Social Security actually favors higher-income households.[6]

ST02-5 SOCIAL SECURITY AND THE TREATMENT OF BLACKS AND WORKING MARRIED WOMEN

When Social Security was established in 1935, the population was growing rapidly, only a few Americans lived to age 65, and the labor-force participation rate of married women was very low. Social Security was designed for this world. But today's world is dramatically different. Several aspects of the system now seem outdated, arbitrary, and in some cases, unfair. Let's consider a couple of these factors.

ST02-5a SOCIAL SECURITY ADVERSELY AFFECTS BLACKS AND OTHER GROUPS WITH BELOW-AVERAGE LIFE EXPECTANCY

Currently, the average retiree reaching age 65 can expect to spend 18 years receiving Social Security benefits, after more than 40 years of paying into the system. But what about those who do not make it into their eighties or even to the normal retirement age of 65? Unlike private financial assets, Social Security benefits cannot be passed on to heirs. Thus, those who die before age 65 or soon thereafter receive little or nothing from their payroll tax payments.

Social Security was not set up to transfer income from some ethnic groups to others, but under its current structure it nonetheless does so. Because of the shorter life expectancy of blacks, the Social Security system adversely affects their economic welfare. Compared with whites and Hispanics, blacks are far more likely to pay a lifetime of payroll taxes and then die without receiving much in the way of benefits. Thus, the system works to their disadvantage. In contrast, Social Security is particularly favorable to Hispanics because of their above-average life expectancy and the progressive nature of the benefit formula. As a result, Hispanics derive a higher return than whites and substantially higher than blacks.[7]

Exhibit 5 presents the expected real returns for those born in 1975, according to gender, marital status, and ethnicity.[8] Single black males born in 1975 can expect to derive a real annual return of negative 1.3 percent on their Social Security tax payments, compared with returns of 0.2 percent for single white males and 1.6 percent for single Hispanic males. Similarly, a two-earner black couple born in 1975 can expect a real return of 0.5 percent, compared with returns

---

[6]See Alan Gustman and Thomas Steinmeier, "How Effective Is Redistribution under the Social Security Benefit Formula?" *Journal of Public Economics* 82 (October 2001): 1–28; and Julia Lynn Coronado, Don Fullerton, and Thomas Glass, "Long Run Effects of Social Security Reform Proposals on Lifetime Progressivity," in Martin Feldstein and Jeffrey B. Liebman, eds., *The Distributional Aspects of Social Security and Social Security Reform* (Chicago: University of Chicago Press, 2002).

[7]For additional details on the redistributive effects of Social Security across ethnic groups, see William W. Beach and Gareth Davis, "More for Your Money: Improving Social Security's Rate of Return," in David C. John, ed., *Improving Retirement Security: A Handbook for Reformers* (Washington, DC: Heritage Foundation, 2000), 25–64; and Martin Feldstein and Jeffrey Liebman, "The Distributional Effects of an Investment-Based Social Security System," in Martin Feldstein and Jeffrey B. Liebman, eds., *The Distributional Aspects of Social Security and Social Security Reform* (Chicago: University of Chicago Press, 2002).

[8]It is common to calculate a rate of return on financial investments by comparing initial investments with the stream of projected future income (or benefits). Social Security is not like a regular financial investment because there is no accumulation of assets and no legal right to benefits. Nonetheless, a rate of return can be calculated by comparing the payroll taxes a worker pays with the future benefits he or she is promised. The rate-of-return figures of Exhibit 5 were derived in this manner. They assume that the current tax level and promised future benefits will be maintained. However, as we noted, projections indicate that current tax rates will cover only about three-fourths of promised benefits by 2030. Thus, higher taxes will be required to maintain the promised benefit levels. In turn, the higher taxes will lower rates of return. Therefore, the figures of Exhibit 5 probably overstate the rates of return for the various groups.

Rates of Return by Gender, Marital Status, and Ethnicity

The earnings of blacks are lower than whites, but blacks have a shorter life expectancy. The latter effect dominates, and therefore blacks derive a lower rate of return from Social Security than whites. In contrast, Hispanics have both lower earnings and a little longer life expectancy than whites. Thus, their returns from Social Security are higher than whites and substantially higher than blacks.

Source: Center for Data Analysis, Heritage Foundation

of 1.2 percent and 2.3 percent for white and Hispanic couples born during the same year. A similar pattern exists when comparisons are made for those born in other years.

The Social Security retirement system also works to the disadvantage of those with life-shortening diseases. People with diabetes, heart disease, AIDS, and other diseases often spend decades paying 10.6 percent of their earnings into the system only to die with loved ones unable to receive benefits from the Social Security taxes they have paid. (People with life-shortening diseases may receive disability insurance, but if they die before retirement they collect nothing from their payments into the retirement system.)

ST02-5b DISCRIMINATION AGAINST MARRIED WOMEN IN THE WORKFORCE

When Social Security was established, relatively few married women worked outside the home. Therefore, individuals were permitted to receive benefits based on either their own earnings or 50 percent of the benefits earned by their spouse, whichever is greater. This provision imposes a heavy penalty on married women in the workforce. In the case of many working married women, the benefits based on the earnings of their spouses are approximately equal to, or in some cases greater than, benefits based on their own earnings. Thus, the payroll tax takes a big chunk of their earnings without providing them with any significant additional benefits.

ST02-6 IS THE STRUCTURE OF SOCIAL SECURITY SUITABLE FOR THE TWENTY-FIRST CENTURY?

When the number of retirees grows more rapidly than the number of workers, pay-as-you-go financing does not work well. The return retirees can expect from their tax payments into the system will be low. As we mentioned, today's typical worker can expect a return of only 2.0 percent from the taxes paid into the Social Security system. By way of comparison, stock market investments have averaged a real return of approximately 7 percent annually for more than a century. Furthermore, when regular investments are made into a diverse holding of

THE WIZARD OF ID

stocks, the variation in the return has been relatively low.[9] Mutual funds now make it feasible for even a small novice investor to invest in a diverse stock portfolio while still keeping administrative costs low. (See Special Topic 3, a feature on the stock market.)

As a result of the changing demographics, the Social Security and Medicare programs now confront huge **unfunded liabilities**, shortfalls between promised future benefits and the revenues that can be expected at current tax rates. The trustees of these two programs project that the unfunded liability of Social Security is $12 trillion, whereas that of Medicare is estimated to be $27 trillion.[10] The sum of these figures is more than three times the current size of the U.S. economy. Predictably, deteriorating financial conditions will lead politicians to look for ways of dealing with this situation. Thus, a combination of factors—low returns from Social Security, a structure that seems outdated, and deteriorating financial conditions—may virtually force Congress to seriously consider modifications in the future.

From an economic viewpoint, the most viable option would be some form of **personal retirement accounts (PRAs)** that would incorporate savings and investment into the financing of retirement. In varying degrees, several countries have already moved in this direction. Beginning in the early 1980s, Chile shifted to a retirement system based on saving and investing through PRAs rather than pay as you go. The Chilean plan was so successful that other Latin American countries, including Mexico, Bolivia, Columbia, and Peru, adopted similar plans in the 1990s. High-income countries have also moved in this direction. In 1986, the United Kingdom began allowing workers to channel 4.6 percentage points of their payroll tax into PRAs in exchange for acceptance of a lower level of benefits from the pay-as-you-go system. The PRA option is currently chosen by nearly three-fourths of British workers. Other countries that now permit at least some substitution of PRAs for payroll taxes and pay-as-you-go benefits include Netherlands, Australia, Sweden, Hungary, Poland, and Germany.

Ownership rights exert a powerful impact on incentives. Personal retirement accounts would provide workers with a property right to the funds contributed into their accounts. The funds paid into a PRA could be passed along to heirs. In contrast with higher taxes, payments into a personally owned investment account that would enhance one's retirement income would not exert a harmful impact on the incentive to work and earn. Furthermore, PRAs would encourage saving and investment, which would help to promote economic growth. They would also reduce the dependency of senior citizens on political officials. There are numerous ways to structure personal retirement accounts. Several plans have already been put forth, and others are sure to arise in the future.

Political debate about the structure of Social Security and how to plan for retirement will continue in the years ahead. This debate is particularly important for younger people because the way it is handled will exert a major impact on their future tax liability and the quality of their life during retirement.

Unfunded liability
A shortfall of tax revenues at current rates relative to promised benefits for a program. Without an increase in tax rates, the promised benefits cannot be funded fully.

Personal retirement account (PRAs)
An account that is owned personally by an individual in his or her name. The funds in the account could be passed along to heirs.

---

[9]See Liqun Liu, Andrew J. Rettenmaier, and Zijun Wang, "Social Security and Stock Market Risk" (NCPA Policy Report No. 244, National Center for Policy Analysis, July 23, 2001).

[10]See *2013 Annual Report of the Boards of Trustees of the Federal Hospital Insurance and Federal Supplementary Medical Insurance Trust Fund*, www.cms.hhs.gov/ReportsTrustFunds/.

KEY POINTS

- Social Security does not follow the saving-and-investment model. Most of the taxes paid into the system are used to finance the benefits of current retirees.

- As the baby-boomers began moving into the retirement phase of life in 2010, the Social Security system shifted from a surplus to a deficit. The deficits will persist and become larger and larger in the decades immediately ahead.

- The previous surpluses of the Social Security system were used to cover current expenditures, and the U.S. Treasury provided the Social Security Administration with nonmarketable bonds. Because the federal government is the payee and the recipient of these bonds, their net asset value to the federal government is zero. They will not reduce the level of future taxes needed to cover the Social Security deficits.

- The major problem resulting from the current pay-as-you-go system is that large tax increases, spending cuts, or additional borrowing will be required to cover the Social Security deficits following the retirement of the baby-boom generation.

- Whereas the Social Security benefit formula favors those with lower lifetime earnings, low-wage workers have a lower life expectancy, begin work at a younger age, and gain less from the spousal benefit provisions of the current system. These latter factors largely, if not entirely, offset the egalitarian effects of the benefit formula.

- Because of their shorter life expectancy, blacks derive a lower rate of return from Social Security than whites and a substantially lower return than Hispanics.

- The demographics of the twenty-first century reduce the attractiveness of pay-as-you-go Social Security. Various plans that would place more emphasis on saving and investment are likely to be considered in the future.

CRITICAL ANALYSIS QUESTIONS

1. Is the Social Security system based on the same principles as private insurance? Why or why not?

2. *Why does the Social Security system face a crisis? Are there real assets in the Social Security Trust Fund that can be used to pay future benefits? Will the trust fund help to avert higher future taxes or benefit reductions or both when the baby-boomers retire? Why or why not?

3. Do you think workers should be permitted to invest all or part of their Social Security taxes into a personal retirement account? Why or why not?

4. How does Social Security affect the economic well-being of blacks relative to whites and Hispanics? Explain.

5. Does the current Social Security system promote income equality? Why or why not?

6. The Social Security payroll tax is split equally between the employee and the employer. Would it make any difference if the entire tax were imposed on employees? Would employees be helped if all the tax were imposed on employers? (Hint: You may want to consult the section on tax incidence in Chapter 4.)

*Asterisk denotes questions for which answers are given in Appendix B.

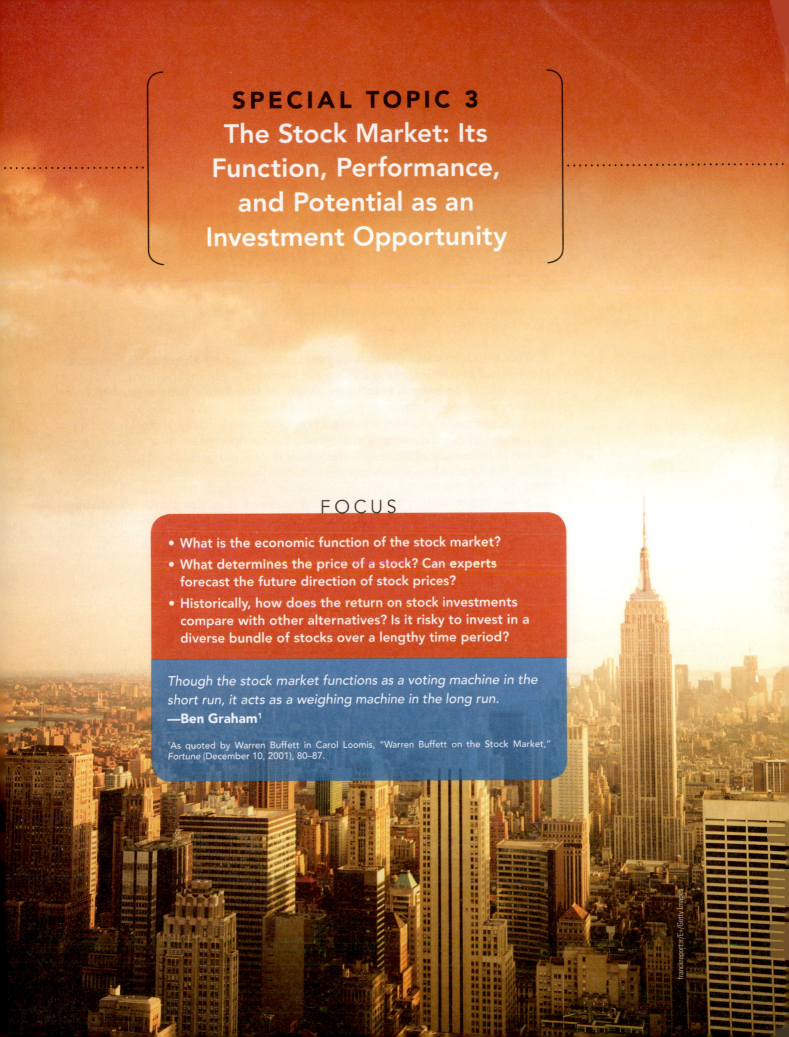

SPECIAL TOPIC 3
The Stock Market: Its Function, Performance, and Potential as an Investment Opportunity

FOCUS

- What is the economic function of the stock market?
- What determines the price of a stock? Can experts forecast the future direction of stock prices?
- Historically, how does the return on stock investments compare with other alternatives? Is it risky to invest in a diverse bundle of stocks over a lengthy time period?

Though the stock market functions as a voting machine in the short run, it acts as a weighing machine in the long run.
—Ben Graham[1]

[1] As quoted by Warren Buffett in Carol Loomis, "Warren Buffett on the Stock Market," *Fortune* (December 10, 2001), 80–87.

The market for corporate shares is called the *stock market*. The stock market makes it possible for investors, including small investors, to share in the profits (and the risks) of large businesses. About one-half of all households now own stock, either directly or indirectly

through shares in an equity mutual fund. In recent years, changes in stock prices have often been front-page news. This feature will focus on the economic functions of the stock market and analyze its potential as an investment tool through which people can build their wealth.

ST03-1 THE ECONOMIC FUNCTIONS OF THE STOCK MARKET

The stock market performs several important functions in a modern economy. Let's consider three of the most important.

1. The stock market provides investors, including those who are not interested in participating directly in the operation of the firm, with an opportunity to own a fractional share of the firm's future profits. As a firm earns profits, its shareholders may gain as the result of both dividend payments and increases in the market value of the stock. Ownership of stock is risky. There is no guarantee that any firm will be profitable in the future. But the shareholders' potential losses are limited to the amount of their initial investment. Beyond this point, shareholders are not responsible for the debts of the corporations that they own.

2. New stock issues are often an excellent way for firms to obtain funds for growth and product development. Essentially, there are three ways for a firm to obtain additional financing. It can use retained earnings (profits earned but not paid out to stockholders), it can borrow money, or it can sell stock. When borrowing, the firm promises to repay the lender a specific amount, including principal and interest. Conversely, new stock issues provide the firm with additional financing, and the owner of the stock acquires an ownership right to a fraction of the future revenues generated by the firm.

Newly issued stocks are sold to the public through specialized firms. A firm that issues new stock sells it in the **primary market**. When news reports tell us about how stock prices are changing, they are referring to **secondary markets**, in which previously issued stocks are traded. Secondary markets make it easy to buy and sell listed stock. This is important to the primary market. The initial buyers want to know that their stock will be easy to sell later. Entry is more attractive when exit will be easy. This will help the corporation issuing new stock to sell it for a higher price.

A stock exchange is a secondary market. It is a place where stockbrokers come to arrange trades for buyers and sellers. The largest and best-known stock market is the New York Stock Exchange, in which more than 2,800 stocks are traded. There are other such markets in the United States, as well as in London, Tokyo, Hong Kong, and other trading centers around the world.

3. Stock prices provide information about the quality of business decisions. Changing stock prices reward good decisions and penalize bad ones. It pays for a stockholder, especially a large one, to be alert to whether the firm's decisions are good or bad. Those who spot a corporation's problems early can sell part or all of their stock in that firm before others notice and lower the price by selling their own stock. Similarly, those who first notice decisions that will be profitable can gain by increasing their holdings of the stock. Stockholder alertness benefits the corporation, too. The firm's board of directors can utilize the price changes resulting from investor vigilance to reward good management decisions. They often do so by tying the compensation of the top corporate officers to stock performance. How? Rather than paying these officers entirely in the form of salaries,

Primary market
The market in which financial institutions aid in the sale of new securities.

Secondary market
The market in which financial institutions aid in the buying and selling of existing securities.

a board of directors can integrate **stock options** into the compensation package of top executives. On the one hand, when good decisions drive the stock price up, the executives' options will be very valuable. On the other hand, if bad decisions cause the stock price to fall, then the options will have little or no value.

ST03-2 STOCK MARKET PERFORMANCE: THE HISTORICAL RECORD

Investors in American stocks have done exceedingly well. Furthermore, this has been true over a lengthy period of time. During the last two centuries, after adjustment for inflation, corporate stocks have yielded an average real return of approximately 7 percent per year, compared with a real return of about 3 percent for bonds. The historic returns derived from savings accounts and money market mutual funds are even lower. A 7 percent real return may not sound particularly good, but when it is compounded, it means that the real value of your investment will double every ten years. In contrast, it will take 23 years to double your money at a 3 percent interest return.[2]

The Standard and Poor's 500 Index (S&P 500) is one measure of the performance of the broad stock market. This index factors in the value of dividends as if they were reinvested in the market. Thus, it provides a measure of the rate of return received by investors in the form of both dividends and changes in share prices. **Exhibit 1** presents data on the real rate of return earned by stockholders each year since 1950 as measured by the changes in the S&P 500 during the year. The compound annual nominal rate of return of the

Stock options
The option to buy a specified number of shares of the firm's stock at a designated price. The designated price is generally set so that the options will be quite valuable if the firm's shares increase in price but of little value if their price falls. Thus, when used to compensate top managers, stock options provide a strong incentive to follow policies that will increase the value of the firm.

EXHIBIT 1

Annual Return for Stocks, 1950–2012

During the past 62 years, the broad S&P 500 indicates that stock investors earned a 10.5 percent compound annual rate of return.

Double-digit returns were earned in 38 of the 62 years, whereas returns were negative during only 14 of the years.

Source: Global Financial Data, www.globalfindata.com; and Standard & Poor's, www.standardandpoors.com.

---

[2]You can approximate the number of years it will take to double your funds at alternative interest rates by simply dividing the yield into 70. This is sometimes referred to as the *rule of 70*.

S&P 500 was 10.5 percent during the 60-year period. Even after adjustment for infla-tion, the real compound annual return was 6.9 percent over this lengthy time period. The returns during the 1980s and 1990s were even higher. Since 2000, however, the returns have not been as high, and during 2008 alone investors experienced a negative 37 percent return.

Exhibit 1 highlights one of the risks that accompanies the ownership of stock: The returns and therefore the value of the stock can be quite volatile. The broad stock market, as measured by the S&P 500, provided double-digit returns during 38 of the 62 years between 1950 and 2012, but the returns were negative during 14 of those years. Stock market inves-tors can never be sure what return they will earn or what the value of their stock holdings will be at a specified time in the future.

But this volatility is a big reason that stocks yield a significantly higher return than savings accounts, money market certificates, and corporate or government bonds, all of which guarantee you a given nominal return in the future. Because most people value the additional certainty in the yields that bonds and savings accounts provide over stocks, the average return on stocks has to be higher to attract investors away from financial assets with more predictable returns.

Given the rather large decline in the stock market in 2008, some might think that the stock market is no longer a good investment. However, even if one would have started a regular monthly investment program at just about the worst possible time in the history of the U.S. stock market—just before the crash of 1929 and the Great Depression of the 1930s in which the value of stocks declined by almost 90 percent—one would still have earned a better return within four years than a person who had invested in U.S. Treasury bills and would have ended up with a 13 percent nominal return (or an 11 percent real return) over the next 30 years.

ST03-3 THE INTEREST RATE, THE VALUE OF FUTURE INCOME, AND STOCK PRICES

The present value of the firm's expected future net earnings (profit) underlies today's price of a firm's stock. What those future profits are worth to an investor today depends on three things: (1) the expected size of future net earnings, (2) when these earnings will be achieved, and (3) how much the investor discounts the future income. The last depends on the interest rate. As we noted in an earlier chapter, the present-value procedure can be used to determine the current value of any future income (or cost) stream. If D represents dividends (and gains from a higher stock price) earned in various years in the future (indi-cated by the subscripts) and i represents the discount or interest rate, the present value of the future income stream is:

$$PV = \frac{D_1}{(1 + i)} + \frac{D_2}{(1 + i)^2} + \cdots + \frac{D_3}{(1 + i)^3}$$

As this formula shows, a higher interest rate will reduce the present value of future rev-enues (returns), including those derived from stocks. This is true even if the size of the future returns is not affected by changes in the interest rate.

Stock analysts often stress that lower interest rates are good for the stock market. This should not be surprising because the lower rates of interest will increase the value of future income (and capital gains). For a specific annual income stream in perpetuity, the present value is equal simply to R/i, where R is the annual revenue stream and i is the interest rate. Thus, for example, when the interest rate is 12.5 percent, the discounted value of $10 of future income to be received each year in perpetuity is $80 ($10 divided by 0.125), eight times the stream of earnings. But when the interest rate is 5 percent, the discounted value of this same income stream is $200 ($10 divided by 0.05), or 20 times the stream of earnings. Therefore, if the $10 represented the expected future income stream from a share of stock, the present value of the income stream would be higher when the interest rate was lower. Other things being constant, lower interest rates will increase the value of future income and thereby increase the market value of stocks.

How can one tell whether stock prices are high or low? The answer to that question depends on both the interest rate and expectations about the future income generated by the stock (or bundle of stocks). The price/earnings (P/E) ratio provides information on the price of a stock relative to its current earnings. It is interesting to look at the historical path of the P/E ratio and observe how it has responded to changes in interest rates and business-cycle conditions. Of course, the latter is likely to influence the future earnings prospects of business firms.

Exhibit 2 presents data on the P/E ratio over the 1950–2012 period for the stocks included in the S&P 500. The P/E ratio average during this lengthy period was 18. From the early 1950s through the mid-1990s, the P/E ratio ranged from a low of 8 to a high of 24. During the 1960s, the economy grew rapidly and both the inflation and interest rates were relatively low. Throughout most of that period, the P/E ratio was near 20. The decade of the 1970s was a period of both high inflation and high interest rates. As we just indicated, high interest rates will reduce the value of future income. Reflecting this factor, the P/E ratio during the 1970s was near 10 throughout the decade, considerably lower than during the 1960s.

EXHIBIT 2

Price/Earnings Ratio, 1950–2012

Since 1950, the average price/earnings ratio of the S&P 500 has been around 18. This ratio was between 8 and 24 throughout the 1951–1997 period. It was persistently near the lower end of this range (between 8 and 10) during the 1970s. It rose during the period 1985–1997 and eventually soared above 30 during the period 1998–2002. A combination of stock price declines and higher earnings as the economy recovered from the 2001 recession caused the price/earnings ratio to recede, but it briefly soared to more than 80 in 2009, primarily because of a sharp decline in earnings during the 2008–2009 recession.

Source: Standard & Poor's, www.standardandpoors.com.

As the economy grew rapidly, and both the inflation rate and interest rates declined and remained at a low level during the 1984–1997 period, the P/E ratio rose sharply. By the mid-1990s, it had risen to the 20 to 25 range, quite high by historical standards. But the stock market continued to boom, and by 1999 the P/E ratio had risen to an extremely high level, 31.7. By the late 1990s, there was considerable talk of a "stock market bubble," high stock prices that could not be maintained because they were out of line with the future earning prospects of business firms. The bubble burst and stock prices fell sharply. As a result, the S&P 500 lost nearly 50 percent of its value during 2000–2002 (see Exhibit 1). As the economy recovered from the recession of 2001, corporate earnings picked up and the P/E ratio receded. By 2005–2006, the P/E ratio had returned closer to its historical average, but briefly soared to more than 80 in 2009. This increase was primarily the result of sharp reductions in earnings and the marking down of bad assets during the 2008–2009 recession.

ST03-4 THE RANDOM WALK THEORY OF THE STOCK MARKET

Random walk theory
The theory that current stock prices already reflect known information about the future. Therefore, the future movement of stock prices will be determined by surprise occurrences. This will cause them to change in a random fashion.

Most economists adhere to the **random walk theory** of stock prices. According to this theory, current stock prices already reflect all available information that is known or can be predicted with any degree of accuracy, including information about the future state of corporate earnings, interest rates, the health of the economy, and other factors that influence stock prices. In other words, current stock prices will already reflect the best information currently available. In the future, the direction of stock prices will be driven by surprise occurrences—things that differ from what people are currently anticipating. By their very nature, these factors are unpredictable. If they were predictable, they would already be reflected in current stock prices.

The random walk theory applies to the price of a specific stock as well as to the market as a whole. The prices of specific stocks will reflect their future earnings prospects. The stock prices of firms with attractive future profit potential will be high relative to their current earnings. Consequently, their current prices will already reflect their attractive future earnings prospects. The opposite will be true for firms with poor future prospects. Although numerous factors affect the future price of any specific stock, changes in the current price will be driven by changes that differ from current expectations. Thus, because the future prices of both specific stocks and the market as a whole are driven by unexpected and unpredictable factors, no one can consistently forecast their future path with any degree of accuracy.

ST03-5 HOW THE ORDINARY INVESTOR CAN BEAT THE EXPERTS

Portfolio
All the stocks, bonds, or other securities held by an individual or corporation for investment purposes.

Equity mutual fund
A corporation that pools the funds of investors, including small investors, and uses them to purchase a bundle of stocks.

Historically, ordinary Americans have often refrained from investing in the stock market because of the risks involved. But there are ways this risk can be reduced, particularly for long-term investments. The value of any specific stock can rise or fall by a huge amount within a relatively short time period. But the risk accompanying these movements can be reduced by holding a diverse **portfolio**, a collection of stocks characterized by relatively small holdings of a large number of companies in different markets and industries. **Equity mutual funds** make this possible. They provide the ordinary investor with a low-cost method of owning a diverse bundle of stocks. An equity mutual fund is a corporation that buys and holds shares of stock in many firms. This diversification puts the law of large numbers to work for you. Whereas some of the investments in a diversified portfolio will do poorly, others will do extremely well. The performance of the latter will offset that of the former, and the rate of return will converge toward the average. Remember, the average real return of equities has been substantially higher than for bonds, savings accounts, and other readily accessible methods of saving.

As **Exhibit 3** shows, there was a huge increase in the quantity of funds flowing into mutual funds during the 1990s. The value of mutual fund investments increased from $239 billion in 1990 to approximately $4 trillion in 1999–2000. Although equity mutual fund investments declined as stock prices fell during 2000–2002, they rebounded and had soared to $6.4 trillion by 2007 before falling more than 43 percent to a value of $3.6 trillion in 2008. Their value rebounded afterward, reaching $5.9 trillion in 2012. They now account for about 30 percent of all publicly traded U.S. stocks.

EXHIBIT 3

Value of Equity Mutual Funds, 1980–2012

The amount of money that people put into U.S. equity mutual funds, in order to hold shares in the ownership of stocks, rose dramatically in the 1990s. Purchasing shares in a mutual fund is a simple way for an individual to buy and hold an interest in a large variety of stocks with one purchase. Due to the recent financial crisis, the value of equity mutual funds fell by 43 percent from 2007 to 2008, before rebounding in 2009–2012.

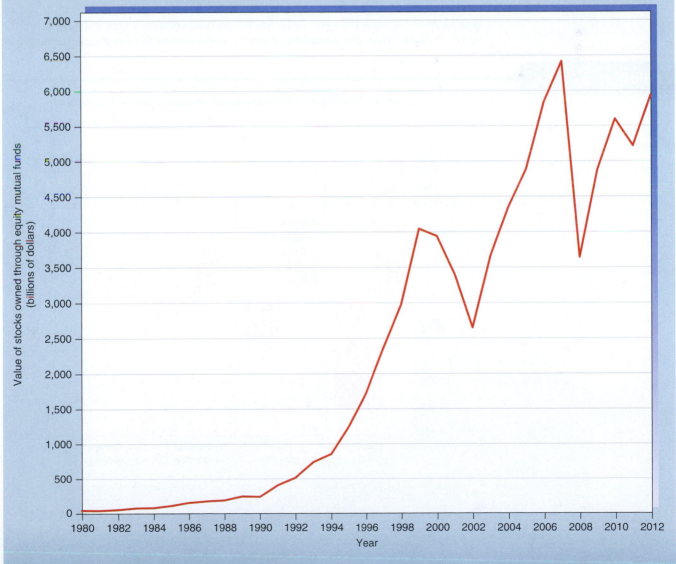

Source: Investor Company Institute, www.ici.org.

A second source of risk facing the stock market investor is the possibility that nearly all stocks in the market can rise or fall together when expectations about the entire economy change. This has happened on several occasions. For example, on October 19, 1987, the stocks listed in the Dow Jones Industrial Average lost more than 22 percent of their value in just one trading day. The high-tech stocks listed on the NASDAQ exchange lost about 70 percent of their value during 2000 and 2001; and most recently the S&P 500 lost about 57 percent of its value between October 2007 and March 2009. However, the risks accompanying such short-term movements can be substantially reduced if an investor either continually adds to or holds a diverse portfolio of stocks over a lengthy period of time, say, 30 or 35 years.

Exhibit 4 illustrates this point. This exhibit shows the highest and lowest real returns (the returns adjusted for inflation) earned from stock market investments for periods of varying lengths between the years 1871 and 2012. The exhibit assumes that the investor paid a fixed amount annually into a mutual fund that mirrored the S&P 500, a basket of stocks thought to represent the market as a whole. Clearly, huge swings are possible when stocks are held for only a short time period. During the 1871–2008 period, the single-year returns of the S&P 500 ranged from 47.2 percent to –40.8 percent. Even over a five-year period, the compound annual returns ranged from 29.8 percent to –16.7 percent. Note that the "best returns" and "worst returns" converged as the length of the investment period increased. When a 35-year period was considered, the compound annual return for the best 35 years between 1871 and 2012 was 9.5 percent, compared with 2.7 percent for the worst 35 years.[3] Thus, the annual real return of stocks during the worst-case scenario was

EXHIBIT 4

Stocks Are Less Risky When Held for a Lengthy Time Period

This exhibit shows the best and the worst annualized real performance for each investment period from 1871 to 2012. It shows that there is less risk of a low or negative return when an investment in a portfolio of stocks (S&P 500) is held for a longer period of time.

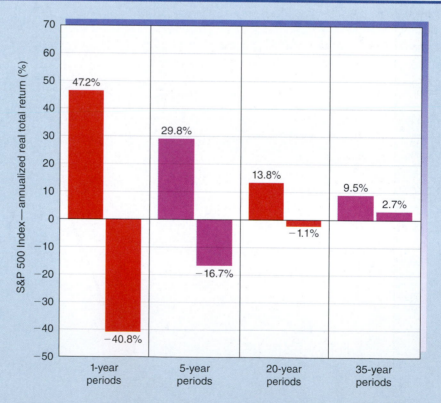

Source: Liqun Liu, Andrew J. Rettenmaier, and Zijun Wang, "Social Security and Market Risk," National Center for Policy Analysis Working Paper Number 244 (July 2001). The returns are based on the assumption that an individual invests a fixed amount for each year in the investment period. Data updated through 2012.

---

[3]Based on Liqun Liu, Andrew J. Rettenmaier, and Zijun Wang, "Social Security and Market Risk" (Working Paper Number 244, National Center for Policy Analysis, Washington, DC, July 2001). Data updated through 2010.

about the same as the real return for bonds. Furthermore, the annual real rate of return from the stock investments during the period was 7 percent—more than twice the comparable rate for bonds.

The bottom line is this: When held over a lengthy period, a diverse portfolio of stocks has yielded a high rate of return, and the variation in that return has been low. Thus, for the long-term investor, such as a person saving for his or her retirement years, a diverse portfolio of stocks is not particularly risky.

ST03-6 THE ADVANTAGES OF INDEXED MUTUAL FUNDS

When purchasing a mutual fund, the investor can choose either a managed or an indexed fund. A **managed equity mutual fund** is one in which an "expert," generally supported by a research staff, tries to pick and choose the stock holdings of the fund in a manner that will maximize its rate of return. In contrast, an **indexed equity mutual fund** merely holds stocks in the same proportion as they exist in a broad stock market index like the S&P 500 or the Dow Jones Industrials.

In the case of indexed funds, neither comprehensive research nor extensive stock trading is needed because the fund merely seeks to mirror the index and earn the rate of return of the broad market that it represents. Thus, because they do not spend much on either research or stock trading, the operating costs of indexed funds are substantially lower than they are for managed funds. Therefore, they are able to charge lower fees, which means that a larger share of the investor's money flows directly into the purchase of stock.

As a result, the average rate of return yielded by a broad indexed fund beats the return of almost all managed mutual funds when comparisons are made over periods of time such as a decade. This is not surprising because, as the random walk theory indicates, not even the experts will be able to forecast consistently the future direction of stock prices with any degree of accuracy. Over the typical ten-year period, the S&P 500 has yielded a higher return than 85 percent of actively managed funds. And over 20-year periods, mutual funds indexed to the S&P 500 have generally outperformed about 98 percent of actively managed funds.[4] Thus, the odds are very low, about 1 in 50, that you or anyone else will be able to select an actively managed fund that will do better than the market average *over the long run*.

Are stocks riskier than bonds? If held for only a short time—five years, for example—stocks are riskier. However, when held over lengthy periods, such as 20 or 30 years, historically the rate of return on stocks has been both higher and less variable than that of bonds. What does this imply for people in their twenties and thirties who are saving for their retirement? Where should they put their funds?

Managed equity mutual fund
An equity mutual fund that has a portfolio manager who decides what stocks will be held in the fund and when they will be bought or sold. A research staff generally provides support for the fund manager.

Indexed equity mutual fund
An equity mutual fund that holds a portfolio of stocks that matches their share (or weight) in a broad stock market index such as the S&P 500. The overhead of these funds is usually quite low because their expenses on stock trading and research are low.

ST03-7 SHOULD YOU INVEST IN A FUND BECAUSE OF ITS PAST PERFORMANCE?

People marketing mutual funds often encourage customers to invest in mutual funds that have yielded high rates of return in the past. This sounds like a good strategy, but history indicates that it is not. Mutual funds with outstanding records over a 5- or 10-year period often perform poorly in the future. The top 20 managed equity funds of the 1990s outperformed the S&P 500 by 3.9 percent per year over the course of the decade. But if investors

---

[4]See Jeremy J. Siegel, *Stocks for the Long Run*, 3rd ed. (New York: McGraw-Hill, 2002), 342–43.

entering the market in 2000 thought they would beat the market by choosing the "hot" funds of the 1990s, they would have been disappointed. The top 20 funds of the 1990s underperformed the S&P 500 by 1.3 percent per year during the 2000s.

Even funds that have persistently been successful in the recent past may do poorly in the future. For example, only 14 out of the more than 1,000 mutual funds were able to beat the S&P 500 for nine consecutive years during 1999–2007. Surely, these were the best managed funds. Nonetheless, only one of the 14 was able to beat the S&P index in 2008.[5]

Why is past performance such an unreliable indicator? Two factors provide insight on the answer to this question. First, some of the mutual funds with above-average returns during a period were merely lucky. After all, if you flip a coin 100 times, you will not always get 50 heads and 50 tails. Sometimes, the coin will come up heads maybe 60 times out of 100. But this does not mean you can expect 60 heads during the next sequence of 100. So it is with stock market mutual funds. Given that there are a large number of funds, some of them will have above-average performance for a time period. But this does not mean that the above-average performance can be expected in the future.

Second, a strategy that works well in one environment, inflationary conditions, for example, is often disastrous when conditions change. For example, mutual funds with substantial holdings of gold-mining companies did exceedingly well during the inflationary 1970s. But their performance was disastrous during the 1980s and 1990s as the inflation was brought under control. Similarly, some mutual funds that performed well during the bull market of the 1990s were among the worst performers during the bear market that began in 2000.

Virtually none of the experts are able to "beat the market average" consistently over lengthy time periods and changing market conditions. Thus, broad market indexes outperform the stock pickers in the long run. This is something you will not often hear from brokerage firms and other experts trying to sell their services to you. But knowing this will make you a smarter investor.

---

[5]Burton G. Malkiel, *A Random Walk Down Wall Street: The Time Tested Strategy for Successful Investing* (New York: W. W. Norton & Company, 2011), 180–83.

KEY POINTS

- The stock market makes it possible for investors without either specialized business skills or the time to become involved in the operation of a business firm to share in the risks and opportunities that accompany the ownership of corporate businesses.

- During the last two centuries, after adjustment for inflation, corporate stocks have yielded a real return of approximately 7 percent per year, compared with a real return of about 3 percent for bonds and even lower yields for savings accounts and money market mutual funds.

- Most economists adhere to the random walk theory of stock prices. According to this theory, current stock prices already reflect all information about factors influencing stock prices that is known or can be forecast with any degree of accuracy. Thus, the future direction of stock prices will be driven by surprise occurrences and, as a result, no one will be able to forecast future stock prices with any degree of accuracy.

- Buying and selling individual stocks without specialized knowledge for a quick profit is very risky. But holding a diverse portfolio of unrelated stocks and holding them for long periods of time greatly reduces the risk of investing in the stock market.

- An equity mutual fund that is tied to a broad stock market index like the S&P 500 provides an attractive method for long-term investors to obtain relatively high yields with minimal risk. Indexed mutual funds have substantially lower operating costs than managed funds because they engage in less trading and have no need for either a market expert or re-search staff.

CRITICAL ANALYSIS QUESTIONS

1. *A friend just inherited $50,000. She informs you of her investment plans and asks for your advice. "I want to put it into the stock market and use it for my retirement in 30 years. What do you think is the best plan that will provide high returns at a relatively low risk?" What answer would you give? Explain.

2. Suppose that more expansionary monetary policy leads to inflation and higher nominal interest rates. How is this likely to affect the value of stocks? Explain.

3. *Google stock rose from $100 in 2004 to more than $900 per share in 2013. Google has made sizable profits but never paid a dividend. Why were people willing to pay such a high price knowing that they might not get dividends for many years?

4. If an investment adviser gives you some hot new stock tip, is it likely to be a "sure thing"? Why or why not? If you have a stockbroker and purchase the stocks promoted by the broker, are you likely to earn a high return on your stock investments? Why or why not?

5. *The stocks of some corporations that have never made a profit, especially those in high-technology industries, have risen in price. What causes investors to be willing to buy these stocks?

6. What is an indexed equity mutual fund? What is a managed equity mutual fund? How will the administrative costs of the two differ?

7. What is the random walk theory of stock prices? What does it indicate about the ability of "experts" to forecast accurately the future direction of stock prices?

8. Are stocks a risky investment? How can one reduce the risk accompanying stock market investments?

*Asterisk denotes questions for which answers are given in Appendix B.

SPECIAL TOPIC 4
Great Debates in Economics: Keynes versus Hayek[1]

FOCUS

- Why are the views of John Maynard Keynes and Friedrich Hayek often compared and contrasted?
- What is the source of economic booms and busts?
- What might be done to reduce the impact of recessions?
- Should the government try to centrally plan the economy?
- Can the political process be counted on to promote economic stability and the efficient allocation of resources?

We've been going back and forth for a century
[Keynes] I want to steer markets,
[Hayek] I want them set free
— **Chorus from Keynes–Hayek video**[1]

[1]Note to instructors: This feature is developed around the Keynes–Hayek video raps (see links in the third paragraph of the following page). It is designed to be a fun exercise that highlights several key points of continuing debate among economists.

John Maynard Keynes and Friedrich August Hayek are two of the most important economists of the twentieth century. Moreover, their scholarly work represents alternative theories and ideas about the central issues of our day, including economic instability, central planning, and the operation of the political process.

Can serious economics be fun? Russell Roberts, a professor of economics at George Mason University, and filmmaker John Papola think it can be. They developed an eight-minute rap video with actors posing as a dueling Hayek and Keynes. The lyrics highlight the contrasting views of Keynes and Hayek on the business cycle, fiscal and monetary policy, and the role of government.

Courtesy of EconStories.tv

©iStockphoto.com/nicoolay

The Roberts–Papola video titled "Fear the Boom and Bust: Keynes versus Hayek" has attracted more than 4 million views. It is available at www.youtube.com/watch?v=d0nERTFo-Sk. Roberts and Papola have also done a follow-up rap, "Fight of the Century: Keynes vs. Hayek Round Two," which is available at www.youtube.com/watch?v=GTQnarzmTOc. Take a break from your studying and have a little fun watching these videos.

The views of Keynes and Hayek provide a vivid contrast on key issues in economics. Nonetheless, both command respect among professional economists. Keynes is widely regarded as the most influential economist of the twentieth century. Hayek was the recipient of the 1974 Nobel Prize in Economics.

Interestingly, Keynes and Hayek were contemporaries at Cambridge University and the London School of Economics in the early 1940s. During World War II, they even spent a night together on the roof of the chapel of King's College, Cambridge looking out for German bombers.

Keynes's *General Theory* provided a reasonable explanation of what went wrong during the Great Depression and what could be done to prevent such an event from occurring in the future. His ideas inspired a generation of economists that transformed macroeconomic analysis. Hayek was born in Vienna in 1899, and he was a rising star in the 1930s. The London School of Economics lured him from Austria, at least partly to counter the influence of Keynes and the reputation he brought to rival Cambridge University. In his 1944 book, the *Road to Serfdom*, Hayek argued that the growth of government was endangering freedom and leading to tyranny in the Western democracies, just as it had done in both Nazi Germany and the Soviet Union.

Keynes and Hayek were polar opposites not only in their economic views but also in their personality characteristics. Keynes was outgoing and dominant. Some charged that he was arrogant, but all recognized that his skills as a persuader were supreme. In contrast, Hayek was quiet and unassuming. While Keynes reveled in policy-making, Hayek was content to remain outside of policy circles. Keynes was optimistic, and his message was well suited for the "We're fixing it" mentality of politicians. On the other hand, Hayek's message was not one political officials like to hear: Policymakers have messed things up and it will take time for the market to correct their errors.

A popular PBS video series, *Commanding Heights* (Episode One: "The Battle of Ideas"), also used the contrasting views of these two economists to illustrate how major trends in economic thinking impacted global economic events during the twentieth century.[2] Following in this tradition, this special topic will use the ideas of Keynes and Hayek, including lyrics from the videos, to explain and contrast their viewpoints and the alternative theories they represent.

---

[2]The PBS series was based on the book by Daniel Yergin and Joseph Stanislaw, *The Commanding Heights: The Battle Between Government and the Marketplace That Is Remaking the Modern World* (New York: Simon and Schuster, 1998).

ST04-1 KEYNES, HAYEK, AND GREAT DEBATES IN ECONOMICS

The lyrics of the Keynes–Hayek videos present alternative views with regard to three of the most important debates in economics. Let's consider these debates and the references to them in the rap lyrics.

ST04-1a WHAT IS THE CAUSE AND CURE FOR THE BUSINESS CYCLE?

The underlying causes of the business cycle and potential effectiveness of policy responses have been a focal point of debate among economists for at least a century. The perspectives of Keynes and Hayek represent alternative viewpoints on this issue.

The Keynesian viewpoint argues that capitalism-based, market economies are inherently unstable. Private investment in particular is fickle and prone to extreme fluctuations driven by changes in business optimism, or what Keynes referred to as "animal spirits." Moreover, the booms and busts will tend to feed on themselves, and therefore a market economy will swing back and forth between a boom that will lead to inflation and a bust that will generate high rates of unemployment. But there is good news in the Keynesian theory. Government can use fiscal and monetary policy to control aggregate demand and thereby promote economic stability. During a recession, government spending should be increased to offset the weak private investment, taxes should be reduced to stimulate consumption, budget deficits should be used to finance these activities, and finally monetary policy should keep interest rates low.

The Hayekian viewpoint argues that booms and busts are caused by perverse government policy and that the economy would be considerably more stable if political decision-makers followed stable policies and refrained from activist interventions. In his research on monetary theory, Hayek argued that economic booms are the result of excessive credit expansion that pushes interest rates to artificially low levels. At the abnormally low interest rates, businesses are induced to undertake investments that will later prove to be both unprofitable and unsustainable.

Hayekians refer to these inefficient investments as malinvestment. In this view, recessions are a "hangover" or adjustment caused by improper government policy during the preceding boom. Once the government has caused the malinvestment, the proper course is to allow market prices to adjust and allow the malinvestment to be cleansed from the system. Government stimulus spending will merely slow the adjustment process and prolong the recession.

Here are some excerpted lyrics from the Keynes versus Hayek rap videos that illustrate their contrasting views on the business cycle.

[Both] There's a boom and bust cycle and good reason to fear it.

[Hayek] Blame low interest rates.

[Keynes] No … it's the animal spirits.
[Keynes] I had a real plan any fool can understand.
The advice, real simple—boost aggregate demand!
C, I, G, all together gets to Y.
Make sure the total's growing, watch the economy fly.
So if that flow is getting low, doesn't matter the reason.
We need more government spending, now it's stimulus season.
The monetary and the fiscal, they're equally correct.
Public works, digging ditches, war has the same effect.
Even a broken window helps the glass man have some wealth.
The multiplier driving higher the economy's health.

[Hayek] The place you should study isn't the bust.
It's the boom that should make you feel leery, that's the thrust
Of my theory, the capital structure is key.

Malinvestments wreck the economy.
The boom gets started with an expansion of credit.
The Fed sets rates low, are you starting to get it?
That new money is confused for real loanable funds
But it's just inflation that's driving the ones
Who invest in new projects like housing construction.
The boom plants the seeds for its future destruction.
So the boom turns to bust as the interest rates rise
With the costs of production, price signals were lies.
The boom was a binge that's a matter of fact.
Now its devalued capital that makes up the slack.
You must save to invest, don't use the printing press
Or a bust will surely follow, an economy depressed.
Your so-called "stimulus" will make things even worse.
It's just more of the same, more incentives perversed.

[Keynes] So what would YOU do to help those unemployed?
This is the question you seem to avoid.
When we're in a mess, would you have us just wait,
Doing nothing until markets equilibrate?

[Hayek] I don't wanna do nothing, there's plenty to do.
The question I ponder is who plans for whom?
Do I plan for myself or I leave it to you?
I want plans by the many, not by the few.
Let's not repeat what created our troubles.
I want real growth not a series of bubbles.
Stop bailing out losers, let prices work.
If we don't try to steer them they won't go berserk.

ST04-1b SHOULD AN ECONOMY BE DIRECTED BY GOVERNMENT CENTRAL PLANNING OR DECENTRALIZED INDIVIDUAL PLANNING AND THE INVISIBLE HAND OF MARKET PRICES?

Clearly, the main chorus of the rap lyrics stresses their differing views, as Keynes says, "I want to steer markets," and Hayek replies, "I want them set free."

The Keynesian viewpoint holds that central planning by wise government officials is needed not only to keep the macroeconomy on track but also to correct market failures and assure an equitable distribution of income. Relying on information derived from economists and other experts, Keynesians believe that policy-makers will be able to selectively intervene into markets (or sometimes outright control them entirely) in ways that will improve on market outcomes.

In contrast, Hayekians argue that central planners do not have sufficient information to direct the economy and their efforts to do so will do more damage than good. Decentralized decision-making, directed by market prices, will be a more reliable method of directing resources into productive projects and away from ones that are counterproductive. Instead of centralized planning, individuals should be left free to make their own plans relying on information and incentives communicated by market prices, competitive forces, and the profit and loss system. According to the Hayekian view, a spontaneous order will emerge from the market process that will coordinate the desires of consumers and producers, and of borrowers and lenders. Hayekians believe this will result in both more economic freedom and more rapid economic progress. Hayek highlights this point in his lyrics: "The question I ponder is who plans for whom? Do I plan for myself or I leave it to you? I want plans by the many, not by the few."

Moreover, dynamic competition provides decision-makers with a strong incentive to discover better ways of doing things, improve technologies, and institute practical innovations that will improve our lives. In this view the information necessary to guide the economy is not known to anyone in total, but is instead generated through the process of decentralized market interaction. According to Hayekians, the proper role of government is simply to provide the rule of law, enforce contracts, and protect property rights, leaving the rest to market forces.

Courtesy of EconStories.tv

Here are some excerpted lyrics from the Keynes versus Hayek rap videos that illustrate these points:

[Hayek] His theory conceals the mechanics of change,
That simple equation, too much aggregation
Ignores human action and motivation.
The economy's not a car. There's no engine to stall.
No experts can fix it. There's no "it" at all.
The economy is us. Put away your wrenches, the economy is organic.

[Keynes] Come on are you kidding?
Don't Wall Street gyrations challenge the world-view of self-regulation?
Even you must admit that lesson we've learned
Is more oversight is needed or else we'll get burned.

[Hayek] Oversight? The government's long been in bed
With those Wall Street execs and the firms that they've bled.
Capitalism is about profit and loss.
You bail out the losers; there is no end to the cost.
The lesson I've learned is how little we know.
The world is complex, not some circular flow.
The economy is not a class you master in college,
To think otherwise is the pretense of knowledge.

ST04-1c CAN DEMOCRATIC DECISION-MAKING BE COUNTED ON TO ALLOCATE RESOURCES EFFICIENTLY?

As we discussed in Chapter 6, public-choice analysis provides insights on the operation of the political process. It indicates that the incentives confronted by voters, interest groups, politicians, and bureaucrats will sometimes conflict with sound policy and the efficient allocation of resources. Even when decisions are made democratically, the political process will often favor well-organized interest groups and shortsighted policies that generate highly visible gains at the expense of costs that are less visible. Predictably, some inefficient use of resources will arise from these forces. Put another way, there is "government failure" as well as "market failure."

The Keynesian perspective seldom directly addresses this issue. Instead, it is assumed that the job of the economists is to figure out the ideal or optimal solutions, and once these are developed, political decision-makers can be expected to adopt them. Moreover, many Keynesians charge that analysis of how the political process works is outside of the scope of economics and therefore those who address this issue are not really addressing economic issues. Keynes himself had great confidence in his ability to convince policy-makers to adopt his advice. Within the Keynesian framework, it is essentially assumed that political decision-makers will implement policies in a proper manner.

The Hayekian perspective argues that the structure of incentives and institutions exert a major impact on how government works. The government failure described within public-choice theory will be a major problem or barrier to implementing good policy. Thus, it is vitally important to adopt institutions and constitutional rules that bring personal self-interest of policy-makers into harmony with growth and prosperity.

The father of economics, Adam Smith, held a similar view. Smith stated,

> *The man of system is apt to be very wise in his own conceit. He seems to imagine that he can arrange the different members of a great society with as much ease as the hand arranges the different pieces upon a chess-board; he does not consider that the pieces upon the chess-board have not another principle of motion besides that which the hand impresses upon them; but that, in the great chess-board of human society, every single piece has a principle of motion of its own, although different from that which the legislature might choose to impress upon it. If those two principles coincide and act in the same direction, the game of human society will go on easily and harmoniously, and is very likely to be happy and successful. If they are opposite or different, the game will go on miserably, and the society must be at all times in the highest degree of disorder.*[3]

Interestingly, Hayek makes a reference to this view of Adam Smith in the rap video.

[Keynes] You've been on your high horse and you are off to the races.
I look at the world on a case-by-case basis.
When people are suffering I roll up my sleeves
And do what I can to cure our disease.
The future's uncertain, our outlooks are frail.
That's why markets are so prone to fail.
In a volatile world we need more discretion
So state intervention can counter depression.

[Hayek] People aren't chessmen you move on a board
At your whim, their dreams and desires ignored.
With political incentives, discretion's a joke.
Those dials are twisting – just mirrors and smoke.
We need stable rules and real market prices
So prosperity emerges and cuts short the crisis.

---

[3]Adam Smith, *The Theory of Moral Sentiments*, Glasgow Edition of Oxford University Press (Indianapolis: Liberty Fund, Inc., [1790] 1976): 233–34. Also available at www.econlib.org/library/Smith,smMS6.html#VI.II.42).

Keynes and Hayek represent two of the most important strands of economic thinking. You will see their views represented in several of the special topics that follow, including the ones on the 2008 financial crisis, the Great Depression, government deficits and debt, and the health care debate.

KEY POINTS

- John Maynard Keynes and Friedrich Hayek are giants in the economics profession. Their theories and ideas represent contrasting views on several of the central issues of economics.

- Keynes believed that market economies were inherently unstable and government intervention in the form of fiscal and monetary stimulus could be used effectively to promote economic stability. Hayek believed that economic instability was primarily the result of malinvestment generated by monetary and credit expansion and that government stimulus would slow market adjustments and the recovery process.

- Keynes believed that government central planning could improve on market outcomes. Hayek believed that policy-makers simply do not have the information or incentives to plan the economy effectively and that their efforts to do so would be far less efficient than allocation through markets.

- Keynesians believe that the job of the economist is to develop policies that will reduce economic instability and correct market failures. Keynesian analysis largely ignores how economic incentives influence the operation of the political process. Hayekians recognize that the political incentive structure often caters to well-organized interest groups and results in the adoption of shortsighted policies. Thus, they stress the importance of legal and political institutions that will provide both market participants and political decision-makers with incentives to engage in productive rather than counterproductive actions.

CRITICAL ANALYSIS QUESTIONS

1. *What* is the underlying message of the following lyrics from Keynes?

   [Keynes] Public works, digging ditches, war has the same effect.
   Even a broken window helps the glass man have some wealth.
   The multiplier driving higher the economy's health.

2. Use the following lyrics to describe the difference between Keynes and Hayek on the role of savings in the economy.

   [Keynes] So forget about saving, get it straight out of your head.
   Like I said, in the long run—we're all dead.
   Savings is destruction, that's the paradox of thrift.
   Don't keep money in your pocket, or that growth will never lift.

   [Hayek] Real savings come first if you want to invest.
   The market coordinates time with interest.
   Your focus on spending is pushing on thread.
   In the long run, my friend, it's your theory that's dead.
   Whether it's the late twenties or two thousand and five
   Booming bad investments, seems like they'd thrive.
   You must save to invest, don't use the printing press
   Or a bust will surely follow, an economy depressed.

3. The following lyrics discuss whether the government stimulus efforts in response to the 2008 financial crisis worked and also argue points about government policy during the Great Depression and the subsequent recovery. What are the major areas of disagreement on these issues as illustrated in the lyrics?

   [Keynes] Are you kidding? My cure works perfectly fine.
   Have a look. The recession ended in '09.
   I deserve credit. Things would have been worse.
   All the estimates prove it. I'll go chapter and verse.
   We could have done better if we'd only spent more.
   Too bad that only happens when there's a world war.
   You can carp all you want about stats and regression.
   Do you deny that world war cut short the Depression?

   [Hayek] Wow. One data point and you're jumping for joy.
   The last time I checked wars only destroy.
   There was no multiplier. Consumption just shrank
   As we used scarce resources for every new tank.
   Pretty perverse to call that prosperity.
   Ration meat. Ration butter. A life of austerity.
   When that war spending ended, your friends cried disaster.
   Yet the economy thrived and grew faster.
   Creating employment is a straightforward craft
   When the nation's at war and there's a draft.
   If every worker were staffed in the army and fleet

We'd have full employment and nothing to eat.
Jobs are a means, not the end in themselves.
People work to live better, to put food on the shelves.
Real growth means production of what people demand.
That's entrepreneurship, not your central plan.

4. The following lyrics discuss the appropriateness of the government bailouts in response to the 2008 financial crisis. Explain why Keynesians generally support these policies while Hayekians do not.

[Hayek] And yet it continues as a justification
For bailouts and payoffs by pols with machi nations.
You provide them with cover to sell us a free lunch,
Then all that we're left with is debt, and a bunch.
If you're living high on that cheap credit hog
Don't look for cure from the hair of the dog.
Let's not repeat what created our troubles.
I want real growth not a series of bubbles.
Stop bailing out losers, let prices work.
If we don't try to steer them they won't go berserk.

SPECIAL TOPIC 5
The Crisis of 2008: Causes and Lessons for the Future

FOCUS

- What impact has the 2008 crisis had on the U.S. economy?
- Why did housing prices rise rapidly during 2001–2005 and then fall in the years immediately following? Did regulation play a role? Did monetary policy contribute to the housing boom and bust?
- What caused the economic Crisis of 2008?
- What lessons should we learn from the Crisis of 2008?

U.S. housing policies are the root cause of the current financial crisis. Other players—"greedy" investment bankers; foolish investors; imprudent bankers; incompetent rating agencies;irresponsible housing speculators; shortsighted homeowners; and predatory mortgage brokers, lenders, and borrowers—all played a part, but they were only following the economic incentives that government policy laid out for them.
—**Peter J. Wallison**[1]

[1]Peter J. Wallison, "Cause and Effect: Government Policies and the Financial Crisis," AEI Financial ServicesOutlook, www.aei.org/publication29015.

The headlines of 2008 were dominated by falling housing prices, rising default and foreclosure rates, failure of large investment banks, and huge bailouts arranged by both the Federal Reserve and the U.S. Treasury. The Crisis of 2008 substantially reduced the wealth of most Americans and generated widespread concern about the future of the U.S. economy. This crisis and the response to it may well be the most important macroeconomic event of our lives. Thus, it is vitally important for each of us to understand what happened, why things went wrong, and the lessons that need to be learned from the experience.

Let's take a closer look at the key events leading up to the crisis and the underlying factors that generated the collapse.

ST05-1 KEY EVENTS LEADING UP TO THE CRISIS

The housing boom and bust during the first seven years of this century are central to understanding the economic events of 2008. As Exhibit 1 shows, housing prices were relatively stable during the 1990s, but they began to increase rapidly toward the end of the decade. By 2002, housing prices were booming. Between January 2002 and mid-year 2006, housing prices increased by a whopping 87 percent. This translates to an annual growth rate of approximately 13 percent. But the housing boom began to wane in 2006. Housing prices leveled off, and by the end of 2006, they were falling. The boom had turned to a bust, and the housing price decline continued throughout 2007 and 2008. By year-end 2008, housing prices were approximately 30 percent below their 2006 peak.

EXHIBIT 1

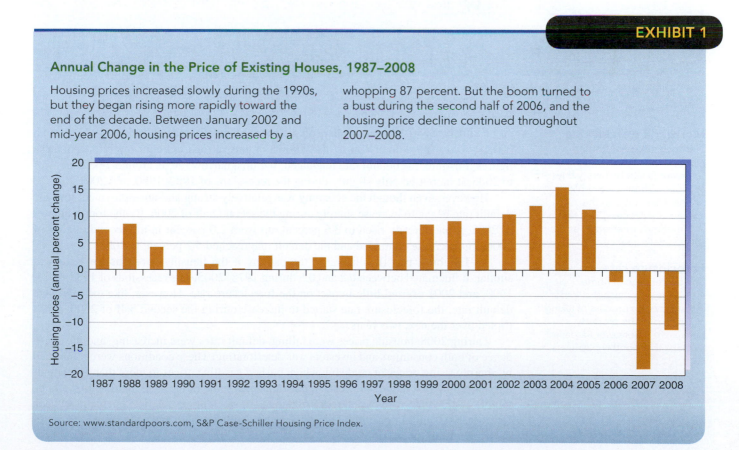

Annual Change in the Price of Existing Houses, 1987–2008

Housing prices increased slowly during the 1990s, but they began rising more rapidly toward the end of the decade. Between January 2002 and mid-year 2006, housing prices increased by a whopping 87 percent. But the boom turned to a bust during the second half of 2006, and the housing price decline continued throughout 2007–2008.

Source: www.standardpoors.com, S&P Case-Schiller Housing Price Index.

EXHIBIT 2

Mortgage Default and Housing Foreclosure Rates, 1979–2008

As part (a) shows, the mortgage default rate fluctuated within a narrow range around 2 percent for more than two decades before 2006. It increased only slightly during the recessions of 1982, 1990, and 2001 but started to increase in the second half of 2006 and soared to more than 5 percent in 2008. As part (b) shows, the foreclosure rate followed a similar pattern. It ranged between 0.2 and 0.5 percent before 2006, before soaring to 1.2 percent in 2008.

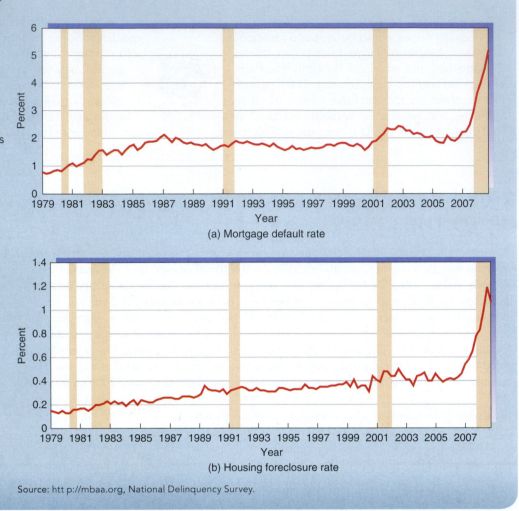

(a) Mortgage default rate

(b) Housing foreclosure rate

Source: htt p://mbaa.org, National Delinquency Survey.

Mortgage default rate
The percentage of home mortgages on which the borrower is late by ninety days or more with the payments on the loan or it is in the foreclosure process. This rate is sometimes referred to as the serious delinquency rate.

Foreclosure rate
The percentage of home mortgages on which the lender has started the process of taking ownership of the property because the borrower has failed to make the monthly payments.

Exhibit 2 part (a) presents data on the **mortgage default rate** from 1979 through 2008. (*Note:* The default rate is also known as the serious delinquency rate.) As these figures illustrate, the default rate fluctuated, within a narrow range, around 2 percent prior to 2006. It increased only slightly during the recessions of 1982, 1990, and 2001.

However, even though the economy was relatively strong and unemployment low, the default rate began to increase sharply during the second half of 2006. By the fourth quarter of 2007, it had already risen to 3.6 percent, up from 2.0 percent in the second quarter of 2006. The increase continued and the default rate reached 5.2 percent in 2008.

As Exhibit 2 part (b) illustrates, the pattern of the housing **foreclosure rate** was similar. It fluctuated between 0.2 and 0.5 during 1978–2005. The recessions of 1982–1983, 1990, and 2001 exerted little impact on the foreclosure rate. However, like the mortgage default rate, the foreclosure rate started to increase during the second half of 2006, and it tripled over the next two years.

During 2008, housing prices were falling, default rates were increasing, and the confidence of both consumers and investors was deteriorating. These conditions were reinforced by sharply rising prices of crude oil, which pushed gasoline prices to more than $4 per gallon during the first half of the year. Against this background, the stock market took a huge tumble. As **Exhibit 3** shows, the S&P 500 index of stock prices fell by 55 percent between October 2007 and March 2009. This collapse eroded the wealth and endangered the retirement savings of many Americans.

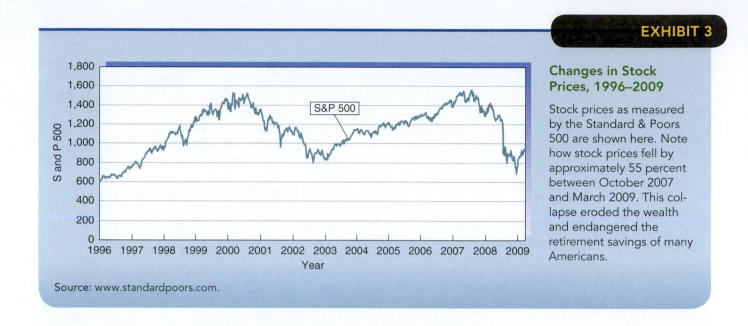

EXHIBIT 3

Changes in Stock Prices, 1996–2009

Stock prices as measured by the Standard & Poors 500 are shown here. Note how stock prices fell by approximately 55 percent between October 2007 and March 2009. This collapse eroded the wealth and endangered the retirement savings of many Americans.

Source: www.standardpoors.com.

ST05-2 WHAT CAUSED THE CRISIS OF 2008?

Why did housing prices rise rapidly, then level off, and eventually collapse? Why did the mortgage default and housing foreclosure rates increase rapidly well before the start of the recession, which did not begin until December 2007? Why are the recent default and foreclosure rates so much higher than the rates of earlier years, including those of prior recessions? Why did large, and seemingly strong, investment banks like Bear Stearns and Lehman Brothers run into financial troubles so quickly? Four factors combine to provide the answers to all of these questions.[2]

ST05-2a FACTOR 1: CHANGE IN MORTGAGE LENDING STANDARDS

The lending standards for home mortgage loans changed substantially beginning in the mid-1990s. The looser lending standards did not just happen. They were the result of federal policy designed to promote home ownership among households with incomes below the median. Home ownership is a worthy goal, but it was not pursued directly through transparent budget allocations and subsidies to homebuyers. Instead, the federal government imposed a complex set of regulations and regulatory mandates that forced various lending institutions to extend more loans to low- and moderate-income households. To meet these mandates, lenders had to lower their standards. By the early years of the twenty-first century, it was possible to borrow more (relative to your income) and purchase a house or condo with a lower down payment than was the case a decade earlier.

The Federal National Mortgage Association and Federal Home Loan Mortgage Corporation, commonly known as Fannie Mae and Freddie Mac, played a central role in this relaxation of mortgage lending standards. These two entities were created by Congress to help provide liquidity in secondary mortgage markets. Fannie Mae, established by the federal

[2]For additional details on the Crisis of 2008, see Thomas Sowell, *The Housing Boom and Bust* (New York: Basic Books, 2009); Stan J. Liebowitz, "Anatomy of a Train Wreck: Causes of the Mortgage Meltdown," in *Housing America: Building Out of a Crisis*, ed. Randall G. Holcombe and Benjamin Powell (New Brunswick, NJ: Transaction Publishers, 2009); Peter J. Wallison, "Cause and Effect: Government Policies and the Financial Crisis," *AEI Financial Services Outlook*, www.aei.org/publication29015; and Lawrence H. White, "How Did We Get Into This Financial Mess?" (Briefing Paper 110, Cato Institute, Washington, DC, November 18, 2008), available at www.cato.org/pub_display.php?pub_id=9788.

government in 1938, was spun off as a *government-sponsored enterprise* (GSE) in 1968. Freddie Mac was created in 1970 as another GSE to provide competition for Fannie Mae.

Fannie Mae and Freddie Mac were privately owned (for-profit) businesses, but because of their federal sponsorship, it was widely perceived that the government would back their bonds if they ever ran into financial trouble. As a result, Fannie and Freddie were able to borrow funds at 50 to 75 **basis points** cheaper than private lenders. This gave them a competitive advantage, and they were highly profitable for many years. However, the GSE structure also meant that they were asked to serve two masters: their stockholders, who were interested in profitability, and Congress and federal regulators, who predictably were more interested in political objectives.

As a result of their GSE structure, Fannie Mae and Freddie Mac were highly political. The top management of Fannie and Freddie provided key congressional leaders with large political contributions and often hired away congressional staffers into high-paying jobs lobbying their former bosses. Between the 2000 and 2008 election cycles, high-level managers and other employees of Fannie Mae and Freddie Mac contributed more than $14.6 million to the campaign funds of dozens of senators and representatives, most of whom were on congressional committees important for the protection of their privileged status.

The lobbying activities of Fannie Mae and Freddie Mac were legendary. Between 1998 and 2008, Fannie spent $79.5 million and Freddie spent $94.9 million on congressional lobbying, placing them among the biggest spenders on these activities. They also set up "partnership offices" in the districts and states of important legislators, often hiring the relatives of these lawmakers to staff these local offices.[3] The politicians, for their part, and the regulators who answered to them fashioned rules that made very high profits possible for the GSEs, at least in the short run. Although it was a relationship that reflected political favoritism (some would say corruption), members of Congress, particularly those involved in banking regulation, were highly supportive of the arrangement.

Fannie Mae and Freddie Mac did not originate mortgages. Instead, they purchased the mortgages originated by banks, mortgage brokers, and other lenders. Propelled by their cheaper access to funds, Fannie Mae and Freddie Mac grew rapidly during the 1990s. As Exhibit 4 shows, the share of all mortgages held by Fannie Mae and Freddie Mac jumped from 25 percent in 1990 to 45 percent in 2001. Their share fluctuated around 40 percent during 2001–2008. Their dominance of the **secondary mortgage market** was even greater. During the decade prior to their insolvency and takeover by the federal government during the summer of 2008, Fannie Mae and Freddie Mac purchased about 90 percent of the mortgages sold in the secondary market. Because of this dominance, their lending practices exerted a huge impact on the standards accepted by mortgage originators.

Responding to earlier congressional legislation, the Department of Housing and Urban Development (HUD) imposed regulations designed to make housing more affordable. The HUD mandates, adopted in 1995, required Fannie Mae and Freddie Mac to extend a larger share of their loans to low- and moderate-income households. For example, under the HUD mandates, 40 percent of new loans financed by Fannie Mae and Freddie Mac in 1996 had to go to borrowers with incomes below the median. This mandated share was steadily increased to 50 percent in 2000 and 56 percent in 2008. Similar increases were mandated for borrowers with incomes of less than 60 percent of the median. Moreover, in 1999, HUD guidelines required Fannie Mae and Freddie Mac to accept smaller down payments and extend larger loans relative to income.

The policies of Fannie Mae and Freddie Mac exerted an enormous impact on the actions of banks and other mortgage lenders. Recognizing that riskier loans could be passed on to Fannie and Freddie, mortgage originators had less incentive to scrutinize

Basis points

One one-hundredth of a percentage point. Thus, 100 basis points are equivalent to one percentage point.

Secondary mortgage market

A market in which mortgages originated by a lender are sold to another financial institution. In recent years, the major buyers in this market have been Fannie Mae, Freddie Mac, and large investment banks.

---

[3]For additional details, see Peter J. Wallison and Charles W. Calomiris, "The Destruction of Fannie Mae and Freddie Mac," American Enterprise Institute, online (posted Tuesday, September 30, 2008). Also see Common Cause, "Ask Yourself Why...They Didn't See This Coming" (September 24, 2008), available at www.commoncause.org/site/pp.asp?c=dkLNK1MQIwG&b=4542875; and Center for Responsive Politics, "Lobbying: Top Spenders" (2008), available at www.opensecrets.org/lobby/top.php?indexType=s.

EXHIBIT 4

The Share of Total Outstanding Mortgages Held by Fannie Mae and Freddie Mac, 1990–2008

Fannie Mae and Freddie Mac dominated the mortgage market for many years. Because of their government sponsorship, they were able to obtain funds cheaper than private firms. They held 45 percent of all mortgages in 2001, up from 25 percent in 1990. During 2001–2008, their share fluctuated around 40 percent. Their dominance of the secondary market, where loans are purchased from originators, is even greater. In July 2008, they were declared insolvent and taken over by the U.S. Treasury.

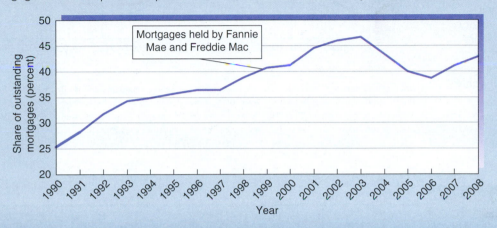

Mortgages held by Fannie Mae and Freddie Mac

Source: Office of Federal Housing Enterprise Oversight, www.ofheo.gov.

the creditworthiness of borrowers and more incentive to reduce the required down payment, in order to sell more mortgages. After all, when the mortgages were soon sold to Fannie or Freddie, the risk was transferred to them also. The bottom line: Required down payments were reduced and the accepted credit standards lowered.

Modifications to the Community Reinvestment Act (CRA) in 1995 also loosened mortgage-lending standards. These changes required banks to meet numeric goals based on the low-income and minority population of their service areas when extending mortgage loans. In order to meet these requirements, many banks, especially those in urban areas, were forced to reduce their lending standards and extend more loans to borrowers who did not meet the conventional credit criteria.

The lower standards resulting from the GSE and CRA regulations reduced lending standards across the board. Lenders could hardly offer low-down-payment loans and larger mortgages relative to housing value on **subprime loans**, without offering similar terms to prime borrowers. As the regulations tightened, the share of loans extended to subprime borrowers steadily increased. Exhibit 5 illustrates this point. Measured as a share of mortgages originated during the year, subprime mortgages rose from 4.5 percent in 1994 to 13.2 percent in 2000 and 20 percent in 2005 and 2006. (*Note:* Bank examiners consider a loan to be subprime if the borrower's **FICO score** is less than 660.) When the **Alt-A loans**, those extended without full documentation, were added to the subprime, a third of the mortgages extended in 2005–2006 were to borrowers with either poor or highly questionable credit records.

As the mortgages extended to those with weak credit soared, so too did the number with little or no down payment. Exhibit 6 shows both the number of loans issued by Fannie Mae and Freddie Mac and the share extended to borrowers with 5 percent or less down payment. Note how the number of new loans financed by the government sponsored corporations increased from less than one hundred thousand in the late 1990s to more than six hundred thousand in 2007. At the same time, the share of mortgages to borrowers making a down payment of 5 percent or less rose from 4 percent in 1998 to 12 percent in 2003 and 23 percent in 2007. Thus, Fannie Mae and Freddie Mac were flooding the market with low-down-payment loans extended to borrowers with weak credit. Meanwhile,

Subprime loan
A loan made to a borrower with blemished credit or one who provides only limited documentation of income, employment history, and other indicators of creditworthiness.

FICO score
A credit score measuring a borrower's likely ability to repay a loan. A person's FICO score will range between 300 and 850. A score of 700 or more indicates that the borrower's credit standing is good. FICO is an acronym for the Fair Isaac Corporation, the creators of the FICO score.

Alt-A loans
Loans extended with little documentation or verification of the borrowers' income, employment, and other indicators of their ability to repay. Because of this poor documentation, these loans are risky.

EXHIBIT 5

Subprime and Alt-A Mortgages as a Share of the Total, 1994–2007

Both subprime and Alt-A mortgages reflect loans to borrowers with a weak credit history. Note how the share of loans to borrowers in these two categories jumped from roughly 10 percent in 2001–2003 to 33 percent in 2005–2006.

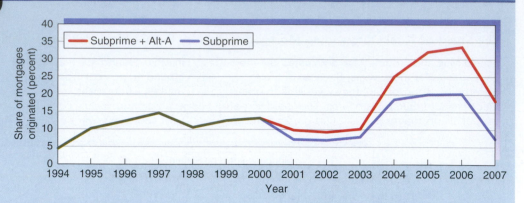

Source: The data for 1994–2000 are from Edward M. Gramlich, Financial Services Roundtable Annual Housing Policy Meeting, Chicago, Illinois (21 May 2004), www.federalreserve.gov/boarddocs/speeches/2004/20040521/default.htm. The data for 2001–2007 are from the Joint Center for Housing Studies of Harvard University, The State of the Nation's Housing 2008, www.jchs.harvard.edu/son/index.htm.

EXHIBIT 6

Growth of Low-down-payment Loans Extended by Fannie Mae and Freddie Mac

Following the 1999 HUD guidelines encouraging Fannie Mae and Freddie Mac to extend more low-down-payment loans, the GSEs both increased the number of their mortgages (left frame) and the share extended with a down payment of 5 percent or less. As the right frame shows, the share of these low down payment mortgages extended by Fannie Mae and Freddie Mac increased from 4 percent in 1998 to 12 percent in 2003 and 23 percent in 2007.

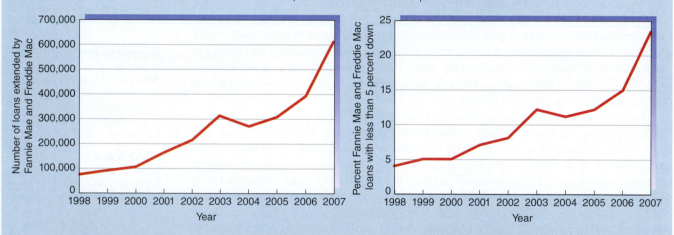

Sources: Russell Robert's, *Gambling With Other Peoples Money*, Mercatus Center, http://mercatus.org/publications/gambling-other-peoples-money.

conventional loans for which borrowers were required to make at least a 20 percent down payment fell from two-thirds of the total in the early 1990s to only one-third in 2005–2006.

The shift from conventional loans to "creative finance" and "flexible standards," as the regulators called the new criteria, is highly important because the default and foreclosure rates for subprime loans ranges from seven to ten times the rate for conventional loans to prime borrowers. This differential is even greater in the case of mortgages with little or no down payment. Initially, this easy credit policy increased demand and pushed housing prices upward. But, the policy was not sustainable and it was predictable where it would lead. Eventually, the growing share of low-down-payment loans extended to those with weak credit would result in substantially higher default and foreclosure rates. This is precisely what happened.

ST05-2b FACTOR 2: PROLONGED LOW-INTEREST RATE POLICY OF THE FED DURING 2002–2004

Following the high and variable inflation rates of the 1970s, Federal Reserve policy focused on keeping the inflation rate low and stable. By the mid-1980s, the inflation rate had been reduced to 3 percent. Throughout 1985–1999, the Fed kept the inflation rate low and avoided abrupt year-to-year changes. In turn, the relative price stability reduced uncertainty and created an environment for both strong growth and economic stability. During this era, it was widely believed that price stability was the only objective that could be achieved with monetary policy, and if this objective was achieved, the monetary policy makers had done their job well.

However, as the lessons of this period began to dissipate, Fed policy makers, including chairman Alan Greenspan, began to focus more on control of real variables such as employment and real GDP. Reflecting this change, Fed policy has been more erratic since 1999. Monetary policy was expansionary just before 2000, restrictive prior to the recession of 2001, and then highly expansionary during the recovery from that recession. As Exhibit 7 shows, the Fed kept short-term interest rates at historic lows throughout 2002–2004. These extremely low short-term rates increased the demand for interest-sensitive goods like automobiles and housing.

The Fed's artificially low short-term rates substantially increased the attractiveness of **adjustable rate mortgages (ARMs)** to both borrowers and lenders. As Exhibit 8 shows, adjustable rate mortgages jumped from 10 percent of the total outstanding mortgages in 2000 to 21 percent in 2005. The low initial interest rates on adjustable rate mortgages made it possible for homebuyers to afford the monthly payments for larger, more expensive homes. This easy credit provided fuel for the housing boom. But the low rates and ARM loans also meant that as short-term interest rates increased from their historic low levels, home buyers would face a higher monthly payment two or three years in the future. Unsurprisingly, this is precisely what happened.

Adjustable rate mortgage (ARM)
A home loan in which the interest rate, and thus the monthly payment, is tied to a short-term rate like the one-year Treasury bill rate. Typically, the mortgage interest rate will be two or three percentage points above the related short-term rate. It will be reset at various time intervals (e.g., annually), and thus the interest rate and monthly payment will vary over the life of the loan.

EXHIBIT 7

Fed Policy and Short-Term Interest Rates, 1995–2009

Here we show the federal funds and one-year Treasury bill interest rates. These short-term rates are reflective of monetary policy. Note how the Fed pushed these rates to historic lows (less than 2 percent) throughout 2002–2004 but then increased them substantially during 2005–2006.

The low rates provided fuel for the housing price boom, but the rising rates led to higher interest rates and monthly payments on adjustable rate mortgage (ARM) loans, which helped push the mortgage default and foreclosure rates upward beginning in the second half of 2006.

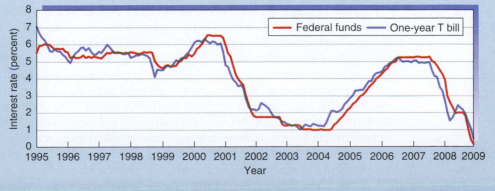

Sources: www.federalreserve.gov and www.economagic.com.

EXHIBIT 8

Adjustable Rate Mortgages (ARMs) as a Share of Total Outstanding Mortgages, 1990–2008

The interest rate and monthly payment on ARMs are tied to a short-term interest rate (e.g., the one-year Treasury bill rate). The Fed's low-interest rate policy of 2002–2004 increased the attractiveness of ARMs. Note how ARM loans increased as a share of total mortgages from 10 percent in 2000 to 21 percent in 2005.

Source: Office of Federal Housing Enterprise Oversight, www.ofheo.gov.

By 2005, the expansionary monetary policy of 2002–2004 was clearly placing upward pressure on the general level of prices. The Fed responded with a shift to a more restrictive monetary policy, which pushed interest rates upward (see Exhibit 7). Many who purchased houses with little or no down payment and adjustable rate loans when interest rates were low during 2002–2004 faced substantially higher monthly payments as interest rates rose and the monthly payments on their ARM loans were reset during 2006 and 2007. These owners had virtually no equity in their homes. Therefore, when housing prices leveled off and began to decline during the second half of 2006, the default and foreclosure rates on these loans began to rise almost immediately (see Exhibits 1 and 2). Some owners with little or no initial equity simply walked away as their outstanding loan exceeded the value of their house.

Essentially, the small down payment and ARMs combination made it possible for homebuyers to gamble with someone else's money. If housing prices rose, buyers could reap a sizable capital gain without risking much of their own investment capital. Based on the rising housing prices of 2000–2005, many of these homebuyers expected to sell the house for a profit and move on in a couple of years. There were even television programs and investment seminars pushing this strategy as the route to riches.

Exhibit 9 shows the foreclosure rates for fixed interest rate and ARM loans for both subprime and prime loans. Compared to their prime borrower counterparts, the foreclosure rate for subprime borrowers was approximately ten times higher for fixed rate mortgages and seven times higher for adjustable rate mortgages. These huge differentials explain why the increasing share of loans to subprime borrowers substantially increased the default and foreclosure rates.

As Exhibit 9 shows, there was no upward trend in the foreclosure rate on fixed interest rate loans for either prime or subprime borrowers during 2000–2008. On the other hand, the foreclosure rate on ARMs soared for both prime and subprime loans during 2006–2008. In fact, the percentage increase in foreclosures on ARM loans was higher for prime than subprime borrowers. This is highly revealing. It illustrates that both prime and subprime borrowers played the low-down-payment, mortgage casino game.

The crisis is often referred to as the *subprime mortgage crisis*. This is true, but it is only part of the story. It was also an ARM loan crisis. Fed policy encouraging

EXHIBIT 9

The Foreclosure Rate of Fixed and Adjustable Rate Mortgages for Subprime and Prime Borrowers, 1998–2008

The foreclosure rates on fixed and adjustable interest rate mortgages are shown here for both subprime (part a) and prime (part b) borrowers. Note how the foreclosure rate was generally seven to ten times higher for subprime loans than for those to prime borrowers. As housing prices leveled off and declined in 2006–2008, the foreclosure rate on fixed interest rate mortgages did not change much. In contrast, the foreclosure rate for ARM loans soared beginning in the second half of 2006, and this was true for ARM loans to both subprime and prime borrowers. Clearly, the increasing share of both subprime and ARM loans during 2000–2005 contributed to the boom and bust of the housing market.

(a) Subprime loans

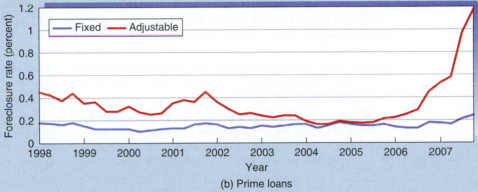

(b) Prime loans

Source: Stan J. Liebowitz, "Anatomy of a Train Wreck: Causes of the Mortgage Meltdown," Ch. 13 in Randall G. Holcombe and Benjamin Powell, eds, *Housing America: Building Out of a Crisis* (New Brunswick, NJ: Transaction Publishers, 2009). We would like to thank Professor Liebowitz for making this data available to us.

ARM loans, the increasing proportion of these loans as a share of the total, and their higher default and foreclosure rates also contributed substantially, first to the housing boom and then to the bust. The combination of the mortgage lending regulations and the Fed's artificially low interest rate policies encouraged decision-makers to borrow more money and make unwise and inefficient investments.

ST05-2c FACTOR 3: THE INCREASED DEBT-TO-CAPITAL RATIO OF INVESTMENT BANKS

A rule change adopted by the Securities and Exchange Commission (SEC) in April 2004 made it possible for **investment banks** to increase the leverage of their investment capital, which eventually led to their collapse. A firm's **leverage ratio** is simply the ratio of its investment

Investment bank
An institution that acts as an underwriter for securities issued by other corporations or lenders. Unlike traditional banks, investment banks do not accept deposits from, or provide loans to, individuals.

Leverage ratios
The ratio of loans and other investments to the firm's capital assets.

holdings (including loans) relative to its capital. Thus, if a firm had investment funds that were twelve times the size of its equity capital, its leverage ratio would be 12 to 1. Prior to the SEC rule change, this was approximately the leverage ratio of both investment and commercial banks.

Essentially, the SEC applied regulations known as Basel I to investment banking. These regulations, which have been adopted by most of the industrial countries, require banks to maintain at least 8 percent capital against assets like loans to commercial businesses. This implies a leverage ratio of approximately 12 to 1. However, the Basil regulations provide more favorable treatment of residential loans. The capital requirement for residential mortgage loans is only 4 percent, which implies a 25 to 1 leverage ratio. Even more important, the capital requirement for low-risk securities is still lower at 1.6 percent. This means that the permissible leverage ratio for low-risk securities could be as high as 60 to 1.

Key investment banking leaders, including Henry Paulson who was CEO of Goldman Sachs at the time, urged the SEC to apply the higher leverage ratio to investment banks. Ironically, Paulson later became Secretary of the Treasury and was in charge of the federal "bailout" of the banks that got into trouble because of the excessive leveraging of their capital.

Following the rule change, large investment banks, like Lehman Brothers, Goldman Sachs, and Bear Stearns, expanded their mortgage financing activities. They bundled large holdings of mortgages together and issued securities for their finance. Because of the diversity of the mortgage portfolio, investment in the underlying securities was thought to involve minimal risk. If the **security-rating** firms provided the **mortgage-backed securities** with a AAA rating, then the investment banks could leverage them up to 60 to 1 against their capital.

The mortgage-backed securities, financed with short-term leveraged lending, were highly lucrative. The large number of mortgages packaged together provided lenders with diversity and protection against abnormally high default rates in specific regions and loan categories. But it did not shield them from an overall increase in mortgage default rates. As default rates increased sharply in 2006 and 2007, it became apparent that the mortgage-backed securities were far more risky than had been previously thought. When the risk of these mortgages became more apparent, the value of the mortgage-backed securities plummeted because it was difficult to know their true value. As the value of the mortgage-backed securities collapsed, the highly leveraged investment banks faced massive short-term debt obligations with little reserves on which to draw. This is why the investment banks collapsed so quickly. In fact, when the Fed financed the acquisition of Bear Stearns by JPMorgan Chase, the leverage ratio of Bear Stearns was an astounding 33 to 1, about two and a half times the historical level associated with prudent banking practices.

Why didn't key Wall Street decision makers see the looming danger? No doubt, they were influenced by the low and relatively stable default rates over the past several decades (see Exhibit 2). Even during serious recessions like those of 1974–1975 and 1982–1983, the mortgage default rates were only a little more than 2 percent, less than half the rates of 2008. But one would still have thought that analysts at investment companies and security-rating firms would have warned that the low historical rates were for periods when down payments were larger, borrowing was more restricted relative to income, and fewer loans were made to subprime borrowers. A few analysts did provide warnings, but their views were ignored by high-level superiors.

However, the incentive structure also helps explain why highly intelligent people failed to see the oncoming danger. The bonuses of most Wall Street executives are closely tied to short-term profitability, and the mortgage-backed securities were highly profitable when housing prices were rising and interest rates were low. If a personal bonus of a million dollars or more is at stake this year, one is likely to be far less sensitive to the long-term dangers.

The incentive structure accompanying the regulation and rating of securities also played an important role. Only three firms—Moody's, Standard & Poors, and Fitch—are legally authorized to rate securities. These rating agencies are paid by the firm requesting the rating. A Triple-A rating was exceedingly important. It made higher leveraging possible, but, even more important, the Triple-A rating made it possible to sell the mortgage-backed securities to institutional investors, retirement plans, and investors around the world looking for relatively safe investments. The rating agencies were paid attractive fees for their ratings, and Triple-A

Security rating
A rating indicating the risk of default of the security. A rating of AAA indicates that the risk of default is low.

Mortgage-backed securities
Securities issued for the financing of large pools of mortgages. The promised returns to the security holders are derived from the mortgage interest payments.

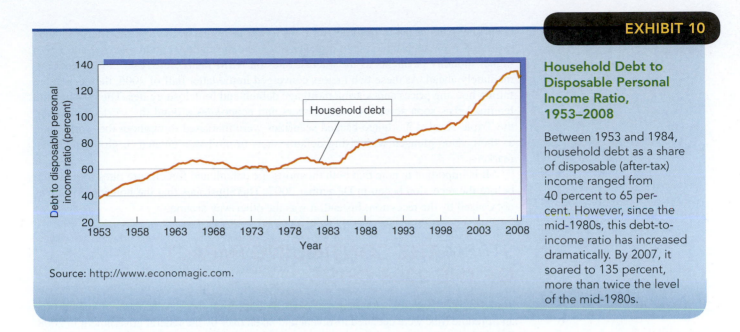

Source: http://www.economagic.com.

EXHIBIT 10

Household Debt to Disposable Personal Income Ratio, 1953–2008

Between 1953 and 1984, household debt as a share of disposable (after-tax) income ranged from 40 percent to 65 percent. However, since the mid-1980s, this debt-to-income ratio has increased dramatically. By 2007, it soared to 135 percent, more than twice the level of the mid-1980s.

approval would mean more business for the rating agencies as well as the investment banks. Clearly, this incentive structure is not one that encourages careful scrutiny and hard-nosed evaluation of the quality of the underlying mortgage bundle. Paradoxically, the shortsighted and counterproductive incentive structures that characterize some of Wall Street's best-known firms contributed to their collapse.

ST05-2d FACTOR 4: HIGH DEBT/INCOME RATIO OF HOUSEHOLDS

During 1985–2007, household debt grew to unprecedented levels. As **Exhibit 10** shows, household debt as a share of disposable (after-tax) income ranged from 40 percent to 65 percent during 1953–1984. However, since the mid-1980s, the debt-to-income ratio of households climbed at an alarming rate. It reached 135 percent in 2007, more than twice the level of the mid-1980s. Unsurprisingly, more debt means that a larger share of household income is required just to meet the interest payments.

Interest payments on home mortgages and home equity loans are tax deductible, but household interest on other forms of debt is not. This incentive structure encourages households to concentrate their debt into loans against their housing. But a large debt against one's housing will mean that housing will be the hardest hit by unexpected events that force major adjustments. This is precisely what occurred in 2006–2008. The rising interest rates and mere leveling off of housing prices soon led to an increase in mortgage defaults and foreclosures, because households were heavily indebted and a huge share of that indebtedness was in the form of mortgages against their housing. As the economy weakened, of course, this situation quickly worsened. Thus, the high level of household indebtedness also contributed to the Crisis of 2008.

ST05-3 HOUSING, MORTGAGE DEFAULTS, AND THE CRISIS OF 2008

The combination of the HUD regulations, low-down-payment requirements, and the Fed's low interest policy of 2002–2004 resulted in the rapid growth of both subprime and ARM loans during the first five years of this century. As is often the case with policy changes, the initial effects were positive—strong demand for housing, rising housing prices, and a construction boom. But the long-term effects were disastrous. The increasing share of subprime loans began to push default rates upward. Similarly, the low short-term interest rates that made adjustable rate mortgages attractive during 2004 soon reversed and led to higher monthly payments as the interest rates on ARM loans were reset in the years immediately ahead. As these two factors converged in the latter half of 2006, they generated falling housing prices and soaring mortgage default and foreclosure rates. The housing and lending crisis soon spread to other sectors and economies around the world. Moreover, the Triple-A rated mortgage-backed securities were marketed throughout the world, and, as their value plunged with rising default rates, turmoil was created in global financial markets.

It is important to note that both the mortgage default and foreclosure rates soared well before the recession began in December 2007. This illustrates that the housing crisis was not caused by the recession. Instead, it was the other way around.

ST05-4 THE CONTINUING IMPACT OF THE 2008 CRISIS

The 2008 financial crisis continues to exert an impact on the U.S. economy. Fannie Mae and Freddie Mac were declared insolvent and taken over by the federal government in 2008. They have received $188 billion in taxpayer funds and still obtain credit at lower interest rates than other potential lenders. The government now dominates the mortgage market. When the mortgage loans of the Federal Housing Administration are added to those of Fannie Mae and Freddie Mac, 90 percent of the new mortgages for housing are currently financed by the federal government. In essence, the mortgage lending business has been nationalized.

Will this dominance of the housing loan market by the federal government persist? Both President Obama and Congress indicate they would like to privatize Fannie Mae and Freddie Mac and reduce the government's role in the housing loan market. However, their incentive to act is relatively weak. In 2012, the net earnings of Fannie Mae and Freddie Mac were positive. While this was good news, it comes with a downside: The inflow of these funds to the Treasury will make it more difficult to privatize them and denationalize the mortgage lending market.

As discussed earlier, regulations that created perverse incentives and undermined sound lending practices were a central cause of the Crisis of 2008. In the aftermath of the Crisis, new regulations designed to prevent the next crisis were adopted. Will these regulations be effective? There is reason for skepticism. History illustrates that regulation is not a cure all. Regulatory agencies will be characterized by "tunnel vision." They will focus on their narrow objectives (e.g., promoting home ownership), and they will largely ignore the secondary effects of their actions. Regulators have a poor record with regard to foreseeing future problems. After all, mortgage lending and banking are two of the most heavily regulated sectors of our economy, but none of their regulators foresaw the problems leading up to the 2008 crisis. With time, a sweetheart relationship will nearly always develop between the regulators and those whom they regulate. All of these factors should cause one to pause before believing that a new regulatory apparatus will head off the next crisis.

To a large degree, the Crisis of 2008 reflects what happens when policies confront people with perverse incentives. Constructive reforms need to focus on getting the incentives right. Consider the following questions. Would the mortgage market work better if loan originators were held responsible for defaults on loans they originated, even if they sold them to another party? Does it really make sense to encourage households to concentrate all of their debt against their house, as current tax policy does? Should high-level corporate managers be provided with a stronger incentive to pursue the long-term success of their company? Incentives related to all of these questions played a role in the Crisis of 2008. Although the precise response is not obvious, the crisis suggests that review of current policy in these areas would be wise.

KEY POINTS

- After soaring during the previous five years, housing prices began to decline during the second half of 2006, and mortgage defaults and housing foreclosures started to increase. As the housing bust spread to other sectors, stock prices plunged, major investment banks experienced financial troubles, unemployment increased sharply, and by 2008 the economy was in a severe recession.

- Fannie Mae and Freddie Mac grew rapidly during the 1990s. Their government sponsorship made it possible for them to obtain funds cheaper than private rivals. Because of their dominance of the secondary market, in which mortgages are purchased from originators, their lending standards exerted a huge impact on the mortgage market.

- Beginning in the mid-1990s, mandates imposed on Fannie Mae and Freddie Mac, along with regulations imposed on banks, forced lenders to reduce their lending standards, extend more mortgages to subprime borrowers, and reduce down payment requirements. The share of mortgages extended to subprime borrowers (including Alt-A loans) rose from 10 percent in 2001–2003 to 33 percent in 2005–2006. Correspondingly, the share of low-down-payment loans extended by Fannie Mae and Freddie Mac soared from 4 percent in 1998 to 23 percent in 2007. These changes were highly important because the default and foreclosure rates on subprime and low-down-payment loans are several times higher than for conventional loans to prime borrowers.

- The historically low interest rate policies of the Fed during 2002–2004 increased the demand for housing and the attractiveness of adjustable rate mortgages. This provided fuel for the soaring housing prices. ARM loans increased from 10 percent of total mortgages in 2000 to 21 percent in 2005. Fed policy pushed interest rates up in 2005–2006 and ARM loans were re-set, pushing monthly payments higher. As a result, the default and foreclosure rates on these loans soared for prime as well as subprime borrowers.

- As a result of regulations adopted in April 2004, investment banks were allowed to leverage their capital by as much as 60 to 1 when financing mortgages with Triple-A rated securities. The rating agencies provided the Triple-A ratings, and the mortgage-backed securities were sold around the world. As the mortgage default rates rose in 2007–2008, Fannie Mae, Freddie Mac, and the major investment banks holding large quantities of these securities quickly fell into financial troubles, and several collapsed.

- The ratio of household debt to personal income increased steadily during 1985–2007, reaching a historic high at the end of that period.

- Low-down-payment requirements, the growth of subprime and ARM loans, the Fed's easy credit policy, highly leveraged mortgage-backed securities, and heavy borrowing by households fueled the run-up in housing prices. With time, however, this was a disastrous combination that provided the ingredients for the recession and Crisis of 2008.

- The Crisis of 2008 reflects the unintended consequences of regulatory and monetary policy and what happens when the incentive structure is polluted by unsound institutions and policies.

CRITICAL ANALYSIS QUESTIONS

1. Why did housing prices rise rapidly during 2002–2005? Why did the mortgage default rate increase so sharply during 2006 and 2007 even before the 2008–2009 recession began?

2. What happened to the credit standards (e.g., minimum down payment, mortgage loan relative to the value of the house, and creditworthiness of the borrower) between 1995 and 2005? Why did the credit standards change? How did this influence the housing price bubble and later the default and foreclosure rates?

3. *If owners have little or no equity in their houses, how will this influence the likelihood that they will default on their mortgage? Why?

4. When did mortgage default and housing foreclosure rates begin to rise rapidly? When did the economy go into recession? Was there a causal relationship between the two? Discuss.

5. *When mortgage originators sell mortgages to Fannie Mae, Freddie Mac, and investment banks the originators have no additional liability for possible default by the borrower. How will this arrangement influence the incentive of the originators to scrutinize the creditworthiness of the borrower? Would the incentive structure be different if the originator planned to hold the mortgage until it was paid off? Why or why not?

6. Some charge that the Crisis of 2008 was caused by the "greed" of Wall Street firms and other bankers. Do you agree with this view? Do you think there was more greed on Wall Street in the first five years of this century than during the 1980s and 1990s? Why or why not?

*Asterisk denotes questions for which answers are given in Appendix B.

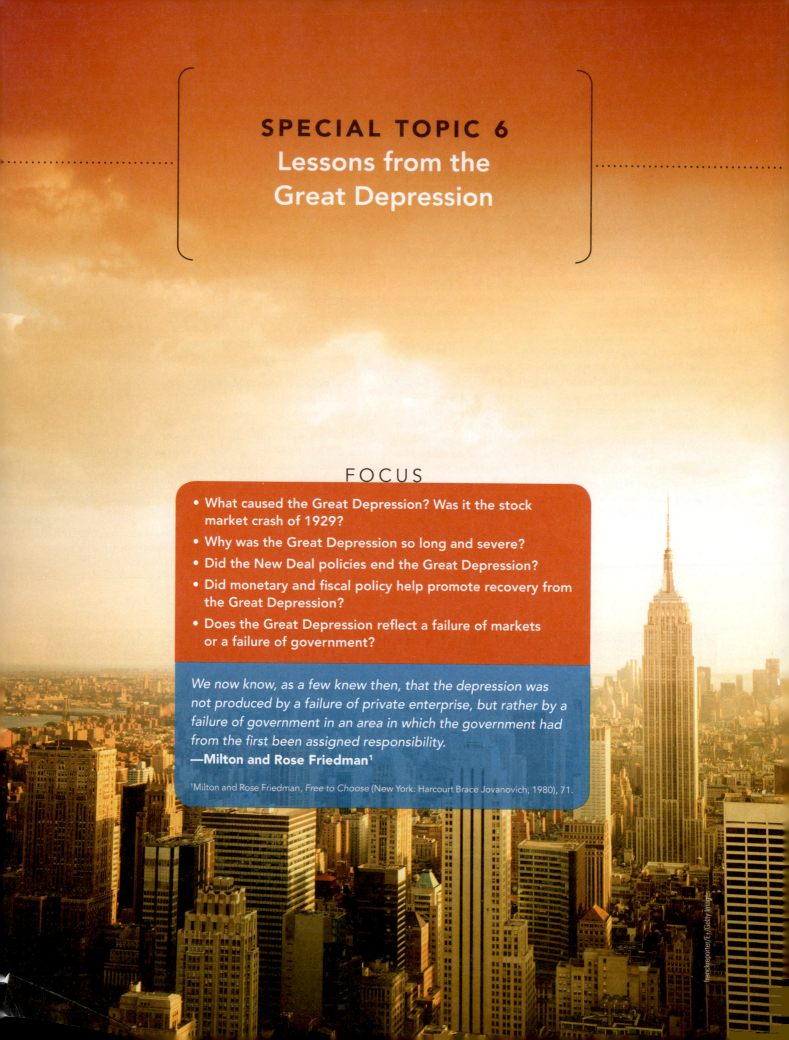

SPECIAL TOPIC 6
Lessons from the Great Depression

FOCUS

- What caused the Great Depression? Was it the stock market crash of 1929?
- Why was the Great Depression so long and severe?
- Did the New Deal policies end the Great Depression?
- Did monetary and fiscal policy help promote recovery from the Great Depression?
- Does the Great Depression reflect a failure of markets or a failure of government?

We now know, as a few knew then, that the depression was not produced by a failure of private enterprise, but rather by a failure of government in an area in which the government had from the first been assigned responsibility.
—Milton and Rose Friedman[1]

[1]Milton and Rose Friedman, *Free to Choose* (New York: Harcourt Brace Jovanovich, 1980), 71.

The Great Depression is perhaps the most catastrophic economic event in American history. It is also one of the most misunderstood. Misconceptions abound with regard to what actually happened. The Great Depression is a tragic story about economic illiteracy and the adverse impact of unsound policies. People who do not learn from the lessons of history are prone to repeat them. If we want to avoid similar experiences in the future, it is vitally important that we understand the factors underlying the tragic events of this era.

ST06-1 THE ECONOMIC RECORD OF THE GREAT DEPRESSION

Exhibit 1 presents data on the change in real GDP and the rate of unemployment during 1929–1940. As part (a) illustrates, real GDP fell by 8.6 percent in 1930, 6.5 percent in 1931, and a whopping 13.1 percent in 1932. By 1933, real GDP was nearly a third less than that in 1929. There was a temporary rebound during 1934–1936, but growth slowed in 1937 and real GDP fell once again in 1938. In 1939, a full decade after the disastrous downturn started, the real GDP of the United States was virtually the same as it had been in 1929.

While output was declining during the depression era, unemployment was soaring. As Exhibit 1, part (b), shows, the rate of unemployment rose from 3.2 percent in 1929 to 8.7 percent in 1930 and 15.9 percent in 1931. During 1932 and 1933, the unemployment rate soared to nearly one-quarter of the labor force. Even though real GDP grew substantially during 1934 and 1935, the unemployment rate remained above 20 percent during both of those years. After declining to 14.3 percent in 1937, the rate of unemployment rose to 19.0 percent during the downturn of 1938, and it was still 17.2 percent in 1939, a full decade after the catastrophic era began. The unemployment rate was 14 percent or more throughout the ten years from 1931 through 1940. By way of comparison, the unemployment rate has averaged less than 6 percent during the past quarter of a century, and it has never reached 11 percent since the Great Depression. Moreover, the statistics conceal the hardship and suffering accompanying the economic disaster. It was an era of farm foreclosures, bank failures, soup kitchens, unemployment lines, and even a sharply declining birthrate. America would never quite be the same after the 1930s.

The Great Depression was a prolonged period of falling incomes, high unemployment, and difficult living conditions. The decline in output and high unemployment were the most severe in American history. Why was the economy so weak for so long?

ST06-2 WAS THE GREAT DEPRESSION CAUSED BY THE 1929 STOCK MARKET CRASH?

The prices of stock shares rose sharply during the 1920s. But this is not surprising because the 1920s were a remarkable decade of innovation, technological advancement, and economic growth. The production of automobiles increased more than tenfold during the 1920s. Households with electricity, telephones, and indoor plumbing spread rapidly throughout the economy. The first regularly scheduled radio programs were broadcast in the early 1920s, providing an amazing new vehicle for mass communication. Air conditioning received a boost from its use in "movie houses," as theaters were called at the time. There is good reason why the decade was known as the "Roaring Twenties." Perhaps more than any other era, the lives of ordinary Americans were

EXHIBIT 1

Real GDP and the Rate of Unemployment, 1929–1940

The change in real GDP (part a) and rate of unemployment (part b) figures during the Great Depression are shown here. These data illustrate both the severity and length of the economic contraction. For four successive years (1930–1933), real output fell. Unemployment soared to nearly one-quarter of the workforce in 1932 and 1933. Although real output expanded and the rate of unemployment declined during 1934–1937, the economy again fell into the depths of a depression in 1938. In 1939, a decade after the economic plunge started, 17.2 percent of the labor force was still unemployed and real GDP was virtually unchanged from the level of 1929.

(a) Change in real GDP

(b) Unemployment rate

Sources: Real GDP growth rates for are from www.bea.gov. The unemployment data are from the Bureau or Labor Statistics (BLS) at www.bls.gov.

transformed during the 1920s. To a large degree, the stock market was merely registering the remarkable growth and development of the decade.[2]

Generations of students have been told that the Great Depression was caused by the stock market crash of October 1929. Is this really true? Let's take a look at the figures. As **Exhibit 2**, part (a), shows, the Dow Jones Industrial Average opened in 1929 at 300, rose to a high of 381 on September 3, 1929, but gradually receded to 327 on Tuesday, October 22. A major sell-off started the following day, and the Dow began to plunge. By October 29, which is known as Black Tuesday, the Dow closed at 230. Thus, in exactly one week, the stock market lost nearly one-third of its value. A couple of weeks later on November 13, the Dow fell to an even lower level, closing at 199.

---

[2]Popular writers often argue that speculators drove the stock market to unsustainable highs in the late 1920s, but this view is an exaggeration. The price/earnings ratio for the Dow was 19 just before the crash. This places it at the upper range of normal but not at an unprecedented high. On October 9, 1929, *The Wall Street Journal* reported that railroad stocks were selling at 11.9 times earnings, which would place their P/E ratio toward the lower range of normal. RCA was the hot "high-tech" company of the era, and it earned $6.15 per share in 1927 and $15.98 per share in 1928. It traded at a high in 1928 of $420. This would imply a P/E ratio of 26, not unreasonable for a growth stock with outstanding future earning prospects.

EXHIBIT 2

(a) Stock prices: 1928 to 1930

(b) Stock prices: 1931 to 1940

Sources: www.finance.yahoo.com and www.analyzeindices.com.

The Stock Market (Dow Jones Industrial Average), 1928–1940

The figures for the Dow Jones Industrial Average (DJIA) are shown here. Clearly, stock prices plunged in September–October 1929, but note how they recovered during the five months from mid-November 1929 through mid-April of 1930. However, this recovery reversed as the Smoot–Hawley tariff bill was debated, passed, and eventually signed into law on June 17, 1930. As part (b) shows, the Dow continued to fall throughout 1931 and 1932 and never reached 200 throughout the remainder of the decade.

However, it is interesting to see what happened during the next five months. From mid-November 1929 through mid-April 1930, the Dow Jones Industrial Average increased every month, and by mid-April the index had risen to 294, regaining virtually all of the losses experienced during the late October crash. This raises an interesting question: If the October crash caused the Great Depression, how can one explain that the stock market had regained most of those losses by April 1930?

But from mid-April throughout the rest of 1930, stock prices moved steadily downward and closed the year at 165. Apparently something happened during May–June 1930, which caused the stock market to head downward. We will return to this issue in a moment. Exhibit 2 part (b) presents data for the Dow Jones Industrials for 1931–1940. The index continued to fall in 1931–1932 and rebounded strongly in 1933 but then fluctuated between 100 and 200 for the remainder of the decade. Note the Dow stood at 131 at year-end 1940, even lower than the closing figure for 1930.

There have been several downturns in stock prices of the magnitude experienced during 1929, both before and after the Great Depression, and none of them resulted in anything like the prolonged unemployment and lengthy contraction of the 1930s. For example, the stock market price declines immediately before and during the recessions of 1973–1975 and 1982–1983 were as large as those of the 1929 crash, approximately 50 percent. But both of these recessions were over in about 18 months. Moreover, in 1987, the Dow Industrials fell from 2640 on October 2 to 1740 on October 19, a decline of 34 percent. Whereas the collapse of stock prices in 1987 was similar to the October 1929 crash, that is where the similarity ends. The 1987 crash did not lead to economic disaster. In fact, it was not even followed by a recession.

Of course, the 1929 decline in stock prices reduced wealth and thereby contributed to the reduction in aggregate demand and real output. But stock prices have fallen by 50 percent or more during other recessions, and the economy nonetheless moved toward a recovery within a year or two at the most. Thus, although the decline in stock prices may well have triggered the initial economic decline, the length and severity of the Great Depression were the result of other factors. We will now consider this issue in more detail.

ST06-3 WHY WAS THE GREAT DEPRESSION SO LENGTHY AND SEVERE?

The length and severity of the Great Depression were the result of bad policies. There were four major policy mistakes that caused the initial downturn to worsen and the depressed conditions to continue on and on. Let's take a closer look at each of them.

1. A sharp reduction in the supply of money during 1930–1933 and again in 1937–1938 reduced aggregate demand and real output. The supply of money expanded slowly but steadily throughout the 1920s. From 1921 through 1929, the money stock increased at an annual rate of 2.7 percent, approximately the economy's long-term real rate of growth. There was even a slight downward trend in the general level of prices during the decade.

In spite of this price stability, the Fed increased the discount rate, the rate it charges banks for short-term loans, four times between January 1928 and August 1929. During this 20-month period, the discount rate was pushed from 3.5 percent to 6 percent. After the October stock market crash, the Fed aggressively sold government bonds, which drained reserves from the banking system and reduced the money supply. As **Exhibit 3** part (a) shows, the money supply fell by 3.9 percent during 1930, by 15.3 percent in 1931, and by 8.9 percent in 1932. As banks failed and the money supply collapsed, the Fed did not inject new reserves into the system. Neither did it act as a lender of last resort. The quantity of money at year-end 1933 was 33 percent less than that in 1929.

Predictably, this huge monetary contraction placed downward pressure on prices. As Exhibit 3 part (b) illustrates, the general level of prices fell by 2.3 percent in 1930, 9.0 percent in 1931, and 9.9 percent in 1932.

Economic activity takes place over time. The deflation during 1929–1933 meant that many people who bought businesses and farms in the late 1920s were unable to pay for them as the prices of their output fell during the 1930s. In essence, the monetary contraction caused unexpected changes in economic conditions. As a result, many people who undertook investments and borrowed funds suffered losses and were unable to fulfill their contracts. As the gains from trade dissipated and aggregate demand plunged, so, too, did output and employment. By 1933, real GDP was 29 percent lower than the 1929 level, and the unemployment rate had soared to nearly 25 percent.

EXHIBIT 3

(a) Change in money supply (M1)

(b) Change in CPI

Sources: Change in the money supply is from December to December. The data are from Milton Friedman, and Anna J. Schwartz, A *Monetary History of the United States, 1867–1960* (Princeton, NJ: Princeton University Press, 1963); for CPI data: www.bls.gov.

The M1 Money Supply and the Change in the General Level of Prices, 1925–1940

Note how the M1 money supply fell sharply during 1930–1933, rose during 1934–1937 but dipped again in 1938 (part a). The general level of prices followed the same pattern (part b). The sharp reduction in the supply of money and deflation during 1930–1933 changed the terms of loans, investments, and other economic activities that take place across time periods. This was a major factor underlying the initial plunge into the Great Depression. Further, the monetary contraction of 1938 stifled the recovery and contributed to still another downturn.

During 1934–1937, the Fed reversed itself and expanded the supply of money. The monetary expansion halted the deflation, and the general level of prices increased. So, too, did the level of economic activity. Real GDP expanded and the unemployment rate fell during 1934–1937. But the Fed doubled the reserve requirements between August 1936 to May 1937, leading to another decline in the money supply and the general level of prices. This caused the economy to falter again and pushed the unemployment rate to almost 20 percent in 1938.

Sound monetary policy is about price stability—following a monetary policy that keeps the inflation rate low and steady. The Federal Reserve totally failed the American people during the 1930s. The severe monetary contraction led to near double-digit deflation. This was followed by a shift to monetary expansion, which generated inflation, but the Fed soon shifted again toward contraction, which caused still more deflation. Essentially,

Senator Reed Smoot and Congressman Willis Hawley (shown here) spearheaded legislation passed in June 1930 that increased tariff rates by an average of more than 50 percent. They thought their bill would "save jobs" and promote prosperity. Instead, it did the opposite, as other nations retaliated with higher tariffs on American products and world trade fell substantially.

Library of Congress, National Photo Company Collection, LC-DIG-mpcc-17371

the monetary instability of the 1930s generated uncertainty and undermined the exchange process.[3]

2. The Smoot–Hawley trade bill of 1930 increased tariffs and led to a huge reduction in the volume of international trade.

Signed into law on June 17, 1930, the Smoot–Hawley trade bill increased tariffs by more than 50 percent on approximately 3,200 imported products. Many of these tariff increases were in dollars per unit, so the subsequent deflation pushed them still higher relative to the price of the product.

Like their protectionist counterparts today, President Herbert Hoover, Senator Reed Smoot, and Congressman Willis Hawley argued that the trade restrictions would "save jobs." As Congressman Hawley put it, "I want to see American workers employed producing American goods for American consumption."[4] The proponents of the Smoot–Hawley legislation also believed the higher tariffs would bring in additional revenue for the federal government.

More than 100 years before the Great Depression, Adam Smith and David Ricardo explained how nations gained when they specialized in the production of goods they could supply at a low cost while trading for those they could produce only at a high cost. Trade makes it possible for both trading partners to generate a larger output and achieve a higher living standard. Moreover, a nation cannot reduce its imports without simultaneously reducing its exports. If foreigners sell less to Americans, then they will earn fewer of the dollars needed to buy from Americans. Thus, a reduction in imports will also lead to a reduction in exports. Jobs created in import competing industries will be offset by jobs lost in exporting industries. There will be no net expansion in employment. The view that import restrictions will generate a net creation of jobs is fallacious.

Having read both Smith and Ricardo, the economists of 1930 were well aware of the benefits derived from international trade and the harm generated by trade restrictions. More than a thousand of them signed an open letter to President Hoover warning of the harmful effects of Smoot–Hawley and pleading with him not to sign the legislation. He rejected their pleas, but history confirmed the validity of their warnings.

The higher tariffs did not generate additional revenue, and they certainly did not save jobs. The import restrictions harmed foreign suppliers, and predictably they retaliated. Sixty countries responded with higher tariffs on American products. By 1932, the volume of U.S. trade had fallen to less than half its earlier level. As a result, the federal government actually derived less revenue at the higher tariff rates. Tariff revenues fell from $602 million in 1929 to $328 million in 1932. Similarly, output and employment declined and the unemployment rate soared. The unemployment rate was 7.8 percent when Smoot–Hawley was passed, but it ballooned to 23.6 percent of the labor force just two years later. Moreover, the "trade war" helped spread the recessionary conditions throughout the world.

There was substantial opposition to the Smoot–Hawley bill, and the Senate vote was close (44–42). Last minute changes in the rate schedules were made in order to gain the final votes needed for passage. Some businesses, seeking to gain advantage at the expense of consumers and foreign rivals, lobbied hard for the legislation. But, like the economists, other business leaders recognized that trade restrictions would harm rather than help the economy.

As we previously discussed, stock prices had increased for five straight months following the November 1929 lows, and by mid-April of 1930, the Dow Jones Industrials had returned to the level just before the October 1929 crash (see Exhibit 2). But as

---

[3]For a comprehensive analysis of monetary policy during the Great Depression, see the chapter on the Great Contraction in Milton Friedman and Anna Schwartz, *A Monetary History of the United States, 1867–1960* (New York: National Bureau of Economic Research, 1963; ninth paperback printing by Princeton University Press, 1993): 411–15.

[4]Frank Whitson Fetter, "Congressional Tariff Theory," *American Economic Review* 23, no. 3 (September 1933): 413–27.

the Smoot–Hawley bill moved through Congress and its prospects for passage improved, stock prices moved steadily downward. In fact, the reduction in stock prices following the debate and passage of Smoot–Hawley was even greater than that of the 1929 October crash. By year-end 1930, recovery was nowhere in sight, and the Dow Jones Industrial index had fallen to 165, down from 294 in mid-April.

The combination of highly restrictive monetary policy and the Smoot–Hawley trade restrictions were enough to push the economy over the cliff, but Congress and the president were not through.

3. A large tax increase in the midst of a severe recession made a bad situation worse.
Before the Keynesian revolution, the dominant view was that the federal budget should be balanced. Reflecting the ongoing economic downturn, the federal budget ran a deficit in 1931, and an even larger deficit was shaping up for 1932. Assisted by the newly elected Democratic majority in the House of Representatives, the Republican Hoover Administration passed the largest peacetime tax rate increase in the history of the United States. As Exhibit 4 indicates, the lowest marginal tax rate on personal income was raised from 1.5 percent to 4 percent in 1932. At the top of the income scale, the highest marginal tax rate was raised from 25 percent to 63 percent. Essentially, personal income tax rates were increased at all levels by approximately 150 percent in one year! This huge tax increase reduced both the after-tax income of households and the incentive to earn and invest.

Fiscal policy analysis indicates that a tax increase of this magnitude in the midst of a severe downturn will be disastrous. Review of Exhibit 1 shows that this was indeed the case. In 1932, real output fell by 13 percent, the largest single-year decline during the Great Depression era. Unemployment rose from 15.9 percent in 1931 to 23.6 percent in 1932.

In 1936, the Roosevelt Administration increased taxes again, pushing the top marginal rate to 79 percent. Thus, during the latter half of the 1930s, high earners were permitted to keep only 21 cents of each additional dollar they earned. Moreover, the 1936 tax legislation also imposed a special tax on the retained earnings of corporations, a major source of funds for business investment. These 1936 tax increases further reduced both income levels and the incentive to earn and invest, prolonging the Great Depression and increasing its severity.

EXHIBIT 4

Marginal Income Tax Rates, 1925–1940

The lowest and highest marginal tax rates imposed on personal income are shown here for the period before, and during, the Great Depression. Note how the top marginal rate was increased from 25 percent in 1931 to 63 percent in 1932. Real GDP fell by 13.3 percent in 1932, and the unemployment rate soared to nearly a quarter of the labor force (see Exhibit 1). In 1935, the top rate was pushed still higher to 79 percent.

Sources: The Tax Foundation, www.taxfoundation.org; and the IRS at www.irs.gov.

The Agricultural Adjustment Act of 1933 sought to increase the prices of farm products by reducing their supply. Under this act, 6 million baby pigs were slaughtered in 1933. Did this help bring the Great Depression to an end?

Cartel

An organization of sellers designed to coordinate supply and price decisions so that the joint profits of the members will be maximized. A cartel will seek to create a monopoly in the market for its product.

4. Price controls, anticompetitive policies, and constant structural changes during the Roosevelt administration generated uncertainty and undermined the normal recovery process. President Roosevelt was elected in 1932, and many history books still credit his New Deal policies with bringing the Great Depression to an end. Numerous policy changes were instituted during the Roosevelt years, and some of them were helpful. In 1933, President Roosevelt revalued the price of gold from $20 per ounce to $35 per ounce, and this contributed to the expansion in the money supply during the years immediately following. The Roosevelt administration also passed the Federal Deposit Insurance program, which provided depositors with protection against bank failures and reduced the occurrence of "bank runs."

However, it is equally clear that many of the major initiatives of the Roosevelt administration were counterproductive and prolonged the Great Depression. Roosevelt perceived that falling prices were a problem, but he failed to recognize that this was because of the monetary contraction. Instead, he tried to keep product prices high by reducing their supply. Under the Agricultural Adjustment Act (AAA) passed in 1933, farmers were paid to plow under portions of their cotton, corn, wheat, and other crops. Potato farmers were paid to spray their potatoes with dye so that they would be unfit for human consumption. Healthy cattle, sheep, and pigs were slaughtered and buried in mass graves in order to keep them off the market. In 1933 alone, 6 million baby pigs were killed under the Roosevelt agricultural policy. The Supreme Court declared the AAA unconstitutional in 1936, but not before it had kept millions of dollars of agricultural products from American consumers.

The National Industrial Recovery Act (NIRA) was another New Deal effort to keep prices high. Under this legislation passed in June 1933, more than 500 industries ranging from automobiles and steel to dog food and dry cleaners were organized into **cartels**. Business representatives from each industry were invited to Washington to work with NIRA officials to set production quotas, prices, wages, working hours, distribution methods, and other mandates for their industry. Once approved by a majority of the firms, the regulations were legally binding, and they applied to all businesses in the industry, regardless of whether they approved or participated in regulations' development. Firms that did not comply were fined and, in some cases, owners were even thrown in jail. A tax was levied on all firms in these industries in order to cover the administrative cost of the act. Before the NIRA, collusive behavior of this type would have been prosecuted as a violation of antitrust laws, but with the NIRA, the government itself provided the organizational structure for the cartels and prosecuted firms that dared to reduce prices or failed to comply with other regulations. Clearly, the NIRA reduced competition, promoted monopoly pricing, and undermined the market process.

Exhibit 5 tracks industrial output before, and during, the NIRA's existence. Interestingly, a recovery had started during the first half of 1933. Industrial output increased sharply and factory employment expanded by 25 percent during the four months before the NIRA took affect. But as the act was implemented in July 1933, industrial output began to decline precipitously. By the end of 1933, output had fallen by more than 25 percent from its mid-summer high. There were some ups and downs during the next year, but industrial output never returned to its pre-NIRA level until after the Supreme Court in a 9–0 vote declared the act unconstitutional in May 1935.[5]

The AAA and NIRA were just part of the persistent policy change during the Roosevelt years. The Wagner Act took labor law out of the courts and assigned it to a new regulatory commission, the National Labor Relations Board. Pro-union appointments to this new board dramatically changed collective bargaining and led to a sharp increase in unionization.

---

[5]For additional details on the impact of the NRA, see Chapter 4 of the recent book by historian Burton Folsom, *New Deal or Raw Deal* (New York: Simon & Schuster, 2008).

The NIRA and Industrial Production, 1932–1936

The change in industrial production before and following the passage of the National Industrial Recovery Act (NIRA) is shown here. Note how industrial output increased sharply during April–July 1933. However, when the implementation of the NIRA began in July, industrial output fell by more than 25 percent over the next six months. It never reached the June 1933 level again until after the Act was declared unconstitutional in May 1935.

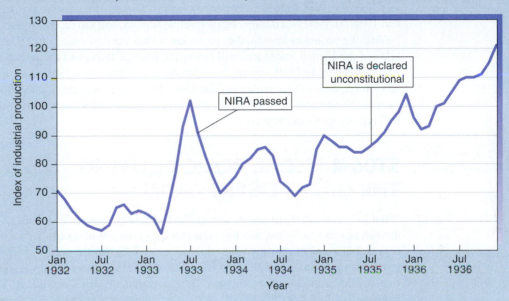

Source: Historical Statistics of the United States. The base period (equal to 100) was the average of the monthly figures during 1923–1925.

The Works Progress Administration (WPA) and Civilian Conservation Corps (CCC) vastly expanded government employment. The Davis–Bacon Act required government contractors to employ higher wage union workers, which, in effect, reduced the employment opportunities of minorities and those with fewer skills. Unprecedented high marginal tax rates, establishment of a minimum wage, pay-as-you-go Social Security, and several other programs changed the structure of the U.S. economy.

This persistent introduction of massive new programs and regulations created what Robert Higgs calls "regime uncertainty," the situation in which people are reluctant to undertake business ventures and investments because the government is constantly changing the "rules."[6] Against this background, business planning was undermined and private investment came to a virtual standstill. Roosevelt's close friend and Treasury Secretary Henry Morgenthau tried to get the president to make a public statement to reassure investors and the business community. He was unsuccessful. Lammont duPont highlighted the uncertainty generated by the constant whirlwind of New Deal policy changes when he stated,

> *Uncertainty rules the tax situation, the labor situation, the monetary situation, and practically every legal condition under which industry must operate. Are taxes to go higher, lower or stay where they are? We don't know. Is labor to be union or non-union? Are we to have inflation or deflation, more government*

---

[6]Robert Higgs, "Regime Uncertainty: Why the Great Depression Lasted So Long and Why Prosperity Resumed After the War," *The Independent Review* 1, no. 4 (Spring 1997).

spending or less? Are new restrictions to be placed on capital, new limits on profits? It is impossible to even guess at the answers.[7]

Did the New Deal policies bring the Great Depression to an end?[8] Through the years, many students have been taught that this was the case. It is difficult to see how anyone could objectively review the data and accept this proposition. Before the Great Depression, recessions lasted only one or two years, three years at the most, and recovery pushed income to new highs. The Great Depression was different. In 1933, the monetary contraction was reversed, and there was evidence of a private-sector recovery. But the NIRA, AAA, and 1936 tax increases dampened productive activity, and the second monetary contraction pushed the economy into another recession within the depression. In 1938, per capita real GDP of the United States was still below the level of 1929, and the rate of unemployment was 19 percent. In 1939, seven years after the beginning of the New Deal, 17 percent of the labor force was still unemployed. The Great Depression was eventually diminished by the increase in demand for military goods of the English and Russians and our own military buildup before World War II.[9]

ST06-4 FISCAL POLICY DURING THE GREAT DEPRESSION

What happened to fiscal policy during the Great Depression? This was, of course, before the Keynesian revolution, and the view that the government should balance its budget, except perhaps during wartime, was widely accepted. **Exhibit 6** part (a) presents the data for government spending as a share of GDP. The size of the government was much smaller as a share of the economy during this era. Total government spending (federal, state, and local) increased from 8 percent of GDP in 1929 to 16 percent in 1933. To a large degree, however, this increase reflected the maintenance of nominal government expenditures during a period of deflation and declining GDP. After 1933, total government spending as a share of GDP remained in the 15 percent to 16 percent range for the rest of the decade, except during 1937, when the ratio fell to 13 percent.

Exhibit 6 part (b) provides the figures for the federal deficit. The budget was in surplus during both 1929 and 1930. After that, the deficit was generally around 2 percent of GDP, except during 1934 and 1936, and in 1937 when a small surplus was present. Measured as a share of the economy, the increases in government spending and federal deficits during the 1930s were relatively small. Thus, there is little reason to believe that fiscal policy exerted much impact on the economy. Certainly, there is no reason to believe that spending increases and budget deficits were a significant source of fiscal stimulus during the era.

---

[7]Quoted in Herman E. Krooss, *Executive Opinion: What Business Leaders Said and Thought on Economic Issues, 1920s–1960s* (Garden City, NY: Doubleday and Co., 1970), 200.

[8]For additional details on the Great Depression, see Gene Smiley, *Rethinking the Great Depression* (Ivan R. Dee, Chicago, IL 2002); Robert J. Samuelson, "Great Depression," in *The Fortune Encyclopedia of Economics*, ed., David R. Henderson (New York: Warner Books, 1993), available online at www.econlib.org; Burton Folsom, *New Deal or Raw Deal?* (New York: Simon & Schuster, 2008); and Amity Shlaes, *The Forgotten Man: A New History of the Great Depression* (New York: HarperCollins Publishers, 2007).

[9]Many argue that the spending increases and large budget deficits of World War II provided sufficient demand stimulus to direct the economy back to full employment and solid growth. Robert Higgs challenges this view. Higgs notes that with 12 million young Americans drafted during the war, this would obviously reduce the unemployment rate to a low level. However, the growth of real GDP is more debatable because almost half of measured output was government spending, and it was added to GDP at cost. Moreover, the income of households was overstated because many goods they would have purchased were unavailable as a result of the price controls. The sharp decline in GDP following the war and the lifting of price controls also imply that the growth of GDP during the war was overstated. Thus, Higgs does not believe that real recovery from the Great Depression occurred until 1946. See Robert Higgs, *Depression, War, and Cold War: Studies in Political Economy* (New York: Oxford University Press, 2006).

EXHIBIT 6

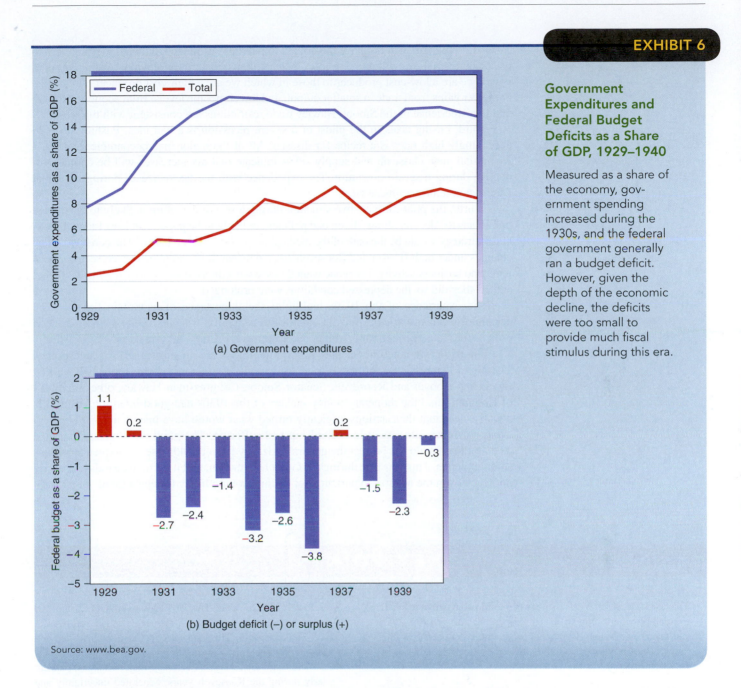

(a) Government expenditures

(b) Budget deficit (−) or surplus (+)

Source: www.bea.gov.

Government Expenditures and Federal Budget Deficits as a Share of GDP, 1929–1940

Measured as a share of the economy, government spending increased during the 1930s, and the federal government generally ran a budget deficit. However, given the depth of the economic decline, the deficits were too small to provide much fiscal stimulus during this era.

ST06-5 LESSONS FROM THE GREAT DEPRESSION

The Great Depression provides several lessons that can help us avoid severe downturns in the future. First, the Great Depression clearly indicates that a prolonged period of monetary contraction will undermine time-dimension economic activity and exert disastrous effects on the economy. We seemed to have learned this lesson well. As the severity of the 2008 downturn increased, the Fed injected abundant reserves into the banking system and shifted to a highly expansionary monetary policy. However, it is also true that Fed policy during 2002–2006 contributed to the housing boom and bust and, thereby, the Crisis of 2008. Monetary and price stability is crucially important for the smooth operation of markets. The Great Depression, along with experience since that era, vividly illustrates this point.

Second, the Great Depression illustrates the fallacy of the "trade restrictions will promote domestic industry" argument. Policies that reduce imports will simultaneously reduce exports. Foreigners will not have the dollars to purchase as much from us if they sell less to us. Trade restrictions will not save jobs. Instead, they will shift employment from sectors in which we are a low-cost producer to those in which we are a high-cost producer. The results are fewer gains from trade, a smaller output, and lower income levels. Both economic theory and the experience of the Smoot–Hawley trade restrictions are consistent with this view.

Third, raising taxes in the midst of a severe recession is a bad idea. Pushing taxes to exceedingly high rates is a recipe for disaster. All of the major macroeconomic theories—Keynesian, new classical, and supply side—indicate that tax increases will be counterproductive during a severe downturn. The experience with the tax increases during the Great Depression reinforces these views.

Fourth, the political incentive structure during a severe downturn is likely to encourage politicians to "do something." Even bad policies are likely to be popular, at least for a while. A better strategy would be the oath of the medical profession, "do no harm." The constant policy changes under both Hoover and Roosevelt created uncertainty and froze private-sector investment and business activity. Everyone waited to see what the next new policy regime would be; and, as they did so, the depressed conditions were prolonged.

The experience of the 1930s highlights the importance of economic literacy. The decadelong catastrophic decline did not have to happen. It was the result of wrong-headed policies based on the economic illiteracy of both voters and policy-makers.

Finally, as we noted in Chapter 1, good intentions are no substitute for sound policy. The Great Depression vividly illustrates this point. There is every reason to believe that Presidents Hoover and Roosevelt, Senator Smoot, Congressman Hawley, other members of Congress, and the monetary policy-makers of the 1930s had good intentions. But, it is equally clear that their actions tragically turned what would have been a normal business cycle downturn into a decade of hardship and suffering. The good intentions of political decision makers do not protect the general citizenry from the adverse consequences of unsound policies. This was true during the Great Depression, and it is still true today. If we do not learn from the adverse experiences of history, we are likely to repeat them.

KEY POINTS

- The Great Depression was a severe economic plunge that resulted in unemployment rates of nearly 25 percent during 1932–1933 and rates of more than 14 percent for an entire decade. It was the longest, most severe period of depressed economic conditions in American history.

- Contrary to a popular view, the Great Depression was not caused by the 1929 stock market crash. We have had similar reductions in stock prices to those of 1929, both before and after the Great Depression, without experiencing prolonged depressed conditions like those of the 1930s.

- There were four major reasons why the Great Depression was long and severe:

  1. Monetary instability: The money supply contracted by 33 percent between 1929 and 1933, and it took another tumble during 1937–1938.

  2. Smoot–Hawley trade bill: This 1930 legislation increased tariffs by more than 50 percent and led to a sharp reduction in world trade.

  3. 1932 tax increase: This huge tax increase reduced demand and undermined the incentive to invest and produce.

  4. Structural policy changes: Persistent major changes, particularly during the Roosevelt years, generated uncertainty and undermined investment and business planning.

- The budget deficits and increases in government spending failed to exert much impact on total demand and the level of economic activity during the 1930s.

- The Great Depression highlights the importance of monetary stability; free trade; avoidance of high tax rates; and avoidance of price controls, entry restraints, and persistent policy changes that generate uncertainty and undermine the security of property rights. Perhaps most important, the Great Depression vividly illustrates that good intentions are not a substitute for sound economic policy.

CRITICAL ANALYSIS QUESTIONS

1. "The Great Depression was caused by the 1929 stock market crash. The 1929 collapse of stock prices was the most severe in U.S. history, and therefore it is not surprising that it caused a prolonged period of economic hardship." Evaluate this statement.

2. Do the length and severity of the Great Depression reflect a defect in the operation of markets? Do they reflect a failure of government policy? Discuss.

3. "Franklin Roosevelt was one of our greatest presidents because it was his New Deal policies that brought the Great Depression to an end." Evaluate this statement.

4. Could the United States ever experience another Great Depression? Why or why not?

5. *"I'm for international trade, but not when it takes jobs from Americans. If the American worker can produce the product, Americans should not buy it from foreigners." Do you agree with this statement? Why or why not?

6. What are the most important lessons Americans should learn from the Great Depression? Do you think we have learned them? Why or why not?

*Asterisk denotes questions for which answers are given in Appendix B.

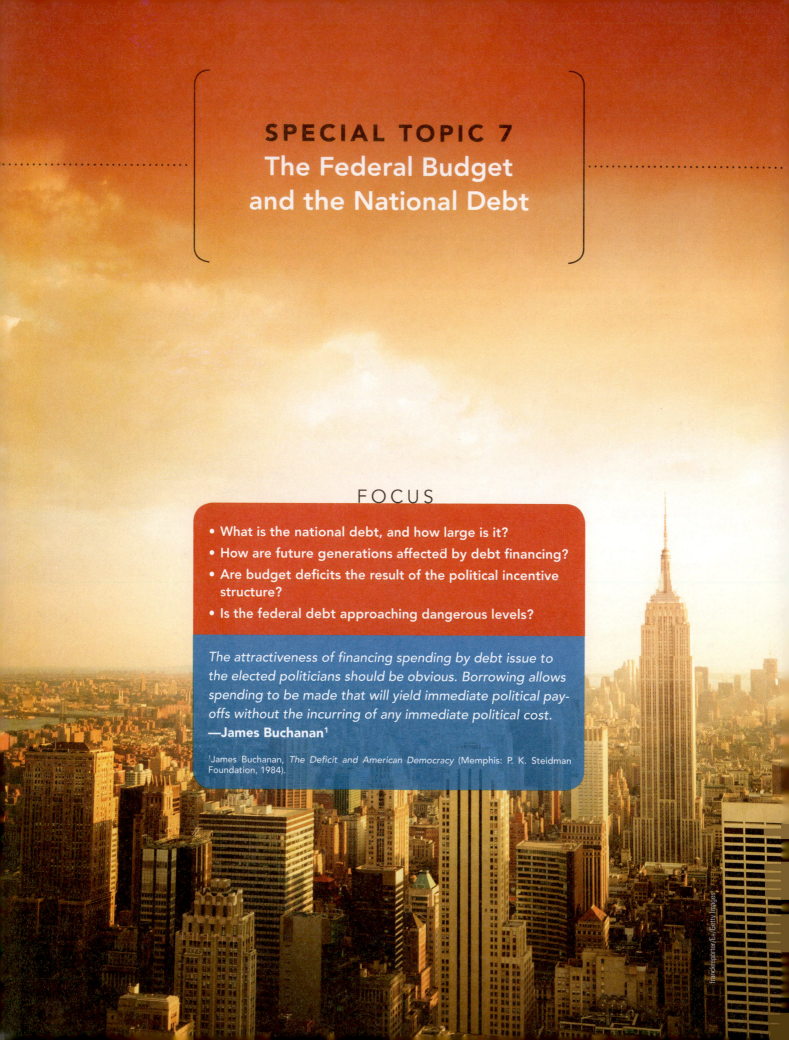

SPECIAL TOPIC 7
The Federal Budget and the National Debt

FOCUS

- What is the national debt, and how large is it?
- How are future generations affected by debt financing?
- Are budget deficits the result of the political incentive structure?
- Is the federal debt approaching dangerous levels?

The attractiveness of financing spending by debt issue to the elected politicians should be obvious. Borrowing allows spending to be made that will yield immediate political pay-offs without the incurring of any immediate political cost.
—James Buchanan[1]

[1]James Buchanan, *The Deficit and American Democracy* (Memphis: P. K. Steidman Foundation, 1984).

Historically, attitudes toward government debt have undergone dramatic swings. Before the 1960s, there was a political consensus that budget deficits were irresponsible and therefore should be avoided, except perhaps during wartime emergencies. The rise of Keynesian economics altered this view. During the 1960–1980 Keynesian era, deficits were perceived as an important policy tool that could be used to stimulate growth and help promote stability. But large budget deficits during the 1980s and since 2001 have again generated concern about the impact of government debt. This feature analyzes both the economics and politics of debt financing.

ST07-1 DEFICITS, SURPLUSES, AND THE NATIONAL DEBT

When the federal government uses debt rather than taxes and user charges to pay for its expenditures, the U.S. Treasury fills this gap by borrowing in the loanable funds market. When borrowing funds, the Treasury generally issues interest-bearing bonds. These bonds compose the **national debt**. In effect, the national debt consists of loans extended by various parties to the general fund of the U.S. Treasury.

The federal budget exerts a direct impact on the national debt. The budget deficit or surplus is a "flow" concept (like water running into or out of a bathtub), whereas the national debt is a "stock" figure (like the amount of water in the tub at a point in time). A budget deficit increases the size of the national debt by the amount of the deficit. Conversely, a budget surplus allows the federal government to pay off bondholders and thereby reduce the size of the national debt. In essence, the national debt represents the cumulative effect of all the prior budget deficits and surpluses.

The creditworthiness of an organization is dependent upon the size of its debt relative to its income base. Therefore, when analyzing the significance of budget deficits, surpluses, and the national debt, it makes sense to consider their size relative to the entire economy.

Exhibit 1 presents data for the 1960–2014 period for both the federal budget deficit and the national debt as a percentage of GDP. Because the defense effort of World War II was largely financed with debt rather than taxes, the national debt was quite large during the period immediately following the war. But the budget deficits were small—less than

National debt
The sum of the indebtedness of the federal government in the form of outstanding interest-earning bonds. It reflects the cumulative impact of budget deficits and surpluses.

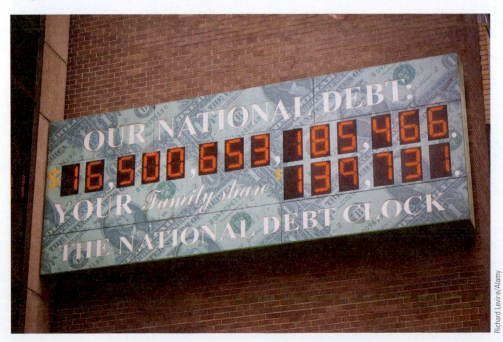

Would you like to know the current level of the national debt? The debt clock will provide you with the answer: http://www.usdebtclock.org/.

EXHIBIT 1

Budget Deficits, Surpluses, and the National Debt as a Percent of GDP, 1960–2014

Between World War II and 1973, federal budget deficits were small as a share of GDP (see part a). During this period, the national debt declined as a proportion of GDP (part b). During 1974–1995, the budget deficits were quite large, causing the national debt to increase as a percent of GDP. After falling during 1996–2001, the national debt increased during 2002–2007, and it soared during and following the recession of 2008–2009. The federal debt to GDP ratio now stands at the highest level since the years immediately following World War II.

(a) Federal budget deficit or surplus as a percent of GDP

(b) Gross and net federal debt as a percent of GDP

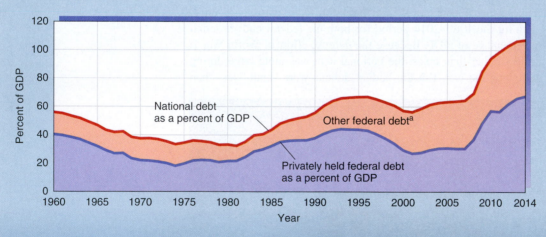

Source: www.whitehouse.gov/omb. The figures for 2013 and 2014 are estimated.
aFederal debt held by U.S. government agencies and Federal Reserve banks.

1 percent—as a share of GDP during the 1950s and 1960s. Historically, real output in the United States has grown at an annual rate of approximately 3 percent. When the budget deficit as a percentage of GDP is less than the growth of real output, the federal debt will decline relative to the size of the economy. This is precisely what happened for a quarter of a century following World War II. Budget deficits were present (see Exhibit 1 part a) and they pushed up the nominal national debt. But the economy grew even more rapidly. As a result, the national debt as a share of GDP fell from 56 percent in 1960 to 34 percent in 1974 (see Exhibit 1 part b).

From the mid-1970s to the mid-1990s, federal deficits were both large and continuous. As Exhibit 1, part (a), shows, budget deficits averaged nearly 4 percent of GDP during 1974–1995. These large deficits pushed the national debt up from 34 percent of GDP in 1974 to 67 percent in 1995. As the economy grew rapidly in the 1990s, the budget deficits were eventually transformed into surpluses, leading to a temporary reduction in the national debt.

However, during the last decade, the budget deficits have been large and the federal debt has grown rapidly, particularly during and following the recession of 2008–2009. As Exhibit 1, part (b), shows, the ratio of federal debt to GDP rose from 57 percent in 2000 to 70 percent in 2008 and then soared to 107 percent in 2014. Measured as a share of the economy, the federal debt is now higher than at any time since the years immediately following World War II.

ST07-2 WHO OWNS THE NATIONAL DEBT?

As Exhibit 2 illustrates, more than a quarter (28.9 percent) of the national debt is held by agencies of the federal government. For example, Social Security Trust Funds were often used to purchase U.S. bonds. When the debt is owned by a government agency, it is little more than an accounting transaction indicating that one government agency (for example, the Social Security Administration) is making a loan to another (the U.S. Treasury). Even the interest payments in this case represent little more than an internal government transfer.

Another 10.9 percent of the public debt is held by the Federal Reserve System. When the Fed purchases U.S. securities, it creates money. The bonds held by the Fed, therefore, are indicative of prior government expenditures that have been paid for with "printing-press" money—money created by the central bank. As in the case of the securities held by

---

EXHIBIT 2

Who Owns the National Debt?

Of the $16.46 trillion national debt (as of December 31, 2012), two-fifths is held by government agencies (primarily the Social Security Trust Fund) and Federal Reserve banks. Of the $9.91 trillion federal debt held privately, a little more than three-fifths is held by foreign investors.

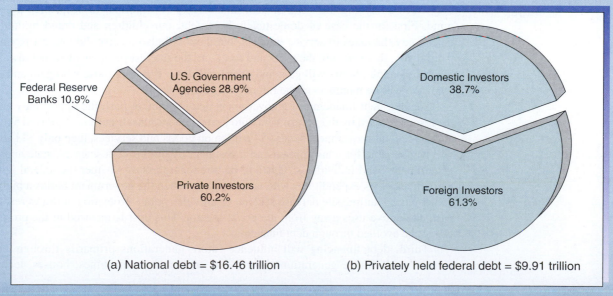

(a) National debt = $16.46 trillion

(b) Privately held federal debt = $9.91 trillion

Source: www.fms.treas.gov/bulletin/index.html.

Privately held government debt
The portion of the national debt owed to domestic and foreign investors. It does not include bonds held by agencies of the federal government or the Federal Reserve.

External debt
The portion of the national debt owed to foreign investors.

government agencies, the interest on the bonds held by the Fed is returned to the Treasury after the Fed has covered its costs of operation. The U.S. Treasury both pays and receives almost all of the interest, approximately $89 billion in 2012, on the bonds held by the Federal Reserve. Thus, the bonds held by the Fed, like those held by U.S. government agencies, do not create a net interest liability for the U.S. Treasury.

In contrast, **privately held government debt** imposes a net interest burden on the federal government. In the case of the privately held debt—that is, the bonds held by individuals, insurance companies, mutual funds, and other investors—the federal government will have to impose taxes to meet the future interest payments on these bonds. Therefore, it is important to distinguish between (1) the total national debt and (2) the privately held government debt. Only the latter imposes a net interest obligation on the federal government. As of December 31, 2012, the privately held portion of the national debt was $9.91 trillion, 60 percent of the $16.46 trillion national debt.

Slightly more than three-fifths of the privately held debt is owned by foreign investors, and this share has been increasing in recent years. This portion is sometimes referred to as **external debt**. In the following section, we will consider how the foreign debt differs from debt financed by borrowing from Americans.

Part (b) of Exhibit 1 presents data on the size of the privately held federal debt for the 1960–2014 period. Measured as a share of GDP, the general pattern of the privately held debt has been similar to that for the national debt as a whole. Like the total debt, the privately held debt has soared in recent years. Driven by the huge deficits of 2008–2014, the privately held debt rose from 37 percent of GDP in 2008 to 49 percent in 2009 and 68 percent in 2014. Clearly, these trends are not sustainable. As we proceed, we will consider their potential impact on the economy.

ST07-3 HOW DOES DEBT FINANCING INFLUENCE FUTURE GENERATIONS?

The impact of the national debt on future generations has been a point of controversy for decades.[2] Opponents of debt financing often charge that we are mortgaging the future of our children and grandchildren—that debt financing permits us to consume today, then send the bill to future generations. In the 1960s and 1970s, the overwhelming bulk of the national debt was held by domestic investors. During this era, Keynesians argued that there was little reason for concern because "We owe it to ourselves."

When analyzing the issue of debt financing, it is important to keep three points in mind. First, in the case of domestically held debt, our children and grandchildren will indeed pay the taxes to service the debt, but they will also receive the interest payments. Admittedly, those paying the taxes and receiving the interest payments will not always be the same people. Some will gain and others will lose. But both those who gain and those who lose will be members of the future generation.

Second, debt financing of a government activity cannot push the opportunity cost of the resources used by the government onto future generations. If current GDP is $15 trillion and the federal government spends $4 trillion on goods and services, then only $11 trillion will be available for consumption and investment by domestic businesses, state and local governments, and individuals. This will be true regardless of whether the federal government finances its expenditures with taxes or debt. When the government builds a highway, constructs an antimissile defense system, or provides police protection, it draws resources with alternative uses away from the private sector. This cost is incurred in the present; it cannot be avoided through debt financing.

Third, debt financing will influence future generations primarily through capital formation. If future generations inherit lots of factories, machines, houses, technical

---

[2]See Richard H. Fink and Jack High, eds., *A Nation in Debt: Economists Debate the Federal Budget Deficit* (Frederick, MD: University Publications of America, 1987), for an excellent set of readings summarizing this debate.

knowledge, and other productive assets, then their productive potential will be high. Alternatively, if the next generation inherits fewer productive assets, then its productive capability will be lower.

The impact of debt financing on capital formation is a point of controversy among economists. If people anticipate the higher future taxes implied by the additional outstanding government debt, as the new classical model implies, they will increase their saving, interest rates will be unchanged, and there will be little impact on private investment. In this case, the quantity of equipment, structures, and other capital assets inherited by future generations will be largely unaffected. However, if borrowing to finance the debt leads to higher interest rates, as the crowding-out model implies, there will be an adverse impact on private investment and fewer capital assets will be passed along to the next generation.

Currently, a little more than three-fifths of the privately held federal debt is financed by borrowing from foreigners. The foreign borrowing will lead to an inflow of financial capital, appreciation of the dollar, and a reduction in net exports. This will lead to a trade deficit and higher levels of current consumption fed by imports. Interestingly, consumption as a share of GDP rose from 69 percent in 2001 to 71 percent in 2012. To the degree that current citizens increase their consumption and future generations pay higher taxes to service the debt to foreigners, the current generation will benefit at the expense of future Americans.

Even in the case of borrowing from foreigners, future generations would not be harmed if the funds were channeled into productive investments that generated sufficient income to cover the interest payments. However, it does not appear that the recent growth of government spending financed by debt has been of this variety. Instead, the additional spending has been directed toward projects designed to stimulate current consumption (for example, extended unemployment benefits, stimulus checks sent to most Americans, and prescription drug benefits for seniors) or projects unlikely to improve the welfare of future generations (for example, subsidies to favored businesses and industries and the wars in Iraq, Afghanistan, and Libya.)

As the United States experienced large budget deficits during 2001–2012, consumption expenditures increased as a share of GDP, private investment was weak, and the trade deficits were large. This pattern indicates that the current generation was the primary beneficiary of the deficits. There is little reason to believe that the deficits enhanced the capital assets that will be available to the next generation of Americans.

ST07-4 GOVERNMENT DEBT: A CROSS-COUNTRY COMPARISON

How does the net government debt of the United States compare with other major industrial nations? Exhibit 3 provides the answer. Among these countries, the net public debt-to-GDP ratio in 2013 was lowest for Australia and Canada. The debt-to-GDP ratio was 50 percent in Germany, 69 percent in France, 78 percent in the United Kingdom, compared to 90 percent for the United States. These figures include the debt of both national and regional governments. The debt-to-GDP ratio exceeded 100 percent in Italy, Greece, and Japan. Thus, the net debt-to-GDP ratio of the United States places it in the upper-middle group among the high-income industrial economies.

A large outstanding debt generally means higher taxes for the financing of the interest payments. This was the case in both Portugal and Italy, in which interest payments as a share of the economy were more than twice the level of the United States. In Japan, however, the interest payments were a relatively small share of GDP, even though the outstanding government debt was large. This occurred because the domestic saving rate of Japan has been exceedingly high, and this has kept domestic interest rates low in recent years.

EXHIBIT 3

Government Debt of Industrial Countries

Measured as a share of the economy, the net public debt of the United States lies in the upper-middle group among the high-income industrial countries.

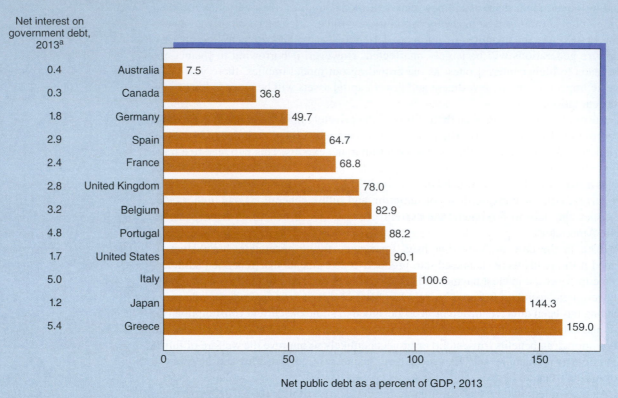

Net interest on government debt, 2013[a]

Net interest	Country	Net public debt as a percent of GDP, 2013
0.4	Australia	7.5
0.3	Canada	36.8
1.8	Germany	49.7
2.9	Spain	64.7
2.4	France	68.8
2.8	United Kingdom	78.0
3.2	Belgium	82.9
4.8	Portugal	88.2
1.7	United States	90.1
5.0	Italy	100.6
1.2	Japan	144.3
5.4	Greece	159.0

Net public debt as a percent of GDP, 2013

[a]As a percent of GDP.

Source: *OECD Economic Outlook*, June 2013, Annex Tables 31 and 33. The figures are estimates for 2013 Net public debt includes debt from all levels of government.

ST07-5 SOCIAL SECURITY, BUDGET DEFICITS, AND THE NATIONAL DEBT

As conventionally measured, the budget deficit includes the revenues and expenditures of government trust funds, including the Social Security Trust Fund. Under legislation adopted in 1983, Social Security payroll tax rates were set at levels designed to generate surpluses for the years before the retirement of the baby boom generation. But, the prior Social Security surpluses have shifted to deficits as the baby boomers begin moving into the retirement phase of life. These deficits will get larger and larger during the next two decades, as more and more baby boomers retire. This will make it even more difficult for the federal government to balance its budget.

Interestingly, the "implicit debt" accompanying the Social Security and Medicare programs is far greater than the national debt. At current tax rates, the revenues flowing into the Social Security system are sufficient to cover only about 75 percent of the promised benefits. Thus, 25 percent of the promised Social Security benefits are unfunded. They cannot be paid without an increase in taxes (or additional borrowing). These unfunded Social Security benefits amount to about $12 trillion. The situation is even worse for Medicare. At current rates, Medicare taxes will fall short of the promised future benefits by an estimated

$27 trillion.[3] Thus, the implicit debt (promised benefits that exceed revenues generated at current tax rates) of the Social Security and Medicare programs is two or three times the national debt.

Like the official federal debt, these unfunded liabilities will mean either higher taxes or broken promises in the future. This is a point that is often overlooked in discussions about the size of the national debt.

ST07-6 THE POLITICAL ECONOMY OF DEBT FINANCING

Before 1960, almost everyone—including the leading figures of both political parties—thought the federal government should balance its budget. In essence, there was widespread implicit agreement, something like a Constitutional rule, that the federal budget should be balanced. Against this political background, both deficits and surpluses were small relative to the size of the economy during times of peace.

The Keynesian revolution changed all of this. Rather than balancing the budget, Keynesians argued that the budget should be shifted toward a deficit when stimulus was needed and toward surplus when there was concern about inflation. In essence, the Keynesian revolution released political decision makers from the discipline imposed by a balanced budget. Freed from this constraint, politicians persistently spent more than they were willing to tax.[4] Since 1960, there have been only two brief periods of budget surplus, one in 1969 and the other in 1998–2001.

From a public-choice viewpoint, the political attractiveness of spending compared to taxation is not surprising. Politicians have a strong incentive to spend money on programs that benefit the voters of their district and special interest groups that will help them win reelection. In contrast, they do not like to levy taxes because they impose a visible cost on voters. Borrowing provides politicians with an attractive alternative. Because they push the taxes into the future, deficits impose a less visible cost than current taxation. Thus, borrowing allows politicians to supply voters with immediate benefits without having to impose a parallel visible cost in the form of higher taxes or user charges.

The same is true for unfunded promises like those of Social Security and Medicare. Like borrowing, this technique makes it possible for politicians to take credit for the promised benefits now without having to levy the equivalent amount of taxes. Thus, the political popularity of both debt financing and unfunded promised benefits is a reflection of the political incentive structure—the desire of elected officials to spend, and their reluctance to tax. Unless the incentive structure is changed—for example, by requiring a two-thirds or three-fourths majority to approve spending measures or additional borrowing—debt financing can be expected to continue.

ST07-7 POLITICS, DEMOGRAPHICS, FEDERAL DEBT, AND THE DANGERS AHEAD

Both the budget deficit and federal debt have soared during the recent financial crisis and recession. During 2009–2010, about 35 percent of federal expenditures were financed by borrowing. The huge recent federal deficits have pushed the federal debt to levels not seen since the years immediately following World War II (see Exhibit 1). The rapid growth of baby-boomer retirees in the decade immediately ahead will mean higher spending levels and larger and larger deficits for both Social Security and Medicare. Moreover, as we discussed in Special Topic 1 (see Exhibits 9 and 10 of Special Topic 1),

---

[3]See *2013 Annual Report of the Boards of Trustees of the Federal Hospital Insurance and Federal Supplementary Medical Insurance Trust Fund*, www.cms.hhs.gov/ReportsTrustFunds/.

[4]See James M. Buchanan and Richard Wagner, *Democracy in Deficit: The Political Legacy of Lord Keynes* (New York: Academic Press, 1977), for a detailed account of the changes wrought by the Keynesian revolution.

more than half of Americans age 18 and older derive benefits from various transfer programs, while paying little or no personal income tax. All of these factors are going to make it extremely difficult to slow the growth of federal spending and keep the debt from ballooning out of control.

What will happen if the federal government does not bring its finances under control? As the size of a nation's debt gets larger and larger relative to income, there will be repercussions in credit markets. Extension of loans to the government of a country with a large debt-to-GDP ratio is risky. As a result, the highly indebted government will have to pay higher interest rates. This happened in Ireland in 1986, Belgium in 1994, and is currently a problem in Greece, Italy, and Portugal. Of course, the higher interest rates will increase the interest cost on the outstanding debt, which will make it still more difficult to control the budget deficit.

Currently, the demand for private investment is weak and the federal government is still able to borrow at low rates of interest. However, if the federal debt continues to rise as a share of the economy, at some point, investors will lose confidence and interest rates will move upward. When a nation's outstanding debt is large, interest payments will increase sharply as interest rates rise. However, even if it is difficult to meet the interest obligations, a country with a central bank, as in the case of the United States, is highly unlikely to default on the payments to the bondholders. Instead, it is far more likely that the government will resort to money creation to service the debt and meet other obligations. But, if lenders even begin to sense that might happen, they will sell their bonds and other dollar denominated assets, the foreign exchange value of the dollar will plunge, and inflation will soar. These factors will lead to an economic crisis.

Historically, this has occurred in other countries that have failed to control government finances, and the United States is not immune to the laws of economics. Greece has already pushed its debt to levels that have undermined its creditworthiness, and other European countries also have dangerously high levels of government debt. In the years immediately ahead, both politics and demographics will be placing upward pressure on government spending and budget deficits in the United States. Nonetheless, controlling the growth of debt during the next decade is vitally important. The future prosperity of Americans may well depend on it.

KEY POINTS

- The national debt is the sum of the outstanding bonds of the U.S. Treasury. Budget deficits increase the national debt, whereas surpluses reduce it. The national debt reflects the cumulative effect of all prior budget deficits and surpluses.

- Approximately two-fifths of the national debt is owned by U.S. government agencies and the Federal Reserve. For this portion of the debt, the government both pays and receives the interest (except for the expenses of the Fed). Only the privately held federal debt—the portion of the national debt owned by domestic and foreign investors—generates a net interest obligation for the government.

- Budget deficits affect future generations through their impact on capital formation. To the extent the deficits reduce capital formation, future generations will inherit fewer capital assets, which will reduce their productivity and income levels.

- During the past couple of decades, the surpluses of the Social Security system reduced the size of the federal deficit. But Social Security will run larger and larger deficits in the next two decades as the baby-boomers retire, and these deficits will enlarge the size of the federal deficit.

- Politicians find debt financing attractive because it allows them to spend without levying the equivalent amount of taxes. Thus, political considerations make it difficult to achieve balanced budgets. This factor, along with increased spending on Social Security and Medicare as the baby-boomers move into the retirement phase of life, will make it difficult to control debt financing in the decade ahead.

- Measured as a share of GDP, the net outstanding debt of the United States falls in the upper-middle group among high-income industrial countries. But the federal debt-to-GDP ratio has soared during 2008–2014, and it now stands at the highest level since the years immediately following World War II. If the upward trend in this ratio is not halted, it will lead to serious economic problems in the future.

CRITICAL ANALYSIS QUESTIONS

1. *Does the national debt have to be paid off at some time in the future? What will happen if it is not?

2. What is the difference between the national debt and privately held federal debt? Why is the distinction between the two important?

3. *When government bonds are held by foreigners, the interest income from the bonds goes to foreigners rather than to Americans. Would Americans be better off if we prohibited the sale of bonds to foreigners?

4. How did the Social Security system influence the size of the budget deficit during 1985–2010? How will it influence the deficit during the next two decades? Is this a cause for concern? Why or why not?

5. *Would you predict that government expenditures would be higher or lower if taxes (or user charges) were required for the finance of all expenditures? Why? Do you think the government would spend funds more or less efficiently if it could not issue debt? Explain.

6. "Given the incentive of elected political officials to spend and their reluctance to tax, two-thirds approval of the House and Senate should be required for both spending measures and increases in government debt." Do you think this is a good idea? Why or why not?

7. Does an increase in the national debt increase the supply of money (M1)? Can the money supply increase when the U.S. Treasury is running a budget surplus?

*Asterisk denotes questions for which answers are given in Appendix B.

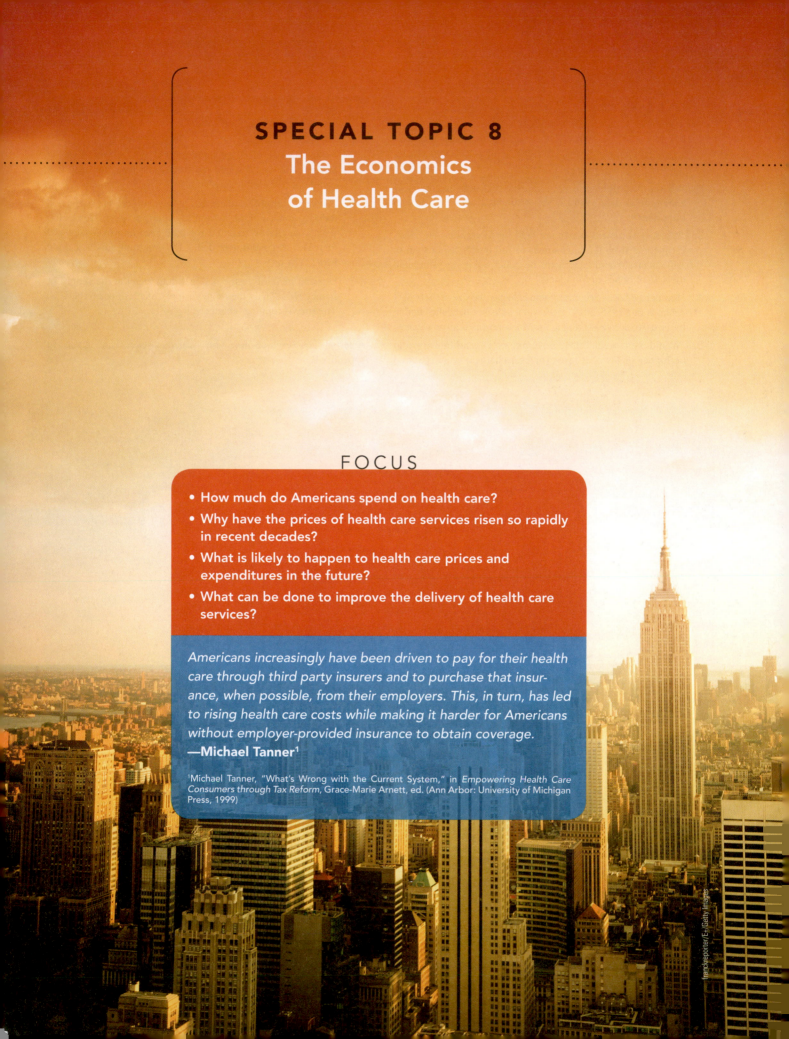

SPECIAL TOPIC 8
The Economics of Health Care

FOCUS

- How much do Americans spend on health care?
- Why have the prices of health care services risen so rapidly in recent decades?
- What is likely to happen to health care prices and expenditures in the future?
- What can be done to improve the delivery of health care services?

Americans increasingly have been driven to pay for their health care through third party insurers and to purchase that insurance, when possible, from their employers. This, in turn, has led to rising health care costs while making it harder for Americans without employer-provided insurance to obtain coverage.
—Michael Tanner[1]

[1]Michael Tanner, "What's Wrong with the Current System," in *Empowering Health Care Consumers through Tax Reform*, Grace-Marie Arnett, ed. (Ann Arbor: University of Michigan Press, 1999)

There is considerable dissatisfaction with the operation of the health care industry in the United States. This is certainly understandable. Both the expenditures on and prices of health care have soared in recent decades. **Exhibit 1** presents the expenditure figures as a share of GDP. Health care spending, including both private and government, jumped from 5.2 percent of GDP in 1960 to 9.2 percent in 1980 and 17.9 percent in 2011. Why has health care spending increased so rapidly? Will the health care legislation passed in 2010 slow the growth of this spending? Is the health care industry in need of fundamental reform? This special topic investigates these questions and related issues.

Some categories of health care spending have substantial public good components. For example, this is true for expenditures on pure research and activities that retard, and in some cases eliminate, the incidence of communicable diseases. In these cases, health care spending can generate spillover benefits for the general populace, and it would be difficult, if not impossible, to exclude nonpaying consumers from the receipt of these benefits. As we discussed in Chapter 5, under these conditions, government action might lead to an improvement in the allocation of resources. The National Institutes of Health and the Centers for Disease Control and Prevention provide examples of government organizations that justify their funding primarily on the basis of the public-good nature of their services. However, the vast majority of health care spending, including that of the government, involves private goods, goods for which the benefits accrue primarily to the consumer. This feature will focus on the provision of these personal consumption health care services.

©iStockphoto.com/nicoolay

EXHIBIT 1

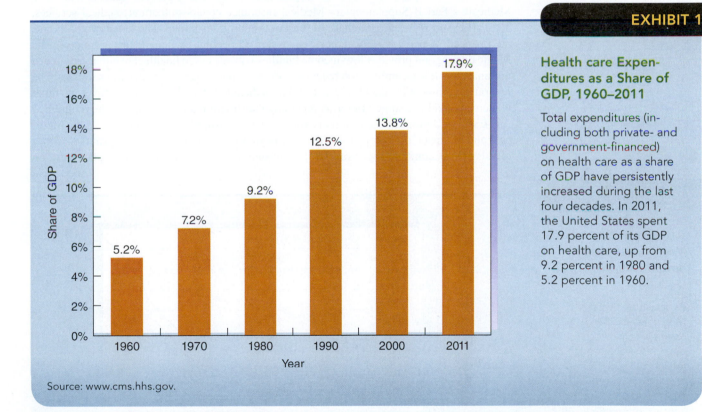

Health care Expenditures as a Share of GDP, 1960–2011

Total expenditures (including both private- and government-financed) on health care as a share of GDP have persistently increased during the last four decades. In 2011, the United States spent 17.9 percent of its GDP on health care, up from 9.2 percent in 1980 and 5.2 percent in 1960.

Source: www.cms.hhs.gov.

ST08-1 THE STRUCTURE OF THE HEALTH CARE INDUSTRY

Goods and services may be produced by either private- or government-operated firms. Correspondingly, they may be paid for by the consumer directly or by the taxpayer or some other third party.

Health care in many countries, including Canada and most of the high-income countries of Europe, is a socialized industry.[2] In these countries, hospitals are operated by the government, and their services are financed through taxes. Physicians, nurses, and other health care workers are government employees. Of course, socialization does not eliminate scarcity, costs, and the need to ration the available supply. Resources must be attracted to the health care industry, and this will involve a cost. No country is able to provide as much health care, free of charge, as its citizens would like. Therefore, when price plays a secondary role, nonprice factors will have to be used to ration health care services. Thus, in these countries, political rules, waiting lists for various treatments, and the absence (or highly restricted availability) of services such as MRIs that involve expensive equipment are used to allocate health care resources.

In the United States, there is widespread use of both private- and government-operated enterprises in the health care industry. Whereas the services of doctors are generally supplied privately, hospitals are often operated by the government, particularly local governments. Many communities, however, also have privately operated hospitals. Some of the privately operated hospitals are for-profit businesses, whereas others are operated by charitable institutions. In contrast with other industries, most health care spending (86 percent) is paid for by a third party, either the taxpayer or a private insurance company.

The Medicare and Medicaid programs have covered the bulk of the health care cost of the elderly and the poor since their establishment in the mid-1960s. Medicare's hospitalization program (Part A) uses a 2.9 percent payroll tax (3.8 percent on all income above $200,000) to finance virtually all of the cost of hospitalization incurred by persons aged 65 and older. Medicare's Part B Supplementary Medical Insurance covers outpatient medical services, and Part D subsidizes the purchase of prescription drug insurance. The latter two programs are financed 75 percent by general revenues and 25 percent by beneficiary premiums. The Medicaid program provides low-income families with access to health care either free or at a nominal cost. It is a combination federal–state program financed from general revenues. The federal government covers 60 percent of the Medicaid costs, whereas states cover the other 40 percent and have some discretion regarding the structure and coverage of the program.

Exhibit 2 presents data for real expenditures (measured in 2011 dollars) on the Medicare and Medicaid programs. From the very beginning, spending on the programs rose rapidly. By 1970, combined spending on the two summed to $71 billion. Real expenditures on

---

EXHIBIT 2

Real Expenditures on Medicare and Medicaid (Measured in 2011 Dollars)

Expenditures on both Medicare and Medicaid have soared in recent decades. Adjusted for inflation, the 2011 expenditures on Medicare are about three times the level of 1990 and 12 times the figure for 1970. The real Medicaid expenditures have also increased rapidly.

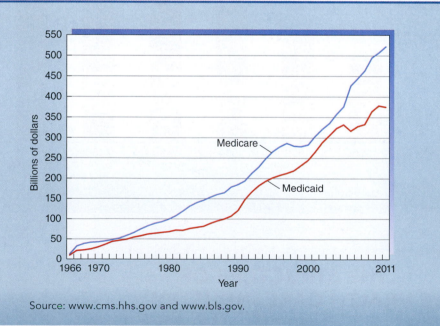

Source: www.cms.hhs.gov and www.bls.gov.

---

[2]For a cross-national comparison of spending on health care, see Uwe E. Reinhardt, "Health Care for Aging Baby Boom: Lessons from Abroad," *Journal of Economic Perspectives* (Spring 2000): 71–83.

the Medicare program doubled between 1970 and 1980 and nearly doubled again between 1980 and 1990. Since 1990, they have increased by another 182 percent. In 2011, the total expenditures on Medicare summed to $522 billion. Spending on Medicaid has also increased rapidly. In 2011, government spending on Medicaid ($375 billion) was more than three times the level of 1990 and 13 times the figure for 1970. As Exhibit 2 shows, spending on Medicaid is now nearly three-fourths that of Medicare.

ST08-1a DISCRIMINATION AGAINST THE DIRECT PURCHASE OF HEALTH INSURANCE

Health insurance is also an integral part of the health care industry in the United States. About two-thirds of nonelderly adults have health insurance through group plans offered by their employers. Employee compensation in the form of health insurance is not subject to taxation. This makes group health insurance programs provided through one's employer particularly attractive.[3] Interestingly, this favorable tax treatment of employer-provided health insurance is a historical relic dating back to the wage and price controls of World War II. Because health insurance benefits were not counted as wages, employers were able to use them as a means to increase compensation and attract additional workers, while still complying with the wage controls imposed during the war.

In contrast with health insurance purchased through one's employer, both personal medical bills and the direct purchase of insurance by an individual or family must be paid for with after-tax dollars. When employees are provided with additional income rather than health insurance benefits, the income is subject to both payroll and personal income taxes. This makes the direct purchase of health insurance far more costly than purchase through an employer. For example, a lower-middle-income family confronting a 15 percent federal income tax and the 15.3 percent payroll tax would have to earn approximately $12,000 of additional income in order to purchase an $8,400 health insurance policy. A family in the 28 percent federal tax bracket would have to earn approximately $14,000 more in order to purchase the policy. When state and local income and payroll taxes are present, these figures are still higher.

This discriminatory tax treatment encourages employees to demand and employers to provide low deductible, small copayment health insurance policies. In essence, health care expenses covered in this manner are tax deductible, whereas those paid for out of pocket or through the direct purchase of health insurance are not.[4] As a result of this distortion, more health care bills are paid for by third-party insurers and fewer are covered directly by the health care consumer or through high-deductible insurance plans. As we will see in a moment, this affects the efficiency of health care delivery.

The linking of health insurance to employment also reduces employee mobility and increases the number of people without any health insurance coverage. When employees lose their job, they also lose their health insurance. Because purchase of a policy with after-tax dollars is so expensive, many unemployed workers remain uncovered until they are able to find a new job. Furthermore, the discriminatory tax treatment of direct purchase policies reduces the competitiveness of the health insurance industry. Unsurprisingly, the industry is dominated by a relatively small number of companies offering primarily "one size fits all" group plans.

ST08-1b THIRD-PARTY PAYMENTS AND HEALTH CARE INFLATION

Following the establishment of the Medicare and Medicaid programs in the mid-1960s, third-party payment of health care expenditures grew rapidly, whereas the share of medical bills paid directly by the consumer declined. As Exhibit 3 shows, 55.2 percent of the

---

[3]In addition to the favorable tax treatment, economies resulting from the group purchase of health insurance may also make employer-provided plans more attractive.

[4]Out-of-pocket health care expenses can only be deducted if the taxpayer files an itemized return. Even in this case, only health care expenses in excess of 7.5 percent of the taxpayer's adjusted gross income are deductible.

EXHIBIT 3

Out-of-Pocket and Third-Party Payments for Medical Care, 1960 and 2011

In 1960, out-of-pocket medical care expenditures of consumers accounted for 55 percent of the total, whereas private insurance and government programs paid 45 percent of the medical bills. By 2011, the out-of-pocket payments had fallen to only 14 percent of expenditures, whereas those covered by a third party had risen to 86 percent of the total. Economic theory indicates that growth of third-party payments will reduce the incentive to economize and lead to both higher prices and expenditure levels.

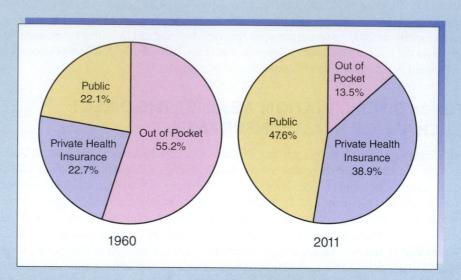

Source: www.cms.hhs.gov. Here, medical care payments are defined as personal health care expenditures.

1960 medical expenditures were paid directly by consumers. Third parties financed only 44.8 percent of the 1960 total. Through the years, the share paid out of pocket has declined, whereas that financed by third parties has risen. By 2011, third-party payments accounted for 86 percent of the medical care purchases, 47.6 percent by the government, and 38.9 percent by private insurers. Only 14 percent of the medical bills in 2011 were paid for directly by consumers.

Economic theory indicates that the growth of subsidies to health care consumers and accompanying expansion in third-party payments will push prices upward. There are two reasons why this will be the case. First, subsidies like those provided by Medicare and Medicaid will increase the demand for medical care. In turn, the stronger demand will lead to higher prices. As we discussed in Chapter 4, when the supply of a good or service is highly inelastic, suppliers will be the primary beneficiaries even if the subsidies are directed toward consumers. This is the case in the health care industry: The supply of most medical service is highly inelastic. As a result, the primary impact of the subsidies will be higher prices and increased returns for health care providers.

Second, the growth of third-party payments weakens the incentive of consumers to economize and shop for low-cost services and for producers to provide the goods at a low price. In a normal market, consumers will shop around and patronize those suppliers that provide the most value per dollar of expenditure. In turn, this shopping by consumers provides suppliers with a strong incentive to control their costs and offer their services at attractive prices. But when someone else is paying all or most of the bill, the incentive to economize is eroded. Rather than search for value relative to cost, consumers will attempt to purchase from the "best available" supplier, pretty much regardless of price.

Perhaps the following example will help explain why the substitution of third-party payments for out-of-pocket spending will lead to higher prices. Suppose that the government, insurance companies, or some other third party was willing to pay 90 percent of the bill of customers purchasing hair-styling services. Think how the behavior of both potential consumers and suppliers in the hair-styling business would be altered. Because someone else is paying most of the bill, many consumers will now get their hair styled more often, search for the very best stylists even if they are quite expensive, and patronize those providing extra services (for example, shoulder massages, pleasant surroundings, and valet parking). The strong demand will make it possible for hair stylists to raise their prices, and many will begin providing the "extras" designed to convince consumers that their services are the best. All of these adjustments will drive the price of hair-styling services upward and cause the third-party expenditures to soar.

Summarizing, economic theory indicates that higher subsidies and increased third-party payments will increase demand for the service, reduce the incentive to economize, and lead to both rising prices and expenditures. Moreover, when the supply of the service is highly inelastic, the producers will be the primary beneficiaries of the subsidies.

The evidence is supportive of this view. **Exhibit 4** shows the ratio of the medical care price index to the overall consumer price index. If the prices of medical services increase more than the prices of other consumer purchases, this ratio will rise. Note that this has been the case year after year. Since the passage of the Medicare and Medicaid programs in 1965, the prices of medical services have more than doubled relative to the general consumer price index. Thus, during this lengthy time span, on average, the prices of health care services rose at more than twice the rate of other consumer items. Furthermore, there is no evidence that the health care inflation is about to subside. In fact, the increase in medical prices relative to the general index of consumer prices has accelerated since 1980. Moreover, the prices of prescription drugs, which rose less than the consumer price index during the 1960s and 1970s, have increased more rapidly than the CPI in recent decades.

As prices and expenditures soar, third-party payees, including both insurance companies and the government, will try to control the growth of their expenditures. They may limit the amount paid for various services, require consumers to patronize only certain providers, make it more difficult to obtain permission for costly procedures, impose delays,

EXHIBIT 4

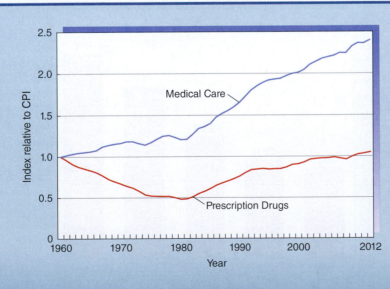

Source: htpp://www.bls.gov.

Ratio of Health care Price Indexes Relative to the Consumer Price Index

The ratio of medical care prices to the general level of consumer prices more than doubled between 1965 and 2012. After declining relative to the Consumer Price Index during 1960–1980, prescription drug prices have increased far more rapidly than the CPI since 1980.

and the like. This is essentially the route taken by the "managed-care movement" of the 1990s. Regulatory controls of this type, however, are difficult to implement successfully because they often conflict with the interest of both consumers and health care providers. As the experience with managed care illustrates, this path will tend to result in unhappy consumers and decisions that, with the benefit of hindsight, were clearly inappropriate and in some cases life-threatening. Controlling costs through rules and regulations imposed by a third party is an imperfect substitute for competition and the choices of consumers spending their own money.

ST08-2 THE GROWTH OF THE ELDERLY POPULATION AND HEALTH CARE

What will happen to the future demand for health care? **Exhibit 5** provides insight on this question. Between 2000 and 2010, the number of Americans age 70 and older expanded by 2.4 million. But the growth of the population in this age category will soar as the baby boomers (the generation born after World War II) reach age 70 in large numbers. This is now happening. During the two decades following 2010, the age 70 and older population of the United States will expand by 20.8 million, a whopping increase of 74 percent.

This huge increase in elderly Americans has enormous implications for the health care industry. Because health care expenses are much higher for people in their seventies than in their sixties and younger, this growth of Americans age 70 and older will increase the demand for both medical services and the share of those services financed by third parties. This will push both health care prices and expenditures upward. It will also cause spending on Medicare and other health care programs to soar and necessitate higher taxes for their finance. Unless reform is undertaken, the health care inflation and spending growth of recent decades will not only continue but also accelerate.

EXHIBIT 5

Growth of the U.S. Population Age 70 and Older, 2000–2040

Between 2000 and 2010, the number of people over age 70 increased by 2.4 million. But, during the two decades that follow, the aging of the baby boom generation will push this group upward by 20.8 million. This rapid growth will place enormous pressure on the Medicare program because the medical expenses of people over age 70 are exceedingly high.

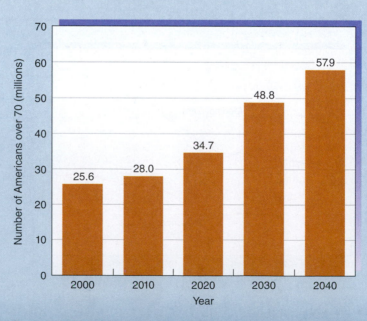

Source: www.census.gov.

The Medicare Trustees estimate that Medicare's unfunded promises—projected spending beyond revenues anticipated at current tax rates—are $27 trillion.[5] That figure is 50 percent more than the official national debt and more than two times the unfunded liability of the Social Security system. Even more important, it is one and a half times the size of the U.S. economy.

ST08-2a WHAT ACCOUNTS FOR THE POOR PERFORMANCE OF THE HEALTH CARE INDUSTRY?

Some charge that market forces have failed in health care and therefore government must intervene. The truth is more nearly the opposite: Government interventions over more than six decades have generated perverse incentives that encourage people to engage in actions that impose costs on others and use resources inefficiently. These incentives clarify the forces underlying both the poor performance of the industry and the rising health care costs. They also provide insight with regard to effective action that would improve outcomes.

There are four major reasons for the poor performance of the health care industry. We will consider each of them.

First, the structure of government programs relies on third-party payments that erode the incentive to economize. Very little health care is purchased directly by consumers. Most is paid for indirectly through taxes or insurance premiums. When someone else is paying the bill, the patient has little reason to conserve on the use of the resource and the provider has little incentive to keep costs low.

Second, the huge tax advantage provided for the purchase of health insurance through one's employer undermines competition and makes it very costly for individuals or families to purchase a health insurance policy that fits their preferences. Rather than allowing consumers to choose, government subsidies and regulations push them into standardized and controlled group plans provided through employers. Moreover, under this system, if you lose your job, you also lose your health insurance. People do not generally buy auto, life, or homeowner insurance through their employer. Why do so many buy health insurance this way? Answer: The tax system subsidizes them to do so and punishes them with higher personal costs if they do not.

Third, state regulations that force insurers operating in the state to cover numerous items such as in vitro fertilization, drug rehabilitation, marriage counseling, acupuncture, and massage therapy also drive up costs and make it still more difficult for consumers to purchase a policy that fits their preferences.[6] Interestingly, the political pressure for this coverage almost always comes from special interest producer associations wanting taxpayers to subsidize the purchase of their services.

Fourth, regulations prevent consumers from purchasing a health insurance plan offered in another state. Thus, if you would like to purchase insurance that would provide you with inexpensive basic coverage at a low cost, but you happen to live in a state that has adopted many of the expensive mandates, you are out of luck. Essentially, the government has organized the health insurance business into separate cartels that operate in each of the 50 states. You can buy most everything ranging from groceries and automobiles to life and auto insurance from providers in other states, but not health insurance.

[5]See *2013 Annual Report of the Boards of Trustees of the Federal Hospital Insurance and Federal Supplementary Medical Insurance Trust Fund*, www.cms.hhs.gov/ReportsTrustFunds/.
[6]Health care insurance premiums are far more economical in states with few mandates than in those that force insurers to cover marginal medical services and to accept persons with known medical problems. For example, the cost of health insurance in states with few mandates like Idaho and Iowa is about half the cost of the premiums in states like Massachusetts, New York, and Rhode Island that mandate broader coverage. The broader set of mandates prevent consumers from buying less expensive coverage tailored to their individual and family needs. Moreover, they also increase the number uninsured because more people will choose to go without insurance when the premiums are higher.

ST08-3 THE AFFORDABLE CARE ACT: MAJOR PROVISIONS AND EXPECTED IMPACT

The rising prices and rapid growth of health care expenditures have generated considerable dissatisfaction with the performance of the health care sector. Moreover, the movement of the huge baby-boom generation into the retirement phase of life beginning in 2010 added another complicating factor. Against this background, the Obama administration pushed hard for action and in 2010 Congress responded with passage of the Patient Protection and Affordable Care Act. This legislation is bringing sweeping changes to both the health care industry and the economy more generally. Let's consider the major provisions of this act and its impact on the economy.

ST08-3a MAJOR PROVISIONS OF THE AFFORDABLE CARE ACT

While the Affordable Care Act is both lengthy (more than 2,000 pages) and complex, the following four provisions summarize the central elements of the program.

Mandated health insurance requirement.   The act requires everyone to have an approved health insurance plan. The legislation imposes a tax penalty on those who fail to comply. In 2016, individuals without coverage will be required to pay a tax penalty of $695 per year, and families will have to pay up to three times that amount ($2,085 or 2.5% of household income, whichever is lowest). This penalty will be phased in according to the following schedule: $95 in 2014, $325 in 2015, and $695 in 2016 for the flat fee or 1.0% of taxable income in 2014, 2.0% of taxable income in 2015, and 2.5% of taxable income in 2016. After 2016, the penalty will be increased annually by the cost-of-living adjustment. Exemptions will be granted for religious objections and a few other special cases.

Mandated provision of health insurance by employers.   Employers with 50 or more employees are required to either provide approved health insurance to their employees or pay a $2,000 fine annually for each full-time equivalent employee. This mandate does not apply to part-time employees—those working less than 30 hours per week. The provision was scheduled to take effect in 2014, but President Obama issued an executive order delaying it for one year.

Health care exchanges and subsidies for the purchase of insurance.   The Affordable Care Act establishes exchanges for the purchase of health care insurance. The exchanges are set up by states or by the federal government. Four alternative plans ranging from low to high coverage are offered through the exchanges. Insurance providers bid on the premiums they are willing to charge for each of the alternative plans. The purchase of health care insurance through the exchanges is subsidized for those earning up to 400 percent of the poverty income threshold, an annual income of about $95,000 in the case of a family of four. Those with incomes less than 134 percent of the poverty level are covered by Medicaid. As incomes increase from 134 percent to 400 percent of the poverty level, the size of the subsidy is scaled downward. The subsidies through the exchanges are complex and vary according to not only income but also age, marital status, and family size. In general, as income increases from 134 percent to 400 percent of the poverty level, the size of the subsidy will be reduced by about 25 percent of additional earnings. Thus, the scaling back of the subsidy pushes the marginal tax rates of these earners up by approximately 25 percentage points.

Expanded coverage.   The act requires insurers to cover children of policyholders up to age 26 and prohibits them from charging higher rates or rejecting anyone because of an existing health condition (e.g. cancer, diabetes, or heart disease).

ST08-3b MAJOR IMPLICATIONS OF THE AFFORDABLE CARE ACT

Regulations providing details on various provisions of the Affordable Care Act are still being processed and released. Thus, there is continuing uncertainty with regard to precisely how the law will evolve and what impact it will have on the economy. Nonetheless, three impacts are highly predictable.

First, part-time employment will grow because employers will not have to pay the $2,000 penalty if health insurance is not provided to employees working less than 30 hours per week. As a result, part-time jobs will expand relative to full-time employment. By 2013, a number of employers were already reducing the weekly time worked of employees below the 30-hour threshold and it was observable in the statistics. During the first seven months of 2013, part-time employment rose by 731,000 (2.7%), but full-time employment increased by only 222,000 (0.2%). Most part-time workers have low earnings and therefore they will qualify for the purchase of health insurance through the exchanges at highly subsidized rates. The taxpayer will be the major loser, as this shift will drive up the overall cost of the program.

Second, many employers with a high proportion of middle- and low-income employees will drop their health insurance coverage. For persons with incomes less than 250 percent of the poverty level, the subsidies for the purchase of insurance through the exchanges will almost always be substantially greater than the tax savings from employer provided health insurance. Thus, low and middle income employees will prefer higher wages rather than the insurance benefits. This situation means that both the employer and employee will be able to gain if the employer drops their provision of health insurance. The situation is just the opposite for high-earning employees because their tax savings will be greater than the subsidies through the health insurance exchanges. Thus, employers with mostly high-income employees will find it advantageous to continue with their employer-provided plan. But, if employer-provided health insurance is offered to some employees, it must be offered to all. As a result, employers will also have an incentive to use contracting out to offload employees with low earnings. While this will involve some cost, it will also make it possible for employers to provide a compensation package that will work better for both low and high wage employees. Once again, this response will increase the number receiving subsidies through the exchanges and drive up the cost of the program to the taxpayer.

Third, when the payroll and income taxes are combined with the phase out of the subsidies for health insurance purchased through the exchanges, the effective marginal tax rate of those making between 134 percent and 400 percent of the poverty income threshold will soar to the 50 percent to 60 percent range. For a family of four, this covers incomes ranging from approximately $35,000 to $95,000 annually. The incomes of tens of millions of Americans fall within this interval. Because they will get to keep only half or less of an increase in earnings, their incentive to develop their skills and take the steps necessary for promotions and movement up the income ladder will be substantially reduced. Moreover, many workers will seek to avoid these high marginal tax rates by working "off the books." As a result, underground (unreported) economic activity will expand and become a larger share of the economy. This has happened in European countries with high marginal tax rates and there is no reason why it will not happen here. In the process, both the efficiency of resource use and economic growth will decline.

ST08-3c IMPACT ON THE COST OF HEALTH CARE

How will the Affordable Care Act influence the cost of health insurance and medical services? The exchanges are designed to increase the competitiveness among health-insurance providers and place downward pressure on the price of health insurance, particularly for those unable to purchase a group plan through an employer. This may well reduce the price of purchasing personal plans. But other aspects of the act will create pressure in the opposite direction. The requirement that insurers must offer their plans to all, regardless of preexisting conditions, provides healthy people with an incentive to game the system: to pay the fine and remain uninsured, knowing that if anything bad happens they will then be able to purchase the insurance. If many people do this, the insurance pools will become disproportionately populated with unhealthy people with high medical expenses. This will place upward pressure on health-insurance premiums, at least partially offsetting the downward pressure achieved through the exchanges.

How will the act affect demand, supply, and the price of medical services? The rapidly rising prices of medical services are driven by the third-party payment system. As long as someone else is paying the bill, neither consumers nor producers will have much incentive to search for and provide value at a low price. If anything, the Affordable Care Act will expand the third-party payment system and the accompanying perverse incentives it creates. Moreover, there is reason to believe that the act will increase the demand for health care service relative to the supply. The legislation is designed to reduce the number without health insurance by 30 million. If substantial progress toward this objective is achieved, the demand for medical services will increase. In addition, the approval process will force providers to offer and consumers to purchase broader, more generous coverage. This, too, will increase demand. On the supply side, there is nothing in the act that will increase the number of doctors or medical suppliers more generally. In fact, there will tend to be a negative impact on the supply of doctors, at least in the short term. The act mandates that patient records be kept electronically. This will require expensive equipment, imposing a sizable cost on many private practices. Additional regulations will lead to still more paper shuffling and secretarial services. Rather than incur the cost of dealing with these issues, many doctors will push their retirement forward, thereby reducing the supply of physician services.

Within the framework of demand and supply, there is little reason to expect that the Affordable Care Act will reduce the growth of medical service prices. The federal government now sets more than 7,000 reimbursement rates for various medical procedures. If the upward pressure on health care prices continues, this price-setting power may well develop into a backdoor system of price controls, and the more lengthy waiting times for medical procedures that are often observed in other countries.

ST08-4 HOW CAN THE PERFORMANCE OF THE HEALTH CARE INDUSTRY BE IMPROVED?

If the provision of health care is to become more efficient and cost-effective, greater reliance must be placed on consumer choice and direct payment of medical expenses. How can this be achieved? Several policy changes would be helpful, but the following six alternatives are particularly important.

1. Equalize the tax treatment of out-of-pocket medical expenses and the direct purchase of health insurance with that of health insurance purchased through an employer. This could be best achieved by providing all taxpayers with a 30-percent refundable tax credit, a tax saving similar to that of employer-provided plans, for expenditures on the direct purchase of medical insurance and out-of-pocket payment of medical bills. This would also make it cheaper for people without access to employer-provided insurance to purchase coverage and pay medical bills directly.

2. Allow the residents of each state to purchase health care from out-of-state providers. This would break up the government-protected cartels now operating in each state and make the health insurance industry more competitive. It would also expand the options available to consumers and make it easier for them to purchase a plan more consistent with their personal preferences.

3. Encourage health savings accounts (HSAS) and the direct payment of medical bills from the accounts.

Beginning in 2004, **health savings accounts** were made more attractive, but they are still treated less favorably than insurance purchased through one's employer. In 2014, HSAS allowed individuals with a high-deductible insurance plan ($1,250 or more) to make tax-deductible contributions of up to $3,300 per year for a single person (or $6,550 for a married couple) into a savings account to cover future medical bills. Employers making contributions into their employees' accounts may take the contributions as a business expense. Individuals have a property right to the account, and their ownership is not dependent upon their employment. Funds can be drawn from these accounts for the direct payment of medical bills not covered by the high-deductible policies. Balances in the accounts can earn interest tax-free and be rolled over from year to year. Accumulated balances can either be used in retirement or passed on to heirs. HSAS reduce the incidence of third-party payments, and with time, as more health care consumers shop for value, medical suppliers will become more cost-sensitive. These accounts have grown substantially in recent years. In 2012, HSAS covered 13 million individuals.

4. Encourage the purchase of catastrophic health insurance and discourage the purchase of policies with first-dollar coverage and small copayments.

HSAS are designed to be used with a high-deductible, modest copayment insurance plan that can be purchased at an economical price. Insurance works well when it compensates people for losses resulting from unpredictable events outside of their control that seldom occur, but when they do, large losses are imposed on the unfortunate parties. Under these circumstances, the premiums of those experiencing little or no damage can be used to compensate those experiencing large losses. Large medical expenses such as those resulting from a severe injury or a catastrophic illness like diabetes or cancer generally fall into this category. It makes sense to promote the purchase of health insurance providing protection against large medical bills from sources like these. High-deductible policies—for example, one that covers most medical expenses in excess of $1,200 per year—are relatively cheap. In 2012, such a policy could be purchased for an annual premium of approximately $4,300. A system of tax credits could be utilized to encourage all (or at least most) citizens to purchase policies of this type.

In contrast, insurance works poorly when the "losses" are widespread among the insurees and when the actions of those insured influence the size of the benefits they derive. Under these circumstances, many insurees will do less to avoid actions that increase the likelihood that events triggering compensation will occur; and, as a result, insurance premiums will be costly relative to the benefits. Many health care costs, including those resulting from routine illnesses (for example, colds and flu), common childhood diseases, minor injuries, and the like, fall into this category. In varying degrees, most everyone can expect to experience such medical problems, and there are several alternative ways of dealing with them, some of which are far less costly than others. Predictably, insurance will work poorly for medical costs of this type. Furthermore, policies requiring only a small copayment for routine medical expenses promote the third-party payment system that retards economizing behavior. Thus, it makes no sense for public policy to promote such schemes.

5. Shift Medicare at least partly from a reimbursement service to a defined-benefit plan.

Under this approach, Medicare recipients would receive a specific amount each year for paying medical bills directly and purchasing private insurance. All Medicare recipients would be required to purchase at least a catastrophic

Health savings accounts Special savings accounts that individuals and families can use for the payment of medical bills and the purchase of a catastrophic (high deductible) health insurance plan.

insurance plan. The funds not used in one year could be rolled over for use in subsequent years. This approach would increase the freedom of Medicare recipients to choose the combination of medical services and method of payment that best fits their personal situation.

6. Place more emphasis on the supply side of the healthcare market. Each year, the government spends several hundred billion dollars subsidizing demand and helping people purchase medical services. Very little is spent encouraging additional supply. However, without additional supply, demand subsidies merely lead to higher prices and a reallocation of healthcare services among consumers. Thus, the primary beneficiaries of the demand-side subsidies are the health care suppliers, who receive the higher prices for their services. Supply-side programs would focus more on the training of health care providers. For example, they might provide more aid for the growth and development of medical schools—only two new medical schools have been established in the United States during the past quarter of a century. Aid to low-income students qualified to attend medical and nursing schools might also be expanded. In contrast with demand subsidies, programs that expand the supply of medical personnel would make it easier to control future costs.

ST08-5 CONCLUDING THOUGHTS

Health care costs so much because consumers directly pay for so little of it. The Affordable Care Act has not changed this situation. When consumers spend their own money, they will choose wisely, and their choices will provide suppliers with a strong incentive to control costs and offer quality service. While the six proposals outlined here will not solve all of the health care problems, economic analysis suggests they are a major move in the right direction. The Affordable Care Act has generated a "great debate" on the structure and future of health care in the United States. As this legislation is fully implemented and the results observed, it is almost certain that this debate will continue.

KEY POINTS

- Spending on health care has soared in recent decades. Measured as a share of the economy, total health care spending has risen from 5.2 percent in 1960 to 9.2 percent in 1980 and 17.9 percent in 2011.

- Following the enactment of Medicare and Medicaid in the mid-1960s, the direct expenditures of health care consumers gradually declined and those of third-party payees expanded. The out-of-pocket spending of consumers accounted for only 14 percent of health care spending in 2011, down from 55 percent in 1960.

- The growth of subsidies to health care consumers and greater reliance on third-party payments of recent decades (1) increased the demand for medical services and (2) reduced the incentive of both health care consumers and providers to economize. Both of these factors have contributed to

the health care inflation and soaring expenditures of recent decades.

- As the baby-boom generation grows older, the number of people aged 70 and older will increase sharply between 2010 and 2030. Under the current Medicare program, this will increase the demand for health care services and the share of medical payments financed by a third party. Unless reform is undertaken, this will mean both more health care inflation and substantially higher taxes for the finance of Medicare.

- Reforms that (1) place more emphasis on direct (rather than third-party) payment of medical bills, (2) increase competition in the health insurance industry, (3) encourage catastrophic insurance protection (but not low deductible, low copayment plans), and (4) expand the supply of health care will help control rising health care expenditures.

CRITICAL ANALYSIS QUESTIONS

1. How does the substitution of third-party payments by insurance companies and the government for the out-of-pocket purchase of health care by consumers influence the demand and price of medical services? Explain.

2. *When an employer provides health insurance benefits as part of the compensation package, does this represent a gift by employers to their employees? Do employees earn these benefits? Why or why not? Justify your response.

3. Do individuals have a right to free health care? Do they have a right to force others to provide them with free health care? Discuss.

4. *How did the Medicare and Medicaid programs influence the cost of medical services purchased by Americans who were neither poor nor elderly? Explain.

5. Consider the six reform proposals suggested by the authors at the end of this feature. Indicate why you believe each is either a good or a bad idea. Explain your answers

6. *Do personal choices influence health care expenditures? If health care is paid for by others or if everyone is charged the same premium for health care, how will this influence the incentive to make healthy lifestyle choices?

7. Suppose the government established a new program that would use revenues from a payroll tax to finance 85 percent of the maintenance and repair cost of automobiles incurred by those who are employed. How would this legislation influence (a) the prices of auto repair and maintenance services, (b) total spending on these services, and (c) the cost of this program in the years immediately ahead? Do you think this program should be adopted? Why or why not?

8. *If the government either provides (or forces insurers to provide) insurance to persons with preexisting adverse health conditions, how will this influence the incentive to purchase insurance when you are healthy?

*Asterisk denotes questions for which answers are given in Appendix B.

SPECIAL TOPIC 9
Earnings Differences between Men and Women

FOCUS

- Why are the earnings of women substantially lower than those of men? Is it because of employment discrimination?

- How has the economic status of women changed in recent decades?

- How have the educational choices and career goals of women changed? Will this affect their future earnings?

> Over the past 25 years, the gender pay gap has narrowed dramatically and women have increasingly entered traditionally male occupations.
>
> **—Francine D. Blau and Lawrence M. Kahn**[1]

[1]Francine D. Blau and Lawrence M. Kahn, "Gender Differences in Pay," *Journal of Economic Perspectives* (Fall 2000): 75.

Sixty years ago, the typical American woman spent most of her time at home caring for her children, preparing food, and doing laundry, cleaning, and other chores for her family. Fewer than one in four married women worked outside the household

in 1950. Today, the situation is dramatically different. Most women, including those who are married, work outside the home. This special topic analyzes earnings differences of men and women and the changing economic role of women.

ST09-1 EMPLOYMENT DISCRIMINATION AND THE EARNINGS OF WOMEN

During the last several decades, there has been a huge shift in the household versus market work choices of women. As **Exhibit 1** shows, the labor force participation rate of women rose from 37.6 percent in 1960 to 58.1 percent in 2011. Married women accounted for most of the increase.

Exhibit 1 also shows that the female–male (F–M) earnings ratio for full-time, year-round workers was approximately 60 percent from 1960 to 1980. In other words, women earned only 60 percent of what men did. Since the early 1980s, though, the earnings of women have steadily increased relative to men. Nevertheless, in 2011, women working full-time, year-round still earned only 77.0 percent as much as their male counterparts. However, among those employed full time, women worked about 5 percent fewer hours

EXHIBIT 1

Labor Force Experience of Women, 1960–2011

Between 1960 and 2011, the labor force participation of women rose from 37.7 to 58.1 percent. However, the female–male earnings ratio for full-time workers fluctuated around 60 percent during the period 1960–1980, before climbing throughout the 1980s and 1990s. By 2011, this ratio had risen to 77 percent. The hourly earnings of women working full-time were a little more than 80 percent those of men in 2011.

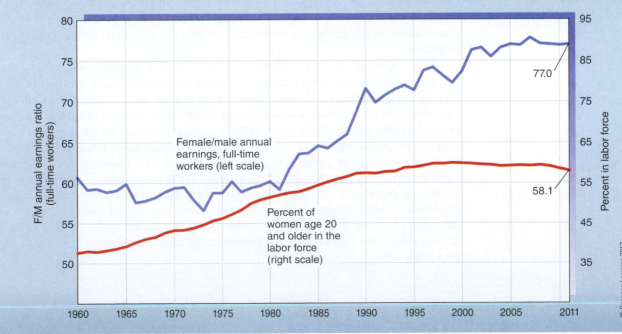

© Cengage Learning 2013

than men. Thus, the hourly earnings of women working full time were a little more than 80 percent of those of full-time male workers in 2011.

Why are the earnings of women so low compared with those of men? Most people blame employment discrimination. Evidence appears to support this view. Key worker characteristics such as age, years of schooling, marital status, location, and language are similar between men and women. So these factors are not the source of the earnings difference according to gender. Women are also crowded into a few low-paying jobs, occupational data show. Until recently, more than half of all women were employed in just four occupations—as clerical workers, teachers, nurses, and food service workers.

Still, attributing all or most of the pay differences between men and women to employment discrimination is an argument that's less than airtight. The very size of the difference makes the argument suspect. If an employer could really hire women who were willing and able to do the same work as men for 15 or 20 percent less, the profit motive would give them a strong incentive to do so. Surely employers (both men and women) who don't consider themselves to be "sexist" would jump at the chance to cut their wage cost so dramatically. Of course, as more and more employers substituted women for men workers, the F–M earnings gap would close.

ST09-2 MARITAL STATUS AND THE EARNINGS OF WOMEN

It might be helpful to think about the problem in a historical light. Before 1980, married men typically pursued paid employment aggressively because they were expected to be the family's primary breadwinners. Because they shouldered most of the responsibility for "bringing home the bacon," they were more likely to (1) participate continuously in the labor force; (2) relocate if necessary to get a higher paying job; and (3) accept jobs with long working hours, uncertain schedules, and out-of-town travel.

In contrast, married women, who were traditionally more responsible for running the households and rearing children, sought part-time work and jobs with more flexible hours.[2] Further, they expected to drop out of the labor force or switch jobs from time to time in order to care for young children, to follow their husband to a new job location, or when their families' financial needs became less burdensome. Because of expected changes in their work status, job skills valued by a large number of employers at most any time and location were particularly valuable to women. Viewed from this perspective, the historical concentration of women in occupations like nursing, teaching, and clerical positions is not surprising.

How important are gender differences when it comes to specialization within the family and pay differences today? **Exhibit 2** shows the median annual earnings of women relative to men in 2010–2011 according to their marital status. Clearly, married women earn substantially less than do married men. Even when working full time, year-round, married women earn only 73 percent as much as men. However, the earnings gap between men and women is substantially less among those who have never married. In 2010–2011, the female–male annual earnings ratio for full-time, year-round workers was 94 percent for those never married. In other words, the earnings gap between men and women was much smaller for those who were never married than for those married or previously married. This implies that although employment discrimination may well contribute to the wage differences between men and women, factors related to marital status, perhaps differences in preferences and past educational choices based on career objectives, are also highly important.

---

[2]For an analysis of how family specialization influences the employment and earnings of women, see James P. Smith and Michael P. Ward, "Women in the Labor Market and in the Family," *Journal of Economic Perspectives* (Winter 1989): 9–23.

EXHIBIT 2

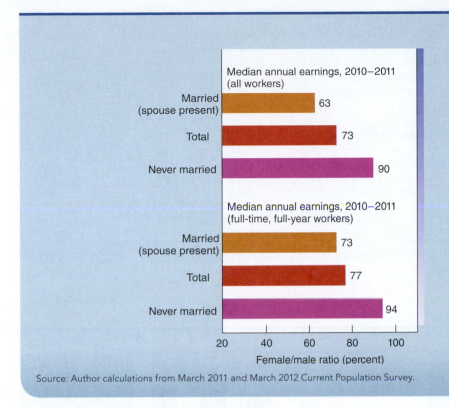

Female–Male Earnings According to Marital Status, 2010–2011

The earnings of women relative to men vary substantially with marital status and time worked. For those working full-time, year-round, the female–male earnings ratio was only 73 percent for married women with spouse present, but it was 94 percent for those never married. This suggests that differences in specialization within the traditional husband–wife family contribute substantially to earnings differentials according to gender.

Source: Author calculations from March 2011 and March 2012 Current Population Survey.

ST09-3 THE CHANGING CAREER OBJECTIVES OF WOMEN

Although the career objectives of men and women have differed substantially in the past, those differences have narrowed in recent years. In 1968, a national survey of women 14 to 24 years of age found that only 27 percent expected to be working at age 35. In contrast, a similar survey of young women in 1979 found that 72 percent expected to be working at that age.[3] These figures show that there was a dramatic increase during the 1970s in the number of young women preparing for a career and lifetime of labor force participation. Although this upward trend may have slowed, it has almost certainly continued during the last three decades.

As the percentage of women planning for a career rose, their educational choices also changed dramatically. In the early 1970s, women were much less likely than men to study and prepare for engineering, medicine, law, and similar high-paying fields traditionally dominated by men. But, as Exhibit 3 shows, the percentage of women earning degrees in these fields and others, such as accounting, veterinary medicine, dentistry, medicine, law, architecture, and pharmacy increased dramatically in the 1970s and 1980s. By the 1990s, parity was achieved in several of these areas. Increasingly, women, like men, are planning for careers in diverse areas, including high-paying professions.

The gender composition of new college graduates also suggests that women are increasingly planning for a career in the marketplace. During the last four decades, the percentage of women as a share of new college graduates has increased dramatically. As Exhibit 4 shows, only 39 percent of those completing an undergraduate degree in 1961 were women. By 1980, that figure had risen to 49 percent, and by 2010 it had jumped to 57 percent. Today, nearly three out of every five graduating seniors are women, compared with less than two out of five four decades ago.

---

[3]See Chapter 7 of the *Economic Report of the President* (1987). The numbers presented here are from tables 7–3 of the report.

EXHIBIT 3

Women as a Percent of People Earning Selected Professional Degrees, 1970–1971, 1987–1988, and 2010–2011

FIELD OF STUDY	1970–1971	1987–1988	2010–2011
Engineering	0.8	15.3	17.2
Dentistry	1.2	26.1	45.5
Optometry	2.4	34.3	64.1
Law	7.3	40.4	47.1
Veterinary Medicine	7.8	50.0	77.4
Medicine	9.2	33.0	48.4
Accounting	10.1	52.6	54.1
Architecture	12.0	38.7	42.1
Pharmacy	25.2	59.7	61.8

Sources: Commission of Professionals in Science and Technology, *Professional Women and Minorities* (Washington, DC: CPST, 1987); and U.S. Department of Education, *Digest of Education Statistics*, 1990 and 2012 (Washington, DC: U.S. Government Printing Office).

EXHIBIT 4

Women as a Percent of People Graduating from College, 1961–2013

Source: U.S. Department of Education, *Digest of Education Statistics*, 2012 (Washington, DC: U.S. Government Printing Office, 2012), table 310. The data are for people graduating with a four-year degree.

The fact that men are now a minority among those currently graduating from college is not particularly surprising. Jobs in fields like construction and heavy manufacturing offer attractive earnings opportunities, but they are also generally physically demanding and require employees to work either outdoors or in a less than ideal environment. Given their greater physical strength and perhaps a stronger preference for outdoor working conditions, men are more likely than women to find these physically demanding jobs attractive. As a result, the opportunity cost of going to college is higher for young men than for young women. Thus, fewer men pursue a college degree.

It is interesting to think about women's career choices in light of societal changes in the United States during the past five decades. In 1962, equal-pay legislation was passed requiring employers to pay equal wage rates to men and women doing the same jobs. In 1964, civil rights legislation was passed prohibiting employers from discriminating on the basis of both gender and race. Nonetheless, in the 1960s and 1970s, there was little change in the earnings of women relative to men. However, as the career objectives of women—perhaps pushed along by earlier legislative actions—began to change during

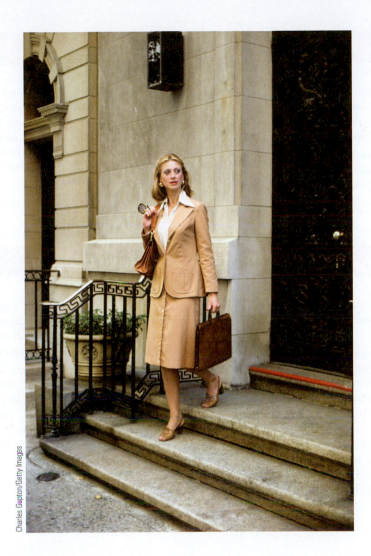

Charles Gupton/Getty Images

During the 1970s, an increasing proportion of women began to plan for full time, long term labor force participation. Reflecting this commitment, the career and educational choices of women shifted toward higher paying professions (see Exhibit 3). As this happened, the earnings of women began to increase steadily relative to men (see Exhibit 1).

the 1970s, the educational choices of men and women started to become more similar (see Exhibit 3).[4] Soon thereafter, the earnings of women began to rise relative to men (see Exhibit 1).

ST09-4 IMPLICATIONS FOR THE FUTURE

Clearly, the increased representation of women during the past several decades among both college graduates and those preparing themselves for careers indicates that women are increasingly committed to working in the marketplace. As the current generation of highly trained, well-educated young women acquires experience and moves into the prime earning years of life, the upward trend in the F–M earnings ratio can be expected to continue in the years ahead.

---

[4]For additional details on recent changes in the male/female earnings gap, see Francine D. Blau and Lawrence M. Kahn, "Gender Differences in Pay," *Journal of Economic Perspectives* (Fall 2000): 75–99; June O'Neill, "The Gender Gap in Wages, circa 2000," *American Economic Review* (May 2003): 309–14; and Francine D. Blau and Lawrence M. Kahn, "The U.S. Gender Pay Gap: Slowing Convergence," *Industrial and Labor Relations Review* (October 2006): 45–66.

KEY POINTS

- The annual earnings of women working full time are approximately 76 percent of those of men. Among full-time workers, the F–M earnings ratio is 73 percent for those married with spouse present but 91 percent for people who never married.

- In addition to employment discrimination, differences in specialization within the family, educational choices, and career goals contribute to the earnings differences between men and women.

- As the educational and career choices of women have become more like those of men during the last two decades, the earnings of women have risen relative to those of men. This trend is likely to continue in the future as more and more women prepare for and acquire experience in high-paying business and professional fields that have traditionally been dominated by men.

CRITICAL ANALYSIS QUESTIONS

1. Is employment discrimination the major cause of earnings differences between men and women? Carefully justify your answer.

2. *Between 1960 and 1990, the labor force participation rate of married women approximately doubled. What impact did this influx of married workers into the labor force have on (a) the average years of work experience of women relative to men, (b) the mean hours of work time of women relative to men, and (c) the female–male earnings ratio?

3. Physical strength is important in some jobs. Do you think differences in physical strength between men and women contribute to earnings differences according to gender? Why or why not? Do they also influence the share of men relative to women who will pursue a college education? Explain.

4. *In 2011, the median earnings of single men working full-time, year-round were only 59 percent of their married counterparts. Does this indicate that employment discrimination existed against single men and in favor of married men?

5. Compared to women, men are overrepresented in occupations like coal mining and construction, in which working conditions are more dangerous. For example, 4,308 American men were killed on the job in 2011, compared to 385 women. How will the more dangerous working conditions of men influence their earnings relative to women? Explain.

*Asterisk denotes questions for which answers are given in Appendix B

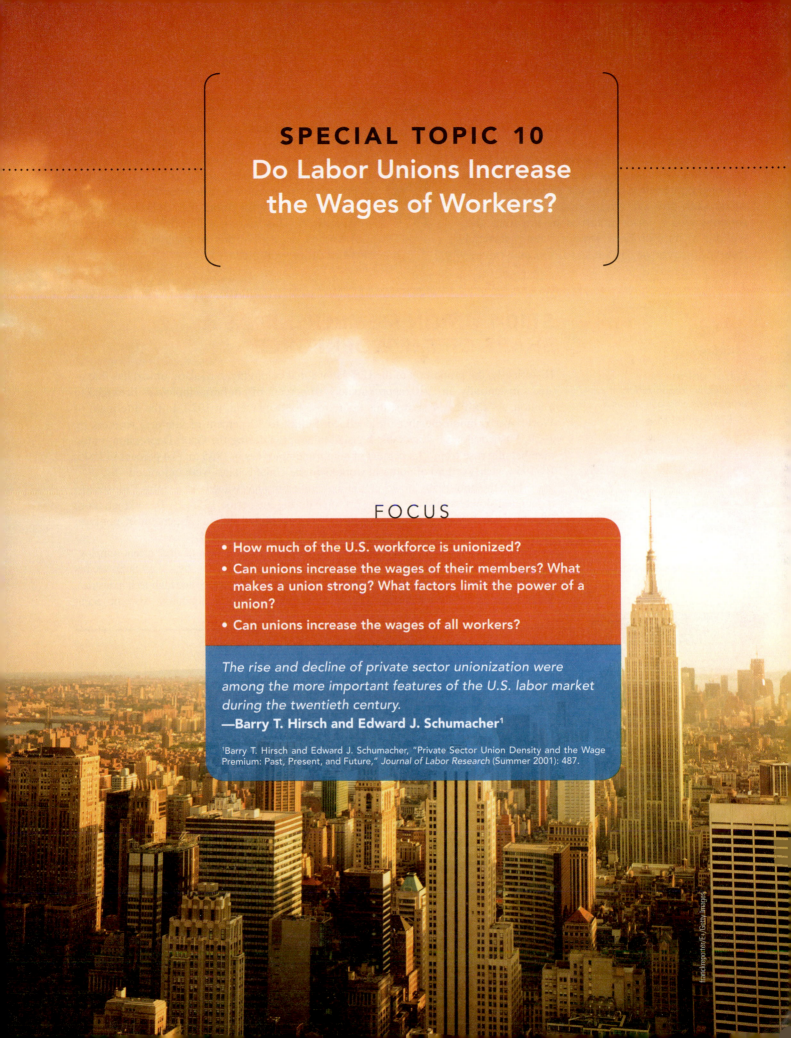

SPECIAL TOPIC 10
Do Labor Unions Increase the Wages of Workers?

FOCUS

- How much of the U.S. workforce is unionized?
- Can unions increase the wages of their members? What makes a union strong? What factors limit the power of a union?
- Can unions increase the wages of all workers?

The rise and decline of private sector unionization were among the more important features of the U.S. labor market during the twentieth century.
—Barry T. Hirsch and Edward J. Schumacher[1]

[1]Barry T. Hirsch and Edward J. Schumacher, "Private Sector Union Density and the Wage Premium: Past, Present, and Future," *Journal of Labor Research* (Summer 2001): 487.

A labor union is an organization of employees, usually working in either the same occupation or same industry, who have consented to joint bargaining with employers about their wages, working conditions, grievance procedures, and other elements of employment. The primary objective of a labor union is to improve the welfare of its members. Unions have historically been controversial. Some see them as a necessary shield protecting workers from employer greed. Others charge that unions are monopolies seeking to provide their members with benefits at the expense of other workers, consumers, and economic efficiency. Still others argue that the economic influence of unions—both for good and for bad—is vastly overrated. This feature will consider the impact of unions on the wages of their members and those of other workers.

ST10-1 UNION MEMBERSHIP AS A SHARE OF THE WORKFORCE

Labor union
A collective organization of employees who bargain as a unit with employers.

Historically, the proportion of the U.S. labor force belonging to a **labor union** has fluctuated substantially. In 1910, approximately 10 percent of nonfarm employees belonged to a union. As **Exhibit 1** shows, this figure rose to 18 percent in 1920. In the aftermath of World War I, union membership declined, falling to 12 percent of nonfarm workers by 1929. Pushed along by favorable legislation adopted during the Great Depression, union membership rose from 13.5 percent of nonfarm employees in 1935 to 30.4 percent in 1945. By 1954, nearly a third of nonfarm workers in the United States were unionized.

Since the mid-1950s, however, union membership has waned. As Exhibit 1 illustrates, it declined slowly as a share of the workforce during the period 1955–1970, and then more rapidly since 1980. By 2012, union members constituted only 11.3 percent of nonfarm employees, down from 24 percent in 1979 (and 32 percent in 1954).

Several factors have contributed to this decline. First, much of the recent employment growth has been in sectors in which unions have been traditionally weak. Such sectors include relatively small firms (fewer than a hundred employees) in service and high-tech industries. Small firms are costly for unions to organize and thus tend to be nonunion. Also, in recent

EXHIBIT 1

Union Membership as a Share of Nonagricultural Employment, 1910–2012

Between 1910 and 1935, union membership fluctuated between 12 percent and 18 percent of nonagricultural employment. During the 1935–1945 period, union membership increased sharply to approximately one-third of the nonfarm workforce. Since the mid-1950s, union membership has declined as a percent of nonfarm employment, and the decline has been particularly sharp since 1979.

Source: Leo Troy and Neil Sheflin, *Union Source Book: Membership, Structure, Finance, Directory* (West Orange, NJ: Industrial Relations and Information Services, 1985); and Barry T. Hirsch, David A. Macpherson, and Wayne G. Vroman, "Estimates of Union Density by State," *Monthly Labor Review*, July 2001.

decades, employment has grown rapidly in the less-organized Sunbelt while stagnating in the more heavily unionized Northeast and upper Midwest. This regional growth pattern has retarded the growth of union membership. Second, competition has eroded union strength in several important industries. Foreign producers have increased their market share in steel, mining, automobiles, and other heavy manufacturing industries. Employment has therefore been shrinking in these areas of traditional union strength. Deregulation in the transportation and communication industries has further reduced the membership of unions. As these industries have become more competitive, unionized firms have faced increased competition from nonunion producers. Finally, union membership has declined, in part, because workers have reduced their demand for unions over time. Consistent with a falling desire for union representation, opinion surveys reveal that workers believe that unions are less effective in improving their lot now than they were in the past.[2]

To some extent, several of these trends reflect the impact of unions on the wages of their members. Business investment and employment will tend to move away from geographic areas, industries, and classes of firms in which wages are high *relative to productivity*. Therefore, when unions increase the wages of their members *relative to nonunion workers of similar productivity*, they will also retard the growth of employment in unionized sectors.

As **Exhibit 2** shows, there is substantial variation in the incidence of union membership across gender, racial, and occupational groups. Men are more likely than women to

EXHIBIT 2

The 2010 Incidence of Union Membership by Sex, Race, Occupation, and Sector

The incidence of unionism is higher among (a) men than women and (b) blacks than whites or Hispanics. Technical, sales, clerical, and service workers are far less likely to be unionized than are craft, operator, and repair workers. As a share of the workforce, unionization among government employees is more than four times that of private-sector workers.

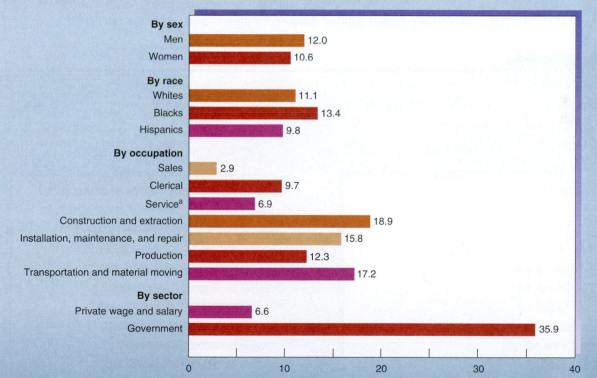

Source: Barry T. Hirsch and David A. Macpherson, *Union Membership and Earnings Data Book: Compilations from the Current Population Survey,* 2013 Edition (Washington, DC: The Bureau of National Affairs, 2013).
[a]Excluding protective service workers.

---

[2]For several recent studies examining the decline in unionism, see "Symposium on the Future of Private Sector Unions in the United States: Part I," *Journal of Labor Research* (Spring 2001); and "Symposium on the Future of Private Sector Unions in the United States: Part II," *Journal of Labor Research* (Summer 2001). Also see Barry T. Hirsch, "Sluggish Institutions in a Dynamic World: Can Unions and Industrial Competition Coexist?" *Journal of Economic Perspectives* (Fall 2007).

belong to a union. In 2012, 12.0 percent of employed men were union members, compared with only 10.6 percent of employed women. The incidence of unionization among blacks (13.4 percent) was higher than for whites (11.1 percent) or Hispanics (9.8 percent). There is substantial variation in unionization according to occupation. Less than 10 percent of the workers in sales, clerical, and service occupations were unionized in 2012. In contrast, more than 12 percent of the workers in construction, extraction, installation, maintenance, repair, production, transportation, and material-moving occupations belonged to a union.

The biggest difference in unionization is found when the private and public sectors are compared. Although only 6.6 percent of the private wage and salary workers are unionized, 35.9 percent of the government employees belong to a union. And whereas the share of the private workforce belonging to a union has been shrinking, unionization has been increasing in the public sector. In fact, the proportion of government employees belonging to a union has more than tripled since 1960. However, there has been a recent legislative trend against public-sector unionism. For example, legislation reducing the bargaining power of public-sector unions was adopted in New Jersey, Ohio, and Wisconsin in 2011.

There is also substantial variation in the rate of unionization among states. **Exhibit 3** indicates the share of wage and salary employees who are unionized for the ten states with the lowest and highest unionization rates. Southern states constitute most of the group of ten with the lowest incidence of union membership. Fewer than 5 percent of employees are unionized in North Carolina, Arkansas, South Carolina, Mississippi, Georgia, Virginia, Idaho, and Tennessee. Heading the list of states with the highest rate of unionization are New York, Alaska, Hawaii, Washington, and Rhode Island. The rate of unionization tends to be high in the industrial states of the Northeast and upper Midwest. All ten states with the lowest incidence of unionization have **right-to-work laws**, legislation that prohibits collective bargaining agreements requiring a worker to join a union as a condition of employment. Employment has grown more rapidly in states with right-to-work laws than in states without such legislation. This generates political pressure for right-to-work legislation. Reflecting these forces,

Right-to-work laws

Laws that prohibit union shops, the requirement that employees must join a union as a condition of employment. Each state has the option to adopt (or reject) right-to-work legislation.

EXHIBIT 3

States with the Lowest and Highest Incidence of Union Members as a Percent of All Wage and Salary Employees, 2012

Ten lowest states

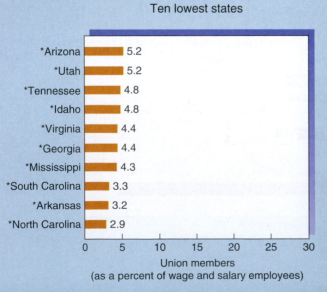

State	Union members (%)
*Arizona	5.2
*Utah	5.2
*Tennessee	4.8
*Idaho	4.8
*Virginia	4.4
*Georgia	4.4
*Mississippi	4.3
*South Carolina	3.3
*Arkansas	3.2
*North Carolina	2.9

Union members
(as a percent of wage and salary employees)

Ten highest states

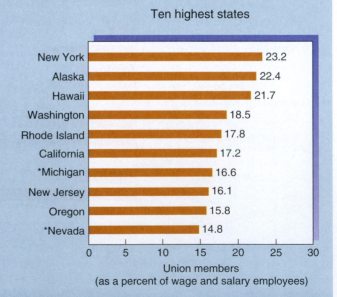

State	Union members (%)
New York	23.2
Alaska	22.4
Hawaii	21.7
Washington	18.5
Rhode Island	17.8
California	17.2
*Michigan	16.6
New Jersey	16.1
Oregon	15.8
*Nevada	14.8

Union members
(as a percent of wage and salary employees)

Source: Barry T. Hirsch and David A. Macpherson, *Union Membership and Earnings Data Book: Compilations from the Current Population Survey,* 2013 Edition (Washington, DC: The Bureau of National Affairs, 2013), table 4a.
*Indicates state has a right-to-work law.

Indiana and Michigan recently adopted right-to-work laws. In contrast, only two of the ten states with the highest rate of union membership has right-to-work legislation.[3]

ST10-2 HOW DO UNIONS INFLUENCE WAGES?

The union–management bargaining process often leaves people with the impression that wages are established primarily by the talents of those sitting at the bargaining table. It might appear that market forces play a relatively minor role. However, as both union and management are well aware, market forces provide the setting in which the bargaining is conducted. They often tip the balance of power one way or the other.

High wages increase the firm's costs. When union employers face stiff competition from nonunion producers or foreign competitors, they will be less able to pass along higher wage costs to their customers. Competition in the product market thus limits the bargaining power of a union. Changing market conditions also affect the balance of power between unions and management. When the demand for a product is strong, the demand for labor will be high, and the firm will be much more willing to consent to a significant wage increase. When demand is weak, however, the product inventory level of the firm (or industry) is more likely to be high. Under these circumstances, wage increases will be more difficult to obtain because the firm will be much less vulnerable to a **strike** on the part of the union. (*Note:* When we speak of wage rates, we are referring to the total compensation package, including both fringe benefits and money wages.)

A union can use three basic strategies to increase the wages of its members: supply restrictions, bargaining power, and increased demand for union labor. We will examine each of these in turn.

Strike
An action of unionized employees in which they (1) discontinue working for the employer and (2) take steps to prevent other potential workers from offering their services to the employer.

ST10-2a SUPPLY RESTRICTIONS

If a union can successfully reduce the supply of competitive labor, higher wage rates will automatically result. Licensing requirements, long apprenticeship programs, immigration barriers, high initiation fees, refusal to admit new members to the union, and prohibition of nonunion workers from holding jobs are all practices that unions have used to limit the supply of labor to various occupations and jobs. Craft unions, in particular, have been able to restrict the supply of workers in various occupations and boost the wages of their members.

Part (a) of **Exhibit 4** illustrates the effect of supply restrictions on wage rates. Successful exclusionary tactics will reduce the supply, shifting the supply curve from S_0 to S_1. Facing the supply curve S_1, employers will consent to the wage rate W_1. Compared to a free-entry market equilibrium, the wage rate has increased from W_0 to W_1, but employment has declined from E_0 to E_1. At the higher wage rate, W_1, an excess supply of labor, AB, will result. The restrictive practices will prevent this excess supply from undercutting the above-equilibrium wage rate. Because of the exclusionary practices, the union will be able to obtain higher wages for E_1 employees. Other employees willing to accept work even at wage rate W_0 will be forced into other areas of employment.

ST10-2b BARGAINING POWER

Must unions restrict entry? Why can't they simply use their bargaining power, enhanced by the threat of a strike, to raise wages? If they have enough economic power, this will be possible. A strike by even a small percentage of vital employees can sometimes halt the flow of production. For example, a work stoppage by airline pilots can force major airlines

---

[3]In 1947, Congress passed the Taft–Hartley Act; Section 14-B allows states to adopt right-to-work laws. Currently, 24 states, mostly in the Sunbelt, have such legislation.

EXHIBIT 4

Supply Restrictions, Bargaining Power, and Wage Rates

The impact of higher wages obtained by restricting supply is very similar to that obtained through bargaining power. As illustrated in part (a), when union policies reduce the supply of one type of labor, higher wages result. Similarly, when bargaining power is used in order to obtain higher wages (1) (part b), employment declines and an excess supply of labor results.

(a) Supply restriction

(b) Bargaining power

© Cengage Learning 2013

to cancel their flights. Because the pilots perform an essential function, an airline cannot operate without their services, even though they constitute only 10 percent of all airline employees.

If the union is able to obtain an above-free-entry wage rate, the effect on employment will be similar to a reduction in supply. As part (b) of Exhibit 4 illustrates, employers will hire fewer workers at the higher wage rate obtained through bargaining power. Employment will decline below the free-entry level (from E_0 to E_1) as a result of the rise in wages. An excess supply of labor, AB, will exist, at least temporarily. More employees will seek the high-wage union jobs than employers will choose to hire. Nonwage methods of rationing jobs will become more important.

ST10-2c INCREASED DEMAND

Unions can attempt to increase the demand for union labor by appealing to consumers to buy only union-produced goods. Union-sponsored promotional campaigns instructing consumers to "look for the union label" or "buy American" are generally designed to increase the demand for union-made products.

Most people, however, are primarily interested in getting the most for their consumer dollar. Thus, the demand for union labor is usually determined primarily by factors outside the union's direct control, such as the availability of substitute inputs and the demand for the product. Unions, though, can sometimes use their political power to increase the demand for their services. They may be able to induce legislators to pass laws that reduce competition from nonunion and/or foreign workers. In some areas, required inspections on construction projects will be undertaken only if the electrical or plumbing services have been performed by "licensed" (mostly union) craft workers. Unions are often supportive of import restrictions designed to increase the demand for products that they produce. In 2009, the steelworkers union, which represents rubber workers, successfully lobbied for higher tariffs restricting the entry of foreign-produced tires. Garment workers have used their political muscle to raise tariffs and reduce import quotas for clothing produced abroad. Practices that increase the demand for goods and services produced by union labor will increase product prices as well as the wages of unionized workers. Thus, it is not surprising that both management and labor of unionized firms often join together to support various restrictions designed to reduce the competitiveness of goods produced by nonunion employees and foreigners.

ST10-3 WHAT GIVES A UNION STRENGTH?

Not all unions are able to raise the wages of their workers. What are the factors that make a union strong? *Simply stated, if a union is to be strong, the demand for its labor must be inelastic. This will enable the union to command large wage increases while suffering only modest reductions in employment.* In contrast, when the demand for union labor is elastic, a substantial rise in wages will mean a large loss in jobs.

There are four major determinants of the demand elasticity for a factor of production: (1) the availability of substitutes, (2) the elasticity of product demand, (3) the share of the input as a proportion of total cost, and (4) the supply elasticity of substitute inputs.[4] We now turn to the importance of each of these conditions as a determinant of union strength.

ST10-3a AVAILABILITY OF GOOD SUBSTITUTE INPUTS

When it is difficult to substitute other inputs for unionized labor in the production of a good, the union is strengthened. The demand for union labor is then more inelastic, and employment cuts tend to be small if the union is able to use its bargaining power and the threat of a strike to push wages up. In contrast, when there are good substitutes for union labor, employers will turn to the substitutes and cut back on their use of union labor as it becomes more expensive. Under these circumstances, higher union wages will price the union workers out of the market and lead to a sharp reduction in their employment.

Some employers may be able to automate various production operations—in effect, substituting machines for union workers if their wages increase. When machines are a good substitute for union labor, the demand for union labor will be elastic, which will reduce the union's ability to push wages above the market level.

The best substitute for union labor is generally nonunion labor. Thus, the power of unions to gain more for their members will be directly related to their ability to insulate themselves from competition with nonunion labor. *When employers are in a position to substitute nonunion labor for unionized workers, the market power of the union will be substantially reduced.*

Within a given plant, a union will negotiate the wages and employment conditions for all workers, both union and nonunion. However, as union wages rise, it may be economical for unionized firms to contract with nonunion firms to handle specific operations or to supply various components used in production. Thus, contracting out often permits employers to substitute nonunion for union workers indirectly. In addition, many large firms in automobile, textile, and other manufacturing industries operate both union and nonunion plants. They may be able to substitute nonunion for union labor by shifting more and more of their production to their nonunion plants, including those located overseas or in right-to-work states, in which unions are generally weaker.

ST10-3b THE ELASTICITY OF DEMAND FOR PRODUCTS PRODUCED BY UNIONIZED FIRMS

Wages are a component of costs. An increase in the wages of union members will almost surely lead to higher prices for goods produced with union labor. Unless the demand for the good produced by union labor is inelastic, the output and employment of unionized firms will decline if the union pushes up wages (and costs). If a union is going to have a significant effect on wages (without undermining employment opportunities), its workers must produce a good for which the demand is inelastic.

Our analysis implies that a union will be unable to increase wages significantly above the free-market rate when producing a good that competes with similar (or

---

[4]Alfred Marshall, *Principles of Economics,* 8th ed. (New York: Macmillan, 1920).

identical) goods produced by nonunion labor or foreign producers. The demand for the good produced by union labor will almost surely be highly elastic when the same product is available from nonunion and foreign producers. Thus, if higher union wages push up costs, the market share of unionized firms will shrink and their employment will fall substantially.

For example, the strength of the Teamsters union was substantially eroded when deregulation subjected the unionized segment of the trucking industry to much more intense competition from nonunion firms in the early 1980s. With deregulation, nonunion firms with lower labor costs entered the industry. Given their labor-cost advantage, many of the new entrants cut their prices and were able to gain a larger market share. In contrast, the output and employment of unionized trucking firms declined. More than 100,000 Teamsters lost their jobs. Given the sharp fall in the employment of their members, the Teamsters eventually agreed to wage concessions and a lower fringe benefit package.[5]

ST10-3c UNIONIZED LABOR AS A SHARE OF THE COST OF PRODUCTION

If the unionized labor input constitutes only a small share of the total production cost of a product, demand for that labor typically will be relatively inelastic. For example, because the wages of plumbers and airline pilots constitute only a small share of the total cost of production in the housing and air travel industries, respectively, a doubling or even tripling of their wages would result in only a 1 percent or 2 percent increase in the cost of housing or air travel. A large increase in the price of these inputs would have little impact on the product price, output, and employment. This factor has sometimes been called "the importance of being unimportant" because when the expenditures on a unionized resource are small relative to total cost, the position of the union is strengthened.

Deregulation of the trucking industry opened the market to nonunion trucking firms. This led to a sharp reduction in the employment of unionized truck drivers (Teamsters) in the early 1980s. Can you explain why?

©Carner/Shutterstock.com

---

[5]A study of the deregulation of the trucking industry found that the wage premium of unionized truckers fell by approximately 30 percent in the regulated sector of the industry. More drivers were employed, but the percentage of drivers who were union members fell from 60 percent before deregulation to 25 percent afterward. See Barry T. Hirsch and David A. Macpherson, "Earnings and Employment in Trucking: Deregulating a Naturally Competitive Industry," in *Regulatory Reform and Labor Markets,* ed. James People (Dordrecht, Netherlands: Kluwer Publishers, 1998).

ST10-3d THE SUPPLY ELASTICITY OF SUBSTITUTE INPUTS

We have just explained that if wage rates in the unionized sector are pushed upward, firms will look for substitute inputs, and the demand for these substitutes will increase. If the supply of these substitutes (like nonunion labor) is inelastic, however, their price will rise sharply in response to an increase in demand. In turn, the higher price will reduce the attractiveness of the substitutes. An inelastic supply of substitutes will thus strengthen the union by making the demand for union labor more inelastic.

ST10-4 THE WAGES OF UNION AND NONUNION EMPLOYEES

The precise effect of unions on the wages of their members is not easy to determine. To isolate the union effect, one must eliminate differences in other factors. Comparisons must be made between union and nonunion workers who have similar productivity (skills) and who are working in similar jobs.

Exhibit 5 provides estimates of the union–nonunion wage differential for private-sector workers adjusted for productivity characteristics.[6] Private-sector union workers received a 28 percent premium compared with similar nonunion workers during the 1983–1984 period. Since the mid-1980s, the private-sector union premium has been shrinking. By 2011–2012, the premium had fallen to 20 percent.

Our theory indicates that some unions will be much stronger than others—that is, better able to achieve higher wages for their members. In some occupations, the size of the union–nonunion differential will be well above the average, whereas in other occupations, unions will have little effect on wages. Strong unions, such as those of electricians, plumbers, tool and die makers, metal craft workers, truckers (before deregulation), and commercial airline pilots, are able to raise the wages of their members substantially more than the average for all unions. Economists have found that the earnings of unionized merchant seamen; postal workers; and rail, auto, and steelworkers, for example, exceed the wages of similarly skilled nonunion workers by 30 percent or more.

EXHIBIT 5

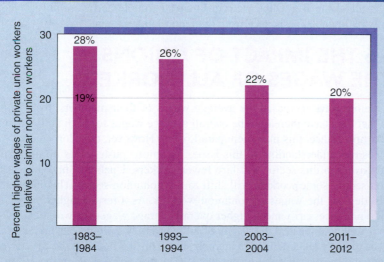

The Wage Premium of Private-Sector Union Workers, 1983–2012

The wages of union workers in the private sector fell relative to similar nonunion workers in the last three decades. In 2011–2012, the estimated union–nonunion differential was 20 percent for private sector workers, down from 28 percent during 1983–1984.

Source: Barry T. Hirsch and David A. Macpherson, *Union Membership and Earnings Data Book: Compilations from the Current Population Survey,* 2013 Edition (Washington, DC: The Bureau of National Affairs, 2013).

[6]Barry T. Hirsch and David A. Macpherson, *Union Membership and Earnings Data Book: Compilations from the Current Population Survey, 2013 Edition* (Washington, DC: The Bureau of National Affairs, 2013). The union wage premium for all wage and salary workers is slightly smaller than for private-sector workers only. The premium for all workers (private sector and public sector) was the following: 1983–1984 (22 percent), 1993–1994 (22 percent), 2003–2004 (18 percent), and 2011–2012 (16 percent).

Unionization appears to have had the least effect on the earnings of cotton/textile, footwear, furniture, hosiery, clothing, and retail sales workers. In these areas, the power of the union has been considerably limited by the existence of a substantial number of nonunion firms. The demands of union workers in these industries are moderated by the fear that unionized employers will be at a competitive disadvantage relative to nonunion employers in the industry.

ST10-5 UNIONS, PROFITABILITY, AND EMPLOYMENT IN THE UNIONIZED SECTOR

If unions increase the wages of unionized firms above the competitive market level, the costs of those firms will rise unless (as seems unlikely) there is a corresponding increase in productivity. In the short run, the higher costs will reduce the profitability of the unionized firm. Research consistently indicates that unions do lower firm profits.[7]

If unions are able to transfer profits from unionized firms to union workers, clearly this is a two-edged sword. For a time, workers enjoy higher wages. In the long run, however, investment will move away from areas of low profitability. Like other mobile resources, capital can be exploited in the short run, but this will not be the case in the long run. Therefore, to the extent that the profits of unionized firms are lower, investment expenditures on fixed structures, research, and development will flow into the nonunion sector and away from unionized firms. As a result, the growth of both productivity and employment will tend to lag in the unionized sector. Investment, production, and employment will all shift away from unionized operations and toward nonunion firms. The larger the wage premium of unionized firms, the greater the incentive will be to shift production toward nonunion operations.

The experience of the United Auto Workers (UAW) vividly illustrates the operation of these forces. The Big Three Detroit-based automakers—General Motors, Ford, and Chrysler—were heavily unionized. For several decades, the UAW was able to increase the wages of workers employed by the Big Three substantially above those of other workers with similar skills. But the higher wages and costs of the Big Three made them more vulnerable to competition from nonunion automakers, primarily foreign-based transplants with manufacturing facilities in southern states. With time, the lower wage transplants gained a larger and larger market share, and the profitability of the Big Three shrank. By 2008–2009, all of the Big Three were in financial trouble and were only saved, at least temporarily, by financial assistance from the federal government.

ST10-6 THE IMPACT OF UNIONS ON THE WAGES OF ALL WORKERS

Although unions have increased the average wages of their members, there is no reason to believe that they have increased the overall average wages for both union and nonunion workers. At first glance, this may seem paradoxical. However, the economic way of thinking enhances our understanding of this issue. As unions push wages up in the unionized sector, employers in this sector will hire fewer workers. Unable to find jobs in the high-wage union sector, some workers will shift to the nonunion sector. This increase in labor supply will depress the wages of nonunion workers. As a result, higher wages for union members do not necessarily mean higher overall average wages for workers.

If labor unions increased the wages of all workers, we would expect labor's share of income to be directly related to union membership. This has not been the case. Even though union membership rose sharply during the 1940s, reached a peak in the 1950s, and has been declining ever since, there was virtually no change in the share of income received by labor (human capital) during this entire period. Similarly, if unions were the primary source of high wages, the real wages of workers would be higher in highly unionized countries, such as Australia, France, and Italy, than they are in the United States. But this is not what we observe.

---

[7]Barry T. Hirsch, "What Do Unions Do for Economic Performance?" *Journal of Labor Research* (Summer 2004): 415–55.

The real source of high wages is high productivity, not labor unions. Increases in the general level of wages are dependent upon increases in productivity per hour. Of course, improvements in (1) technology, (2) the machines and tools available to workers (physical capital), (3) worker skills (human capital), and (4) the efficiency of economic organization provide the essential ingredients for higher levels of productivity. ***Higher real wages can be achieved only if the production of goods and services is expanded. Although unions can increase the wages of union workers, they cannot increase the wages of all workers unless their activities increase the total productivity of labor.***

KEY POINTS

- Union membership as a share of nonfarm employees fluctuated substantially during the last century. During the 1910–1935 period, union workers constituted between 12 and 18 percent of nonfarm employees. Unionization increased rapidly during the two decades following 1935, however, soaring to one-third of the workforce in the mid-1950s. Since then, union membership has waned, falling to only 11.3 percent of employees in 2012.

- A union can use three basic methods to increase the wages of its members: (1) restrict the supply of competitive inputs, including nonunion workers; (2) apply bargaining power enforced by a strike or threat of one; and (3) increase the demand for the labor service of union members.

- If a union is going to increase the wages of its members without experiencing a significant reduction in employment, the demand for union labor must be inelastic. The strength of a union is enhanced if (1) there is an absence of good substitutes for the services of union employees, (2) the demand for the product produced by

the union labor is highly inelastic, (3) the union labor input is a small share of the total cost of production, and (4) the supply of available substitutes is highly inelastic. An absence of these conditions weakens the power of the union.

- Studies suggest that the wage premium of private-sector union members relative to similar nonunion workers has fallen during the last three decades. In the period 2011–2012, private-sector union workers earned about 20 percent more, on average, than similar nonunion workers.

- Even though unions have increased the average wage of their members, there is no indication that they have increased either the average wage of all workers or the share of national income going to labor (human capital rather than physical capital).

- The real wages of workers are a reflection of their productivity rather than the share of the workforce that is unionized.

CRITICAL ANALYSIS QUESTIONS

1. *Suppose that Florida's migrant workers are effectively unionized. What will be the effect of the unionization on (a) the price of Florida oranges? (b) the profits of Florida fruit growers in the short run and in the long run? (c) the mechanization of the fruit-picking industry? (d) the employment of migrant farm workers?

2. Assume that the primary objective of a union is to raise the wages of its members.

   a. Discuss the conditions that will help the union achieve this objective.

   b. Why might a union be unable to meet its goal?

3. "If a union is unable to organize all the major firms in an industry, it is unlikely to exert a major effect on the wages of union members." Indicate why you either agree or disagree.

4. Evaluate the following statements.

   a. "An increase in the price of steel will be passed along to consumers in the form of higher prices for automobiles, homes, appliances, and other products made with steel." Do you agree or disagree?

   b. "An increase in the price of craft union labor will be passed along to consumers in the form of higher prices

of homes, repair and installation services, appliances, and other products that require craft union labor." Do you agree or disagree?

   c. Are the interests of labor unions in conflict primarily with the interests of union employers? Explain.

5. *"Unions provide the only protection available to working men and women. Without unions, employers would be able to pay workers whatever they wanted." True or false?

6. *A survey of firms in your local labor market reveals that the average hourly wage rate of unionized production workers is $1.50 higher than the average wage rate of nonunion production workers. Does this indicate that unionization increases the wage rates of workers in your area by $1.50? Why or why not?

7. *Even though the wage scale of union members is substantially greater than the minimum wage, unions have generally been at the forefront of those lobbying for higher minimum rates. Why do you think unions fight so hard for a higher minimum wage?

*Asterisk denotes questions for which answers are given in Appendix B.

SPECIAL TOPIC 11
The Question of Resource Exhaustion

FOCUS

- Why have there been repeated forecasts that the world will run out of key resources? Why have these forecasts been consistently wrong?

- Are proved reserves the same thing as the total future supply of a resource?

- What do prices indicate has happened to resource availability? Will that trend continue?

- Why is there a major misallocation problem for a few key resources like water?

The massive scale of the global drilling sector, combined with its technological prowess, gives us every reason to believe that we will have cheap, abundant, reliable supplies of oil and gas for many years to come. —**Robert Bryce**[1]

[1]Robert Bryce, "New Technology For Old Fuels: Innovation in Oil and Natural Gas Production Assures Future Supplies," Energy Policy & the Environment Report No. 12 (New York: Manhattan Institute, April 2013), http://www.manhattan-institute.org/html/eper_12.htm#.UWnReBnlV1g.

For centuries, various social commentators have argued that the world is about to run out of vital minerals and various sources of energy. Economic growth and the technological advances that help to fuel it have accelerated the use of many natural resources. Population growth has added to the rate of resource use.

Nonetheless, as the quote from Robert Bryce indicates, future depletion of energy resources is unlikely to be a problem, at least in the case of oil and gas. This feature examines the economic forces affecting the availability of natural resources and explains why the numerous forecasts of resource exhaustion throughout history have been wrong.

ST11-1 FORECASTS OF RESOURCE EXHAUSTION

As recently as 2011, scientists worried about "peak oil"—the claim that at some point the world will not be able to increase its oil production, and output will fall.[2] Natural gas, too, seemed headed for permanent decline. The CEO of ExxonMobil, the biggest energy company in the world, said in 2005 that "gas production has peaked in North America."[3] But just as *Science* magazine was reporting "peak oil production may already be here," the situation was changing. Oil and gas production went up dramatically in 2012. In fact, in 2012, as the Wall Street Journal phrased it, the "U.S. production gain of 1.04 million barrels a day surpassed the earlier biggest annual increase of 640,000 barrels per day recorded in 1967."[4] Once again, forecasts of declining future resource availability had proven to be incorrect.

In sixteenth-century England, fear arose that the supply of wood—widely used as a source of energy—would soon disappear. Higher wood prices, however, encouraged conservation and led to the development of coal. The wood crisis soon dissipated.

In the middle of the nineteenth century, fear arose that the United States was about to run out of whale oil, at that time the primary fuel for artificial lighting. As the demand for whale oil increased, many predicted that all the whales would soon be gone and that Americans would face long nights without light. Whale-oil prices rose sharply from $0.23 per gallon in 1820 to $1.42 per gallon in 1850. The higher prices motivated consumers and entrepreneurs to seek alternatives, which included distilled vegetable oils, lard oil, and coal gas. By the early 1850s, coal oil (kerosene) had won out. A little later, petroleum replaced coal as the primary resource used to produce kerosene. As for whale oil, by 1896 its price had fallen to $0.40 per gallon, and even at that price few people used it.

As people switched to petroleum, dire predictions about its future exhaustion arose almost immediately. In 1914, the Bureau of Mines reported that the total U.S. supply of oil was 6 million barrels, an amount less than the United States now produces each year. In 1926, the Federal Oil Conservation Board announced that oil would be depleted in the United States within seven years. The Interior Department predicted in 1939 that petroleum supplies in this nation would run out within 20 years. And in 1949, the Secretary of the Interior proclaimed that the end of oil supplies was near.[5]

Perhaps the most stunning prediction of disaster came in 1972 with the publication of *The Limits to Growth*.[6] This book made projections of resource depletion based on large computer models and received widespread publicity in the *New York Times* and major national

[2]Richard A. Kerr, "Peak Oil Production May Already Be Here," *Science*, March 25, 2011, p. 1510.

[3]Reuters, "Exxon CEO Says,"America Gas Production Has Peaked," June 21, 2005, http://www.reuters.com/article/Utilities/idUSN2163310420050621.]

[4]Keith Johnson and Russell Gold, "U.S. Oil Notches Record Growth," *Wall Street Journal*, June 12, 2013, http://online.wsj.com/article/ SB10001424127887324049504578541601909939628.html.

[5]Predictions are cited from Wallace Kaufman, *No Turning Back* (New York: Basic Books, 1994), 24; and from Charles Maurice and Charles Smithson, *The Doomsday Myth, 10,000 Years of Economic Crises* (Stanford, CA: Hoover Institution Press, 1987), 12.

[6]Donella H. Meadows, Dennis L. Meadows, and William W. Behrens, *The Limits to Growth* (New York: Universe Books, 1972).

magazines. As statistician and environmentalist Bjorn Lomborg explained in 2013, the 1972 book had tapped into the grim pessimism of the day—the anxiety surrounding the Vietnam War, the stagnating economy, mounting concerns about pollution, and what seemed to be out-of-control population growth. "The genius of *The Limits to Growth*," he wrote, "was to fuse these worries with fears of running out of stuff. We were doomed, because too many people were consuming too much." The authors of *The Limits to Growth* predicted that prior to 2013 "the world would run out of aluminum, copper, gold, lead, mercury, molybdenum, natural gas, oil, silver, tin, tungsten, and zinc."[7] Of course, this didn't happen.

ST11-2 WHY HAVE THE FORECASTS OF RESOURCE CRISES BEEN WRONG?

Technology has revolutionized the production of both oil and gas. The new buzzword in energy production is "fracking," an innovative extraction method developed in Texas in the 1990s. Based on techniques that have been used for decades, fracking facilitates the extraction of a much larger share of oil from existing pools than was previously possible. "The dramatic increase in oil and gas resources is the result of a century of improvements to older technologies such as drill rigs and drill bits, along with better seismic tools, advances in materials science, better robots, more capable submarines, and, of course, cheaper computing power," writes Robert Bryce in a paper on energy industry innovations.[8] The development of technology and its application to the extraction of mineral resources crucially depends on economic forces—specifically, incentives.

The incentives generated by markets provide the means for the expansion of supply, and thus they explain why the forecasts of resource supply crisis have always been wrong, when markets are allowed to work. Think about what happens when a resource becomes less available. This might happen because of either a reduction in supply or an increase in demand. In either case, the price of the resource will rise. In turn, the higher price will cause (1) users of the resource to cut back on their usage, (2) suppliers to figure out how to supply more of it or perhaps to recycle, and (3) both users and potential suppliers to search for substitutes. Each of these factors will tend to increase future supply relative to demand. The larger the initial increase in the price of a resource, the greater the incentive to cut back on usage, expand the future supply, and develop substitutes.

These adjustments will keep usage rates of the resource pretty much in line with the expected future supply. With time, they can often bring relief in the form of a lower future price. The key point is this: Although the price of a resource may increase sharply during some periods, the structure of incentives accompanying the price increase makes depletion highly unlikely and provides the seeds for future reversal.

As an analysis of the resource crisis forecasts indicates, we have seen these forces work again and again. Think about the actions producers, resource users, and consumers will take when oil prices go up. The higher prices will provide petroleum producers with a stronger incentive to search for and find new fields. They will also provide them with incentive to use technology to extract a larger share of the oil from existing fields. Up to 70 percent of the oil can now be extracted from highly productive wells that in prior decades would have yielded much less. When sustained price increases are large enough, generating expectations they will be sufficient to cover the higher-cost production methods, it becomes economical to produce petroleum products from exceedingly abundant, but less-rich petroleum resources. These include oil shale and tar sands and, indeed, such production has already begun.

[7]Bjorn Lomborg, "The Limits of Panic," Project Syndicate, June 17, 2013, http://www.project-syndicate.org/commentary/economic-growth-and-its-critics-by-bj-rn-lomborg.

[8]Robert Bryce, "New Technology for Old Fuels: Innovation in Oil and Natural Gas Production Assures Future Supplies," Energy Policy & the Environment Report No. 12 (New York: Manhattan Institute, April 2013), www.manhattan-institute.org/html/eper_12.htm#.UWnReBnlV1g.

When the price of gasoline increases substantially, many consumers will turn to more fuel-efficient cars like this Toyota Prius, a hybrid that combines a gas engine with an electric motor and a battery.

On the demand side, higher oil prices also provide users with a strong incentive to reduce their consumption of petroleum. Electric power–generating firms will search for and some will shift to alternatives like coal and nuclear power. Manufacturers of plastics and other products that use petroleum as a resource will face higher costs; they, too, will seek to shift to substitute resources and cut back on their future use of petroleum. For their part, consumers will use less of the oil-intensive products and adjust their behavior accordingly, purchasing more fuel-efficient cars and trucks, commuting less, and finding other ways to economize on oil-intensive products.

These adjustments and many more on both the supply and the demand sides of the crude oil market will tend to reduce demand over time, increase supply, and thus moderate price increases. This has happened for oil and other resources many times, and these constructive pressures will continue to do so whenever resource availabilities change and market forces are permitted to work.

ST11-3 PROVED RESERVES AND RUNNING OUT OF RESOURCES

Geologists use the term **proved reserves** to mean the specific mineral deposits that have been shown by scientific examination and cost calculation to be extractable and deliverable to the market for use at a cost that users can pay, using known technologies under expected market conditions. Proved reserves have often been used by doomsday forecasters to calculate the future time when we will run out of a resource. But this is a misapplication of the concept. Proved reserves are quite different than the total quantity of a resource in the ground. Put simply, proved reserves are the verified quantity that can be extracted, given investors' expectations of developing technologies and expected prices.

We have seen how improvements in technology and higher future prices can increase proved reserves. **Exhibit 1** shows the proved reserves for several minerals. While existing reserves are constantly being used up, in most cases, they are amply replaced with the "proving" of new reserves in the ground. For example, in 1950, there were 100 million metric tons of known copper ore reserves in the world. Over the next 50 years, 339 million tons of copper ore reserves were mined and used. Yet, in 2000, the reserves stood at 340 million tons, and by 2012 the reserves had reached 680 million tons. Additional reserves had been discovered and technology had advanced, so that the existing known reserves were larger in 2000 than

Proved reserves
Specific mineral deposits that have been shown by scientific examination and cost calculation to be extractable and deliverable to the market for use, with current technology and expected market conditions.

World Reserves and Cumulative Production of Selected Minerals, 1950 to 2012 (Millions of Metric Tons)

For most mineral resources, existing proved reserves are constantly being used up but are being amply replaced by the "proving" of new reserves from existing resources in the ground.

MINERAL	RESERVES 1950	PRODUCTION 1950–2000	RESERVES 2000	RESERVES 2012
Tin	6	11	10	4.9
Copper	100	339	340	680
Iron Ore	19,000	37,583	140,000	170,000
Lead	40	150	64	89
Zinc	70	266	190	190

Source: Sue Anne Batey Blackman and William J. Baumol, "Natural Resources," in *The Concise Encyclopedia of Economics*, 2nd ed., ed. David R. Henderson (Indianapolis: Liberty Fund), available online at http://econlib.org/library/Enc/NaturalResources.html; and Department of the Interior, USGS, Mineral Commodity Surveys (2013), http://minerals.usgs.gov/minerals/pubs/mcs/.

50 years earlier, even after 50 years of steady depletion. The other minerals listed show similar trends, except for tin. In 1950, the world had 6 million tons of tin ore reserves. Fifty years later, after 11 million tons of production, reserves had grown to 10 million. Since then, however, reserves have declined substantially, to 4.9 million tons. Why? Not because we are running out of tin. We know there is no long-term shortage because the price of tin, which has fluctuated over the past six decades, shows no consistent upward trend. Given the cost of finding and proving reserves, it has not been worthwhile for suppliers to expand reserves. And, since world production of tin is under 250,000 tons per year, existing reserves will supply that production for at least two decades.

It is important to note that in shorter time periods, it is not uncommon for world reserves of a natural resource to fall. World tin reserves fell from 10 million tons in 2000 to 5 million tons in 2010, while reserves of the other four minerals in Exhibit 1 all rose. The forces described earlier do not guarantee that resource prices must fall, but as we will see in the following in more detail, when those forces have been allowed to operate, the results have tended to make natural resources more available to us, even as their physical abundance in nature declines.

For producers, proved reserves are like an inventory of cars to an auto dealer. They are the quantity that can be available quickly for sale. Just as it is costly for an auto dealer to hold more inventory, it is costly for a firm to discover and sufficiently research a mineral deposit to qualify it as proved reserves. Producers who buy or develop proved reserves do not want to pay for them farther in advance than needed, just as an auto dealer wants to have cars available in stock but not too far ahead of the time they can be sold.

As with inventories, it is costly to develop and hold proved reserves for lengthy time periods. If it takes an auto dealer five weeks from the time of a new car order to receive the cars, the dealer may want something close to a ten-week supply of cars, relative to expected sales, on the car lot and available for customers to see and buy. Similarly, if it takes two years, say, for a user of iron ore to replace iron ore reserves that they have used, then a four-year supply of those reserves might be a desired amount to have available. Just as inventories are a poor indicator of the total future supply of a good like cars, proved reserves are a poor indicator of the total future supply of a mineral resource. Proved reserves will always be a small fraction of what they could be simply because proving and holding them are costly.

ST11-4 ARE RESOURCES BECOMING LESS ABUNDANT?

If the supply of a resource decreases relative to demand, its price will rise. If a resource is increasing in supply relative to demand and is becoming less costly to supply, its price will fall. Therefore, resource price trends provide information about how the availability of various resources is changing.

What have resource prices been telling us? During the past century and more, ending in 2000, the real price of most mineral resources fell. A classic study by Harold Barnett and Chandler Morse illustrates this point.[9] Using data from 1870 to 1963, Barnett and Morse found that the real price of resources declined during that long period. A later study by William Baumol and Sue Anne Batey Blackman buttresses this view. They cite a composite mineral price index, corrected for inflation and published by the U.S. Geological Survey, showing a decline in the price index from 185 in 1905 to 100 in 2000. Thus, the real price of minerals fell, on average, by 46 percent in 95 years, even as the use of those minerals had greatly expanded.[10]

As **Exhibit 2** left panel shows, the real price of crude oil trended downward during the 1950s and 1960s, rose during the 1970s, before falling again during most of the 1980s and 1990s. During the past 15 years, crude oil prices have risen sharply. Measured in 2005 dollars, however, the price of oil rose from $13 per barrel in 1998 to $83 in 2012. Prior to 2008, the pattern of natural gas prices was similar to that of crude oil. But during the last five years, the situation has changed dramatically. The price of natural gas has plunged from $7.39 per thousand cubic feet in 2008 to $2.33 in 2012 (right panel). Fracking provides the explanation. Fracking has facilitated a substantial increase in the production of natural gas.

Some environmentalists are concerned about possible pollution from this technique. While such problems are "challenging," a 2011 report from MIT indicates they are also manageable.[11] As Robert Nelson explains in a column for *Forbes*, it is unlikely that fracking itself, usually thousands of feet beneath the surface, can affect land or usable water aquifers, which are almost always located much nearer the surface. However, after the

---

EXHIBIT 2

Real Crude Oil and Natural Gas Prices, 1949 to 2012 (Real Year 2005 Dollars)

The real prices of crude oil and natural gas show a similar pattern of rising in the 1970s, falling in the 1980s and 1990s, and rising sharply again in the 2000s. However, recent technological innovations in fracking technology have greatly expanded natural gas reserves and production, resulting in natural gas prices declining sharply in recent years to less than one-third of the real 2008 price, while the real price of crude oil has remained high.

(a) Crude Oil

(b) Natural Gas

Source: Energy Information Administration, http://www.eia.gov/dnav/pet/hist/LeafHandler/ashx?n=pet&s=f000000_3&f=a and http://www.eia.gov/dnav/ng/hist/n9190us3A.htm.

---

[9]Harold Barnett and Chandler Morse, *Scarcity of Growth: The Economics of Natural Resource Availability* (Baltimore: The Johns Hopkins University Press for Resources for the Future, 1963). See also Julian L. Simon, *The State of Humanity* (Cambridge, MA: Blackwell Publishers, 1995), Part III, Natural Resources.

[10]Quoted by Sue Anne Batey Blackman and William J. Baumol, "Natural Resources," in *The Concise Encyclopedia of Economics*, 2nd ed., ed. David R. Henderson (Indianapolis: Liberty Fund, Inc., 2007), available online at http://econlib.com/library/Enc/NaturalResources.html.

[11]MIT Energy Initiative, The Future of Natural Gas. Cambridge, MA: Massachusetts Institute of Technology, June 2011, http://mitei.mit.edu/system/files/NaturalGas_ExecutiveSummary.pdf.

APPLICATIONS IN ECONOMICS

Is It Smart to Bet on Higher Resource Prices?

Rapid rises in prices of oil and other commodities in the 1970s led to widespread anxiety that the world was running out of major resources. In 1980, economist Julian Simon argued that this run-up was temporary and that, over time, prices were likely to fall. Simon offered a $1,000 bet that any raw materials selected in 1980 would be lower ten years later after adjustment was made for inflation. Environmentalist Paul Ehrlich took up the bet. He and his associates chose five metals (chrome, copper, nickel, tin, and tungsten), put $200 on each, and bet that the inflation-adjusted prices in 1990 would be higher.

Simon easily won the bet. During the decade, the real prices declined not only for the bundle but also for each of the five minerals chosen by Ehrlich. In 1990, Ehrlich wrote a check to Simon to pay off the bet. (The wager became famous after an article about it appeared in *The New York Times*.)

In 2005, a student and a professor at Michigan State University analyzed whether Simon would have won the bet had it extended over the entire twentieth century. Using U.S. Geological Survey price data for basic metals, they examined the change in prices from 1900 to 1999. "The person who took Simon's position would have won over the entire century," wrote David McClintick and Ross B. Emmett. "If someone invested $200 at 1900 metals' prices in each of these five metals, the inflation-adjusted value of the same bundle of metals in 1999 would have been 53-percent lower."[1] Of course, resource prices did not go down during every decade of the twentieth century, but they went down during most decades and for the century as a whole. Thus, history suggests that it is not too smart to bet on rising resource prices.

[1]David McClintick and Ross B. Emmett, "Betting on the Wealth of Nature," *PERC Reports* (September 2005), www.perc.org/perc.php?subsection=5&id=588.

©iStockphoto.com/sorendls

---

shale is fractured, some of the water returns to the surface. This "flowback water" contains both natural contaminants and the chemicals used in the fracturing. Writes Nelson: "The water must therefore be disposed of safely or—as is increasingly the case—be cleaned up and recycled for use in the next well."[12] Nelson points out that some environmental abuses have occurred, such as dumping this water into rivers and streams. "As a result of increasing regulation, however, and growing recognition within the gas industry that its future depends on public acceptance, the treatment of flowback water has improved greatly."

Resource prices fluctuate from month to month and year to year, but the trends have been mainly downward, often with the assistance of technical changes like fracking. For the bigger picture, see the box feature, "Is It Smart to Bet on Rising Resource Prices?"

ST11-5 RENEWABLE RESOURCES

Nonrenewable resources
Those that are not created or renewed naturally at a significant rate.

Renewable resources
Those that are renewed in nature, like water flows, or grown, like timber.

To this point, we have focused on **nonrenewable resources**—those that are not created or renewed at a significant rate, and therefore they could potentially be used up over time. Our analysis, however, indicates that this is unlikely to be the case in a market setting. What about **renewable resources**, like timber, that can be continually replanted and replenished? Those resources, too, can become less abundant and more expensive in a market depending on (1) the ability of users to find substitutes and reduce the quantity demanded and, over time, the demand and (2) producers' ability to produce more output at the higher price and to find substitute products to bring to market for buyers.

Forests are an example of a renewable resource for which there has been concern about future availability. Deforestation can lead to a loss of timber, wildlife habitat, watershed regulation, and recreational services. Are concerns about serious deforestation justified? Rivers, lakes, and other sources of freshwater are other important renewable resources for

---

[12]Robert Nelson, "Ernest Moniz and Fracking Drive Environmentalists Off of the Rails," *Forbes*, March 26, 2013, http://www.forbes.com/sites/realspin/2013/03/26/ernest-moniz-and-fracking-drive-environmentalists-off-of-the-rails.

which depletion is a serious concern. What can economic thinking and a careful look at history tell us about these two concerns?

ST11-6 ARE FORESTS DISAPPEARING?

Use of land has changed dramatically over the centuries. When colonists arrived in what is now the United States, about half the land was forested. In parts of the world today, significant areas of woodlands, including tropical areas of Brazil and Southeast Asia, are being turned into farmland or logged for wood products. How serious are the loss of timber and the loss of wildlife habitat?

Not all the world's forests are in well-functioning market economies (that is, economies with property rights, the rule of law, and minimal corruption). Where strong market economies do exist, however, the forces of supply and demand are protecting forests from significant decline.

The United States has about the same amount of land devoted to forest as it did in 1920—and far more timber is growing on it. A study by two natural resource economists (Roger Sedjo and Marion Clawson) found that timber volume in the temperate climates, including countries such as the United States, the former Soviet Union, and Canada, is growing rapidly.[13]

A recent U.S. Forest Service study of the northern United States (20 states stretching from Maine to Minnesota) reported that during the 100 years between 1907 and 2007, forest land in that region increased by 28 percent. During the past 50 years, timber production from the region expanded by 138 percent (from 104 to 248 billion cubic feet).[14] Clearly, the nation is not running out of wood. Furthermore, Bill McKibben, writing for the *Atlantic Monthly*, said that the "mostly unnoticed renewal of the rural and mountainous East" is "the great environmental story of the United States."[15] This has come about through market forces, as New England farms revert to forest and former cotton plantations in the South become more attractive as woodlands.

Even Latin America, Sedjo and Clawson reported, is undergoing a major transition, with an increase in tree plantations, in which trees are being grown as crops. These changes reflect the response to demand for wood and put less pressure on the existing tropical rainforest.

ST11-7 TECHNOLOGY AND LAND MANAGEMENT

Technology is helping to preserve land in its wooded state as well. Chemical fertilizers, pesticides, and other technologies—"high-tech" farming—do have some negative environmental impacts, but they have also freed a great deal of land from use for farming. By raising productivity per acre, technology reduces the amount of land required to produce food and fiber.

Indur M. Goklany has estimated that if agricultural technology had been frozen at 1961 levels, the 1998 level of food production would have required more than double the amount of land used today for farming.[16] That means that 76 percent of the world's land would be used for agriculture, compared with only 38 percent in 1998! Not only would farmland have taken up space, much of it now available as wildlife habitat, but the added land would probably have been less productive. Farmers are already cultivating the best acres among

---

[13]See Roger A. Sedjo and Marion Clawson, "Global Forests Revisited," in *The State of Humanity*, ed. Julian Simon (Cambridge, MA: Blackwell Publishers, 1995).

[14]Stephen R. Shifley et al., "Forests of the northen United States," General Technical Report NRS-90 (Newtown Square, PA: U.S. Department of Agriculture, Forest Service, Northern Research Station, 2012).

[15]Bill McKibben, "An Explosion of Green," *The Atlantic Monthly* (April 1995), 61–83.

[16]This fact and others used in this section are from Indur M. Goklany, "The Pros and Cons of Modern Farming," in *PERC Reports* (March 2001), available online at www.perc.org/perc.php?id5307.

those acres not committed to other, more valuable uses. Greater land productivity enabled by new technologies has kept down the cost and price of food in world markets.

When resource users and suppliers are free to innovate and respond to changes in prices and in technologies as market participants, and when property rights hold them accountable for the cost of what they use while allowing them personally to reap benefits from fruitful innovations, the result has been economic progress in increasing prosperity from one generation to the next. Each generation has less in the way of physical natural resources in Earth, but successive new resource discoveries and improved technology allow the old resource base to deliver more services for a smaller sacrifice because it is better used and with less waste.

ST11-8 NATURAL RESOURCES WHEN MARKETS ARE NOT ALLOWED TO FUNCTION FULLY

When natural resources are not traded, or when markets are not allowed to function as well as the previously described markets, problems of waste and shortages are common.

ST11-8a WATER MARKETS

"As we enter a new decade, water is the new oil: the less abundant resource worth fighting over. In arid parts of the world, the fight for water has always been a fight for survival. One-third of the world's population lives where their water supply is either a stress or a crisis." Thus began an MSNBC online story in 2010.[17] The article predicted that developing nations would experience "water shortages, crop failures, and conflict over shrinking lakes and rivers." News stories like this and the more formal studies they often cite are more frequent as demands for water increase.

The world is not going to run out of water in a literal sense—the world has the same amount of moisture that it always did. And, in the words of economist Terry L. Anderson, Earth "has more than enough water to meet human demands." But, he says, "Water is often found in the wrong place at the wrong time."[18] Water supply problems reflect the fact that in most situations, water markets are missing or are incomplete. Therefore, the smoothly functioning market that might bring more effective cooperation among users and suppliers, or buyers and sellers, seldom exists.

Throughout the world, the sources of water—lakes, rivers, and streams—are often kept under tight control by governments, preventing transferable ownership that would allow supply and demand to operate. This approach is defended on the grounds that water, which is necessary for life, needs to be treated differently. To establish a system of transferable property rights is complicated by the fact that changing a water use in one place on a stream can influence everyone downstream also. But it is also true that the difficulty of obtaining a property right to water provides a less certain water supply than market trades could make available. Progress is possible, and in some places where water is extremely valuable, some progress toward more trading is being made. The net benefits are being reaped by participants, in particular, and by the economy more generally.

In some places, people do own a right to water or at least the right to use some water from a lake or stream. In the arid western United States, for example, a person may own a right to divert a specific amount of water from a stream in order to irrigate crops. But state and federal laws may prevent that person from selling the right for use elsewhere or even changing its use in its current location. Other uses of the water may be far more valuable, but the owner cannot sell the water or the right to use it. The market mechanism that allocates

---

[17]Mark Strassmann, "Preview: America's Water Crisis," January 8, 2010, accessed Sept. 1, 2011, from www.cbsnews.com/8301-500803_162-6071729-500803.html.
[18]Terry L. Anderson, "Water Options for the Blue Planet," in *The True State of the Planet*, ed. Ronald Bailey (New York: Free Press, 1995), 275.

copper and tin efficiently and prevents waste, shortages, or total depletion is very often missing in the case of water. Government subsidies to current water uses and users may also distort the allocation of this key resource.

Consider, for example, the federally funded Central Utah Project (CUP), which delivers water to farms from dams built on rivers. It illustrates the lack of complete and tradable property rights in water as well as the distortions caused by subsidies. According to the Department of the Interior, the annual cost of delivering CUP water is $161 per acre-foot (326,000 gallons), not counting the cost of building and maintaining the dam. But farmers pay less than $30 per acre-foot. Taxpayers cover the rest ($131 per acre-foot). The farmers have the politically awarded right to the water and the subsidy, but they cannot sell the right and other potential users cannot bid the water away from the farmers. Meanwhile, cities and other water users in the region face shortages and are making plans to increase their own water supplies by costly means. Water trading could help buyers and sellers to reap large mutual gains from trade, but the trades are not allowed.

Some water-short cities near the ocean or other saltwater bodies are considering desalination, which uses massive amounts of energy and special equipment to make saltwater into freshwater at a cost of up to $2,000 per acre-foot. Others are seeking permission (and federal subsidies) to build more dams dedicated to storing water for their own use. The economic and environmental costs of building more dams are very high, but water is quite valuable once a shortage develops. In fact, when droughts occurred in California in 1991 and 2009, trading through the mechanism of "water banking" reduced the damage. The state of California bought water from farmers, who, in return for cash, fallowed their land or used water more efficiently. The water they saved was sold to drought-stricken farmers and municipalities. The water bank was not a genuine market, because the state of California set the price (it bought at $125 an acre-foot and sold at $175), but it shows the direction that could be taken to ease shortages and save money. If farmers in northern California could sell their water rights to southern California municipalities, water would be moved away from low marginal value in agriculture toward higher marginal valued municipal uses, improving economic efficiency and making both parties better off.[19]

---

[19]The source for these examples is Terry L. Anderson, Brandon Scarborough, and Lawrence R. Watson, *Tapping Water Markets, 2012,* (New York: Routledge 2012), 22, 71, 73–4.

KEY POINTS

- Forecasts that the world will soon run out of various key resources have been made for centuries. These forecasts have consistently been wrong.

- Resource prices fluctuate from month to month and year to year, but for long periods, the trends have been mainly downward. See the Applications of Economics feature, "Is It Smart to Bet on Rising Resource Prices?"

- When resources are allocated by markets, decreased availability leads to higher prices. The higher prices will strengthen the incentive for (1) users to reduce their consumption, (2) suppliers to search for ways to expand future supply, and (3) both producers and users to search for substitutes. All of these adjustments will increase future supply relative to demand and make it highly unlikely that the resource will be depleted.

- Proved reserves are the verifiable quantity of a resource available at current prices and technology. They are not the total supply of the resource that will be available in the future. Proved reserves can be expanded with improvements in technology and increases in prices.

- The trend in the price of resources has been downward for at least a century, indicating that the relative availability of most resources has been increasing.

- When property rights are poorly defined or when regulations make a resource nontradable, waste will result because the resource will often be directed toward less valuable uses.

CRITICAL ANALYSIS QUESTIONS

1. If the world were about to run out of a highly valued resource, what would happen to its price? How would this affect the future supply of the resource relative to demand?

2. "If China and India continue their economic expansion, the world cannot provide enough raw materials without terrible shortages worldwide." Evaluate this statement.

3. In the industrial nations, have succeeding generations, each with a higher income than before, left the world resource-poor, with only low-grade mineral ores left, for example? Have they been "consuming the birthright" of future generations? Explain your answer.

4. Why have cotton fields retreated and forests returned in many areas of the southeastern United States? With fewer acres farmed, will the nation continue to be able to provide food and fiber for itself? Explain.

5. *"Water is a necessity of life. It should not be bought and sold, or traded in markets!" Use the economic way of thinking to evaluate this statement.

*Asterisk denotes questions for which answers are given in Appendix B.

SPECIAL TOPIC 12
Difficult Environmental Cases and the Role of Government

FOCUS

- Why do people seek governmental regulation to improve the environment in a market economy?

- What can economics tell us about an effective policy on global warming and climate change? Will economic growth help with this problem or make matters worse?

- How can the government utilize marketlike policies to reduce the cost of environmental policy?

- Why does federal ownership of our national parks pose problems for park managers serving the public? Are there ways to lessen those problems?

A little richer is a lot safer. —**Aaron Wildavsky**[1]

[1]Aaron Wildavsky and Adam Wildavsky, "Risk and Safety," in *The Concise Encyclopedia of Economics,* 2nd ed., ed. David R. Henderson (Indianapolis, IN: Liberty Fund, Inc., 2007), available online at http://econlib.com/library/Enc/RiskandSafety.html.

rivate property rights can promote prosperity and cooperation and at the same time protect the environment, but do they protect the environment sufficiently? In recent years, people have increasingly turned to the government to achieve additional environmental improvements. Sometimes people turned to government because property rights failed to hold polluters accountable for the costs they were imposing on others.

In other instances, people with strong desires for various environmental amenities (for example, green spaces, hiking trails, and wilderness lands) want the government to force others to help pay for them. In this special topic, we look more closely at the possibilities for achieving environmental goals through governmental control of pollution and of natural resources, as well as the problems that arise from government action in these areas.

ST12-1 GOVERNMENT REGULATION: GOOD FOR THE ENVIRONMENT?

In the middle of the twentieth century, Americans became increasingly concerned about pollution of air and water. While there had been pollution in the past, it had not been a major public issue. Indeed, active smoke stacks were often viewed favorably as a sign of job-creating factories. In addition, court actions had often kept severe pollution at bay by protecting property rights, as we noted in Chapter 2. For example, in 1903, ranchers in Montana sued the Anaconda Smelting Co., for destroying their grass and killing livestock with the smelter's sulfur emissions. The ranchers won, so the company had to compensate the ranchers for past damages and for any future damages traceable to them. To reduce future damages, they built what was for many years the tallest smoke stack in the world. By the time the plume from the stack reached the ground, it was so dilute that concentrations were very low.[2]

In Wisconsin in the nineteenth century, paper companies routinely bought miles of downstream property to avoid polluting others. Their wastewater emissions, which were costly to control, could be diluted by water from tributary streams before reaching others' downstream properties. If they had not done so, the high initial concentrations could have subjected the companies to litigation. By owning the land located well below their production facility, paper companies were imposing costs on themselves, not on others.[3]

Clearly, property rights, properly enforced, help optimize decisions to produce greater net social benefits from activities that also pollute. But it is difficult—if not impossible—to define, establish, and fully protect property rights when there are a large number of polluters or a large number of people harmed by the emissions, or both. Consider the air quality in a large city such as Los Angeles or Denver. Millions of people can be harmed when the pollutants are put into the air. Yet many of those affected people also contribute to the pollution as they drive their cars and operate industrial and commercial establishments. In such cases, high transaction costs make it hard to rely on the protection of rights (from damage to one's body or to one's property) to clean up the air. Who, exactly, would sue whom? Under these circumstances, the Wisconsin rivers common-law solution would not be a practical option.

Such large-number problems were growing during the last century, and in the 1960s the resulting public frustrations gave birth to the modern environmental movement and a push for federal legislation. A series of environment acts were passed, including the Clean Air Act of 1970 and the Clean Water Act of 1972, followed by many others.

Although government regulation is an alternative method of protecting the environment, the regulatory approach also has a number of deficiencies. First, government regulation is often sought precisely because the harms are uncertain and the source of the

[2]Department of the Interior, National Park Service, "The Butte-Anaconda District," National Register of Historic Places Registration Form (n.d.), 84, http://www.nps.gov/nhl/designations/samples/mt/Butte-Anaconda.pdf
[3]Peter Davis, "Theories of Water Pollution Litigation." *Wisconsin Law Review*. 3 (1971): 738–816, at 777–80.

problem cannot be demonstrated in a court of law, so relief from the courts is difficult to obtain. But when the harms are uncertain and thus speculative, so too are the benefits of reducing them. The costs of reducing them, however, are real and often large.

Second, by its very nature, regulation overrides or ignores the information and incentives provided by market signals. Accountability of regulators for the costs they impose is lacking, just as accountability for polluters is missing in the market sector when secure and tradable property rights are not in place. The tunnel vision of regulators, each assigned to oversee a small part of the economy, is not properly constrained by readily observable costs.

Third, regulation allows special interests to use political power to achieve objectives that may be quite different from the environmental goals originally announced. The global warming issue illustrates all of these problems and the uncertainties that they generate. Let's take a closer look at this high-profile issue.

ST12-2 THE ECONOMICS OF GLOBAL WARMING

The highly publicized issue of global warming generates a legitimate reason for considering governmental intervention. But the global nature of the problem and the scientific uncertainties associated with it also illustrate the problems that come with regulation.

Burning fuels such as coal, oil, and natural gas emits carbon dioxide. These emissions cause no direct harm, unlike traditional pollutants such as particulates and sulfur dioxide. While carbon dioxide is not a pollutant in the normal sense, long-term concern about its effects on the atmosphere caused the U.S. Environmental Protection Agency (EPA) to begin regulating it as a pollutant in 2009. This made it possible for the EPA to restrict carbon dioxide emissions of factories. In 2012 President Barack Obama agreed with the leaders of seven industrialized nations that they would try to cut carbon emissions by 80 percent by the year 2050, but no specific targets were set.

As the world has become warmer and more industrialized, more carbon dioxide has been building up in the atmosphere. Although carbon dioxide represents a tiny part of the atmosphere, it is a "greenhouse" gas (GHG). It contributes to the formation of an invisible blanket that traps some heat on Earth that would otherwise be radiated into space.

Coal-fired power generators put large amounts of visible steam and invisible carbon dioxide into the air. Carbon dioxide is a greenhouse gas that may be warming the earth significantly.

Harry Waller/Index Stock Imagery/PhotoLibrary

Interestingly, carbon dioxide is a "greenhouse gas" in another sense as well. It is purchased in compressed gas form by owners of greenhouses as a fertilizer for their plants because it spurs their growth.

Higher levels of carbon dioxide may have contributed to the 1.4 degree Fahrenheit increase in the Earth's temperature over the past century. Further increases in carbon dioxide levels might cause the Earth to warm more dramatically, changing weather patterns and perhaps leading to rising sea levels around the globe. If the "worst-case scenarios" suggested by some scientists were to materialize, certain communities would face flooding of their lands and serious ecological disruption. Reports of extreme weather and melting glaciers add to the alarm surrounding this issue.

In recent years, predictions of runaway rising temperatures, based on the work of some scientists, have been strongly endorsed by national environmental groups and extensively discussed in the media. But the Earth's temperatures have been flat since 1998. The Earth did get warmer in the last third of the twentieth century, but by 2013 it had remained at roughly the level it reached in 1998. This occurred even though the world produced a lot more carbon dioxide—about 100 billion tons of carbon between 2000 and 2013. Taking note of these figures, the *Economist* magazine commented that the "mismatch between rising greenhouse-gas emissions and not-rising temperatures is among the biggest puzzles in climate science just now."[4]

Most predictions of significant temperature increases are based on giant computer models of Earth's atmosphere, but these models are full of information gaps. The effects of clouds and water vapor in warming or cooling Earth and the role of oceans in absorbing carbon dioxide are especially important in the models, because the projected warming effect depends heavily on water vapor and clouds. The models assume that water vapor and clouds will increase the warming effect. Indeed, in the models, they are assumed to be 10 to 20 times as important in raising future temperatures as is carbon dioxide itself. But it is quite possible that the water vapor won't increase with carbon dioxide in the way that the models assume and that changes in clouds, on balance, will do little to add to warming or might even be, on balance, a force for cooling. Scientists do agree that, by reflecting sunlight back into space clouds tend to cool Earth, while clouds also trap heat from below them, thus warming Earth.

Is a world that is warmer by one or two degrees better on the whole or worse? Climate researcher Indur Goklany points out that since 1920, as carbon dioxide emissions increased with industrialization and Earth's temperature rose, deaths per million people from all extreme weather events (droughts, floods, temperature extremes, etc.) fell globally by 98 percent.[5] Burning fossil fuel may have played a part in raising the Earth's temperature, but it also resulted in enormous increases in people's well-being. In the same chapter, Goklany details the many roles fossil fuels have played in helping people globally to prosper mightily and be healthier as a result. His work adds hard evidence to the simple observation that when people retire from their jobs and have more freedom to live where they wish, large numbers of them move south—to Florida, for example, seeking more warmth and less rigorous winters.

Costs also matter. The opportunity cost of attempting to slow the warming trend by reducing greenhouse gas emissions (the "carbon footprint") would be extremely high—economic growth would be substantially reduced. According to two MIT researchers, it would be "impossible to achieve the desired emission reductions while simultaneously maintaining reasonable economic growth unless, in addition, the energy efficiency of the economy improves at a rate significantly above the historical trend."[6]

---

[4]*Economist*, "A Sensitive Matter," March 30, 2013, http://www.economist.com/news/science-and-technology/21574461-climate-may-be-heating-up-less-response-greenhouse-gas-emissions.

[5]Indur M. Goklany, "Economic Development in Developing Countries: Advancing Human Well-Being and the Capacity to Adapt to Global Warming," in *Climate Coup* (Washington, DC: Cato Institute, 2011).

[6]Richard Lester and Ashley Finan, "Quantifying the Impact of Proposed Carbon Emission Reductions on the U.S. Energy Infrastructure," MIT-IPC-Energy Innovation Working Paper 09-004 (Cambridge, MA, July 2009).

Ironically, however, carbon dioxide emissions have fallen in the United States. According to data released in 2013 by the U.S. Department of Energy, previously rising U. S. emissions fell by 12 percent between 2007 and 2012.[7] While that reduction was due in part to the 2008–2009 recession, few (if anyone) had anticipated it. But the main reason for the drop, says Jeffrey Frankel—an economist at the Harvard Kennedy School—is fracking. This is the production of natural gas (or oil) from shale rock using horizontal drilling and hydraulic fracturing of the rock. Through this process, Frankel points out, the output of natural gas has increased substantially. Because natural gas emits less carbon dioxide per unit of energy produced than coal, the increasing replacement of coal by natural gas in the U.S. has caused the drop in total emissions of carbon dioxide.[8]

The surging production of gas and oil in parts of the United States is already reducing the nation's reliance on coal, but fracking faces opposition, primarily from environmental groups, as discussed in the previous Special Topic. Frankel concedes there maybe be some local water contamination but, overall, he says, "one must compare the risks of fracking with the risks of the alternative," citing pollution caused by oil, nuclear, and coal production. Even so, fear of fracking is strong enough that New York State (and France as well) have banned it, at least as of 2013.

Meanwhile, the developing countries are not reducing their carbon dioxide emissions. China is the largest emitter at 8.7 trillion metric tons (in 2011), compared with the U.S., which is next, with 5.5 trillion metric tons that year. Any impact from reducing U.S. emissions is likely to be swamped by the output of developing countries.[9]

Political action will reflect special interest politics and global warming policy is no exception. Interest groups will use global warming and other environmental concerns in an effort to obtain policies providing them with a competitive advantage relative to rivals. For example, wind and solar producers will lobby for subsidies and tax breaks, favor tighter restrictions on carbon emissions, and oppose fracking in order to gain an advantage relative to natural gas, petroleum, and coal producers. Similarly, producers of corn-based ethanol will use environmental arguments to lobby for subsidies and mandates expanding the use of their product in the production of gasoline. Clearly, regulation and political allocation will not guarantee sound policy in this area.

ST12-3 MITIGATION VERSUS ADAPTATION STRATEGY

The estimated costs, the special-interest involvement, and the scientific uncertainties leave many economists unwilling to recommend strong regulations to reduce emissions of carbon dioxide. But given the possibility of serious harm from global warming, what should be done? Until recently, the most talked-about approach was *mitigation*—reducing carbon emissions in order to keep global temperatures from rising as much as they otherwise would. Adaptation, making changes when and if actual problems begin to occur, provides an alternative approach.

Climate change researcher Indur M. Goklany suggests that adaptation is the superior strategy. He examines four risk factors—hunger, malaria, water shortages, and coastal flooding—that might worsen if global temperatures increase significantly. He concludes that taking action now to address these already serious problems, independent of global warming, would cost far less than trying to reduce temperature increases, and the payoff in improved human lives would be achieved long before any significant benefits were derived

---

[7]U.S. Energy Information Administration, "Carbon Dioxide Emissions From Energy Consumption by Source," Monthly Energy Review (April 2013), Table 12.2, http://www.eia.gov/totalenergy/data/monthly/pdf/sec12.pdf.

[8]Jeffrey Frankel, "Frack to the Future," Project Syndicate, April 16, 2013, http://www.project-syndicate.org/blog/frack-to-the-future.

[9]U.S. Energy Information Administration, "International Energy Statistics," http://www.eia.gov/cfapps/ipdproject/IEDIndex3.cfm?tid=90&pid=44&aid=8.

from greenhouse gas reductions.[10] Economic logic suggests that a larger payoff obtained sooner for a smaller cost is the better bet.

Instead of forcing a smaller carbon footprint, which would greatly reduce national income, nations might be better off dealing with the uncertainties of global warming through growth and development. As Aaron Wildavsky implied in the quotation at the opening of this special topic, wealthier people can better handle all sorts of risks. They purchase better healthcare, make available more emergency transport and care facilities, drive safer cars, and pay for routine safety measures of all sorts. A more prosperous country is more resilient when faced with major threats, whether from a new disease, an earthquake, an asteroid striking Earth, or global warming. In fact, economist Donald Coursey estimates that a rise of 1 percent in a population's income produces a 2.5 percent increase in that group's willingness and ability to pay for environmental improvements.[11]

A strong economy allows its citizens to help not only themselves but also others. For example, when an earthquake and tsunami hit northern Japan and killed thousands of people in March of 2011, it took Americans less than two weeks to give more than $161 million in private donations to assist the victims in Japan. The U.S. Department of Defense had a naval presence in the area, and those ships quickly began delivering food and other emergency supplies. The U.S. Agency for International Development also participated, and within nine days, USAID and the U.S. military had put more than $23 million into those supply efforts. A poor society has fewer options and less resilience. Also, richer people are far more willing and able to make sacrifices to gain greater environmental quality of all sorts. Economic development accomplishes all these goals on behalf of health and environmental safety. In contrast, reducing one risk at a large cost to economic growth makes us more vulnerable to other risks, including those that were not anticipated.

ST12-4 MARKETLIKE SCHEMES: REDUCING THE COST OF SPECIFIC REGULATIONS

Policy-makers realize that action on global warming would be costly. There are two major marketlike approaches to the control of pollution. We now turn to the consideration of each.

1. Cap and trade. Some emitters of carbon dioxide, however, can cut back on their emissions at much lower cost than others, and that fact suggests that an approach to cutting carbon emissions called "cap-and-trade" might be useful. Under "cap-and-trade," a pollution-control authority, such as the Environmental Protection Agency (EPA) in the United States, sets the total amount of emissions, in effect setting "caps" on emissions. Then it issues tradeable permits allowing each emitter a set amount of pollution.

Such a program gives each emitter an incentive to reduce or even eliminate its emissions. A company that can cheaply reduce emissions below its allowed level, can sell emissions permits ("credits") to other companies that face higher costs. The total reduction in pollution will not change, but the overall costs of achieving it will probably be much lower. The result at that point is greater efficiency in attaining any specified overall emissions level.

The Clear Air Act Amendments of 1990 established what is perhaps the best-known "cap-and-trade" program in the United States. The act authorized the EPA to set up a nationwide system for trading sulfur dioxide emission reductions among power plants. The utilities that face the highest cost of emission control can purchase permits from those who

[10]Indur M. Goklany, "Relative Contributions of Global Warming to Various Climate Sensitive Risks, and Their Implications for Adaptation and Mitigation," *Energy & Environment* 14 (2003): 797–822.
[11]Donald Coursey, "The Demand for Environmental Quality," a booklet published by the John M. Olin School of Business, Washington University, St. Louis, December 1992.

can more easily control emissions. This program has lowered the long-run costs to electric utilities of meeting the legislated targets.

Such schemes can play a useful role, but difficulties remain. One is how to set the appropriate amount of pollution reduction? Or put another way, "How clean is 'clean enough?'" And a second is how much should be spent to achieve it? Policy analysts familiar with the negotiations over the 1990 Act say that the standard chosen, a national reduction of 10 million tons of sulfur dioxide per year, was arbitrary, not backed by well-estimated, clearly relevant health and aesthetic standards. So even though the trades reduced the total cost of meeting the standard, the standard may have been unreasonably strict—or, for that matter, too lax. Because the major problem the program addressed—acid rain—turned out to be smaller than many people expected, the overall program was probably unnecessarily costly in spite of the gains allowed by trading of emission rights among pollution sources.[12]

Setting the pollution levels at the ideal level, where the costs of additional emissions reduction are equal to the benefits, would require information that is unavailable to government officials. When enforceable property rights exist and are exchanged in workable markets, this kind of information is generated through voluntary trades—by individuals knowing their own costs of selling, and buyers judging for themselves the benefits expected from a purchase—that determine prices.

When courts decide who has the property rights in environmental matters—when, for example, a court decides that a factory must cut pollution to protect a farmer's property rights—trades are still possible. The farmer might prefer a cash payment to being entirely free of pollution. But such negotiations are not allowed when the issue is decided by direct regulation of each emitter.

2. Pollution charges or taxes. Pollution charges or taxes can also be used to change the incentives of polluters. Under this approach, the government levies fees on polluters. Ideally—in order to achieve efficiency—these charges would just equal the costs of pollution borne by others downwind or downstream. Facing a pollution tax, a polluter has an incentive to reduce the contaminants it is putting into the air or water or soil. As emissions decrease, the payment of the pollution tax by the company will also decrease. The incentive to reduce emissions continues only to the point at which the cost of cutting back further would exceed the cost savings from the reduced emission charges. At that point, the company will pay tax on the remaining emissions.

This process will result in efficient emission controls only if the emission charges properly represent the marginal cost of the pollutant to those harmed. But it is difficult or impossible for the regulator to know this cost without market trades to provide information. In a true property-rights situation, would-be polluters could negotiate with those who would be harmed by the pollution and decide whether to stop the pollution or compensate those harmed. As indicated at the beginning of this Special Topic, owners of early paper mills in Wisconsin bought land for miles downstream so that the effluent from their manufacturing would not violate the property rights of others. Thus, any harm from emissions would be borne by the owners—who are now also the emitters. These transactions internalized the costs of pollution and thereby avoided the external cost problem.

Only a few pollution charges have been adopted in the United States. Companies oppose these fees because they are an added cost of doing business (just as being forced to reduce emissions would be). Governments are not happy with them, either. If the emission charge does reduce pollution, the government will get less revenue over time. Reluctance on the part of governments to impose them has held back their implementation. There are no costless solutions to current pollution problems, which is why we continue to seek better solutions.

---

[12]Robert W. Crandall, "Is There Progress in Environmental Policy?" *Contemporary Economic Policy* 12, no. 1 (1994): 80–83.

ST12-5 PROPERTY RIGHTS AS A TOOL FOR GOVERNMENT POLICY

When the government recognizes the power of private property rights, there is potential for successful government policy. Ocean fisheries are one example in which progress is being made.

ST12-5a OCEAN FISHERIES: A LACK OF PROPERTY RIGHTS CAUSES OVERFISHING[13]

Overfishing in the oceans is a classic example of overexploitation of a resource that is not privately owned. This is typically called the "tragedy of the commons."[14] Without ownership of the fish or of fishing rights, each fisher has little to gain from holding back, because others will get most of the fish left in the water by any one fisher. To cope with this tragedy of the commons, governments try to institute regulations that protect the fish. Since the 1970s, the U.S. government has regulated fishing in coastal waters. Even so, at least a third of U.S. fisheries are known to be overfished.

One reason is that the regulations encouraged a wasteful and dangerous "race to fish." To preserve the stock of fish, governments reduced the length of the fishing seasons (often to just a few days) and set limits on the kinds of gear that could be used. This sometimes meant that boats went out to sea in dangerous weather, took all the fish they could, even immature fish, and faced accidents and capsizing as their gear became entangled with other fishers' gear.

Property-rights strategies are increasingly used around the world instead of limits on season length. A prominent example is the adoption of individual transferable quotas (ITQs), which give fishers ownership of a portion of the annual allowable catch. For example, as economist Don Leal puts it in one case, "an individual who holds a 0.1-percent share in the South Atlantic wreckfish fishery is entitled to 7,400 pounds of wreckfish for the season if the total allowable catch is 7,400,000 pounds."[15] Regulators could be mistaken in setting the quota, of course. However, unlike the case of air pollution, the fishery itself will give them rapid feedback. If the stock of fish falls, regulators can drop the total allowable catch to let the fishery recover. When they own ITQs, fishers support such limits to maintain the value of their fishing rights over time. Leal reports that in the United States, the number of federal fisheries adopting rights-based approaches has grown from 4 in 1995 to 15 in 2010, with more in the planning stage. At the global level however, less than 2 percent of the world's fisheries have adopted rights-based strategies.

ST12-6 GOVERNMENT OWNERSHIP OF RESOURCES AND PROVISION OF SERVICES

Much government intervention in environmental matters has to do with establishing regulations to control pollution. But the government also owns many natural resources and seeks to protect environmental quality through parks, refuges, and other lands it owns. When resources are not privately owned and traded in open markets, however, the vital flow of information and incentives that prices bring is missing. That is the case with our

---

[13]This section is based in large part on information found in Donald R. Leal, *Homesteading the Oceans: The Case for Property Rights in U.S. Fisheries*, www.perc.org/perc.php?subsection=6&id=188, and from personal communications with Leal.

[14]Garrett Hardin, "The Tragedy of the Commons," *The Concise Encyclopedia of Economics*, Library of Economics and Liberty, www.econlib.org/library/Enc/TragedyoftheCommons.html.

[15]Donald R. Leal, "Fencing the Fishery—A Primer on Ending the Race for Fish," www.perc.org/perc.php?subsection=3&id=120. The data for ITQ numbers are found at www.perc.org/articles/article1271.php.

national parks.[16] Government ownership stops the flow of information and incentives provided by dynamic market data. In complex ecosystems and in a world in which incomes, scientific understanding, and resource values all are constantly changing, the absence of up-to-date knowledge, including the desires of the tax-paying public, can lead to mismanagement. That is true even with management provided by highly qualified, well-intended professionals.

Most of the funds for the national parks are tax dollars appropriated by Congress. Park visitors pay only a small fraction of the cost of the services they receive, although fees have increased since the adoption of a fee demonstration program in the late 1990s, which became law in 2004. In 1995, for example, proceeds from national park recreation fees covered only 7.5 percent of the cost of park operations. Thus, park managers had little information about how much the various services were worth to visitors. Without good information about what visitors wanted, park managers didn't know whether to improve the roads, buildings and sewers, hire more rangers for interpretive programs, or keep campgrounds open longer and add new ones. And even today, because the National Park Service's funding is dependent upon decisions in Congress, it spends more time figuring out what the relevant congressional representatives want than what park visitors want.

Even when park managers have good information, the proper incentive to use it may not be present. This was the case in 1996 when the superintendent of Yellowstone Park closed a campground. The park was short on cash, and the superintendent was trying to reduce his spending. In fact, the campground in question was profitable—that is, it earned more than it cost to operate. The problem was that although his budget paid the cost of keeping the campground open, the revenues went to the U.S. Treasury, not to Yellowstone. So the superintendent closed the campground to save money, even though doing so deprived visitors of a campground that was providing net earnings for the Treasury.

In contrast, for owners of private forests, campgrounds, amusement parks, museums, and other attractions that also draw visitors, information is always flowing, and managers always have an incentive to respond to that information. These owners must pay for the resources they use, and they collect the needed revenue from customers. If people don't come to a private museum, its revenues fall. In response, its owners must do something to attract customers who are willing to pay the full cost (or, alternatively, philanthropists who will cover the costs for them), or they will have to close their doors.

The National Park Service may be starting to realize that it needs better information and better incentives. The law that raised fees in 2004 also required that 80 percent of the fees be kept in the specific parks where they were collected and that they be used for projects in those parks—rather than flowing into the U.S. Treasury to be spent according to congressional mandate. "With greater accountability to those most impacted by the parks, the program is funding projects that otherwise might sit on a shelf," wrote one commentator about the fee program.[17]

While the National Park Service and several other government agencies own a great deal of protected land, much of the protection of nature is coming about through a different source: technology. As we saw in the previous Special Topic, forests have regrown in the United States. British scientist and author Matt Ridley recently wrote that the story is even more dramatic in Great Britain, which has "three times as much forest as it did 100 years ago." And in North England in the 1970s, he recalls, "otters had vanished, salmon were gone from the River Tyne because of pollution, and hawks and falcons had disappeared due to DDT." But today "otters are thriving, salmon are back, and seabirds on the nearby Farne Islands have doubled in numbers."

The improvement comes about through what Ridley calls "land sparing." Thanks to technology—from modern farming equipment to new crop varieties—less land is needed

---

[16]Many of the facts and much of the data for this section come from Donald R. Leal and Holly L. Fretwell, "Back to the Future to Save Our Parks," *PERC Policy Series*, no. PS-10 (June 1997), www.perc.org/perc .php?subsection=6&id=654.

[17]Brian Yablonski, "The National Parks: America's Best Idea," *PERC Reports*, 27, no. 3 (Fall 2009), www.perc .org/articles/article1191.php.

to produce food (and the same is true of fiber and fuel). That allows more and more land to return to a wild state. Says Ridley: "What is really making a positive dent in the environmental arena is the unintended effects of technology rather than nature reserves or exhortations to love nature."[18] If Ridley is right, then one of the most effective ways that government can protect nature is to allow technology to thrive.

ST12-7 CONCLUSION

People turn to government to get what they can't get in markets. In many cases, they are seeking to get what they want with a subsidy from others. Government can provide protection from harms, as in regulation that reduces pollution, or production of goods and services, as in the provision of national parks. Government can indeed shift the cost of services from some citizens to others, and can do the same with benefits from its programs. There is little reason, however, to expect a net increase in efficiency when government steps in. That is true in environmental matters, as well as in many other areas of citizen concern.

---

[18]Matt Ridley, "Ecology or Economics: Which Has Done More?" *PERC Reports* 31, no. 1 (Winter 2013): 22–27, http://perc.org/articles/ecology-or-economics-which-has-done-more-our-environmental-future.

KEY POINTS

- When it is difficult to assign and enforce private property rights, markets often result in outcomes that are inefficient. This is often the case when large numbers of people engage in actions that impose harm on others. Government regulation has some promise but also poses some problems of its own.

- Global warming could exert a sizable adverse impact on human welfare, but there is considerable uncertainty about both its cause and the potential gains that might be derived from regulations that require reductions in emissions of carbon dioxide. Global temperature changes have been observed previously; we do not know for certain if the current warming stems primarily from human

activity. We do not even know whether, on balance, a warming would exert an adverse impact. These uncertainties increase the attractiveness of adaptation as an option to regulation.

- Marketlike schemes can reduce the costs of reaching a chosen environmental goal, but the programs provide little help in choosing the right goal.

- Federal ownership of national parks, as with other lands, has brought troublesome results along with benefits, but there seems to be progress in moving closer to market solutions that provide better information and incentives for federal managers.

CRITICAL ANALYSIS QUESTIONS

1. *The movie *The Perfect Storm* was set in a situation in which a very short fishing season forces the fishers to go to sea despite the dangerous conditions. Explain how a move to ITQs could solve that problem.

2. "The national parks belong to us all. No one should be charged money to enter." Evaluate, using the economic way of thinking.

3. *"The buildup of carbon dioxide and other gases in the air threatens to warm the planet and cause enormous damage worldwide. We must immediately stop this buildup for the

sake of future generations." Why do many economists disagree with this statement? Are they not concerned about the future? Explain.

4. *"Unlike a marketplace in which pollution is profitable, government control of resources and pollution can take into account the desires of all the people." Evaluate, using economic thinking.

*Asterisk denotes questions for which answers are given in Appendix B.

APPENDIX A

General Business and Economics Indicators for the United States

Section 1

						Real GDP		
Year	Personal Consum Expend	Gross Private Domestic Invest	Govt Consumpand Gross Invest	Net Exports	Gross Domestic Product	2005 Prices	Annual Real Rate	Real GDP Per Capita
1960	$331.8	$78.9	$111.5	$4.2	$526.4	$2,830.9	2.5	$15,661
1961	342.2	78.2	119.5	4.9	544.8	2,896.9	2.3	15,766
1962	363.3	88.1	130.1	4.1	585.7	3,072.4	6.1	16,466
1963	382.7	93.8	136.4	4.9	617.8	3,206.7	4.4	16,940
1964	411.5	102.1	143.2	6.9	663.6	3,392.3	5.8	17,675
1965	443.8	118.2	151.4	5.6	719.1	3,610.1	6.4	18,576
1966	480.9	131.3	171.6	3.9	787.7	3,845.3	6.5	19,559
1967	507.8	128.6	192.5	3.6	832.4	3,942.5	2.5	19,836
1968	558.0	141.2	209.3	1.4	909.8	4,133.4	4.8	20,590
1969	604.5	173.6	240.4	1.4	1,019.9	4,707.9	13.9	23,222
1970	647.7	170.1	254.2	4.0	1,075.9	4,717.7	0.2	23,003
1971	701.0	196.8	269.3	0.6	1,167.8	4,873.0	3.3	23,463
1972	769.4	228.1	288.2	−3.4	1,282.4	5,128.8	5.2	24,432
1973	851.1	266.9	306.4	4.1	1,428.5	5,418.2	5.6	25,565
1974	932.0	274.5	343.1	−0.8	1,548.8	5,390.2	−0.5	25,200
1975	1,032.8	257.3	382.9	16.0	1,688.9	5,379.5	−0.2	24,907
1976	1,150.2	323.2	405.8	−1.6	1,877.6	5,669.3	5.4	25,996
1977	1,276.7	396.6	435.8	−23.1	2,086.0	5,930.6	4.6	26,922
1978	1,426.2	478.4	477.4	−25.4	2,356.6	6,260.4	5.6	28,120
1979	1,589.5	539.7	525.5	−22.5	2,632.1	6,459.2	3.2	28,694
1980	1,754.6	530.1	590.8	−13.1	2,862.5	6,443.4	−0.2	28,295
1981	1,937.5	631.2	654.7	−12.5	3,210.9	6,610.6	2.6	28,741
1982	2,073.9	581.0	710.0	−20.0	3,345.0	6,484.3	−1.9	27,923
1983	2,286.5	637.5	765.7	−51.7	3,638.1	6,784.7	4.6	28,953
1984	2,498.2	820.1	825.2	−102.7	4,040.7	7,277.2	7.3	30,784
1985	2,722.7	829.6	908.4	−114.0	4,346.7	7,585.7	4.2	31,805
1986	2,898.4	849.1	974.5	−131.9	4,590.1	7,852.1	3.5	32,624
1987	3,092.1	892.2	1,030.8	−144.8	4,870.2	8,123.9	3.5	33,453
1988	3,346.9	937.0	1,078.2	−109.4	5,252.6	8,465.4	4.2	34,544
1989	3,592.8	999.7	1,151.9	−86.8	5,657.7	8,777.0	3.7	35,479
1990	3,825.6	993.5	1,238.4	−77.9	5,979.6	8,945.4	1.9	35,756
1991	3,960.2	944.3	1,298.2	−28.6	6,174.0	8,938.9	−0.1	35,258
1992	4,215.7	1,013.0	1,345.4	−34.8	6,539.3	9,256.7	3.6	36,029
1993	4,471.0	1,106.8	1,366.1	−65.2	6,878.7	9,510.8	2.7	36,540
1994	4,741.0	1,256.5	1,403.7	−92.5	7,308.7	9,894.7	4.0	37,557
1995	4,984.2	1,317.5	1,452.2	−89.8	7,664.0	10,163.7	2.7	38,125
1996	5,268.1	1,432.1	1,496.4	−96.4	8,100.2	10,549.5	3.8	39,114
1997	5,560.7	1,595.6	1,554.2	−102.0	8,608.5	11,022.9	4.5	40,383
1998	5,903.0	1,735.3	1,613.5	−162.7	9,089.1	11,513.4	4.4	41,692
1999	6,316.9	1,884.2	1,726.0	−261.4	9,665.7	12,071.4	4.8	43,216
2000	6,801.6	2,033.8	1,834.4	−380.1	10,289.7	12,565.2	4.1	44,495
2001	7,106.9	1,928.6	1,958.8	−369.0	10,625.3	12,684.4	0.9	44,472
2002	7,385.3	1,925.0	2,094.9	−425.0	10,980.2	12,909.7	1.8	44,832
2003	7,764.4	2,027.9	2,220.8	−500.9	11,512.2	13,270.0	2.8	45,660
2004	8,257.8	2,276.7	2,357.4	−614.8	12,277.0	13,774.0	3.8	46,968
2005	8,790.3	2,527.1	2,493.7	−715.7	13,095.4	14,235.6	3.4	48,094
2006	9,297.5	2,680.6	2,642.2	−762.4	13,857.9	14,615.2	2.7	48,910
2007	9,744.4	2,643.7	2,801.9	−709.8	14,480.3	14,876.8	1.8	49,311
2008	10,005.5	2,424.8	3,003.2	−713.2	14,720.3	14,833.6	−0.3	48,708
2009	9,842.9	1,878.1	3,089.1	−392.2	14,417.9	14,417.9	−2.8	46,927
2010	10,201.9	2,100.8	3,174.0	−518.5	14,958.3	14,779.4	2.5	47,710
2011	10,711.8	2,232.1	3,158.7	−568.7	15,533.8	15,052.4	1.8	48,239
2012	11,149.6	2,475.2	3,167.0	−547.2	16,244.6	15,470.7	2.8	49,226

Source: http://www.bea.gov

Section 2

Year	GDP Deflator Index (2005 = 100)	Annual Percentage Change	Consumer Price Index Index	Percentage Change
1960	20.2	1.4	29.6	1.0
1961	20.5	1.1	29.9	1.1
1962	20.7	1.4	30.3	1.2
1963	21.0	1.1	30.6	1.2
1964	21.3	1.6	31.0	1.3
1965	21.7	1.8	31.5	1.6
1966	22.3	2.8	32.5	3.0
1967	23.0	3.1	33.4	2.8
1968	23.9	4.3	34.8	4.3
1969	23.6	−1.5	36.7	5.5
1970	24.8	5.3	38.8	5.8
1971	26.1	5.1	40.5	4.3
1972	27.2	4.3	41.8	3.3
1973	28.7	5.4	44.4	6.2
1974	31.3	9.0	49.3	11.1
1975	34.2	9.3	53.8	9.1
1976	36.0	5.5	56.9	5.7
1977	38.3	6.2	60.6	6.5
1978	41.0	7.0	65.2	7.6
1979	44.3	8.3	72.6	11.3
1980	48.4	9.0	82.4	13.5
1981	52.9	9.4	90.9	10.3
1982	56.1	6.1	96.5	6.1
1983	58.3	3.9	99.6	3.2
1984	60.4	3.6	103.9	4.3
1985	62.3	3.2	107.6	3.5
1986	63.6	2.0	109.6	1.9
1987	65.2	2.4	113.6	3.7
1988	67.4	3.5	118.3	4.1
1989	70.1	3.9	124.0	4.8
1990	72.7	3.7	130.7	5.4
1991	75.1	3.3	136.2	4.2
1992	76.8	2.3	140.3	3.0
1993	78.6	2.4	144.5	3.0
1994	80.3	2.1	148.2	2.6
1995	82.0	2.1	152.4	2.8
1996	83.5	1.8	156.9	2.9
1997	84.9	1.7	160.5	2.3
1998	85.8	1.1	163.0	1.6
1999	87.0	1.4	166.6	2.2
2000	89.0	2.3	172.2	3.4
2001	91.1	2.3	177.1	2.8
2002	92.5	1.5	179.9	1.6
2003	94.3	2.0	184.0	2.3
2004	96.9	2.7	188.9	2.7
2005	100.0	3.2	195.3	3.4
2006	103.1	3.1	201.6	3.2
2007	105.8	2.7	207.3	2.8
2008	107.8	1.9	215.3	3.8
2009	108.7	0.8	214.5	−0.4
2010	110.0	1.2	218.1	1.6
2011	112.2	2.0	224.9	3.1
2012	114.2	1.7	229.6	2.1

Source: http://www.bea.gov and http://www.bls.gov

Section 3

Year	Civilian Pop	Civilian Labor Force	Civilian Labor Force Participation	Civilian Employment/ Population	Unemployment Rates			
					All	Age 16 to 19	Men Age 20+	Women Age 20+
1960	117.2	69.6	59.4	56.1	5.5	14.7	4.7	5.1
1961	118.8	70.5	59.3	55.4	6.7	16.8	5.7	6.3
1962	120.2	70.6	58.8	55.5	5.5	14.7	4.6	5.4
1963	122.4	71.8	58.7	55.4	5.7	17.2	4.5	5.4
1964	124.5	73.1	58.7	55.7	5.2	16.2	3.9	5.2
1965	126.5	74.5	58.9	56.2	4.5	14.8	3.2	4.5
1966	128.1	75.8	59.2	56.9	3.8	12.8	2.5	3.8
1967	129.9	77.3	59.6	57.3	3.8	12.9	2.3	4.2
1968	132.0	78.7	59.6	57.5	3.6	12.7	2.2	3.8
1969	134.3	80.7	60.1	58.0	3.5	12.2	2.1	3.7
1970	137.1	82.8	60.4	57.4	4.9	15.3	3.5	4.8
1971	140.2	84.4	60.2	56.6	5.9	16.9	4.4	5.7
1972	144.1	87.0	60.4	57.0	5.6	16.2	4.0	5.4
1973	147.1	89.4	60.8	57.8	4.9	14.5	3.3	4.9
1974	150.1	91.9	61.3	57.8	5.6	16.0	3.8	5.5
1975	153.2	93.8	61.2	56.1	8.5	19.9	6.8	8.0
1976	156.2	96.2	61.6	56.8	7.7	19.0	5.9	7.4
1977	159.0	99.0	62.3	57.9	7.1	17.8	5.2	7.0
1978	161.9	102.3	63.2	59.3	6.1	16.4	4.3	6.0
1979	164.9	105.0	63.7	59.9	5.8	16.1	4.2	5.7
1980	167.7	106.9	63.8	59.2	7.1	17.8	5.9	6.4
1981	170.1	108.7	63.9	59.0	7.6	19.6	6.3	6.8
1982	172.3	110.2	64.0	57.8	9.7	23.2	8.8	8.3
1983	174.2	111.6	64.0	57.9	9.6	22.4	8.9	8.1
1984	176.4	113.5	64.4	59.5	7.5	18.9	6.6	6.8
1985	178.2	115.5	64.8	60.1	7.2	18.6	6.2	6.6
1986	180.6	117.8	65.3	60.7	7.0	18.3	6.1	6.2
1987	182.8	119.9	65.6	61.5	6.2	16.9	5.4	5.4
1988	184.6	121.7	65.9	62.3	5.5	15.3	4.8	4.9
1989	186.4	123.9	66.5	63.0	5.3	15.0	4.5	4.7
1990	189.2	125.8	66.5	62.8	5.6	15.5	5.0	4.9
1991	190.9	126.3	66.2	61.7	6.8	18.7	6.4	5.7
1992	192.8	128.1	66.4	61.5	7.5	20.1	7.1	6.3
1993	194.8	129.2	66.3	61.7	6.9	19.0	6.4	5.9
1994	196.8	131.1	66.6	62.5	6.1	17.6	5.4	5.4
1995	198.6	132.3	66.6	62.9	5.6	17.3	4.8	4.9
1996	200.6	133.9	66.8	63.2	5.4	16.7	4.6	4.8
1997	203.1	136.3	67.1	63.8	4.9	16.0	4.2	4.4
1998	205.2	137.7	67.1	64.1	4.5	14.6	3.7	4.1
1999	207.8	139.4	67.1	64.3	4.2	13.9	3.5	3.8
2000	212.6	142.6	67.1	64.4	4.0	13.1	3.4	3.6
2001	215.1	143.7	66.8	63.7	4.7	14.7	4.2	4.1
2002	217.6	144.9	66.6	62.7	5.8	16.5	5.2	5.1
2003	221.2	146.5	66.2	62.3	6.0	17.5	5.4	5.1
2004	223.4	147.4	66.0	62.3	5.5	17.0	4.9	4.9
2005	226.1	149.3	66.0	62.7	5.1	16.6	4.5	4.6
2006	228.8	151.4	66.2	63.1	4.6	15.4	4.1	4.1
2007	231.9	153.1	66.0	63.0	4.6	15.7	4.1	4.0
2008	233.8	154.3	66.0	62.2	5.8	18.7	5.4	4.9
2009	235.8	154.1	65.4	59.3	9.3	24.8	9.6	7.5
2010	237.8	153.9	64.7	58.5	9.6	25.9	9.8	8.0
2011	239.6	153.6	64.1	58.4	8.9	24.4	8.7	7.9
2012	243.3	155.0	63.7	58.6	8.1	24.0	7.5	7.3

Source: www.bls.gov

Section 4

Year	M1	Annual Change	M2	Annual Change	Aaa Bonds	Federal Budget Fiscal Year Outlays	Fiscal Year Receipts	Surplus/ Deficit	National Debt[1] Billions of Dollars	Percent of GDP
1960	$140.3	–0.1	$304.3	3.8	4.4	$92.2	$92.5	$0.3	$210.3	40.5%
1961	143.1	2.0	324.8	6.7	4.4	97.7	94.4	(3.3)	211.1	39.8%
1962	146.5	2.4	350.1	7.8	4.3	106.8	99.7	(7.1)	218.3	38.5%
1963	150.9	3.0	379.6	8.4	4.3	111.3	106.6	(4.8)	222.0	37.0%
1964	156.8	3.9	409.4	7.8	4.4	118.5	112.6	(5.9)	222.1	34.6%
1965	163.5	4.2	442.5	8.1	4.5	118.2	116.8	(1.4)	221.7	32.2%
1966	171.0	4.6	471.4	6.5	5.1	134.5	130.8	(3.7)	221.5	29.3%
1967	177.7	3.9	503.6	6.8	5.5	157.5	148.8	(8.6)	219.9	27.1%
1968	190.1	7.0	545.3	8.3	6.2	178.1	153.0	(25.2)	237.3	27.3%
1969	201.4	5.9	578.7	6.1	7.0	183.6	186.9	3.2	224.0	23.6%
1970	209.1	3.8	601.4	3.9	8.0	195.6	192.8	(2.8)	225.5	22.3%
1971	223.2	6.7	674.4	12.1	7.4	210.2	187.1	(23.0)	237.5	22.0%
1972	239.0	7.1	758.1	12.4	7.2	230.7	207.3	(23.4)	251.0	21.3%
1973	256.4	7.2	831.8	9.7	7.4	245.7	230.8	(14.9)	265.7	20.3%
1974	269.2	5.0	880.7	5.9	8.6	269.4	263.2	(6.1)	263.1	18.3%
1975	281.4	4.5	963.7	9.4	8.8	332.3	279.1	(53.2)	309.7	19.8%
1976	297.2	5.6	1,086.6	12.8	8.4	371.8	298.1	(73.7)	382.7	22.0%
1977	320.0	7.7	1,221.4	12.4	8.0	409.2	355.6	(53.7)	444.1	22.5%
1978	346.3	8.2	1,322.4	8.3	8.7	458.7	399.6	(59.2)	491.6	22.2%
1979	372.7	7.6	1,425.8	7.8	9.6	504.0	463.3	(40.7)	524.7	21.0%
1980	395.7	6.2	1,540.4	8.0	11.9	590.9	517.1	(73.8)	591.1	21.7%
1981	424.9	7.4	1,679.6	9.0	14.2	678.2	599.3	(79.0)	664.9	21.8%
1982	453.0	6.6	1,831.4	9.0	13.8	745.7	617.8	(128.0)	790.1	24.5%
1983	503.2	11.1	2,054.8	12.2	12.0	808.4	600.6	(207.8)	981.7	28.5%
1984	538.6	7.0	2,219.3	8.0	12.7	851.8	666.4	(185.4)	1,151.9	30.0%
1985	587.0	9.0	2,416.7	8.9	11.4	946.3	734.0	(212.3)	1,337.5	32.3%
1986	666.4	13.5	2,613.5	8.1	9.0	990.4	769.2	(221.2)	1,549.8	35.2%
1987	743.5	11.6	2,783.8	6.5	9.4	1,004.0	854.3	(149.7)	1,677.7	36.1%
1988	774.8	4.2	2,933.4	5.4	9.7	1,064.4	909.2	(155.2)	1,822.4	36.4%
1989	782.2	1.0	3,056.1	4.2	9.3	1,143.7	991.1	(152.6)	1,970.6	36.5%
1990	810.6	3.6	3,223.6	5.5	9.3	1,253.0	1,032.0	(221.0)	2,177.1	38.0%
1991	859.0	6.0	3,342.2	3.7	8.8	1,324.2	1,055.0	(269.2)	2,430.4	41.0%
1992	965.9	12.5	3,403.6	1.8	8.1	1,381.5	1,091.2	(290.3)	2,703.3	43.3%
1993	1,078.5	11.7	3,438.0	1.0	7.2	1,409.4	1,154.3	(255.1)	2,922.7	44.4%
1994	1,145.2	6.2	3,482.1	1.3	8.0	1,461.8	1,258.6	(203.2)	3,077.9	44.1%
1995	1,143.1	–0.2	3,552.7	2.0	7.6	1,515.7	1,351.8	(164.0)	3,230.3	44.0%
1996	1,106.5	–3.2	3,722.8	4.8	7.4	1,560.5	1,453.1	(107.4)	3,343.1	43.3%
1997	1,070.1	–3.3	3,909.8	5.0	7.3	1,601.1	1,579.2	(21.9)	3,347.8	40.8%
1998	1,080.6	1.0	4,188.9	7.1	6.5	1,652.5	1,721.7	69.3	3,262.9	37.7%
1999	1,102.3	2.0	4,496.9	7.4	7.0	1,701.8	1,827.5	125.6	3,135.7	34.1%
2000	1,103.6	0.1	4,769.3	6.1	7.6	1,789.0	2,025.2	236.2	2,898.4	29.5%
2001	1,140.3	3.3	5,179.4	8.6	7.1	1,862.8	1,991.1	128.2	2,785.5	27.2%
2002	1,196.7	4.9	5,562.4	7.4	6.5	2,010.9	1,853.1	(157.8)	2,936.2	27.8%
2003	1,273.8	6.4	5,950.1	7.0	5.7	2,159.9	1,782.3	(377.6)	3,257.3	29.7%
2004	1,344.3	5.5	6,236.0	4.8	5.6	2,292.8	1,880.1	(412.7)	3595.2	30.8%
2005	1,371.6	2.0	6,504.3	4.3	5.2	2,472.0	2,153.6	(318.3)	3855.9	31.0%
2006	1,374.7	0.2	6,845.3	5.2	5.6	2,655.1	2,406.9	(248.2)	4060.0	30.7%
2007	1,372.6	–0.1	7,267.1	6.2	5.6	2,728.7	2,568.0	(160.7)	4255.5	30.7%
2008	1,434.9	4.5	7,763.7	6.8	5.6	2,982.5	2,524.0	(458.6)	5311.9	37.1%
2009	1,637.7	14.1	8,385.3	8.0	5.3	3,517.7	2,105.0	(1,412.7)	6775.5	48.5%
2010	1,742.3	6.4	8,593.4	2.5	5.0	3,457.1	2,162.7	(1,294.4)	8207.2	57.2%
2011	2,010.0	15.4	9,221.3	7.3	4.6	3,603.1	2,303.5	(1,299.6)	8463.5	56.7%
2012	2,310.9	15.0	10,006.9	8.5	3.7	3,537.1	2,450.2	(1,087.0)	9635.8	62.0%

Source: www.economagic.com and www.whitehouse.gov/omb/

[1]National debt is debt held by private investors.

Section 5

Year	SIZE OF GOVERNMENT AS A PERCENT OF GDP[1]				
	EXPENDITURES	REVENUES	PURCHASES	NONDEFENSE	TRANSFER
1960	31.8	25.9	23.0	14.9	5.3
1961	33.2	25.9	23.8	15.7	5.9
1962	33.2	26.1	24.1	15.8	5.6
1963	33.1	26.6	23.9	15.8	5.6
1964	32.4	25.5	23.4	15.7	5.3
1965	31.8	25.5	22.9	15.4	5.3
1966	32.7	26.2	23.7	15.6	5.3
1967	34.8	26.5	25.0	16.1	6.0
1968	35.2	28.1	24.9	16.0	6.4
1969	33.6	28.1	23.6	15.5	6.3
1970	35.1	27.0	23.6	16.0	7.2
1971	35.2	26.4	23.1	16.0	7.9
1972	34.8	27.5	22.5	15.9	8.0
1973	33.8	27.7	21.4	15.5	8.1
1974	35.2	28.2	22.2	16.4	8.8
1975	37.2	26.5	22.7	17.1	10.1
1976	35.8	27.3	21.6	16.4	9.8
1977	34.7	27.6	20.9	15.9	9.4
1978	33.8	27.7	20.3	15.5	8.9
1979	33.6	28.0	20.0	15.3	9.0
1980	35.5	28.2	20.6	15.7	9.8
1981	35.7	28.9	20.4	15.3	9.9
1982	37.9	28.4	21.2	15.7	10.6
1983	37.8	27.7	21.0	15.6	10.5
1984	36.6	27.8	20.4	15.1	9.8
1985	37.1	28.2	20.9	15.6	9.7
1986	37.5	28.4	21.2	15.9	9.7
1987	37.2	29.1	21.2	15.8	9.5
1988	36.3	28.9	20.5	15.3	9.4
1989	36.2	29.0	20.4	15.3	9.5
1990	36.9	28.9	20.7	15.8	9.9
1991	37.7	28.8	21.0	16.0	10.2
1992	38.4	28.5	20.6	15.9	11.6
1993	37.7	28.6	19.9	15.5	11.7
1994	36.5	28.9	19.2	15.2	11.5
1995	36.5	29.2	18.9	15.2	11.5
1996	35.7	29.7	18.5	14.9	11.5
1997	34.6	30.0	18.1	14.7	11.1
1998	33.6	30.4	17.8	14.6	10.8
1999	33.1	30.4	17.9	14.7	10.5
2000	32.6	30.8	17.8	14.8	10.4
2001	33.7	29.7	18.4	15.4	11.0
2002	34.6	27.3	19.1	15.8	11.6
2003	35.0	26.7	19.3	15.7	11.8
2004	34.7	26.8	19.2	15.6	11.7
2005	34.7	28.2	19.0	15.4	11.7
2006	34.8	29.1	19.1	15.5	11.8
2007	35.5	29.2	19.3	15.7	12.1
2008	37.2	27.7	20.4	16.4	13.0
2009	40.6	25.8	21.4	17.2	15.1
2010	40.8	26.1	21.2	16.9	15.4
2011	39.7	26.3	20.3	16.1	15.0
2012	38.4	26.4	19.5	15.5	14.7

Source: http://www.bea.gov

[1]There are some differences across reporting agencies with regard to accounting procedures and the treatment of government enterprises. This results in some differences in statistical measures of the size of government.

Section 6

Year	Top 1	Top 5	Top 10	Next 40	Bottom 50
1980	19.1	36.8	49.3	43.7	7.0
1981	17.6	35.1	48.0	44.6	7.5
1982	19.0	36.1	48.6	44.1	7.3
1983	20.3	37.3	49.7	43.1	7.2
1984	21.1	38.0	50.6	42.1	7.4
1985	21.8	38.8	51.5	41.4	7.2
1986	25.7	42.6	54.7	38.9	6.5
1987	24.8	43.3	55.6	38.3	6.1
1988	27.6	45.6	57.3	37.0	5.7
1989	25.2	43.9	55.8	38.4	5.8
1990	25.1	43.6	55.4	38.8	5.8
1991	24.8	43.4	55.8	38.7	5.5
1992	27.5	45.9	58.0	36.9	5.1
1993	29.0	47.4	59.2	36.0	4.8
1994	28.9	47.5	59.4	35.8	4.8
1995	30.3	48.9	60.7	34.6	4.6
1996	32.3	51.0	62.5	33.2	4.3
1997	33.2	51.9	63.2	32.5	4.3
1998	34.8	53.8	65.0	30.8	4.2
1999	36.2	55.5	66.5	29.5	4.0
2000	37.4	56.5	67.3	28.8	3.9
2001	33.9	53.3	64.9	31.1	4.0
2002	33.7	53.8	65.7	30.8	3.5
2003	34.3	54.4	65.8	30.7	3.5
2004	36.9	57.1	68.2	28.5	3.3
2005	39.4	59.7	70.3	26.6	3.1
2006	39.9	60.1	70.8	26.2	3.0
2007	40.4	60.6	71.2	25.9	2.9
2008	38.0	58.7	70.0	27.3	2.7
2009	36.7	58.7	70.5	27.3	2.3

APPENDIX B

Answers to Selected Critical Analysis Questions

CHAPTER 1: THE ECONOMIC APPROACH

4. For most taxpayers, the change will reduce the after-tax cost of raising children. Other things being constant, one would predict an increase in the birthrate.

5. False. Intentions do not change the effect of the policy. If the policy runs counter to sound economics, it will lead to a counterproductive outcome even if that was not the intention of the policy. Bad policies are often advocated by people with good intentions.

8. Money has nothing to do with whether an individual is economizing. Any time a person chooses, in an attempt to achieve a goal, he or she is economizing.

9. Positive economics can help one better understand the likely effects of alternative policies. This will help one choose alternatives that are less likely to lead to disappointing results.

10. Association is not causation. It is likely that a large lead, near the end of the game, caused the third team to play more, rather than the third team causing the lead.

14. This is a question that highlights the importance of marginal analysis. In responding to the question, think about the following. After pollution has already been reduced substantially, how much will it cost to reduce it still more? If the quality of air and water were already high, how much gain would result from still less pollution?

CHAPTER 2: SOME TOOLS OF THE ECONOMIST

2. This is an opportunity cost question. Even though the productivity of brush painters has changed only slightly, rising productivity in other areas has led to higher wages in other occupations, thereby increasing the opportunity cost of being a house painter. Because people would not supply house-painting services unless they were able to meet their opportunity costs, higher wages are necessary to attract house painters from competitive (alternative) lines of work.

8. Yes. This question highlights the incentive of individuals to conserve for the future when they have private ownership rights. The market value of the land will increase in anticipation of the future harvest as the trees grow and the expected day of harvest grows closer. Thus, with transferable private property, the tree farmer will be able to capture the value added by his planting and holding the trees for a few years, even if the actual harvest does not take place until well after his death.

9. In general, it sanctions all forms of competition except for the use of violence (or the threat of violence), theft, or fraud.

12. Those who get tickets at the lower price gain, whereas those who are prevented from offering a higher price to ticket holders may not get a ticket even though both the prospective buyer and some ticket holders would have gained from the exchange at the higher price. Ticket holders may simply break the law or may sell at the regulated price only to buyers willing to provide them with other favors. Price controls, if they are effective, always reduce the gains from trade.

17. The opportunity cost of those individuals will rise, and they will likely consume less leisure.

CHAPTER 3: SUPPLY, DEMAND, AND THE MARKET PROCESS

1. Choices (a) and (b) would increase the demand for beef; (c) and (d) would affect primarily the supply of beef, rather than the demand; (e) leads to a change in quantity demanded, not a change in demand.

4. Prices reflect marginal value, not total value. The marginal value of a good is the maximum amount a consumer would be willing to pay for a specific unit. The height of the

demand curve reflects the value that consumers place on each unit. The total value is the total benefit consumers derive from all units consumed. The area under the demand curve for the number of units consumed reflects the total value. Water provides an example of a good with high total value but low marginal value. With regard to the last question, are there more nurses or professional wrestlers?

8. Neither markets nor the political process leaves the determination of winners and losers to chance. Under market organization, business winners and losers are determined by the decentralized choices of millions of consumers who use their dollar votes to reward firms that provide preferred goods at a low cost and penalize others who fail to do so. Under political decision-making, the winners and losers are determined by political officials who use taxes, subsidies, regulations, and mandates to favor some businesses and penalize others.

10. **a.** Profitable production increases the value of resources owned by people and leads to mutual gain for resource suppliers, consumers, and entrepreneurs. **b.** Losses reduce the value of resources, which reduces the well-being of at least some people. There is no conflict.

12. The supply curve is constructed under the assumption that other things are held constant. A reduction in the supply of oranges such as would occur under adverse weather conditions would lead to both a higher price and smaller total quantity supplied. This is perfectly consistent with economic theory.

CHAPTER 4: SUPPLY AND DEMAND: APPLICATIONS AND EXTENSIONS

1. An increase in demand for housing will also increase the demand for the resources required for its production, including the services of carpenters, plumbers, and electricians. This will lead to higher wages and an increase in employment for people in these groups.

4. Agreement of both buyer and seller is required for an exchange. Price ceilings push prices below equilibrium and thereby reduce the quantity sellers are willing to offer. Price floors push prices above equilibrium and thereby reduce the quantity consumers wish to buy. Both decrease the actual quantity traded in the market.

6. **a.** Decreases; **b.** Increases; **c.** Decreases; **d.** Increases

11. The deadweight loss is the loss of the potential gains of buyers and sellers emanating from trades that are squeezed out by the tax. It is an excess burden because even though the exchanges that are squeezed out by the tax impose a cost on buyers and sellers, they do not generate tax revenue (because the trades do not take place).

12. The employment level of low-skilled workers with large families would decline. Some would attempt to conceal the presence of their large family in order to get a job.

14. No. As the tax rate approaches the revenue maximum point, the higher rates substantially reduce the number of trades that take place. This is why the higher rates do not raise much additional revenue. As rates increase toward the revenue maximum point, the lost gains from trade are large and the additions to revenue are small. Thus, rates in this range are highly inefficient.

CHAPTER 5: DIFFICULT CASES FOR THE MARKET, AND THE ROLE OF GOVERNMENT

1. When payment is not demanded for services, potential customers have a strong incentive to attempt a "free ride." However, when the number of nonpaying customers becomes such that the sales revenues of sellers are diminished (and in some cases eliminated), the sellers' incentive to supply the good is thereby reduced (or eliminated).

9. By reducing output below the efficient level, sellers of toasters would no longer pro- duce or exchange some units of the good, despite the fact that the consumers value the marginal units more than it costs to produce them.

11. A public good reflects the characteristics of the good, not the sector in which it is provided. Elementary education is not a public good because it is relatively easy to exclude nonpaying customers and to establish a one-to-one link between payment for and receipt of the good.

CHAPTER 6: THE ECONOMICS OF COLLECTIVE DECISION-MAKING

2. Corporate officers, although they surely care about the next few months and the profits dur- ing that time, also care about the value of the firm and its stock price. If the stock price rises sufficiently in the next few months—as it will if investors believe that current investments in future-oriented projects (planting new trees, for example) are sound—then the officers will find their jobs secure even if current profits do not look good. Rights to the profits from those (future) trees are salable now in the form of the corporation's stock. There is no such mechanism to make the distant fruits of today's investments available to the political entrepreneurs who might otherwise fight for the future-oriented project. Only if the project appeals to today's voters, and only if they are willing to pay today for tomorrow's benefits, will the program be a political success. In any case, the wealth of the political official is not directly enhanced by his or her successful fight for the project.

4. The problem is not so much that the "wrong guys" won the last election as it is the incentive structure confronted by political decision-makers. Even if the "right people" were elected, they would be unlikely to improve the efficiency of government, at least not very much, given the strong incentive to support special-interest and shortsighted policies and the weak incentives for operational efficiency when decisions are made by the political process.

8. It is difficult for the voter to know what a candidate will do once elected, and the rationally ignorant voter is usually unwilling to spend the time and effort required to understand issues because the probability that any single vote will decide the issue is exceedingly small. Special-interest voters, in contrast, will know which candidate has promised them the most on their issue. Also, the candidate who is both competent and prepared to ignore special interests will have a hard time getting these facts to voters without financial support from special-interest groups. Each voter has an incentive to be a "free rider" on the "good government" issue. Interestingly, controlling govern- ment on behalf of society as a whole is a public good. As in the case of other public goods, there is a tendency for too little of it to be supplied.

10. No. The government is merely an alternative form of organization. Government organization does not permit us to escape either scarcity or competition. It merely affects the nature of the competi- tion. Political competition (for example, voting, lobbying, political contributions, and politically determined budgets) replaces market competition. Neither is there any reason to believe that gov- ernment organization modifies the importance of personal self-interest.

12. When the welfare of a special-interest group conflicts with that of a widely dispersed, unorganized majority, the legislative political process can reasonably be expected to work to the benefit of the special interest.

CHAPTER 7: TAKING THE NATION'S ECONOMIC PULSE

1. Choices (a), (c), (f), (g), and (h) will exert no effect on GDP; (b) and (d) will increase GDP by the amount of the expenditure; and (e) will increase GDP by $250 (the com- mission on the transaction).

3. Because the furniture was produced last year, the sale does not affect GDP this year. It reduces inventory investment by $100,000 and increases consumption by $100,000, leaving GDP unchanged.

7. $8.31
9. **a.** $1,000; **b.** $600; **c.** $200; **d.** 0; **e.** $20,000
11. **a.** False. Inventory investment indicates whether the holdings of unsold goods are rising or falling. A negative inventory investment merely indicates that there was a reduction in the size of inventories during the period. **b.** False. If gross investment is less than the depreciation of capital goods during the period, net investment would be negative. Net investment in the United States was negative for several years during the Great Depression of the 1930s. **c.** Not necessarily. Rather, it may be the result of an increase in prices, population, or hours worked.
12. Neither the receipts nor the expenditures on payouts would count toward GDP because they are merely transfers—they do not involve production. However, expenditures on operations, administration, and government-provided goods and services from lottery proceeds would add to GDP.
16. **a.** $2,30.1 billion; **b.** $4,272.8 billion; **c.** 47.8; **d.** $5,800.5 billion; **e.** 88.6; **f.** $12,638.4 billion; **g.** $13,591.7 billion

CHAPTER 8: ECONOMIC FLUCTUATIONS, UNEMPLOYMENT, AND INFLATION

2. Job seekers do not know which employers will offer them the more attractive jobs. They find out by searching. Job search is "profitable" and consistent with economic efficiency as long as the marginal gain from search exceeds the marginal cost of searching. The job search process will lead to a better match between the skills of employees and the requirements of the available jobs.
3. Individuals (e) and (f) would be classified as employed; (a), (b), and (c) would be classified as unemployed; (d) is not in the labor force.
6. When the actual unemployment rate is equal to the natural rate of unemployment, cyclical unemployment is absent and potential GDP is at its sustainable rate.
7. **a.** 60 percent; **b.** 8.3 percent; **c.** 55 percent
8. No. It means that there were no jobs available at wage rates acceptable to the potential workers who were unemployed. Thus, they continued to search for more attractive opportunities.
13. The wages people earn are also prices (prices for labor services) and, like other prices, they usually rise as the general level of prices increases. The statement ignores this factor. It implicitly assumes that money wages are unaffected by inflation—that they would have increased by the same amount (6 percent) even if prices would have been stable. Generally, this will not be the case.

CHAPTER 9: AN INTRODUCTION TO BASIC MACROECONOMIC MARKETS

4. When the price level is higher than anticipated, real wages will decline and employment expands. Profit rates will be higher than normal, and the actual rate of unemployment will fall below the natural rate. The abnormally high rate of output will not be sustainable, because the real wage rates will rise when the long-term contracts expire and are renegotiated.
6. An increase in the real interest rate will make it more attractive for foreigners to purchase bonds and make other investments in the United States. As a result, there will be an increase in the inflow of capital from abroad.
10. They are all equal.
12. $10,000; $20,000
15. **a.** 5,700; **b.** No, because the actual price level will be 110, higher than what was

anticipated. **c.** Actual unemployment will be less than the natural rate because the un-expected high level of prices will improve profit margins, reduce real wage rates, and cause the firms to expand output in the short run.

CHAPTER 10: DYNAMIC CHANGE, ECONOMIC FLUCTUATIONS, AND THE *AD–AS* MODEL

1. Choice (a) would decrease *AD*; (b), (c), and (d) would increase it; and (e) would leave it unchanged. For the "why" part of the question, see the Factors That Shift Aggregate Demand section at the beginning of the chapter.
2. Choices (a), (b), (c), and (d) will reduce *SRAS*; (e) will increase it.
8. Tightness in resource markets will result in rising resource prices relative to product prices, causing the *SRAS* to shift to the left. Profit margins will decline, output rates will fall, and long-run equilibrium will be restored at a higher price level. The above-normal output cannot be maintained because it reflects input prices that people would not have agreed to and output decisions they would not have chosen if they had antici-pated the current price level (and rate of inflation). Once they have a chance to correct these mistakes, they do so; output returns to the economy's long-run potential.

CHAPTER 11: FISCAL POLICY: THE KEYNESIAN VIEW AND HISTORICAL PERSPECTIVE

3. The multiplier principle is the concept that a change in one of the components of ag-gregate demand—investment, for example—will lead to a far greater change in the equilibrium level of income. Because the multiplier equals $1/(1 - MPC)$, its size is de-termined by the marginal propensity to consume. The multiplier makes stabilizing the economy more difficult, because relatively small changes in aggregate demand have a much greater effect on equilibrium income.
6. Either an increase in government expenditures or a reduction in taxes should be em-ployed to shift the budget toward a larger deficit (or smaller surplus).

CHAPTER 12: FISCAL POLICY, INCENTIVES, AND SECONDARY EFFECTS

2. The crowding-out effect is the theory that budget deficits will lead to higher real interest rates, which retard private spending. The crowding-out effect indicates that fiscal policy will not be nearly as potent as the simple Keynesian model implies. The new classical theory indicates that anticipation of higher future taxes (rather than higher interest rates) will reduce private spending when government expenditures are financed by debt.
10. In the Keynesian model, investment is determined by factors other than the interest rate. Thus, budget deficits would not exert much effect on capital formation. In the crowding-out model, capital formation would be reduced because the budget deficits would lead to higher interest rates, which would crowd out private investment. In the new classical model, households will save more, and, as a result, budget deficits could be financed without either an increase in the interest rate or a reduction in capital formation.
13. Yes. Only the lower rates would increase the incentive to earn marginal income and thereby stimulate aggregate supply.
15. No. If it takes more workers to generate a specific amount of energy with wind power, this implies that wind power is a more costly method of generating energy than either coal or natural gas. Thus, the implications of the statement are exactly the opposite of what the wind energy proponents imply.

CHAPTER 13: MONEY AND THE BANKING SYSTEM

1. A liquid asset is one that can easily and quickly be transformed into money without experiencing a loss of its market value. Assets such as high-grade bonds and stocks are highly liquid. In contrast, illiquid assets cannot be easily and quickly converted to cash without some loss of their value. Real estate, a family-owned business, business equipment, and artistic works are examples of illiquid assets.

3. Money is valuable because of its scarcity relative to the availability of goods and services. The use of money facilitates (reduces the cost of) exchange transactions. Money also serves as a store of value and a unit of account. Doubling the supply of money while holding output constant would simply cause its purchasing power to fall without enhancing the services that it performs. In fact, fluctuations in the money supply generally create uncertainty about the future value of money and thereby reduce its ability to serve as a reliable store of value, accurate unit of account, and medium of exchange for time-dimension contracting.

6. **a.** There is no change; currency held by the public increases, but checking deposits decrease by an equal amount. **b.** Bank reserves decrease by $100. **c.** Excess reserves decrease by $100, minus $100 multiplied by the required reserve ratio.

8. Answers (b), (e), and (f) will reduce the money supply; (a) and (c) will increase it. If the Treasury's deposits (or the deposits of people who receive portions of the Treasury's spending) are considered part of the money supply, then (d) will leave the money supply unchanged.

10. Whereas the transformation of deposits into currency does not directly affect the money supply, it does reduce the excess reserves of banks. The reduction in excess reserves will cause banks to reduce their outstanding loans and thereby shrink the money supply. Therefore, an increase in the holding of currency relative to deposits will tend to reduce the supply of money.

12. There are two major reasons. First, the money supply can be altered quietly via open market operations, whereas a reserve requirement change focuses attention on Fed policy. Second, open market operations are a fine-tuning method, whereas a reserve requirement change is a blunt instrument. Generally, the Fed prefers quiet, marginal changes to headline-grabbing, blunt changes that are more likely to disrupt markets.

16. **a.** Money supply increases by $100,000; **b.** $80,000; **c.** $500,000; **d.** no; there will be some leakage in the form of additional currency holdings by the public and additional excess reserve holdings by banks.

18. **a.** Money supply will increase by $2 billion; **b.** $1.8 billion; **c.** $20 billion.

CHAPTER 14: MODERN MACROECONOMICS AND MONETARY POLICY

2. Choices (a) and (c) would increase your incentive to hold money deposits; (b) and (d) would reduce your incentive to hold money.

3. **a.** The cost of obtaining the house is $100,000. **b.** The cost of holding it is the interest forgone on the $100,000 sales value of the house. **c.** The cost of obtaining $1,000 is the amount of goods one must give up in order to acquire the $1,000. For example, if a pound of sugar sells for 50 cents, the cost of obtaining $1,000 in terms of sugar is 2,000 pounds. **d.** As in the case of the house, the cost of holding $1,000 is the interest forgone.

7. **a.** Bank reserves will decline; **b.** Real interest rates will rise; **c.** Spending on consumer durables will fall; **d.** The dollar will appreciate because the higher interest rates will attract bond purchases by foreigners; **e.** Exports will decline because the appreciation of the dollar will make U.S. goods more expensive for foreigners; **f.** The higher real interest rates will tend to reduce real asset prices; **g.** Real GDP will fall.

10. If the time lag is long and variable (rather than short and highly predictable), it is less likely that policy makers will be able to time changes in monetary policy so that they

will exert a countercyclical effect on the economy. The policy makers will be more likely to make mistakes and thereby exert a destabilizing influence.

11. Association does not reveal causation. Decision-makers, including borrowers and lenders, will eventually anticipate a high rate of inflation and adjust their choices accordingly. As the expected rate of inflation increases, the demand for loanable funds will increase and the supply will decrease. This will lead to higher nominal interest rates. Thus, economic theory indicates that the causation tends to run the opposite direction from that indicated by the statement.

CHAPTER 15: STABILIZATION POLICY, OUTPUT, AND EMPLOYMENT

2. Compared with earlier periods, the United States has experienced less economic instability since 1960. This has been particularly true during the past twenty-five years. An increase in the stability of monetary policy deserves much of the credit for the more stable economic conditions of recent decades.

5. For (a) and (b), the actual and natural rates of unemployment will be equal. For (c), the actual rate will be less than the natural rate. For (d), the actual rate will exceed the natural rate.

11. **a.** Keep the inflation rate at a low and highly predictable level; **b.** No; **c.** Both nominal interest rates and the general level of prices will rise.

CHAPTER 16: CREATING AN ENVIRONMENT FOR GROWTH AND PROSPERITY

3. If poor countries follow sound policies and provide an attractive economic environment, foreigners will be willing to supply investment funds. Propelled by foreign investment, some poor countries have achieved exceedingly high rates of both investment and growth during recent decades.

8. When considering the answer to this question, think about the following: Is there an opportunity cost of the capital used by government firms? Do government firms have a strong incentive to keep costs low? Are government firms innovative?

12. The increase in diversity provides consumers with more options and thereby improves their welfare. For the most part, the GDP figures fail to capture the impact of this factor.

13. Regulations such as price ceilings, price floors, and mandated product characteristics will generally reduce the volume of gains from trade. Simultaneously, they will encourage rent-seeking activities, which will increase the contributions available to political officials.

CHAPTER 17: INSTITUTIONS, POLICIES, AND CROSS-COUNTRY DIFFERENCES IN INCOME AND GROWTH

6. Gains from trade, technological improvements, discovery of high value products (relative to cost) and lower-cost production methods, and capital formation are the major sources of economic growth. Institutions that protect property rights, enforce contracts in an even-handed manner, and promote open markets are crucial to the realization of the gains from the key sources of growth. Countries that adopt sound institutions and policies grow, while those that fail to do so stagnate.

8. It is hard to see how the less-developed economies could have grown so rapidly without borrowing technologies and ideas from the high-income countries. The high-income countries also provided both investment capital and markets for the sale of products for the LDCs. Historical growth records buttress this view. The per capita incomes of several economies including Hong Kong, Singapore, South Korea, and China have

grown at annual rates of 5 percent or more over periods of twenty-five years or more. Prior to 1960, no country was able to achieve long-term growth anywhere near such a rate. By way of comparison, per capita income in the United Kingdom and the United States grew at an annual rate of approximately 1 percent during the nineteenth century when countries with significantly higher incomes were absent.

10. A country does not have to be democratic in order to be economically free. Hong Kong illustrates this point. Neither does democracy guarantee economic freedom. India was democratic, but it was one of the world's least free economies prior to 1990.

12. Quality of the legal system: Does it protect property rights and enforce contracts fairly; tax rates; freedom to trade with others; onerous regulations, to list a few of the factors.

13. Poor economic institutions and policies provide the primary reason.

14. Because citizens can move elsewhere at a low cost. When significant numbers vote with their feet by leaving an area, the tax base will erode, and this confronts politicians with an incentive to change their ways.

CHAPTER 18: GAINING FROM INTERNATIONAL TRADE

2. Availability of goods and services, not jobs, is the source of economic prosperity. When a good can be purchased cheaper abroad than it can be produced at home, a nation can expand the quantity of goods and services available for consumption by specializing in the production of those goods for which it is a low-cost producer and trading them for the cheap (relative to domestic costs) foreign goods. Trade restrictions limiting the ability of Americans to purchase low-cost goods from foreigners stifle this process and thereby reduce the living standard of Americans.

4. Statements (a) and (b) are not in conflict. Because trade restrictions are typically a special-interest issue, political entrepreneurs can often gain by supporting them even when they promote economic inefficiency.

6. True. The primary effect of trade restrictions is an increase in domestic scarcity. This has distributional consequences, but it is clear that, as a whole, a nation will be harmed by the increased domestic scarcity that accompanies the trade restraints.

10. In thinking about this issue, consider the following points. Suppose that the Japanese were willing to give products such as automobiles, electronic goods, and clothing to us free of charge. Would we be worse off if we accepted the gifts? Should we try to keep the free goods out? What is the source of real income—jobs or goods and services? If the gifts make us better off, doesn't it follow that partial gifts would also make us better off?

12. Although trade reduces employment in import-competing industries, it expands employment in export industries. On balance, there is no reason to believe that trade either promotes or destroys jobs. The major effect of trade is to permit individuals, states, regions, and nations to generate a larger output by specializing in the things they do well and trading for those things that they would produce only at a high cost. A higher real income is the result.

16. True. If country A imposes a tariff, other countries will sell less to A and therefore acquire less purchasing power in terms of A's currency. Thus, they will have to reduce their purchases of A's export goods.

CHAPTER 19: INTERNATIONAL FINANCE AND THE FOREIGN EXCHANGE MARKET

4. On February 2, the dollar appreciated against the British pound and depreciated against the Canadian dollar.

5. Scenarios (a) and (g) would cause the dollar to appreciate; (b), (c), (d), (e), and (h) would cause the dollar to depreciate; (f) would leave the exchange rate unchanged.

8. Some people fear that foreign investment makes the United States vulnerable because foreigners might decide to sell their assets and leave suddenly. When you consider this argument, it is important to recognize that foreign and domestic investors are influenced by pretty much the same considerations. Anything that would cause foreigners to withdraw funds would also cause domestic investors to do likewise. In fact, the vulnerability runs the other way. If foreign investors were to leave, the assets financed by their funds would remain. Thus, they would be in a weak position to impose harm on the U.S. economy.

9. Each of the changes would reduce the size of the current-account deficit.

13. False. Flexible exchange rates bring the sum of the current and capital accounts into balance, but they do not necessarily lead to balance for either component.

14. **a.** No. The exchange rate will bring the overall purchases and sales into balance, but there is no reason to expect the imports and exports to any given country to be in balance. **b.** The United States imports large quantities of goods Japan and China produce at a low cost (for example, electronic products, and labor intensive goods like toys and textiles), but it is not a major exporter of goods purchased intensively by these countries (natural resources, building materials, and inexpensive consumer items).

15. These purchases increase the foreign exchange value of the dollar, which makes imports cheaper relative to exports and thereby enlarges the trade deficit. Politicians often charge that this reduces output and employment. However, the bond purchases are an inflow of capital that will also result in lower U.S. interest rates, which will tend to stimulate output and employment. Thus, there is little reason to believe that the net effect will be either substantial or harmful.

CHAPTER 20: CONSUMER CHOICE AND ELASTICITY

2. If your opportunity cost of time is more than $15, it will make sense to take the plane. Thus, Kathy will take the bus and Rachel the plane.

3. It is likely that the income effect of cigarette price changes is much larger for low-income smokers than for high-income smokers, perhaps because expenditures on cigarettes are a larger proportion of the household budget for those with lower incomes. Thus, the income effect will be larger for this group.

6. Both income and time constrain our ability to consume. Because, in a wealthier society, time becomes more binding and income less binding, time-saving actions will be more common in a wealthier society. As we engage in time-saving actions (fast food, automatic appliances, air travel, and so on) in order to shift the time restraint outward, our lives become more hectic.

10. The answer to the first question is "No." Even for things we like, we will experience diminishing returns. Eventually, the cost of additional units of pizza will exceed their benefits. And, in answer to the second question, perfection in any activity is generally not worth the cost. For example, reading every page of this text three, four, or five times may improve your grade, but it may not be worth it. One function of a text is to structure the material (highlighted points, layout of graphs, and so on) so that the reader will be able to learn quickly (at a lower cost).

11. Carole

12. **a.** −0.33; inelastic **b.** −1.67 elastic

CHAPTER 21: COSTS AND THE SUPPLY OF GOODS

2. **a.** The amount paid for the course is a sunk cost. It is not directly relevant to whether one should attend the lectures. **b.** There is an opportunity cost of one's house even if it is paid for. **c.** The decline in the price of the stock is a sunk cost and therefore it is not

directly relevant to whether or not to sell at this time. **d.** There is an opportunity cost of public education even if it is provided free to the consumer.

5. True. If it could produce the output at a lower cost, its profit would be greater.

7. At low output, the firm's plant (a fixed cost) is underutilized, implying a high average cost. As output rises toward the designed output level, average cost falls, but then rises as the designed or optimal output for that size plant is surpassed and diminishing returns set in.

11. Because owners receive profits, clearly profit maximization is in their interest. Managers, if they are not owners, have no property right to profit and therefore no direct interest in profit maximization. Because a solid record of profitability tends to increase the market value (salary) of corporate managers, they do have an indirect incentive to pursue profits. However, corporate managers may also be interested in gaining power, having nice offices, hiring friends, expanding sales, and other activities, which may conflict with profitability. Thus, owners need to provide incentives for managers to seek profits and to monitor the results.

12. **a.** The interest payments; **b.** The interest income forgone. The tax structure encourages debt rather than equity financing because the firm's tax liability is inversely related to its debt–equity ratio.

14. Check list. Did your marginal cost curve cross the *ATC* and *AVC* curves at their low points? Does the vertical distance between the *ATC* and *AVC* curves get smaller and smaller as output increases? If not, redraw the three curves correctly. See Exhibit 6b.

17. $2,500: the $2,000 decline in market value during the year plus $500 of potential interest on funds that could be obtained if the machine were sold new. Costs associated with the decline in the value of the machine last year are sunk costs.

18. Because they believe they will be able to restructure the firm and provide better management so that the firm will have positive net earnings in the future. If the firm is purchased at a low enough price, this will allow the new owners to cover the opportunity cost of their investment and still earn an economic profit. Alternatively, they may expect to sell off the firm's assets, receiving more net revenue than the cost of purchasing the firm.

CHAPTER 22: PRICE TAKERS AND THE COMPETITIVE PROCESS

1. In a highly competitive industry such as agriculture, lower resource prices might improve the rate of profit in the short run, but in the long run, competition will drive prices down until economic profit is eliminated. Thus, lower resource prices will do little to improve the long-run profitability in such industries.

2. The market price will decline because the profits will attract new firms (and capital investment) into the market and supply will increase, driving down the price until the profits are eliminated.

5. **a.** Increase; **b.** Increase; **c.** Increase: firms will earn economic profit; **d.** Rise (compared with its initial level) if coffee is an increasing-cost industry, but return to initial price if it is a constant-cost industry; **e.** Increase even more than it did in the short run; **f.** Economic profit will return to zero.

6. **a.** Decline; **b.** Increase; **c.** Decline; **d.** Decline

9. Competition virtually forces firms to operate efficiently and produce goods and services that consumers value highly relative to cost. Firms that fail to do so will find it difficult to compete and eventually losses will drive them from the market.

11. **a.** The reduction in supply led to higher prices. **b.** Because demand is inelastic, the total revenue from sales increased. **c.** Overall, the profitability of farming increased, although some of the producers that were hardest hit by the drought experienced losses because of their sharp reduction in output.

15. **b.** Six or seven tons—$250 profit; **c.** seven or eight tons—$600 profit; **d.** five or six tons—$50 loss. Because the firm can cover its variable cost, it should stay in business if it believes that the low ($450) price is temporary.

CHAPTER 23: PRICE-SEARCHER MARKETS WITH LOW ENTRY BARRIERS

3. The amount of variety is determined by the willingness of consumers to pay for variety relative to the cost of providing it. If consumers value variety highly and the added costs of producing different styles, designs, and sizes is low, there will be a lot of variety. Alternatively, if consumers desire similar products, or if variation can be produced only at a high cost, little variety will be present. Apparently, consumers place a substantial value (relative to cost) on variety in napkins but not in toothpicks.

7. No. A firm that maximizes *total* revenue would expand output as long as marginal revenue is positive. When marginal costs are positive, the revenue-maximizing price would be lower (and the output greater) than the price that would maximize the firm's profits.

8. In any of these cases, the answer is competition. To survive, a given type and size of firm must be able to produce at a low cost. Those firms with high per-unit cost will be driven from the market.

10. Building the new resort is more risky (and less attractive) because if the market analysis is incorrect, and demand is insufficient, it probably will be difficult to find other uses for the newly built resort. If the airline proves unprofitable, however, the capital (airplanes) should be extremely mobile. However, the resort would have one offsetting advantage: If demand were stronger than expected, and profits larger, it would take competitors longer to enter the market (build a new resort), and they would be more reluctant to make the more permanent investment.

12. In a competitive setting, only the big firms will survive if economies of scale are important. When economies of scale are unimportant, small firms will be able to compete effectively.

14. Competition provides the answer. If McDonald's fails to provide an attractively priced, tasty sandwich with a smile, people will turn to Burger King, Wendy's, Dairy Queen, and other rivals. If Walmart does not provide convenience and value, people will turn to Kmart, Target, and other retailers. Similarly, as recent experience has shown, even a firm as large as General Motors will lose customers to Ford, Honda, Toyota, Chrysler, Volkswagen, and other automobile manufacturers if it fails to please the customer as much as rival suppliers do.

17. **a.** Total revenue: $0; $8,000; $14,000; $18,000; $20,000; $20,000; Total cost: $0; $5,000; $10,000; $15,000; $20,000; $25,000; Economic profit: $0; $3,000; $4,000; $3,000; $0; $5,000 (loss). **b.** Marginal revenue: $8,000; $6,000; $4,000; $2,000; $0; Marginal cost: $5,000; $5,000; $5,000; $5,000; $5,000. **c.** Profit-maximizing price: $7,000. **d.** Rod will sell two boats at the profit-maximizing price of $7,000. **e.** Rod's economic profits will be $4,000 per week. Sales volume will be 2. **f.** Yes, boats 1 and 2 are the only boats for which marginal revenue is higher than marginal cost. **g.** Because of the existence of economic profit, more boat dealers will open up in the area. This will result in more competition and lower prices. The entry will continue until boat dealers' economic profits fall to zero. **h.** When demand is elastic, lowering price increases total revenue; thus, Rod's demand is elastic between the prices of $9,000 and $5,000. When demand is unitary elastic, lowering price leaves revenue unchanged; thus, Rod's demand is unitary elastic between the prices of $5,000 and $4,000. One could also assume that Rod's demand would eventually become inelastic below a price of $4,000 because the elasticity of demand keeps falling as one moves down along a demand curve. When this happens, Rod's total revenue will begin to fall as he contin-

ues to lower price. For example, at a price of $3,000, Rod may sell six boats per week, resulting in only $18,000 in revenue, which is less than the revenue Rod receives at a price of $4,000.

CHAPTER 24: PRICE-SEARCHER MARKETS WITH HIGH ENTRY BARRIERS

1. The statement is true. Profits cannot exist in the long run without barriers to entry because without barriers new entrants seeking the profits would increase supply, drive down price, and eliminate the profits. But barriers to entry are no guarantee of profits. Sufficient demand is also a necessary condition.

3. No; No; No.

8. Because use of product variation and quality improvements to obtain a larger share of the market will be more difficult to monitor and control than a simple price reduction.

11. Reductions in the cost of transportation generally increase competition because they force firms to compete with distant rivals and permit consumers to choose among a wider range of suppliers. As a result, the U.S. economy today is generally more competitive, in the rivalry sense, than it was hundred years ago.

12. The stock price, when the uncle bought the stock, no doubt reflected the well-known profits. The previous owners of the stock surely would not have sold it at a price that failed to reflect its high expected rate of future profit. Thus, there is no reason to believe that the stock purchase will earn a high rate of return for the uncle.

13. **a.** $15, profit = $140,000; **b.** $10.

CHAPTER 25: THE SUPPLY OF AND DEMAND FOR PRODUCTIVE RESOURCES

3. **a.** Five; **b.** $350; **c.** Four. The firm will operate in the short run, but it will go out of business in the long run unless the market prices rise.

4. Yes. General increases in the productivity of the labor force will cause a general increase in wages. The higher general wage rates will increase the opportunity cost of barbering and cause the supply of barbers to decline. The reduction in the supply of barbers will place upward pressure on the wages of barbers, even if technological change and worker productivity have changed little in barbering.

6. The job opportunities outside of teaching are more attractive for people with math and science training than for those with English and history degrees. Therefore, the same salary that attracts a substantial number of English and history teachers will be insufficient to attract the required number of math and science teachers.

8. No. The dressmaker needs to employ more capital and less labor because the marginal dollar expenditures on the former are currently increasing output by a larger amount than the latter.

12. **a.** MP 14; 12; 11; 9; 7; 5; 4. TR 70; 130; 185; 230; 265; 290; 310. MRP 70; 60; 55; 45; 35; 25; 20. **b.** 4; **c.** Employment would decline to 3.

CHAPTER 26: EARNINGS, PRODUCTIVITY, AND THE JOB MARKET

2. U.S. workers are more productive. By investing in human capital, the laborers are somewhat responsible, but the superior tools and physical capital that are available to U.S. workers also contribute to their higher wages.

6. Although this statement, often made by politicians, sounds true, in fact, it is false. Output of goods and services valued by consumers, not jobs, is the key to economic progress and a high standard of living. Real income cannot be high unless real output is high. If job creation were the key to economic progress, it would be easy to create millions of jobs. For example, we could prohibit the use of farm machinery. Such a prohibition would create millions of jobs in agriculture. However, it would also reduce output and our standard of living.

9. False. Several additional factors, including differences in preferences (which would influence time worked, the trade-off between money wage and working conditions, and evaluation of alternative jobs), differences in jobs, and imperfect labor mobility, would result in variations in earnings.

11. Hourly wages will be highest in B because the higher wages will be necessary to compensate workers in B for the uncertainty and loss of income during layoffs. Annual earnings will be higher in A in order to compensate workers in A for the additional hours they will work during the year.

CHAPTER 27: INVESTMENT, THE CAPITAL MARKET, AND THE WEALTH OF NATIONS

1. All the changes would increase interest rates in the United States.

4. No. The average outstanding balance during the year is only about half of $1,000. Therefore, the $200 interest charge translates to almost a 40 percent annual rate of interest.

6. *Hints:* Which has been considered to be more risky—purchasing a bond or a stock? How does risk influence the expected rate of return?

8. 6 percent.

10. **a.** Mike; **b.** Yes, people who save a lot are able to get a higher interest rate on their savings as the result of people with a high rate of time preference; **c.** Yes, people who want to borrow money will be able to do so at a lower rate when there are more people (like Alicia) who want to save a lot.

11. They are helped. This question is a lot like prior questions involving Alicia and Mike. Potential gains from trade are present. If obstacles do not restrain trade, the low-income countries will be able to attract savings (from countries with a high saving rate) at a lower interest rate than would exist in the absence of trade. Similarly, people in the high-income countries will be able to earn a higher return than would otherwise be possible. Each can gain because of the existence of the other.

12. **a.** Approximately $1.277 million; **b.** Yes; **c.** The lottery earnings are less liquid. Because there is not a well-organized market transforming lottery earnings into present income, the transaction costs of finding a "buyer" (at a price equal to the present value of the earnings) for the lottery earnings "rights" may be higher than for the bond, if one wants to sell in the future.

14. No. The present value of the $500 annual additions to earnings during the next ten years is less than the cost of the schooling.

16. Consider the following when answering this question: Whose money is being invested by each of the two entities? If a private investment project goes bad, who is hurt? If a private project is successful, who reaps the gain? Answer the same two questions for political officials.

CHAPTER 28: INCOME INEQUALITY AND POVERTY

2. Differences in family size, age of potential workers, nonmoney "income," taxes, and cost-of-living among areas reduce the effectiveness of annual money income as a measure of economic status. In general, high-income families are larger, are more likely to be headed by a prime-age worker, have less nonmoney income (including leisure), pay

more taxes, and reside in higher-cost-of-living areas (particularly large cities). Thus, money income comparison between high- and low-income groups often overstates the economic status of the former relative to the latter.

4. If there were no intergenerational mobility, the diagonal numbers would all be 100 percent. If there were complete equality of opportunity and outcomes, the numbers in each column and row would be 20 percent.

6. No. The increase in marginal tax rates will reduce the incentive of the poor to earn income. Therefore, their income will rise by $1,000 minus the reduction in their personal earnings due to the disincentive effects of the higher marginal tax rates.

7. 67 percent

SPECIAL TOPIC 1: GOVERNMENT SPENDING AND TAXATION

1. Taxes reduce economic efficiency because they eliminate some exchanges and thereby reduce the gains from these transactions. Because of (a) the deadweight losses accompanying the elimination of exchanges and (b) the cost of collecting taxes, the costs of additional tax revenue will be greater than the revenue transferred to the government. Studies indicate that it costs between $1.20 and $1.30 for each dollar of tax revenue raised by the government.

5. As we discussed in Chapter 6, the political process works better when there is a close relationship between who pays for and who benefits from government programs. An increase in the number of people who pay no income taxes is likely to weaken this relationship. Whereas those with low incomes pay payroll taxes, the revenues from this tax are earmarked for the finance of the Social Security and Medicare programs. Thus, expansions in government are financed primarily by the personal income tax. In the future, exemption of large numbers of people from this tax is likely to make it more difficult to control the growth of government. If you do not have to help pay for more government spending, why would you oppose it?

SPECIAL TOPIC 2: THE ECONOMICS OF SOCIAL SECURITY

2. The pay-as-you-go Social Security system is facing a crisis because the inflow of tax revenue is insufficient to cover the promised benefits. Although the Social Security Trust Fund has bonds, they are merely an IOU from the Treasury to the Social Security Administration. To redeem these bonds and provide additional funds to finance Social Security benefits, the federal government will have to raise taxes (or pay the interest on additional Treasury bonds it sells), or cut other expenditures, or both. Thus, the presence of the SSTF bonds does not do much to alleviate the crisis.

SPECIAL TOPIC 3: THE STOCK MARKET: ITS FUNCTION, PERFORMANCE, AND POTENTIAL AS AN INVESTMENT OPPORTUNITY

1. History shows that in the U.S. stock market, fairly high returns can be gained at a relatively low risk by people who hold a diverse portfolio of stocks in unrelated industries for a period of twenty years or more. An indexed equity mutual fund is an option that would allow a person to purchase a diverse portfolio while keeping commission costs low.

3. The expectation of high profits in the future drove up the price of the stock, despite the lack of a dividend payment in the first years of the firm. Investors are equally happy

with high dividends or the equivalent in rising stock value due to the firm's retaining its profits for further investment.

5. Investors are buying such a stock for its rising value (price), which reflects expected future earnings and dividends.

SPECIAL TOPIC 4: GREAT DEBATES IN ECONOMICS: KEYNES VERSUS HAYEK

1. Keynes is arguing that it does not matter much how the government spends stimulus funds. According to the Keynesian view, the key consideration is to spend the funds so they will generate income for those undertaking the project, and as those funds are spent, a multiple expansion in income and aggregate demand will result.

SPECIAL TOPIC 5: THE CRISIS OF 2008: CAUSES AND LESSONS FOR THE FUTURE

3. The less equity the owner has in his or her house, the more likely he or she will default. This is particularly true in the United States because most home mortgages here are nonrecourse loans: The owner is not responsible for the debt beyond turning the property over to the lender in case of default. The lender has no legal claim on assets of the borrower beyond the asset that was mortgaged. Thus, when the value of a house falls below the outstanding loan, the borrower will often gain by simply abandoning the property. This is precisely what many have done in recent years.

5. The incentive to evaluate the borrower's creditworthiness carefully is reduced. If the mortgage originator had to keep the loan until it was repaid, there would be greater incentive for the lender to evaluate the creditworthiness of the borrower more diligently.

SPECIAL TOPIC 6: LESSONS FROM THE GREAT DEPRESSION

5. The statement reflects a failure to recognize the secondary effects of limiting imports. If we buy less from foreigners, they will have fewer dollars that are required for the purchase of our exports. Therefore, a reduction in imports will also reduce exports and there is no reason to expect any net increase in employment. Instead, trade restraints lead to less output and lower incomes.

SPECIAL TOPIC 7: THE FEDERAL BUDGET AND THE NATIONAL DEBT

1. No. Both private corporations and governments can, and often do, have continual debt outstanding. Borrowers can continue to finance and refinance debt as long as lenders have confidence in their ability to pay. This will generally be the case as long as the interest liability is small relative to income (or the potential tax base).

3. No. Remember, trade is a positive-sum game. Bonds are sold to foreigners because they are offering a better deal (acceptance of a lower interest rate) than is available elsewhere. Prohibiting the sale of bonds to foreigners would result in higher real interest rates and less investment, both of which would adversely affect Americans.

5. Lower; voters do not enjoy paying taxes and, therefore, voter dissatisfaction places a restraint on higher taxes, which would also restrain expenditures if the budget had to be

balanced. More efficiently, the restraint of tax increases would tighten the budget constraint and make the reality of opportunity cost more visible to both voters and politicians.

SPECIAL TOPIC 8: THE ECONOMICS OF HEALTH CARE

2. Health insurance benefits are a component of the employee's compensation package. Unless the employer values the services of the employee by an amount greater than or equal to the total cost of the employee's compensation, the worker will not be hired. Thus, like other components of the compensation package, health insurance benefits are earned by employees.

4. Medicare and Medicaid increased both total health care spending and the share of that spending paid by a third party. Both of these factors increased the demand for and prices of medical services, thereby making them more expensive for people who do not qualify for these programs.

6. Personal choices exert a major impact on health care expenditures. Individuals who smoke, consume alcohol, and eat excessively; fail to exercise and control their weight; use recreational drugs; and engage in other risky behavior will have higher health care costs. Under systems in which all are charged the same premium, the incentive to adopt a healthy lifestyle is reduced. Persons who make choices that promote good health are forced to subsidize those who do not. This perverse incentive structure also pushes health care costs upward.

8. The incentive to purchase insurance when you are healthy will be reduced.

SPECIAL TOPIC 9: EARNINGS DIFFERENCES BETWEEN MEN AND WOMEN

2. **a.** The average years of work experience of women relative to men would decline because many of the women entering the labor force would have little prior work experience. **b.** The average hours of work of women would also decline because many of the married women would be looking for part-time employment and hours that were complementary with their historic household responsibilities. **c.** The increased labor force participation of married women would cause the female–male earnings ratio to fall.

4. Not necessarily. Compared with married men, single men tend to be younger, have fewer dependents, be more likely to drop out of the labor force, and be less likely to receive earnings-enhancing assistance from another person. All these factors will reduce their earnings relative to married men.

SPECIAL TOPIC 10: DO LABOR UNIONS INCREASE THE WAGES OF WORKERS?

1. If the union is able to raise the wages of the farm workers: (a) The cost of Florida oranges will rise, causing supply to decline and price to rise in the long run; (b) profits of the Florida orange growers will decline in the short run, but in the long run they will return to the normal rate; (c) mechanization will be encouraged; and (d) the employment of fruit pickers will decline—particularly in the long run.

3. If only part of an industry is unionized, if the union pushes up the wages of the unionized firms, this will increase their cost and make it difficult for them to compete effectively with their nonunion rivals. Thus, the union will be unable to increase wages much without experiencing a substantial reduction in the employment of its members.

5. False. Competition constrains both employers and employees. Employers must compete with other employers for labor services. To gain the labor services of an employee, an employer must offer a compensation package superior to one that the employee can get elsewhere. If the employer does not offer a superior package, the employee will work for a rival employer or choose self-employment. Similarly, employees must compete with other employees. Therefore, their ability to demand whatever wage they would like is also restrained. Thus, competition prevents both the payment of low (below-market) wages by employers and the imposition of high (above-market) wages by employees.

6. Not necessarily. Adjustment must be made for differences in (a) the productivity characteristics of the union and nonunion workers and (b) the types of jobs they occupy (for example, work environment, job security, likelihood of layoff, and so on). Adjustment for these factors may either increase or reduce the $1.50 differential.

7. Remember, union members compete with other workers, including less-skilled workers. An increase in the minimum wage makes unskilled, low-wage workers more expensive. A higher minimum wage increases the demand for high-skilled employees who are good substitutes for the low-skilled workers. Union members are overrepresented among the high-skilled group helped by an increase in the minimum wage. Therefore, although union leaders will generally pitch their support for a higher minimum wage in terms of a desire that all workers be paid a "decent wage," the effect of the legislation on union members suggests that self-interest rather than altruism underlies their support for the legislation.

SPECIAL TOPIC 11: THE QUESTION OF RESOURCE EXHAUSTION

2. When demand expands in resource markets, prices send signals and provide the incentives that will reduce future demand relative to supply. These forces will avoid lasting shortages.

5. If any resource, including water, is bought and sold, then market signals will automatically be provided to signal the desires of users to have, and the abilities of suppliers to supply, more. A market provides productive incentive to all concerned. Users conserve more when a market price rises, suppliers provide more, and there is greater incentive to develop and use substitutes for the higher priced resource. If markets are not used to allocate a resource, these benefits will be lost.

SPECIAL TOPIC 12: DIFFICULT ENVIRONMENTAL CASES AND THE ROLE OF GOVERNMENT

1. The ITQ would allow fishers to fish at their own speed without fear of losing their quota to others.

3. The cost of stopping the buildup would be very large. Avoiding the buildup would be very costly. That large opportunity cost could accomplish instead much else that would help future generations. The forecasted risks are only speculatively the result of the buildup and would occur mostly far in the future. And a warmer world has advantages as well as disadvantages.

4. In a market with strong property rights in place, a polluter would have to be concerned about harming others and being sued by them for damages. Without strong property rights in place, regulation might help. Or it might not. In any case, regulators need information available only in a market to judge how tightly to regulate if the regulator is seeking efficiency.

GLOSSARY

A

Absolute advantage A situation in which a nation, as the result of its previous experience and/or natural endowments, can produce more of a good (with the same amount of resources) than another nation.

Accounting profits The sales revenues minus the expenses of a firm over a designated time period, usually one year. Accounting profits typically make allowances for changes in the firm's inventories and depreciation of its assets. No allowance is made, however, for the opportunity cost of the equity capital of the firm's owners, or other implicit costs.

Activists Economists who believe that discretionary changes in monetary and fiscal policy can reduce the degree of instability in output and employment.

Adaptive-expectations hypothesis The hypothesis that economic decision-makers base their future expectations on actual outcomes observed during recent periods. For example, according to this view, the rate of inflation actually experienced during the past two or three years would be the major determinant of the rate of inflation expected for the next year.

Administrative lag The time period after the need for a policy change is recognized but before the policy is actually implemented.

Aggregate demand curve A downward-sloping curve showing the relationship between the price level and the quantity of domestically produced goods and services all households, business firms, governments, and foreigners (net exports) are willing to purchase.

Aggregate supply curve The curve showing the relationship between a nation's price level and the quantity of goods supplied by its producers. In the short run, it is an upward-sloping curve, but in the long run the aggregate supply curve is vertical.

Anticipated change A change that is foreseen by decision-makers in time for them to make adjustments.

Anticipated inflation An increase in the general level of prices that was expected by most decision-makers.

Appreciation An increase in the value of the domestic currency relative to foreign currencies. An appreciation increases the purchasing power of the currency over foreign goods.

Automatic stabilizers Built-in features that tend automatically to promote a budget deficit during a recession and a budget surplus during an inflationary boom, even without a change in policy.

Automation A production technique that reduces the amount of labor required to produce a good or service. It is beneficial to adopt the new labor-saving technology only if it reduces the cost of production.

Average fixed cost Total fixed cost divided by the number of units produced. It always declines as output increases.

Average product The total product (output) divided by the number of units of the variable input required to produce that output level.

Average tax rate (ATR) Tax liability divided by taxable income. It is the percentage of income paid in taxes.

Average total cost Total cost divided by the number of units produced. It is sometimes called *per-unit cost*.

Average variable cost The total variable cost divided by the number of units produced.

B

Balance of merchandise trade The difference between the value of merchandise exports and the value of merchandise imports for a nation. It is also called simply the *balance of trade* or *net exports*. The balance of merchandise trade is only one component of a nation's total balance of payments and its current account.

Balance of payments A summary of all economic transactions between a country and all other countries for a specific time period, usually a year. The balance-of-payments account reflects all payments and liabilities to foreigners (debits) and all payments and obligations received from foreigners (credits).

Balance on current account The import–export balance of goods and services, plus net investment income earned abroad, plus net private and government transfers. If the value of the nation's export-type items exceeds (is less than) the value of the nation's import-type items plus net unilateral transfers to foreigners, a current-account surplus (deficit) is present.

Balance on goods and services The exports of goods (merchandise) and services of a nation minus its imports of goods and services.

Balanced budget A situation in which current government revenue from taxes, fees, and other sources is just equal to current government expenditures.

Bank reserves Vault cash plus deposits of banks with Federal Reserve banks.

Barriers to entry Obstacles that limit the freedom of potential rivals to enter and compete in an industry or market.

Black market A market that operates outside the legal system in which either illegal goods are sold or legal goods are sold at illegal prices or terms.

Budget deficit A situation in which total government spending exceeds total government revenue during a specific time period, usually one year.

Budget surplus A situation in which total government spending is less than total government revenue during a time period, usually a year.

Business cycle Fluctuations in the general level of economic activity as measured by variables such as the rate of unemployment and changes in real GDP.

C

Capital Human-made resources (such as tools, equipment, and structures) used to produce other goods and services. They enhance our ability to produce in the future.

Capital account The record of transactions with foreigners that involve either (1) the exchange of ownership rights to real or financial assets or (2) the extension of loans.

Capitalism An economic system in which productive resources are owned privately and goods and resources are allocated through market prices.

Cartel An organization of sellers designed to coordinate supply and price decisions so that the joint profits of the members will be maximized. A cartel will seek to create a monopoly in the market for its product.

Central bank An institution that regulates the banking system and controls the supply of a country's money.

Ceteris paribus A Latin term meaning "other things constant" that is used when the effect of one change is being described, recognizing that if other things changed, they also could affect the result. Economists often describe the effects of one change, knowing that in the real world, other things might change and also exert an effect.

Choice The act of selecting among alternatives.

Civilian labor force The number of people 16 of age and over who are either employed or unemployed. To be classified as unemployed, a person must be looking for a job.

Collective decision-making The method of organization that relies on public-sector decision making (voting, political bargaining, lobbying, and so on) to resolve basic economic questions; the use of the political process (voting, taxes, government spending, regulation, political bargaining, lobbying, and so on) to make decisions and allocate resources. In a democratic setting, the votes of citizens and their representatives will determine the actions undertaken.

Collusion Agreement among firms to avoid various competitive practices, particularly price reductions. It may involve either formal agreements or merely tacit recognition that competitive practices will be self-defeating in the long run. Tacit collusion is difficult to detect. In the United States, antitrust laws prohibit collusion and conspiracies to restrain trade.

Commercial banks Financial institutions that offer a wide range of services (for example, checking accounts, savings accounts, and loans) to their customers. Commercial banks are owned by stockholders and seek to operate at a profit.

Comparative advantage The ability to produce a good at a lower opportunity cost than others can produce it. Relative costs determine comparative advantage.

Compensating wage differentials Wage differences that compensate workers for risk, unpleasant working conditions, and other undesirable nonpecuniary aspects of a job.

Competition as a dynamic process Rivalry or competitiveness between or among parties (for example, producers or input suppliers) to deliver a better deal to buyers in terms of quality, price, and product information.

Competitive price-searcher market A market in which the firms have a downward-sloping demand curve, and entry into and exit from the market are relatively easy.

Complements Products that are usually consumed jointly (for example, bread and butter, hot dogs and hot dog buns). A decrease in the price of one will cause an increase in demand for the other.

Constant returns to scale Unit costs that are constant as the scale of the firm is altered. Neither economics nor diseconomies of scale are present.

Constant-cost industry An industry for which factor prices and costs of production remain constant as market output is expanded. The long-run market supply curve is therefore horizontal in these industries.

Consumer price index (CPI) An indicator of the general level of prices. It attempts to compare the cost of purchasing the market basket bought by a typical consumer during a specific period with the cost of purchasing the same market basket during an earlier period.

Consumer sentiment index A measure of the optimism of consumers based on their responses to a set of questions about their current and expected future personal economic situation. Conducted by the University of Michigan, it is based on a representative sample of U.S. households.

Consumer surplus The difference between the maximum price consumers are willing to pay and the price they actually pay. It is the net gain derived by the buyers of the good.

Contestable market A market in which the costs of entry and exit are low, so a firm risks little by entering. Efficient production and zero economic profits should prevail in a contestable market.

Corporation A business firm owned by shareholders who possess ownership rights to the firm's profits, but whose liability is limited to the amount of their investment in the firm.

Countercyclical policy A policy that tends to move the economy in an opposite direction from the forces of the business cycle. Such a policy would stimulate demand during the contraction phase of the business cycle and restrain demand during the expansion phase.

Creative destruction The replacement of old products and production methods by innovative new ones that consumers judge to be superior. The process generates economic growth and higher living standards.

Credit Funds acquired by borrowing.

Credit unions Financial cooperative organizations of individuals with a common affiliation (such as an employer or a labor union). They accept deposits, including checkable deposits, pay interest (or dividends) on them out of earnings, and lend funds primarily to members.

Crony capitalism A situation where the institutions of markets are maintained, but the allocation of resources, and the profit and loss of businesses, are determined by political decision-making rather than consumer purchases and market forces. To a large degree, the activities of business firms are directed and controlled by government spending and regulation. In turn, many of the business firms will use contributions and other forms of political support to compete for government favors.

Crowding-out effect A reduction in private spending as a result of higher interest rates generated by budget deficits that are financed by borrowing in the private loanable funds market.

Currency Medium of exchange made of metal or paper.

Currency board An entity that (1) issues a currency with a fixed designated value relative to a widely accepted currency (for example, the U.S. dollar), (2) promises to continue to redeem the issued currency at the fixed rate, and (3) maintains bonds and other liquid assets denominated in the other currency that provide 100-percent backing for all currency issued.

Current account The record of all transactions with foreign nations that involve the exchange of merchandise goods and services, current income derived from investments, and unilateral gifts.

Cyclical unemployment Unemployment due to recessionary business conditions and inadequate labor demand.

D

Deadweight loss The loss of gains from trade to buyers and sellers that occurs when a tax is imposed. The deadweight loss imposes a burden on both buyers and sellers over and above the actual payment of the tax.

Decreasing-cost industry An industry for which costs of production decline as the industry expands. The market supply is therefore inversely related to price. Such industries are atypical.

Demand deposits Non–interest-earning checking deposits that can be either withdrawn or made payable on demand to a third party. Like currency, these deposits are widely used as a means of payment.

Demand for money A curve that indicates the relationship between the interest rate and the quantity of money people want to hold. Because higher interest rates increase the opportunity cost of holding money, the quantity of money demanded will be inversely related to the interest rate.

Democracy A form of political organization in which adult citizens are free to participate in the political process (vote, lobby, and choose among candidates), elections are free and open, and majority voting, either directly or by elected representatives, decides outcomes.

Deposit expansion multiplier The multiple by which an increase in reserves will increase the money supply. It is inversely related to the required reserve ratio.

Depository institutions Businesses that accept checking and savings deposits and use a portion of them to extend loans and make investments. Banks, savings and loan associations, and credit unions are examples.

Depreciation (of assets) The estimated amount of physical capital (for example, machines and buildings) that is worn out or used up producing goods during a period.

Depreciation (of currency) A reduction in the value of a currency relative to foreign currencies. A depreciation reduces the purchasing power of the currency over foreign goods.

Depression A prolonged and very severe recession.

Derived demand The demand for a resource; it stems from the demand for the final good the resource helps produce.

Differentiated products Products distinguished from similar products by characteristics like quality, design, location, and method of promotion.

Discount rate The interest rate the Federal Reserve charges banking institutions for short-term loans.

Discounting The procedure used to calculate the present value of future income, which is inversely related to both the interest rate and the amount of time that passes before the funds are received.

Discretionary fiscal policy A change, in laws or appropriation levels, that alters government revenues and/or expenditures.

Division of labor A method that breaks down the production of a product into a series of specific tasks, each performed by a different worker.

Dumping Selling a good in a foreign country at a lower price than it's sold for in the domestic market.

E

Earmarking The direction of budgeted funds to specific projects, programs, and locations. The technique is costly but provides major benefits to business firms and other concentrated constituent groups, and to the districts where the spending takes place. The benefits are often targeted to those willing to make substantial campaign contributions.

Economic efficiency A situation that occurs when (1) all activities generating more benefit than cost are undertaken, and (2) no activities are undertaken for which the cost exceeds the benefit.

Economic freedom Method of organizing economic activity characterized by (1) personal choice, (2) voluntary exchange coordinated by markets, (3) freedom to enter and compete in markets, and (4) protection of people and their property from aggression by others.

Economic profit The difference between the firm's total revenues and its total costs, including both the explicit and implicit cost components.

Economic theory A set of definitions, postulates, and principles assembled in a manner that makes clear the "cause-and-effect" relationships.

Economies of sale Reductions in the firm's per-unit costs associated with the use of large plants to produce a large volume of output.

Economizing behavior Choosing the option that offers the greatest benefit at the least possible cost.

Employment discrimination Unequal treatment of people on the basis of their race, gender, or religion, restricting their employment and earnings opportunities compared with others of similar productivity. Employment discrimination may stem from the prejudices of employers, customers, fellow employees, or all three.

Employment/population ratio The number of people 16 years of age and older employed as civilians divided by the total civilian population 16 years of age and older. The ratio is expressed as a percentage.

Entrepreneur A person who introduces new products or improved technologies and decides which projects to undertake. A successful entrepreneur's actions will increase the value of resources and expand the size of the economic pie.

Equation of exchange $MV = PY$, where M is the money supply, V is the velocity of money, P is the price level, and Y is the output of goods and services produced in an economy.

Equilibrium A state in which the conflicting forces of supply and demand are in balance. When a market is in equilibrium, the decisions of consumers and producers are brought into harmony with one another, and the quantity supplied will equal the quantity demanded.

Excess burden of taxation Another term for deadweight loss. It reflects losses that occur when beneficial activities are forgone because they are taxed.

Excess reserves Actual reserves that exceed the legal requirement.

Exchange rate The price of one unit of foreign currency in terms of the domestic currency. For example, if it takes $1.50 to purchase an English pound, the dollar–pound exchange rate is 1.50.

Expansionary fiscal policy An increase in government expenditures and/or a reduction in tax rates, such that the expected size of the budget deficit expands.

Expansionary monetary policy A shift in monetary policy designed to stimulate aggregate demand. Injection of additional bank reserves, lower short-term interest rates, and acceleration in the growth rate of the money supply are indicators of a more expansionary monetary policy.

Expenditure multiplier The ratio of the change in equilibrium output to the independent change in investment, consumption, or government spending that brings about the change. Numerically, the multiplier is equal to 1 *divided by* (1 − MPC) when the price level is constant.

Explicit costs Payments by a firm to purchase the services of productive resources.

Exports Goods and services produced domestically but sold to foreigners.

External benefits Spillover effects that generate benefits for nonconsenting third parties.

External costs Spillover effects that reduce the well-being of nonconsenting third parties.

Externalities Spillover effects of an activity that influence the well-being of nonconsenting third parties.

F

Fallacy of composition Erroneous view that what is true for the individual (or the part) will also be true for the group (or the whole).

Federal Deposit Insurance Corporation (FDIC) A federally chartered corporation that insures the deposits held by commercial banks, savings and loans, and credit unions.

Federal funds market A loanable funds market in which banks seeking additional reserves borrow short-term funds (generally for seven days or less) from banks with excess reserves. The interest rate in this market is called the *federal funds rate*.

Federal Open Market Committee (FOMC) A committee of the Federal Reserve System that establishes Fed policy with regard to the buying and selling of government securities—the primary mechanism used to control the money supply. It is composed of the seven members of the Board of Governors and the twelve district bank presidents of the Fed.

Federal Reserve System The central bank of the United States; it carries out banking regulatory policies and is responsible for the conduct of monetary policy.

Fiat money Money that has neither intrinsic value nor the backing of a commodity with intrinsic value; paper currency is an example.

Final market goods and services Goods and services purchased by their ultimate user.

Fiscal policy The use of government taxation and expenditure policies for the purpose of achieving macroeconomic goals.

Fixed exchange rate An exchange rate that is set at a determined amount by government policy.

Flexible exchange rates Exchange rates that are determined by the market forces of supply and demand. They are sometimes called *floating exchange rates*.

Foreign exchange market The market in which the currencies of different countries are bought and sold.

Fractional reserve banking A system that permits banks to hold reserves of less than 100 percent against their deposits.

Franchise A right or license granted to an individual to market a company's goods or services or use its brand name. The individual firms are independently owned but must meet certain conditions to continue to use the name.

Free rider A person who receives the benefit of a good without paying for it. Because it is often virtually impossible to restrict the consumption of public goods to those who pay, these goods are subject to free-rider problems.

Frictional unemployment Unemployment due to constant changes in the economy that prevent qualified unemployed workers from being immediately matched up with existing job openings. It results from imperfect information and search activities related to suitably matching employees with employers.

Fringe benefits Benefits other than normal money wages that are supplied to employees in exchange for their labor services. Higher fringe benefits come at the expense of lower money wages.

Full employment The level of employment that results from the efficient use of the labor force taking into account the normal (natural) rate of unemployment due to information costs, dynamic changes, and the structural conditions of the economy. For the United States, full employment is thought to exist when approximately 95 percent of the labor force is employed.

G

Game theory A tool used to analyze the strategic choices made by competitors in a conflict situation like the decisions made by firms in an oligopoly.

GDP deflator A price index that reveals the cost during the current period of purchasing the items included in GDP relative to the cost during a base year (currently 2005). Unlike the consumer price index (CPI), the GDP deflator also measures the prices of capital goods and other goods and services purchased by businesses and governments.

General Agreement on Tariffs and Trade (GATT) An organization formed after World War II to set the rules for the conduct of international trade and reduce trade barriers among nations.

Going out of business The sale of a firm's assets and its permanent exit from the market. By going out of business, a firm is able to avoid its fixed costs, which would continue during a shutdown.

Goods and services market A highly aggregated market encompassing the flow of all final-user goods and services. The market counts all items that enter into GDP. Thus, real output in this market is equal to real GDP.

Government failure A situation in which the structure of incentives is such that the political process, including democratic political decision-making, will encourage individuals to undertake actions that conflict with economic efficiency.

Gross domestic product (GDP) The market value of all final goods and services produced within a country during a specific period.

Gross national product (GNP) The total market value of all final goods and services produced by the citizens of a country. It is equal to GDP minus the net income of foreigners.

H

Human resources The abilities, skills, and health of human beings that contribute to the production of both current and future output. Investment in training and education can increase the supply of human resources.

I

Impact lag The time period after a policy change is implemented but before the change begins to exert its primary effects.

Implicit costs The opportunity costs associated with a firm's use of resources that it owns. These costs do not involve a direct money payment. Examples include wage income and interest forgone by the owner of a firm who also provides labor services and equity capital to the firm.

Implicit marginal tax rate The amount of additional (marginal) earnings that must be paid explicitly in taxes or implicitly in the form of lower income supplements. The marginal tax rate establishes the fraction of an additional dollar earned that an individual is permitted to keep, so it is an important determinant of the incentive to work and earn.

Import quota A specific limit or maximum quantity (or value) of a good permitted to be imported into a country during a given period.

Imports Goods and services produced by foreigners but purchased by domestic consumers, businesses, and governments.

Income effect That part of an increase (decrease) in amount consumed that is the result of the consumer's real income being expanded (contracted) by a reduction (rise) in the price of a good.

Income elasticity The percentage change in the quantity of a product demanded divided by the percentage change in consumer income that caused the change in quantity demanded. It measures the responsiveness of the demand for a good to a consumer's change in income.

Income mobility Movement of individuals and families either up or down income distribution rankings when comparisons are made at two different points in time. When substantial income mobility is present, a person's current position in the rankings will not be a very good indicator of what his or her position will be a few years in the future.

Increasing-cost industry An industry for which costs of production rise as output is expanded. In these industries, even in the long run, higher market prices will be needed to induce firms to expand total output. As a result, the long-run market supply curve in these industries will slope upward to the right.

Index of leading indicators An index of economic variables that historically has tended to turn down prior to the beginning of a recession and turn up prior to the beginning of a business expansion.

Indirect business taxes Taxes that increase a business firm's costs of production and, therefore, the prices charged to consumers. Examples are sales, excise, and property taxes.

Inferior good A good that has a negative income elasticity, so that, as consumer income rises, the demand for the good falls.

Inflation An increase in the general level of prices of goods and services. The purchasing power of the monetary unit, such as the dollar, declines when inflation is present.

Inflationary premium A component of the money interest rate that reflects compensation to the lender for the expected decrease, due to inflation, in the purchasing power of the principal and interest during the course of the loan. It is determined by the expected rate of future inflation.

Innovation The successful introduction and adoption of a new product or process; the economic application of inventions and marketing techniques.

Institutions The legal, regulatory, and social constraints that affect the security of property rights and enforcement of contracts. They exert a major impact on transaction costs between parties, particularly when the trading partners do not know each other.

Intermediate goods Goods purchased for resale or for use in producing another good or service.

International Monetary Fund (IMF) An international banking organization, currently with more than 180 member nations, designed to oversee the operation of the international monetary system. Although it does not control the world supply of money, it does hold currency reserves for member nations and makes currency loans to national central banks.

Invention The creation of a new product or process, often facilitated by the knowledge of engineering and science.

Inventory investment Changes in the stock of unsold goods and raw materials held during a period.

Investment The purchase, construction, or development of capital resources, including both nonhuman capital and human capital. Investments increase the supply of capital.

Investment in human capital Expenditures on training, education, skill development, and health designed to increase human capital and people's productivity.

Invisible hand principle The tendency of market prices to direct individuals pursuing their own interests to engage in activities promoting the economic well-being of society.

L

Labor force participation rate The number of people in the civilian labor force 16 years of age or older who are either employed or actively seeking employment as a percentage of the total civilian population 16 years of age and older.

Laffer curve A curve illustrating the relationship between the tax rate and tax revenues. Tax revenues will be low at both very high and very low tax rates. When tax rates are quite high, lowering them can increase tax revenue.

Law of comparative advantage A principle that states that individuals, firms, regions, or nations can gain by specializing in the production of goods that they produce cheaply (at a low opportunity cost) and exchanging them for goods they cannot produce cheaply (at a high opportunity cost).

Law of demand A principle that states there is an inverse relationship between the price of a good and the quantity of it buyers are willing to purchase. As the price of a good increases, consumers will wish to purchase less of it. As the price decreases, consumers will wish to purchase more of it.

Law of diminishing marginal utility The basic economic principle that as the consumption of a product increases, the marginal utility derived from consuming more of it (per unit of time) will eventually decline.

Law of diminishing returns The postulate that as more and more units of a variable resource are combined with a fixed amount of other resources, using additional units of the variable resource will eventually increase output only at a decreasing rate. Once diminishing returns are reached, it will take successively larger amounts of the variable factor to expand output by one unit.

Law of supply A principle that states there is a direct relationship between the price of a good and the quantity of it producers are willing to supply. As the price of a good increases, producers will wish to supply more of it. As the price decreases, producers will wish to supply less.

Less-developed countries Countries with low per capita incomes, low levels of education, widespread illiteracy, and widespread use of production methods that are largely obsolete in high-income countries. They are sometimes referred to as developing countries.

Licensing A requirement that one obtain permission from the government in order to perform certain business activities or work in various occupations.

Liquid asset An asset that can be easily and quickly converted to money without loss of value.

Loanable funds market A general term used to describe the market that coordinates the borrowing and lending decisions of business firms and households. Commercial banks, savings and loan associations, the stock and bond markets, and insurance companies are important financial institutions in this market.

Logrolling The exchange between politicians of political support on one issue for political support on another.

Long run (in production) A time period long enough to allow the firm to vary all of its factors of production.

Loss A deficit of sales revenue relative to the opportunity cost of production. Losses are a penalty imposed on those who produce goods even though they are valued less than the resources required for their production.

M

M1 (money supply) The sum of (1) currency in circulation (including coins), (2) checkable deposits maintained in depository institutions, and (3) traveler's checks.

M2 (money supply) Equal to M1 plus (1) savings deposits, (2) time-deposits (accounts of less than $100,000) held in depository institutions, and (3) money market mutual fund shares.

Macroeconomics The branch of economics that focuses on how human behavior affects outcomes in highly aggregated markets, such as the markets for labor or consumer products.

Marginal Term used to describe the effects of a change in the current situation. For example, a producer's marginal cost is the cost of producing an additional unit of a product, given the producer's current facility and production rate.

Marginal benefit The maximum price a consumer will be willing to pay for an additional unit of a product. It is the dollar value of the consumer's marginal utility from the additional unit, and therefore it falls as consumption increases.

Marginal cost The change in total cost required to produce an additional unit of output.

Marginal product (MP) The increase in the total product resulting from a unit increase in the employment of a variable input. Mathematically, it is the ratio of the change in total product to the change in the quantity of the variable input.

Marginal propensity to consume (MPC) Additional current consumption divided by additional current disposable income.

Marginal revenue (MR) The change in a firm's total revenue that results from the production and sale of one additional unit of output.

Marginal revenue product (MRP) The change in the total revenue of a firm that results from the employment of one additional unit of a resource. The marginal revenue product of an input is equal to its marginal product multiplied by the marginal revenue of the good or service produced.

Marginal tax rate (MTR) The additional tax liability a person faces divided by his or her additional taxable income. It is the percentage of an extra dollar of income earned that must be paid in taxes. It is the marginal tax rate that is relevant in personal decision-making.

Marginal utility The additional utility, or satisfaction, derived from consuming an additional unit of a good.

Market An abstract concept encompassing the forces of supply and demand and the interaction of buyers and sellers with the potential for exchange to occur.

Market failure A situation in which the structure of incentives is such that markets will encourage individuals to undertake activities that are inconsistent with economic efficiency.

Market organization A method of organization in which private parties make their own plans and decisions with the guidance of unregulated market prices. The basic economic questions of consumption, production, and distribution are answered through these decentralized decisions.

Market power The ability of a firm that is not a pure monopolist to earn persistently large profits, indicating that it has some monopoly power. Because the firm has few (or weak) competitors, it has a degree of freedom from vigorous competition.

Means-tested income transfers Transfers that are limited to people or families with an income below a certain cutoff point. Eligibility is thus dependent upon low-income status.

Medium of exchange An asset that is used to buy and sell goods or services.

Microeconomics The branch of economics that focuses on how human behavior affects the conduct of affairs within narrowly defined units, such as individual households or business firms.

Middleman A person who buys and sells goods or services or arranges trades. A middleman reduces transaction costs.

Minimum wage Legislation requiring that workers be paid at least the stated minimum hourly rate of pay.

Monetary base The sum of currency in circulation plus bank reserves (vault cash and reserves with the Fed). It reflects the purchases of financial assets and extension of loans by the Fed.

Monetary policy The deliberate control of the money supply, and, in some cases, credit conditions, for the purpose of achieving macroeconomic goals.

Money interest rate The percentage of the amount borrowed that must be paid to the lender in addition to the repayment of the principal. The money interest rate overstates the real cost of borrowing during an inflationary period. When inflation is anticipated, an inflationary premium will be incorporated into this rate. The money interest rate is often called the *nominal interest rate*.

Money market mutual funds Interest-earning accounts that pool depositors' funds and invest them in highly liquid short-term securities. Because these securities can be quickly converted to cash, depositors are permitted to write checks (which reduce their share holdings) against their accounts.

Money rate of interest The rate of interest in monetary terms that borrowers pay for borrowed funds. During periods when borrowers and lenders expect inflation, the money rate of interest exceeds the real rate of interest.

Money supply The supply of currency, checking account f and traveler's checks. These items are counted as because they are used as the means of payment for p

Monopolistic competition A term often used by economists to describe markets characterized by a large number of sellers that supply differentiated products to a market with low barriers to entry. Essentially, it is an alternative term for a competitive price-searcher market.

Monopoly A market structure characterized by (1) a single seller of a well-defined product for which there are no good substitutes and (2) high barriers to the entry of any other firms into the market for that product.

N

National income The total income earned by a country's nationals (citizens) during a period. It is the sum of employee compensation, self-employment income, rents, interest, and corporate profits.

Natural monopoly A market situation in which the average costs of production continually decline with increased output. In a natural monopoly, the average costs of production will be lowest when a single, large firm produces the entire output demanded by the marketplace.

Natural rate of unemployment The "normal" unemployment rate due to frictional and structural conditions in labor markets. It is the unemployment rate that occurs when the economy is operating at a sustainable rate of output. The current natural rate of unemployment in the United States is thought to be approximately 5 percent.

Net exports Exports minus imports.

Net income of foreigners The income that foreigners earn by contributing labor and capital resources to the production of goods within the borders of a country minus the income the nationals of the country earn abroad.

New classical economists Economists who believe that there are strong forces pushing a market economy toward full-employment equilibrium and that macroeconomic policy is an ineffective tool with which to reduce economic instability.

Nominal GDP GDP expressed at current prices. It is often called *money GDP*.

Nominal values Values expressed in current dollars.

Nonactivists Economists who believe that discretionary macro policy adjustments in response to cyclical conditions are likely to increase, rather than reduce, instability. Nonactivists favor steady and predictable policies regardless of business conditions.

Nonhuman resources The durable, nonhuman inputs used to produce both current and future output. Machines, buildings, land, and raw materials are examples. Investment can increase the supply of nonhuman resources. Economists often use the term *physical capital* when referring to nonhuman resources.

Nonpecuniary job characteristics Working conditions, prestige, variety, location, employee freedom and responsibilities, and other nonwage characteristics of a job that influence how employees evaluate the job.

Normal good A good that has a positive income elasticity, so that, as consumer income rises, demand for the good rises, too.

Normal profit rate Zero economic profit, providing just the competitive rate of return on the capital (and labor) of owners. An above-normal profit will draw more entry into the market, whereas a below-normal profit will lead to an exit of investors and capital.

Normative economics Judgments about "what ought to be" in economic matters. Normative economic views cannot be proved false because they are based on value judgments.

North American Free Trade Agreement (NAFTA) A comprehensive trade agreement between the United States, Mexico, and Canada that went into effect in 1994.

O

Objective A fact based on observable phenomena that is not influenced by differences in personal opinion.

Official reserve account The record of transactions among central banks.

Oligopoly A market situation in which a small number of sellers constitutes the entire industry. It is competition among the few.

Open market operations The buying and selling of U.S. government securities and other financial assets in the open market by the Federal Reserve.

Opportunity cost The highest valued alternative that must be sacrificed as a result of choosing an option.

Opportunity cost of production The total economic cost of producing a good or service. The cost component includes the opportunity cost of all resources, including those owned by the firm. The opportunity cost is equal to the value of the production of other goods sacrificed as the result of producing the good.

Opportunity cost of equity capital The rate of return that must be earned by investors to induce them to supply financial capital to the firm.

Other checkable deposits Interest-earning deposits that are also available for checking.

P

Paradox of thrift The idea that when many households simultaneously try to increase their saving, actual saving may fail to increase because the reduction in consumption and aggregate demand will reduce income and employment.

Partnership A business firm owned by two or more individuals who possess ownership rights to the firm's profits and are personally liable for the debts of the firm.

Pegged exchange rate system A commitment to use monetary and fiscal policy to maintain the exchange rate value of the domestic currency at a fixed rate or within a narrow band relative to another currency (or bundle of currencies).

Per capita GDP Income per person. Increases in income per person are vital for the achievement of higher living standards.

Personal consumption Household spending on consumer goods and services during the current period. Consumption is a flow concept.

Phillips curve A curve that illustrates the relationship between the rate of inflation and the rate of unemployment.

Pork-barrel legislation A package of spending projects benefiting local areas financed through the federal government. The costs of the projects typically exceed the benefits in total, but the projects are intensely desired by the residents of a particular district who get the benefits without having to pay much of the costs.

Positive economics The scientific study of "what is" among economic relationships.

Positive rate of time preference The desire of consumers for goods now rather than in the future.

Potential deposit expansion multiplier The maximum potential increase in the money supply as a ratio of the new reserves injected into the banking system. It is equal to the inverse of the required reserve ratio.

Potential output The level of output that can be achieved and sustained in the future, given the size of the labor force, its expected productivity, and the natural rate of unemployment consistent with the efficient operation of the labor market. Actual output can differ from the economy's potential output.

Poverty threshold income level The level of money income below which a family is considered to be poor. It differs according to family characteristics (e.g., number of family members) and is adjusted when consumer prices change.

Present value (PV) The current worth of future income after it is discounted to reflect the fact that revenues in the future are valued less highly than revenues now.

Price ceiling A legally established maximum price sellers can charge for a good or resource.

Price controls Government-mandated prices that are generally imposed in the form of maximum or minimum legal prices.

Price discrimination A practice whereby a seller charges different consumers different prices for the same product or service.

Price elasticity of demand The percentage change in the quantity of a product demanded divided by the percentage change in the price that caused the change in quantity. The price elasticity of demand indicates how responsive consumers are to a change in a product's price.

Price elasticity of supply The percentage change in quantity supplied, divided by the percentage change in the price that caused the change in quantity supplied.

Price floor A legally established minimum price buyers must pay for a good or resource.

Price searchers Firms that face a downward-sloping demand curve for their product. The amount the firm is able to sell is inversely related to the price it charges.

Principal–agent problem The incentive problem that occurs when the purchaser of services (the principal) lacks full information about the circumstances faced by the seller (the agent) and cannot know how well the agent performs the purchased services. The agent may to some extent work toward objectives other than those sought by the principal paying for the service.

Private investment The flow of private-sector expenditures on durable assets (fixed investment) plus the addition to inventories (inventory investment) during a period. These expenditures enhance our ability to provide consumer benefits in the future.

Private-property rights Property rights that are exclusively held by an owner and protected against invasion by others. Private property can be transferred, sold, or mortgaged at the owner's discretion.

Producer surplus The difference between the price that suppliers actually receive and the minimum price they would be willing to accept. It measures the net gains to producers and resource suppliers from market exchange. It is not the same as profit.

Production possibilities curve A curve that outlines all possible combinations of total output that could be produced, assuming (1) a fixed amount of productive resources, (2) a given amount of technical knowledge, and (3) full and efficient use of those resources. The slope of the curve indicates the amount of one product that must be given up to produce more of the other.

Productivity The average output produced per worker during a specific time period. It is usually measured in terms of output per hour worked.

Profit An excess of sales revenue relative to the opportunity cost of production. The cost component includes the opportunity cost of all resources, including those owned by the firm. Therefore, profit accrues only when the value of the good produced is greater than the value of the resources used for its production.

Progressive tax A tax in which the average tax rate rises with income. People with higher incomes will pay a higher percentage of their income in taxes.

Property rights The rights to use, control, and obtain the benefits from a good or resource.

Proportional tax A tax in which the average tax rate is the same at all income levels. Everyone pays the same percentage of income in taxes.

Proprietorship A business firm owned by an individual who possesses the ownership right to the firm's profits and is personally liable for the firm's debts.

Public goods Goods for which rivalry among consumers is absent and exclusion of nonpaying customers is difficult.

Public-choice analysis The study of decision-making as it affects the formation and operation of collective organizations, like governments. In general, the principles and methodology of economics are applied to political science topics.

Purchasing power parity method (PPP) Method in which the relative purchasing power of each currency is determined by comparing the amount of each currency required to purchase a common bundle of goods and services in the domestic market. This information is then used to convert the GDP of each nation to a common monetary unit like the U.S. dollar.

Pure competition A market structure characterized by a large number of small firms producing an identical product in an industry (market area) that permits complete freedom of entry and exit. Also called *price-taker markets*.

Q

Quantity theory of money A theory that hypothesizes that a change in the money supply will cause a proportional change in the price level because velocity and real output are unaffected by the quantity of money.

Quartile A quarter (25 percent) of a group. The quartiles are often arrayed on the basis of an indicator like income or degree of economic freedom.

R

Rational ignorance effect Because it is highly unlikely that an individual vote will decide the outcome of an election, a rational individual has little or no incentive to search for and acquire the information needed to cast an informed vote.

Rational-expectations hypothesis The hypothesis that economic decision-makers weigh all available evidence, including information concerning the probable effects of current and future economic policy, when they form their expectations about future economic events (like the probable future inflation rate).

Rationing Allocating a limited supply of a good or resource among people who would like to have more of it. When price performs the rationing function, the good or resource is allocated to those willing to give up the most "other things" in order to get it.

Real earnings Earnings adjusted for differences in the general level of prices across time periods or geographic areas. When real earnings are equal, the same bundle of goods and services can be purchased with the earnings.

Real GDP GDP adjusted for changes in the price level.

Real interest rate The interest rate adjusted for expected inflation: It indicates the real cost to the borrower (and yield to the lender) in terms of goods and services.

Real rate of interest The money rate of interest minus the expected rate of inflation. The real rate of interest indicates the interest premium in terms of real goods and services that one must pay for earlier availability.

Real values Values that have been adjusted for the effects of inflation.

Recession A downturn in economic activity characterized by declining real GDP and rising unemployment. In an effort to be more precise, many economists define a recession as two consecutive quarters in which there is a decline in real GDP.

Recognition lag The time period after a policy change is needed from a stabilization standpoint but before the need is recognized by policy-makers.

Regressive tax A tax in which the average tax rate falls with income. People with higher incomes will pay a lower percentage of their income in taxes.

Rent-seeking Actions by individuals and groups designed to restructure public policy in a manner that will either directly or indirectly redistribute more income to themselves or the projects they promote.

Repeat-purchase item An item purchased often by the same buyer.

Required reserve ratio The ratio of reserves relative to a specified liability category (for example, checkable deposits) that banks are required to maintain.

Required reserves The minimum amount of reserves that a bank is required by law to keep on hand to back up its deposits. If reserve requirements were 15 percent, banks would be required to keep $150,000 in reserves against each $1 million of deposits.

Residual claimants Individuals who personally receive the excess, if any, of revenues over costs. Residual claimants gain if the firm's costs are reduced or revenues increase.

Resource An input used to produce economic goods. Land, labor, skills, natural resources, and human-made tools and equipment provide examples. Throughout history, people have struggled to transform available, but limited, resources into things they would like to have—economic goods.

Resource market A highly aggregated market encompassing all resources (labor, physical capital, land, and entrepreneurship) contributing to the production of current output. The labor market is the largest component of this market.

Resource markets Markets in which business firms demand factors of production (for example, labor, capital, and natural resources) from household suppliers. The resources are then used to produce goods and services. These markets are sometimes called factor markets or input markets.

Resource mobility The ease with which factors of production are able to move among alternative uses. Resources that can easily be transferred to a different use or location are said to be highly mobile. Resources with few alternative uses are immobile.

Restrictive fiscal policy A reduction in government expenditures and/or an increase in tax rates such that the expected size of the budget deficit declines (or the budget surplus increases).

Restrictive monetary policy A shift in monetary policy designed to reduce aggregate demand and put downward pressure on the general level of prices (or the rate of inflation). A reduction in bank reserves, higher short-term interest rates, and a reduction in the growth rate of the money supply are indicators of a more restrictive monetary policy.

Ricardian equivalence The view that a tax reduction financed with government debt will exert no effect on current consumption and aggregate demand because people will fully recognize the higher future taxes implied by the additional debt.

Rule of 70 If a variable grows at a rate of x percent per year, $70/x$ will approximate the number of years required for the variable to double.

S

Samaritan's dilemma The dilemma that occurs when assisting low-income citizens with transfers reduces the opportunity cost of choices that lead to poverty. Providing income transfers to the poor and discouraging behavior that leads to poverty are conflicting goals.

Saving The portion of after-tax income that is not spent on consumption. Saving is a "flow" concept.

Savings and loan associations Financial institutions that accept deposits in exchange for shares that pay dividends. Historically, these funds were channeled into residential mortgage loans, but today they offer essentially the same services as a commercial bank.

Scarcity Fundamental concept of economics that indicates that there is less of a good freely available from nature than people would like.

Scientific thinking Developing a theory from basic principles and testing it against events in the real world. Good theories are consistent with and help explain real-world events. Theories that are inconsistent with the real world are invalid and must be rejected.

Secondary effects The indirect impact of an event or policy that may not be easily and immediately observable. In the area of policy, these effects are often both unintended and overlooked.

Shirking Working at less than the expected rate of productivity, which reduces output. Shirking is more likely when workers are not monitored, so that the cost of lower output falls on others.

Short run (in production) A time period so short that a firm is unable to vary some of its factors of production. The firm's plant size typically cannot be altered in the short run.

Shortage A condition in which the amount of a good offered for sale by producers is less than the amount demanded by buyers at the existing price. An increase in price would eliminate the shortage.

Shortsightedness effect The misallocation of resources that results because public-sector action is biased (1) in favor of proposals yielding clearly defined current benefits in exchange for difficult-to-identify future costs and (2) against proposals with clearly identifiable current costs that yield less concrete and less obvious future benefits.

Shutdown A temporary halt in the operation of a firm. Because the firm anticipates operating in the future, it does not sell its assets and go out of business. The firm's variable cost is eliminated by the shutdown, but its fixed costs continue.

Socialism A system of economic organization in which (1) the ownership and control of the basic means of production rest with the state, and (2) resource allocation is determined by centralized planning rather than market forces.

Special-interest issue An issue that generates substantial individual benefits to a small minority while imposing a small individual cost on many other citizens. In total, the net cost to the majority might either exceed or fall short of the net benefits to the special-interest group.

Store of value An asset that will allow people to transfer purchasing power from one period to the next.

Structural unemployment Unemployment due to the structural characteristics of the economy that make it difficult for job seekers to find employment and for employers to hire workers. Although job openings are available, they generally require skills many unemployed workers do not have.

Subjective An opinion based on personal preferences and value judgments.

Subsidy A payment the government makes to either the buyer or seller, usually on a per-unit basis, when a good or a service is purchased or sold.

Substitutes Products that serve similar purposes. An increase in the price of one will cause an increase in demand for the other (examples are hamburgers and tacos, butter and margarine, Microsoft Xbox and Sony PlayStation, Chevrolets and Fords).

Substitution effect That part of an increase (decrease) in amount consumed that is the result of a good being cheaper (more expensive) in relation to other goods because of a reduction (increase) in price.

Sunk costs Costs that have already been incurred as a result of past decisions. They are sometimes referred to as historical costs.

Supply shock An unexpected event that temporarily increases or decreases aggregate supply.

Supply-side economists Economists who believe that changes in marginal tax rates exert important effects on aggregate supply.

Surplus A condition in which the amount of a good offered for sale by producers is greater than the amount that buyers will purchase at the existing price. A decline in price would eliminate the surplus.

T

Tariff A tax levied on goods imported into a country.

Tax base The level or quantity of an economic activity that is taxed. Higher tax rates reduce the level of the tax base because they make the activity less attractive.

Tax incidence The way the burden of a tax is distributed among economic units (consumers, producers, employees, employers, and so on). The actual tax burden does not always fall on those who are statutorily assigned to pay the tax.

Tax rate The per-unit amount of the tax or the percentage rate at which the economic activity is taxed.

Team production A production process in which employees work together under the supervision of the owner or the owner's representative.

Technological advancement The introduction of new techniques or methods that increase output per unit of input.

Technology The technological knowledge available in an economy at any given time. The level of technology determines the amount of output we can generate with our limited resources.

Total cost The costs, both explicit and implicit, of all the resources used by the firm. Total cost includes a normal rate of return for the firm's equity capital.

Total fixed cost The sum of the costs that do not vary with output. They will be incurred as long as a firm continues in business and the assets have alternative uses.

Total product The total output of a good that is associated with each alternative utilization rate of a variable input.

Total variable cost The sum of those costs that rise as output increases. Examples of variable costs are wages paid to workers and payments for raw materials.

Tournament pay A form of compensation in which the top performer (or performers) receives much higher rewards than other competitors, even if the others perform at only a slightly lower level.

Trade deficit The situation when a country's imports of goods and services are greater than its exports.

Trade surplus The situation when a country's exports of goods and services are greater than its imports.

Transaction costs The time, effort, and other resources needed to search out, negotiate, and complete an exchange.

Transfer payments Payments to individuals or institutions that are not linked to the current supply of a good or service by the recipient.

U

Unanticipated change A change that decision-makers could not reasonably foresee. The choices they made prior to the change did not take it into account.

Unanticipated inflation An increase in the general level of prices that was not expected by most decision-makers.

Underground economy Unreported barter and cash transactions that take place outside recorded market channels. Some are otherwise legal activities undertaken to evade taxes. Others involve illegal activities, such as trafficking drugs and prostitution.

Unemployed The term used to describe a person not currently employed who is either (1) actively seeking employment or (2) waiting to begin or return to a job.

Unemployment rate The percentage of unemployed people in the labor force. Mathematically, it is equal to the number of people unemployed divided by the number of people in the labor force.

Unit of account A unit of measurement used by people to post prices and keep track of revenues and costs.

User charges Payments users (consumers) are required to make if they want to receive certain services provided by the government.

Utility The subjective benefit or satisfaction a person expects from a choice or course of action.

V

Value marginal product (VMP) The marginal product of a resource multiplied by the selling price of the product it helps produce. For a price-taker firm, marginal revenue product (MRP) will be equal to the value marginal product (VMP).

Velocity of money The average number of times a dollar is used to purchase final goods and services during a year. It is equal to GDP divided by the stock of money.

W

World Trade Organization (WTO) The new name given to GATT in 1994; the WTO is currently responsible for monitoring and enforcing multilateral trade agreements among its 153 member countries.

INDEX

Note: "n" after a page number indicates information in a footnote on that page.

The Evolution of

1776

Adam Smith (1723–1790)

Smith's book *An Inquiry into the Nature and Causes of the Wealth of Nations* provided the first comprehensive analysis of wealth and prosperity and introduced "the invisible hand" principle. It also explained that the wealth of a nation was determined by its production of goods and services, not by its gold and silver.

1817

David Ricardo (1772–1823)

In his book *On the Principles of Political Economy and Taxation*, Ricardo developed the law of comparative advantage and used it to explain why trade leads to mutual gains.

1871

William Stanley Jevons (1835–1882)

Along with Carl Menger and Leon Walras, Jevons (in *The Theory of Political Economy*) introduced (1) the idea that the value of goods is determined subjectively rather than by the labor required for production, and (2) the law of diminishing marginal utility. Independently, the same concepts were developed by Menger in *Grundsätze* (1871) and Walras in *Elements of Pure Economics* (1874). These two concepts are still an integral part of modern analysis.

1890

Alfred Marshall (1842–1924)

In his book *The Principles of Economics*, Marshall introduced and developed many of the key concepts of modern microeconomics, including concepts like supply and demand, equilibrium, short run and long run, elasticity, and consumer and producer surplus. The book went through eight editions between 1890 and 1920.